Computers

Computers
7th Edition

Larry Long

Nancy Long

PRENTICE HALL Upper Saddle River, New Jersey 07458

Acquisitions Editor: David Alexander
Managing Editor: Lucinda Gatch
Assistant Editor: Lori Cerreto
Editor-in-Chief: Mickey Cox
Director Strategic Marketing: Nancy Evans
Sales Specialists: Kris King, Dana Simmons, Sharon Turkovich, Iain MacDonald, Matt Denham, Linda Pham, Greg Christofferson
Senior Production Editor: Anne Graydon
Assoc. Managing Editor/Production: Sondra Greenfield
Copy Editor: Nancy Marcello
Senior Manufacturing Supervisor: Paul Smolenski
Senior Manager, Manufacturing and Prepress: Vincent Scelta
Senior Designer: Cheryl Asherman
Design Manager: Pat Smythe
Interior & Cover Designer: Amanda Kavanagh/Ark Design
Illustrator (Interior): Batelman Illustration/York Production Services
Cover Art: Cary Henrie

Library of Congress Cataloging in Publication Data
Long, Larry E.
Computers/Larry Long, Nancy Long.—7th edition
528pp.
ISBN 0–13–083190–5
1. Computers. 2. Electronic data processing. I. Long, Nancy
II. Title.
QA76.L576 1999
004—dc21
99–32131
CIP

Prentice Hall International (UK) Limited, London
Prentice Hall of Australia Pty. Limited, Sidney
Prentice Hall of Canada Inc., Toronto
Prentice Hall Hispanoamericano, S.A., Mexico
Prentice Hall of India Private Limited, New Delhi
Prentice Hall of Japan, Inc., Tokyo
Prentice Hall (Singapore) Pte. Ltd.
Editora Prentice Hall do Brasil, Ltda., Rio de Janeiro

Printed in the United States of America
10 9 8 7 6 5 4 3 2 1

Dedication

To our children,
Troy and Brady—
the motivation for all we do.

Contents Overview

Information Technology Concepts

1 Information Technology in Perspective 2
Focus on IT: The History of Computing 40

2 Using the PC: Popular Productivity Software 50

3 Inside the Computer 82
Focus on IT: The Computer on a Chip 108

4 Storing and Retrieving Information 114

5 Information Input and Output 146

6 Networks and Networking 180

7 Going Online 214

8 The Windows Environment 250
Focus on IT: PC Buyer's Guide 280

Living in an Information Society

9 PC Software for Every Application 2

10 Computers in Society: Today 38
Focus on IT: Robots and Robotics 76

11 Computers in Society: Tomorrow 82

Business Information Systems

12 Information Systems 2

13 Developing Business Information Systems 32

The seventh edition of *Computers* is a modular book that can be custom published to meet curriculum needs. This book may contain the Information Technology Concepts (I) module with none or any combination of the other two modules: Living in an Information Society (S), and Business Information Systems (B).

Contents

Preface to the Student xvii
Preface to the Instructor xix

Information Technology Concepts

Information Technology in Perspective 2

1.1 The Information Society 4

R_x for Cyberphobia: Information Technology Competency 4 *The Technology Revolution* 5 *Looking Back a Few Years* 6 *Data: Foundation for Our Information Society* 7 *This Course: Your Ticket to the Computer Adventure* 8

1.2 Networking: Bringing People Together 9

The Global Village 9 *The Internet and Information Services: Going Online* 10

1.3 Computers: The Essentials 12

Conversational Computerese: Basic Terms and Definitions 12 *Computer Systems: Commuters to Wide-Bodies* 13 *The House of Software* 14

1.4 Personal Computers to Supercomputers 18

Personal Computers 18 *Workstations: The Hot Rods of Computing* 23 *Mainframe Computers: Corporate Workhorses* 25 *Supercomputers: Processing Giants* 26

1.5 A Computer System at Work 28

Processing Payroll: Payday 28 *What Can a Computer Do?* 29 *The Computer's Strengths* 31

1.6 How Do We Use Computers? 32

Information Systems 32 *Personal Computing* 32 *Communication* 34 *Science, Research, and Engineering* 34 *Education and Reference* 34 *Entertainment and Edutainment* 35

Focus on IT
The History of Computing 40

2 Using the PC: Popular Productivity Software 50

2.1 Personal Computing with Popular Productivity Packages 52

The seventh edition of *Computers* is a modular book that can be custom published to meet curriculum needs. This book may contain the Information Technology Concepts (I) module with none or any combination of the other two modules: Living in an Information Society (S), and Business Information Systems (B).

2.2 Word Processing: The Most Popular PC Application 52

Word Processing Concepts and Features 53 Putting Word Processing to Work 56

2.3 Desktop Publishing: Freedom of the Press 60

Desktop Publishing and Word Processing: What's the Difference? 61 Desktop Publishing Concepts and Features 61

2.4 Presentation Software: Putting on the Show 62

2.5 Spreadsheet: The Magic Matrix 66

Spreadsheet Concepts and Features 67 Putting Spreadsheet Software to Work 69

2.6 Database: A Dynamic Data Tool 72

Database Software and Spreadsheet Software: What's the Difference? 72 Database Concepts and Features 73

3 Inside the Computer 82

3.1 Going Digital 84

Binary Digits: 1 and 0 84 Encoding Systems: Bits and Bytes 85

3.2 The PC System Unit: Looking in the Box 88

Why It's Important to Know What's Inside Your PC 88 The Motherboard 88 Computer on a Chip: The Microprocessor 90 Putting It All Together 95 PC Growth: Adding Capabilities 99

3.3 Describing the Processor 101

Word Size 101 Processor Speed 101 Memory Capacity 102 Differences in Processor Personality 103

3.4 Processor Design 103

CISC and RISC: More Is Not Always Better 103 Parallel Processing: Computers Working Together 103 Neural Networks: Wave of the Future? 104

Focus on IT
The Computer on a Chip 108

4 Storing and Retrieving Information 114

4.1 Mass Storage and Files 116

Storage Technologies 116 The Many Faces of Files 116

4.2 Magnetic Disks 119

Hardware and Storage Media 119 PC Magnetic Disk Drives and Media 121 Magnetic Disk Organization 123 Disk Access Time: Seek and Transmit 127 Disk Caching: Speed Boost 127 Diskette Care: Do's and Don'ts 127 Computer Viruses: The Plague of Magnetic Disks 128

4.3 Backup: Better Safe than Sorry 130

Backup to Magnetic Tape 130 Backup to Interchangeable Disks 132

4.4 Optical Laser Disks: High-Density Storage 133

CD-ROM and DVD: Moby Dick, Mozart, and the Cinemania 134 WORM Disks 141 What's the Best Mix of Storage Options? 141

4.5 Storage Forecast: Is There a Disk in Your Future? 142

5 Information Input and Output 146

5.1 I/O Devices: Let's Interface 148

5.2 Traditional Input Devices 149

The Keyboard 149 Point-and-Draw Devices 151

5.3 Source-Data Automation 154

Scanners 155 Magnetic Stripes and Smart Cards 157 Speech Recognition: Getting on Speaking Terms with Computers 158 Vision-Input Systems: Computer Eyes 160 Digital Cameras: Look, No Film 161 Handheld Data Entry Devices 162

5.4 Output Devices 163

Monitors and Graphics Adapters 163 Desktop Printers: Lots of Choices 168 Presentation Graphics: Be Persuasive 172 Voice-Response Systems: Say It with Bits 172

5.5 Terminals: Input and Output 174

Dumb and Smart Terminals 174 Telephone Terminals and Telephony 175 Special-Function Terminals: ATMs and POSs 176

6 Networks and Networking 180

6.1 Our Weird, Wild, Wired World 182

Digital Convergence: Coming Together as Bits and Bytes 182 Connectivity: Getting to the Information 183 The Beginning of an Era: Cooperative Processing 184

6.2 Data Communications Hardware: Making It Happen 185

The Modem: Digital to Analog to Digital 187 Network Interface Cards 187 Special-Function Communications Devices: Help along the Line 187 Routers: Bridging the Gap 188

6.3 The Data Communications Channel: Data Highways 190

Transmission Media: Wires and Wireless 190 Common Carriers 194 Data Transmission in Practice 195

6.4 Networks: Connecting Nodes 196

Network Topologies: Star, Ring, and Bus 197 Computer Systems Working Together: Client/Server Computing 198 Network Line Control: Rules for Data Transmission 199

6.5 Networks: The WAN, MAN, LAN, and TAN 201

Types of Networks 201 LAN Overview 205 LAN Software 208

7 Going Online 214

7.1 The Online World 216

7.2 Information Services: America Online, CompuServe, and More 216

7.3 The Internet: A World Wide Web of Computers and Information 217

What Is the Internet? 217 From ARPANET to the Internet: Some Historical Perspective 217 Who Governs the Internet? 219 The Link to the Internet 220 Retrieving and Viewing Information 222 Uniform Resource Locator: The Internet Address 223

7.4 Browsers: The Information Tool 225

Concepts and Features 226 Browser Summary 229

7.5 Internet Resources and Applications 230

Using the Browser to Find Resources and Information on the Net 230 Internet Applications: The Web, FTP, and More 232 Communicating with People: E-Mail, Newsgroups, Mailing Lists, and More 236

7.6 Internet Issues 246

8 The Windows Environment 250

8.1 The Operating System: Directing the Action 252

Operating System Objectives and Orientation 253 Living on a Budget: Allocating Computer Resources 253 The Graphical User Interface: "Gooie" 254

8.2 Platforms: Homes for Software 255

PC Platforms 256 Platform Problems: Interoperability and Cross-Platform Technologies 257

8.3 Windows Concepts and Terminology 259

Understanding Windows 98: Help 259 Non-Windows versus Windows Applications 260 Differences between Windows 95 and Windows 98/2000 260 The Desktop 263

8.4 Sharing Information among Windows Applications 270

The Clipboard: The Information Way Station 270 Object Linking and Embedding: OLE 270 A Thousand Look-Alikes 272 Migrating to Windows 2000 272

8.5 Interacting with the PC and Its Software 273

Computer Operation: Getting Started 273 Entering Commands and Data: Computers Can Be Very Picky 277

Focus on IT
PC Buyer's Guide 280

Living in an Information Society

9 PC Software for Every Application 2

9.1 Graphics and Multimedia Software 4

Graphics Software 4 Multimedia 13

9.2 Personal Information Management Software 19

9.3 Home and Family Software 19

9.4 Education and Edutainment Software 24

9.5 Reference Software 25

9.6 Business and Management Software 29

9.7 Utility Software 34

10 Computers in Society: Today 38

10.1 The Information Technology Paradox 40

Are We Ready for Information Technology? 40 *Do We Really Want Information Technology?* 40 *Reaching the Point of No Return* 42

10.2 Working in the Information Society 43

Opportunities for IT Specialists 44 *Career Opportunities for IT-Competent Minority* 48 *Our Jobs Are Changing* 49

10.3 The Work Place: Ergonomics and Green Computing 51

Ergonomics and Workplace Design 51 *Reasons for Concern* 51 *Workplace Design: An Evaluation* 52 *Green Computing* 53

10.4 The Question of Ethics 54

Standards of Conduct: A Code of Ethics 55 *The Misuse of Personal Information* 56 *Computer Monitoring* 58 *Computer Crime* 60 *Computers and the Law* 60

10.5 Computer, Internet, and System Security 66

Computer-Center Security 66 *Information Systems Security* 70 *PC Security* 70 *Level of Risk* 71

Focus on IT
Robots and Robotics 76

11 Computers in Society: Tomorrow 82

11.1 The Virtual Frontier 84

11.2 The Wake Up Call 86

11.3 Artificial Intelligence 89

Categories of Artificial Intelligence 89 *The Commercialization of Artificial Intelligence* 91

11.4 Down the Road: The Information Superhighway 92

Travelers along the Information Superhighway 92 *The Information Superhighway: Getting There* 108

11.5 Your Challenge 110

Business Information Systems

12 Information Systems 2

12.1 An End to Business as Usual 4

12.2 Information and Decision Making 5

Qualities of Information 5 *Making Decisions to Produce Products and Services* 6 *Filtering Information: Getting the Right Information to the Right Person* 8 *Decisions: Easy Ones and Tough Ones* 10

12.3 All about Information Systems 11

The Information System: What Is It? 11 *The Information System: What*

Can It Do? 11 *The Manual System: Opportunities for Automation* 13 *Function-Based and Integrated Information Systems* 13 *Getting Data into the System: Data Entry Concepts* 14

12.4 Data Processing Systems 16

12.5 Management Information Systems 16

The Management Information System: What Is It? 16 *The MIS versus the Data Processing System* 17 *Characteristics of Management Information Systems* 17 *The MIS in Action* 18

12.6 Decision Support Systems 18

The Decision Support System: What Is It? 18 *The DSS versus the MIS* 19 *Characteristics of Decision Support Systems* 19 *The DSS Tool Box* 19 *Executive Information Systems: The Executive's DSS* 22

12.7 Expert Systems 23

The Expert System: What Is It? 23 *An Expert System Example: Technical Support* 24 *Are Expert Systems in Your Future?* 25

12.8 Intelligent Agents: Working for Us 28

13 Developing Business Information Systems 32

13.1 The System Life Cycle 34

Stages of the Life Cycle 34 *Applications Software: Whether to Make It or Buy It* 34

13.2 System Development Techniques and Concepts 36

Structured System Design 36 *Data Flow Diagrams* 37 *Entity Relationship Diagrams* 40 *Flowcharting* 40

13.3 Computer-Aided Software Engineering: The CASE Tool Kit 41

Design Tools 42 *Information Repository Tools* 43 *Program Development Tools* 43

13.4 Prototyping: Creating a Model of the Target System 43

The Emergence of Prototyping 44 *The Prototype System* 45 *Rapid Application Prototyping* 45 *The Prototyping Process* 45

13.5 System Conversion and Implementation: Making the Transition 49

Systems and Acceptance Testing 49 *Approaches to System Conversion* 50 *The System Becomes Operational* 51

13.6 Programming: Making It Happen 53

Software in Perspective 53 *Types of Programming Languages* 56 *Writing the Program* 58 *Programming and You* 59

Answers to Section Self-Checks S1

Glossary G1

Index Idx1

Special Interest Sidebars

Chapter 1
Emerging IT: Online Shopping: Let Your Fingers Do the Walking 16
IT Ethics: The Spam Dilemma 8

Chapter 2
Emerging IT: Getting Help with Getting Started 74
IT Ethics: E-mail Etiquette 59

Chapter 3
IT Ethics: Should PC Ownership Be an Entrance Requirement for Colleges? 95

Chapter 4
Emerging IT: Electronic Publishing: Saving the Trees 135
IT Ethics: Accessibility to E-mail Archives 131

Chapter 5
Emerging IT: Computers: The Enabling Technology for the Disabled 164
IT Ethics: ATM Fees 175

Chapter 6
Emerging IT: WORKING@HOME 202
IT Ethics: Telecommuting 194

Chapter 7
Emerging IT: Cybertalk: A New Way to Communicate 240
IT Ethics: Prescreening of Online Communications 223

Chapter 8
Emerging IT: Tailoring PCs to the Needs of Mobile Workers 274
IT Ethics: The Quality of Software 258

Chapter 9
IT Ethics: Term-Paper Fraud 25

Chapter 10
Emerging IT: Who Knows What About You? 62
IT Ethics: Hate Sites on the Internet; Monitoring of E-mail 60, 57

Chapter 11
Emerging IT: The Promise of Virtual Reality 104
IT Ethics: Addiction to the Internet; Inappropriate Usage of the Internet at Work 99, 96

Chapter 12
Emerging IT: The Millennium Bug: Y2K 26
IT Ethics: Predicting Election Returns 11

Chapter 13
Emerging IT: Twenty-First Century Case 54
IT Ethics: Collecting and Distributing Personal Information 51

Preface to the Student

Welcome to the computer and information technology revolution. You've taken the first step toward information technology (IT) competency, the bridge to an amazing realm of adventure and discovery. Once you have read and understood the material in this text and have acquired some hands-on experience with computers, you will be poised to play an active role in this revolution.

- You'll be an intelligent consumer of PCs and related products.
- You'll be better prepared to travel the Internet and take advantage of its wealth of resources and services.
- You'll become a participant when conversations at work and school turn to computers and technology.
- You'll be better able to relate your computing and information processing needs to those who can help you.
- You'll know about a wide variety of software and services that can improve your productivity at work and at home, give you much needed information, expand your intellectual and cultural horizons, amaze you, your family, and your friends, and give you endless hours of enjoyment.

Achieving IT competency is the first step in a lifelong journey toward greater knowledge and interaction with more and better applications of IT. IT competency is your ticket to ride. Where you go, how fast you get there, and what you do when you arrive is up to you.

LEARNING AIDS

Computers is supported by a comprehensive learning assistance package that includes these helpful learning aids:

The Long and Long INTERNET BRIDGE

The Long and Long INTERNET BRIDGE at http://www.prenhall.com/long is a Companion Web site on the Internet that is accessible from any PC with Internet access. The site, which is designed to help you make the transition between textbook learning and real-world understanding, has a variety of learning aids, including these three main components.

- *Internet Exercises.* The INTERNET BRIDGE invites you to go online and explore the wonders of the Internet through a comprehensive set of Internet exercises. These entertaining exercises invite you to learn more about the topics in this book and to do some "serendipitous [just-for-fun] surfing."
- *Interactive Study Guide (ISG).* The INTERNET BRIDGE's comprehensive Interactive Study Guide gives you an opportunity to sharpen your problem-solving skills and to gauge your understanding of the material in the chapter. For each chapter, the ISG has multiple-choice, true/false, matching, and essay quizzes. The built-in grading feature gives you immediate feedback in the form of a report. The report also includes a question-by-question summary with an explanation or hint, your response, and the correct response (if needed).
- *Monthly Technology Update.* The printed book alone is no longer sufficient to keep you abreast of a rapidly advancing technology. The INTERNET

BRIDGE's Monthly Technology Update section helps you bridge this technology gap. Each month the authors post a chapter-by-chapter update to the INTERNET BRIDGE. The monthly update includes summaries of important technological events that occurred during the previous month.

The WEB icons in the margins throughout the book relate material in the book to applicable INTERNET BRIDGE exercises, *Interactive Study Guide* chapters, and technology updates.

WebCT.long: Distance Learning with Computers

WebCT.Long at http://www.prenhall.com/WebCT.long is a demo site for the optional online course for this information technology concepts book. The site lets you take computer competency courses via distance learning or allows you to enhance your classroom experience with online learning. That is, you logon to the *WebCT.long page* on the Internet to interact with instructors and classmates, go over chapter summaries, evaluate your understanding of course material, participate in online discussion groups, take quizzes and tests, gain access to class information (schedule, homework, and so on), make inquiries about your grades, and much more.

Computers, Seventh Edition, Interactive CD-ROM

An optional interactive version of the seventh edition of *Computers* integrates the book's content, a variety of learning tools, and access to the resources of the Internet on a CD-ROM. This electronic book makes it easy for you to navigate between computer and information technology topics in the book and various learning aids, including the interactive labs on the CD-ROM and the interactive Internet-based study guide.

YOU, COMPUTERS, AND THE FUTURE

Whether you are pursuing a career as an economist, a social worker, a politician, an attorney, a dancer, an accountant, a computer specialist, a sales manager, or virtually any other career, the knowledge you gain from this course ultimately will prove beneficial. Keep your course notes and your book; they will prove to be valuable references in other courses and in your career.

Even though computers are all around us, we are seeing only the tip of the information technology iceberg. You are entering the IT era in its infancy. Each class you attend and each page you turn will present a learning experience to help you advance one step closer to an understanding of how computers and IT are making the world a better place in which to live and work.

Preface to the Instructor

THE PARADIGM SHIFT

The rules are changing. The criteria by which we make decisions, the way we do things, and even what we do are changing dramatically. Affordable PCs with tremendous power can reach around the world via the Internet, a rapidly expanding worldwide network of computers. Each increment in PC power and Internet resources adds fuel to the personal computing phenomena, accelerating the pace of change. We are now members of an interconnected society where we can shop at online Wal-Mart Supercenters, research our family tree, take virtual tours of thousands of sites from the White House to the pyramids, take courses for college credit, and much, much more, all from a linked PC.

This paradigm shift is causing radical changes in all facets of society, including the way we teach and learn. We are entering a new era of education in which technology plays an increasingly significant role. This is especially true of introductory information technology courses where the integration of the technology is a natural extension of the learning process. After all, the best place to learn about computers is at the computer.

THE INTRO COURSE

The introductory IT course poses tremendous teaching challenges. To be effective, we must continually change our lecture style and even the vehicle by which we convey content and interact with students. Throughout the term we are continually changing hats. Sometimes we are historians. Much of the time we are scientists presenting technical material. On occasion we are sociologists commenting on social issues. In the same course we now toggle between lecture, lab, and, for some, distance learning via the Internet. If that's not enough, we teach an ever-increasing amount of material to students with a wide range of career objectives and technical abilities. We, and Prentice Hall, have done everything we can to help you meet this challenge.

Opportunity, challenge, and competition are forcing all of us to become IT-competent and to prepare ourselves for a more interconnected world. The seventh edition of *Computers,* its mixed-media components, and its ancillary materials provide a launch pad toward these objectives. The target course for this text and its teaching/learning system:

- *Provides overview coverage of computing/IT concepts and applications for introductory courses.* The seventh edition of *Computers* comes in three versions so that you can get the best fit for your course's educational objectives.
- *Accommodates students from a broad spectrum of disciplines and interests.*
- *May or may not include a laboratory component.* Prentice Hall offers an extensive array of optional learning resources for hands-on laboratories.

COMPUTERS, SEVENTH EDITION: A FAST-PACED INTRODUCTION TO THE WORLD OF COMPUTING

About 6 Internet years pass in one real-time year—the elapsed time between the sixth and seventh editions. This new edition is a major *technology update* intended to bring *Computers* abreast with a rampaging technology. For the past 17 years, your peers have told us that we consistently publish the most up-to-date IT concepts textbook. We take great pride in your confidence in us and are committed to presenting a current and forward-looking picture of IT innovations and issues. But, this seventh edition is much more than a technology update.

The seventh edition has been reorganized and largely rewritten. We have listened to your feedback and feel that this new edition strikes a good balance between *efficiency of presentation* and *content that holds the student's interest and invites learning*.

- *Efficient presentation.* To achieve our *efficiency-of-presentation* goal, we cover only material that is critical to general IT competency. We avoid dated concepts; we don't cover basic concepts from every angle; and we're careful not to present topics at depths inconsistent with introductory learning. We feel that students at this stage of their IT competency journey need a breadth of understanding that is applicable *today* and in the *future*. Also, we present only information that will have an impact on students' ability to cope with the IT revolution, avoiding superfluous information that might dampen students' interest in technology.
- *Interesting and inviting content.* The text and all supplements are written in a style that remains pedagogically sound while communicating the energy and excitement of IT to students. We used every writing tool and pedagogical technique in our arsenal to entice students to turn the page and learn more. Throughout the book we make learning about IT a very personal experience by relating terms or concepts to their personal and professional lives. Students make the effort to learn when they can see why it's important to them.

The seventh edition presents a body of knowledge that students need in order to become active participants in this exciting new era of technological innovation and application. The book's content runs the gamut from motherboard technologies, such as USB, to ethical issues, such as spam. Our guiding objective during the writing of the seventh edition was to impart this crucial and substantial body of information in a manner that can be absorbed, retained, and enjoyed.

NEW FEATURES IN THE SEVENTH EDITION OF *COMPUTERS*

The seventh edition reflects thousands of changes in content, style, organization, and presentation. Here's a summary of these changes:

- *Conversational writing style.* The book now "talks" to the student in a manner that is more consistent with their everyday conversation.
- *New design.* The seventh edition has a new "reader-friendly" face that is more inviting to today's students.
- *One less chapter and no appendices.* In keeping with the book's new fast-paced presentation, the book is slightly condensed to better fit the reality of what can be accomplished in a college course.
- *New chapter on Windows.* A whole chapter is devoted to "the Windows environment" to better present the interface and interactive concepts that are embodied in the Windows 9x/NT/2000 operating systems and most modern PC software.
- *Productivity software presentation streamlined.* The presentation of office suite–type applications is consolidated in a single chapter, rather than two, in which the focus is more on overall functionality than on operation.
- "*Why This Chapter Is Important to You" section.* A section that personalizes the students' learning experience begins each chapter.

- *Section self-checks.* Generally, the number of self-check questions for each chapter has doubled or tripled, and now they're conveniently placed at the end of each section. Self-Check answers follow Chapter 13.
- *All-new software screen captures.* All of the screen-capture images have been updated to reflect the latest releases and innovations in software.
- *Many new colorful photo images.* The photo images have been updated to give the student a better feel for state-of-the-art hardware and applications.
- *All-new online examples.* All of the many Internet and America Online examples have been updated.
- *Capacities and speeds updated.* The numbers for modems, disks, RAM, processors, printers, the Internet, and so on are updated to reflect 2000–2001.
- *Expanded coverage of the Internet.* The coverage of the Internet throughout the book reflects its increased presence in society and in our lives.
- *Currency-plus.* The seventh edition actually anticipates emerging technology. If it's current and it's within the IT-competency body of knowledge, it's in this book. It has the latest on the Internet: online publishing, portals, videophones, flaming, firewalls, extranets, spam, and more. The software is right out of the box: Office 2000 and many more innovative applications. The latest hardware is here, too: infrared ports, CD-RW, SuperDisk, iMac, Pentium III, and more. And, of course, it's current with the acronyms: USB, AGP, SDRAM, OLE, RAD, OOP, WPNG, DVD, and all the rest.

Even with all these changes, the seventh edition of *Computers* was written to enable a smooth, seamless transition for those colleges moving from the fifth or sixth edition to the seventh edition.

POPULAR FEATURES RETAINED IN THE SEVENTH EDITION

- *Applications oriented.* The continuing theme throughout the text is applications. Hundreds of applications are presented from online universities to telemedicine to robotics.
- *Readability.* All elements (photos, figures, sidebars, and so on) are integrated with the textual material to complement and reinforce learning.
- *Flexibility.* The text and its mixed-media teaching/learning system are organized to permit maximum flexibility in course design and in the selection, assignment, and presentation of material.
- *Analogies.* Analogies are used throughout the book to relate information technology concepts to concepts students already understand, such as airplanes (computer systems), audio CDs (random processing), and cars/parking lots (files/disks).
- *Colorful Focus on ITs.* The Focus on IT feature combines dynamic photos with an in-depth discussion of topics that are of interest to students, such as the history of computers, how chips are made, and how to buy a PC.
- *Walk-through illustrations.* Every attempt has been made to minimize conceptual navigation between the running text and figures. This was done by including relevant information within the figures in easy-to-follow numbered walk-throughs.
- *Mixed-media margin icons.* The WEB and PHitLAB (Computers Interactive Labs) icons in the margin point students to interactive multimedia learning resources on the INTERNET BRIDGE and the PHitLAB CD-ROM. The WEB icons invite students to check out the Monthly Technology Update, do applicable Internet exercises, and use the Interactive Study Guide to assess their grasp of the material. The PHitLAB icons identify applicable laboratory exercises that let students interactively explore IT concepts.

- *Chapter pedagogy.* Chapter organization and pedagogy are consistent throughout the text. Each chapter is prefaced by *Learning Objectives* and *Why This Chapter Is Important to You*. In the body of the chapter, all major headings are numbered. (1.1, 1.2, and so on) to facilitate selective assignments and to provide an easy cross-reference to all related material in the supplements. Important terms and phrases are highlighted in **boldface** type. Words and phrases to be emphasized appear in *italics*. Informative boxed features (*Emerging IT* and *IT Ethics*), photos, and *Memory Bits* (outlines of key points) are positioned strategically to complement the running text. A *Section Self-Check* gives students an opportunity to assess their understanding at the end of each numbered section. Margin icons direct students to applicable WEB and PHitLAB CD-ROM–based lab activities. Each chapter concludes with a *Summary and Key Terms* section and *Discussion and Problem Solving* exercises.

A MIXED-MEDIA LEARNING TOOL

This textbook is one component of a *mixed-media learning tool*. Although it can be used as a stand-alone resource, its effectiveness is enhanced when used in conjunction with the Long and Long INTERNET BRIDGE or WebCT.long (companion Internet sites), PHitLABs (CD-ROM–based courseware), Image Library (multimedia lecture aid), and other media-based ancillaries. The mixed-media orientation of this edition of *Computers* gives students a power boost up the learning curve and instructors an innovative vehicle for delivery of course content. The margin icons throughout the book direct students to applicable INTERNET BRIDGE and PHitLAB activities.

We've designed the seventh edition of *Computers* mixed-media resources to give you maximum flexibility in course design and instruction. Use these resources to offer IT competency education in whatever formats meet your student and curriculum needs. We are proud that *Computers* has been and remains the standard of excellence for traditional classroom/lab instruction through seven editions. Now it has emerged as the standard for courses offered completely online via distance learning.

Throughout all aspects of this mixed-media approach to learning, we play to students' sense of exhilaration by projecting the excitement of the age of information. We have attempted to include something on every printed page, every Internet page, and every CD-ROM–based laboratory that will tickle their senses and inspire them to learn more. Eventually anxieties and fears fade away as students recognize the dawning of a new era in their life, an era bursting with opportunity.

A *COMPUTERS* EDITION FOR EVERY COURSE

Computers is organized into three modules.

- *Information Technology Concepts module.* These *eight core chapters* introduce students to the world of computing; concepts relating to interaction with computers; fundamental hardware, software, and communications concepts; going online (the Internet, online information services); and the Windows environment. This module includes three Focus on IT segments: computer history, the making of integrated circuits, and a PC buyer's guide.
- *Living in an Information Society module.* These *three chapters* are intended to give students greater insight into personal computing and our information society. Chapter 9 introduces students to a variety of PC software that can enrich their personal computing experience. The other two issue-oriented chapters discuss computing in context with society, addressing the many issues raised by the coming of the Information Age. Also, in these chapters

students travel the information superhighway, making frequent stops to discuss current and future applications. This module has one Focus on IT: Robots and Robotics.

- *Business Information Systems module.* This *two-chapter* module introduces students to the various types of information systems (MIS, DSS, expert systems, intelligent agents, and so on) and includes an overview of the latest approaches to system development.

The Right PHit program offers a complete solution for introductory computer courses, from concepts to applications. Components of the Prentice Hall Applications Series can be bound with the seventh edition of *Computers* via Prentice Hall's Right PHit program. Office 97 and Office 2000 titles are available in this custom-binding program and comprise part of the most extensive array of hands-on laboratory materials offered by any textbook publisher. These hands-on manuals can be bound together with *Computers* or, if you prefer, bound separately and shrink-wrapped as a package so students can carry them to the lab one at a time. Your Prentice Hall representative will be happy to work with you to identify that combination of student support materials and packaging that best meets the needs of your lab environment.

THE *COMPUTERS* TEACHING/LEARNING SYSTEM

The seventh edition of *Computers* continues the Long and Long tradition of having the most comprehensive, innovative, and effective support package on the market. The teaching/learning system includes the following components.

Long and Long INTERNET BRIDGE

The Long and Long INTERNET BRIDGE at http://www.prenhall.com/long is designed to help students studying Long and Long resources make the transition between textbook learning and real-world understanding. To use this resource, the student connects to the Internet, navigates to the INTERNET BRIDGE, and clicks on the *Computers*, seventh edition, image. The site offers a variety of activities and services, including these main components:

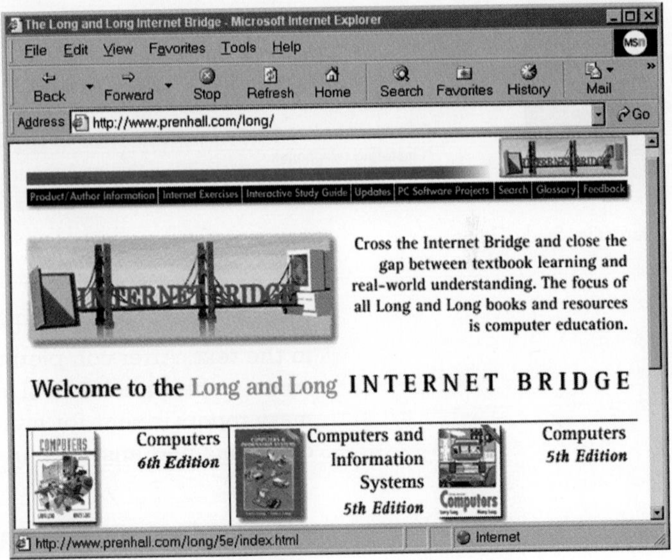

Long and Long Internet Bridge

Internet Exercises

The Internet exercises encourage students to fully explore IT competency topics while familiarizing themselves with the Internet. The student selects a specific chapter to begin an online adventure that will take him or her around and into the exciting world of computing. The student's journey will include many stops that can increase his or her understanding and appreciation of the technologies that change and embellish our lives.

Each chapter has from one to seven topics (for example, Printers, Telecommuting, Multimedia, Artificial Intelligence), at least one of which is Serendipitous Surfing (for example, movies, sports, or popular culture). Each topic has from three to seven Internet exercises. For each exercise, the student: (1) reads the exercise; (2) searches for, then navigates to, the applicable Internet site(s); (3) notes the source(s) title(s) and URL(s); (4) finds the requested information; and (5) returns to the topic page and enters the requested information in the response box. When

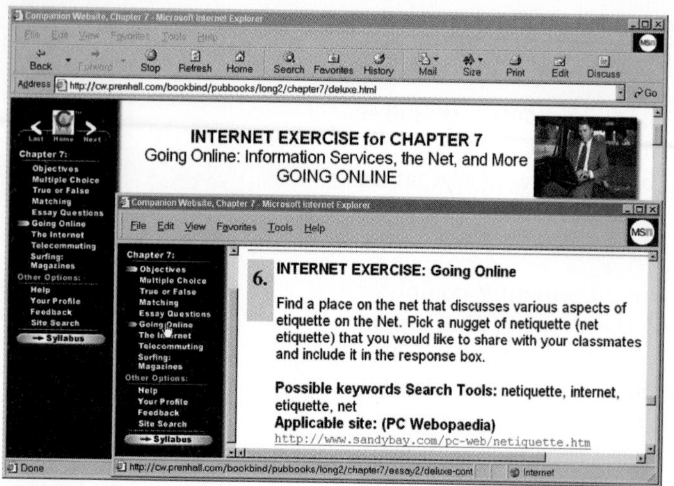

Internet Exercises

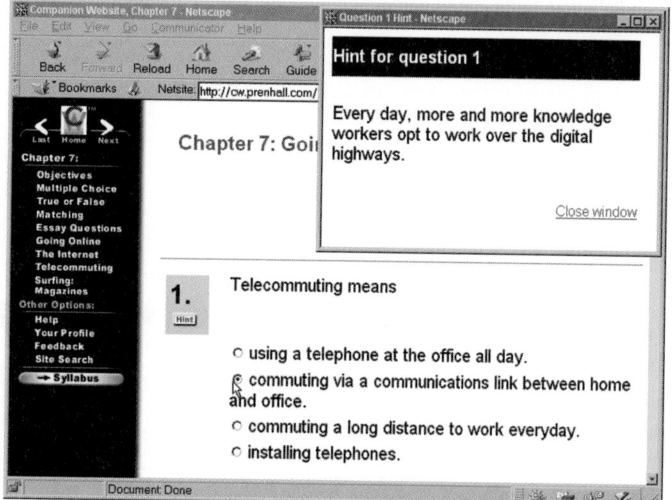

Interactive Study Guide

all Internet exercises are completed for a given topic, the student clicks the "Submit for Grade" button to e-mail the responses to his or her instructor/grader.

Interactive Study Guide

The Internet-based Interactive Study Guide (ISG) helps the student learn and retain concepts presented in the text. After navigating to the applicable chapter, the student can view the chapter learning objectives, then choose from four skills quizzes: multiple choice, true or false, matching, or essay. These quizzes are designed to give students the opportunity to sharpen their problem-solving skills and assess their grasp of concepts.

- *Multiple Choice.* When taking the multiple-choice quiz the student simply clicks the radio button for the correct response for each question. After answering all of the questions, the student submits the answers for automatic grading. A summary report is returned to the student within seconds. The summary report includes the percentage correct, the number of incorrect answers, and the number of unanswered questions. The report also includes a question-by-question summary with an explanation, the student's response, and the correct response (if needed).
- *True or False.* The true/false interface and summary report is like that of a multiple-choice quiz.
- *Matching.* The student matches terms with applicable descriptions by selecting a response from a drop-down box.
- *Essay Questions.* The essay exam includes a text-response box for each question into which the student inserts the answer.

Most questions have hints or they provide a reference to the applicable section in the text. After completing a quiz, the student has the option of routing the answers to his or her e-mail address and/or to that of his or her instructor. The summary report is sent for multiple-choice, true/false, and matching quizzes, and the questions and answers are sent for the essay exams.

Monthly Technology Update

Each month we compile a summary of important changes and happenings in the world of computing and IT. These summaries, which are keyed to chapters, are intended to help keep the student's learning experience current with a rampaging technology.

Syllabus Manager

The Syllabus Manager component of the INTERNET BRIDGE is a free utility for instructors and students who use our book/Web site products. Faculty can easily build and maintain one or more syllabi on the Web. The course syllabus is readily available to students from any PC with Internet access.

Instructor's Resource Page on the INTERNET BRIDGE

The INTERNET BRIDGE includes a frequently updated, password-protected Instructor's Resource page that is available to all instructors who adopt the Long and Long package. The Instructor's Resource Page contains a variety of downloadable resources, including supplementary images, the *IRM*, crossword puzzles, PowerPoint Slides, a buyer's guide worksheet, supplementary PC exercises, PDF format transparencies, applicable material contributed by colleagues, and other helpful teaching/learning aids.

WebCT.long: Distance Learning via the Internet

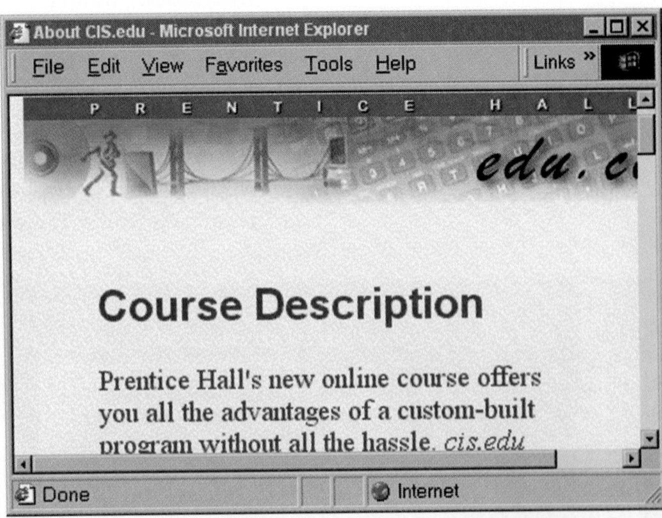

WebCT.long for Online Learning

WebCT.long at http://www.prenhall.com/WebCT.long is Prentice Hall's demonstration site supporting online IT competency courses for colleges using this book. Prentice Hall's complete galley of WebCT courses can be found at www.prenhall.com/WebCT. WebCT offers you and your colleagues all the advantages of a custom-built program, but without the hassle. If you are considering offering all or part of your course via distance learning, then WebCT.long can help you create and implement a high-quality course with relative ease. If you already offer an online course, then WebCT.long can assist you in formalizing your course. WebCT.long gives you the flexibility to integrate your custom material with the continuously updated Long and Long content. The course is packaged within the WebCT course-authoring tool so that you can customize the content to meet the most demanding curriculum requirements. Whether you are off and running or this is your first online course, WebCT.long can save you countless hours of preparation and course administration time.

This resource includes these and many other features in each of its learning modules: an introduction, objectives, summaries of key concepts, online activities that use the Internet, offline activities that integrate the texts with Web content, self-check exercises, online quizzes (auto-scored and recorded), test item database and test preparation tools (auto-scored and recorded), e-mail accounts for students and instructors, and a bulletin board primed with interesting discussion topics.

A wizard program guides you through the initial stages of course development, including the creation of a password-protected course home page. The *Course Management* feature automatically grades online tests and records scores in your electronic grade book. The *Progress Tracking* feature lets you monitor individual and overall student progress. The *Content Tracking* feature tells you how often and for how long each and every student visits a *WebCT.long* page. The WebCT shell also lets you integrate files without using HTML.

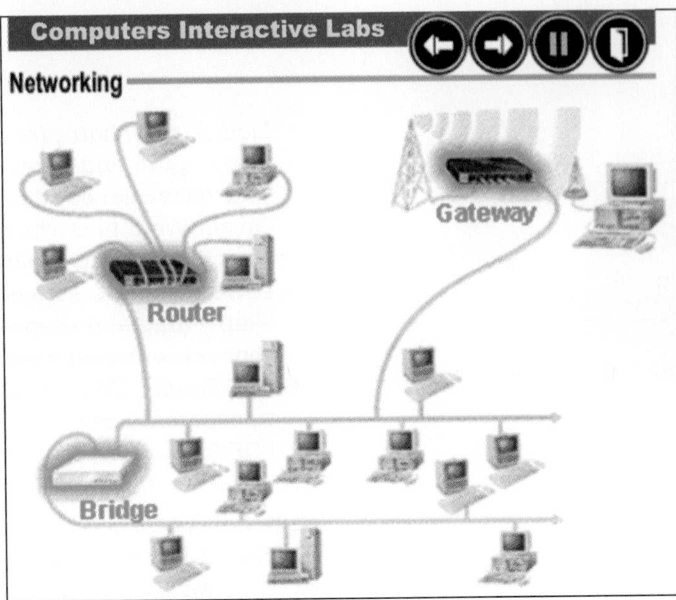

PHitLAB (Computers Interactive Labs)

Computers, Seventh Edition, Interactive CD-ROM

The interactive version is an innovative discovery-based learning tool that offers multimedia explorations of key textbook topics, seamless integration of the World Wide Web, and more! Key features include the following:

- *Computers,* seventh edition, becomes interactive, enabling easy and intuitive navigation with Internet Explorer™ or Netscape Communicator®.
- PHitLABs offer students the opportunity to experience many of the concepts covered in the text. Each lab includes sound, video, interactive review questions, and a hands-on exercise for a complete learning experience. Sample interactive lab topics are input and output, computer architecture, disk fragmentation, binary numbers, and multimedia and virtual reality, word processing, spreadsheets, databases, networking, programming, e-mail, World Wide Web and Internet tools, Web pages and HTML, Web servers, and Y2K issues.
- PHitNotes allows students to build a personal study guide by cutting and pasting text or by adding their own materials.
- End-of-chapter Review Exercises link to the text's Companion Web site Interactive Study Guide. Students can then e-mail results to their instructor.

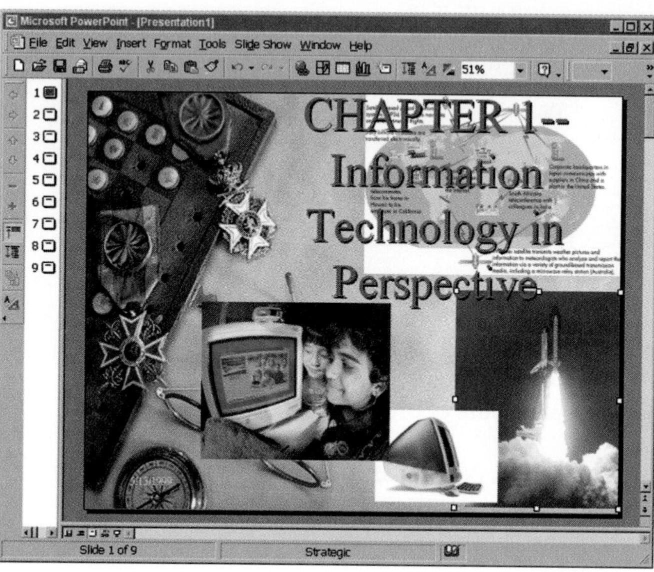

Image Library

The Instructor's One-Stop CD-ROM Resource

A variety of helpful instructor resources are distributed on a single CD-ROM, that includes an Image Library with PowerPoint slides and images from the text, Windows PH Test Manager, Test Item File, Instructor's Resource Manual, and Transparency Masters. Please see below for detailed descriptions of each. (ISBN 013-085076–4)

Image Library with PowerPoint Presentations

The *Image Library* is a wonderful resource for creating vibrant lecture presentations. The *Image Library* includes the following:

- *PowerPoint Slides.* Several hundred colorful and illustrative PowerPoint slides are available for use with Microsoft PowerPoint. The chapter-by-chapter PowerPoint slides can easily be customized to meet lecture needs.
- *Figures and Photos from the Textbook.* The *Image Library* contains just about every figure and photo in the text, all organized by chapter and section for your convenience. Caption/notes are supplied for each image within a Microsoft Word file, which can be copied or exported to a spreadsheet or database. These images and caption/notes can easily be integrated into Microsoft PowerPoint to create new presentations, or to add to existing presentations. Simply drag-and-drop slides and images in PowerPoint to sequence them for your presentation needs.
- *PDF-Format Color Transparency Masters.* Approximately one-hundred color transparency masters, which support material in the text, are provided in PDF format for protection via Acrobat Reader. Acrobat Reader lets you zoom in on those portions of the image discussed.

Windows PH Test Manager and Test Item File

Windows PH Test Manager is an integrated PC-compatible test-generation and classroom-management software package. The package permits instructors to design and create tests, to maintain student records, and to provide online practice testing for students. The accompanying *Test Item File* contains thousands of multiple-choice, true/false, matching, and essay questions. The questions are organized by numbered section head. (Windows PH Test Manager ISBN 0-13-085074-8; Test Item File ISBN 013-085071-3)

Instructor's Resource Manual (IRM)

The *IRM,* which is available in hard copy, is also included in Microsoft Word format on the Instructor's One-Stop CD-ROM and on the INTERNET BRIDGE in the Instructor's Resource Section. The *IRM* contains teaching hints, references to other resources, PowerPoint and acetate images, lecture notes, key terms with definitions, solutions to review exercises, and much more. (Print *IRM*: ISBN 013-084933-2)

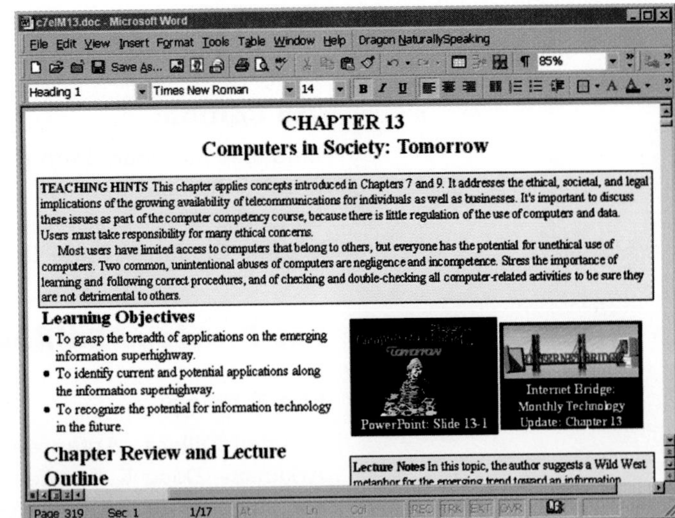

Instructor's Resource Manual

Color Transparency Acetates

Approximately one hundred color transparency acetates, which support material in the text, are available to adopters to facilitate in-class explanation. Transparency masters are also provided in PDF format for viewing on Acrobat Reader. (ISBN 0-13-085072-1)

Author Link

If you have questions about the text, its package, or course planning, call us (see the *IRM* for number) or e-mail us via the INTERNET BRIDGE authors' page or the Feedback page.

ACKNOWLEDGMENTS

Several hundred people have contributed to the making of this seventh edition of *Computers* and its many mixed-media ancillaries. The considerable talents of my family at Prentice Hall in editorial, production, marketing, research, and sales are evident throughout this book. We wish that every author had an Acquisitions Editor like David Alexander to bring harmony, purpose, and passion to his or her project. Also, in Editorial we are particularly grateful to Keith Kryszczun, Lori Cerreto, Lucinda Gatch, Mickey Cox, and P. J. Boardman for their continued encouragement and for helping in so many small and big ways. And to the miracle workers in Production and Manufacturing, Anne Graydon, Cheryl Asherman, Richard Bretan, Paul Smolenski, Vinnie Scelta, Michael Weinstein, and their colleagues, we say, "Way to go"—again! Nancy Evans, Kris King, Dana Simmons, Sharon Turkovich, Iain MacDonald, Matt Denham, Linda Pham, and Greg Christofferson in Marketing and Patty Arneson in Research have provided us with the insight we need to fine-tune content to meet course needs. The artistic gifts of Nancy Welcher and Grace Walkus in New Media are embedded in our Web and mixed-media supplements. And for our most beautiful and effective design—ever—we thank Cary Henrie (cover) and Amanda Kavanagh of Ark Design (interior design). In addition, we would like to thank Gretchen Miller at York Production Services for her patience and attention to detail in the production process.

We would like to thank those who created key ancillaries for *Computers:* Henry Rowe *(Instructor's Resource Manual),* C. Norman Hollingsworth of Georgia Perimeter College *(PowerPoint slides),* and Jack Pesci of Owens Community College *(Interactive Study Guide and Test Item File).*

The feedback from numerous college professors, both invited and voluntary, has proven invaluable in refining this new edition to better serve their course needs. We would like to extend our heartfelt gratitude to these professors for their insight on this and previous editions of *Computers*.

7th Edition:

LindaLee Massoud, Mott Community College; Robert Spear, Prince George's Community College; Behrooz Saghafi, Chicago State University; Home Ghajar, Oklahoma State University; Ruth Schmitz, University of Nebraska at Kearney; Gloria Melara, California State University at Northridge.

For Previous Editions, Reviewers include:

6th Edition:

Wendell Dillard, Arkansas State University; Ken Giffin, University of Central Arkansas; Doug K. Lauffer, Community College of Beaver County; Dori McPherson, Schoolcraft College; Tom Gorecki, Charles County Community College; Dan Everett, University of Georgia; Carol Mull, Asheville-Buncombe Technical Community College; Marian Schwartz, North Central Technical College; Cindy Hanchey, Oklahoma Baptist University; Dr. Emmanuel Opara, Prairie View A&M University; Rajiv Malkan, Montgomery College; Focus Group for *Computers,* 6th ed.; Jeanann Boyce, University of Maryland; Nancy Cosgrove, University of Central Florida; Barbara Ellestad, Montana State University; Shirley Fedorovich, Embry-Riddle Aeronautical University; Wayne Headrick, New Mexico State University; Suzanne Konieczny, Marshall University; Gary Mattison, Strayer College; Rick Parker, College of Southern Idaho; Judy Scholl, Austin Community College.

5th Edition:

Amir Afzal, Strayer College; Gary R. Armstrong, Shippensburg University; Shira L. Broschat, Washington State University; James Frost, Idaho State University; Jorge Gaytan, University of Texas, El Paso; Helene Kershner, SUNY, Buffalo; Ruth Malmstrom, Raritan Valley Community College; Michael A. McNeece, Strayer College; John F. Sharlow, Eastern Connecticut State University; John Stocksen, Kansas City Kansas Community College.

4th Edition:

Suzanne Baker, Lakeland Community College; Amanda Bounds, Florida Community College at Jacksonville; Don Cartlidge, New Mexico State University (emeritus); Stephanie Chenault, The College of Charleston; Eli Cohen, Wichita State University; William Cornette, Southwest Missouri State University; Timothy Gottlebeir, North Lake College; Vernon Griffin, Austin Community College; Sandra Brown, Finger Lakes Community College; Mike Michaelson, Palomar College; Domingo Molina, Texas Southmost College; Joseph Morrell, Metropolitan State College of Denver; Patricia Nettnin, Finger Lakes Community College; Anthony Nowakowski, State University of New York College at Buffalo; Michael Padbury, Arapahoe Community College; Carl Ubelacker, Cincinnati State Technical and Community College.

3rd Edition:

Ray Fanselau, American River College; Fred Homeyer, Angelo State University; Robert Keim, Arizona State University; Carl Clavadetscher, California Polytechnic State University, Pomona; Barry Floyd, California Polytechnic State University, San Luis Obispo; Dr. Diane Visor, University of Central Oklahoma; Dr. Diane Fischer, Dowling College; Dr. Adolph Katz, Fairfield University; Constance Knapp, Pace University; Dr. John Sanford, Philadelphia College of Textiles and Science; Peter Irwin, Richland College; Al Schroeder, Richland College; Amir Afzal, Strayer College; James Johnson, Valencia Community College.

2nd Edition:

Michael J. Belgard, Bryant and Stratton College; Roy Bunch, Chemeketa Community College; Marvin Daugherty, Indiana Vocational Technical College; Joyce Derocher, Bay de Noc Community College; Kirk L. Gibson, City College of San Francisco; Randy Goldberg, Marist College; Don Hall, Manatee Community College; Seth Hock, Columbus State Community College; Dr. M. B. Kahn, California State University at Long Beach; Michael A. Kelly, City College of San Francisco; Constance K. Knapp, CSP, Pace University; Sandra Lehmann, Moraine Park Technical College; William McTammany, Florida Community College at Jacksonville; Margaret J. Moore, Coastal Carolina Community College; Thomas H. Miller, University of Idaho; Anne L. Olsen, Wingate College; Verale Phillips, Cincinnati Technical College; Mark Seagroves, Wingate College; Bari Siddique, Texas Southmost College; Dr. Joseph Williams, University of Texas at Austin; Larry B. Wintermeyer, Chemeketa Community College; Floyd Jay Winters, Manatee Community College.

1st Edition:

Sally Anthony, San Diego State University; Harvey Blessing, Essex Community College; Wayne Bowen, Black Hawk Community College; Michael Brown, DeVry Institute of Technology, Chicago; J. Patrick Fenton, West Valley College; Ken Griffin, University of Central Arkansas; Nancy Harrington, Trident Technical College; Grace C. Hertlein, California State University; Shirley Hill, California State University; Cynthia Kachik, Santa Fe Community College; Sandra Lehmann, Morraine Park Technical Institute; Michael Lichtenstein, DeVry Institute of Technology, Chicago; Dennis Martin, Kennebec Valley Vocational Technical Institute; William McDaniel, Jr., Northern Virginia Community College at Alexandria; Edward Nock, DeVry Institute of Technology, Columbus; Lewis Noe, Ivy Technical Institute; Frank O'Brien, Milwaukee Technical College; Alvin Ollenburger, University of Minnesota; Beverly Oswalt, University of Central Arkansas; James Phillips, Lexington Community College; Nancy Roberts, Lesley College; Richardson Siebert, Morton College; Bob Spear, Prince George's Community College; Thomas Voight, Franklin University.

Finally, we wish to thank the professionals from over one hundred companies who have contributed resources (information, photos, software, and images) to this book and its supplements.

Larry Long, Ph.D. **Nancy Long, Ph.D.**

About the Authors

Dr. Larry Long and **Dr. Nancy Long** have written more than 30 books, which have been used in hundreds of colleges throughout the world. Larry is a lecturer, author, consultant, and educator in the information technology fields. He has served as a consultant to all levels of management in virtually every major type of industry. He has over 25 years of classroom experience at IBM, the University of Oklahoma, Lehigh University, and the University of Arkansas. Nancy has teaching and administrative experience at all levels of education.

Information Technology Concepts

1 Information Technology in Perspective
Focus on IT The History of Computing

2 Using the PC: Popular Productivity Software

3 Inside the Computer
Focus on IT The Computer on a Chip

4 Storing and Retrieving Information

5 Information Input and Output

6 Networks and Networking

7 Going Online

8 The Windows Environment
Focus on IT PC Buyer's Guide

Information Technology in Perspective

Learning Objectives

1.1 Become aware of the scope of computer understanding needed by someone living in an information society.

1.2 Describe the implications of computer networks on organizations and on society.

1.3 Grasp essential hardware, software, and computer system terminology.

1.4 Demonstrate awareness of the relative size, scope, uses, and variety of available computer systems.

1.5 Describe the fundamental components and the operational capabilities of a computer system.

1.6 Identify and describe uses of the computer.

chapter 1

Value Learning

WHY THIS CHAPTER IS IMPORTANT TO YOU

Welcome! To the computer revolution, that is. We'll be using this "Value Learning" space to make this book very personal—to show you why studying computers and information technology is important you, now and in the future. We're all members of a rapidly maturing information society. In this dynamic new society, people at home and in schools, institutions, and businesses are engaged in an ever-growing partnership with computers and information technology, called *IT*. Whether we like it or not, for good or bad, computers and technology are part of just about everything we do, during both work and play. And the fact is, computers will play an even greater role in our lives next month and in years to come.

In the 1960s, mainstreamers considered people who had anything to do with computers, especially the techies who actually touched them, to be different, even a little weird. Through the 1970s, computer illiterate people led happy and productive lives, not knowing the difference between a system bug and a byte. Well, those days are gone.

Today we're all part of an exploding information society—you, us, and the rest of the world. Computer-knowledgeable people are considered mainstream, even cool in some circles. The rest are on the outside looking in. By reading this book and taking this course, you're telling your family, friends, and, perhaps, your colleagues at work that you want to participate—to be an insider.

It's amazing how achieving information technology competency can help you keep in touch, help you learn, help make many of life's little chores easier and more fun, help you earn more money, and that's the tip of the iceberg. Upon successful completion of this course, you will be information technology competent. In most fields, this competency is considered critical to *getting* and *keeping* a good job. Your adventure into this amazing world of technology begins right here. Have fun!

1.1 THE INFORMATION SOCIETY

Monthly Technology Update Chapter 1

Where will you be and what will you be doing in the year 2010? This is a tough question even for technology experts who are reluctant to speculate more than a few months into the future. Things are changing too quickly. A continuous stream of exciting new innovations in **information technology (IT)** continues to change what we do and how we think. We use the term *IT* to refer to the integration of computing technology and information processing.

Most of us are doing what we can to adapt to this new **information society** where **knowledge workers** channel their energies to provide a cornucopia of computer-based information services. A knowledge worker's job function revolves around the use, manipulation, and dissemination of information. Your knowledge of computers will help you cope with and understand today's technology so you can take your place in the information society, both at the workplace and during your leisure time.

R_x for Cyberphobia: Information Technology Competency

Not too long ago, people who pursued careers in almost any facet of business, education, or government were content to leave computers to computer professionals. Today these people are knowledge workers. In less than a generation, **information technology competency (IT competency)** has emerged in virtually any career from a *nice-to-have skill* to a *job-critical skill.*

If you're afraid of computers, information technology competency is a sure cure. IT competency will allow you to be an active and effective participant in the emerging information society. You and other IT-competent people will:

- *Feel comfortable using and operating a computer system.*
- *Be able to make the computer work for you.* The IT-competent person can use the computer to solve an endless stream of life's problems, from how to pass away a couple of idle hours to how to increase company revenues.
- *Be able to interact with the computer—that is, generate input to the computer and interpret output from it.* **Input** is data entered to a computer system for processing. **Output** is the presentation of the results of processing (for example, a printed résumé or a tax return).

Jurassic Technology Computers and information technology enliven our information society in many ways. Technology makes it possible for us to go back in time and experience the Jurassic period. At Universal Studios Hollywood theme park, the Jurassic Park River Adventure ride is completely automated. It was designed with the help of paleontologists, robotics engineers, and many other "knowledge workers." The ride includes "animatronic" dinosaurs that roar, lunge, and even spit at riders in passing boats.
Photo courtesy of Intel Corporation: Photo by Dana Fineman-Appel, Hollywood, California.

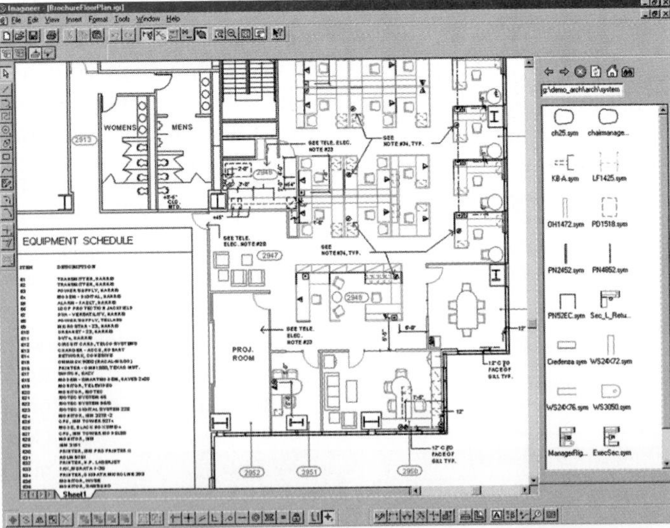

Technology in Our Jobs Twenty years ago, college curricula in architecture included little or no study in the area of computers. Today, architects rely on information technology for everything from design to cost analysis. Architects used computers to prepare this drawing and a visual perspective for a proposed renovation project. The computer has dramatically changed the way architects do their jobs. The same is true for hundreds of other professions.
Courtesy of Intergraph Corporation

- *Be comfortable in cyberspace.* Cyberspace is a nonphysical world made possible by a worldwide network of computer systems. Once in cyberspace, you can communicate with one another and literally travel the virtual world, visiting Walt Disney World in Florida, the Louvre Museum in Paris, and a million other interesting places.
- *Understand the impact of computers on society, now and in the future.* Automation is having such a profound impact on society that we must position ourselves to act responsibly to ensure that these changes are in the right direction.
- *Be an intelligent consumer of computers and computer equipment, collectively called* **hardware.** Smart computer shoppers usually get what they need, not what they think they need. And, they can save a lot of money.
- *Be an intelligent consumer of software and other nonhardware-related computer products and services.* **Software** refers to a collective set of instructions, called **programs,** that can be interpreted by a computer. The programs cause the computer to perform desired functions, such as flight simulation (a computer game), the generation of business graphics, or word processing.
- *Be conversant in the language of computers and information technology.* In this book, you will learn those terms and phrases that not only are the foundation of computer terminology but also are very much a part of everyday conversation at school, home, and work.

The Technology Revolution

In an information society, the focus of commerce becomes the generation and distribution of information. A technological revolution is changing our way of life: the way we live, work, and play. The cornerstone of this revolution, the *computer,* is transforming the way we communicate, do business, and learn.

Personal computers, or **PCs,** offer a vast array of *enabling technologies.* Enabling technologies help us do things. For example, PCs have maps that pinpoint your location to help you navigate the streets of the world. They have presentation tools that help you make your point when you get there. Already, you need go no farther than your home computer to get the best deal on a new car, send your congressperson a message, order tickets to the theater, play chess with a grand master in Russia, or listen to a radio station in New Zealand.

- Millions of people can be "at work" wherever they are as long as they have their portable personal computers—at a client's office, in an airplane, or at home. The *mobile worker*'s personal computer provides electronic links to a vast array of information and to clients and corporate colleagues.
- Increasingly, the computer is the vehicle by which we communicate, whether with our colleagues at work through **electronic mail (e-mail)** or with our friends through **newsgroups.** Both electronic mail and newsgroups allow us to send/receive information via computer-to-computer hookups.
- Comic strips routinely rely on cybertalk for laughs, especially Dilbert, which is set in a corporate cubicle city. In one Dilbert strip (written by Scott Adams), the clueless pointy-haired boss commented, "I don't see why our Web pages need URLs. Get rid of them." Engineer Dilbert responds with "Give me a month and I'll replace our URLs with Uniform Resource Locators." The IT-savvy reader, knowing that URLs and Uniform Resource Locators are one in the same, will laugh. Others won't get it or hundreds of other comic strip punch lines.

Exploring Internet Possibilities The Mediadome℠ web site <www.mediadome.com> introduced visitors to Dilbert and Dogbert in a completely different dimension. Mediadome, which shows people what is possible on Internet-linked PCs, has the first ever Internet-based, interactive, walking, talking 3-D Dilbert and Dogbert. Dilbert, the United Feature Syndicate comic strip, first became popular in the world of personal computing in January 1995 when creator Scott Adams published his personal e-mail address in his comic strip. Three months later, Dilbert became the first nationally syndicated comic strip to appear on America Online and the Internet.
Photo courtesy of Intel Corporation

That's today. *Tomorrow,* the next wave of enabling technologies will continue to cause radical changes in our lives. For example, if you're in the market for a new home, you will be able to "visit" any home for sale in the country from the comfort of your own home or office via computer. All you will need to do is tell the computer what city to look in and then enter your search criteria (price range, house style, and so on). The electronic realtor will then list those houses that meet your criteria, provide you with detailed information on the house and surrounding area, then offer to take you on a tour of the house—inside and out. After the virtual tour, you will be able to "drive" through the neighborhood, looking left and right as you would in your automobile. Such systems may seem a bit futuristic, but virtually all of California's real estate listings can be viewed on your computer. Systems that permit neighborhood drive-throughs are under active development!

Each day new applications, such as a national multilist for real estate, as well as thousands of companies, schools, and individuals, are being added to the world's information infrastructure. The infrastructure, sometimes called the **information superhighway,** encompasses a network of electronic links that eventually will connect virtually every facet of our society, both public (perhaps the local supermarket) and private (perhaps to Aunt Minnie's daily schedule).

Looking Back a Few Years

To put the emerging information society into perspective, let's flash back a half century and look *briefly* at the evolution of computing.

- Fifty years ago, our parents and grandparents built ships, kept financial records, and performed surgery, all without the aid of computers. Indeed, everything they did was without computers. There were no computers!

A World without Computers The industrial society evolved in a world without computers. The advent of computers and automation has changed and will continue to change the way we do our jobs. In the automobile industry, those assembly-line workers who used to perform repetitive and hazardous jobs now program and maintain industrial robots to do these jobs.
GM Assembly Division, Warren, Michigan
Courtesy of Ford Motor Company

- In the 1960s, mammoth multimillion-dollar computers processed data for those large companies that could afford them. These computers, the domain of highly specialized technical gurus, remained behind locked doors. In "the old days," business computer systems were designed so a computer professional served as an intermediary between the **user**—someone who uses a computer—and the computer system.
- In the mid-1970s, computers became smaller, less expensive, and more accessible to smaller companies and even individuals. This trend resulted in the introduction of personal computers. During the 1980s, millions of people from all walks of life purchased these miniature miracles. Suddenly, computers were for everyone!
- Today, one in two Americans has a computer at home or work more powerful than those that processed data for multinational companies during the 1960s. The widespread availability of computers has prompted an explosion of applications. At the individual level, we can use our PCs to go on an electronic fantasy adventure or hold an electronic reunion with our scattered family. At the corporate level, virtually every business has embraced information technology. Companies in every area of business are using IT to offer better services and gain a competitive advantage.

Data: Foundation for Our Information Society

Data (the plural of *datum*) are just raw facts. Data are all around us. Every day we generate an enormous amount of data. **Information** is data that have been collected and processed into a meaningful form. Simply, information is the meaning we give to accumulated facts (data). Information as we now know it, though, is a relatively new concept. Just 50 short years ago, *information* was the telephone operator who provided directory assistance. Around 1950, people began to view information as something that could be collected, sorted, summarized, exchanged, and processed. But only during the last decade have computers allowed us to begin tapping the potential of information.

Computers are very good at digesting data and producing information. For example, when you call a mail-order merchandiser, the data you give the sales representative (name, address, product number) are entered directly into the merchandiser's computer. When you run short of cash and stop at an automatic teller machine, all data you enter, including that on the magnetic stripe of your bankcard, are processed immediately by the bank's computer system. A computer system eventually manipulates your *data* to produce *information*. The information could be an invoice from a mail-order house or a bank statement.

IT Ethics

THE SPAM DILEMMA

As we all know, Spam is a popular Hormel meat product. By some unlucky quirk of fate unsolicited e-mail was given the same name—spam. To Netizens, citizens of the Internet, spam is the Internet equivalent of junk mail and those dreaded telemarketing calls. To the senders of junk e-mail, spam is simply bulk e-mail, usually some kind of advertisement and/or an invitation to try some service or product. Spam may be unsolicited religious, racial, or sexual messages, as well. Such messages can be especially irritating. Generally, Internet users loathe spamming because spammers (those who send spam) use the shotgun approach, broadcasting their message to large numbers of people. Inevitably, enough of these messages find a welcome audience, prompting spammers to send more spam.

Those who receive e-mail consider their e-mail boxes a personal and costly resource. They feel that spam wastes their time, violates their electronic mailbox, and in some cases insults their integrity. On the other hand, spammers cite free speech and the tradition of a free flow of information over the Internet as justification for broadcasting their messages. Spam renews the conflict between free speech and the individual's right to privacy.

Discussion: Currently laws favor the spammers, that is, there is little an individual can do to thwart the barrage of junk mail. Do you believe legislation should be enacted to control unsolicited e-mail over the Internet? Explain.

Traditionally, we have thought of data in terms of numbers (account balance) and letters (customer name), but recent advances in information technology have opened the door to data in other formats, such as visual images. For example, dermatologists (physicians who specialize in skin disorders) use digital cameras to take close-up pictures of patients' skin conditions. Each patient's **record** (information about the patient) on the computer-based **master file** (all patient records) is then updated to include the digital image. During each visit, the dermatologist recalls the patient record, which includes color images of the skin during previous visits. Data can also be found in the form of sound. For example, data collected during noise-level testing of automobiles include digitized versions of the actual sounds heard within the car.

The relationship of data to a computer system is much like the relationship of gasoline to an automobile. Data provide the fuel for a computer system. Your car won't get you anywhere without gas, and your computer won't produce any information without data.

This Course: Your Ticket to the Computer Adventure

You are about to embark on a journey that will stimulate your imagination, challenge your every resource, from physical dexterity to intellect, and alter your sense of perspective on technology. Learning about computers is more than just education. It's an adventure!

Gaining information technology competency is just the beginning—your computer adventure lasts a lifetime. Information technology is changing every minute of the day. Every year, hundreds of new IT-related buzz words, concepts, applications, and hardware devices will confront you. Fortunately, you will have established a base of IT knowledge (information technology competency) upon which you can build and continue your learning adventure.

Self-Check

SECTION SELF-CHECK

1-1.1 To be IT-competent, you must be able to write computer programs. (T/F)

1-1.2 Data are the raw facts from which information is derived. (T/F)

1-1.3 Hardware refers collectively to computers and computer equipment. (T/F)

1-1.4 The term used to describe the integration of computing technology and information processing is: (a) information technology, (b) information handling, (c) software, or (d) data tech.

1-1.5 A person whose job revolves around the use, manipulation, and dissemination of information is called: (a) an office wunderkind, (b) a knowledge worker, (c) a data expert, or (d) an info being.

1-1.6 Generally, what is the presentation of the results of processing called: (a) output, (b) printout, (c) outcome, or (d) download?

Global Village

1.2 NETWORKING: BRINGING PEOPLE TOGETHER

So far we know that computers are extremely good at bringing together data to produce information. Computers also bring together people, from all over the world, resulting in improved communication and cooperation.

The Global Village

In 1967 Marshall McLuhan said, "The new electronic interdependence recreates the world in the image of a global village." His insightful declaration is now clearly a matter of fact. At present, we live in a *global village* in which computers and people are linked within companies and between countries (see Figure 1.1). The global village is an outgrowth of the **computer network.** Most existing computers are linked electronically to a network of one or more computers to share resources and information. When we tap into networked computers, we can hold

The Global Village Computer-based communication is turning the world into a global village. We can communicate electronically with people on the other side of the world as easily as we might have a conversation with a neighbor.

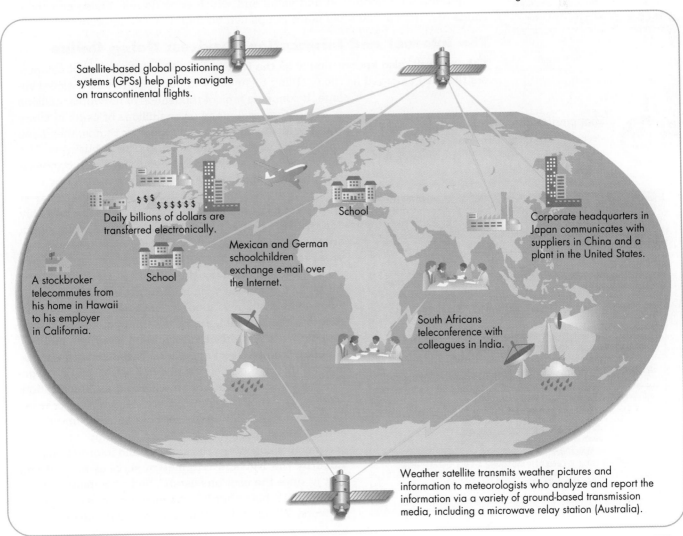

Satellite-based global positioning systems (GPSs) help pilots navigate on transcontinental flights.

$ $ $ $ $ $ $ $ $

Daily billions of dollars are transferred electronically.

School

Corporate headquarters in Japan communicates with suppliers in China and a plant in the United States.

Mexican and German schoolchildren exchange e-mail over the Internet.

A stockbroker telecommutes from his home in Hawaii to his employer in California.

School

South Africans teleconference with colleagues in India.

Weather satellite transmits weather pictures and information to meteorologists who analyze and report the information via a variety of ground-based transmission media, including a microwave relay station (Australia).

electronic meetings with widely dispersed colleagues, retrieve information from the corporate database, make hotel reservations, and much, much more.

On a more global scale, computer networks enable worldwide airline reservation data to be entered in the Bahamas and American insurance claims to be processed in Ireland. Securities can be traded simultaneously on the New York Stock Exchange and other exchanges around the world by people in Hong Kong, Los Angeles, and Berlin. Computer networks can coordinate the purchases of Korean electronics, American steel, and Indonesian glass to make cars in Japan, and can then be used to track sales of those cars worldwide. Lotteries are no longer confined to a state, or even the nation. Internet-based lotteries draw players from the entire world, paying huge pots to the winners.

Thanks to computer networks, we are all part of a global economy, in which businesses find partners, customers, suppliers, and competitors around the world. The advent of this global economy is changing society across the board, often in subtle ways. For example, customer service may continue to improve as companies realize how quickly an irate customer can broadcast messages vilifying a company or a particular product to millions of potential customers via the information superhighway. Computers, related hardware, and software products are especially vulnerable to such customer attacks. If a product does not stand up to advertised capabilities, the computing community will quickly expose its shortcomings to potential buyers. This same level of scrutiny will ultimately be applied to other products and services. For example, there are hundreds of newsgroups devoted exclusively to discussions of restaurants in various cities and countries. In these cities and countries, you can be sure that frequent diners know which restaurants offer good food and value and which ones do not. These and thousands of other special-topic newsgroups can be found on the Internet.

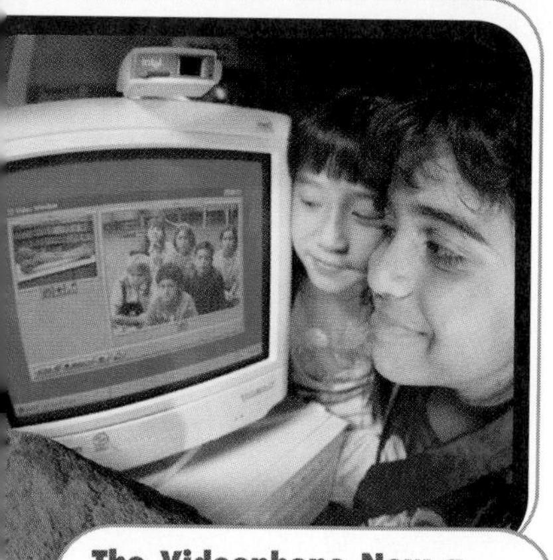

The Videophone Now a Reality These schoolchildren in India are videoconferencing with children in the United States. This type of videophone link lets you check out a blind date, attend a virtual family reunion, speak with your business associate in another city, or say good night to your kids "in person" while away on a business trip. To make videophone calls, you need videophone software, an analog or digital camera, a PC, an Internet access, and a link to a standard telephone line. Photo courtesy of Intel Corporation

The Internet and Information Services: Going Online

The Internet, also known simply as **the Net,** is a worldwide network of computers that has emerged as *the* enabling technology in our migration to a global village. It connects tens of thousands of networks, millions of computers, and many more millions of users in every country. Most colleges are on the Net; that is, they have an Internet account. The same is true of business. The Internet can be accessed by people in these organizations with established links to the Internet and by individuals with PCs. If you have access to a computer at work or at a college computer lab, the PCs are probably "on the Net" (see Figure 1.2). Typically, individuals gain access to the Internet by subscribing to an **Internet service provider (ISP).** For a monthly fee, you can link your PC to the ISP's computer, thus gaining access to the Net. An ISP is a company with an Internet account that provides individuals and organizations access to, or presence on, the Internet. As an alternative, you can subscribe to a commercial **information service,** such as **America Online** (see Figure 1.3). These and other commercial information services have one or several large computer systems that offer a wide range of information services over their proprietary network, which, of course, is linked to the Net. **AOL** services include up-to-the-minute news and weather, electronic shopping, e-mail, and much, much more. The services and information provided by the Net and information services are **online;** that is, once the user has established a communications link between his or her PC, the user becomes part of the network. When online, the user interacts directly with

Shopping on the Internet You can shop the electronic malls of the information superhighway to get bargains on everything from pasta makers to homes.

America Online Channels
America Online has many channels, or interest areas (upper left corner), from which to choose, plus a variety of other services. Shown here are the main choice screens for the *Sports* and the *People Connection* channels, plus the current weather and a buddy list that alerts you when one of your buddies logs on so you can chat.

the computers in the information network to obtain desired services. When the user terminates the link, the user goes **offline.**

The Internet emerged from a government-sponsored project to promote the interchange of scientific information. This spirit of sharing continues as the overriding theme over the Internet. For example, aspiring writers having difficulty getting read or published can make their writing available to thousands of readers, including agents and publishers, in a matter of minutes. Unknown musicians also use the Internet to gain recognition. *Surfers* on the Internet (Internet users) desiring to read a story or listen to a song, **download** the text or a digitized version of a song (like those on an audio CD) to their personal computer, then read it or play it through their personal computer. Downloading is simply transmitting information from a remote computer (in this case, an Internet-based computer) to a local computer (in most cases a PC). Information (perhaps a story or a song) going the other way, from a local computer to a remote computer, is said to be **uploaded.**

This spirit of sharing has prompted individuals and organizations all over the world to make available information and databases on a wide variety of topics. This wonderful distribution and information-sharing vehicle is, of course, a boon for businesses. Thousands of publishers, corporations, government agencies, colleges, and database services give Internet users access to their information—some provide information gratis and some charge a fee. Over the next few years look for more and more businesses to use the Internet to generate revenue.

Services and capabilities of the Internet and commercial information services are growing daily. For example, a hungry traveler on the Internet can now order a pizza via the Net from a large number of online pizza delivery services. It works pretty much like a telephone order, except you enter the information on your PC, and it is routed immediately to the pizza shop nearest you. Usually, the order is displayed for the pizza chef within seconds. Of course, you can't download a pizza—it has to be delivered in the traditional manner. Already you can order almost any consumer item from tulips to trucks through the electronic malls (see Figure 1.2).

Services available from the publicly available Internet and the subscription-based information services play a major role in shaping our information society. We'll discuss both in considerable detail throughout the book.

SECTION SELF-CHECK

Self-Check

1-2.1 Uploading on the Internet is transmitting information from an Internet-based host computer to a local PC. (T/F)

1-2.2 A global network called the Internet links millions of computers throughout the world. (T/F)

1-2.3 Mail sent electronically is called: (a) snail mail, (b) quick mail, (c) e-mail, or (d) e-news.

1-2.4 A computer network links computers to enable the: (a) linking of terminals and HDTV hookups, (b) sharing of resources and information, (c) distribution of excess processor capabilities, or (d) expansion of processing capabilities.

1-2.5 When the user terminates the link with a commercial information service, the user goes: (a) offline, (b) on-log, (c) out-of-site, or (d) online.

1.3 COMPUTERS: THE ESSENTIALS

Almost everyone in our information society has a basic understanding of what a computer is and what it can do. This book is designed to add a little depth to what you already know.

Conversational Computerese: Basic Terms and Definitions

The **computer,** also called a **processor,** is *an electronic device that can interpret and execute programmed commands for input, output, computation, and logic operations.* That's a mouthful. But computers aren't as complicated as you might have been led to believe. A **computer system** has only four basic components: *input, processor, output,* and *storage* (see Figure 1.4). Note that the processor, or computer, is just one component in a computer system. It gives the computer system its intelligence, performing all computation and logic operations. In everyday conversation people simply say "computer" when they talk about a computer system. We'll do this as well throughout this book. We'll refer specifically to the processor when discussing that part of the computer system that does the processing.

Each of the components in a computer system can take on a variety of forms. For example, *output* (the results of processing) can be routed to a televisionlike **monitor,** audio speakers (like those on your stereo system), or a **printer** (see Figure 1.4). The output on a monitor, which is temporary, is called **soft copy.** Printers produce **hard copy,** or printed output which can be physically handled, folded, and so on. Data can be entered to a computer system for processing (input) via a **keyboard** (for keyed input), a microphone (for voice and sound input), or a **point-and-draw device,** such as a **mouse** (see Figure 1.4).

Storage of data and software in a computer system is either *temporary* or *permanent.* **Random-access memory (RAM,** rhymes with *ham*) provides temporary storage of data and programs during processing within solid-state **integrated circuits.** Integrated circuits, or **chips,** are tiny (about .5 inch square) silicon chips into which thousands of electronic components are etched. The processor is also a chip. Permanently installed and interchangeable **disks** provide permanent storage for data and programs (see Figure 1.4). Information is read from and written to a variety of disks. Because the surface of circular, spinning disks is coated with easily magnetized elements, such as nickel, they sometimes are called *magnetic disks.* A computer system is comprised of its internal components (for example, RAM and special features) and its **peripheral devices** (printer, various disk-storage devices, monitor, and so on).

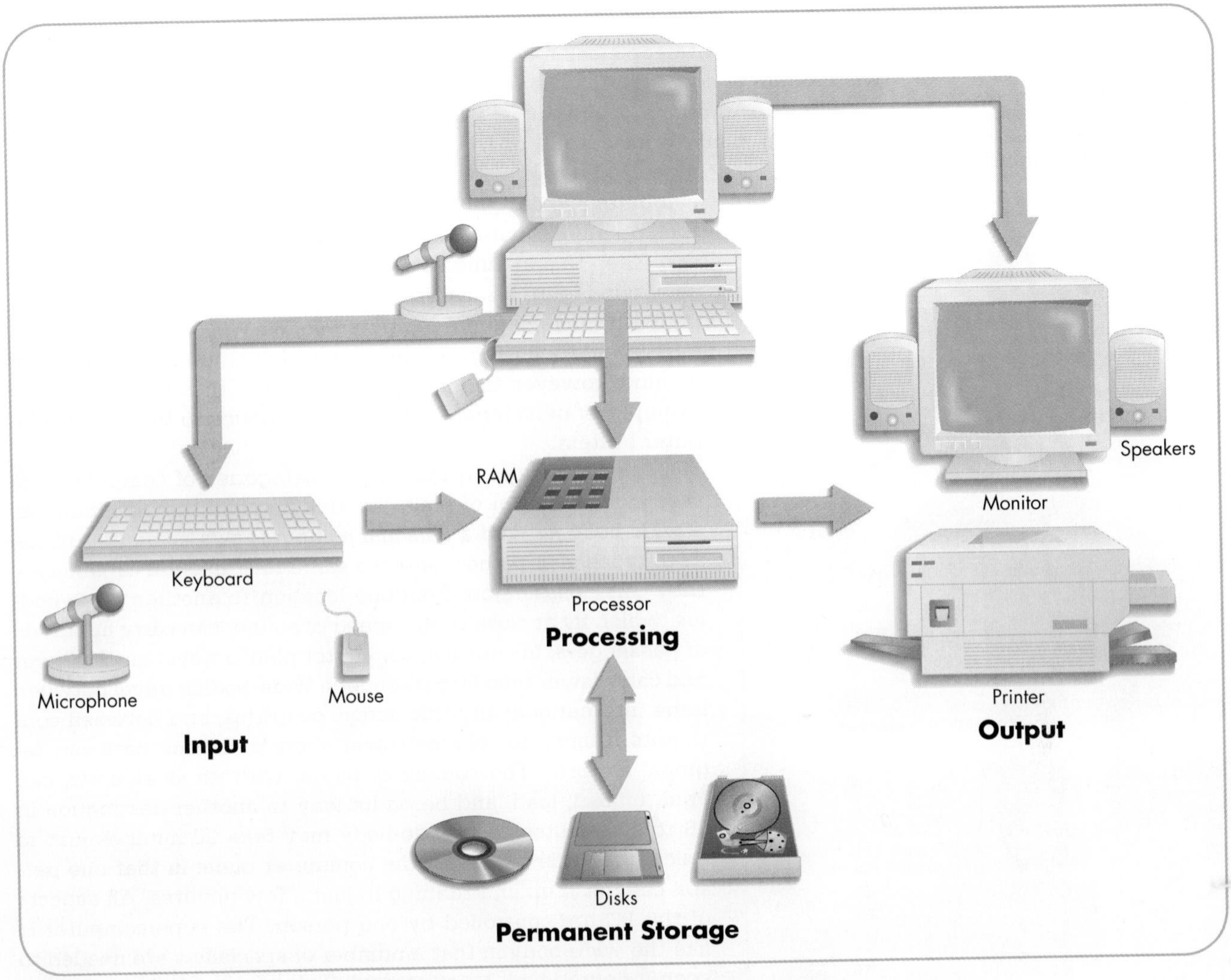

The Four Fundamental Components of a Personal Computer System In a personal computer system, the storage and processing components are often contained in the same physical unit. In the illustration, the disk-storage medium is inserted into the unit that contains the processor.

Computer Systems: Commuters to Wide-Bodies

Computers can be found in a variety of shapes, from cube-shaped to U-shaped to cylindrical to notebook-shaped. However, the most distinguishing characteristic of any computer system is its *size*—not its physical size, but its *computing capacity.* Loosely speaking, size, or computing capacity, is the amount of processing that can be accomplished by a computer system per unit of time. **Mainframe computers** have greater computing capacities than do personal computers, which are also called **microcomputers.** Mainframe computers vary greatly in size from midsized mainframes serving small companies to large mainframes serving thousands of people. And **supercomputers,** packing the most power, have greater computing capacities than do mainframe computers. Depending on its sophistication, a **workstation**'s computing capacity falls somewhere between that of a PC and a midsized mainframe. Some vendors are not content with pigeonholing their products into one of these four major categories, so they have created new niches, such as *desktop mainframes.* In this book, we will limit our discussion to these

Categories of Computers

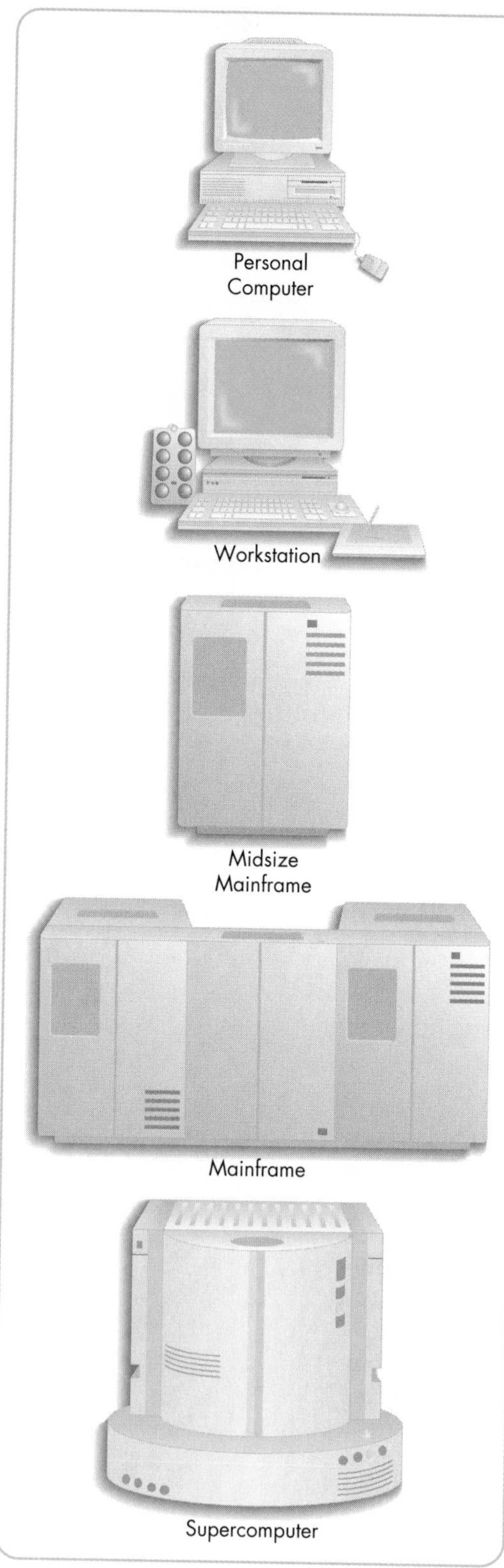

four major categories (see Figure 1.5). We should emphasize that these categories are relative. What people call a personal computer system today may be called a workstation at some time in the future.

PCs, workstations, mainframes, and supercomputers are computer systems. Each offers many **input/output,** or **I/O,** alternatives—ways to enter data to the system and to present information generated by the system. All computer systems, no matter how small or large, have the same fundamental capabilities—*input, processing, output,* and *storage.* Keep this in mind as you encounter the computer systems shown in Figure 1.5 in this book, at school, and at work. In keeping with conversational computerese, we will drop the word *system* when discussing the categories of computer systems. Keep in mind, however, that a reference to any of these categories (for example, supercomputer) implies a reference to the entire computer system.

The differences in the various categories of computers are very much a matter of scale. Try thinking of a *supercomputer* as a *wide-body jet,* and a *personal computer* as a *commuter plane.* Both types of airplanes have the same fundamental capability—they carry passengers from one location to another. Wide-bodies, which fly at close to the speed of sound, can carry hundreds of passengers. In contrast, commuter planes travel much slower and carry fewer than 50 passengers. Wide-bodies travel between large international airports, across countries, and between continents. Commuter planes travel short distances between regional airports. The commuter plane, with its small crew, can land, unload, load, and be on its way to another destination in 15 to 20 minutes. The wide-body may take 30 minutes just to unload. A PC is much like the commuter plane in that one person can get it up and running in just a few minutes. All aspects of the PC are controlled by one person. The supercomputer is like the wide-body in that a number of specialists are needed to keep it operational. No matter what their size, airplanes fly and carry passengers and computers process data and produce information. Besides obvious differences in size, the various types of computers differ mostly in how they are used. The following section should give you insight into when and where a particular system might be used.

The House of Software

Software refers to any program that tells the computer system what to do. Of course, there are many different types of software. The more you understand about the scope and variety of available software, the more effective you will be as a user. Actually, understanding software is a lot like being in a big house—once you know its layout, you're able to move about the house much easier.

Once but a cottage, the house of software is now a spacious eight-room house (in a few years, it will be a mansion). Figure 1.6 shows the blueprint for today's house of software, with the rooms arranged by function. The entryway in the house of software consists of **system software.** When you turn on the computer, the first actions you see are directed by system software. It takes control of the PC on start up, and then plays a central role in all interactions with the computer. The

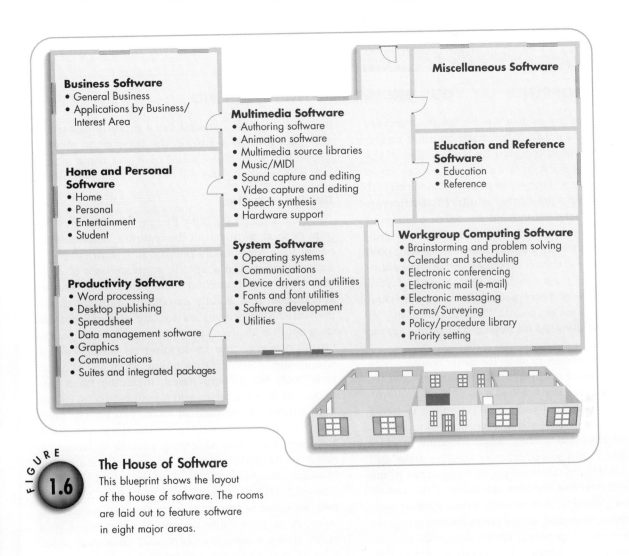

Business Software
- General Business
- Applications by Business/Interest Area

Home and Personal Software
- Home
- Personal
- Entertainment
- Student

Productivity Software
- Word processing
- Desktop publishing
- Spreadsheet
- Data management software
- Graphics
- Communications
- Suites and integrated packages

Multimedia Software
- Authoring software
- Animation software
- Multimedia source libraries
- Music/MIDI
- Sound capture and editing
- Video capture and editing
- Speech synthesis
- Hardware support

System Software
- Operating systems
- Communications
- Device drivers and utilities
- Fonts and font utilities
- Software development
- Utilities

Miscellaneous Software

Education and Reference Software
- Education
- Reference

Workgroup Computing Software
- Brainstorming and problem solving
- Calendar and scheduling
- Electronic conferencing
- Electronic mail (e-mail)
- Electronic messaging
- Forms/Surveying
- Policy/procedure library
- Priority setting

FIGURE 1.6

The House of Software
This blueprint shows the layout of the house of software. The rooms are laid out to feature software in eight major areas.

software from the other rooms, collectively known as **applications software,** is designed and created to perform specific personal, business, or scientific processing tasks, such as word processing, tax planning, or interactive gaming. We'll visit every room in the house by the time you finish this book.

SECTION SELF-CHECK

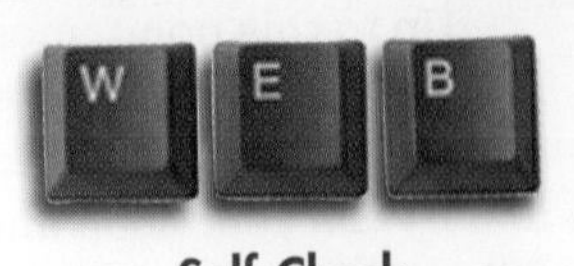

Self-Check

1-3.1 Output on a monitor is soft copy and output on a printer is hard copy. (T/F)

1-3.2 Supercomputers have greater computing capacity than mainframe computers. (T/F)

1-3.3 Only personal computers offer a variety of I/O alternatives. (T/F)

1-3.4 Applications software takes control of a PC on start up and then controls all system software activities during the computing session. (T/F)

1-3.5 A printer is an example of which of the four computer system components: (a) input, (b) output, (c) processor, or (d) storage?

1-3.6 Integrated circuits are also called: (a) slivers, (b) chips, (c) flakes, or (d) electronic sandwiches?

1-3.7 Which component of a computer system executes the program: (a) input, (b) output, (c) processor, or (d) storage?

ONLINE SHOPPING: LET YOUR FINGERS DO THE WALKING

How would you like to do a week's worth of grocery shopping in 10 minutes? Purchase gourmet chocolates without being tempted by the goodies in the candy counter? Book your airline and motel reservations without making a dozen calls? Check out job openings in your area of the country? Send flowers (virtual and real)? Trade stocks online? Do your banking transactions from home? Rather than loading the kids into the SUV or minivan on shopping day, you can send them out to play and do your shopping and other business from the comfort of your home. Millions of busy people have traded their shopping carts for keyboards. They log on to the Internet, a new channel for buying and selling goods and services.

People go online to shop for many reasons. The reason cited most often is that the stores are always open. People love the convenience of shopping anytime—day or night. People also go online to avoid traffic, crowds, lines, and the never-ending search for a parking place. Other reasons include product availability and the opportunity to save time and money. Currently, the most popular consumer items purchased over the Internet are books, CDs, and all computer products. Action on Internet auction sites also is brisk. However, online shoppers can purchase toys, electronics, greeting cards, automobiles, groceries, securities, houses, just about anything that Wal-Mart stocks, and a lot more.

Popularity of Online Retailing Is Growing Fast

In a few years, according to projections, commerce in cyberspace will be just as important as in-person, mail, and telephone sales. If businesses are not planning for this real-time economy, they may not be doing business to the fullest (if at all) in the twenty-first century.

Up to this point, most Internet commerce is done from business-to-business. Forecasters predict U.S. online business-to-business sales to be over $100 billion by the year 2000 and triple that in the two years following. Online retailing (business-to-consumer) is less than half that size, but it's exploding in popularity. A variety of sources report online shopping is escalating at rates from 400 percent a year to 400 percent a month. And, the rate of growth is expected to accelerate next year. Any business that hopes to stay in business in the next millennium is offering or planning to offer its products and/or services online. If there is a demand for a product or service, there is probably a site on the Internet to meet it. These few examples should give you some insight into what we have and can expect in the near future.

Groceries Online

"Smart Shopping for Busy People"® is Peapod's slogan. Peapod, a grocer on the Internet, has made life easier for a great many people. Although Peapod is not yet national in scope, it is giving us a glimpse into the future of retailing—the *virtual store.* Peapod is a pioneer in a rapidly expanding industry that is dedicated to enabling us to buy almost anything from our PCs. Peapod subscribers go shopping at the virtual grocery store by logging on to the Peapod site on the Internet. Once online, they can shop interactively for grocery items, including fresh produce, deli, bakery, meat, and frozen products. Rather than running from aisle to aisle, you simply point and click around the screen for the items you want.

Peapod's online shopping system is linked directly to its partner stores' computer systems (for example, Safeway in San Francisco and Jewel in Chicago). When you send your shopping list to Peapod, an order is transmitted to the nearest partner store. A professionally trained shopper takes your order, grabs a shopping cart, and does your shopping for you. The professional shopper takes a fraction of the time you would take because the list is ordered by aisle and the shopper knows exactly what to get. You can redeem your coupons when the shopper/delivery person arrives with your food. Food is delivered in temperature-controlled containers. Peapod is far from alone as others, including Wal-Mart, have begun to offer online grocery services. This is one of many interactive online approaches to shopping that can help take the hassle out of shopping.

Books and CDs Online

If you've traveled in the World Wide Web at all, you've probably run across Amazon.com, one of the most well-known online stores. Intrigued by the amazing growth in use of the Internet, Jeff Bezos founded Amazon.com, Inc. in 1994 and it opened its virtual doors in 1995. The mission was to use the Internet to offer products that educate, inform, and inspire. The company wanted to build an online store that would be customer-friendly and easy to navigate and would offer the broadest possible selection.

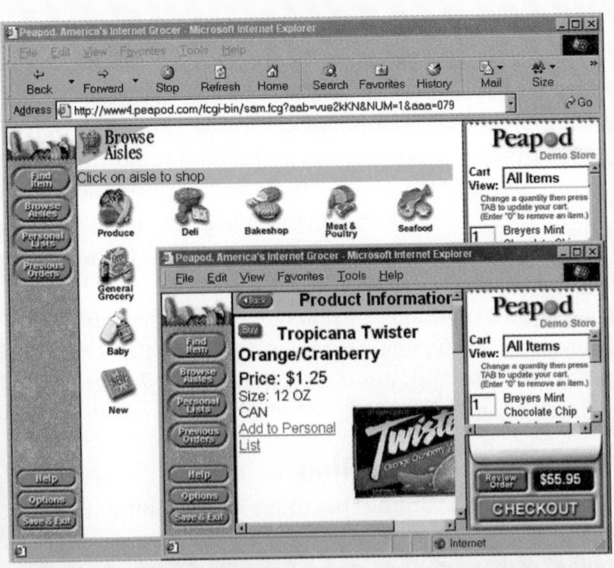

Virtual Grocery Store

Grocery shoppers now have another option—going online. The Peapod system lets subscribers point and click their way around a virtual supermarket. Now, shopping online means never having to leave your home.

Amazon.com is more than just a bookstore. Today it offers 3 million books, CDs, audiobooks, DVDs, computer games, and more, including customer reviews, personal recommendations, best-seller lists, musical chart toppers, and gift suggestions. From alternative to Zydeco, Hip-hop to Bebop, Amazon.com's customers will find everything from the latest releases to hard-to-find gems in nearly 300 musical genres. You can even be an Amazon.com Associate and earn money by selling books from your own Web site.

Stocks and Bonds Online

Why would you want to make online investments electronically through an online brokerage service instead of through a full-service broker? Those who do cite price and the ability to make their own trading decisions as the main reasons they go online. To date, online companies have been very competitive on price, a serious motivator to savvy investors. Generally an online trading charge is much less than that of a traditional broker (from under $10 to $30, sometimes less than 10% that of a similar trade through a traditional broker). Frequent users of online brokerage services enjoy the autonomy of having the information resources they need to do their own research.

Currently only about 4 percent of U.S. households are involved in online finance. This includes

securities trading and online banking. However, online trading companies are experiencing tremendous growth in trading volume as more and more investors switch to online trading.

Online trading companies, such as E-Trade Group Inc., Charles Schwab & Co. Inc., and Datek

(continues on next page)

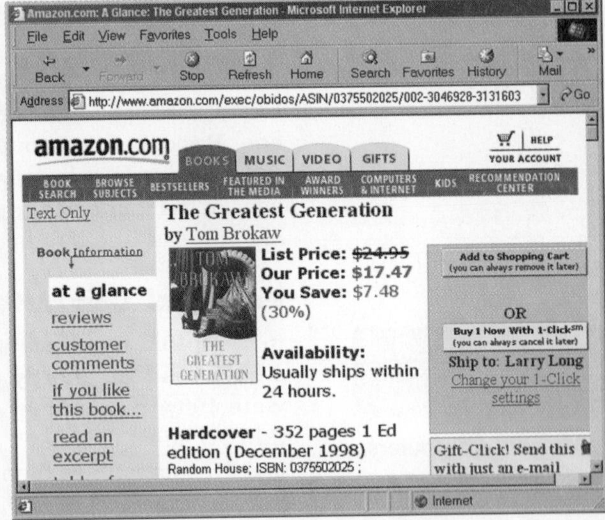

Amazon.com

In a few short years, Amazon.com, selling exclusively on the Net, became a serious competitor to industry giant Barnes and Noble. In only a few years, Amazon.com reached $1 billion in sales, becoming one of e-commerce's (electronic commerce) early success stories.

Emerging IT *continued*

Online Brokerage Services Corporation, are providing online discount brokerage services, including automated order placement, portfolio tracking and related market information, news, and other information services 24 hours a day, 7 days a week. Online services offer essentially the same order options as their full-service cousins, including limit, stop, and stop limit orders for all securities trading on U.S. exchanges. And, the services usually are free. The investor pays only a relatively small fee to place the order.

Online Auctions: Going. Going. Gone!

You can be part of a live auction 24 hours a day when you visit the eBay or ONSALE sites. Just enter "online auctions" into an Internet search engine and you'll be amazed at what can be traded, bought, and sold.

Every day ONSALE opens a new set of auctions where you will find thousands of items on which to bid. You set the price on the merchandise. ONSALE offers such goods and services as computers, peripherals, consumer electronics, sporting goods, gourmet foods, and vacation packages.

eBay boasts itself as the world's largest personal online trading community with more than 1 million registered users. Individuals can use eBay to buy and sell items in more than 1000 categories, including collectibles, antiques, sports memorabilia, computers, toys, Beanie Babies, dolls, figures, coins, stamps, books, magazines, music, pottery, glass, photography, electronics, jewelry, gemstones, and much more. Users can find the unique and the interesting on eBay—everything from china to chintz chairs, teddy bears to trains, and furniture to figurines.

Even Universal Studios has online auctions of exclusive celebrity memorabilia and collectibles direct from popular movies, television shows, and entertainment in Hollywood.

The Future of Retailing

The future of online retailing and selling is very bright, but what about traditional approaches to sales? What will become of our department stores, specialty stores, bookstores, and so on? It is unlikely that any of these would disappear anytime soon; however, it's apparent that people are shopping and buying more at the virtual store and less at the bricks and mortar store. Each approach has its advantages. It looks like we'll still have the option to shop downtown or online for the foreseeable future.

1.4 PERSONAL COMPUTERS TO SUPERCOMPUTERS

Every 10 hours, more computers are sold than existed in the entire world 30 years ago. Back then, computers came in one size—big and expensive. Today, computers come in a variety of sizes. In this section we discuss the capabilities and uses of the four basic categories of computers: personal computers, workstations, mainframes, and supercomputers.

Personal Computers

Personal Computers

In 1981, IBM introduced its **IBM PC** and it legitimized the personal computer as a business tool. Shortly after that, other manufacturers began making PCs that were 100% compatible with the IBM PC; that is, they basically worked like an IBM PC. Most of today's personal computers (over 80%) evolved from these original PC-compatibles. Long removed from the IBM PC, they are also called **Wintel PCs** because they use the Microsoft *Windows 9x/NT/2000* (a collective reference to Microsoft *Windows 95®*, *Windows 98®*, *Windows NT®*, or *Windows® 2000*) control software and an Intel Corporation or Intel-compatible processor. Each of the Microsoft Windows 9x/NT/2000 family of **operating systems** controls all hardware and software activities on Wintel PCs.

The Wintel PC represents the dominant PC platform. A **platform** defines a standard for which software is developed. Specifically, a platform is defined by two key elements:

- The processor (for example, Intel® Pentium® II, Intel® Pentium III®, Intel® Celeron™, Motorola® PowerPC®, and so on)
- The operating system (for example, Windows® 2000, Mac® OS X, Unix®, and so on)

Generally, software created to run on one platform is not compatible with any other platform. Most of the remaining personal computers are part of the Apple *Macintosh®* line of computers or the Apple *iMac™* line of computers. The Macintosh uses the *Mac® OS* operating system and new iMac uses Apple's next-generation operating system, the *Mac® OS X*. Both are powered by Motorola® *PowerPC®* processors.

One person at a time uses a PC. The user turns on the PC, selects the software to be run, enters the data, and requests the information. The PC, like other computers, is very versatile and has been used for everything from communicating with business colleagues to controlling household appliances. Computerese is like spoken English in that more than one term can be coined to describe something. For example, the terms *personal computer, PC, microcomputer,* and *micro* are used interchangeably in practice. The personal computer is actually a family of computers, some conventional and some unconventional.

Categories of Computer Systems

- Personal computers (PCs)
- Workstations
- Mainframe computer systems
  —Enterprise-wide systems
  —Input/output-bound applications
- Supercomputer systems
  —Engineering and scientific computing
  —Processor-bound applications

Conventional PCs: Pockets, Laptops, Desktops, and Towers

Conventional personal computers have a full keyboard, a monitor, and can function as stand-alone systems. These PCs can be categorized as *pocket PCs, laptop PCs, desktop PCs,* and *tower PCs* (see Figure 1.7).

Pocket and Laptop PCs **Pocket PCs** and **laptop PCs** are light (a few ounces to about eight pounds), compact, and are called "portable" because they have batteries and can operate with or without an external power source. The pocket PC, sometimes called a **palmtop PC,** literally can fit in a coat pocket or a handbag. Laptops, which weigh from three to eight pounds, often are called **notebook PCs** because they are about the size of a one-inch-thick notebook.

The power of a PC may not be related to its size. A few laptop PCs can run circles around some tower PCs. Some user conveniences, however, must be sacrificed to achieve portability. For instance, input devices, such as keyboards and point-and-draw devices, are given less space in portable PCs and may be more cumbersome to use. This is particularly true of pocket PCs, in which miniaturized keyboards make data entry and interaction with the computer difficult and slow. The display screen on some pocket PCs is monochrome (as opposed to color) and may be difficult to read under certain lighting situations. Portable computers take up less space and, therefore, have a smaller capacity for permanent storage of data and programs. Laptop battery life can be as little as a couple of hours for older models to 20 hours for state-of-the-art rechargeable lithium batteries.

Computer Fundamentals

The 2-in-1 PC can be used as both a notebook and a desktop PC. It has two parts: a fully functional *notebook PC* and a **docking station.** Two-in-one PCs have a configuration that allows users to enjoy the best of both worlds—portability and the expanded features of a desktop. The notebook, which supplies the processor, is simply inserted into or removed from the docking station, depending on the needs of the user. The docking station can be *configured* to give the docked notebook PC the look and feel of a desktop PC. That is, the docking station can expand the notebook's capabilities and might include more disk storage, a CD-ROM drive, several interchangeable disk options, a full-size keyboard, a large monitor, and expansion slots into which still other features can be added to the system (for example, circuitry that would enable television programming to be viewed on the PC's monitor). Usually, docking stations provide a direct link to the corporate network.

Another notebook option, called the **port replicator,** works like the docking station in that the notebook PC is inserted into it and removed as needed. Once inserted the notebook can use the port replicator **ports** and whatever is connected

FIGURE 1.7

Conventional PCs

The iMac Desktop The iMac™ brings back Apple Computer's all-in-one concept and then some. Under the hood, the iMac sports an impressive list of features, including a powerful processor, plenty of memory, stereo sound, and network and Internet capabilities. In its first year (1998), the iMac emerged as the best-selling PC. It comes in blueberry (shown here), strawberry, tangerine, grape, and lime.
Courtesy of Apple Computer, Inc.

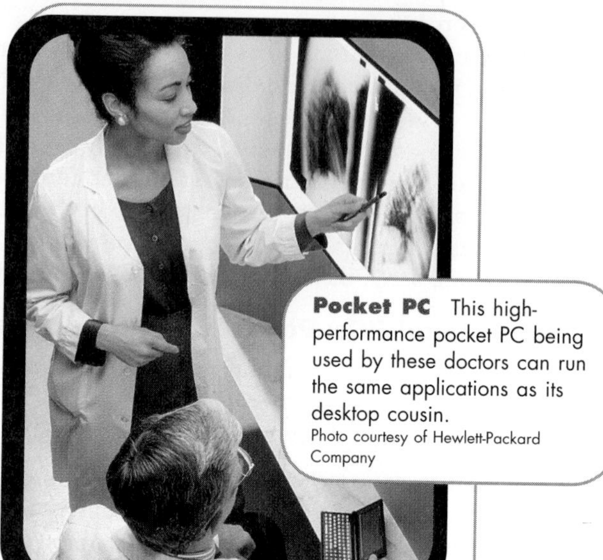

Pocket PC This high-performance pocket PC being used by these doctors can run the same applications as its desktop cousin.
Photo courtesy of Hewlett-Packard Company

Traditional Desktop PC Although most new PCs are either tower or laptop, millions of people still use desktop PCs, like this classic Compaq Presario.
Reprinted with permission of Compaq Computer Corporation. All Rights Reserved.

Tower PC This IBM Aptiva tower PC can sit under, beside, or on top of a desk.
Courtesy of International Business Machines Corporation

Laptop PC When searching for a personal computer, this executive identified portability and flexibility as her primary criteria, so she chose a laptop PC. Laptop users can now ask for SuperDisk drives (shown here) to be built into new notebooks for convenient, interchangeable, and high-capacity storage (over 100 characters of data on a SuperDisk the size of a traditional floppy disk).
Photo courtesy of Imation Corporation

to them. Ports are electronic interfaces through which devices like the keyboard, monitor, mouse, printer, and so on are connected. Port replicators also provide bigger speakers and an AC power source, and some include a network connector.

Desktop PCs and Tower PCs **Desktop PCs** and **tower PCs** are not considered portable because they rely on an outside power source and are not designed for frequent movement. Typically, the desktop PC's monitor is positioned on top of the processing component. The processing component of the tower PC is designed to sit upright, like a desktop PC's processing component standing on its end. The taller towers (over two feet) are usually placed beside or under a desk, and the smaller mini-tower may be placed in any convenient location (on a nearby shelf, on the desk, or on the floor).

Of the two, the tower has emerged as the most popular, primarily because it has a smaller *footprint* (the surface space used by the unit). The laptop, which cost about twice that of a comparable tower PC, is gaining ground. About one in three PCs sold are laptops.

The Extended PC Family: Slate PCs, PDAs, and NCs

The conventional members of the PC family have several unconventional cousins (see Figure 1.8). These personal computers may be designed for special applications or for use in a particular computing environment.

Slate Computers Mobile workers in increasing numbers are using portable **slate PCs.** Slate PCs, sometimes called **pen-based PCs,** use electronic pens in conjunction with a combination monitor/drawing pad instead of keyboards. Users select options, enter data, and draw with the pen. United Parcel Service (UPS) couriers use slate PCs when they ask you to sign for packages on a pressure-sensitive display screen with an electronic stylus.

Slate computers are poised to make an entry into the world of many mobile professionals. Handwritten text is interpreted by handwriting-recognition software, then entered into the system. **Speech-recognition** software, which allows the user to enter spoken words into the system, is being integrated into high-end slate PCs. Insurance agents and claims adjusters who need to work at accident or disaster scenes have found slate computers more suitable to their input needs, which may include both text and drawings.

Personal Digital Assistants **Personal digital assistants (PDAs),** or **handheld PCs,** may take on many forms and are called by many names, from *connected organizers* to *personal communicators* to *mobile business centers* to *Web phones.* PDAs are smaller than slate PCs, usually weighing less than half a pound. They can include a built-in cellular phone that enables the wireless sending/receiving of faxes and access to the Internet (including e-mail). Their built-in wireless communications capabilities give their users immediate access to the Internet, colleagues and clients, and needed information, virtually anytime, anywhere. PDA interaction can be via the pen (like a slate PC) or by touching the keys on an on-screen keyboard or a reduced-key keyboard.

Generally, PDAs support a variety of **personal information management** systems. A **PIM** might include appointment scheduling and calendar, e-mail, fax, phone-number administration, to-do lists, tickler files, "Post-it" notes, diaries, and so on. Some PDAs can support a variety of PC-type applications, such as spreadsheets and personal financial management. Also, PDAs are designed to be easily connected to other computers and printers for data transfer, network access, and printing. Coca-Cola and Pepsi-Cola distributors equip their salespeople with PDAs, which enable them to manage their territories better.

Network Computers In contrast to the conventional PC, the **network computer,** or **NC,** is designed to function only when it is linked to a server computer (normally an organization's internal network of computers). The NC looks similar to a PC but with several major configuration differences. First, it has a relatively

FIGURE 1.8

Extended PC Family

Palm III Connected Organizer This executive's address list is just one of many applications on his Palm III organizer. This device can store some 4000 addresses, 4 years of appointments (approximately 2400), 750 to-do items, 750 memos, and 100 e-mail messages. The executive can use a stylus or a PC keyboard to enter data. Also, it's easy to exchange information with a desktop or laptop PC.
3Com and the 3Com logo are registered trademarks. Palm III™ and the Palm III™ logo are trademarks of Palm Computing, Inc., 3Com Corporation, or its subsidiaries.

Wearable PC This maintenance worker uses a hands-free, paperless computer system while making repairs. Rockwell's Trekker™ system is worn on a belt or shoulder strap and includes a display worn on the head like a headset. The Trekker is a wearable, voice-controlled personal computer that frees technicians and others from bulky manuals. This man simply navigates to needed information by voice interface, then glances at the display. Rockwell is developing systems that will allow interactive questioning and problem solving.
Courtesy of Rockwell International Corporation

Futuristic Concept PCs Intel Corporation is working with PC manufacturers to build better, simpler, and more effective personal computers. Shown here are several Intel Concept PCs that showcase the possibilities and benefits of drastically redesigned, legacy-free, easily upgradable personal computers. These prototype PCs are not meant for production but are intended to spark alternative visions for future PCs.
Photo courtesy of Intel Corporation: Photos for Intel by Court Mast, Mast Photography, San Francisco

Apple Newton Messagepad This student is using the handwriting-recognition capability of the Apple Newton® Messagepad® to jot down a few notes between classes. Courtesy of Apple Computer, Inc.

Network Computer During the last half of the 1990s, industry observers have predicted that network computers, such as this HDS @workStation Network Computer, might replace PCs in the workplace. NCs eliminate the hassle associated with configuring and maintaining software on PCs. NC software is retrieved from a central network computer as it is needed.
Courtesy of HDS Network Systems, Inc.

small processor and considerably less RAM than modern personal computers. Second, it does not have a permanently installed disk. And, of course, it is less expensive than a stand-alone PC.

The NC depends on a central network server computer to do much of the processing and for permanent storage of data and information. Here is the way an NC works: The network computer user has access to a wide range of applications; however, the software applications and data are downloaded as they are needed to the NC from a network's central computer. Whether or not to buy into the NC concept is one of the major debates in the information technology community. Exchanging PCs for NCs will eliminate the expensive and time-consuming task of installing and maintaining PC-based software, but it will make all NCs dependent on the server computer. If the server goes down, all NCs depending on it go down.

Configuring a PC: Putting the Pieces Together

PC users often select, configure, and install their own system. The configuration of a PC or what you put into and attach to your computer can vary enormously. Common configuration options are shown in Figure 1.9.

Nowadays, the typical off-the-shelf PC is configured to run multimedia applications. **Multimedia applications** integrate text, sound, graphics, motion video, and/or animation. Computer-based encyclopedias, such as Microsoft® *Encarta*®, and games, such as Broderbund's Carmen Sandiego™ series, provide a good example of multimedia applications. *Encarta* can take you back to July 20, 1969, and let you see motion video of the Apollo 11 lunar module *Eagle* landing on the moon at the Sea of Tranquility. If you wish, you can listen to Commander Neil Armstrong proclaim, "That's one small step for [a] man, one giant leap for mankind" as he steps on the moon. Of course, the electronic encyclopedia contains supporting text that explains that he intended to say "a man." The typical multimedia-configured PC (see Figure 1.4) includes the following components.

1. A microcomputer (the processor and other electronic components)
2. A keyboard for input
3. A point-and-draw device for input (usually a mouse)
4. A monitor for *soft-copy* (temporary) output
5. A printer for *hard-copy* (printed) output
6. A permanently installed high-capacity **hard-disk drive** for permanent storage of data and programs
7. A **floppy disk drive** into which an interchangeable **diskette,** or **floppy disk,** is inserted
8. A **CD-ROM drive** into which an interchangeable **CD-ROM,** which looks like an audio CD, is inserted
9. A microphone (audio input)
10. A set of speakers (audio output)

Virtually all PCs give users the flexibility to configure the system with a variety of peripheral devices (input/output and storage). A PC system is configured by linking any of a wide variety of peripheral devices to the processor component. Figure 1.9 shows the more common peripheral devices that can be configured with a PC. Many other peripherals can be linked to a PC, including video cameras, telephones, image scanners (to enter images to the system), other computers, security devices, and even a device that will enable you to watch your favorite television show on the PC's monitor.

Types of Personal Computers

- Conventional PCs
  - —Pocket PC or palmtop PC
  - —Laptop PC or notebook PC
  - —Desktop PC
  - —Tower PC
  - —2-in-1 PC (notebook with docking station)
- Extended PC family
  - —Slate or pen-based PC
  - —Personal digital assistant (PDA)
  - —Network computer (NC)

Workstations: The Hot Rods of Computing

What looks like a PC but isn't? It's a *workstation* and it's very fast. Speed is one of the characteristics that distinguishes workstations from PCs. In fact, some people talk of workstations as "souped-up" PCs. The PC was fine for word processing, spreadsheets, and games, but for real "power users"—engineers doing

Workstations

The Personal Computer and Common Peripheral Devices
A wide range of peripheral devices can be connected to a PC. Those shown here and others are discussed in detail in later chapters.

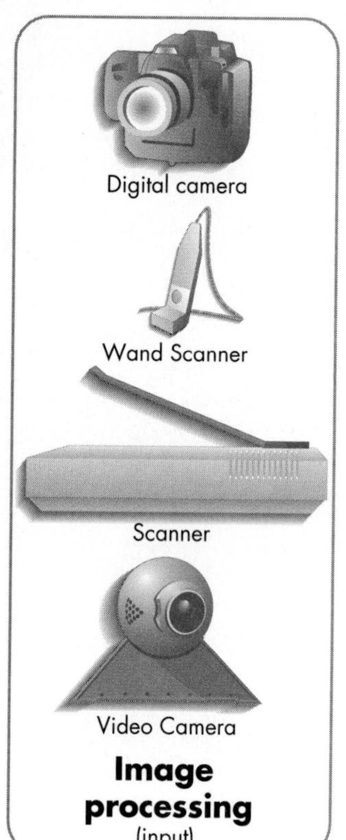

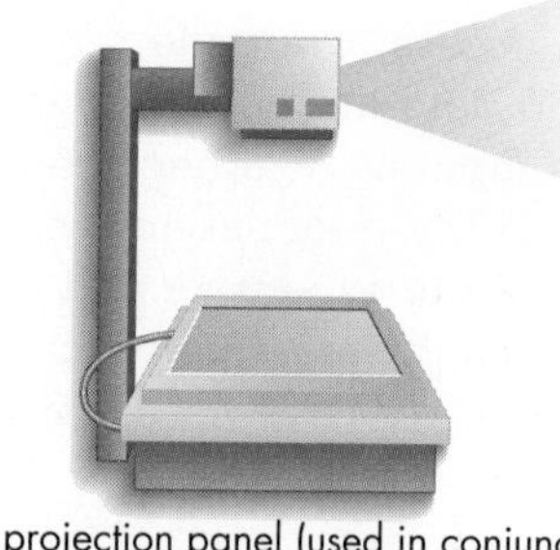

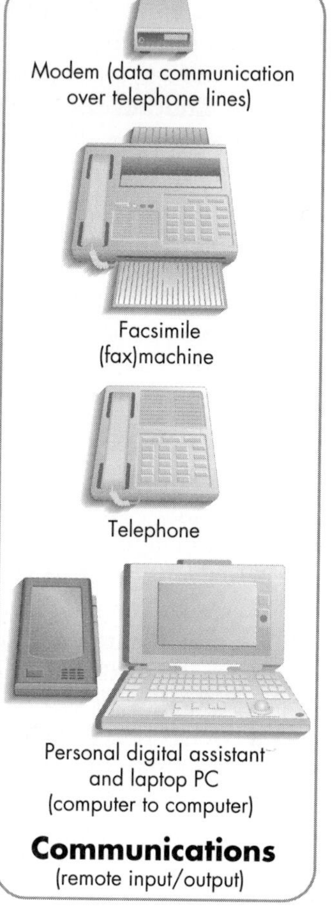

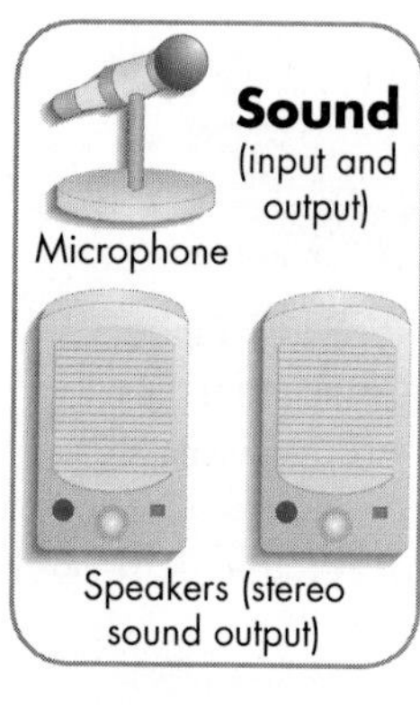

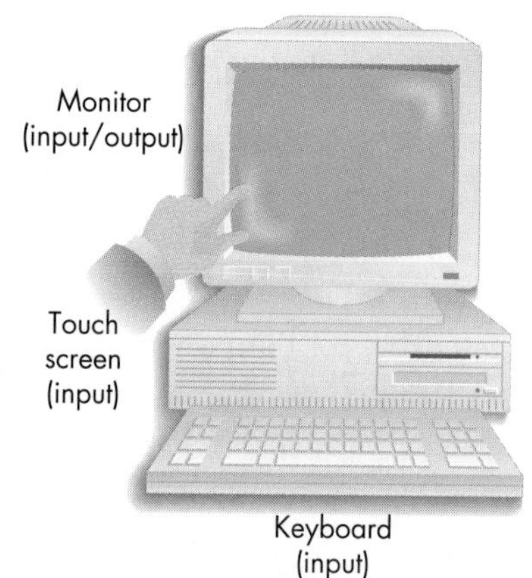

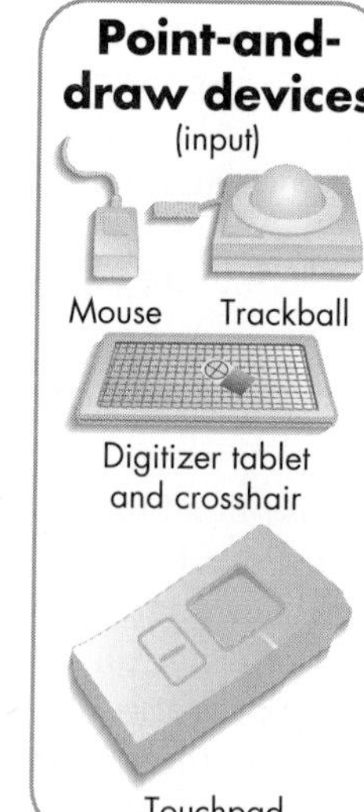

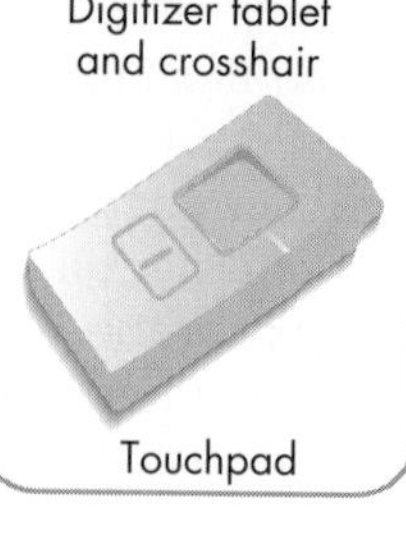

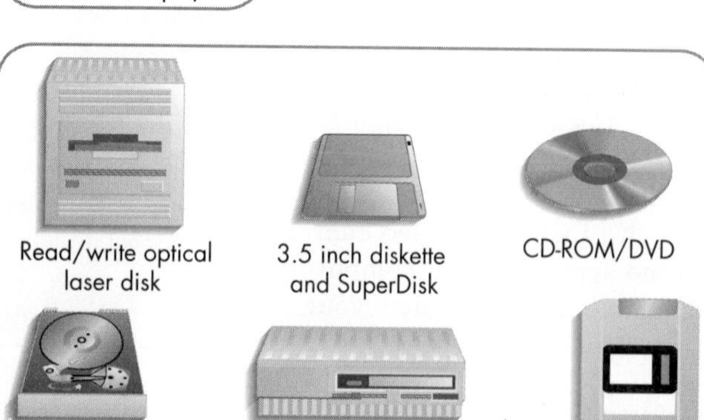

Video Production Workstation Intergraph's StudioZ™ GT workstation is designed for use by video production professionals who create content such as commercials, television programs, TV station promos, and corporate videos. Courtesy of Intergraph Corporation

computer-aided design, or **CAD** (using the computer in the design process), scientists and researchers who do a lot of "number crunching," graphics designers, multimedia content developers, and so on—the PC sometimes falls short.

The workstation's input/output devices also set it apart from a PC. A typical workstation will sport a large-screen color monitor capable of displaying high-resolution graphics. **Resolution** refers to the clarity of the image on the monitor's display. For pointing and drawing, the workstation user can call on a variety of specialized point-and-draw devices that combine the precision of a gun sight with the convenience of a mouse. Add-on keypads can expand the number of specialized function keys available to the user.

The capabilities of today's high-end PCs are very similar to those of low-end workstations. In a few years, the average PC will have workstation capabilities. Eventually the distinctions between the two will disappear, and we will be left with a computer category that is a cross between a PC and a workstation. Time will tell whether we call it a PC, a workstation, or something else.

Mainframe Computers: Corporate Workhorses

Mainframe Computers

Mainframe computers, with their expanded processing capabilities, provide a computing resource that can be shared by many people. Mainframes are usually associated with **enterprise-wide systems**—that is, computer-based systems that service departments, plants, warehouses, and other entities throughout an organization. For example, human resources management, accounting, and inventory management tasks may be enterprise-wide systems handled by mainframe-based networks. Typically, users communicate with one or more centralized mainframes, called **host computers,** through a PC or a **terminal.** A terminal has a keyboard for input and a monitor for output. Terminals are standard equipment at airline ticket counters. Depending on the size of the organization, a dozen people or 10,000 people can share system resources (for example, information and software) by interacting with their PCs, terminals, workstations, NCs, PDAs, and other communications devices.

Until the late 1960s, all computers were mainframe computers, and they were expensive—too expensive for all but the larger companies. Large companies shelled out $1.5 million and more for mainframe computers with less power than today's $1000 PCs. In the late 1960s, computer vendors introduced smaller, slightly "watered down" computers that were more affordable for smaller companies. The industry dubbed these small computers **minicomputers.** The term was used until recently, when the distinction between minis and mainframes began to blur. Today the term is seldom used. Smaller mainframes are called midsized computers.

Mainframe computers are *designed specifically* for the multiuser environment, in contrast to PCs and workstations, which frequently are used as stand-alone computers. Mainframes are oriented to **input/output-bound applications;** that is, the amount of work that can be performed by the computer system is limited primarily by the speeds of the I/O and storage devices. Administrative data processing jobs, such as generating monthly statements for checking accounts at a bank, require relatively little calculation and a great deal of input and output. In I/O-bound applications, the computer's processor is often waiting for data to be entered or for an output device to complete its current task.

It is unlikely that you would find two mainframe computers configured in exactly the same way. For example, a large municipal government generates a tremendous amount of *external output* (output that is directed to persons not affiliated with city government, such as utility bills and tax notices) and would require several high-speed page printers. In contrast, a software development company might enter and process all data from terminals with relatively little hard-copy output.

Supercomputers: Processing Giants

Supercomputers

During the early 1970s, administrative data processing dominated computer applications. Bankers, college administrators, and advertising executives were amazed by the blinding speed at which million-dollar mainframes processed their data. Engineers and scientists were grateful for this tremendous technological achievement, but they were far from satisfied. When business executives talked about unlimited capability, engineers and scientists knew they would have to wait for future enhancements before they could use computers to address truly complex problems. Automotive engineers were still not able to create three-dimensional prototypes of automobiles inside a computer. Physicists could not explore the activities of an atom during a nuclear explosion. A typical scientific job involves the manipulation of a complex mathematical model, often requiring trillions of operations to resolve. During the early 1970s, some complex scientific processing jobs would tie up large mainframe computers at major universities for days at a time. This, of course, was unacceptable. The engineering and scientific communities had a desperate need for more powerful computers. In response to that need, computer designers began work on what are now known as supercomputers.

Supercomputer The CRAY T90™ supercomputer is one of the most powerful general-purpose computers. General-purpose computers are capable of handling a wide range of applications.
Courtesy of E-Systems, Inc.

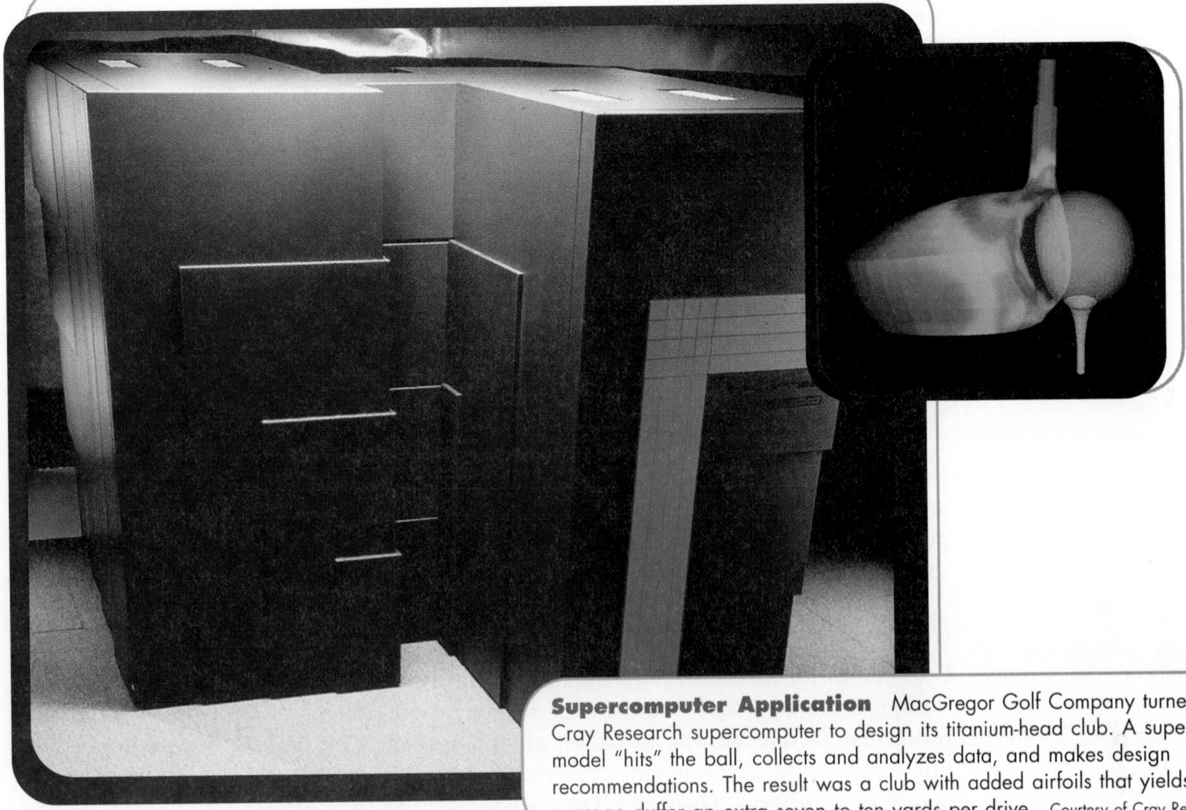

Supercomputer Application MacGregor Golf Company turned to a Cray Research supercomputer to design its titanium-head club. A supercomputer model "hits" the ball, collects and analyzes data, and makes design recommendations. The result was a club with added airfoils that yields the average duffer an extra seven to ten yards per drive. Courtesy of Cray Research, Inc.

Supercomputers primarily address **processor-bound applications,** which require little in the way of input or output. In processor-bound applications, the amount of work that can be done by the computer system is limited primarily by the speed of the computer. Such applications involve highly complex or vastly numerous calculations, all of which require processor, not I/O, work.

Supercomputers are known as much for their applications as they are for their speed or computing capacity, which may be 100 times that of a large mainframe computer. These are representative supercomputer applications:

- Supercomputers enable the simulation of airflow around an airplane at different speeds and altitudes.
- Auto manufacturers use supercomputers to simulate auto accidents on video screens. (It is less expensive, more revealing, and safer than crashing the real thing.)
- Meteorologists employ supercomputers to study how oceans and the atmosphere interact to produce weather phenomena such as El Niño.
- Hollywood production studios use supercomputers to create the advanced graphics used to create special effects for movies such as *Star Wars: Episode I–The Phantom* and for TV commercials.
- Supercomputers sort through and analyze mountains of seismic data gathered during oil-seeking explorations.
- Medical researchers use supercomputers to simulate the delivery of babies.

All of these applications are impractical, if not impossible, on mainframes.

Self-Check

SECTION SELF-CHECK

1-4.1 The power of a PC is directly proportional to its physical size. (T/F)

1-4.2 The four size categories of conventional personal computers are miniature, portable, notebook, and business. (T/F)

1-4.3 Workstation capabilities are similar to those of a low-end PC. (T/F)

1-4.4 Mainframes are usually associated with enterprise-wide systems. (T/F)

1-4.5 What has I/O capabilities and is designed to be linked remotely to a host computer: (a) terminal, (b) printer, (c) port, or (d) mouse?

1-4.6 Supercomputers are oriented to what type of applications: (a) I/O-bound, (b) processor-bound, (c) inventory management, or (d) word processing?

1-4.7 A 2-in-1 PC is in two parts, a fully functional notebook PC and a: (a) slate, (b) port hole, (c) runway, or (d) docking station.

1-4.8 What is the name given those applications that combine text, sound, graphics, motion video, and/or animation: (a) videoscapes, (b) motionware, (c) multimedia, or (d) anigraphics?

1.5 A COMPUTER SYSTEM AT WORK

Now that we know a little about the basic types of computer systems, let's examine what a computer can and cannot do. To get a better idea of how a computer system actually works, let's look at how it might do the processing of a payroll system.

Processing Payroll: Payday

One computer-based system makes us happy each and every payday. It's called a *payroll system.* Just about every organization that has employees and a computer maintains a computer-based payroll system. The payroll system enables input and processing of pertinent payroll-related data to produce payroll checks and a variety of reports. The payroll system walkthrough in Figure 1.10 illustrates how data are entered into a network of personal computer systems and how the four system components (input, processing, output, and storage) interact to produce payroll checks and information (in our example, a year-to-date overtime report).

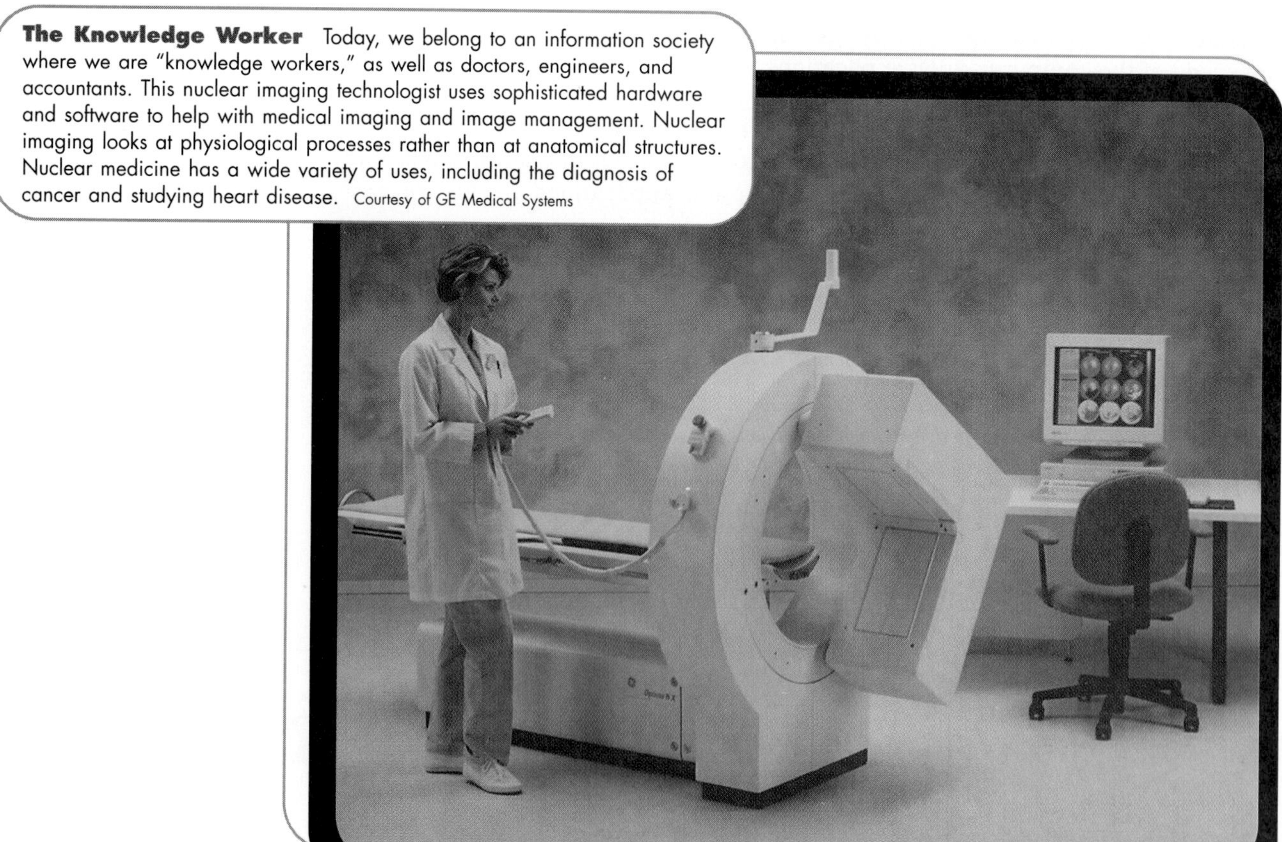

The Knowledge Worker Today, we belong to an information society where we are "knowledge workers," as well as doctors, engineers, and accountants. This nuclear imaging technologist uses sophisticated hardware and software to help with medical imaging and image management. Nuclear imaging looks at physiological processes rather than at anatomical structures. Nuclear medicine has a wide variety of uses, including the diagnosis of cancer and studying heart disease. Courtesy of GE Medical Systems

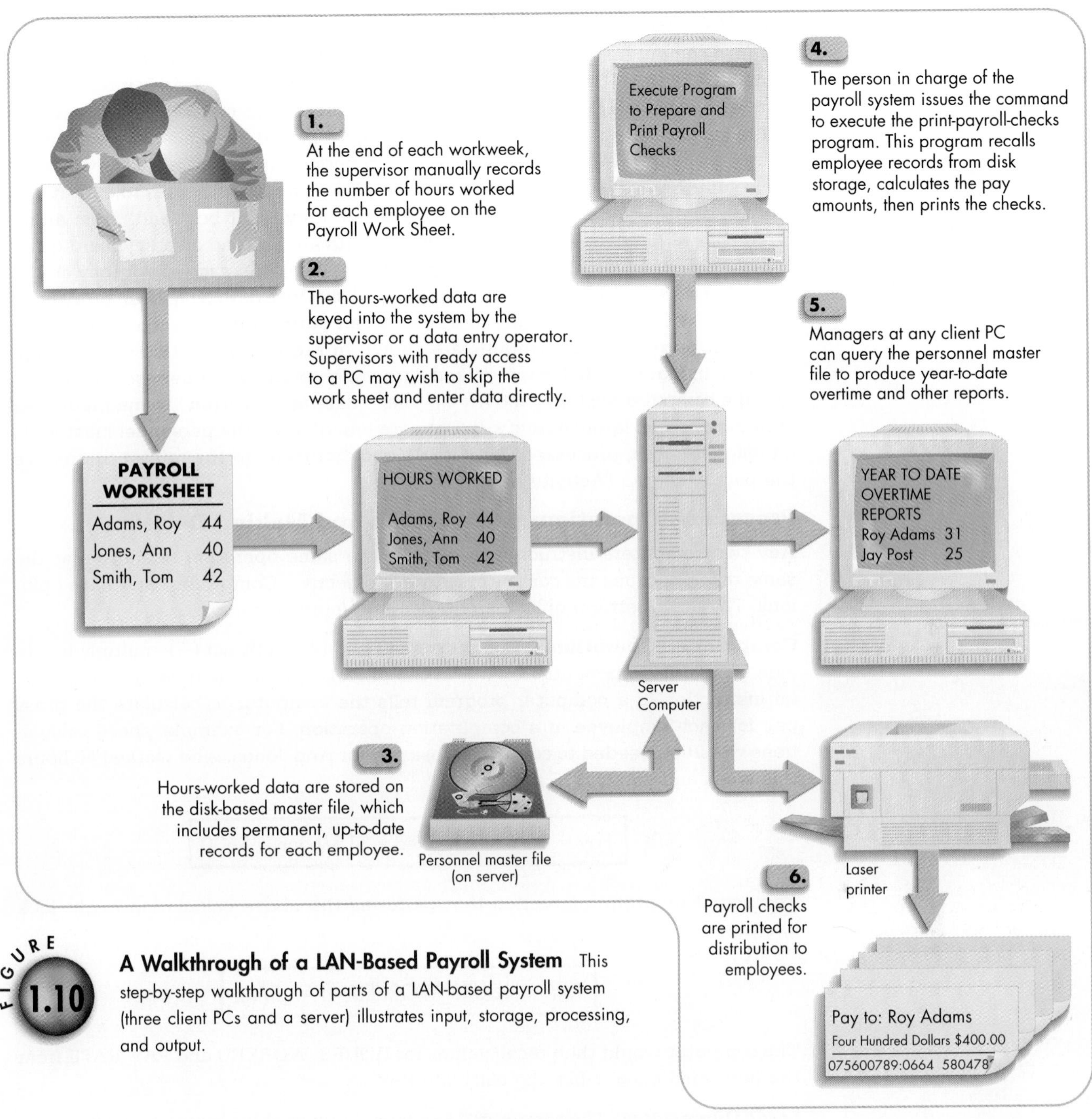

1.
At the end of each workweek, the supervisor manually records the number of hours worked for each employee on the Payroll Work Sheet.
2.
The hours-worked data are keyed into the system by the supervisor or a data entry operator. Supervisors with ready access to a PC may wish to skip the work sheet and enter data directly.
Execute Program to Prepare and Print Payroll Checks
4.
The person in charge of the payroll system issues the command to execute the print-payroll-checks program. This program recalls employee records from disk storage, calculates the pay amounts, then prints the checks.
5.
Managers at any client PC can query the personnel master file to produce year-to-date overtime and other reports.
PAYROLL WORKSHEET
Adams, Roy 44
Jones, Ann 40
Smith, Tom 42
HOURS WORKED
Adams, Roy 44
Jones, Ann 40
Smith, Tom 42
YEAR TO DATE OVERTIME REPORTS
Roy Adams 31
Jay Post 25
Server Computer
3.
Hours-worked data are stored on the disk-based master file, which includes permanent, up-to-date records for each employee.
Personnel master file (on server)
Laser printer
6.
Payroll checks are printed for distribution to employees.
Pay to: Roy Adams
Four Hundred Dollars $400.00
075600789:0664 580478

FIGURE 1.10

A Walkthrough of a LAN-Based Payroll System This step-by-step walkthrough of parts of a LAN-based payroll system (three client PCs and a server) illustrates input, storage, processing, and output.

In the walkthrough of Figure 1.10, the payroll system and other company systems are supported on a **local area network (LAN).** A LAN connects PCs or workstations that are relatively near one another, such as in a suite of offices or a building. In most LANs, one central computer, called a **server computer,** performs a variety of functions for the other computers on the LAN, called **client computers.** One such function is the storage of data and applications software. In Figure 1.10, client PCs throughout the company are linked to a server computer. In the example, the server computer is a tower PC, but the server computer can be any type of computer, from a notebook PC to a supercomputer.

What Can a Computer Do?

Computers perform two operations: input/output operations and processing operations.

Input/Output Operations: Movement in a Computer System

Within a computer system, information is continuously moved from one part of the system to another. This movement is controlled by the processor. It interprets information from the keyboard (a tapped key), moves it to memory and eventually to the monitor's display, the printer, or, perhaps a stored file. This movement is referred to as input/output, or I/O for short. In performing input/output operations, the computer *reads* from input and storage devices and then *writes* to output and storage devices. Before data can be processed, they must be "read" from an input device or data storage device. Typically, data are entered on a *keyboard* or via *speech recognition* (spoken words entered to the computer system), or they are retrieved from data storage, such as a magnetic disk. Once data have been processed, they are "written" to a magnetic disk or to an output device, such as a printer.

Input/output (I/O) operations are shown in the payroll-system walkthrough example in Figure 1.10. Hours-worked data are entered by a supervisor, or "read," into the computer system (Activity 2). These data are "written" to magnetic disk storage for recall later (Activity 3). Data are "read" from the personnel master file on magnetic disk, processed (Activity 4), and "written" to the printer to produce the payroll checks (Activity 6).

Processing Operations: Doing Math and Making Decisions

Any two computers instructed to perform the same operation will arrive at the same result because the computer is totally objective. Computers can't have opinions. They can perform only *computation* and *logic operations.*

Computation Operations Computers can add (+), subtract (−), multiply (*), divide (/), and do exponentiation (^). In the payroll system example of Figure 1.10, an instruction in a computer program tells the computer to calculate the gross pay for each employee in a computation operation. For example, these calculations would be needed to compute gross pay for Ann Jones, who worked 40 hours this week and makes $15 per hour:

Pay = 40 hours worked * $15/hour = $600

The actual program instruction that performs the above calculation might look like this:

```
PAY = HOURS_WORKED * PAY_RATE
```

The computer would then recall values for HOURS_WORKED and PAY_RATE from the personnel master file and calculate PAY.

Logic Operations The computer's logic capability enables comparisons between numbers and between words. Based on the result of a comparison, the computer performs appropriate functions. In the example of Figure 1.10, Tom Smith and Roy Adams had overtime hours because they each worked more than 40 hours (the normal workweek). The computer must use its *logic capability* to decide if an employee is due overtime pay. To do this, hours worked are compared to 40.

Are hours worked > (greater than) 40?

For Roy Adams, who worked 44 hours, the comparison is true (44 is greater than 40). A comparison that is true causes the difference (4 hours) to be credited as overtime and paid at time and a half. The actual instruction that would perform the logical operation might look like this.

```
IF HOURS_WORKED > 40 THEN PAY_OVERTIME
```

MEMORY

Computer Operations

- Input/output
  - —Read
  - —Write
- Processing
  - —Computation
  - —Logic

The Computer's Strengths

In a nutshell, computers are fast, accurate, consistent, and reliable. They don't forget anything, and they don't complain.

Speed: 186 Miles per Millisecond

Computers perform various activities by executing instructions, such as those discussed in the previous section. These operations are measured in **milliseconds, microseconds, nanoseconds,** and **picoseconds** (one thousandth, one millionth, one billionth, and one trillionth of a second, respectively). To place computer speeds in perspective, consider that a beam of light travels down the length of this page in about one nanosecond. During that time a mainframe computer can perform the computations needed to complete a complex tax return.

Accuracy: Zero Errors

Computers are amazingly accurate, and their accuracy reflects great *precision.* Computations are accurate within a penny, a micron (a millionth of a meter), a picosecond, or whatever level of precision is required. Errors do occur in computer-based information systems, but precious few can be directly attributed to the computer system itself. Most can be traced to a program logic error, a procedural error, or erroneous data. These are *human errors.*

Consistency: All Strikes, No Balls

Baseball pitchers try to throw strikes, but often end up throwing balls. Computers always do what they are programmed to do—nothing more, nothing less. If we ask them to throw strikes, they throw nothing but strikes. This ability to produce the consistent results gives us the confidence we need to allow computers to process *mission-critical* information (information that is necessary for continued operation of an organization, a space shuttle, and so on).

Reliability: No Downtime

Computer systems are the most reliable workers in any company, especially when it comes to repetitive tasks. They don't take sick days or coffee breaks, and they seldom complain. Anything below 99.9% *uptime,* the time when the computer system is in operation, is usually unacceptable. For some companies, any *downtime* is unacceptable. These companies provide **backup** computers that take over automatically should the main computers fail.

Memory Capability: Virtually Unlimited

Computer systems have total and instant recall of data and an almost unlimited capacity to store these data. A typical mainframe computer system will have

MEMORY bits

Fractions of a Second

- Millisecond = 0.001 second (one thousandth of a second)
- Microsecond = 0.000001 second (one millionth of a second)
- Nanosecond = 0.000000001 second (one billionth of a second)
- Picosecond = 0.000000000001 second (one trillionth of a second)

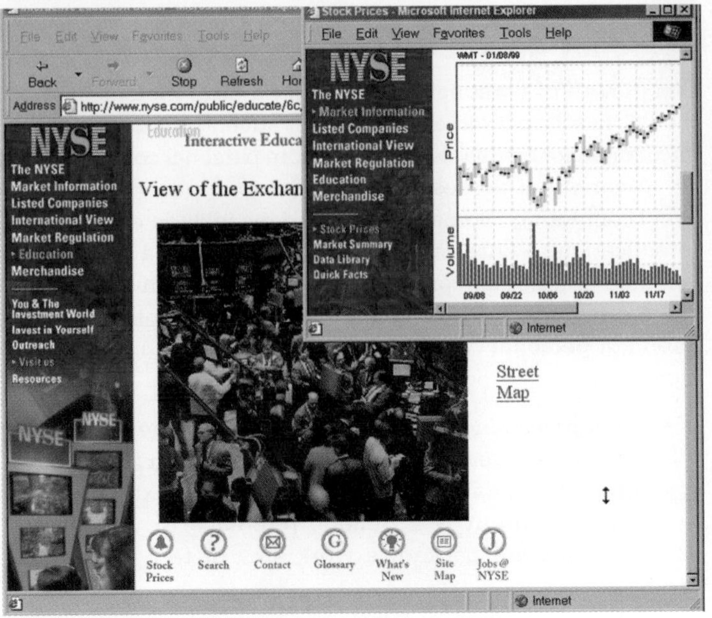

Trillions of Dollars Traded without Error At the New York Stock Exchange, literally trillions of dollars' worth of securities are routinely bought and sold with nary a penny lost, a testament to the accuracy of computers. The trading floor scene is one of many that can be found at the NYSE's Visitors Center tour on its Internet site <http://www.nyse.com/public/visit/vistour.html>

trillions of characters and millions of images stored and available for instant recall. A typical PC will have immediate access to billions of characters of data and thousands of images. To give you a benchmark for comparison, this book contains approximately 1.5 million characters and about 500 images.

SECTION SELF-CHECK

Self-Check

1-5.1 On a LAN, the client computer stores all data and applications software used by the server computer. (T/F)

1-5.2 The operational capabilities of a computer system include the ability to do both logic and computation operations. (T/F)

1-5.3 A microsecond is 1000 times longer than a nanosecond. (T/F)

1-5.4 Downtime is unacceptable in some companies. (T/F)

1-5.5 In a LAN, a server computer performs a variety of functions for its: (a) client computers, (b) subcomputers, (c) LAN entity PC, or (d) work units.

1-5.6 Which of the following would be a logic operation: (a) TODAY<BIRTHDATE, (b) GROSS-TAX-DEDUCT, (c) HOURS*WAGE, or (d) SALARY/12?

1-5.7 Spoken words are entered directly into a computer system via: (a) key entry, (b) OCR, (c) Morse code, or (d) speech recognition?

NASA Information System
Each launch of the space shuttle creates enormous activity in the NASA-based information system that supports the shuttle and the International Space Station. The system is continuously collecting and analyzing data, then providing feedback to scientists and the automated systems that guide the spacecraft. The information system encompasses everything from monitoring space resources (fuel, oxygen, and so on) to more earth-based concerns such as inventory and logistics.
Courtesy NASA

1.6 HOW DO WE USE COMPUTERS?

The uses of computers are like the number of melodies available to a songwriter—limitless. If you can imagine it, there is a good chance that computers can help you do it. This section provides an overview of potential computer applications, which should give you a feel for how computers are affecting your life. These applications, however, are but a few of the many applications presented throughout the book.

Information Systems

The bulk of existing computer power is dedicated to **information systems.** This includes all uses of computers that support the administrative aspects of an organization, such as airline reservation systems, student registration systems, hospital patient-billing systems, and countless others. We combine *hardware, software, people, procedures,* and *data* to create an information system. A computer-based information system provides an organization with *data processing* capabilities and the knowledge workers in the organization with the *information* they need to make better, more informed decisions.

Personal Computing

The growth of **personal computing,** an environment in which one person controls the PC, has surpassed even the most adventurous forecasts of a decade ago. It's not uncommon for companies to have more personal computers than they do telephones.

A variety of domestic and business applications form the foundation of personal computing. Domestic applications include everything from personal finance to education to entertainment. PC software is available to support thousands of common and not-so-common personal and business applications.

A growing family of software for personal or business productivity is the foundation of personal computing in the home and in the business world. These are some of the most popular productivity tools.

Serendipitous Surfing: The Movies

- *Word processing.* **Word processing software** enables users to create, edit (revise), and format documents in preparation for output (for example, printing, displaying locally or over the Internet, faxing, or sending via e-mail). The term **document** is a generic reference to whatever is currently displayed in a software package's work area or to a permanent file, perhaps a disk,

The Personal Computing Experience Personal computing provides a much richer experience than just a few years ago. After receiving a box of chocolates for Valentine's Day, this man immediately called his fiancée to show his appreciation. Through a videophone Internet hookup, she is able to see and hear his expression of joy. She sent him a digital image of her with the roses she received from him.
Photo courtesy of Intel Corporation

containing document contents (perhaps a report or an outline). Word processing documents can include anything that can be printed (for example, text and graphic images). When viewed on a computer, displayed documents can include objects other than graphic images. Generally, an **object** is anything within a document that can be selected and manipulated. For example, animations, video, and sound objects can be embedded in displayed word processing documents.

- *Desktop publishing.* **Desktop publishing software** allows users to produce camera-ready documents (ready to be printed professionally) from the confines of a desktop. People routinely use desktop publishing to create newsletters, advertisements, procedures manuals, and for many other printing needs.
- *Spreadsheet.* **Spreadsheet software** permits users to work with the rows and columns of data.
- *Database.* **Database software** permits users to create and maintain a database and to extract information from the database. In a database, data are organized for ease of manipulation and retrieval.
- *Presentation.* **Presentation software** lets you create professional-looking images for group presentations, self-running slide shows, reports, and for other situations that require the presentation of organized, visual information. The electronic images may include multimedia elements, such as sound, animation, and video.
- *Communications.* **Communications software** is a family of software applications that enable users to send e-mail and faxes, tap the Internet, log on to an information service, and link their PC with a remote computer.
- *Personal information management.* PIM software is an umbrella term that encompasses a variety of personal management and contact information programs. A particular PIM package might include calendar applications (appointment scheduling and reminders), communications applications (e-mail and fax), and databases that help you organize your phone numbers, e-mail addresses, to-do lists, notes, diary entries, and so on.

Multimedia Impact As we witnessed firsthand in the O. J. Simpson "trial of the century," multimedia presentations are beginning to revolutionize courtroom litigation techniques. This law firm uses a multimedia system to capture video, audio, and text information. Once captured, the system assists lawyers in mixing video depositions, animated simulations, graphs, and other physical evidence into a multimedia package for courtroom presentations.
Courtesy of Dynatech Corporation

Communication

Computers are communications tools that give us the flexibility to communicate electronically with one another and with other computers. For example, we can set up our computers to send e-mail birthday greetings to our friends and relatives automatically. We can log on to a commercial information service (like America Online or CompuServe) to chat online (via keyed-in text) with one person or a group of people. Recent software innovations allow us to talk to, and see, people in remote locations, using only our PCs and a link to the Internet. Communications applications and concepts are discussed and illustrated in detail throughout the book.

Science, Research, and Engineering

Engineers and scientists routinely use the computer as a tool in *experimentation, design,* and *development.* There are at least as many science and research applications for the computer as there are scientists and engineers. One of these applications is computer-aided design (CAD), which involves using the computer in the design process. CAD systems enable the creation and manipulation of an on-screen graphic image. CAD systems provide a sophisticated array of tools, enabling designers to create three-dimensional objects that can be flipped, rotated, resized, viewed in detail, examined internally or externally, and much more. Photographs in this chapter and throughout the book illustrate a variety of CAD applications, such as automobile design and architectural design.

Education and Reference

Students at all levels, from kindergarten to professional adult education, are embracing a new approach to learning. Learning resources are being developed and delivered on CD-ROM and via the Internet to relatively inexpensive personal com-

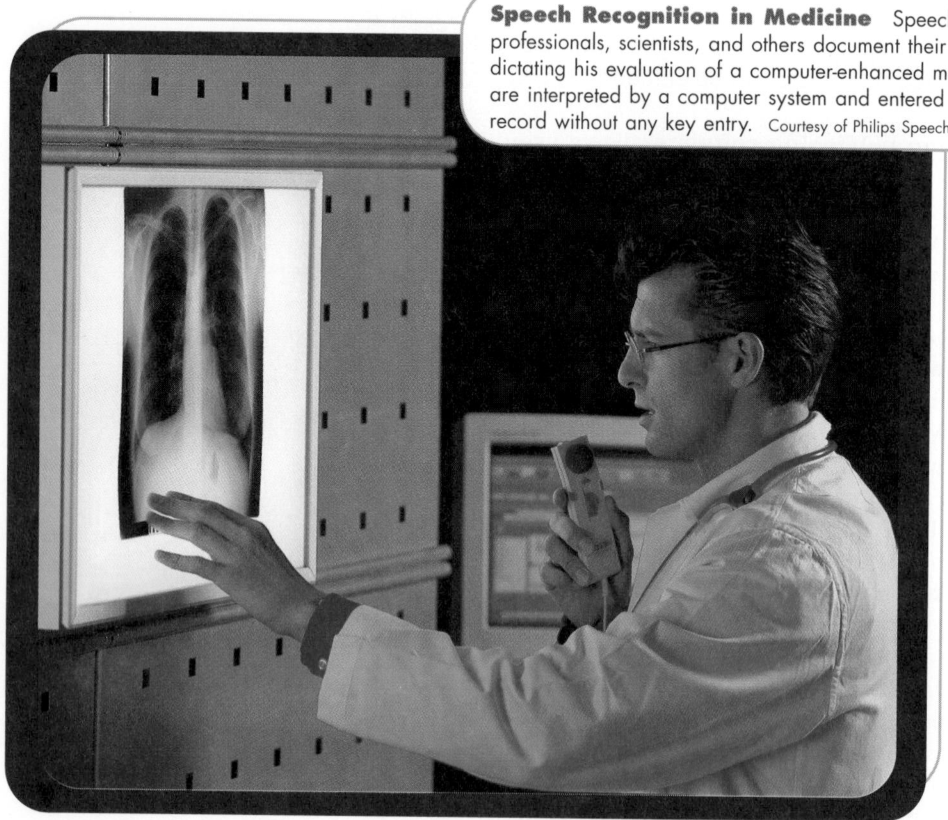

Speech Recognition in Medicine Speech recognition is changing the way professionals, scientists, and others document their work. Here, a radiologist is dictating his evaluation of a computer-enhanced medical image. The words he speaks are interpreted by a computer system and entered directly into the patient's medical record without any key entry. Courtesy of Philips Speech Processing

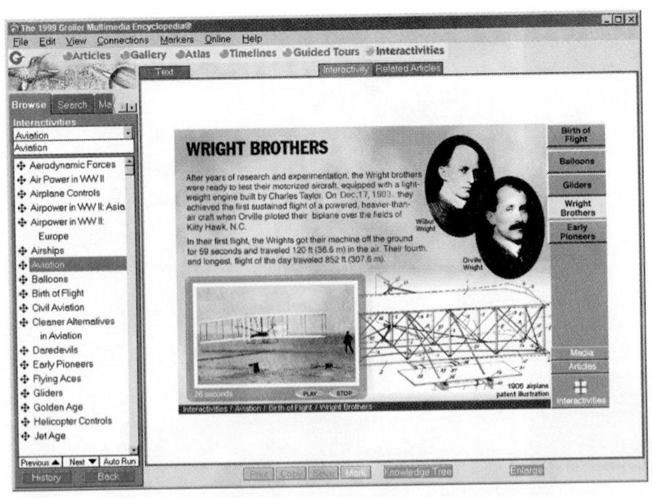

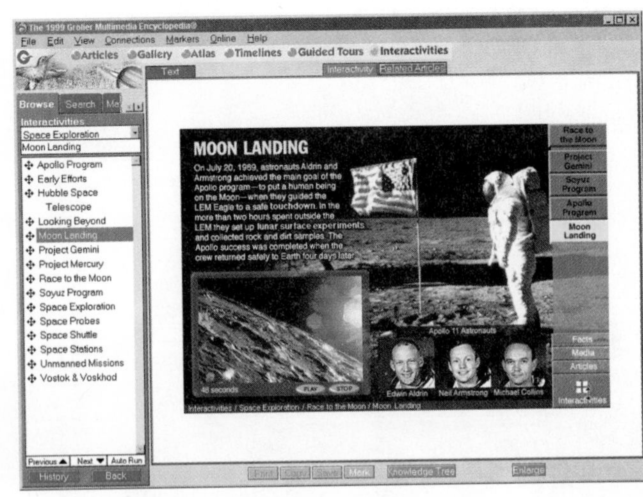

The Multimedia Encyclopedia The multimedia encyclopedia is a good place to start your multimedia adventure. The *Grolier Multimedia Encyclopedia*® (shown here) contains millions of words about thousands of persons, places, and things. The CD-ROM encyclopedia uses the full capabilities of multimedia to enrich the presentation of information. For example, you can travel through time using maps that chart journeys filled with sights, sounds, and motion. How would you like to sail with Magellan or march with General Robert E. Lee? The encyclopedia offers narrated essays that use photos, music, and sound to explore such topics as the human body and space exploration. "Thumbing" through an encyclopedia will never be the same. You can view motion videos of one of the Wright Brothers' early flights, and then fast forward to 1969 to watch Neil Armstrong walk on the Moon.

puters, each capable of multidimensional communication (sound, print, graphics, video, and animation). The result is a phenomenal growth of technology as an educational tool in the home, in the classroom, and in business. Computer-based education and online classes will not replace teachers, but educators agree that CD-ROM-based *computer-based training (CBT)* and information-based *distance learning* is having a profound impact on traditional modes of education. Available CBT programs can help you learn keyboarding skills, increase your vocabulary, study algebra, learn about the makeup of the atom, practice your Russian, and learn about computers. Colleges and even high schools offer thousands of courses online via distance learning. You can now get an MBA, a law degree, and bachelors degrees in most disciplines without attending a single traditional classroom lecture. These are just the tip of the CBT/distance learning iceberg.

Entertainment and Edutainment

More applications are being created that tickle our fancy and entertain us. You can play electronic golf. You can buy a computer chess opponent in the form of a board, chess pieces, and a miniature robotic arm that moves the pieces (you have to move your own pieces). You can "pilot" an airplane to Paris and battle Zorbitrons in cyberspace. Carmen Sandiego, the debonair thief of computer games and television fame, thrills children with the chase to find her and her accomplices, while teaching them history and geography. Software that combines *edu*cation and enter*tainment,* such as "Carmen Sandiego," has been dubbed *edutainment software.*

The amount of computing capacity in the world is doubling every two years. The number and sophistication of applications are growing at a similar pace. Tomorrow, there will be applications that are unheard of today.

She wanted to visit a hot spot, the Sun King's palace at Versailles.
FRANCE
Where did the suspect go?
Tell me about the suspect.
Thank you, goodbye.
• France 12:07 PM
"She's in over her head in a European country that would be half underwater without dykes and dams."
Page 4 of 4

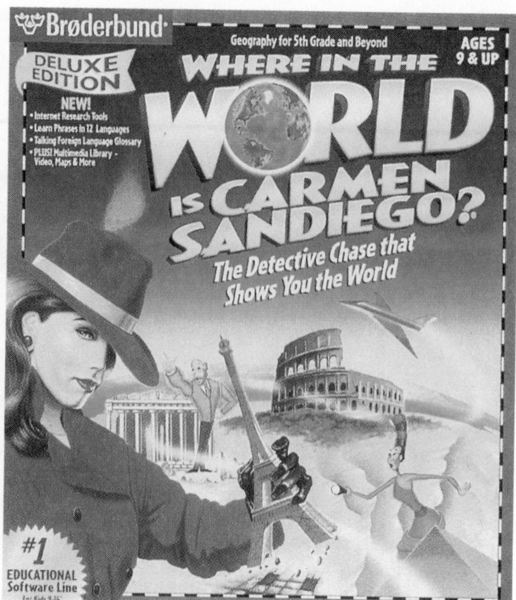
Brøderbund
Geography for 5th Grade and Beyond
AGES 9 & UP
DELUXE EDITION
WHERE IN THE WORLD IS CARMEN SANDIEGO?
The Detective Chase that Shows You the World
#1 EDUCATIONAL Software Line

Where in the World Is Carmen Sandiego™? Carmen Sandiego, an elegant thief, is the title character of the popular edutainment software that gives players clues that can lead them to the stolen goods. As players home in on the whereabouts of Carmen Sandiego, they learn a lot about geography. Courtesy of Broderbund Software, Inc.

SECTION SELF-CHECK

Self-Check

Interactive Study Guide Chapter 1

1-6.1 Desktop publishing refers to the capability of producing camera-ready documents from the confines of a desktop. (T/F)

1-6.2 More computing capacity is dedicated to information systems than to CBT. (T/F)

1-6.3 The PC productivity tool that manipulates data organized in rows and columns is called a: (a) database record manager, (b) presentation mechanism, (c) word processing document, or (d) spreadsheet.

1-6.4 What type of software combines education and entertainment: (a) video games, (b) Nintendo, (c) edutainment, or (d) click-and-learn?

1-6.5 Which PC productivity tool would be helpful in writing a term paper: (a) word processing, (b) presentation, (c) spreadsheet, or (d) communications?

SUMMARY AND KEY TERMS

1.1 The information society

In an **information society** (4), **knowledge workers** (4) focus their energies on providing a myriad of information services. The knowledge worker's job function revolves around the use, manipulation, and dissemination of information. Learning about computers is an adventure that will last a lifetime because **information technology (IT)** (4), the integration of computing technology and information processing, is changing daily.

Information technology competency (IT competency) (4) is emerging as a universal goal in the information society. IT-competent people know how to purchase, use, and operate a computer system, and how to make it work for them. The IT-competent person is also aware of the computer's impact on society and is conversant in the language of technology.

Software (5) refers collectively to a set of machine-readable instructions, called **programs** (5), that causes the computer to perform desired functions.

Computers and computer equipment, which accept **input** (4) and provide **output** (4), are called **hardware** (5).

The computer revolution is transforming the way we communicate, do business, and learn. This technological revolution is having a profound impact on the business community and on our private and professional lives. For example, increasingly, we communicate with our colleagues at work through **electronic mail (e-mail)** (6) or with our friends through **newsgroups** (6).

After the turn of the century we can anticipate traveling the **information superhighway** (6), a network of high-speed data communications links that eventually will connect virtually every facet of our society. Today, millions of people have a **personal computer (PC)** (5). This widespread availability has resulted in an explosion of applications for computers.

Through the 1970s, **users** (7) related their information needs to computer professionals who would then work with the computer system to generate the necessary information. Today, users work directly with their PCs to obtain the information they need.

Data (7), which all of us create and use every day, are the raw facts from which information is derived. **Information** (7) consists of data collected and processed into a meaningful form. The data in a computer-based system are stored on the **master file** (8), which is made up of **records** (8).

1.2 Networking: Bringing people together

We now live in a global village in which computers and people are linked within companies and between countries. Most existing computers are part of a **computer network** (9) that shares resources and information.

The Internet (10) links millions of users in a global network. **The Net** (10) can be accessed by people in organizations with established links to the Internet and by individuals with PCs often via **Internet service providers (ISPs)** (10). Commercial **information services** (10), such as **America Online (AOL)** (10), offer a wide range of information services, including up-to-the-minute news and weather, electronic shopping, e-mail, and much more. When the user terminates this **online** (10) link, the user goes **offline** (11). Internet users can **download** (11) text or a digitized version of a song directly to their PC, then read it or play it through their PC. Information is **uploaded** (11) from a local computer to a remote computer.

1.3 Computers: The essentials

The **computer** (12), or **processor** (12), is an electronic device capable of interpreting and executing programmed commands for input, output, computation, and logic operations.

Output on a computer can be routed to a **monitor** (12) or a **printer** (12). The output on a monitor is temporary and is called **soft copy** (12). Printers produce **hard-copy** (12) output. Data can be entered via a **keyboard** (12) or a **mouse** (12), a **point-and-draw device** (12).

Random-access memory (RAM) (12) provides temporary storage of data and programs during processing within solid-state **integrated circuits** (12), or **chips** (12). Permanently installed and interchangeable **disks** (12) provide permanent storage for data and programs. A computer system can include a variety of **peripheral devices** (12).

The differences in the various categories of computers are very much a matter of scale. **Mainframe computers** (13) have greater computing capacities than do PCs, or **microcomputers** (13). And **supercomputers** (13) have greater computing capacities than mainframe computers. Depending on its sophistication, a **workstation**'s (13) computing capacity falls somewhere between that of a PC and a midsized mainframe. All **computer systems** (12), no matter how small or large, have the same fundamental capabilities—*processing, storage, input,* and *output*. Each offers many **input/output** (14), or **I/O** (14), alternatives.

System software (14) takes control of the PC on start up, and then plays a central role in all interactions with the computer. **Applications software** (15) performs specific personal, business, or scientific processing tasks.

1.4 Personal computers to supercomputers: Capabilities and uses

In 1981, IBM introduced its **IBM PC** (18), defining the original PC-compatible machine, now also called a **Wintel PC** (18) because of its use of Windows 9x/NT/2000 **operating systems** (18) and the Intel processors. The Apple iMac, with its Mac OS X and Motorola PowerPC processor, is the other major **platform** (18). Conventional personal computers come in four different physical sizes: **pocket PCs (palmtop PCs)** (19), **laptop PCs** (also called **notebook PCs**) (19), **desktop PCs** (21), and **tower PCs** (21). Pocket and laptop PCs are considered portable. A 2-in-1 PC that can be used as both a notebook and a desktop has two parts: a fully functional *notebook PC* and a **docking station** (19). Two-in-one PCs allow users to enjoy the best of both worlds: portability and the expanded features of a desktop. The **port replicator** (19) works like the docking station in that the notebook PC is inserted into it and removed as needed to enable access to the port replicator **ports** (19) and whatever is connected to them.

Slate PCs (21), sometimes called **pen-based PCs** (21), use electronic pens instead of keyboards. **Speech-recognition** (21) software is being integrated into high-end slate PCs. **Personal digital assistants (PDAs)** (21), or **handheld PCs** (21), are handheld personal computers that support a variety of personal information systems. PDAs support a variety of **personal information management (PIM)** (21) systems, including appointment scheduling and to-do lists. The **network computer** (21), or **NC** (21), is designed to work only when linked to a network. The diskless NC has a relatively small processor and less RAM than modern personal computers.

Multimedia applications (23) combine text, sound, graphics, motion video, and/or animation. The typical multimedia-configured PC includes a microcomputer; a keyboard and a point-and-draw device for input; a monitor and a printer for output; a **hard-disk drive** (23) and a **floppy disk drive** (23) into which an interchangeable **diskette** (23), or **floppy disk** (23), is inserted; a **CD-ROM drive** (23) into which an interchangeable **CD-ROM** (23) is inserted; and a microphone and a set of speakers for audio I/O.

The workstation's speed and input/output devices set it apart from a PC. A typical workstation will have a high-**resolution** (25) monitor and a variety of specialized point-and-draw devices. A common use of workstations is for **computer-aided design (CAD)** (25).

Mainframe computers are usually associated with **enterprise-wide systems** (25); that is, computer-based systems that service entities throughout the company. Users communicate with a centralized mainframe, called a **host computer** (25), through their **terminals** (25) and other communications devices. The term **minicomputer** (25) was used until recently, when the distinction between minis and mainframes began to blur. Mainframes are oriented to **input/output-bound applications** (26). Supercomputers primarily address **processor-bound applications** (27).

1.5 A Computer system at work

A **local area network (LAN)** (29) connects PCs or workstations in close proximity. The LAN's **server computer** (29) performs a variety of functions for other computers on the LAN, called **client computers** (29).

Computer system capabilities are either input/output or processing. Processing capabilities are subdivided into computation and logic operations.

Computers perform input/output (I/O) operations by reading from input and storage devices and writing to output devices.

The computer is fast, accurate, consistent, and reliable, and has an enormous memory capacity. Computer operations are measured in **milliseconds** (31), **microseconds** (31), **nanoseconds** (31), and **picoseconds** (31). When downtime is unacceptable, companies provide **backup** (31) computers that take over automatically should the main computers fail.

1.6 How do we use computers?

There are many applications of computers, including the following:

- *Information systems.* The computer is used to process data and produce business information. Hardware, software, people, procedures, and data are combined to create an **information system** (32).
- *Personal computing.* The PC is used for **personal computing** (32) by individuals for a variety of business and domestic applications, including such productivity tools as **word processing software** (32), **desktop publishing software** (33), **spreadsheet software** (33), **database software** (33), **presentation software** (33), and **communications software** (33). An **object** (33) is anything within a **document** (32) that can be selected and manipulated.
- *Communication.* Computers are communications tools that give us the flexibility to communicate electronically with one another and with other computers.
- *Science, research, and engineering.* The computer is used as a tool in experimentation, design, and development.
- *Education and reference.* The computer interacts with students to enhance the learning process.
- *Entertainment and edutainment.* Every day, computer applications are being designed and created just to entertain us. Software that combines *edu*cation and enter*tainment* has been dubbed edutainment software.

DISCUSSION AND PROBLEM SOLVING

1.1 **a.** Information technology has had far-reaching effects on our lives. How has the computer and IT affected your life?

b. What is your concept of information technology competency? In what ways do you think achieving information technology competency will affect your domestic life? Your business life?

c. At what age should information technology competency education begin? Is society prepared to provide IT education at this age? If not, why?

d. Describe the relationship between data and information. Give an example.

e. Discuss how the complexion of jobs will change as we evolve from an industrial society into an information society. Give several examples.

1.2 **a.** Comment on how information technology is changing our traditional patterns of personal communication.

b. If you are a current user of the Internet, describe four Internet services that have been of value to you. If not, in what ways do you think the Internet might be a benefit to you?

c. What might you want to download over the Internet?

1.3 **a.** List as many computer and information technology terms as you can (up to 30) that are used in everyday conversations at the office and at school.

b. Describe an ideal applications software package that might help you meet your personal or business information processing needs.

1.4 **a.** If you could purchase only one personal computer, which would you buy, a notebook PC or a tower PC? Why?

b. Explain circumstances that would cause you to choose a docking station over a port replicator.

c. Speculate on how one of these professionals would use a slate PC: a police officer, an insurance adjuster, a delivery person for a courier service, or a newspaper reporter.

d. Management at a large company with 1000 three-year-old PCs, all on a network, is debating whether to replace the PCs with network computers or with new PCs. Each has its advantages. Name the single most important advantage for each option.

e. Give at least two reasons that a regional bank might opt to buy two mainframe computers rather than one supercomputer.

1.5 **a.** Discuss the relationship between the server computer and its client computers.

b. Compare the information processing capabilities of human beings to those of computers with respect to speed, accuracy, reliability, consistency, and memory capability.

c. Within the context of a computer system, what is meant by *read* and *write*?

d. Identify and briefly describe five computation and five logic operations that might be performed by a computer during the processing of college students throughout the academic year.

1.6 **a.** The use of computers tends to stifle creativity. Argue for or against this statement.

b. Comment on how computers are changing our traditional patterns of recreation.

c. Of the productivity software described in this chapter, choose the two that will have (or currently have) the most impact on your productivity. Explain why you chose these two.

THE HISTORY OF COMPUTING

The history of computers and computing is of special significance to us, because many of its most important events have occurred within our lifetime. Historians divide the history of the modern computer into generations, beginning with the introduction of the UNIVAC I, the first commercially viable computer, in 1951. But the quest for a mechanical servant—one that could free people from the more boring aspects of thinking—is centuries old.

Why did it take so long to develop the computer? Some of the "credit" goes to human foibles. Too often brilliant insights were not recognized or given adequate support during an inventor's lifetime. Instead, these insights would lay dormant for as long as 100 years until someone else rediscovered—or reinvented—them. Some of the "credit" has to go to workers, too, who sabotaged labor-saving devices that threatened to put them out of work. The rest of the "credit" goes to technology; some insights were simply ahead of their time's technology. Here, then, is an abbreviated history of the stops and starts that have given us this marvel of the modern age, the computer.

3000 B.C.: The Abacus

The abacus is probably considered the original mechanical counting device (it has been traced back 5000 years). It is still used in education to demonstrate the principles of counting and arithmetic and in business for speedy calculations. The Computer Museum, Boston, MA

1623–1662: Blaise Pascal

Although inventor, painter, and sculptor Leonardo da Vinci (1425–1519) sketched ideas for a mechanical adding machine, it was another 150 years before French mathematician and philosopher Blaise Pascal (1623–1662) finally invented and built the "Pascaline" in 1642 to help his father, a tax collector. Although Pascal was praised throughout Europe, his invention was a financial failure. The hand-built machines were expensive and delicate; moreover, Pascal was the only person who could repair them. Because human labor was actually cheaper, the Pascaline was abandoned as impractical. Courtesy of International Business Machines Corporation

Computer History

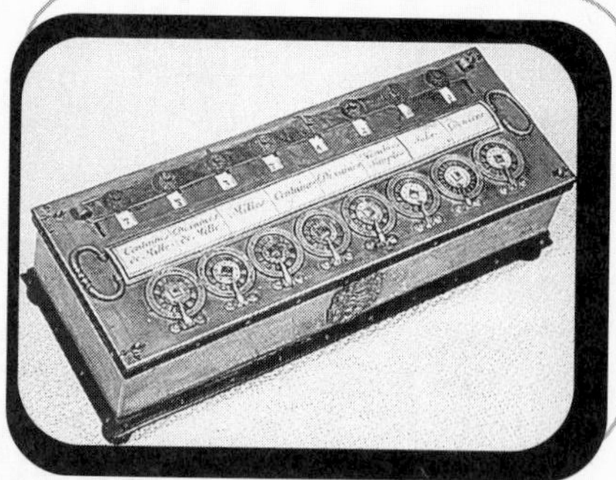

1642: The Pascaline

The Pascaline used a counting-wheel design: Numbers for each digit were arranged on wheels so that a single revolution of one wheel would engage gears that turned the wheel one tenth of a revolution to its immediate left. Although the Pascaline was abandoned as impractical, its counting-wheel design was used by all mechanical calculators until the mid-1960s, when they were made obsolete by electronic calculators. Courtesy of International Business Machines Corporation

3000 B.C. City of Troy first inhabited

1639 First North American printing press

1793–1871: Charles Babbage

Everyone, from bankers to navigators, depended on mathematical tables during the bustling Industrial Revolution. However, these hand-calculated tables were usually full of errors. After discovering that his own tables were riddled with mistakes, Charles Babbage (1793–1871) envisioned a steam-powered "differential engine" and then an "analytical engine" that would perform tedious calculations accurately. Although Babbage never perfected his devices, they introduced many of the concepts used in today's general-purpose computer. Courtesy of International Business Machines Corporation

1801: Jacquard's Loom

A practicing weaver, Frenchman Joseph-Marie Jacquard (1753–1871) spent what little spare time he had trying to improve the lot of his fellow weavers. (They worked 16-hour days, with no days off!) His solution, the Jacquard loom, was created in 1801. Holes strategically punched in a card directed the movement of needles, thread, and fabric, creating the elaborate patterns still known as Jacquard weaves. Jacquard's weaving loom is considered the first significant use of binary automation. The loom was an immediate success with mill owners because they could hire cheaper and less skilled workers. But weavers, fearing unemployment, rioted and called Jacquard a traitor. Courtesy of International Business Machines Corporation

1842: Babbage's Difference Engine and the Analytical Engine

Convinced his machine would benefit England, Babbage applied for—and received—one of the first government grants to build the difference engine. Hampered by nineteenth-century machine technology, cost overruns, and the possibility his chief engineer was padding the bills, Babbage completed only a portion of the difference engine (shown here) before the government withdrew its support in 1842, deeming the project "worthless to science." Meanwhile, Babbage had conceived of the idea of a more advanced "analytical engine." In essence, this was a general-purpose computer that could add, subtract, multiply, and divide in automatic sequence at a rate of 60 additions per second. His 1833 design, which called for thousands of gears and drives, would cover the area of a football field and be powered by a locomotive engine. Babbage worked on this project until his death. In 1991 London's Science Museum spent $600,000 to build a working model of the difference engine, using Babbage's original plans. The result stands 6 feet high, 10 feet long, contains 4000 parts, and weighs 3 tons. New York Public Library Picture Collection

1801 Thomas Jefferson elected President

1838 Samuel F. B. Morse develops Morse Code

1816–1852: Lady Ada Augusta Lovelace
The daughter of poet Lord Byron, Lady Ada Augusta Lovelace (1816–1852) became a mentor to Babbage and translated his works, adding her own extensive footnotes. Her suggestion that punched cards could be prepared to instruct Babbage's engine to repeat certain operations has led some people to call her the first programmer. Ada, the programming language adopted by Department of Defense as a standard, is named for Lady Ada Lovelace.
The Bettman Archive/BBC Hulton

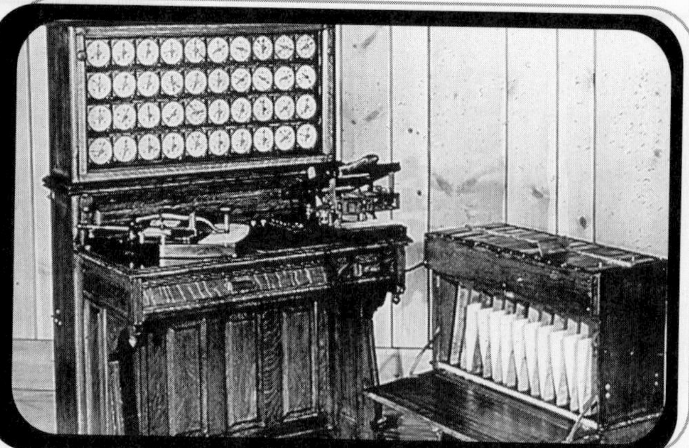

1890: Hollerith's Tabulating Machine
Hollerith's *punched-card tabulating machine* had three parts. Clerks at the U.S. Bureau of the Census used a hand punch to enter data onto cards a little larger than a dollar bill. Cards were then read and sorted by a 24-bin sorter box (right) and summarized on numbered tabulating dials (left), which were connected electrically to the sorter box. Ironically, Hollerith's idea for the punched card came not from Jacquard or Babbage but from "punch photography." Railroads of the day issued tickets with physical descriptions of a passenger's hair and eye color. Conductors punched holes in the ticket to indicate that a passenger's hair and eye color matched those of the ticket owner. From this, Hollerith got the idea of making a punched "photograph" of every person to be tabulated.
Courtesy of International Business Machines Corporation

1860–1929: Herman Hollerith
With the help of a professor, Herman Hollerith (1860–1929) got a job as a special agent helping the U.S. Bureau of the Census tabulate the head count for the 1880 census—a process that took almost eight years. To speed up the 1890 census, Hollerith devised a punched-card tabulating machine. When his machine outperformed two other systems, Hollerith won a contract to tabulate the 1890 census. Hollerith earned a handsome income leasing his machinery to the governments of the United States, Canada, Austria, Russia, and others; he charged 65 cents for every 1000 people counted. (During the 1890 U.S. census alone, he earned more than $40,000—a fortune in those days.) Hollerith may have earned even more selling the single-use punched cards. But the price was worth it. The bureau completed the census in just 2 $\frac{1}{2}$ years and saved more than $5 million.
Courtesy of International Business Machines Corporation

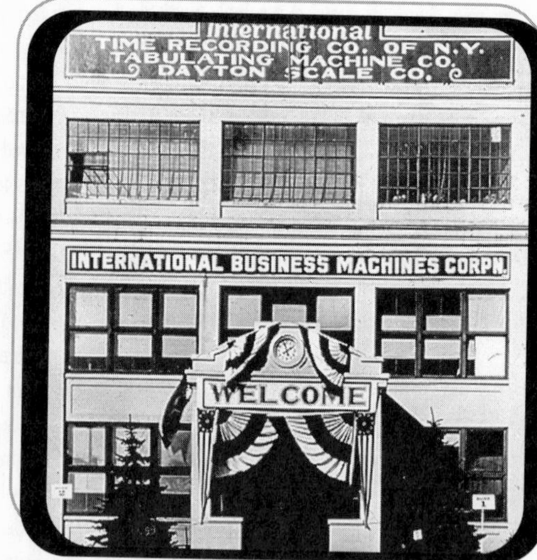

1924: IBM's First Headquarters Building
In 1896 Herman Hollerith founded the Tabulating Machine Company, which merged in 1911 with several other companies to form the Computing-Tabulating-Recording Company. In 1924 the company's general manager, Thomas J. Watson, changed its name to International Business Machines Corporation and moved into this building. Watson ran IBM until a few months before his death at age 82 in 1956. His son, Thomas J. Watson, Jr., lead IBM into the age of computers.
Courtesy of International Business Machines Corporation

1883 Brooklyn Bridge completed in NYC

1923 Zworykin patents first TV transmission tube

1920s–1950s: The EAM Era

From the 1920s throughout the mid-1950s, punched-card technology improved with the addition of more punched-card devices and more sophisticated capabilities. The *electromechanical accounting machine (EAM)* family of punched-card devices includes the card punch, verifier, reproducer, summary punch, interpreter, sorter, collator, and accounting machine. Most of the devices in the 1940s machine room were "programmed" to perform a particular operation by the insertion of a prewired control panel. A machine-room operator in a punched-card installation had the physically challenging job of moving heavy boxes of punched cards and printed output from one device to the next on hand trucks.

Courtesy of International Business Machines Corporation

1903–1995: Dr. John V. Atanasoff

In 1939 Dr. John V. Atanasoff, a professor at Iowa Sate University, and graduate student Clifford E. Berry assembled a prototype of the *ABC* (for *Atanasoff Berry Computer*) to cut the time physics students spent making complicated calculations. A working model was finished in 1942. Atanasoff's decisions—to use an electronic medium with vacuum tubes, the base-2 numbering system, and memory and logic circuits—set the direction for the modern computer. Ironically, Iowa State failed to patent the device and IBM, when contacted about the ABC, airily responded, "IBM will never be interested in an electronic computing machine." A 1973 federal court ruling officially credited Atanasoff with the invention of the automatic electronic digital computer.

Courtesy of Iowa State University

1942: The First Computer: The ABC

During the years 1935 through 1938, Dr. Atanasoff had begun to think about a machine that could reduce the time it took for him and his physics students to make long, complicated mathematical calculations. The ABC was, in fact, born of frustration. Dr. Atanasoff later explained that one night in the winter of 1937, "nothing was happening" with respect to creating an electronic device that could help solve physics problems. His "despair grew," so he got in his car and drove for several hours across the state of Iowa and then across the Mississippi River. Finally he stopped at an Illinois roadhouse for a drink. It was in this roadhouse that Dr. Atanasoff overcame his creative block and conceived ideas that would lay the foundation for the evolution of the modern computer. Courtesy of Iowa State University

1931 Empire State building becomes tallest in world

1939–1945 World War II

1944: The Electromechanical Mark I Computer
The first electromechanical computer, the *Mark I*, was completed by Harvard University professor Howard Aiken in 1944 under the sponsorship of IBM. A monstrous 51 feet long and 8 feet high, the MARK I was essentially a serial collection of electromechanical calculators and was in many ways similar to Babbage's analytical machine. (Aiken was unaware of Babbage's work, though.) The Mark I was a significant improvement, but IBM's management still felt electromechanical computers would never replace punched-card equipment. Courtesy of International Business Machines Corporation

1946: The Electronic Eniac Computer
Dr. John W. Mauchly (middle) collaborated with J. Presper Eckert, Jr. (foreground) at the University of Pennsylvania to develop a machine that would compute trajectory tables for the U.S. Army. (This was sorely needed; during World War II, only 20% of all bombs came within *1000 feet* of their targets.) The end product, the first fully operational electronic computer, was completed in 1946 and named the *ENIAC* (Electronic Numerical Integrator and Computer). A thousand times faster than its electromechanical predecessors, it occupied 15,000 square feet of floor space and weighed 30 tons. The ENIAC could do 5000 additions per minute and 500 multiplications per minute. Unlike computers of today that operate in binary, it operated in decimal and required 10 vacuum tubes to represent one decimal digit.

The ENIAC's use of vacuum tubes signaled a major breakthrough. (Legend has it that the ENIAC's 18,000 vacuum tubes dimmed the lights of Philadelphia whenever it was activated.) Even before the ENIAC was finished, it was used in the secret research that went into building the first atomic bomb at Los Alamos. United Press International Photo/AT&T Technology

1947 Chuck Yeager breaks sound barrier

1951: The UNIVAC I and the First Generation of Computers
The first generation of computers (1951–1959), characterized by the use of vacuum tubes, is generally thought to have begun with the introduction of the first commercially viable electronic digital computer. The Universal Automatic Computer (*UNIVAC I* for short), developed by Mauchly and Eckert for the Remington-Rand Corporation, was installed in the U.S. Bureau of the Census in 1951. Later that year, CBS News gave the UNIVAC I national exposure when it correctly predicted Dwight Eisenhower's victory over Adlai Stevenson in the presidential election with only 5% of the votes counted. Mr. Eckert is shown here instructing news anchor Walter Cronkite in the use of the UNIVAC I.
Courtesy of Unisys Corporation

1954: The IBM 650
Not until the success of the UNIVAC I did IBM make a commitment to develop and market computers. IBM's first entry into the commercial computer market was the *IBM 701* in 1953. However, the *IBM 650* (shown here), introduced in 1954, is probably the reason IBM enjoys such a healthy share of today's computer market. Unlike some of its competitors, the IBM 650 was designed as a logical upgrade to existing punched-card machines. IBM management went out on a limb and estimated sales of 50—a figure greater than the number of installed computers in the entire nation at that time. IBM actually installed 1000. The rest is history.
Courtesy of International Business Machines Corporation

1953 Hillary and Norgay climb Mt. Everest

1907–1992: "Amazing" Grace Murray Hopper

Dubbed "Amazing Grace" by her many admirers, Dr. Grace Hopper was widely respected as the driving force behind COBOL, the most popular programming language, and a champion of standardized programming languages that are hardware-independent. In 1959 Dr. Hopper led an effort that laid the foundation for the development of COBOL. She also helped to create a compiler that enabled COBOL to run on many types of computers. Her reason: "Why start from scratch with every program you write when a computer could be developed to do a lot of the basic work for you over and over again?"

To Dr. Hopper's long list of honors, awards, and accomplishments, add the fact that she found the first "bug" in a computer—a real one. She repaired the Mark II by removing a moth that was caught in Relay Number II. From that day on, every programmer has *debugged* software by ferreting out its *bugs*, or errors, in programming syntax or logic. Official U.S. Navy Photo

1959: The Honeywell 400 and the Second Generation of Computers

The invention of the transistor signaled the start of the second generation of computers (1954–1964). Transistorized computers were more powerful, more reliable, less expensive, and cooler to operate than their vacuum-tubed predecessors. Honeywell (its *Honeywell 400* is shown here) established itself as a major player in the second generation of computers. Burroughs, Univac, NCR, CDC, and Honeywell—IBM's biggest competitors during the 1960s and early 1970s—became known as the BUNCH (the first initial of each name). Courtesy of Honeywell, Inc.

1958: The First Integrated Circuit

If you believe that great inventions revolutionize society by altering one's lifestyle or by changing the way people perceive themselves and their world, then the integrated circuit is a great invention. The integrated circuit is at the heart of all electronic equipment today. Shown here is the first integrated circuit, a phase-shift oscillator, invented in 1958 by Jack S. Kilby of Texas Instruments. Kilby (shown here in 1997 with his original notebook) can truly say to himself, "I changed how the world functions." Texas Instruments Incorporated

1963: The PDP-8 Minicomputer

During the 1950s and early 1960s, only the largest companies could afford the six- and seven-digit price tags of *mainframe* computers. In 1963 Digital Equipment Corporation introduced the *PDP-8* (shown here). It is generally considered the first successful *minicomputer* (a nod, some claim, to the playful spirit behind the 1960s miniskirt). At a mere $18,000, the transistor-based PDP-8 was an instant hit. It confirmed the tremendous demand for small computers for business and scientific applications. By 1971 more than 25 firms were manufacturing minicomputers, although Digital and Data General Corporation took an early lead in their sale and manufacture. Courtesy of Digital Equipment Corporation

1957 *Sputnik* launched

1964 Beatlemania develops in U.S.

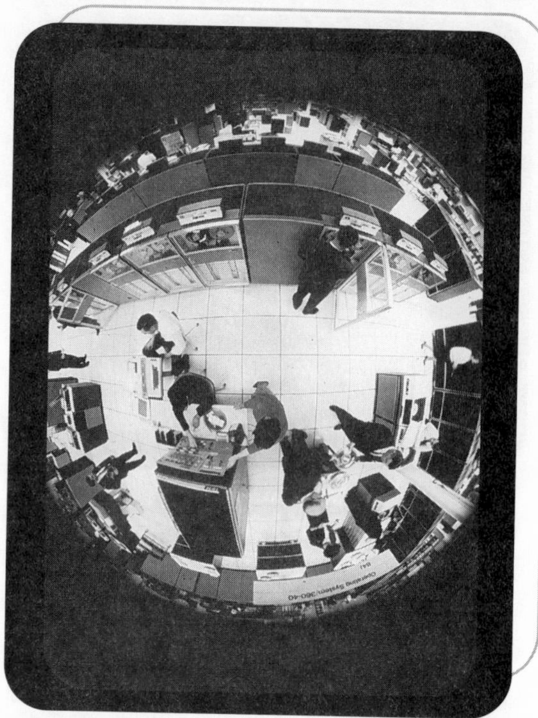

1964: The IBM System/360 and the Third Generation of Computers

The third generation was characterized by computers built around integrated circuits. Of these, some historians consider IBM's *System/360* line of computers, introduced in 1964, the single most important innovation in the history of computers. System/360 was conceived as a family of computers with *upward compatibility;* when a company outgrew one model it could move up to the next model without worrying about converting its data. System/360 and other lines built around integrated circuits made all previous computers obsolete, but the advantages were so great that most users wrote the costs of conversion off as the price of progress.
Courtesy of International Business Machines Corporation

1964: Basic—More than a Beginner's Programming Language

In the early 1960s, Dr. Thomas Kurtz and Dr. John Kennedy of Dartmouth College began developing a programming language that a beginner could learn and use quickly. Their work culminated in 1964 with BASIC. Over the years, BASIC gained widespread popularity and evolved from a teaching language into a versatile and powerful language for both business and scientific applications. BASIC is supported on more computers than any other language—from micros to mainframes. Courtesy of True BASIC, Inc.

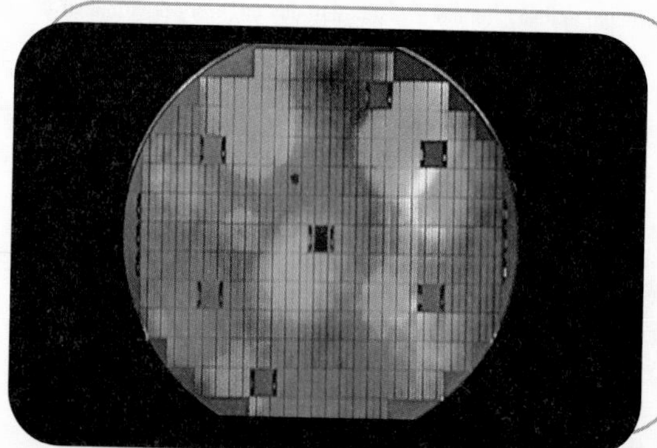

1971: Integrated Circuits and the Fourth Generation of Computers

Although most computer vendors would classify their computers as fourth generation, most people pinpoint 1971 as the generation's beginning. That was the year large-scale integration of circuitry (more circuits per unit of space) was introduced. The base technology, though, is still the integrated circuit. This is not to say that two decades have passed without significant innovations. In truth, the computer industry has experienced a mind-boggling succession of advances in the further miniaturization of circuitry, data communications, and the design of computer hardware and software. Courtesy of International Business Machines Corporation

1969 *Apollo 11* lands on moon

1975: Microsoft and Bill Gates

In 1968, seventh grader Bill Gates and ninth grader Paul Allen were teaching the computer to play monopoly and commanding it to play millions of games to discover gaming strategies. Seven years later, in 1975, they were to set a course that would revolutionize the computer industry. While at Harvard, Gates and Allen developed a BASIC programming language for the first commercially available microcomputer, the MITS Altair. After successful completion of the project, the two formed Microsoft Corporation, now the largest and most influential software company in the world. Microsoft was given enormous boost when its operating system software, MS-DOS®, was selected for use by the IBM PC. Gates, now richest man in America, provides the company's vision on new product ideas and technologies.
Courtesy of Microsoft Corporation

1981: The IBM PC

In 1981, IBM tossed its hat into the personal computer ring with its announcement of the IBM Personal Computer, or IBM PC. By the end of 1982, 835,000 had been sold. When software vendors began to orient their products to the IBM PC, many companies began offering *IBM-PC compatibles* or *clones*. Today, the IBM PC and its clones have become a powerful standard for the microcomputer industry.
Courtesy of International Business Machines Corporation

1977: The Apple II

Not until 1975 and the introduction of the *Altair 8800* personal computer was computing made available to individuals and very small companies. This event has forever changed how society perceives computers. One prominent entrepreneurial venture during the early years of personal computers was the Apple II® computer (shown here). Two young computer enthusiasts, Steven Jobs and Steve Wozniak (then 21 and 26 years of age, respectively), collaborated to create and build their Apple II computer on a makeshift production line in Jobs' garage. Seven years later, Apple Computer earned a spot on the Fortune 500, a list of the 500 largest corporations in the United States. Courtesy of Apple Computer, Inc.

1976 USA's 200th birthday

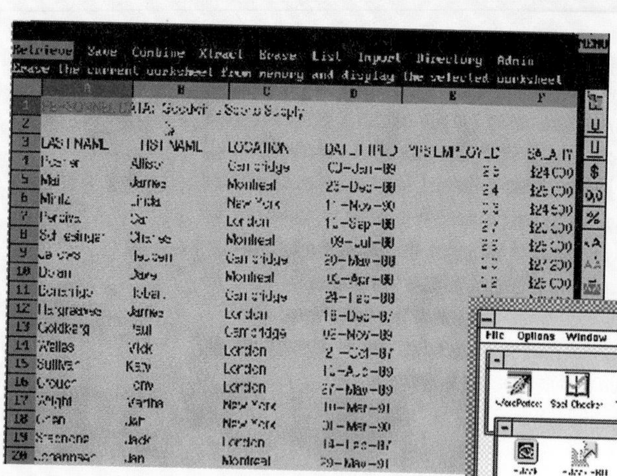

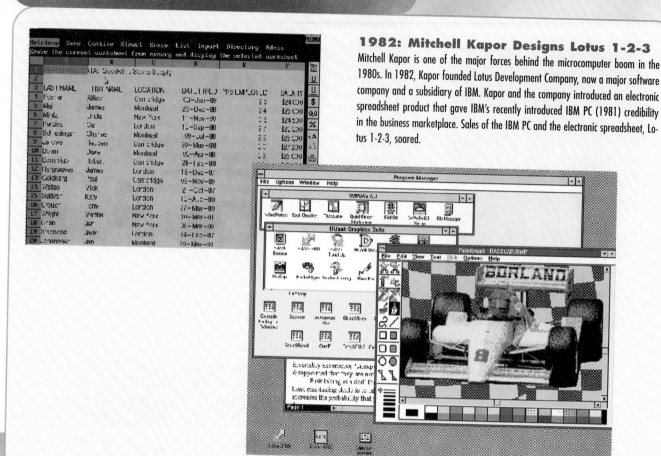

1982: Mitchell Kapor Designs Lotus 1-2-3

Mitchell Kapor is one of the major forces behind the microcomputer boom in the 1980s. In 1982, Kapor founded Lotus Development Company, now a major software company and a subsidiary of IBM. Kapor and the company introduced an electronic spreadsheet product that gave IBM's recently introduced IBM PC (1981) credibility in the business marketplace. Sales of the IBM PC and the electronic spreadsheet, Lotus 1-2-3, soared.

1985-Present: Microsoft® Windows®

Microsoft introduced Windows®, a GUI for IBM-PC compatible computers in 1985; however, Windows did not enjoy widespread acceptance until 1990 with the release of Windows 3.0. Windows 3.0 gave a huge boost to the software industry because larger, more complex programs could now be run on IBM-PC compatibles. Subsequent releases, including Windows® 95, Windows® NT, Windows® 98, and Windows® 2000 made personal computers even easier to use, fueling the PC explosion of the 1990s.

1984: The Macintosh and Graphical User Interfaces

In 1984 Apple Computer introduced the Macintosh® desktop computer with a very "friendly" graphical user interface—proof that computers can be easy and fun to use. Graphical user interfaces (GUIs) began to change the complexion of the software industry. They have changed the interaction between human and computer from a short, character-oriented exchange modeled on the teletypewriter to the now familiar WIMP interface—Windows, Icons, Menus, and Pointing devices.

Courtesy of Apple Computer, Inc.

1983 Compact disk (CD) introduced for recording music

1993: The Pentium Processor and Multimedia

The IBM-PC–compatible PCs started out using the Intel® 8088 microprocessor chip, then a succession of ever more powerful chips, including the Intel 80286, 80386, or 80486 chips. But not until the Intel® Pentium® (shown here) and its successors, the Pentium Pro and Pentium II, did PCs do much with multimedia, the integration of motion video, animation, graphics, sound, and so on. The emergence of the high-powered Pentium processors and their ability to handle multimedia applications changed the way we view and use PCs. Photo courtesy of Intel Corporation

1993: The World Wide Web and the Internet Browser

The 1995 bombing of the Murrah Federal Building in Oklahoma City stirred the emotions of the people throughout the world. This picture by Liz Dabrowski, staff photographer for *The Oklahoma Daily* (the student voice of the University of Oklahoma in Norman), speaks volumes about what happened and reminds us that we must never forget. In retrospect, we now view 1993 through 1995 as turnaround years for the Internet when millions of people began to tune into it for news of the bombing and other events and for a wealth of other information and services. Two things happened to encourage greater use of the Internet. The World Wide Web, one of several Internet-based applications, came of age as Web traffic grew 341,634% in its third year, 1993. The Web was unique in that it enabled "Web pages" to be linked across the Internet. Second, a number of Internet browsers were introduced during this time, including the Prodigy (a commercial information service) browser shown here and Netscape Navigator. These browsers enabled users to navigate the World Wide Web with ease. Today, the World Wide Web is the foundation for most Internet communications and services.

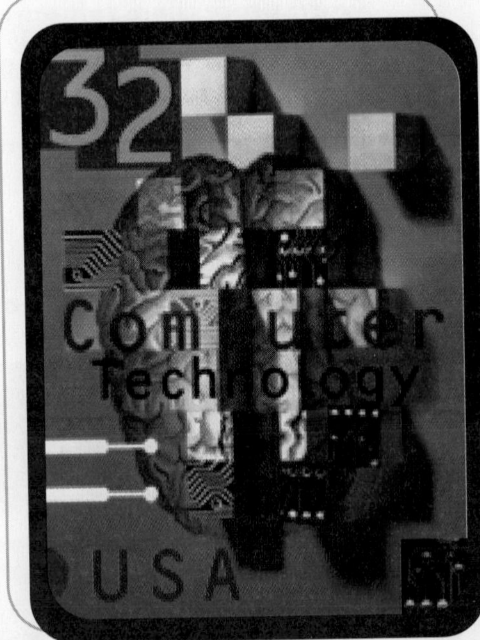

1996: U.S. Stamp Commemorates Half Century of Computing

The dedication of this U.S. Postal Service stamp was unique in that it was the first to be broadcast live over the Internet so that stamp collectors throughout the world could see and hear the ceremony. The USPS issued the stamp to commemorate the fiftieth anniversary of the ENIAC (the first full-scale electronic computer) and the 50 years of computer technology that followed. The dedication was held at Aberdeen Proving Ground, Maryland, the home of the ENIAC.

1989 Berlin Wall falls

1995 Bombing of the Murrah Federal Building in Oklahoma City

Using the PC: Popular Productivity Software

Learning Objectives

2.1 Become familiar with mainstream personal productivity software.

2.2 Understand the function and applications of word processing software.

2.3 Understand the function and applications of desktop publishing software.

2.4 Understand the function and applications of presentation software.

2.5 Understand the function and applications of spreadsheet software.

2.6 Understand the function and applications of database software.

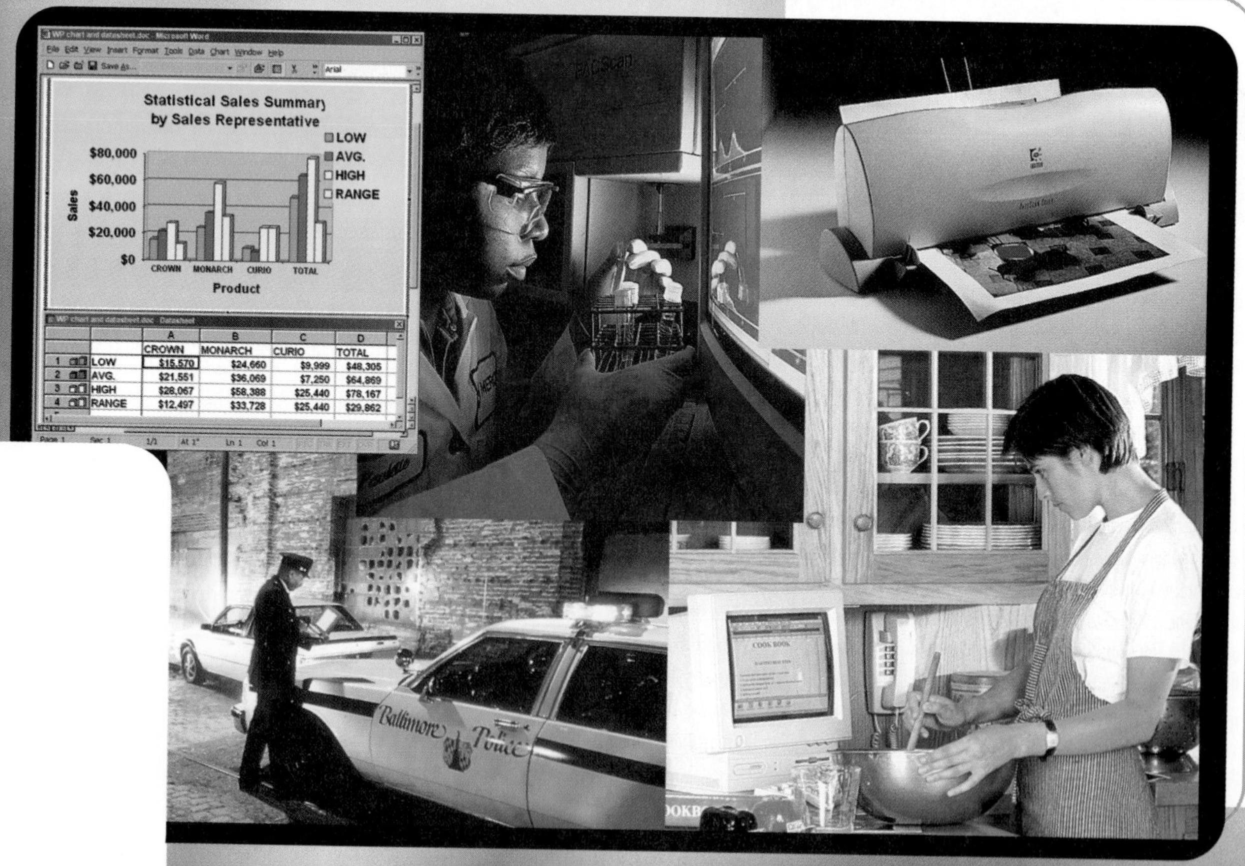

chapter 2

WHY THIS CHAPTER IS IMPORTANT TO YOU

Any computer, whether it supports video games or an enterprise-wide information system, does nothing until given exact, step-by-step instructions by a human. We provide these instructions in the form of a computer *program.* Programs comprise the system's software. How many instructions fit into a single program? The program in a multifunction digital wristwatch has about 5000 instructions. The programs that control the space shuttle during flight have about the same number of instructions as those for a cash register—about 1 million. Word processing and spreadsheet programs have several million instructions.

Instructions can be sequenced to perform just about any business or scientific procedure. And they have. The PC software story has no end. As you read this, tens of thousands of people are inventing new and better ways to use PCs through imaginative programming. Today, there are more than half a million commercial software products that cover everything from astrology to zoology.

Although this text is filled with examples of software and how it is used, these examples don't adequately convey the vast number of applications software packages available to us. What we do in this book is give you a carefully selected overview of what the PC software world has to offer. This chapter introduces you to the most commonly used applications software, generally those contained in popular software suites, such as Microsoft Office 2000. Communications software, including Internet browsers, is covered in Chapter 7. Operating systems and utility software are covered in Chapter 8. Chapter 9 illustrates some of the rest (personal information management, education, reference, home and personal, business, graphics, entertainment, edutainment, and other software).

This chapter gives you an overview understanding of word processing, desktop publishing, presentation, spreadsheet, and database software. You'll learn that almost anything involving the manipulation of text and images can be done more easily and professionally with word processing and desktop publishing software. You'll learn that you can prepare professional looking visual aids that can bolster the effectiveness of any presentation. You'll learn how spreadsheet and database software can help you organize, analyze, and present all kinds of information. Perhaps, most importantly, you learn that tools exist that can save you lots of time, make you more productive, and help you present yourself in a more professional manner.

Value Learning

2.1 PERSONAL COMPUTING WITH POPULAR PRODUCTIVITY PACKAGES

Monthly Technology Update

Personal computing encompasses everything from 3-D games, to going online, to computer-based education, to music composition. A seemingly endless number of software packages adds variety to the personal computing experience. However, over the history of personal computing, word processing software, desktop publishing software, presentation software, spreadsheet software, database software, and, more recently, Internet browser software and graphics software have formed the foundation of personal computing. Software packages in these categories have won unanimous user acceptance because of their tremendous contribution to personal productivity. This chapter provides a conceptual and functional overview of the first five of these mainstream applications. The newcomers, browser and graphics software, are covered later in the book.

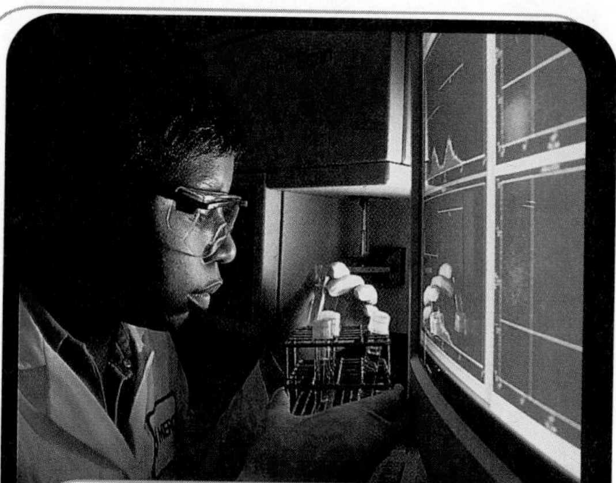

PC Skills Critical Most jobs require a fair amount of writing, drawing, and/or working with stored information. This is true for architects, teachers, lawyers, insurance agents, executives, and it is true for this Merck & Company medical researcher. Word processing skills will benefit her as she writes up her findings, and spreadsheet software helps her organize and analyze resulting data. Courtesy of Merck & Co., Inc.

After reading this chapter, you'll understand what these software packages are and, generally, what they can do. To learn how to perform basic word processing operations in Microsoft Word 2000, PowerPoint 2000, or some other productivity package, you'll need some hands-on laboratory work. Over time, through experience and experimentation, you will learn how to take advantage of all that these packages have to offer. Microsoft Office 2000, a software suite, is the basis for the examples in this chapter (Word 2000, Publisher 2000, PowerPoint 2000, Excel 2000, and Access 2000). **Software suites** are bundles of complementary software that include, to varying degrees, several or all of the software featured in this chapter. The various programs within a given software suite have a common interface and are integrated for easy transfer of information among programs. Corel®, WordPerfect® 9, and Lotus SmartSuite® 9 are the other major suites.

SECTION SELF-CHECK

Self-Check

2-1.1 The foundation of personal computing over the last decade has been 3-D computing games. (T/F)

2-1.2 Various programs within a given software suite have a common interface. (T/F)

2-1.3 Which of the following is not a software suite: (a) Borland's Pathmaker Online Navigator, (b) Corel WordPerfect 9, (c) Lotus SmartSuite 9, or (d) Microsoft Office 2000?

2.2 WORD PROCESSING: THE MOST POPULAR PC APPLICATION

Word Processing/DTP

At work, at home, at school, and even during leisure activities, we spend much of our time writing. At work we send e-mail and write procedures manuals. At home we keep to-do lists and prepare party announcements. At school we write reports and essays. During leisure time, we keep diaries, write letters to our family and friends, and prepare newsletters for our club associations (see Figure 2.1). These are just a few of the many day-to-day writing activities that can be made easier and more presentable through the use of word processing software. Today's sophisticated *word processing software* packages do much more than text-oriented word processing. For example, popular packages, like Microsoft Word and WordPerfect, not only let you integrate images with text for *printed documents,* but they let you integrate audio, such as voice annotations, and even video within documents designed for *on-screen viewing.*

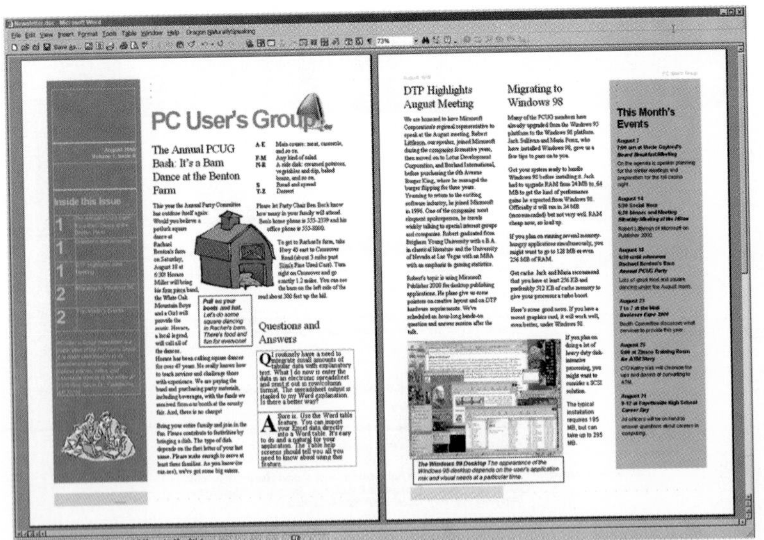

FIGURE 2.1

Word Processing Newsletter

This Microsoft Word 2000–based newsletter illustrates many of the features of word processing. The newsletter includes text columns, shaded sidebars, embedded images, headings, a variety of fonts, and much more.

Word Processing Concepts and Features

In Chapter 1 we learned that word processing software lets us create, edit (revise), and format documents in preparation for output. Output can be a document that is printed, displayed on a monitor, faxed, e-mailed, or, perhaps, posted to the Internet for worldwide access. If you were to use word processing to prepare a report, you would key in the full draft only once. Revisions and corrections are made to a computer-based file before the finalized report is printed or output in some other way. If you forget a word or need to add a paragraph, you do not have to retype a page or, in the worst case, the whole report. For example, the original text for this book was keyed in only once. The authors then made many editorial changes before the final manuscript was submitted to the publisher. Word processing is a lot more than an automated pen and paper. It checks your grammar and spelling, helps you find the right word, and assists you in formatting your document (margins, typeface, headings, and so on). You, however, must supply the words and images.

Creating and Saving a Document

Word Processing

You'll probably learn the process and techniques of preparing a word processing document in a lab or, perhaps, via interactive computer-based training. To create an original document, such as a résumé (see Figure 2.2), you simply begin entering text from the keyboard and, as needed, enter format commands that enhance the appearance of the document when it is printed or displayed (spacing, italics, and so on). You can insert images, such as the photo in Figure 2.2, then resize and/or reposition them anywhere within the word processing document. If you wish to work with the document later, you will need to save it to disk storage for later recall. When you recall a document from disk storage, you can *edit* (revise) it, then save the revised version of the document to disk storage. Once you are satisfied with the content and appearance of the document, you are ready to print, send, or display it.

Formatting a Document You format a word processing document by specifying what you wish the general appearance of the document to be when it is printed. Typically, the preset format, or *default settings,* fit most word processing applications. For example, the size of the output document is set at letter size ($8\frac{1}{2}$ by 11 inches); the left, right, top, and bottom margins are set at 1 inch; tabs are set every $\frac{1}{2}$ inch; and line spacing is set at 6 lines per inch. The default font might be 12 point Arial. Arial is one of dozens of available **typefaces** you can use in documents. A typeface refers to a set of characters of a particular design (*Shelley Script*, Plantin, Calligraphy, and so on are typefaces). A **font** is described by its typeface, its height in points (8, 10, 14, 24, and so on; there are 72 points to the

Word Processing Résumé
Mallory Brooks used Microsoft Word 2000 to help her make a good first impression with prospective employers. The result is this professional-looking résumé that emphasizes her strengths. The use of color adds flair to any document. This and other modern word processing packages are WYSIWYG (pronounced *"WIZ e wig"*), short for "What you see is what you get." What you see on the screen is essentially what the document will look like when it is printed—the font, graphics, and all.

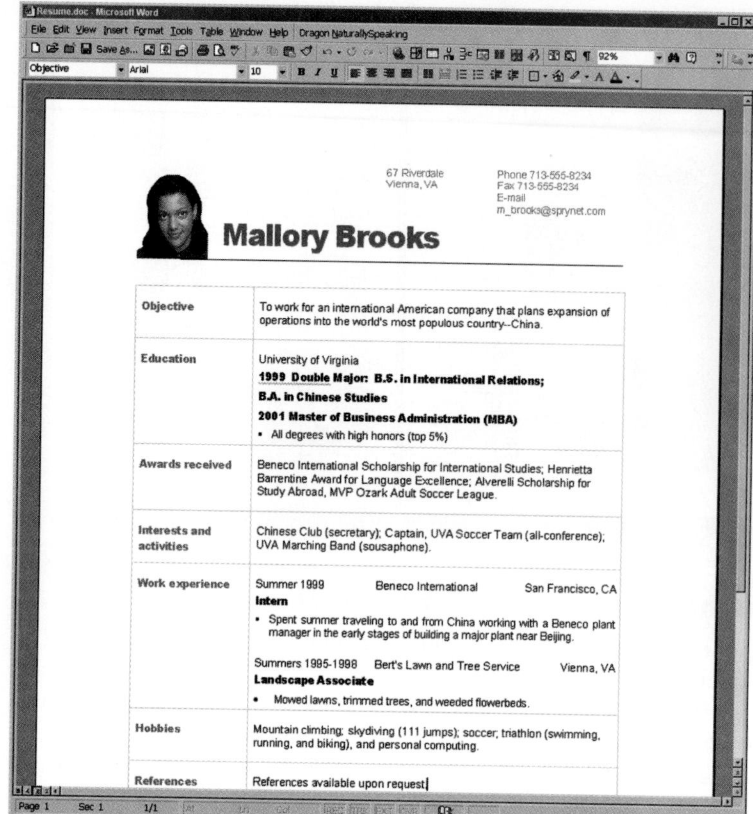

67 Riverdale
Vienna, VA

Phone 713-555-8234
Fax 713-555-8234
E-mail
m_brooks@sprynet.com

Mallory Brooks

Objective	To work for an international American company that plans expansion of operations into the world's most populous country--China.
Education	University of Virginia **1999 Double Major: B.S. in International Relations;** **B.A. in Chinese Studies** **2001 Master of Business Administration (MBA)** • All degrees with high honors (top 5%)
Awards received	Beneco International Scholarship for International Studies; Henrietta Barrentine Award for Language Excellence; Alverelli Scholarship for Study Abroad, MVP Ozark Adult Soccer League.
Interests and activities	Chinese Club (secretary); Captain, UVA Soccer Team (all-conference); UVA Marching Band (sousaphone).
Work experience	Summer 1999 Beneco International San Francisco, CA **Intern** • Spent summer traveling to and from China working with a Beneco plant manager in the early stages of building a major plant near Beijing. Summers 1995-1998 Bert's Lawn and Tree Service Vienna, VA **Landscape Associate** • Mowed lawns, trimmed trees, and weeded flowerbeds.
Hobbies	Mountain climbing; skydiving (111 jumps); soccer; triathlon (swimming, running, and biking), and personal computing.
References	References available upon request.

inch), and its presentation attribute (roman [or normal], **bold,** *italic,* underline, and so on). If you are planning a three-column newsletter or would prefer something other than the defaults, you would want to revise the format specifications.

What You Can Do with Word Processing: The Features Package

Typically, text is entered in a word processing or other type of document via *keyboard* or *speech recognition.* In speech recognition, you simply speak into a microphone and the words are interpreted by speech-recognition software and entered in the document. Word processing packages are **WYSIWYG** (pronounced "*WIZ e wig*"), short for "What you see is what you get." What you do to a document, whether entering text or inserting an image, is reflected on the screen showing you what the document will look like when it is printed. Word processing software has many features that help you create exactly what you want. The specifics of these features are left to the hands-on lab, but Figure 2.3 gives you a good visual summary of word processing features and capabilities. As you can see, you can mix the size and style of fonts, add headers and footnotes, create outlines, make text run vertical, draw images, place text in columns, and much more.

The word processing *find* feature lets us search our entire word processing document and identify all occurrences of a particular search string. For example, when you could find (search) for "January", the cursor is placed at the first occurrence of "January". The *replace* feature enables replacement either selectively or globally. For example, you can replace any or all occurrences of "January" with "February".

Writing Tools: Dotting the i's and Crossing the t's

Word processing programs offer several helpful writing tools.

- *Spelling checker.* The **spelling checker** checks every word in the text against an **electronic dictionary** and alerts you if a word is not in the dictionary. Some systems automatically correct misspelled words as they are entered.

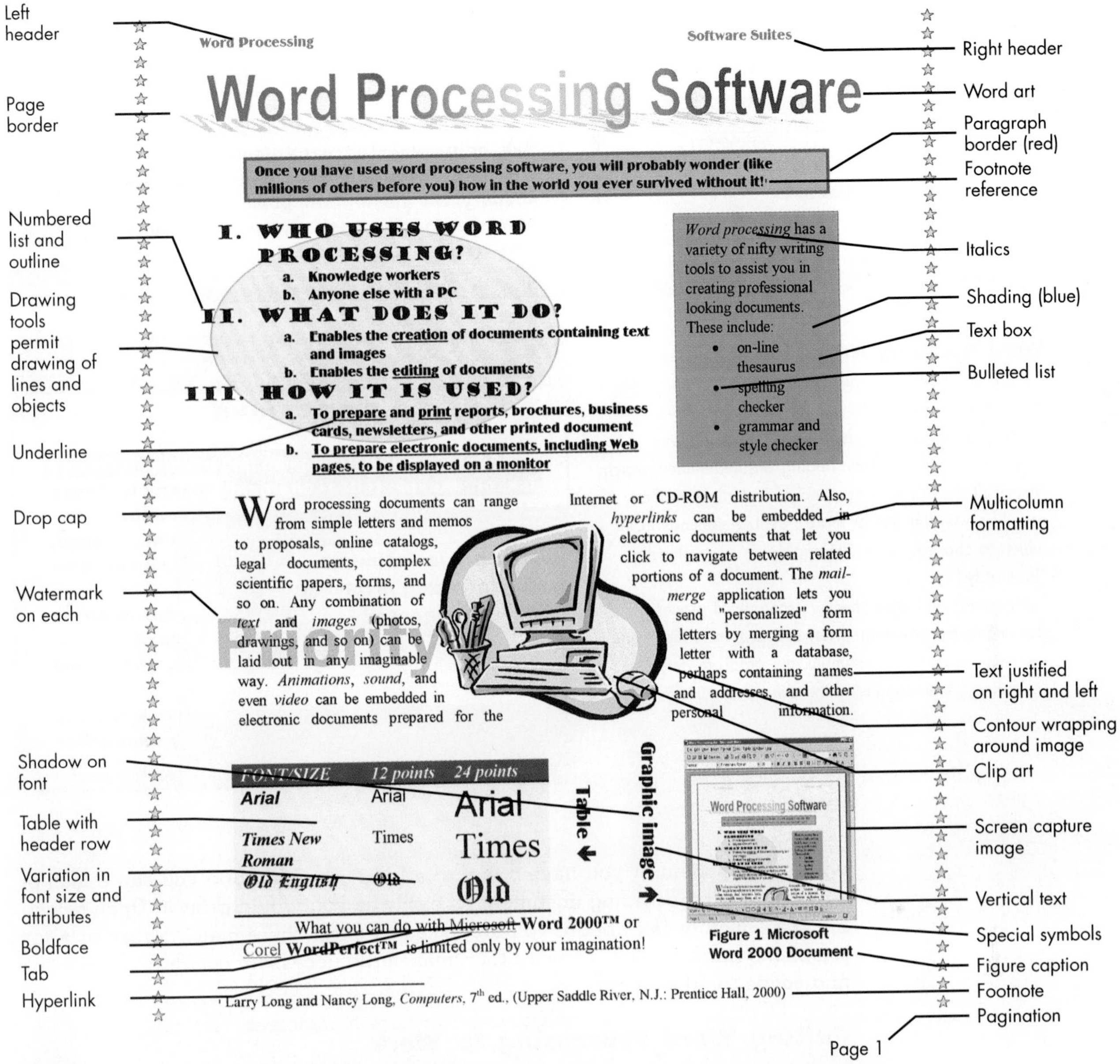

Left header

Word Processing

Software Suites

Right header

Word Processing Software

Word art

Page border

Paragraph border (red)

Once you have used word processing software, you will probably wonder (like millions of others before you) how in the world you ever survived without it![1]

Footnote reference

Numbered list and outline

I. WHO USES WORD PROCESSING?

a. Knowledge workers

b. Anyone else with a PC

II. WHAT DOES IT DO?

a. Enables the <u>creation</u> of documents containing text and images

b. Enables the <u>editing</u> of documents

III. HOW IT IS USED?

a. To <u>prepare</u> and <u>print</u> reports, brochures, business cards, newsletters, and other printed document

b. <u>To prepare electronic documents, including Web pages, to be displayed on a monitor</u>

Drawing tools permit drawing of lines and objects

Underline

Word processing has a variety of nifty writing tools to assist you in creating professional looking documents. These include:

- on-line thesaurus
- spelling checker
- grammar and style checker

Italics

Shading (blue)

Text box

Bulleted list

Drop cap

Word processing documents can range from simple letters and memos to proposals, online catalogs, legal documents, complex scientific papers, forms, and so on. Any combination of *text* and *images* (photos, drawings, and so on) can be laid out in any imaginable way. *Animations*, *sound*, and even *video* can be embedded in electronic documents prepared for the Internet or CD-ROM distribution. Also, *hyperlinks* can be embedded in electronic documents that let you click to navigate between related portions of a document. The *mail-merge* application lets you send "personalized" form letters by merging a form letter with a database, perhaps containing names and addresses, and other personal information.

Priority

Multicolumn formatting

Watermark on each

Text justified on right and left

Contour wrapping around image

Clip art

Shadow on font

Table with header row

Variation in font size and attributes

FONT/SIZE	*12 points*	*24 points*
Arial	Arial	Arial
Times New Roman	Times	Times
Old English	Old	Old

Table ➔

Graphic image ➔

Figure 1 Microsoft Word 2000 Document

Screen capture image

Vertical text

Special symbols

Figure caption

What you can do with Microsoft **Word 2000™** or <u>Corel</u> **WordPerfect™** is limited only by your imagination!

Boldface

Tab

Hyperlink

[1] Larry Long and Nancy Long, *Computers*, 7th ed., (Upper Saddle River, N.J.: Prentice Hall, 2000)

Footnote

Pagination

Page 1

Word Processing Features Overview This word processing document illustrates features common to most word processing software. Note that you can create special effects with the *drawing tool* and *border* features. The *watermark* feature lets you add a drawing, a company logo, headline-sized text (such as the "PRIORITY" in this example), or any image behind the printed document text. In the electronic world, documents are "networked" with hyperlinks (references to different sections of an electronic document or to other related electronic documents). Even the *callouts*, which label the features, are a word processing feature. Not shown is the *editing* feature that lets you add editorial remarks and make corrections to an original document. This feature is helpful when several people review a document prior to publication.

- *Thesaurus.* Most commercial word processing packages have an **online thesaurus** to help you find the right word.
- *Grammar and style checkers.* A **grammar and style checker** highlights grammatical concerns and deviations from conventions.

Figure 2.4 illustrates the use of these tools in a typical document.

Printing a Document or Sending an E-mail or Fax To print a document, ready the printer and select the *print* option on the main menu. If your PC is configured

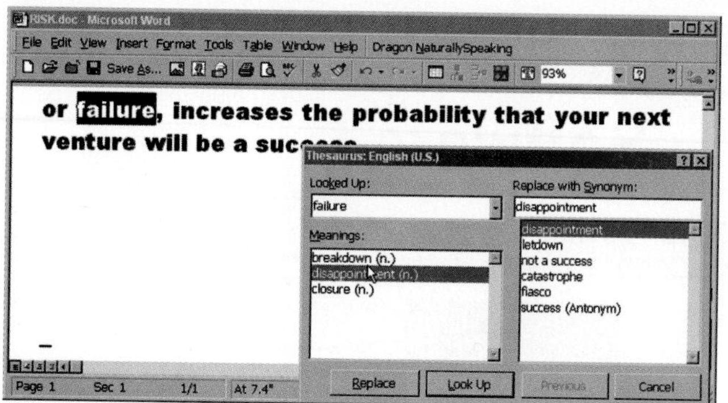

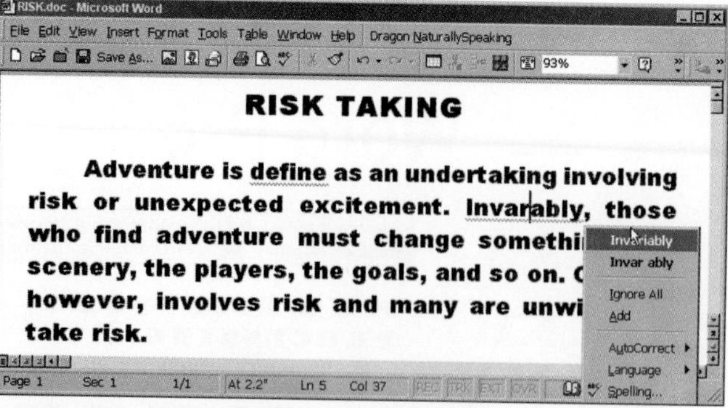

Word Processing Writing Tools The thesaurus feature helps you find the right word. In the example, the user requested synonyms for the word *failure.*

The spelling checker does as its name implies—checks the spelling. Upon finding an unidentified word, Microsoft Word's spelling checker underlines it, then usually gives you one or more possible spellings from which to choose. Here, "Invariably" is suggested for "Invarably."

Grammar and style checkers scan word processing documents for grammar, style, usage, punctuation, and spelling errors. In the example, the program detected "is define," then suggested the past tense, "defined."

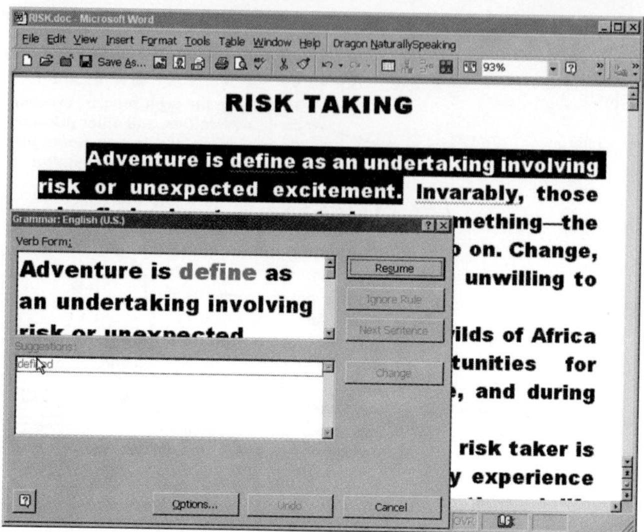

with a fax modem or you have a link to a local area network, you can e-mail or fax your word processing document as easily as you would print it. Upon selecting the e-mail or fax option, you are asked to enter the e-mail address or a fax telephone number. The software then makes the necessary communications link and sends the document.

Putting Word Processing to Work

Word processing is extremely versatile, offering you a wide range of capabilities. Here are a few more applications for word processing. You will find many more as you gain experience with this, the most used of all software applications.

Merging Documents with a Database

Word processing software allows you to merge data in a database with the text of a document. The most common use of this capability is the *mail-merge* application, illustrated in Figure 2.5. In the example, Winnie Winnowski, the president of the PC User's Group, decided to send personalized letters to the club's new members. To do so, Winnie created a *form letter* file. The form letter contains references to entries in a *database file,* a separate word processing file containing a table. She then used the *merge* feature to combine the information in the table with the form letter to generate separate letters for each new member, thus produce the "personalized letters." This handy, timesaving process is illustrated and explained in Figure 2.5.

The mail-merge example is a good illustration of the use of **boilerplate.** Boilerplate is existing text that can be reused and customized for a variety of word processing applications. One nice feature of word processing is that you can accumulate documents on disk storage that eventually will help you meet other

FirstName	LastName	JobTitle	Company	Address	City	State	Zip	Memberdate	Work Phone	Email
Mike	Quinn	Sports Editor	Ozark Times	766 Second Ave.	Eureka Springs	AR	72766	7/20/2000	444-8586	quinn@ozarktimes.com
Rita	Cole	Marketing Mgr.	Evco Limited	1583 E. Star Rd.	Fayetteville	AR	72702	7/12/2000	231-5567	rcole@evco.com
Linda	Mench	Soccer Coach	State University	1 Ivy St. Apt A4	Fayetteville	AR	72703	7/07/2000	231-0080	lmench@stateu.edu
Jim	Best	Plant Manager	Best, Inc.	324 Market Dr.	Fayetteville	AR	72701	6/29/2000	555-5677	jbest@best.com
Frank	Lee	Prosecuting Attorney	Washington County	564 N. Town St.	Springdale	AR	72777	6/14/2000	799-3421	frl@wash.ar.gov

Winnie Winnowski created the *database file* by entering new member information into the PC User's Group member database, actually a word processing table with rows and columns. She then used a *sort* feature (descending by Memberdate, or date of membership) to select only the new members from the database. The database file contains *records* for each member, which are made up of related *fields*. Each record has eleven fields, each of which is described in its field name at the top of the database display. This database file is merged with the *form file* (the letter) to generate the personalized letters.

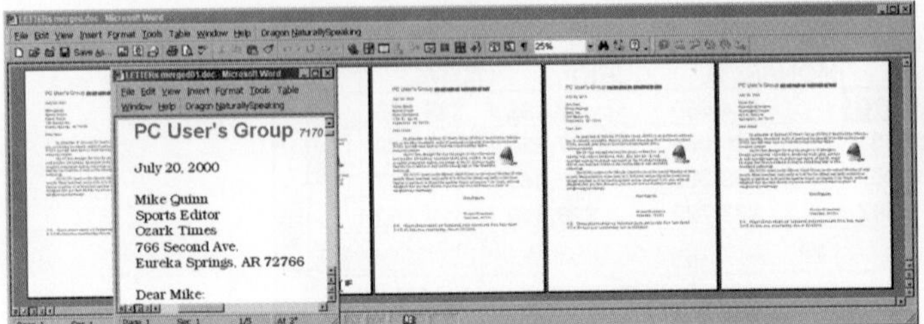

During the merge process the letter document in the *form file* is merged with each record in the *database file* to create a *merge file* containing personalized letters to each new member. The example illustrates what happens when the records are merged with the form file letter. The resulting document, which contains all personalized letters, is ready to print. The address of the first letter is exploded to show how database information is merged with the first letter. The PCUG member database file can be merged with an envelope form file to print the envelopes.

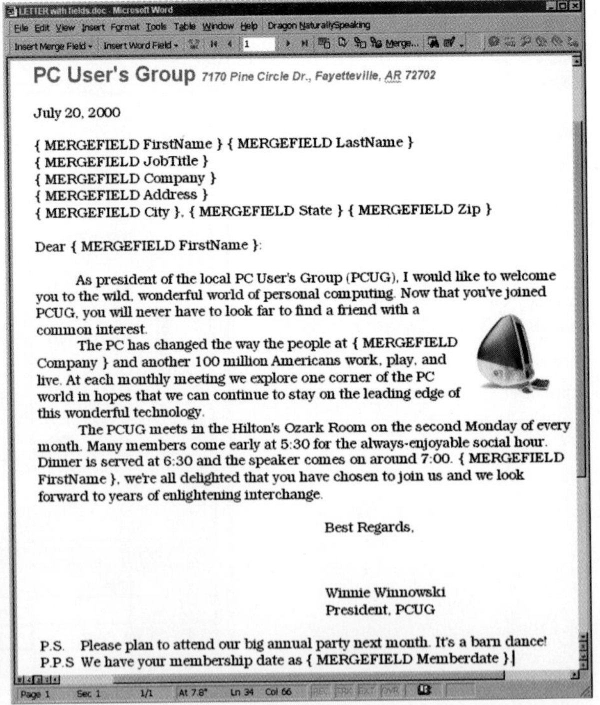

PC User's Group *7170 Pine Circle Dr., Fayetteville, AR 72702*

July 20, 2000

{ MERGEFIELD FirstName } { MERGEFIELD LastName }
{ MERGEFIELD JobTitle }
{ MERGEFIELD Company }
{ MERGEFIELD Address }
{ MERGEFIELD City }, { MERGEFIELD State } { MERGEFIELD Zip }

Dear { MERGEFIELD FirstName }:

As president of the local PC User's Group (PCUG), I would like to welcome you to the wild, wonderful world of personal computing. Now that you've joined PCUG, you will never have to look far to find a friend with a common interest.

The PC has changed the way the people at { MERGEFIELD Company } and another 100 million Americans work, play, and live. At each monthly meeting we explore one corner of the PC world in hopes that we can continue to stay on the leading edge of this wonderful technology.

The PCUG meets in the Hilton's Ozark Room on the second Monday of every month. Many members come early at 5:30 for the always-enjoyable social hour. Dinner is served at 6:30 and the speaker comes on around 7:00. { MERGEFIELD FirstName }, we're all delighted that you have chosen to join us and we look forward to years of enlightening interchange.

Best Regards,

Winnie Winnowski
President, PCUG

P.S. Please plan to attend our big annual party next month. It's a barn dance!
P.P.S. We have your membership date as { MERGEFIELD Memberdate }.

To prepare the *form file,* Winnie created and formatted this form letter, inserting merge codes in the text of the letter to indicate where the data are to be merged. Information from the database file is merged with the form file in the inside address, the salutation, the body of the letter, and the postscript section.

Word Processing Mail-Merge Application Winnie Winnowski used the mail-merge capability to send personalized letters to all the new members of her club. Two specially formatted document files must be created to merge data with a text document: the *database file* and the *form file*. The two are merged to create the personalized letters.

word processing needs. You can even *buy* boilerplate (for example, text for business letters). The legal profession offers some of the best examples of the use of boilerplate. Simple wills, uncontested divorces, individual bankruptcies, real estate transfers, and other straightforward legal documents may be as much as 95% boilerplate. The use of boilerplate is common in all areas of business, education, government, and personal endeavor.

Integrating Charts with Documents

The word processing *chart* feature lets you generate a variety of charts from spreadsheet-like data in a Microsoft® Word 2000 *datasheet.* Figure 2.6 shows how the information in a "Statistical Sales Summary" datasheet can be dynamically graphed within a word processing document. The bar graph in Figure 2.6 was created automatically from the data in the datasheet. Once data have been entered into the datasheet, you can change values and observe their effect on the chart.

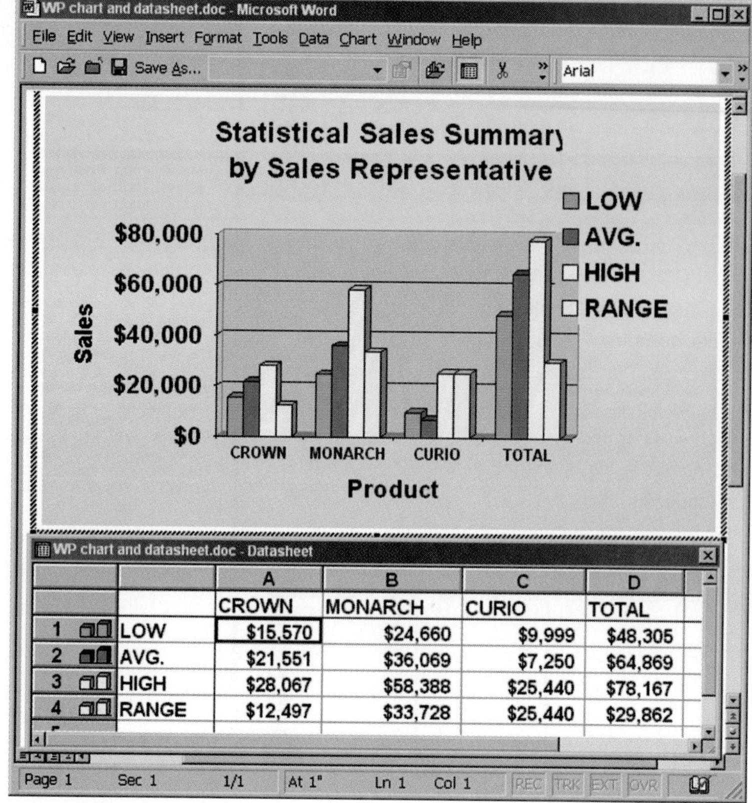

		A	B	C	D
		CROWN	MONARCH	CURIO	TOTAL
1	LOW	$15,570	$24,660	$9,999	$48,305
2	AVG.	$21,551	$36,069	$7,250	$64,869
3	HIGH	$28,067	$58,388	$25,440	$78,167
4	RANGE	$12,497	$33,728	$25,440	$29,862

FIGURE 2.6

Word Processing Table and Chart The word processing *chart* feature makes it easy to generate professional looking charts within documents. In Microsoft Word 2000, data are entered into a datasheet (much like a spreadsheet). The data in the Word datasheet can be presented in a variety of charts.

Embedded Hyperlinks

Not all word processing documents are designed to be printed. For example, many companies are opting to put their reference materials in electronic, rather than printed, documents. Electronic versions of product catalogs, procedures manuals, personnel handbooks, and so on are now common in the business community. They are easier to create, maintain, and distribute. One of the main reasons for this trend toward online documents is the ability to place **hyperlinks** in documents.

Hyperlinks let you tie parts of a document or different documents together. Words or phrases within documents can be highlighted as hyperlinks (see Figure 2.7). When you encounter a hyperlink entry, you can jump (link) to another place in the same document or to another document on your PC's hard disk, on a local area network, or on the Internet for more information. In Windows-based programs, hyperlinks usually are displayed in a color (often blue or green) and underlined (see Figure 2.7). Hyperlinks make it easy to skip around within or between documents to find what you want.

Creating Web Pages

If you can create a word processing document, you can create a Web page on the **World Wide Web,** the primary application used for viewing information on the Internet. Information on **the Web,** which may be graphics, audio, video, animation, and text, is viewed in **Web pages.** A Web page is retrieved from an Internet server computer, just as the word processing document is retrieved from a PC's hard disk. To a large extent, the explosion of information made available over the Internet can be attributed to the fact that word processing software lets users save documents in a format compatible with transmission over the Internet's World Wide Web. Now, anyone with word processing skills can contribute to the wealth of information on the Internet. What you see in a word processing document is essentially what you would see when viewing it as a Web page on an Internet browser.

IT Ethics

E-MAIL ETIQUETTE

As a knowledge worker, you may spend an hour or more each day composing or responding to e-mail. E-mail is now as much a part of the business world as the paycheck. How we present ourselves in our e-mails can play a role in how effective we are in business and what people think of us. You can leave a good or bad impression with your correspondents depending on *what* you say in your message and *how* you say it. During face-to-face conversations we use vocal inflections or body movements that clarify words or phrases. E-mail is just words, leaving the door open for misinterpretation of our intended message. Anyone composing e-mail should be aware that it's electronic and could be easily forwarded, printed, and even broadcast to others. Broadcasting sensitive information could be very embarrassing to you and to others. Every e-mailer should be careful what he or she writes and follow the basic tenents of e-mail etiquette. For example, you should inform senders when you forward their e-mail. A good e-mail message includes a subject, has a logical flow, and concludes with a signature (name, association, and contact information).

Discussion: What would be considered good e-mail etiquette?

Word Processing: Working Faster and Smarter

Word processing is the perfect example of how automation can be used to increase productivity and foster creativity. It reduces the effort you must devote to the routine aspects of writing so you can focus your attention on its creative aspects. As a result, most word processing users will agree that their writing styles have improved. The finished product is less verbose, better organized, free from spelling errors, and, of course, more visually appealing.

Self-Check

SECTION SELF-CHECK

2-2.1 Preset format specifications are referred to as *concrete settings.* (T/F)

2-2.2 Modern word processing packages let you integrate audio, such as voice annotations, and video within documents designed for on-screen viewing. (T/F)

2-2.3 An online thesaurus can be used to suggest synonyms for a word in a word processing document. (T/F)

2-2.4 Hyperlinks have been important in the trend of online documentation. (T/F)

2-2.5 The word processing form letter contains references to entries in a database file. (T/F)

Word Processing Hyperlinks
Microsoft Word and other Microsoft Office 2000 applications let you embed hyperlinks within documents. When clicked with a mouse, the hyperlinks can link to another Word or Microsoft Office 2000 document or to a page on the Internet. In this example, the user clicked on the hyperlink "IBM" to open the associated Internet page (IBM Corporation's home page at <www.ibm.com>) within the Internet Explorer browser. After viewing the linked document, the user can opt to return to the original document.

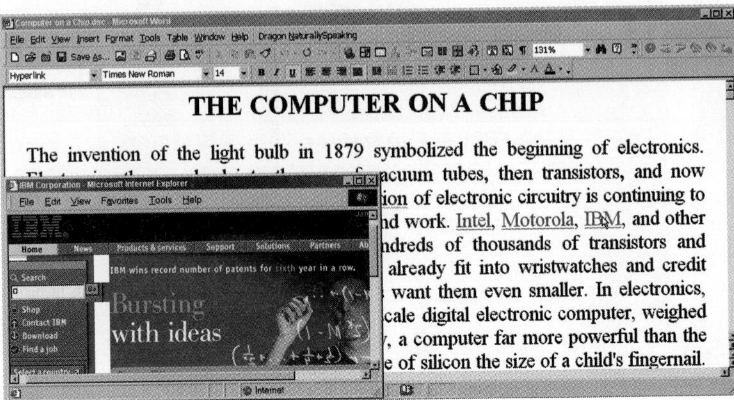

2-2.6 Boilerplate is existing text that can in some way be reused and customized for a variety of word processing applications. (T/F)

2-2.7 In a word processing document, different documents can be tied together by: (a) cybertext links, (b) hydratext links, (c) hydrolinks, or (d) hyperlinks.

2-2.8 The spelling checker checks every word in the text against a(n): (a) online thesaurus, (b) hyperlink, (c) datasheet, or (d) electronic dictionary.

2-2.9 Which of these terms is not normally associated with the default settings on word processing software: (a) merge sequence, (b) document size, (c) margins, or (d) font?

2-2.10 Word processing writing tools include all but which of the following: (a) spelling checker, (b) thesaurus, (c) electronic pencil, or (d) grammar and style checker?

2.3 DESKTOP PUBLISHING: FREEDOM OF THE PRESS

Word processing can handle just about any document generation task, but some people need to produce documents with complicated layouts and documents that are ready to be printed professionally. For these people, the application of choice is *desktop publishing.* Instead of being tied to the typesetter and a commercial print shop, millions of users now create newsletters, brochures, user manuals, pamphlets, flyers, restaurant menus, periodicals, greeting cards, graduation certificates, and thousands of other printed and published items. Desktop publishing refers to the capability of producing *camera-ready documents* (ready to be printed professionally) from the confines of a desktop. The resulting documents are then reproduced by a variety of means, from duplicating machines to offset printing (a commercial printing process used for high-volume printing). The files/documents resulting from desktop publishing are compatible with hardware used in offset printing. Desktop publishing software can help you produce every conceivable type of printed matter, from business cards to catalogs, and is changing the way organizations and individuals meet their printing needs. Consider these examples.

- PTA parents use desktop publishing to prepare flyers for school fund-raisers (see Figure 2.8).
- Marketing managers use desktop publishing to prepare ad pieces.

FIGURE 2.8

Desktop Publishing Fund-Raising Flyer This flyer for a school fund-raiser was produced with Microsoft® Publisher 2000. The adjacent image illustrates how desktop publishing documents are composed of rectangular frames (each frame is outlined and has little squares in its corners). Frames hold text and images and can be resized and repositioned to meet layout needs.

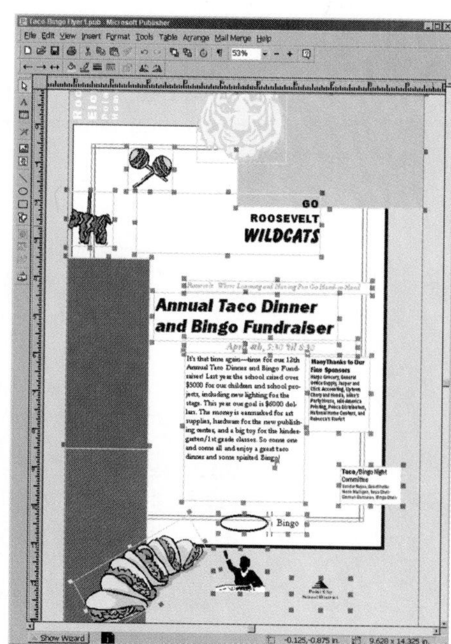

- Restaurant owners use desktop publishing to create menus.
- Personnel directors use desktop publishing to publish employee handbooks.

Desktop Publishing and Word Processing: What's the Difference?

Both desktop publishing and word processing software assist you in creating documents, but the end result and the way you get there can be quite different. In word processing, the emphasis is on *words,* the text that makes up the documents. In word processing, we fill the document with words, then add images, borders, shading, and so on around the running text. The text runs from the beginning to the end of the letter, handbook, or whatever document is being created. In desktop publishing, the emphasis is on overall *document composition.* Various types of *objects* are pulled together and laid out on a page. An object can be a block of text, an image, a border, an area of shading, and so on (see the explosion of objects in Figure 2.7). Desktop publishing's page layout capabilities, combined with its precision, have made desktop publishing the choice of professional designers of publication materials.

Creating and editing text within a desktop publishing program can be cumbersome, so most seasoned desktop publishers prepare their text using word processing software. Once the page layout is established, the text is *copied* (from the word processing document) and *pasted* (inserted) into the desktop publishing document at the appropriate location. Both desktop publishing and word processing allow you to save documents in a format compatible with the World Wide Web.

Desktop Publishing Concepts and Features

The quality of the desktop publishing–produced output depends on the quality of available input and output devices. The typical office will have hardware (scanners, printers, and so on) that is sufficient for most printing needs; however, professional graphics studios with very high-resolution hardware are needed for some jobs, like this book.

Creating a document, such as the fund-raiser flyer in Figure 2.8, with desktop publishing software involves going through the *document-composition process.* This process involves integrating graphics, photos, text, and other resources into a visually appealing *document layout.* Follow these steps to produce finished, professional-looking documents.

1 *Prepare text.* Generally, the text to be placed in desktop publishing documents is prepared with a word processing program.
2 *Prepare or identify nontext-related resources.* A number of resources are pulled together in a typical desktop publishing–produced document, such as a newsletter. These resources might include the text files; original artwork, photographs, and hard-copy graphics to be scanned; screen displays that have been captured into files; and clip art. All modern desktop publishing programs come with a healthy supply of **clip art.** Clip art refers to prepackaged electronic images stored on disk to be used as needed. The tacos and castanets images in Figure 2.8 are clip art, as are the tiger and the bingo player. The typical desktop publishing program will come with several thousand pieces of clip art, all searchable by keyword ("taco" or "tiger"). Had the document in the Figure 2.8 example required original art, the art would have been prepared using a separate illustration program.
3 *Lay out the document page(s).* Set up the page(s), indicating margins, number of columns, and so on. When you set up the page, *layout guides* are displayed to help you, but these will not appear in the printed document.
4 *Fill in the text frames.* Each resource is assigned to a rectangular **frame** (see the image in Figure 2.8 with the frames exploded for easy viewing). Generally, frames are classified as either *text frames* or *picture frames.* Text is

Image Scanner The components required for desktop publishing include a PC, document-composition software (for example, Microsoft® Publisher 2000), a printer, clip art, multimedia resources, illustration software (if you intend to create original illustrations), and image scanner (shown here). Relatively inexpensive page image scanners have opened the door for more people to get into desktop publishing.
Courtesy of Epson America, Inc.

placed in text frames. Note that a frame can be positioned within a frame or it can overlap a frame. For publications that require little text, enter the text directly into the text frame.

5 *Fill in the picture frames.* All types of images, from clip art to scanned photographs, are placed in picture frames. The example in Figure 2.8 includes several picture frames filled with images. Note that the taco frame is rotated about 45 degrees.

6 *Fine-tune the layout.* If what you see is not what you want, then you can use the mouse to reposition and/or resize frames containing text and pictures to the desired locations and sizes.

7 *Print the camera-ready document.* Once the display shows what you want, use a desktop page printer or commercial imagesetter (a typesetting device) to produce the finished camera-ready document.

8 *Publish the document.* Reproduce the camera copy for distribution.

SECTION SELF-CHECK

Self-Check

2-3.1 Desktop publishing software enables users to produce camera-ready documents for reproduction. (T/F)

2-3.2 Text in a desktop publishing file usually is entered first in spreadsheet software then moved. (T/F)

2-3.3 In desktop publishing, the emphasis is on overall document composition, pulling together various objects. (T/F)

2-3.4 Frames generally are classified as text frames and picture frames. (T/F)

2-3.5 The first step to producing desktop publishing documents is to: (a) print the camera copy, (b) fine-tune the layout, (c) prepare text, or (d) fill in the text frames?

2-3.6 During the document-composition process, each file is assigned to a rectangular: (a) frame, (b) image scanner, (c) clip-art file, or (d) hyperlink file?

2-3.7 Prepackaged electronic images stored on disk to be used as needed in documents are called: (a) text frames, (b) clip art, (c) camera copy, or (d) imagesetters?

2.4 PRESENTATION SOFTWARE: PUTTING ON THE SHOW

Serendipitous Surfing: Humor

During the past decade, PC-based *presentation software* has replaced overhead projectors and carousel projectors as the presentation tool of choice, whether at the lectern or the pulpit. Presentation software lets you create highly stylized images for group presentations, self-running slide shows (for example, PC-based information displays at trade shows), reports, and any other situation that requires the presentation of organized, visual information (see Figure 2.9). The software, such as Microsoft® PowerPoint® 2000, gives you a rich assortment of tools to help you create a variety of charts, graphs, and images and to help you make the presentation.

A progressive sales manager would never consider reporting a sales increase in tabular format on computer printout paper. A successful year that otherwise would be hidden in rows and columns of sales figures will be vividly apparent in a colorful PowerPoint bar graph. Those in other areas of business also want to "put their best foot forward." To do so, they use PC-based presentation software, often with an LCD projector, capable of projecting images onto a screen for all to see.

A number of studies confirm the power of presentation software. These studies uniformly support the following conclusions:

- People who use presentation software are perceived as being better prepared and more professional than those who do not.

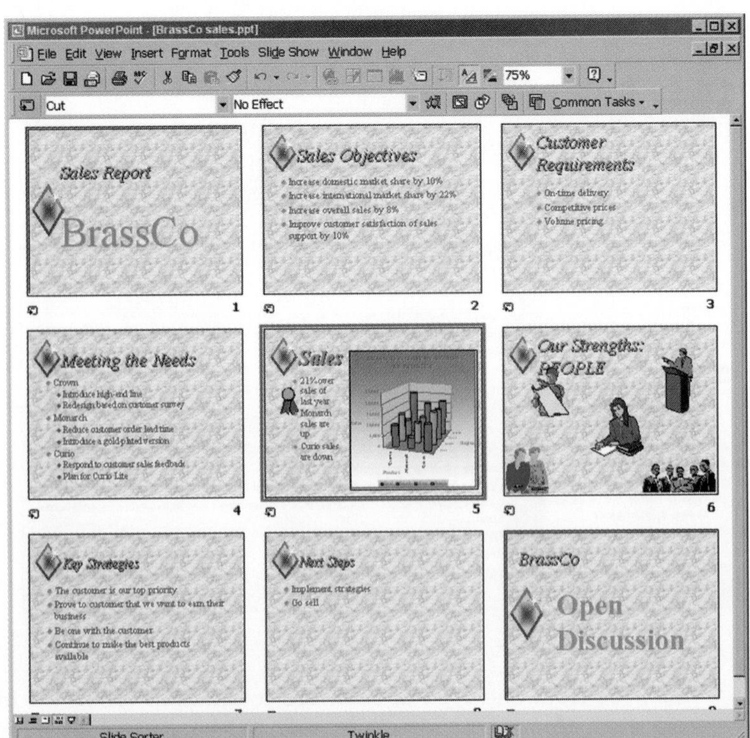

PowerPoint Slide Sorter View Microsoft PowerPoint 2000 helps you prepare and present slides for presentations. PowerPoint has a variety of slide templates from which you can choose. You can work with the entire presentation or with a single chart (see Figure 2.10). Slides are easily rearranged by simply dragging a slide to a new position.

- Presentation software can help persuade attendees or readers to adopt a particular point of view.
- Judicious use of presentation software tends to make meetings shorter and more effective.

Follow these steps to prepare a presentation using presentation software.

1 *Select a template.* Presentation software comes with many handy **templates.** Generically, a template is a form, mold, or pattern used as a guide to making something. All productivity software packages have templates to give us a leg up when creating documents. Templates can be real time-savers. In word processing, there are templates for business letters, faxes, memos, reports, and so on. We add the content. PowerPoint 2000, the industry standard for presentation software, has two types of templates: *design templates* and *content templates.* Design templates are predesigned formats and complementary color schemes with preselected background images you can apply to any content material (the outline) to give your slides a professional, customized appearance. A **slide** is one of the images to be displayed. A design template was used for Figure 2.9. Content templates go one step further and suggest content for specific subjects (for example, business plan, project overview, employee orientation, and many others).

2 *Create an outline for the presentation.* PowerPoint's tri-pane view lets you view the *slide, outline,* and *notes* at the same time (see Figure 2.10). This view makes it easy to add new slides, edit text, and enter notes while creating a presentation. The outline feature helps you organize your presentation material into a multilevel outline. What you include in the outline is automatically formatted into slides based on the selected design template. In the slides, the main points (first-level headings in the outline) become slide titles and their subordinate items become subheadings and subpoints. People often *import* their outline from a word processing document. Each software package produces its own unique files. However, with so much overlap in functionality between popular productivity software, files can be

Projectors Enhance Presentations The presenter is using a Proxima screen image projector to project carefully prepared electronic slides onto a screen for all to see. Transparency acetates and 35-mm slides were the presentation aids of choice for decades, but they now take a backseat to slide projection hardware and software.
Courtesy of Proxima Corporation

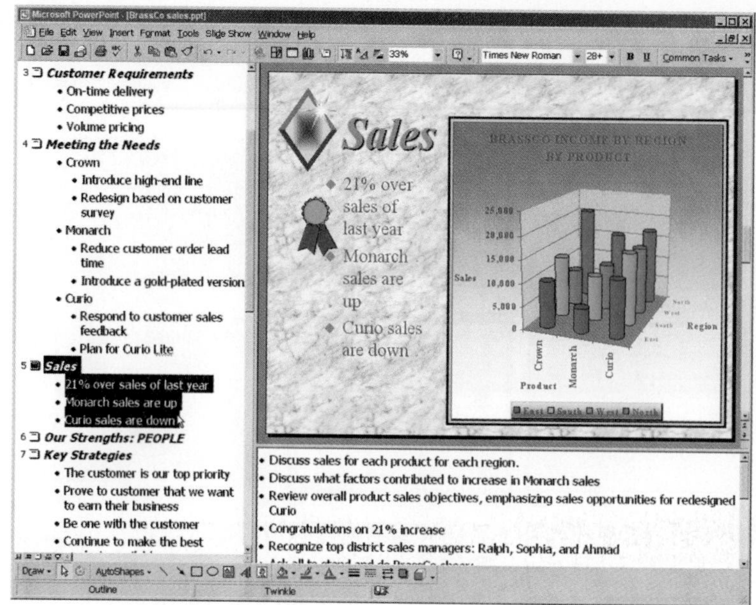

PowerPoint Tri-Pane View

The PowerPoint 2000 tri-pane view shows the *slide, outline,* and *notes* so you can work with all the elements of the presentation at once.

imported from one type of software to another. When we **import** a file, we convert it from its foreign format to a format that is compatible with the current program. For example, people frequently import Microsoft Word 2000 outlines into the PowerPoint 2000 outline feature. Microsoft® Excel spreadsheets can be imported directly into the PowerPoint chart feature. When we **export** a file, we convert a file in the current program to a format that can be read directly by another program.

3 *Compile and create other nontext resources.* Text alone, no matter how well formatted, may fall short of what is needed for a quality presentation. A good slide presentation will include some or all of the following: *photo images, charts* and *graphs,* original *drawings,* a variety of eye-catching *clip art, audio clips,* and even *full-motion video* captured with a digital camera. Obviously, not all presentations will comprise every capability, but at a minimum there is clip art available for every presentation situation (for example, the blue ribbon in Figure 2.10). A company can add another dimension to a sales summary bar chart by topping the bars with clip art that represents the product being sold (a bar of soap, an airplane, a refrigerator). Also, it's a good idea to use audio to introduce or highlight critical points. A slide on a new bonus plan can be introduced with the "ca-chink" sound of a cash register.

With presentation software you can create a variety of charts from data imported from a spreadsheet or a database, or you can enter the data into a PowerPoint table (see Figure 2.11). Usually the data needed to produce a graph already exist in a spreadsheet or a database. Among the most popular charts are *pie charts* and *bar charts.* You have many other charting options, including *line charts, bubble charts, range charts, doughnut charts,* and *area charts,* each of which can be presented in two or three dimensions and annotated with *titles, labels,* and *legends*

Besides traditional business charts, presentation software allows you to prepare *organization charts* showing the hierarchical structure of an organization (see Figure 2.12) and *maps* showing demographic information in context with geographic location.

4 *Integrate resources.* Once all text and visual resources have been compiled, it is time to integrate them into a visually appealing presentation. Typically, people work from the slides generated from the outline, inserting clip art, charts, and so on as needed. Some slides may include only a title and

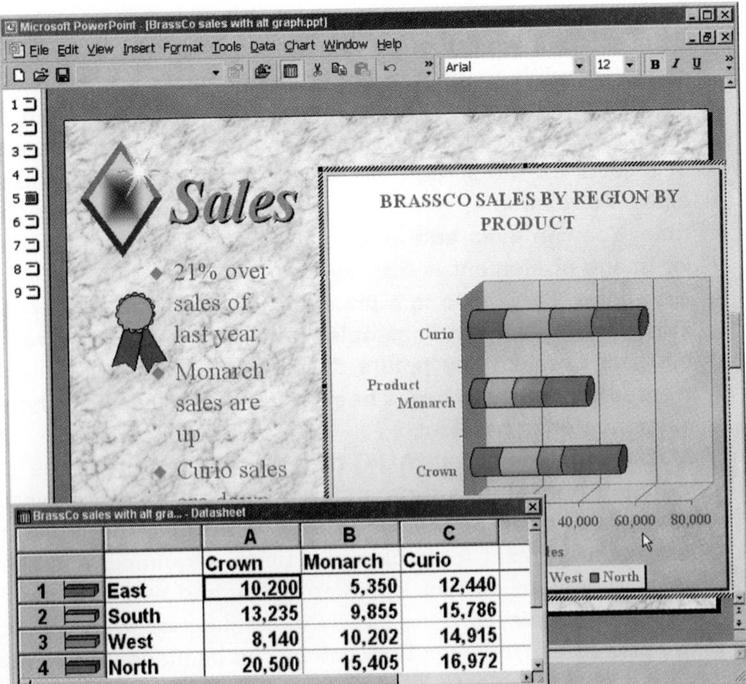

		A	B	C
		Crown	Monarch	Curio
1	East	10,200	5,350	12,440
2	South	13,235	9,855	15,786
3	West	8,140	10,202	14,915
4	North	20,500	15,405	16,972

PowerPoint Table and Chart

Shown here is a PowerPoint 2000 chart along with the table containing the data for chart. This horizontal stacked bar chart with a cylindrical shape portrays the same information as the 3-D bar chart of Figure 2.10.

images, such as the sixth slide in Figure 2.9. The PowerPoint *slide sorter* view gives you an overview of the presentation. The slide sorter shows thumbnail images to enable the viewing of all or much of a presentation in sequence on a single screen. A **thumbnail** is a miniature display of an image or perhaps a page (document or Web). The slide sorter makes it easy to add or delete slides and to rearrange them to meet presentation needs.

5 *Add special effects.* With PowerPoint you can give the audience a little candy for the eyes by introducing visually interesting transitions between slides during a PC-based presentation. For example, the current graph or image can be made to *fade out* (dissolve to a blank screen) while the text is

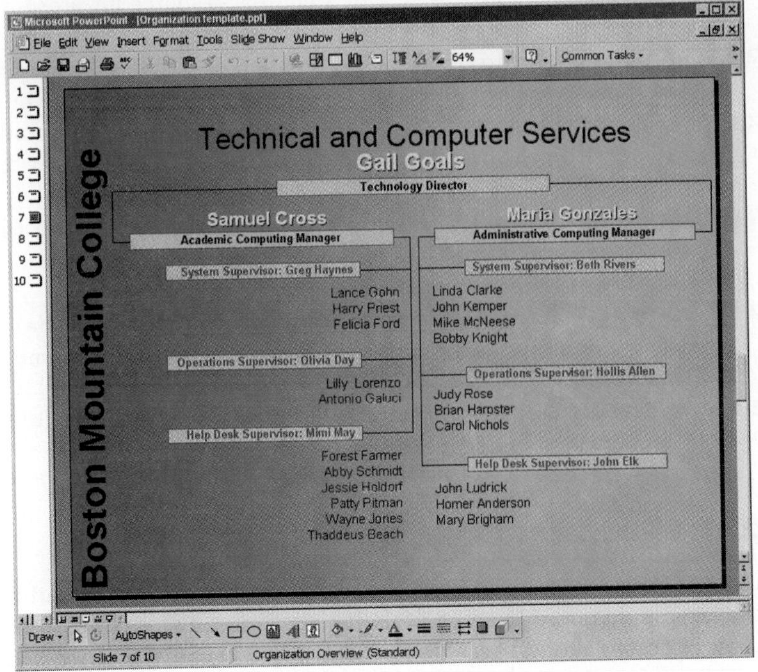

PowerPoint Organization Chart

fading in. Or, the current image can be *wiped* away with the next. PowerPoint offers a variety of transitions, each of which adds an aura of professionalism while helping to hold the audience's attention. Also, text and objects can be animated. For example, text and objects can be made to fly in from the perimeter of the screen a word or a letter at a time. Any number of objects on the screen can be animated, even individual elements on a chart. For example, you can introduce the bars on a bar chart one bar at a time. You can even add an applause sound that is played when a particular image or element is displayed.

6. *Add notes.* Each slide in a presentation can have corresponding notes (see Figure 2.10). Frequently, people make notes for themselves to help them remember to make key points during a presentation. Sometimes, notes are created for the audience. The notes and the slides can be printed together as an audience handout.
7. *Make the presentation.* A PC-based presentation can be made to an individual or a small group on a single PC, or it can be projected onto a large screen. Or, it can be fashioned as a self-running information center where screens are preset to display in a timed sequence. A presentation may involve slides, an outline, speaker notes, and even handouts. Typically the slides are displayed dynamically in conjunction with a PC under control of the presenter. However, they can be can be made into 35-mm slides (for use with a 35-mm projector) or transparency acetates (for use with an overhead projector) for use in more traditional settings.

Whether you're preparing a report, a speech, a newsletter, or any other form of business, academic, or personal communication, it pays—immediately and over the long term—to take full advantage of presentation software.

SECTION SELF-CHECK

Self-Check

2-4.1 Presentation software allows users to create charts, graphs, and images for use during presentations. (T/F)

2-4.2 An image to be displayed in a PC-based presentation is called a preselected format. (T/F)

2-4.3 The presentation software slide sorter lets users add or delete slides and rearrange them to meet presentation needs. (T/F)

2-4.4 Audio clips are an example of a nontext resource for presentation software. (T/F)

2-4.5 A pattern used to facilitate the creation of a slide presentation is called a: (a) guide word, (b) demographic datum link, (c) template, or (d) hyperlink?

2-4.6 Which of the following is a commercial example of presentation software: (a) Microsoft Excel, (b) Microsoft PowerPoint 2000, (c) Lotus 1–2–3, or (d) Print House?

2-4.7 When we convert a file from its foreign format to a format that is compatible with the current program: (a) import the file, (b) export the file, (c) bypass the file, or (d) link the file?

2-4.8 A typical slide in a slide presentation would not include: (a) photo images, charts, and graphs, (b) clip art, audio clips, (c) content templates, or (d) full-motion video?

2-4.9 Which of these is a presentation software special effect: (a) fade out, (b) thumbnail, (c) notes, or (d) export file?

2.5 SPREADSHEET: THE MAGIC MATRIX

The spreadsheet, which is simply a grid for entering rows and columns of data, has been a common business tool for centuries. Before computers, the ledger (a book of spreadsheets) was the accountant's primary tool for keeping records of financial transactions. Instructors' grade books are also in spreadsheet format, with student names labeling the rows and quiz scores labeling the columns.

Spreadsheet software is an electronic alternative to thousands of traditionally manual tasks. We are no longer confined to using pencils, erasers, and hand calculators to deal with rows and columns of data. Think of anything that has rows and columns of data and you have identified an application for spreadsheet software: income (profit-and-loss) statements, personnel profiles, demographic data, home inventories, and budget summaries, just to mention a few.

Spreadsheets

Spreadsheet/Database

Spreadsheet Concepts and Features

We will use the March sales summary, shown in Figure 2.13, to demonstrate spreadsheet concepts. The national sales manager for BrassCo Enterprises, a manufacturer of an upscale line of brass coat hanger products (the Crown, the Monarch, and the Curio), compiles monthly sales summaries using a spreadsheet software template. The template, simply a spreadsheet model, contains the layout and formulas needed to produce the summary illustrated in Figure 2.13. The manager entered only the data for the current month (the *sales amounts* for each salesperson for March) and the spreadsheet template performed all of the necessary calculations (the *totals* and the *commissions*).

Organization: Rows and Columns

Spreadsheets are organized in a *tabular structure* with *rows* and *columns.* The intersection of a particular row and column designates a **cell.** As you can see in Figure 2.13, the rows are *numbered,* and the columns are *lettered.*

Data are entered and stored in a cell. During operations, data are referred to by their **cell address,** which identifies the location of a cell in the spreadsheet by its column and row, with the column designator first. For example, in the monthly sales summary of Figure 2.13, C4 is the address of the column heading for product Crown, and D5 is the address of the total amount of Monarch sales for R. Rosco ($30,400).

In the spreadsheet work area (the rows and columns), a movable highlighted area "points" to the *current cell.* The current cell is highlighted with either a different background color or a dark border (see the dark border around Cell A1, the current cell, in the first example in Figure 2.13). This highlighted area, called the **pointer,** can be moved around the spreadsheet with the arrow keys or the mouse. The address and content of the current cell are displayed in the cell content portion of the spreadsheet above the work area. The content or value resulting from a formula of each cell is shown in the spreadsheet work area.

Ranges: Groups of Cells

Many spreadsheet operations ask you to designate a **range** of cells. These are highlighted in Figure 2.13: *cell range* (a single cell); *column range* (all or part of a column of adjacent cells), *row range;* and *block range* (a rectangular group of cells). A particular range is indicated by the addresses of the endpoint cells separated by a colon, such as the row range C14:E14.

Cell Entries

To make an entry in the spreadsheet, simply move the pointer to the appropriate cell, and key in the data. The major types of entries are *label* entry, *numeric* entry, and *formula* entry, shown in Figure 2.13. A label entry is a word, a phrase, or any string of alphanumeric text (spaces included) that occupies a particular cell. In Figure 2.13, "NAME" in Cell A4 is a label entry, as is "COMMISSION" in G4.

In Figure 2.13, the dollar sales values in the range C5:E10 are *numeric.* The dollar sales values in the ranges F5:G10 and C12:G12 are results of *formulas.* Cell F5 contains a formula, but it is the numeric result (for example, 61150 in Figure 2.13) that is displayed in the spreadsheet work area. With the pointer positioned at F5, the formula appears in the cell contents box. The formula value in F5 computes the total sales made by the salesperson in Row 5 for all three products (that

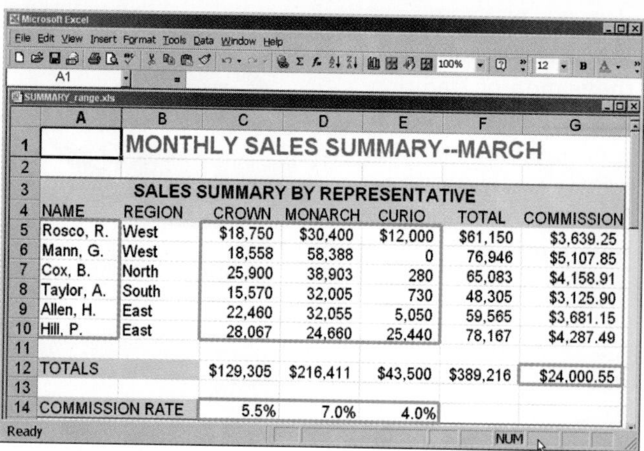

	A	B	C	D	E	F	G
1		MONTHLY SALES SUMMARY--MARCH					
2							
3		SALES SUMMARY BY REPRESENTATIVE					
4	NAME	REGION	CROWN	MONARCH	CURIO	TOTAL	COMMISSION
5	Rosco, R.	West	$18,750	$30,400	$12,000	$61,150	$3,639.25
6	Mann, G.	West	18,558	58,388	0	76,946	$5,107.85
7	Cox, B.	North	25,900	38,903	280	65,083	$4,158.91
8	Taylor, A.	South	15,570	32,005	730	48,305	$3,125.90
9	Allen, H.	East	22,460	32,055	5,050	59,565	$3,681.15
10	Hill, P.	East	28,067	24,660	25,440	78,167	$4,287.49
11							
12	TOTALS		$129,305	$216,411	$43,500	$389,216	$24,000.55
13							
14	COMMISSION RATE		5.5%	7.0%	4.0%		

Spreadsheet ranges. The highlighted cells in this spreadsheet illustrate the four types of ranges: cell (G12), column (A5:A10), row (C14:E14), and block (C5:E10).

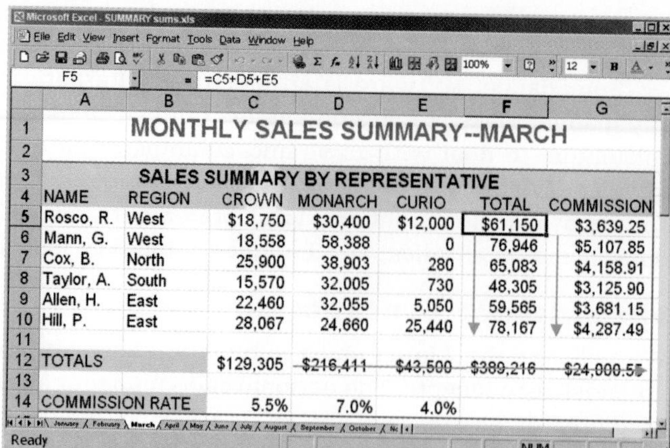

F5 =C5+D5+E5

	A	B	C	D	E	F	G
1		MONTHLY SALES SUMMARY--MARCH					
2							
3		SALES SUMMARY BY REPRESENTATIVE					
4	NAME	REGION	CROWN	MONARCH	CURIO	TOTAL	COMMISSION
5	Rosco, R.	West	$18,750	$30,400	$12,000	$61,150	$3,639.25
6	Mann, G.	West	18,558	58,388	0	76,946	$5,107.85
7	Cox, B.	North	25,900	38,903	280	65,083	$4,158.91
8	Taylor, A.	South	15,570	32,005	730	48,305	$3,125.90
9	Allen, H.	East	22,460	32,055	5,050	59,565	$3,681.15
10	Hill, P.	East	28,067	24,660	25,440	78,167	$4,287.49
11							
12	TOTALS		$129,305	$216,411	$43,500	$389,216	$24,000.55
13							
14	COMMISSION RATE		5.5%	7.0%	4.0%		

Copying formulas. The actual content of F5 is the formula in the cell contents box (=C5+D5+E5). The result of the formula (61150) appears in the spreadsheet at F5, formatted as currency ($61,150). In creating the spreadsheet template for the monthly sales summary, the national sales manager for BrassCo entered only three formulas (see cell contents summary below).

- The formula in F5 to sum the product sales for each salesperson was copied to the range F6:F10.
- The formula in G5: =$C$14*C5+$D$14*D5+$E$14*E5 to compute the commission for each salesperson was copied to the range G6:G10.
- The formula in C12: =SUM(C5:C10) to sum the sales for each product was copied to the range D12:G12.

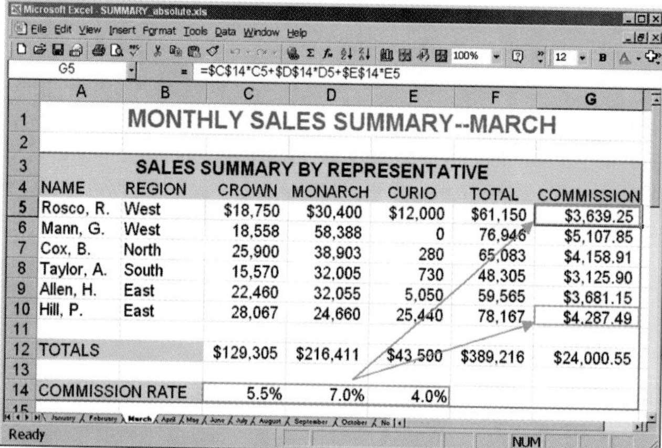

G5 =$C$14*C5+$D$14*D5+$E$14*E5

	A	B	C	D	E	F	G
1		MONTHLY SALES SUMMARY--MARCH					
2							
3		SALES SUMMARY BY REPRESENTATIVE					
4	NAME	REGION	CROWN	MONARCH	CURIO	TOTAL	COMMISSION
5	Rosco, R.	West	$18,750	$30,400	$12,000	$61,150	$3,639.25
6	Mann, G.	West	18,558	58,388	0	76,946	$5,107.85
7	Cox, B.	North	25,900	38,903	280	65,083	$4,158.91
8	Taylor, A.	South	15,570	32,005	730	48,305	$3,125.90
9	Allen, H.	East	22,460	32,055	5,050	59,565	$3,681.15
10	Hill, P.	East	28,067	24,660	25,440	78,167	$4,287.49
11							
12	TOTALS		$129,305	$216,411	$43,500	$389,216	$24,000.55
13							
14	COMMISSION RATE		5.5%	7.0%	4.0%		

Copying formulas that include absolute cell addresses. Each of the commission computation formulas in the range G5:G10 has the same multipliers — the commission rates in the range C14:E14. Because the *relative* positions between the commission formulas in G5:G10 and the commission rates in C14:E14 vary from row to row, the commission rates are entered as *absolute* cell addresses. If the contents of a cell containing a formula are copied to another cell, the relative cell addresses in the copied formula are revised to reflect the new position (perhaps a new row), but the absolute cell addresses are unchanged. Notice in the cell contents summary below how the absolute addresses ($C$14, $D$14, and $E$14) in the copied formulas (G6:G10) remained the same in each formula and the relative addresses were revised to reflect the applicable row. If a dollar sign precedes the letter and/or number in a cell address, such as $C$14, the column and/or row reference is absolute.

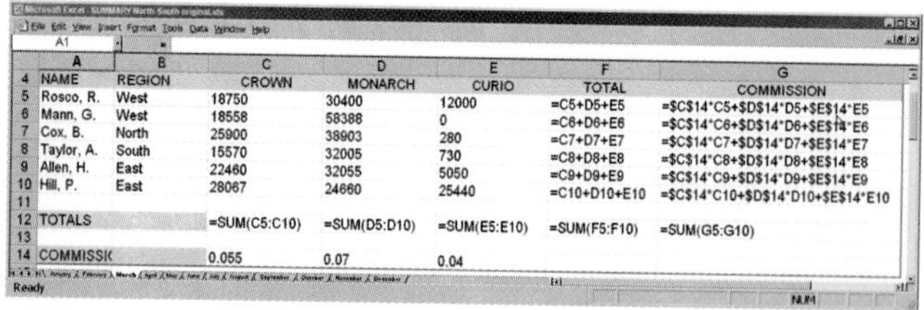

	A	B	C	D	E	F	G
4	NAME	REGION	CROWN	MONARCH	CURIO	TOTAL	COMMISSION
5	Rosco, R.	West	18750	30400	12000	=C5+D5+E5	=$C$14*C5+$D$14*D5+$E$14*E5
6	Mann, G.	West	18558	58388	0	=C6+D6+E6	=$C$14*C6+$D$14*D6+$E$14*E6
7	Cox, B.	North	25900	38903	280	=C7+D7+E7	=$C$14*C7+$D$14*D7+$E$14*E7
8	Taylor, A.	South	15570	32005	730	=C8+D8+E8	=$C$14*C8+$D$14*D8+$E$14*E8
9	Allen, H.	East	22460	32055	5050	=C9+D9+E9	=$C$14*C9+$D$14*D9+$E$14*E9
10	Hill, P.	East	28067	24660	25440	=C10+D10+E10	=$C$14*C10+$D$14*D10+$E$14*E10
11							
12	TOTALS		=SUM(C5:C10)	=SUM(D5:D10)	=SUM(E5:E10)	=SUM(F5:F10)	=SUM(G5:G10)
13							
14	COMMISSIK		0.055	0.07	0.04		

Cell contents summary. This cell contents summary illustrates the actual content of the cells in the above spreadsheet.

Spreadsheet Template Showing a Monthly Sales Summary Spreadsheets can be formatted to better portray the information (for example, the use of color, font size, and shading). Also, you can draw over a spreadsheet. The red markings are included here to help illustrate spreadsheet concepts.

Microsoft Excel - World Population.xls

B218 =SUM(B2:B217)

	A	B	C	D
1	COUNTRY/REGION	TOTAL POP	TOTAL MALE	TOTAL FEMALE
2	China	1,130,510,638	581,820,407	548,690,231
3	India	849,638,000	440,455,000	409,183,000
4	United States	257,907,937	125,897,610	132,010,327
5	Indonesia	179,247,783	89,375,677	89,872,106
6	Brazil	150,367,000	74,992,000	75,375,000
7	Russian Federation	148,310,174	69,562,474	78,747,700
8	Japan	124,451,938	61,095,667	63,356,271
216	Falkland Islands	2,050	1,095	955
217	Vatican City (Holy See)	1,000		
218	TOTAL POPULATION	5,157,461,605	2,542,068,266	2,506,944,452

Spreadsheet Scrolling to View Large Spreadsheets To view spreadsheets larger than the application window, scroll left or right using the scroll bars. Use the split-screen feature, shown here, to view different portions of the same spreadsheet.

is, total sales is +C5+D5+E5). The actual numeric value appears in the spreadsheet work area (see Figure 2.13).

Spreadsheet formulas use standard notation for **arithmetic operators:** + (add), − (subtract), * (multiply), / (divide), ^ (raise to a power, or exponentiation). The formula in F5 computes the total sales for R. Rosco. The range F6:F10 contains similar formulas that apply to their respective rows (+C6+D6+E6, +C7+D7+E7, and so on). For example, the formula in F6 computes the total sales for G. Mann. The last image in Figure 2.13 provides a summary of the actual unformatted cell contents for all cells.

Viewing a Spreadsheet

In Windows 9x/NT/2000, one or more applications run in **windows**—rectangular areas displayed on the screen. Depending on the size of a window, the entire document may not be visible. Spreadsheets can be large, sometimes thousands of rows and dozens of columns (for example, an employee database). When document content is more than can be displayed in a window, the window is outfitted with **vertical** and/or **horizontal scroll bars.** The world population summary shown in Figure 2.14 illustrates the use of scroll bars. Each bar contains a **scroll box** and two **scroll arrows.** Use the mouse or keyboard to move a box up/down or left/right on a scroll bar to display other parts of the application. This movement is known as **scrolling.** Scrolling through a spreadsheet is much like looking through a magnifying glass as you move it around a newspaper page. The figure also shows how the screen can be split to show both the beginning and the end of the summary. Portions of the split screen can be scrolled independently. The screen is split horizontally and/or vertically, as needed.

Putting Spreadsheet Software to Work

The possibilities of what you can do with spreadsheet software and PCs are endless. Find any set of numbers and you have identified a potential application for spreadsheet software.

Spreadsheet Templates: Models

The spreadsheet in Figure 2.13 is a *template,* or a model, for a monthly sales summary. All the manager has to do is enter the sales data for the current month in the range C5:E10. All other data are calculated with formulas.

Most spreadsheet applications eventually take the form of a spreadsheet template. Once created, the template becomes the basis for handling a certain type of data (for example, monthly sales data). Spreadsheet templates are modified easily. For example, any of these modifications of Figure 2.13 would require only a few minutes:

- Add another column to accommodate a new product.
- Delete a row to handle one less salesperson.
- Compute the standard deviation for Crown sales data.

- Change the rate of commission for the Crown from 5.5% to 6.0%.
- Sort the sales summary portion (A5:G10) alphabetically by name.
- Sort the sales summary portion (A5:G10) in descending order by commission.

Templates often are created to portray the income statement (see Figure 2.15). The income statement describes a business's financial position. The vice president of Finance at BrassCo uses an income statement template to do financial planning. The income statement is essentially a record of a company's operating activities over an entire year. The template in Figure 2.15 shows information for the past two years and contains a column that allows him to produce a *pro rata income statement* for next year based on figures in the income statement for the preceding year(s) and on project sales and expenses (see rows 21 through 24). The VP can change any or all of these variables to see the impact on next year's estimated net profit (B19): projected change in sales (C22), projected change in cost of goods sold (C23), and projected change in administrative expenses (C24). Figure 2.15 also shows actual cell content for the pro rata income statement, including formulas.

The use of predefined functions can save a lot of time. The Three-Year Summary Data in rows 26 through 31 of Figure 2.15 demonstrate the use of spreadsheet functions. The summary uses three common statistical functions: average (=AVERAGE(B3:D3) in B28), minimum (=MIN(B3:D3) in C28), and maximum (=MAX(B3:D3) in D28). Other spreadsheet functions include trigonometric functions, square roots, comparisons of values, manipulations of strings of data, computation of net present value and internal rate of return, and a variety of techniques for statistical analysis.

MEMORY

bits

Spreadsheet Organization

- Tabular structure
  - —Numbered rows
  - —Lettered columns
- Row/column intersect at cell
- Cell address locates cell
- Pointer highlights current cell
- Common cell entry types
  - —Label
  - —Numeric
  - —Formula

Spreadsheet Graphics

Spreadsheet packages let you generate a variety of charts from spreadsheet data. The spreadsheet template in Figure 2.16 presents an Income Summary by Region by Product for BrassCo. The income figures for each region (Range C4:E7) are

FIGURE 2.15

Spreadsheet Template Showing a Pro Rata Income Statement The "Next Year" pro rata income statement is extrapolated from the data in the "This Year" income statement and the values of forecast variables in the range C22:C24. Actual cell content, including formulas, is shown in the second screen image.

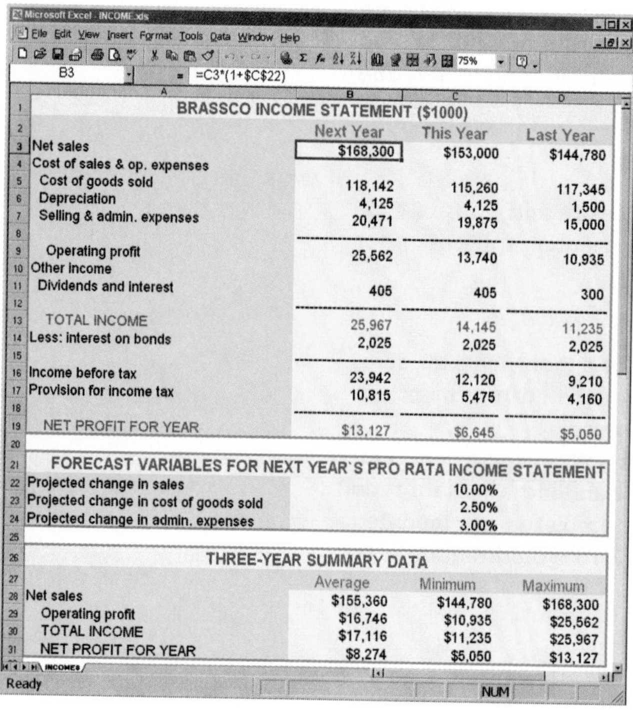

Microsoft Excel - INCOME.xls

B3 = =C3*(1+$C$22)

	A	B	C	D
1	BRASSCO INCOME STATEMENT ($1000)			
2		Next Year	This Year	Last Year
3	Net sales	$168,300	$153,000	$144,780
4	Cost of sales & op. expenses			
5	Cost of goods sold	118,142	115,260	117,345
6	Depreciation	4,125	4,125	1,500
7	Selling & admin. expenses	20,471	19,875	15,000
9	Operating profit	25,562	13,740	10,935
10	Other income			
11	Dividends and interest	405	405	300
13	TOTAL INCOME	25,967	14,145	11,235
14	Less: interest on bonds	2,025	2,025	2,025
16	Income before tax	23,942	12,120	9,210
17	Provision for income tax	10,815	5,475	4,160
19	NET PROFIT FOR YEAR	$13,127	$6,645	$5,050
21	FORECAST VARIABLES FOR NEXT YEAR'S PRO RATA INCOME STATEMENT			
22	Projected change in sales		10.00%	
23	Projected change in cost of goods sold		2.50%	
24	Projected change in admin. expenses		3.00%	
26	THREE-YEAR SUMMARY DATA			
27		Average	Minimum	Maximum
28	Net sales	$155,360	$144,780	$168,300
29	Operating profit	$16,746	$10,935	$25,562
30	TOTAL INCOME	$17,116	$11,235	$25,967
31	NET PROFIT FOR YEAR	$8,274	$5,050	$13,127

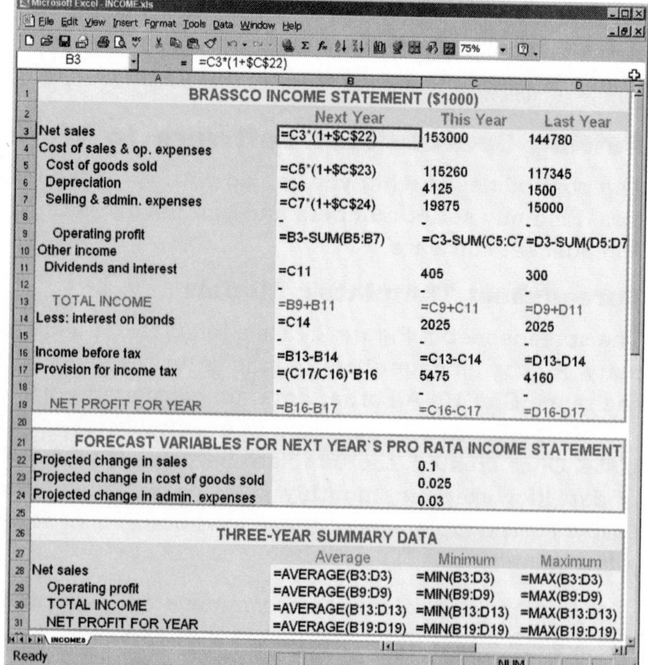

Microsoft Excel - INCOME.xls

B3 = =C3*(1+$C$22)

	A	B	C	D
1	BRASSCO INCOME STATEMENT ($1000)			
2		Next Year	This Year	Last Year
3	Net sales	=C3*(1+$C$22)	153000	144780
4	Cost of sales & op. expenses			
5	Cost of goods sold	=C5*(1+$C$23)	115260	117345
6	Depreciation	=C6	4125	1500
7	Selling & admin. expenses	=C7*(1+$C$24)	19875	15000
9	Operating profit	=B3-SUM(B5:B7)	=C3-SUM(C5:C7	=D3-SUM(D5:D7
10	Other income			
11	Dividends and interest	=C11	405	300
13	TOTAL INCOME	=B9+B11	=C9+C11	=D9+D11
14	Less: interest on bonds	=C14	2025	2025
16	Income before tax	=B13-B14	=C13-C14	=D13-D14
17	Provision for income tax	=(C17/C16)*B16	5475	4160
19	NET PROFIT FOR YEAR	=B16-B17	=C16-C17	=D16-D17
21	FORECAST VARIABLES FOR NEXT YEAR'S PRO RATA INCOME STATEMENT			
22	Projected change in sales		0.1	
23	Projected change in cost of goods sold		0.025	
24	Projected change in admin. expenses		0.03	
26	THREE-YEAR SUMMARY DATA			
27		Average	Minimum	Maximum
28	Net sales	=AVERAGE(B3:D3)	=MIN(B3:D3)	=MAX(B3:D3)
29	Operating profit	=AVERAGE(B9:D9)	=MIN(B9:D9)	=MAX(B9:D9)
30	TOTAL INCOME	=AVERAGE(B13:D13)	=MIN(B13:D13)	=MAX(B13:D13)
31	NET PROFIT FOR YEAR	=AVERAGE(B19:D19)	=MIN(B19:D19)	=MAX(B19:D19)

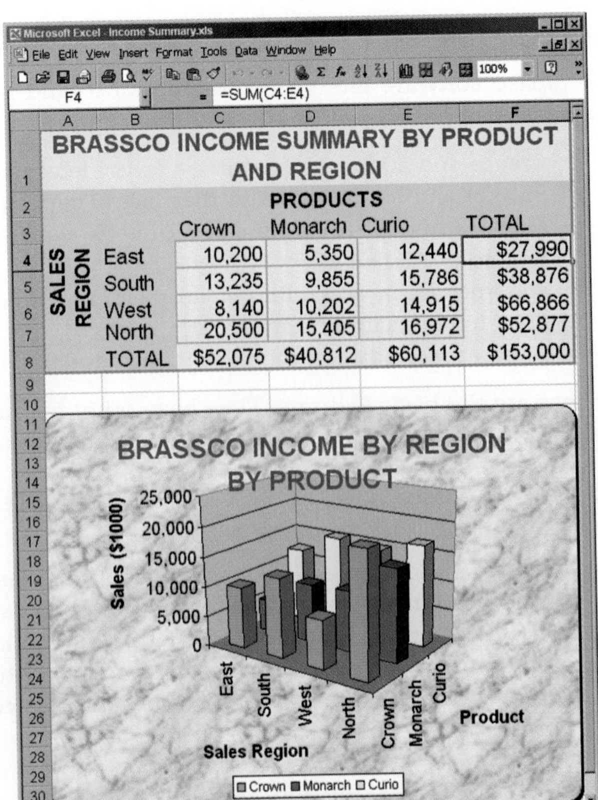

Spreadsheet Graphs

Regional income for each of the three products (range C4:E7) are graphically illustrated in this 3-dimensional bar chart.

plotted by product in a 3-dimensional bar chart. To spreadsheet data into a chart, the BrassCo VP needed only to respond to a series of prompts from the spreadsheet program. The first prompt asked him to select the type of graph to be generated. He then identified the source of the data, entered labels and titles, and so on. The resulting graph permits him to better understand the regional distribution of income by product.

SECTION SELF-CHECK

Self-Check

2-5.1 D20:Z40 and Z20:D40 define the same spreadsheet range. (T/F)

2-5.2 The term *spreadsheet* was coined at the beginning of the personal computer boom. (T/F)

2-5.3 The intersection of a particular row and column in a spreadsheet designates a cell. (T/F)

2-5.4 Spreadsheet software works only with numbers and doesn't generate charts. (T/F)

2-5.5 A model of a spreadsheet designed for a particular application is sometimes called a template. (T/F)

2-5.6 Panning a spreadsheet to view different parts of the document is called: (a) panning, (b) scrolling, (c) rolling, or (d) grid pasting?

2-5.7 If the formula +B1+B2−B3 in cell B4 was copied to C4, the formula in C4 would be: (a) +B1+B2−B3, (b) +C1+C2−C3, (c) +A1+A2−A3, or (d) −B1−B2+B3?

2-5.8 The spreadsheet pointer highlights the: (a) relative cell, (b) status cell, (c) current cell, or (d) merge cell?

2-5.9 Data in a spreadsheet are referred to by their cell: (a) box, (b) number, (c) address, or (d) code?

2-5.10 Which of these is not a range in a spreadsheet: (a) block range, (b) row range, (c) column range, or (d) grazing range?

2.6 DATABASE: A DYNAMIC DATA TOOL

Serendipitous Surfing: Money Management

Database software lets you enter, organize, and retrieve stored data. With Microsoft Access, featured here, and other database software packages you can:

- Create and maintain a database (add, delete, and revise records)
- Extract and list information that meets certain conditions
- Make inquiries (for example, "What is the total amount owed by all customers in Alabama?")
- Sort records in ascending or descending sequence by key fields (for example, alphabetical by last name)
- Generate formatted reports with subtotals and totals

These are the basic features. They have other features as well, including spreadsheet-type computations, presentation graphics, and programming.

Database Software and Spreadsheet Software: What's the Difference?

Both database and spreadsheet software packages let you work with data as rows and columns in a spreadsheet and as records in a database. Spreadsheet software gives you greater flexibility in the manipulation of rows and columns of data. Everything relating to spreadsheet-based data is easier with spreadsheet software—creating formulas, generating charts, what-if analysis (for example, "What if revenue increases by 10% next year?"), and so on. Database software offers greater flexibility in the organization and management of records within a database. Everything relating to a database is easier with database software—

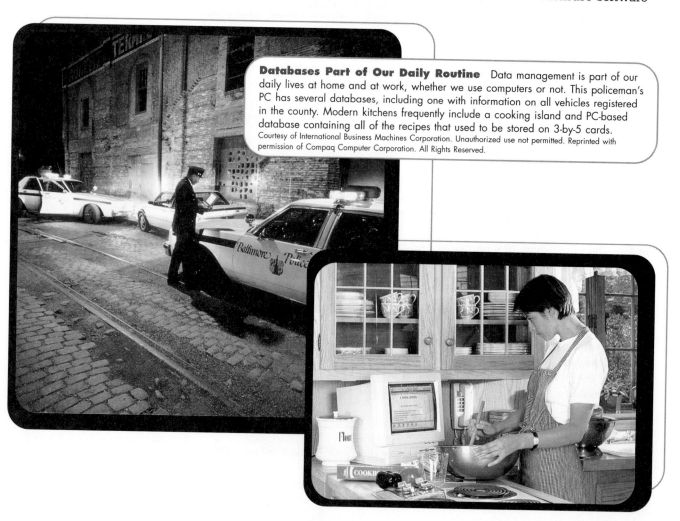

Databases Part of Our Daily Routine Data management is part of our daily lives at home and at work, whether we use computers or not. This policeman's PC has several databases, including one with information on all vehicles registered in the county. Modern kitchens frequently include a cooking island and PC-based database containing all of the recipes that used to be stored on 3-by-5 cards. Courtesy of International Business Machines Corporation. Unauthorized use not permitted. Reprinted with permission of Compaq Computer Corporation. All Rights Reserved.

queries, data entry, linking databases, report generation, programming to create systems, and so on.

In short, spreadsheet packages are great number crunchers and are very helpful for small database applications. Database software packages may be too cumbersome for any serious number crunching, but they are terrific for creating any kind of personal or business information system.

Databases

Database Concepts and Features

The concepts and features of database software packages are very similar. The Microsoft® Access 2000 example in this section is generally applicable to all database software.

Creating a Database with Database Software

In a database, related *fields,* such as student, course ID, and major, are grouped to form *records* (for example, the student record in the STUDENTS table in Figure 2.17). PC-based database packages use the *relational* approach to database management, which organizes data into *tables* in which a *row* is equivalent to a *record* that contains *fields* (set apart by columns). As you can see, the database *table* is conceptually the same as a *file.* One or more tables comprise a **relational database,** which refers to all of the tables in the database and the relationships between them.

The best way to explain the concepts of database software is by example. The chairperson of the Computer Information Systems (CIS) department uses Microsoft Access to help her with record-keeping tasks and to provide valuable information. She has created an education database with two tables: COURSE and STUDENT (see Figure 2.17). The COURSE table contains a record for each course offered in the CIS Department. Each record (row) in the COURSE table contains the following fields:

- COURSE ID
- COURSE TITLE
- TYPE of course (lecture, lab, or lecture/lab)
- INSTRUCTOR name
- CREDIT hours awarded for completion of course

The STUDENT table contains a record for each student who is enrolled in or has taken a CIS course. The table has only a few students to enable ease of demonstration of concepts, but it works just the same with hundreds of students.

COURSE : Table

COURSE ID	COURSE TITLE	TYPE	INSTRUCTOR	CREDIT
CIS 100	Telecommunications	lecture	Babbage	3
CIS 101	Database Management	lecture/lab	Babbage	2
CIS 110	Intranets and Extranets	lab	Gates	3
CIS 150	Mgt. Info. Systems	lecture	Eckert	3
CIS 202	Visual Basic Programming	lecture/lab	Wang	4
CIS 310	Network Administration	lecture	Gates	4
CIS 320	Desktop Publishing	lab	Eckert	3
CIS 330	Information Retrieval	lecture/lab	Wang	3
CIS 350	Web Site Design	lab	Gates	1
CIS 401	Local Area Networks	lecture/lab	Wang	3

Record: 1 of 10

STUDENT : Table

STUDENT	COURSE ID	MAJOR	DATE ENROLLED	STATUS
Adler, Phyllis	CIS 401	Marketing	2/10/1999	withdraw
Austin, Jill	CIS 330	Finance	1/12/1999	incomplete
Bell, Jim	CIS 330	Marketing	1/12/1999	complete
Day, Elizabeth	CIS 310	Accounting	3/18/1999	complete
Fitz, Paula	CIS 310	Finance	4/4/1999	complete
Johnson, Charles	CIS 100	Marketing	1/10/1999	withdraw
Klein, Ellen	CIS 100	Accounting	1/10/1999	complete
Massey, Rose	CIS 101	Management	2/14/1999	incomplete
Mendez, Carlos	CIS 150	Accounting	1/15/1999	incomplete
Targa, Phil	CIS 330	Finance	1/12/1999	complete
Targa, Phil	CIS 100	Finance	1/4/1999	complete

Record: 1 of 11

Education Database: COURSE Table and STUDENT Table The Microsoft Access 2000 Education database is comprised of these two tables. The COURSE table contains a record for each course offered by the Computer Information Systems Department. The STUDENT table contains a record for each student who is enrolled in or has taken a course. The COURSE ID field links the two tables.

Emerging IT

GETTING HELP WITH GETTING STARTED

Just as there's no reason to reinvent the wheel, there are relatively few circumstances where we must start from scratch to create a document, database, or presentation. Much of what we want to do has already been done before, whether it's an expense statement spreadsheet, a fax form, or an important market report presentation. Building on what has worked in the past, developers of productivity software such as word processing, desktop publishing, spreadsheet, database, and presentation software have done all they can to help you get a head start on whatever project you might be doing.

Each of the major productivity software packages offers a variety of templates. A template is simply a document or file that is already formatted or designed for a particular task. For example, a template might be a fax form that includes your name, address, and fax number, but no content. You add the content.

- *Word processing templates.* Templates can be a big help for a variety of word processing tasks. Word processing software may come with templates for brochures (see Microsoft Word 2000 inset), e-mail messages, letters, Web pages, faxes, different legal pleadings, memos, calendars, résumés, directories, manuals, and even academic theses.
- *Desktop publishing templates.* Desktop publishing has templates for many publishing needs. For example, you can choose templates for newsletters (see Microsoft Publisher inset), colorful flyers, business cards, catalogs, signs, menus, Web sites, and even books.
- *Spreadsheet templates.* In spreadsheets you have templates for expense statements, purchase orders, grade books, and for many other row-and-column documents.
- *Database software.* Database software, such as Microsoft Access 2000, includes templates for many database applications such as asset tracking, contact management, inventory control, order entry, resource scheduling, students and classes, video collections, wine lists, and so on.
- *Presentation software templates.* Presentation software offers two types of templates. The content template includes slides formatted with bulleted points for a particular type of presentation. Available content templates might include those for a brainstorming session (see Microsoft PowerPoint 2000 inset), business plan, financial overview, employee orientation, project overview, marketing plan, training program, and even one for communicating bad news. PowerPoint users can choose from many interesting design templates. The design template defines the background image, all colors and fonts, and uses of animation.

Typically, most of what is included in a template is appropriate; however, invariably you will want to modify the basic template to meet your application needs and esthetic tastes. For example, you might wish to add a "personal interest" section in your résumé, add another field to the wine list database, or add a "Great Ideas" slide for the brainstorming session.

Each record contains the following fields:

- STUDENT (name of student; last name first)
- COURSE ID (provides a link to the COURSE table)
- MAJOR
- DATE ENROLLED
- STATUS (course status: incomplete, withdrew, complete)

No single field in the STUDENT table uniquely identifies each record. However, the combined STUDENT and COURSE ID fields do identify each record. Therefore, to access a particular record in the STUDENT table, the chairperson must specify both the STUDENT and COURSE ID (for example, Targa, Phil, CIS 330). The COURSE and STUDENT tables can be linked because they have the COURSE ID field in common.

Generally, you provide content, but if you look around you might find help with content, too. For example, you can liven up any document, database, or presentation with clip art, audio clips, video clips, and animation. Office suites, such as Microsoft Office 2000, include a healthy library from which to choose. Also, third-party vendors offer a mountain of boilerplate for just about any occasion. Boilerplate is existing text that can be reused and customized as needed. In word processing, boilerplate is available for most common legal documents, for business letters/e-mail suitable for most occasions, and for many other writing needs.

And, once content is added to your modified template, you can check all text for spelling and grammatical errors. It pays to take advantage of all that the system has to offer. Judicious use of templates and other canned and automated resources can save you a lot of valuable time.

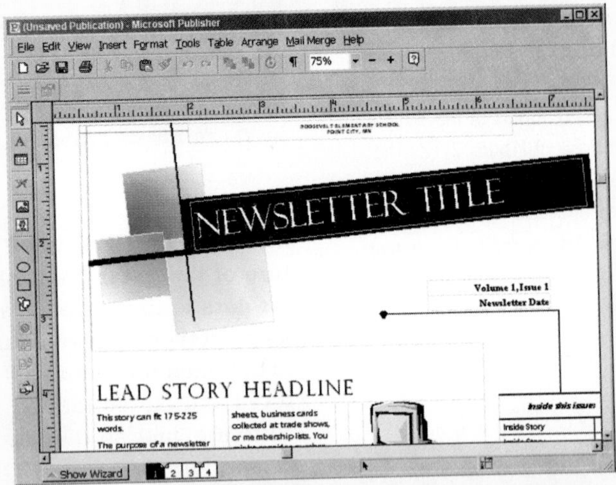

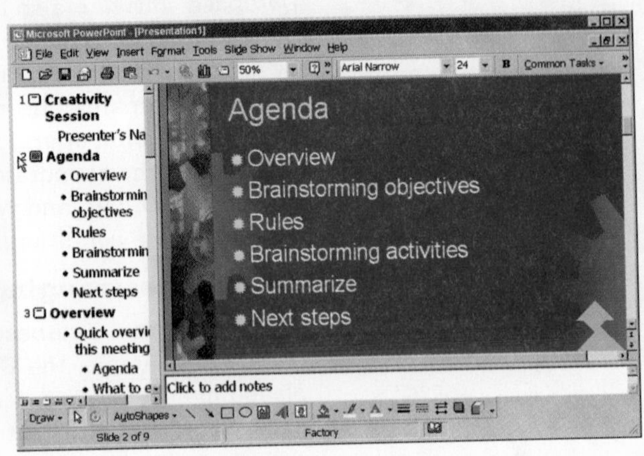

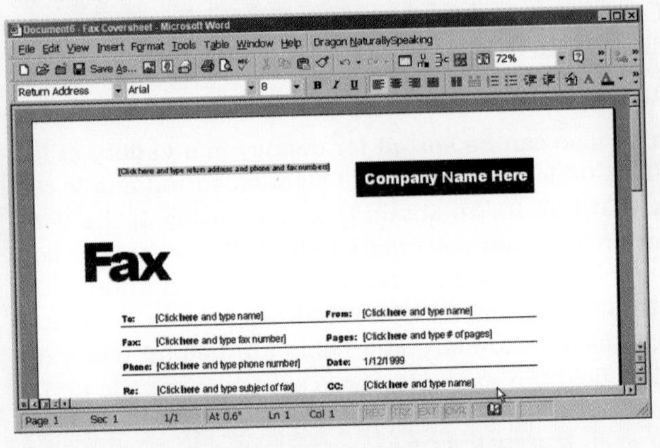

Templates for Every Occasion
Microsoft Office 2000 offers a wide variety of templates, including fax forms (Word 2000), newsletters (Publisher 2000), and brainstorming slides (PowerPoint 2000).

The Structure of the Database Table The first thing you do to set up a database table is to specify its structure by identifying the characteristics of each field in it. This structuring is done interactively, with the system prompting you to enter the field name, the field type, and so on. For example, in the first row of Figure 2.18 the *field name* is COURSE ID; the *data type* is "text"; and the *field size,* or field length, is seven positions. The field names for the COURSE and STUDENT tables are listed at the top of each table in Figure 2.17 (COURSE ID, COURSE TITLE, TYPE, and so on). Content for a *text* field can be a single word or any alphanumeric (numbers, letters, and special characters) phrase. For *number* field types, you can specify the number of decimal positions that you wish to have displayed (none in the example because credit hours are whole numbers).

Structure of the Education Database This display shows the structure of the COURSE and STUDENT tables of the education database of Figure 2.17. The COURSE record (left) has four *text* fields and one *number* field. The STUDENT record has four *text* fields and one *date/time* field.

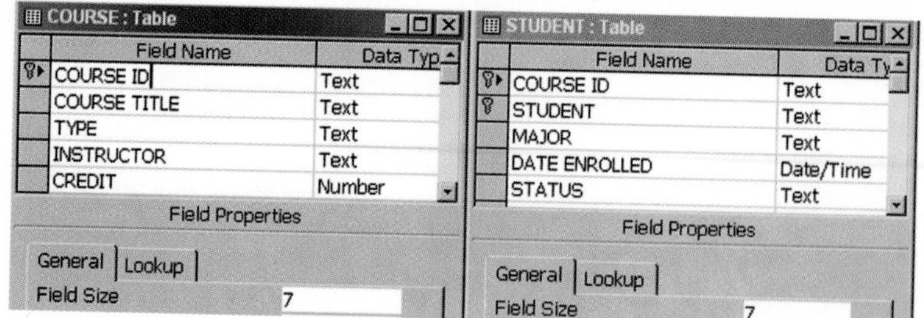

COURSE : Table

Field Name	Data Type
COURSE ID	Text
COURSE TITLE	Text
TYPE	Text
INSTRUCTOR	Text
CREDIT	Number

Field Properties

General | Lookup

Field Size 7

STUDENT : Table

Field Name	Data Type
COURSE ID	Text
STUDENT	Text
MAJOR	Text
DATE ENROLLED	Date/Time
STATUS	Text

Field Properties

General | Lookup

Field Size 7

Entering and Editing Data in a Database Once you have defined the structure of the database table, you are ready to enter the data. The best way to enter data is to create a *screen format* that allows convenient data entry. The data entry screen format is analogous to a hard-copy form that contains labels and blank lines for you to fill in (for example, a medical questionnaire). Data are entered and edited (added, deleted, or revised) one record at a time with database software, just as they are on hard-copy forms. Figure 2.19 shows the data entry screen format for the COURSE table.

Query by Example

Database software also lets you retrieve, view, and print records based on **query by example.** In query by example, you set conditions for the selection of records by composing one or more example *relational expressions.* A relational expression normally compares one or more field names to numbers or character strings using the **relational operators** (= [equal to], > [greater than], < [less than], and combinations of these operators). Several conditions can be combined with **logical operators** (*AND, OR,* and *NOT*). Figure 2.20 demonstrates three types of query by example—one condition, using logical operators, and two conditions.

Sorting: Rearranging Records

The records in a database table also can be sorted for display in a variety of formats. For example, the COURSE table in Figure 2.17 has been sorted and is displayed in ascending order by COURSE ID. To obtain this sequencing of the database records, the department chairperson selected COURSE ID as the *key field* and *ascending* (versus descending) as the sort order. To get a presentation of the COURSE table sorted by COURSE ID within INSTRUCTOR, she needs to identify a *primary* and a *secondary key field.* Secondary key fields are helpful when duplicates exist in the primary key field (for example, there are three records for INSTRUCTOR=Gates). She selects INSTRUCTOR as the primary key field, but she wants the courses offered by each INSTRUCTOR to be listed in ascending order by COURSE ID (see Figure 2.21).

Data Entry Screen Format The screen format for entering, editing, and adding records to the COURSE table is illustrated.

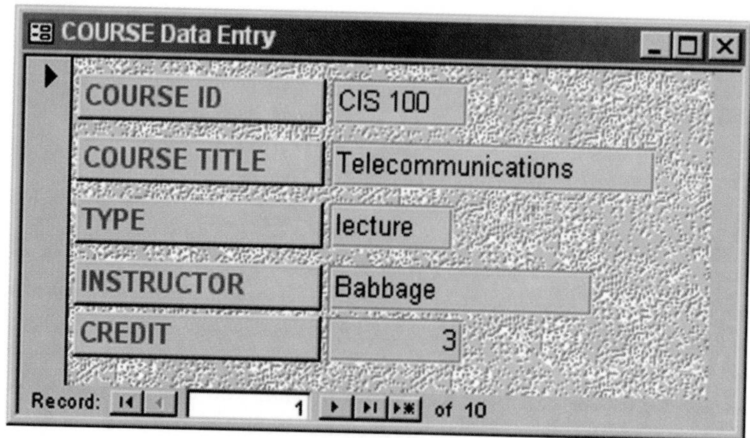

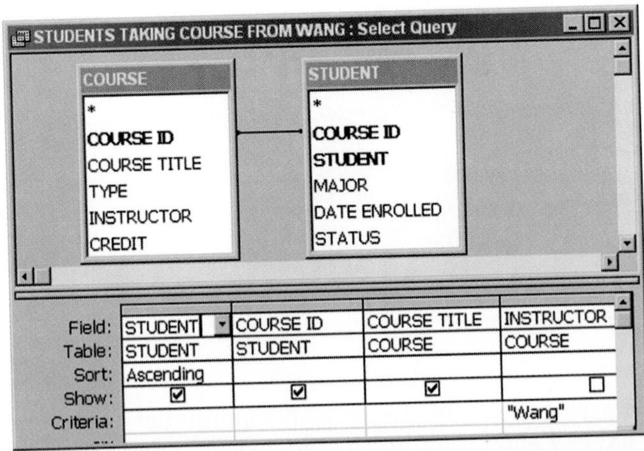

STUDENTS TAKING COURSE FROM WANG : Select Query

STUDENT	COURSE ID	COURSE TITLE
Adler, Phyllis	CIS 401	Local Area Networks
Austin, Jill	CIS 330	Information Retrieval
Bell, Jim	CIS 330	Information Retrieval
Targa, Phil	CIS 330	Information Retrieval

Record: 1 of 4

QBE: One Condition The department chairperson wanted a listing of all students taking courses from Professor Wang. She requested a list of all courses that meet the condition INSTRUCTOR=*Wang* (see Figure 2.17). All records that meet this condition (see criteria query box shown here) are displayed in the answer window in ascending alphabetical order by student name. She selected only three fields to be included in the results display (checked boxes in figure). Notice that the query needed information from both tables.

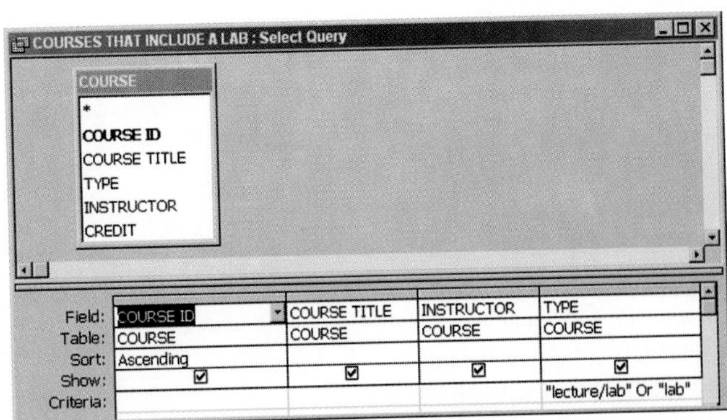

COURSES THAT INCLUDE A LAB : Select Query

COURSE ID	COURSE TITLE	INSTRUCTOR	TYPE
CIS 101	Database Management	Babbage	lecture/lab
CIS 110	Intranets and Extranets	Gates	lab
CIS 202	Visual Basic Programming	Wang	lecture/lab
CIS 320	Desktop Publishing	Eckert	lab
CIS 330	Information Retrieval	Wang	lecture/lab
CIS 350	Web Site Design	Gates	lab
CIS 401	Local Area Networks	Wang	lecture/lab

Record: 1 of 7

QBE: Using Logical Operators To produce the results shown here, the department chairperson set up her query by example to select only those courses that include a lab; that is, the criteria is (course) TYPE=*lab* OR *lecture/lab* (see Figure 2.17). The OR operator can be applied between fields (see example) or within fields. Only the COURSE table is needed for the query.

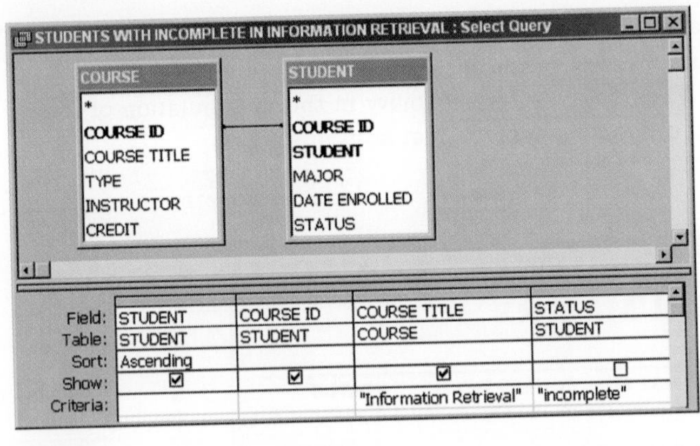

QBE: Two Conditions The query in this example is set up to list those students who have an incomplete (STATUS=*incomplete*) in the course entitled Information Retrieval (COURSE ID=*Information Retrieval*). The query requires the use of both tables in the database.

Query by Example

Generating Reports

A database is a source of information, and database software helps you get the information you need. A *report* is the presentation of information derived from one or more databases. The simple listings of selected and ordered records in Figure 2.20 are "quick and dirty" reports. Such reports are the bread and butter of database capabilities and can be easily copied or imported into word processing or desktop publishing documents.

FIGURE 2.21

COURSE Table Sorted by COURSE ID within INSTRUCTOR This display is the result of a sort operation on the COURSE table with the INSTRUCTOR field as the primary key field and the COURSE ID field as the secondary key field. Notice that the COURSE ID field entries are in alphabetical order by instructor; that is, the three "Gates" records are in sequence by COURSE ID (CIS 110, CIS 310, CIS 350).

COURSE BY ID WITHIN INSTRUCTOR : Select Query

INSTRUCTOR	COURSE ID	COURSE TITLE	TYPE	CREDIT
Babbage	CIS 100	Telecommunications	lecture	3
Babbage	CIS 101	Database Management	lecture/lab	2
Eckert	CIS 150	Mgt. Info. Systems	lecture	3
Eckert	CIS 320	Desktop Publishing	lab	3
Gates	CIS 110	Intranets and Extranets	lab	3
Gates	CIS 310	Network Administration	lecture	4
Gates	CIS 350	Web Site Design	lab	1
Wang	CIS 202	Visual Basic Programming	lecture/lab	4
Wang	CIS 330	Information Retrieval	lecture/lab	3
Wang	CIS 401	Local Area Networks	lecture/lab	3

Record: 1 of 10

Database software allows you to create customized reports and to design their *layout*. This design capability allows you to change spacing and to include titles, subtitles, column headings, separation lines, and other elements that make a report more readable. Managers often use this capability to generate periodic reports, such as the Course Status Summary report shown in Figure 2.22.

Database: The Next Step

The database capabilities illustrated and discussed in this section merely "scratch the surface" of the potential of database software. For example, with relative ease, you can generate sophisticated reports that involve subtotals, calculations, and programming. In addition, data can be presented as a graph. You can even change the structure of a database (for example, add another field). Database software's programming capability has enabled users to create thousands of useful information systems, including student information systems, inventory management systems, hospital patient accounting systems, and cinema management systems.

SECTION SELF-CHECK

Self-Check

2-6.1 If the COURSE database table in Figure 2.17 is sorted in descending order by ID, the third course record would be Local Area Networks. (T/F)

2-6.2 Database software gives you greater flexibility in the manipulation of rows and columns of data than does spreadsheet software. (T/F)

Customized Report To obtain this Course Status Summary report, the CIS Department chairperson needed both the COURSE and STUDENT tables of Figure 2.17 from the education database.

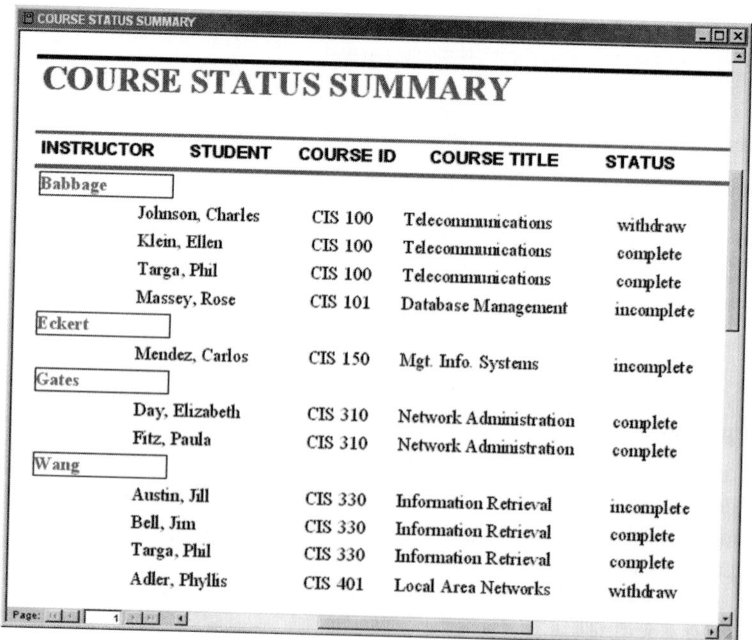

COURSE STATUS SUMMARY

INSTRUCTOR	STUDENT	COURSE ID	COURSE TITLE	STATUS
Babbage				
	Johnson, Charles	CIS 100	Telecommunications	withdraw
	Klein, Ellen	CIS 100	Telecommunications	complete
	Targa, Phil	CIS 100	Telecommunications	complete
	Massey, Rose	CIS 101	Database Management	incomplete
Eckert				
	Mendez, Carlos	CIS 150	Mgt. Info. Systems	incomplete
Gates				
	Day, Elizabeth	CIS 310	Network Administration	complete
	Fitz, Paula	CIS 310	Network Administration	complete
Wang				
	Austin, Jill	CIS 330	Information Retrieval	incomplete
	Bell, Jim	CIS 330	Information Retrieval	complete
	Targa, Phil	CIS 330	Information Retrieval	complete
	Adler, Phyllis	CIS 401	Local Area Networks	withdraw

Page: 1

2-6.3 AND and OR are relational operators. (T/F)

2-6.4 In a database, related fields are grouped to form records. (T/F)

2-6.5 The definition of the structure of a database table would not include which of the following: (a) field names, (b) field sizes, (c) data types, or (d) pointer cell?

2-6.6 Files are sorted, merged, and processed by: (a) a key field, (b) an ISBN, (c) columnar index, or (d) a lock entry?

2-6.7 The relational operator for greater than or equal to is: (a) > OR =, (b) < AND=, (c) < NOT=, or (d) < OR =?

2-6.8 Which record(s) would be selected from the COURSE table in Figure 2.17 for the condition TYPE=lecture/lab: (a) 100, 330, 110, 401, (b) 101, 202, 330, 401, (c) 202, 150, 320, 350 or (d) 110, 150, 320, 350?

2-6.9 Which record(s) would be selected from the STUDENT table in Figure 2.17 for the condition STATUS=complete AND MAJOR=marketing: (a) Targa, Phil/330, (b) Targa, Phil/100, (c) Johnson, Charles/100, (d) Bell, Jim/330?

2-6.10 Which student record(s) would be displayed if the selection condition for the STUDENT table (Figure 2.17) were DATE ENROLLED > 3/1/1999 AND MAJOR=Finance: (a) Adler, Phyllis, (b) Targa, Phil, (c) Paula, Fitz, or (d) Massey, Rose?

2-6.11 Which of these is normally not associated specifically with database terminology: (a) table, (b) query by example, (c) relational, or (d) audio clip?

Database Inquiries

Query by example (create relational expressions with)

- Relational operators (=, >, <)
- Logical operators (AND, OR, NOT)

Sorts (identify)

- Primary key field
- Secondary key field (if needed)

Interactive Study Guide Chapter 2

SUMMARY AND KEY TERMS

2.1 Personal computing with popular productivity packages

Although there are many software packages that add variety to the potential of personal computing, the traditional foundation of personal computing has been software in these categories: word processing, desktop publishing, presentation software, spreadsheet, and database. Internet browser and graphics software have been added to the foundation in recent years.

2.2 Word processing: The most popular PC application

Word processing lets you create text-based documents into which you can integrate images. In nonprinted documents, audio and video can be included as well.

When you format a document, you are specifying the size of the page to be printed and how you want the document to look when it is printed. The preset format, or *default settings,* may fit your word processing application. A **font** (53), which refers to the style, appearance, and size of print, is described by its **typeface** (53). Most word processing packages are considered **WYSIWYG** (54), short for "What you see is what you get." The find and replace features make all word processing documents searchable.

Several helpful writing tools are designed to enhance the functionality of word processing programs: the **spelling checker** (54) (using an **electronic dictionary** [54]), an **online thesaurus** (55), and a **grammar and style checker** (55).

Word processing has a variety of features that enable users to enhance the appearance and readability of their documents, including footnoting, numbered and bullet lists, outline, drawing tools, borders, integration of images, multicolumn text, and more. You can print or fax a document by selecting the print option on the main menu.

Word processing software provides the capability of merging data in a database with the text of a document. The *mail-merge* application is an example. Here you merge a *database file* with a *form file.* **Boilerplate** (56) is existing text that can in some way be reused and customized for a variety of word processing applications.

Hyperlinks (58) let you tie parts of a document or different documents together. Word processing packages also let you enter tabular data so that you can create charts within documents.

Convert word processing documents to create **Web pages** (58) on the **World Wide Web (the Web)** (58), the primary application used for viewing information on the Internet.

2.3 Desktop publishing: Freedom of the press

Desktop publishing refers to the capability of producing *camera-ready documents* from the confines of a desktop. In word processing software, the emphasis is on *words,* and in desktop publishing, the emphasis is on overall *document composition.*

The quality of the desktop publishing–produced output depends on the quality of available input and output devices. The document-composition process involves integrating graphics, photos, text, and other elements into a visually appealing document layout. The steps are (1) prepare text, (2) prepare or identify nontext-related resources, (3) lay out the document page(s), (4) fill in the text frames, (5) fill in the picture frames, (6) fine-tune the layout, (7) print the camera-ready document, and (8) publish the document.

A number of resources are pulled together in a typical desktop publishing–produced document: text files, **clip art** (61), original artwork, photographs and hard-copy graphics, and screen displays. During the document-composition process, each file is assigned to a rectangular **frame** (61). A frame holds the text or an image of a particular file.

2.4 Presentation software: Putting on the show

Presentation software enables you to create a wide variety of visually appealing and informative presentation graphics. These steps are used with presentation software: (1) *Select a template* (63). Microsoft's PowerPoint 2000 offers both *design templates* and *content templates.* (2) *Create an outline for the presentation.* PowerPoint's tri-pane view lets you view the *slide, outline,* and *notes* at the same time. (3) *Compile and create other nontext resources.* A slide presentation may include text, photo images, charts and graphs, original drawings, clip art, audio clips, and even full-motion video. Among the most popular charts are the pie and bar charts. Presentation software also permits the preparation of organization charts and maps. (4) *Integrate resources.* The PowerPoint *slide sorter* view gives you an overview of the presentation via **thumbnail** (65) images. (5) *Add special effects.* With PowerPoint you can have an image fade out, be wiped away, show animation, or add sound, to name a few. (6) *Add notes.* (7) *Make the presentation.*

2.5 Spreadsheet: The magic matrix

Spreadsheet software provides an electronic alternative to thousands of traditionally manual tasks that involve rows and columns of data. The intersection of a particular row and column in a spreadsheet designates a **cell** (67). During operations, data are referred to by their **cell addresses** (67). The **pointer** (67) can be moved around the spreadsheet to any cell address.

To make an entry, to edit, or to replace an entry in a spreadsheet, move the pointer to the appropriate cell. Revise the entry in much the same way you would revise the text in a word processing document. The appearance of data in a spreadsheet can be modified to enhance readability.

The four types of **ranges** (67) are a single cell, all or part of a column of adjacent cells, all or part of a row of adjacent cells, and a rectangular block of cells. A particular range is depicted by the addresses of the end-point cells (for example, C5:E10).

Three major types of entries to a cell are label, numeric, and formula. A label entry is any string of alphanumeric text (spaces included) that occupies a particular cell. A numeric entry is any number. A cell may contain a formula, but it is the numeric results that are displayed in the spreadsheet. Spreadsheet formulas use standard programming notation for **arithmetic operators** (69).

In Windows 9x/NT/2000, applications run in **windows** (69)—rectangular areas displayed on the screen. Windows are outfitted with **vertical** (69) and/or **horizontal scroll bars** (69). Each bar contains a **scroll box** (69) and two **scroll arrows** (69). Use the mouse or keyboard to move a box up/down or left/right on a scroll bar to display other parts of the application. This movement is known as **scrolling** (69).

A spreadsheet template can be used over and over for different purposes by different people. If you change the value of a cell in a spreadsheet, all other affected cells are revised accordingly. Spreadsheet packages also can let you generate a variety of charts from spreadsheet data.

2.6 Database: A dynamic data tool

Database software lets you enter, organize, and retrieve stored data. Once the database is created, its data can be deleted or revised, and other data can be added to it.

Both database and spreadsheet software packages enable us to work with tabular data and records in a database. Spreadsheet software works better with tabular data and database software is better at the manipulation of records within a database.

Database software uses the **relational database** (73) approach to data management. Relational databases are organized in tables in which a row is a record and a column is a field.

In database software, the user-defined structure of a database table identifies the characteristics of each field in it. Related fields are grouped to form records.

Database software also permits you to retrieve, view, and print records based on **query by example** (76). To make a query by example, users set conditions for the selection of records by composing a relational expression containing **relational operators** (76) that reflects the desired conditions. Several expressions can be combined into a single condition with **logical operators** (76).

Records in a database can be sorted for display in a variety of formats. To sort the records in a database, select a primary key field and, if needed, a secondary key field. Database software can create customized, or formatted, reports.

DISCUSSION AND PROBLEM SOLVING

2.1 **a.** Explain why software packages in a software suite are complementary.

b. The dominant software suite is Microsoft Office, in its various versions. However, some analysts claim that alternative software suites are as good as or better than it. Under what circumstances would a company with 5000 PCs opt to go with a Microsoft competitor?

2.2 **a.** List five ways that you might use word processing software at school or work. And five more ways at home.

b. Name five format considerations for a word processing document.

c. What is meant when a document is formatted to be justified on the right and on the left? Give three examples where type of justification is used.

d. Customer-service representatives at BrassCo Enterprises spend almost 70% of their day interacting directly with customers. Approximately one hour each day is spent preparing courtesy follow-up letters based on boilerplate, primarily to enhance good will between BrassCo and its customers. Do you think the "personalized" letters are a worthwhile effort? Why or why not?

e. Describe a real-life example of when you might issue a global replace command within a word processing document.

f. Give an example of how hyperlinks can be used in an online word processing document.

g. Identify at least one print document in each of the following environments that would be more effective if distributed as an electronic document: federal government, your college, and any commercial organization.

2.3 **a.** Describe when you might use a text frame and a picture frame in a desktop publishing document.

b. Speculate on what type of peripheral devices you might need to do desktop publishing.

c. Identify five organizations and give one example of how each might use desktop publishing software.

d. With the advent of desktop publishing, the number of printed items bearing the company logo has increased dramatically. Many companies require that all such documents be approved by a central desktop publishing review board prior to distribution. What concerns prompted these managers to establish the review board?

2.4 **a.** Name five types of charts that can be created with presentation software and illustrate three of them.

b. Describe a situation in which you may need to export a presentation software file to a different type of document (for example, word processing). Do the same for importing a file into a presentation software file.

c. Create a series of bulleted text charts (manually or with presentation software) that you might use to make a presentation to the class on the capabilities and benefits of presentation software.

2.5 **a.** Identify three applications for spreadsheet software. Then for each application describe the layout specifying at least three column entries and generally what would be contained in the rows.

b. Use the examples in this section as your guide, and create a formula that might be used in one of the spreadsheet applications you identified in the above question (or another of your choosing). Briefly describe the entries in the formula.

c. Give an example of each of the four types of ranges. Also, list an alternative way to define the range A4:P12.

d. Describe how you might use the pro rata income statement template in Figure 2.15 to do what-if analysis.

2.6 **a.** Describe the relationship between a field, a record, and the structure of a database table.

b. If you were asked to create a PC-based inventory management system for a privately owned retail shoe store, would you use spreadsheet software, database software, or both? Why?

c. Describe two types of inquiries to a student database that involve calculations.

d. Under what circumstances is a graphic representation of data more effective than a tabular presentation of the same data?

e. Give examples and descriptions of at least two other fields that might be added to the record for the STUDENT table (Figure 2.17).

f. Name two possible key fields for an employee file. Name two for an inventory file.

g. Use appropriate relational and logical operators to set conditions for displaying STUDENT, COURSE TITLE, and MAJOR for all courses *completed* by *marketing* or *accounting* majors that include a *lecture*. Illustrate the results showing column headings and the appropriate entries sorted by student.

Inside the Computer

Learning Objectives

3.1 Understand how data are stored and represented in a computer system.

3.2 Identify and describe the function of and relationships between the internal components of a personal computer, including the motherboard, processor, RAM and other memories, ports, buses, expansion boards, and PC cards.

3.3 Distinguish processors by their word size, speed, and memory capacity.

3.4 Explain several approaches to processor design.

chapter 3

WHY THIS CHAPTER IS IMPORTANT TO YOU

A PC card here, a DVD drive there, a few hundred MHz, and all of a sudden you're talking big bucks. A modern mid-level, communications-ready PC configured with a "standard" set of peripheral devices will run you about two grand. Hang on a few extras and add a little power and you're over $3,000. And that's just the hardware! With Mom, Dad, and the kids all wanting their own PC, it's not unusual for expenditures on hardware to top that of the family car. With a significant portion of your budget at stake, you want to make informed decisions when purchasing PCs.

When you purchase a car, you know that it will perform its basic function—to carry people over roadways from point to point. Not so with PCs. PCs have thousands of functions and when you purchase one, you want to be sure that it will do what you want it to do. Most of us can easily grasp the variables involved in buying a house or a car. The average car buyer can assess functionality and style relative to his or her budget constraints and aesthetic tastes, then make a reasonably informed decision. However, to get what you want and need in a PC, and to get the most for your money, you need to have an overall understanding of the essential elements of a computer.

One tower PC looks about like another, with perhaps a little variation in color, style, and size. The same can be said of laptops. Look inside, however, and they are vastly different. Similar-looking PC boxes can be mansions or efficiency apartments on the inside. One might have a 600-MHz processor and another a much slower 350-MHz processor. Differences in processor speed, cache and RAM capacity, type of RAM, speed of the modem, what's embedded on the motherboard, the type of bus, and so on, dictate overall system performance. If you understand these essential elements, you'll be able to make informed decisions when purchasing PCs—and that may be as often as once or twice a year for work and family. Those people who depend on advice from the PC salesperson may end up spending far more than necessary to get what they want.

3.1 GOING DIGITAL

Monthly Technology Update

A computer is an entertainment center with hundreds of interactive games. It's a virtual university providing interactive instruction and testing. It's a painter's canvas. It's a video telephone. It's a CD player. It's a home or office library. It's a television. It's the biggest marketplace in the world. It's the family photo album. It's a print shop. It's a wind tunnel that can test experimental airplane designs. It's a recorder. It's an alarm clock that can remind you to keep an appointment. It's an encyclopedia. It can perform thousands of specialty functions that require specialized skills, such as preparing taxes, drafting legal documents, counseling suicidal patients, and much more.

In all of these applications, the computer deals with everything as electronic signals. Electronic signals come in two flavors—**analog** and **digital.** Analog signals are *continuous* wave forms in which variations in frequency and amplitude can be used to represent information from sound and numerical data. The sound of our voice is carried by analog signals when we talk on the telephone. Computers use digital signals where everything is described in two states: the circuit is either *on* or *off.* Generally, the *on* state is expressed or represented by the number 1 and the *off* state by the number 0. Anymore, just about everything in the world of electronics and communication is *going digital.*

So how do you go digital? You simply need to **digitize** your material. To digitize means to convert data, analog signals, and images into the discrete format (1s and 0s) that can be interpreted by computers. For example, Figure 3.1 shows how music can be digitized. Once digitized, you can use a computer to work with (revise, copy, and so on) the music recording, data, image, shape, and so on. Old recordings of artists from Enrico Caruso to the Beatles have been digitized and then digitally reconstructed on computers to eliminate unwanted distortion and static. Some of these reconstructed CDs are actually better than the originals!

Binary Numbers

Binary Digits: 1 and 0

The electronic nature of the computer makes it possible to combine the two digital states—*on* and *off*—to represent letters, numbers, colors, sounds, images, shapes, and even odors. An "on" or "off" electronic state is represented by a **bit,** short for *binary digit.* In the **binary** numbering system (base 2), the *on-bit* is a 1 and the *off-bit* is a 0. Physically, these states are achieved in a variety of ways.

Going Digital with Compact Discs The recording industry has gone digital. To create a master CD, analog signals are converted to digital signals that can be manipulated by a computer and written to a master CD. The master is duplicated and the copies are sold through retail channels.

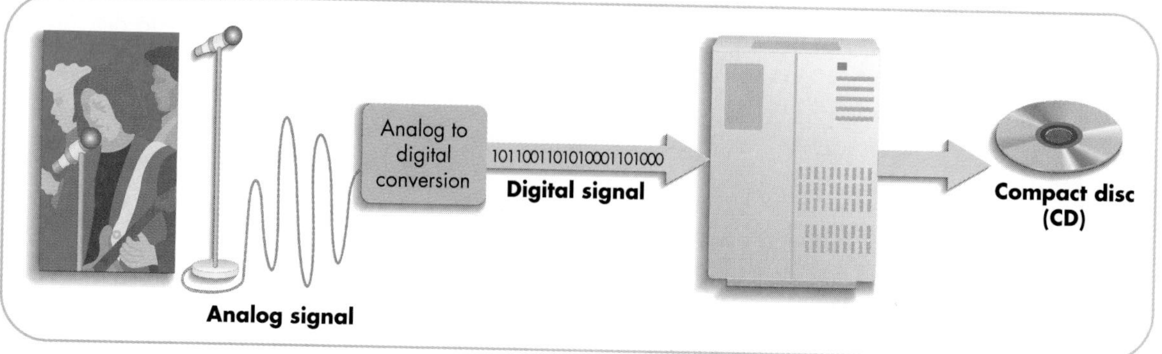

Making PCs at Dell Dell Computer Corporation, founded in 1984, is the world's leading direct-sales computer-systems company. Shown here is one of the company's manufacturing facilities, where it makes the Dell OptiPlex® desktop computers. Courtesy of Dell Computer Corporation

ASCII Codes This figure shows the ASCII codes for upper-case letters, numbers, and several special characters. The ASCII codes for upper-case and lower-case letters are similar. Replace the second binary digit with a 1 to get the lowercase equivalent (*A* is 1000001 and *a* is 1100001).

Character	ASCII Code
A	100 0001
B	100 0010
C	100 0011
D	100 0100
E	100 0101
F	100 0110
G	100 0111
H	100 1000
I	100 1001
J	100 1010
K	100 1011
L	100 1100
M	100 1101
N	100 1110
O	100 1111
P	101 0000
Q	101 0001
R	101 0010
S	101 0011
T	101 0100
U	101 0101
V	101 0110
W	101 0111
X	101 1000
Y	101 1001
Z	101 1010
0	011 0000
1	011 0001
2	011 0010
3	011 0011
4	011 0100
5	011 0101
6	011 0110
7	011 0111
8	011 1000
9	011 1001
Space	010 0000
.	010 1110
(	010 1000
+	010 1011
&	010 0110
$	010 0100
*	010 1010
)	010 1001
;	011 1011
,	010 1100
-	101 1111
?	011 1111
:	011 1010
=	011 1101

- In RAM (temporary storage), the two electronic states often are represented by the presence or absence of an electrical charge in an integrated circuit—a computer chip.
- In disk storage (permanent storage), the two states are made possible by the magnetic arrangement of the surface coating on magnetic disks.
- In CDs and CD-ROMs, digital data are stored permanently as microscopic pits.
- In fiber optic cable, binary data flow through as pulses of light.

Bits may be fine for computers, but human beings are more comfortable with letters and decimal numbers (the base-10 numerals 0 through 9). We like to see colors and hear sounds. Therefore, the letters, decimal numbers, colors, and sounds we input into a computer system while doing word processing, graphics, and other applications must be translated into 1s and 0s for processing and storage. The computer translates the bits back into letters, decimal numbers, colors, and sounds for output on monitors, printers, speakers, and so on.

Encoding Systems: Bits and Bytes

Computers don't speak to one another in English, Spanish, or French. They have their own languages, which are better suited to electronic communication. In these languages, bits are combined according to an **encoding system** to represent letters (**alpha** characters), numbers (**numeric** characters), and special characters (such as *, $, +, and &), collectively referred to as **alphanumeric** characters.

ASCII and ANSI

ASCII (*A*merican *S*tandard *C*ode for *I*nformation *I*nterchange—pronounced "*AS-key*") is the most popular encoding system for PCs and data communication. In ASCII, alphanumeric characters are *encoded* into a bit configuration on input so that the computer can interpret them. This coding equates a unique series of 1s and 0s with a specific character. Figure 3.2 shows the ASCII bit string of commonly used characters. Just as the words *mother* and *father* are arbitrary English-language character strings that refer to our parents, 1000010 is an arbitrary ASCII

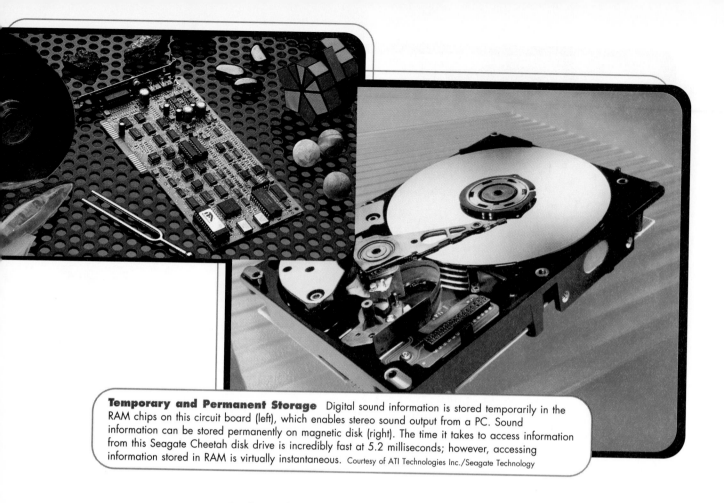

Temporary and Permanent Storage Digital sound information is stored temporarily in the RAM chips on this circuit board (left), which enables stereo sound output from a PC. Sound information can be stored permanently on magnetic disk (right). The time it takes to access information from this Seagate Cheetah disk drive is incredibly fast at 5.2 milliseconds; however, accessing information stored in RAM is virtually instantaneous. Courtesy of ATI Technologies Inc./Seagate Technology

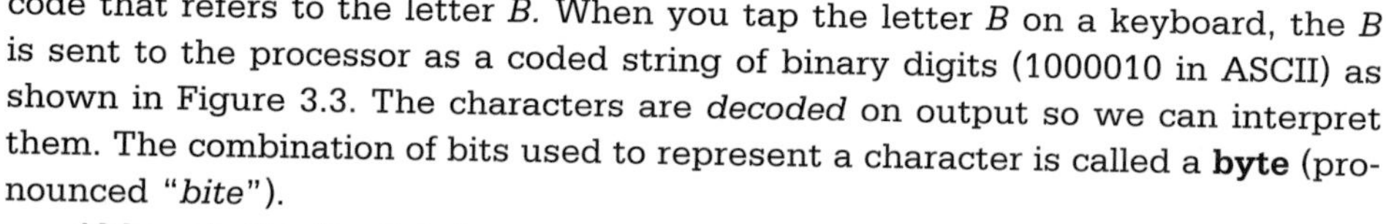

code that refers to the letter *B*. When you tap the letter *B* on a keyboard, the *B* is sent to the processor as a coded string of binary digits (1000010 in ASCII) as shown in Figure 3.3. The characters are *decoded* on output so we can interpret them. The combination of bits used to represent a character is called a **byte** (pronounced "*bite*").

Encoding

Although the English language has considerably fewer than 128 printable characters, the extra bit configurations are needed to represent additional common and not-so-common special characters (such as - [hyphen]; @ [at]; | [a broken vertical bar]; and ~ [tilde]) and to signal a variety of activities to the computer (such as ringing a bell or telling the computer to accept a piece of datum).

The 7-bit ASCII code can represent up to 128 characters (2^7), but the PC byte is 8 bits. There are 256 (2^8) possible bit configurations in an 8-bit byte. Hardware and software vendors accept the 128 standard ASCII codes and use the extra 128 bit configurations to represent control characters (such as ringing a bell) or non-

FIGURE 3.3

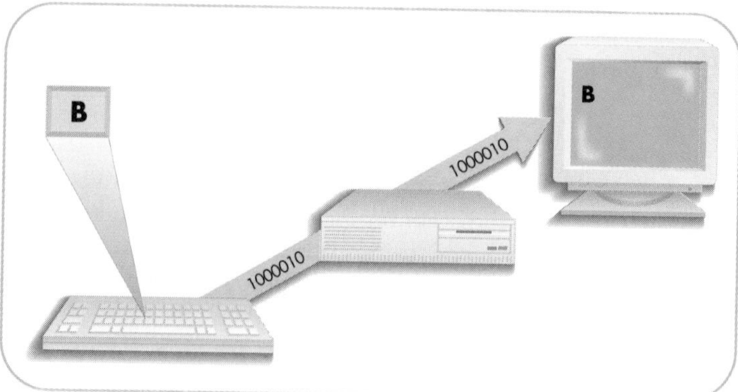

Encoding When you tap the B key on the keyboard, a binary representation of the letter *B* is sent to the processor. The processor sends the encoded *B* to the monitor, which interprets and displays a **B.**

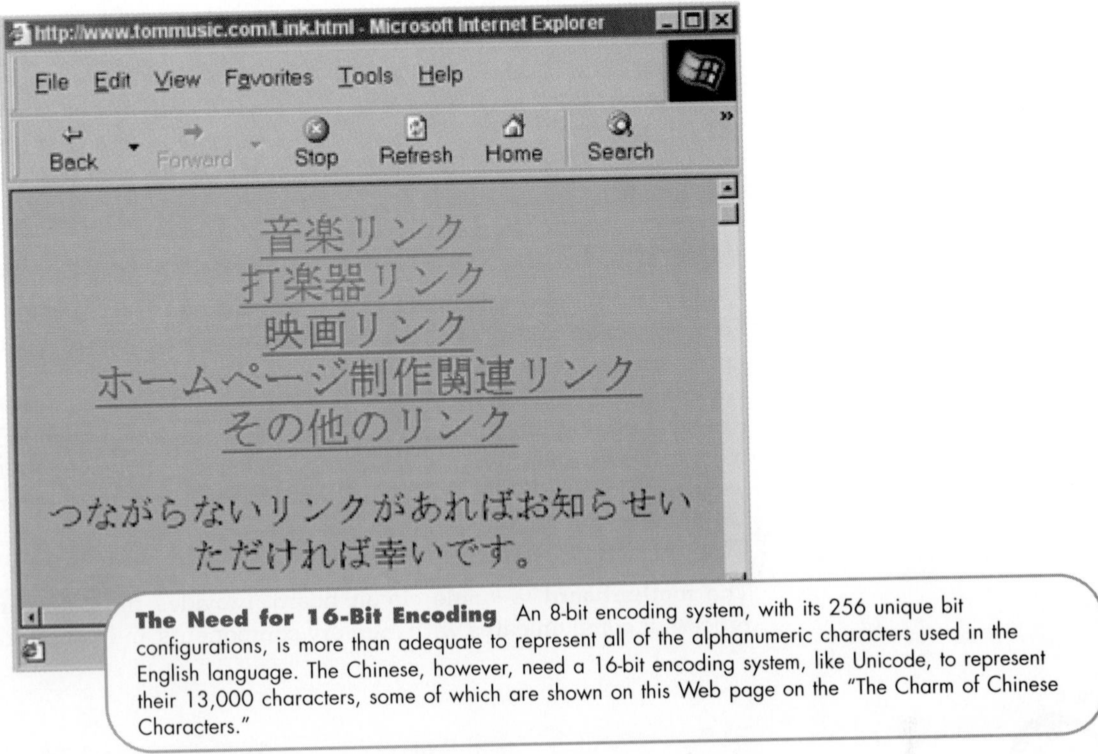

The Need for 16-Bit Encoding An 8-bit encoding system, with its 256 unique bit configurations, is more than adequate to represent all of the alphanumeric characters used in the English language. The Chinese, however, need a 16-bit encoding system, like Unicode, to represent their 13,000 characters, some of which are shown on this Web page on the "The Charm of Chinese Characters."

character images to complement their hardware or software product. Microsoft Windows uses the 8-bit **ANSI** encoding system (developed by the *A*merican *N*ational *S*tandards *I*nstitute) to enable the sharing of text between Windows applications. The first 128 ANSI codes are the same as the ASCII codes, but the next 128 are defined to meet the specific needs of Windows applications.

Unicode: 65,536 Possibilities

ASCII, with 128 character codes, is sufficient for the English language, but we're now a global economy and ASCII falls far short of the Japanese language requirements. The relatively new **Unicode,** a 16-bit encoding system, will enable computers and applications to talk to one another more easily and will handle most languages of the world (including Hebrew, Japanese, and Greek). Unicode's 16-bit code allows for 65,536 characters (2^{16}). Eventually, Unicode may be adopted as a standard for information interchange throughout the global computer community. Universal acceptance of the Unicode standard would make international communication in all areas easier, from monetary transfers between banks to e-mail.

SECTION SELF-CHECK

Self-Check

3-1.1 Bit is the singular of byte. (T/F)

3-1.2 Data are stored permanently on magnetic storage devices, such as magnetic disk. (T/F)

3-1.3 Binary data flow through fiber optic cable as pulses of light. (T/F)

3-1.4 What are the two kinds of electronic signals: (a) analog and digital, (b) binary and octal, (c) alpha and numeric, or (d) bit and byte?

3-1.5 The base of the binary number system is: (a) 2, (b) 8, (c) 16, or (d) 32?

3-1.6 The combination of bits used to represent a character is called a: (a) bits on/off, (b) binary config, (c) 0–1 string, or (d) byte?

3-1.7 The 16-bit encoding system is called: (a) Unicorn, (b) Unicode, (c) Hexacode, or (d) 10 plus 6 code?

3-1.8 How many ANSI bytes can be stored in a 32-bit word: (a) 2, (b) 4, (c) 6, or (d) 8?

Chips

The processor, RAM, and a variety of other electronic components are housed in the **system unit,** usually a metal and plastic upright box (the tower), or inside the laptop's shell. In this section, we'll look inside the box at the major electronic components of a computer system. Figure 3.4 lets you peek inside the system unit of a PC.

Why It's Important to Know What's Inside Your PC

If you want to take advantage of ever-advancing PC technology, get the most for your PC dollar, and allow your PC to grow with your capabilities, you need to know what's inside your PC. You need to know because personal computing is very personal. You are the decision maker. A little knowledge about what's inside can save you big bucks and make you a more effective user. Someday we won't have to worry about what's inside a PC. That day, however, will not be any time soon. So, let's start with the component that ties it all together, the *motherboard.*

The Motherboard

The **motherboard,** a single circuit board, provides the path through which the processor communicates with memory components and peripheral devices. Think

System Unit and Motherboard The system unit is this box and its content—the computer system's electronic circuitry, including the motherboard with the processor and various expansion boards (added capabilities discussed later in this chapter), and various storage devices.

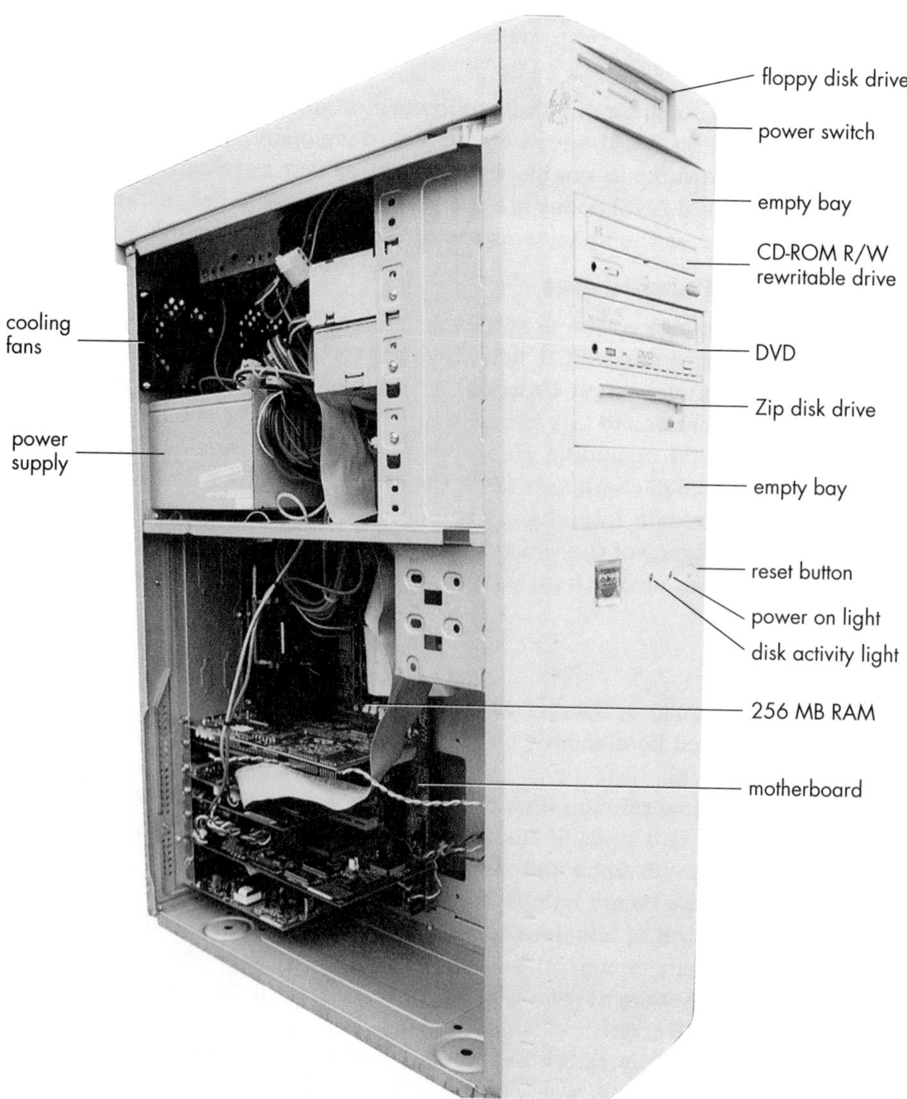

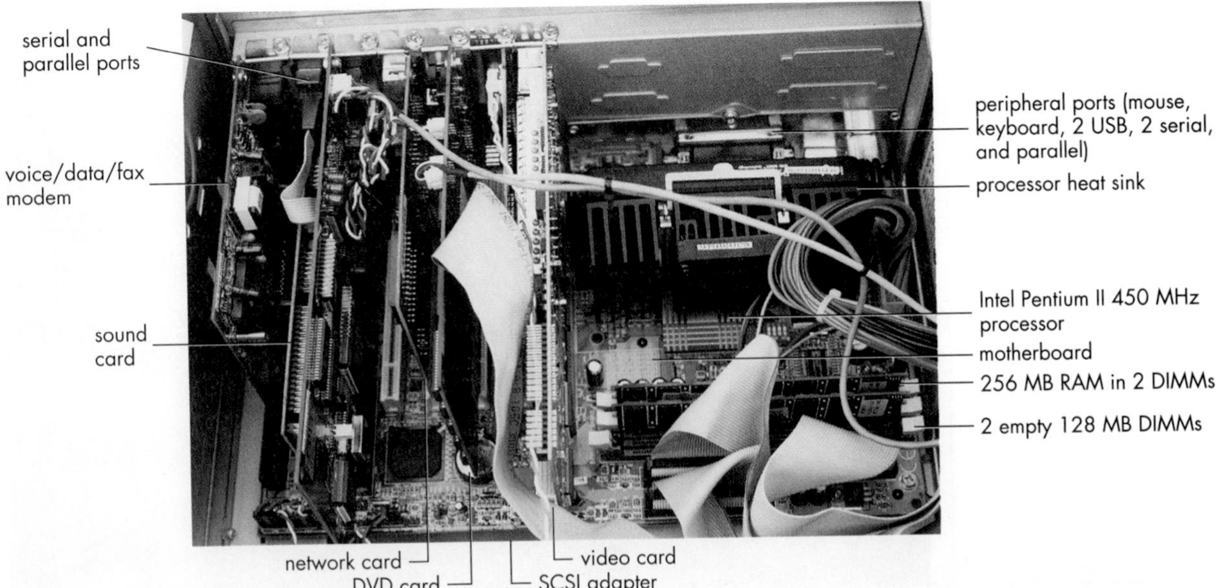

FIGURE 3.5 **Motherboard with Components** Here a motherboard is configured with a processor, memory, and various expansion cards (discussed later). It has a 450-MHz Intel Pentium II processor, 512 K of cache memory, plus three ISA expansion slots, three PCI local bus slots, and one AGP slot for video for adding capabilities, such as a voice/data/fax modem. The motherboard has four DIMMs that can accept 512 MB of SDRAM. It also has mouse and keyboard ports, two serial ports, one parallel port, and two USB ports.

of the processor as the PC's brain and the motherboard as the PC's central nervous system. The motherboard's **chipset** is its intelligence and controls the flow of information between system components connected to the board. The chipset is important because it determines what features are supported on the system (including types of processors and memory). In a personal computer, the following are attached to the motherboard:

- Microprocessor (main processor)
- Support electronic circuitry (for example, one chip handles input/output signals from the peripheral devices)
- Memory chips (for example, RAM and other types of memory)
- Expansion boards (optional circuit boards, such as a fax/modem)

The various chips have standard-sized pin connectors that allow them to be attached to the motherboard and, therefore, to a common electrical **bus** that enables data flow between the various system components.

Just as big cities have mass transit systems that move large numbers of people, the computer has a similar system that moves millions of bits a second. Both transit systems use buses, although the one in the computer doesn't have wheels. All electrical signals travel on a common electrical bus. The term *bus* was derived from its wheeled cousin because passengers on both buses (people and bits) can get off at any stop. In a computer, the bus stops are the control unit, the arithmetic and logic unit, RAM and other types of internal memory, and the **device controllers** (small computers) that control the operation of the peripheral devices (see Figure 3.5).

Ultimately, the type of processor and the amount of RAM placed on the motherboard define the PC's speed and capacity. The central component of the motherboard, the processor, is generally not made by the manufacturers of PCs. It is made by companies that specialize in the development and manufacture of

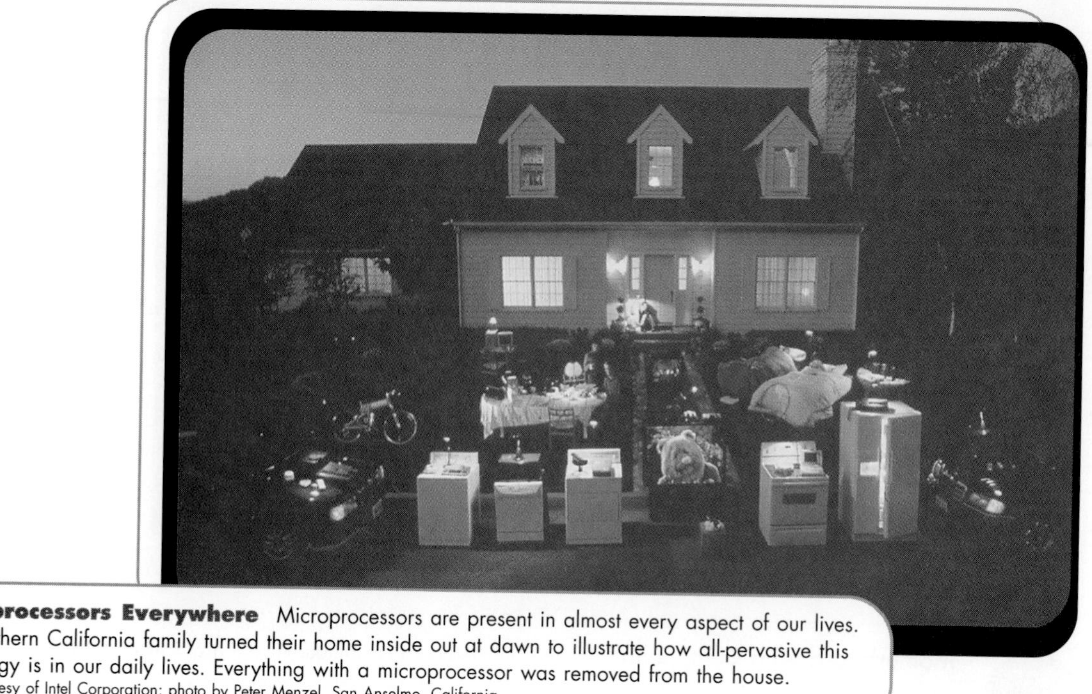

Microprocessors Everywhere Microprocessors are present in almost every aspect of our lives. This northern California family turned their home inside out at dawn to illustrate how all-pervasive this technology is in our daily lives. Everything with a microprocessor was removed from the house.
Photo courtesy of Intel Corporation; photo by Peter Menzel, San Anselmo, California

microprocessors. A number of companies make PC microprocessors, including Intel, Motorola, Advanced Micro Devices (AMD), Cyrix, and IBM. Within the context of a PC, the terms *microprocessor* and *processor* are used interchangeably.

Computer on a Chip: The Microprocessor

What is smaller than a postage stamp and found in wristwatches, sewing machines, and CD players? The answer is a **microprocessor.** The processor component of personal computer systems is a microprocessor, or simply a small processor. The microprocessor is literally a "computer on a chip." We use the term *chip* to refer to any self-contained integrated circuit. The size of chips varies from fingernail size to postage-stamp size (about 1-inch square). Microprocessors have been integrated into thousands of mechanical and electronic devices—even elevators, band saws, and ski-boot bindings. In a few years, virtually everything mechanical or electronic will incorporate microprocessor technology into its design.

The motherboard for the original (1981) and most of the *IBM-PC–compatible* microcomputers manufactured through 1984 used the Intel 8088 microprocessor chip. Since then, Intel has introduced a succession of increasingly more advanced processors to power the IBM-PC compatible PCs, called *PC compatibles* or, simply, *PCs.* The Intel "286" (Intel 80286), "386," and "486" processors took us into the 1990s followed by the Intel **Pentium®** and **Pentium® Pro** series. Most new system units have an Intel **Pentium® II, Pentium® III,** or **Celeron®** processor inside. The more expensive Pentium II-based PCs offer the greatest performance whereas the less expensive Celeron-based PCs offer good value with reduced performance.

The Processor

The processor runs the show and is the nucleus of any computer system. Regardless of the complexity of a processor, sometimes called the **central processing unit** or **CPU,** it has only two fundamental sections: the *control unit* and the *arithmetic and logic unit.* These units work together with random-access memory (RAM) and other internal memories to make the processor—and the computer system—go. Figure 3.6 illustrates the interaction between computer system components.

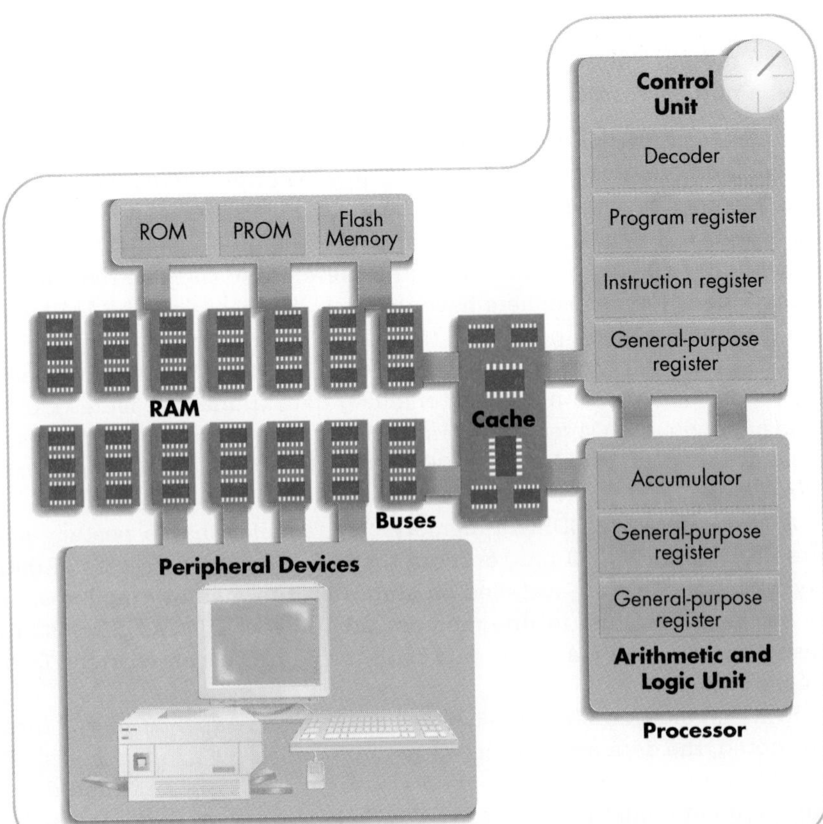

Interaction between Computer System Components During processing, instructions and data are passed between the various types of internal memories, the processor's control unit and arithmetic and logic unit, and the peripheral devices over the common electrical bus. A system clock paces the speed of operation within the processor and ensures that everything takes place in timed intervals.

The Control Unit Just as the processor, or CPU, is the nucleus of a computer system, the **control unit** is the nucleus of the processor. It has three primary functions:

- To read and interpret program instructions
- To direct the operation of internal processor components
- To control the flow of programs and data in and out of RAM

During program execution, the first in a sequence of program instructions is moved from RAM to the control unit, where it is decoded and interpreted by the **decoder.** The control unit then directs other processor components to carry out the operations necessary to execute the instruction.

The processor contains high-speed working storage areas called **registers** that can store no more than a few bytes (see Figure 3.6). Because registers reside on the processor chip, they handle instructions and data at very high speeds and are used for a variety of processing functions. One register, called the **instruction register,** contains the instruction being executed. Other general-purpose registers store data needed for immediate processing. Registers also store status information. For example, the **program register** contains the location in RAM of the next instruction to be executed. Registers facilitate the processing and movement of data and instructions between RAM, the control unit, and the arithmetic and logic unit.

The Arithmetic and Logic Unit The **arithmetic and logic unit** performs all computations (addition, subtraction, multiplication, and division) and all logic operations (comparisons). The results are placed in a register called the **accumulator.** Examples of *computations* include the payroll deduction for social security, the day-end inventory level, and the balance on a bank statement. A *logic* operation compares two pieces of data, either alphabetic or numeric. Based on the result of the comparison, the program "branches" to one of several alternative sets of program instructions. For example, in an inventory system each item in stock is

Central Processing Unit

compared to a reorder point at the end of each day. If the inventory level falls below the reorder point, a sequence of program instructions is executed that produces a purchase order.

RAM RAM, a *read-and-write memory,* enables data to be both read and written to memory. RAM is *solid state*; that is, it is electronic circuitry with no moving parts. Electrically charged points in the RAM chips represent the bits (1s and 0s) that comprise the data and other information stored in RAM. RAM is attached to the motherboard, like the processor, and therefore to the electronic bus. Over the past two decades, researchers have given us a succession of RAM technologies, each designed to keep pace with ever-faster processors. Most new PCs are being equipped with **synchronous dynamic RAM (SDRAM).** SDRAM is able to synchronize itself with the processor, enabling data transfer at more than twice the speed of previous RAM technologies. With the next generation of processors, we'll probably move to **Rambus DRAM (RDRAM),** which is six times faster than SDRAM.

A state-of-the-art SDRAM memory chip, smaller than a postage stamp, can store about 128,000,000 bits, or more than 12,000,000 characters of data! Physically, memory chips are installed on **single in-line memory modules,** or **SIMMs,** and on the newer **dual in-line memory modules,** or **DIMMs.** SIMMs are less expensive but have only a 32-bit data path to the processor, whereas DIMMs have a 64-bit data path.

RAM is **volatile memory.** That is, when the electrical current is turned off or interrupted, the data are lost. In contrast to permanent storage on disk, RAM provides the processor only with *temporary* storage for programs and data. All programs and data must be transferred to RAM from an input device (such as a keyboard) or from disk before programs can be executed and data can be processed. Once a program is no longer in use, the storage space it occupied is assigned to another program awaiting execution. Programs and data are loaded to RAM from disk storage because the time required to access a program instruction or piece of datum from RAM is significantly less than from disk storage. RAM is essentially a high-speed holding area for data and programs. In fact, *nothing really happens in a computer system until the program instructions and data are moved from RAM to the processor.*

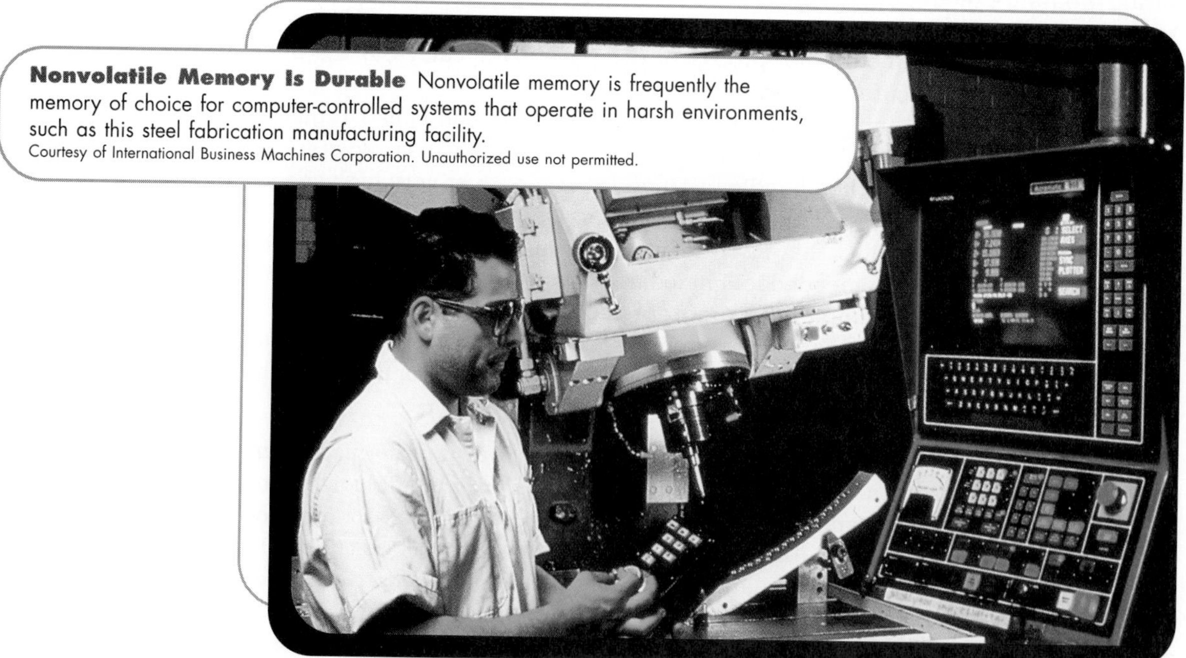

Nonvolatile Memory Is Durable Nonvolatile memory is frequently the memory of choice for computer-controlled systems that operate in harsh environments, such as this steel fabrication manufacturing facility.
Courtesy of International Business Machines Corporation. Unauthorized use not permitted.

The data in RAM are manipulated by the processor according to program instructions. A program instruction or a piece of datum is stored in a specific RAM location called an **address.** RAM is analogous to the rows of boxes you see in post offices. Just as each P.O. box has a number, each byte in RAM has an address. Addresses permit program instructions and data to be located, accessed, and processed. The content of each address changes frequently as different programs are executed and new data are processed.

Other High-Speed Memories Data and programs are being continually moved in and out of RAM at electronic speeds. But that's not fast enough. To achieve even faster transfer of instructions and data to the processor, computers are designed with **cache memory** (see Figure 3.6). Cache memory is used by computer designers to increase computer system throughput. **Throughput** refers to the rate at which work can be performed by a computer system.

Like RAM, cache is a high-speed holding area for program instructions and data. However, cache memory uses internal storage technologies that are much faster (and much more expensive) than conventional RAM. With only a fraction of the capacity of RAM, cache memory holds only those instructions and data that are *likely* to be needed next by the processor. Cache memory is effective because, in a typical session, the same data or instructions are accessed over and over. The processor first checks cache memory for needed data and instructions, thereby reducing the number of accesses to the slower RAM.

Another special type of internal memory, called *read-only memory (ROM),* cannot be altered by the user (see Figure 3.6). The contents of **ROM** (rhymes with "mom"), are "hard-wired" (designed into the logic of the memory chip) by the manufacturer and can be "read only." When you turn on a microcomputer system, a program in ROM automatically readies the computer system for use and produces the initial display-screen prompt. A variation of ROM is **programmable read-only memory (PROM).** PROM is ROM into which you, the user, can load read-only programs and data.

Flash memory is a type of PROM that can be altered easily by the user. Flash memory, a feature of new processors, I/O devices, and storage devices, is **nonvolatile memory** that retains its contents after an electrical interruption. The logic capabilities of these devices can be upgraded by simply downloading new software from the Internet or a vendor-supplied disk to flash memory. Upgrades to early processors and peripheral devices required the user to replace the old circuit board or chip with a new one. The emergence of flash memory has eliminated this time-consuming and costly method of upgrade.

MEMORY

Internal Storage

Volatile memory
- Registers
- Synchronous dynamic RAM (SDRAM)
- Rambus DRAM (RDRAM)
- Cache

Nonvolatile memory
- ROM and PROM
- Flash memory

What Happens Inside: Unraveling the Mystery

BASIC is a popular programming language. The simple BASIC program in Figure 3.7 computes and displays the sum of any two numbers (22 and 44 in the example). The instructions in this example program are intuitive; that is, you don't really need to know BASIC to understand what is happening. Figure 3.7 gives you insight into how a processor works by showing the interaction between RAM, the control unit, and the arithmetic and logic unit during the execution of this program. There is actually more going on in the processor, but this example captures the essence of what's happening. Figure 3.7 uses only 10 RAM locations, and only for data. In practice, both programs and data would be stored in RAM, which usually has a minimum of 64 million storage locations.

The statement-by-statement walkthrough in Figure 3.7 illustrates generally what happens as each BASIC instruction is executed. More complex arithmetic and input/output tasks involve further repetitions of these fundamental operations. Logic operations (greater than, less than, equal to, and so on) are similar, with values being compared between RAM locations, the accumulator, and the various registers (see Figure 3.6).

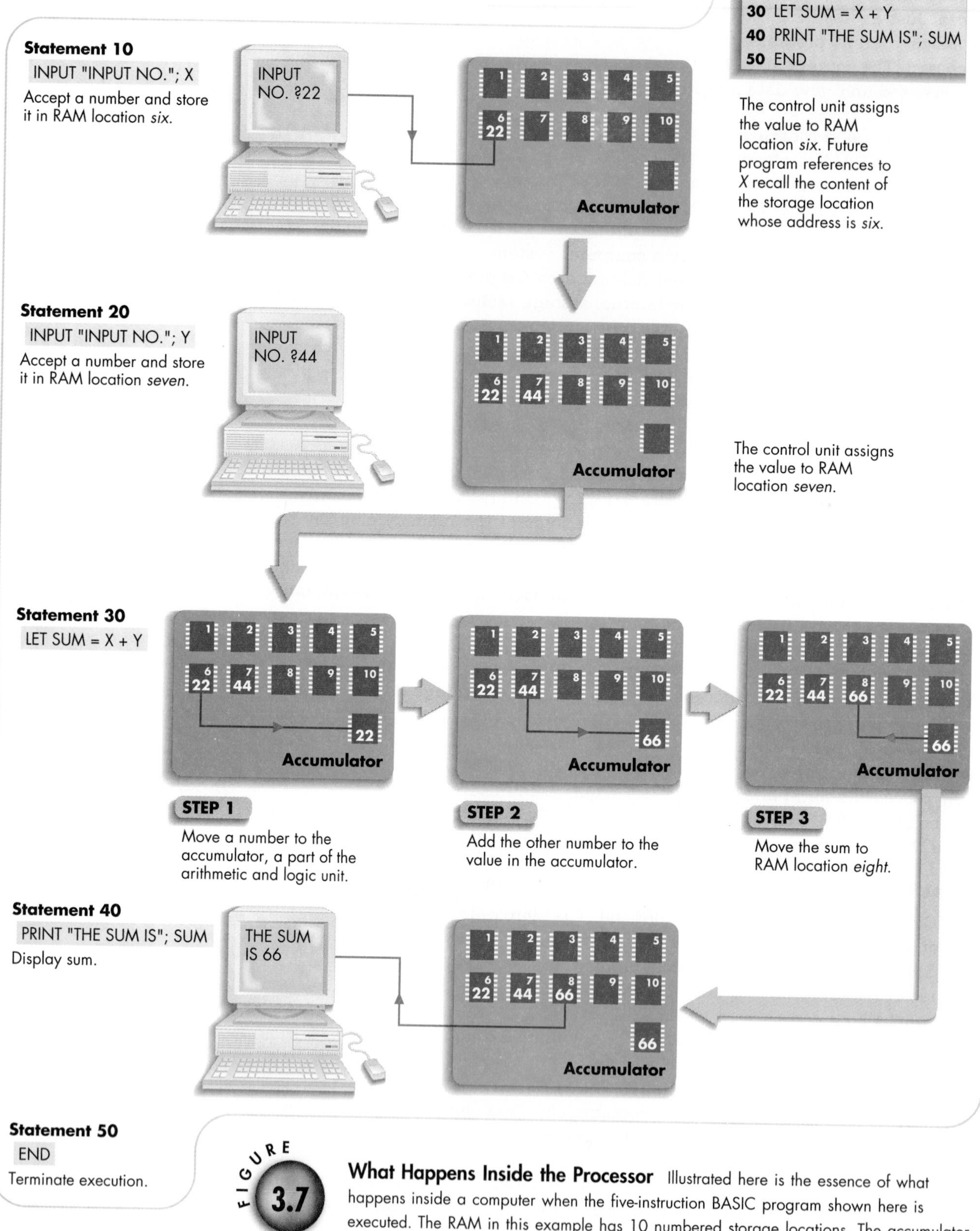

10 INPUT "INPUT NO."; X
20 INPUT "INPUT NO."; Y
30 LET SUM = X + Y
40 PRINT "THE SUM IS"; SUM
50 END
Statement 10
INPUT "INPUT NO."; X
Accept a number and store it in RAM location six.
INPUT NO. ?22
Accumulator
The control unit assigns the value to RAM location six. Future program references to X recall the content of the storage location whose address is six.
Statement 20
INPUT "INPUT NO."; Y
Accept a number and store it in RAM location seven.
INPUT NO. ?44
Accumulator
The control unit assigns the value to RAM location seven.
Statement 30
LET SUM = X + Y
Accumulator
STEP 1
Move a number to the accumulator, a part of the arithmetic and logic unit.
STEP 2
Add the other number to the value in the accumulator.
STEP 3
Move the sum to RAM location eight.
Statement 40
PRINT "THE SUM IS"; SUM
Display sum.
THE SUM IS 66
Accumulator
Statement 50
END
Terminate execution.

FIGURE 3.7

What Happens Inside the Processor Illustrated here is the essence of what happens inside a computer when the five-instruction BASIC program shown here is executed. The RAM in this example has 10 numbered storage locations. The accumulator is part of the arithmetic and logic unit.

IT Ethics

SHOULD PC OWNERSHIP BE AN ENTRANCE REQUIREMENT FOR COLLEGES?

As the job market tightens, colleges are looking to give their students a competitive edge. With computer knowledge becoming a job prerequisite for many positions, hundreds of colleges have made the purchase of a personal computer a prerequisite for admission. Personal computers are versatile in that they can be used as stand-alone computers or they can be linked to the college's network, the Internet, or other personal computers in a classroom. At these colleges, PCs are everywhere—in classrooms, lounges, libraries, and other common areas.

Wouldn't it be great to run a bibliographic search from your dorm room or home? Make changes to a report without retyping it? Run a case search for a law class? Use the computer for math homework calculations?

Instead of making hard copies of class assignments, some instructors key in their assignments, which are then "delivered" to each student's electronic mailbox. At some colleges, student PCs are networked during class enabling immediate distribution of class materials. Students can correspond with their instructors through their computer to get help with assignments. They can even "talk" to other students at connected colleges.

Discussion: If your college does not require PC ownership for admission, should it? If it does, should the policy be continued?

The Interactive Networked Classroom

Owning a PC is a prerequisite for admission to the University of Oklahoma's College of Engineering. OU students, shown here, use PCs with wireless technology that lets them connect to the Internet anywhere within the engineering complex. During class, students and the instructor can easily create a wireless local area network to link all PCs. Students can do the same for a linked study group.

Courtesy of *Sooner Magazine*, University of Oklahoma

The Machine Cycle: Making the Rounds

We communicate with computers by telling them what to do in their native tongue—the machine language. You may have heard of computer programming languages such as BASIC (in Figure 3.7) and C++. Dozens of these languages are in common usage, but all need to be translated into the only language that a computer understands—its own **machine language.** Typically, each instruction in a human-oriented language, like BASIC, is translated into several machine language instructions. As you might expect, machine language instructions are represented inside the computer as strings of binary digits.

These instructions are executed within the framework of a **machine cycle.** The speed of a processor is sometimes measured by how long it takes to complete a machine cycle. The timed interval that comprises the machine cycle is the total of the *instruction time*, or *I-time*, and the *execution time*, or *E-time*. The actions that take place during the machine cycle are shown in Figure 3.8.

Putting It All Together

The motherboard, with its processor and memory, is ready for work. Alone, though, a motherboard is like a college with no students. The motherboard must be linked to I/O, storage, and communication devices to receive data and return the results of processing.

The Machine Cycle

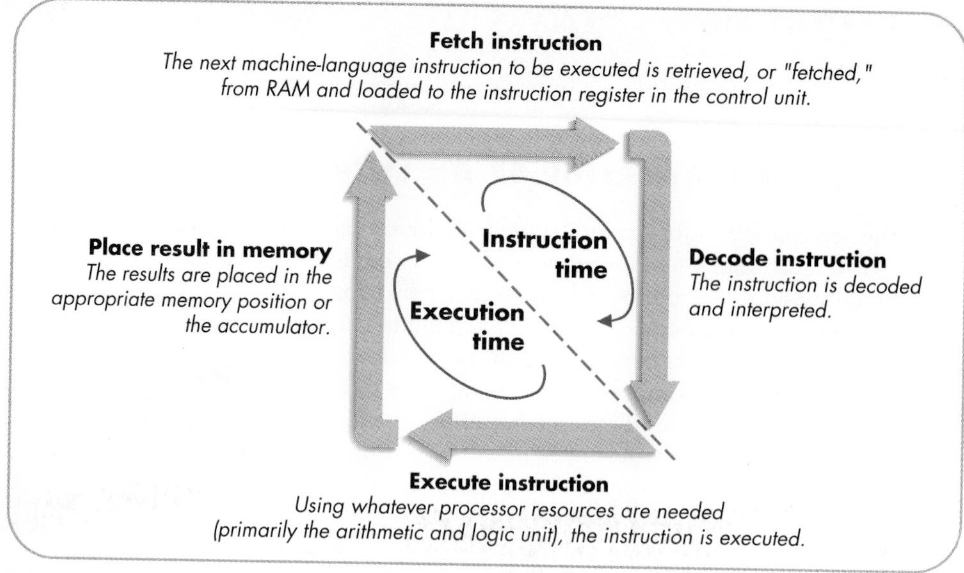
Fetch instruction
The next machine-language instruction to be executed is retrieved, or "fetched," from RAM and loaded to the instruction register in the control unit.
Decode instruction
The instruction is decoded and interpreted.
Execute instruction
Using whatever processor resources are needed (primarily the arithmetic and logic unit), the instruction is executed.
Place result in memory
The results are placed in the appropriate memory position or the accumulator.
Instruction time
Execution time

Ports

In a PC, external peripheral devices (such as a printer and a mouse) usually come with a cable and a multipin connector. To link a device to the PC, you plug its connector into a socket in much the same way you plug a lamp cord into an electrical outlet. The socket, called a *port*, provides a direct link to the PC's common electrical bus on the motherboard. Ports on a typical PC are shown in Figure 3.9.

External peripheral devices and other computers can be linked to the processor via cables or a wireless connection. The motherboard is designed with several port options, including at least one serial port and parallel port each, a keyboard port, a mouse port, plus a couple of USB ports.

- *Serial ports*–**Serial ports** allow the serial transmission of data, one bit at a time (see Figure 3.10). Imagine a line of fans going single-file through a turnstile at a high school football game. An external modem might be connected to a serial port. The standard for PC serial ports is the 9-pin or 25-pin (male or female) **RS-232C connector.** One of the 9 or 25 lines carries the serial signal to the peripheral device, and another line carries the signal from the device. The other lines carry control signals.
- *Parallel ports*–**Parallel ports** allow the parallel transmission of data; that is, several bits are transmitted simultaneously. Figure 3.10 illustrates how 8-bit bytes travel in parallel over 8 separate lines. Imagine 8 lines of fans going through 8 adjacent turnstiles at an NFL football game. Extra lines carry control signals. Parallel ports use the same 25-pin RS-232C connector or the 36-pin **Centronics connector.** These ports provide the interface for such devices as high-speed printers, external magnetic tape or disk backup units, and other computers.
- *SCSI port*–The **SCSI port** provides a parallel interface that enables faster data transmission than serial and parallel ports. Also, up to 15 peripheral devices can be daisy-chained to a single SCSI port; that is, they are connected along a single cable. The typical off-the-shelf PC compatible may not come with a **SCSI controller,** the add-on circuitry needed for a SCSI port.
- *USB port*–The **USB port** (Universal Serial Bus port) is the most recent innovation in high-speed device interfaces. Up to 127 peripheral devices can be daisy-chained to a single USB port. USB ports are ideal for digital cameras, scanners, and high-speed modems.
- *Dedicated keyboard and mouse ports*–These two ports have a round 5-pin connector.

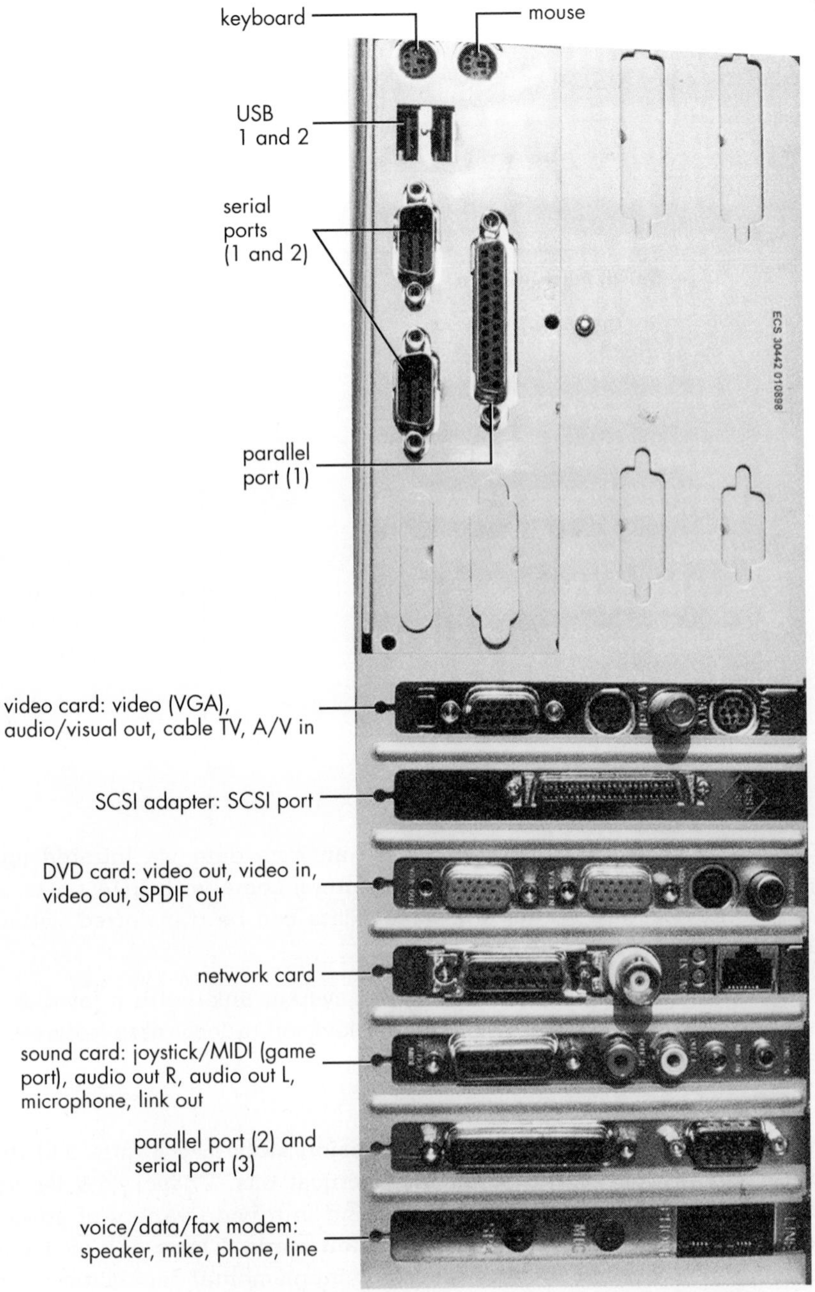

Making the Connection to the System Unit Typically, external connections to the motherboard and expansion cards are made to the ports at the rear of the system unit. The various ports are labeled in the first illustration. Several of the many possible cables that can be connected to the ports are shown, left to right (SCSI to scanner and parallel to printer in inset, SCSI to adapter, USB, coaxial network cable, keyboard, mouse, video, parallel, L and R speakers, microphone, headset, serial). Also shown is the hodgepodge of wires that result when devices are linked to the system unit. As you can see, a large number of devices using a variety of connectors and cables can be linked to a PC.

keyboard

mouse

USB
1 and 2

serial
ports
(1 and 2)

parallel
port (1)

ECS 30442 010898

video card: video (VGA),
audio/visual out, cable TV, A/V in

SCSI adapter: SCSI port

DVD card: video out, video in,
video out, SPDIF out

network card

sound card: joystick/MIDI (game
port), audio out R, audio out L,
microphone, link out

parallel port (2) and
serial port (3)

voice/data/fax modem:
speaker, mike, phone, line

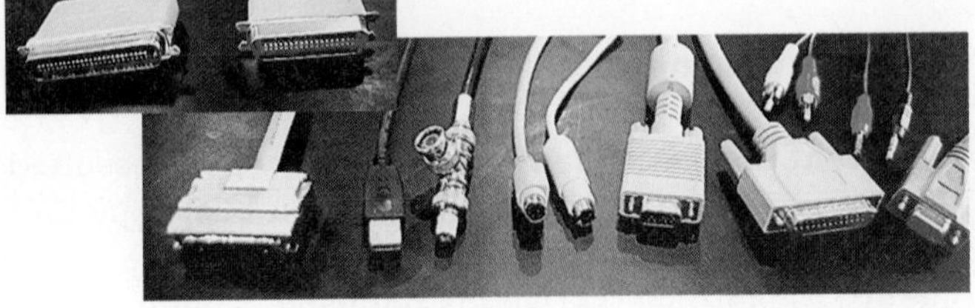

Serial and Parallel Data Transmission In serial transmission, outgoing and incoming bits flow one-at-a-time through a single line. In parallel transmission, bytes flow together over eight separate lines.

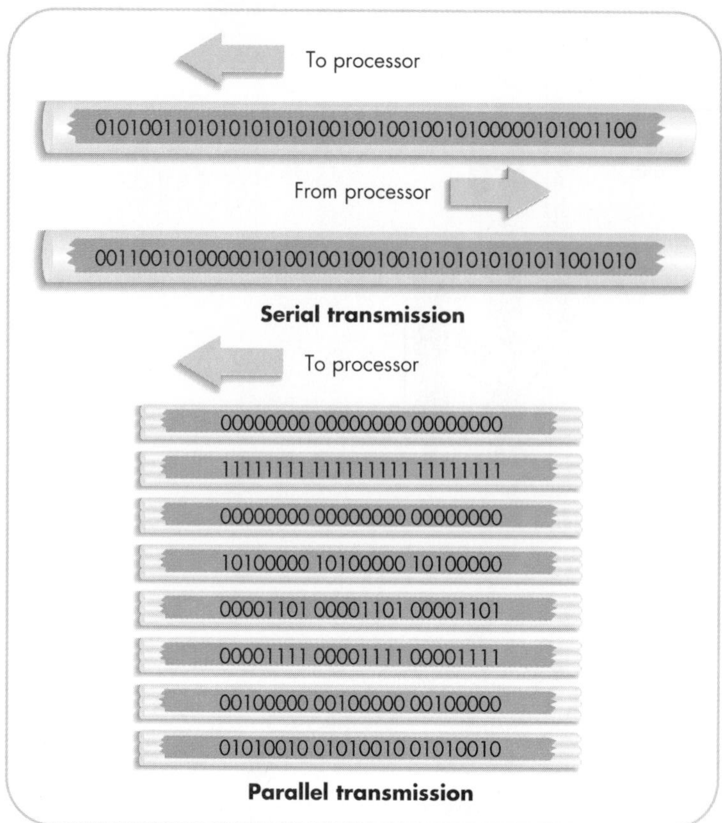

Peripherals World Record This Intel engineer connected 111 peripheral devices to single PC via a USB port, setting a new world record. The feat was staged before a live audience at Fall COMDEX, an industry trade show. Peripherals ranged from mice, joysticks, and keyboards to digital speakers and video conferencing systems.
Photo courtesy of Intel Corporation

- *IrDA port*–The **IrDA port, infrared port,** transmits data via infrared light waves. Many PCs and devices, such as printers, come with IrDA ports. As long as the devices are within a few feet, data can be transferred without the use of cables.

A variety of ports shown in Figure 3.9 enables system links with a joystick or MIDI music device (via the *game port*), cable television, a local area network, a telephone line, the monitor, and other devices.

A Fleet of Buses

The motherboard includes several empty **expansion slots** (see Figure 3.5) that provide direct connections to the common electrical bus. These slots let you expand the capabilities of a basic PC by plugging in a wide variety of special-function **expansion boards,** also called **expansion cards.** These add-on circuit boards contain the electronic circuitry for many supplemental capabilities, such as extra ports, a modem, or video capture capability. Expansion boards are made to fit a particular type of bus. These are the more popular types of buses for PC compatibles:

- *ISA bus.* The most common expansion bus is the **ISA bus.** It's also the oldest and slowest.
- *PCI local bus.* Recent innovations in bus technology have resulted in linking expansion boards directly to the system's common bus, sometimes referred to as the **local bus.** The **PCI local bus** improves performance for today's high-speed peripherals. Modern motherboards normally include both the popular ISA bus and the PCI local bus.
- *SCSI bus.* The **SCSI bus,** or "scuzzy" bus, provides an alternative to the expansion bus. Up to 15 SCSI peripheral devices can be daisy-chained to a SCSI interface expansion card via the SCSI port. That is, the devices are connected along a single cable, both internal and external, with multiple SCSI connectors (see Figure 3.11).

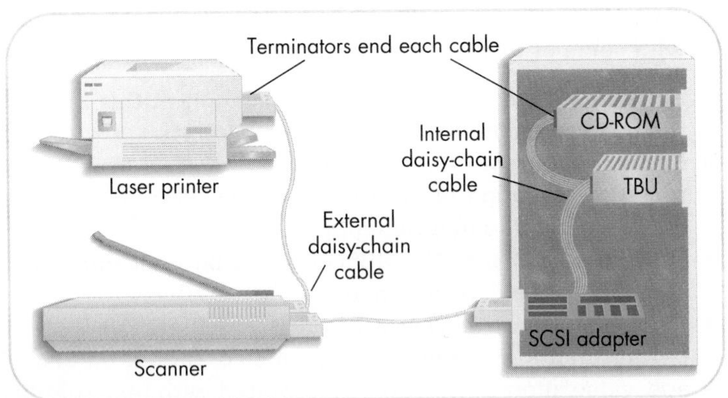

SCSI Bus Two external devices, a printer and a scanner, are daisy-chained on the SCSI's external cable. Two internal devices, the CD-ROM and the tape backup unit, are daisy-chained on the SCSI's internal cable. Terminators are attached at the end of each cable to denote the end of the chain.

- *Universal Serial Bus.* The **Universal Serial Bus (USB)** is a relatively new bus standard that permits up to 127 peripheral devices to be connected to a USB port. The USB will eliminate the hassle of installing expansion cards. PC peripheral devices are designed to connect to the USB port on the motherboard. The USB **hot plug** feature allows peripheral devices to be connected to or removed from the USB port while the PC is running.

Buses
ISA bus
PCI local bus
SCSI bus
Universal Serial Bus (USB)

Serendipitous Surfing: Online Shopping

PC Growth: Adding Capabilities

Today's PCs are designed such that they can grow with your personal computing needs. Initially you purchase what you need and/or can afford, then purchase and install optional capabilities as required.

Expansion: Slots for Boards

The *expansion slots* associated with expansion buses (ISA), local buses (PCI), and the *SCSI adapter* let you add features to your PC by adding *expansion boards*. The number of available expansion slots varies from computer to computer (see Figure 3.5). Keep in mind that an expansion board and/or peripheral device is designed for use with a particular type of expansion bus (PCI, SCSI, and so on). There are literally hundreds of expansion boards from which to choose. You will find these on most PCs:

- *Graphics adapter.* These adapters permit interfacing with video monitors. The VGA (video graphics array) board and the newer **AGP (accelerated graphics port) board** enable the interfacing of high-resolution monitors with the processor.
- *Sound.* The sound card, which is included on most new PCs, makes two basic functions possible. First, it enables sounds to be captured and stored on disk. Second, it enables sounds, including music and spoken words, to be played through external speakers. The sound card can add realism to computer games with stereo music and sound effects. It also allows us to insert spoken notes within our word processing documents. The typical sound card will have receptacles for a microphone, a headset, an audio output, and a joystick.
- *Data/voice/fax modem.* A **modem** permits communication with remote computers via a telephone-line link. The **data/voice/fax modem** performs the same function as a regular modem, plus it has added capabilities. It enables you to receive and make telephone calls, and it enables your PC to emulate a **fax** machine. Fax machines transfer images of documents via telephone lines to another location. A different type of modem, the **cable modem,** is connected to the TV cable.

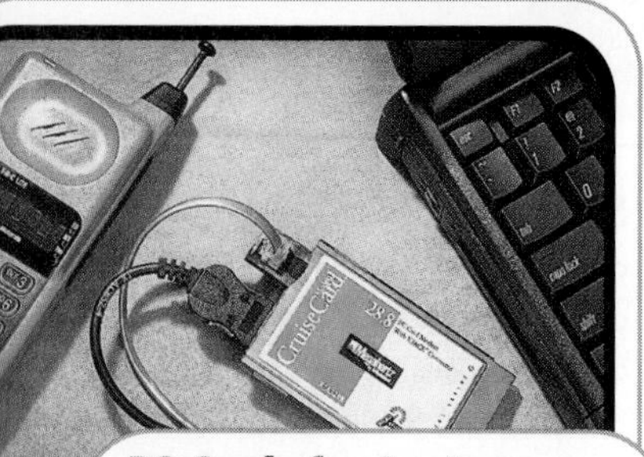

PC Cards for Laptops
Notebook PCs, because of their compact size, have fewer expansion slots than desktop PCs. For this reason, notebook PCs are designed with PCMCIA expansion slots. PC cards are plugged into PCMCIA expansion slots to give the system added capability. This U.S. Robotics PC card contains a voice/data/fax modem.
U.S. Robotics Mobile Communications Corporation

Depending on your applications needs, you might wish to enhance your system with some of these expansion boards:

- *Extra serial and parallel ports.* Installation of this board provides access to the bus via auxiliary serial and parallel ports.
- *Network interface card.* The network interface card (NIC) enables and controls the exchange of data between the PCs in a local area network. Each PC in a network must be equipped with an NIC.
- *SCSI interface card.* The SCSI bus can be built into the motherboard or installed as an expansion board.
- *Video capture card.* This card enables full-motion color video with audio to be captured and played on a monitor or stored on disk. Once on disk storage, video information can be integrated with text, graphics, and other forms of presentation.

PC Cards: PCMCIA Technology

The **PCMCIA card,** sometimes called a **PC card,** is a credit-card–sized removable expansion module that is plugged into an external PCMCIA expansion slot. The PC card functions like an expansion board in that it offers a wide variety of capabilities. PC cards can be expanded RAM, programmable nonvolatile flash memory, network interface cards, SCSI adapters, data/voice/fax modems, hard-disk cards, and much more. For example, one PC card comes in the form of a mobile **GPS (global positioning system).** The Mobile GPS card can be used to pinpoint the latitude and longitude of the user within a few feet, anywhere on or near earth. Business travelers use GPS cards in conjunction with computer-based road maps to help them get around in unfamiliar cities.

Virtually all new portable computers are equipped with a PCMCIA-compliant interface. PDAs (personal digital assistants) and notebook PCs do not have enough space for as many expansion slots as do their desktop cousins. Interchangeable PC cards let laptop users insert capabilities as they are needed. For example, a user can insert a data/voice/fax modem PC card to send e-mail, then do a *hot swap* (PC remains running) with a hard-disk card to access corporate maintenance manuals.

SECTION SELF-CHECK

Self-Check

3-2.1 The control unit is that part of the processor that reads and interprets program instructions. (T/F)

3-2.2 The arithmetic and logic unit controls the flow of programs and data in and out of main memory. (T/F)

3-2.3 PC cards can be hot swapped while the PC is running. (T/F)

3-2.4 The RS-232C connector provides the interface to a port. (T/F)

3-2.5 The rate at which work can be performed by a computer system is called: (a) system spray, (b) throughput, (c) push through, or (d) volume load.

3-2.6 Which of the following memory groups are in order based on speed (slowest to fastest): (a) registers, cache, RAM, (b) cache, RAM, registers, (c) cache, registers, RAM, or (d) RAM, cache, registers?

3-2.7 The timed interval that comprises the machine cycle is the total of the instruction time and: (a) execution time, (b) I-time, (c) X-time, or (d) delivery time?

3-2.8 Which one of the following would not be attached to a motherboard: (a) RAM, (b) microprocessor, (c) FLOP, or (d) expansion board?

3-2.9 Which port enables the parallel transmission of data within a computer system: (a) serial, (b) parallel, (c) Centronics, or (d) speaker?

3-2.10 PC components are linked via a common electrical: (a) train, (b) bus, (c) car, or (d) plane?

3-2.11 Which two buses enable the daisy chaining of peripheral devices: (a) USB and SCSI, (b) SCSI and infrared, (c) USB and PCI local bus, or (d) PCI local bus and ISA?

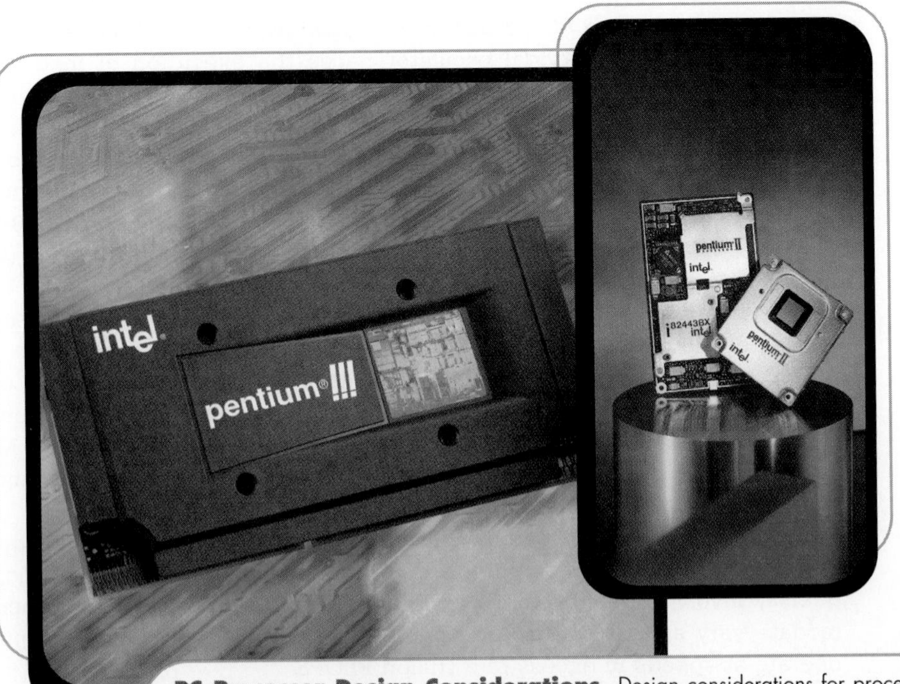

PC Processor Design Considerations Design considerations for processors used in desktop PCs, such as the Pentium III (left), and laptop PCs are different. For example, the mobile Intel Pentium II processor (right) has a feature that drops the processor power consumption to .4 watts when the laptop is idle or inactive to preserve battery life. Laptop processors must also be designed to dissipate heat within smaller enclosures. Photos courtesy of Intel Corporation

3.3 DESCRIBING THE PROCESSOR

Serendipitous Surfing: Popular Culture

How do we distinguish one computer from the other? Much the same way we'd distinguish one person from the other. When describing someone we generally note gender, height, weight, and age. When describing computers or processors we talk about *word size, processor speed,* and the *memory capacity*. For example, a computer might be described as a 64-bit, 500-MHz, 384-MB PC. Let's see what this means.

Word Size

Just as the brain sends and receives signals through the central nervous system, the processor sends and receives electrical signals through its common electrical bus a word at a time. A **word** describes the number of bits that are handled as a unit within a particular computer system's bus or during internal processing. Internal processing involves the movement of data and commands between registers, the control unit, and the arithmetic and logic unit (see Figure 3.6). Many popular computers have 64-bit internal processing but only a 32-bit path through the bus. The word size for internal processing for most modern PCs is 64 bits (eight 8-bit bytes). Workstations, mainframes, and supercomputers have 64-bit word sizes and up.

Processor Speed

A tractor can go 12 miles per hour (mph), a minivan can go 90 mph, and a sling-shot drag racer can go 240 mph. These speeds, however, provide little insight into the relative capabilities of these vehicles. What good is a 240-mph tractor or a 12-mph minivan? Similarly, you have to place the speed of computers within the context of their design and application. Generally, PCs are measured in *MHz,* workstations and mainframes are measured in *MIPS,* and supercomputers are measured in *FLOPS.*

Supercomputer at National Laboratory This engineer at Sandia National Labs is inspecting a connection in one of the 86 cabinets that house the 9,200 Pentium Pro processors contained in the Intel supercomputer during its final installation at the labs in New Mexico. The collective power of thousands of processors enables this supercomputer to perform at more than 1 trillion FLOPS (TERAFLOPS), giving Sandia scientists the tool they need to solve previously unsolvable problems. This supercomputer is used to ensure the safety, reliability, and effectiveness of the U.S. nuclear stockpile through computer simulation instead of nuclear testing. It is used for other scientific applications, as well, such as evaluating the effect of a kilometer-wide comet striking the Atlantic Ocean.
Photo courtesy of Intel Corporation

- *Megahertz: MHz.* The PC's heart is its *crystal oscillator* and its heartbeat is the *clock cycle.* The crystal oscillator paces the execution of instructions within the processor. A micro's processor speed is rated by its frequency of oscillation, or the number of clock cycles per second. Most modern personal computers are rated between 400 and 700 **megahertz,** or **MHz** (millions of clock cycles). The elapsed time for one clock cycle is 1 divided by the frequency. For example, the time it takes to complete one cycle on a 500-MHz processor is 1/500,000,000, or 0.000000002 seconds or 2 nanoseconds (2 billionths of a second). Normally several clock cycles are required to fetch, decode, and execute a single program instruction. The shorter the clock cycle, the faster the processor.
- *MIPS.* Processing speed may also be measured in **MIPS,** or *m*illions of *i*nstructions *p*er *s*econd. Although frequently associated with workstations and mainframes, MIPS is also applied to PCs. Computers operate up to 1000 MIPS. Figure 3.12 illustrates relative performance (speed) of past, present, and future Intel microprocessors in MIPS.
- *FLOPS.* Supercomputer speed is measured in **FLOPS**—*fl*oating point *op*erations *p*er *s*econd. Supercomputer applications, which are often scientific, frequently involve floating point operations. Floating point operations accommodate very small or very large numbers. State-of-the-art supercomputers operate at speeds in excess of a trillion FLOPS.

Memory Capacity

The capacity of RAM, cache, and other memories are stated in terms of the number of bytes they can store. Memory capacity for most computers is stated in terms of **megabytes (MB).** One megabyte equals 1,048,576 (2^{20}) bytes. Memory capacities of modern PCs range from 32 MB to 512 MB. High-speed cache memory capacities usually are measured in **kilobytes (KB),** the most common being 512 KB of cache. One kilobyte is 1024 (2^{10}) bytes of storage.

Some high-end mainframes and supercomputers have more than 8000 MB of RAM. Their RAM capacities are stated as **gigabytes (GB)**—about one billion bytes. It's only a matter of time before we state RAM in terms of **terabytes (TB)**—about one trillion bytes. GB and TB are frequently used in reference to high-capacity disk storage. Occasionally you will see memory capacities of individual chips

The Intel® Family of Processors The Intel family of processors have been installed in 9 of every 10 PCs in use today. This chart is an approximation of the relative speeds of popular Intel processors. It also compares these to one that reflects anticipated technology at the turn of the century. This processor will have about 10,000 times the speed of the Intel 8088 (2000 MIPs to .2 MIPs), the processor that ushered in the age of personal computing. Note that this chart is logarithmic, so MIPs increase by a factor of 10 at each labeled interval.

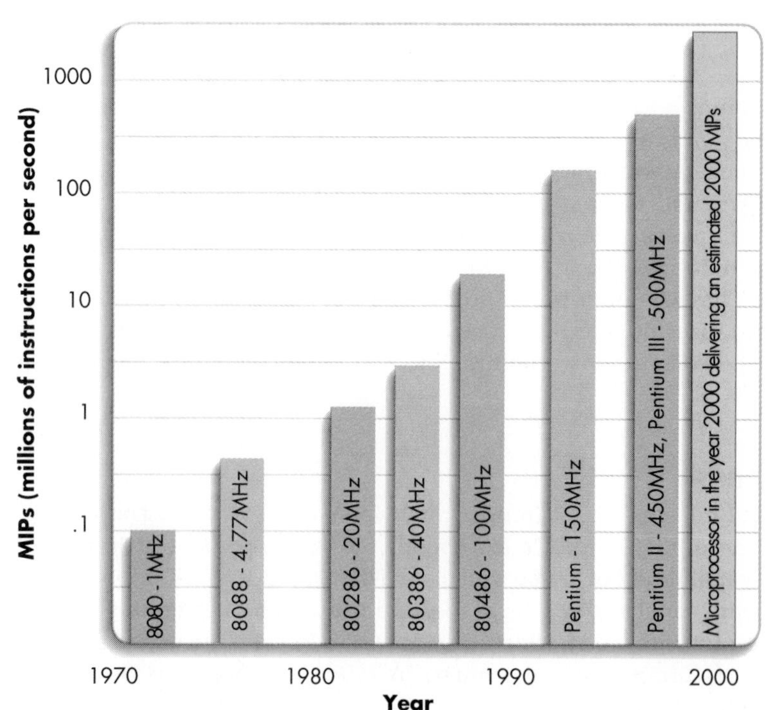

stated in terms of **kilobits (Kb)** and **megabits (Mb).** Figure 3.13 should give you a feel for KBs, MBs, GBs, and TBs.

Differences in Processor Personality

Word size, speed, and *memory capacity* are the primary descriptors of processors. However, computers, like people, have their own "personalities." That is, two similarly described computers might possess attributes that give one more capability than the other. For example, one 64-bit, 500-MHz, 512-MB PC might have 1 MB of cache memory and another only 512 KB. Remember this: When you buy a PC, the basic descriptors tell most of but not the entire story.

Self-Check

SECTION SELF-CHECK

3-3.1 The word size of all PCs is 32 bits. (T/F)

3-3.2 *MIPS* is an acronym for "millions of instructions per second." (T/F)

3-3.3 A gigabyte of RAM has more storage capacity than a megabit of RAM. (T/F)

3-3.4 Which has the most bytes: (a) a kilobyte, (b) a gigabyte, (c) a megabyte, or (d) a big byte?

3-3.5 We describe computers in terms of what three characteristics: (a) processor speed, memory, and word size; (b) word meaning, layer width, and memory; (c) memory, cache, and register size; or (d) SDRAM, E-time, and bus length?

3-3.6 The time it takes to complete one cycle on a 400-MHz processor is: (a) 1/400,000,000 seconds, (b) .000000004 seconds, (c) 4 microseconds, or (d) 4 thousandths of a second?

How Much Is a KB, an MB, a GB, and a TB?

Compare the number of characters in the Gettysburg Address to 1 KB (Kilobyte)

Compare the number of characters in this book to 1 MB (Megabyte)

Compare the number of people in China to 1 GB (Gigabyte)

Compare the number of gallons of water consumed each day in North America to 1 TB (Terabyte)

3.4 PROCESSOR DESIGN

Researchers in IT are continually working to create new technologies that will make processors faster and, thereby, improve system throughput.

CISC and RISC: More Is Not Always Better

Most processors in mainframe computers and personal computers have a **CISC** (*c*omplex *i*nstruction *s*et *c*omputer) design. A CISC computer's machine language offers programmers a wide variety of instructions from which to choose (add, multiply, compare, move data, and so on). Computer designers, however, are rediscovering the beauty of simplicity. Computers designed around much smaller machine language instruction sets (fewer instructions) can realize significantly increased throughput for certain applications, especially those that involve graphics (for example, computer-aided design or CAD). These computers have **RISC** (*r*educed *i*nstruction *s*et *c*omputer) design. The RISC processor shifts much of the computational burden from the hardware to the software. Proponents of RISC design feel that the limitations of a reduced instruction set are easily offset by increased processing speed and the lower cost of RISC microprocessors.

Parallel Processing: Computers Working Together

In a single processor environment, the processor addresses the programming problem sequentially, from beginning to end. Today, designers are building computers that break a programming problem into pieces. Work on each of these pieces is then executed simultaneously in separate processors, all of which are part of the same computer system. The concept of using multiple processors in the same computer system is known as **parallel processing.** In parallel processing, one main processor examines the programming problem and determines what portions, if any, of the problem can be solved in pieces (see Figure 3.14). Those pieces that can be addressed separately are routed to other processors and solved. The individual pieces are then reassembled in the main processor for further computation, output, or storage. The net result of parallel processing is better throughput.

FIGURE 3.14

Parallel Processing In parallel processing, auxiliary processors solve pieces of a problem to enhance system throughput.

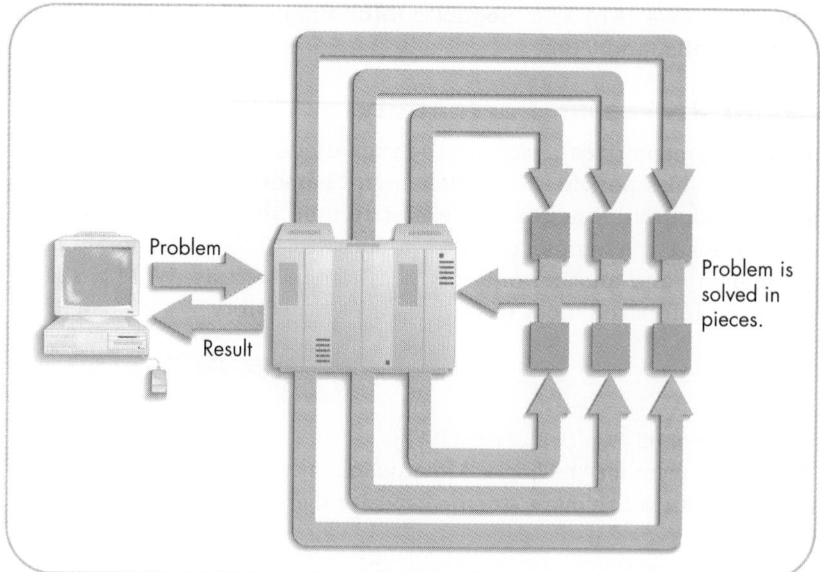

MEMORY bits

Processor Description

- Word size: Bits handled as a unit
- Speed
  PCs: MHz (clock cycles)
  PCs, workstations, and mainframes: MIPS
  Supercomputers: FLOPS
- Capacity
  Kilobyte (KB), kilobit (Kb)
  Megabyte (MB), megabit (Mb)
  Gigabyte (GB)
  Terabyte (TB)

Computer designers are creating mainframes and supercomputers with thousands of integrated microprocessors. Parallel processing on such a large scale is referred to as **massively parallel processing.** These superfast supercomputers have sufficient computing capacity to attack applications that have been beyond that of computers with traditional computer designs. For example, researchers can now simulate global warming with these computers.

Neural Networks: Wave of the Future?

Most of us interact with digital computers. Digital computers are great at solving structured problems involving computations and logic operations. However, most of the challenges we face from day to day can't be solved with these capabilities. For example, several times each year we are confronted with this problem: to find a pair of shoes that fits. This is a very human problem, better suited to the workings of the human brain than for digital computers. Such problems involve unstructured input and outcomes that are unclear, so we use the best available processor—our brain. Scientists are studying the way the human brain works and are attempting to build computers that mimic the incredible human mind. The base technology for these computers is **neural networks.**

The neural network computer employs hundreds, even thousands, of small, interconnected processors, called *processing units*. The neural network works by creating connections and maintaining relationships between these processing units, the computer equivalent of neurons in the brain. Working within a specific sphere of knowledge (for example, worldwide agriculture strategies), the neural network computer can draw from its human-supplied knowledge base, learn through experience, and make informed decisions in an unstructured environment. Here are but a few of an increasing number of neural network applications: playing chess, improving automobile engine efficiency, enabling improved vision technology, planning crop rotation strategies, and forecasting financial market fluctuations.

RISC Computer Software developers rely on this high-power RISC-based workstation to create software for a variety of applications. Courtesy of Intergraph Corporation

The primary difference between traditional digital computers and neural networks is that digital computers process *structured data sequentially* whereas neural networks process *unstructured information simultaneously*. Digital computers will always be able to outperform neural networked computers and the human brain when it comes to fast, accurate numeric computation. However, if neural networks live up to their potential, they will be able to handle tasks that are currently very time-consuming or impossible for conventional computers, such as recognizing a face in the crowd.

SECTION SELF-CHECK

Self-Check

3-4.1 The instruction set for RISC computers is smaller than that for CISC computers. (T/F)

3-4.2 In a single processor environment, the processor addresses the programming problem sequentially. (T/F)

3-4.3 Parallel processing on such a large scale is referred to as massively trapezoidal processing. (T/F)

3-4.4 The concept of using multiple processors in the same computer system is known as: (a) massive processing, (b) acute processing, (c) parallel processing, or (d) perpendicular processing.

3-4.5 The base technology for computers that mimic the human mind is called: (a) HAL, (b) neural network, (c) human brain focus, or (d) interconnected processing.

3-4.6 Neural networks process unstructured information: (a) intermittently, (b) sequentially, (c) simultaneously, or (d) as time permits.

Interactive Study Guide
Chapter 3

SUMMARY AND KEY TERMS

3.1 Going digital

The two kinds of electronic signals are **analog** (84) and **digital** (84). To make the most effective use of computers and automation, the electronics world is going digital. The music industry **digitizes** (84) the natural analog signals that result from recording sessions, then stores the digital version on CDs. Computers are digital and, therefore, work better with digital data.

The two digital states of the computer—on and off—are each represented by a **bit** (84), short for *binary digit*. These electronic states are compatible with the **binary** (84) numbering system. Letters and decimal numbers are translated into bits for storage and processing on computer systems.

Data are stored temporarily during processing in RAM and permanently on devices such as disk drives.

Alphanumeric (85) [**alpha** (85) and **numeric** (85)] characters are represented in computer storage by unique bit configurations. Characters are translated into these bit configurations, also called **bytes** (86), according to a particular coding scheme, called an **encoding system** (85).

The 7-bit **ASCII** (85) encoding system is the most popular encoding system for PCs and data communication. An extended version of ASCII, an 8-bit encoding system, offers 128 more codes. Microsoft Windows uses the 8-bit **ANSI** (87) encoding system.

Unicode (87), a uniform 16-bit encoding system, will enable computers and applications to talk to one another more easily and will accommodate most of the world's languages.

3.2 The PC system unit: Looking in the box

The processor, RAM, and other electronic components are housed in the **system unit** (88). The **microprocessor** (90) is literally a "computer on a chip." The processor in a PC is the microprocessor. It, the electronic circuitry for handling input/output signals from the peripheral devices, and the memory chips are mounted on a single circuit board called a **motherboard** (88). The motherboard's **chipset** (89) controls the flow of information between system components.

The **bus** (89) is the common pathway through which the processor sends/receives data and commands to/from RAM and disk storage and all I/O peripheral devices. Like the wheeled bus, the bus provides data transportation to all processor components, memory, and **device controllers** (89).

Most new system units have an Intel **Pentium® II** (90), **Pentium® III** (90), or **Celeron®** (90) processor inside, but many older systems with **Pentium®** (90) and **Pentium® Pro** (90) processors continue to be workhorses.

The processor is the nucleus of any computer system. A processor, which is also called the **central processing unit** or **CPU** (90), has only two fundamental sections, the **control unit** (91) and the **arithmetic and logic unit** (91), which work together with RAM to execute programs. The control unit's **decoder** (91) interprets instructions and then the control unit directs the arithmetic and logic unit to perform computation and logic operations. During execution, instructions and data are passed between very high-speed **registers** (91) [for example, the **instruction register** (91), the **program register** (91), and the **accumulator** (91)] in the control unit and the arithmetic and logic unit.

RAM, or random-access memory, provides the processor with temporary storage for programs and data. Physically, memory chips are installed on **single in-line memory modules (SIMMs)** (92) and on **dual in-line memory modules (DIMMs)** (92). Most new PCs are being equipped with **synchronous dynamic RAM (SDRAM)** (92). However, an even faster RAM, **Rambus DRAM (RDRAM)** (92), may be the de facto standard in the near future.

In RAM, each datum is stored at a specific **address** (93). Most of today's computers use SDRAM technology for RAM. SDRAM is **volatile memory** (92) [contrast with **nonvolatile memory** (93)]; that is, the data are lost when the electrical current is turned off or interrupted. All input/output, including programs, must enter and exit RAM. Other variations of internal storage are **ROM** (93), **programmable read-only memory (PROM)** (93), and **flash memory** (93), a nonvolatile memory.

Some computers employ **cache memory** (93) to increase **throughput** (93) (the rate at which work can be performed by a computer system). Like RAM, cache is a high-speed holding area for program instructions and data. However, cache memory holds only those instructions and data likely to be needed next by the processor.

Every **machine language** (95) has a predefined format for each type of instruction. During one **machine cycle** (95), an instruction is "fetched" from RAM, decoded in the control unit, and executed, and the results are placed in memory. The machine cycle time is the total of the instruction time (I-time) and the execution time (E-time).

In a PC, external peripheral devices come with a cable and a multipin connector. A port provides a direct link to the PC's common electrical bus. External peripheral devices can be linked to the processor via cables through either a **serial port** (96), **parallel port** (96), **SCSI port** (96) on the **SCSI controller** (96), **USB port** (96), or **IrDA (infrared) port** (98). The standard for PC serial ports is the **RS-232C connector** (96). The RS-232C and **Centronics connectors** (96) are used with parallel ports.

The motherboard includes several empty **expansion slots** (98) so you can purchase and plug in optional capabilities in the form of **expansion boards** (98) or **expansion cards** (98).

The most common PC expansion boards plug into a 16-bit **ISA bus** (98). The expansion bus accepts the expansion boards that control the video display, disks, and other peripherals. Recent innovations have resulted in linking expansion boards directly to the system's **local bus** (98). The **PCI local bus** (98) offers a local bus solution to the data stream bottleneck in PCs. The **SCSI bus** (98), or "scuzzy" bus, allows up to 15 SCSI peripheral devices to be daisy-chained to a SCSI interface expansion card. The **Universal Serial Bus (USB)** (99) permits up to 127 USB peripheral devices to be **hot plugged** (99) to the PC.

Popular expansion boards include graphics adapters such as the **AGP** or **Accelerated Graphics Port board** (99), sound, **modem** (99) (permits communication with remote computers via a telephone-line link), **data/voice/fax modem** (99) [enables emulation of a **fax** (99) machine], **cable modem** (99), peripheral device interface, serial and parallel ports, network interface, SCSI interface card, and video capture.

The **PCMCIA card** (100), sometimes called a **PC card** (100), provides a variety of interchangeable add-on capabilities in the form of credit-card–sized modules. The PC card is especially handy for the portable environment. A mobile **GPS (global positioning system)** (100) can be a PC card.

3.3 Describing the processor

A processor is described in terms of its word size, speed, and memory capacity.

A **word** (101) is the number of bits handled as a unit within a particular computer system's common electrical bus or during internal processing.

Personal computer speed is measured in **megahertz (MHz)** (102). High-end PC, workstation, and mainframe speed is measured in **MIPS** (102). Supercomputer speed is measured in **FLOPS** (102).

Memory capacity is measured in **kilobytes (KB)** (102), **megabytes (MB)** (102), **gigabytes (GB)** (102), and **terabytes (TB)** (102). Chip capacity is sometimes stated in **kilobits (Kb)** (103) and **megabits (Mb)** (103).

3.4 Processor design

Most mainframes and PCs use **CISC** (103) architecture. Those using **RISC** (103) architecture realize increased throughput for certain applications.

In **parallel processing** (104), one main processor examines the programming problem and determines what portions, if any, of the problem can be solved in pieces. Those pieces that can be addressed separately are routed to other processors, solved, then recombined in the main processor to produce the result. Parallel processing on a large scale is referred to as **massively parallel processing (MPP)** (104).

Neural networks (104) mimic the way the human brain works. The neural network computer uses many small, interconnected processors to address problems that involve *unstructured information.*

DISCUSSION AND PROBLEM SOLVING

3.1 **a.** Generally, computers are digital and human beings are analog, so what we say, hear, and see must be converted, or digitized, for processing on a computer. Speculate on how a family photograph might be digitized for storage and processing on a computer system.

b. Create a 5-bit encoding system to be used for storing upper-case alpha characters, punctuation symbols, and the apostrophe. Discuss the advantages and disadvantages of your encoding system in relation to the ASCII encoding system.

c. How many characters can be represented with a 12-bit encoding system?

d. Write your first name as an ASCII bit configuration.

3.2 **a.** List at least 10 products that are smaller than a toaster oven and use microprocessors. Select one and describe the function of its microprocessor.

b. Describe the advantages of a USB port over a parallel port. Also, describe the advantages of a parallel port over a serial port.

c. Distinguish between RAM and flash memory. Be specific.

d. Which two functions does the arithmetic and logic unit perform? Give a real-life example for each function.

e. Explain the relationship between a microprocessor, a motherboard, and a PC.

f. Generally describe the interaction between the processor's control unit, registers, and RAM.

g. Give one example of where each of these memory technologies might be used in a personal computer system.

h. Illustrate the interaction between the user RAM and the accumulator in the arithmetic and logic unit for the following basic program. Use the model shown in Figure 3.7.

```
INPUT "Enter ages for 3 children"; A, B, C
LET AVGAGE=(A+B+C)/3
PRINT "The average age is"; AVGAGE
END
```

i. List three expansion boards you would like to have on your own PC. How would you use these added capabilities?

j. Describe a hot swap as it relates to a PCMCIA-compliant interface.

k. Why do you suppose PC motherboards are designed to accommodate several types of buses?

3.3 **a.** Assume a move data instruction requires five clock cycles. Compute the time it takes, in nanoseconds, to execute a move data instruction on a 600-MHz processor.

b. Convert 5 MB to KB, Mb, and Kb. Assume a byte contains eight bits.

3.4 **a.** Describe the computer you use at home, at work, or in the PC laboratory.

b. What are the trade-offs between CISC and RISC processor designs?

c. Speculate on an application that might be appropriate for parallel processing and one that might be appropriate for a neural network–based system.

THE COMPUTER ON A CHIP

The invention of the lightbulb in 1879 symbolized the beginning of electronics. Electronics then evolved into the use of vacuum tubes, then transistors, and now integrated circuits. Today's microminiaturization of electronic circuitry is continuing to have a profound effect on the way we live and work. The increased speed and capability of computers influence all the many services we may take for granted. Where would telecommunications, speech recognition, advanced software applications, and the Internet be without this technology?

Current chip technology permits the placement of hundreds of thousands of transistors and electronic switches on a single chip. Chips already fit into wristwatches and credit cards, but electrical and computer engineers want them even smaller. In electronics, smaller is better. The ENIAC, the first full-scale digital electronic computer, weighed 50 tons and occupied an entire room. Today, a computer far more powerful than the ENIAC can be fabricated within a single piece of silicon the size of a child's fingernail.

Chip designers think in terms of nanoseconds (one billionth of a second) and microns (one millionth of a meter). They want to pack as many circuit elements as they can into the structure of a chip. This is called *scaling*, or making the transistor, and the technology that connects them, smaller. High-density packing reduces the time required for an electrical signal to travel from one circuit element to the next—resulting in faster computers. Circuit lines on early 1980s PC processors were 10 microns wide. Today's are less than .2 microns. The latter holds 50 million transistors and is hundreds of times more powerful than the initial processors. The .1 micron barrier may be just around the corner.

As transistors become smaller, the chip becomes faster, conducts more electricity, and uses less power. Also, it costs less to produce as more transistors are packed on a chip. The computer revolution will continue to grow rapidly into the twenty-first century as long as researchers find ways to make transistors faster and smaller, make wiring that links them less resistive to electrical current, and increase chip density. Each year, researchers have developed radically new techniques for manufacturing chips. For example, IBM recent began developing a logic chip and processor using silicon-on-insulator (SOI) technology, an innovative approach to the chip-making process. The process presented here provides a general overview that is representative of the various techniques used by chip manufacturers.

Chips are designed and manufactured to perform a particular function. One chip might be a microprocessor, or the "brains," for a personal computer. Another, such as a memory chip, might be for temporary random-access storage (RAM). Logic chips are used in beverage vending machines, televisions, refrigerators, cell phones, and thousands more devices. Microprocessors, memory, and logic chips are three of the most common kinds of chips.

The development of integrated circuits starts with a project review team made up of representatives from design, manufacturing, and marketing. This group works together to design a product the customer needs. Next, they go through prototype wafer manufacturing to resolve potential manufacturing problems. Once a working prototype is produced, chips are manufactured in quantity and sent to computer, peripheral, telecommunications, and other customers.

DESIGN

1. Using CAD for Chip Design ▶

Chip designers use computer-aided design (CAD) systems to create the logic for individual circuits. Although a chip can contain up to 30 layers, typically there are 10 to 20 patterned layers of varying material, with each layer performing a different purpose. In this multilayer circuit design, each layer is color-coded so the designer can distinguish between the various layers. Some of the layers lie within the silicon wafer and others are stacked on top. Photo courtesy of Micron Semiconductors, Inc.

The manufacturing of integrated circuits involves a multistep process using various photochemical etching and metallurgical techniques. This complex and interesting process is illustrated here with photos, from silicon to the finished product. The process is presented in five steps: design, fabrication, packaging, testing, and installation.

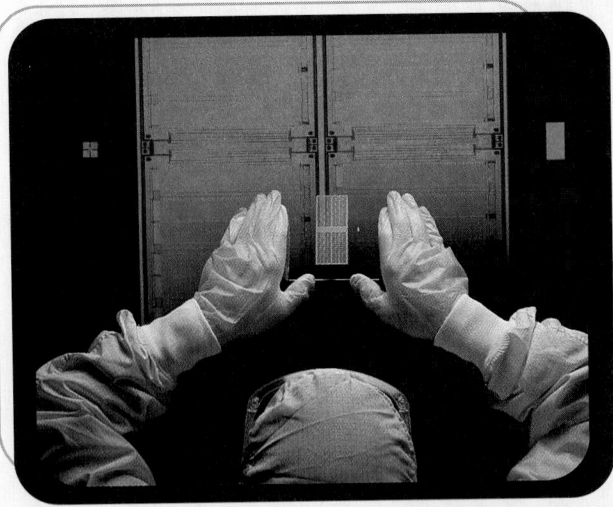

2. Creating a Mask

The product designer's computerized drawing of each circuit layer is transformed into a *mask*, or *rectile*, a glass or quartz plate with an opaque material (such as chrome) formed to create the pattern. The process used to transfer a pattern or image from the masks to a wafer is called *photolithography*. The number of layers depends on the complexity of the chip's logic. The Intel Pentium processor, for example, contains 20 layers. When all these unique layers are combined, they create the millions of transistors and circuits that make up the architecture of the processor. Needless to say, the manufacturing process forming this sequence of layers is a very precise one! Photo courtesy of Micron Semiconductor, Inc.

FABRICATION

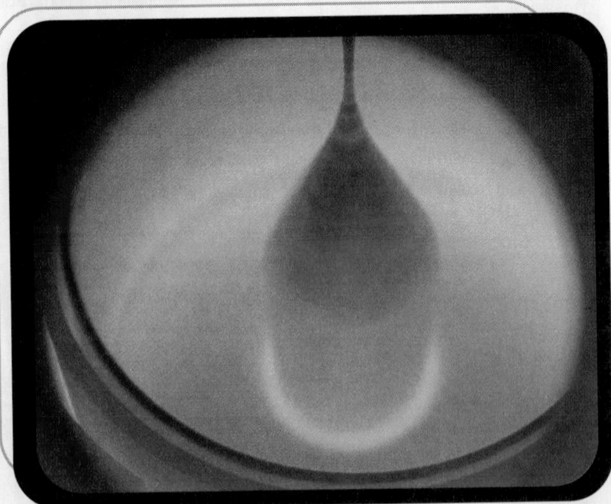

3. Creating Silicon Ingots

Molten silicon is spun into cylindrical ingots, usually from six to eight inches in diameter. Because silicon, the second most abundant substance, is used in the fabrication of integrated circuits, chips are sometimes referred to as "intelligent grains of sand." M/A-COM, Inc.

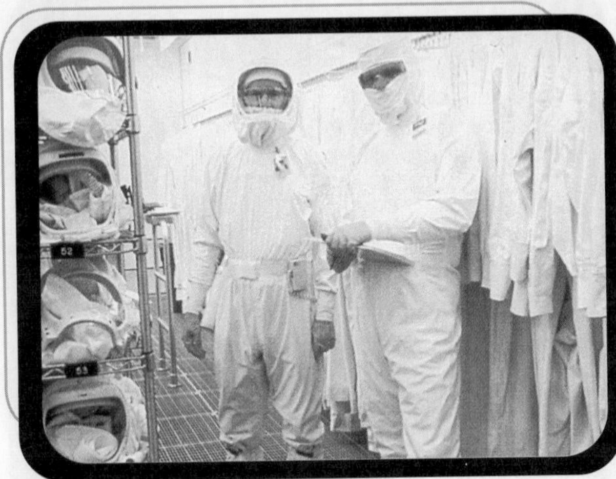

5. Wearing Bunny Suits

To help keep a clean environment, workers wear semi-custom-fitted Gortex® suits. They follow a 100-step procedure when putting the suits on. Courtesy of Intel Corporation

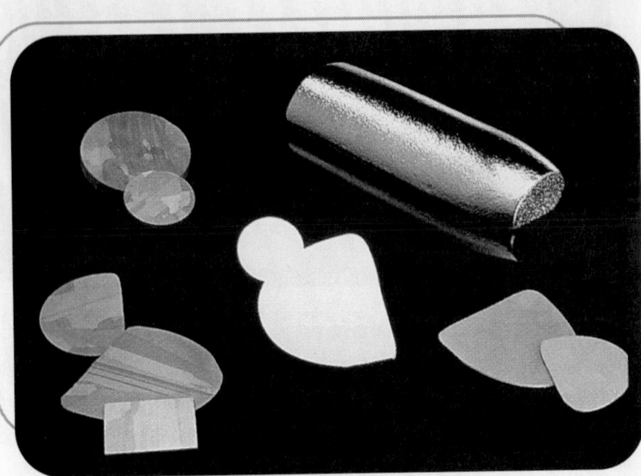

4. Cutting the Silicon Wafers

The ingot is shaped and prepared prior to being cut into silicon wafers. Once the wafers are cut to about the thickness of a credit card, they are polished to a perfect finish. M/A-COM, Inc.

6. Keeping a Clean House

Clean air continuously flows from every pore of the ceiling and through the holes in the floor into a filtering system at the manufacturing plant. A normal room contains some 15 million dust particles per cubic foot. A clean, modern hospital has about 10,000 dust particles per cubic foot. A class 1 clean room (the lower the rating, the cleaner the facility) contains less than 1 dust particle per cubic foot. All of the air in a "clean room" is replaced seven times every minute.

Portions of the microchip manufacturing process are performed in yellow light because the wafers are coated with a light-sensitive material called "photoresist" before the next chip pattern is imprinted onto the surface of the silicon wafer. Courtesy of Intel Corporation

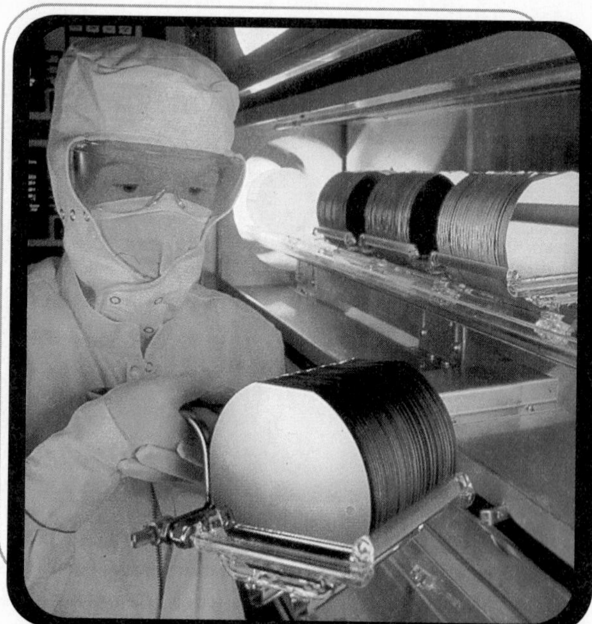

7. Coating the Wafers

Silicon wafers that eventually will contain several hundred chips are placed in an oxygen furnace at 1200 degrees Celsius. In the furnace the wafer is coated with other minerals to create the physical properties needed to produce transistors and other electronic components on the surface of the wafer. Gould Inc.

8. Etching the Wafer

A photoresist is deposited onto the wafer surface creating a film-like substance to accept the patterned image. The mask is placed over the wafer and both are exposed to ultraviolet light. In this way the circuit pattern is transferred onto the wafer. The photoresist is developed, washing away the unwanted resist and leaving the exact image of the transferred pattern. Plasma (superhot gases) technology is used to etch the circuit pattern permanently into the wafer. This is one of several techniques used in the etching process. The wafer is returned to the furnace and given another coating on which to etch another circuit layer. The procedure is repeated for each circuit layer until the wafer is complete.

Some of the layers include aluminum or copper interconnects, which leave a fine network of thin metal connections or wires for these semiconductor chips. The wires are used to link the transistors. Aluminum has long been the standard for semiconductor wiring, but recent innovations with the use of copper wiring, a better conductor of electricity, will help create the next generation of semiconductors. AT&T Technologies

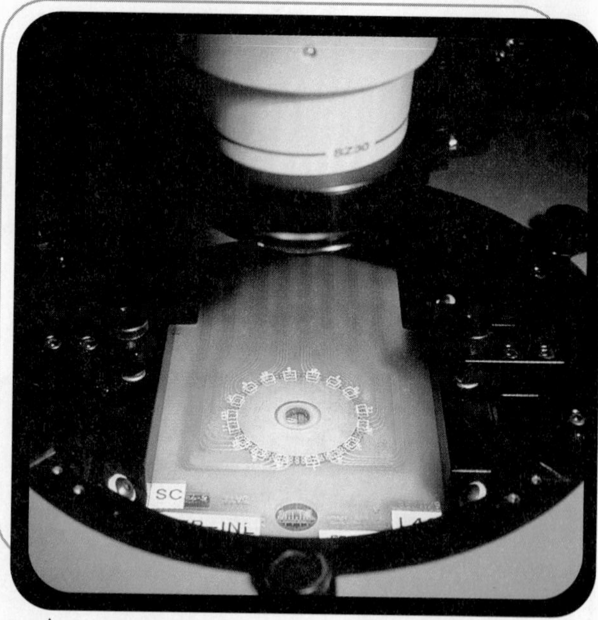

9. Tracking the Wafers

Fabrication production control takes wafers through the fabricating process and measures layers at certain manufacturing stages to determine layer depth and chemical structure. These measurements assess process accuracy and facilitate real-time modifications. Courtesy of Micron Technology, Inc.

◀ **10. Drilling the Wafers**

It takes only a second for this instrument to drill 1440 tiny holes in a wafer. The holes enable the interconnection of the layers of circuits. Each layer must be perfectly aligned (within a millionth of a meter) with the others.
Courtesy of International Business Machines Corporation

▲
13. Dicing the Wafers

A diamond-edged saw, with a thickness of a human hair, separates the wafer into individual processors, known as die, in a process called *dicing*. Water spray keeps the surface temperature low. After cutting, high-pressure water rinses the wafer clean. In some situations, special lasers are used to cut the wafers.
Courtesy of Micron Technology, Inc.

PACKAGING

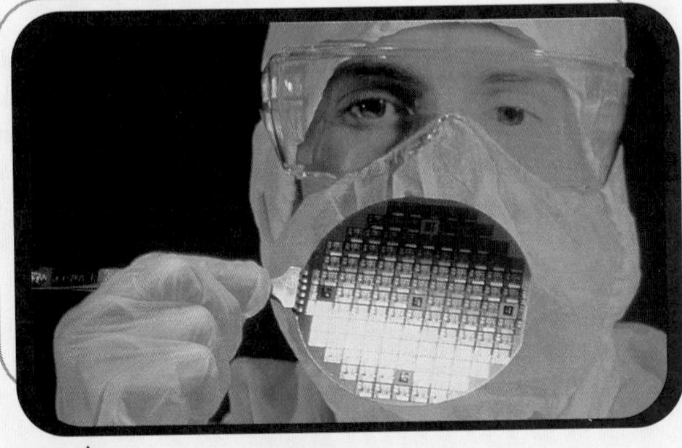

▲
11. Removing the Etched Wafers

The result of the coating/etching process is a silicon wafer that contains from 100 to 400 integrated circuits, each of which includes millions of transistors.
National Semiconductor Corporation

▲
12. Mounting the Wafer

Each wafer is vacuum mounted onto a metal-framed sticky film tape. The wafer and metal frame are placed near the tape, then all three pieces are loaded into a vacuum chamber. A vacuum forces the tape smoothly onto the back of the wafer and metal frame. Courtesy of Micron Technology, Inc.

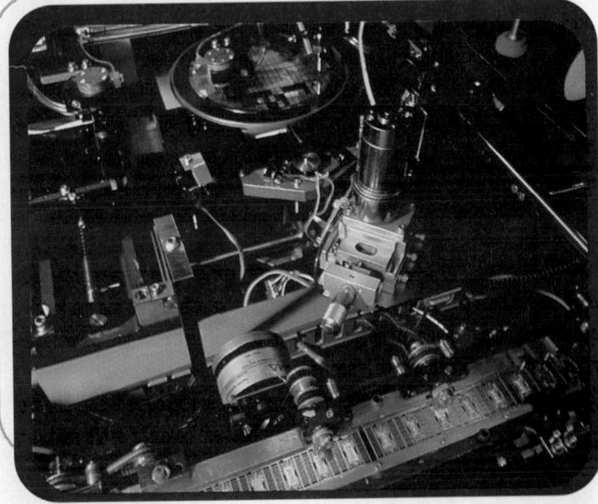

▲
14. Attaching the Die

Individual die are attached to silver epoxy on the center area of a lead frame. Each die is removed from the tape with needles plunging up from underneath to push the die while a vacuum tip lifts the die from the tape. Lead frames are then heated in an oven to cure the epoxy. The wafer map created in probe tells the die-attach equipment which die to place on the lead frame. Courtesy of Micron Technology, Inc.

◀ **15. Packaging the Chips**

The chips are packaged in protective ceramic or metal carriers. The carriers have standard-sized electrical pin connectors that allow the chip to be plugged conveniently into circuit boards. Because the pins tend to corrode, the pin connectors are the most vulnerable part of a computer system. To avoid corrosion and a bad connection, the pins on some carriers are made of gold.
Courtesy of International Business Machines Corporation

TESTING

◀ **16. Testing the Chips**

Each chip is tested to assess functionality and to see how fast it can store or retrieve information. Chip speed (or access time) is measured in nanoseconds (a billionth, 1/1,000,000,000th of a second). The precision demands are so great that as many as half the chips are found to be defective. A drop of ink is deposited on defective chips. Courtesy of Micron Technology, Inc.

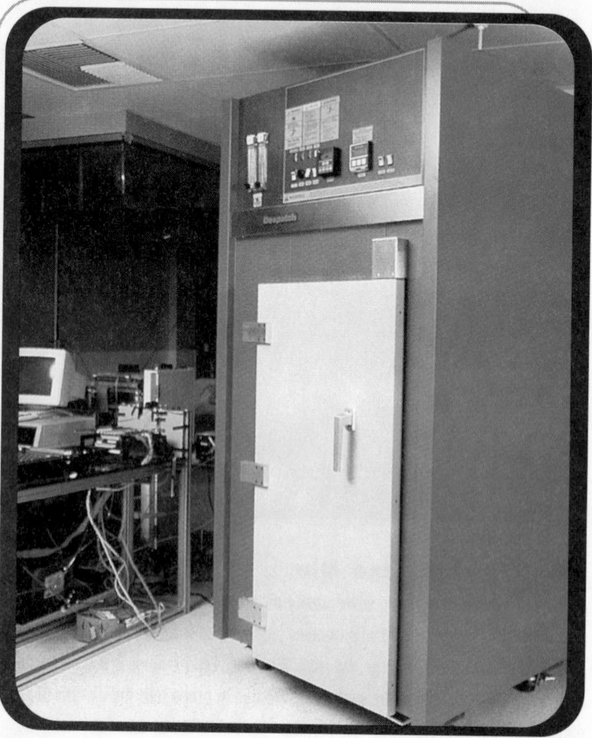

◀ **17. Burning In**

This burn-in oven runs performance tests on every chip simulating actual usage conditions. Each chip is tested by feeding information to the chip and querying for the information to ensure the chip is receiving, storing, and sending the correct data.
Courtesy of Micron Technology, Inc.

18. Scanning

All chips are scanned, using optics or lasers, to discover any bent, missing, or incorrectly formed leads. Courtesy of Micron Technology, Inc.

▼

INSTALLATION

◀ **19. Creating Circuit Boards**
Pick and place equipment precisely positions various chips on the solder and contacts. Completed boards are then heated in the reflow ovens, allowing the lead coating and solder to melt together, affixing the chips to the printed circuit board. Courtesy of Micron Technology, Inc.

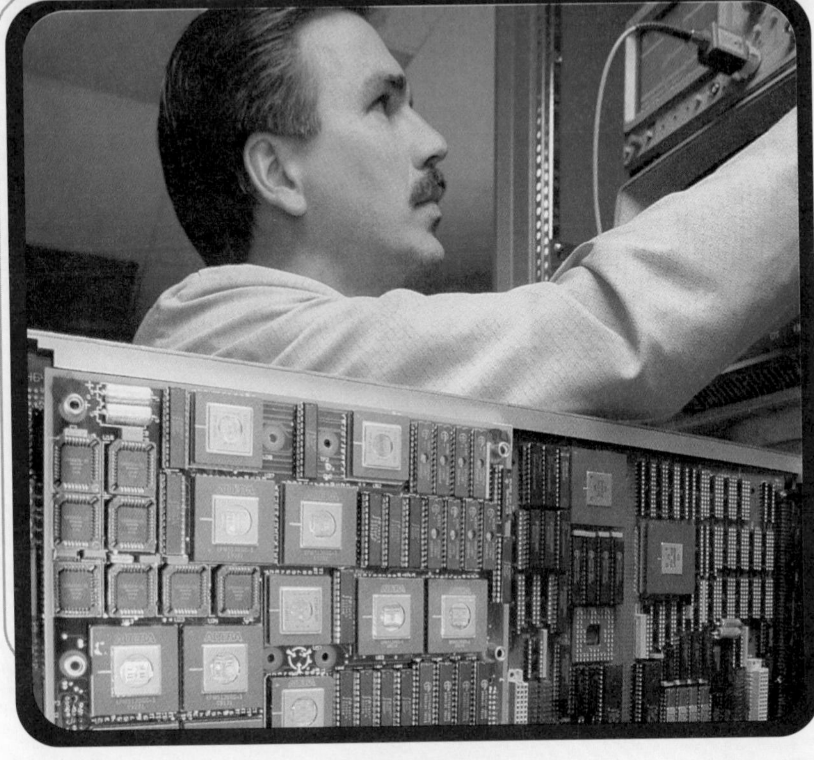

◀ **20. Installing the Finished Chips**
The completed circuit boards are installed in computers and thousands of other computer-controlled devices. Courtesy of E-Systems

Storing and Retrieving Information

Learning Objectives

4.1 Understand the relationship between mass storage and the various types of files.

4.2 Describe the various types of magnetic disk devices and media, including organization, principles of operation, maintenance, performance considerations, and security concerns.

4.3 Describe procedures for backing up disk files to tape data cartridges or to diskettes.

4.4 Discuss the operational capabilities and applications for the various types of optical laser disk storage.

4.5 Gain insight into the future of storage technologies.

chapter

WHY THIS CHAPTER IS IMPORTANT TO YOU

Not too long ago we stored things in file drawers, hall closets, family photo albums, notebooks, recipe boxes, keepsake boxes, calendars, Rolodex name and address files, and many other places. We also had bookshelves filled with all kinds of reference books, from the phone book to encyclopedias. We had wire frame holders to store long-play record albums (LPs). Most of us still store things in these same places, but to a far lesser extent. The family photo album may be scanned and stored on a rewritable CD-ROM. Personal information software is rapidly replacing the Rolodex file. Young families are opting to buy an interactive encyclopedia on CD-ROM rather than an expensive 20-volume set. Music is now available from many electronic sources. You get the idea. Much of what used to be physical and tangible is now stored permanently in electronic form on various storage media.

This chapter gives you an overview of electronic storage media and devices. In a nutshell, media used for storage of data and various forms of information can be classified as disk, tape, or optical (such as a CD-ROM). Each has its advantages and disadvantages. For example, the functionality of the removable Zip® disks and SuperDisks is similar, but speed and compatibility considerations may sway you toward one or the other. After studying this chapter, you'll be better prepared to answer the always popular question, "How much hard-disk space do I need." Pointers throughout the chapter will help you protect your valuable data and information from electronic vandals and accidental loss.

Unfortunately, the somewhat confusing array of storage options makes us all vulnerable to making big mistakes when purchasing and using computer systems. This chapter should help you sort out the options and give you some insight as to what (and how much) to buy. Plus, it will help you to know when and how to use the various storage alternatives.

4.1 MASS STORAGE AND FILES

Monthly Technology Update

Did you ever stop to think about what happens behind the scenes when you

- Request a telephone number through directory assistance?
- Draw money from your checking account at an ATM?
- Check out at a supermarket?
- Download a file on the Internet?

Needed information—such as telephone numbers, account balances, item prices, or stock summary files on the Internet—is retrieved from rapidly rotating disk-storage media and loaded to random-access memory (RAM) for processing. Untold terabytes (trillions of characters) of information, representing millions of applications, are stored *permanently* for periodic retrieval in magnetic and optical storage media, such as hard disk. There they can be retrieved in milliseconds. For example, as soon as the directory assistance operator keys in the desired name, the full name and number are retrieved from disk storage and displayed. Moments later, a digitized version of voice recordings of numbers is accessed from disk storage and played in response to the caller's request: "The number is five, zero, one, five, five, five, two, two, four, nine."

Storage Technologies

Storage Devices

Within a computer system, programs and information in all forms (text, image, audio, video) are stored in both *RAM* and permanent **mass storage,** such as *magnetic disk and tape* (see Figure 4.1). Programs and information are retrieved from mass storage and stored *temporarily* in high-speed RAM for processing. In this section we examine two common types of mass storage, magnetic disk and magnetic tape.

Over the years, manufacturers have developed a variety of permanent mass storage devices and media. Today the various types of **magnetic disk drives** and their respective storage media are the state of the art for permanent storage. **Magnetic tape drives** complement magnetic disk storage by providing inexpensive *backup* capability and *archival* storage. Later in the chapter, **optical laser disk,** a rapidly emerging alternative to magnetic storage drives, is introduced. First, let's take a look at the files stored on these drives.

The Many Faces of Files

We have talked in general about the *file* in previous chapters. The **file** is simply a recording of information. It is the foundation of permanent storage on a computer system. To a computer, a file is a string of 0s and 1s (digitized data) that are stored and retrieved as a single unit.

Types of Files: ASCII to Video

There are many types of files, most of which are defined by the software that created them (for example, a word processing document or spreadsheet). Popular files are listed on page 117.

RAM and Mass Storage
Programs and data are stored permanently in mass storage and temporarily in RAM.

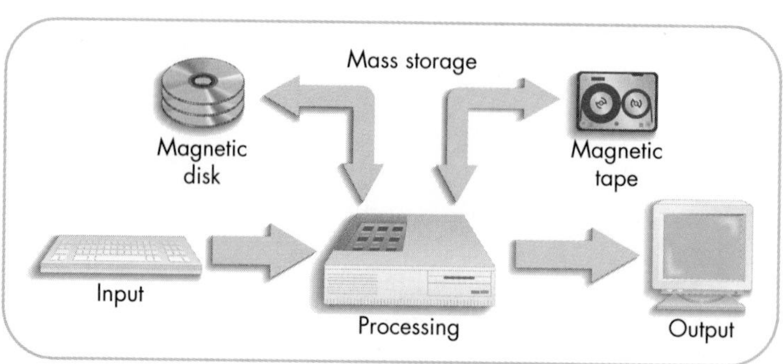

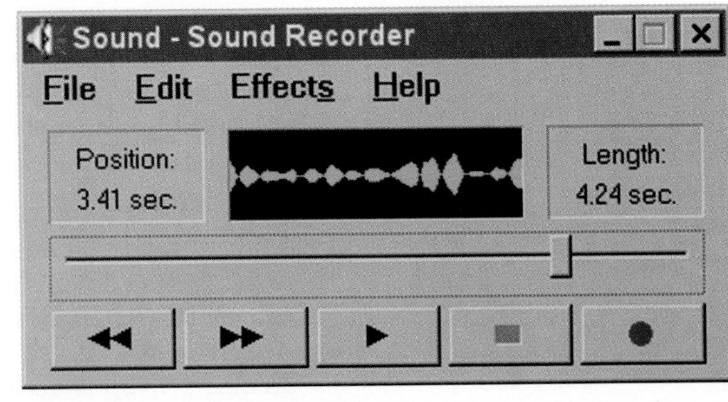

Storing Digitized Resources Anything we digitize and store permanently takes up space on a disk. This clip art (top left) is representative of thousands available for use in documents—hard-disk storage requirement is 23 KB. A 4.24-second digital recording of an audio greeting (top right) can be attached to and sent with an e-mail message—hard-disk storage requirement is 92 KB. This surreal scene (bottom) is all the more remarkable for the way the computer artist has used graphics techniques to model light, shadow, and reflections, mimicking a photograph's realism—hard-disk storage requirement is 4.7 MB. Courtesy of Electric Image, Inc.

- *ASCII file.* An **ASCII file** is a text-only file that can be read or created by any word processing program or text editor.
- *Data file.* A **data file** contains data organized into records.
- *Document file.* All word processing and desktop publishing **document files** contain text and, often, images.
- *Spreadsheet file.* A **spreadsheet file** contains rows and columns of data.
- *Web page file.* A **Web page file** is compatible with the World Wide Web and Internet browsers.
- *Source program file.* A **source program file** contains user-written instructions to the computer. These instructions must be translated to machine language prior to program execution.
- *Executable program file.* An **executable program file** contains executable machine language code.
- *Graphics file.* A **graphics file** contains digitized images.
- *Audio file.* An **audio file** contains digitized sound.
- *Video file.* A **video file** contains digitized video frames that when played rapidly (for example, 30 frames per second) produce motion video.

Files and Parking Lots

Mass storage is much like a parking lot for files. In a parking lot, a variety of vehicles—cars, buses, trucks, motorcycles, and so on—are put in parking places to be picked up later. Similarly, all sorts of files are "parked" in individual spots in mass storage, waiting to be retrieved later. To help you find your vehicle, large parking lots are organized with numbered parking places in lettered zones. The same is true with files and mass storage. Files are stored in numbered "parking places" on disk for retrieval. Fortunately, we do not have to remember the exact location of the file. The operating system does that for us. All we have to know is the name of the file. We assign user names to files, then recall or store them by name. Filenames in the Windows environment can include spaces, but some special characters, such as the slash (/) and colon (:), are not permitted. An optional three-character extension identifies the type of file.

- *Readme.txt* is an ASCII file.
- *Student-Course.mdb* is a Microsoft Access data file.
- *Letter.doc* is a Microsoft Word document file.
- *Income Statement.xls* is a Microsoft Excel spreadsheet file.
- *Adams School Home Page.htm* is a Web page file.
- *Module 1-1.vbp* is a Visual Basic source program file.
- *Play Game.exe* is an executable program file.
- *Family album.gif, Vacation Banff.bmp, Logo.jpg, Sarah.wmf, Project A.pcx* are graphic files.
- *My_song.wav* is an audio file.
- *Introduction Sequence.mov* is a video file.

What to Do with a File

Everything we do on a computer involves a file and, therefore, mass storage. But what do we do with files?

- *We create, name, and save files.* We create files when we name and save a letter, a drawing, a program, or some digital entity (an audio clip) to mass storage.
- *We copy files, move files, and delete files.* We copy files from CD-ROMs and diskettes to a hard disk to install software. We move files during routine file management activities. When we no longer need a file, we delete it.
- *We retrieve and update files.* We continuously retrieve and update our files (such as when we update the entries in a spreadsheet or revise a memo).
- *We display, print, or play files.* Most user files that involve text and graphics can be *displayed* and *printed.* Audio and video files are *played.*
- *We execute files.* We execute program files to run our software. In the Windows environment, executable filenames end in EXE, COM, BAT, and PIF.
- *We download and upload files.* We download useful files from the Internet to our PCs. We sometimes work on, then upload updated files to our company's server computer.
- *We export/import files.* The *file format*, or the manner in which a file is stored, is unique for each type of software package. When we import a file, we convert it from its foreign format (perhaps WordPerfect, a word processing program) to a format that is compatible with the current program (perhaps Microsoft Word, also a word processing program). We export files when we want to convert a file in the current program to a format needed by another program.
- *We compress files.* When the air is squeezed out of a sponge, it becomes much smaller. When you release it, the sponge returns to its original shape—nothing changes. **File compression** works in a similar fashion. File formats for most software packages are inefficient, resulting in wasted space on mass storage when you save files. Using file compression, a repeated pattern, such as the word *and* in text documents, might be replaced by a one-byte descriptor in a compressed file, saving two bytes for each occurrence of *and.* For example, "A band of sand stands grand in this land" might be compressed to "A bδ of sδ stδs grδ in this lδ," where the symbol "δ" replaces "and" in the stored file. One technique used when compressing graphics files replaces those portions of an image that are the same color with a brief descriptor that identifies the color only once and the area to be colored. Depending on the type and content of the file, file compression can create a compressed file that takes 10% to 90% less mass storage (the average is

about 50%). Compressed files are decompressed when loaded to RAM for processing.

- *We protect files.* We can protect sensitive files by limiting access to authorized persons. For example, a human resources manager might want to limit access to the company's personnel file that might contain salary, health, and other sensitive information.

SECTION SELF-CHECK

Self-Check

4-1.1 Data are retrieved from temporary mass storage and stored permanently in RAM. (T/F)

4-1.2 An ASCII file is a text-only file that can be read or created by any word processing program or text editor. (T/F)

4-1.3 A file is to mass storage as a vehicle is to a parking lot. (T/F)

4-1.4 WINTER.SALES and .ADD are valid filenames in the Windows environment. (T/F)

4-1.5 When we import a file, we convert a file in the current program to a format needed by another program. (T/F)

4-1.6 One way to reduce the size of a graphics file is called file: (a) deflation, (b) compression, (c) downsizing, or (d) decreasing?

4-1.7 We do all of the following to files except: (a) create files, (b) update files, (c) throw files, or (d) execute files?

4-1.8 Which of the following is not a type of file: (a) audio, (b) spreadsheet, (c) source program, or (d) book?

4-1.9 Magnetic tape storage provides inexpensive (a) archival storage, (b) random-access storage, (c) direct-access storage, or (d) cache storage?

4.2 MAGNETIC DISKS

Magnetic Disk

Magnetic disks have *random-* or *direct-access* capabilities as well as *sequential-access* capabilities. You are quite familiar with these access concepts, but you may not realize it. Suppose you have Paul Simon's classic album, *The Rhythm of the Saints,* on CD. The first four songs on this CD are: (1) "The Obvious Child," (2) "Can't Run But," (3) "The Coast," and (4) "Proof." Now suppose you also have this album on a tape cassette. To play the third song on the cassette, "The Coast," you would have to wind the tape forward and search for it sequentially. To play "The Coast" on the CD, all you would have to do is select track number 3. This simple analogy demonstrates the two fundamental methods of storing and accessing data—*sequential* and *random.*

For a mechanical device magnetic disks are very fast, able to seek and retrieve information quicker than a blink of an eye (in milliseconds). This direct-access flexibility and speed have made magnetic disk storage the overwhelming choice of computer users, for all types of computers. A variety of magnetic disk drives, the *hardware device,* and magnetic disks, the *medium* (the actual surface on which the information is stored), are manufactured for different business requirements.

Hardware and Storage Media

There are two fundamental types of magnetic disks: interchangeable and fixed.

- **Interchangeable magnetic disks** can be stored offline and loaded to the magnetic disk drives as they are needed.
- **Fixed magnetic disks,** also called hard disks, are permanently installed, or fixed. All hard disks are rigid and are usually made of aluminum with a surface coating of easily magnetized elements, such as iron, cobalt, chromium, and nickel. Today's integrated systems and databases are stored on hard

FIGURE 4.2

Magnetic Disk Drives and Media

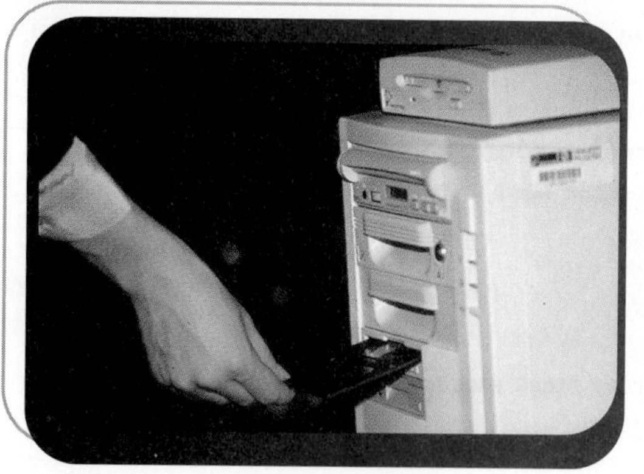

SuperDisk Shown here is a comparison highlighting a 120 MB SuperDisk's capacity in terms of the traditional floppy disk. The SuperDisk is being inserted into an internal drive and a companion external SuperDisk drive (top of unit). The SuperDisk drive is compatible with the traditional 1.44 MB diskette. Courtesy of Imation Corporation

Zip Disk An alternative high-capacity interchangeable disk is the 100 MB Zip disk, shown here with an external Zip drive. Courtesy of Iomega Corporation

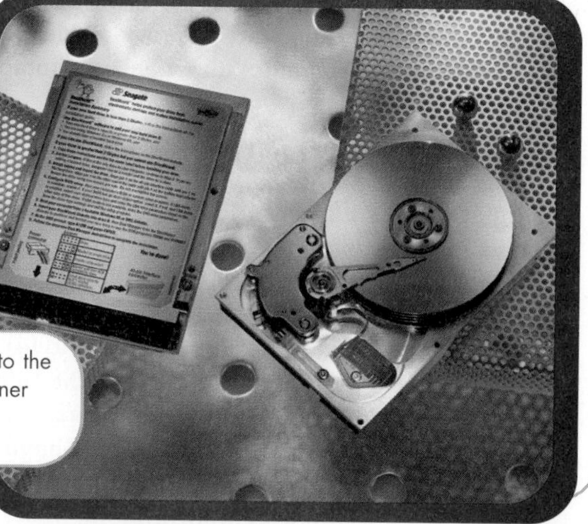

Hard Drive The 8.6 GB hard drive is pictured as it is delivered to the manufacturer (in a sealed enclosure) and broken down to show its inner workings (four platters with eight read/write heads).
Courtesy of Seagate Technology

Microdrive IBM unveiled the world's smallest and lightest hard-disk drive with a disk platter that will fit into an egg. The IBM Microdrive weighs less than an AA battery and holds 340 MB. The device is designed for use in PDAs and palmtop PCs.
Courtesy of International Business Machines Corporation

PC Card Hard Drive This 420 MB hard drive on a PCMCIA card, which can be inserted into a PCMCIA slot on a laptop PC, provides added storage capacity.
Courtesy of Integral Peripherals

disk, especially those used in workgroup computing. Such systems and databases require all data and programs to be online (accessible to the computer for processing) at all times.

Figure 4.2 shows the different types of interchangeable magnetic disks and fixed disks. As you can see, the drives for the various magnetic disk media are available in a wide variety of shapes and storage capacities. The type you (or a company) should use depends on the volume of data you have and the frequency with which those data are accessed.

PC Magnetic Disk Drives and Media

Virtually all PCs sold today are configured with at least one hard-disk drive and one interchangeable disk drive. Having two disk drives increases system flexibility and throughput. The interchangeable disk drive provides a means for the distribution of data and software and for backup and archival storage. The high-capacity hard-disk storage has made it possible for today's PC users to enjoy the convenience of having their data and software readily accessible at all times.

The Diskette

Three types of interchangeable disk drives are commonly used on PCs. These disk drives accept interchangeable magnetic disks, such as the traditional *diskette* and the new high-capacity *SuperDisk* and *Zip disk.*

- *Diskette and SuperDisk.* The traditional 3.5-inch diskette, or *floppy disk*, is a thin, mylar disk that is permanently enclosed in a rigid plastic jacket. The widely used standard for traditional diskettes permits only 1.44 MB of storage, not much in the modern era where 4 MB images or 30 MB programs are common place. A state-of-the-art version, called the **SuperDisk,** can store 120 MB of information. Both the diskette and the SuperDisk are the same size but have different disk densities. **Disk density** refers to the number of bits that can be stored per unit of area on the disk-face surface. In contrast to a hard disk, a diskette and SuperDisk are set in motion only when a command is issued to read from or write to the disk. The 120 MB Superdisk combines floppy and hard-disk technology to read and write to specially formatted floppy-size disks. The SuperDisk drive reads from and writes to the traditional diskette as well.
- *Zip disk.* The **Zip® drive** reads and writes to 100 MB **Zip® disks**. The Zip disk and SuperDisk have storage capacities of 70 and 83 floppy diskettes, respectively.

The diskette-based floppy disk drive is still standard equipment on most PCs and will remain so during this transition period to a new higher-density interchangeable disk, such as the Zip disk or the SuperDisk. The iMac™ from Apple Computer doesn't come with a floppy disk drive, relying instead on CD-ROMs, local area networks, and the Internet as vehicles for the transfer of information and programs.

The Hard Disk

Hard disk manufacturers are working continuously to achieve two objectives: (1) to put more information in less disk space and (2) to enable a more rapid transfer of that information to/from RAM. Consequently, hard-disk storage technology is forever changing. There are two types of hard disk, those that are permanently installed and those that are interchangeable.

- *Permanently installed hard disks.* Generally, the 1- to 5.25-inch (diameter of disk) permanent PC-based hard disks have storage capacities from about 4 GB (gigabytes) to over 30 GB. A 30 GB hard disk stores about the same amount of data as 20,000 floppies.

Fixed Hard Disk with Four Platters and Eight Recording Surfaces A cylinder refers to similarly numbered concentric tracks on the disk-face surfaces. In the illustration, the read/write heads are positioned over Cylinder 0012. At this position, the data on any one of the eight tracks numbered 0012 are accessible to the computer on each revolution of the disk. The read/write heads must be moved to access data on other tracks/cylinders.

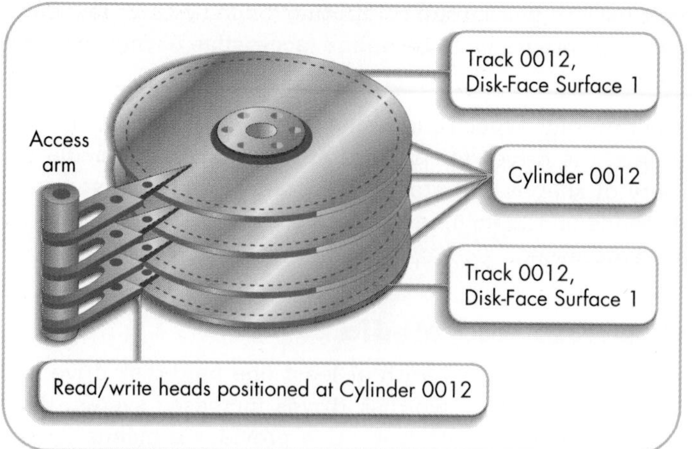

A hard disk contains several disk platters stacked on a single rotating spindle. Data are stored on all *recording surfaces.* For a disk with four platters, there are eight *recording surfaces* on which data can be stored (see Figure 4.3). The disks spin continuously at a high speed (from 3600 to 10,000 revolutions per minute) within a sealed enclosure. The enclosure keeps the disk-face surfaces free from contaminants (see Figure 4.4), such as dust and cigarette smoke. This contaminant-free environment allows hard disks to have greater density of data storage than the interchangeable diskettes.

The rotation of a magnetic disk passes all data under or over a **read/write head,** thereby making all data available for access on each revolution of the disk (see Figure 4.3). A fixed disk will have at least one read/write head for each recording surface. The heads are mounted on **access arms** that move together and literally float on a cushion of air over (or under) the spinning recording surfaces. The tolerance is so close that a particle of smoke from a cigarette will not fit between these "flying" heads and the recording surface!

- *Interchangeable hard disks.* The majority of hard disks are permanently installed in the same physical unit as the processor and diskette drive. This, however, is changing with the introduction of interchangeable hard disks, such as Iomega's **Jaz® drive.** The 3.5-inch **Jaz® cartridge,** which can store up to 1 GB of information, is inserted and removed as easily as the 3.5-inch floppy. The Jaz cartridges are about the size of a stack of four floppies. The Jaz drive's performance is almost as good as that of a permanently installed hard disk.

One of the most frequently asked questions is "How much hard drive capacity do I need?" The answer you hear most is "As much as you can afford." Disk space is like closet space—you never seem to have enough. If it's there, you tend to fill it with something.

Disk Read/Write Head Flying Distance When the disk is spinning at 7200 rpm, the surface of the disk travels across the read/write head at approximately 300 mph.

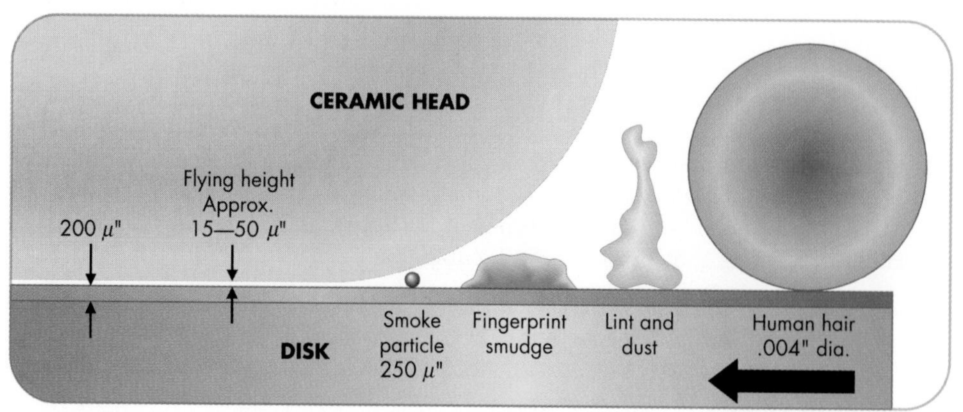

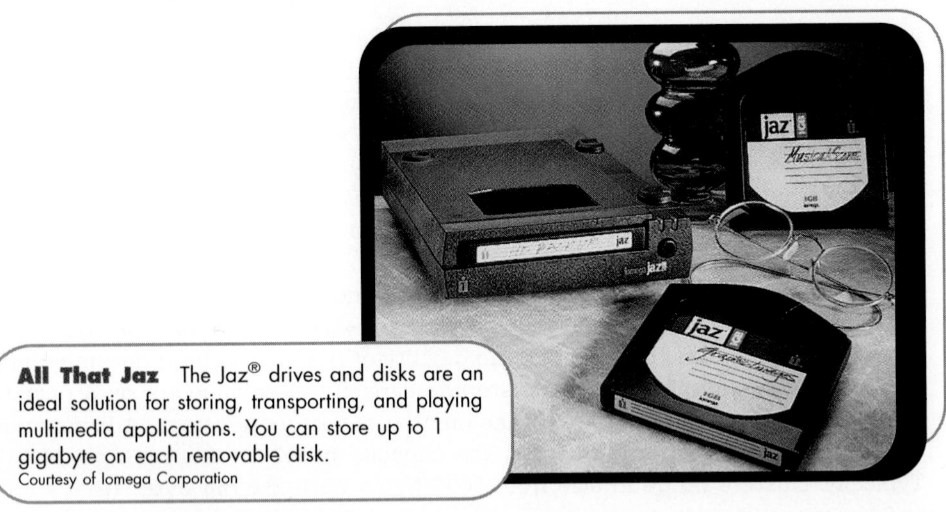

All That Jaz The Jaz® drives and disks are an ideal solution for storing, transporting, and playing multimedia applications. You can store up to 1 gigabyte on each removable disk.
Courtesy of Iomega Corporation

Magnetic Disk Organization

The way in which data and programs are stored and accessed is similar for both hard and interchangeable disks. Conceptually, a floppy disk looks like a hard disk with a single platter. Both media have a thin film coating of one of the easily magnetized elements (cobalt, for example). The thin film coating on the disk can be magnetized electronically by the read/write head to represent the absence or presence of a bit (0 or 1).

Tracks and Sectors: A Disk Floor Plan

Data are stored in concentric **tracks** by magnetizing the surface to represent bit configurations (see Figure 4.5). Bits are recorded using *serial representation;* that

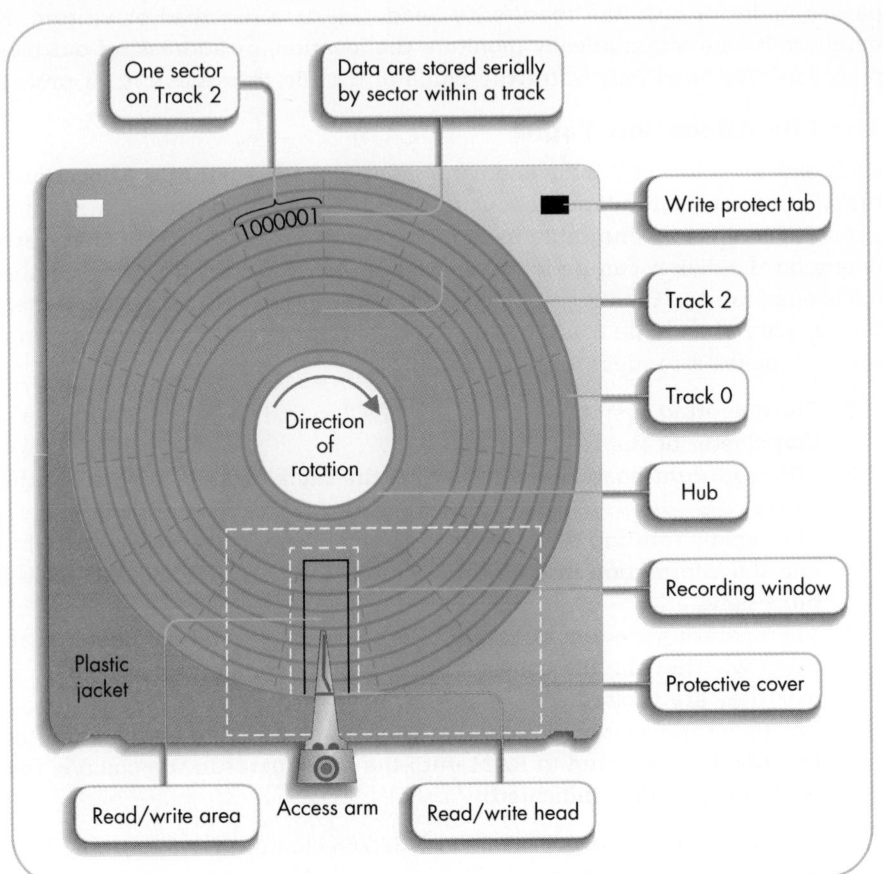

Cutaway of a Diskette The access arm on this 3.5-inch disk drive is positioned at a particular track (Track 2 in the example). Data are read or written serially in tracks within a given sector.

Bits on the Surface of a Magnetic Disk This highly magnified area of a magnetic disk-face surface shows elongated information bits recorded serially along 8 of the disk's 1774 concentric tracks. One square inch of this disk's surface can hold 22 million bits of information.
Courtesy of International Business Machines Corporation

is, bits are aligned in a row in the track. The number of tracks varies greatly between disks, from as few as 80 on a diskette to thousands on high-capacity hard disks. The spacing of tracks is measured in **tracks per inch,** or **TPI.** The 3.5-inch diskettes are rated at 135 TPI. The TPI for hard disks can be in the thousands. The *track density* (TPI) tells only part of the story. The *recording density* tells the rest. Recording density, which is measured in *kilobits per inch (k bps),* refers to the number of bits (1s and 0s) that can be stored per inch of track. High-density hard disks have densities in excess of 250 k bps.

PC disks use **sector organization** to store and retrieve data. In sector organization, the recording surface is divided into pie-shaped **sectors** (see Figure 4.5). The number of sectors depends on the density of the disk. A hard disk may have hundreds of sectors. Typically, the storage capacity of each sector on a particular track is 512 bytes, regardless of the number of sectors per track. Adjacent sectors are combined to form **clusters,** the capacity of which is a multiple of 512. Typically, clusters range in size from 4096 bytes up to 32,768 bytes (that's 8 up to 64 sectors). The cluster is the smallest unit of disk space that can be allocated to a file, so every file saved to disk takes up one or more clusters.

Each disk cluster is numbered, and the number of the first cluster in a file comprises the **disk address** on a particular file. The disk address represents the physical location of a particular file or set of data on a disk. To read from or write to a disk, an access arm containing the read/write head is moved, under program control, to the appropriate *track* or *cylinder* (see Figures 4.3 and 4.5). A particular **cylinder** refers to the same-numbered tracks on each recording surface (for example, Track 0012 on each recording surface–see Figure 4.3). When reading from or writing to a hard disk, all access arms are moved to the appropriate *cylinder.* For example, each recording surface has a track numbered 0012, so the disk has a cylinder numbered 0012. If the data to be accessed are on Recording Surface 01, Track 0012, then the access arms and the read/write heads for all eight recording surfaces are moved to Cylinder 0012. When the cluster containing the desired data passes under or over the read/write head, the data are read or written. Fortunately, software automatically monitors the location, or address, of our files and programs. We need only enter the name of the file to retrieve it for processing.

The File Allocation Table

Each disk used in the Windows environment has a **Virtual File Allocation Table (VFAT)** in which information about the clusters is stored (it was a FAT in early operating systems). The table includes an entry for each cluster that describes where on the disk it can be found and how it is used (for example, whether the file is open or not). Clusters are *chained* together to store information larger than the capacity of a single cluster. Here's what happens when you or a program on your PC makes a request for a particular file.

1. The operating system searches the VFAT to find the physical address of the first cluster of the file.
2. The read/right heads are moved over the track/cylinder containing the first cluster.
3. The rapidly rotating disk passes the cluster under/over the read/right head and the information in the first cluster is read and transmitted to RAM for processing.
4. The operating system checks an entry within the initial cluster that indicates whether the file consists of further clusters, and if so, where on the disk they are located.
5. The operating system directs that clusters continue to be read and their information transmitted to RAM until the last cluster in the chain is read (no further chaining is indicated).

A 100 KB file being stored on a disk with 32,768 clusters would require four clusters (three clusters will store only 98,304 bytes). Most of the space in the fourth cluster is wasted disk space. Large clusters may improve overall system performance, but they tend to make more space inaccessible. The trade-off between system performance and efficient use of disk space is a major consideration during the disk design process.

Sooner or later your PC will give you a "lost clusters found" message, indicating that the hard disk has orphan clusters that don't belong to a file. Typically, lost clusters are the result of an unexpected interruption of file activity, perhaps a system crash or loss of power. Utility programs are available that scan the disk for lost clusters and let you return them to the available pool of usable clusters.

Defragmentation: Rearranging Clusters to Enhance Performance

The easiest and least expensive way to get a performance boost out of your PC (make it run faster) is to run a utility program that consolidates files into contiguous clusters; that is, the clusters for each file are chained together on the same or adjacent tracks (see Figure 4.6). Each file stored on a disk is a single cluster or a chain of clusters. A 5 MB file may require thousands of linked clusters. Ideally all files would be stored on disk in contiguous clusters, but such is not the case with computing. Over time, files are added, deleted, and modified such that, eventually, files must be stored in noncontiguous clusters. When clusters are scattered, the read/write heads must move many times across the surface of a disk to access a single file. This excess mechanical movement slows down the PC because it takes longer to load a file to RAM for processing.

Disk Fragmentation

The mechanical movement of the disk read/write heads is the Achilles heel of a PC system—the greater the fragmentation of files, the slower the PC. Fortunately, we can periodically reorganize the disk such that files are stored in contiguous clusters. This process, appropriately called **defragmentation,** is done with a handy utility program. How often you run a "defrag" program depends on how much you use your PC. The fragmentation problem and the defragmentation solution are illustrated in Figure 4.6. In the example, five files are loaded to a disk, each in contiguous clusters. A file is modified, another is deleted, and another is added, resulting in fragmentation of several files and a need for defragmentation. The defragmentation process rewrites fragmented files into contiguous clusters (see Figure 4.6).

Formatting: Preparing a Disk for Use

A new disk is coated with a surface that can be magnetized easily to represent data. However, before the disk can be used, it must be **formatted.** The formatting procedure causes the disk to be initialized with a recording format for your operating system. Specifically, it:

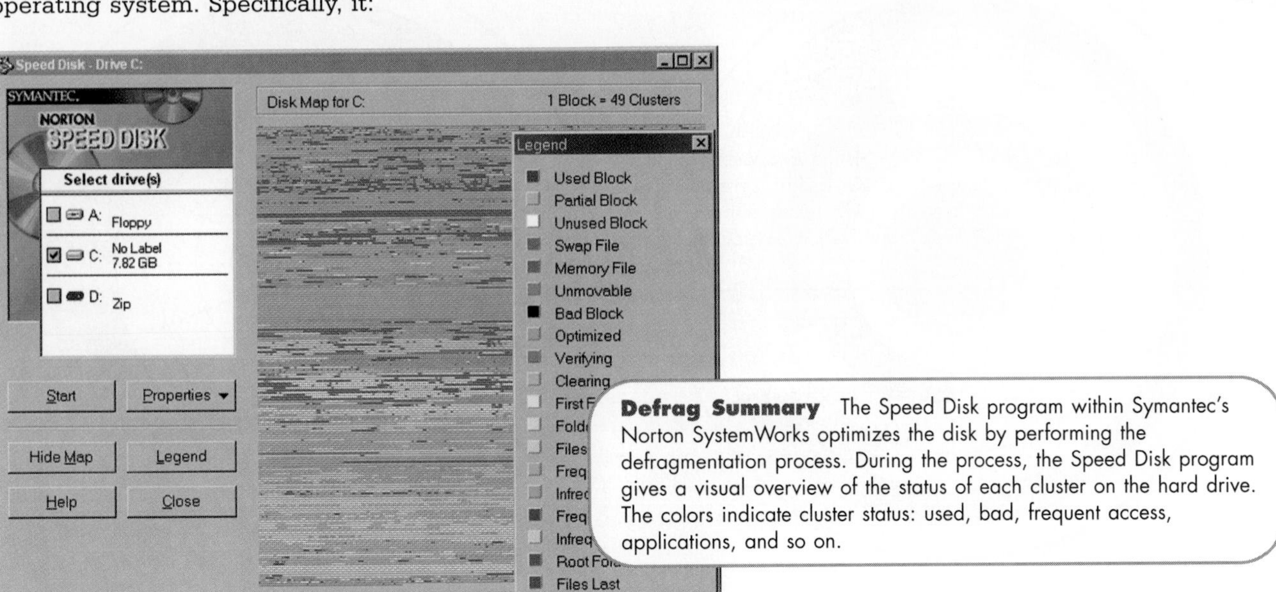

Defrag Summary The Speed Disk program within Symantec's Norton SystemWorks optimizes the disk by performing the defragmentation process. During the process, the Speed Disk program gives a visual overview of the status of each cluster on the hard drive. The colors indicate cluster status: used, bad, frequent access, applications, and so on.

- Creates sectors and tracks into which data are stored.
- Sets up an area for the file allocation table.

If you purchased a PC today, the hard disk probably would be formatted and ready for use. However, if you added a hard disk or upgraded your existing hard disk,

Disk Defragmentation (a) Initially, five files are stored ideally in contiguous clusters. (b) The user adds a few objects to a graphics file (blue), increasing its size and the number of clusters needed to store it. Note that file clusters are no longer contiguous. Then, a file (green) is deleted. (c) A new file (gray) is stored in noncontiguous clusters. (d) The disk is defragmented, resaving all files in contiguous clusters.

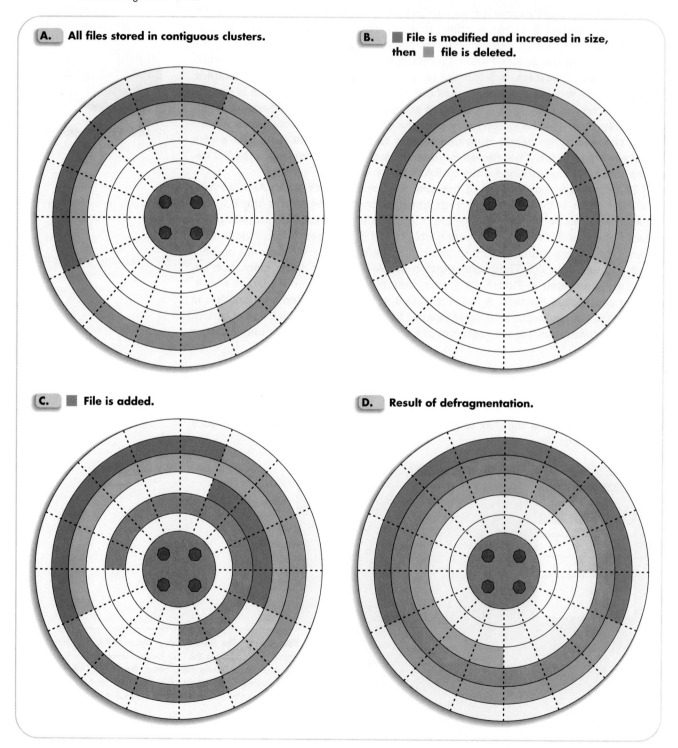

A. All files stored in contiguous clusters.

B. File is modified and increased in size, then file is deleted.

C. File is added.

D. Result of defragmentation.

the new disk would need to be formatted. Diskettes can be purchased as formatted or unformatted. Unformatted diskettes cost less, but they must be formatted prior to use.

Disk Access Time: Seek and Transmit

Access time is the interval between the instant a computer makes a request for the transfer of data from a disk-storage device to RAM and the instant this operation is completed. The read/write heads on the access arm in the illustration of Figure 4.3 move together. Some hard disks have multiple access arms, some with two read/write heads per disk-face surface. Having multiple access arms and read/write heads results in less mechanical movement and faster access times.

The access of data from RAM is performed at electronic speeds—approximately the speed of light. But the access of data from disk storage depends on the movement of mechanical apparatus (read/write heads and spinning disks) and can take from 6 to 10 milliseconds—still very slow when compared with the microsecond-to-nanosecond internal processing speeds of computers.

Disk Caching: Speed Boost

The **data transfer rate** is the rate at which data are read from mass storage to RAM or written to mass storage from RAM. Even though the data transfer rate from magnetic disk to RAM may be 80 million bytes per second, the rate of transfer between one part of RAM to another is much faster. **Disk caching** (pronounced *"cashing"*) is a technique that improves system speed by taking advantage of the greater transfer rate of data within RAM. With disk caching, programs and data that are *likely* to be called into use are moved from a disk into a separate disk-caching area of RAM. When an application program calls for the data or programs in the disk cache area, the data are transferred directly from RAM rather than from the slower magnetic disk. Updated data or programs in the disk cache area eventually must be transferred to a disk for permanent storage. All modern PCs take full advantage of disk caching.

Diskette Care: Do's and Don'ts

A blank interchangeable disk has a very modest value. But once you save your files on it, its value, at least to you, increases greatly. Such a valuable piece of property should be handled with great care. Following are a few guidelines for handling interchangeable disks.

Do's

- *Do* store disks at temperatures between 50 and 125 degrees Fahrenheit.
- *Do* keep a backup of disks containing important data and programs.
- *Do* remove disks from disk drives before you turn off the computer.
- *Do* clean diskette drive read/write heads periodically with a diskette cleaning kit (available at most computer retailer locations).
- *Do* slide the *write-protect tab* to its open position on all important 3.5-inch disks intended for read-only use (see Figure 4.5).

Don'ts

- *Don't* force a disk into the disk drive. It should slip in with little or no resistance.
- *Don't* touch the disk surface.
- *Don't* place disks near a magnetic field, such as magnetic paper-clip holders, tape demagnetizers, telephones, or electric motors.
- *Don't* expose disks to direct sunlight for a prolonged period.
- *Don't* insert or remove a disk from a disk drive if the "drive active" light is on.

MEMORY bits

Characteristics of Magnetic Disk

Media: Fixed (hard) and interchangeable disks
Type access: Direct (random) or sequential
Data representation: Serial
Storage scheme: Clusters on tracks

Computer Viruses: The Plague of Magnetic Disks

Computers can get sick just like people. A variety of highly contagious "viruses" can spread from computer to computer, much the way biological viruses do among human beings. Just as a virus can infect human organs, a **computer virus** can infect programs and databases. It can also hide duplicates of itself within legitimate programs, such as an operating system or a word processing program. These viruses, which are programs, reside on and are passed between magnetic disks.

Most people who write and circulate virus programs fall into two groups. The first group uses viruses to show off for their peers. They are harmless. The second, and far more dangerous group, creates viruses with malicious intent. These people are just plain mean and want their viruses to result in property damage and cause human suffering.

Types of Computer Viruses: Bad and Worse

There are lots of viruses. Some act quickly by erasing user programs and files on disk. Others grow like a cancer, destroying small parts of a file each day. Some act like a time bomb. They lay dormant for days or months but eventually are activated and wreak havoc on any software on the system. Many companies warn their PC users to back up all software prior to every Friday the thirteenth, a favorite date of those who write virus programs. Some viruses attack the hardware and have been known to throw the mechanical components of a computer system, such as disk-access arms, into costly spasms.

Sources of Computer Viruses

In the PC environment, there are three primary sources of computer viruses (see Figure 4.7).

- *The Internet.* The most common source of viral infection is the very public Internet on which people download and exchange software. All too often, a user logs on to the Internet and downloads a game, a utility program, or some other enticing piece of freeware from an unsecured site, but gets the software with an embedded virus instead. Sometimes viruses are attached to e-mails. A good rule is to know the sender before opening a program sent with an e-mail.
- *Diskettes.* Viruses are also spread from one system to another via common interchangeable disks. For example, a student with an infected application disk might unknowingly infect several other laboratory computers with a virus, which, in turn, infects the applications software of other students. Software companies have unknowingly distributed viruses with their proprietary software products. Ouch!
- *Computer networks.* Viruses can spread from one computer network to another.

How serious a problem are viruses? They have the potential of affecting an individual's career and even destroying companies. For example, a company that loses its accounts receivables records—records of what the company is owed—could be a candidate for bankruptcy. Antiviral programs, also called *vaccines,* exist, but a persistent (and malicious) programmer can circumvent them. The best way to cope with viruses is to recognize their existence, then take precautionary measures. Your chances of living virus free are greatly improved if you periodically check for viruses and are careful about what you load to your system's hard disk. If you catch a virus, your best chance of surviving is backing up all important data and programs.

Self-Check

SECTION SELF-CHECK

4-2.1 Magnetic disks have sequential-access capabilities only. (T/F)

4-2.2 Virtually all PCs sold today are configured with at least one DVD drive and one interchangeable disk drive. (T/F)

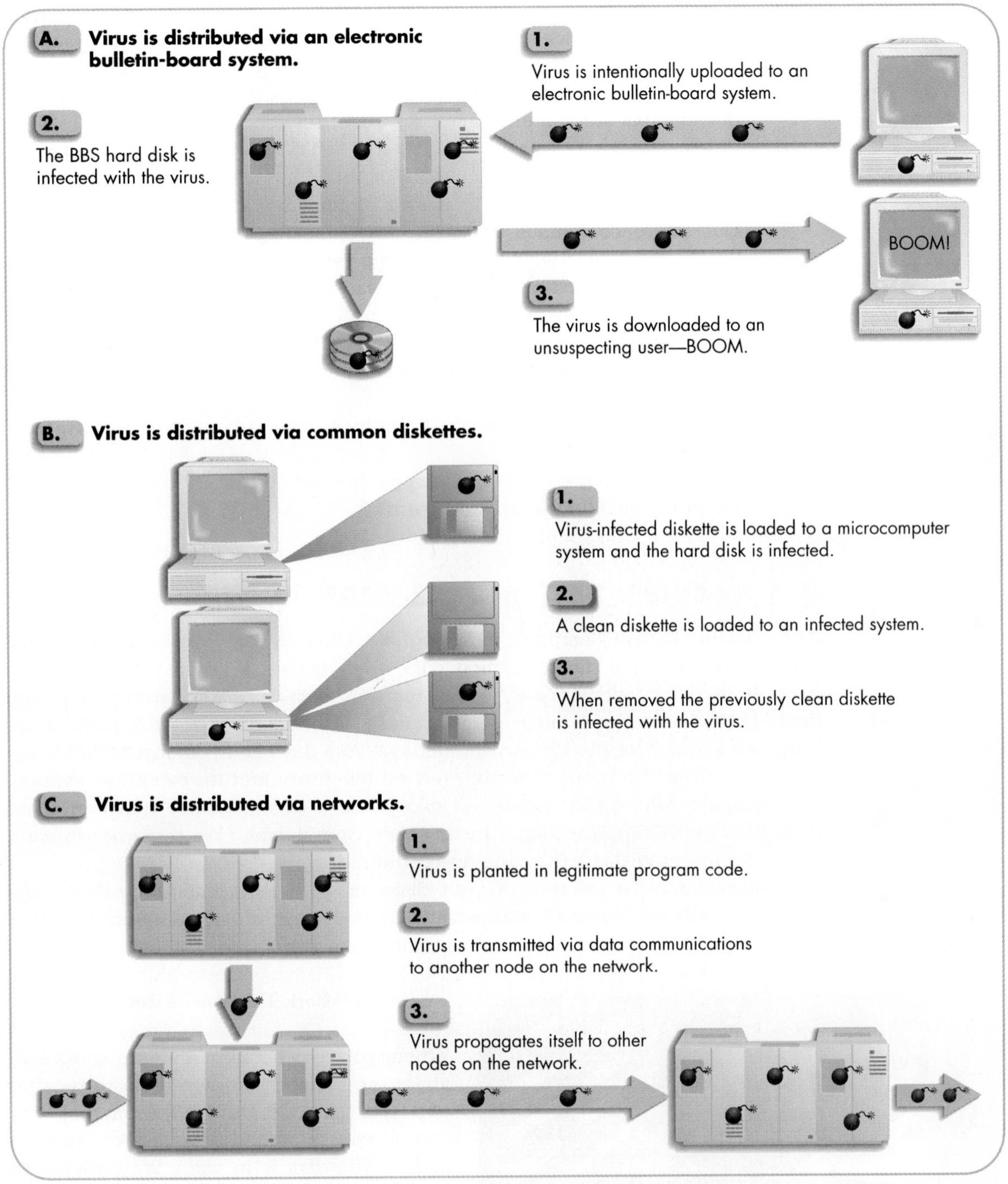

A. Virus is distributed via an electronic bulletin-board system.

1. Virus is intentionally uploaded to an electronic bulletin-board system.

2. The BBS hard disk is infected with the virus.

3. The virus is downloaded to an unsuspecting user—BOOM.

BOOM!

B. Virus is distributed via common diskettes.

1. Virus-infected diskette is loaded to a microcomputer system and the hard disk is infected.

2. A clean diskette is loaded to an infected system.

3. When removed the previously clean diskette is infected with the virus.

C. Virus is distributed via networks.

1. Virus is planted in legitimate program code.

2. Virus is transmitted via data communications to another node on the network.

3. Virus propagates itself to other nodes on the network.

How Viruses Are Spread

4-2.3 Both the diskette and the SuperDisk are the same size but have different disk densities. (T/F)

4-2.4 Information on interchangeable disks cannot be stored offline. (T/F)

4-2.5 The Zip disk has a greater capacity for storage than the SuperDisk. (T/F)

4-2.6 TPI stands for tracks per inch. (T/F)

4-2.7 The capacity of clusters is based on a multiple of 521 bytes. (T/F)

4-2.8 In a disk drive, the read/write heads are mounted on an access arm. (T/F)

4-2.9 Before a disk can be used, it must be formatted. (T/F)

4-2.10 Which has the greatest storage capacity: (a) the traditional floppy, (b) the Zip disk, (c) the SuperDisk, (d) or the CD-RW disk?

4-2.11 Which of these statements is not true: (a) The rotation of a magnetic disk passes all data under or over a read/write head; (b) the heads are mounted on access arms; (c) The 3.5-inch Jaz cartridge is permanently installed in the same physical unit as the processor; (4) a hard disk contains several disk platters stacked on a single rotating spindle?

4-2.12 The standard size for common diskettes is: (a) 3.25 inches, (b) 3.5 inches, (c) 3.75 inches, or (d) 5.25 inches?

4-2.13 The defragmentation process rewrites fragmented files into: (a) contiguous clusters, (b) continuous clusters, (c) circular clusters, (d) Cretan clusters?

4-2.14 The VFAT is searched by the operating system to find the physical address of the: (a) first cluster of the file, (b) read/write head, (c) microprocessor, (d) mid-sector of the file?

4-2.15 What denotes the physical location of a particular file or set of data on a magnetic disk: (a) cylinder, (b) data compression index, (c) CD-R, or (d) disk address?

4-2.16 TPI refers to: (a) sector density, (b) cylinder overload, (c) track density, or (d) bps thickness?

4-2.17 The disk-caching area is (a) on floppy disk, (b) in RAM, (c) on hard disk, or (d) on the monitor's expansion board?

4.3 BACKUP: BETTER SAFE THAN SORRY

At the Skalny Basket Company, in Springfield, Ohio, Cheryl Hart insisted on daily backups of the small family-owned company's accounts receivables files. The backups were inconvenient and took 30 minutes each day. Cheryl took the backup home each day in her briefcase, just in case. On December 23, she packed her briefcase and left for the Christmas holidays. Five days later, Skalny Basket Company burned to the ground, wiping out all inventory and its computer system. The company was up in smoke, all except for a tape cassette that contained records of its $600,000 accounts receivables. Cheryl said, "We thought we were out of business. Without the tape, we couldn't have rebuilt."

Safeguarding the content of your disks may be more important than safeguarding hardware. After all, you can always replace your computer, but you often cannot replace your lost files. The first commandment in computing, at any level, is

Back Up Your Files.

When you create a document, a spreadsheet, or a graph and you wish to recall it at a later time, you *store* the file on disk. You can, of course, store many files on a single disk. If the disk is in some way destroyed (scratched, demagnetized, burned, and so on) or lost, you have lost your files unless you have a backup.

If your system is configured with a tape backup unit, then you easily can back up all files on a system. However, if you do not have a TBU, you still can back up critical files to diskettes.

Automatic Retrieval Tape Storage This robotic tape storage and retrieval unit holds hundreds of high-density tape cartridges, each with a capacity of 25 GB (gigabytes). The tape cartridges are automatically loaded and unloaded to a tape drive as they are needed for processing. Companies use tape storage and retrieval systems to back up massive master files on magnetic disk storage.
Courtesy of International Business Machines Corporation

Back Up to Magnetic Tape

During the 1950s and 1960s, the foundation of many information systems was *sequential processing* using *magnetic tape* master files. Today, magnetic tape storage

IT Ethics

ACCESSIBILITY TO E-MAIL ARCHIVES

E-mail may be the corporate Achilles heel when it comes to lawsuits. Attorneys can subpoena e-mail archives on disk or tape relative to pending lawsuits. Among the thousands of e-mail messages sent each day in a typical medium-sized company, attorneys are likely to find statements that support their cause. People tend to be conversational when writing e-mail messages. People don't write e-mail with the thought that it might be shown as evidence in a court of law. To avoid the potential for litigation, many companies routinely purge e-mail archives. Had the people at Microsoft Corporation been more diligent about purging their e-mail, U.S. government prosecutors would not have been able to subpoena the company's e-mail. The e-mail they eventually found was critical to the government's antitrust suit against Microsoft.

Discussion: Should companies save e-mail? If so, for how long? Should attorneys be allowed to subpoena e-mail archives?

is no longer used for routine processing; however, it has three other important functions.

- *Protection against loss of valuable files.* Magnetic tape is used primarily as a backup medium for magnetic disk storage.
- *Archiving files.* Important files no longer needed for active processing can be archived to magnetic tape. For example, banks archive old transactions (checks and deposits) for a number of years.
- *File portability between computers.* Large amounts of information can be transferred between computers by writing to magnetic tape at the source site and reading from the tape at the destination site.

Magnetic tape drives are called **tape backup units (TBUs).** They use a $\frac{1}{4}$-inch cartridge (QIC), also called a **data cartridge.** A data cartridge (the medium) can be loaded conveniently to a TBU (the hardware device) for processing. The data cartridge is self-contained and is inserted into and removed from the tape drive in much the same way you would load or remove videotape from a VCR. When processing is complete, the tape is removed for offline storage until it is needed again for processing.

If your backup requirements exceed 1 GB per day, you are a candidate for a tape backup unit. Anything under 1 GB can be handled with diskettes or the high-capacity SuperDisk or Zip disk. The relatively inexpensive TBU is a good investment for the active PC user and for all administrators of local area networks (LANs).

Tape Backup Methods

You can choose from three common backup methods.

Full backup	A full backup copies all files on a hard disk to magnetic tape.
Selective backup	Only user-selected files are backed up to magnetic tape.
Modified files, only, backup	Only those files that have been modified since the last backup are backed up to magnetic tape.

Tape Backup Rotation: Six Tapes This six-tape backup rotation is common in small businesses and with individuals whose files have high volatility. Two total backups are done every Monday, one of which is taken to an off-site location. Only files that are modified on a given day are backed up for each of the other weekdays. If all files are lost on Friday, the total backup from Monday is restored to the hard disk, then modified backups are restored for Tuesday through Thursday.

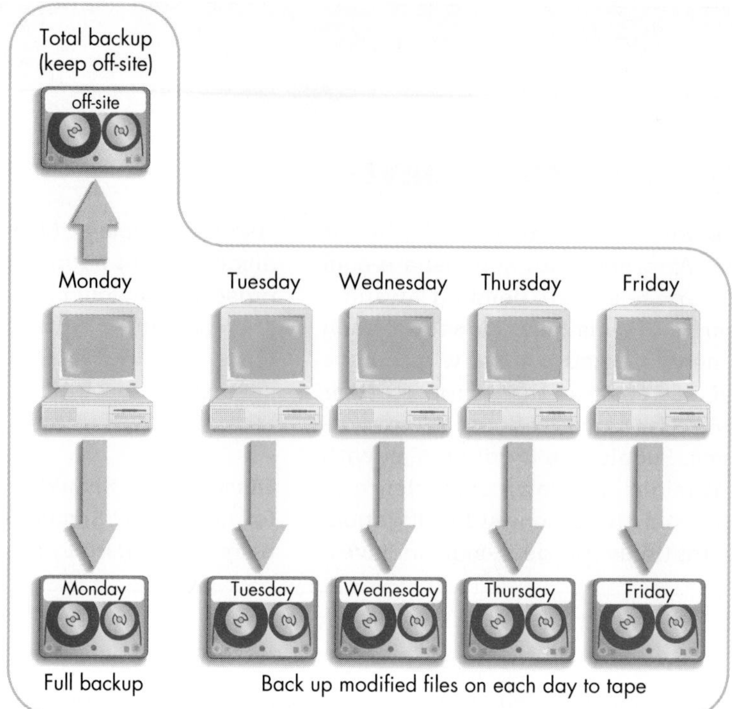

The frequency with which files are backed up depends on their *volatility,* or how often you update the files on the disk. If you spend time every day working with files, you should back them up each day. Others should be backed up no more often than they are used. Figure 4.8 illustrates a six-tape backup rotation.

At one time or another, just about everyone who routinely works with computers has experienced the trauma of losing work for which there was no backup. It is no fun seeing several days (or weeks) of work disappear, but it does emphasize the point that it is well worth the effort to make backup copies of your work.

Restoring Files

If you lose your data or programs, you will need to restore the backed-up file to disk. If you use a backup system similar to the one shown in Figure 4.8, then some updating will occur between total backup runs. To re-create your files, then, you need to use the last total backup and incorporate all subsequent partial backups. For example, assume a virus wiped your hard drive clean at the end of the day on Thursday. To restore the backup files, you would restore the full backup tape from Monday, then the modified backup from Tuesday, and finally the modified backup tape from Wednesday. Then you would need to redo any processing that was done on Thursday prior to the virus striking.

Back Up to Interchangeable Disks

What if you do not have a tape backup unit? If you do not have a TBU (which is usually the case), then you will need to back up your files to diskettes, available on every PC, or to SuperDisks or Zip disks. Backing up a complete hard disk to diskette is impractical because it would require hundreds, perhaps thousands, of diskettes. However, you should back up critical files to diskette. If you have a SuperDisk or Zip disk drive, then you can back up your entire system to 120 MB or 100 MB disks, respectively. For the casual PC user, high-capacity interchangeable disks provide an excellent alternative to tape backup units.

Figure 4.9 illustrates and explains a backup procedure for critical files that are used daily. The procedure is the same whether your critical files are main-

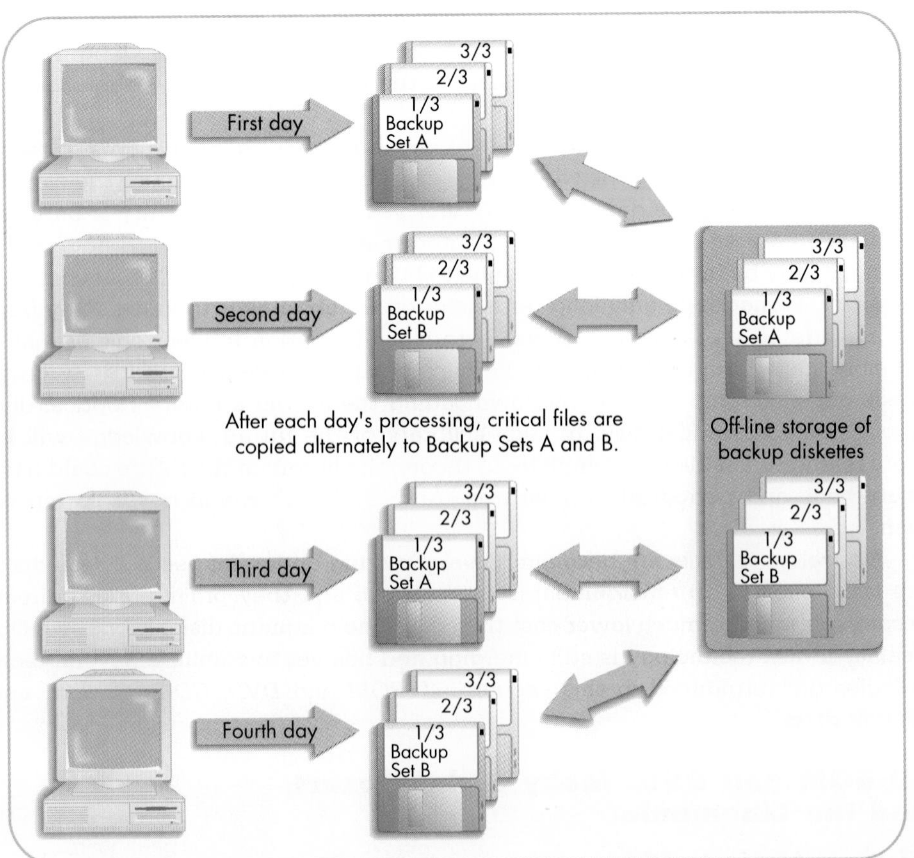

Interchangeable Disk Backup Rotation: Two Backup Sets After each day's processing, critical disk files are copied alternately to Backup Sets A and B. In this manner, one backup set (possibly several diskettes) is always current within a day's processing. If the critical work files and the most recent backup are accidentally destroyed, a third backup is current within two days' processing. Backup Sets A and B are alternated as the most current backup.

tained on a hard disk or on one or more interchangeable disks. In the figure, two generations of backup are maintained on Backup Sets A and B. Critical disk files are copied alternately to Backup Sets A and B each day. This technique is popular with individual users, especially those in an office setting.

SECTION SELF-CHECK

Self-Check

4-3.1 The frequency with which a work disk is backed up depends on its volatility. (T/F)

4-3.2 Tape backup units store data on QIC tape cartridges. (T/F)

4-3.3 Any systems with weekly backup requirements under 100 MB are candidates for TBUs. (T/F)

4-3.4 Which of the following generally is not an application for magnetic tape storage: (a) routine information processing, (b) backup for disk storage, (c) archival storage, or (d) medium for transfer between computers?

4-3.5 In the full backup method: (a) only user-selected files are backed up, (b) only those files that have been modified since the last backup are backed up, (c) only volatile files are backed up, or (d) all files are backed up?

4-3.6 When performing backup using interchangeable disks, it is best to maintain at least: (a) one generation, (b) two generations, (c) four generations, or (d) eight generations?

4.4 OPTICAL LASER DISKS: HIGH-DENSITY STORAGE

Some industry analysts have predicted that *optical laser disk* technology eventually may make magnetic disk and tape storage obsolete. With this technology, two lasers replace the read/write head used in magnetic storage. One laser beam

Optical Storage

writes to the recording surface by scoring microscopic *pits* in the disk, and another laser reads the data from the light-sensitive recording surface. A light beam is easily deflected to the desired place on the optical disk, so a mechanical access arm is not needed.

Optical technology opens the door to new and exciting applications. Already this technology is leading the way to the library of the future. Because the world's output of knowledge is doubling every four years, the typical library is bursting at the seams with books and other printed materials. With library budgets declining, it may be impractical to continue to build structures to warehouse printed materials. Perhaps the only long-term solution for libraries is to move away from storing printed materials and toward storing information in electronic format—possibly some form of optical disk. Perhaps in the not-too-distant future we will check out electronic "books" by downloading them from a library's optical disk to our personal optical disk. In such a library of the future, knowledge will be more readily available and complete. In theory, the library of the future could have every book and periodical ever written. And, a "book" would never be out on loan.

Optical laser disks are becoming a very inviting option for users. These disks are less sensitive to environmental fluctuations, and they provide more direct-access storage at a much lower cost than does the magnetic disk alternative. Optical laser disk technology is still emerging and has yet to stabilize. Several technologies are introduced in this section: *CD-ROM* and *DVD, CD-R, CD-RW*, and *WORM disks.*

CD-ROM and DVD: Moby Dick, Mozart, and the Cinemania

History: Audio to Video

Introduced in 1980 for stereo buffs, the extraordinarily successful CD, or compact disk, is an optical laser disk designed to enhance the reproduction of recorded music. To make a CD recording, the analog sounds of music are digitized and stored on a 4.72-inch optical laser disk. Seventy-four minutes of music can be

CD-ROMs, DVDs, and Multimedia The CD-ROM is the foundation technology for an explosion of multimedia applications. Multimedia kiosk information centers are popping up everywhere, including retail stores (shown here), office buildings, museums, and music stores. The information provided by the interactive kiosks is frequently stored on CD-ROM or DVD.
Courtesy of International Business Machines Corporation

Emerging IT

ELECTRONIC PUBLISHING: SAVING THE TREES

For centuries, the words and images of the world were published and viewed on paper. That's changing. The ability to store and retrieve massive amounts of information from online storage (various types of disk) and the ability to make that information available through the Internet and networking has resulted in enthusiastic acceptance and use of electronic publishing.

Historically, word processing and desktop publishing software have been used to produce documents that can be physically distributed in hard copy—letters, periodicals, magazines, books, reports, manuals, and many other forms of written communication and documentation. However, more and more of what we write never makes it to paper. Look at written correspondence. A few years ago, we wrote letters and memos, but today e-mail outnumbers print correspondence 200 to 1.

An alternative to producing hard-copy documents is *electronic publishing.* In electronic publishing, *electronic documents* are created that can be retrieved from disk storage. Electronic documents, also called *online documents,* are normally found on a hard disk (the PC's, the network server's, or an Internet server's). Electronic documents are also distributed on CD-ROM or DVD. All such documents are designed to be viewed on a monitor and most are interactive.

The business world is now linked via the Internet, intranets (an Internet within an organization), and extranets (an intranet that is partially accessible to authorized outsiders, such as suppliers and customers). This linking of the world has revolutionized the way we enter, retrieve, send, maintain, and view information. This worldwide networking has made it possible for business to move toward greater use of electronic publishing.

The Advantages of Electronic Publishing

When compared to print publishing, the advantages of electronic publishing become overwhelming for many publishing needs. Just about every printing need is a candidate for electronic publishing. Restaurant menus, college textbooks, magazines, romance novels, corporate sales manuals, civic club newsletters, annual reports, travel brochures, IRS forms, and many more traditional print documents are being published electronically.

- **Electronic documents are good for the environment** Electronic publishing has eliminated the need to use trees to produce billions of printed pages. Electronic documents are being composed and distributed as bits. The fossil fuel, as well as the human effort, required to distribute millions of pounds of personnel manuals, reports, policy statements, newsletters, and many other types of printed material can be put to better use.
- **Electronic documents are easily updated** A company may print thousands of sales manuals. But when the company changes product prices, the printed sales manuals become out of date. The federal government routinely prints large quantities of informational documents. However, printed government documents are often inaccurate because of frequent changes in regulations and laws. In a world that is in constant change, print documents have become simply too difficult to maintain. In contrast, companies, the government, and anyone else can produce online documents that can be easily updated to reflect current circumstances. There is only one copy of an electronic document to change, and it is distributed electronically on demand.
- **Electronic documents offer a much richer form of communication** An electronic format enables the integration of audio clips, video clips, and even animation, with the text and graphics. Print documents include only text and graphics. Electronic travel advertisements frequently include video clips that take you on visual tours of the local sites. The illustrations in online technical manuals are brought to life via an added dimension—animation. Animation can also be used to simplify complex diagrams.
- **Electronic documents can be interactive** Electronic documents permit interactivity. Electronic documents can include forms, pop-up boxes, and buttons that allow the user to enter information to a system. For example, the exercises associated with the Internet Bridge, the companion Internet site for this book, are interactive. Each exercise is followed by a response box that allows the student to enter an answer to the exercise. Student answers to the exercises are sent via e-mail to the instructors.
- **Electronic documents facilitate navigation** In the electronic environment, it is easy to move between areas of the documents. In a print document, you go to the table of contents or the index to obtain a page number for the topic of interest. Then you physically flip through the pages to find the topic. In an electronic document, the user simply

clicks on the desired topic and the topic is immediately displayed for viewing.

- **Electronic documents are searchable** Electronic documents are electronically searchable. An automobile parts sales representative can use the *find* feature to locate all references to a particular part in an online sales manual. The representative does this by entering a part name, a part number, or, possibly, the characteristics of the part (for example, water pump, Mercedes 380SL, 1985).
- **Electronic documents are tied together by hyperlinks** The hyperlink feature enables electronic links between different sections of an electronic document, or to other related electronic documents. In the print world, documents stand alone. In the electronic world, documents are "networked." A viewer has only to click on a hyperlink (usually highlighted text, an image, or a graphic icon) to navigate to and view related material. These hyperlinks enable a single electronic document to reach far beyond what you see on the screen.

Creating Electronic Documents

The three most popular formats for electronic documents are *word processing, HTML,* and *portable document.* Adjacent illustrations show how the material can be presented in each of these three formats. For each type of document, the user must have a PC, a workstation, or a terminal and be running the software that permits viewing of the electronic document.

- **Word processing documents** During the early 1990s, word processing was used extensively to create both print and online documents. The online documents, however, were created for use within the confines of a particular organization. This is because the viewer for such documents is the word processing software used to create them. This type of online document works well as long as all users have the same word processing program. This lack of portability, though, limits the effectiveness of word processing–based electronic documents. The trend is to online documents that are platform-independent. In short, that means Internet technologies.
- **HTML documents** The most popular format for electronic documents is HTML (HyperText Markup Language). HTML provides a description of how the information is to be presented on the screen. All Internet browsers, including Netscape Communicator and Microsoft Internet Explorer, can retrieve HTML documents from their servers and display them for viewing. Companies and individuals who wish to make publications available via World Wide Web Internet servers must create HTML-compliant documents.

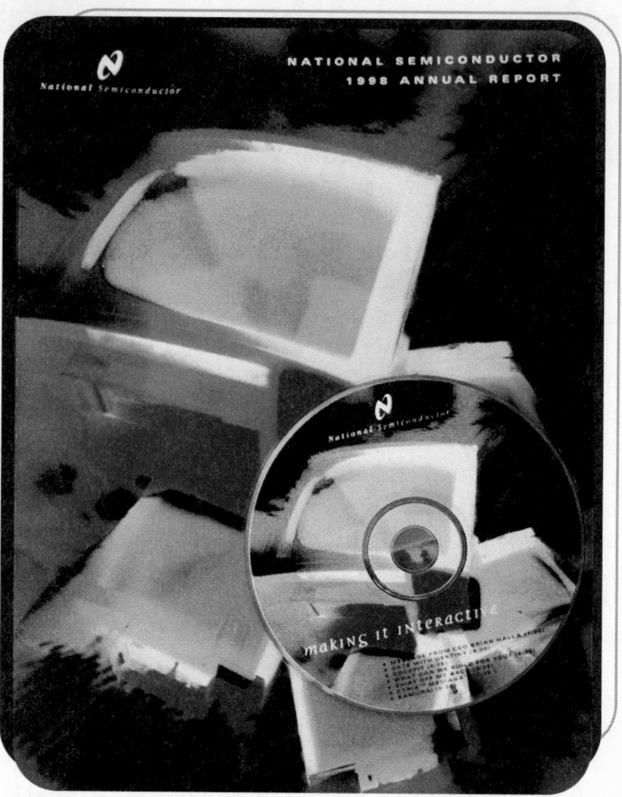

Annual Report on CD-ROM
Each year corporations distribute millions of printed annual reports to shareholders. Some companies, such as National Semiconductor (shown here), also distribute an interactive version on CD-ROM.

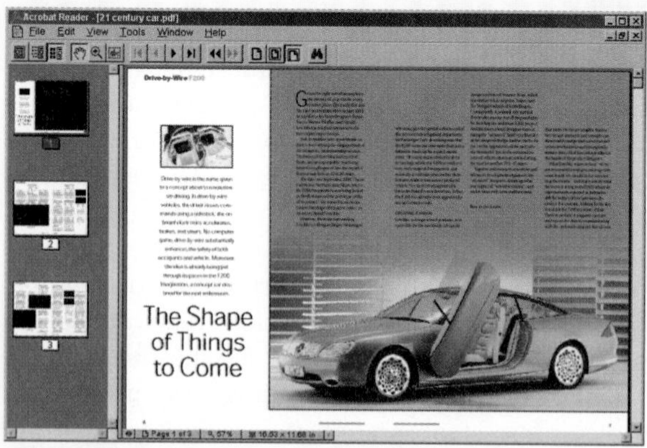

PDF Format
Mercedes-Benz used PDF format to distribute research information on its futuristic drive-by-wire automobile. The information pamphlet can be downloaded on the Internet and viewed with Adobe Acrobat Reader (shown here).

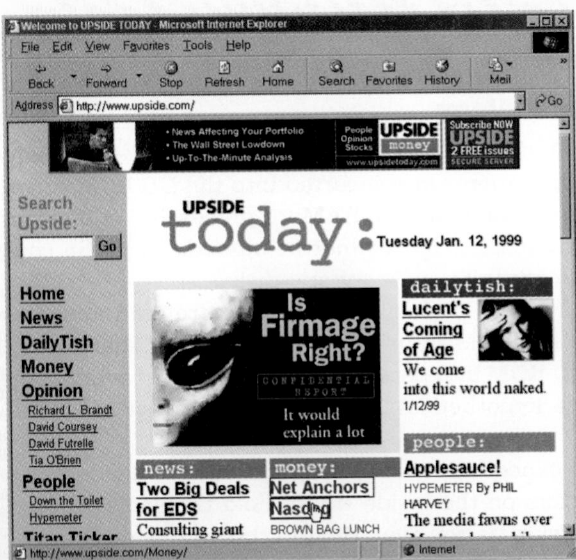

E-zines

Shown here is *Upside,* an electronic magazine, or e-zine. You can find many e-zines on the Internet, all of which can be continuously updated to reflect breaking events and news.

- **Portable documents** You can pass a *portable document* around the electronic world as you would a print document in the physical world. It can be embedded in HTML-based World Wide Web pages on the Internet, attached to e-mail messages, distributed on a CD-ROM, and generally made available in any computing environment. The most popular format is the *portable document format,* or *PDF* (created by Adobe Corporation). The PDF file has emerged as the standard for portable documents, including contracts, financial reports, advertising brochures, personnel forms, and many other publishing needs. Millions of Internet users have downloaded the Adobe Acrobat Reader (for free), the software needed to view PDF documents. PDF documents are created with a variety of proprietary products from Adobe Corporation, including Acrobat and Acrobat Capture.

The PDF format is ideal for Internet publishing because it integrates the viewing of PDF files directly into Web browsers. PDF files can be highly compressed (more information in smaller files), thereby reducing the time required to send them to the end user. Also, a PDF file looks the same on all platforms. In contrast, similar HTML-based content can take longer to transmit, and its appearance may vary depending on the platform on which it is viewed.

Distribution of Electronic Documents

Most electronic documents are distributed over the Internet, intranets, or extranets. Online documents meant for public consumption are placed on the Internet. Those designed for internal use, such as employee benefits manuals, are made available over intranets. Portable documents are frequently uploaded, downloaded, and attached to e-mail. Some applications call for distribution of documents via CD-ROM or DVD. For example, many companies now distribute their annual reports via print and/or CD-ROM.

Converting Print Documents to Electronic Documents

Software vendors are aware of the trend to electronic publishing and are working diligently to create products that make it easier for us to produce online documents from existing print-oriented documents. Several products enable us to export word processing documents directly to HTML or PDF format. That means that the countless existing documents can be easily converted for use in the electronic environment. One popular product enables scanned hard-copy documents to be converted to fully searchable PDF documents that look just like the original. That means that a flashy marketing brochure, a census form, or any other hard-copy document can be easily converted for online distribution.

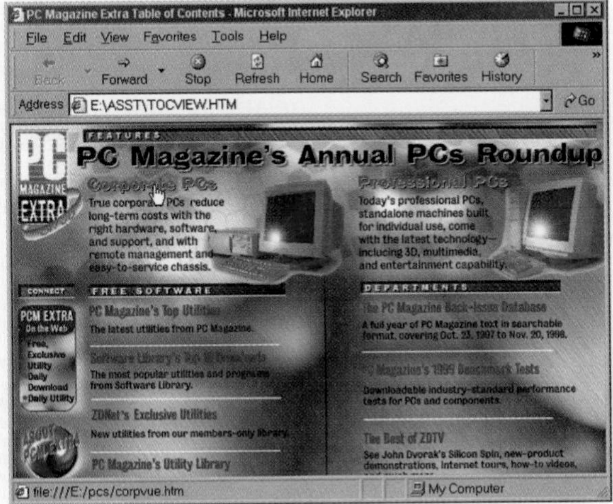

Magazines on CD-ROM

Magazines take on a new look when reformatted for electronic publishing. This *PC Magazine Extra,* which is written in HTML format and distributed on CD-ROM, is viewed on a browser such as Internet Explorer. It contains the complete text of all issues of the magazine published during the past year, plus motion video, animation, and much more.

recorded on each disk in digital format in 2 billion bits. (A bit is represented by the presence or absence of a pit on the optical disk.) With its tremendous storage capacity per square inch, computer industry entrepreneurs immediately recognized the potential of optical laser disk technology. In effect, anything that can be digitized can be stored on optical laser disk: data, text, voice, still pictures, music, graphics, and motion video.

CD-ROM and DVD: The Technology

CD-ROM, a spinoff of audio CD technology, stands for *compact disk–read-only memory.* The name implies its application. Once inserted into the *CD-ROM drive,* the text, video images, and so on can be read into RAM for processing or display. However, the data on the disk are fixed—*they cannot be altered.* This is in contrast, of course, to the read/write capability of magnetic disks.

What makes CD-ROM so inviting is its vast capacity to store data and programs. The capacity of a single CD-ROM is up to 680 MB—about that of 477 diskettes. To put the density of CD-ROM into perspective, the words in every book ever written could be stored on a hypothetical CD-ROM that is 8 feet in diameter.

Magnetic disks store data in concentric tracks, each of which is divided into sectors (see Figure 4.5). The sectors on the inside tracks hold the same amount of information as those on the outside tracks, even though the sectors on the outside tracks take up more space. In contrast, CD-ROMs store data in a single track that spirals from the center to the outside edge (see Figure 4.10). The ultrathin track spirals around the disk thousands of times.

Data are recorded on the CD-ROM's reflective surface in the form of *pits* and *lands.* The pits are tiny reflective bumps that have been burned in with a laser. The lands are flat areas separating the pits. Together they record read-only binary (1s and 0s) information that can be interpreted by the computer as text, audio, images, and so on. Once the data have been recorded, a protective coating is applied to the reflective surface (the nonlabel side of a CD-ROM).

Popular CD-ROM drives are classified simply as 24X, 32X, and 40X. These spin at 24, 32, and 40 times the speed of the original CD standard. The speed at which a given CD-ROM spins depends on the physical location of the data being read. The data pass over the movable laser detector at the same rate, no matter where the data are read. Therefore, the CD-ROM must spin more quickly when accessing data near the center.

The laser detector is analogous to the magnetic disk's read/write head. The relatively slow spin rates make the CD-ROM access time much slower than that of its magnetic cousins. A CD-ROM drive may take 10 to 50 times longer to ready

CD-ROM Organization A laser beam detector interprets pits and lands, which represent bits (1s and 0s), located within the sectors in the spiraling track on the CD-ROM reflective surface.

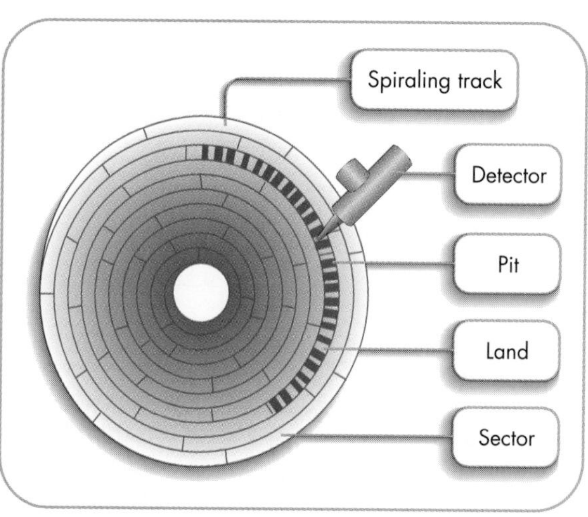

itself to read the information. Once ready to read, the transfer rate also is much slower.

The introduction of *multidisk CD-ROM player/changers* enables ready access to vast amounts of online data. This device is like a CD audio player/changer in that the desired CD-ROM can be loaded to the CD-ROM disk drive under program control. These CD-ROM player/changers, sometimes called **jukeboxes,** can hold from 6 to more than 500 CD-ROMs. The larger jukeboxes have multiple drives so that network users can have simultaneous access to different CD-ROM resources.

Just as CD-ROMs become mainstream equipment, **DVDs** are poised to replace them. The DVD **(digital videodisk)** looks like the CD and the CD-ROM, but it can store from seven to fourteen times as much information (up to about 10 gigabytes). A DVD can store the video for a full-length movie. DVD drives are *backwards compatible;* that is, they can play all of your CD-ROMs and CDs. DVDs probably will replace videotapes and CDs in a few years. Already there is a wide selection of DVD-based movies available at the neighborhood video store.

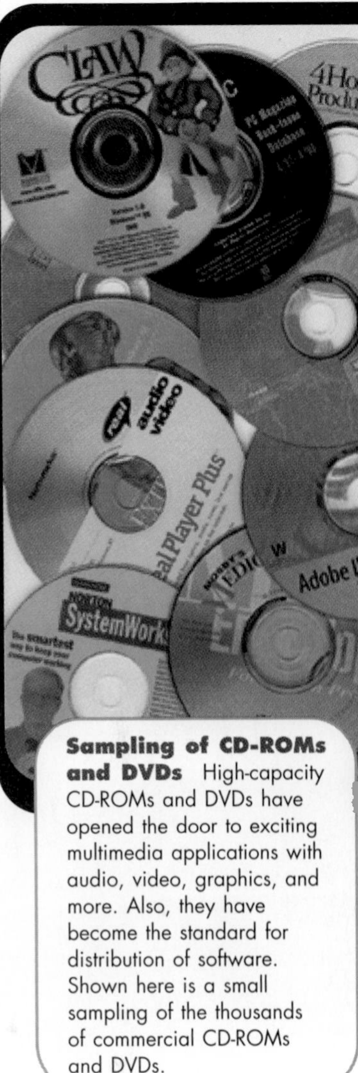

Sampling of CD-ROMs and DVDs High-capacity CD-ROMs and DVDs have opened the door to exciting multimedia applications with audio, video, graphics, and more. Also, they have become the standard for distribution of software. Shown here is a small sampling of the thousands of commercial CD-ROMs and DVDs.

CD-ROM and DVD Applications

The tremendous amount of low-cost direct-access storage made possible by optical laser disks has opened the door to many new applications. The most visible application for CD-ROM is that it has emerged as the media-of-choice for the distribution of software. CD-ROM has the capacity to store massive sound, graphics, motion video, and animation files needed for multimedia applications. Many of the thousands of commercially produced CD-ROM disks contain reference material. The following is a sampling of available CD-ROM disks.

- *The Grolier Multimedia Encyclopedia®* (including text, thousands of still photos, motion video sequences, and sounds)
- *The Oxford English Dictionary*
- *Microsoft® Bookshelf® 98 for Windows* (dictionary, thesaurus, almanac, atlas, book of facts, and more)
- The 1990 U.S. Census (county level)
- The text of 450 titles (including *Moby Dick,* the *King James version of the Bible, Beowulf, The Odyssey,* and many more)
- Multilingual dictionaries (one disk contains translation dictionaries for 12 languages)
- Scientific writings for the Apple Macintosh
- *Microsoft® Cinemania®* (thousands of movie reviews from 1914 to present, actor biographies, movie stills, and more)
- *Great Cities of the World* (narratives, facts, photos, hotel and transportation information)
- Need for Speed™ III (3-D motor car racing game)
- Sound effects (thousands of sound clips)
- The Animals (multimedia zoo with 225 animals)
- World Atlas (thousands of maps and graphs, flags, audio of anthems, and more)
- *Desert Storm: The War in the Persian Gulf* (chronological multimedia presentation)

The cost of commercially produced CD-ROMs varies considerably from as little as a couple of dollars to several thousand dollars. Sales of commercial CD-ROM titles are doubling each year.

Creating CD-ROMs for Mass Distribution

Most CD-ROMs and DVDs are created by commercial enterprises and sold to the public for multimedia applications and reference. Application developers gather and create source material, then write the programs needed to integrate the material into a meaningful application. The resulting files are then sent to a mastering facility. The master copy is duplicated, or "pressed," at the factory, and the copies are distributed with their prerecorded contents (for example, the complete works of Shakespeare or *Gone with the Wind*). Depending on the run quantity, the cost of producing and packaging a CD-ROM for sale can be less than a dollar apiece! CD-ROM is a very inexpensive way to distribute applications and information.

CD-R: Creating CD-ROMs Locally

Most of the world's PCs have CD-ROM drives. This rapid and universal acceptance of CD-ROM has given rise to another technology—**CD-R, compact disk–recordable.** A few years ago, the capability to record on CD-ROM media cost over $100,000 dollars. CD-R, at less than $200, brings that capability into small businesses and homes.

Locally produced CD-R disks, which will play in any CD-ROM drive, are created on CD writers. **CD writers** are peripheral devices that can write once to a CD-R disk to create an audio CD or a CD-ROM. CD writers offer a low-cost alternative to the mastering of CD-ROMs. For a few hundred dollars, commercial enterprises can expand the capabilities of a PC to create one-of-a-kind CDs or CD-ROMs at a fraction of the cost of low-volume pressed disk manufacturing. A growing number of organizations are using CD-R and CD writers to create their own CD-ROMs. These are used primarily for internal reference applications and for archiving. Already there is a trend among manufacturing companies to replace their printed sales manuals with CD-ROM–based manuals. Sales manuals, which can span thousands of pages, are compressed to a single CD-ROM that can be easily updated each quarter. Relatively inexpensive low-volume **CD production stations** are used to duplicate locally produced CD-ROMs.

First the CD-ROM, Then CD-R, Now CD-RW

People are still celebrating the arrival of CD-R and a new CD technology is introduced—**CD-ReWritable (CD-RW).** This technology goes one step further, allowing users to rewrite to the same CD media, just as is done on magnetic disk media. The manufacturers believe that the new CD-RW will replace the CD-ROM drives that are currently installed on most new PCs. With the cost of CD-R and CD-RW technologies converging, CD-R may disappear as people opt to pay a few dollars more for rewritable capability.

Writable CD-ROM The HP SureStore CD-Writer 4020i is an internal compact disk record-once system that comes with a complete software suite for creating custom CDs, along with the necessary media, cards, and cables to begin recording immediately.
Photo courtesy of Hewlett-Packard Company

High Capacity CD-ROM This researcher at Merck's Clinical & Regulatory Development (CARD) department displays a CD-ROM. A four-inch stack of these CD-ROMs can store printed documentation that, if stacked, would be 2.5 times the height of the World Trade Center. CARD is supporting the use of the electronic medium as a means of both a faster delivery and review of its drug submissions to regulatory agencies and as a better use of Merck resources. Courtesy of Merck & Co., Inc.

WORM Disks

Write once, read many optical laser disks, or **WORM disks,** are used by end user companies to store their own proprietary information. As with CD-ROMs, once the data have been written to the medium, they can only be read, not updated or changed. **WORM disk cartridges** can store greater volumes of information than can a CD-ROM. Typically, WORM applications involve image processing or archival storage. A single mainframe-based 200-gigabyte (GB) WORM disk can store more than 3 million digitized images the size of this page. A good example of an image processing application is an "electronic catalog." The retailer digitizes images of items for sale and stores these images for ready access on WORM disks. A customer can see the item while reading about it when perusing a retailer's Internet-based electronic catalog. And, with a few keystrokes, the customer can order the item as well. The Library of Congress is using WORM technology to help alleviate a serious shelf-space problem and to make more material available over the Internet.

What's the Best Mix of Storage Options?

The choice of which technologies to choose for a system or an application is often a trade-off between storage capacity, cost (dollars per megabyte), and speed (access time). You can never really compare apples to apples when comparing storage media because one might have an advantage in access time, portability, random access, nonvolatility, and so on. Solid-state storage (RAM) is the fastest and most expensive (about $1 per MB), but it's volatile. You can get 1 MB of storage for a fraction of a penny with interchangeable CD-ROM, but it is read-only and slow. Hard disk offers fast, permanent storage for about $.10 per MB. A well-designed system will have a mix of storage options. Each time you purchase a PC, you should spend a little extra time assessing your application needs so you can configure your system with an optimum mix of storage options.

MEMORY

Optical Laser Disk Technology

- CD-ROM (read only)
- DVD (digital videodisk)
- CD-R (recordable)
- CD-RW (ReWritable)
- WORM disks (write once, read many)

SECTION SELF-CHECK

Self-Check

- **4-4.1** CD-ROM is a spinoff of audio CD technology. (T/F)
- **4-4.2** CD-ROM is read-only. (T/F)
- **4-4.3** CD writers are peripheral devices that can write once to a hard disk. (T/F)
- **4-4.4** CD-ROM stores data in spiraling tracks. (T/F)
- **4-4.5** Jukebox refers to a player/changers that can handle multiple CD-ROMs. (T/F)
- **4-4.6** A WORM disk cartridge has less capacity than a CD-ROM. (T/F)
- **4-4.7** CD-RW technology is: (a) rewritable, (b) read-only, (c) write-only, or (d) non-writable?
- **4-4.8** The CD-ROM drive specifications 24X, 32X, and 40X refer to its: (a) speed, (b) diameter, (c) number of platters, or (d) sector groupings?
- **4-4.9** Which of these is poised to replace the CD-ROM: (a) VVV, (b) jukebox, (c) CD-R, or (d) DVD?

4.5 STORAGE FORECAST: IS THERE A DISK IN YOUR FUTURE?

Storage is like money: No matter how much you have, you always want more. Each year, improvements are made in existing mass storage devices as the storage industry strives to meet our craving for more storage.

Some scientists believe that holographic technology may give users everything they want in a storage device. Holographic memory systems enable the stacking of data on the recording surface. The different layers are read by changing the angle of the laser beam used for reading the data. Holographic memory systems will enable the entire *Encyclopedia Britannica* to be stored in a space the size and thickness of a penny.

Rotating storage media may go the way of the steam engine when low-cost solid-state memory (RAM) can store as much in less space. If nonvolatile chip technology continues to improve at the current pace, the entire *Encyclopedia Britannica* will fit into 8 tiny memory chips in the near future. Already, flash memory chips are being developed that will have 16 times more storage capacity than the largest flash chips currently available. The 30 MB flash memory chips could be used in place of hard drives in portable PCs. Perhaps someday the only moving parts on PCs will be the cooling fan. If 1 GB flash memory chips emerge as predicted within a few years, then rotating storage may very quickly be relegated to archival storage.

Interactive Study Guide Chapter 4

What does being able to store more information in less space mean to you? It means videophones that can be worn like wristwatches. It means that you can carry a diskette-sized reader and all your college "textbooks" in your front pocket. We can expect at least one big leap in storage technology within a couple of years. That leap will forever change much of what we do and how we do it.

SECTION SELF-CHECK

Self-Check

- **4-5.1** Holographic memory systems enable the stacking of data on the recording surface. (T/F)
- **4-5.2** Rotating storage media are the newest rave in storage. (T/F)
- **4-5.3** In the future, hard disks might be replaced by which of these in laptop PCs: (a) flashbulbs, (b) flash memory, (c) SDRAM, or (d) CD-R?

4.1 Mass storage and files

Data and programs are stored in **mass storage** (116) for permanent storage. **Magnetic disk drives** (116) and **magnetic tape drives** (116) are popular devices for mass storage. **Optical laser disk** (116) technology is emerging as an alternative to magnetic disks and magnetic tapes.

The **file** (116) is the foundation of permanent storage on a computer system. Filenames in the Windows environment can include spaces, but some special characters are not permitted. An optional three-character extension identifies the type of file (for example, *myphoto.gif* is a graphics file). Popular file types include the **ASCII file** (117) (txt), **data file** (117) (mdb for Access), **document file** (117) (doc for Word), **spreadsheet file** (117) (xls for Excel), **Web page file** (117) (htm), **source program file** (117) (vbp for Visual Basic), **executable program file** (117) (exe), **graphics file** (117) (gif, bmp, jpg, wmf, and pcx), **audio file** (117) (wav), and **video file** (117) (mov).

Everything we do on a computer has to do with a file and, therefore, mass storage. We can create, name, save, copy, move, delete, retrieve, update, display, print, play, execute, download, upload, export, import, compress, and protect files. **File compression** (118) is used to economize on storage space.

4.2 Magnetic disks

Data are retrieved and manipulated either sequentially or randomly. There are two types of magnetic disk: **interchangeable magnetic disks** (119) and **fixed magnetic disks** (119). Magnetic disk drives enable random- and sequential-processing capabilities.

Popular types of interchangeable magnetic disks include the 3.5-inch diskette, also called a floppy disk, the 120 MB **SuperDisk** (121), and the 100 MB **Zip disk** (121), which is inserted into a **Zip drive** (121). The floppy disk and SuperDisk are the same size but have different **disk densities** (121).

Permanently installed hard disks contain several disk platters stacked on a single rotating spindle. The rotation of a magnetic disk passes all data under or over **read/write heads** (122), which are mounted on **access arms** (122). The **Jaz drive** (122) uses an interchangeable **Jaz cartridge** (122).

The way in which data and programs are stored and accessed is similar for both hard and interchangeable disks. Data are stored via serial representation in concentric **tracks** (123) on each recording surface. The spacing of tracks is measured in **tracks per inch (TPI)** (124). In **sector organization** (124), the recording surface is divided into pie-shaped **sectors** (124), and each sector is assigned a number. Adjacent sectors are combined to form **clusters** (124).

Each disk cluster is numbered and the number of the first cluster in a file comprises the **disk address** (124) on a particular file. The disk address designates a file's physical location on a disk. A particular **cylinder** (124) refers to every track with the same number on all recording surfaces.

Each disk used in the Windows environment has a **Virtual File Allocation Table (VFAT)** (124) in which information about the clusters is stored. Clusters are *chained* together to store file information larger than the capacity of a single cluster. The **defragmentation** (125) process rewrites fragmented files into contiguous clusters.

Before a disk can be used, it must be **formatted** (125). Formatting creates *sectors* and *tracks* into which data are stored and establishes an area for the VFAT.

The **access time** (127) for a magnetic disk is the interval between the instant a computer makes a request for transfer of data from a disk-storage device to RAM and the instant this operation is completed.

The **data transfer rate** (127) is the rate at which data are read from (written to) mass storage to (from) RAM. **Disk caching** (127) improves system speed.

Apply the dictates of common sense to the care of diskettes (avoid excessive dust, avoid extremes in temperature and humidity, and so on).

A **computer virus** (128) is a program that "infects" other programs and databases upon contact. Three primary sources of computer viruses are the Internet, diskettes, and computer networks. Antiviral programs, also called vaccines, exist to help fight viruses.

4.3 Backup: Better safe than sorry

Today, magnetic tape storage, which is sequential access only, is no longer used for routine processing; however, it has three other important functions. It is used for backup, for archiving files, and for file portability between computers.

Magnetic tape drives are called **tape backup units (TBUs)** (131). They use a $\frac{1}{4}$-inch cartridge (QIC), also called a **data cartridge** (131). Three common backup methods for TBUs are full backup, selective backup of files, or backup of modified files only. If you do not have a TBU, then you will need to back up your files to diskettes, available on every PC, or to SuperDisks or Zip disks. The frequency with which files are backed up depends on their volatility. It is common practice to maintain two generations of backup when rotating backup among interchangeable disks.

4.4 Optical laser disks: High-density storage

Optical laser disk storage is capable of storing vast amounts of data. The main categories of optical laser disks are CD-ROM and DVD, CD-R, CD-RW, and WORM disks.

A CD-ROM is inserted into the CD-ROM drive for processing. Most of the commercially produced read-only CD-ROM disks contain reference material or support multimedia applications. Multidisk player/changers are called **jukeboxes** (139).

The **DVD (digital videodisk)** (139) looks like the CD and the CD-ROM, but it can store up to about 10 gigabytes. DVD drives can play CD-ROMs and CDs.

A blank **compact disk-recordable (CD-R)** (140) disk looks like a CD-ROM and once information is recorded on it, it works like a CD-ROM. Locally produced CD-R disks are created on **CD writers** (140). Relatively inexpensive low-volume **CD production stations** (140) are used to duplicate locally produced CD-ROMs. **CD-ReWritable (CD-RW)** (140) allows users to rewrite to the same CD media.

WORM disks (141) are used by end user companies to store their own proprietary information. **WORM disk cartridges** (141) can store greater volumes of information than can a CD-ROM. WORM applications involve image processing or archival storage.

The choice of which technologies to choose for a system or an application is often a trade-off between storage capacity and cost (dollars per megabyte).

4.5 Storage forecast: Is there a disk in your future?

Each year, improvements are made in existing mass storage devices as the storage industry strives to meet our craving for more storage.

DISCUSSION AND PROBLEM SOLVING

4.1 **a.** Describe seven personal activities that might result in information being read from or written to magnetic disk (for example, buying a candy bar at Wal-Mart).

b. Name and briefly describe applications for four different types of files.

c. Describe file compression and why and how it might be used.

4.2 **a.** Traditionally personal computers have had a floppy disk drive. However, some recent personal computers no longer come with a floppy drive. Is the floppy drive needed anymore? Explain.

b. A program issues a "read" command for data to be retrieved from hard disk. Describe the resulting mechanical movement and the movement of data.

c. What happens during formatting? Why must hard disks and diskettes be formatted?

d. List six content areas that are distributed commercially on CD-ROM (for example, electronic encyclopedias).

e. What name is given to programs intended to damage the computer system of an unsuspecting victim? Name three sources of these. What would be appropriate punishment for the originator of a virus that destroyed the user files of thousands of people?

f. A floppy disk does not move until a read or write command is issued. Once it is issued, the floppy begins to spin. It stops spinning after the command is executed. Why is a hard disk not set in motion in the same manner? Why is a floppy not made to spin continuously?

g. The SuperDisk and Zip disk serve similar purposes on a computer system. The SuperDisk drive is compatible with the traditional floppy diskette, but the Zip disk reads and writes data more rapidly. Costs are comparable. Which one would you choose and why?

h. What would determine the frequency with which you would need to defragment your hard drive? Explain.

4.3 **a.** Describe how a tape backup unit might be used in a small company with a local area network serving 28 users.

b. Every Friday night a company makes backup copies of all master files and programs (over 8 GB). Why is this necessary? The company has both tape and disk drives. Which storage medium would you suggest for the backup? Why?

c. How many diskettes would you need to do a daily backup of the files (2 MB total) you created for a college course?

4.4 **a.** Describe the potential impact of optical laser disk technology on public and university libraries. On home libraries.

b. Describe at least two applications where CD-ReWritable would be preferred over hard disk for storage.

c. The DVD drive is compatible with CD-ROM. Currently the DVD drive is more expensive than CD-ROM, but prices are converging. Speculate on when or if DVD will replace CD-ROM.

4.5 The only internal mechanical movement in a typical laptop PC is associated with the disk and CD-ROM drives. Someday soon both may be replaced with solid-state nonvolatile memory. Speculate on how this might change how we use and what we do with laptop PCs.

Information Input and Output

Learning Objectives

5.1 Recognize the role played by input/output devices in our lives.

5.2 Explain alternative approaches to and devices for providing input to a system.

5.3 Describe methods and devices used for source-data automation.

5.4 Describe the operation and application of common output devices.

5.5 Describe the use and characteristics of the different types of terminals.

chapter 

Value Learning

WHY THIS CHAPTER IS IMPORTANT TO YOU

When PCs arrived as a viable consumer product in the late 1970s, choices for input were limited. Input was mostly via the standard QWERTY keyboard. Output was a 14-inch low-resolution monitor, printer A or B, and a tinny little speaker that made annoying sounds when you tapped the wrong key. Now we've got ergonomic keyboards or, if you prefer, speech recognition that lets you talk to your PCs. Monitors come in a jillion different shapes, sizes, and qualities. Near-photo-quality color printers are common in the home.

There's an endless array of input/output devices you can connect to a PC for what seems to be an infinite number of applications. You can scan in photographs. You can capture real-time video images from your camcorder. You can enter the TV signal directly to your PC for recording or viewing. An innovative input device can even give PCs a sense of smell. New and exciting I/O devices are being announced every month.

Today, you are the person who makes the decisions about which input/output devices you hang on your PC. If you have a good grasp of the depth and breadth of available input/output devices, you will be able to take full advantage of your PC system. Did you know the mouse is but one of many options for point-and-draw devices? Did you know you could enjoy videophone conversations with your friends across town or around the world? Did you know you would need OCR software if you wish to use your scanner to scan in text from printed documents? Did you know that carefully selected I/O options, such as ergonomic keyboards and speech-recognition software, could reduce neuromuscular problems associated with entering data to a computer? The knowledge you gain from this chapter should prove helpful when it comes time to configure and purchase a PC.

It's surprisingly easy to foul up when purchasing peripheral I/O devices. Perhaps an off-brand printer doesn't work well with your PC. The speakers don't work without the optional AC adapter. The scanner is monochrome and won't give your spouse the color she needs for the family newsletter. The system's video board doesn't meet the minimum requirements for the kids' game software. You bought a headset that isn't compatible with your speech-recognition software. You get a $500 color printer on clearance for $400 only to learn that the new feature-rich model sells for $295! The warranty on your broken video camera doesn't cover labor after 30 days.

When it comes to buying a PC or related hardware, you're generally on your own. Realistically, you can't depend on salespeople or friends to make these important monetary decisions for you. This and the previous two chapters should help you get the biggest bang for your PC buck.

5.1 I/O DEVICES: LET'S INTERFACE

Monthly Technology Update Chapter 5

Just about everyone routinely communicates directly or indirectly with a computer, even people who have never sat in front of a PC. Perhaps you have had one of these experiences.

- Have you ever been hungry and short of cash? No problem. Just stop at an automatic teller machine (ATM) and ask for some "lunch money." The ATM's keyboard and monitor enable you to hold an interactive conversation with the bank's computer. The ATM's printer provides you with a hard copy of your transactions when you leave. Some ATMs talk to you as well.
- Have you ever called a mail-order merchandiser and been greeted by a message like this: "Thank you for calling BrassCo Enterprises Customer Service. If you wish to place an order, press one. If you wish to inquire about the status of an order, press two. To speak to a particular person, enter that person's four-digit extension or hold and an operator will process your call momentarily." The message is produced by a computer-based voice-response system, which responds to the buttons you press on your telephone keypad.

We communicate with these computers through input/output devices. *Input devices* translate our data and communications into a form that the computer can

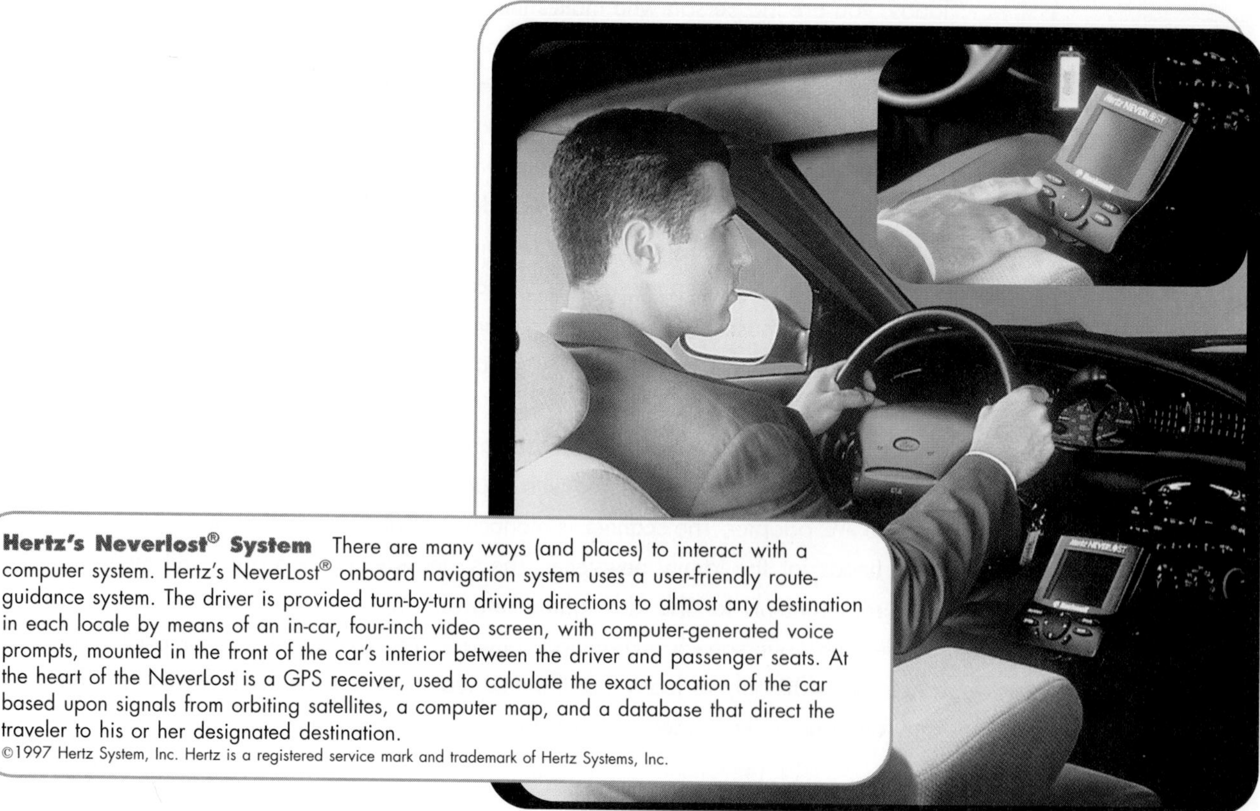

Hertz's Neverlost® System There are many ways (and places) to interact with a computer system. Hertz's NeverLost® onboard navigation system uses a user-friendly route-guidance system. The driver is provided turn-by-turn driving directions to almost any destination in each locale by means of an in-car, four-inch video screen, with computer-generated voice prompts, mounted in the front of the car's interior between the driver and passenger seats. At the heart of the NeverLost is a GPS receiver, used to calculate the exact location of the car based upon signals from orbiting satellites, a computer map, and a database that direct the traveler to his or her designated destination.

understand. The computer then processes these data, and an *output device* translates them back into a form we can understand. In our two examples, the ATM's keyboard and monitor and the telephone keypad serve as input devices, and the ATM's monitor and printer and the voice-response system serve as output devices.

Input/output devices are quietly playing an increasingly significant role in our lives. The number and variety of I/O devices are expanding even as you read this, and some of these devices are fairly exotic. For example, AromaScan markets an electronic nose that can measure and digitally record smells. Perhaps the AromaScan smelling device may revolutionize aroma analysis in the food, drink, and perfume industries and enable better environmental monitoring. However, its cost, about that of a BMW, may force us to do our sniffing around the house the old-fashioned way.

SECTION SELF-CHECK

Self-Check

5-1.1 Input devices translate data into a form that can be interpreted by a computer. (T/F)

5-1.2 The primary function of I/O peripherals is to facilitate computer-to-computer data transmission. (T/F)

5-1.3 An ATM's input/output capabilities are: (a) input only, (b) output only, (c) both input and output, or (d) customer input only?

5.2 TRADITIONAL INPUT DEVICES

The primary input devices found on all PCs, workstations, and many terminals are the *keyboard* and a *point-and-draw device.*

The Keyboard

The most common device for transferring user input to the computer system is the keyboard. There are two basic types of keyboards: alphanumeric keyboards and special-function keyboards.

Traditional Alphanumeric Keyboards

The *keyboard* remains the primary input for entering data and issuing commands. One of the most widely used keyboards is the 101-key keyboard with the traditional *QWERTY* (the first five letters on the third row) key layout, 12 function keys, a numeric keypad, a variety of special-function keys, and dedicated cursor-control keys (see Figure 5.1). PC, workstation, and terminal keyboards vary considerably in appearance. Portable computers have a simple QWERTY keyboard with a minimum number of special-function keys. Desktop computers frequently are configured with a 124-key PC keyboard that includes an extended set of function keys and extra unlabeled keys that can be programmed to perform user-defined keystroke sequences (macros) when tapped. When tapped, the keyboard's **function keys** trigger the execution of some type of software activity. For example, HELP (context-sensitive user assistance) is often assigned to F1 (Function Key 1). Function keys are numbered and assigned different functions in different software packages.

The cursor-control keys, or "arrow" keys, can be used to select options from a **menu,** which is simply a list of options for the user. These keys also allow you to move the **text cursor** *up* (↑) and *down* (↓), usually a line at a time, and *left* (←) and *right* (→), usually a character at a time. The text cursor always shows the location of where the next keyed-in character will appear on the screen. The text cursor can appear as several shapes depending on the application, but frequently you will encounter a blinking vertical line (|). Other important keys common to most keyboards are illustrated and described in Figure 5.1.

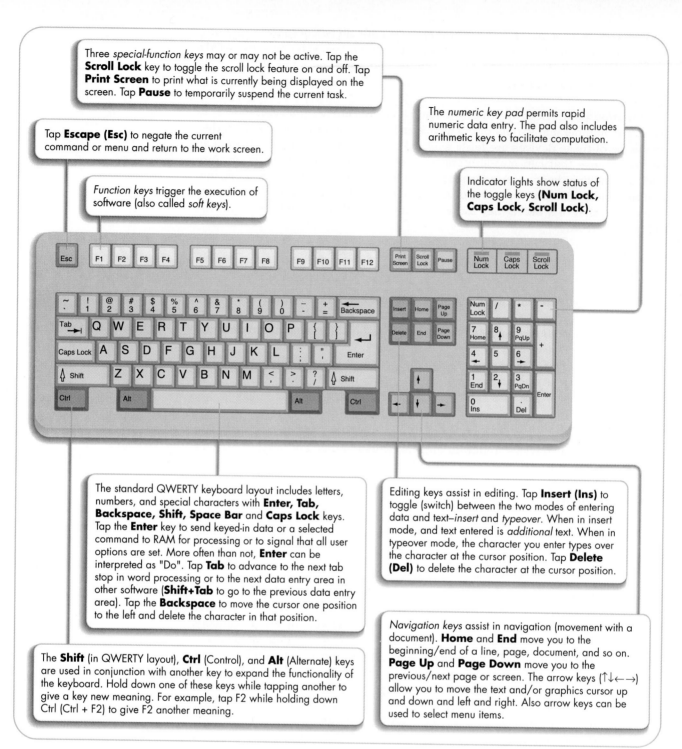

Three *special-function keys* may or may not be active. Tap the **Scroll Lock** key to toggle the scroll lock feature on and off. Tap **Print Screen** to print what is currently being displayed on the screen. Tap **Pause** to temporarily suspend the current task.

Tap **Escape (Esc)** to negate the current command or menu and return to the work screen.

Function keys trigger the execution of software (also called *soft keys*).

The *numeric key pad* permits rapid numeric data entry. The pad also includes arithmetic keys to facilitate computation.

Indicator lights show status of the toggle keys **(Num Lock, Caps Lock, Scroll Lock)**.

The standard QWERTY keyboard layout includes letters, numbers, and special characters with **Enter, Tab, Backspace, Shift, Space Bar** and **Caps Lock** keys. Tap the **Enter** key to send keyed-in data or a selected command to RAM for processing or to signal that all user options are set. More often than not, **Enter** can be interpreted as "Do". Tap **Tab** to advance to the next tab stop in word processing or to the next data entry area in other software (**Shift+Tab** to go to the previous data entry area). Tap the **Backspace** to move the cursor one position to the left and delete the character in that position.

Editing keys assist in editing. Tap **Insert (Ins)** to toggle (switch) between the two modes of entering data and text–*insert* and *typeover*. When in insert mode, and text entered is *additional* text. When in typeover mode, the character you enter types over the character at the cursor position. Tap **Delete (Del)** to delete the character at the cursor position.

The **Shift** (in QWERTY layout), **Ctrl** (Control), and **Alt** (Alternate) keys are used in conjunction with another key to expand the functionality of the keyboard. Hold down one of these keys while tapping another to give a key new meaning. For example, tap F2 while holding down Ctrl (Ctrl + F2) to give F2 another meaning.

Navigation keys assist in navigation (movement with a document). **Home** and **End** move you to the beginning/end of a line, page, document, and so on. **Page Up** and **Page Down** move you to the previous/next page or screen. The arrow keys (↑↓←→) allow you to move the text and/or graphics cursor up and down and left and right. Also arrow keys can be used to select menu items.

A Representative PC Keyboard

Special-Function Keyboards: Tap the French Fry Key

Some keyboards are designed for specific applications. For example, the cash-register-like terminals at most fast-food restaurants have special-purpose keyboards. Rather than key in the name and price of an order of French fries, attendants need only press the key marked "French fries" to record the sale. Such keyboards help shop supervisors, airline ticket agents, retail sales clerks, and many others interact more quickly with their computer systems.

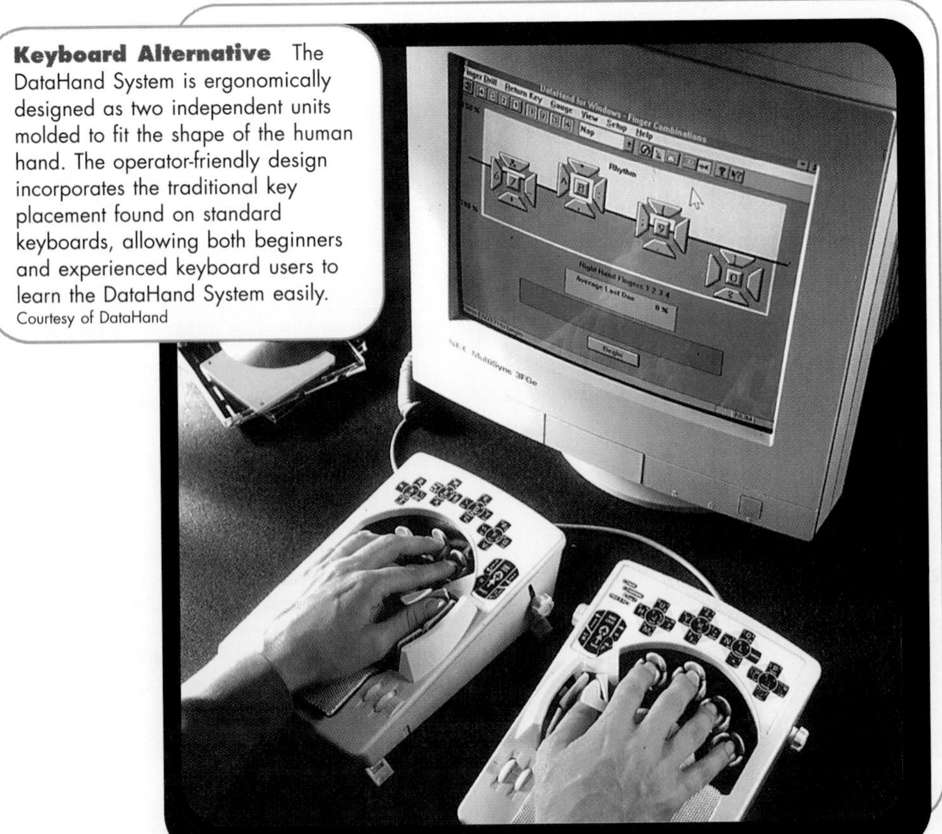

Keyboard Alternative The DataHand System is ergonomically designed as two independent units molded to fit the shape of the human hand. The operator-friendly design incorporates the traditional key placement found on standard keyboards, allowing both beginners and experienced keyboard users to learn the DataHand System easily.
Courtesy of DataHand

Point-and-Draw Devices

The keyboard is too cumbersome for some applications, especially those that rely on a graphical user interface (GUI) or require the user to point or draw. Interaction with all Windows 9x/NT/2000 operating systems is via a **graphical user interface (GUI).** The user-friendly GUI lets you *point and click* with the mouse to navigate between and within programs and to issue commands. The effectiveness of GUIs depends on the user's ability to make a rapid selection from a screen full of menus or graphic icons (each of which represents a program or user option). In these instances a point-and-draw device, such as a mouse, can be used to *point* to and select (click) a particular user option quickly and efficiently. Also, such devices can be used to *draw.* For example, computer artists use mice to create images.

The handheld mouse, or something like it, is a must-have item on any PC or workstation. When the mouse is moved across a desktop, the **mouse cursor** on the display moves accordingly. The mouse cursor can be positioned anywhere on the screen. It is displayed as a bracket ([), an arrow (→), a crosshair (+), or a variety of other symbols (for example, %), depending on the current application and its position on the screen. The text and mouse cursors may be displayed on the screen at the same time in some programs, such as word processing. The mouse is either attached to the computer by a cable (the mouse's "tail") or linked via a wireless connection (either infrared or radio wave).

Mice and other point-and-draw devices have one or more buttons. The Macintosh mouse has one button, and the PC-compatible mouse normally has a left and right button (see Figure 5.2). The **wheel mouse** also has "wheel" to facilitate scrolling. You tap, or **click,** the left button (left click) to select a menu item or a program represented by an icon. The function of the right button (right click) varies between software packages, but often it is used to call up a menu of

The graphics cursor, or pointer, is initially at Position 1 on the display screen. The artist moves the mouse up (toward monitor) to position the pointer over the image to be moved (Position 2).

The artist clicks (taps the left mouse button) on the sun image to highlight the area containing the sun image (rectangular box).

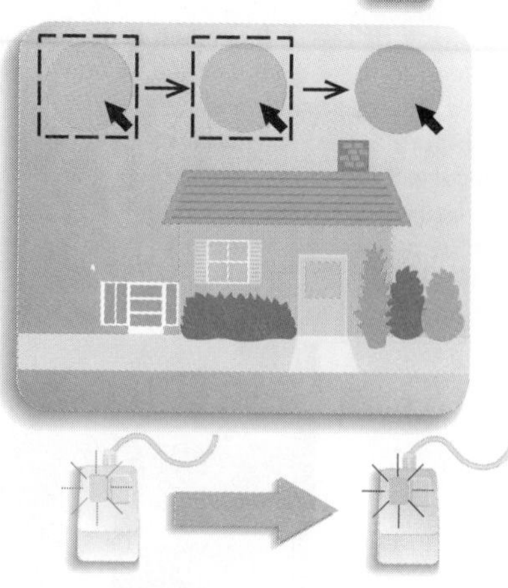

The artist drags the image to the desired location (Position 3) by pressing and holding the mouse's left button and moving the mouse. The artist releases the button to complete the drag operation.

The Mouse and the Mouse Cursor In the example, a computer artist repositions the mouse cursor on the sun, and then moves the sun image from the left to the right side of the screen.

options germane to the current activity. A **double-click,** which is tapping a button twice in rapid succession, gives each button a different meaning.

Press and hold a button to **drag** the mouse cursor across the screen. When using a graphics software program, you drag the mouse cursor across the screen to create the image. When using a word processing program, you highlight a block of text by dragging the mouse cursor from the beginning to the end of the text block. In a GUI, you can point to an object, perhaps an icon, then drag (move) it to a new position. Click and drag operations are demonstrated in Figure 5.2 within the context of a graphics software package. In the example, a computer artist uses a mouse to reposition the sun in the drawing.

For the moment, the mouse remains the most popular point-and-draw device. However, a variety of devices are available that move the mouse cursor to point and draw, and each has its advantages and disadvantages. Here are a few of the more popular ones (see Figure 5.3).

- *Trackball.* The **trackball** is a ball inset in a small external box or adjacent to and in the same unit as the keyboard. The ball is "rolled" with the fingers to move the mouse cursor. Some people find it helpful to think of a trackball as an upside-down mouse with a bigger ball on the bottom.
- *Trackpad.* The **trackpad** has no moving parts. Simply move your finger about a small touch-sensitive pad to move the mouse cursor.
- *Trackpoint.* **Trackpoints** usually are positioned in or near a laptop's keyboard. They function like miniature joysticks but are operated with the tip of the finger.
- *Digitizer tablet and pen.* The **digitizer tablet and pen** is a pen and a touch-sensitive tablet whose *X–Y* coordinates correspond with those on the computer's display screen. Some digitizing tablets also use a crosshair device instead of a pen.
- *Joystick.* The **joystick** is a vertical stick that moves the mouse cursor in the direction the stick is pushed. Video arcade wizards are no doubt familiar with the joystick, which is used mostly for gaming.

Point-and-Draw Devices

Trackpad This laptop PC is equipped with a trackpad that allows you to move the cursor with the tip of your finger, as well as a disk drive that is compatible with the SuperDisk and the floppy. Photo courtesy of Imation Corporation

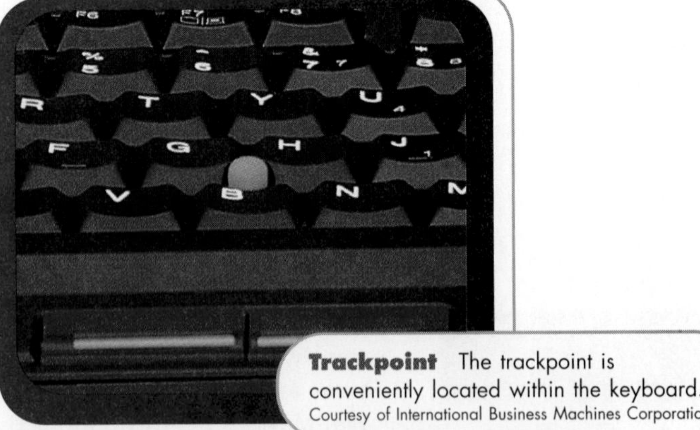

Trackpoint The trackpoint is conveniently located within the keyboard. Courtesy of International Business Machines Corporation

Trackball This Canon notebook PC comes with a trackball. Courtesy of Canon Computer Systems, Inc.

Pen with Touch-Sensitive Display The ViA II, shown here, is a full-function wearable PC (only 22 oz.). This man is using a pen with the PC's touch-sensitive display to enter information. It provides input via speech recognition as well. Courtesy of ViA, Inc.

Digitizer Tablet and Pen The digitizer tablet and pen is used by artists. Courtesy Houston Instrument Div. AMETEK, Inc.

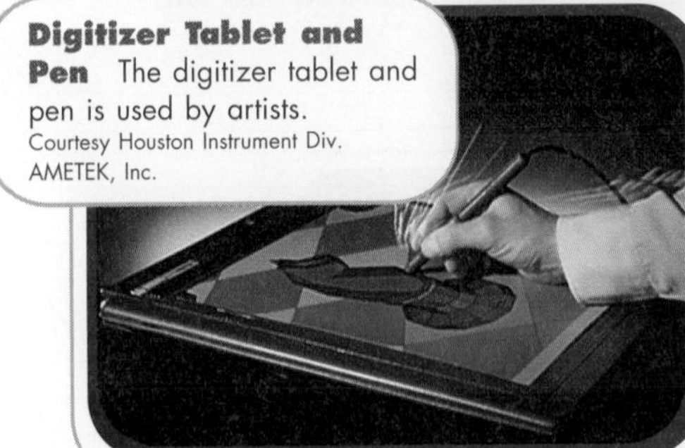

Joystick and Game Pad The Thrustmaster XFighter (joystick) and the Gravis Stinger (game pad) are designed specifically for PC action games and flight simulation programs. They move airplanes, aliens, and monsters, as well as cursors. Courtesy of Thrustmaster/Courtesy of Advanced Gravis Computer Technology Ltd.

SECTION SELF-CHECK

Self-Check

5-2.1 Use the keyboard's keypad for rapid numeric data entry. (T/F)

5-2.2 The wheel on the wheel mouse makes it easier to drag icons. (T/F)

5-2.3 Only those keyboards configured with laptop PCs have function keys. (T/F)

5-2.4 To drag the mouse cursor across the screen: (a) press and hold a mouse button, (b) click once then hold a mouse button, (c) simultaneously click both buttons, or (d) tap and click the buttons alternately?

5-2.5 Which of the following is not a point-and-draw device: (a) joystick, (b) document scanner, (c) trackpad, or (c) trackpoint?

5-2.6 User interaction with the Windows 2000 operating systems is via a: (a) GUI, (b) Gooie, (c) mouse interface, or (d) user-friendly menu?

5.3 SOURCE-DATA AUTOMATION

Input

The trend in data entry has been toward entering data more quickly and efficiently. As a result, more people are entering data as close to the source as possible and, if possible, when the transaction occurs. For example, each sale at Wal-Mart stores throughout the world is recorded immediately, keeping sales and inventory information up to the minute.

Today, inefficient key-driven data entry is being eliminated whenever possible. In the push toward speed and efficiency, data entry is relying more on **source-data automation.** For example, the preprinted **bar codes** on consumer products have eliminated the need for most key entry at checkout counters. Checkers need only pass the product over the *laser scanner.* The price is entered into the store's computer system, and the shelf inventory is updated as well.

Data entry is an area in which enormous potential exists for increases in productivity. The technology of data entry devices is constantly changing. New and improved methods of transcribing raw data are being invented and put on the market each month. Scanner technology has spawned an explosion of source-data automation applications. One of the more innovative applications of source-data automation is along toll roads. Frequent users of toll roads in a particular region (for example, Oklahoma) pay tolls in advance and receive electronic labels for their cars. Scanners along the toll road read these labels as cars pass at highway speeds. The electronic toll booths transmit the data directly to a central computer system. At the central site, the drivers' accounts are debited the amount of the toll.

Source-Data Automation in Retail Retailers have worked hard to create information systems and automate the checkout process. The portable Shopping System™ uses a hand-held scanner. Customers pick up the Portable Shopper when entering the store and use it to scan and tally their purchases while shopping. As customers finish shopping, they return their scanner to the rack, where they receive an automatically dispensed barcoded ticket. With ticket in hand, they proceed to an express checkout station where the cashier scans the ticket and accepts any coupons. Customers pay as usual, receive their receipt and are on their way. Courtesy of Symbol Technologies, Inc.

Scanners

A variety of **scanners** read and interpret information on printed matter and convert it to a format that can be stored and/or interpreted by a computer. For example, you are probably familiar with one of the oldest scanner technologies, optical mark scanners. These scanners scan preprinted multiple-choice test answer forms, comparing the position of the "sense marks" with a master to grade the test.

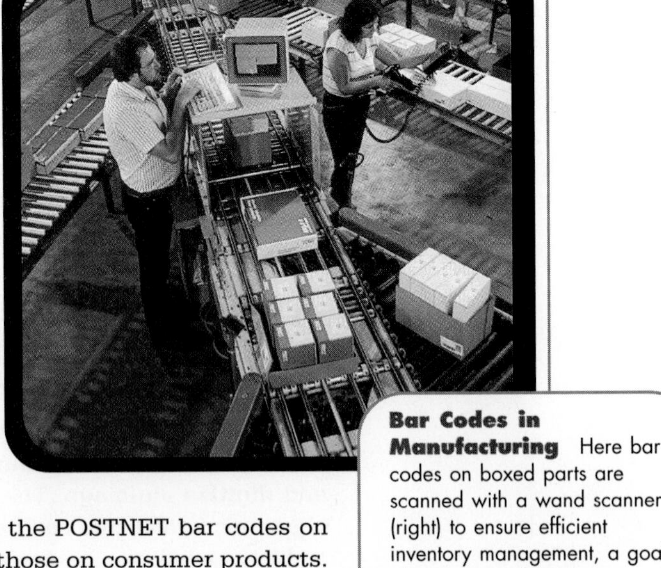

Bar Codes in Manufacturing Here bar codes on boxed parts are scanned with a wand scanner (right) to ensure efficient inventory management, a goal of every manufacturing company. Courtesy TRW, Inc.

OCR and Bar Codes

OCR (optical character recognition) is the ability of scanners to read text information into a computer system. This ability includes reading your handwriting, as well. More commonly, scanners read bar codes. Bar codes represent alphanumeric data by varying the size of adjacent vertical lines. There are a variety of bar-coding systems. Compare the POSTNET bar codes on metered mail with those on packing labels and with those on consumer products. One of the most visible bar-coding systems is the Universal Product Code (UPC). The UPC, originally used for supermarket items, is now being printed on other consumer goods.

The United States Postal Service relies on both OCR and bar code scanning to sort most mail. At the Postal Service, light-sensitive scanners read and interpret the ZIP code and POSTNET bar code on billions of envelopes each day. The ZIP information is then sent to computer-based sorting machines that route the envelopes to appropriate bins for distribution.

Are there advantages to using OCR over bar codes or bar codes over OCR? The advantage of bar codes over OCR is that the position or orientation of the code being read is not as critical to the scanner. In a supermarket, for example, the UPC can be recorded even when a bottle of ketchup is rolled over the laser scanner.

OCR and Bar Code Scanners and Applications

Two types of OCR and bar code scanners—*contact* and *laser*—read information on labels and various types of documents. Both bounce a beam of light off an image, then measure the reflected light to interpret the image. Handheld contact scanners make contact as they are brushed over the printed matter to be read. Laser-based scanners are more versatile and can read data passed near the scanning area. Scanners of both technologies can recognize printed characters and various types of bar codes. Scanners used for OCR or bar code applications can be classified into three basic categories.

Stationary Laser Scanners Supermarket checkout systems are now an established cost-saving technology. The automated systems use stationary laser scanners to read the bar codes that identify each item. Price and product descriptions are retrieved from a database and recorded on the sales slip. Courtesy of International Business Machines Corporation

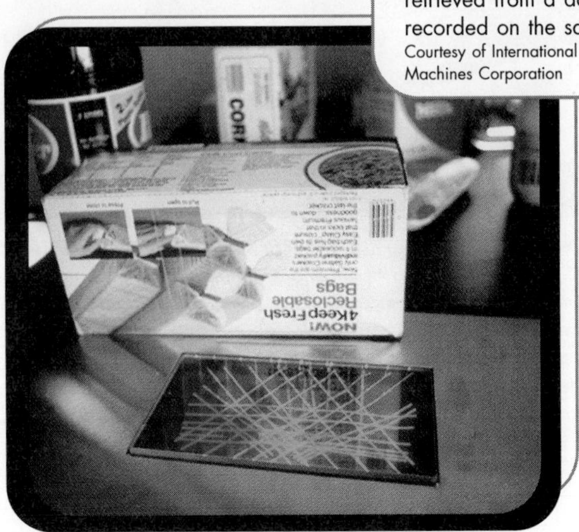

- *Handheld label scanners.* These devices read data on price tags, shipping labels, inventory part numbers, book ISBNs, and the like. Handheld label scanners, sometimes called **wand scanners,** use either contact or laser technology. You have probably seen both types used in libraries and various retail stores. Wand scanners also are used to read package labels in shipping and receiving and in inventory management.
- *Stationary label scanners.* These devices, which rely exclusively on laser technology, are used in the same types of applications as wand scanners. Stationary scanners are common in grocery stores and discount stores.

- *Document scanners.* Document scanners are capable of scanning documents of varying sizes. Document scanners read envelopes at the U.S. Postal Service, and they also read turnaround documents for utility companies. A **turnaround document** is computer-produced output that we can read and is ultimately returned as computer-readable input to a computer system. For example, when you pay your utility bills, you return a check and a stub for the invoice (the turnaround document). The stub is scanned, and payment information is entered automatically to the utility company's system.

Most retail stores and distribution warehouses, and all overnight couriers, are seasoned users of scanner technology. Salespeople, inventory management personnel, and couriers would much prefer to wave their "magic" wands than enter data one character at a time.

Image Scanners and Processing

Source-data automation allows direct entry of graphic information, as well as text-based information, via scanners. An **image scanner** uses laser technology to scan and **digitize** an image. The hard-copy image is scanned and translated into an electronic format that can be interpreted by and stored on computers. The image to be scanned can be a photograph, a drawing, an insurance form, a medical record—anything that can be digitized. Once an image has been digitized and entered to the computer system, it can be retrieved, displayed, modified, merged with text, stored, sent via data communications to one or several remote computers, and even faxed. Manipulating and managing scanned images, known as **image processing,** is becoming increasingly important, especially with recent advances in optical storage technologies (for example, rewritable CD-ROM). Organizations everywhere are replacing space-consuming metal filing cabinets and millions of hard-copy documents, from tax returns to warrantee cards, with their electronic equivalents. Image processing's space-saving incentive, along with its ease of document retrieval, is making the image scanner a must-have peripheral in most offices.

Page and Hand Image Scanners Image scanners are of two types: *page* and *hand.* Virtually all modern scanners can scan in both black and white images and color images. *Page image scanners* work like desktop duplicating machines. That

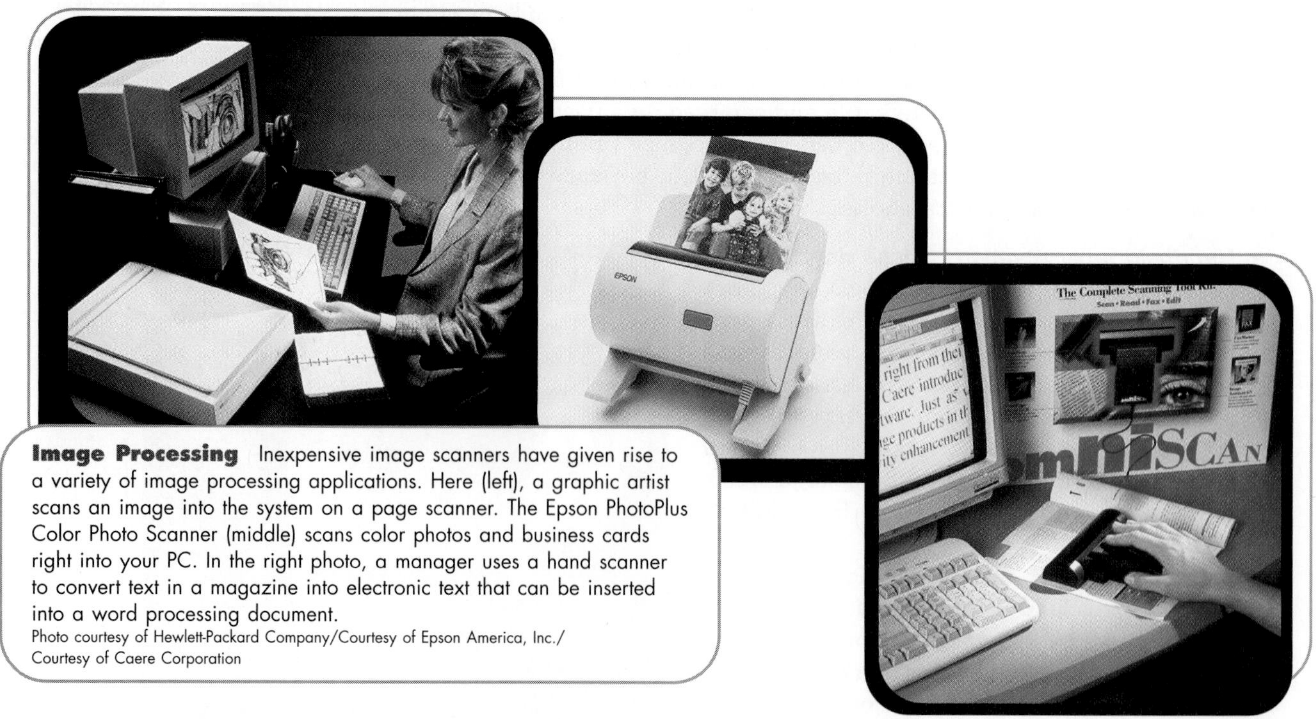

Image Processing Inexpensive image scanners have given rise to a variety of image processing applications. Here (left), a graphic artist scans an image into the system on a page scanner. The Epson PhotoPlus Color Photo Scanner (middle) scans color photos and business cards right into your PC. In the right photo, a manager uses a hand scanner to convert text in a magazine into electronic text that can be inserted into a word processing document.
Photo courtesy of Hewlett-Packard Company/Courtesy of Epson America, Inc./ Courtesy of Caere Corporation

is, the image to be scanned is placed face down on the scanning surface, covered, then scanned. The result is a high-resolution digitized image. Inexpensive page scanners weighing less than two pounds accept the document to be scanned in a slot. The *hand image scanner* is rolled manually over the image to be scanned. About five inches in width, hand image scanners are appropriate for capturing small images or portions of large images.

In addition to scanning photos and other graphic images, image scanners can also scan and interpret the alphanumeric characters on regular printed pages. People use page scanners to translate printed hard copy to computer-readable format. For applications that demand this type of translation, page scanners can minimize or eliminate the need for key entry. Today's image scanners and the accompanying OCR software are very sophisticated. Together they can read and interpret the characters from most printed material, such as a printed letter or a page from this book.

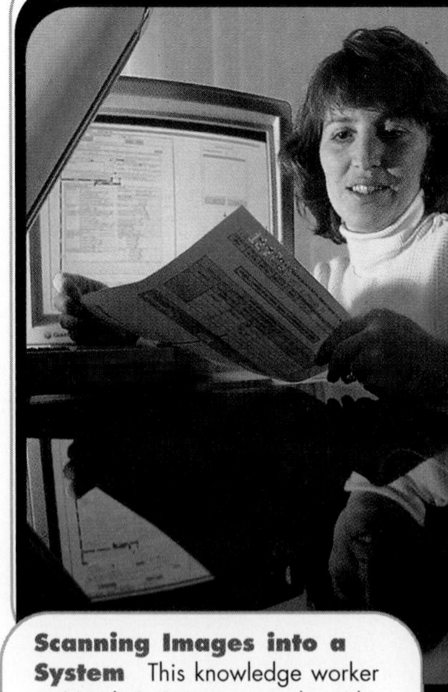

Scanning Images into a System This knowledge worker at Merck & Company works with an image processing application in which she scans images of case reports from clinical studies into a database. The application helps facilitate the FDA drug approval processes. Courtesy of Merck & Co., Inc.

Image Processing: Eliminating the Paper Pile Companies and even individuals are becoming buried in paper, literally. In some organizations, paper files take up most of the floor space. Moreover, finding what you want may take several minutes to hours. Or, you may never find what you want. Image processing applications scan and index thousands, even millions, of documents. Once these scanned documents are on the computer system, they can be easily retrieved and manipulated. For example, banks use image processing to archive canceled checks and to archive documents associated with mortgage loan servicing. Insurance companies use image processing in claims processing applications.

Images are scanned into a digital format that can be stored on disk, often optical laser disk because of its huge capacity. For example, decades worth of hospital medical records can be scanned and stored on a handful of optical laser disks that fit easily on a single shelf. The images are organized so they can be retrieved in seconds rather than minutes or hours. Medical personnel who need a hard copy can simply print one out in a matter of seconds.

The State of Louisiana Department of Public Safety routinely supplies driver information to other state agencies and to outside organizations, such as insurance companies, and is a perfect example of how image processing can reduce the need for paper while making records more accessible. The department has the dual problem of keeping up with thousands of documents received each week and with servicing thousands of requests for driver information, mostly for problem drivers. The amount of paperwork involved could be staggering. However, because this department has gone to image processing for driver information, other state agencies have direct access to the image bank over communication lines, and the department has no trouble handling outside requests for information. The department's long-range plan calls for using image processing to minimize or eliminate paper and microfilm in as many applications as possible.

Intelligent Plastic Smart cards have a variety of applications, including banking, medical records, security, and more. Some smart cards allow access to information if they are given the correct password. In the photo a person is about to insert her Gemplus smart card into a telephone capable of reading and transmitting information on her smart card. Courtesy of Gemplus

The real beauty of image processing is that the digitized material can be easily manipulated. For example, any image can be easily faxed to another location (without being printed). A fax is sent and received as an image. The content on the fax or any electronic image can be manipulated in many ways. OCR software can be used to translate any printed text on the stored image to an electronic format. For example, a doctor might wish to pull selected printed text from various patient images into a word processing document to compile a summary of a patient's condition. The doctor can even select specific graphic images (X-rays, photos, or drawings) from the patient's record for inclusion in the summary report.

Magnetic Stripes and Smart Cards

The magnetic stripes on the back of charge cards and badges offer another means of data entry at the source. The magnetic stripes are encoded with data appropriate for specific applications. For example, your account number and personal identification number are encoded on a card for automatic teller machines.

Magnetic stripes contain much more data per unit of space than do printed characters or bar codes. Plus, because they cannot be read visually, they are perfect for storing confidential data, such as a personal identification number. Employee cards and security badges often contain authorization data for access to physically secured areas, such as a computer center. To gain access, an employee inserts a card or badge into a **badge reader.** This device reads and checks the authorization code before permitting the individual to enter a secured area. When badge readers are linked to a central computer, that computer can maintain a chronological log of people entering or leaving secured areas.

The **smart card** looks like any garden-variety charge card, but with a twist. It has an embedded microprocessor with up to 32 KB of nonvolatile memory. Because the smart card can hold more information, has processing capability, and is almost impossible to duplicate, smart cards may soon replace cards with magnetic stripes. Already, smart cards are gaining widespread acceptance in Europe and in the United States, especially smart cards with *stored value.* The dual-function stored-value smart card serves as a credit card and as a replacement for cash. Customers with these cards can go to automatic teller machines to transfer electronic cash from their checking or savings account to the card's memory. They are used like cash at the growing number of stores that accept stored-value cards. Each time the card is used, the purchase amount is deducted from the card's stored value. To reload the card with more electronic cash, the card's owner must return to an automatic teller machine. The stored-value smart card is another big step toward the inevitable elimination of cash.

Speech Recognition: Getting on Speaking Terms with Computers

Speech recognition has been possible for over 20 years, but only when the words were spoken in discrete speech (slowly, one word at a time) to an expensive, room-sized mainframe computer. The power of PCs has finally caught up with speech-recognition technology. With the modern speech-recognition software and

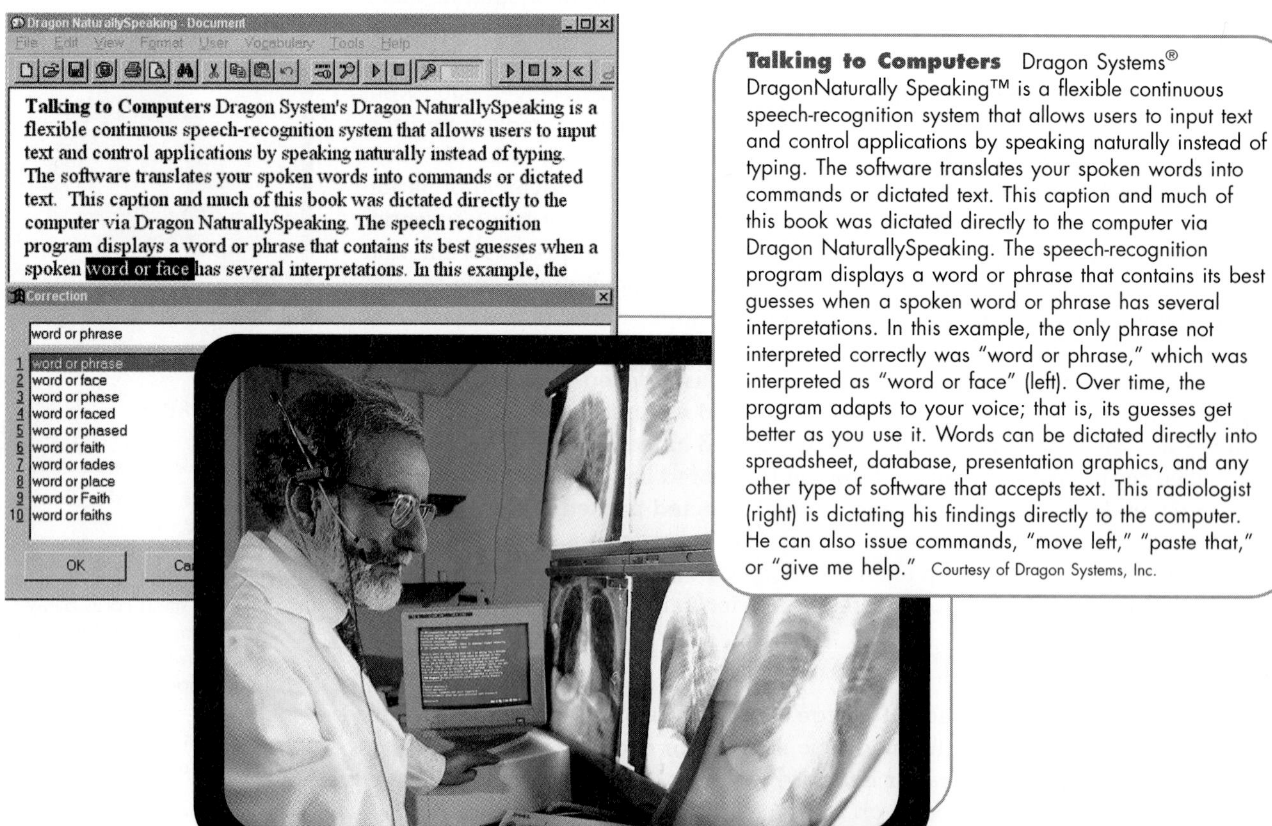

Talking to Computers Dragon Systems® DragonNaturally Speaking™ is a flexible continuous speech-recognition system that allows users to input text and control applications by speaking naturally instead of typing. The software translates your spoken words into commands or dictated text. This caption and much of this book was dictated directly to the computer via Dragon NaturallySpeaking. The speech-recognition program displays a word or phrase that contains its best guesses when a spoken word or phrase has several interpretations. In this example, the only phrase not interpreted correctly was "word or phrase," which was interpreted as "word or face" (left). Over time, the program adapts to your voice; that is, its guesses get better as you use it. Words can be dictated directly into spreadsheet, database, presentation graphics, and any other type of software that accepts text. This radiologist (right) is dictating his findings directly to the computer. He can also issue commands, "move left," "paste that," or "give me help." Courtesy of Dragon Systems, Inc.

a microphone, the typical off-the-shelf PC is able to accept spoken words in continuous speech (as you would normally talk) at speeds of up to 125 words a minute. Authors can dictate their books. Much of the manuscript for this book was dictated to a PC using Dragon NaturallySpeaking Professional, speech-recognition software from Dragon Systems, Inc. Quality-control personnel, for example, must use their hands to describe defects as they are detected. Speech recognition has made hands-free interaction possible for surgeons during operations. Many executives now dictate, rather than keyboard, their e-mail messages. Also, speech recognition is a tremendous enabling technology for the physically challenged.

Speech recognition is emerging as the newest *killer application*. In the PC world, a killer application has a profound impact on personal computing. The "killer app" handle places speech-recognition systems alongside some pretty good company: word processing, spreadsheet, database, and Internet browser applications.

If you were to purchase a **speech-recognition system** for your PC, you would receive software, a generic vocabulary database, and a high-quality microphone with noise-canceling capabilities. Successful speech recognition depends on a strong, clear signal from the microphone. Popular systems include IBM's ViaVoiceType, Dragon System's Dragon NaturallySpeaking, and Kurzweil Applied Intelligence's Kurzweil VOICE. The microphone, which is mounted on a headset, filters out general office noise, including ringing phones and slamming doors. The size of the vocabulary database ranges from 30,000 words for general dictation to more than 300,000 words for technical, legal, or medical dictation.

Once you have installed the hardware and software, you are ready to speak to the computer. The basic steps involved in speech recognition are illustrated in Figure 5.4. The system will accept most of your spoken words. However, you can *train* the system to accept virtually all of your words. It helps to train the system to recognize your unique speech patterns. We all sound different, even to a computer. To train the system, simply talk to it for about an hour—the longer the better. Even if a word is said twice in succession, it will probably have a different inflection or nasal quality. The system uses artificial intelligence techniques to learn our speech patterns and update the vocabulary database accordingly. The typical speech-recognition system never stops learning, for it is always fine-

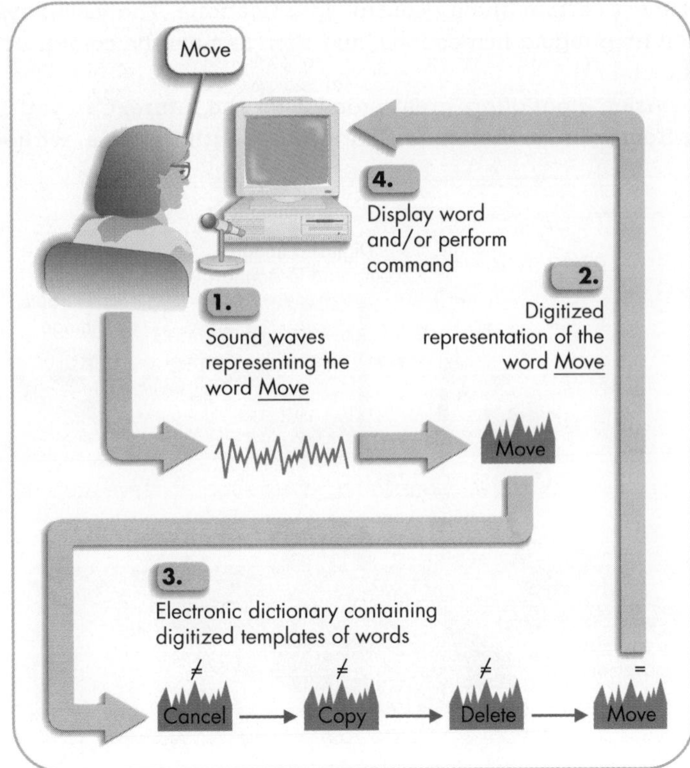

Speech Recognition The sound waves created by the spoken word *Move* are digitized by the computer. The digitized template is matched against templates of other words in the electronic dictionary. When the computer finds a match, it displays a written version of the word.

tuning the vocabulary so it can recognize words with greater speed and accuracy. Each user on a given PC would need to customize his or her own vocabulary database. To further customize our personal vocabulary database, we can add words that are unique to our working environment.

Some speech-recognition systems are speaker-independent; that is, they can accept words spoken by anyone. Such systems are restricted to accepting only a limited number of words and tasks. Despite its limitations, speaker-independent speech recognition has a number of applications. For example, salespeople in the field can enter an order simply by calling in to the company's computer and stating the customer number, item number, and quantity. Some telephone companies have implemented systems that permit customers to speak numbers and a few commands.

It is only a matter of time before we all will be communicating with our PCs in spoken English rather than through time-consuming keystrokes. Already, thousands of attorneys, doctors, journalists, and others who routinely do dictation and write are enjoying the benefits of speech recognition.

Vision-Input Systems: Computer Eyes

Some data are best entered and processed visually. However, the simulation of human senses, especially vision, is extremely complex. A computer does not actually see and interpret an image the way a human being does. Computers need cameras for their "eyesight." To create a visual database, a vision system, via a camera, digitizes the images of all objects to be identified, then stores the digitized form of each image in the database. When the system is placed in operation, the camera enters each newly "seen" image into a digitizer. The system then compares the digitized image to be interpreted with the prerecorded digitized images in the computer's database, much like a speech-recognition system does with speech input. The computer identifies the image by matching the structure of the input image with those images in the database. This process is illustrated by the digital vision-inspection system in Figure 5.5.

As you can imagine, **vision-input systems** are best suited to very specialized tasks in which only a few images will be encountered. These tasks are usually simple, monotonous ones, such as inspection. For example, in Figure 5.5 a digital vision-inspection system on an assembly line rejects those parts that do not meet certain quality-control specifications. The vision system performs rudimentary gauging inspections, and then signals the computer to take appropriate action.

Vision input offers great promise for the future. Can you imagine traveling by car from your hometown to Charleston, South Carolina, without the burden of ac-

Digital Vision-Inspection System In this digital vision-inspection system, the system examines parts for defects. If the digitized image of the part does not match a standard digital image, the defective part is placed in a reject bin.

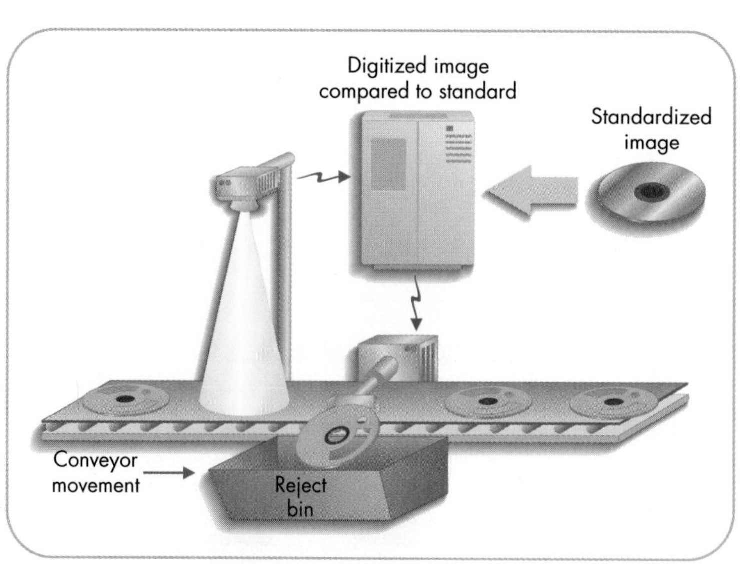

tually driving? Sound far-fetched? Not really. Mercedes-Benz, the German automobile maker, is actively developing a system that will allow you to do just that. The copilot system is a step up from cruise control, freeing the driver from both the accelerator pedal and the steering wheel. Like cruise control, the driver would remain behind the wheel, even when the system is operational. The foundation technology is vision input. When traveling down the German autobahn, the system "sees" the lines on either side of the lane and makes minor adjustments in direction to keep the automobile centered in the lane. This part of the system works well; however, Mercedes-Benz engineers have many hurdles to overcome (exit ramps, pedestrians, and so on) before you see this feature in showroom automobiles. Someday the safest drivers on the road won't be driving at all.

Digital Cameras: Look, No Film

Most of us take photographs in the traditional manner—with a camera and film. We drop off our rolls of film for developing, and then we enjoy the results in the form of prints and slides. Some people use image scanners to digitize photos for use in newsletters, magazines, and so on. This process may change forever as the price of **digital cameras** continues to plummet (currently priced from $200 to $5000). When you take a picture with a digital camera, a digitized image goes straight to 3.5-inch diskette, CD-R, or to onboard flash memory. Once on disk or in memory, it can be uploaded to a PC and manipulated (viewed, printed, modified, and so on) as you would other graphic images.

There are many applications for digital cameras. Customers from all over the world make special requests to a designer jewelry store. Store personnel take photos of available merchandise from various angles, and then they e-mail the photos to the customer. An automobile repair center takes photos of all major repair jobs to show customers exactly what the problem was and for training purposes. To help them to adjust braces better, orthodontists use digital cameras to track the migration of patients' teeth. Online retailers use digital cameras when preparing product Web pages, thereby skipping the film developing and scanning process altogether. One of the most popular applications is expanding the family photo album. Typically, photos are stored permanently on hard disk, CD-R or CD-RW, or on high-density interchangeable disks.

Once you own a digital camera, the cost of photography plummets because the costly, time-consuming developing processing is eliminated. With digital cameras you can take all the photos you want and just keep the really good ones. With the cost of high-resolution digital cameras close to that of a quality 35-mm camera, a lot more people are going digital for photography.

Digital Photography We may be entering an era of filmless photography. This image was taken with a digital camera, such as the one in the inset. You can capture, view, print, store, and transmit almost any image. Images are stored on interchangeable memory cards or diskettes, then uploaded to a PC and used in countless applications, from the family photo album to training software. Toshiba America, Inc.

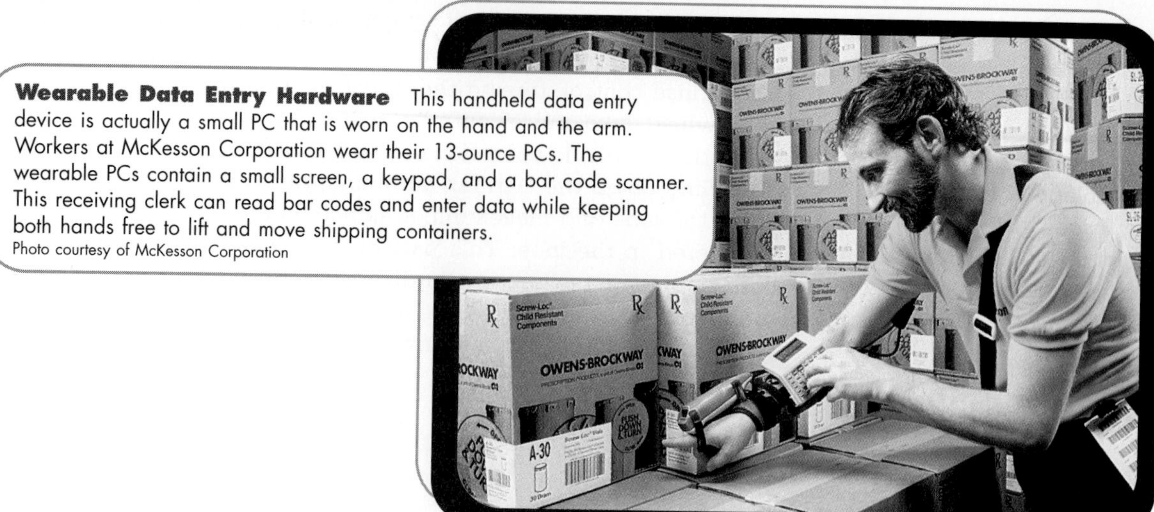

Wearable Data Entry Hardware This handheld data entry device is actually a small PC that is worn on the hand and the arm. Workers at McKesson Corporation wear their 13-ounce PCs. The wearable PCs contain a small screen, a keypad, and a bar code scanner. This receiving clerk can read bar codes and enter data while keeping both hands free to lift and move shipping containers.
Photo courtesy of McKesson Corporation

Handheld Data Entry Devices

Some close-to-the-source data entry tasks still require the use of some keystrokes and are best performed on handheld data entry devices. The typical *handheld data entry device,* which is actually a small computer, has the following:

- A limited external keyboard or a soft keyboard (displayed on a touch-sensitive screen)
- A small display that may be touch sensitive
- Some kind of storage capability for the data, usually solid-state nonvolatile flash memory
- A scanning device, capable of optical character recognition

After the data have been entered, the portable data entry device is linked with a central computer, and data are *uploaded* (transmitted from the data entry device to a central computer) for processing.

Stock clerks in department stores routinely use handheld devices to collect and enter reorder data. As clerks visually check the inventory level, they identify the items that need to be restocked. They first scan the price tag (which identifies the item), and then enter the number to be ordered on the keyboard.

Handheld slate PCs and PDAs (personal digital assistants), introduced in Chapter 1, frequently are used as data entry devices. Slate PCs have pressure-sensitive writing pads that recognize hand-printed alphanumeric characters. Also, they permit the entering of graphic information. For example, police officers use slate PCs to document accidents, including recording the handwritten signatures of the participants.

MEMORY

bits

Input Devices

- Keyboard
- Point-and-draw devices
- Scanners
- Image scanners (*page* and *hand*)
- Badge reader (for magnetic stripes and smart cards)
- Speech-recognition systems
- Vision-input systems
- Digital cameras
- Handheld data entry devices

SECTION SELF-CHECK

Self-Check

5-3.1 Vision-input systems are best suited to generalized tasks in which a wide variety of images will be encountered. (T/F)

5-3.2 Optical character recognition is a means of source-data automation. (T/F)

5-3.3 The preprinted bar codes on consumer products have actually increased the number of keystrokes at supermarket checkout counters. (T/F)

5-3.4 The United States Postal Service uses OCR to sort most mail. (T/F)

5-3.5 Speech-recognition systems can be trained to accept words not originally in the dictionary. (T/F)

5-3.6 Portable data entry devices are linked to a central computer to download collected data for processing. (T/F)

5-3.7 In speech recognition, the computer's electronic dictionary of words contains: (a) firmware, (b) synonyms, (c) digitized phonemes, or (d) digitized templates?

5-3.8 The Universal Product Code (UPC) was originally used by which industry: (a) supermarket, (b) hardware, (c) mail-order merchandising, or (d) steel?

5-3.9 Image scanners are either page or: (a) arm, (b) hand, (c) footer, or (d) header?

5-3.10 The enhanced version of cards with a magnetic stripe is a: (a) badge card, (b) intelligent badge, (c) smart card, or (d) debit card?

5-3.11 Which is not generally considered a source-data automation technology: (a) keyboard, (b) OCR, (c) speech recognition, or (d) UPC?

5-3.12 Which of these is not a type of scanner: (a) document scanner, (b) stationary label scanner, (c) wand scanner, or (d) magnetic scanner?

5-3.13 Manipulating and managing scanned images is called: (a) image processing, (b) parallel processing, (c) scanner management, or (d) image administration?

5-3.14 Memory on smart cards is: (a) volatile, (b) nonvolatile, (c) inert, or (d) never more that 1024 bits?

5-3.15 Which of the following is not true of digital cameras: (a) uses the same film as 35-mm cameras, (b) digitized images are uploaded from the camera, (c) uses disk or flash memory to store photos, or (d) can be purchased for as little as $400?

5.4 OUTPUT DEVICES

Output

Output devices translate bits and bytes into a form we can understand. These devices include monitors, printers, plotters, multimedia projectors, and voice-response systems.

Monitors and Graphics Adapters

The output device we are most familiar with is the televisionlike monitor, which displays alphanumeric and graphic output. We describe monitors and their capabilities in terms of the following:

- Graphics adapter (the electronic link between the processor and the monitor)
- Size (diagonal dimension of the display screen)
- Resolution (detail of the display)
- Display quality

Graphics Adapters

The **graphics adapter** is the device controller for the monitor. Graphics adapters can be inserted into an expansion slot on the motherboard. Newer motherboards equipped with an *AGP bus slot* can take advantage of AGP technology. The monitor cable is plugged into the graphics adapter board to link the monitor with the processor. All display signals en route to the monitor pass through the graphics adapter, where the digital signals are converted to analog signals compatible with the monitor's display capabilities.

Most existing graphics adapters have their own RAM, called **video RAM** or **VRAM,** where they prepare monitor-bound images for display. The size of the video RAM is important in that it determines the number of possible colors and resolution of the display, as well as the speed at which signals can be sent to the monitor. A minimum of two megabytes of video RAM is recommended to accommodate the complexities of modern graphics-based software. The newer AGP graphics adapters enjoy much better performance by using the PC system's RAM directly.

COMPUTERS: THE ENABLING TECHNOLOGY FOR THE DISABLED

Computer technology is having a profound effect on physically challenged people. With the aid of computers they now are better prepared to take control of their environments.

On the Move

Paraplegic walks A little over a decade ago, Nan Davis stunned the world. A paraplegic since an automobile accident on the night of her high school graduation, she walked to the podium to receive her college diploma—with the help of a rehabilitative tool that uses FES, or functional electrical stimulation.

FES uses low-level electrical stimulation to restore or supplement the minute electrical currents the nervous system generates to control different parts of the body. This electrical stimulation is controlled by a microprocessor—a computer—that uses feedback from the body to adjust the electrical stimulation's length and intensity.

In Nan's case, FES took the form of electrodes to stimulate her leg muscles; a sensory feedback system; and a small, portable computer. The sensory feedback system tells the computer the position and movement of the legs so that it knows which muscles it must electrically stimulate next to produce a coordinated gait.

Grasping the Technology
This person, whose hands are paralyzed due to a spinal cord injury, uses an implanted FES system that causes her finger muscles to contract and allows her to grasp the telephone. Courtesy of MetroHealth Medical Center, Cleveland, Ohio

Paraplegic Walks
The Parastep® System is a microcomputer controlled functional neuromuscular stimulation (FNS) device that enables people paralyzed with spinal cord injuries to stand and walk. This system comes from the medical engineering sciences known as neuroprosthetics.

The Parastep stimulator generates sequences of electrical pulses passed to target peripheral nerves through electrodes placed over muscles and nerves of the lower extremities. The user controls stimulation through a keypad on the stimulator unit or with control switches on the walker. Courtesy of Sigmedics, Inc.

FES comes of age Although the use of FES to restore one's ability to stand, walk, and use the arms and hands is still in the experimental stage, many other FES applications are accepted medical practice. The best-known application is the cardiac pacemaker that is attached directly to a faulty heart with electrodes. FES can also be used to control chronic pain, correct spinal deformities, improve auditory defects, and pace the rise and fall of the diaphragm during breathing.

FES can also be used as a therapeutic tool to strengthen muscles idled by paralysis. Without exercise, muscles atrophy, circulation becomes sluggish, cardiovascular fitness declines, and pressure sores develop. These FES devices, which look like high-tech exercise bicycles, use a microprocessor to coordinate a system of electrodes and feedback sensors, allowing the user to push the pedals and turn a hand crank. Like anyone who engages in a regular exercise program, users of the FES devices report noticeable improvements in muscle tone, mass, and cardiovascular fitness. These devices cannot restore function, of course, but they can help the paralyzed to maintain their bodies while researchers continue to seek ways to help them walk again. In the meantime, many are thrilled just to see their bodies move again.

At Work
The nature of the work and the availability of specially designed workstations have made computer careers particularly inviting to the physically disabled. The man in the photo works as a database administrator at a computer services company. Boeing Computer Services

Scaling the Barriers at Work

For most disabled workers—especially those with physical impairments—the barriers to gainful employment have been as steep as the stairs flanking many public buildings. This is changing thanks to federal legislation and revolutionary advances in computer hardware and software.

The Americans with Disabilities Act of 1990 This legislation prohibits discrimination that might limit employment or access to public buildings and facilities. In fact, many call the law a bill of rights for people with physical limitations, mental impairments, and chronic illnesses. The legislation promises to benefit the nation, too. Of the approximately 43 million disabled workers, only about 28% hold full- or part-time jobs at a time when experts are projecting labor shortages and a shrinking pool of *skilled* workers.

Enabling technology Under the law, employers cannot discriminate against any employee who can perform a job's "essential" responsibilities with "reasonable accommodations." Increasingly, these "accommodations" take the form of a personal computer with special peripherals and software. All told, almost 20,000 technology-based products are available for the disabled.

For example, getting a complete impression of the contents of a computer screen is a problem for the visually impaired, as is the ability to maneuver around such features as pull-down windows and click-on icons. The partially sighted can benefit from adaptive software packages that create large-type screen displays, while voice synthesizers can let the blind "read" memos, books, and computer screens.

For the hearing impaired, voice mail and a computer's beeps can be translated into visual cues, such as a screen display of text or flashing icons. Advancing communications and video technologies have made it possible for users to sit in front of their respective computer screens and have sign language conversations.

Virtually any type of physical movement can be used to input commands and data to a computer. This is good news for people with limited use of their arms and hands. Alternative input devices can range from a standard trackball (instead of a mouse) to the relatively slow sip-and-puff devices to speech-recognition systems. There are even software programs that allow keystroke combinations to be entered one key at a time.

Several studies, including ones by the U.S. Department of Labor and private firms, concluded that 80% of all accommodations would cost less than $1000 per employee. Text-to-speech software, for example, can be purchased for as little as $30 and sophisticated continuous speech-recognition software costs as little as $100. Some PC-based accommodations are more costly, of course. A PC modified for a blind word processor can cost double that of a standard PC. Still, the prices of these technologies, like the prices of PCs themselves, continue to drop. The cost of a "reading" device, for example, fell from $40,000 to $1000 in about a decade. Furthermore, employers who provide "assistive technologies" to their employees are eligible for tax incentives. Employers benefit, too, by gaining highly motivated and productive workers. A study at a major chemical company found that workers with and without disabilities were equal or closely matched on safety and performance.

Personal Reader
This personal reader allows visually impaired people to "hear" books and typewritten material. An optical scanner reads the words into the computer system, where they are converted into English speech using a speech synthesizer (a device that produces electronic speech). Users can request any of nine different voices (including male, female, and child). Xerox Imaging Systems/Kurzweil, a Xerox Company

Monitor Size

Display screens vary in size from 5 to 30 inches (measured diagonally). The monitor size for newly purchased desktop PCs has inched up from 9 inches to 17 inches over the past 10 years and is now moving toward 19 inches.

Monitor Resolution: Pixels and Dot Pitch

Monitors vary in their quality of output, or **resolution.** Resolution depends on the *number of pixels that can be displayed,* the *number of bits used to represent each pixel,* and the *dot pitch of the monitor.* A **pixel** is an addressable point on the screen, a point to which light can be directed under program control. The typical monitor is set to operate with 786,432 addressable points in 1024 columns by 768 rows; however, most can be set at resolutions ranging from 640 by 480 to 1600 by 1200. The 1600 by 1200 setting has almost 2 million addressable points.

Each pixel, short for *picture elements* (see Figure 5.6), can be assigned a color or, for monochrome monitors, a shade of gray. **Gray scales** refer to the number of shades of a color that can be shown on a monochrome monitor's screen. Most color monitors mix red, green, and blue to achieve a spectrum of colors, and are called **RGB monitors.** One of the user options is the number of bits used to display each pixel. In 8-bit color mode, 256 colors are possible ($2^8 = 256$). The 16-bit mode *high color* mode yields 65,536 colors. *True color* options, either 24-bit or 32-bit modes, provide photo-quality viewing with over 16 million colors. There is a trade-off between resolution and system performance. Greater resolutions demand more of the processor, leaving less capacity for other processing tasks.

A monitor's resolution also is affected by its **dot pitch,** or the distance between the centers of adjacent pixels. Any dot pitch equal to or less than .28 mm (millimeters) provides a sharp image. The crispness of the image improves as the dot pitch gets smaller. When you have an opportunity, use a magnifying glass to examine the pixels and observe the dot pitch on your computer's monitor.

Display Quality: Be Flicker Free

There are two more characteristics that affect the quality of the display—the *refresh rate* and whether the monitor is *interlaced.* The phosphor coating on a mon-

The Pixels This photo of newlyweds Brian and Alyson illustrates how computers use picture elements, or pixels, to portray digital images. Thousands (even millions) of pixels, each a single point on a graphics image, are arranged in rows and columns to create the image. In the inset image, the pixels are so close together they portray continuous color. The blowup highlights the individual pixels.

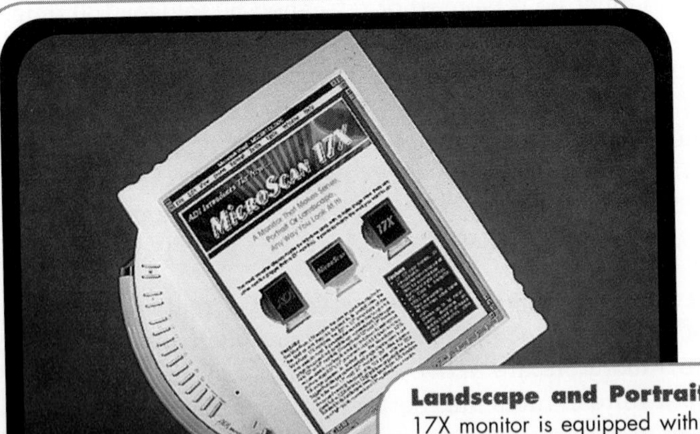

Special-Purpose Monitors This Advanced Remote Control for Videoshow system enables the presentation of spectacular multimedia shows. The remote control includes a full-color LCD screen so that presenters can face their audience and still see what is on the big screen.
Courtesy General Parametrics Corporation

Landscape and Portrait Monitors The Microscan 17X monitor is equipped with a pivoting capability. It's ideal for business professionals and computing enthusiasts who work with page-oriented document processing, oversized spreadsheets, and graphics design applications. Users can switch easily between landscape and portrait viewing.
Courtesy of ADI Systems, Inc.

Durable Monitors In video arcades, the action takes place on large, durable monitors. Photo courtesy of Intel Corporation

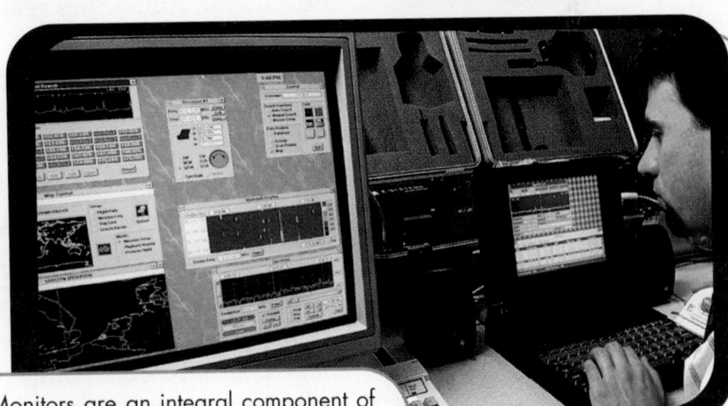

CAD Monitors Monitors are an integral component of virtually all computer-based applications. An engineer at E-Systems needs a large high-resolution monitor for computer-aided design (CAD) applications. His laptop PC has an LCD flat-panel monitor. Courtesy of E-Systems

World's Smallest Monitor Kopin Corporation's CyberDisplay™ is the world's smallest high-performance, high-resolution, full-function information display. It's especially designed for portable products, such as with cellular phone applications (videophone, e-mail, and so on) and with pagers. Courtesy of Kopin Corporation

Touch Screen Monitors A growing number of ATMs (shown here) and public information kiosks use touch screen monitors with input/output capabilities.
Courtesy of Diebold, Incorporated

itor's CRT (cathode-ray tube) must be repainted or refreshed 50 to over 100 times each second (Hz) to maintain clarity of the image. Generally, monitors with faster refresh rates have fewer flickers and are easier on the eyes. Interlacing will also affect screen flicker. Less expensive monitors are interlaced; that is, they paint every other horizontal line on the screen, then fill in the rest on a second pass (TVs are interlaced). Interlacing may result in some flicker. In contrast, *noninterlaced monitors* minimize flicker by painting the whole screen in one pass.

Flat-Panel Monitors: Thin Is In

Laptop PCs use space-saving **flat-panel monitors,** some less that ½-inch thick. Flat-panel monitors use a variety of technologies, the most common being *LCD* (*l*iquid *c*rystal *d*isplay). LCD monitors are *active matrix* or *passive matrix.* Active matrix monitors have higher refresh rates and better contrast, making for a more brilliant display. Millions of transistors are needed for color active matrix LCD monitors. Color monitors need three transistors for each pixel: one each for red, green, and blue. Active matrix LCD displays are more expensive than passive matrix displays; therefore, active matrix LCD displays are usually associated with high-end notebook PCs.

Touch Screen Monitors: Natural Monitors

Touch screen monitors permit input as well as output. Pressure-sensitive overlays are placed over monitor screens that can detect pressure and the exact location of that pressure. Users simply touch the desired icon or menu item with their finger. Educators realize that we are born with an ability to point and touch, and are beginning to use touch screen technology in the classroom to teach everything from reading to geography. Interactive touch screen systems are installed in shopping centers, zoos, airports, grocery stores, post offices, and many other public locations.

Desktop Printers: Lots of Choices

Printers

Printers produce hard-copy output, such as college term papers, management reports, cash register receipts, labels, memos, and payroll checks. Hundreds of printers are produced by dozens of manufacturers. There is a printer manufactured to meet the hard-copy output requirements of any individual or company, and almost any combination of features can be obtained. You can specify its size (some weigh less than a pound), speed, quality of output, color requirements, and even noise level. PC printers sell for as little as a pair of shoes or for as much as a minivan. High-speed, high-volume mainframe printers that produce utility bills, credit-card charge summaries, and the like can cost as much as a house.

Any person or company about to purchase a printer must consider:

- What's the budget?
- Is color needed or will black and white do?
- What will be the volume of output (pages per hour, day, or week)?
- How important is the quality of the output?
- What special features are needed (ability to print envelopes, on legal size paper, on multi-part forms, and so on)?
- If the printer is to be shared on a network, what do the other users want?

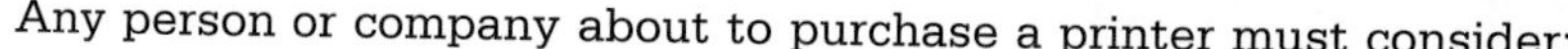

Think about these considerations as you read about various printer options. Keep in mind that color, additional features, and each increment in speed and quality of output add to the cost of the printer.

Printer technology is ever changing. Three basic technologies dominate the PC printer arena: page, ink-jet, and dot-matrix. The advantages and disadvantages of these technologies are summarized in Figure 5.7. All PC printers have the capability of printing graphs and charts and offer considerable flexibility in the size and style of print. All printers also can print in portrait or landscape format. **Portrait** and **landscape** refer to the orientation of the print on the page. Portrait format is like the page of this book—the lines run parallel to the shorter sides

The Do-It-All Printer This multifunction printer acts as a copier, a fax machine, and a printer, providing small office and home PC users with a range of capabilities.
Photo courtesy of Hewlett-Packard Company

Color Printers By the mid-1990s, the price of color printers plummeted to the point that they were economically feasible for virtually all computing environments, including the home. Now users can add color to their everyday business (memos, reports, spreadsheets, graphs) and home (banners, invitations) printing needs. The Hewlett-Packard color notebook (top left), color ink-jet (top right), and color laser (bottom left) printers provide high-quality color output. The notebook printer allows wireless printing from up to three feet away from a PC.
Photos courtesy of Hewlett-Packard Company

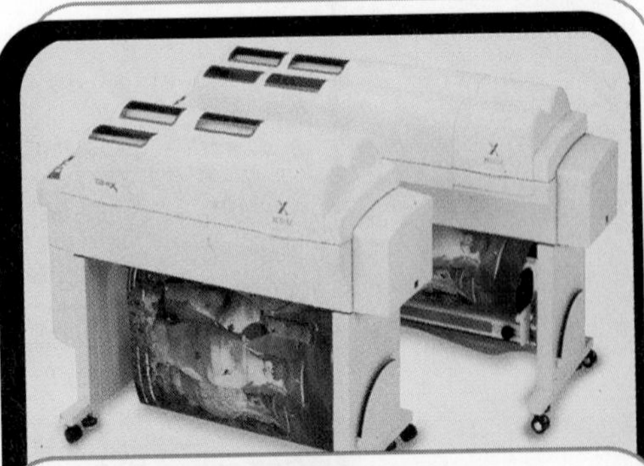

Large-Format Printers Typical applications for the Xerox Colorgraphx large-format ink-jet printers (bottom right) include point-of-sale displays, billboards, banners, backlit signs, backdrops for photography or video, and trade-show graphics. Large-format prints are typically 22 inches and larger.
Courtesy of Xerox Corporation

of the page. In contrast, landscape output runs parallel to the longer sides of the page. Landscape is frequently the orientation of choice for spreadsheet outputs with many columns.

Page Printers: A Page at a Time

Nonimpact **page printers** use laser, LED (*l*ight-*e*mitting *d*iode), LCS (*l*iquid *c*rystal *s*hutter), and other laser-like technologies to achieve high-speed hard-copy output by printing *a page at a time.* Page printers are also referred to simply as **laser printers.** The operation of a laser-based page printer is illustrated in Figure 5.8. Most of the laser printers in use print shades of gray; however, color laser printers are becoming increasingly popular as their price continues to drop.

Economically priced desktop page printers have become the standard for office printing. These printers, which print at speeds of 4 to 32 pages per minute (ppm) for text-only printing, can run through up to 6 feet of paper during a business day. Printing in color (when available) and/or printing graphic images may slow down output to about 25% the rated monochrome text-only output speed. Most page printers print on standard letter and legal paper.

All desktop page printers are capable of producing *near-typeset-quality (NTQ)* text and graphics. The resolution (quality of output) of the low-end desktop page printer is *600 dpi* (dots per inch). High-end desktop page printers, which are sometimes called *desktop typesetters,* are capable of at least 1200 dpi. The dpi qualifier refers to the number of dots that can be printed per linear inch, horizontally or vertically. That is, a 600-dpi printer is capable of printing 360,000 (600 times 600) dots per square inch. Commercial typesetting quality is a minimum of 1200 dpi and is usually in excess of 2000 dpi. Desktop page printers are also quiet (an

Printer Summary

	Page Printers	Ink-Jet Printers	Dot-Matrix Printers
Pros	• High-resolution output (up to 1200 dpi) • Fast (4 to 32 ppm–text only) • Quiet • Many choices from which to choose (from under $400 for low-speed home/office models up to $10,000 for sophisticated shared printers) • Low cost per page (1 to 4 cents)	• High-resolution output (but less than that of page) • Quiet • Small (footprint can be smaller than a sheet of paper) • Energy efficient • Many choices from which to choose (black and white from $90 to full color (from $100 to $1500)	• Inexpensive • Can print multi-part forms • Can print on narrow and wide fanfold paper • Low per page cost (less than a penny per page) • Energy efficient
Cons	• Cost • Limited to cut sheet media • Slow for graphics output	• Higher cost per page than page (2 to 6 cents) • Slower than page (4 to 12 ppm) • Special paper required for highest resolution output • Limited to cut sheet media	• Noisy • Low-resolution output that gets worse as the ribbon ages • Slow (40 to 450 cps) • Poor quality graphics output • Requires add-on to handle cut sheets and envelopes • Limited font flexibility
Color	Color page models produce high-resolution color output. At $.30 to $1.00 per color page, they can be expensive to operate.	Color ink-jet models may take over the low-end color market. Models under $200 are available that produce 720 to 1440 dpi color output. Color output costs from $.10 to $1.20 per page.	Color ribbons can be used for highlighting.
Outlook	High-speed, high-quality page printers will remain the mainstay of office printing for the foreseeable future. This is especially true for shared printers.	Ink-jet offers low-cost high-quality output. Home PC buyers with low volume output requirements may opt for color models in large numbers.	Dot-matrix technology is fading except for situations that require printing on multi-part forms.

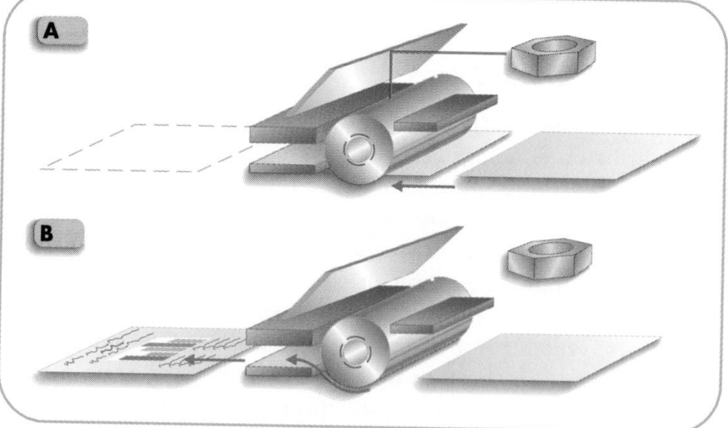

Desktop Page Printer Operation The enclosure of a desktop page printer is removed to expose its inner workings. (a) Prior to printing, an electrostatic charge is applied to a drum. Then laser beam paths to the drum are altered by a spinning multisided mirror. The reflected beams selectively remove the electrostatic charge from the drum. (b) Toner is deposited on those portions of the drum that were affected by the laser beams. The drum is rotated and the toner is fused to the paper to create the image.

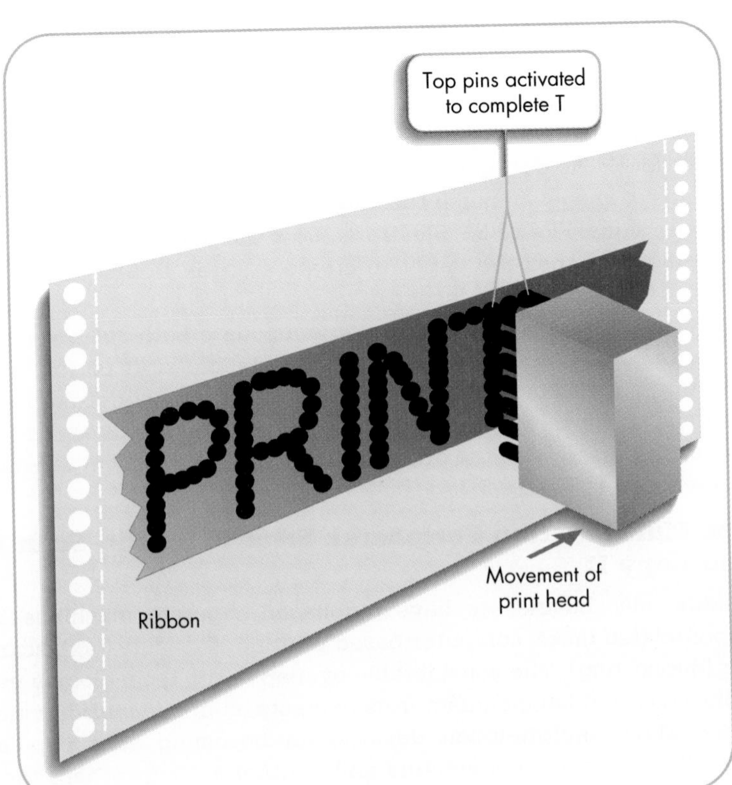

Dot-Matrix-Printer Character Formation Each character is formed in a matrix as the print head moves across the paper. The bottom pins are used for lowercase letters that extend below the line (for example, *g* and *p*). Notice how dots are overlapped to increase the density and, therefore, the quality of the image.

important consideration in an office setting). Other pros and cons of page printers are summarized in Figure 5.7.

Ink-jet Printers: Popular in SOHO

To the naked eye, there is little difference between the print quality of nonimpact **ink-jet printers** and page printers. Although the output quality of ink-jet printers is more in line with page printers, their mechanical operation is more like that of the dot-matrix printer (see Figure 5.9) because they have a print head that moves back and forth across the paper to write text and create the image. Several independently controlled injection chambers squirt ink droplets on the paper. The droplets, which dry instantly as dots, form the letters and images. Resolutions for the typical ink-jet printer are about that of page printers (600 dpi and up). Print speeds range from 4 to 12 ppm.

The color ink-jet printer is emerging as the choice for budget-minded consumers. SOHO (small office/home office) buyers also are opting for color ink-jet printers by the millions. The cost of color ink-jet printers ranges from about $100 to about $1500. The pros and cons of home/office ink-jet printers are summarized in Figure 5.7.

Large-Format Ink-jet Printers: Seeing the Big Picture

Page, ink-jet, and dot-matrix printers are capable of producing page-size graphic output, but are limited in their ability to generate large-scale, high-quality, perfectly proportioned graphic output. For example, on a blueprint, the sides of a 12-foot-square room must be exactly the same length. Architects, engineers, graphics artists, city planners, and others who routinely generate high-precision, hard-copy graphic output of widely varying sizes use another hard-copy alternative—**large-format ink-jet printers,** also called **plotters.** Plotters use ink-jet technology to print on roll-feed paper up to 4 feet wide and 50 foot in length. Plotters can be used for large printing needs, such as commercial posters or blueprints, or they can be used to produce continuous output, such as plotting earthquake activity or a five-year project activity chart.

Output Devices

Monitors

- Described by graphics adapter, size, resolution (pixels, bits per pixel, and dot pitch), color (gray scales, RGB), and display quality
- Types of monitors
  - —Televisionlike
  - —Flat-panel
  - —Touch screen

Printers

- Page printers (color option)
- Ink-jet printers (color option)
- Large-format ink-jet printers (color option)
- Dot-matrix printers
- Multifunction peripherals

Multimedia projectors

Voice-response systems

- Recorded voice
- Speech synthesis

Dot-Matrix Printers: Walking into the Sunset

The **dot-matrix printer** forms images *one character at a time* as the print head moves across the paper. The dot-matrix printer is an *impact printer;* that is, it uses from 9 to 24 tiny *pins* to hit an ink ribbon and the paper, much as a typewriter does. The dot-matrix printer arranges printed dots to form characters and all kinds of images in much the same way as lights display time and temperature on bank signs. Figure 5.9 illustrates how the dots can form characters as a print head moves across the paper to create a letter. Dot-matrix printers print up to 450 cps (characters per second).

Most dot-matrix printers can accommodate both *cut-sheet paper* and *fanfold paper* (a continuous length of paper that is folded at perforations). The *tractor-feed* that handles fanfold paper is standard with most dot-matrix printers. Impact printers, as opposed to nonimpact printers, touch the paper and can produce carbon copies along with the original. Other pros and cons of dot-matrix printers are summarized in Figure 5.7.

The Multifunction Peripheral: Print It, Fax It, Scan It, and Copy It

Traditionally, businesses have purchased separate machines to handle these paper-related tasks: computer-based printing, facsimile (fax), scanning, and copying (duplicating). The considerable overlap in the technologies used in these machines has enabled manufacturers to create all-in-one *multifunction peripheral devices.* These multifunction devices are becoming very popular in the small office/home office environments and in other settings where the volume for any of their functions is relatively low.

Presentation Graphics: Be Persuasive

Businesspeople have found that sophisticated and colorful graphics add an aura of professionalism to any report or presentation. This demand for *presentation graphics* has created a need for corresponding output devices. Computer-generated graphic images can be re-created on paper and transparency acetates with printers. Graphic images also can be captured on 35-mm slides, displayed on a monitor, or projected onto a large screen.

The need for overhead transparencies and 35-mm slides is beginning to fade as presenters discover the ease with which they can create and deliver dynamic multimedia presentations. They do this with the help of **multimedia projectors.** These output devices fall into two categories: *LCD panels* and *LCD projectors.* The LCD panels, which are about the size of a notebook PC, are used with overhead projectors. The LCD panels are placed directly on the overhead projector as you would a transparency acetate. The light from the overhead projector is directed through an LCD panel and whatever image is on its display is shown on a large screen for all to see. The LCD projectors use their own built-in lens and light source to project the image on the screen.

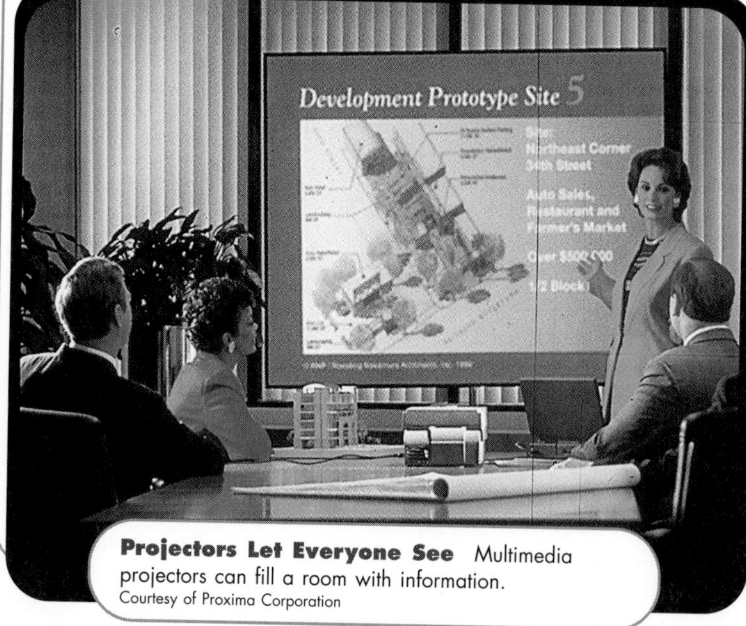

Projectors Let Everyone See Multimedia projectors can fill a room with information.
Courtesy of Proxima Corporation

Voice-Response Systems: Say It with Bits

Anyone who has used a telephone has heard "If you're dialing from a touch-tone phone, press 1." You may have driven a car that advised you to "fasten your seat belt." These are examples of "talking computers" that use output from a voice-response system. There are two types of **voice-response systems:** One uses a *reproduction* of a human voice and other sounds, and the other uses **speech synthesis.** Like monitors, voice-response systems provide temporary, soft-copy output.

The first type of voice-response system selects output from a digitized audio recording of words, phrases, music, alarms, or anything you might record, just as a printer would select characters. In these recorded voice-response systems, the actual analog recordings of sounds are converted into digital data, then permanently stored on disk or in a memory chip. When output occurs, a particular sound is converted back into analog before being routed to a speaker. Sound chips are mass-produced for specific applications, such as output for automatic teller machines, microwave ovens, smoke detectors, elevators, alarm clocks, automobile warning systems, video games, and vending machines, to mention only a few. When sounds are stored on disk, the user has the flexibility to update them to meet changing application needs.

Speech synthesis systems, which convert raw data into electronically produced speech, are popular in the PC environment. All you need to produce speech on a PC are a sound expansion card, speakers (or headset), and appropriate software. Such software often is packaged with the sound card. To produce speech, sounds resembling the phonemes (from 50 to 60 basic sound units) are combined to make up speech. The existing technology produces synthesized speech with only limited vocal inflections and phrasing, however. Despite the limitations, the number of speech synthesizer applications is growing. For example, a visually impaired person can use the speech synthesizer to translate printed words into spoken words. Translation systems offer one of the most interesting applications for speech synthesizers and speech-recognition devices. Researchers are making progress toward enabling conversations among people who are speaking different languages. A prototype system has already demonstrated that three people, each speaking a different language (English, German, and Japanese), can carry on a computer-aided conversation. Each person speaks and listens to his or her native language.

SECTION SELF-CHECK

Self-Check

5-4.1 Ink-jet printers are nonimpact printers. (T/F)

5-4.2 Dot-matrix printers generate graphs with greater precision than plotters do. (T/F)

5-4.3 The graphics adapter is the device controller for a high-resolution speech synthesizer. (T/F)

5-4.4 The passive matrix LCD monitor provides a more brilliant display than those with active matrix technology. (T/F)

5-4.5 You would be more likely to print a spreadsheet in landscape format than in portrait format. (T/F)

5-4.6 The tractor-feed on dot-matrix printers enables printing on what kind of paper: (a) cut-sheet paper, (b) fanfold paper, (c) landscape paper, (d) portrait paper?

5-4.7 What type of printer would you be most likely to find in a busy office: (a) laser printer, (b) ink-jet printer, (c) multifunction duplicator systems, or (d) glovebox printer?

5-4.8 What technology converts raw data into electronically produced speech: (a) voice response, (b) reproduction analysis, (c) speech synthesis, or (d) sound duping?

5-4.9 Which of these is not one of the capabilities of a multifunction peripheral device: (a) duplicating, (b) faxing, (c) scanning, or (d) vision input?

5-4.10 Which of these does not play a part in determining a monitor's resolution: (a) the number of colors mixed within a pixel, (b) number of pixels, (c) number of bits that represent a pixel, or (d) dot pitch?

5-4.11 Which type of graphics adapter improves system performance by using the PC system's RAM: (a) AGP, (b) GAP, (c) PAG, or (d) APG?

5-4.12 Which of these would not be a pixel density option for monitors: (a) 1024 by 768, (b) 640 by 480, (c) 123 by 84, or (d) 1600 by 1200?

5-4.13 Most flat-panel monitors are used in conjunction with: (a) server computers, (b) tower PCs, (c) laptop PCs, or (d) desktop PCs?

5-4.14 Which of these I/O devices produces hard-copy output: (a) monitor, (b) printer, (c) multimedia projector, or (d) voice-response system?

5-4.15 Which kind of printer is used to print originals with carbon copies: (a) ink-jet, (b) large-format ink-jet, (c) dot-matrix, or (d) laser?

5-4.16 All other things being equal on a monitor, which dot pitch would yield the best resolution: (a) .24 dot pitch, (b) .26 dot pitch, (c) .28 dot pitch, or (d) .31 dot pitch?

5.5 TERMINALS: INPUT AND OUTPUT

Terminals

A variety of terminals enable both *input to* and *output from* a remote computer system. Interactions via a terminal form the foundation for a wide variety of applications, from airline reservations to point-of-sale systems in retail outlets.

Dumb and Smart Terminals

Terminals come in all shapes and sizes and have a variety of input/output capabilities. The most popular general-purpose terminal is the traditional **video display terminal (VDT)** that you see in hospitals and airports. The primary input mechanism on the *VDT,* or simply the *terminal,* is a *keyboard.* Output is displayed on a *monitor.* Most of these terminals are dumb; that is, they have little or no intelligence (processing capability). Typically, they provide text-only output (no graphics).

Some terminals, called **Windows terminals,** have processing capabilities and RAM comparable to some PCs; however, they are not designed for stand-alone operation. The Windows terminal is so named because the user interacts with a Windows 9x/NT/2000 graphical user interface (GUI). All Windows terminals are configured with some type of point-and-draw device, such as a mouse, to permit efficient interaction with the GUI.

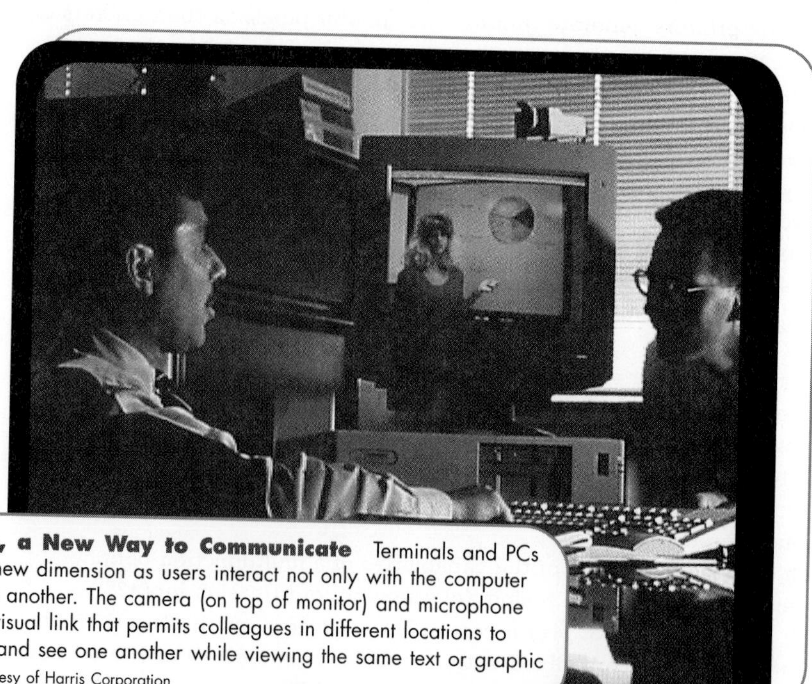

Talk and See, a New Way to Communicate Terminals and PCs are taking on a new dimension as users interact not only with the computer but also with one another. The camera (on top of monitor) and microphone enable an audiovisual link that permits colleagues in different locations to literally talk with and see one another while viewing the same text or graphic information. Courtesy of Harris Corporation

IT Ethics

ATM FEES

Generally, banks don't charge their own customers for using the bank's automatic teller machines (ATMs). In fact, they would like to encourage greater ATM usage. A transaction involving a human teller costs the bank about a dollar, but an ATM transaction costs only a dime. Banks may charge noncustomers from $1 to $5 per transaction. The high-end charges are in entertainment areas, such as casinos. People who routinely use their own bank's ATMs may be unaware of the stiff charges levied by other banks.

Discussion: Some banks charge substantial fees when nonbank customers use their ATMs. Is it ethical to do so without warning them first?

Telephone Terminals and Telephony

The telephone's widespread availability is causing greater use of it as a terminal. You can enter alphanumeric data on the touch-tone keypad of a telephone or by speaking into the receiver (voice input via speech recognition). You would then receive computer-generated voice output from a voice-response system. Salespeople use telephones as terminals for entering orders and inquiries about the availability of certain products into their company's mainframe computer. Brokerage firms allow their clients to tap into the firm's computers via telephone. After entering a password, clients can request a wide variety of services and information by working through a hierarchy of spoken menus. For example, they can request account balances and stock quotes. They can even request that a specific company's earnings report be sent to their fax machines.

Terminals for Doctors
Terminals are being created to meet a variety of needs. This doctor at the Florida Hospital in Orlando is dictating into a dictation terminal. The terminal makes it easy for radiologists and other physicians to dictate findings into a central system.
Courtesy of Harris Corporation

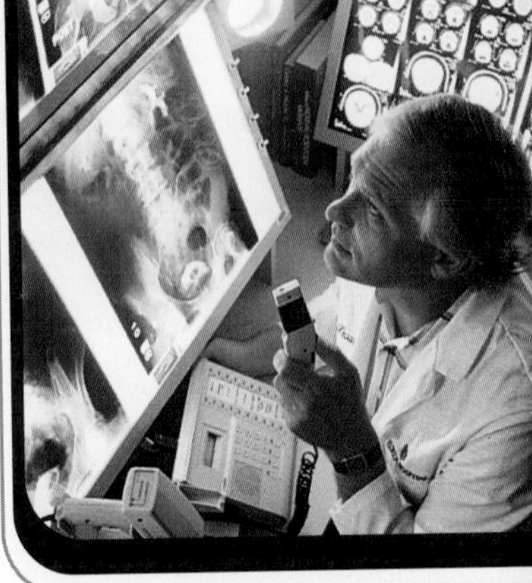

The telephone by itself has little built-in intelligence; however, when linked to a computer, potential applications abound. **Telephony** is the integration of computers and telephones, the two most essential instruments of business. In telephony, the computer, perhaps a PC, acts in concert with the telephone. For example, a PC can analyze incoming telephone calls and take appropriate action (take a message, route the call to the appropriate extension, and so on). The telephone is a terminal, but with only 12 buttons. In effect, telephony augments these 12 buttons to include a PC-based GUI. Consider these telephony applications.

- A mail-order house keeps customer records by customer telephone number. When a customer calls to phone in an order, the system detects the customer's telephone number (caller ID), routes the call to an available salesperson (or the one with the shortest wait time), and, finally, displays the customer's record on the salesperson's monitor before anyone says hello. If the salesperson is busy, the customer is given an opportunity to enter the order directly from a telephone.
- A school district uses telephony to reschedule district events. Here is how it works. A computer system can announce a last-minute change of time for a school board meeting via the telephone system. Upon being prompted by a user, the system automatically announces the change to the participants and the media community. The telephony system even negotiates scheduling conflicts with participants to arrive at an acceptable time for all concerned—all automatically.

Telephony promotes efficient interactions. As it matures, look for many routine communications to be handled entirely by computers (for example, scheduling of meetings). Much of what has to be done in a typical business phone call can be accomplished between cooperating computers. If and when we are needed, we will be asked to join the conversation.

FIGURE 5.10

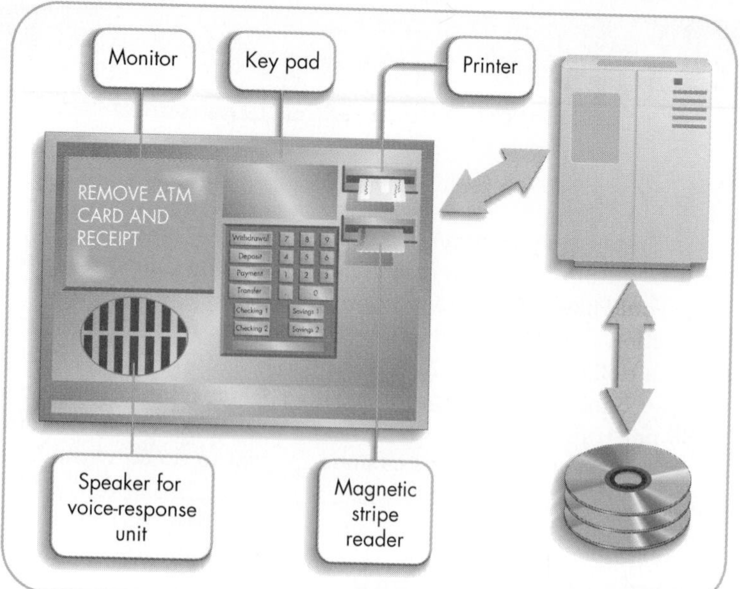

Terminals for Banking Customers: Automatic Teller Machines The widely used automatic teller machine (ATM) supports a variety of input/output methods. The magnetic stripe on the ATM card contains identification and security information that, when read, is sent to the bank's computer system. The ATM responds with instructions via its monitor. The customer enters an identification number and data via a keypad. In the figure, the computer processes the customer's request, and then provides instructions for the customer via the monitor and verbally with a voice-response unit.

Special-Function Terminals: ATMs and POSs

The number and variety of special-function terminals are growing rapidly. Special-function terminals are designed for a specific application, such as convenience banking. You probably are familiar with the *automatic teller machine (ATM)* and its input/output capabilities (see Figure 5.10). A badge reader (magnetic stripe) and a keypad enable input to the system. A monitor and a printer (for printing transaction receipts) provide output. Some ATMs use voice response as a monitor backup to alert people when to perform certain actions (for example, "Take your receipt").

The ATM idea has caught on for other applications. A consortium of companies is installing thousands of ATM-like terminals that will let you order and receive a wide variety of documents on the spot. For example, you can now obtain an airline ticket, your college transcript, and an IRS form electronically, and many more applications are on the way.

Another widely used special-function terminal is the *point-of-sale (POS)* terminal. POS terminals are used by clerks and salespeople in retail stores, restaurants, and other establishments that sell goods and services. POS terminals have a keypad for input, at least one small monitor, and a printer to print the receipt. Some have other input/output devices, such as a badge reader for credit cards, a wand or stationary scanner to read price and inventory data, and/or a printer to preprint checks for customers.

During the late 1980s, a number of grocery stores had POS terminals with voice-response systems that verbally confirmed the price on each item. The unnecessary noise caused by these systems added confusion to the checkout process without any increase in value to the store or the customer. These systems are now a part of computing history. That's the way it is with technology, especially input/output. Sometimes you have to try it to see if it works. Over the next few years we'll be confronted with many I/O experiments.

MEMORY

Terminals

General-purpose
- Video display terminal (VDT)
- Windows terminal
- Telephone

Special-function
- Automatic teller machine (ATM)
- Point-of-sale (POS) terminal

SECTION SELF-CHECK

Self-Check

5-5.1 Special-function terminals can be found in most department stores. (T/F)

5-5.2 ATMs are now available in some areas of the country that will let you order and receive Internal Revenue Service (IRS) forms and airline tickets. (T/F)

5-5.3 The telephone is considered a terminal. (T/F)

5-5.4 Some terminals are dumb and some are smart. (T/F)

5-5.5 Which terminal permits system interaction via a GUI: (a) a dumb terminal, (b) a Windows terminal, (c) a text-based terminal or (d) a traditional VDT?

5-5.6 The integration of computers and telephones is known as: (a) telecommunications, (b) telephony, (c) autophony, or (d) IT phoning?

5-5.7 The primary input/output on the VDT is: (a) the mouse and microphone, (b) the keyboard and speaker, (c) a hard disk and monitor, or (d) the keyboard and monitor?

Interactive Study Guide
Chapter 5

SUMMARY AND KEY TERMS

5.1 I/O devices: Let's interface

A variety of input/output (I/O) peripheral devices provide the interface between us and the computer.

5.2 Traditional input devices

There are two basic types of keyboards: traditional alphanumeric keyboards and special-function keyboards. A widely used keyboard layout is the 101-key keyboard with the traditional *QWERTY* key layout, 12 **function keys** (149), a numeric keypad, a variety of special-function keys, and dedicated cursor-control keys. The cursor-control keys can be used to select **menu** (149) options or to move the **text cursor** (149). Some special-function keyboards are designed for specific applications. The mouse and its cousins enable interaction with the operating system's **graphical user interface (GUI)** (151) and they help us to draw. These include the **trackball** (152), **trackpoint** (152), **trackpad** (152), **digitizer tablet and pen** (152), and **joystick** (152). When these point-and-draw devices are moved, the **mouse cursor** (151) on the display moves accordingly. Along with buttons, the **wheel mouse** (151) also has a "wheel" for scrolling. **Click** (151) the left button to select a menu item. Tap the mouse button twice to **double-click** (152). Press and hold a button to **drag** (152) the mouse cursor.

5.3 Source-data automation

The trend in data entry has been toward **source-data automation** (154).

A variety of **scanners** (155) read and interpret information on printed matter and convert it to a format that can be interpreted by a computer. **OCR (optical character recognition)** (155) is the ability to read printed information into a computer system. **Bar codes** (154) represent alphanumeric data by varying the size of adjacent vertical lines. Two types of OCR or bar code scanners—*contact* and *laser*—read information on labels and various types of documents. Scanners used for OCR or bar code applications can be classified into three basic categories—handheld label scanners [called **wand scanners** (155)], stationary label scanners, and document scanners [which are often used with **turnaround documents** (156)].

An **image scanner** (156) uses laser technology to scan and **digitize** (156) an image. Image scanners provide input for **image processing** (156). Image scanners are of two types: *page* and *hand*.

Magnetic stripes, **smart cards** (158), and badges provide input to **badge readers** (158).

Speech-recognition systems (159) can be used to enter spoken words in continuous speech at speeds of up to 125 words a minute by comparing digitized representations of words to similarly formed templates in the computer system's electronic dictionary.

Vision-input systems (160) are best suited to very specialized tasks in which only a few images will be encountered.

Digital cameras (161) are used to take photos that are represented digitally (already digitized).

Handheld data entry devices have a limited external keyboard or a soft keyboard; a small display that may be touch sensitive; nonvolatile RAM, and often a scanning device.

5.4 Output devices

Output devices translate bits and bytes into a form we can understand. The most common "output only" devices include monitors, printers, plotters, multimedia projectors, and voice-response systems.

Monitors are defined in terms of their (1) **graphics adapter** (163) (which has **video RAM** or **VRAM** [163]); (2) size; (3) **resolution** (166) (number of **pixels** [166], number of bits used to represent each pixel, and **dot pitch** [166]); (4) display quality. The quality of the display is affected by the *refresh rate* and whether the monitor is *interlaced*.

Gray scales (166) are used to refer to the number of shades of a color that can be shown on a monochrome monitor's screen. **RGB monitors** (166) mix red, green, and blue to achieve a spectrum of colors.

Flat-panel monitors (168) are used with laptop PCs, many of which use LCD technology. **Touch screen monitors** (168) permit input as well as output.

Three basic PC printer technologies include page, ink-jet, and dot-matrix. Printers can print in **portrait** (168) or **landscape** (168) format. Nonimpact **page printers** (169) (**laser printers** [169]) use several technologies to achieve high-speed hard-copy output by printing a page at a time. The color option is available in laser and ink-jet printers.

Nonimpact **ink-jet printers** (171) have print heads that move back and forth across the paper squirting ink droplets to write text and create images. The color ink-jet printer is emerging as the choice for home and small office consumers.

Large-format ink-jet printers (171), also called **plotters** (171), use ink-jet technology to print on roll-feed paper up to four feet wide.

The **dot-matrix printer** (171), an impact printer, forms images one character at a time as the print head moves across the paper.

Multifunction peripheral devices are available that handle several paper-related tasks: computer-based printing, facsimile (fax), scanning, and copying.

The demand for presentation graphics has created a need for corresponding output devices, such as a **multimedia projector** (172).

Voice-response systems (172) provide recorded or synthesized audio output (via **speech synthesis** [172]).

5.5 Terminals: Input and output

Terminals enable interaction with a remote computer system. The general-purpose terminals are the **video display terminal (VDT)** (174) and the *telephone.* Terminals come in all shapes and sizes and have a variety of input/output capabilities.

Terminals that have little or no intelligence are called dumb terminals. **Windows terminals** (174) with processing capabilities enable the user to interact via a graphical user interface. **Telephony** (175) is the integration of computers and telephones.

A variety of special-function terminals, such as automatic teller machines and point-of-sale terminals, are designed for a specific application.

DISCUSSION AND PROBLEM SOLVING

5.1 **a.** Describe two instances during the past 24 hours in which you had indirect communication with a computer; that is, something you did resulted in computer activity.

b. Describe an automated telephone system with which you are familiar that asks you to select options from a series of menus. Discuss the advantages and disadvantages of this system.

5.2 **a.** Name four types of point-and-draw devices. Which one do you think you would prefer? Explain your reasoning.

b. What is the relationship between a trackpad and a mouse cursor? Between a trackpad and a text cursor?

c. The QWERTY keyboard, which has been the standard on typewriters and keyboards for decades, was actually designed to keep people from typing so rapidly. Speculate on why built-in inefficiency was a design objective.

5.3 **a.** Today's continuous speech-recognition systems are able to interpret spoken words more accurately when the user talks in phrases. Why would this approach be more accurate than discrete speech where the user speaks one word at a time with a slight separation between words?

b. In the next generation of credit cards, the familiar magnetic stripe probably will be replaced by embedded microprocessors in smart cards. Suggest applications for this capability.

c. Some department stores use handheld label scanners, and others use stationary label scanners to interpret the bar codes printed on the price tags of merchandise. What advantages does one scanner have over the other?

d. Compare today's vision-input systems with those portrayed in such films as *2001* and *2010.* Do you believe we will have a comparable vision technology by the year 2001?

e. What is a turnaround document? Describe at least one instance in which you have used a turnaround document.

f. Today, literally billions of pages of documentation are maintained in government and corporate file cabinets. Next year, the contents of millions of file cabinets will be digitized via image processing. Briefly describe at least one situation with which you are familiar that is a candidate for image processing. Explain how image processing can improve efficiency at this organization.

g. Describe how your photographic habits might change if you owned a digital camera.

5.4 **a.** What input/output capabilities are available at your college or place of work? Describe the input/output characteristics of a workstation/PC that would be desirable for engineers doing computer-aided design (CAD).

b. Four PCs at a police precinct are networked and currently share a 200-cps impact dot-matrix printer. The captain has budgeted enough money to purchase one page printer (15 ppm) or two more 200-cps dot-matrix printers. Which option would you suggest the precinct choose and why?

c. A large company can save up to $200 per employee by purchasing small, low-quality monitors. In the long run, however, health and overall efficiency implications of this decision may result in costs that far exceed any savings. Explain.

d. In five years, forecasters are predicting flat-panel monitors less than .25-inch thick may be placed everywhere around the home and office. Speculate on how these ultra-thin monitors might be used in the home and in the office.

e. Would a multifunction peripheral be appropriate in your home or would you prefer purchasing separate devices for the various document-handling functions (duplicating, faxing, printing, scanning)? Explain your reasoning.

f. Describe the benefits of using a laptop PC in conjunction with a multimedia projector during a formal business presentation as opposed to the traditional alternative (transparency acetates and overhead projector).

g. People are calling PC-based speech-recognition software a "killer app." Why?

5.5 **a.** Identify all input and output methods used by automatic teller machines in your city.

b. Dumb terminals linked to mainframe computers remain the standard at airport ticketing counters. Speculate on why the airlines have not replaced these terminals with more user-friendly Windows terminals.

Networks and Networking

Learning Objectives

6.1 Describe the concept of connectivity.

6.2 Detail the function and operation of data communications hardware.

6.3 Describe alternatives and sources of data transmission services.

6.4 Illustrate the various kinds of network topologies and show an understanding of client/server computing.

6.5 Identify the various types of networks and show an overview understanding of local area network hardware and software.

chapter 6

WHY THIS CHAPTER IS IMPORTANT TO YOU

Ten years ago, the number-one reason people purchased a PC was for word processing. Now people buy PCs for many reasons, but frequently they do so to get on the Internet. Everyone wants to logon and travel through cyberspace, soaking up all it has to offer. Each day our world is becoming increasingly connected—electronically. If you aren't already online, you, too, will eventually want to be connected. When you do, you can save yourself both time and money by knowing the basics of data communications.

Data communications was relatively new in the mid-1960s. During the first 25 years of the communications era, data communications experts purchased, installed, and maintained multimillion-dollar communications hardware and channels. Now, most of the connected computer systems are personal computers owned by people like you. Relatively few of us are blessed with a technical support staff at our beck-and-call, so we, the users, are the people who purchase, install, and maintain our own communications hardware and channels—not the experts. Usually the hardware is no more involved than a modem and a telephone line. However, this is beginning to change as homes and small offices begin to network multiple PCs and install higher-capacity lines.

This chapter introduces you to data communications concepts that will prove helpful at home and make you a more informed employee at work. You'll learn about communications-related hardware and be introduced to various delivery alternatives, including transmission options over traditional voice-grade telephone lines, cable TV lines, and wireless alternatives. Many people have literally thrown up their hands in frustration when dealing with communications tasks and issues. Hopefully, what you learn from this chapter will help eliminate some of that frustration.

Value Learning

6.1 OUR WEIRD, WILD, WIRED WORLD

Monthly Technology Update Chapter 6

Serendipitous Surfing: Online Books

Millions of people are knowledge workers by day and Internet surfers by night. As knowledge workers, we need ready access to information. In the present competitive environment, we cannot rely solely on verbal communication to get that information. Corporate presidents cannot wait until the Monday morning staff meeting to find out whether production is meeting demand. Field sales representatives can no longer afford to play telephone tag with headquarters personnel to get answers for impatient customers. The president, the field rep, and the rest of us now rely on *computer networks* to retrieve and share information quickly. Of course, we will continue to interact with our co-workers, but computer networks simply enhance the efficiency and effectiveness of that interaction.

As surfers, we surf the Internet, America Online, CompuServe, or any of scores of commercial information services. Once logged on to one of these networks, cybersurfers can chat with friends, strangers, and even celebrities. We can go shopping, peruse electronic magazines, download interesting photos and songs, plan a vacation, play games, buy and sell stock, send e-mail, and generally hang out. It's official: We now live in a weird, wild, wired world where computer networks are networked to one another. This chapter is devoted to concepts relating to computer networks and communications technology. Once you have a grasp of this technology, you will find it easier to understand the different uses and applications of networks.

Digital Convergence: Coming Together as Bits and Bytes

We are going through a period of **digital convergence.** That is, TVs, PCs, telephones, movies, college textbooks, newspapers, and much, much more are converging toward digital compatibility. For example, movies that are now frames of cellulose are in the process of digital convergence. The 200,000 frames required for a full-length movie will converge to 16 billion bits on a single DVD. Already hundreds of movies have been released on DVD. Major components of this book's

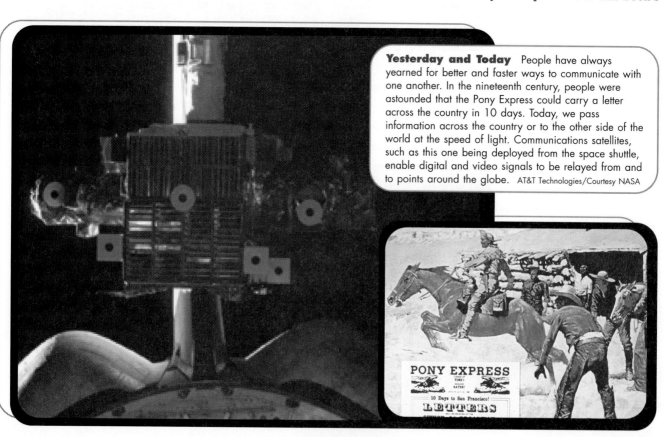

Yesterday and Today People have always yearned for better and faster ways to communicate with one another. In the nineteenth century, people were astounded that the Pony Express could carry a letter across the country in 10 days. Today, we pass information across the country or to the other side of the world at the speed of light. Communications satellites, such as this one being deployed from the space shuttle, enable digital and video signals to be relayed from and to points around the globe. AT&T Technologies/Courtesy NASA learning system are on CD-ROM and the Internet. Future editions will follow the trend toward digital convergence with an increasing portion of the material being distributed digitally. And, perhaps the ultimate example of digital convergence is that you can go online and purchase the digital equivalent of United States Postal Service postage stamps.

Digital convergence, combined with an ever-expanding worldwide network of computers, is enabling our society to take one giant leap into the future. Already the TV, PC, video game, stereo system, answering device, and telephone are on a collision course that will meld them into communications/information centers by the end of the century. We'll have video-on-demand such that we can view all or any part of any movie ever produced at any time, even in a window on our office PC. Instead of carrying a billfold, we might carry a credit-card-sized device that would contain all the typical billfold items such as money, credit cards, pictures, driver's license, and other forms of identification. These items will all be digital. When we buy a pizza in the future, we might simply enter a code into our electronic billfold to automatically order and pay for the pizza. The possibilities are endless.

Digital convergence is more than a convergence of technologies. Information technology is the enabling technology for the convergence of industries, as well. In a recent survey, 95 percent of the CEOs in the entertainment, telecommunications, cable, and computer industries agreed that their industries are converging.

With half the industrial world (and many governments) racing toward digital convergence, there is no question that we are going digital over the next few years. Our photo album will be digital. Our money will be digital. Already, digitized movies are being transmitted to theaters where they are shown via high-definition projection units.

Connectivity: Getting to the Information

All of this convergence is happening so that information will be more accessible to more people. To realize the potential of a universe of digital information, the business and computer communities are continually seeking ways to interface, or connect, a diverse set of hardware, software, and databases. This increased level of **connectivity** brings people from as close to the next room and as far as the other side of the world closer together.

- Connectivity means that a marketing manager can use a PC to access information in the finance department's database.
- Connectivity means that a network of PCs can route output to a shared page printer.
- Connectivity means that a manufacturer's server computer can communicate with a supplier's server.
- Connectivity means that you can send your holiday newsletter via e-mail.
- Connectivity means that the appliances, including PCs, in your home can be networked.

Connectivity is implemented in degrees. We can expect to become increasingly connected to computers and information both at work and at home during the coming years. Thirty years ago there were tens of thousands of computers. Today there are hundreds of *millions* of them! Computers and information are everywhere. Our challenge is to connect them.

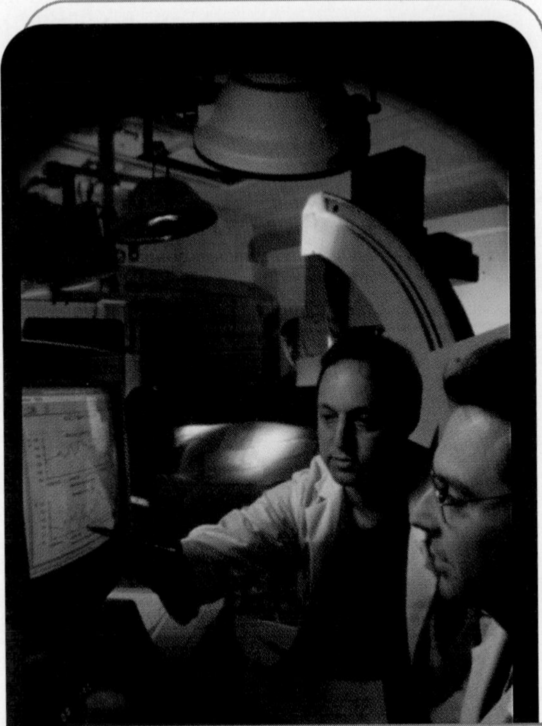

Hospitals Link Up The workstations and PCs at this hospital are linked to a server computer, which is connected via a high-speed communications line. A computerized patient records system allows physicians to easily access up-to-date patient chart information from workstations throughout the hospital. Courtesy of Harris Corporation

The Beginning of an Era: Cooperative Processing

We are living in an era of **cooperative processing.** Companies have recognized that they must cooperate internally to take full advantage of company resources, and that they must cooperate externally with one another to compete effectively in a world market. To promote internal cooperation, businesses are setting up *intracompany networking* (see Figure 6.1). These networks allow people in, say, the sales department to know the latest information from the production department. Companies cooperate externally (with customers and other companies) via **intercompany networking** (Figure 6.1) or, more specifically, via **electronic data interchange (EDI).** EDI relies on computer networks to transmit data electronically between companies. Invoices, orders, and many other intercompany transactions can be transmitted from the computer of one company to the computer of another. For example, at major retail chains, such as Wal-Mart, over 90% of all orders are processed directly between computers via EDI. Much of that will be via a traditional EDI, but an increasing amount of business between companies will be moved to the Internet. More specifically, it will be moved to a company's *intranet* with actual commerce taking place over their *extranets.* An **intranet** is essentially a closed or private version of the Internet. An intranet looks and feels like the Internet, but is accessible only by those people within the company. An **extranet** is simply an extension of an intranet such that it is partially accessible to authorized outsiders, such as customers and suppliers. In time, EDI will be replaced entirely by Internet-based solutions to intercompany commerce. Figure 6.2 contrasts the traditional interactions between a customer and supplier company with interactions via EDI and extranets. Business-to-business commerce is expected to grow to a whopping $1.3 trillion by 2003, almost 10% of all U.S. business trade!

The phenomenal growth of the use of PCs in the home is causing companies to expand their information system capabilities to allow linkages with home and portable PCs. This form of cooperative processing increases system efficiency while lowering costs. For example, home banking customers use their personal computers to link to the bank's mainframe computer system to pay bills, transfer funds, and ask about account status.

Intracompany and Intercompany Networking

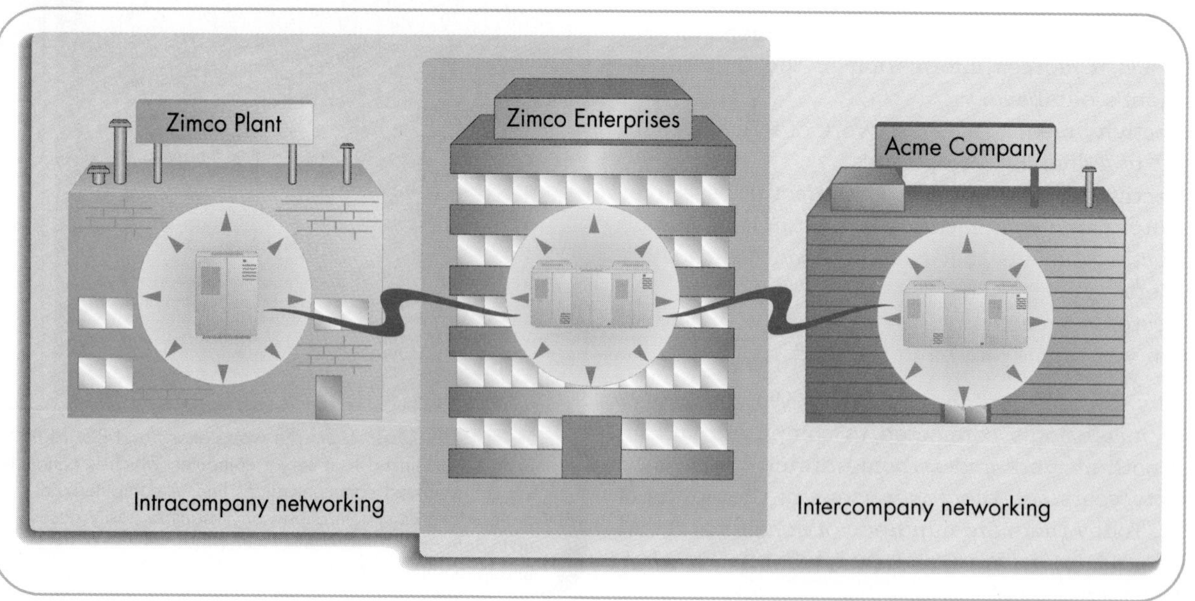

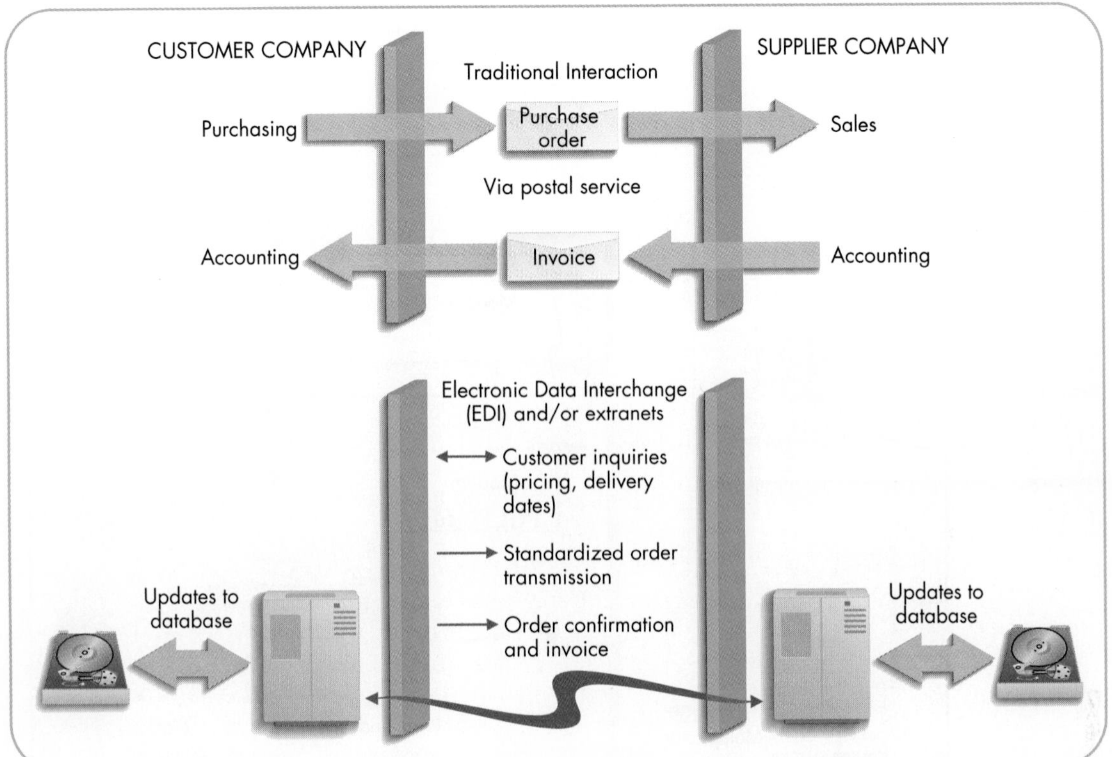

FIGURE 6.2 **Interactions between Customer and Supplier** In the figure, the traditional interaction between a customer company and a supplier company are contrasted with similar interactions via electronic data interchange (EDI) and/or extranets.

SECTION SELF-CHECK

Self-Check

6-1.1 We are going through a period of digital convergence. (T/F)

6-1.2 EDI eventually will replace the extranet for electronic communication between companies. (T/F)

6-1.3 A company either has connectivity or it doesn't, with no in-between. (T/F)

6-1.4 One approach to using computers to transmit data electronically between companies is called: (a) EDI, (b) DIE, (c) DEI, or (d) DIT?

6-1.5 A closed or private version of the Internet is called: (a) a fishnet, (b) an intranet, (c) an overnet, or (d) an addnet?

6.2 DATA COMMUNICATIONS HARDWARE: MAKING IT HAPPEN

Data communications, or **telecommunications,** is the electronic collection and distribution of information between two points. Information can appear in a variety of formats—numeric data, text, voice, still pictures, graphics, and video. As we have already seen, raw information must be digitized before we can input it into a computer. For example, numerical data and text might be translated into their corresponding ASCII codes. Once the digitized information has been entered into a computer, that computer can then transfer the information to other computers connected over a network. Ultimately, all forms of digitized information are transmitted over the transmission media (for example, fiber optic cable) as a series of binary bits (1s and 0s).

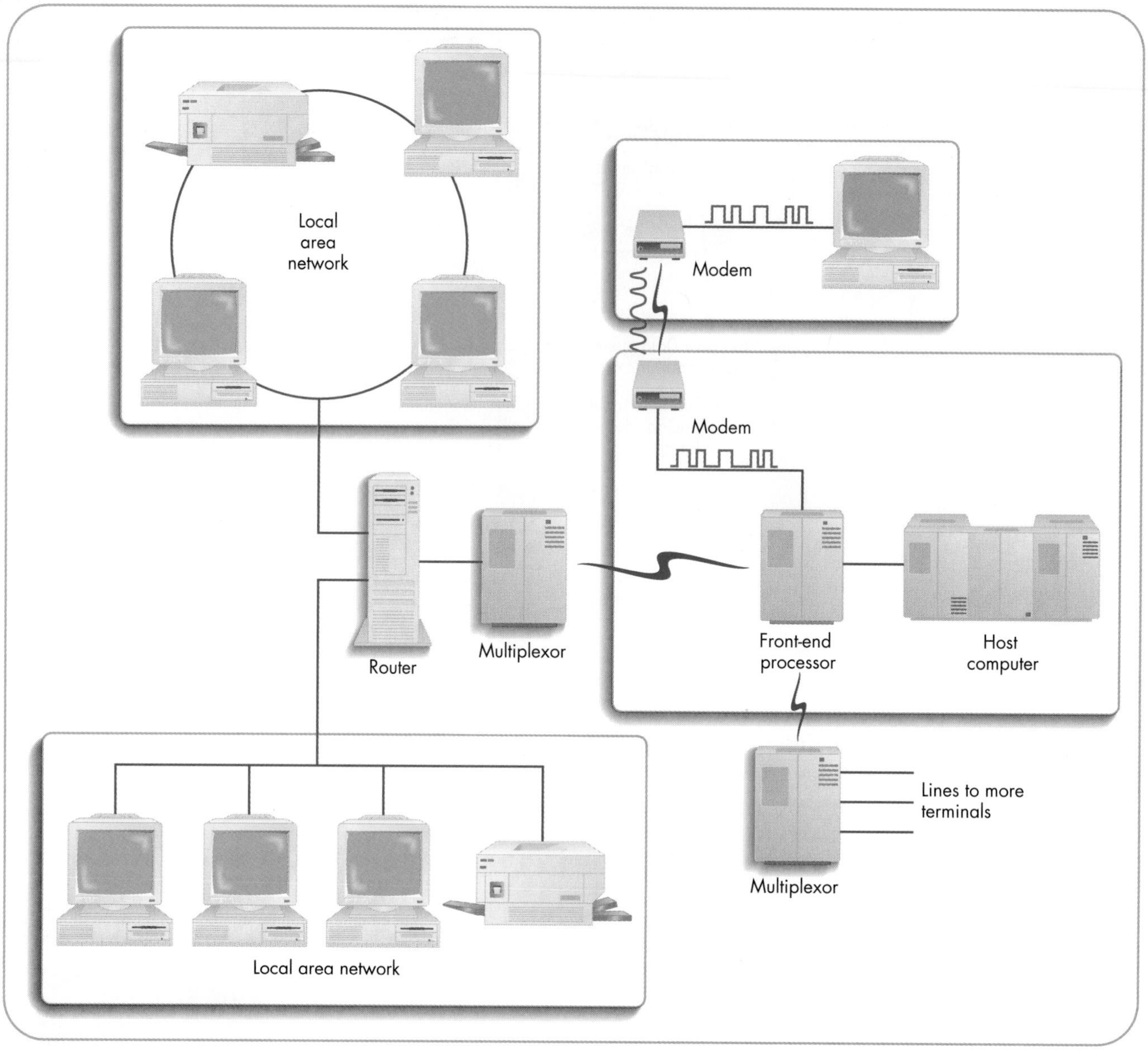

Local area network
Modem
Modem
Router
Multiplexor
Front-end processor
Host computer
Lines to more terminals
Multiplexor
Local area network

Hardware Components in Data Communications Devices that handle the movement of data in a computer network are the modem, the multiplexor, the front-end processor, the router, network interface cards (expansion cards in the local area network–based PCs), and the host computer. Also in the figure, electrical digital signals are modulated (via a modem) into analog signals for transmission over telephone lines and then demodulated for processing at the destination. The lightning bolts indicate transmission between remote locations.

Data communications hardware is used to transmit digital information between terminals and computers or between computers and other computers. There is a vast array of communications and networking hardware. Figure 6.3, which shows the integration of some of these devices with terminals and computer systems, is a representative computer network. With so much networking hardware, networks are a lot like snowflakes—no two are alike. Unlike snowflakes, however, networks never melt. Once created, networks seem to have a life of their own, growing with the changing needs of the organization.

With the trend toward digital convergence, the number and variety of network hardware components that enable data communications continue to evolve, with new devices being introduced almost monthly. There are *concentrators, switching hubs, bridges, routers, brouters* (combination bridges and routers), *network interface cards, front-end processors, multiplexors, modems,* and many more special-function devices that route, pass along, convert, package and repackage, and format and reformat bits and bytes traveling along communications links. Most of these are beyond the scope of an introductory study of IT. We will, however, talk about a couple of the more personal devices: the modem, a device that comes with every new PC, and the network interface card, a device found on most corporate PCs. Also, we will talk about a few other devices to help you better understand the fundamental terminology of data communications.

The Modem: Digital to Analog to Digital

Even if your PC is not connected to a corporate local area network with a digital line to cyberspace, you can establish a communications link between it and any remote computer system in the world, assuming you have the authorization to do so. However, you must first have ready access to a telephone line, and your PC must be equipped with a *modem.*

Telephone lines were designed to carry *analog signals* for voice communication, not the binary *digital signals* (1s and 0s) needed for computer-based data communication. The modem (*mo*dulator-*dem*odulator) converts *digital* signals into *analog* signals so data can be transmitted over telephone lines (see Figure 6.3). The digital electrical signals are modulated to make sounds similar to those you hear on a touch-tone telephone. Upon reaching their destination, these analog signals are demodulated into computer-compatible digital signals for processing. A modem is always required for two computers to communicate over a telephone line. It is not needed when the PC is wired directly to a computer network.

There are two types of modems for PCs and terminals: *internal* and *external.* Most PCs have internal modems; that is, the modem is on an optional add-on circuit board that is simply plugged into an empty expansion slot in the PC's motherboard. Laptops typically use modems on interchangeable PC cards. The external modem is a separate component, as illustrated in Figure 6.3, and is connected via a serial interface port. To make the connection with a telephone line and either type of modem, you simply plug the telephone line into the modem just as you would when connecting the line to a telephone.

The typical modem is a voice/data/fax modem. Besides the data communications capabilities, it allows you to make telephone calls through your PC and modem hookup (using a microphone, speakers, and/or a headset). The fax component enables a PC to simulate a *facsimile* or *fax* machine. Instead of sending a document to a printer, you simply send it to the fax modem along with a destination fax number.

Network Interface Cards

The **network interface card (NIC),** which we introduced in Chapter 3, "Inside the Computer," is an add-on board or PC card (for laptops) that enables and controls the exchange of data between the PCs in a LAN. Each PC in the LANs in Figure 6.3 must be equipped with an NIC. The cables or wireless transceivers that link the PCs are physically connected to the NICs. Whether as an add-on board or a PC card, the NIC is connected directly to the PC's internal bus.

Special-Function Communications Devices: Help along the Line

In Figure 6.3, there is a *host computer,* or server computer, that is responsible for the overall control of the network and for the execution of applications (for example, a hotel reservation system). To improve the efficiency of a computer system, the *processing load* is sometimes *distributed* among several other special-function processors. The two communications-related processors in the network of Figure 6.3, the front-end processor and the multiplexor, are under the control

Communications Hardware The applications of communications hardware are far more exciting than their appearance. Shown here are a wide variety of modems (internal, external, rack-mounted, PC card) and other communications hardware made by Multi-Tech Systems.
Courtesy of Multi-Tech Systems, Inc.

of and subordinate to the host. In Figure 6.3, the host computer is a large server computer; however, the host could just as well be a PC or a supercomputer, depending on the size and complexity of the network.

The terminal or computer sending a **message** is the *source.* The terminal or computer receiving the message is the *destination.* The **front-end processor** establishes the link between the source and destination in a process called **handshaking.** The term *front-end processor* has evolved to a generic reference for a computer-based device that relieves the host computer of a variety of communications-related processing duties. These duties include the transmission of data to and from remote terminals and other computers. The host can instead concentrate on overall system control and the execution of applications software.

If you think of messages as mail to be delivered to various points in a computer network, the front-end processor is the post office. Each computer system and terminal/PC in a computer network is assigned a **network address.** The front-end processor uses these addresses to route messages to their destinations. The content of a message could be a prompt to the user, a user inquiry, a program instruction, an "electronic memo," or any type of information that can be transmitted electronically—even the image of a handwritten report.

The **multiplexor** is an extension of the front-end processor. It is located downline from the host computer—at or near a remote site. The multiplexor collects data from several low-speed devices, such as terminals and printers. It then "concentrates" the data and sends them over a single communications channel (see Figure 6.4) to the front-end processor. The multiplexor also receives and distributes host output to the appropriate remote terminals. Using one high-speed line to connect the multiplexor to the host is considerably less expensive than is using several low-speed lines to connect each terminal to the host. For example, an airline reservation counter might have 10 terminals, and it would be very slow and very expensive to connect each directly to the host computer. Instead, each terminal would be connected to a common multiplexor, which in turn would be connected to the central host computer.

Routers: Bridging the Gap

Computer networks are everywhere—in banks, in law offices, and in the classroom. In keeping with the trend toward greater connectivity, computer networks are themselves being networked and interconnected to give users access to a greater variety of applications and to more information. For example, the typical

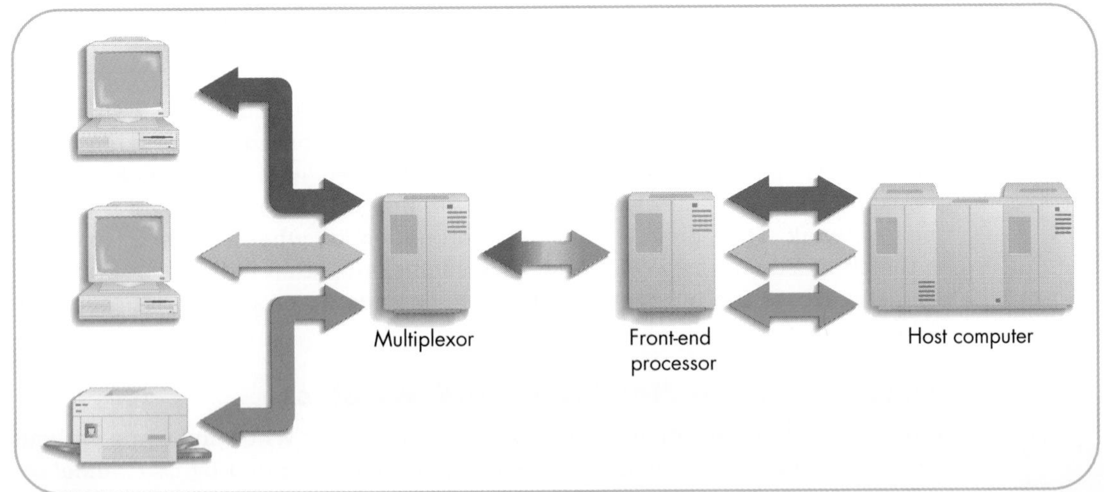

Concentrating Data for Remote Transmission The multiplexor concentrates the data from several low-speed devices for transmission over a single high-speed line. At the host site, the front-end processor separates the data for processing. Data received from a front-end processor are interpreted by the multiplexor processor and routed to the appropriate device.

medium-to-large company links several PC-based networks to the company's enterprise-wide mainframe network. This enables end users on all networks to share information and resources.

Communications protocols are rules established to govern the way data are transmitted in a computer network. Because networks use a variety of communications protocols and operating systems, incompatible networks cannot "talk" directly to one another. The primary hardware/software technology used to alleviate the problems of linking incompatible computer networks is the **router.** Routers help to bridge the gap between incompatible networks by performing the necessary protocol conversions to route messages to their proper destinations.

Organizations that are set up to interconnect computer networks do so over a **backbone.** The backbone is a collective term that refers to a system of routers and the associated transmission media (cables, wires, and wireless links) that link the computers in an organization.

Serendipitous Surfing: Government

SECTION SELF-CHECK

Self-Check

6-2.1 The electronic collection and distribution of information between two points is referred to as telecommunications. (T/F)

6-2.2 Another name for a server is a multiplexor. (T/F)

6-2.3 The typical modem is a voice/data/fax modem. (T/F)

6-2.4 Each PC in the LANs in Figure 6.3 must be equipped with an NIC. (T/F)

6-2.5 A communications device establishes the link between the source and destination in a process called: (a) handshaking, (b) greeting, (c) hello–good bye, or (d) messaging?

6-2.6 The communications device that facilitates the interconnection of dissimilar networks is: (a) a server, (b) a client, (c) an ISDN line, or (d) a router?

6-2.7 What device converts digital signals into analog signals for transmission over telephone lines: (a) router, (b) brouter, (c) modem, or (d) client/server?

6-2.8 Each computer system and PC in a computer network is assigned: (a) a network address, (b) a mailbox, (c) a P.O. address, or (d) an alphabetic identifier?

6.3 THE DATA COMMUNICATIONS CHANNEL: DATA HIGHWAYS

A **communications channel** is the medium through which digital information must pass to get from one location in a computer network to the next. Most people use colloquial terms for communications channel, such as *line, link,* or *pipe.* Communications channels link PCs, servers, and other devices in an organization's network. They provide links between networks, whether across, down, or on the other side of the world. And, they enable you, other individuals, and companies to access the Internet, which, itself, is made up of a variety of communications links.

Transmission Media: Wires and Wireless

Transmission Media

A variety of communication channels, some made up of wires and some without wires, carry digital signals between computers. Each is rated by its *channel capacity* or *bandwidth.* The channel capacity is the number of bits a channel can transmit per second. Channel capacities vary from 56,000 **bits per second (bps),** or 56 K bps (thousands of bits, or kilobits, per second) to 622 M bps (millions of bits, or megabits, per second). In practice, the word **baud** is often used interchangeably with *bits per second.* Technically speaking, however, it is quite different. But if someone says *baud* when talking about computer-based communications, that person probably means bits per second.

Twisted-Pair Wire: Still Growing in Capability

Twisted-pair wire is just what we think of as regular telephone wire. Each twisted-pair wire is actually two insulated copper wires twisted around each other. At least one twisted-pair line provides **POTS** (plain old telephone services) to just about every home and business in the United States. Telephone companies offer different levels of twisted-pair service (see Figure 6.5). All companies offer voice-grade service. The other two services listed below may or may not be available in your area.

- *POTS.* When you call the telephone company and request a telephone line, it installs POTS. This analog line permits voice conversations and digital transmissions with the aid of a modem. Traditional modem technology permits data transmission up to 56 K bps.
- *ISDN.* Some applications demand a higher channel capacity than that available over voice-grade lines. One alternative, which can be delivered over a POTS line, is **Integrated Services Digital Network (ISDN),** a digital service. The ISDN line terminates at an **ISDN modem** (internal or external). The ISDN modem is then connected to a port on the computer. The ISDN line enables data transmission at 128 K bps, more than twice the speed of the fastest analog modem. The ISDN modem allows the line's channel capacity to be split such that one channel can carry a voice conversation while the other

Popular Internet Access Options for Individual Users
The overwhelming majority of users still link to the Internet via POTS at a maximum speed of 56 K bps, but increasing numbers are moving to higher-speed options as they become available at reasonable prices.

Transmission Media	Service and/or Channel Capacity		
Twisted-pair	POTS (56 K bps)	ISDN (128 K bps)	ADSL (1 to 9 M bps)
Cable TV	1 to 10 M bps (one way or two way high-speed)		
Satellite	500 K bps to 48 M bps (one way or two way high-speed)		

supports an electronic link between computers. ISDN lines have become popular for telecommuters who work at home but need to be networked to their office's computer system.

- *ADSL.* Another technology, **Asymmetric Digital Subscriber Line (ADSL),** has made it possible to receive data over POTS lines at 1.5 to 9 M bps (the **downstream rate** in megabits per second). In a few years, the downstream rate will be 52 M bps. The **upstream rate** (sending) is 16 to 640 K bps. Like ISDN, ADSL requires a special modem. ADSL opens the door for some amazing applications to be delivered over POTS lines. Applications include support for full-motion video, very high-speed transfer of graphics, and real-time applications involving a group of online participants.

Coaxial Cable

Most people know coaxial cable as the cable in "cable television." **Coaxial cable,** or "coax," contains electrical wire (usually copper wire) and is constructed to permit high-speed data transmission with a minimum of signal distortion. It is laid along the ocean floor for intercontinental voice and data transmission; it's used to connect terminals and computers in a "local" area (from a few feet to a few miles); and it delivers TV signals to close to 100 million homes in America alone. Coaxial cable has a very "wide pipe." That is, it is a high-capacity channel that can carry digital data at up to 10 M bps, as well as more than 100 analog TV signals. Internet access via cable TV coax cable is hundreds of times faster than POTS and 100 times faster than ISDN service.

Cable television systems originally were designed to deliver television signals to subscribers' homes. However, this same coaxial cable can be used to provide high-speed Internet access at reasonable prices. All over the United States, cable companies are updating their cable infrastructure to enable them to offer Internet access to subscribers. Initially cable Internet access companies are offering 1 M bps to 10 M bps service, significantly faster than POTS service and only

Copper Wire and Fiber Optic Cable At one time, New York City was laced with copper wire. Today, the more versatile fiber optic cable has replaced the telephone poles and the wire. Laser-generated light pulses are transmitted through glass fibers. A pair of optic fibers can simultaneously carry 1344 voice conversations and interactive data communications sessions.
AT&T Technologies/Courtesy of International Business Machines Corporation

slightly more expensive. A 10 megabits per second channel capacity is very inviting to the millions of people who are chugging along at 56 K bps over POTS lines (see Figure 6.5). Linking to cable TV for Internet access requires a *cable modem.*

Fiber Optic Cable: Light Pulse

Twisted-pair wire and coaxial cable carry data as electrical signals. **Fiber optic cable** carries data as laser-generated pulses of light. Made up of bundles of very thin, transparent, almost hair-like fibers, fiber optic cables transmit data more inexpensively and much more quickly than do copper wire transmission media. The Internet backbone, the primary channels for Internet transmissions, is mostly fiber optic cable. In the time it takes to transmit a single page of *Webster's Unabridged Dictionary* over twisted-pair copper wire (about 3 seconds), the entire dictionary could be transmitted over a single optic fiber!

Each time a communications company lays a new fiber optic cable, the world is made a little smaller. In 1956, the first transatlantic cable carried 50 voice circuits. Then, talking to someone in Europe was a rare and expensive experience. Today, a single fiber can carry over 32,000 voice and data transmissions, the equivalent of 2.5 billion bits per second. Nowadays, people call colleagues in other countries or link up with international computers as readily as they call home.

Another of the many advantages of fiber optic cable is its contribution to data security. It is much more difficult for a computer criminal to intercept a signal sent over fiber optic cable (via a beam of light) than it is over copper wire (an electrical signal).

High-Speed Wireless Communication

High-speed communications channels do not have to be wires or fibers. Data can also be transmitted via **microwave signals** or **radio signals.** Transmission of these signals is line-of-sight; that is, the signal travels in a straight line from source to destination.

Microwave signals are transmitted between transceivers. Because microwave signals do not bend around the curvature of the earth, signals may need to be relayed several times by microwave repeater stations before reaching their destination. Repeater stations are placed on the tops of mountains, tall buildings, and towers, usually about 30 miles apart.

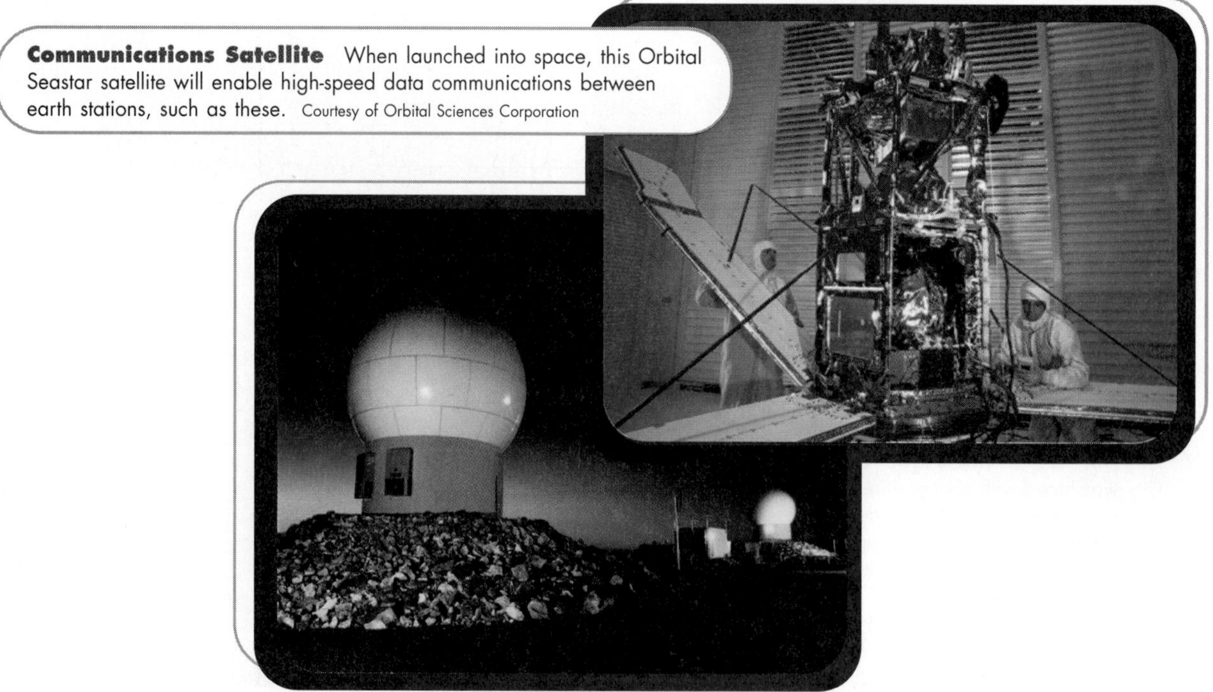

Communications Satellite When launched into space, this Orbital Seastar satellite will enable high-speed data communications between earth stations, such as these. Courtesy of Orbital Sciences Corporation

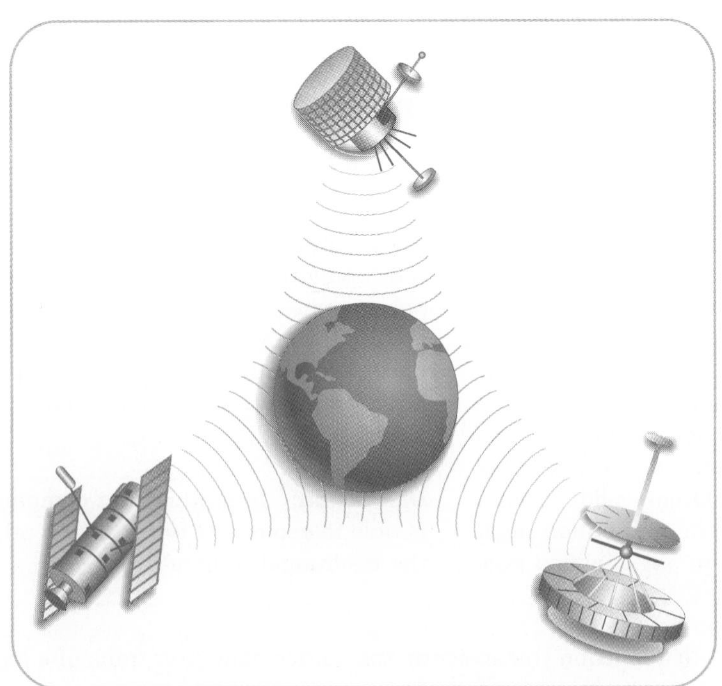

Satellite Data Transmission
Three satellites in geosynchronous orbit (staying over the same point on earth) provide worldwide data transmission service.

Satellites eliminate the line-of-sight limitation because microwave signals are bounced off satellites, avoiding buildings, mountains, and other signal obstructions. One of the advantages of satellites is that data can be transmitted from one location to any number of other locations anywhere on (or near) our planet. Satellites are routinely launched into orbit for the sole purpose of relaying data communications signals to and from earth stations. A satellite, which uses microwave signals and is essentially a repeater station, is launched and set in a **geosynchronous orbit** 22,300 miles above the earth. A geosynchronous orbit permits the communications satellite to maintain a fixed position relative to the earth's surface. Each satellite can receive and retransmit signals to slightly less than half of the earth's surface; therefore, three satellites are required to cover the earth effectively (see Figure 6.6). Internet access via satellite is available to companies and to individuals at speeds up to 48 M bps.

PCs Communicating without Wires

PCs in the office and on the road can be linked via wireless connections. One of the greatest challenges and biggest expenses in a computer network is the installation of the physical links between its components. The **wireless transceiver** provides an alternative to running a permanent physical line (twisted-pair wire, coaxial cable, or fiber optic cable). Two PC-based wireless transceivers, each about the size of a thick credit card, replace a physical line between any source and destination. For example, wireless communication is routinely used to link these devices:

- Desktop PC and laptop PC
- PC and local area network (LAN)
- PC and mainframe computer
- Terminal and multiplexor
- Laptop PC and page printer

The wireless transceiver hooks into a serial port or PCMCIA slot. Transceivers, which have a limited range (about 50 feet), link computers via omnidirectional (traveling in all directions at once) radio waves. In actuality, you can use transceivers only locally to connect computers in adjacent rooms or even on different floors.

IT Ethics

TELECOMMUTING

Ten years ago companies would set aside one day each year when workers could come to work in casual clothes. That day was so well received by employees that some companies decided to do it once each month, then once a week. Now, casual professional dress is the norm at many companies. The same thing is happening with telecommuting. Ten years ago a few people with special circumstances were allowed to telecommute. Others said, "I want to do it too." Now, the telecommuting option must be in place in some industries to get qualified people to interview. Still, very few companies offer the telecommuting option to all employees. Typically, only people at certain levels of management or in certain jobs, especially high-tech jobs, can telecommute and work at home at least part time. Those not permitted that option often are upset with management.

Discussion: Is it ethical for companies to let some people telecommute while asking others to continue the traditional commute?

When using transceivers, the source computer transmits digital signals to its transceiver, which, in turn, retransmits the signals over radio waves to the other transceiver. Transceivers provide users with tremendous flexibility in the location of PCs and terminals in a network; however, the flexibility advantage is offset by the transceivers' limited channel capacity (about 115 K bps). Also, the number of terminals/PCs that can be linked via transceivers is limited by the frequencies allotted for this purpose.

The 1998 Olympics in Nagano were the perfect venue for widespread use of wireless networks. Many sites at the games were temporary or difficult to wire and were thus made-to-order situations for wireless networks. Wireless networks allowed judges, statisticians, and journalists to move with the action within and between venues.

Common Carriers

It is impractical for individuals and companies to string their own fiber optic cable between distant locations, such as Hong Kong and New York City. It is also impractical for them to set their own satellites in orbit, although some have. There-

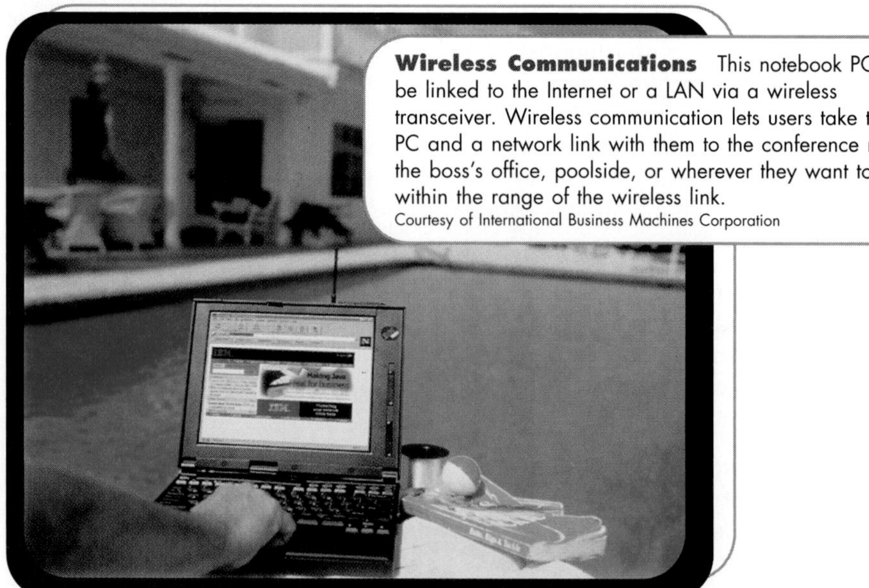

Wireless Communications This notebook PC can be linked to the Internet or a LAN via a wireless transceiver. Wireless communication lets users take the PC and a network link with them to the conference room, the boss's office, poolside, or wherever they want to go within the range of the wireless link.
Courtesy of International Business Machines Corporation

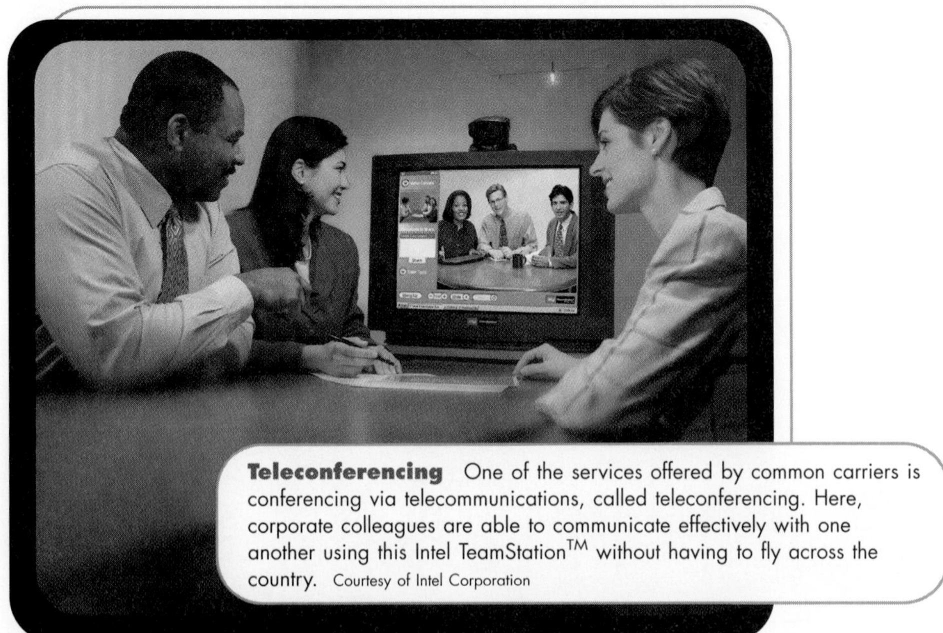

Teleconferencing One of the services offered by common carriers is conferencing via telecommunications, called teleconferencing. Here, corporate colleagues are able to communicate effectively with one another using this Intel TeamStation™ without having to fly across the country. Courtesy of Intel Corporation

fore, most people and companies turn to communications **common carriers,** such as AT&T, MCI, and Sprint, to provide communications channels for data transmission. Organizations pay communications common carriers, which are regulated by the Federal Communications Commission (FCC), for *private* or *switched* data communications service.

A **private line** (or **leased line**) provides a dedicated data communications channel between any two points in a computer network. The charge for a private line is based on channel capacity (bps) and distance.

A **switched line** (or **dial-up line**) is available strictly on a time-and-distance charge, similar to a long-distance telephone call. You (or your computer) make a connection by "dialing up" a computer, then a modem sends and receives data. Switched lines offer greater flexibility than do private lines because they allow you to link up with any communications-ready computer. A regular telephone line is a switched line.

The number and variety of common carriers is expanding. For example, cable TV companies are entering the market. Data rates offered by common carriers range from voice-grade POTS (up to about 56 K bps with a modem) to the widest of all pipes, the massive 622 M-bps channel.

MEMORY bits

Transmission Media

Twisted-pair wire
- POTS
- ISDN
- ADSL

Coaxial cable

Fiber optic cable

Wireless
- Microwave
- Radio signals

Data Transmission in Practice

A communications channel from Computer A in Seattle, Washington, to Computer B in Orlando, Florida (see Figure 6.7), usually would consist of several different transmission media. The connection between Computer A and a terminal in the same building is probably coaxial cable or twisted-pair wire. The Seattle company might use a common carrier company such as AT&T to transmit the data. AT&T would then send the data through a combination of transmission facilities that might include copper wire, fiber optic cable, microwave signals, and radio signals.

SECTION SELF-CHECK

6-3.1 It is more difficult for a computer criminal to tap into a fiber optic cable than a copper telephone line. (T/F)

6-3.2 The wireless transceiver replaces the physical link between the source and the destination in a network. (T/F)

Self-Check

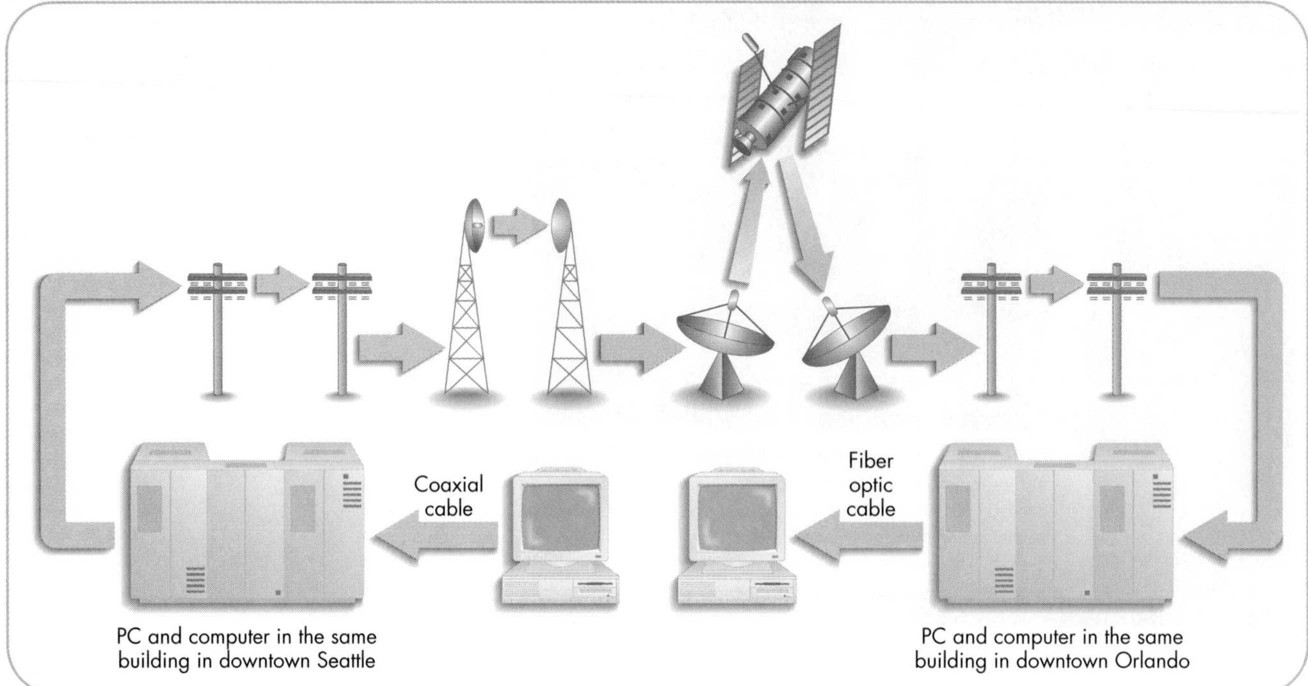

Data Transmission Path It's more the rule than the exception that data are carried over several transmission media between source and destination.

6-3.3 The terminal sending a message over a network is the source and the computer receiving the message is the destination. (T/F)

6-3.4 The two basic types of service offered by common carriers are a private line and a switched line. (T/F)

6-3.5 Microwave relay stations are located approximately 500 miles apart. (T/F)

6-3.6 The ISDN service channel capacity is about 100 times that of cable TV digital service. (T/F)

6-3.7 A 56,000 bits-per-second channel is the same as a: (a) 56 kps pipe, (b) 56 K-bps line, (c) dual 28000X2 K-bps line, or (d) single-channel ADSL?

6-3.8 The unit of measure for the capacity of a data communications channel is: (a) bps, (b) bytes per second, (c) RAM units, or (d) megabits?

6-3.9 Which of these terms is not used to refer to a communications channel: (a) link, (b) pipe, (c) tunnel, or (d) line?

6-3.10 Which of these communications services is not distributed over twisted-pair wire: (a) cable TV with digital service, (b) POTS, (c) ISDN, or (d) ADSL?

6.4 NETWORKS: CONNECTING NODES

Networking

Each time you use the telephone, you use the world's largest computer network—the telephone system. A telephone is an endpoint, or a **node,** connected to a network of computers that routes your voice signals to any one of the 500 million telephones (other nodes) in the world. In a computer network the node can be a terminal, a computer, or any destination/source device (for example, a printer, an automatic teller machine, or even a telephone). Within an organization, computer networks are set up to meet the specific requirements of that organization. Some have five nodes; others have 10,000 nodes. We have already seen the hardware and transmission media used to link nodes in a network. In this section we put it all together and explain how networks are actually created and how they function.

Network Topologies: Star, Ring, and Bus

Networks

A **network topology** is a description of the possible physical connections within a network. The topology is the configuration of the hardware and shows which pairs of nodes can communicate. The basic computer network topologies—star, ring, and bus—are illustrated in Figure 6.8. However, a pure form of any of these three basic topologies is seldom found in practice. Most computer networks are *hybrids*—combinations of these topologies.

Star Topology

The **star topology** involves a centralized host computer connected to several other computer systems, which are usually smaller than the host. The smaller computer systems communicate with one another through the host and usually share the host computer's database. The host could be anything from a PC to a supercomputer. Any computer can communicate with any other computer in the network. Banks often have a large home-office computer system with a star network of smaller mainframe systems in the branch banks.

Ring Topology

The **ring topology** involves computer systems of approximately the same size, with no one computer system as the focal point of the network. When one system routes a message to another system, it is passed around the ring until it reaches its destination address.

Bus Topology

The **bus topology** permits the connection of terminals, peripheral devices, and microcomputers along a common cable called a **network bus.** The term *bus* is used

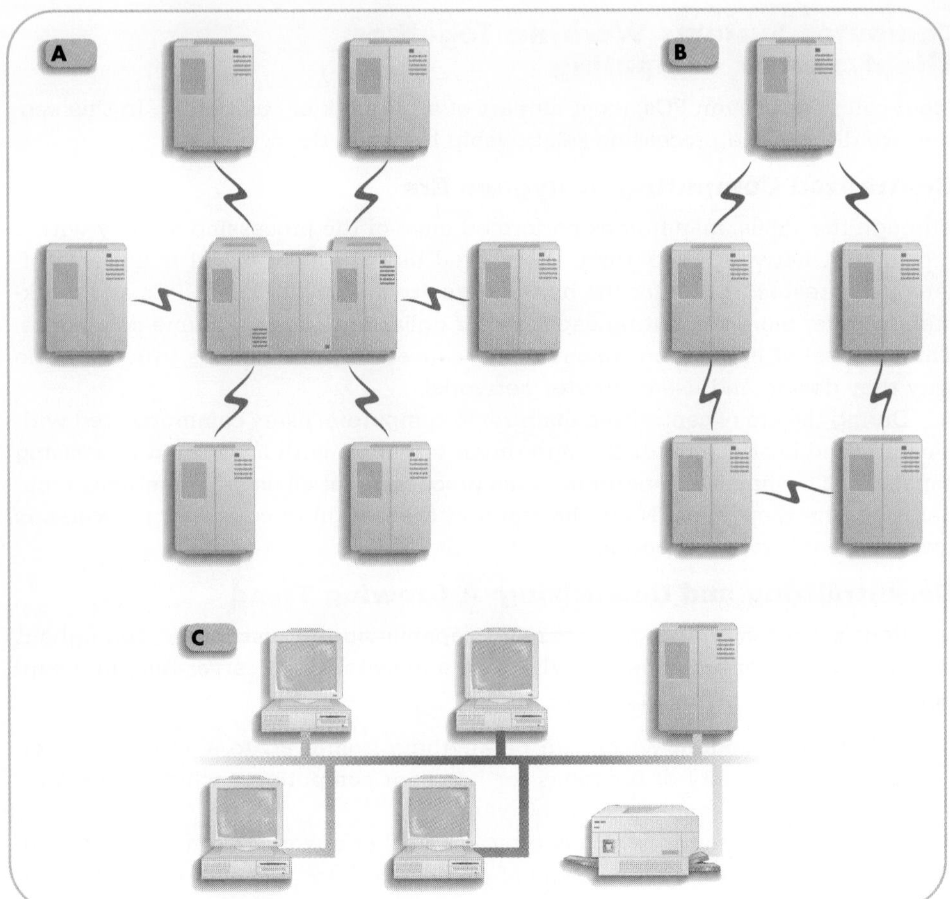

Network Topologies Network topologies include (a) star, (b) ring, and (c) bus.

Network Control Center This Global Network Control Center controls the entire ORBCOMM satellite constellation. ORBCOMM's mission is to revolutionize the way companies and individuals use wireless data communications. The satellites envelop the earth in low-altitude orbits, which allows messages to be sent and received by small, low-power access devices.
Courtesy of Orbital Sciences Corporation

because people on a bus can get off at any stop along the route. In a bus topology a signal is broadcast to all nodes, but only the destination node responds to the signal. It is easy to add devices or delete them from the network, as devices are simply daisy-chained along the network bus. Bus topologies are most appropriate when the linked devices are physically close to one another.

Computer Systems Working Together: Client/Server Computing

Most computers, even PCs, exist as part of a network of computers. In this section we discuss the processing relationship between them.

Centralized Computing: A Bygone Era

Through the 1980s, mainframes performed most of the processing activity within a computer network. Back then, the shared use of a centralized mainframe offered the greatest return for the hardware/software dollar. Today, PCs and workstations offer more computing capacity per dollar than do mainframe computers. This reversal of hardware economics has caused IT professionals to rethink the way they design and use computer networks.

During the era of centralized mainframe computers, users communicated with a centralized host computer through dumb terminals with little or no processing capability. The mainframe performed the processing for all users, sometimes numbering in the thousands. Now, the trend in the design of computer networks is toward *client/server computing.*

Decentralizing and Downsizing: A Growing Trend

In **client/server computing,** processing capabilities are distributed throughout the network, closer to the people who need and use them. A *server computer* supports many *client computers.*

- A **server computer,** which can be anything from a PC to a supercomputer, performs a variety of functions for its client computers, including the storage of data and applications software.
- The **client computer,** which is typically a PC or a workstation, requests processing support or another type of service (perhaps printing or remote communication) from one or more server computers.

Client/Server Computing This company is moving toward a client/server–computing environment. The users at client PCs in this office access a common database on this Compaq PC server computer (foreground).

In the client/server environment, both client and server computers perform processing to optimize application efficiency. For example, the client computer system might run a database application *locally* (on the client computer) and access data on a *remote* (not local) server computer system. In client/server computing, applications software has two parts—*the front end* and *the back end.*

- The client computer runs **front-end applications software,** which performs processing associated with the user interface and applications processing that can be done locally (for example, database and word processing).
- The server computer's **back-end applications software** performs processing tasks in support of its client computers. For example, the server might accomplish those tasks associated with storage and maintenance of a centralized corporate database.

In a client/server database application (see Figure 6.9), users at client PCs run front-end software to *download* (server-to-client) parts of the database from the server for processing. Upon receiving the requested data, perhaps sales data on customers in the mid-Atlantic region, the client user runs front-end software to work with the data. After local processing, the client computer may *upload* (client-to-server) updated data to the server's back-end software for processing. The server then updates the customer database. The database application is popular in client/server computing, but the scope and variety of applications are growing daily.

There is a mass migration *toward client/server computing* and *away from host-based networks.* Already over 70% of all PCs are clients linked to at least one server computer, and most workstations are either clients or servers. Because client computers have their own software and processing capability, they request only needed data, resulting in reduced traffic over communications channels and increased speed and efficiency throughout the network.

Network Line Control: Rules for Data Transmission

Communications Protocols: Transmitting by the Rules

Communications protocols describe how data are transmitted in a computer network. Communications protocols are defined in *layers,* the first of which is the

A Walkthrough of a Client/Server Database Application

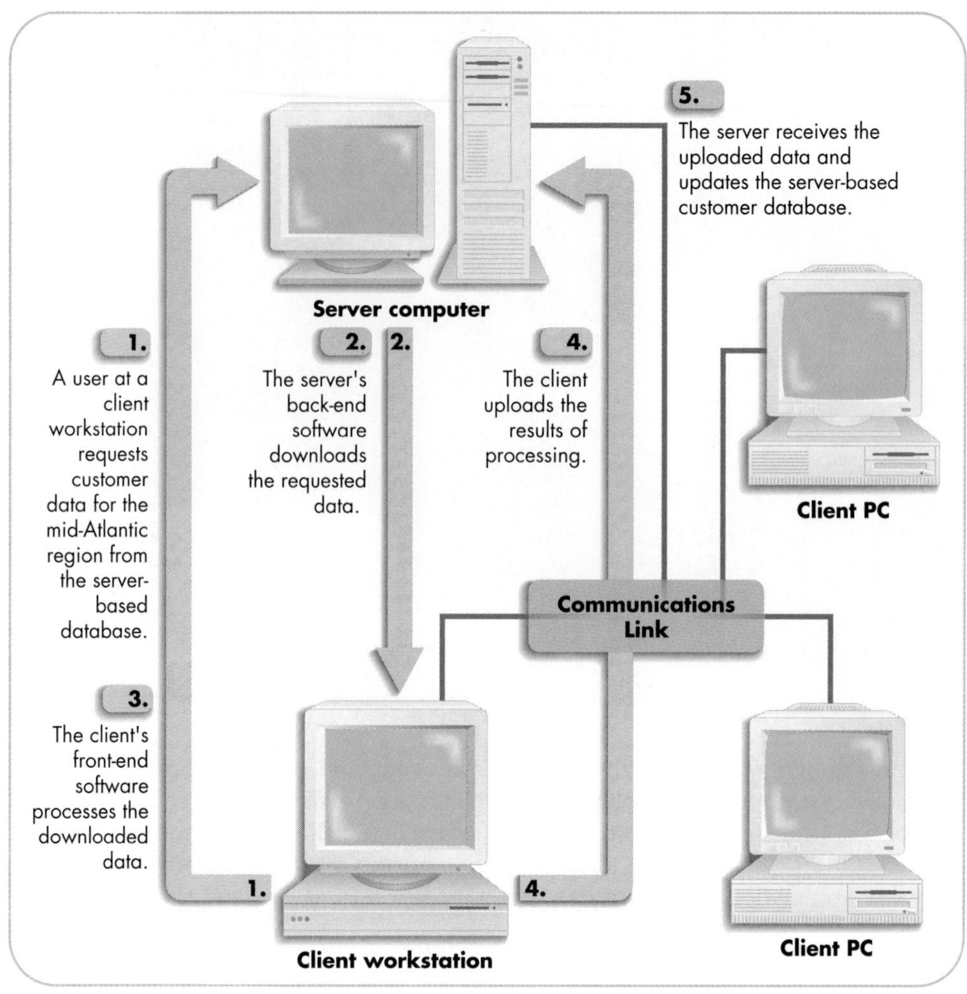

physical layer. The physical layer defines the manner in which nodes in a network are connected to one another. Subsequent layers, the number of which vary between protocols, describe how messages are packaged for transmission, how messages are routed through the network, security procedures, and the manner in which messages are displayed. A number of different protocols are in common use. The protocol you hear about most often is TCP/IP, which actually is a collective reference to the protocols that link computers on the Internet (TCP and IP).

Server computer
5.
The server receives the uploaded data and updates the server-based customer database.
1.
A user at a client workstation requests customer data for the mid-Atlantic region from the server-based database.
2.
The server's back-end software downloads the requested data.
4.
The client uploads the results of processing.
3.
The client's front-end software processes the downloaded data.
Communications Link
Client PC
Client PC
Client workstation

Asynchronous and Synchronous Transmission

Protocols fall into two general classifications: *asynchronous* and *synchronous* (see Figure 6.10). In **asynchronous transmission,** data are transmitted at irregular intervals on an as-needed basis. A modem is usually involved in asynchronous transmission. *Start/stop bits* are appended to the beginning and end of each message. The start/stop bits signal the receiving terminal/computer at the beginning and end of the message. In PC data communications, the message is a single byte or character. Asynchronous transmission, sometimes called *start/stop transmission,* is best suited for data communications involving low-speed I/O devices, such as serial printers and PCs functioning as remote terminals.

In **synchronous transmission,** the source and destination operate in timed synchronization to enable high-speed data transfer. Start/stop bits are not required in synchronous transmission. Data transmission between computers, routers, multiplexors, and front-end processors is normally synchronous.

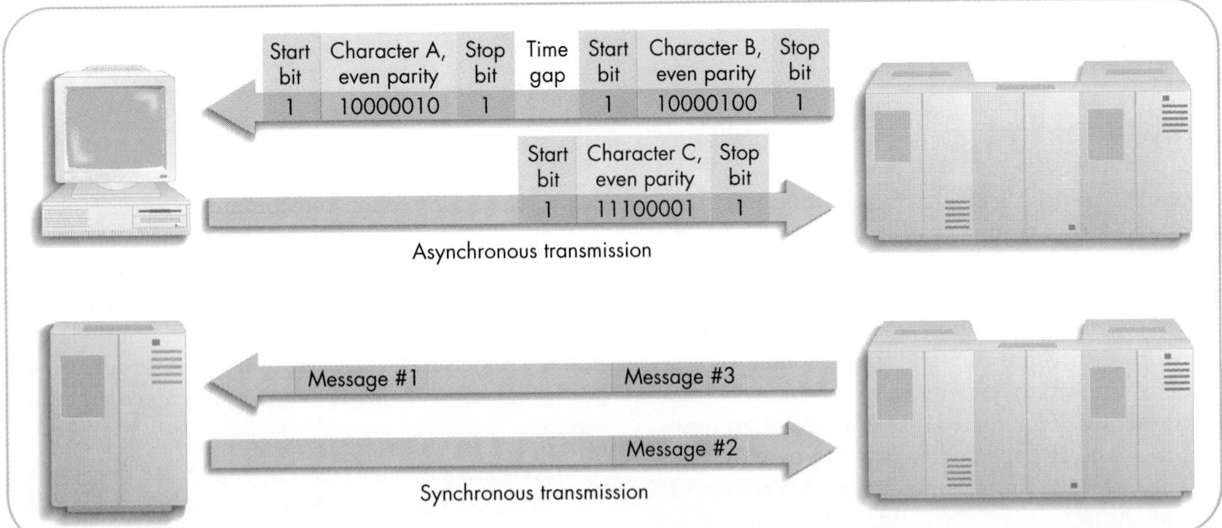

Asynchronous and Synchronous Transmission of Data Asynchronous data transmission takes place at irregular intervals. In asynchronous transmission, the message is typically a single character. Sending characters with an even number of on-bits, or even parity, ensures transmission accuracy. Synchronous data transmission requires timed synchronization between sending and receiving devices. The message is typically a block of characters.

SECTION SELF-CHECK

Self-Check

6-4.1 Synchronous transmission is best suited for data communications involving low-speed I/O devices. (T/F)

6-4.2 The client computer runs front-end applications software. (T/F)

6-4.3 Communications protocols describe how data are transmitted in a computer network. (T/F)

6-4.4 An endpoint in a network of computers is called a: (a) break point, (b) stop bit, (c) node, or (d) PC?

6-4.5 The central cable called a network bus is most closely associated with which network topology: (a) ring, (b) star, (c) bus, or (d) train?

6-4.6 The trend in the design of computer networks is toward: (a) distributed transmission, (b) client/server computing, (c) CANs, or (d) centralized mainframe computers?

6-4.7 A client computer requests processing support or another type of service from one or more: (a) sister computers, (b) server computers, (c) customer computers, or (d) IT managers?

6.5 NETWORKS: THE WAN, MAN, LAN, AND TAN

In this section, we introduce the various types of networks. LANs, the most popular type of network, are discussed in more detail.

Types of Networks

Networks tend to be classified by the proximity of their nodes.

- *The WAN.* A **WAN,** or **wide area network,** connects nodes in widely dispersed geographic areas, such as cities, states, and even countries. The WAN will normally depend on the transmission services of a common carrier to transmit signals between nodes in the network.

WORKING@HOME

Traditionally, people get up in the morning, get dressed, and fight through rush hour to go to the office because that's where their work is. All this, however, is changing. People who work at home have accounted for more than half of all new jobs since 1987. In 1990, 2 million Americans telecommuted to work. Telecommuting is "commuting" to work via data communications. In 1998, that number jumped to 26 million and is expected to grow to over 30 million by the new millenium. Analysts predict that over 40% of all American workers will telecommute at least part time by 2005.

For many knowledge workers, work is really at a PC or over the telephone, whether at the office or at home. PCs and communications technology make it possible for these people to access needed information, communicate with their colleagues and clients, and even deliver their work (programs, stories, reports, or recommendations) in electronic or hard-copy format. More and more people are asking: "Why travel to the office when I can telecommute?" The trend toward PCs and networks has also fueled the growth of cottage industries where people work exclusively from their home offices.

The Trend to Telecommuting

Millions of people are working at home full time: stockbrokers, financial planners, writers, programmers, buyers, teachers (yes, some teachers and professors work exclusively with online students), salespeople, and graphic artists, to mention a few. A larger group is working at home at least one day a week: engineers, lawyers, certified public accountants, company presidents, mayors, and plant managers, to mention some. Anyone who needs a few hours, or perhaps a few days, of uninterrupted time to accomplish tasks that do not require direct personal interaction is a candidate for telecommuting. Through the early 1990s, telecommuting was discouraged. Management was reluctant to relinquish direct control of workers. Managers were concerned that workers would give priority to personal, not business, objectives. Now we know that telecommuters are not only more productive, but they tend to work more hours. A Gartner Group study reported increases in productivity between 10% and 16% per telecommuter (as measured by employers). According to the study, each telecommuter experienced a 2-hour increase in work time per day and saved the company about $4000 in annual facilities costs. It is only a matter of time before all self-motivated knowledge workers at all levels and in a variety of disciplines are given the option of telecommuting at least part of the time. Look at what companies are already doing.

- AT&T is encouraging its employees to telecommute on Tuesdays. Among other reasons, AT&T management is trying to support the lifestyle people think is desirable.
- The Canadian government hopes to save taxpayers hundreds of millions of dollars by encouraging telecommuting for public servants. Those who participated in a government-sponsored telecommuting pilot project reported a 73% increase in productivity.
- Compaq Computer Corporation realized productivity increases from 15 to 45%.
- Pacific Bell offered telecommuting to its workers following the 1994 earthquake in Los Angeles. Ninety percent of the workers who took advantage of the "telecommuting relief package" were still working at home nine months after the earthquake. Half of those who opted to telecommute had not considered it before. Now half of those work at home five days a week. More than half of those are managers.
- Telecommuters at American Express handled 26% more calls and produced 43% more business than their office-based counterparts.

The Pros and Cons of Working at Home

Why Work at Home? Everyone has a different reason for wanting to telecommute. A programmer with two school-age children says, "I want to say good-bye when the kids leave for school and greet them when they return." A writer goes into the office once a week, the day before the magazine goes to press. She says, "I write all of my stories from the comfort of my home. An office that puts out a weekly magazine is not conducive to creative thinking." A company president states emphatically, "I got sick and tired of spending nights up in my office. By telecommuting, I'm at least within earshot of my wife and kids."

These are the most frequently citing reasons for working at home.

- *Increased productivity.* Telecommuters get more done at home than at the office.
- *Better retention of employees.* Having the telecommuting option attracts and helps to retain top talent. Telecommuters cite improved morale and job satisfaction.
- *Greater flexibility.* Telecommuters can optimize the scheduling of life events. For example, they can work late on Monday and take off for a few hours to exercise on Tuesday.
- *Money savings on office space.* Companies can reduce required office space.
- *Improved relations with family.* Telecommuters spend more time with or around their family.
- *No commute.* The average commuter in a major metropolitan area spends the equivalent of one working day a week traveling to and from work. The telecommuter eliminates transportation expenses associated with the commute and gains valuable time that can be used more productively.
- *More comfortable and cheaper clothes.* Men willingly trade ties for T-shirts and women prefer sneakers to heels.
- *Reduction of sick time.* Telecommuters miss fewer days of work as a result of sickness, thus lowering overall health-care–related costs (an average of five days per year at the city of Los Angeles).

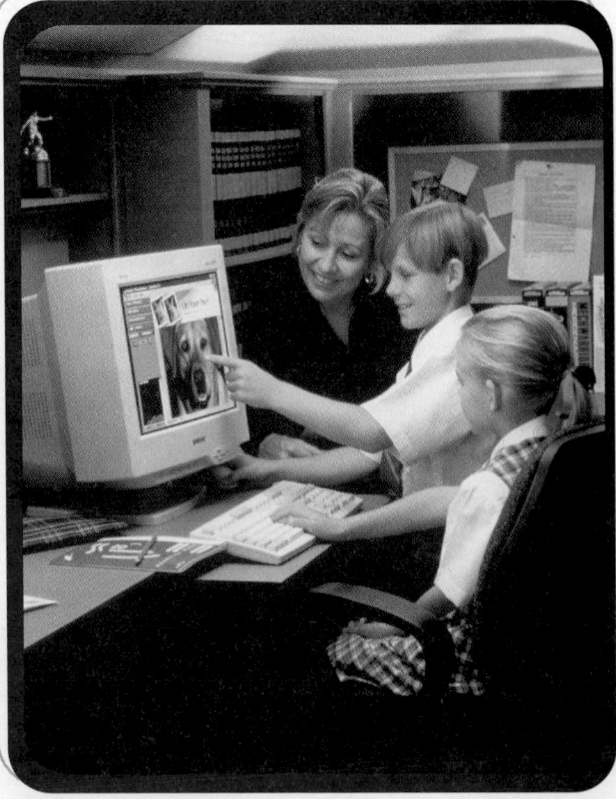

Working at Home
Sometimes telecommuters get a little "help" from the kids. The familiar surroundings of home inspire some people to do their best work. Others, however, are more comfortable working in a traditional office setting.

Arguments against Working at Home. Working at home is not the answer for all workers. Some people are easily distracted and need the ready access to management and the routine of the office to maintain a business focus. Telecommuting is not possible when job requirements demand daily face-to-face meetings (for example, bank tellers and elementary school teachers). Telecommuters routinely interact with clients and colleagues over the telephone and e-mail. They even participate in online group meetings via groupware. However, those arguing against telecommuting say that this type of interaction does not permit "pressing of the flesh" and the transmittal of the nonverbal cues that are essential to personal interaction. These arguments, though valid, have done little to hamper the emergence of telecommuting as a mainstream business strategy.

- *The MAN.* The **MAN,** or **metropolitan area network,** is a network designed for a city. MANs are more encompassing than local-area networks (LANs), but smaller than wide-area networks (WANs).
- *The LAN.* The *local area network (LAN),* or **local net,** connects nodes in close proximity, such as in a suite of offices or a building. The local net, including all data communications channels, is owned by the organization using it. Because of the proximity of nodes in local nets, a company can install its own communications channels (such as coaxial cable, fiber optic cable, or wireless transceivers). Therefore, LANs do not need common carriers. LANs, the most popular type of network, are more fully explained later in this section.
- *The TAN.* **TAN,** or **tiny area network,** is a term coined to refer to very small LANs—perhaps two, three, or four nodes. For example, TANs are popular in home computing. They enable households to share resources (printer, modem, files) among the kids' PC, the parents' PC, and perhaps a parent's laptop from the office.

When we refer to WANs, MANs, LANs, and TANs, we refer to all hardware, software, and communications channels associated with them.

The focus of this section is the LAN, the most common network. Strictly speaking, any type of computer can be part of a LAN, but, in practice, PCs and workstations provide the foundation for local area networks. PCs in a typical LAN are linked to each other and share resources such as printers and disk storage. The distance separating devices in the local net may vary from a few feet to a few miles. As few as two and as many as several hundred PCs can be linked on a single local area network.

Most corporate PCs are linked to a LAN to aid in communication among knowledge workers. LANs make good business sense because these and other valuable resources can be shared.

- *Applications software.* The cost of a LAN-based word processing program (for example, Word for Windows) is far less than the cost of a word processing program for each PC in the LAN.
- *Links to mainframes.* The mainframe becomes an accessible resource. It is easier to link the mainframe to a single LAN than to many individual PCs.
- *Communications capabilities.* Many users can share a dedicated communications line or a modem.
- *I/O devices.* With a little planning, a single page printer, plotter, or scanner can support many users on a LAN with little loss of office efficiency. In a normal office setting, a single page printer can service the printing needs of up to 20 LAN users.
- *Storage devices.* Databases on a LAN can be shared. For example, some offices make a CD-ROM–based national telephone directory available to all LAN users.
- *Add-on boards.* Add-on boards, such as a video capture boards, can be shared by many PCs.

Like computers, automobiles, and just about everything else, local nets can be built at various levels of sophistication. At the most basic level, they permit the interconnection of PCs in a department so that users can send messages to one another and share files and printers. The more sophisticated local nets permit the interconnection of mainframes, PCs, and the spectrum of peripheral devices throughout a large but geographically constrained area, such as a cluster of buildings.

In some offices, you plug a terminal or PC into a network just as you would plug a telephone line into a telephone jack. This type of data communications capability is being installed in the new "smart" office buildings.

Automobile LANs A semiconductor chip set provides local area network (LAN) capabilities within an automobile, solving the problems created by increasingly complex, space-consuming electrical wiring. Courtesy of Harris Corporation

LAN Overview

Local net, or LANs, are found in just about any office building. The basic hardware components in a PC-based LAN are the network interface cards, or NICs, in the PCs; the transmission media that connect the nodes in the network; and the servers. LANs may also have routers, modems, and other previously mentioned network hardware.

LAN Access Methods

Only one node on a LAN can send information at any given time. The other nodes must wait their turn. The transfer of data and programs between nodes is controlled by the access method embedded in the network interface card's ROM. The two most popular access methods are *token* and *Ethernet.*

Token Access Method When a LAN with a *ring* topology uses the **token access method,** an electronic *token* travels around a ring of nodes in the form of a header. Figure 6.11 demonstrates the token-passing process for this type of LAN. The header contains control signals, including one specifying whether the token is "free" or carrying a message. A sender node captures a free token as it travels from node to node, changes it to "busy," and adds the message. The resulting *message frame* travels around the ring to the addressee's NIC, which copies the message and returns the message frame to the sender. The sender's NIC removes the message frame from the ring and circulates a new free token. When a LAN with a *bus* topology uses the token access method, the token is broadcast to the nodes along the network bus. Think of the token as a benevolent dictator who, when captured, bestows the privilege of sending a transmission.

Ethernet In the popular **Ethernet** access method, nodes on the LAN must contend for the right to send a message. To gain access to the network, a node with a message to be sent automatically requests network service from the network software. The request might result in a "line busy" signal. In this case the node waits a fraction of a second and tries again, and again, until the line is free. Upon assuming control of the line, the node sends the message and then relinquishes control of the line to another node. Ethernet LANs operate like a conversation between polite people. When two people begin talking at the same time, one must wait until the other is finished.

Moving the Data: LAN Transmission Media

Three kinds of cables can be connected to the network interface cards: twisted-pair wire (the same wire used to connect telephones in a home), coaxial cable,

The Token Access Method in a LAN with a Ring Topology

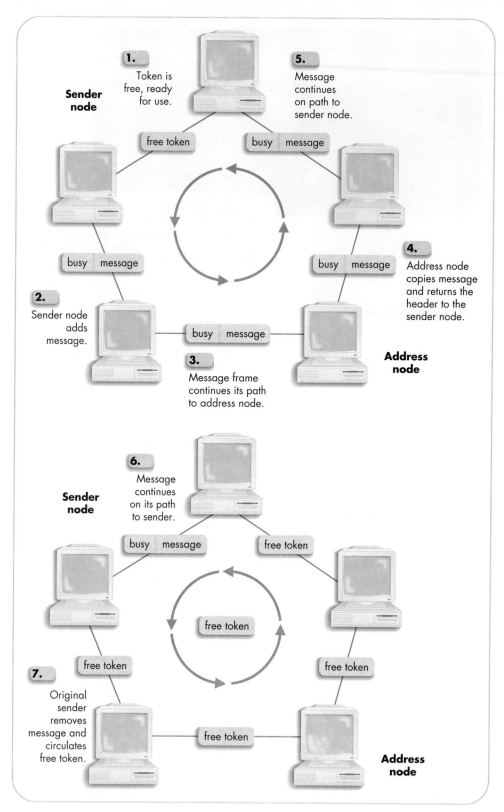

Sender node

1. Token is free, ready for use.

free token

5. Message continues on path to sender node.

busy message

busy message

2. Sender node adds message.

busy message

3. Message frame continues its path to address node.

busy message

4. Address node copies message and returns the header to the sender node.

Address node

Sender node

6. Message continues on its path to sender.

busy message

free token

free token

free token

free token

7. Original sender removes message and circulates free token.

free token

Address node

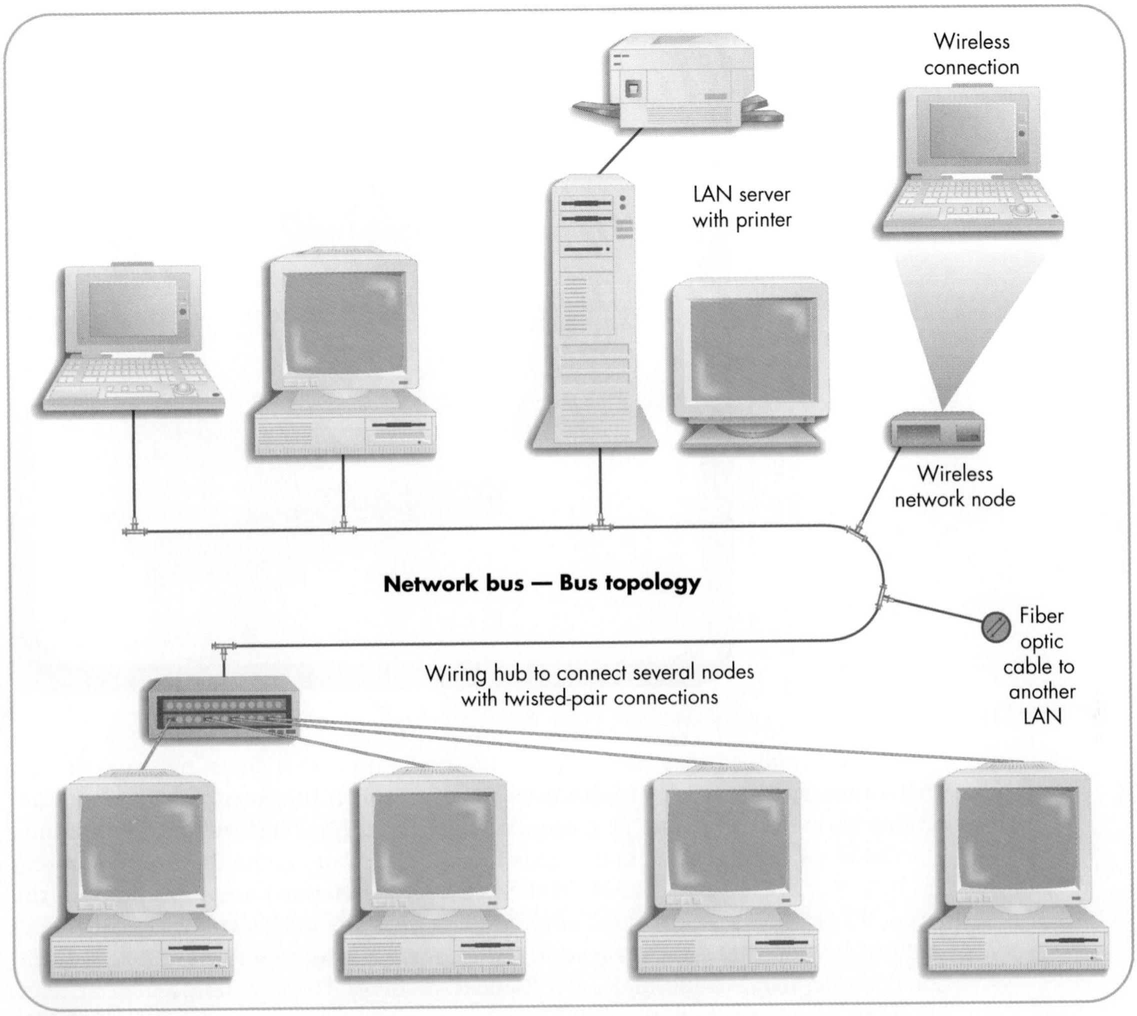

LAN Links In this figure, nodes in a LAN are linked via a bus topology. One of the nodes is linked to a wiring hub that enables several PCs to be connected to the network bus. The wiring hub acts like a multiplexor, concentrating transmissions from several nodes. The LAN is linked to other LANs with fiber optic cable.

and fiber optic cable. In wireless transmission, the cable runs from the transceiver to the NIC. Figure 6.12 illustrates how nodes in a LAN are connected in a bus topology with a wiring hub at the end that allows several more nodes to be connected to the bus.

Servers: Serving the LAN

In a LAN, a *server* is a component that can be shared by users on the LAN. The three most popular servers are the **file server,** the **print server,** and the **communications server.**

The *file server* normally is a dedicated PC with a high-capacity hard disk for storing the data and programs shared by the network users. For example, the master customer file, word processing software, spreadsheet software, and so on would be stored on the server disk. When a user wants to begin a spreadsheet session, the spreadsheet software is downloaded from the file server to the user's RAM.

The *print server* typically is housed in the same dedicated PC as the file server. The print server handles user print jobs and controls at least one printer. If needed, the server *spools* print jobs; that is, it saves print jobs to disk until the requested printer is available, then routes the print file to the printer.

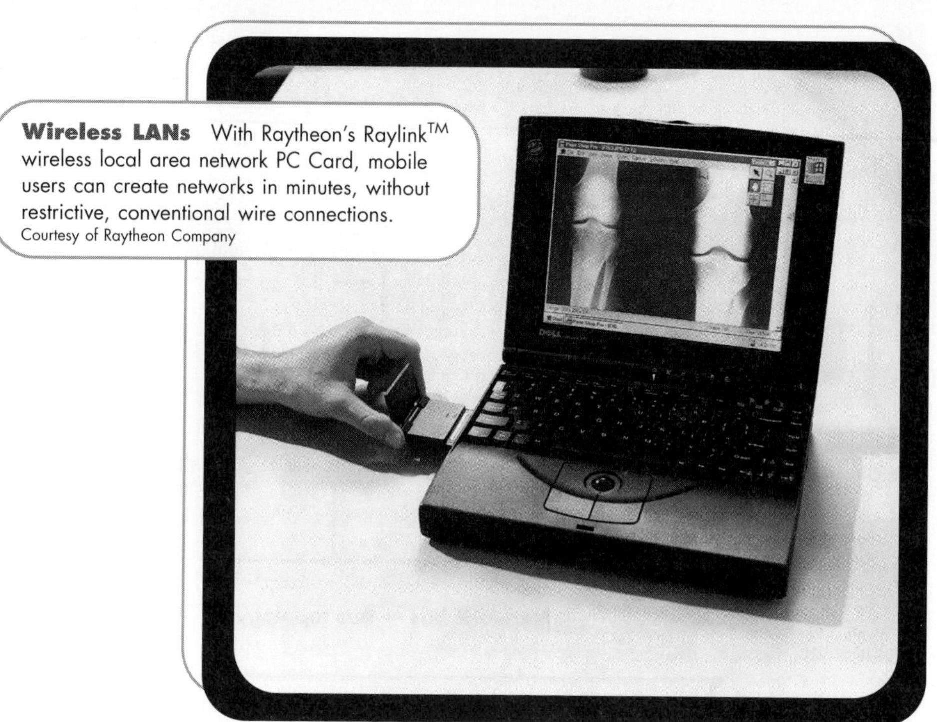

Wireless LANs With Raytheon's Raylink™ wireless local area network PC Card, mobile users can create networks in minutes, without restrictive, conventional wire connections.
Courtesy of Raytheon Company

The *communications server* provides communication links external to the LAN—that is, links to other networks. To accomplish this service, the communications server controls one or more modems, or perhaps access to an ADSL line.

These server functions may reside in a single PC or can be distributed among the PCs that make up the LAN. When the server functions are consolidated, the server PC usually is *dedicated* to servicing the LAN. Some PCs are designed specifically to be dedicated **LAN servers.** Until recently, you would purchase a traditional single-user PC and make it a dedicated server. Using a single-user PC continues to be an option with small- to medium-sized LANs, but not in large LANs with 100 or more users. Now, PC vendors manufacture powerful PCs designed, often with multiple processors, specifically as LAN servers. LAN servers are configured with enough RAM, storage capacity, and backup capability to handle the resource needs of hundreds of PCs.

LAN Software

In this section we explore LAN-based software, including LAN operating systems alternatives and a variety of applications software.

Network Operating Systems

LAN operating systems, the nucleus of a local net, come in two formats: *peer-to-peer* and *dedicated server.* In both cases, the LAN operating system is actually several pieces of software. Each processing component in the LAN has a piece of the LAN operating system resident in its RAM. The pieces interact with one another to enable the nodes to share resources and communication.

The individual user in a LAN might appear to be interacting with an operating system, such as Windows 2000. However, the RAM-resident LAN software *redirects* certain requests to the appropriate LAN component. For example, a print request would be redirected to the print server.

Peer-to-Peer LANs In a **peer-to-peer LAN,** all PCs are peers, or equals. Any PC can be a client to another peer PC or any PC can share its resources with its peers. Peer-to-peer LANs are less sophisticated than those that have one or more dedicated servers. Because they are relatively easy to install and maintain, peer-to-peer LANs are popular when small numbers of PCs are involved (for example, from 2 to 20). PCs running the Windows 95, Windows 98, Windows 2000, or Windows NT operating system can be linked together in a peer-to-peer LAN.

LANs with Dedicated Servers In LANs with dedicated servers, the controlling software resides in the file server's RAM. LANs with dedicated servers can link hundreds of PCs in a LAN while providing a level of system security that is not possible in a peer-to-peer LAN. Control is distributed among the PCs in the LAN. Popular LAN operating systems are Novell's *NetWare* and Microsoft's *Windows NT Server.*

Applications Software for LANs

LAN-based PCs can run all applications that stand-alone PCs can run plus those that involve electronic interaction with groups of people.

Shared Applications Software LANs enable the sharing of general-purpose software, such as any Microsoft Office 2000 application (word processing, spreadsheet, and so on). LAN-based applications software is licensed for sharing. The PCs on the LAN with a dedicated central server interact with a file server to load various applications programs. When a LAN-based PC is booted, software that enables the use of the network interface card, communication with the file server, and interaction with the operating system is loaded from the PC's hard disk to RAM. Depending on how the LAN system administrator configured the LAN, you may see a graphical user interface that lists software options or you may see a prompt from the operating system. When you select a software package, it is downloaded from the LAN's file server to your PC's RAM for processing. You can then work with shared files on the file server or with your own local files (those stored on your PC).

Groupware: Software for the Group LANs have opened the door to applications that are not possible in the one-person, one-computer environment. For ex-

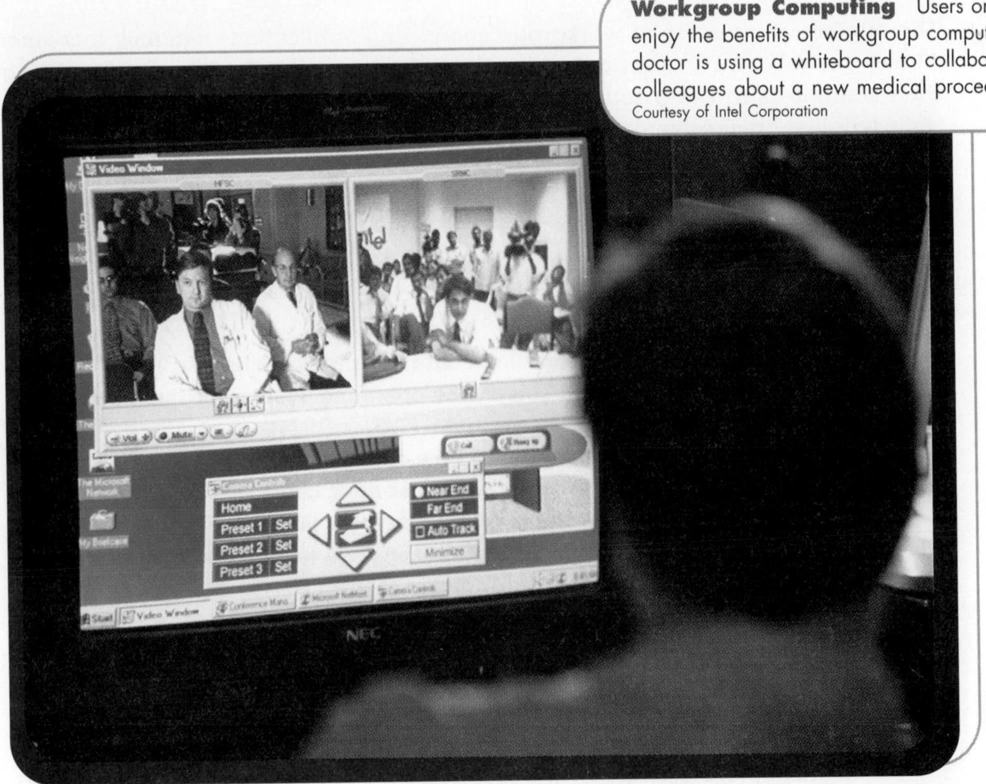

Workgroup Computing Users on a LAN can enjoy the benefits of workgroup computing. Here, a doctor is using a whiteboard to collaborate with colleagues about a new medical procedure.
Courtesy of Intel Corporation

ample, users linked together via a LAN can send electronic mail to one another. Scheduling meetings with other users on the LAN is a snap. This type of multiuser software designed to benefit a group of people is called *groupware.* Local area networks and groupware provide the foundation for *workgroup computing.* The breadth of workgroup computing encompasses any application that involves groups of people linked by a computer network. The following is a sampling of workgroup computing applications.

- *Electronic mail (e-mail).* E-mail enables people on a LAN to route messages to one another's electronic mailbox.
- *Calendar and scheduling.* People can keep online calendars and schedule meetings automatically. The scheduling software automatically checks appropriate users' electronic calendars for possible meeting times, schedules the meeting, and informs the participants via electronic mail.
- *Brainstorming and problem solving.* A LAN enables collaborative brainstorming and problem solving.
- *Shared whiteboarding.* Shared whiteboards permit a document or image to be viewed simultaneously by several people on the network. All people involved can make drawing or text annotations directly on the shared whiteboard. The annotations appear in the color associated with a particular participant.
- *Setting priorities.* Groupware is available that enables LAN users to establish priorities for projects through collective reasoning.
- *Electronic conferencing.* Conferencing groupware lets LAN users meet electronically.
- *Electronic forms.* American businesses and government spend over $400 billion each year to distribute, store, and update paper forms. Electronic forms groupware lets LAN users create forms for gathering information from other LAN users.

MEMORY

Networking

Network topologies
- Star
- Ring
- Bus
- Hybrid

Client/server computing

Types of networks
- Wide area network (WAN)
- Metropolitan area network (MAN)
- Local area network (LAN)
- Tiny area network (TAN)

Local area network
- Also called LAN or local net
- Hardware components: NICs, transmission media, and servers

Networks on the Fly

The number and variety of workgroup computing applications can only increase. Already, notebook PC users are creating networks on the fly. That is, they bring their computers to the meeting and attach them to a common cable or activate their wireless transceivers to create a peer-to-peer LAN. In effect, we have progressed from the *portable computer* to the *portable network.* Once part of a LAN, users can enjoy the advantages of networking and groupware.

SECTION SELF-CHECK

Self-Check

Interactive Study Guide Chapter 6

6-5.1 A LAN is designed for "long-haul" data communications. (T/F)

6-5.2 In a LAN with a dedicated server, the operating system for the entire LAN resides in the server processor's RAM. (T/F)

6-5.3 In a peer-to-peer LAN, any PC can be a client to another peer PC. (T/F)

6-5.4 Twisted-pair wire, coaxial cable, and fiber optic cable can be used to connect nodes on a LAN via the network interface cards. (T/F)

6-5.5 Which LAN access method passes a token from node to node: (a) token, (b) Ethernet, (c) contention, or (d) parity checking?

6-5.6 Which of the following doesn't fit: (a) WAN, (b) LAN, (c) DAN, or (d) MAN?

6-5.7 Which would not be a type of LAN server: (a) communications server, (b) file server, (c) print server, or (d) scan server?

6-5.8 Which of these applications permits a document or image to be viewed simultaneously by several people on the network: (a) scheduling, (b) whiteboarding, (c) electronic forms, or (d) brainstorming?

SUMMARY AND KEY TERMS

6.1 Our Weird, Wild, Wired World

We rely on *computer networks* to retrieve and share information quickly; thus the current direction of **digital convergence** (182). **Connectivity** (183) facilitates the electronic communication between companies and the free flow of information within an enterprise.

This is the era of **cooperative processing** (184). To obtain meaningful, accurate, and timely information, businesses have decided that they must cooperate internally and externally to take full advantage of available information. To promote internal cooperation, businesses are promoting intracompany and **intercompany networking** (184). Much of the business conducted between companies is done via **electronic data interchange (EDI)** (184) and over **extranets** (184). An extranet is an extension of an **intranet** (184), a closed or private version of the Internet.

6.2 Data communications hardware: Making it happen

Data communications (185) (also called **telecommunications** [185]) is the electronic collection and distribution of information from and to remote facilities. Data communications hardware is used to transmit digital information between terminals and computers or between computers. These hardware components include the modem, the **network interface card (NIC)** (187), the **front-end processor** (188), the **multiplexor** (188), and the **router** (189).

Voice/data/fax modems, both internal and external, modulate and demodulate signals so that data can be transmitted over telephone lines. Besides the data communications capabilities, they let you make telephone calls via your PC and simulate a *facsimile* or *fax* machine.

The front-end processor establishes the link between the source and destination in a process called **handshaking** (188), then sends the **message** (188) to a **network address** (188). The front-end processor relieves the host computer of communications-related tasks. The multiplexor concentrates data from several sources and sends it over a single communications channel.

Communications protocols (189) are rules established to govern the way data are transmitted in a computer network. The primary hardware/software technology used to enable the interconnection of incompatible computer networks is the *router*. A **backbone** (189) is composed of one or more routers and the associated transmission media.

6.3 The data communications channel: Data highways

A **communications channel** (190) is the facility through which digital information must pass to get from one location in a computer network to the next. A channel's capacity is rated by the number of bits it can transmit per second **(bits per second** or **bps)** (190). In practice, the word **baud** (190) is often used interchangeably with *bits per second;* in reality, they are quite different.

A channel may be composed of one or more of the following transmission media: telephone lines of copper **twisted-pair wire** (190), **coaxial cable** (191), **fiber optic cable** (191), **microwave signals** (191), **radio signals** (191), and **wireless transceivers** (193). Satellites are essentially microwave repeater stations that maintain a **geosynchronous orbit** (193) around the earth. Three services are made available over twisted-pair wire: **POTS** (plain old telephone services) (190), **Integrated Services Digital Network (ISDN)** (190), a digital service that requires an **ISDN modem** (190); and **Asymmetric Digital Subscriber Line (ADSL)** (191). The **downstream rate** (191) is in megabits per second, and the **upstream rate** (191) (receiving) (sending) is in k bps. Some cable television systems offer high-speed Internet access over coaxial cable.

Communications **common carriers** (195) provide communications channels to the public, and lines can be arranged to suit the application. A **private,** or **leased, line** (195) provides a dedicated communications channel. A **switched,** or **dial-up, line** (195) is available on a time-and-distance-charge basis.

6.4 Networks: Connecting nodes

Computer systems are linked together to form a computer network. In a computer network the **node** (196) can be a terminal, a computer, or any other destination/source device. The basic patterns for configuring computer systems within a computer network are **star topology** (197), **ring topology** (197), and **bus topology** (197). The bus topology permits the connection of nodes along a **network bus** (197). In practice, most networks are actually hybrids of these **network topologies** (197).

In **client/server computing** (198), processing is distributed throughout the network. The **client computer** (198) requests processing or some other type of service from the **server computer** (198). Both client and server computers perform processing. The client computer runs **front-end applications software** (199), and the server computer runs the **back-end applications software** (199).

Asynchronous transmission (200) begins and ends each message with start/stop bits and is used primarily for low-speed data transmission. **Synchronous transmission** (200) permits the source and destination to communicate in timed synchronization for high-speed data transmission.

6.5 Networks: The WAN, MAN, LAN, and TAN

A **WAN,** or **wide area network** (201), connects nodes in widely dispersed geographic areas. The **local area network (LAN),** or **local net** (204), connects nodes in close proximity and does not need a common carrier. The **MAN,** or **metropolitan area network** (204), is a network designed for a city. A **TAN,** or **tiny area network** (204), is a very small LAN. The physical transfer of data and programs between LAN nodes is controlled by the access method embedded in the network interface card's ROM, usually the **token access method** (205), or **Ethernet** (205). The three most popular servers are the **file server** (207), the **print server** (207), and the **communications server** (207). These server functions may reside in a dedicated **LAN server** (208).

The **LAN operating system** (208) is actually several pieces of software, a part of which resides in each LAN component's RAM. In a **peer-to-peer LAN** (208), all PCs are equals. Any PC can share its resources with its peers. In LANs with dedicated servers, the controlling software resides in the file server's RAM.

LANs and *groupware* provide the foundation for *workgroup computing.* The breadth of workgroup computing encompasses any application that involves groups of people linked by a computer network. Workgroup computing applications include electronic mail, calendar and scheduling, brainstorming and problem solving, shared whiteboarding, and others.

DISCUSSION AND PROBLEM SOLVING

6.1 **a.** Discuss ways that the trend toward digital conversion has changed your life over the last two years. Speculate on ways that it might change your life during the next five years.

b. Select a type of company and give an example of what information might be made available over the company's Internet, its intranet, and its extranet.

6.2 **a.** Explain why you must use a modem to send data over a plain old telephone line.

b. Describe how a multiplexor can be used to save money.

c. A variety of communications hardware, including a router, are needed to link local area networks that use different communications protocols. Why aren't all LANs designed to use the same standards for communication so that communications hardware tasks can be simplified?

6.3 **a.** It's getting crowded in space with so many companies and countries launching communications satellites into geosynchronous orbit. Is there a danger of having too many satellites hovering above the earth?

b. Describe circumstances in which a leased line would be preferred to a dial-up line.

c. The cost of a dial-up connection with unlimited access to the Internet costs anywhere from $15 to $30. How much more would you pay to get Internet access via cable TV that is hundreds of times faster? Explain.

d. Speculate on the different types of transmission media that might be used to transmit data for a one-hour Internet session.

6.4 **a.** Identify the type and location of at least five different types of nodes in your college's network.

b. The basis for many high-profile information systems, such as airline reservation systems, is still one or several centralized mainframe computers servicing a large number of terminals. With the trend to client/server computing, why haven't these systems been converted?

c. Discuss the advantages of client/server computing over that of a network with a centralized mainframe computer system.

6.5 **a.** Describe how information can be made readily accessible to many people in a company, but only on a need-to-know basis.

b. The five PCs in the purchasing department of a large consumer-goods manufacturer are used primarily for word processing and database applications. What would be the benefits associated with connecting the PCs in a local area network?

c. The mere fact that PCs on a LAN are networked poses a threat to security. Why?

d. Some metropolitan area networks are completely private; that is, communications common carrier services are not used. Network nodes can be distributed throughout large cities. How do companies link the nodes on the network without common carrier data communications facilities?

e. Describe at least one situation in academe or the business world where creating a portable network would be inappropriate. That is, a situation where people with laptop PCs link them in a network by attaching them to a common cable or by using wireless transceivers. Briefly describe what the network might do.

Going Online

Learning Objectives

7.1 Be aware of what you must do to go online.

7.2 Understand the scope and features offered by online information services.

7.3 Demonstrate knowledge of Internet concepts.

7.4 Gain a basic understanding of Internet browser concepts and operation.

7.5 Describe the scope of Internet resources and the various types of Internet applications.

7.6 Identify and discuss important Internet issues.

chapter 7

WHY THIS CHAPTER IS IMPORTANT TO YOU

The Internet is a new door in our lives that was simply not there a few years ago. For many people, that door is there, but it remains locked. This chapter is the key to that door. Use it to open the door and enter the cyberworld. In this chapter you'll learn about online information services and the Internet, what you will need to do to get on, what you'll find when you get there, and how you travel to what seems to be an endless variety of cybersites.

To say that the Internet has had a profound impact on our lives is truly an understatement. What we do at work, how we work, how we learn, and what we do during leisure time has changed dramatically during the short-lived public Internet era. The virtual classroom, where students can attend classes online, is remaking our college and university system. Each year millions more people choose to telecommute to work from their homes. Many more people make their résumé available to millions by posting it to the Internet, then using searchable jobs databases to find employment throughout the world. Many people stay connected to the Internet all day long, taking advantage of its latest resources to get help with many daily activities—planning a vacation, getting the best deal on an airline ticket, communicating with friends via e-mail or videophone, and so on. More and more, we rely on the Internet to get our news and weather, and even to play games with other cybersurfers.

For those of you who have not had an opportunity to browse the Internet, this chapter should open your eyes and that previously locked door to information and services beyond your imagination. The typical response from a first-time visitor to the Internet, called a newbie, is something like, "Wow, I had no idea!"

Value Learning

7.1 THE ONLINE WORLD

Monthly Technology Update Chapter 7

Your PC and your willingness to explore are central to unlocking the door to the online world. To open the door and go online, you will need to connect your PC to the global network we call the Internet. That can be done in a variety of ways. You can enter using cable modems connected to cable TV, using ISDN or ADSL (both over twisted-pair telephone wire), wireless satellite links, and direct links via LANs. However, most of us enter cyberspace by simply plugging the phone line into our PC's modem and running our communications software.

Once online, you can talk (just as you would on the telephone) with friends in Europe, send Grandma a picture, schedule a meeting with your co-workers, pay your utility bill, play games with people you've never met, listen to a live audio broadcast of a sporting event, or conduct research for a report. Every day a growing number of online capabilities continues to change the way we live our lives.

The online world offers a vast network of resources, services, and capabilities. To go online, people with PCs generally subscribe to a commercial information service, such as America Online (AOL), or open an account with a company that will provide access to the Internet. This chapter explores these and other online options and shows how you, too, can become a part of this global community.

SECTION SELF-CHECK

Self-Check

7-1.1 One way to go online is to subscribe to a commercial information service. (T/F)

7-1.2 Which of the following is not a link to the Internet: (a) interstate bonds, (b) ISDN, (c) cable TV, or (d) wireless satellite?

7.2 INFORMATION SERVICES: AMERICA ONLINE, COMPUSERVE, AND MORE

Serendipitous Surfing: Magazines

Commercial information services have an array of powerful server computer systems that offer a variety of online services, from hotel reservations to daily horoscopes. More and more PC users are subscribing to commercial information services. About one-third of the American households with PCs subscribe to America Online (AOL) and other major information services, such CompuServe, an AOL subsidiary. Generally, other information services such as LEXIS-NEXIS, Dow Jones Business Information Service, and DialogWeb cater to niche markets, providing specific services to customers with special information needs (legal, financial, and so on). Information services have grown at a rate of 30% per year since 1990 and there's still plenty of room to grow.

To take advantage of information services, you need a communications-equipped PC (that is, one with a modem and communications software) and a few dollars. Most services have a *monthly service charge.* The monthly service charge for the most popular services is usually a flat rate of $15 to $30 for unlimited usage. Some usage information services bill based on time online. The charges can be substantial for business-oriented services, perhaps as much as a dollar a minute for medical and legal services. Initially, you get:

- *Communications software.* Some information services, such as AOL, give you communications software packages designed specifically to interface with their information service network. Others rely on Internet **browsers** to deliver the service. Browsers are programs that let you go to and view the various Internet resources.
- *A username and password.* To obtain authorization to connect with the online information service, you need to enter your username and a password to **logon,** or make the connection with the remote computer.

- *A user's guide.* A user's guide provides an overview of services and includes telephone numbers that can be dialed to access the information service's private network. America Online is a worldwide network, something like the Internet but on a smaller scale. (Except for small towns, the AOL telephone number you dial is usually local.) Most information services deliver their services entirely over the Internet.

Figure 7.1 on pages 218–220 takes you on a visual tour of America Online, the most popular information service. This walkthrough figure shows you a few of the well-traveled roads on this stretch of the information highway, but it does not begin to show the true breadth and scope of America Online (or any other major information service). If you were to spend every waking minute of the next year logged on to AOL, you would not be able to explore all of its features, forums (like newsgroups), databases, download opportunities, and information services. In fact, you would probably fall behind. Existing services are updated and new services are added on AOL and all of the other information services every day.

SECTION SELF-CHECK

Self-Check

7-2.1 The monthly service charge for most commercial information services is set by law at $5 per month for unlimited usage. (T/F)

7-2.2 America Online has a private worldwide network. (T/F)

7-2.3 Which of the following does not come with a subscription to an information service: (a) communications software, (b) a username, (c) a PC, or (d) password?

7-2.4 Which of the following is not an online commercial information service: (a) Dow Jones Business Information Service, (b) the Web, (c) AOL, or (d) CompuServe?

7-2.5 You would look for a forum on your favorite hobby in which AOL channel: (a) Shopping, (b) Personal Finance, (c) Interests, or (d) News?

7.3 THE INTERNET: A WORLDWIDE WEB OF COMPUTERS AND INFORMATION

The Internet

America Online (AOL), an information service, is one of the many beautiful stars in cyberspace. Now imagine being able to explore an entire universe with millions of beautiful stars, each offering databases, forums for discussion, e-mail, files of every conceivable type, information services, and more. That's *the Internet.*

What Is the Internet?

The Internet is a worldwide collection of *inter*connected *net*works. It's actually comprised of thousands of independent networks at academic institutions, military installations, government agencies, commercial enterprises, and other organizations. Once on the Internet, cybersurfers can tap into a vast array of information resources, have access to millions of retrievable files, "talk" on thousands of worldwide newsgroups, send e-mail to close to hundreds of millions of people in every country, and take advantage of thousands of free and pay-for-use information services.

Just how big is the Internet? The Net, the Internet's nickname, links a million networks with even more Internet host server computers in every country in the world. Internet hosts are connected to the Internet 24 hours a day. Thousands more join this global network each month. The number of people using the Internet is in the hundreds of millions moving toward a billion.

From ARPANET to the Internet: Some Historical Perspective

A lot happened in 1969, including Woodstock and the first landing on the moon. Amidst all of this activity, the birth of what we now know as the Internet went virtually unnoticed. A small group of computer scientists on both coasts of the

Touring America Online

Sign on to America Online When you sign on to America Online, now used by over 20 million Americans, you enter a screen name, usually an alias, like SkyJockey or PrincessLea, and a password. The software dials the AOL number, makes the connection, and displays the AOL main menu (see example), which is divided into channels.

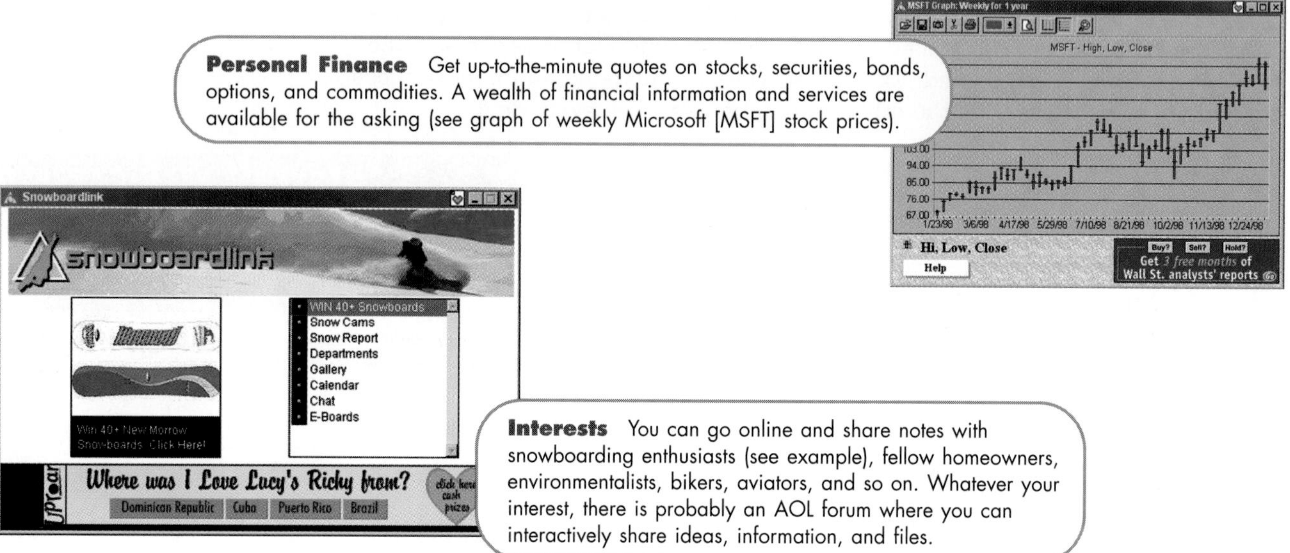

Personal Finance Get up-to-the-minute quotes on stocks, securities, bonds, options, and commodities. A wealth of financial information and services are available for the asking (see graph of weekly Microsoft [MSFT] stock prices).

Interests You can go online and share notes with snowboarding enthusiasts (see example), fellow homeowners, environmentalists, bikers, aviators, and so on. Whatever your interest, there is probably an AOL forum where you can interactively share ideas, information, and files.

United States were busy creating a national network that would enable the scientific community to share ideas over communications links. At the time, this network was truly a giant leap because computers were viewed more as number crunchers than as aids to communication.

The Department of Defense's Advanced Research Project Agency (ARPA) sponsored the project, named ARPANET, to unite a community of geographically dispersed scientists by technology. The first official demonstration linked UCLA with Stanford University, both in California. Ironically, this historic event had no reporters, no photographers, and no records. No one remembered the first message, only that it worked. By 1971, the ARPANET included more than 20 sites, including Harvard and MIT. By 1981, the ARPANET linked 200 sites. A few years later, this grand idea of interconnected networks caught on like an uncontrolled forest fire, spreading from site to site throughout the United States. Other countries wanted in on it, too.

ARPANET broke new ground. The diversity of computers and the sites forced ARPA to develop a standard protocol (rules of data communications) that would enable communication between diverse computers and networks. ARPANET eventually lost its reason to exist, as other special-interest networks took its place. In 1990, ARPANET was eliminated, leaving behind a legacy of networks that evolved into the Internet. At that time, commercial accounts were permitted access to what had been a network of military and academic organizations.

What we now know as the Internet is one of the federal government's success stories. Although the Internet, along with its policies and technologies, is now pushed along by market forces, the United States government remains active in promoting cooperation between communications, software, and computer companies. The current administration would like for the Internet to emerge as

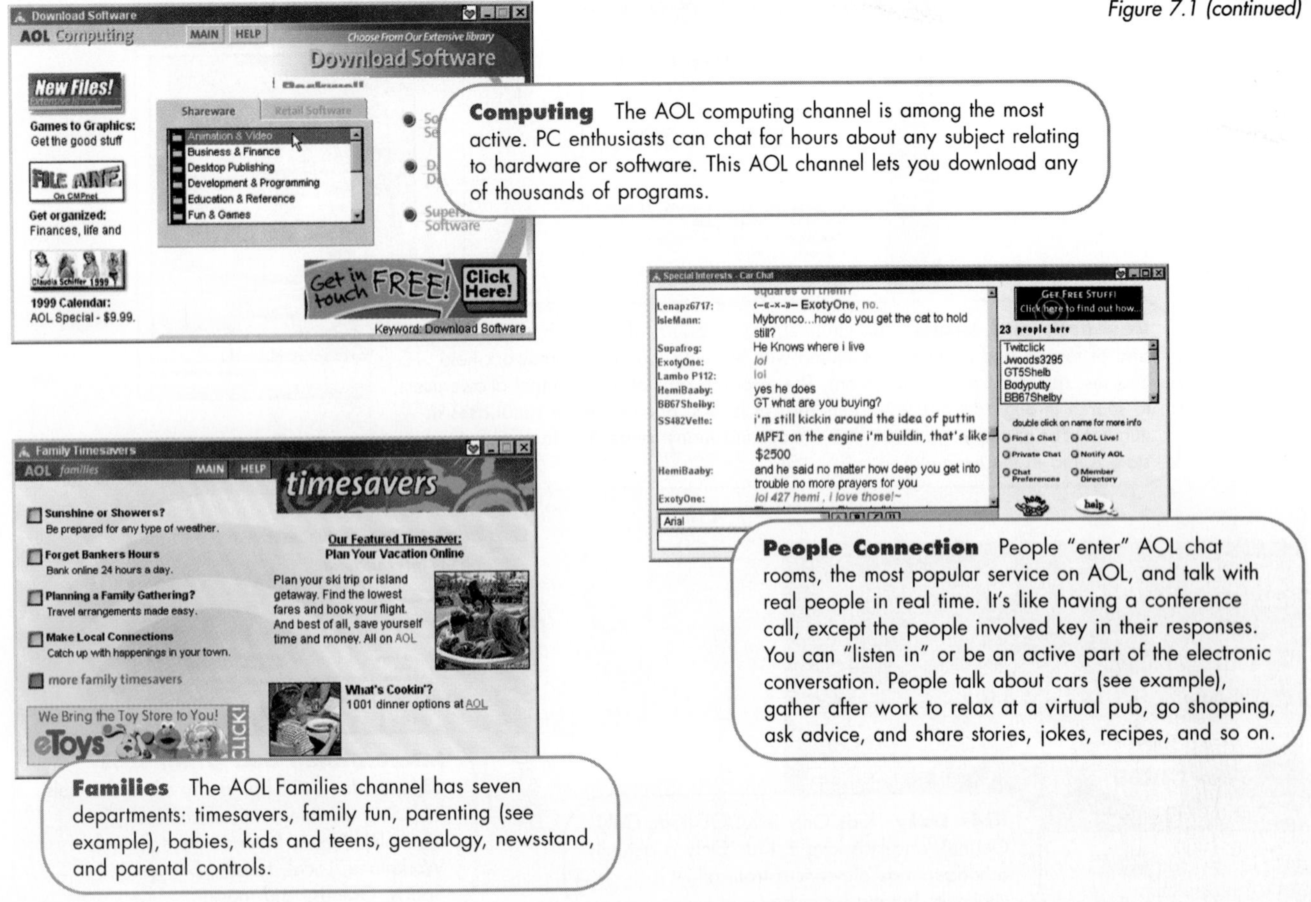

Computing The AOL computing channel is among the most active. PC enthusiasts can chat for hours about any subject relating to hardware or software. This AOL channel lets you download any of thousands of programs.
People Connection People "enter" AOL chat rooms, the most popular service on AOL, and talk with real people in real time. It's like having a conference call, except the people involved key in their responses. You can "listen in" or be an active part of the electronic conversation. People talk about cars (see example), gather after work to relax at a virtual pub, go shopping, ask advice, and share stories, jokes, recipes, and so on.
Families The AOL Families channel has seven departments: timesavers, family fun, parenting (see example), babies, kids and teens, genealogy, newsstand, and parental controls.

Figure 7.1 (continued)

a *National Information Infrastructure (NII)* that may someday link schools, libraries, hospitals, corporations, agencies at all levels of government, and much more as we enter the twenty-first century.

Who Governs the Internet?

When the ARPANET was conceived, one objective of its founders was to create a network in which communications could continue even if parts of the network crashed. To do this, it was designed with no central computer or network. This is still true today. The U.S. Internet *backbone,* the major communications lines and nodes to which thousands of host computers are connected, crisscrosses the United States with no node being the central focus of communications.

Unlike AOL, CompuServe, and other information services, the Internet is coordinated (not governed) by volunteers from many nations serving on various advisory boards, task groups, steering committees, and so on. There is no single authoritative organization. The volunteer organizations set standards for and help coordinate the global operation of Internet. Each autonomous network on the Internet makes its own rules, regulations, and decisions about which resources to make publicly available. Consequently, the Internet is being re-invented almost daily by the people who run these independent networks.

InterNIC, an organization funded by a cooperative agreement from the National Science Foundation, provides registration services for the Internet community. Any person or organization desiring to connect a computer to the Net must register its computer with InterNIC. Besides keeping track of the computers connected to the Net (site names and addresses), it also provides assistance to users concerning policy and the status of their existing registrations. Registered Internet hosts must pay an amount based on Internet usage to support the Internet's backbone.

Figure 7.1 (continued)

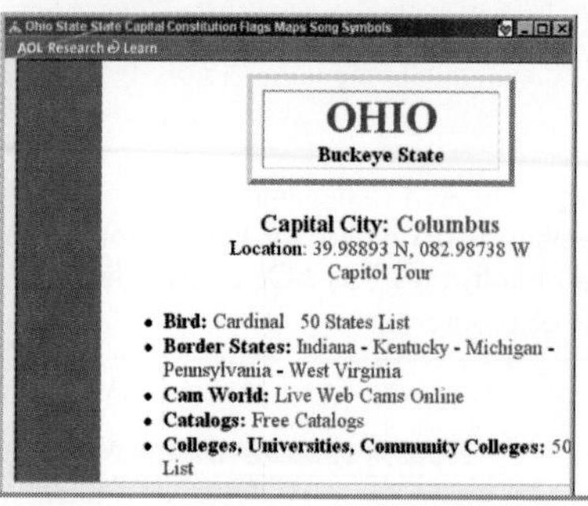

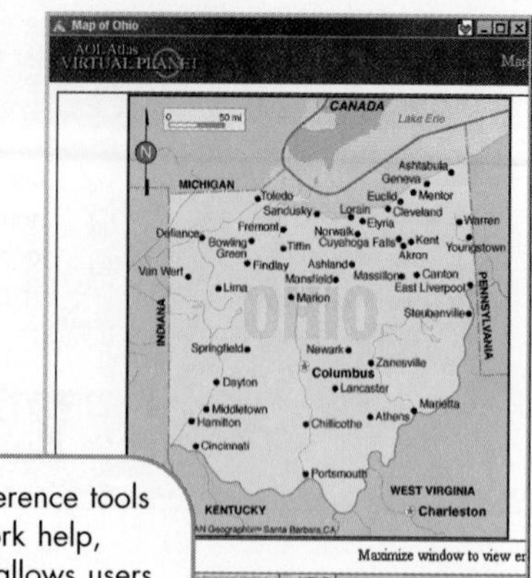

Research and Learn This channel is a potpourri of research/reference tools and of forums and activities associated with learning (careers, homework help, courses, reference desk, and so on). The research part of this channel allows users to search through dozens, even hundreds of books, documents, or databases in minutes. For example, you can find a map and many interesting facts about a state (Ohio in the example).

Kids Only Kids Only is KOOL (Kids Only OnLine), and kids love it. Kids Only is actually a hodgepodge of services from all AOL channels, but just for kids.

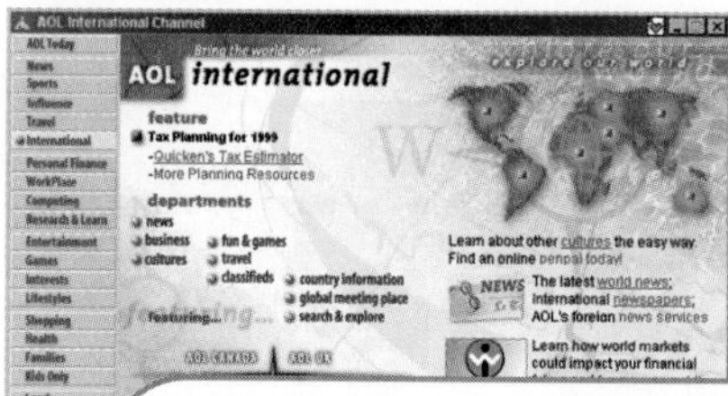

International and Other AOL Channels AOL has many other channels, including the International channel (see example), News, Entertainment, Travel, Workplace, Local, Health, Shopping, Sports, Games, and more.

The Link to the Internet

How do you get on the Internet? In this section we talk about connecting to the Internet and, also, we unravel the mystery of how information is packaged and sent over the Internet.

Making the Internet Connection

There are three levels at which you can connect your PC to the Internet (see Figure 7.2):

Connect via an Information Service Gateway One way to gain access to the Internet is to subscribe to a commercial information service, such as America Online. This level one connection method is a popular choice for people working from their home or small business and for those who wish to link their home PC to the Internet. AOL and the other major information services are themselves large self-contained networks. Each provides an electronic *gateway* to the Net; that is, you are linked to the information services network that, in turn, links you to the Internet.

Connect via an Internet Service Provider At the second level of Internet service, you would make the connection via a *dialup connection* through an *Internet service provider.* This type of connection gives you direct access to the Internet. A **dialup connection** is a temporary connection established using a modem to dialup the number (over a telephone line or a digital ISDN or ADSL line) for a line linked to a remote computer with Internet access. An **Internet service provider (ISP)** is any company that provides individuals and organizations with access to, or presence on, the Internet. ISPs do not offer the extended information services offered by commercial information services, such as CompuServe and AOL, although some information services double as Internet service providers. There are thousands of Internet service providers, ranging from local elementary schools making unused line capacity available to students and parents to major communications companies, such as AT&T and Sprint.

Direct via Network Connection A level three direct connection to the Internet generally is preferable to a dialup link (levels one and two above) because it normally gives you faster interaction with the Internet. At this level, your PC is wired directly into the Internet, usually via a local area network (LAN). A LAN will normally have a high-speed digital link to the Internet, which is shared by the users on the LAN. Depending on the size of the LAN and the extent of Internet usage, the LAN may be connected to an ISDN (128 K bps), an ADSL line (up to 9 M bps [megabits per second]), a **T-1 line** (1.544 M bps), or a **T-3 line** (44.736 M bps) line. A faster connection means you don't have to wait so long to retrieve information, execute commands, or just connect to the Internet. A dialup connection can take from 15 seconds to about 45 seconds to establish, whereas a direct connection via a LAN is almost immediate, and it's available 24 hours a day. To have a direct connection, your PC must be connected to a LAN that is linked directly to an Internet host. This is the case with most businesses and many college computer labs.

Ready Access to the Internet

Do you want to be a **newbie?** Newbies are what seasoned Internet surfers (those who regularly travel or "surf" from Internet site to Internet site) call novice In-

Ways to Connect to the Internet

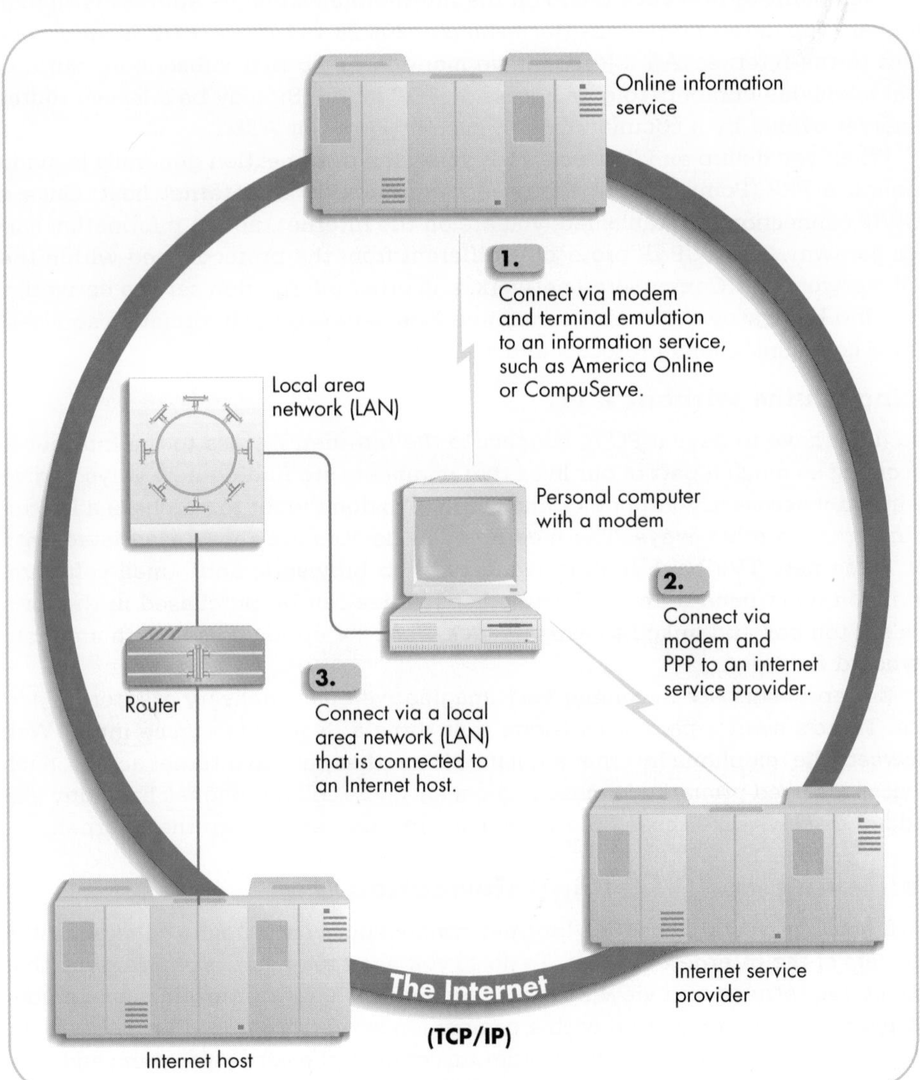

ternet users. If you do, there is a good chance that your college or company's computer network is linked to the Internet. Obtaining access may be as easy as asking your boss, instructor, or the network administrator to assign you an Internet address (username) and password.

TCP/IP and Packets

The **Transmission Control Protocol/Internet Protocol (TCP/IP)** is the communications protocol that permits data transmission over the Internet. Any modern operating system (for example, Window 9x/NT/2000 or Mac OS) comes with the software needed to handle TCP/IP communications. Communications over the Net are built around this two-layer protocol. A *protocol* is a set of rules computers use to talk to each other.

The *Transmission Control Protocol* (the TCP of the TCP/IP) sets the rules for the packaging of information into **packets.** Each message, file, and so on to be sent over the Internet is disassembled and placed into packets for routing over the Internet. The *Internet Protocol* (the IP of the TCP/IP) handles the address, such that each packet is routed to its proper destination. Here is how it works. When you request a file from an Internet server computer, the TCP layer divides the file into one or more packets, associates a number with each packet, and then routes them one-by-one through the IP layer. Each packet has the same destination *IP address,* but they may take different paths through the Internet to their destination. At the destination, the TCP layer waits until all the packets arrive, reassembles them, and then forwards them to users as a single file.

Each **point-of-presence** (POP) on the Internet has a unique address with four numbers separated by periods (for example, 206.28.104.10). A **POP** is an access point to the Internet. An ISP may have many POPs so that subscribers can dial local telephone numbers to gain access. A POP for an ISP may be a leased router or server owned by a common carrier, such as Sprint or AT&T.

When you dialup an ISP's local POP, your dialup connection generally is made through a *PPP* (Point-to-Point Protocol) connection to an Internet host. Once a TCP/IP connection is established, you are on the Internet, not an information service gateway. The TCP/IP protocol is different from the protocol used within the AOL network, the CompuServe network, and other information service networks. Their Internet gateways enable communication between the information services' native communications protocols and TCP/IP.

Going Online without a PC

You don't have to have a PC to connect to the Internet. Access to the Internet is becoming so much a part of our lives that engineers are finding new ways to give us Internet access. Cyberphobics and those who don't want to purchase a PC can gain access in other ways. The most popular devices are those associated with TV. Some new TVs have built-in modems, Web browsers, and e-mail software. Or, if you don't need a new TV, these capabilities can be purchased in the form of a set-top box and linked to existing TVs. Each TV option comes with a remote keyboard for input.

Entrepreneurs are becoming very imaginative about delivery of Internet service. There's even a plug-in cartridge that turns a Sega video game into a Web browser. The telephone Internet appliance is another path to Internet access. Such devices are used primarily for checking e-mail. Some cellular phones have tiny embedded displays, like those on a video camera, that let you tap the Internet.

Retrieving and Viewing Information

Once you have established an Internet connection, you're ready to explore the wonders of the Internet—almost. To do so you need to open a *client program* that will let you retrieve and view Internet resources. A **client program** runs on your PC and works in conjunction with a companion **server program** that runs on the Internet host computer. The client program contacts the server program, and they

IT Ethics

PRESCREENING OF ONLINE COMMUNICATIONS

Millions of people have access to and participate in the bulletin boards and online forums. Some information services feel obligated to give their subscribers an environment that is free of offensive language. These information services use an electronic scanner to "read" each message before it is posted to a bulletin board or a forum. In a split second the scanner flags those words and phrases that do not comply with the information service's guidelines. The scanner even catches words or phrases that may be disguised with asterisks and so on. Generally the guidelines are compatible with accepted norms in a moral society. These include the use of grossly repugnant material, obscene material, solicitations, and threats. The scanner also scans for text that may be inappropriate for a public discussion, such as the use of pseudonyms, attempts at trading, presentation of illegal material, and even speaking in foreign languages. Messages that do not pass the prescreening process are returned automatically to the sender.

Some might cry that their rights to freedom of expression are violated. This, of course, is a matter that may ultimately be decided in a court of law. In the meantime, those who wish a more open discussion have plenty of opportunities. On some national bulletin boards and information services, anything goes.

Discussion: Is prescreening of electronic communications a violation of freedom of expression?

work together to give you access to the resources on the Internet server. Client programs are designed to work with one or more specific kinds of server programs (for example, the Microsoft Internet Explorer client software works with the companion Internet Explorer server software). A single server computer might have several different server programs running on it, enabling it to accommodate a variety of clients.

A *browser* is one kind of client. Browsers are application software that present you with a graphical interactive interface (GUI) for searching, finding, viewing, and managing information over any network. Microsoft Internet Explorer and Netscape Communicator are the two most popular browsers. Both are used in the examples throughout this book. Most information on the Internet is accessed and viewed in the workspace of browser client programs. You give the browser an Internet address, called the *URL,* and it goes out over your Internet connection, finds the server site identified in the URL, then downloads the requested file(s) for viewing on your browser. The operation of browsers is discussed later in this chapter.

Uniform Resource Locator: The Internet Address

The **URL,** or **uniform resource locator** (pronounced *"U-R-L"* or *"earl"*), is the Internet equivalent of an address. Just as postal addresses progress from general to specific (country, state, city, to street address), URLs do the same. The URL gives those who make information available over the Internet a standard way to designate where Internet elements, such as server sites, documents, files, newsgroups, and so on, can be found. Let's break down one of the following URLs from the Long and Long INTERNET BRIDGE, the companion Internet site for this book.

http://www.prenhall.com/long/7e/main.html

- *Access method*—**http:***//www.prenhall.com/long/7e/main.html.* That portion of the URL before the first colon (http in the example) specifies the access method. This indicator tells your client software how to access that particular file. The http tells the software to expect an **http (HyperText Transport Protocol)** file. Http is the primary access method for interacting with the

Internet. Other common access methods include *ftp* (File Transfer Protocol) for transferring files, *news* for newsgroups, and *gopher* for accessing information via a Gopher menu tree. When on the Internet, you will encounter URLs like these.

ftp://ftp.prenhall.com/ (Prentice Hall ftp site)
http://www.yahoo.com/ (Internet portal and search engine)
news://alt.tennis (tennis newsgroup)
gopher://wiretap.spies.com/00/Library/Classic/twocity.txt (African National Congress Information)

- *Domain name—http://***www.prenhall.com/***long/7e/main.html.* That portion following the double forward slashes (//), *www.prenhall.com,* is the server address, or the domain name. The **domain name,** which is a unique name that identifies an Internet host site, will always have at least two parts, separated by dots (periods). This host/network identifier adheres to rules for the domain hierarchy. The part to the right of the domain name is the most general and that part on the left is the most specific.

  At the top of the domain hierarchy (the part on the right) is the country code for all countries except the United States. For example, the address for the Canadian Tourism Commission is info.ic.gc.ca. Other common country codes are au (Australia), dk (Denmark), fr (France), and jp (Japan). Within the United States, the country code is replaced with a code denoting affiliation categories. Colleges are in the edu category. Other categories are shown in Figure 7.3. The next level of the domain hierarchy identifies the host network or host provider, which might be the name of a business or college (prenhall or stateuniv). Large organizations might have networks within a network and need subordinate identifiers. The example Internet address cis.stateuniv.edu identifies the cis local area network at stateuniv. The Physics Department LAN at State University might be identified as physics.stateuniv.edu.

FIGURE 7.3

United States Top-level Domains

U.S. Top-level Domain Affiliation ID	Affiliation
com	Commercial
edu	Education
firm	Businesses
gov	Government
info	Purveyors of information
int	International
mil	Military
net	Network resources
nom	Users desiring personal nomenclature
org	Usually nonprofit organizations
rec	Entities dealing in recreational activities
store	Retailers
web	Businesses related to the web

- *Directory—http://www.prenhall.com/***long/7e***/main.html.* What follows the domain name is a directory containing the resources for a particular topic. The resource directory long/ in this example refers to the Long and Long INTERNET BRIDGE (the companion Internet site for all Prentice Hall books by Larry and Nancy Long). Several books are covered within this INTERNET BRIDGE resource, so subordinate directories are needed to reference a specific book (7e, implying *Computers*, seventh edition).
- *Filename—http://www.prenhall.com/long/7e/***main.html.** At the end of the URL is the specific filename of the file that is retrieved from the server (www.prenhall.com in this example) and sent to your PC over the Internet. The html extension (after the dot) in the filename main.html indicates that this is an html file. **HTML (HyperText Markup Language)** is the language used to compose and format most of the content

you see when cruising the Net. HTML documents are text (ASCII) files that can be created with any text editor or word processing package. In HTML each element in the electronic document is tagged and described (for example, justification). Elements include title, headings, tables, paragraphs, lists, and so on. In this example, the title and a paragraph are tagged.

⟨TITLE ALIGN=CENTER⟩A Centered Title of an Electronic Document⟨/TITLE⟩
⟨P⟩This paragraph is displayed in standard paragraph format.⟨P⟩

Tags always come in pairs, with the last one including a forward slash (/). Tags can include attributes, which further describe the presentation of the element. For example, the title in the example is to be centered on the screen (ALIGN=CENTER). The HTML language also permits the identification of inline (inline with the text) graphic images to be inserted in the document. Inline images are retrieved from the server and inserted as per the HTML instructions (position and size).

For those people who are not used to programming, HTML can be rather cryptic. Fortunately, there are a number of good WYSIWYG development tools that allow you to generate HTML documents using drag-and-drop techniques along with fill-in-the-blank dialog boxes. The tags are inserted automatically for you.

SECTION SELF-CHECK

Self-Check

7-3.1 These communications channels are listed by capacity (from least to most): T-1, ADSL, ISDN, and T-3. (T/F)

7-3.2 The Internet is like AOL, a commercial information service. (T/F)

7-3.3 ARPANET was the first commercially available communications software package. (T/F)

7-3.4 To eliminate the spread of viruses, the uploading of files is no longer permitted on the Internet. (T/F)

7-3.5 A newbie is anyone with a fear of cyberspace. (T/F)

7-3.6 In an Internet address, levels in the host/network identifier are separated by a: (a) period, (b) comma, (c) @, or (d) colon?

7-3.7 Which of these is not a U.S. top-level domain affiliation ID: (a) moc, (b) edu, (c) gov, or (d) org?

7-3.8 In the URL, http://www.abccorp.com/pr/main.htm, the domain is: (a) http, (b) www.abccorp.com, (c) pr/main.htm, or (d) www?

7-3.9 TCP/IP is the communications protocol for: (a) the Net, (b) sending faxes, (c) all internal e-mail, or (d) spherical LANs?

7-3.10 What type of company provides people with access to the Internet: (a) PSI, (b) ISP, (c) SPI, or (d) IPS?

7-3.11 In the e-mail address, mickey_mouse@disney.com, the username is: (a) mickey_mouse, (b) mouse, (c) disney.com, or (d) @?

7-3.12 The Internet is short for (a) International Network, (b) interconnected networks, (c) internal net e-mail terminal, or (d) inner net?

7.4 BROWSERS: THE INFORMATION TOOL

There's a good chance that you will spend a good deal of time with an Internet browser once you get a taste of the Internet. The Internet browser, or *Web browser,* is a software tool that makes it possible for you to tap the information resources of the electronic world and to communicate with those living in the electronic world. Browsers have several main functions.

- They enable us to retrieve and view information from World Wide Web, Gopher, and FTP server computers on the Internet, on internal (within an organization) intranets, and on any disk medium with HTML-based content (for example, *PC Magazine* distributes electronic versions of the magazine in HTML format on CD-ROM).

- They allow us to interact with server-based systems and to submit information to these systems.
- They are the foundation tool for viewing electronic documents.
- They let us download digital information, then view and/or hear the downloaded video, images, music, and so on. They let us upload information, as well.
- They allow us to send and receive e-mail.
- They allow us to participate with online newsgroups.

The emphasis in this section is on the basic elements of browser software and its relationship to the Internet. E-mail and newsgroups are covered later.

The viewing area of a browser can be filled with documents containing any combination of text, images, motion video, and animation. The visual information can be enhanced with real-time audio. These various forms of communication are presented within HTML documents. The browser opens an HTML document and displays the information according to HTML instructions embedded in the document. The HTML document pulls together all the necessary elements, including image files, audio streams, and small programs, called **applets.** The browser accepts the applets, then interprets and executes them. These applets frequently contain the instructions for an animation sequence. Browsers can be used with or without an Internet connection; however, an Internet link is needed to access files other than those on your PC or your local area network. We will discuss browsers within the context of the Internet. With browsers you can:

- Visit the museums of the world.
- Listen to the very latest song from your favorite group.
- Do your grocery shopping.
- Track the progress of the space shuttle.
- Tune in to a radio station in Australia.
- Send and receive holiday greetings to/from friends and family.
- Make an inquiry regarding the status of an order.
- Study from an interactive book in preparation for an exam.
- Chat with colleagues and friends.
- Send digital business materials, such as contracts and portable documents.
- Participate in ongoing discussions about your favorite celebrity.
- Learn more about almost anything.

These are just a few of the many things you can do with browsers.

Concepts and Features

We interact with word processing, desktop publishing, presentation, spreadsheet, and database software to create some kind of a document. Browser software is different in that there is no resulting document. Browsers let you retrieve and view information as well as interact with server computers. Compared to the other productivity tools, browsers are easy to use, almost intuitive. It's not unusual for IT-competent people, unfamiliar with browsers, to be cruising the Internet within minutes after their first exposure to the software.

To use browsers successfully, you will need to understand the basic makeup of the Internet and the browser's navigational tools. Internet **search engines,** Internet-based capabilities that help you find information on the Internet, are discussed in the next section.

The Internet: A Public Network

The vast majority of the Internet resources made available by millions of participating networks can be accessed by anyone, anywhere. To take advantage of these resources, you will need a browser and an Internet connection. Most knowledge workers now have access to the Internet through their employers' networks. Families and individuals can obtain dialup connections via Internet service providers (ISPs) or commercial information services.

Internet Organization Fortunately, the Internet has a straightforward organization. At the top of the organization are the Internet servers, the computers that provide on-demand distribution of information. Each server has one or more home pages. When you navigate to a particular Web site (perhaps that of your college), the first page you will normally view is the site's **home page.** Information on the Web, which may be graphics, audio, video, animation, and text, is viewed in **pages.** A Web page can contain text plus any or all of these multimedia elements.

Think of a Web page as a page in an alternative type of book, one with nonsequential linked documents at a Web site. The home page is the table of contents for the resources at a server site. A home page will have links to many other pages, some associated with the home page and located on the same server and others that may be elsewhere on the Internet. The home page for this book ⟨http://www.prenhall.com/long⟩ has hundreds of pages and links to other pages. The home page for Prentice Hall ⟨http://www.prenhall.com/⟩, the publisher of this book, has thousands of pages and links to other pages. A page has no set length and can be a few lines of text, or it can be thousands of lines with many graphic images. *Hyperlinks,* in a form of *hypertext* (highlighted and underlined text), *hot images,* or *hot icons,* permit navigation between pages and between other resources on the Internet. All hyperlinks are hot; that is, when you click on one with your mouse, the linked page is retrieved for viewing. An image or icon is hot if the cursor pointer turns into a hand image when positioned over it.

Each Web page is actually a file with its own URL. Typically, you will start at a Web site's home page, but not always. A college's home page might be at URL http://stateuniv.edu, but each college or department might have a home page as well (for example, http://stateuniv.edu/cis for the Computer Information Systems Department's home page). A page is a scrollable file; that is, when it is too large for the viewing area, you can scroll up or down to view other parts of the page.

Web Servers

Internet Servers and Addresses The World Wide Web (WWW), or Web server, with its multimedia capability, has emerged as the dominant server type on the Internet. The FTP server facilitates the transfer of files between computers, and the Gopher servers provide a hierarchical storehouse of information. FTP and Gopher sites are being rapidly integrated in the more user-friendly Web server format. Browsers accommodate information retrieval for any type of Internet server.

We navigate to an address on the Internet just as we drive to a street city. These Internet addresses are called URLs. Let's review. The address for the Prentice Hall server is http://www.prenhall.com/. Each Web server's address begins with http:// (for HyperText Transfer Protocol) and is followed by a unique *domain name,* usually the name of or an abbreviation for the organization sponsoring the Internet server (prenhall for Prentice Hall). URLs must begin with: http:// (WWW site), ftp:// (FTP site), gopher:// (Gopher site), mail:, or news:. The domain name is usually prefaced by www to designate a World Wide Web server.

Web Pages and HTML

The pages at a server site are set up within a hierarchy of URLs. At the top in the example on the next page is the company URL, for example, Prentice Hall. Special-topic directories, such as home pages for various Prentice Hall authors (Kotler, Long, Macionis, and Morris in the following example), are subordinate to the company URL but have their own URLs. These directories have subdirectories, which may also have subdirectories, and so on, all of which have their own unique URL. Here's the good news. For most of your navigation around the Internet, you'll simply click on a named hyperlink to go to a URL. Occasionally, you will need to enter a URL, usually a home page. The subset, at the top of page 228, of some of the URLs at the Prentice Hall server site illustrates one hierarchy of URLs.

http://www.prenhall.com/ (Prentice Hall home page URL)

- http://www.prenhall.com/kotler/ (home page URL for Kotler books)
- http://www.prenhall.com/long/ (the Internet Bridge, home page URL for all Long books)
  - http://www.prenhall.com/long/6e/index.html (the opening page for a Long book)
    - http:// . . . (other pages associated with the above book)
  - http://www.prenhall.com/long/7e/index.html (the opening page for another Long book)
    - http:// . . . (other pages associated with the above book)
- http://www.prenhall.com/macionis (home page URL for Macionis books)
- http://www.prenhall.com/morris (home page URL for Morris books)

The above hierarchy of URLs is illustrated in Figure 7.4.

Navigating the Internet

Microsoft Internet Explorer and Netscape Communicator, the dominant browsers, are shown in Figure 7.5. Their appearance is similar and they have the same basic elements.

The Menu Bar The menu bar at the top of the user command interface is used to select file options (print, save, and so on), to select edit options (including copy, cut, and paste), and to set and change a variety of options (for example, how buttons are displayed, color options, font choices, and so on). As with most menu bars, the Help pull-down menu is the last option.

The Toolbar In a typical browser session, most of your interaction is with the toolbar and the hot links in the Web pages. These are the navigation buttons on the Internet Explorer toolbar (Netscape Communicator's toolbar has similar functions).

- *Back.* During the course of a browser session you will normally view several pages, one after another. This button takes you back to the last site that you visited.
- *Forward.* Use this button if you clicked on the back button and would like to go forward to the next site in the string of sites you have viewed.
- *Stop.* Use the stop button to abort any transfer of information to/from the server. The browser displays the last fully viewed site.
- *Refresh.* This button refreshes (reloads) the current document into the browser. Information on some pages is volatile and may need to be updated.
- *Home.* This button takes you to the URL that you have selected as your default home page, perhaps that of your college or company.

The Hierarchy of URLs at a Server Site This figure shows three levels of URLs at the Prentice Hall server site. In the background is the Prentice Hall home page ⟨http://www.prenhall.com/⟩. The Internet Bridge, the Web URL for all books written by Larry and Nancy Long, is ⟨http://www.prenhall.com/long⟩. In front and at the bottom is the main page for a 1999 title, *Computers,* sixth edition ⟨http://www.prenhall.com/long/6e/index.htm⟩.

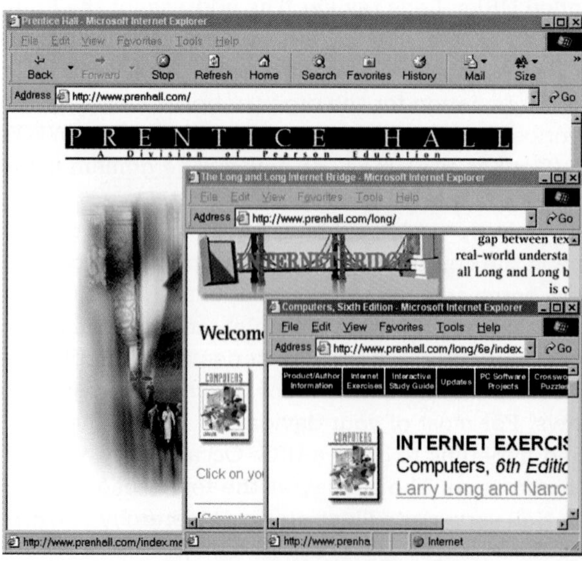

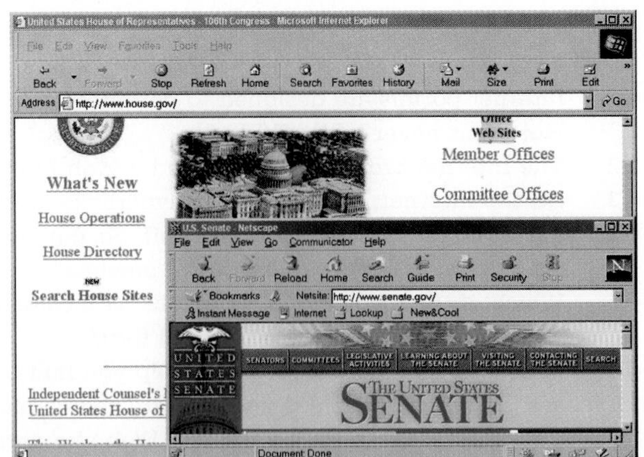

Netscape Communicator (foreground) and Microsoft Internet Explorer (background) Browsers

- *Search.* This button calls up the Internet portal that you have selected as your default search site, usually an Internet portal. A **portal** is a Web site that offers a broad array of information and services, including a menu tree of categories, a tool that lets you search for specific information on the Internet, and a variety of services from up-to-the minute stock quotes to horoscopes. Infoseek, Excite, and Yahoo are portals.
- *Favorites.* Click on the favorites button to view a list of your favorite sites. Browsers let you create and modify this list.

The browser logo symbol to the right of the toolbar is animated when your browser is transferring or waiting for information from the server.

The URL Bar The URL bar, containing the URL of the current page, serves three purposes.

- It allows you to key in (or paste in) the URL (the address or "location") of the desired server site.
- It displays the URL of the page being displayed in the workspace.
- It includes a drop-down box that includes a list of previously visited URLs. To return to one of these sites, simply select it.

The Workspace The workspace is that area in which the document is displayed. You can view documents by scrolling or by using the page up and page down keys. Position the mouse cursor over a hyperlink, a hot image, or a hot icon, and click the left mouse button to navigate to and view another Web document. Click on the right mouse button to call up a menu that includes such options as adding the site to your favorite list, saving the current document, downloading the image, and so on.

The Status Bar The status bar is found below the workspace. This area displays the status of transmissions to and from Internet servers ("Finding site: www.prenhall.com," "Connecting to site," "Web site found. Waiting for reply," "Opening picture: logo.gif at www.prenhall.com," and so on). When transmission is complete, the status bar may display other information or instructions relating to the use of the browser. The transmission status box gives you a visual reference of transmission progress.

Browser Summary

The function and use of Internet browsers are changing as quickly as the applications on the Internet. At this writing, there are a number of complementary applications, called plug-ins, which can be used to enhance the functionality of browsers. These plug-ins may give your browser the ability to accept and play audio streams or to run applets written in different programming languages. These and other capabilities, however, will be integrated into future releases of major browsers. Browsers will continue to change with the technology, but most industry observers feel that browsers will remain intuitive and, perhaps, become even easier to use.

SECTION SELF-CHECK

Self-Check

7-4.1 Internet portals are designed to permit searches by category or by keyword, but never both. (T/F)

7-4.2 The Internet browser is also called a Web browser. (T/F)

7-4.3 On the Internet, only hypertext hyperlinks are hot. (T/F)

7-4.4 Small programs embedded in HTML documents are called: (a) apples, (b) applets, (c) applications, or (d) omelets?

7-4.5 Which of the following labels might be included with an Internet address: (a) ⟨bps⟩, (b) ULS, (c) http://, or (d) fpt://?

7-4.6 Internet-based capabilities that help you find information on the Internet are: (a) seek portals, (b) find files, (c) search motors, or (d) search engines?

7-4.7 The opening page for a particular Web site normally is the: (a) opener page, (b) home page, (c) flip-flop page, or (d) master page?

7-4.8 A URL that begins with http:// begins the address for what type of Internet server: (a) Web, (b) Gopher, (c) file transfer protocol, or (d) news?

7-4.9 Which of the following buttons is not one of the main buttons on a browser toolbar: (a) back, (b) forward, (c) refresh, or (d) house?

7.5 INTERNET RESOURCES AND APPLICATIONS

The Internet offers a broad spectrum of resources, applications, and capabilities. In this section, we'll discuss how to find what you need, the major Internet applications, and ways you can use the Internet to communicate with people, including e-mail.

Using the Browser to Find Resources and Information on the Net

Going Online

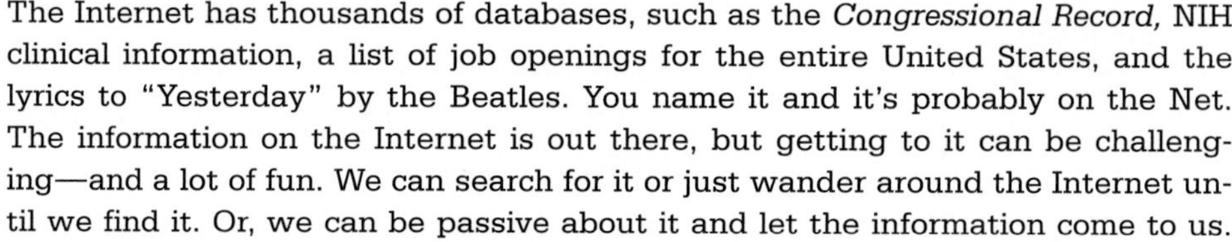

The Internet has thousands of databases, such as the *Congressional Record,* NIH clinical information, a list of job openings for the entire United States, and the lyrics to "Yesterday" by the Beatles. You name it and it's probably on the Net. The information on the Internet is out there, but getting to it can be challenging—and a lot of fun. We can search for it or just wander around the Internet until we find it. Or, we can be passive about it and let the information come to us.

There are three ways to search the Internet: *browse, search,* or *ask someone.* The function of a browser is to take you someplace in the electronic world. Where you go and how you get there is entirely up to you. There are two basic approaches to using a browser: *browsing* and *searching.* The difference between browsing and searching is best explained through an analogy to a print book. When you leaf through a book, you're browsing. When you select a topic from the index and open the book to the indicated page, you're searching.

Browsing the Net

Browsers let you poke around the Internet with no particular destination in mind—this is browsing. Some people just get on the Internet and travel to wherever their heart leads them. All the popular portals on the Net offer a menu tree of categories. These include Yahoo, Infoseek, AltaVista, Excite, WebCrawler, Lycos, Search.com, Snap, Magellan, and others. An Internet portal is always a good place to start. These portal sites divide the wealth of resources on the Internet into about a dozen major categories (for example, arts, business, computers, education, entertainment, health, and so on). Click on one of these main categories, each a hyperlink, to view subcategories (for art: animation, architecture, art history, and so on). You may navigate through several levels of categories before reaching the pages you want.

Most of us have at least one general interest area in mind, even when browsing. For example, let's say you want to go shopping for holiday gifts. You can do this by going to the various "shopping" categories, moving from virtual store to virtual store. Whether shopping or just surfing the Internet, browsing is always fun because you never know what you will find or where you will end up. Many pages have banner ads that entice us to click on them and travel to a totally unrelated site.

Using Search Engines to Search the Net

You can browse the Net or you can search it. If you knew that you wanted to buy your parents sterling silver candlesticks for their twenty-fifth anniversary, then you would want to go directly to a site that sells them—the quicker the better.

The Net helps those who help themselves. Each major portal, such as Excite, provides a resource discovery tool, called a *search engine,* to help you find the information or service you need. Most of them let you find information by keyword(s) searches. You can search the Net by keying in one or more keywords, or perhaps a phrase, that best describes what you want (perhaps, information on "Julia Roberts" or who might offer a "masters degree biomedical engineering"). The rules by which you enter the keywords and phrases vary slightly between the search engines (see Figure 7.6). The results of the search are seldom exhaustive; so, you may need to go to one of the listed sites, then follow the hyperlinks to find the information you need. These hints may reduce your search time.

- *Read the search rules.* Each search engine has different rules for formulating the inquiry. Click on "help" and read the instructions first.
- *If you don't get results with one search engine, try another.* The results vary significantly between search engines, because their databases are compiled in completely different manners. For example, Yahoo's database is organized by category, encouraging topical searches such as "White House AND press room." Infoseek's database is created from actual content on the Web, enabling searches for specific phrases, such as "Penn State Nittany Lions."
- *The results of the search are seldom exhaustive.* You may need to go to one of the listed sites, and then follow the hyperlinks to find the information you need.

An Internet Search Engine Yahoo, shown here, is a popular Internet search engine. Internet users can enter keywords or phrases ("bed and breakfast" AND California in the example), and the search engine scans its database, and then lists applicable pages (see inset window). Clicking on the "Bed & Breakfast California" hyperlink (see hand) took the user to the linked Web site. Yahoo also allows users to navigate to desired sites through a menu tree of categories and subcategories.

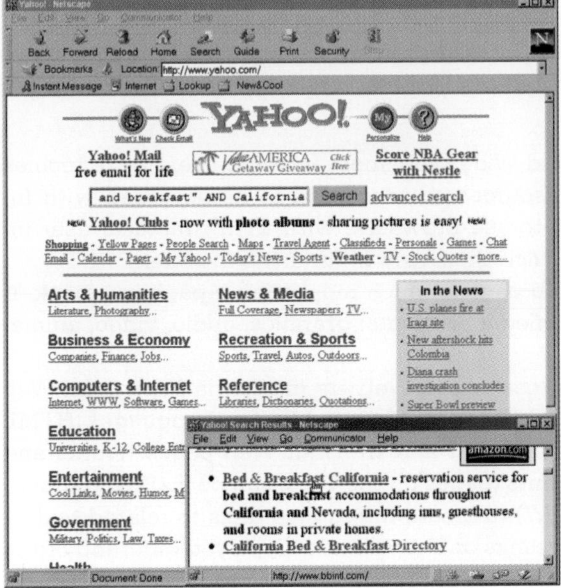

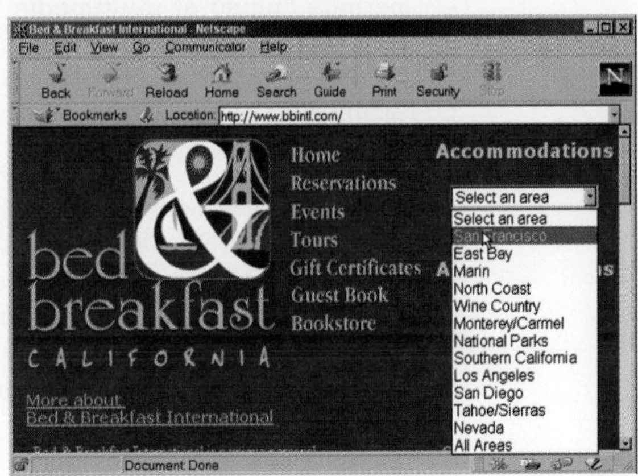

- *Choose search words carefully.* The keywords and phrases you enter are critical to the success of your search. Choose them carefully and try to be as specific as you can.
- *Be persistent.* Many of your searches will result in something like "Search item not found." This doesn't mean that the information you need is not on the Internet. It means only that you need to extend your search to other search criteria and/or other search engines.

The Internet browser is your ticket to ride on the information superhighway. The highway has millions of interesting stops, many of which are featured throughout this book.

Generally, these search engines are business ventures. Keep in mind that the companies sponsoring these widely used portals make money by selling advertising and by selling priority rights to a particular word or phrase. For example, if you enter the keywords "long-distance telephone," the company that purchased the rights to these words or this phrase would be listed in a priority position (first or possibly alone). It pays to tap into several portals to get the best deal or most impartial information.

Asking Someone

People on the Net are a family, ready to help those in need. Don't hesitate to post an inquiry to the people in cyberworld via a topical newsgroup when you need help. Also, the Net is full of **FAQ** (frequently asked questions) pages and files that you can view or download. Your question has probably been asked and answered before.

Internet Applications: The Web, FTP, and More

Internet Tools

World Wide Web servers have emerged as the choice for cruising the Internet; however, other not-so-user-friendly types of servers contain useful information still not available from World Wide Web sources. These systems, which pre-date the World Wide Web, include *FTP, Gopher, Telnet,* and *Webcasting.* Critical resources on these servers are being reformatted and modernized for distribution via World Wide Web servers, but this may take a while. In the meantime these resources remain available from these effective but old-fashioned servers. This section describes modern and traditional servers on the Internet.

WWW: World Wide Web

The World Wide Web, affectionately called *the Web,* is an Internet system that permits linking of multimedia documents among servers on the Internet. By establishing a linked relationship between Web documents, related information becomes easily accessible. These linked relationships are completely independent of physical location. These attributes set Web servers apart from other Internet servers.

- *User-friendly.* Prior to the World Wide Web, most Internet users were techies and IT professionals. Web resources are designed to be accessed with Internet browsers. These easy-to-use browsers, with their graphical user interfaces, let users point-and-click their way around the Internet.
- *Multimedia documents.* A Web page is much more than a page in a book. It can contain all of these multimedia elements: graphics, audio, video, animation, and text.
- *Hyperlinks.* Multimedia resources on the Web are linked via *hyperlinks.* Web documents are created using HTML (HyperText Markup Language). HTML is the "tag" language used to format and transmit Web pages. Words and phrases within HTML documents (pages on the Web) can be marked (tagged) and highlighted (see Figure 7.7) to create interactive links to related text or multimedia information. Hyperlinks on the Web are displayed differently from accompanying text, usually as colored (often blue) and underlined text. Links need not be limited to text, though. Any multimedia object on the page (im-

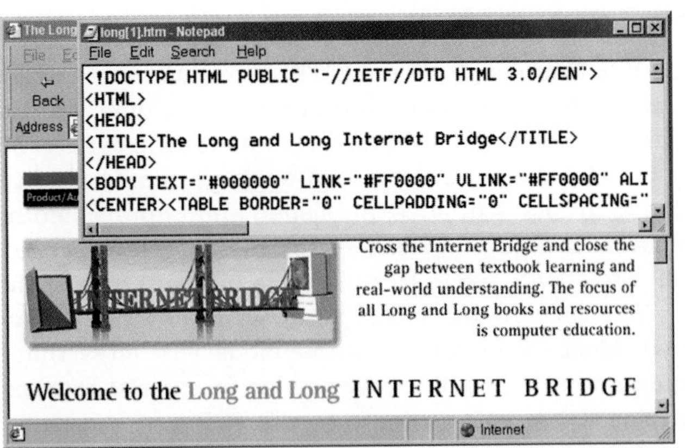

A Web Page and Its HTML Source Document

ages, animated objects, and so on) can be a hyperlink. When the cursor is positioned over a hyperlink, it changes to a hand with a pointing finger. When you click on the link (the highlighted word[s] or image), you are electronically whisked away to the URL (uniform resource locator) address specified in the HTML document. The link could take you to another location in the same document or to another document on the same Web server or to a Web server on another continent. The transition between hyperlinks appears seamless to the Web user.

- *Interactive.* The Web system, with its pages, enables interactivity between users and servers. There are many ways to interact with the Web. The most common form of interactivity is clicking on hyperlinks to navigate around the Internet. Some pages have input boxes into which you can enter textual information. You can click on radio buttons to select desired options. **Radio buttons** are circle bullets in front of user options that when selected include a dot in the middle of the circle. Each time you enter information in a text box or make selections, you will normally have to click on a submit button to transmit the information to the server computer.
- *Frames.* Some Web sites present some or all of their information in frames. The **frames** feature enables the display of more than one independently controllable section on a single Web page (see Figure 7.8). When you link to a Web page that uses frames, the URL of that page is that of a master HTML file that defines the size, position, and content of the frames. Ultimately your request for a frames page results in multiple HTML files being returned from the Web server. The frames capability may be used to display the main site options in one small frame and the primary information page in another larger frame. Sometimes a third frame displays context-sensitive instructions.

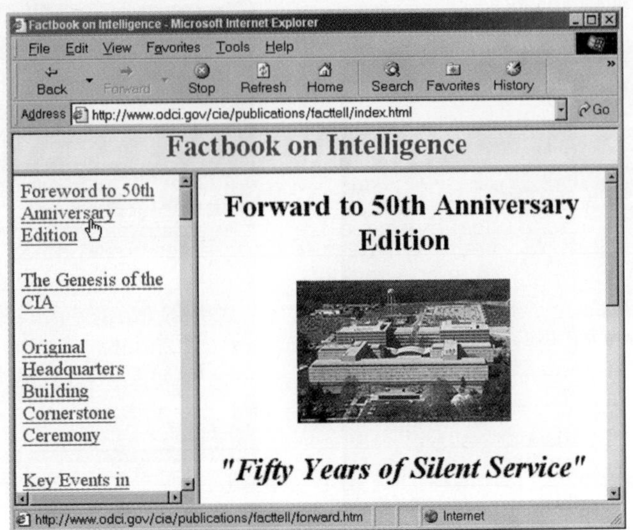

A Web Page with Frames

See your taxpayer dollars at work on the CIA Web site, which has frames for more convenient viewing. The site contains some very interesting information on the CIA mission, current maps and several online books including the most recent *The Factbook on Intelligence* and *The World Fact Book,* with comprehensive information on every country in the world.

FTP: Downloads for the Asking

The **File Transfer Protocol (FTP)** allows you to download and upload files on the Internet. FTP has been around for a long time, so thousands of FTP sites offer millions of useful files—most are free for the asking. FTPing is a popular activity on the Net. You can download exciting games, colorful art, music from up-and-coming artists, statistics, published and unpublished books, maps, photos, utility and applications programs—basically anything that can be stored digitally. Many FTP sites invite users to contribute (upload) files of their own.

You must be an authorized user (know the password) to access many FTP sites. Most, however, are anonymous FTP sites that maintain public archives. **Anonymous FTP** sites allow anyone on the Net to transfer files without prior permission. Once you navigate to the FTP site, you will be asked to enter a username and a password. Don't panic. Just enter "anonymous" or "ftp" at the username prompt and enter your e-mail address (or just tap the enter key) at the password prompt. Although most files on an FTP server might be restricted to the host computers and its users, often there is a public or "pub" directory that contains files accessible by all Internet users.

The trick to successful FTPing is knowing where to look. Fortunately, you can connect to FTP sites using a Web browser. Figure 7.9 demonstrates the hierarchical organization of FTP files.

Gopherspace: Go-for Information

Gopherspace is the home of thousands of Gopher servers throughout the world. The **Gopher** system, which pre-dates the World Wide Web, was developed at the University of Minnesota, the home of the Golden Gophers. Think of the Gopher system as a huge menu tree that allows you to keep choosing menu items until you find the information you want. Gopher resources can also be accessed through Internet browsers. Figure 7.10 illustrates the results of a gopherspace search.

Telnet: Remote Login

Telnet refers to a class of Internet application programs that lets you log into a remote computer using the Telnet communication protocol. **Telnet** is a *terminal*

FTPing on the Internet The browser image illustrates how you might navigate through the directories of an anonymous FTP site. The user proceeded from the /graphics/ directory to the /graphics/train/ directory to the /graphics/train/steam/ directory to the 011075_3.GIF file (the locomotive engine). The FTP site shown here, however, has been converted to a user-friendlier World Wide Web format (right). Other major FTP sites have or are undergoing a similar transformation.

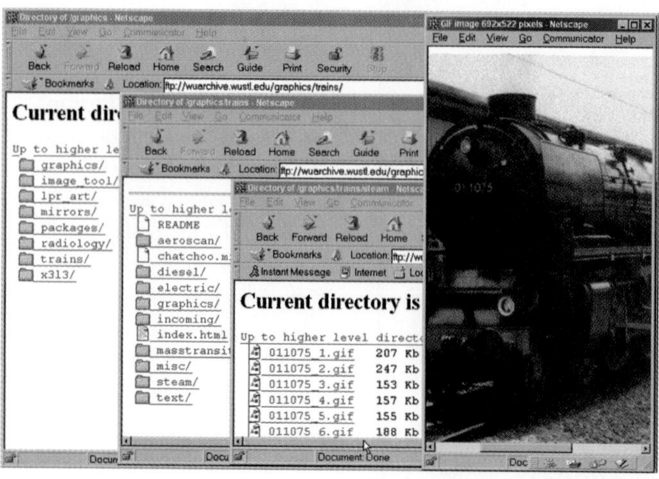

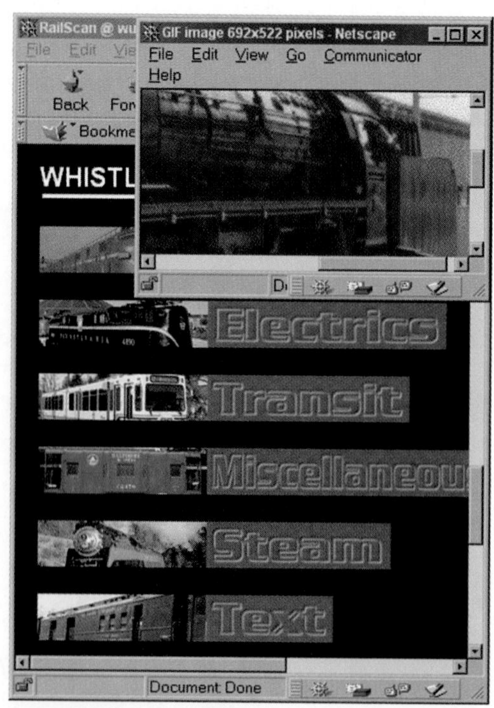

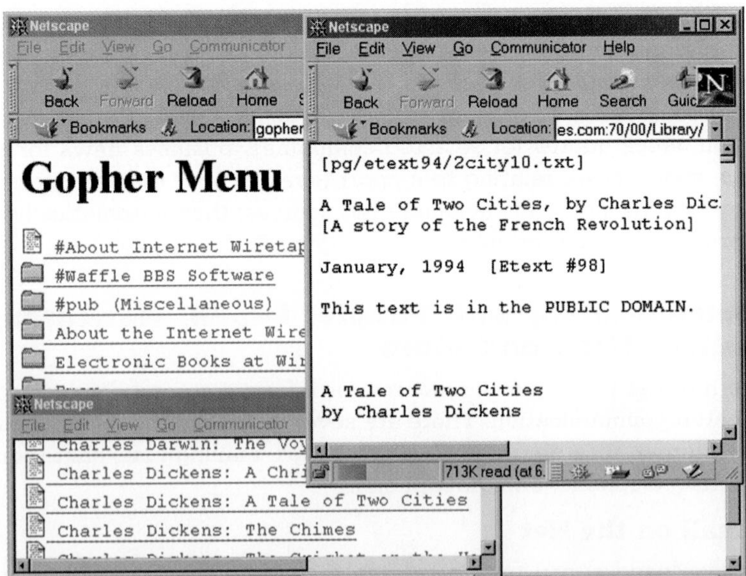

The Results of a Gopher Search The Wiretap Gopher site contains a little bit of everything, including the complete text of many books in the public domain. Here, the user navigated *A Tale of Two Cities* by Charles Dickens.

emulation protocol that allows you to work from a PC as if it were a terminal linked directly to a host computer. Thousands of Internet sites around the world have Telnet interfaces. Once online to one of these sites, you can run a normal interactive session as if you were sitting at an on-site terminal. You can run programs, search databases, execute commands, and take advantage of many special services. For example, you can search through the county library's electronic card catalog or run programs to analyze data from an experiment.

Webcasting: Internet Broadcasting

Until recently, all Internet sites were more or less passive, waiting for Net surfers to find them. It's now apparent that the Internet can be a broadcast medium as well. For example, thousands of radio stations now **webcast** their audio signals over the Internet (see Figure 7.11). If you have an Internet connection and a multimedia PC, there is no reason for you to miss the radio broadcast of any of your favorite team's games. To tune in to the game, simply use your browser to navigate to the webcasting radio station's Internet site, then request a *real-time audio stream* of the game. You may need a program, such as RealNetworks' RealPlayer G2, to receive and play the audio or video stream. RealPlayer G2 lets listeners preset "stations" and scan them, much as you would in a car radio. Can TV broadcasting be far behind?

Generally, Internet applications are based on **pull technology** where the user requests information via a browser. Broadcast applications employ **push technology,**

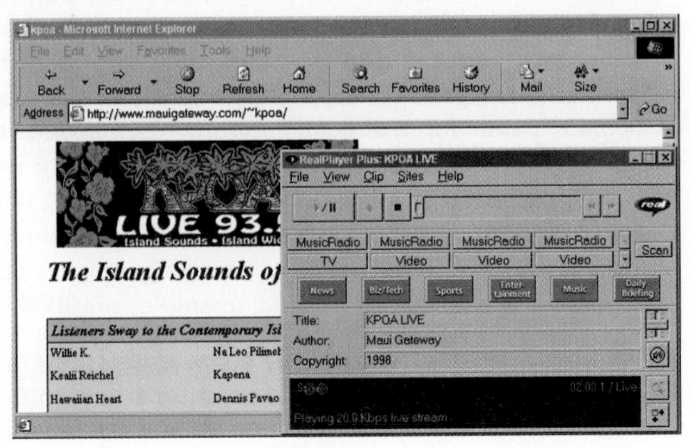

Webcasting on the Internet This figure shows a real-time audio stream from a webcasting radio station in Hawaii. The Internet program RealPlayer (shown in lower right window) plays real-time streaming audio in stereo.

where information is sent automatically to a user. Several companies, including PointCast, broadcast news and other information that can be customized to your information needs. For example, you can request news on a particular topic (personal computing, politics) or from a particular country, weather for a particular region, stock quotes for selected companies, business news for selected industries, sports news relating to a sport (even to your teams), and so on. The company periodically scans available net sources, then automatically downloads the information to you for viewing (see Figure 7.12).

E-mail

Communicating with People: E-mail, Newsgroups, Mailing Lists, and More

The Internet is not just a resource for information and services; it is also an aid to better communication. There are several ways for people to communicate over the Internet, including e-mail, newsgroups, mailing lists, chat rooms, audio mail, Internet telephone, and videophone.

E-mail on the Net

You can send e-mail to and receive it from anyone with an Internet e-mail address, which is just about everyone who uses the Internet. Each Internet user has an electronic mailbox to which e-mail is sent. E-mail sent to a particular person can be "opened" and read by that person. To send an e-mail message, the user simply enters the address (for example, *TroyBoy@mindspring.com*) of the recipient, keys in a message, adds a subject in the subject line, and clicks the send icon to place the message in the recipient's electronic mailbox.

Internet e-mail is like company e-mail, but with a great many more electronic mailboxes. You can send an e-mail message to anyone on the Net, even the President of the United States *(president@whitehouse.gov).* You can even use Internet e-mail to give your congressperson a few political hints. Figure 7.13 illustrates the use of Internet e-mail.

Your Internet e-mail address is your online identification. Once you get on the Internet, you will need to let other users and other computers know how to find you. All of your interaction will be done using your Internet address. Think of an Internet address as you would your mailing address. Each has several parts with the most encompassing part at the end. When you send mail outside the country, you note the country at the end of the address. The Internet address has two parts and is separated by an @ symbol. Consider this example Internet address for Kay Spencer at State University in CIS:

kay_spencer@cis.stateuniv.edu

- *Username*—**kay_spencer**@*cis.stateuniv.edu.* On the left side of the @ separator is the username (usually all or part of the user's name). Organizations often standardize the format of the username so users don't have to memorize so many usernames. One of the most popular formats is simply the first and last name separated by an underscore (kay_spencer). Some organizations prefer an abbreviated format to help minimize strokes. For example, some have adopted a username format in which the first five letters of the last name are prefaced by the first letter of the first name (kspenc).
- *Domain name for the host/network—kay_spencer*@**cis.stateuniv.edu.** That portion to the right of the @ identifies the host or network that services your e-mail, sometimes called the **e-mail server.** This is normally the Internet address for your Internet service provider (for example, worldnet.com), information service (for example, aol.com), your college (for example, stateuniv.edu), or your company (for example, prenhall.com).

The e-mail client software is the software that interacts with the e-mail server to enable sending and receiving of e-mail. Early e-mail client software packages limited messages to simple ASCII text. However, most modern e-mail client soft-

PointCast: Push Technology PointCast gathers news according to preset user specifications and then delivers it periodically via the Internet.

ware lets you embed graphics and do fancy formatting as you might in a word processing document. Also, you can attach files to an e-mail message. For example, you might wish to send a program or a digitized image along with your message. The **attached file** is routed to the recipient's e-mail server computer along with the message. It and the message are downloaded to your PC when you ask for your e-mail.

The typical e-mail client software has some very handy features. For example, you can send copies of your e-mail to interested persons. Or, you can forward to another person(s) e-mail messages that you received. Another feature lets you send a single e-mail to everyone on a particular distribution list (for example, workers in a particular department or players on a soccer team). You can even send your e-mail to a fax machine. E-mail features and services continue to grow. One of the information services translates e-mail messages posted in French and German into English, and vice versa.

POP stands for both point-of-presence on the Internet (discussed earlier in this chapter) and **Post Office Protocol.** Post Office Protocol refers to the way your e-mail client software gets your e-mail from the server. When you get a PPP access from an Internet service provider, you also get a Post Office Protocol account. When you set up your e-mail client software, you will need to specify this account name to get your mail (usually your username).

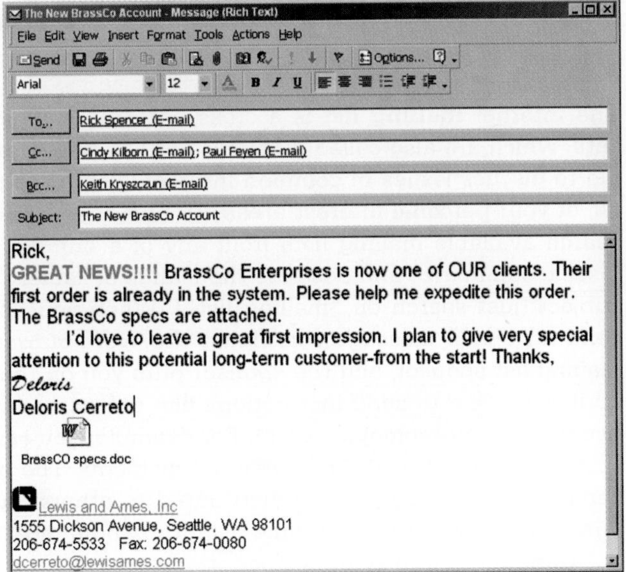

E-mail on the Internet The e-mail format for Microsoft Outlook 2000 (shown here) is representative of other Internet e-mail formats: to, cc (copy to), bcc (blind copy to), subject, text of message, and an attached file. The attached file is sent with the message. This e-mail client software (the software you use to receive and send e-mail) permits messages to be sent and viewed in rich text format, that is, with variations in font attributes and embedded graphics. The optional "personal information" placed automatically at the end of each message is called a signature. People usually include name, address, company (if appropriate), and communications information into the signature.

The United States Postal Service is losing ground to electronic communications. As more people send birthday invitations and greeting cards via e-mail and business communications continues its trend away from "snail mail" to e-mail, look for substantial increases in e-mail volume and commensurate decreases in traditional mail. E-mail has resulted in tremendous changes in the business world, as did the invention of the telephone. The telephone, however, is essentially one-to-one communication, but e-mail can be one-to-one, one-to-many, or many-to-many—and it's written.

Newsgroups: Electronic Bulletin Boards

A **newsgroup** is the cyberspace version of a bulletin board. A newsgroup can be hosted on Internet servers and on USENET servers. **USENET** is a worldwide network of servers that can be accessed over the Internet. "Newsgroups" is a misnomer in that you seldom find any real news. They are mostly electronic discussion groups. Tens of thousands of newsgroups entertain global discussions on thousands of topics, including your favorite celebrities. If you're unable to reach celebrities via e-mail, you can talk about them on an Internet newsgroup. For example, *alt.fan.letterman* (the newsgroup's name) is a David Letterman newsgroup. Sometimes Dave joins the fun. If Letterman is not your cup of tea, you can join another newsgroup and talk about Madonna *(alt.fan.madonna)* or Elvis *(alt.fan.elvis-presley).* Real Elvis fans can learn about recent Elvis sightings on the *alt.elvis.sighting* newsgroup.

Newsgroups are organized by topic. The topic, and sometimes subtopics, is embedded in the newsgroup name. Several major topic areas include: news, *rec* (recreation), *soc* (society), *sci* (science), and *comp* (computers). For example, *rec.music.folk* is the name of a music-oriented newsgroup in the recreation topic area whose focus is folk music. Another example is *rec.sport.tennis.*

You need *newsreader client software* or similar software that is built into most Internet browser clients. Generally newsgroups are public, but if you wish to keep up with the latest posting in a particular newsgroup, you will want to subscribe to it (at no charge). The newsreader software lets you read previous postings (messages), add your own messages to the newsgroup, respond to previous postings, and even create new newsgroups. Figure 7.14 illustrates interaction with a newsgroup.

People who frequent newsgroups refer to the original message and any posted replies to that message as a **thread.** The newsreader sorts and groups threads according to the original title. For example, a thread that begins with a message titled "Pete Sampras's forehand" includes all of the replies titled "RE: Pete Sampras's forehand." If you post a message with an original title or reply to a message and change the title, you start a new thread. For example, posting a reply titled "Pete Sampras's backhand" begins a new thread.

Mailing Lists: Listserv's

The Internet **mailing list** is a cross between a newsgroup and e-mail. Mailing lists, which are also called *listserv's,* are like newsgroups in that they allow people to discuss issues of common interest. There are mailing lists for most, if not all, of your personal interest areas. To find one of the interest areas, you scan or search available mailing lists from any of a number of sources. Portals, like Infoseek, summarize and describe thousands of listserv's by description, name, and subject (just search on "mailing list"). When you find one you like, you simply send an e-mail message containing the word *subscribe* plus your name to the mailing list sponsor, and the sponsor puts you on the list. Mailing lists have two addresses, one to send instructions like subscribe (and unsubscribe) to the list, usually listserv@someplace.com. For example, you can subscribe to the Women's History mailing list at listserv@h-net.msu.edu. The other address is where you send e-mail messages to be distributed to others on the list. Computerized administrators with the username listserv handle most mailing lists automatically.

Generally there is no subscription fee. Once on the list, you receive every e-mail message sent to that list by other subscribers. Sending mail to the list is

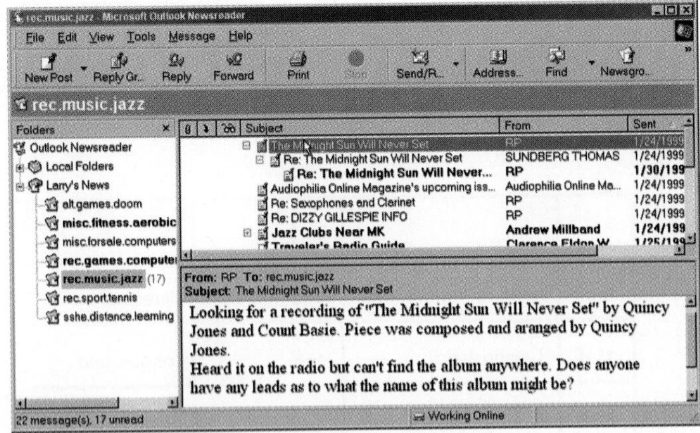

Newsgroups on the Internet People frequenting the highlighted newsgroup (rec.music.jazz) post messages related to jazz music. This person has subscribed to this and six other newsgroups (see list in folders window). In the example, a newsgroup subscriber was looking for a recording of "The Midnight Sun Will Never Set." The reply (also shown) will be sent and added to the "The Midnight Sun Will Never Set" thread for all subscribers to see.

as easy as sending an e-mail message to its mailing list address. Subscribing to a mailing list can be stimulating and, possibly, overwhelming. Remember, each message posted is broadcast to all on the list. If you subscribe to a couple of active mailing lists, your Internet mailbox could be filled with dozens if not hundreds of messages—each day! So, if you can't get enough of David Letterman through a newsgroup, you can subscribe to a mailing list whose theme is Letterman.

Internet Relay Chat: Chit-Chat

The **Internet Relay Chat (IRC)** protocol allows users to join and participate in group chat sessions. A chat session is when two or more Internet users carry on a typed, real-time, online conversation. Chatting is a favorite pastime of millions of cybernauts. They do this by establishing a link with a chat server; that is, an Internet server that runs the IRC protocol.

Chat servers let users join chat sessions called *channels.* A single chat server can have dozens, even thousands, of chat channels open at the same time. The name of the channel will usually reflect the general nature of the discussion. Usually channel names are unchanged, but topics on the channels are continuously changing. For example, in a channel called "Personal Computing," the topic might be "Macintosh tips" one day and "Windows 98 trouble-shooting" the next day.

The channel operator creates or moderates the channel and sets the topic. This way, chat participants can exchange ideas about common interests. Chats are ideal for group discussions. For example, many organizations schedule chat sessions as a way to exchange information between employees and customers. Universities schedule chat sessions to exchange technical information and advice. When you log into a chat session, you can "talk" by keying in messages that are immediately displayed on the screens of other chat participants (see Figure 7.15 on page 241). Any number of people can join a channel discussion. The rate at which you communicate is, of course, limited by your keyboarding skills.

Audio Mail: Just Say It

E-mail is just text. But with audio mail software you speak your message instead of typing it. Users send sound files over the Internet (rather than e-mail), thus producing a form of worldwide audio messaging. Proponents of **audio mail** tout it as a faster and more effective way to communicate over the Internet. It eliminates the need to key in, edit, and spell-check text before sending a message, a

Emerging IT

CYBERTALK: A NEW WAY TO COMMUNICATE

When online, we key in, rather than speak, our words and emotions. People who frequent bulletin boards and online forums have invented keyboard shortcuts and "emoticons" (emotion icons), called smileys, to speed up the written interaction and convey emotions. These are among the most frequently used keyboard shortcuts.

AFJ	April fool's joke
AFK	Away from keyboard
BRB	Be right back
BTW	By the way . . .
F2F	Face-to-Face
FAQ	Frequently asked questions
<GG>	Grin
IMHO	In my humble opinion
IRL	In real life
LOL	Laughing out loud
ROFL	Rolling on the floor laughing
TPTB	The powers that be
TTYL	Talk to you later
<VBG>	Very big grin
WAG	A guess
Wizard	A gifted or experienced user
YKYBHTLW	You know you've been hacking too long when . . .

To shout online, key in entries in all capital letters. Do this only when you really wish to make a point.

In cyberspace there is no eye contact or voice inflection, so cybernauts use smileys to express emotions. They must be effective because many couples who meet on the information highway are eventually married. Their courtship may have involved some of these smileys.

*****	Kiss	**:~)**	User with a cold
:-)	Smiling	**:-@**	Screaming
:'-(	Crying (sad)	**:-&**	Tongue tied
:'-)	Crying (happy)	**:-Q**	Smoker
:-(	Sad	**:-D**	Laughing
<:(	Dunce	**:-/**	Skeptical
:-o	Amazed	**O:-)**	Angel
:-|	Bored	**;-)**	Wink
:-I	Indifferent	**;c)**	Pigheaded
8-)	Wearing sunglasses	**@-->-->--**	A rose
::-)	Wearing glasses	**[[[***]]]**	Hugs and kisses

Creating smileys has emerged as a pop art. These smileys were created by online users with a sense of humor. Turn the page sideways and see if you recognize any familiar faces.

:-)X	Sen. Paul Simon
+-(:-)	The Pope
==:-D	Don King
[8-]	Frankenstein
==):-)=	Abe Lincoln
@@@@@@@@:)	Marge Simpson
/:-)	Gumby
7:-)	Ronald Reagan
\\ 8-]	FDR
***<(:')**	Frosty the Snowman
(8-o	Mr. Bill
~8-)	Alfalfa
@;^[)	Elvis

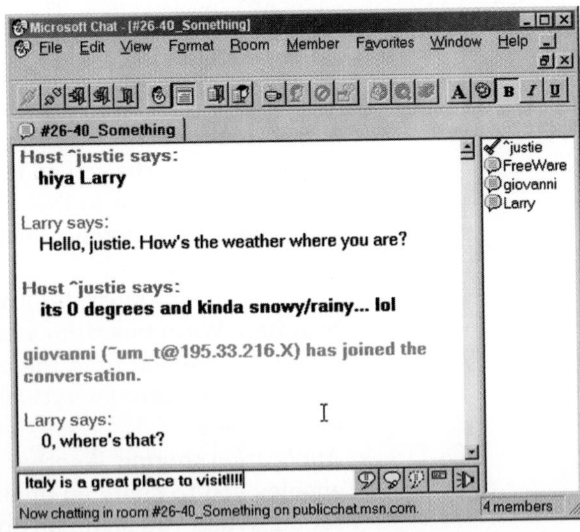

FIGURE 7.15 **An IRC Chat Session on the Internet** Shown here is Microsoft Chat, a popular Internet chat program that gives you the option of conversing inside a comic strip. Chat programs let you "enter" a chat room on an Internet server and have real-time conversations with other people from all over the world. With Microsoft Chat, you can pick a cartoon character to represent you, and your conversation appears as word balloons inside the frames of a comic strip. As a cartoon character, you can express a wide range of emotions, send "thoughts," and even whisper to a single recipient. You can also view the chat session in text format (see inset).

time-consuming task for many of us. Also, audio mail conveys humor and other emotions that may be lost in e-mail messages. Audio mail is just evolving, but it's inevitable that this system of worldwide audio messaging will continue to grow and mature.

The Internet Telephone: A Great Long-Distance Plan

To make a phone call we simply pick up a telephone, which is linked to a worldwide communications network, and speak into its microphone and listen through its speaker. Guess what? Millions of Internet users with multimedia PCs have these same capabilities: access to a worldwide network (the Internet), a mike, and a speaker. The only other thing needed to make telephone calls via the Internet is Internet telephone software. The Internet phone capability lets you call people at other computers on the Internet. These computers must have the same capabilities. By now you are probably wondering about cost. There is no added cost over the cost of your PC and your Internet connection. People routinely use this capability to talk for hours on international calls!

Here is how the Internet telephones work. First, you establish a connection with the Internet, then open your Internet telephone software. The software automatically notifies the host server supporting the **User Location Service (ULS)** that you selected in your software. The ULS is simply an Internet-based listing of Internet users who are currently online and ready to receive Internet telephone calls. If you and your brother, who lives in Germany, wanted to talk via Internet telephone, you would both have to be online with Internet telephone software running and be registered with the same ULS. When you make an Internet call you speak just as you would on a regular speakerphone. Whether your Internet phone conversation is *half-duplex* or *full-duplex* depends primarily on the capabilities of your sound card and the speed of your PC. Half-duplex conversations require that one party stop speaking before the other can speak.

The Internet telephone conversation can be a much richer experience than a regular telephone call. This is because both parties have the capabilities of the

Internet and their PCs at their fingertips. These capabilities can take place during the conversation.

- *Conferencing.* A two-way voice telephone conversation can be expanded to a conference that lets others listen in and add to the conversation via a chat box (an area on the screen that allows text entry). Those participants in chat mode provide input to the conversation by entering text in the chat box. All people in the conference hear the spoken words and see all textual entries simultaneously.
- *Whiteboarding.* Most Internet phone software packages support whiteboarding. **Whiteboarding** enables participants to sketch and illustrate ideas. When one person runs the whiteboard option, it automatically appears on everyone's screen. Everything that is drawn on the whiteboard is displayed for all to see.
- *Application sharing.* Another very helpful feature of Internet phone software enables you to share an application with others participating in the conversation. When you share an application (for example, a spreadsheet), you can work alone while others in the conference watch you work, or you can allow them to take turns working on the application.

The Videophone: Videoconferencing

The next dimension in Internet communications is the videophone, and it's here now! People who have a multimedia PC with a relatively inexpensive digital camera (around $70), dialup access to the Internet, and videophone software can see each other while talking. While they are talking they can continue to browse the Web, exchange electronic photos, or even play games. Commercial videoconferencing has been available for many years, but it could cost hundreds of dollars an hour. Now you can see and hear your family members, friends, and colleagues during conversations for pennies (see Figure 7.16). It's quite possible that video-based Internet communications will be as mainstream as e-mail in a few years!

The videophone is far from the last word in personal communications over the Internet. In the mid-1990s relatively few people even used the Internet and those who did communicated with one another by text-based e-mail and newsgroups. These remain the most popular means of personal communications over the Internet, but now we have other choices: audio mail, chat, Internet phone, and Internet videophone. If recent history is an indication, we will have even more and better options next year.

Cruising the Net

Vast, enormous, huge, immense, massive—none of these words is adequate to describe the scope of the Internet. Perhaps *the Internet* may someday emerge as a euphemism for anything that is almost unlimited in size and potential. There are

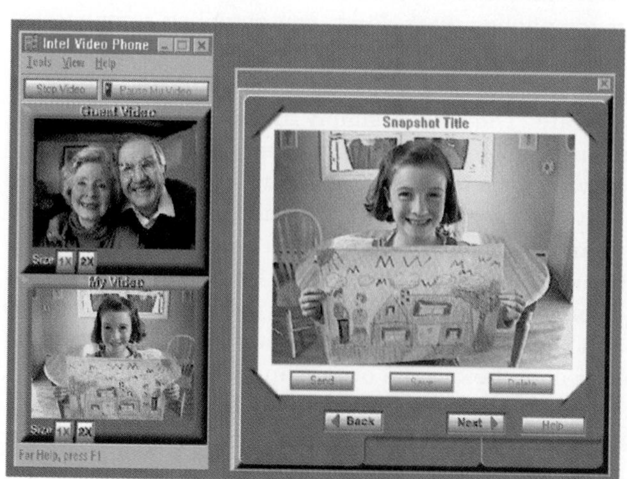

Internet Videophone Capability When this schoolgirl talks with her grandparents about her class project, she can see them and show them her project.

at least as many applications on the Internet as there are streets in Moscow. To truly appreciate Moscow, you would need to learn a little of the Russian language and the layout of the city. Navigating the Internet also requires a little bit of knowledge. Gaining this knowledge takes time and a lot of practice. In this brief space, we can hope to expose you to only some of the thoroughfares. As you gain experience and confidence, you can veer off onto the Internet's side streets. These stops along the cyberstreets of the Internet should give you a feel for what to expect.

On The Internet

Accessing Information and Services

- World Wide Web (the Web)
- FTP
- Gopher
- Telnet
- Webcasting

Communicating with People

- E-mail
- Newsgroups
- Mailing list (listserv)
- IRC (chat)
- Audio mail
- Internet telephone
- Videophone

- *MUDers on the Internet.* One of the exits on the Internet highway leads to MUD (Multi-User Domain), online role-playing adventure games. MUDs are challenging games that provide text descriptions of circumstances and situations rather than the graphic images of video games. Think of them as the online version of Dungeons and Dragons. A player explores his or her realm by entering simple commands such as "go," "east," "west," and so on. As you might expect, not-so-nice creatures occupy the same realm and are out to get you.
- *Love and war.* The Internet is a romance connection. Many married couples met and courted over the Net. Talk show host Rush Limbaugh had an electronic courtship that led to matrimony. Of course, where there is marriage there is divorce. Some couples prefer to negotiate their divorce settlement over Internet e-mail. This written approach to arbitration allows parties to choose their words more carefully and to keep records of exactly what has been said.
- *The electronic confessional.* Confess your sins over the Internet. To do so, choose a sin from a menu, enter the date of your last confession, and then receive your penance.
- *Be an informed traveler.* Savvy travelers often shop around for the best deal on a hotel room, make their own reservations, and get information on local attractions and nearby restaurants—all over the Net.
- *Subscription services.* The Net offers subscription services for just about every interest area. Subscription services are available for the international intelligence community, podiatrists, CD-ROM manufacturers, tennis players, high school football coaches, and hundreds of other groups. The services supply e-mail, newsletters, reports, scores, images, or whatever the service is designed to provide.
- *E-mail and geography.* A Wisconsin teacher encourages her fifth graders to correspond with e-mail pen pals in all 50 states. The teacher conceived the idea to help students learn geography and practice communication skills. Kids ask their "pen pals" about everything from pizza prices to politics.

As you can see, the Internet offers a vast treasure trove of information and services. Emotions of newbies (those new to the Internet) run high when they enter the Net for the first time. They simultaneously are shocked, amazed, overwhelmed, appalled, and enlightened. The Internet is so vast that seasoned users experience these same emotions. Figure 7.17 includes examples of a few of the millions of stops along the Internet.

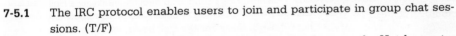

SECTION SELF-CHECK

Self-Check

7-5.1 The IRC protocol enables users to join and participate in group chat sessions. (T/F)

7-5.2 Yahoo is a site on Internet that can be used to browse the Net by content category. (T/F)

7-5.3 Subscribing to a popular mailing list would result in more Internet e-mail than posting a message to a newsgroup. (T/F)

7-5.4 All Internet search engines have the same rules for formulating the inquiry. (T/F)

7-5.5 The Gopher system pre-dates the World Wide Web. (T/F)

7-5.6 A file attached to an e-mail is routed to the recipient's e-mail server computer along with the message. (T/F)

FIGURE 7.17

Surfing the World Wide Web

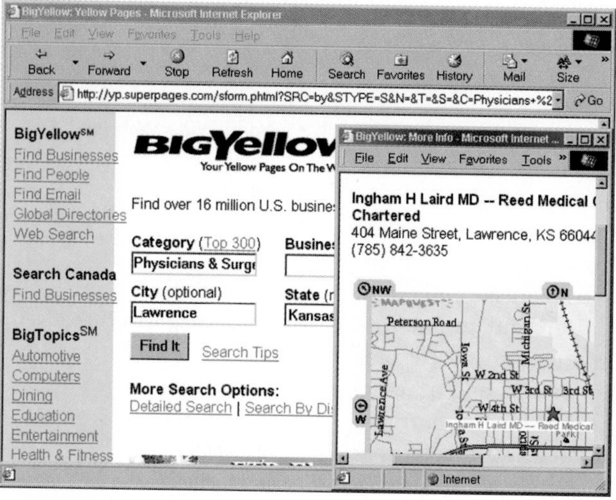

The Yellow Pages Use the BigYellow pages on the Net to quickly find any business in the United States. A search "Physicians & Surgeons," "Lawrence," and "Kansas" listed Dr. H. Laird Ingham (shown here) and 130 other Lawrence physicians. Clicking on Dr. Ingham's listing calls up a street map to his office.

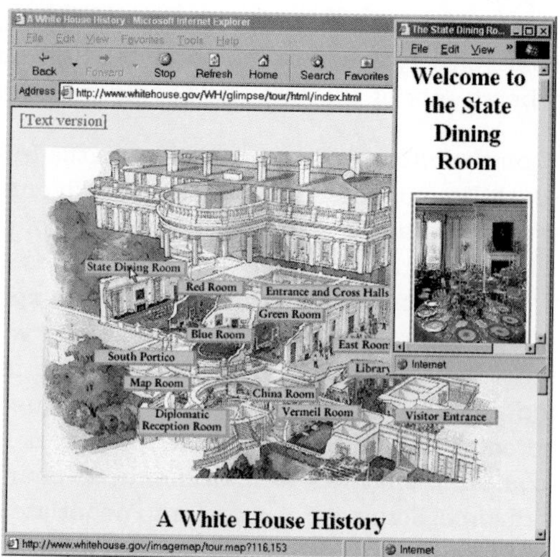

White House Tour When you take your cybertour of the White House be sure to sign the guest book. During the tour, you can listen to the comments of the President and the Vice President, meet the first family, and see the White House. In the breakout of the White House, you just click on a room to learn more about it.

At the Movies The Internet has just about everything but the movie (and that will change someday soon). You can read and view in-depth information about past, current, and future movies, including reviews by professionals and people who just like movies.

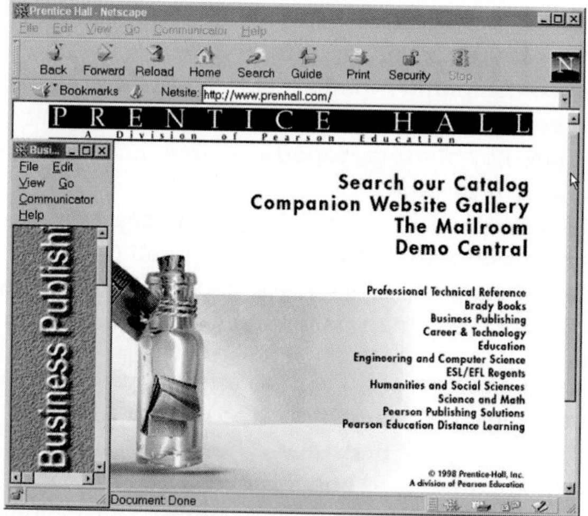

Commercial Web Presence Most businesses, including the publisher of this book, Prentice Hall, have a presence on the Internet. Prentice Hall has a comprehensive Web site over which students and professors can communicate with one another and download important class materials. Users can thumb through the Prentice Hall College Division's catalog to obtain information about any book it offers. Many Prentice Hall books, including this one, have a companion Web site. These are accessed from the Companion Website Gallery.

Shopper's Paradise The Internet is becoming a shopper's paradise, whether for retail or the excitement of an auction. Online auctions are going on 24 hours a day with thousands of items up for bid, including this $19,000 bracelet. Auctions take place over a few minutes or as much as two days.

Figure 7.17 (continued)

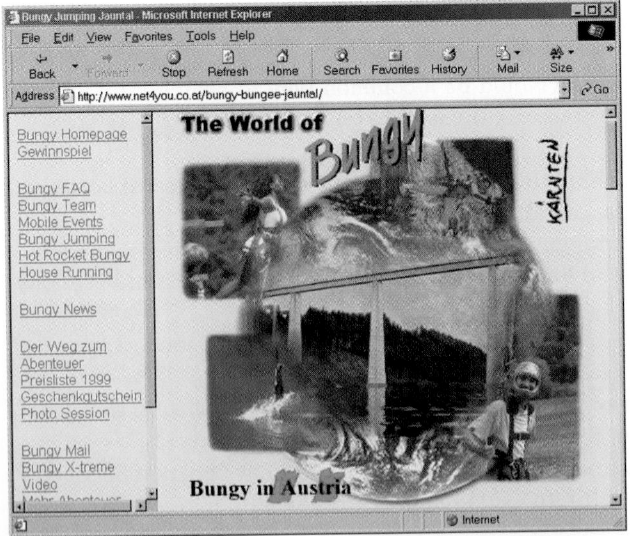

Special Interest Pages No matter what your interests or hobbies, whether bungee jumping or basket weaving, there is a wealth of information, including images, about it (or them) on the Internet.

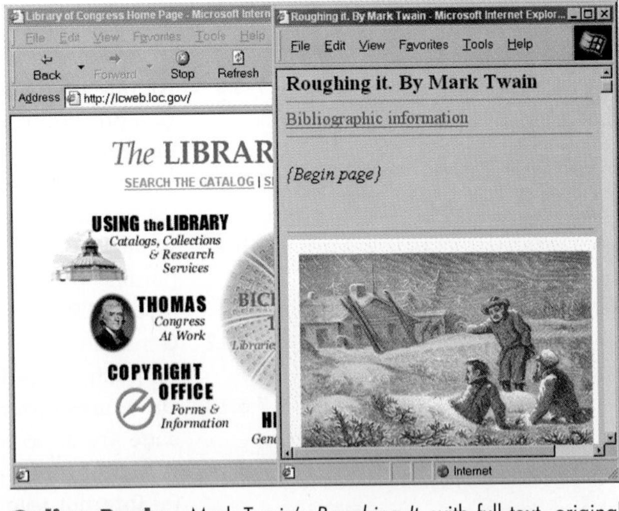

Online Books Mark Twain's *Roughing It*, with full text, original illustrations (shown in background window), and early reviews can be found at a number of Internet sites, including the Library of Congress. Thousands of public domain works of literature from *Beowulf* to the complete works of Shakespeare can be found on the Net.

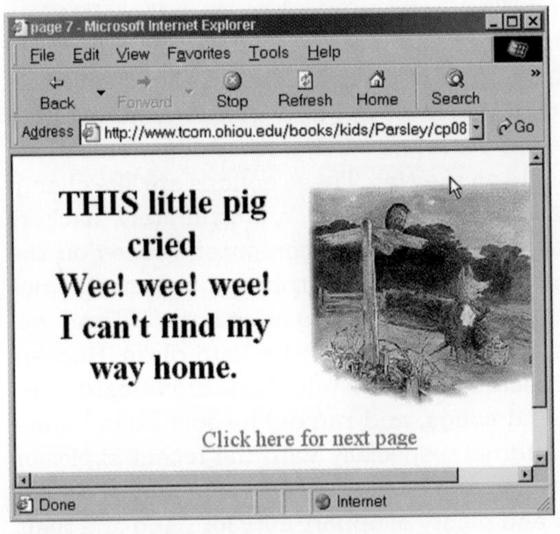

Story Hour There is something for children of all ages on the Net. The Internet Public Library offers a story hour section that contains many wonderful illustrated stories, including the *Cecily Parsley's Nursery Rhymes* by Beatrix Potter (shown here).

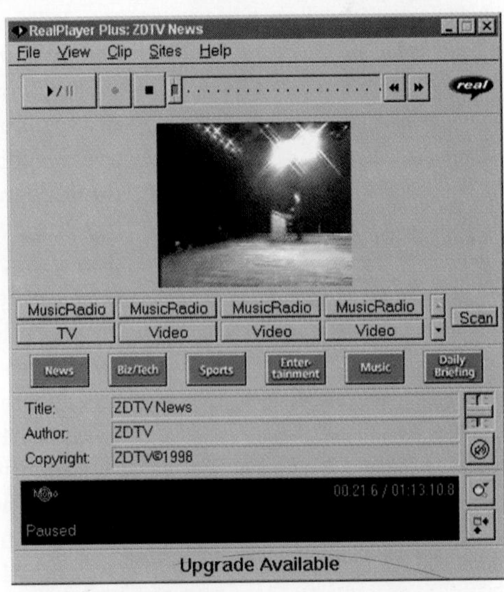

Streaming Video Not all that comes over the Internet is viewed on a browser. Much of the Internet's "streaming video" (with audio) is created for viewing on RealPlayer Plus. Bill Gates' keynote address at the annual Comdex Conference was broadcast live over the Internet. Mr. Gates is the chairman of Microsoft.

The Ultimate Travel Brochure The Internet has emerged as "the" source for travel information. It's easy to get information about any destination, including Sydney, Australia (shown here), the site of the 2000 Olympics.

Online Newspapers *USA Today*, The *Washington Post*, the *Los Angeles Times* and many other newspapers, even weekly newspapers in small towns, sponsor Internet Web sites. Some, such as *USA Today*, have comprehensive up-to-the-minute news by category as well as a variety of other information-based services, such as a continuously updated daily chart of the Dow index (inset window).

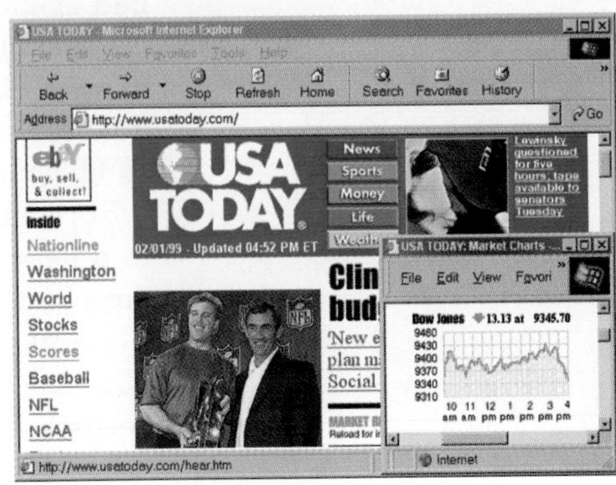

7-5.7 Which server on the Internet offers hyperlinks: (a) News, (b) Web, or (c) Gopher, or (d) ftp?

7-5.8 Which of these would not be considered an Internet portal: (a) Yahoo, (b) Infoseek, (c) Webcast, or (d) Excite?

7-5.9 All but which one of these would be a common way to search for information on the Internet: (a) browse, (b) search, (c) push/pull, or (d) ask someone on the Net?

7-5.10 What Web features enable the display of more than one page: (a) borders, (b) windows, (c) frames, or (d) structures?

7-5.11 What FTP feature allows anyone on the Net to use FTP sites without prior permission: (a) unsigned FTP, (b) secret FTP, (c) unnamed FTP, or (d) anonymous FTP?

7-5.12 Generally, today's Internet applications are based on what technology: (a) push, (b) pull, (c) place, or (d) draw?

7-5.13 On a newsgroup, the original message and any posted replies to that message are a: (a) needle, (b) thread, (c) pinpoint, or (d) tapestry?

7-5.14 Which of these applications is associated with the User Location Service: (a) Internet telephone, (b) IRC, (c) e-mail, or (d) newsgroups?

7.6 INTERNET ISSUES

Telecommuting

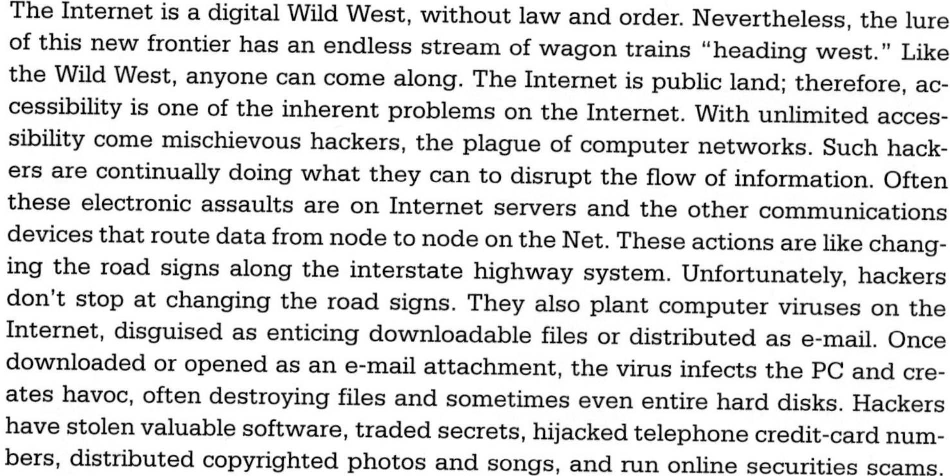

The Internet is a digital Wild West, without law and order. Nevertheless, the lure of this new frontier has an endless stream of wagon trains "heading west." Like the Wild West, anyone can come along. The Internet is public land; therefore, accessibility is one of the inherent problems on the Internet. With unlimited accessibility come mischievous hackers, the plague of computer networks. Such hackers are continually doing what they can to disrupt the flow of information. Often these electronic assaults are on Internet servers and the other communications devices that route data from node to node on the Net. These actions are like changing the road signs along the interstate highway system. Unfortunately, hackers don't stop at changing the road signs. They also plant computer viruses on the Internet, disguised as enticing downloadable files or distributed as e-mail. Once downloaded or opened as an e-mail attachment, the virus infects the PC and creates havoc, often destroying files and sometimes even entire hard disks. Hackers have stolen valuable software, traded secrets, hijacked telephone credit-card numbers, distributed copyrighted photos and songs, and run online securities scams.

Security is a serious issue on the Internet, especially with the recent explosion of **e-commerce.** E-commerce is simply conducting business online and, that, of course, means the electronic transfer of money and plenty of opportunity for fraud and theft. Organizations have been forced to return to the days of walled forts and castles to protect themselves from cyberthieves. One approach is to set up *intranets* within enterprises that permit access to the Internet through a firewall. A **firewall** is software that is designed to restrict access to an organization's network or its intranet. The firewall screens electronic traffic in both directions so that organizational security is maintained. The screening process can be adjusted to various levels of security.

People on the Internet reflect real life—most are good and a few are bad. The bad elements deal in garbage. Some Internet newsgroups are dominated by bigots and cranks who push everything from neo-Nazi propaganda to pornographic images. Electronic lechers sometimes hound women on the Internet, and the language spoken in the heat of a passionate electronic debate can range from rude to libelous. Fortunately, responsible people are fighting back. When somebody posts something outlandish, inappropriate, or out of phase with the societal norms to a newsgroup or mailing list, he or she gets **flamed.** Flaming results in a barrage of scathing messages from irate Interneters.

And then there's spam, what we used to think of as junk mail, except that now it's in the cyberworld as well. **Spam** is unsolicited junk e-mail, mostly advertising for commercial products or services. Occasionally **spammers,** or those who send spam, spam unsuspecting people with political messages. Though most of us would prefer not to be spammed, it's as difficult to rid the public Internet of spam as it is to rid our mailboxes of junk mail. Just like at home, we must sort through the spam to find our legitimate e-mail. Also, people are concerned that spam is taking up valuable bandwidth on the Internet, stressing the information capacity of the Net. As you might have guessed by now, the origin of the term *spam* is the popular lunch meat of the same name.

The Internet rivals the towering majesty of Mount Everest, but there is a dark side of every mountain. At the foot of this great mountain of information is a rocky pasture. Watch your step as you cross this pasture, then enjoy the climb up Mount Internet.

Self-Check

SECTION SELF-CHECK

Interactive Study Guide Chapter 7

7-6.1 The Internet is now secure and no longer vulnerable to malicious hackers. (T/F)

7-6.2 Conducting business online is called: (a) electronic business, (b) cyber commerce, (c) e-commerce, or (d) cyber business?

7-6.3 Unsolicited junk e-mail is called: (a) spam, (b) pam, (c) weanies, or (d) flames?

SUMMARY AND KEY TERMS

7.1 The online world

The online world offers a vast network of resources, services, and capabilities. Most of us enter it simply by plugging the phone line into our PC's modem and running our communications software.

7.2 Information services: America Online, CompuServe, and more

When you subscribe to a commercial information service such as America Online or CompuServe, you get communications software, a username and password (required for **logon** [216]), and a user's guide. The communications software may be designed specifically to work with an information service network or it may be an Internet **browser** (216). Information services are continually updating and adding new services.

7.3 The Internet: A Worldwide Web of computers and information

The Internet (a worldwide collection of *inter*connected *net*works) is comprised of thousands of independent networks in virtually every type of organization. The Department of Defense's ARPANET project was the genesis of the Internet. Volunteers from many nations coordinate the Internet. InterNIC provides registration services for the Internet community.

There are three levels at which you can connect your PC to the Internet. The easiest way to gain access is through a commercial information service's gateway. Or you can make the connection via a **dialup connection** (220) through an **Internet service provider (ISP)** (220). At the third level, there is direct connection to the Internet where your PC is wired directly into the Internet. Such connections often use an ISDN (128 K bps), an ADSL line (up to 9 M bps), a **T-1 line** (221) (1.544 M bps), or a **T-3 line** (221) (44.736 M bps).

The **Transmission Control Protocol/Internet Protocol (TCP/IP)** (222) is the communications protocol that permits data transmission over the Internet. The *Transmission Control Protocol* sets the rules for the packaging of information into the **packets** (222). The *Internet Protocol* handles the address, such that each packet is routed to its proper destination. When you dialup an ISP's local **POP (point-of-presence)** (222), your dialup connection is made through a PPP connection to an Internet host. As long as you or a **newbie** (221) has a TCP/IP connection and appropriate hardware, you can go online with appliances other than a PC, such as a TV.

A **client program** (222) runs on your PC and works in conjunction with a companion **server program** (222) that runs on the Internet host computer. The client program contacts the server program, and they work together to give you access to the resources on the Internet server. A *browser* is one kind of client.

The **URL (uniform resource locator)** (223), which is the Internet equivalent of an address, progresses from general to specific. That portion of the URL before the first colon (usually http) specifies the access method. The http tells the software to expect an **http**

(HyperText Transport Protocol) (223) file. That portion following the double forward slashes (//) is the server address, or the **domain name** (224). It has at least two parts, separated by dots (periods). What follows the domain name is a directory containing the resources for a particular topic. At the end of the URL is the specific filename of the file that is retrieved from the server. **HTML (HyperText Markup Language)** (224) is the language used to compose and format most files on the Net.

7.4 Browsers: The information tool

Internet browser, or Web browser, software lets us tap the information resources of the electronic world. It enables us to retrieve and view information from server computers, interact with server-based systems, view electronic documents, pass digital information between computers, send and receive e-mail, and join newsgroups. The browser opens an HTML document and displays the information according to HTML instructions embedded in the document. The HTML documents may reference **applets** (226), or small programs.

We learned that the Internet is a worldwide collection of *inter*connected *net*works. At the top of the Internet organization scheme are the Internet servers. Each World Wide Web server has one or more **home pages** (227), the first page you will normally view when traveling to a particular site. Web resources, which may be graphics, audio, video, animation, and text, are viewed in **pages** (227). Each Web page is actually a file with its own URL. We navigate to an address on the Internet just as we drive to a street address. Hyperlinks, in a form of *hypertext, hot images,* or *hot icons,* permit navigation between pages and between other resources on the Internet. The pages at a server site are set up within a hierarchy of URLs. Internet **search engines** (226) can help you find information on the Internet.

The basic elements used for server navigation and viewing include the menu bar, the toolbar, the URL bar, the workspace, and the status bar.

Portals (229) are Web sites that offer a broad array of information and services, including a menu tree of categories and a capability that help us find online resources.

The appearance of the dominant browsers, Microsoft Internet Explorer and Netscape Communicator, is similar with the same basic elements: a menu bar, a toolbar, a URL bar, a workspace, and a status bar.

7.5 Internet resources and applications

There are three ways to search the Internet: *search, browse,* or *ask someone.* You can search using a variety of resource discovery tools or you can browse through menu trees of *categories.* People on the Net are ready to help those in need. There are also **FAQ** (232) pages and files.

The World Wide Web is an Internet application that permits linking of multimedia documents among Web servers on the Internet. By establishing a linked relationship between Web documents, related information becomes easily accessible. Web resources are designed to be accessed with easy-to-use browsers. Web pages are linked via *hyperlinks.* The Web enables interactivity between users and servers. For example, you can click on **radio buttons** (233) to select desired options. Some Web sites present some or all of their information in **frames** (233).

The **File Transfer Protocol (FTP)** (234) allows you to download and upload files on the Internet. Most are **anonymous FTP** (234) sites. The **Gopher** (234) system is a huge menu tree that allows you to keep choosing menu items until you find the information you want. **Telnet** (234) is a *terminal emulation* protocol that allows you to work from a PC as if it were a terminal linked directly to a host computer.

Webcasting (235) (Internet broadcasting) has emerged as a popular Internet application. With **pull technology** (235) the user requests information via a browser. With **push technology** (235) information is sent automatically to a user.

The Internet is an aid to better communication. You can send e-mail to and receive it from anyone with an Internet e-mail address. The Internet e-mail address has two parts and is separated by an @ symbol, the username and the domain name. The latter identifies the **e-mail server** (236). An **attached file** (237) can be sent with an e-mail message. **Post Office Protocol** (237) refers to the way your e-mail client software gets your e-mail from the server.

A **newsgroup** (238) can be hosted on Internet servers and on **USENET** (238) servers. People who frequent newsgroups refer to the original message and any posted replies to that message as a **thread** (238). The Internet **mailing list** (listserv) (238) is a cross between a newsgroup and e-mail.

The **Internet Relay Chat (IRC)** (239) protocol allows users to participate in group chat sessions. A chat session is when two or more Internet users carry on a typed, real-time, online conversation.

Audio mail (239) lets you speak your Internet message instead of typing it.

The Internet phone capability lets you call people at other computers on the Internet. The telephone software automatically notifies the host server supporting the **User Location Service (ULS)** (241) when you are ready to talk. Other Internet telephone capabilities include *conferencing,* **whiteboarding** (242), and *application sharing.* The next dimension in Internet communications, the videophone, permits videoconferencing.

7.6 Internet issues

The Internet is a digital Wild West. With **e-commerce** (246) growing so rapidly, security is an important issue on the Internet. **Firewalls** (246) are being implemented to restrict access to an organization's network or its intranet.

People who send discourteous communications over the Net are frequently **flamed** (246). **Spammers** (246) send **spam** (246), the electronic equivalent of junk mail.

The Internet offers a vast treasure trove of information and services, and it will always be encircled by critical issues.

DISCUSSION AND PROBLEM SOLVING

7.1 **a.** Describe at least three things you do now without the aid of online communications that may be done in the online environment in the near future.

b. What kind of work would you like to be doing in five years? Explain how you might telecommute to accomplish part or all of your work.

c. The federal government is calling for "universal service" such that everyone has access to the "information superhighway." Is this an achievable goal? Explain.

7.2 **a.** Discuss how you would justify spending $15 to $25 a month to subscribe to an online information service.

b. Which two America Online channels would be of most interest to you? Explain.

7.3 **a.** What is the organizational affiliation of these Internet addresses: smith_jo@mkt.bigco.com; politics@washington.senate.gov; and hugh_roman@anthropology.stuniv.edu.

b. Expand and discuss the meaning of the following acronyms: TCP/IP, ISP, http, and URL.

c. Briefly describe one of the three levels at which you can connect your PC to the Internet.

7.4 **a.** Some Web sites create and store a text file on the user's PC called a *cookie*. Each time the user accesses that Web site the personal information in the cookie is sent to the Web server. The cookie may contain your name, perhaps your password to access that Web site, and personal preferences. Discuss the advantages and disadvantages of cookies from the perspective of the Web site sponsor.

b. Discuss the advantages and disadvantages of cookies (see above) from the perspective of the user.

7.5 **a.** In what ways is the World Wide Web different from other servers on the Internet?

b. Describe circumstances for which you would prefer browsing the Net over using a search engine.

c. Discuss the pros and cons of FTPing on the Internet.

d. Videophones are available on the Internet now. In all probability they will be available to the mass market in the near future. Is this new innovation in personal communications something you are looking forward to or dreading? Explain.

e. Would you prefer to receive traditional e-mail or audio mail? Explain.

f. Describe five things you would like to do on the Internet.

7.6 **a.** The Internet is a digital Wild West. Should access be more tightly controlled to help bring law and order to the Internet?

b. Gambling could be one of the most profitable computer applications ever. Americans spent 70 times as much on gambling last year as they spent on movies. Gambling is being proposed as a possible application on the Internet. Argue for or against this proposal.

c. The Internet is public and much of the readily accessible content on the Internet is considered inappropriate for viewing by young people. Should legislation be enacted to control Internet content?

d. Dissatisfied customers routinely create Web sites devoted to criticizing a company's product or services. The company's name usually is embedded in the domain name in a derogatory manner. Companies being attacked are seeking legislative relief. Should the government get involved?

The Windows Environment

Learning Objectives

8.1 Detail the purpose and objectives of an operating system.

8.2 Describe what constitutes a platform.

8.3 Understand the concepts and terminology integral to the use and operations of Windows 9x/NT/2000 operating systems.

8.4 Describe how information is passed between and shared among applications in the Windows environment.

8.5 Grasp concepts related to interaction with PCs and PC software.

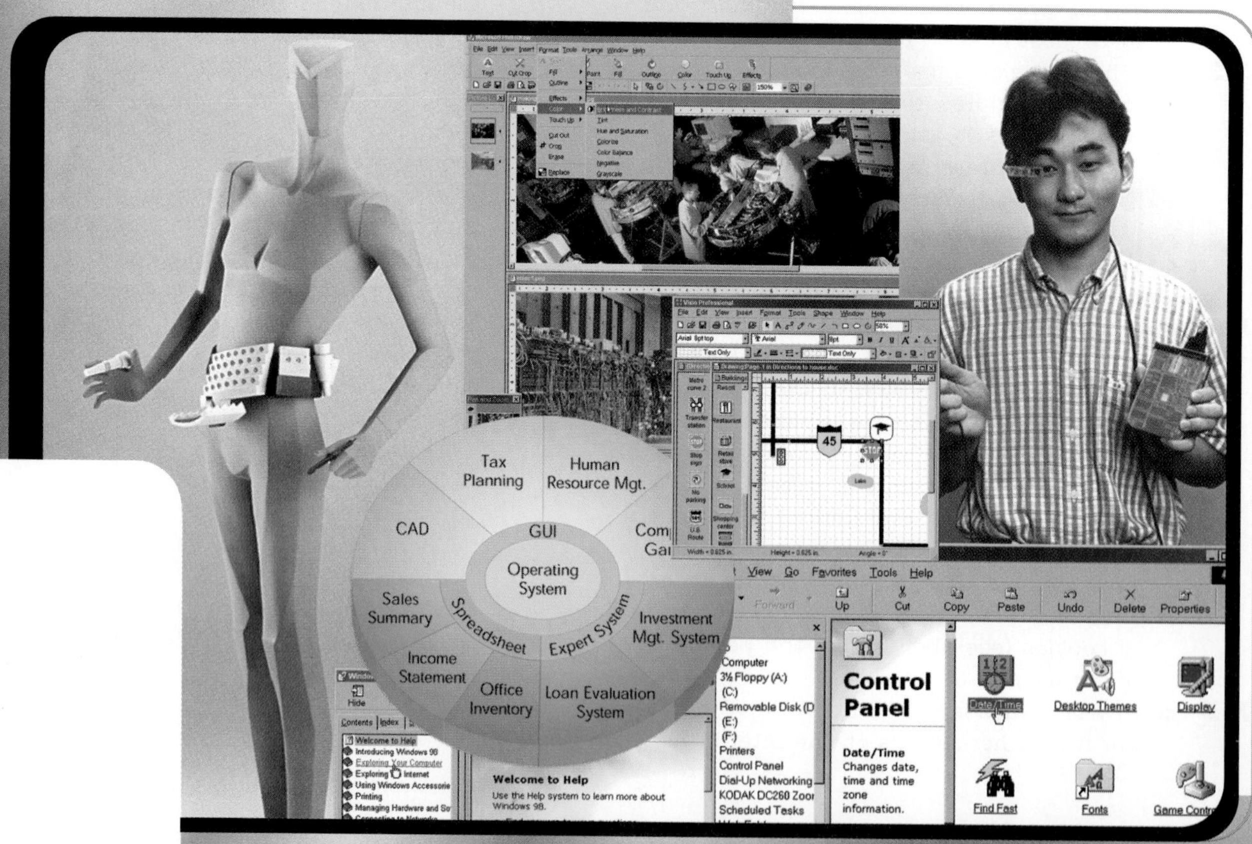

chapter

Value Learning

WHY THIS CHAPTER IS IMPORTANT TO YOU

Computing has a language all its own. It's called *computerese*. Terms used with software, including the operating system, are no exception. Fortunately, many of the words and phrases are simply old words being applied to software concepts (for example, menus, background, and help). Some terms evolved out of the need to abbreviate verbal and written communication (for example, GUI, pronounced "gooie"). Others are buzzwords that may convey different meanings to different people (for example, interoperability and user interface). When you consider that computing knowledge is doubling every two years, it is no wonder that its language is filled with buzzwords, acronyms, and the like. Even with its shortcomings, computerese provides a surprisingly efficient mechanism for communication. Our challenge is to learn these terms, then to keep up with the inevitable changes.

To be conversant with a personal computer, you must know your way around its operating system, such as the popular Microsoft Windows operating systems. Once you have read and studied this chapter, you'll be better prepared to interact effectively with the Windows environment, something that most knowledge workers do many hours each day.

8.1 THE OPERATING SYSTEM: DIRECTING THE ACTION

Monthly Technology Update Chapter 8

Operating Systems

When we go out to a movie we see only a few of those responsible for making the film—the actors. We don't see the director, the producers, the writers, the editors, and many others. Perhaps it's because of this visual link that we, the audience, tend to become adoring fans of glamorous actors. We tend to forget the others involved in the film, even the director who is the person who ties it all together and makes it happen. It's much the same with software. As software users we tend to shower our praise on that which we see most often—the *applications software.* However, *system software,* like the film director, stays in the background and ties it all together. The most prominent of these behind-the-scenes players is the operating system.

The *operating system* and its *graphical user interface* (*GUI*), both system software, are at the heart of the software action (see Figure 8.1). All other software depends on and interacts with the operating system, the software that controls everything that happens in a computer. Its graphical user interface (GUI) provides a user-friendly interface to the operating system. *System software* encompasses those programs that manage, maintain, and control computer resources. Programs designed to be used by the end user are *applications software.* Figure 8.1 illustrates examples of and the relationship between system and applications software.

Just as the processor is the nucleus of the computer system, the *operating system* is the nucleus of all software activity (see Figure 8.1). Windows 2000, Windows 98, Windows NT, Mac OS X, and Unix are popular operating systems for PCs and workstations. The operating system is actually a family of *system software* programs that monitor and control all I/O and processing activities within a computer system. The computer system vendor supplies the operating system when you buy a computer. One of the operating system programs, often called the **kernel,** loads other operating system and applications programs to RAM as they are needed. The kernel is loaded to RAM on system start up and remains *resident*—available in RAM—until the system is turned off.

All hardware and software are under the control of the operating system. Among other things, the operating system:

- Determines how valuable RAM is allotted to programs
- Performs tasks related to file management
- Sets priorities for handling tasks
- Manages the flow of information to and from the processor

To be an effective PC or workstation user, you will need a working knowledge of your computer's operating system.

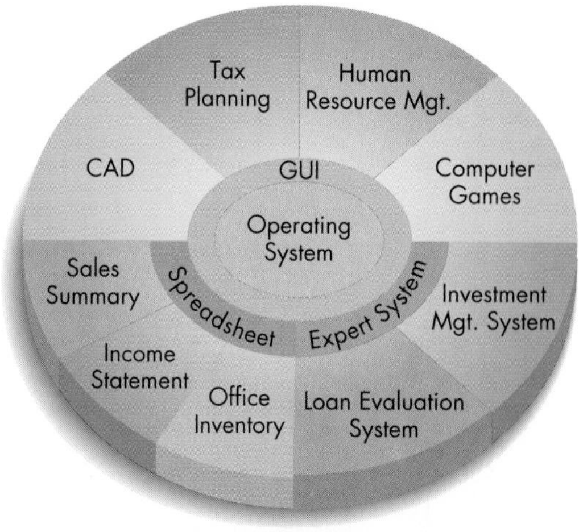

Relationship between the Operating System, the GUI, and Applications Software The operating system coordinates all software activity within a computer system. Our interaction with the operating system is through the graphical user interface, the GUI. With applications software packages, such as spreadsheet and expert systems, we can address a variety of problems. For example, a manager can use spreadsheet software to create *templates* (models) for summarizing sales and maintaining the office's fixed inventory. A knowledge engineer can use expert system software to create a loan evaluation system to assist a bank's loan officers in making better, more consistent decisions.

Operating System Objectives and Orientation

The operating system is what gives a *general-purpose computer,* such as a PC or a company's Internet server, its flexibility to tackle a variety of jobs. Most *dedicated computers,* such as those that control appliances and arcade games, are controlled by a single-function program and do not need a separate operating system.

Operating Systems

One of the best ways to understand an operating system is to understand its objectives. These objectives are listed and explained in Figure 8.2. All operating systems are designed with the same basic objectives in mind. However, mainframe and PC operating systems differ markedly in complexity and orientation. On the mainframe, *multi-user operating systems* coordinate a number of special-function processors and monitor interaction with hundreds, even thousands, of terminals and PCs in a network. Most PC operating systems are designed primarily to support a *single user on a single micro.* This PC may or may not be linked to a network.

Living on a Budget: Allocating Computer Resources

We all must live within our means, and the same goes for computers. A conscientious shopper can stretch the value of a dollar, and a good operating system can get the most from its limited resources. Any computer system's most precious resource is its processor. Operating systems get the most from their processors

Objectives of an Operating System

Operating System Objectives	
1. To facilitate communication between the computer system and the people who run it.	The interface through which users issue system-related commands is part of the operating system.
2. To facilitate communication among computer system components.	The operating system facilitates the movement of internal instructions and data between peripheral devices, the processor, programs, and the computer's storage.
3. To maximize throughput.	The operating system coordinates system resources to maximize throughput, the amount of processing per unit of time.
4. To minimize the time needed to execute a user command.	In today's interactive systems, even small decreases in user wait time pay big dividends in user efficiency.
5. To optimize the use of computer system resources.	The operating system is continually looking at what tasks need to be done and what resources (processor, RAM, and peripheral devices) are available to accomplish these tasks. The incredible speed of a computer system dictates that resource-allocation decisions be made at computer speeds. Each millisecond the operating system makes decisions about what resources to assign to which tasks.
6. To keep track of all files in disk storage.	The operating system and its file and disk management utility programs enable users to perform such tasks as making backup copies of work disks, erasing disk files that are no longer needed, making inquiries about the number and type of files on a particular disk, and preparing new disks for use. The operating system also handles many file- and disk-oriented tasks that are *transparent* (invisible) to the end user. For example, operating systems keep track of the physical location of disk files so that we, as users, need only refer to them by name (for example, myfile or year-end-summary) when loading them from disk to RAM.
7. To provide an envelope of security for the computer system.	The operating system can allow or deny user access to the system as a whole or to individual files. Specific security measures, such as passwords, are discussed later in the book.
8. To monitor all systems capabilities and alert the user of system failure or potential problems.	The operating system is continually checking system components for proper operation. Any problems are brought immediately to the attention of the user.

through multitasking. **Multitasking** is the *concurrent* execution of more than one program at a time. Actually, a single computer can execute only one program at a time. However, its internal processing speed is so fast that several programs can be allocated "slices" of computer time in rotation, making it appear that several programs are being executed at once.

The great difference in processor speed and the speeds of the peripheral devices makes multitasking possible. The speed of a 22-page-per-minute printer doesn't come close to pushing the processor of a low-end PC. The computer's processor is continually waiting for peripheral devices to complete such tasks as retrieving a record from disk storage or printing a report. During these waiting periods, the processor just continues processing other programs. The operating system ensures that the most appropriate resources are allocated to competing tasks in the most efficient manner.

Modern personal computing is done in a multitasking environment, where one or more programs run concurrently and are controlled and assigned priorities by the operating system. For example, you can prepare a graphics presentation in PowerPoint 2000 while faxing an Excel 2000 spreadsheet document via the fax modem. The **foreground** is that part of RAM containing the active or current program (PowerPoint 2000 in this example) and is usually given priority by the operating system. Other lower-priority programs, such as the fax transmittal in the example, are run in the **background** part of RAM. The operating system rotates allocation of the processor resource between foreground and background programs, with the foreground programs receiving the lion's share of the processor's attention.

The Graphical User Interface: "Gooie"

To better appreciate the impact of graphical user interfaces (GUIs), it helps if you know what preceded them.

Text-Based Software

Through the 1980s, the most popular microcomputer operating system, **MS-DOS,** was strictly *text-based, command-driven* software. That is, we issued commands directly to DOS (the MS–DOS nickname) by entering them on the keyboard, one character at a time. For example, if you wished to issue a command to copy a word processing document from one disk to another for your friend, you might have entered "copy c:\myfile.txt a:\yourfile.txt" via the keyboard at the DOS prompt, "C:\⟩".

C:\⟩ copy c:\myfile.txt a:\yourfile.txt

When using command-driven, text-based software you must be explicit. In the previous example, you could not just enter "copy" or even "copy MYFILE". You would have to enter the command that tells the PC where to find MYFILE and where to make the copy. If you omitted necessary information in a command or the format of the command was incorrect, you would get one of those dreaded error messages. Command-driven DOS, in particular, demanded strict adherence to command **syntax,** which are the rules for entering commands, such as word spacing, punctuation, and so on (see Figure 8.3).

Graphics-Based Software

Today, relatively few computers run with purely text-based operating systems. For the past decade, the trend in PC operating systems has been toward a user-friendly, graphics-oriented environment—the graphical user interface, or GUI (pronounced *"G-U-I"* or *"gooie"*). Graphical user interfaces rely on graphics-based software, which permits the integration of text with graphic images (see Figure 8.3).

All modern operating systems, including the *Windows 9x/NT/2000* operating systems, provide GUIs. GUI users interact with the operating system and other software packages by using a pointing device (perhaps a mouse on desktop PCs

```
A:\>del *.*
All files in directory will be deleted!
Are you sure (Y/N)?y

A:\>c:

C:\>copy c:\myfile.txt a:\yourfile.txt
        1 file(s) copied

C:\>a:

A:\>dir

 Volume in drive A has no label
 Volume Serial Number is 245C-7321
 Directory of A:\

YOURFILE TXT            14  02-05-99  9:48a yourfile.txt
         1 file(s)              14 bytes
         0 dir(s)        1,226,240 bytes free
```

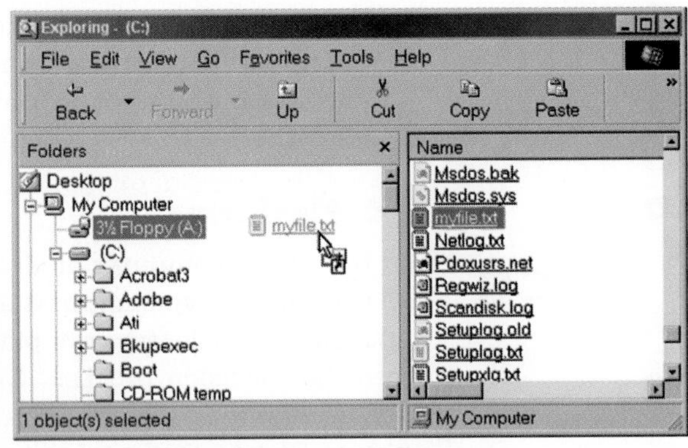

Text-Based and Graphics-Based Interfaces MS-DOS (shown here), the primary PC operating system for the first 15 years of personal computing, has a text-based, command-driven interface. Windows 98 has a graphical user interface (GUI) in which files can be dragged with a mouse between disk icons. Each has its pros and cons. For example, MS-DOS demands knowledge of syntax, but the GUI may require more operations (myfile.txt would need to be renamed to yourfile.txt after the drag operation).

or a trackpad on notebook PCs) and a keyboard to issue commands. Rather than enter a command directly, as in a command-driven interface, the user chooses from options displayed on the screen. The equivalent of a syntax-sensitive operating system command is entered by pointing to and choosing one or more options from menus or by pointing to and choosing a graphics image, called an **icon.** An icon is a graphic rendering that represents a processing activity or a file. For example, the file folder icon represents processing activities associated with file management. Users might choose the "trash can" icon to delete a file from disk storage.

GUIs have eliminated the need for us to memorize and enter cumbersome commands. For example, in GUIs all we have to do to copy a file from one disk to another disk is to reposition the file's icon from one area on the screen to another.

SECTION SELF-CHECK

Self-Check

8-1.1 MS-DOS is a state-of-the-art operating system. (T/F)

8-1.2 The kernel is loaded to RAM on system start up. (T/F)

8-1.3 All computers, including computers dedicated to a particular application, have operating systems. (T/F)

8-1.4 The concurrent execution of more than one program at a time is called: (a) double duty, (b) multitasking, (c) multilayering, or (d) multiple kerneling?

8-1.5 A GUI is: (a) text-based, (b) graphics-based, (c) label-based, or (d) paste-based?

8-1.6 Programs designed to be used by the end user are: (a) system software, (b) systemware, (c) personware, or (d) applications software?

8.2 PLATFORMS: HOMES FOR SOFTWARE

In Chapter 1 we learned that a *platform* is defined by a *processor* and an *operating system.* Software created to run on a specific platform won't run on other platforms. The typical computer system, large or small, runs under a single platform. However, some can run several platforms. A multiplatform computer runs its native platform and *emulates* other platforms.

The selection of a platform is important because it sets boundaries for what you can and cannot do with your computer system. Before choosing a platform, consider the following:

- *Availability* of appropriate commercial applications software for the platform.
- *Compatibility* of platform with existing hardware, software, and expertise (a big investment in one platform often deters people from switching to another).

MEMORY

PC Platforms

- Legacy PC-Compatible
  - —MS-DOS
  - —MS-DOS with Windows
  - —Windows 95 and Windows 98
  - —Windows NT (client/server)
- Current PC-Compatible
  - —Windows 2000 (client/server)
  - —Windows CE (handheld and pocket PC)
- Apple Macintosh with Mac OS
- Unix
- Linux

PC Platforms

In the server computer environment, choosing a platform is the responsibility of IT specialists. Typically, in the PC environment, you—the individual user—are responsible for selecting the platform. The following discussion will provide insight into that decision process. Our discussion will focus on the most common personal computing environments, that is, one characterized by PC-compatible computers. The Apple line of computers, including the Apple Macintosh series of computers and the iMac, define another common single-user platform.

Windows with PC Compatibles

The PC-compatible platforms of the modern era are the Microsoft Windows family of operating systems: Windows 95, Windows 98, Windows 2000, Windows NT, and Windows CE. However, two other operating systems ruled the PC-compatible environment for 15 years: *MS-DOS* and *Windows.* Through 1990, the platform of choice for the majority of PC users was defined by PCs that were functionally compatible with the 1984 IBM PC-AT architecture (the Intel family of microprocessors) and ran under MS-DOS. Although the wide popularity of the modern Windows family and its user-friendly graphical user interface has all but eliminated the use of MS-DOS for modern computing, there are still a few loyal DOS fans.

The original Microsoft Windows, which introduced the GUI to the PC-compatible environment, was introduced in 1987 and made obsolete with the introduction of Windows 95 in 1995. It, however, is still used by many individuals and companies who have chosen not to make the upgrade. MS-DOS programs that do not conform to Windows standards can still be run within Windows, though. These programs, called *non-Windows* programs, are no less effective when run within Windows, but they don't take full advantage of the Windows capabilities.

The PC/Windows Platforms: 95, 98, 2000, NT, and CE

The PC/Windows platforms—Windows 95, 98, 2000, NT, and CE—offer many advantages over their predecessors, including **plug-and-play** capability. Plug-and-play refers to making a peripheral device or an expansion board immediately operational by simply plugging it into a port or an expansion slot. Users no longer have to juggle limited system resources, such as I/O ports, to eliminate system-level conflicts. Another major advantage of Windows 95 is its ability to run 32-bit programs; that is, programs that use the full 32-bit data paths in the processor. (MS-DOS and the original Windows are 16-bit operating systems.) All members of the PC/Windows family have a similar look and feel.

Each member of the Windows family of operating systems plays an important role in Microsoft's strategy for the future of personal computing. The following descriptions of the family members should provide some insight into the roles that they play.

Windows 95 and Windows 98 Windows 95 and Windows 98 are operating systems designed to bridge the technology gap between the original Windows and Windows NT. Most individuals and companies were not technologically prepared or willing to jump directly to Windows NT, the most sophisticated of the Windows family of operating systems. Bill Gates, the founder of Microsoft, has made it clear that " . . . Windows 95 was a milestone, not a destination." The primary difference between Windows 95 and Windows 98 is that the latter integrates the Internet into the operating system.

Windows NT Is Now Windows 2000 Windows 2000 is the future of the PC/Windows family of operating systems. Windows 2000 replaces Windows NT and reflects a push for Windows 95 and Windows 98 users to migrate (move to) Windows 2000. Windows NT has been Microsoft's high-end operating system, used primarily in networked businesses. Ultimately, Microsoft would like all Windows users to move to the Windows 2000 environment. The Microsoft Office suite is called Microsoft Office 2000.

Windows 2000 is a powerful client/server operating system that is emerging as the choice for businesses doing client/server computing. Windows 2000 has two components: **Windows 2000 Professional,** the client-side operating system, and **Windows 2000 Server,** the server-side portion of the operating system (which runs on the server computer). The two work together to make client/server computing possible.

Windows 2000 Professional has the look and feel of Windows 98, but it has a number of additional features, most of which have to do with security and networking. The Windows 2000 Professional system's requirements are greater than those for Windows 95 and Windows 98.

Windows 2000 is among the new wave of client/server platforms supporting LAN-based *workgroup computing.* Workgroup computing allows people on a network to use the network to foster cooperation and the sharing of ideas and resources. Groupware, such as electronic messaging, calendar, brainstorming, and scheduling, is developed to run under workgroup platforms.

The Palm Computing Platform Not all handheld PCs have adopted the Window CE platform, even though it offers a breadth of features. The Palm Computing Platform is the foundation for the market-leading PalmPilot organizers. This platform enables you to "beam" data, notes, schedules, applications, even your business card, to other PalmPilot users via an infrared link.

3Com and the 3Com logo are registered trademarks. PalmIII™ and the PalmIII™ logo are trademarks of Palm Computing, Inc., 3Com Corporation, or its subsidiaries.

Windows CE The **Windows CE** operating system is designed for handheld and pocket PCs. Its look and feel are similar to the other members of the family. Windows CE users can share information with other Windows-based PCs. And, they can connect to the Internet.

The Macintosh/Mac OS Platform The Apple family of microcomputers (including the Macintosh, Powerbook, and iMac computers) and its operating system, **Mac OS** (see Figure 8.4), define another major platform. About one in every 10 PCs runs under this platform. The Apple line of microcomputers is based on the Motorola family of microprocessors. One inviting feature of Apple's Mac OS is that it can be adjusted to fit the user's level of expertise.

PC Platform Options: Which to Choose? Several personal computing platform options, including the **UNIX** and **Linux** (a Unix spin-off) operating systems, await new and existing PC users, but which one is right for you? Your choice depends on your circumstances (knowledge, compatibility with office PCs, existing configuration, budget, and so on) and personal preferences.

Platform Problems: Interoperability and Cross-Platform Technologies

Many companies purchase and maintain a fleet of automobiles for use by employees. Companies routinely exchange entire fleets of Chevys for Fords (and vice

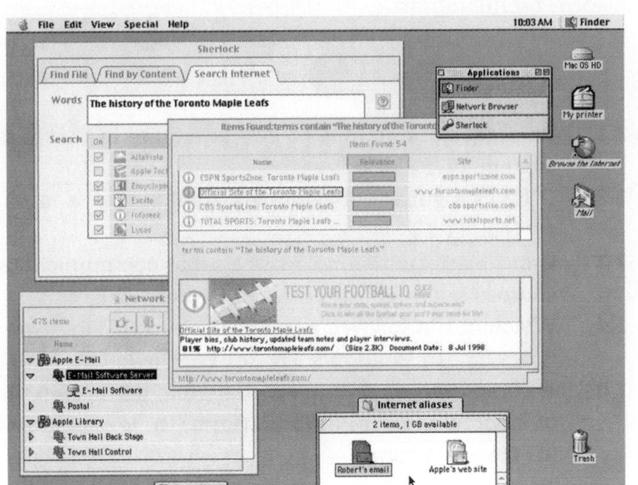

FIGURE 8.4

The Mac OS Apple Computer Company introduced the GUI concept in the mid-1980s, and the Mac OS operating system (shown here) continues the GUI tradition.

IT Ethics

THE QUALITY OF SOFTWARE

The software market is highly competitive even though Microsoft dominates the operating system and productivity software markets. Competition and other market pressures have forced software vendors, including Microsoft, into rushing their products to market, bugs and all. Some industry observers have argued that the quality of software is declining with an increasingly higher percentage of bugs being left intact within commercial software. The end result of this rush to market is that customers lose time and money coping with pesky bugs. Information technology and those who make software decisions are putting pressure on software vendors to raise the quality of their software. Generally, they want a clean product, even if they have to wait for it.

Discussion: What can software vendors do within the context of competition and economic reality to improve software quality? What can those who buy commercial software do to improve software quality?

versa) without any loss of functionality. Employees simply come to work in a Chevy and drive away in a Ford. This decision doesn't commit a company over the long term. The choice of a computer platform, however, does.

When you decide on a particular platform, you begin to purchase and create resources for that platform. The investment required in selecting a platform demands a long-term commitment—at least five years. This type of commitment makes choosing a platform at the individual or company level a very important decision.

All companies have platform problems, although some to a lesser extent than others. Those that standardize on platforms can enjoy the benefits of easily shared resources (from data to printers). Those that do not must do some work to achieve interoperability. **Interoperability** refers to the ability to run software and exchange information in a **multiplatform environment** (a computing environment of more than one platform). Enabling technologies that allow communication and the sharing of resources between different platforms are called **cross-platform technologies.** Multiplatform organizations use cross-platform technologies, both hardware and software, to link PCs, workstations, LANs, mainframes, and so on. Multiplatform environments are more the rule than the exception in medium-sized and large organizations. Whenever possible, companies try to minimize the number of platforms represented in the company. The fewer the number of platforms, the less the hassle and expense associated with installing and maintaining cross-platform technologies.

SECTION SELF-CHECK

Self-Check

8-2.1 The Macintosh family of PCs is unique in that it does not need an operating system. (T/F)

8-2.2 UNIX is a subset of Windows 2000 Server, a more sophisticated operating system. (T/F)

8-2.3 Cross-platform technologies enable communication and the sharing of resources between different platforms. (T/F)

8-2.4 Which of the following is not in the PC/Windows platform family: (a) Windows 98, (b) Windows TN, (c) Windows CE, or (d) Windows 2000?

8-2.5 A computing environment that runs more than one platform is what type of environment: (a) high platform, (b) low platform, (c) multiplatform, or (d) cross-platform?

8-2.6 Making an expansion board immediately operational by simply plugging it into an expansion slot is referred to as: (a) plug-and-play, (b) cap-and-cork, (c) pop-and-go, or (d) plug-and-go?

8-2.7 The future of the PC/Windows family of operating systems is: (a) Windows 95, (b) Windows 98, (c) Windows 2000, or (d) Windows 2002?

8.3 WINDOWS CONCEPTS AND TERMINOLOGY

The Windows Environment

Windows 95, Windows 98, Windows NT, and *Windows 2000,* all operating systems from Microsoft Corporation, dominate the PC-compatible environment. The Microsoft master plan has all Windows users eventually migrating to Windows 2000. Today's new PCs come with a Windows 98 or Windows 2000 operating system installed on the hard disk. Windows 98 works well in the home or the office, but Windows NT, with its security and networking capabilities, is better suited for networking on a local area network (LAN). Windows 2000 has the best features of both and works in all environments.

The terms, concepts, and features discussed in this chapter generally apply to Windows 9x/NT/2000; however, the examples show the most recent home/office version as of this edition—Windows 98. The name *Windows* describes basically how the software functions. The GUI-based Windows series runs one or more applications in *windows*—rectangular areas displayed on the screen. The Windows operating system series has introduced a number of new concepts and terms, all of which apply to the thousands of software packages that have been and are being developed to run on the Windows platforms.

Understanding Windows 98: Help

Books, like this one, and tutorial software are *complementary* learning tools. Hands-on activity with Windows 98, Windows 2000, or any other software package is essential to learning. The explanations in the following sections will make more sense once you begin interacting with Windows 9x/2000. We recommend that you visit your college's PC lab and run *Help* to learn more about your Windows 9x/2000 operating system (see Figure 8.5). That is, click on the *Start* button in the *taskbar* (usually positioned at the bottom of the screen), then click Help. In addition, if you have Windows 98, you can take advantage of its excellent Web-based feature, called Web Help. This feature provides online access to comprehensive, continually updated Help information. The Windows 9x/2000 Help capabilities include step-by-step tutorials that lead you through numerous common Windows 9x/2000 procedures. Also, the Windows 9x/2000 CD-ROM has several excellent multimedia tutorials that provide general competency instruction for information technology, as well as specifics on how to use Windows 9x/2000, the mouse, and the keyboard.

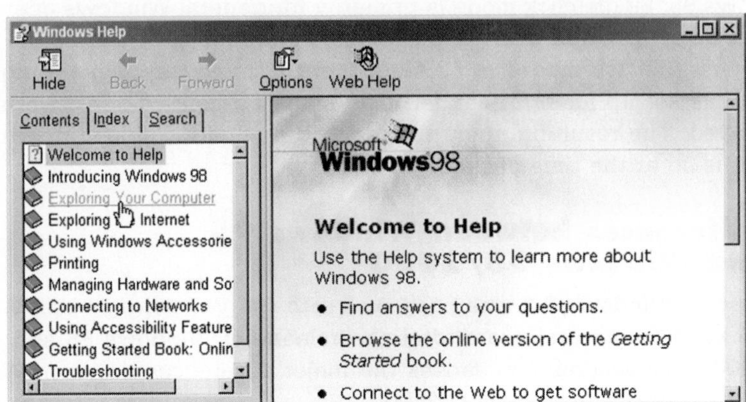

The Windows 98 Help Feature The Help feature lets you find help by scanning a hierarchical table of *Contents*. Click on the *Index* tab to search an index similar to one you would find in a book (but without page references). Click on the *Search* tab to search the help files by keyword. Click on the *Web Help* button for Internet-based Windows 98 help and technical support.

Non-Windows versus Windows Applications

Non-Windows Applications

Any software application that does not adhere to the Microsoft Windows standard is a **non-Windows application.** Non-Windows applications will run under Windows 9x or Windows 2000, but these software packages do not take advantage of the many helpful Windows 9x/2000 features. Generally, non-Windows programs are legacy software created for the earlier MS-DOS and Windows 3.1 platforms.

Windows Applications

Programs that adhere to Windows conventions are **Windows applications.** These conventions describe:

- Type and style of window
- Arrangement and style of menus
- Use of the keyboard and mouse
- Format for screen image display

Virtually all new software for the PC environment is designed to run on the Windows 9x/2000 platform. The GUI for Windows versions of Word, Quicken, Adobe Illustrator, and all other Windows applications have the same look and feel. *When you learn the GUI for Windows 9x/2000, you also learn the GUI for all Windows 9x/2000–based software packages.*

The Windows 9x/2000 graphical user interfaces use both a keyboard and a point-and-draw device for input. The point-and-draw device is often a mouse, but is increasingly a touchpad or some other such device. Such devices also are called **cursor control devices (CCDs)**. Interaction with Windows 9x/2000 or an application is most efficient when options are chosen with a mouse and characters are entered via the keyboard.

When working with the keyboard:

- Enter text as needed (for example, a path for a file: "C:\Program Files\Microsoft Office\Office\winword.exe").
- Activate the current menu bar by tapping the ALT key.
- Enter the underlined letter of the menu option in the active menu to choose that option.
- Use the arrow keys to highlight menu options in an active menu.
- Use the **shortcut key,** which can be a key or a key combination (for example, ALT+F4 to *Exit* and CTRL+C to *Copy*) to issue commands within a particular application without activating a menu.
- Use the **hotkey,** also a key or key combination, to cause some function to happen in the computer, no matter what the active application.

Input via a CCD, such as a mouse, is slightly different in Windows 95 and in Windows 98/2000. When performing operating system functions in Windows 98, you can opt for the single-click mode or the traditional double-click mode of Windows 95. Single-click mode is primarily for general Windows operations and may not be available in many applications. Figure 8.6 summarizes the differences between the two modes of clicking. *Right clicking* (tapping the right button on a mouse set up for right-handed use) causes a context-sensitive menu to be displayed. The resulting menu relates to the window, object, or whatever the cursor is on at the time of the right click.

Differences between Windows 95 and Windows 98/2000

Just as Windows 3.1 was used well into the Windows 9x era, Windows 95 will be used for several years after the release of Windows 98 and even Windows 2000. This section summarizes the major differences between Windows 95 and its successors, Windows 98/2000.

Windows 9x/2000 Task	Double-Click Mode Windows 9x/2000	Single-Click Mode Windows 98/2000 only
Select an item	Point and click on item (an icon, a filename, a task bar program, and so on)	Point to item.
Open (or choose) an item	Double-click on the item.	Click on the item.
Select a range of items	Press and hold the SHIFT key, then **click** the first and last items in a group of items (for example, files or words in a paragraph).	Press and hold the SHIFT key, and **point to** the first and last items in the group.
Select multiple individual items	Press and hold the CTRL key, and **click** individual items in a group.	Press and hold down the CTRL key, and **point to** individual items in the group.
Drag and drop item	Point to an item, press and hold the mouse button, and drag the item to new location.	Same as double-click mode.

FIGURE 8.6

Double-Click and Single-Click Modes for the Windows 9x/2000 Operating Systems

The Windows 95 GUI looks very much like that of Windows 98/2000. What you see, however, tells only part of the story. The underlying software for Windows 98/2000 reflects three to five years of improved and changing technology. The following summary of Windows 98/2000 features highlights of the differences between the operating systems.

Easier to Use

With Windows 98/2000 users can manage their files and move between applications in the same intuitive way they browse the Internet. This new *Web page–oriented interface* may be the most significant visual difference between Windows 95 and Windows 98/2000. Windows 95 users can enjoy this feature by downloading and installing the most recent version of Internet Explorer, the Microsoft Internet browser, from the Microsoft Web site ⟨http://www.microsoft.com⟩. The browser look is embedded in the functionality of the Windows 98/2000 operating system. This integration of the operating system and the browser was one of the main reasons for the federal government's recent antitrust action against Microsoft. In most Windows 98/2000 user activities, an Internet or intranet connection is just a click away. It does not matter whether your files or applications are local (on the PC's hard disk), on a LAN server, or on the Internet; the user interface is the same.

Several enhancements to the user interface make navigation easier. For example, being able to click the forward/backward buttons on the Web page interface provides rapid navigation between application views. The cumbersome double-clicking to open (choose) files in Windows 95 is replaced with a single-clicking option (see Figure 8.6). With Windows 98/2000, users simply point to an icon to select it.

Improved Performance

Windows 98/2000 is a newer, faster, and more feature-rich operating system. It boots, loads applications, and shuts down more quickly. It includes many new user-friendly tools that assist users in preparing their computer to run faster (for example, optimizing the location of frequently used files on the hard disk). A Maintenance **Wizard** (see Figure 8.7) monitors your system, then suggests ways you can improve your system's performance. Wizards lead you step by step through many common user procedures, such as installing new software or hardware.

Fully Integrated with the Internet

With the Internet Explorer interface now a part of Windows 98/2000, Internet access and viewing is integrated within any common office application (word

The Windows 98 Maintenance Wizard The Windows Maintenance Wizard is one of many wizards that can guide you through common procedures. This wizard can help you make your programs run faster, check your hard disk for problems, and free up hard-disk space.

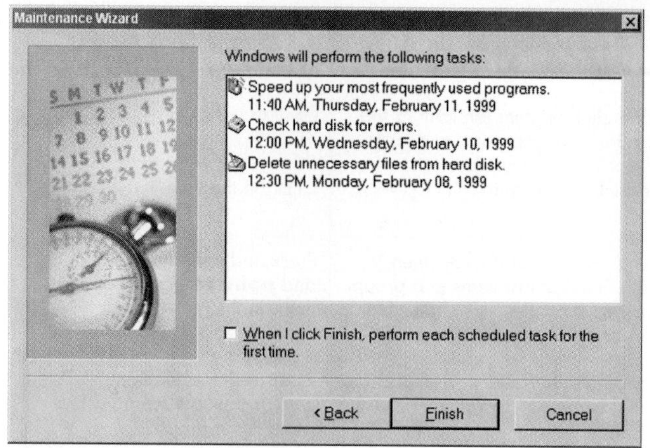

processing, spreadsheet, e-mail, and so on). An Internet Connection Wizard even helps you get connected to an ISP (Internet service provider) so you can logon to the Internet. Besides Internet Explorer, two other major Internet-based applications are distributed with Windows 98/2000 including Outlook Express (for e-mail and newsgroups) and NetMeeting (for chat, Internet telephony, video conferencing, and application sharing over the Internet).

Enhanced Reliability

Windows 98/2000 is more reliable than Windows 95. Windows 98/2000 actually looks for system concerns and either alerts you or fixes the problem automatically. Windows Update (see Figure 8.8), an Internet-based Microsoft resource site, will help you keep your system up-to-date and running smoothly with the latest **drivers** (the software that enables interaction between the operating system and peripheral devices) and operating system files.

Operational Features

Windows 98/2000 provides support for recent hardware standards like Universal Serial Bus (USB), DVD, and the Accelerated Graphics Port (AGP) video accelerator cards. The USB is an advance over plug-and-play technology. With USB, you no longer need to reboot your PC to use new hardware. For gamers, Windows 98/2000 surely enhances the entertainment experience with new digital audio capabilities, support for forced-feedback joysticks, and support for multiple monitors. The multiple monitor feature lets you connect up to eight monitors to a single PC, enabling a substantial increase in the size of your desktop (the viewing area). The Broadcast Architecture feature enables PCs to receive **enhanced television.** An enhanced TV presentation combines video, HTML (the language of the World Wide Web on the Internet), and general programming from broadcast, satellite, and cable networks.

Keeping Windows 98 Up-to-Date The Windows Update feature helps you keep your Windows 98/2000 system tuned and up-to-date by automating driver and system updates via the Internet. The registered user simply navigates to the Windows Update page then downloads appropriate files.

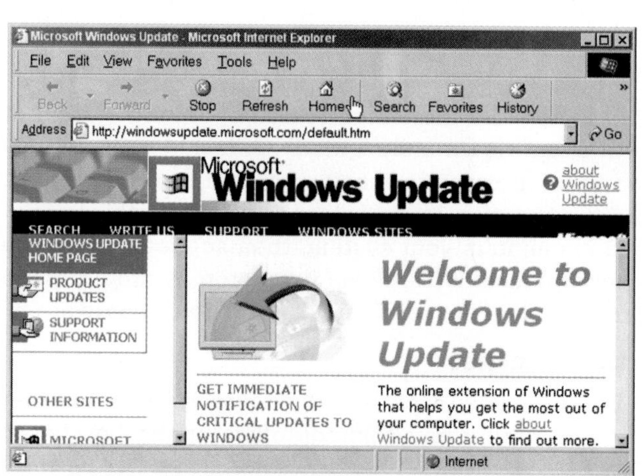

If your PC is on a LAN, the *Network Neighborhood* icon provides ready access to its resources.

Windows 98 provides support for plug-and-play and USB peripherals. This means your system can grow with your computing needs with considerably less effort on your part. All you have to do to add a new device, such as a video camera, is "plug" and "play" it.

A *Channel Bar* provides users with an opportunity to go directly to and subscribe to some of the more popular sites on the Internet.

Program icons, files, and folders (groups of related files) can be displayed directly on the desktop. The *My Computer* icon provides access to all files and folders.

The *Shortcut Bar* gives you single-click access to user-selected programs.

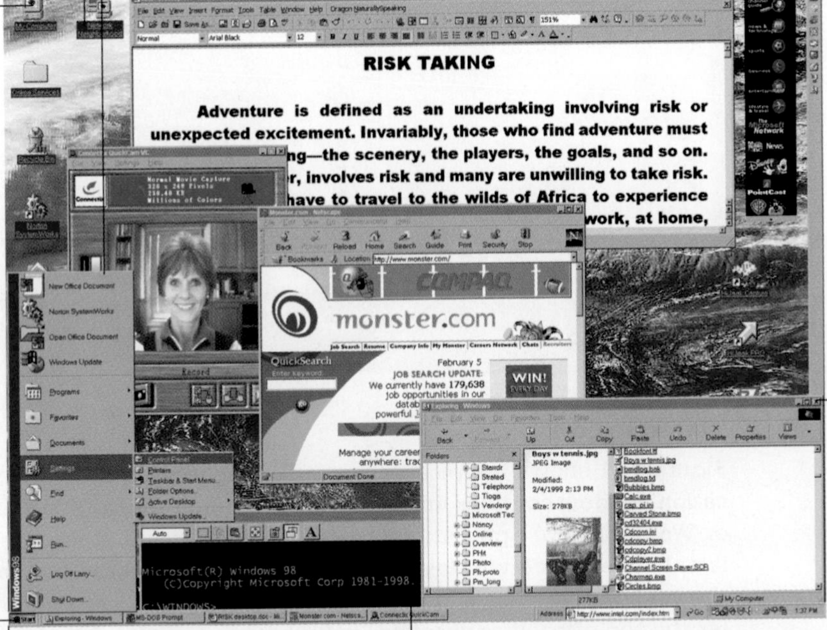

The Window 98 *Explorer* (the file management program) redefines user-friendliness, especially in the Web page format shown here, where files and folders are shown hierarchically and pictorially. Windows 9x/2000 enables descriptive names for files and folders.

A handy Start button provides easy access to most of the Windows tools and applications.

The *taskbar* keeps you abreast of active applications. Just click on the application button to switch to that application.

Windows 98 eliminates the need for MS-DOS (the original PC-compatible operating system) but offers complete backward compatibility for all MS-DOS and Windows 3.x software.

The Windows 9x/2000 Desktop The appearance of this Windows 98 desktop depends on the user's application mix and visual needs at a particular time. Windows 9x/2000 enables sophisticated multitasking, that is, running several programs at one time. This feature allows you to work on a word processing document while backing up files and checking e-mail on the Internet. The taskbar lists all open applications.

The Desktop

The screen upon which icons, windows, and so on are displayed is known as the **desktop.** The Windows 9x/2000 desktop may contain a *background, one active window, one or more inactive windows, icons,* and *various bars showing processing options* (see Figure 8.9). The background can be anything from a single-color screen to an elaborate image, such as the satellite view of Hurricane Danielle in Figure 8.9. All windows and icons are superimposed over the background, be it plain or an artistic image. The Windows desktop reflects the user's personality as well as processing and information needs, so no two are the same.

The Taskbar

Typically, a Windows session begins with the **Start button** in the taskbar. The **taskbar,** which can be displayed all the time or hidden, as desired, shows what programs are running and available for use. Click the *Start* button in the taskbar to display the Start menu and open the door to the resources on your PC. An application window can be opened in several ways, but usually people point and click on the desired application icon in the *Programs* option on the Start menu (see Figure 8.10). Highlighting the Programs option presents a pop-out menu with either application options or folders containing other options. A Windows **folder** is a logical grouping of related files and subordinate folders.

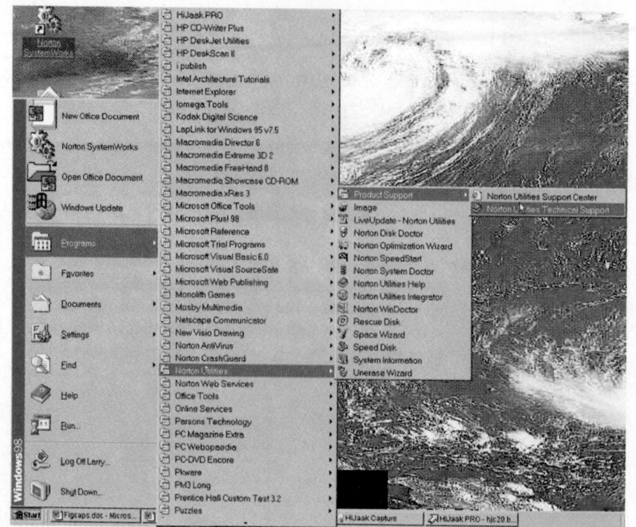

The Start Menu with Pop-out Menus The *Start* menu *Program* option is selected, prompting a display of available programs. Then, the *Norton Utilities* folder is highlighted causing its contents (fourteen applications and one subordinate folder) to be displayed. Highlighting the folder shows two more application options.

The Window

Figure 8.11 shows a typical rectangular Windows **application window.** An application window contains an **open application** (a running application), such as Paint or Word. Several applications can be open or running simultaneously, but there is only one **active window** at any given time. Application commands issued via the keyboard or mouse apply to the active window. The active window's title bar (at the top of each application) is highlighted. There is no active window in Figure 8.9 because the user has clicked on the Start button to open another program. The elements of an application window are: the workspace, the scroll bars, the title bar, the menu bar, the toolbar, the ruler bar, and the corners and borders. Each is described in the following sections and illustrated in Figure 8.11.

Workspace The application **workspace** is the area in a window below the title bar, menu bar, or toolbar. Everything that relates to the application noted in the title bar is displayed in the workspace. In the example in Figure 8.11, two **document windows** are displayed in the parent application window's workspace. Both are photo images and each is shown in a document window. The workspace of a word processing program might contain one or more word processing documents. If only one file/document is displayed in the workspace, then its filename appears in the title bar. If multiple files/documents are displayed, then filenames

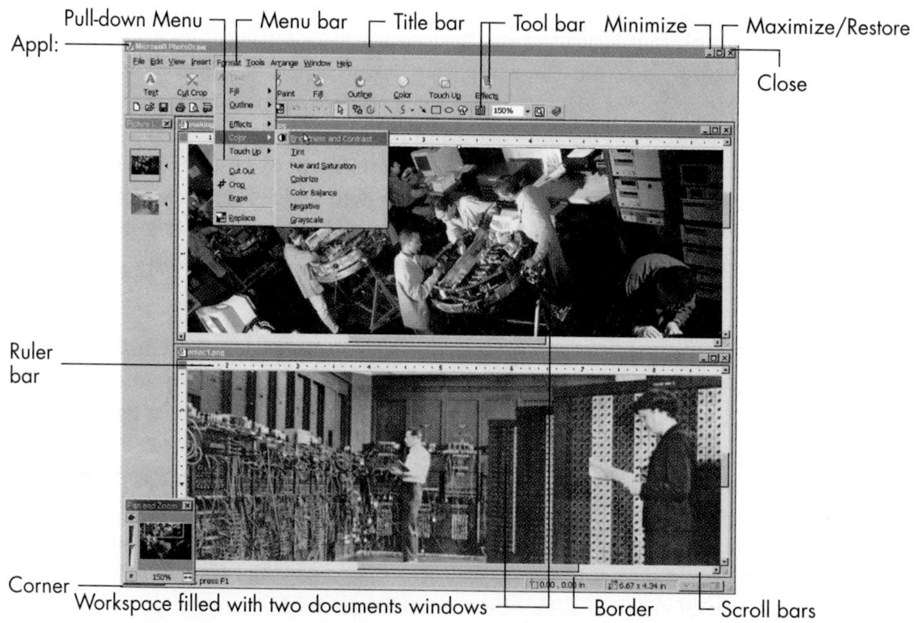

Elements of an Application Window In this example display, the workspace in this Microsoft PhotoDraw application has two open document windows, one showing the making of a communications satellite and the other the making of the ENIAC, the first electronic computer. The window with the highlighted title bar, "making of satellite Orbital.jpg", is the active document window.

appear in the title bars of their windows (making of satellite Orbital.jpg and eniac1.png in the Figure 8.11 work area).

The *vertical* and/or *horizontal scroll bars* (see Figure 8.11) are shown when the entire document can't be displayed in the window. Adjust the view by dragging the *scroll box* and clicking on the up/down *scroll arrows.*

Title Bar The horizontal **title bar** at the top of each window runs the width of the window from left to right (see Figure 8.11). The elements of the title bar include the *application icon, window title, minimize button, maximize/restore button, close button,* and the *title area.* Point and click/drag on these elements to change the presentation of the window.

- *Application icon in title bar.* The application icon is a miniature visual representation of the application and is displayed on the left end of the title bar. Double-click on it to close the application. Click on it to display a pull-down control menu for the associated application. Control menu options vary, depending on the type of application being displayed in the window.
- *Window title.* The title bar displays the title of the application ("Microsoft PhotoDraw" in Figure 8.11).
- *Maximize/minimize/restore buttons.* Point and click on the minimize button (—), maximize or restore button (☐ or ❐), or the close button (✕) at the right end of the title bar in Figure 8.11.

  Minimize (—) The *Minimize* option shrinks the active window to a button in the taskbar (see Figure 8.11). That is, the application in the window is deactivated and the window disappears from the screen, but the application remains open in the form of a button.

  Maximize (☐) The *Maximize* option enlarges the active window to fill the entire screen. The maximize button is dimmed if not available to the user.

  Restore (❐) When maximized, the restore button (❐) replaces the maximize button in the title bar. Click it to restore an enlarged window to its previous size.

  Close (✕) Choosing *Close* deactivates and removes the active window (and its application) from the desktop.
- *Title area.* To *move* a window, the user simply points to the window title area (the band between the application icon and the minimize button) and drags the window to the desired location.

Menu Bar The menu bar for an application window runs the width of the window just below the title bar (see Figure 8.11). The menu bar lists the menus available for that application. Choosing an option from the menu bar results in a pull-down menu. The *File, Edit, View,* and *Help* menus are available for most applications. Other menu options depend on the application. When you select an item from the menu bar, a subordinate **pull-down menu** (see Figure 8.11) is "pulled down" from the selected menu bar option and displayed as a vertical list of menu options.

Certain conventions apply to user interactions with any menu.

- *Only the boldface options can be chosen.* Dimmed options are not available for the current circumstances. For example, the *Copy* option would not be available in an Edit menu if nothing had been selected to be copied.
- *Corresponding shortcut keys are presented adjacent to many options in Windows menus.* For example, the *Open* option on the File menu for most applications can be executed by the Ctrl+O shortcut key combination.
- *Choosing a menu option followed by an arrow (▶)* results in a pop-out menu. The *Color* menu option on Figure 8.11 demonstrates the resulting **pop-out menu.**
- *A user-recorded check mark (√) to the left of the menu option indicates that the option is active and applies to any related commands.* For example, many programs have a toolbar, a ruler, and a status bar that are hidden or displayed depending on whether or not these items in the *View* option are checked.

- *There are three ways to choose a menu option.*
  1. Point and click the mouse on the option.
  2. Enter the underlined letter key, called a **mnemonic** (pronounced *"neh MON ik"*), of the menu option in combination with the Alt key on a keyboard (Alt+v for the *View* menu in Figure 8.11). Tap the underlined letter of a pull-down menu option to choose that option (*l* for *Color* in Figure 8.11).
  3. Once the menu is activated (by mouse click or keyboard), you can use the keyboard cursor-control keys to select (highlight) the desired option and tap the Enter key to choose it.
- *Choosing a menu option followed by an ellipsis (. . .) results in a dialog box.* The pop-up **dialog box** that would result from an action in a Figure 8.11 menu would ask the user to choose parameters or enter additional information.

You'll encounter a variety of menus, including the pop-up and floating menus. The context-sensitive **pop-up menu** is displayed when you right click the mouse. The pop-up menu gives you options appropriate for whatever you're doing at the time. The **floating menu** "floats" over the display and can be dragged with a mouse to any position on the work area.

Toolbar A software package's menu bar is but the tip of a hierarchy of menus that may contain as many as 200 menu item options. You might go for years and not choose some of these options. Others you might use every day. **Toolbars** have been created to give you ready access to these frequently used menu items. Toolbars contain a group of rectangular graphics that represent a frequently used menu option or a command (see Figure 8.11). To execute a particular command, simply click on the button. The graphics on the buttons are designed to represent actions of the command. You can customize your toolbars to meet your processing needs.

Ruler Bar Typically, the **ruler bar** shows the document window's content relative to the printed page. It is usually in inches and is based on standard letter-sized paper (see Figure 8.11).

Corners and Borders To resize a window, use a CCD and point to a window's border or corner. The mouse cursor changes to a double arrow when positioned over a border or corner. Drag the border or corner in the directions indicated by the double arrow to the desired shape.

The Dialog Box

Often, you, the user, must okay or revise entries in the *dialog box* before a command can be executed. The dialog box may contain any of these elements.

- *Tabs.* The tabs enable similar properties to be grouped within a dialog box (for example, *Appearance* and *Background* in Figure 8.12).
- *Text box.* Enter text information in the text box or accept the default entry that is displayed (see Figure 8.12).
- *Command buttons.* Point and click on the *OK* command button to carry out the command with the information provided in the dialog box. Choose *Cancel* to retain the original information (see Figure 8.12).
- *List boxes.* A list box displays a list of available choices for a particular option (see Figure 8.12). Long lists will have a vertical scroll bar.
- *Drop-down list boxes.* The drop-down list box is an alternative to the list box (see Figure 8.12) when the dialog box is too small for a list box to be displayed.
- *Drop-down color palette.* The drop-down color palette displays a matrix of available font, line, and fill colors (see Figure 8.12).
- *Radio buttons.* Circular option buttons, called radio buttons, preface each item in a list of mutually exclusive items (only one can be activated). Point and click a button to insert a black dot in the button and activate the option.
- *Scroll bar adjustment.* The scroll bar adjustment enables users to change parameters, such as the speed at which the cursor blinks or speaker volume.

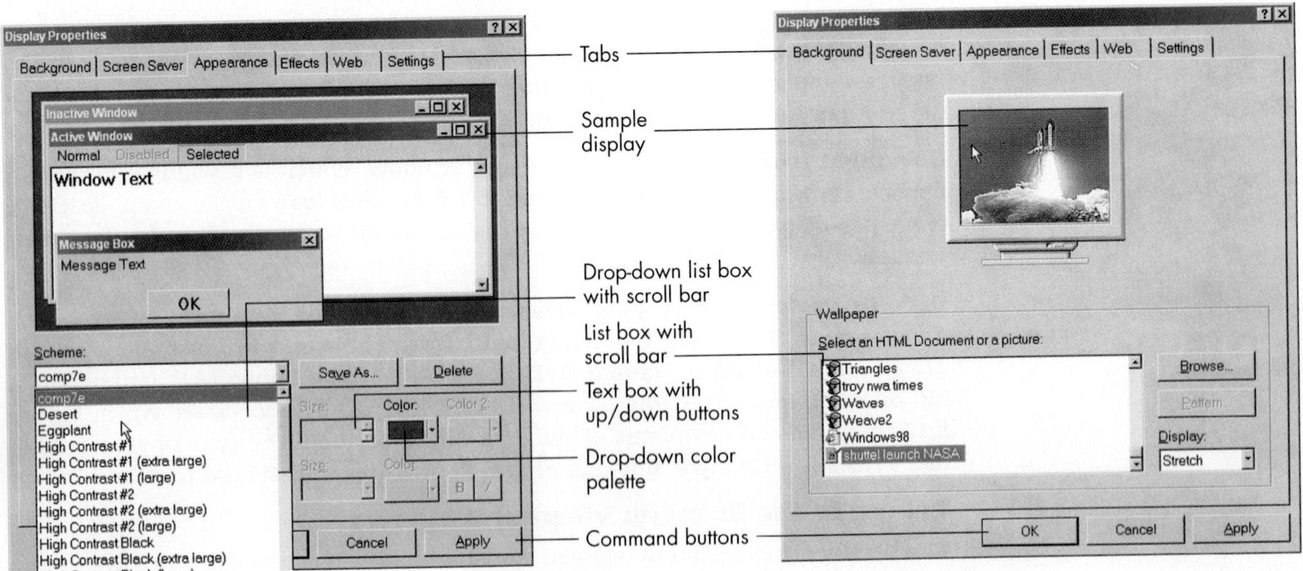

Elements of a Dialog Box Many common dialog box elements are shown in the Display Properties dialog box. Not shown are the radio button and scroll bar adjustment elements.

Icons

Icons, the graphical representation of a Windows element, play a major role in the Windows 9x/2000 GUI. Commonly used icons include *application icons, shortcut icons, document icons,* and *disk drive icons.* The **Windows Explorer** in Figure 8.13 shows the use of these icons. Use the Windows Explorer to perform file management tasks such as creating folders, copying files, moving files, deleting files, and other folder/file–related tasks. In Windows 9x/2000, named folders are created to hold document and program files.

Application Icons An active application window can be minimized to a button on the taskbar (see Figure 8.9), thereby making it inactive. The **application icon,** usually a graphic rendering of the software package's logo, is positioned on the button. Point and click (or double-click in Windows 95) on the button or icon to restore the window and the application to active status. Typically, you would minimize application windows that may not be needed for a while to make room on the desktop for other windows.

Shortcut Icons A **shortcut icon** to any application, document, or printer can be positioned on the desktop, in a folder (Font icon in Figure 8.13), or on a shortcut

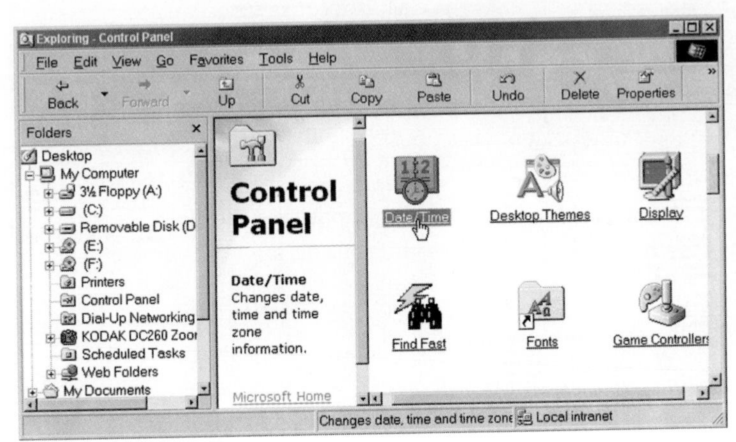

The Windows 98 Explorer
The Windows 98 Explorer makes resources on the computer readily accessible to the user. The plus sign to the left of the icon indicates that the item has subordinate folders. Click the disk or folder icon to show its content or click on an application icon to open the application.

bar (see icons on the right edge of Figure 8.9). The shortcut icon has an arrow in its lower left corner. Shortcuts are clicked (or double-clicked in Windows 95) to begin an application. They have other uses as well. For example, you can drag a file to a printer shortcut to print the file.

Document Icons The active document window, which is a window within an application window, can be minimized to a **document icon** within an application's workspace. Point and double-click on the document icon to restore the document window.

Disk Drive Icons The **disk drive icons** graphically represent several disk drive options: floppy, hard, network (hard), removable disk (for example, Zip disk drive), and CD-ROM (including DVD and CD-RW). The floppy (A), hard-disk (C), Zip disk (D), and CD-ROMs (E, a DVD, and F, a CD-RW) icons shown in Figure 8.13 resemble the faceplates of the disk drives or show the type of storage media. Typically, PCs have only one or two floppy drives, assigned to A and B.

Taking in the Scenery: Viewing Windows

The Windows environment lets you view multiple applications in windows on the desktop display. Once open, a window can be resized, minimized (and restored), maximized (and restored), and, finally, closed.

Essentially, any applications software for the Windows 9x/NT/2000 environment can be:

- Viewed and run in a window, the shape and size of which is determined by you, the user.
- Run full-screen (maximized); that is, filling the entire screen, with no other application windows or icons showing.

Some non-Windows applications run only as full-screen applications and cannot be run in a window. When multiple applications are running, the user can use the *Move* and *Resize* capabilities to arrange and size the windows to meet viewing needs. Of course, open windows can be minimized to free viewing space on the desktop.

Within a given application window, such as Microsoft Word 2000, multiple document windows can be sized, shrunk, and arranged by the user within the workspace. As an alternative, the user can request that the document windows be automatically presented as **cascading windows** or **tiled windows** (see Figure 8.14). Choose these options from the *Windows* menu option in the menu bar of any Windows application. The *Cascade* option overlaps open document windows

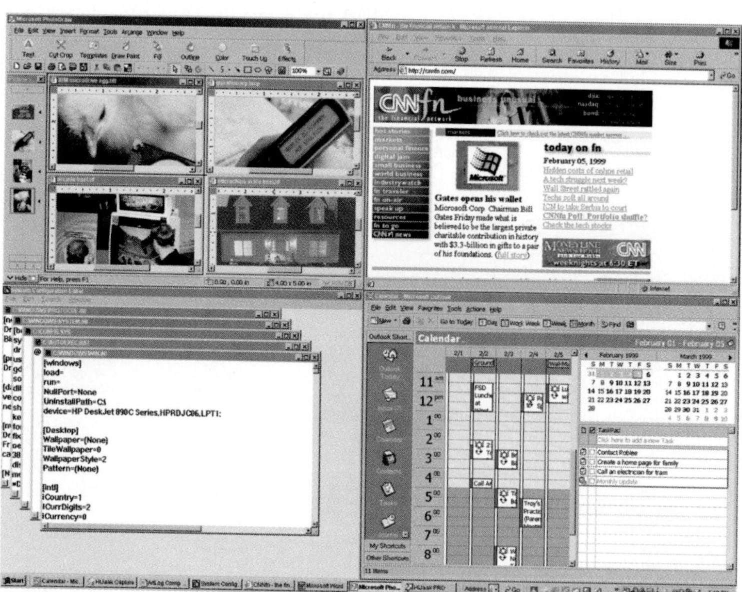

Arrangement of Windows

Here, four open applications are tiled on the Windows 98 desktop (clockwise from top left: Microsoft PhotoDraw, Internet Explorer, System Configuration Editor, and Outlook 2000). The applications, as well as documents within an application's workspace, can be presented as tiled documents (in top left Microsoft PhotoDraw images) or cascading (bottom left documents are overlapped such that all title bars are visible).

so that all title bars are visible. The *Tile* option fills the workspace in such a way that no document window overlaps another. Scroll bars are provided on those document windows for which the space is not adequate to display the window's content.

Switching between Windows

In the Windows environment, users can open as many applications as available RAM will permit. The active window is always highlighted in the **foreground.** When located in the foreground all parts of the window are visible. Other open windows are in the **background,** or behind the foreground (see Figure 8.9). Do the following to switch between open applications.

- Point and click anywhere on the desired inactive window
- Point and click (double-click in Windows 95) the desired application button in the taskbar or an application icon.

Moving On: Terminating an Application and a Windows Session

Perform three operations before ending a Windows session.

1. *Save your work.* The *Save* option in the *File* menu updates the existing file to reflect the changes made during the session. The *Save as* option allows users to save the current file under another filename.
2. *Close all open windows.* After saving your work, exit each window by pointing and clicking the close button in the title bar. You may also exit a Windows application through its menu bar (*File* then *Exit*).
3. *Shut down Windows 9x/2000.* Click *Start* in the taskbar, then select on the *Shut Down* radio button, the OK, in the Windows Shut-down dialog box.

SECTION SELF-CHECK

Self-Check

8-3.1 Any software application that does not adhere to the Microsoft Windows standard is a non-Windows application. (T/F)

8-3.2 In Windows, wizards lead you step by step through many common user procedures. (T/F)

8-3.3 In Windows 98/2000, Internet viewing is integrated within common office applications. (T/F)

8-3.4 In the Windows environment, the active window is highlighted in the background. (T/F)

8-3.5 The cascading windows option fills the workspace in such a way that no document window overlaps another. (T/F)

8-3.6 The Close button in a Windows application is indicated with a letter "Y."

8-3.7 A Windows folder can contain either files or subordinated folders, but not both. (T/F)

8-3.8 When you press and hold a mouse button, what do you do to the graphics cursor: (a) drag it, (b) draw it, (c) pull it, or (d) tug it?

8-3.9 Which is not considered a common menu format: (a) floating, (b) pop-out, (c) pop-up, or (d) pop-down?

8-3.10 Which of these is a cursor control device: (a) printer, (b) CD-ROM, (c) mouse, or (d) scanner?

8-3.11 The shortcut key for Copy is: (a) ALT+C, (b) SHIFT+C, (c) TAB+C, or (d) CTRL+C?

8-3.12 The software that enables interaction between the operating system and peripheral devices is called a: (a) passenger, (b) back seater, (c) driver, or (d) shotgun?

8-3.13 Document windows are displayed in the parent application window's: (a) system window, (b) title bar, (c) scroll area, or (d) workspace?

8-3.14 Which of these would not be found in a dialog box: (a) list boxes, (b) tabs, (c) television buttons, or (d) text boxes?

8.4 SHARING INFORMATION AMONG WINDOWS APPLICATIONS

One of the most inviting aspects of the Windows environment is the ability to copy and move information (text, graphics, sound clips, video clips, or a combination) from one application to another. Windows offers several methods for sharing information.

The Clipboard: The Information Way Station

The most common method of sharing information among applications is to use the Windows **clipboard** and the *Edit* option in the menu bar. Think of the clipboard as an intermediate holding area for information. The information in the clipboard can be en route to another application or it can be copied anywhere in the current document. *Edit* is an option in the menu bar of most Windows applications. Choosing Edit results in a pull-down menu from the menu bar. Options common to most Edit menus are *Cut, Copy, Paste,* and *Delete.* The **source application** and **destination application** can be one and the same or they can be entirely different applications.

The procedure for transferring information via the clipboard is demonstrated in Figure 8.15. This example illustrates the *Copy* procedure. Choosing the *Cut* option causes the specified information to be removed from the source application and placed on the Windows clipboard. Whether *Copy* or *Cut* is chosen, the clipboard contents remain unchanged until the next copy/cut and can be pasted as many times as needed.

Object Linking and Embedding: OLE

Another way to link applications is through **object linking and embedding** or **OLE.** Loosely, an **object** is the result of any Windows application. The object can be a block of text, all or part of a graphic image, or even a sound or video clip. OLE gives us the capability to create a **compound document** that contains one or more objects from other applications. A document can be a word processing newsletter, a Visio Professional drawing, a spreadsheet, and so on. The object originates in a **server application** and is linked to a destination document of a **client application.** For example, when a Visio Professional (server application) drawing (object) is linked to a Word (client) note (destination document), the result is a compound document (see Figure 8.16).

Object Linking: Dynamic Connection

OLE lets you *link* or *embed* information. When you link information, the link between source and destination documents is dynamic; that is, any change you make in the source document is reflected in the destination document. Object linking is demonstrated in Figure 8.16. Linking doesn't actually place the object into the destination document: It places a pointer to the source document (a disk-based file). In linking, the object is saved as a separate file from the source document. The source document must accompany the destination to maintain the integrity of the destination document (a compound document); that is, if you give a friend a copy of the destination document, you must also give the friend the source as well. Your friend's PC must have both the server and client application software to display the compound document. Linking is helpful when the object is used in several destination documents because when you change the source, it is updated in all documents to which it is linked.

Object Embedding: Implant Operation

When you embed information, you insert the actual object, not just a pointer. Where linking is dynamic, embedding is not. You can change the source within the destination document, but the original (if there is one) is unchanged. A source document is not required in object embedding.

Copy and Paste via the Clipboard This walkthrough demonstrates the procedure for transferring information among multiple Windows applications: Paint (a paint program), Word (a word processing program), and a CD-ROM–based encyclopedia. In the example, the Niagara Falls image in a Paint document is marked and copied (to the clipboard), then pasted to a Word document. Supporting text in the *1999 Grolier Multimedia Encyclopedia* is marked and copied to the same Word document via the clipboard.

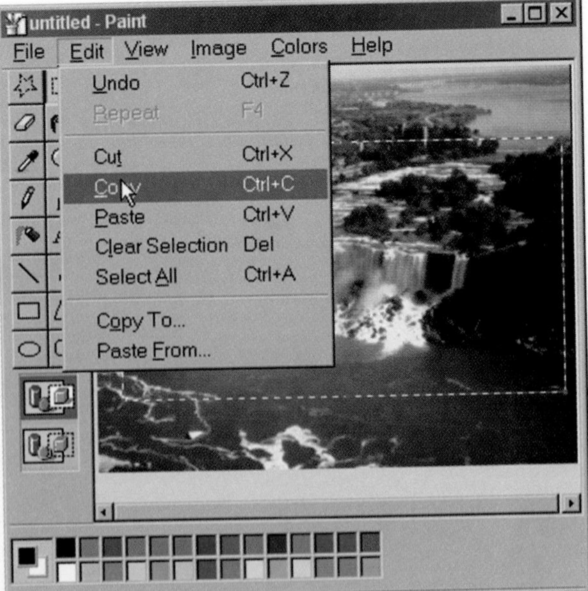

1. *Mark the information.* Drag the select cursor (the Pick tool in Paint) from one corner of the information to be copied to the opposite corner of the area and release the mouse button. The information to be transferred is highlighted.

2. *Copy the marked information to the clipboard.* Choose Edit in the source application's (Paint) menu bar to display the options. Choose Copy to place the specified information on the Windows clipboard, leaving the source application unchanged.

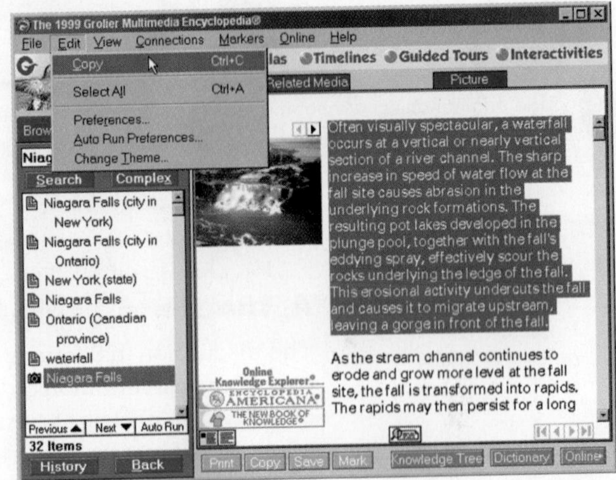

3. *Switch to the destination application and place the graphics cursor at the desired insertion point.*

4. *Paste the marked information.* Choose Edit in the destination application's (Word) menu bar to display the applicable options. Choose the Paste option to copy the contents of the clipboard to the cursor position in the destination application.

5. *Mark the information.* Use the cursor to highlight the information to be copied in the source application (*1999 Grolier Multimedia Encyclopedia*).

6. *Copy the marked information to the clipboard.*

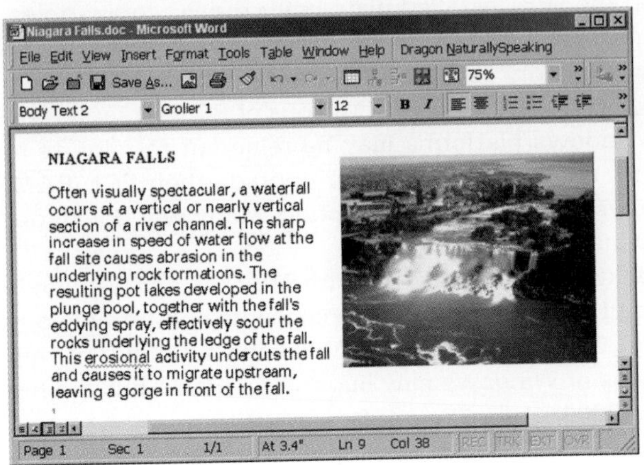

7. *Switch to the destination application and place the graphics cursor at the desired insertion point.*

8. *Paste the marked information.*

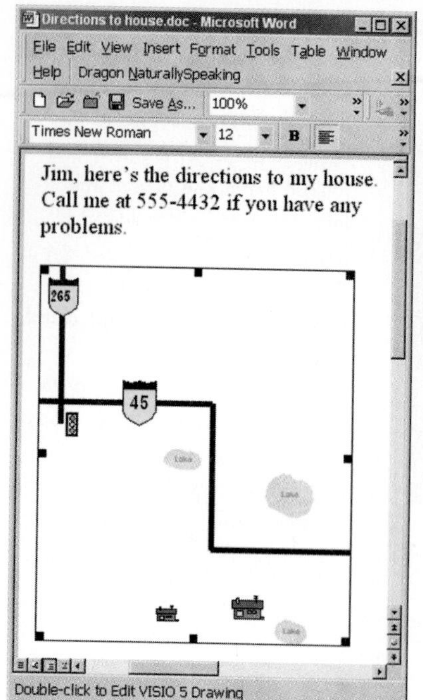

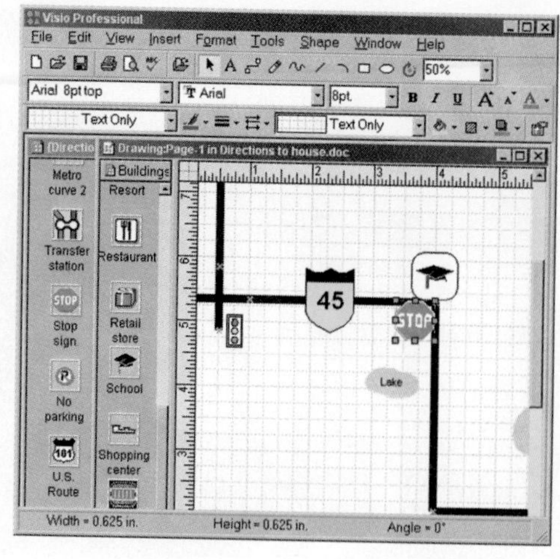

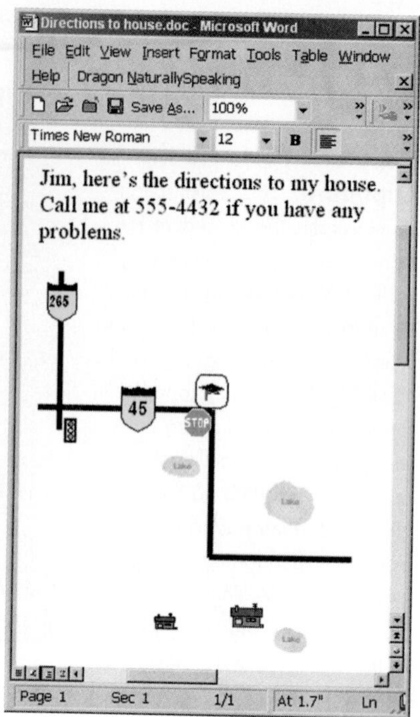

Object Linking An image is linked to a Word document (left) to create a compound document. The original object did not include the school image or the stop sign image. The image was modified in Visio Professional (middle), and the linked object was updated automatically in Word (right).

A Thousand Look-Alikes

The discussion in Sections 8.3 and 8.4 is intended to introduce you to fundamental concepts and terminology associated with the Windows environment. Thousands of software packages written specifically for the Windows environment have adopted these same concepts and terminology and are designed to take advantage of Windows capabilities. Once you understand the Windows environment, you will feel comfortable with the user interfaces of all software written for this environment.

Migrating to Windows 2000

All Microsoft upgrade strategies lead to Windows 2000, both for home and LAN-based business PCs. However, more than seven years transpired before the original Microsoft Windows passed the 50% installed plateau for the PC compatibles. After seven years on the market, 50% of the users still preferred MS-DOS, the original PC operating system. If history repeats itself, acceptance of Windows 2000 may be slow in coming for Windows 9x users. Millions of PC users who feel comfortable with the earlier Windows platforms may be reluctant to migrate to Windows 2000. Some users with older PCs must either upgrade their PCs, RAM, and/or hard disk before Windows 2000 becomes an option. Many will opt to get a new PC with Windows 2000 installed.

Windows 2000 has full backward compatibility with MS-DOS and Windows programs. Windows 9x users will find that most of the concepts and terminology they learned apply to Windows 2000 as well. They will also find a number of very enticing features. Earlier versions of Windows may linger for a while, but the migration has begun to Windows 2000.

Self-Check

8-4.1 You must always paste to the source application. (T/F)

8-4.2 In OLE, the object originates in a server application. (T/F)

8-4.3 Object linking doesn't actually place the object into the destination document. (T/F)

8-4.4 In the Windows environment, an intermediate holding area for information is the: (a) clipboard, (b) chalkboard, (c) bulletin board, or (d) white board?

8-4.5 What kind of document contains one or more objects from other applications: (a) hyperlinked, (b) composite, (c) complex, or (d) compound?

8-4.6 All Microsoft upgrade strategies lead to: (a) Windows CE, (b) Windows 98, (c) Windows 2000, or (d) Windows Millennium?

8.5 INTERACTING WITH THE PC AND ITS SOFTWARE

Serendipitous Surfing: Travel

The thesaurus lists these synonyms for the word *interact: blend, associate, hobnob, mingle, combine, mix, stir,* and *socialize.* To some extent we do all of these, even socialize, when we interact with PCs and their software. Most of us will interact directly with a personal computer or a workstation that may or may not be linked to a network or the Internet. To interact effectively with a computer and its software, you need to be knowledgeable in four areas.

1. General software concepts
2. The operation and use of the hardware over which you have control
3. The function and use of the computer's operating system and/or its graphical user interface (GUI), both of which provide a link between you, the computer system, and the various applications programs
4. The specific applications programs you are using

The first three areas are *prerequisites* to the fourth. That is, you will need a working knowledge of software concepts, hardware, and the operating system and/or a GUI before you can make effective use of Quicken 99 (personal finance), PowerPoint 2000 (presentation graphics), Excel 2000 (database), or any of the thousands of software packages on the market today.

Computer Operation: Getting Started

Who operates computers? Probably you do. End users, especially those of PCs and workstations, routinely do everything from unpacking boxes of hardware to installing and using the software.

Installing Hardware and Software

When you purchase a computer system, typically you will receive several boxes containing the various components of the system. Unless it is a portable computer, your system will come in several pieces: a keyboard, a mouse, a monitor, a printer, and a processor unit that houses the magnetic disk drives. Normally you can complete the installation of the hardware simply by linking the pieces of the system with the various types of cables. A computer, however, does nothing without software.

PCs are sold with the operating system and, perhaps, a few applications already installed (stored on the hard disk and ready to run). If not, you must install the software. Even if your new system includes some software, you will likely install other software as well. **Software installation** involves copying the program and data files from the vendor-supplied master disks or CD-ROMs to the permanently installed hard disk. Software installation is a two-step process for the operating system and all applications software packages.

TAILORING PCs TO THE NEEDS OF MOBILE WORKERS

Wearable PCs Thousands of mobile workers could benefit from using a computer if only the computer were lighter, freed their hands, and didn't tether them to a desk or a power outlet. Now a new generation of wearable computers promises to extend the trend begun by laptop, notebook, and pen-based computers.

Wearable computers, long a staple of science fiction, are here. In an effort to create truly personal computers that meld a computer and its user, designers have divided the wearable PC's components into cable-connected modules that fit into headsets, drape across shoulders, hang around the neck, and fasten around the waist, forearm, or wrist. Lightweight (two pounds or less), the components are covered in soft plastic and strapped on with Velcro.

Manufacturers of these wearable PCs combine existing or emerging technologies to create customized PCs for specific types of workers. The TLC (Tender Loving Care) PC for paramedics is a good example. At an accident scene, speech-recognition software lets the paramedic dictate symptoms and vital signs into a slender microphone hanging from a headset. The computer, draped across the medic's shoulders like a shawl, compares this data to a CD-ROM medical directory in the shoulder unit. The computer then projects possible diagnoses and suggested treatments onto the headset's miniature display. The TLC unit improves upon the two-way radio medics now use to communicate with emergency-room doctors. Instead of describing symptoms over a two-way radio, medics could use a trackball-operated video camera and body sensor strapped to their palm to *show* doctors the patients' condition. The video and additional data would be beamed to the doctors by a satellite link. Headphones would let the medics get feedback and additional advice from the waiting doctors.

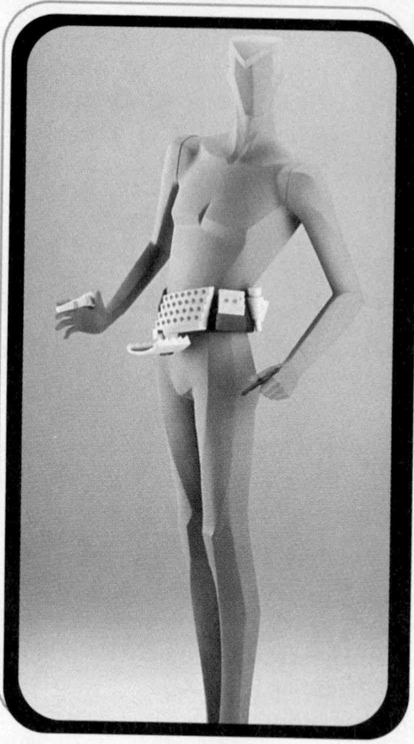

The Future of PCs?
At NEC a handful of engineers and designers are creating what they believe to be the future of PCs—wearable PCs. Their objective is to blend the machine with the body. Courtesy NEC Corporation, Tokyo, Japan

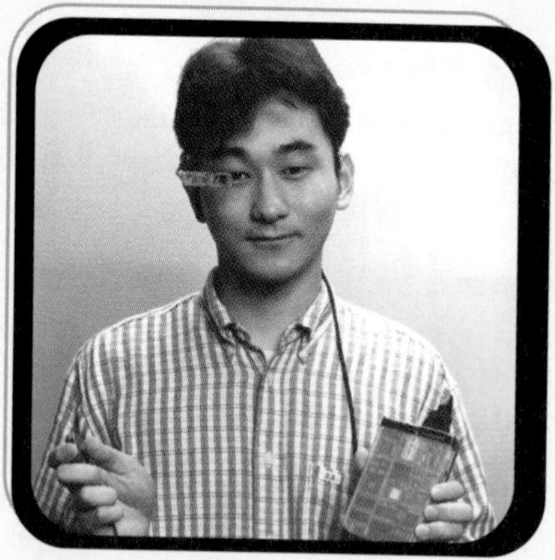

Wearable PC
IBM's 10.5-ounce Wearable PC fits in your pocket and is completely portable, yet offers enough power to run the Windows operating system and IBM's Via Voice speech-recognition software. This hands-free computer's headset provides audio output and a miniature eye-level display for viewing.
Courtesy of International Business Machines Corporation

The Electronic Fashion Statement Certainly the trend is toward increasingly smaller PCs. Some say that an emerging trend is toward increasingly wearable PCs. If this trend holds, it's inevitable that vendors will be as concerned with fashion as they are with functionality. Power and size have always been critical elements of PCs, but now design is of growing importance. We may be entering an era of fashion wars where we may have to upgrade our PC to keep up with the latest fashion fad! With everyone drawing from essentially the same pool of microprocessors, is it possible that technical innovation may someday take a back seat to fashion?

Body Nets Perhaps the most intriguing concept in wearable computers is the Body Net. The Body Net will be a network of wearable computers strategically located over the body. For example, the shoe-based computer might detect your location, then transmit appropriate location-specific information for viewing on your eyeglasses computer. Perhaps by the twenty-first century, the PC will become as much an essential part of one's wardrobe as an indispensable business tool.

Software Installation Step 1: Install or Set Up Software Most new commercial software is distributed on *CD-ROM* (some of the smaller programs are available on 3.5-inch diskettes). This normally straightforward installation process can take up to an hour depending on the complexity of the software, the distribution media, and the speed of the PC. Most installations, however, last only a few minutes. Installing programs from CD-ROM is a relatively standard and straightforward procedure.

- *Insert the CD-ROM.* If installing within Windows 9x/2000, enter D:setup or D:install (where *D* is the letter of the CD-ROM drive) at the Run command line (click on the Start button, then select Run). Typically, the software is installed on hard-disk Drive C unless you indicate otherwise.
- *Respond to install inquiries.* An *installation wizard* (see Figure 8.17) leads you through the installation process. Depending on the software, you may be asked to respond to several questions, including whether or not you are willing to accept the software's license agreement.

Many CD-ROM–based applications, especially games, are designed to be run entirely, or at least in part, from the CD-ROM. However, because CD-ROM is relatively slow, critical programs are loaded to the hard disk during installation to speed up the running of the overall software package. Most business programs, such as word processing, presentation graphics, and so on, are copied in their entirety to hard disk.

Software Installation Step 2: Set System Information Applications software is installed to accommodate the "typical" PC. You may need to revise some of the standard settings to better fit your PC's specific configuration. You may be prompted to make some of these changes automatically during software installation. Also, you may wish to customize an application to better meet your processing needs. If so, you will probably need to revise certain **default options** (standard settings), such as location of data files, display colors, and so on.

HELP!

Many programs come with an online tutorial that demonstrates the use of the software's common features (see Figure 8.17). These tutorials are helpful, but when you have specific questions, help is never farther away than your keyboard.

Installation Wizards and Application Tutorials The installation wizard leads you through the installation process (DeLorme Street Atlas 6.0 in the example), prompting you for information along the way. Street Atlas and other modern programs have informative tutorials that introduce you to the software's features.

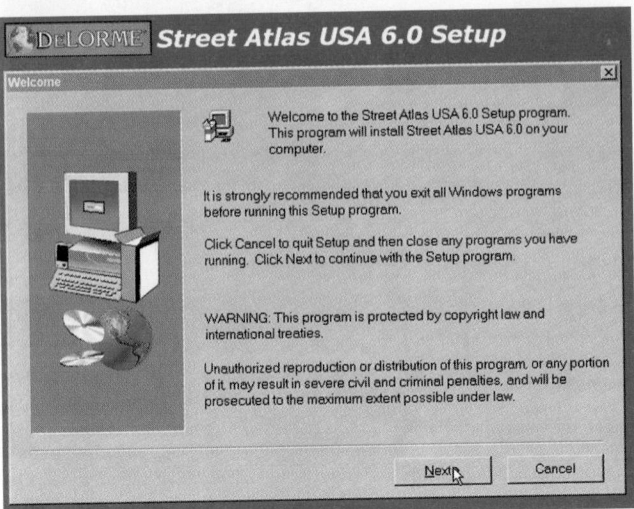

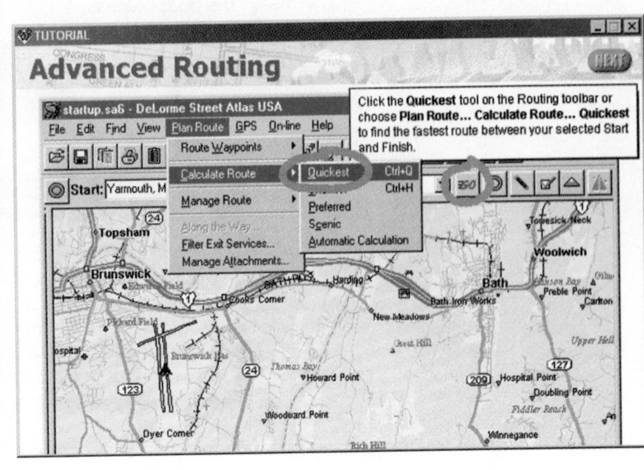

A handy feature available on nearly all modern software packages is the **help command.** When you find yourself in need of a more detailed explanation or instructions on how to proceed, tap the *Help* key, often assigned to Function Key 1 (F1), or choose *Help* from the main menu. The resulting explanation relates to what you were doing when you entered the command because help is usually context-sensitive. When you are finished reading the help information, the system returns you to your work at the same point you left it.

Power Up/Shut Down

Computers are similar to copy machines, toasters, and other electrical devices—you must turn them on by applying electrical power. The power-on procedure on almost any computer is straightforward—flip the on/off switch on the processor unit to *on.* It is good practice to turn on needed input/output devices before turning on the processor.

When you **power up** you also **boot** the system. The booting procedure is so named because the computer "pulls itself up by its own bootstraps." When you boot the system, a ROM (read-only memory) program performs a **system check,** readies the computer for processing, and loads the operating system to RAM (see Figure 8.18). Although the boot procedure officially ends with the display of the **system prompt** (for example, C:\> for MS-DOS) or the Windows 9x/2000 desktop, the operating system may execute predefined user instructions, such as running an antivirus program.

Unlike electrical appliances, computers are not simply turned off when you're done using them. You must **shut down** your computer in an orderly manner. Shutting down involves a normal exit from all active applications programs before shutting off the power. All applications programs have an **exit routine.** *Exit routines perform some administrative processing that, if bypassed, can result in loss of user data and problems during subsequent sessions.*

The Boot Procedure

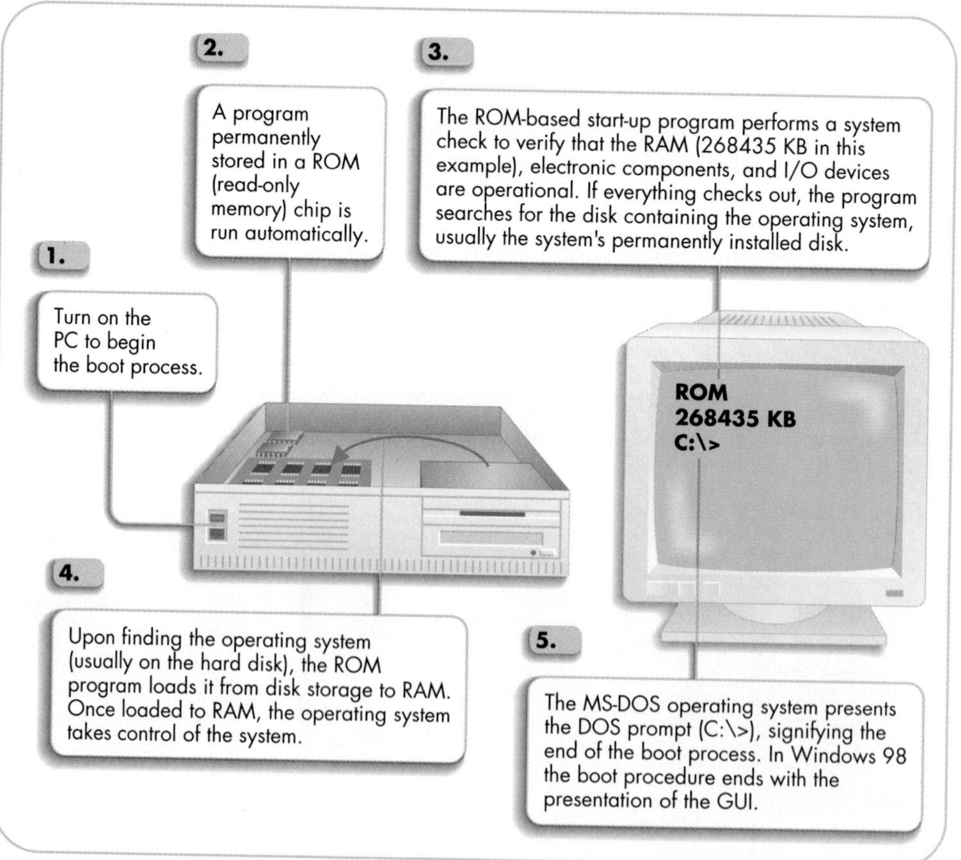

1.
Turn on the PC to begin the boot process.
2.
A program permanently stored in a ROM (read-only memory) chip is run automatically.
3.
The ROM-based start-up program performs a system check to verify that the RAM (268435 KB in this example), electronic components, and I/O devices are operational. If everything checks out, the program searches for the disk containing the operating system, usually the system's permanently installed disk.
ROM
268435 KB
C:\>
4.
Upon finding the operating system (usually on the hard disk), the ROM program loads it from disk storage to RAM. Once loaded to RAM, the operating system takes control of the system.
5.
The MS-DOS operating system presents the DOS prompt (C:\>), signifying the end of the boot process. In Windows 98 the boot procedure ends with the presentation of the GUI.

Entering Commands and Data: Computers Can Be Very Picky

Computers do *exactly* what you tell them to do—no more, no less. If you tell a computer to add the numbers in the "Sales" column in a spreadsheet, then that is what it does. The computer knows only what you tell it, not that you have given it an erroneous command to find the lowest sales figure rather than the total. All computers can do is interpret and do what you tell them to do.

Generally, if you make a mistake, the worst that can happen is that you get an error message or inaccurate results. Fortunately, most software packages have built-in safeguards that ask for confirmation before executing a command that might significantly alter or erase your work.

SECTION SELF-CHECK

Self-Check

8-5.1 Help commands can be context-sensitive. (T/F)

8-5.2 Most new commercial software is distributed on 3.5-inch diskettes. (T/F)

8-5.3 Windows 9x/2000 discourages the use of exit routines when leaving a Windows application. (T/F)

8-5.4 All games are designed to be run entirely from the CD-ROM with no programs installed on the hard drive. (T/F)

8-5.5 A computer user must do what to the system to load the operating system to RAM: (a) kick it, (b) boot it, (c) punt it, or (d) dribble it?

8-5.6 At the end of the MS–DOS boot procedure, what is displayed to signal the user that the system is ready to accept a user command: (a) system prompt, (b) decoy item, (c) semicolon, or (d) OK button?

8-5.7 The standard settings for an application or feature are its: (a) preference options, (b) default options, (c) user-defined options, or (d) baseline options?

SUMMARY AND KEY TERMS

8.1 The operating system: Directing the action

The operating system is the nucleus of all software activity. One of the operating system programs, called the **kernel** (252), loads other operating system and applications programs to RAM as they are needed.

All operating systems are designed with the same basic objectives in mind. Perhaps the most important objectives are to facilitate communication between the computer system and the people who run it and to optimize the use of computer system resources.

Operating systems get the most from their processors through **multitasking** (254), the concurrent execution of more than one program at a time. High-priority programs run in the **foreground** (254) part of RAM and the rest run in the **background** (254).

Through the 1980s, the most popular microcomputer operating system, **MS-DOS** (254), was strictly *text-based, command-driven* software that required strict adherence to command **syntax** (254). The trend now is toward GUIs that use graphical **icons** (255). All modern operating systems have adopted the GUI concept.

8.2 Platforms: Homes for software

MS-DOS and/or Windows was the platform of choice for PC compatibles through 1990. The original Microsoft Windows, with its GUI, was made obsolete with the introduction of Windows 95. A platform defines a standard for which software packages are developed. The modern PC/Windows platforms include PC-compatible computers with Windows 95, Windows 98, Windows 2000, Windows NT, and **Windows CE** (257) (for handheld and pocket PCs). These PC/Windows platforms offer many advantages, including **plug-and-play** (256) capability and an ability to run 32-bit programs. The Windows 95 and Windows 98 operating systems are designed to bridge the technology gap between the original Windows and Windows NT, now called Windows 2000. Windows 2000 is a powerful client/server operating system for client/server computing. Windows 2000 has two components: **Windows 2000 Professional** (257) (for the client side) and **Windows 2000 Server** (257) (for the server side). The two work together to enable client/server computing.

The Apple family of microcomputers and **Mac OS** (257) define another major platform.

Those companies that do not standardize on a platform must work to achieve **interoperability** (258), which refers to the ability to run software and exchange information in a **multiplatform environment** (258). Enabling technologies that allow communication and the sharing of resources between different platforms are called **cross-platform technologies** (258).

UNIX (257) and **Linux** (257) define other PC platforms.

8.3 Windows concepts and terminology

Windows 95, Windows 98, Windows NT, and *Windows 2000* dominate the PC-compatible environment. The Windows 9x/2000 *Help* capabilities include step-by-step tutorials that lead you through numerous common procedures.

Any software application that does not adhere to the Microsoft Windows standard is a **non-Windows application** (260). Programs that adhere to Windows conventions are **Windows applications** (260).

The latest **drivers** (262), the software that enables interaction between the operating system and the peripheral devices, can be downloaded via Windows Update.

The Windows 9x/2000 graphical user interfaces rely on **cursor control devices (CCDs)** (260), such as a mouse. The **shortcut key** (260) and the **hotkey** (260) help speed up interaction on the keyboard.

The Windows 95 GUI looks very much like that of Windows 98/2000. However, Windows 98/2000 users can manage their files and move between applications in the same intuitive way they browse the Internet. A Maintenance **Wizard** (261) monitors your system to improve performance and reliability. The Internet Explorer interface is part of Windows 98/2000. Windows 98/2000 provides support for recent hardware standards like Universal Serial Bus (USB) and enables PCs to receive **enhanced television** (262).

The screen upon which icons, windows, and so on are displayed is known as the **desktop** (263). Typically, a Windows session begins with the **Start button** (263) in the **taskbar** (263). An active application window can be minimized to a button on the taskbar. You may open a Windows **folder** (263), which contains a logical grouping of related files and subordinated folders, to obtain a work file.

A rectangular **application window** (264) contains an **open application** (264) (a running application). Several applications can be open, but there is only one **active window** (264) at any given time.

Everything that relates to the application noted in the title bar is displayed in the **workspace** (264). Several **document windows** (264) can be displayed in the parent application window's workspace.

The horizontal **title bar** (265) at the top of each window has these elements: application icon, window title, minimize button, maximize/restore button, close button, and the title area.

When you select an item from the menu bar, a subordinate **pull-down menu** (265) is "pulled down." Use the left/right or up/down arrow keys, to enter the **mnemonic** (266), or use the mouse to position the mouse cursor at the desired option. Further selection may result in a **pop-out menu** (265) or a pop-up **dialog box** (266). The context-sensitive **pop-up menu** (266) is displayed when you right click the mouse. The **floating menu** (266) "floats" over the display.

Toolbars (266), containing rectangular graphics, give you ready access to frequently used menu items. The **ruler bar** (266) shows the document window's content relative to the printed page.

The **Windows Explorer** (267), which can include commonly used icons such as **application icons** (267), **shortcut icons** (267), **document icons** (268), and **disk drive icons** (268), performs file management tasks such as creating folders, copying files, moving files, deleting files, and other folder/file–related tasks.

The Windows environment lets you view multiple applications that can be sized, shrunk, and arranged by the user within the workspace. Or, they can be arranged as **cascading windows** (268) or **tiled windows** (268).

The active window is always highlighted in the **foreground** (269). Other open windows are in the **background** (269).

8.4 Sharing information among Windows applications

The most common method of sharing information among applications is to use the Windows **clipboard** (270) and the *Edit* option in the menu bar. The **source application** (270) and **destination application** (270) for a copy or move operation can be one and the same or they can be entirely different applications.

Applications can be linked through **object linking** (270) **and embedding** (270) or **OLE** (270). An **object** (270) is the result of any Windows application. We can create **compound documents** (270) that contain one or more objects from other applications. The object originates in a **server application** (270) and is linked to a destination document of a **client application** (270).

OLE lets you *link* or *embed* information. When you link information, the link between source and destination documents is dynamic. When you embed information, you insert the actual object, not just a pointer.

All Microsoft upgrade strategies lead to Windows 2000, both for home and LAN-based business PCs.

8.5 Interacting with the PC and its software

The effective user will understand general computer software concepts, how to operate and use the hardware, the operating system and/or a graphical user interface (GUI), and one or more applications programs.

When you purchase a computer system, you receive several components. Hardware installation involves linking the pieces of the system with the various types of cables. **Software installation** (273) involves copying the program and data files from the vendor-supplied CD-ROM (or diskettes) to the permanently installed hard disk. Software installation is a two-step process for the operating system and all applications software packages: Copy files to the permanently installed hard disk; and set system information, revising **default options** (275) (standard settings) as needed. Use the **help command** (276), which is usually context-sensitive, when you need assistance.

When you **power up** (276) a computer, you **boot** (276) the system. First, a program in read-only memory (ROM) initializes the system and runs a **system check** (276). Next, the operating system is loaded to random-access memory (RAM), takes control of the system, and presents the user with a **system prompt** (276) or a GUI screen full of options. RAM provides temporary storage of data and programs during processing.

You must **shut down** (276) your computer in an orderly manner using the program's **exit routine** (276).

DISCUSSION AND PROBLEM SOLVING

8.1 **a.** Some people contend that the traditional text-based, command-driven operating system interface has some advantages over the modern graphical user interface. Speculate on what these advantages might be.

b. Multitasking allows PC users to run several programs at a time. Describe a PC session in which you would have at least two applications running at the same time.

8.2 **a.** Why is the selection of a platform such an important decision to an organization?

b. A popular platform for the handheld and pocket PCs is Windows CE. Why don't these devices use Windows 98/2000 like other personal computers?

8.3 **a.** Describe the Windows desktop. Where would you put the taskbar—at the top, at the bottom, or on one of the sides? What else would you do to personalize your desktop?

b. List and briefly describe four elements of the Windows application window.

c. In the Windows 98/2000 environment, how is an item, such as an application program or a menu option, selected with a mouse? How is the item opened?

d. Describe the relationship between a Windows menu bar, a pop-out menu, and a menu item followed by an ellipsis (. . .).

e. There are two camps when it comes to learning a software package. Some prefer to read the instructions carefully before attempting to create a document. Others prefer to begin using the software, tapping context-sensitive help as needed. In which camp would you feel most comfortable? Why?

8.4 **a.** Describe three situations in which you might use the clipboard to *copy* or *move* information within or between applications.

b. Briefly describe at least one advantage gained by linking information via OLE. Give an example for which object linking might be appropriate.

c. Some organizations may delay their migration from an earlier version of Windows to Windows 2000 for several years. What do they lose and what do they gain by delaying this decision?

8.5 **a.** Software vendors list minimum system requirements (processor, RAM, etc.) to run their software. Frequently, however, a minimal PC may not permit any real user interaction with the software (too slow, poor graphics, and so on). Why don't vendors publish more realistic system requirements for their software?

b. You can end a personal computing session by simply turning off the power. However, this approach bypasses exit routines if you have open software. In the long run, exiting "gracefully" is recommended. Why?

PC BUYER'S GUIDE

Millions of people like you are continuously involved in the process of buying a PC, PC peripherals, and PC software. They also subscribe to information service providers (for Net connections) and/or commercial information services, plus they subscribe to related print magazines and/or electronic magazines on the Net or on CD-ROM. During the last few years, PC-related expenses have emerged as the third most expensive item for the typical family—right behind homes and automobiles. The process is always an adventure, whether you're a first-time buyer or you're buying a replacement system. What you read in the next few pages will help you enjoy your adventure and spend your money wisely.

The emphasis in this PC Buyer's Guide is on the actual buying process. Hardware and software concepts are discussed in detail in other sections of the book.

A PC Is a Great Gift

Generally, a new PC is ready to run right out of the box. Simply connect the cords, plug it in, and turn it on. Photo courtesy of Intel Corporation

STEPS IN BUYING PC HARDWARE, SOFTWARE, AND SERVICES

Buying a PC can be a harrowing experience, or it can be a thrilling and fulfilling one. It depends on your approach. If you approach the purchase of a PC haphazardly, expect the former. If you go about the acquisition methodically and with purpose, expect the latter. Follow this 11-step procedure to get the biggest bang for your buck.

Step 1: Achieve Information Technology Competency

You don't buy an automobile before you learn how to drive, and you really shouldn't buy a PC without a good understanding of its capabilities and how you intend to use it. Every college offers courses leading to information technology competency.

- In effect, this book is a comprehensive buyer's guide. The informed buyer will understand its content.

Step 2: Decide How Much You Are Willing to Spend

Assess your circumstances and decide how much you are willing to commit to the purchase of a PC system. Get as much quality as your pocketbook will allow. If you don't and you are a typical user, you will end up replacing or upgrading it sooner than you think. You can pay now or pay later. If you must buy a smaller system, make sure it is easily upgradable to the next level.

- Generally, purchase the best system you can afford.

Step 3: Determine Your Information and Computing Needs

Your goal is to figure out where you want to go by answering this question: "How can I use a PC to simplify my work, increase my pleasure, or both?"

For most people, this means deciding which types of software packages they want to use. The choices here truly are vast, including office suites (word processing, spreadsheet, database, presentation, and so on), data communications, personal finance, graphics, edutainment, games, and much more. This is an important decision because software needs frequently determine hardware needs.

- If you don't know where you are going, any road will get you there.

Step 4: Assess the Availability and Quality of Software and Information Services

Determine what software, information service providers (ISPs), and commercial information services, such as AOL, are available to meet your needs. Good sources of this type of information include general computer periodicals (*PC Magazine, Byte,* and *MacWorld,* to name a few), salespeople at computer stores, your computer/software instructor, members of the local PC club, your colleagues at work, and knowledgeable acquaintances. If you have access to the Internet and/or an online information service, you can request information from vendors and tap into the thoughts of those who have used the software or information service. Thousands of software packages are available commercially, and they vary greatly in capability and price.

- Considering the amount of time you might spend using PC software, any extra time you devote to evaluating the software will pay dividends in the future.

Step 5: Choose a Platform

At this point in the PC decision process you will need to decide on a platform. Platforms are important because software is written to run under a particular platform. The various platforms are discussed in detail in Chapter 8, "The Windows Environment." Essentially, for full-function PCs, you have the "Wintel" options with PC compatibles running Windows 9x/NT/2000 or the Apple Computer Company alternatives (including the iMac). Pocket PCs or handheld organizers represent other platforms. Of course, you will need to select a platform that supports your software and information needs (Step 4).

- When making the platform decision, consider compatibility with the other PCs in your life: your existing PC (if you have one), the one at work/home, and/or the one in your college lab.

The iMac Fac

In its first year, the Apple iMac emerged as a major platform. At the Apple "iMac Fac" (iMac Factory), iMac computers are "burned in" for several days before shipment. This lowers infant mortality rates so that you can be assured that your new computer will work when you plug it in. Courtesy of Apple Computer, Inc.

Step 6: Identify the Desired Type of PC

PCs come in many flavors. You can choose from the conventional members of the PC family: pocket PCs, notebook PCs, desktop PCs, and tower PCs. Or, you can select one from the extended PC family: slate PCs (pen-based PCs), PDAs, and NCs (network computers). All are discussed in Chapter 1, "Information Technology in Perspective."

- Choose the PC that fits your lifestyle, your pocketbook, and your application needs.

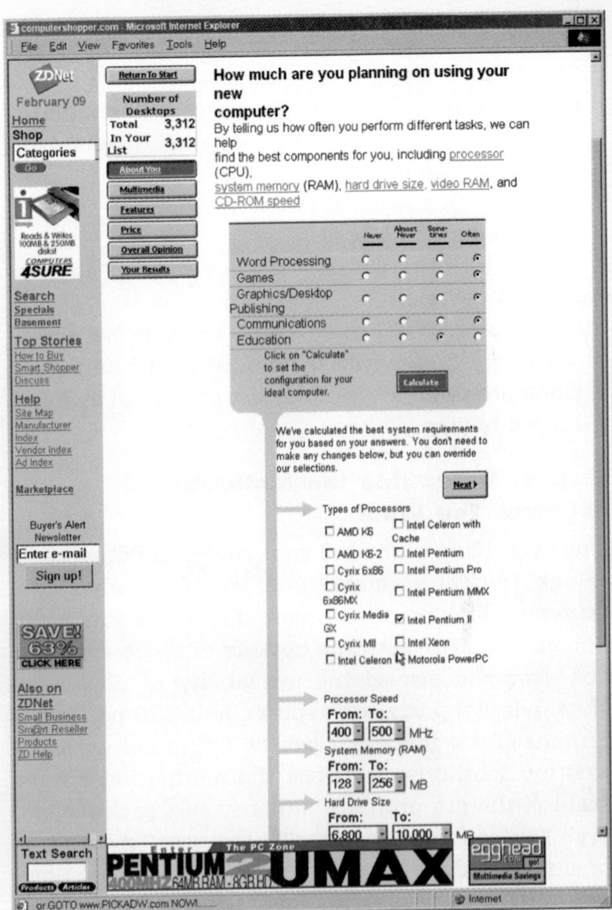

The Online Buyer's Guide

Several Internet sites, including the Computer Shopper, offer online buyer's guides that help you find the right PC. You select the features you want by selecting options from drop-down boxes or clicking on radio buttons (usage profile, processor type, price range, RAM, and so on). The Computer Shopper buyer's guide searches its PC database (3312 PCs in the example), then lists only those systems that meet your requirements.

Step 7: Identify One or More PC Systems for Further Examination

If your software needs are typical, you will have a number of PC alternatives available to you within a given platform. Identify one or more that meet criteria established in the first six steps.

Virtually all new desktop and tower PCs will be configured to handle the system requirements for modern software packages, including multimedia and data communication applications. Nevertheless, you should check each alternative against these *minimum hardware requirements for PC compatibles.*

- 450 MHz Pentium II–level processor (500 Pentium III is desirable)
- 128 MB RAM (256 MB or greater is desirable)

- Hard-disk drive (8 GB for portable PCs and 16 GB for others)
- CD-ROM drive (32-speed or faster is desirable)
- Super VGA monitor (1024 by 768 pixels with 16 million colors)
- Sound card, speakers, and a microphone
- Fax modem (56 k bps)
- Mouse (or other point-and-draw device) and enhanced keyboard

Virtually all new PC compatibles are sold with Windows 98 or Windows 2000 installed on the hard disk.

- Compare the features and cost of several systems before buying.

Step 8: Determine the Motherboard Features You Want

Once you have narrowed your choice of PC systems to one, two, or perhaps three, you are ready to determine which processor-related features you want. Become familiar with the options of these systems. For example, assess the availability of expansion slots, parallel ports, serial ports, and USB ports. Determine if the processor can be upgraded with the existing motherboard. Does the motherboard have state-of-the-art graphics support and cache memory? You can go with a basic processor (see Step 7) or, if your budget allows, you can select a more powerful processor and add a few "bells and whistles."

- Expect to pay for each increase in convenience, quality, and speed.

Step 9: Determine the Peripheral Devices You Want

Peripheral devices come in a wide variety of speeds, capacities, and qualities. The peripherals you select depend on your specific needs, volume of usage, and the amount of money you are willing to spend. If you plan on doing a lot of graphics work, you might wish to consider getting a color image scanner. You might want to pay a little more to get a 22 GB hard disk. Over the past few years the DVD drive and the CD-RW drive have been listed as optional storage devices, but as the prices continue to drop, they are being configured with mainline PCs. A large monitor (17 inches or bigger) can relieve eyestrain. You can pay as little as $100 or as much as $7000 for a printer. This choice depends on the anticipated volume of hard-copy output, the quality of the output, and whether you need color output. See Chapter 4, "Storing and Retrieving Information," and Chapter 5, "Information Input and Output," for detailed information on peripheral devices.

- A good mix of peripheral devices can really spice up your computing experience.

Step 10: "Test Drive" Several Alternatives

Once you have selected several software and hardware alternatives, spend enough time with them to gain some familiarity. Do you prefer one keyboard over another? Is the word processing system compatible with the one used at the office? Is one help facility easier to understand than another?

Many software packages are distributed with an interactive tutorial (usually on the program CD-ROM). When you run the tutorial, an instructional program interactively "walks you through" the features and use of the software. It is a good idea to work through the tutorial to get a feeling for the product's features and ease of use.

Frequently, software is bundled with a PC, thus confusing the issue. You might like the software bundled with your second choice PC. If this is the case, don't hesitate to ask the vendor about the possibility of bundling the software you want with the PC you want.

Salespeople at most retail stores are happy to give you a "test drive," so just ask. Use these sessions to answer any questions you might have about the hardware or software.

- Kick the tires and take both the hardware and software for a spin around the block.

Step 11: Select and Buy Your System

Apply your criteria, select, and then buy your hardware and software. Keep in mind that PCs with similar functionality may differ as much as 40% in price.

- Don't let a fancy talker or a flashy ad campaign distract you from what should be your primary considerations—functionality and price.

FACTORS TO CONSIDER WHEN BUYING A PC

Future computing needs What will your personal computing needs be in the future? Make sure the system you select can grow with your needs. For example, the difference between a 16 GB and a 22 GB hard disk may be several hundred dollars. However, if you estimate your disk-storage needs to be in excess of 16 GB within a year or so, you may be better off in the long run buying the 22 GB disk.

Who will use the system? Plan not only for yourself but also for others in your home or office who will use the system. Get their input and consider their needs along with yours. For example, if you're purchasing for a home with teenagers, you might want to consider a joystick, game pad, or, perhaps, bigger speakers.

Service Computing hardware is very reliable. Even so, the possibility exists that one or several of the components eventually will fail and have to be repaired. Before buying a PC, ask the retailer, whether local or on the Internet, to tell you exactly what you must do to get your system repaired.

Most retailers or vendors will offer a variety of maintenance contracts from same-day, on-site repairs that cover all parts and service to a carry-in service that does not include parts. Most home users treat their PCs like their televisions and cars: When the warranty runs out, they pay for repairs as they are needed. Usually this strategy will prove the least expensive. Business users are sometimes willing to pay extra for the convenience of an on-site maintenance contract.

Service extends beyond hardware maintenance. Service is also an organization's willingness to respond to your inquiries before *and* after the sale. For example, some retailers and vendors offer classes in the use of the hardware and software they sell.

Hardware and Software Packaging

Anymore, it's not unusual to purchase software, such as IBM's ViaVoice speech recognition software (shown here), and get hardware, too. In this case you get a high-quality headset with a directional microphone that picks up the user's voice, but not the ever-present noises around the office and home.

Courtesy of International Business Machines Corporation. Unauthorized use not permitted.

Fully Configured PC

This telecommuter has a tower PC with all the trimmings, including an all-in-one HP LaserJet printer, fax, copier, and scanner. Multifunction printers are ideal for the home or small offices where volume for any single function is low.

Photo courtesy of Hewlett-Packard Company

Most hardware and software vendors offer a *technical support hot line.* The extent of the hot-line service varies considerably. Some companies provide their licensed users with a toll-free 24-hour hot line—free of charge for as long as they own the product. At the other end of the spectrum, companies charge their users as much as $50 an hour for talking with their technical support personnel. Typically, companies will provide hot-line service for a limited period of time (six months or a year), then charge after that. Some vendors offer other tech support options including a free Web site (with online tech support, answers to frequently asked questions, and solutions to common problems) and fax support (automated fax-back of documentation and solutions to common problems).

Hardware obsolescence In 2000 you can buy a PC that costs half as much and offers a 15000% improvement in performance over a 1990 PC. If you decide to wait until the price goes down a little more, you may never purchase a computer. If you wait another six months, you probably will be able to get a more powerful PC for less money, but what about the lost opportunities?

There is also a danger in purchasing a PC that is near the end of its life cycle. If you are planning on using a PC frequently at school, home, or work, focus your search on PCs with state-of-the-art technology. You may get a substantial discount on a PC with dated technology, but will it run next year's software?

Software obsolescence Software can become obsolete as well. Software vendors are continually improving their software packages. Make sure you are buying the most recent release of a particular software package. A software package that offers online updates is a plus.

Product documentation (internal and external) PC products are consumer items and are distributed with printed or electronic user manuals, just like automobiles and VCRs. In most cases, the person who purchases the product installs it and uses it. To install it and use it, you will need effective product documentation. Inevitably you will spend many hours with the product's documentation. Make sure that it is good.

Other costs The cost of the actual PC system is the major expense, but there are many incidental expenses that can mount up and influence your selection of a PC. If you have a spending limit, consider the estimated incidental costs shown in the table. The cost ranges listed are for a first-time user.

WHERE TO BUY

PC Retailers

Fifteen years ago PCs were considered high-tech specialty items and were sold almost exclusively through PC retail outlets. Today, PCs and PC software have emerged as popular consumer items. PCs and associated hardware and software can be purchased at thousands of convenient locations.

Computer retailers Several national retail chains and many regional retail chains specialize in the sale of PC hardware and/or software. Most market and service a variety of small computer systems. There are also thousands of computer stores, some that make their own line of computers, that are not affiliated with a national or regional chain.

Other retail stores PCs and PC software are sold in the computer/electronics departments of most department stores and discount warehouse stores. Also, many office supply stores, college bookstores, audio/video stores, and other specialty retailers sell computers and computer products.

	ONE-TIME COST	ANNUAL COST
Software	\$100–\$1500	\$100–\$500
Cables	\$0–\$50	
Supplies (printer cartridges, paper, diskettes, Zip disks, SuperDisks, CD-RW blanks, tape cartridges, and so on)	\$100–\$200	\$100–\$500
Subscriptions (information services, Internet service providers, magazines)		\$250–\$1000 (includes basic Internet service)
Telephone (long distance)		\$0–\$300
Furniture and Accessories	\$30–\$500	\$50–\$150
Maintenance		\$0–\$500
Insurance		\$0–\$200
TOTAL ESTIMATED INCIDENTAL EXPENSES	\$230–\$2250	\$500–\$3150

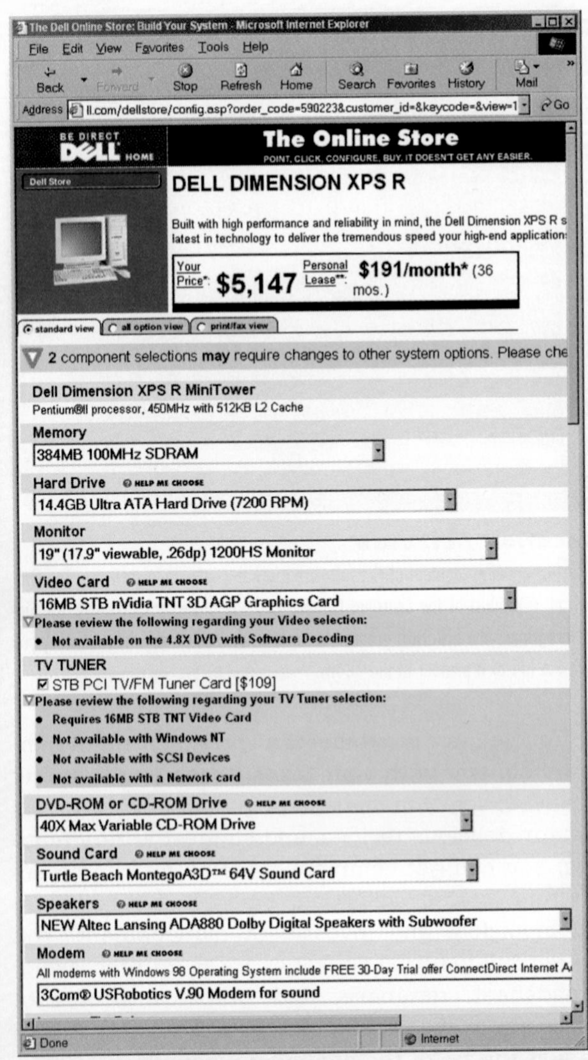

The Online Store

Dell Computer Corporation is a direct marketer with a Web site that provides detailed information about any available system. The customer can go to the Dell Online Store to customize and purchase a system entirely online. In this example, the customer configured a high-end system with lots of extras, including a scanner, a color printer, and a CD-RW drive.

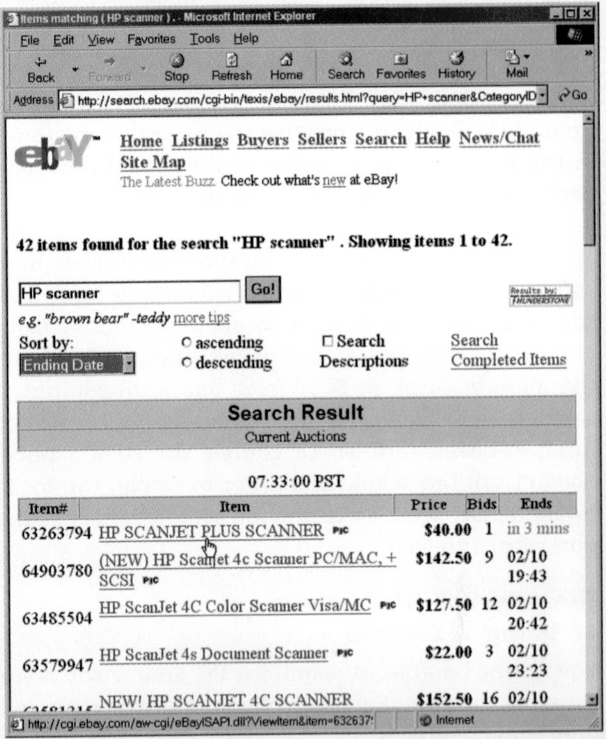

The Online Auction

One of eBay's major auction categories is "Computers." Here the user was interested in bidding on an "HP scanner" (see search box). At the time of the request, 44 HP scanners are on the auction block. At any given time, literally hundreds of PCs, software, and peripherals are up for sale on eBay, one of the Internet's most popular auction sites.

Online Internet and mail-order sales The alternative to buying a computer and related products at a retail outlet is to purchase them online over the Internet or from a mail-order service. Most major mail-order houses support online sales, and vice versa. Some Internet sales organizations offer interactive Internet-based buyer's guides that help you select the best product for your needs. Internet and mail-order sales are a great way to shop if you buy from reputable dealers. But, be wary of fly-by-night organizations that won't be there when you need service. The best mail-order/Internet services offer at least a 30-day unconditional money-back guarantee on all merchandise. Accept nothing less.

Direct marketers Some manufacturers of PC hardware and/or software are direct marketers; that is, they sell directly to the customer. For the most part, the direct marketer's "store window" is an advertisement in a PC trade magazine or a site on the Internet. The customer telephones, faxes, or mails the order, or the order can be entered via the Internet. The direct marketer sends the requested product(s) by return mail.

Used-computer retailers The used-computer retailer was as inevitable as the used-car dealer. A computer that is no longer powerful enough for one user may have more than enough power for another.

Online auctions A great source for anything used is an online auction. PCs and electronics are among the most popular items up for auction on the Internet. Online auctions go on 24 hours a day with people all over the world registering bids on selected items during a specific time frame. And, like any auction, the item goes to the highest bidder.

Classified ads Frequently, people wishing to upgrade will opt to advertise their existing systems in the classified ad sections of their local newspapers and in Internet-based classified ads.

The sale price of a PC, a peripheral device, or a software package may vary substantially from one source to another. It pays to shop around. A software suite may be offered at list price ($599) from the manufacturer, at $350 from one local computer retailer, at $299 from another, and at $259 from an Internet-based retailer. Of course, the selling price doesn't tell the whole story. For example, the local retailers may promise to provide some technical support after the sale.

The "Perks" of Employment or Being a Student

You might be able to acquire a PC and/or software through your employer or college. Many companies offer their employees a "PC perk." In cooperation with vendors, companies and colleges make volume purchases of PCs and software at discount rates, then offer them to employees and students at substantial savings. The employee-purchase program is so popular in some organizations that they set up internal computer stores.

Downloadable Software

Thousands of software authors have created a wide variety of excellent programs, from business graphics to trivia games. However, most of these creative authors do not have the funds needed to launch their creations in the commercial software marketplace. The alternative is to make their software available as *shareware.* Shareware is software made readily available to PC users via download on the Internet or online services (AOL, CompuServe, and so on).

When you download shareware, it is implied that you will register the software with the developer if you like it and intend to use it. The registration fees vary from $10 for utility programs to $100 for full-featured CAD packages. Software developers use several methods to encourage registration of their software. The shareware may be a limited-feature version or it may cease to load after a 30-day trial period. At a minimum, developers provide technical support and update information to registered users.

Education Software

The fastest growing segment of the software market is education software. The Oregon Trail, a product of the Learning Company, is one of many innovative edutainment programs. The historical program entertains and educates while allowing you to live the life of a pioneer in the 1840s. Courtesy of The Learning Company

You can get programs that print signs and banners, help you with your taxes, teach you to speak Japanese, help you manage projects, provide access to many delicious recipes, and suggest lottery numbers. You can get complete systems for church accounting, stamp collection, small business billing and invoicing, and investment management. You can get full-featured packages for word processing, spreadsheet, database, and graphics. Scores of games are available from golf to martial arts. These are just the tip of the shareware iceberg.

Most software vendors, such as Microsoft and IBM, maintain a Web site with lots of free downloadable software. Many of the downloads may be updates to commercial software, but many excellent stand-alone packages, ranging from games to Web authoring tools to videoconferencing software, are included as well.

INSTALLATION TIPS

- *Select a good location.* The location you select for your computer system should be away from people traffic; have access to a telephone line (for communications applications); have plenty of nonglare lighting; and be within a controlled environment (temperature, dust, and humidity).
- *Create an ergonomically designed workplace.* Chapter 10, "Computers in Society: Today," con-

tains a section on workplace design considerations.

- *Plan for growth.* It's inevitable that your space requirements will grow (more CD-ROMs, peripherals, books, manuals, and so on).
- *Complete and send registration cards for all hardware and software.* Product registration is important for warranty protection and for access to technical support. Most modern software packages let you submit your registration online during installation. If not, complete the registration card. Write down the product serial number on the inside covers of the user's manual or CD-ROM covers. You will need it if you reinstall the software.
- *Read and consolidate all manuals.* Read installation instructions before beginning any installation procedure. Keep all manuals together and readily accessible.
- *Keep shipping material for at least the period of the warranty.*
- *Clearly label all external connectors.* Some, but usually not all, connectors are labeled by the manufacturer. You may need to label extra serial ports, sound card connectors, and so on.

SYSTEM MAINTENANCE TIPS

- *Back up critical files.* The critical element in any computer system is the hard disk because that is where you keep your program and data files. Everything else can be replaced. Back up these files regularly to interchangeable disks, such as SuperDisk, Zip disk, or CD-RW. Magnetic tape is a good backup medium, too.
- *Keep your hard disk healthy.* Periodically use disk management software to reorganize fragmented files for faster operation and to check for and fix disk problems. The Windows 98/2000 Maintenance Wizard will help you set up your system for routine disk maintenance. This maintenance includes defragmentation and deleting unused files.
- *Clean all interchangeable disk drives.* Periodically use a disk-cleaning kit to clean read/write heads and other mechanical elements of disk drives.
- *Enable an antivirus program.* Activate an antivirus program such that it periodically scans your disks to maintain a virus-free operation.
- *Clean the monitor.* Use the special cloth distributed with your monitor to maintain a dust-free screen for better viewing.
- *Replace the printer cartridge as needed.* Output quality usually dictates the need for a new cartridge.
- *Upgrade software.* It's a good idea to upgrade the operating system and frequently used programs as new releases become available.
- *Upgrade hardware.* Once you purchase and begin to use a PC, the buying doesn't stop. It is inevitable that your PC will grow with the technology and your ever-expanding processing needs. This growth means that occasionally you may need to upgrade the PC. The upgrade might involve switching processors (for example, an Intel Pentium II to an Intel Pentium III), adding a hard drive, adding an expansion board (for example, 56 k-bps voice/data/fax modem), upgrading to a color printer, or adding peripherals (for example, a Zip disk).

Disk Drive Maintenance
To keep interchangeable disk and CD-ROM drives at peak performance, you will need to clean them periodically with a cleaning kit. Courtesy of Kensington Technology Group

PC BUYER'S WORKSHEET

After you have looked at two or three systems, their features, options, and specifications tend to blur in your mind. It is difficult to remember whether the first system had a 300 MHz processor or 300-day money-back warranty. The best way to make an informed purchase decision is to capture pertinent information in a way that will allow an easy comparison between alternatives. You can use the PC Buyer's Worksheet on the following page to *gather information on proposed systems* and/or to *document the ideal system for your needs.*

PC BUYER'S WORKSHEET

Vendor ______________________________

Contact person ______________ Telephone number (__) __________ ext. ______

PRODUCT	MAKE	MODEL	WARRANTY	COST
Processor unit				$
Processor speed in MHz:				
RAM in MB				
Cache in KB				
BUS # 1 type: *No. of slots:*				
BUS # 2 type: *No. of slots:*				
Serial ports: *Parallel ports:* *USB ports:*				
Special feature # 1:				
Special feature # 2:				
Keyboard				$
Point-and-draw device				$
Monitor				$
Size: *Resolution:* *Dot pitch:*				
Hard-disk drive				$
Capacity: *Access time:* *Transfer rate:*				
Zip disk or SuperDisk				$
CD-ROM or DVD drive				$
Access time: *Transfer rate:*				
Tape backup unit or CD/RW				$
Capacity: *Transfer rate:*				
Printer				$
Type: *Speed:* *Resolution:*				
Sound card				$
Speakers				$
Fax modem				$
K bps: *Fax software:* *Voice software:*				
Other I/O Device # 1:				$
Specs:				
Other I/O Device # 2:				$
Specs:				
Total System Cost	$			

PROGRAM		VERSION	COST
Name:	*Description:*		$
Name:	*Description:*		$
Name:	*Description:*		$
Name:	*Description:*		$
	Total Software Cost $		

Living in an Information Society

9 PC Software for Every Application

10 Computers in Society: Today
Focus on IT Robots and Robotics

11 Computers in Society: Tomorrow

PC Software for Every Application

Learning Objectives

9.1 Understand graphics and multimedia concepts and gain overview knowledge of related software.

9.2 Gain overview knowledge of personal information management software.

9.3 Gain overview knowledge of home and family software.

9.4 Gain overview knowledge of education and edutainment software.

9.5 Gain overview knowledge of reference software.

9.6 Gain overview knowledge of business and management software.

9.7 Gain overview knowledge of utility software.

chapter 9

WHY THIS CHAPTER IS IMPORTANT TO YOU

Most new computer systems are bundled with a software suite, often the latest version of Microsoft Office, and a few other programs such as an electronic encyclopedia and a few games. After that, additions and changes to your software portfolio are your responsibility. A software portfolio is simply the mix of applications software you have on your PC. Somewhere among the over 500,000 commercial software packages rests the answers to many of your processing and information needs, as well as plenty of opportunities to have a great time.

Today's powerful personal computers generally are underused, both at home and at work, often because PC users don't know where to begin building their software portfolio. The most popular software is word processing, browser, and e-mail. These are the applications that people use first and most often during their personal computing sessions. For many, these are the only applications they use. There's a world of software out there that can enhance your productivity and your enjoyment of personal computing. And, there's some software that you should be using to protect your system and, possibly, your children. Specific mainstream software packages are introduced to demonstrate capabilities, but be aware that each of these packages has plenty of competition.

This chapter is all about software, the software that you will purchase and install over and above that which comes with most new systems. This chapter is designed to put you on the right pathway toward exploring the software possibilities so you can take those first few steps toward building a cost-effective and helpful software portfolio.

Value Learning

9.1 GRAPHICS AND MULTIMEDIA SOFTWARE

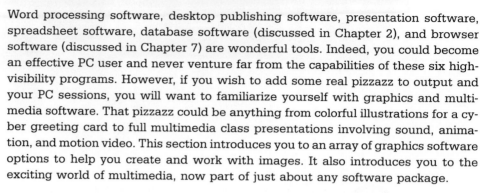

Monthly Technology Update Chapter 9

Word processing software, desktop publishing software, presentation software, spreadsheet software, database software (discussed in Chapter 2), and browser software (discussed in Chapter 7) are wonderful tools. Indeed, you could become an effective PC user and never venture far from the capabilities of these six high-visibility programs. However, if you wish to add some real pizzazz to output and your PC sessions, you will want to familiarize yourself with graphics and multimedia software. That pizzazz could be anything from colorful illustrations for a cyber greeting card to full multimedia class presentations involving sound, animation, and motion video. This section introduces you to an array of graphics software options to help you create and work with images. It also introduces you to the exciting world of multimedia, now part of just about any software package.

Graphics Software

Graphics

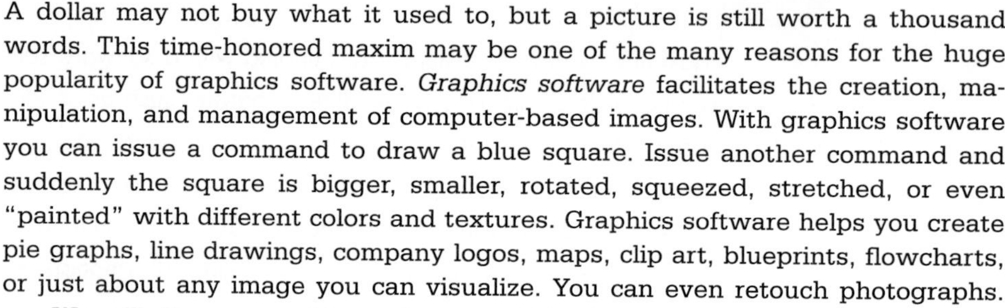

A dollar may not buy what it used to, but a picture is still worth a thousand words. This time-honored maxim may be one of the many reasons for the huge popularity of graphics software. *Graphics software* facilitates the creation, manipulation, and management of computer-based images. With graphics software you can issue a command to draw a blue square. Issue another command and suddenly the square is bigger, smaller, rotated, squeezed, stretched, or even "painted" with different colors and textures. Graphics software helps you create pie graphs, line drawings, company logos, maps, clip art, blueprints, flowcharts, or just about any image you can visualize. You can even retouch photographs.

We will discuss graphics software within the context of five common capabilities:

- Painting
- Drawing
- Photo illustration
- Drag-and-drop
- Animation

Commercial graphics software often includes two or more of these capabilities. Before you can fully understand graphics software, you first need to know the fundamentals of how images are displayed.

Displaying and Printing Graphic Images

Graphic images can be maintained as **bit-mapped graphics, vector graphics,** or in a **metafile** format. In bit-mapped graphics, the image is composed of patterns of dots called *picture elements* or *pixels*. In vector graphics, the image is composed of patterns of lines, points, and other geometric shapes (vectors). The metafile format is a class of graphics that combines the components of bit-mapped and vector graphics formats. The naked eye cannot distinguish one method of graphics display from another; however, the differences are quite apparent when you try to manipulate images in the various formats.

Bit-Mapped Graphics Bit-mapped graphics, displayed as dot patterns, are created by digital cameras, fax machines, scanners, graphics paint software, and when you capture an image on a screen. The term *bit-mapped* is used because the image is projected, or "mapped," onto the screen based on binary bits. Dots, or pixels, on the screen are arranged in rows and columns. The typical PC monitor has about 1.3 million pixels in 1024 rows and 1280 columns. Each dot or pixel on a monitor is assigned a number that denotes its position on the screen grid (120th row and 323rd column) and its color.

As with all internal numbers in a computer system, the numbers that describe the pixel attributes (position and color) are binary bits (1s and 0s). The number of bits needed to describe a pixel increases with the monitor's resolution and the number of colors that can be presented (from 256 colors in 8-bit color mode to

32-bit color mode with millions of colors). The term **raster graphics** is also used to describe *bit-mapped* images. Images are stored according to a **file format** that specifies how the information is organized in the file. Most of the popular programs that create graphic images have their own file formats. There are dozens of commonly used formats. The bit-mapped file format for a specific file is noted by its file name extension (for example, myfile.bmp or myfile.gif).

- *BMP*. **BMP** is the most common format used in the Microsoft Windows environment.
- *GIF*. **GIF,** a patented format, is used in Web pages and for downloadable online images.
- *TIFF and TIF*. **TIFF,** or **TIF,** is the industry standard for high-resolution bit-mapped images used in print publishing.
- *PCX*. **PCX** was introduced for PC Paintbrush (distributed with Windows) but is supported by many graphics packages and by scanners and faxes.
- *PNG*. **PNG** provides a patent-free replacement for GIF.
- *JPEG or JPG*. **JPEG,** or **JPG,** is commonly used on Web pages and in digital photography.

Vector Graphics Vectors, which are lines, points, and other geometric shapes, are configured to create the vector graphics image. The vector graphics display, in contrast to the bit-mapped graphics display, permits the user to work with objects, such as a drawing of a computer. Computer-aided design (CAD) software, which is used by engineers and scientists, uses vector graphics to meet the need to manipulate individual objects on the screen. Figure 9.1 illustrates a vector graphics image. Notice how the screen portion of the overall image is actually made up of many objects. Think of a vector graphics screen image as a collage of one or more objects.

Vector graphics images take up less storage space than do bit-mapped images. Each pixel in the bit-mapped image must be fully described internally to the computer, including the background colors, which requires a good deal of

Adobe Illustrator: A Draw Program Adobe® Illustrator®, shown here, is a vector graphics program. The user draws, then integrates, objects to create the drawing. This avant-garde drawing of a TV is made up of several vector objects. Some of the many objects that make up the drawing are moved and highlighted to demonstrate what makes up a vector graphics drawing. In the exploded example, each object is highlighted in blue. Adobe Illustrator's interface is similar to Paint's (see Figure 9.2); however, its drawing features are much more sophisticated.

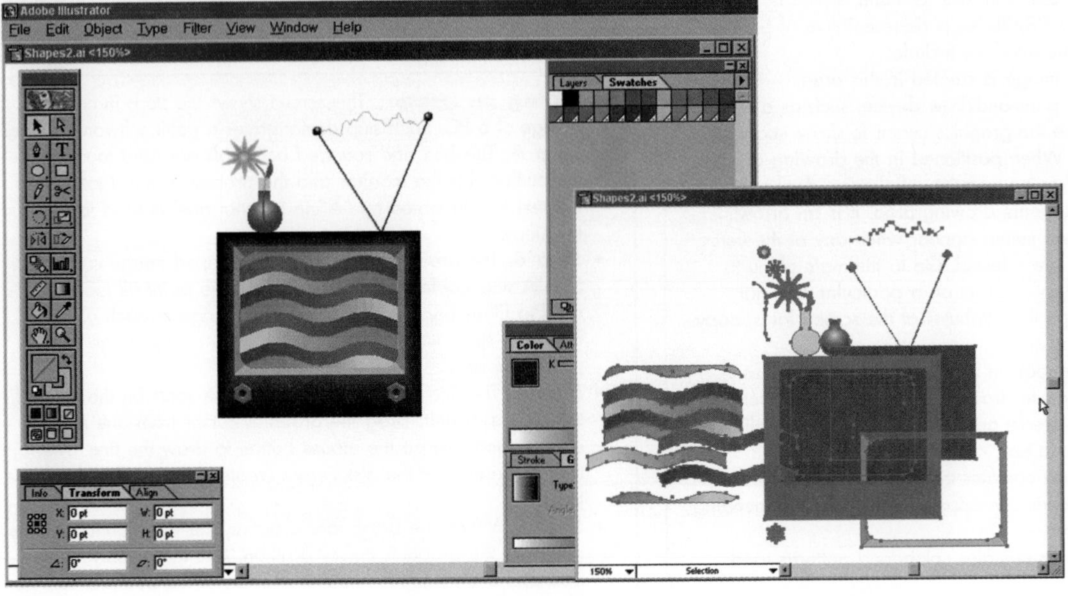

memory. Vector graphics are defined in geometric shapes, each of which can define the attributes of many pixels. For example, a vector graphics image of a blue square may encompass thousands of pixels when displayed, but the image is stored with a few simple descriptors: location of one of the corners, angle to horizontal, length of a side, and color. Vector graphics images provide more flexibility in that individual objects within the drawing can be resized, moved, stretched, and generally manipulated without affecting the rest of the drawing. **CGM** and **EPS** are widely supported vector graphics file formats. A popular metafile format, **WMF,** is used for exchanging graphics between Windows applications.

Graphics Conversion Unfortunately, there are no standards for the way graphic images are stored, so those formats discussed earlier and many others are used in practice. However, not all graphics programs support all formats. But most will support common bit-mapped formats such as BMP, WMF, GIF, PNG, and JPEG (JPG). This means that you can read or copy an image, such as myfile.bmp, into a graphics program's workspace, then save it in another format (for example, myfile.jpg). This graphics file format conversion capability enables graphics files to be passed between programs.

Specialized *graphics conversion programs* provide dozens of conversion options. For example, you can convert a DXF image created with AutoCAD® (a popular vector-based CAD program created by Autodesk®) into a PNG bit-mapped image for pixel-level editing. You also can convert images on Web pages (usually

Paint: A Paint Program

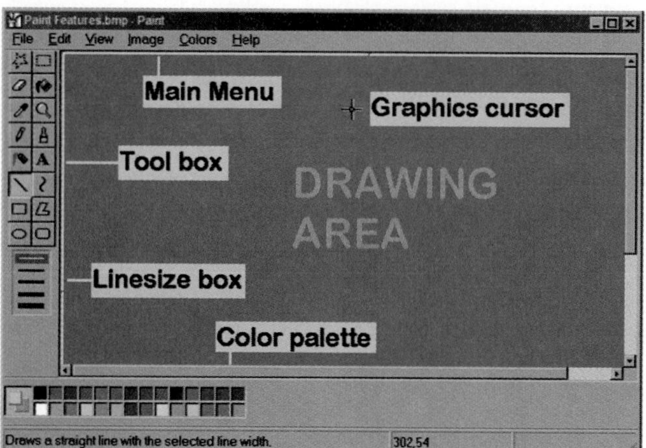

User Interface The user interface for Paint, which is distributed with Windows 98/2000, is representative of paint programs. The parts of the interface include:

- ***Drawing area.*** The image is created in this area.
- ***Graphics cursor.*** A point-and-draw device, such as a mouse, is used to move the graphics cursor to draw images and to select options. When positioned in the drawing area, the graphics cursor takes on a variety of shapes, depending on the tool selected. Outside the drawing area, it is an arrow.
- ***Main menu.*** Pull-down menus appear when any of the items in the main bar menu are selected. Go to the main menu to load and save drawings, zoom in on a particular area for detailed editing, change the attributes of the screen fonts, copy parts of the screen, and so on.
- ***Tool box.*** One of the tools in the tool box is active at any given time. Use the tools to draw; to move, copy, or delete parts of the screen; to create geometric shapes; to fill defined areas with colors; to add text; and to erase.
- ***Linesize box.*** This box contains the width options for the drawing line. Other boxes can appear in this space depending on which tool is selected.
- ***Color palette.*** This box contains colors and patterns used with the drawing tools.

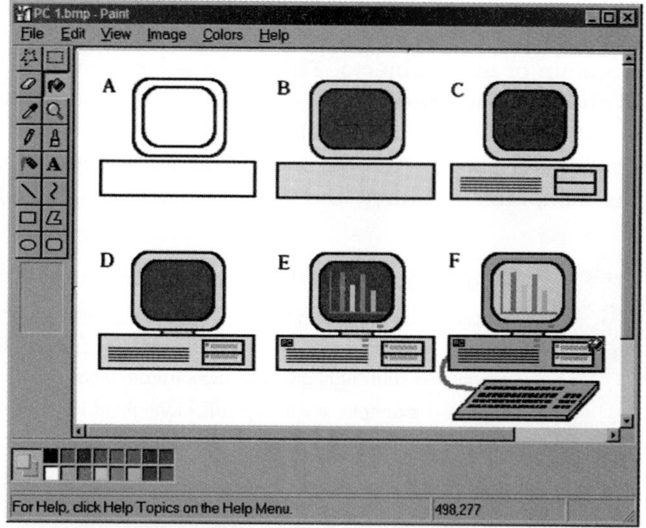

Creating an Image This screen shows the steps in creating an image of a PC. Each step demonstrates a paint software feature.

- ***Step A.*** The *box* and *rounded box tools* are used to create the outlines for the monitor and the processor unit. Notice that the *text tool* (denoted by "A" in the tool box) is used to label the steps.
- ***Step B.*** The area containing the bit-mapped image created in Step A was *copied* to position B, then the *paint fill tool* was used to fill in *background colors.* The image in each of the following steps was created from a copy of the image of the preceding step.
- ***Step C.*** The *line tool* is used to draw the vents on the front of the processor unit. Drag the graphics cursor from one point to another and release the mouse button to draw the line. The two box areas for the disks were created with the box and line tools.
- ***Step D.*** When the *brush tool* is active, the *foreground color* is drawn at the graphics cursor position. Use the brush tool for freehand drawing, such as the addition of the pedestal for the

in JPG or GIF bit-mapped file formats) into a format that is compatible with your word processing or desktop publishing program. If you do much work with graphics files, a good graphics conversion program is invaluable.

Paint Software

Paint software provides the user with a sophisticated electronic canvas for the creation of bit-mapped images. Figure 9.2 illustrates the Windows® 98 Paint program, which is a paint program distributed with Microsoft's Windows series of operating systems. Figure 9.2 shows you what the common tools on the program interface are and explains how to use the program. Although we use Paint in the example, the user interfaces of all paint programs are similar. The enlarged view shown in Figure 9.2 illustrates the pixel makeup of the original image.

Although you can perform amazing feats with paint software, one important similarity remains between it and the traditional canvas: Whatever you draw on either one becomes part of the whole drawing. Because the canvas is a *bit map*, you must erase or draw over any individual part with which you are dissatisfied. For example, suppose you draw a green circle. You would not be able simply to replace the circle with a blue square. The paint software does not remember the circle or any other representation of an object on the screen; it just remembers the pixel placement. To replace the circle with the square, you would have to draw the square over the pixels that make up the green circle or erase those pixels and then draw in the blue square.

MEMORY bits

Graphic Images

- Bit-mapped (raster) graphics
  - —Image as pixels
  - —Bit-mapped image
- Vector graphics
  - —Image as line patterns and geometric shapes
  - —Permits manipulation of objects within image
- Metafiles
  - —Combination of bit-mapped and vector

monitor. The disk slots and the disk-active lights were drawn with the line tool. Notice that the line width and the foreground color were changed to draw the disk slots and the lights.

- ***Step E.*** A logo (upper-left corner of processor box) and a bar graph are added. The *PC* in the black logo box was drawn one pixel at a time. The *zoom* feature explodes a small segment of the draw area to enable the user to draw one pixel at a time (see the next screen). The bar graph was drawn with the line tool. Notice that each line was drawn with a different color from the color palette.
- ***Step F.*** In this final step, the beige color is *erased* to gray. Paint software permits the user to selectively switch one color for another within a user-defined area or in the entire drawing area. The keyboard was drawn with the box, line, and erase tools, then *tilted* for a three-dimensional look.

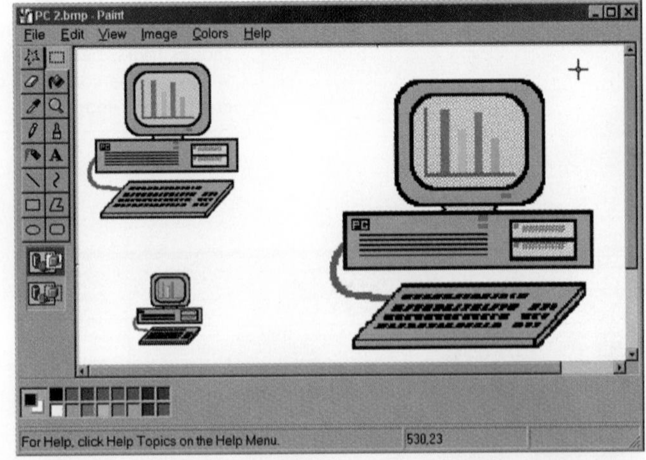

The Shrink/Grow Feature The PC image in the upper-left corner was copied from Step F in the previous image. The original image was selected with the *pick tool*, then copied to the clipboard. The clipboard contents were then loaded to a clean drawing area. The PC image in Step F is reduced and enlarged with the shrink/grow feature of paint software. Notice that image resolution suffers when the image is shrunk or enlarged (for example, the disk slots).

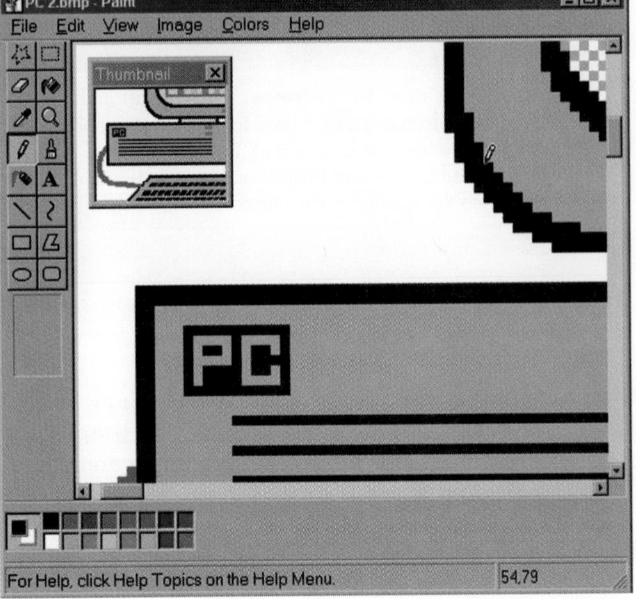

Zoom Feature In the illustration, the paint software user has zoomed in on the upper-left corner of the processor box in the completed PC image (Step F). Each square is a pixel. Any changes made in the enlarged version of the image are reflected in the window in the upper-left corner of the work area. The window reflects the size of the image, as it would normally appear on the screen.

Photo Illustration Software Photo illustration software, such as Microsoft® PhotoDraw® (shown here), lets you work with digital images, such as those resulting from a digital photograph and scan of an image. With photo illustration software you can touch up your photographs and apply a wide variety of special effects to all or portions of your images. Once you're satisfied with your artistic work, you can post them to the Internet or print them on greeting cards, T-shirts, calendars, and so on.

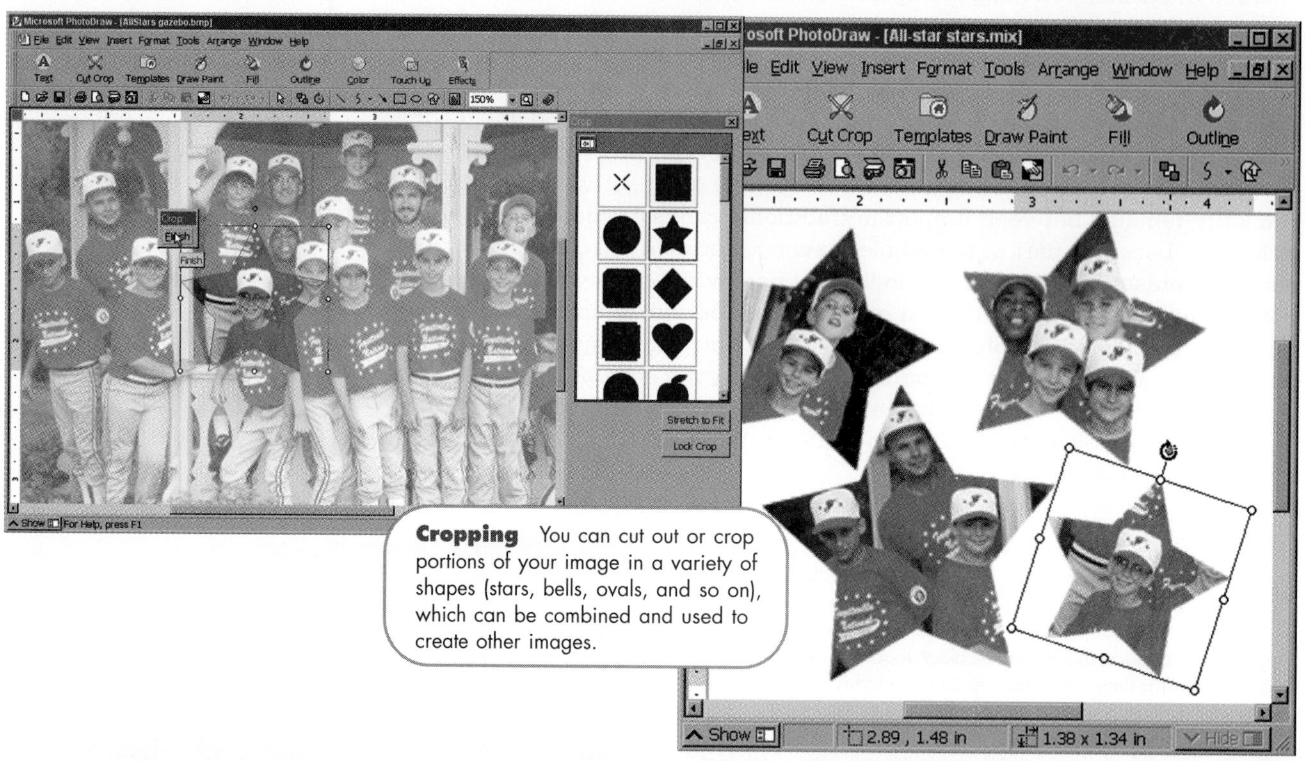

Cropping You can cut out or crop portions of your image in a variety of shapes (stars, bells, ovals, and so on), which can be combined and used to create other images.

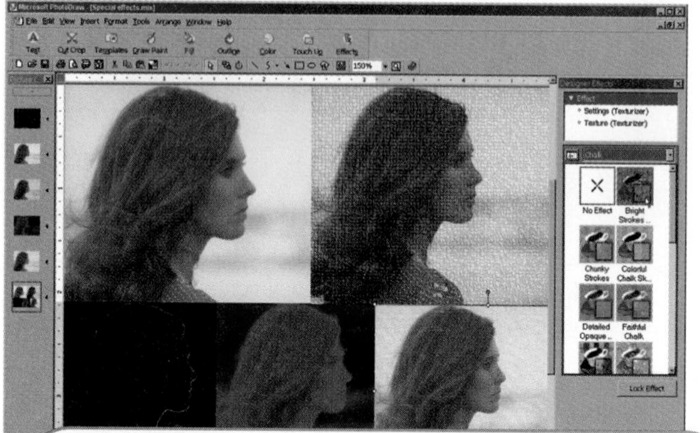

Special Effects The special effects shown here are but a few of the many that can be applied to give your digital images an artistic touch. Clockwise from the original image in the top left, they are the *mosaic*, *texturizer*, *neon glow*, and *glowing edges* effects.

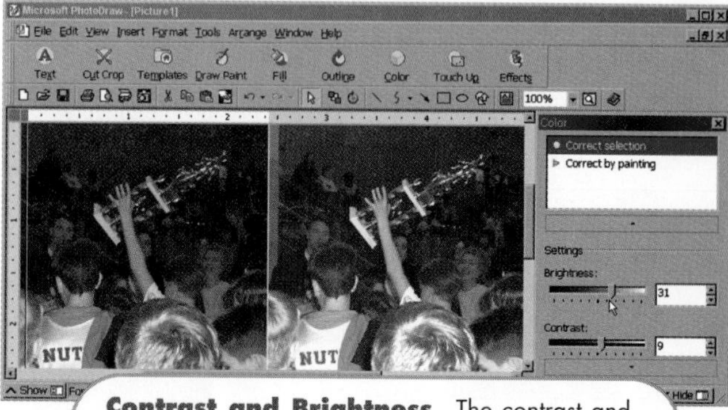

Contrast and Brightness The contrast and brightness feature can be used to save photographs that may otherwise be too dark (or light) in spots. Here, the contrast and brightness are adjusted to enhance the quality of the photo.

Draw Software

Both paint and **draw software** enable users to create imaginative images, but draw software relies on vector graphics instead of the bit-mapped graphics of paint software. As a result, draw software gives you greater flexibility and allows you to alter images more easily. For example, with draw software a specific object can be moved, copied, deleted, rotated, tilted, flipped horizontally or vertically, stretched, and squeezed (see Figure 9.1).

Recall the example of the green circle we wanted to replace with the blue square. With paint software, we had to erase or paint over one image to replace it with a new one. Because draw software uses vector graphics and manipulates objects, not pixels, replacing an image is made far simpler. All you need to do is delete the entire green circle at once and copy a blue square to that position.

Photo Illustration Software

Photo illustration software enables you to create original images as well as to dress up existing digitized images, such as photographs and electronic paintings. Images can be retouched with special effects to dramatically alter the way they appear (see Figure 9.3). Photo illustration software is to an image as word processing software is to text. A word processing package allows you to edit, sort, copy, and generally do whatever can be done to electronic text. Photo illustration software allows you to do just about anything imaginable to digitized photos or drawings. The result of a photo illustrator's effort is a composite image with stunning special effects. For example, you can show the changes that take place as one image is modified to become an entirely different image. This process is called **morphing,** a term derived from the word *metamorphosis*. You also can feather images to blend with their surroundings, enter artistic text over the image, change colors, include freehand drawings, isolate objects for special treatment, distort specific objects (for example, *glass blocking*), and much more.

An interesting application of what photo illustration software can do is the electronic aging of missing children. Artists combine a child's snapshot with a database of measurements showing how human facial dimensions change in a fairly predictable way over time. Such retouched snapshots have helped find hundreds of children since the mid-1980s.

Drag-and-Drop Software

Paint and draw software demand that the user possess considerable drawing skills. That is, it is not enough to understand the use of the software; you also must be able to create the image from scratch. **Drag-and-drop software** is designed for those who have an ongoing need to create drawings and diagrams but are not graphics specialists and artists. With drag-and-drop software, users drag ready-made shapes from application-specific stencils to the desired position on the drawing area (see Figure 9.4). Each stencil addresses a particular application. For example, the user can select stencils for flowcharting, organizational charts, network diagrams, landscaping, maps, plant layout, bath and kitchen planning,

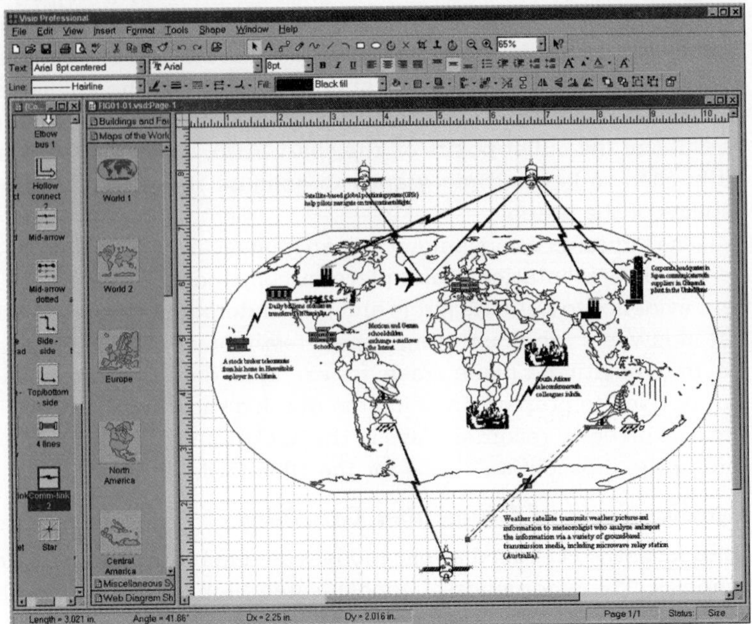

Drag-And-Drop Software

Visio®, a product of Visio Corporation, lets you create professional-looking drawings. Visio templates are opened to the left of the drawing area. Images are chosen from these templates, then dragged to the drawing area and dropped. Once positioned on the drawing area, images can be moved and resized to meet user needs. In this drawing, a world map image was dragged to the viewing area and enlarged to fill the screen. Other images were dragged from the templates and dropped on the map. Various connectors link the images. This Visio drawing was the authors' original drawing for Figure 1.1 in Chapter 1.

Animation Macromedia®, a software company, practices what it preaches. Here, the movie feature found in Director® is used to create an animated example that demonstrates the software's "Ink Effects" (window in lower right).

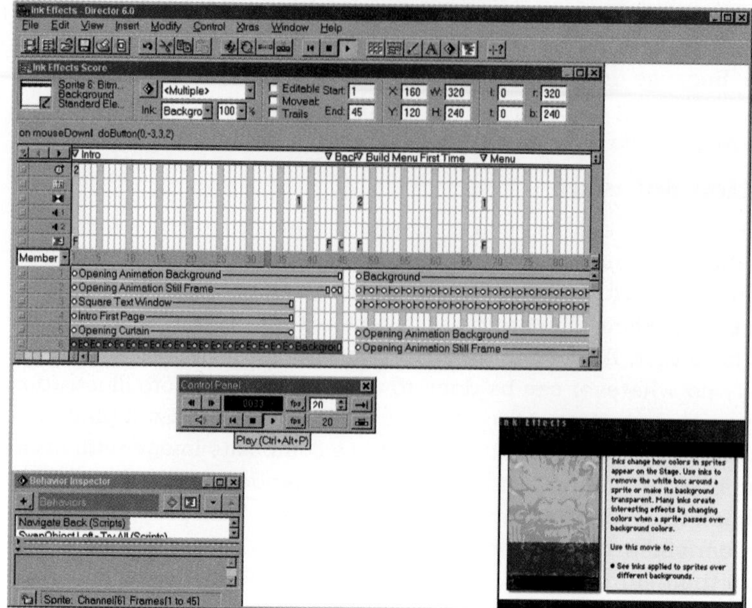

various engineering schematics, marketing, project management, vehicle accident reporting, business graphics, and many more. Even stencils with dinosaurs and castles are available.

In drag-and-drop software, the shapes are intelligent; that is, they can take on different forms, proportions, colors, and other properties, depending on the context in which they are used. Drag-and-drop software enables you to *glue* the shapes together such that the shapes stay connected even if one of them is moved.

Animation

The next step up from a static display of images is a dynamic display—that is, one that features movement within the display. **Animation,** or movement, is accomplished by the rapid repositioning (moving) of objects on the display screen. For example, animation techniques give life to video-game characters.

Animation involves the rapid movement of an object, perhaps the image of a dollar sign, from one part of the screen to another (see Figure 9.5). The animation is accomplished by moving the object in small increments in rapid succession, giving the illusion of movement. The object may gradually change shape, as well. Most presentation software packages, which are discussed in Chapter 2, have several built-in animation features that help you include simple animation in the slides used in the presentation. For example, the *animated bullet build* feature can be applied to a simple text chart to integrate animation into the presentation of the bullet points on the chart. Also, the *animated charting* feature can be applied to bar and pie graphs to animate the presentation of the important aspects of the graph.

The judicious use of animation can enliven any presentation. Some of the most important presentations take place in courtrooms. How can a lawyer best present evidence to help the judge and jury understand the case? An increasing number of lawyers are illustrating expert testimony with animated computer graphics. In re-creating a plane crash, for example, data from the plane's data recorder can be used to prepare an animated graphic showing the exact flight path, while the cockpit voice recorder plays in the background. Several animations were used during the prosecution's case for the 1995 O. J. Simpson trial.

Applications of Computer Graphics

Until recently, PC-based applications were limited to numbers, letters, and crude graphics. The emergence of sophisticated high-resolution graphics has resulted in an avalanche of new applications in almost every area of endeavor. Figure 9.6 provides a sampling of some of these exciting applications.

FIGURE 9.6 Applications of Graphics Software

Computer Graphics in Industry Computer-aided design software enables plant designers to build electronic prototypes that can be viewed and even tested for functionality, all within the confines of a computer system. It's much less expensive to correct a mistake made with bits and bytes than it is one with steel girders. Courtesy of Intergraph Corporation

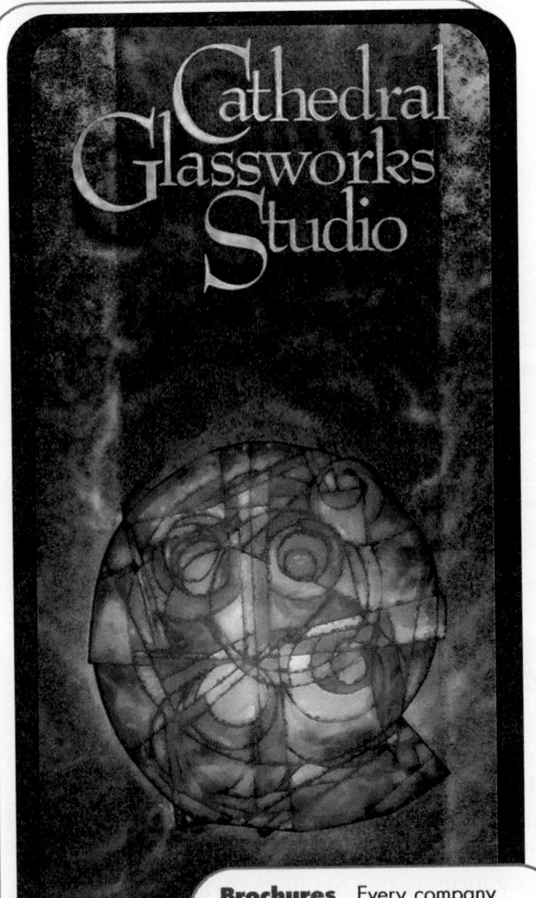

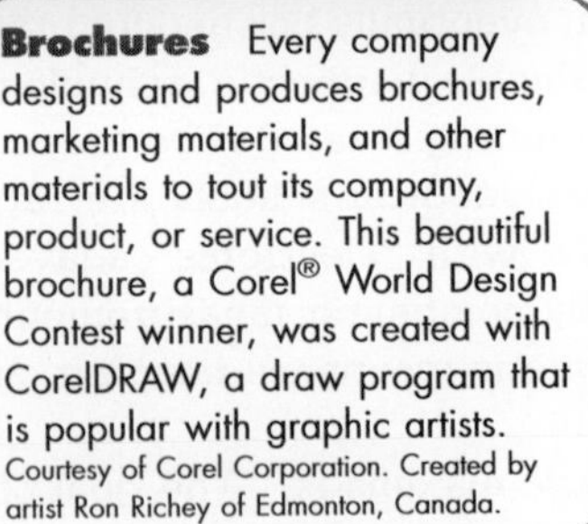

Brochures Every company designs and produces brochures, marketing materials, and other materials to tout its company, product, or service. This beautiful brochure, a Corel® World Design Contest winner, was created with CorelDRAW, a draw program that is popular with graphic artists. Courtesy of Corel Corporation. Created by artist Ron Richey of Edmonton, Canada.

Adding Color to Black-and-White Classics This movie is just one of many black-and-white films that has been *colorized* with the aid of computer graphics technology. The colorizing process uses an electronic scanner to break each frame into 525,000 dots the computer can store and manipulate. The art director reviews the frames at the beginning, middle, and end of the scene and selects a specific color for every object. A computer graphics artist then uses a digitizing tablet to "hand paint" these frames as per the art director's instructions. Computer software then colors the remaining frames. Mobile Image Canada Limited

Preparing for Surgery Preparation and accuracy are especially important for any surgery. This doctor is using computer graphics to better prepare himself in making more informed decisions before and during surgery. Photo courtesy of Intel Corporation

(Figure 9.6 continues on next page)

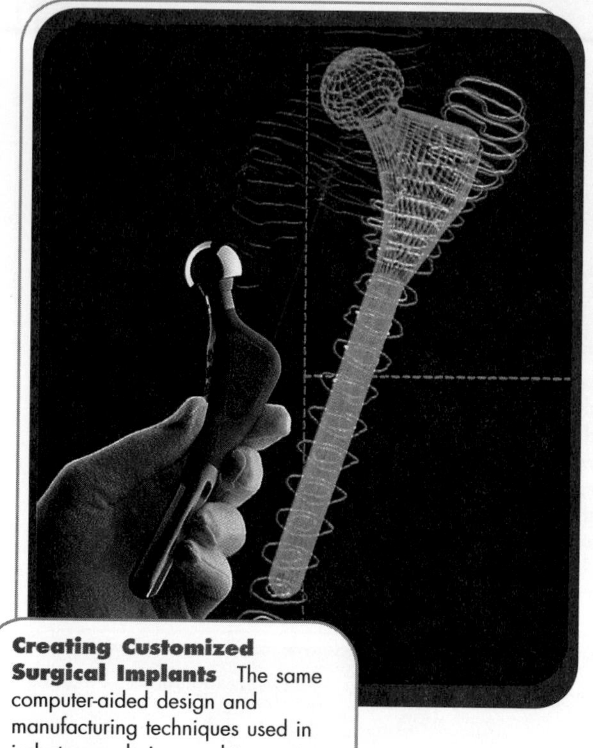

Creating Customized Surgical Implants The same computer-aided design and manufacturing techniques used in industry are being used to create artificial hips and other replacement bones and joints. Special software translates CAT scans and other medical images of a patient's body into a precise drawing, which doctors and medical engineers use to create a final design. The software then uses this design to control the manufacture of the finished implant. Similar techniques are being used to create other medical devices, such as replacement heart valves. Courtesy Techmedica

The Origin of Myst Island All of the 2500 pieces of art in Myst, a popular game, are original. Myst was two years in the making and nothing in Myst is photo-based. Courtesy of Strata, Inc.

The emergence of computer graphics has not only changed what we see on the screen, but what we do as well. For example, computer graphics applications can now be found in almost every phase of medical training, diagnosis, and treatment. In fact, scholars of medical ethics predict that doctors who don't use these and other computer-based aids might eventually be sued for providing inadequate medical treatment. One especially valuable diagnostic technology is computed axial tomography, or the CAT scan, a rotating X-ray device that constructs a three-dimensional view of body structures. Medical schools are replacing traditional anatomy lessons and dissection labs with "electronic cadavers," databases of three-dimensional images created by combining measurements taken from human cadavers with CAT scans, magnetic resonance imaging, and still and video photographic images.

One of the computer world's basic maxims is, "The goal of computing is insight, not numbers." The same could be said of scientific research, where a wealth of data is both a blessing and a curse. Computer graphics are now helping scientists of every type gain new insights. Consider just these few examples.

- *Archaeology*. A blend of database technology and three-dimensional computer mapping, modeling, and imaging have helped researchers reconstruct and preserve the ruins and artifacts of Pompeii. Like modern architects, archaeologists can now tour electronic models of ancient buildings and get a better idea of how the Pompeiians lived and died.
- *Astrophysics*. With the help of extremely powerful computers, researchers have been able to create three-dimensional simulations of the sun's surface that will help them understand the structure of the sun and the physical processes within it.
- *Entertainment*. The stars of more and more movies are animated characters. Computer-based graphics have given us new ways to entertain ourselves. Life-like arcade and PC-based video games give us that *you-are-there* feeling.

- *Oceanography*. Computer-enhanced graphics can be used to plot millions of pieces of raw data collected by satellite, creating three-dimensional color-coded maps that help oceanographers envision the interplay of water temperature and movement with the terrain of the ocean floor.
- *Aviation*. Flight simulators that combine wrapped-around graphic images with sound and motion provide pilots an opportunity to practice their skills at handling in-flight emergencies, but without the risk.
- *Retailing*. Have you ever wandered through a store looking for a particular product or someone who could point you in the right direction? Kiosks are being installed in stores all over the world to help us find what we need. The graphic images on the kiosk screen show us where we are and how to get to the product's location.

Computer graphics has emerged as one of the most exciting tools for computer users in all fields. Computer graphics is playing an increasing role in almost everything we do, whether it's driving a car, studying for a test, or watching TV. Some automobiles have monitors that display descriptive computer graphics, including our exact location on a map. Much of the material in college textbooks is being presented within the context of computer graphics, rather than print pages. Already a few television shows are interactive, with graphic images and interactivity on the Internet interlaced with traditional television programming.

Multimedia

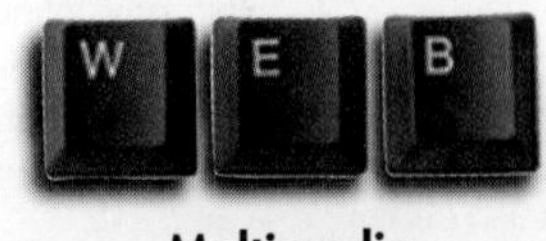

Multimedia

One of the most exciting computer "buzzwords," *multimedia,* applies to most modern software. Multimedia is the capability that enables the integration of computer-based text, high-resolution still graphics, motion visuals, animation, and sound. In the mid-1990s, software that used multimedia was relatively new and multimedia PCs, still a bit pricey, were rare. Today, all PCs are multimedia-ready and most software packages and the Web take advantage of multimedia capabilities. Consider the *show biz* appeal of these few examples.

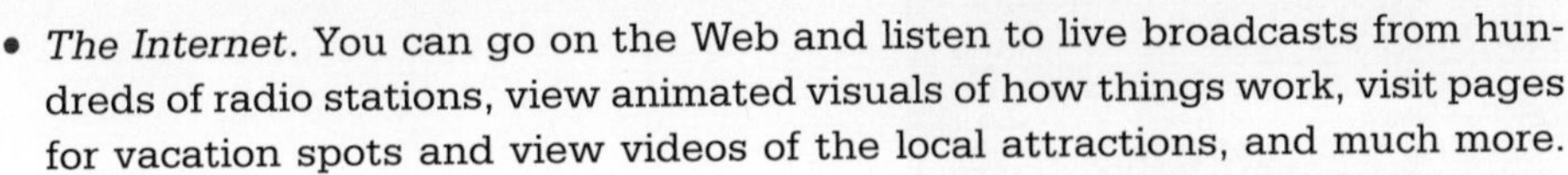

- *The Internet*. You can go on the Web and listen to live broadcasts from hundreds of radio stations, view animated visuals of how things work, visit pages for vacation spots and view videos of the local attractions, and much more.
- *Presentations*. Multimedia has allowed presenters to graduate from the overhead projector to full multimedia productions with orchestral fanfares and exploding rockets.
- *Kiosks*. Interactive kiosks with touch-sensitive screens provide public users with detailed information about a city, a company, a product, events, and so on.
- *Tutorials*. Multimedia is rapidly becoming the foundation of computer-based training. For example, companies prepare interactive tutorials to introduce newcomers to company procedures. Thousands of workers are now learning Word, Excel, and other popular applications via interactive multimedia tutorials that are enlivened with music, graphics, and motion. A Department of Defense study concluded that such tutorials take about a third less time, cost about a third less, and are more effective than traditional training methods.
- *Online reference*. CD-ROM–based multimedia alternatives are beginning to replace encyclopedias, technical reference manuals, product information booklets, and the like. Electronic versions of reference materials are easier to use and much, much lighter to carry.
- *Interactive publications*. Books, magazines, and newspapers are already being distributed as multimedia publications on CD-ROM and online via the Internet. The printed page will never be able to share moving visuals and sounds.

Multimedia

With multimedia, the combined use of text, sound, images, motion video, and animation transforms a PC into an exciting center for learning, work, or play (see Figure 9.7).

Multimedia Applications

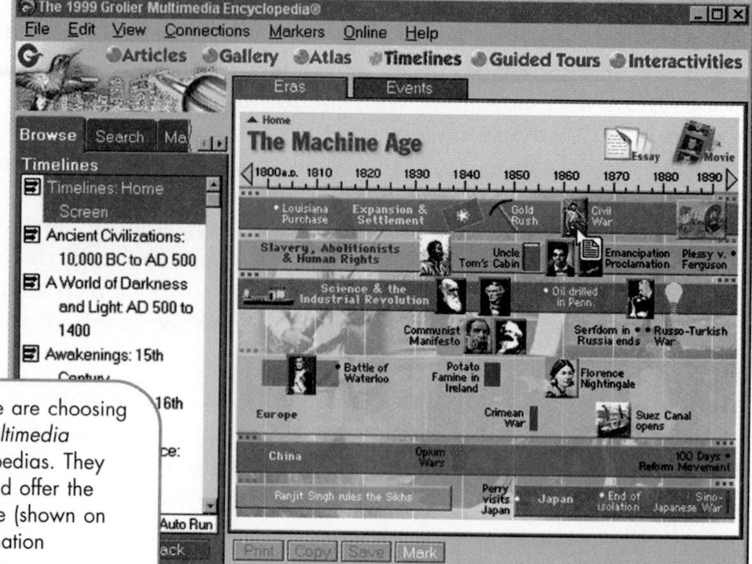

The Multimedia Encyclopedia Far more people are choosing multimedia encyclopedias, such as the *1999 Grolier Multimedia Encyclopedia* shown here, than traditional print encyclopedias. They cost considerably less, are about 100 pounds lighter, and offer the advantages of multimedia. As you travel along a timeline (shown on the screen, here), you can enjoy audio, video, and animation presentations that are not possible in print encyclopedias.

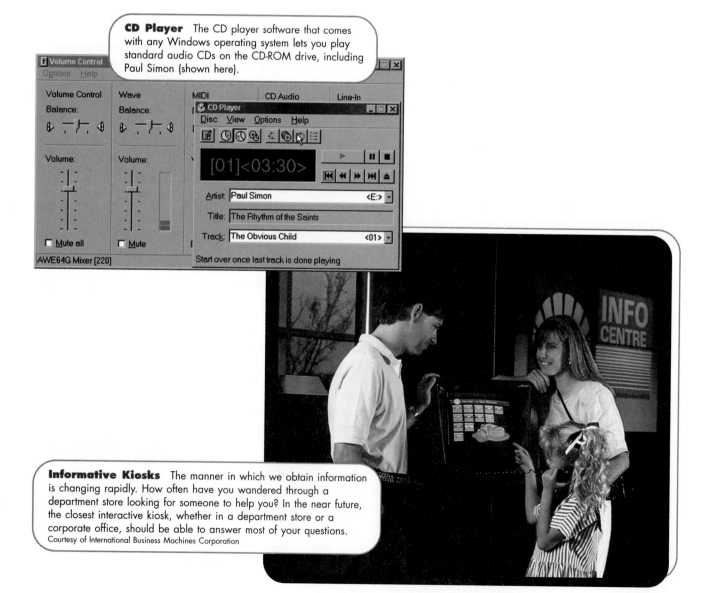

CD Player The CD player software that comes with any Windows operating system lets you play standard audio CDs on the CD-ROM drive, including Paul Simon (shown here).

Informative Kiosks The manner in which we obtain information is changing rapidly. How often have you wandered through a department store looking for someone to help you? In the near future, the closest interactive kiosk, whether in a department store or a corporate office, should be able to answer most of your questions.

Multimedia in the Home Virtually all new PCs purchased for home use have full multimedia capability. Many are equipped with a digital camera (on top of monitor). Here, a grandmother is putting on the finishing touches before capturing her image and broadcasting it to her grandchildren over the Internet.
Photo courtesy of Intel Corporation

Corporate Training To save network technicians critical time in off-site training, this telephone company uses multimedia training courses that can be accessed directly from the individual's PC or workstation. Courtesy of Dynatech Corporation

Multimedia and Education People retain 10% of the information they see; 20% of what they hear; 50% of what they see and hear; and 80% of what they see, hear, and do. These statistics present a strong argument for interactive learning via multimedia. With the right software, this multimedia-capable Power Macintosh can answer student's questions and guide them through the learning process.
Courtesy of Apple Computer, Inc. (Jeff Haeger, photographer)

The best way to understand multimedia is to experience it firsthand on a PC. No verbal description can do it justice. The most we can say is that multimedia is more sensual than traditional PC applications in that it tickles our senses while presenting us with information.

Growing with Multimedia

The typical off-the-shelf PC is multimedia ready. The next stage of multimedia growth comes when you decide to *develop* sophisticated multimedia applications—either your own multimedia title, an interactive tutorial, or an information kiosk. At this point, you or your company may need to invest in some or all of the following hardware and software.

- *Video camera, videocassette recorder/player, audiocassette player, CD-audio player, and television.* These electronic devices are emerging as staples in many households and companies. The video camera lets you capture motion video source material that can be integrated with multimedia applications. The videocassette recorder/player and audiocassette player are needed to edit prerecorded motion video and sounds for inclusion in an application. The CD-audio player is handy when combining CD-based audio material with CD-ROM source material. The television provides an alternative output device.
- *Synthesizer.* A good synthesizer can reproduce a variety of special effects and sounds, including those of almost any musical instrument. A synthesizer with a keyboard can be played to create source music for inclusion in a multimedia application.
- *Video capture card.* This expansion card lets you capture and digitize full-motion color video with audio. The digitized motion video can then be used as source material for a CD-ROM–based multimedia application.
- *Color scanner.* A color scanner lets you capture color images from hard-copy source material.
- *Digital camera.* A digital camera captures high-resolution digital images that can be integrated into multimedia applications.
- *CD-RW.* CD-rewritable technology lets you write and rewrite to the same high-capacity CD media. Multimedia applications generally have huge storage requirements and usually are distributed on CD-ROM.
- *Applications development software.* If you plan to develop sophisticated multimedia applications, you will need to upgrade to professional application development tools and high-level authoring software. **Authoring software** lets you create multimedia applications that integrate sound, motion, text, animation, and images.
- *PC source library.* The source library contains digitized "clips" of art, video, and audio that you can use as needed to complement a multimedia application.

Multimedia Resources

Multimedia applications draw content material from a number of sources.

Text Files A little over a decade ago, most computer-based applications were designed strictly around text and numbers. However, this has changed. An animation of how the human heart works is far more effective than is a textual description of how it works.

Database Files Many CD-ROM titles involve the use of databases. For example, one CD-ROM title contains information on every city in the United States (name, population, major industries, and so on) stored and sorted in a database.

Sound Files Sound files are of two types: *waveform* and *nonwaveform*. The waveform files, or **wave files,** contain the digital information needed to reconstruct the analog waveform of the sound so it can be played through speakers. The Windows waveform files are identified with the WAV extension (for example, SOUNDFIL.WAV).

Digital Audio Sequencer and MIDI Digital Orchestrator Pro™ (a software product from Voyetra Turtle Beach, Inc.) is one of the most popular digital audio sequencers. The program lets you create multitrack recordings from external audio sources, such as the output from a keyboard synthesizer or an audio CD. Digital audio and MIDI tracks exist side by side in perfect sync, making song editing a snap. This image is one of the many views in the intuitive user interface that allows users to edit virtually any facet of a song.

The nonwaveform file contains instructions as to how to create the sound, rather than a digitized version of the actual sound. For example, an instruction might tell the computer the pitch, duration, and sound quality of a particular musical note. The most common nonwaveform file, which is primarily for recording and playing music, is known as the **MIDI file.** MIDI files are identified with the MID extension (for example, MUSICFIL.MID). MIDI stands for *M*usical *I*nstrument *D*igital *I*nterface. MIDI provides an interface between PCs and electronic musical instruments, such as the synthesizer. A typical application involving MIDI files has the PC recording notes played by a musician on a synthesizer. The musician then adds additional instruments to the original track (layering) to create a full orchestral sound (see Figure 9.8).

Image Files Multimedia is visual, so it uses lots of images. We have already seen and discussed the most common sources of images. They include:

- *You.* You can create your own images using the graphics software and techniques discussed earlier in this chapter.
- *Clip art.* Anyone serious about creating multimedia material will have a hefty clip art library of up to 100,000 images.
- *Scanned images.* If you have a scanner, you can scan and digitize any hard-copy image (photographs, drawings, and so on).
- *Photo images.* Photo image libraries are available commercially (on CD-ROM) and as downloadable files over the Internet and information services. And, you can create your own with a digital camera.

Animation Files You can create your own animation using software, such as Macromedia® Director®, or you can purchase a commercial animation library. The latter contains animation templates that can be applied to different presentation needs.

Motion Video Files Obtaining relevant motion video for a particular multimedia application can be a challenge. You will need a video camera and a video capture board to produce original motion video for inclusion in a multimedia application. Depending on your presentation, you may need actors, props, and a set, as well. For example, you will frequently see video clips of on-screen narrators in multimedia presentations and tutorials. Videos are produced as you would any video product (set, actor, and so on), then digitized for storage on a CD-ROM or hard disk.

FIGURE 9.9

Multimedia Presentations
Microsoft® PowerPoint® 2000, one of the most popular presentation graphics programs, helps you prepare and present multimedia slides for formal presentations. PowerPoint has a variety of slide templates from which you can choose. You can work with the entire presentation (slide sorter view in the background window) or with a single chart and the presentation outline. Slides are easily rearranged by simply dragging a slide to a new position in the slide sorter view.

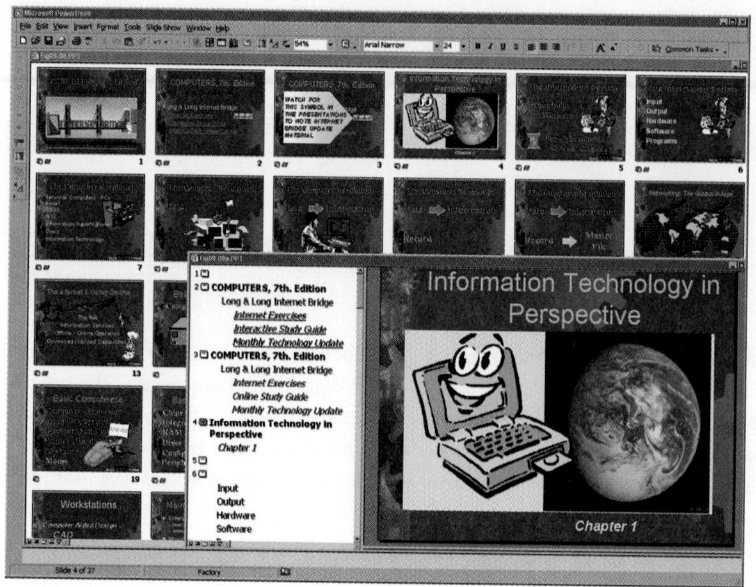

Creating a Multimedia Application: Putting the Resources Together

Once you have prepared and/or identified the desired sight and sound resource material, you're ready to put it together. A wide variety of software packages is available to help you accomplish this task.

- *Presentation software.* As we have already seen, presentation software such as PowerPoint (see Figure 9.9) can help you prepare and create stimulating multimedia presentations.
- *Authoring programs.* To create interactive multimedia tutorials and titles, you will need an authoring program, such as Toolbook from Asymetrix or Macromedia Director.
- *Multimedia programming.* The creation of sophisticated commercial multimedia titles, such as the multimedia encyclopedia, may require the use of several multimedia development tools, including high-end authoring programs and programming languages, such as Visual Basic and C++.

MEMORY bits

Multimedia Resources
- Text files
- Database files
- Sound files
- Image files
- Animation files
- Motion video files

Multimedia possibilities stretch the human imagination to its limits. Already we see that multimedia will change the face of publishing. Many feel that *interactive books* based on multimedia technology have the potential to be more accessible and effective than traditional books, especially as learning tools. Early indications are that passive entertainment, such as TV and movies, may have to move aside to make way for interactive multimedia entertainment that involves the viewer in the action.

SECTION SELF-CHECK

Self-Check

9-1.1 As a rule of thumb, you cannot be an effective user of presentation software without knowing something about multimedia software. (T/F)

9-1.2 Draw software relies on vector graphics to enable the manipulation of specific objects within an image. (T/F)

9-1.3 The video synthesizer expansion card lets you capture and digitize full-motion color video with audio. (T/F)

9-1.4 An EPS bit-mapped file can be converted to other types of bit-mapped file formats. (T/F)

9-1.5 JAZZ.MID is a filename for a video file. (T/F)

9-1.6 In bit-mapped graphics, the image is composed of patterns of: (a) vectors, (b) pictures, (c) dots, or (d) objects?

9-1.7 Which of the following would not be a tool in a paint program's tool box: (a) rectangle tool, (b) color palette, (c) add text tool, or (d) line tool?

9-1.8 What photo illustration process takes place as one image is modified to become an entirely different image: (a) morphing, (b) transforming, (c) morphic, or (d) transformer?

9-1.9 Which of the following would not be considered one of the major elements of multimedia: (a) sound, (b) sequential access, (c) the opportunity for interaction, or (d) animation?

9-1.10 What type of program lets you create multimedia applications that integrate sound, motion, text, animation, and images: (a) authoring, (b) writer, (c) integrator, or (d) direction?

9-1.11 MIDI files are: (a) waveform files, (b) nonwaveform files, (c) minidigital files, or (d) minifiles?

9-1.12 Another term for bit-mapped graphics is: (a) raster, (b) vector, (c) faster, or (d) geometric?

9-1.13 Which type of graphics software package provides a computer-based version of the painter's canvas: (a) draw, (b) paint, (c) illustrator, or (d) sketch?

9-1.14 What class of graphics combines the components of bit-mapped and vector graphics formats: (a) metafiles, (b) raster files, (c) text files, or (d) MIDI files?

9-1.15 Which of the following pairs of file formats are used in Web page design: (a) JPG and BMP, (b) TIF and PCX, (c) JPG and GIF, or (d) TIF and PNG?

9.2 PERSONAL INFORMATION MANAGEMENT SOFTWARE

Personal information management or *PIM* software is a catch-all phrase that generally refers to messaging and personal information management software that helps you manage your messages, appointments, contacts, and tasks. PIM software, such as Microsoft® Outlook®, may include *calendar* applications for appointment scheduling and reminders; communications applications such as *e-mail*, *phone dialer*, and *fax;* and *databases* for organizing telephone numbers, e-mail addresses, to-do lists, notes, diary entries, and so on. Figure 9.10 gives you an overview of Microsoft Outlook personal information management software.

SECTION SELF-CHECK

Self-Check

9-2.1 The foundation application of PIM software is e-mail. (T/F)

9-2.2 PIM software can display daily hour-by-hour listings of appointments. (T/F)

9-2.3 Personal information management is concerned with messages, appointments, contacts, and tasks. (T/F)

9-2.4 Which of these is not a PIM application: (a) phone dialer, (b) e-mail, (c) fax, or (d) edutainment?

9-2.5 Which of these is messaging and personal information management software: (a) IMP, (b) PIM, (c) MIP, or (d) IPM?

9-2.6 PIM software databases include all but which of the following: (a) to-do lists, (b) virus list, (c) notes, or (d) diary entries?

9.3 HOME AND FAMILY SOFTWARE

For the first decade of personal computing, the only home or personal applications were those that could be created within a word processing or spreadsheet document. This changed quickly as personal computers made their way into the home. Now, over half the homes in America have at least one PC. Many have one for the parent's home office and one for the kids. Some have tiny area networks, linking all home computers. Today, a wide range of software is available for these home PCs that can help us with the many activities of day-to-day living, as well as some of the chores of life.

Microsoft Outlook: Personal Information Management Software Microsoft® Outlook® is a handy time-management tool that you can use on your own or as part of a group.

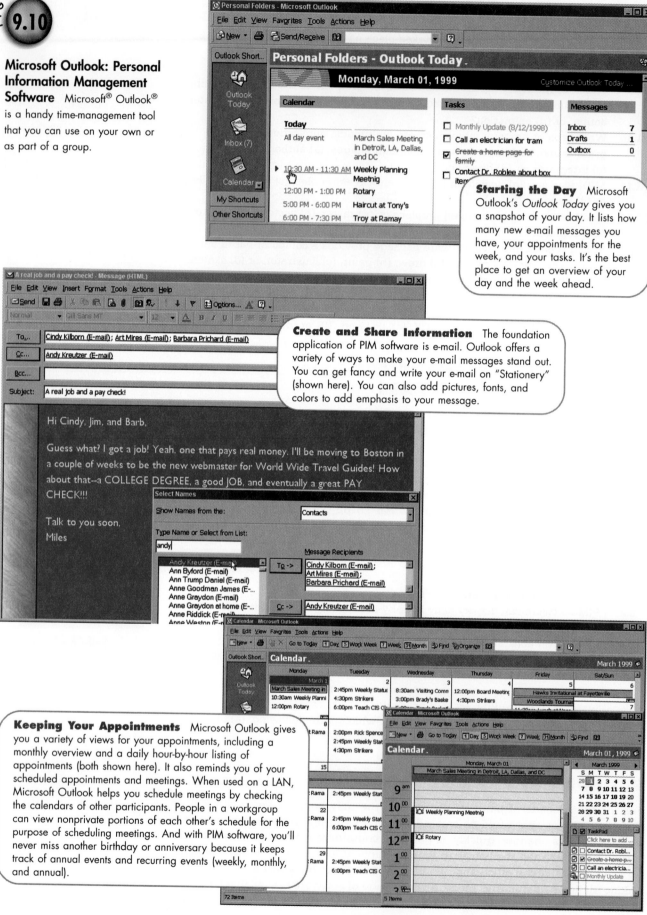

Starting the Day Microsoft Outlook's *Outlook Today* gives you a snapshot of your day. It lists how many new e-mail messages you have, your appointments for the week, and your tasks. It's the best place to get an overview of your day and the week ahead.

Create and Share Information The foundation application of PIM software is e-mail. Outlook offers a variety of ways to make your e-mail messages stand out. You can get fancy and write your e-mail on "Stationery" (shown here). You can also add pictures, fonts, and colors to add emphasis to your message.

Keeping Your Appointments Microsoft Outlook gives you a variety of views for your appointments, including a monthly overview and a daily hour-by-hour listing of appointments (both shown here). It also reminds you of your scheduled appointments and meetings. When used on a LAN, Microsoft Outlook helps you schedule meetings by checking the calendars of other participants. People in a workgroup can view nonprivate portions of each other's schedule for the purpose of scheduling meetings. And with PIM software, you'll never miss another birthday or anniversary because it keeps track of annual events and recurring events (weekly, monthly, and annual).

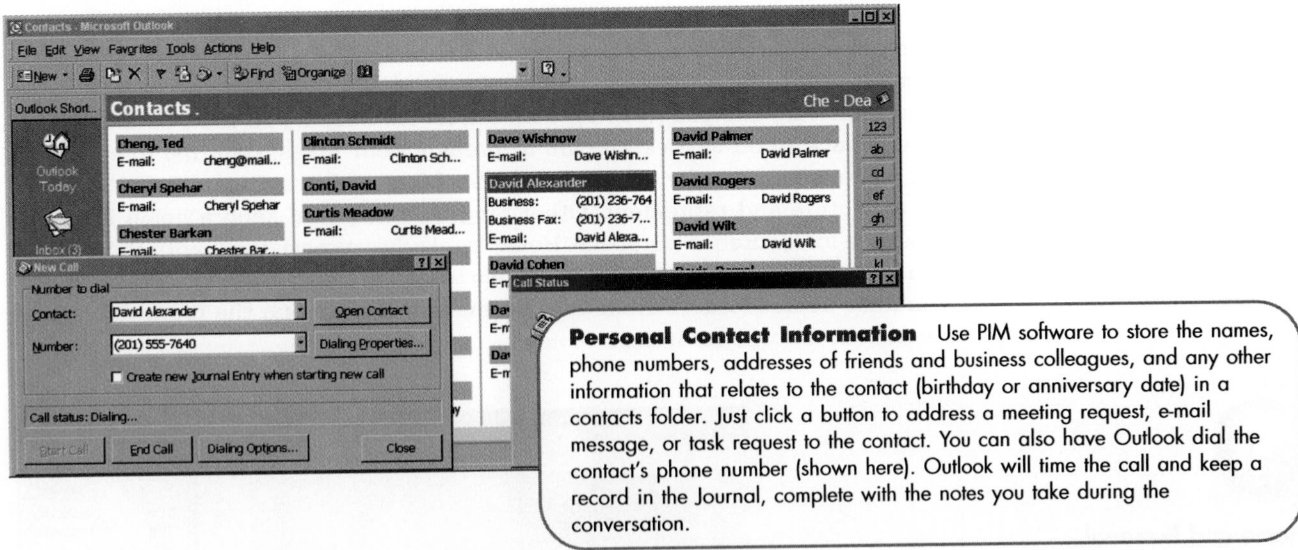

Personal Contact Information Use PIM software to store the names, phone numbers, addresses of friends and business colleagues, and any other information that relates to the contact (birthday or anniversary date) in a contacts folder. Just click a button to address a meeting request, e-mail message, or task request to the contact. You can also have Outlook dial the contact's phone number (shown here). Outlook will time the call and keep a record in the Journal, complete with the notes you take during the conversation.

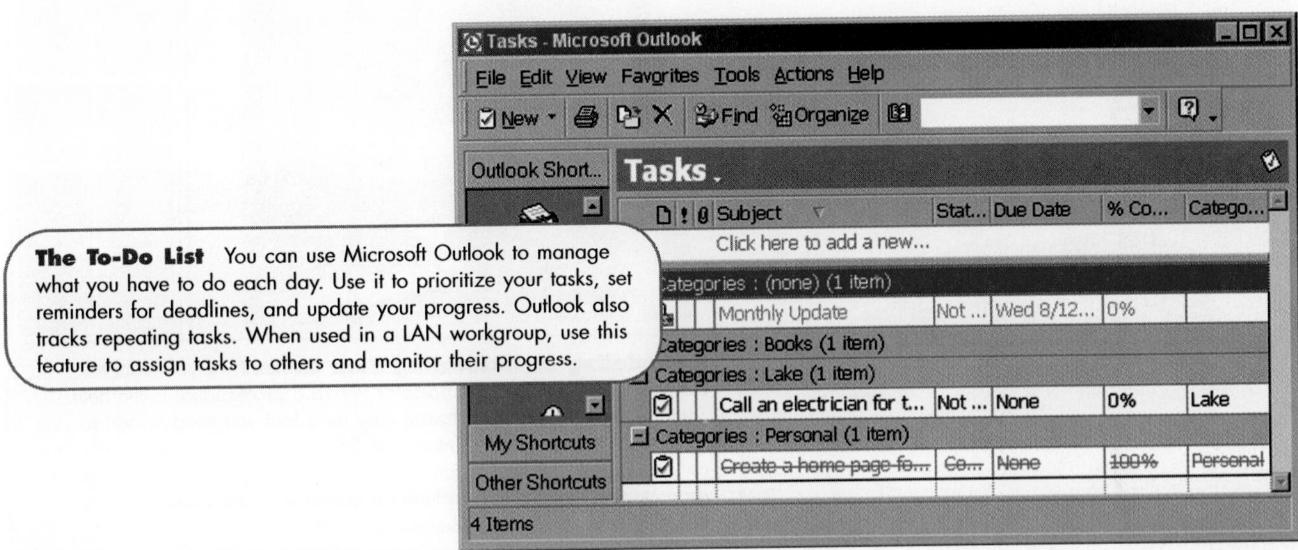

The To-Do List You can use Microsoft Outlook to manage what you have to do each day. Use it to prioritize your tasks, set reminders for deadlines, and update your progress. Outlook also tracks repeating tasks. When used in a LAN workgroup, use this feature to assign tasks to others and monitor their progress.

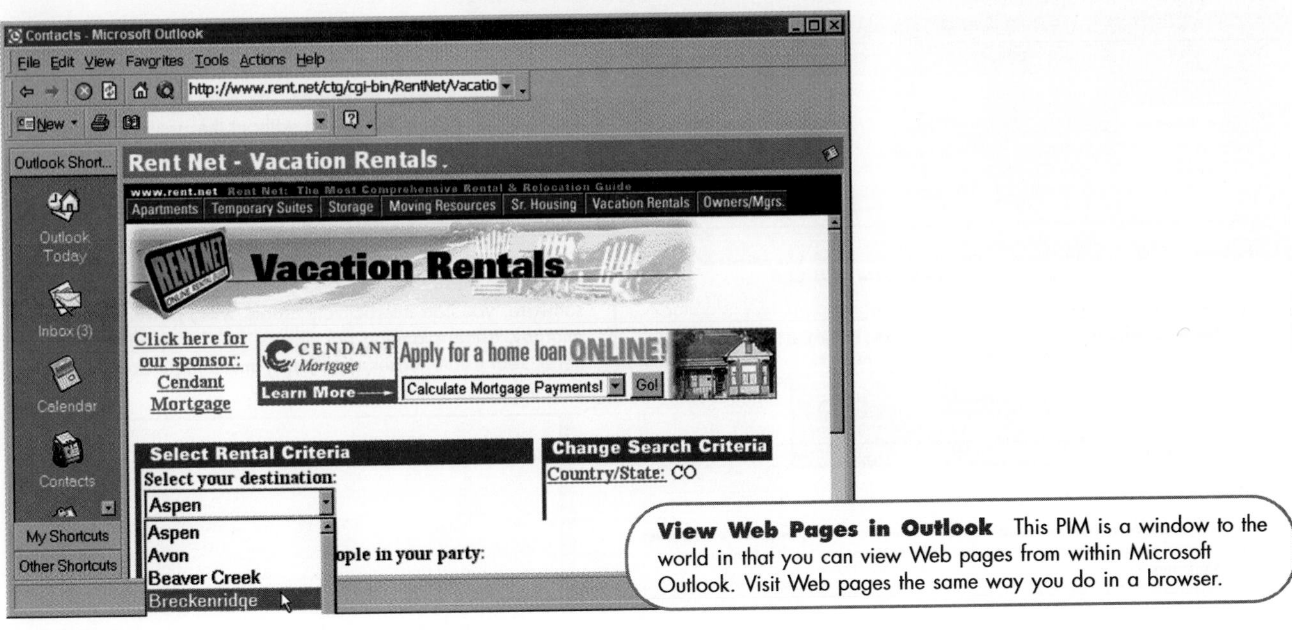

View Web Pages in Outlook This PIM is a window to the world in that you can view Web pages from within Microsoft Outlook. Visit Web pages the same way you do in a browser.

Figure 9.11 illustrates but a few of the thousands of software applications that you might find around the home. For example, one of the most popular applications helps us with the creation of greeting cards and banners. Tax preparation software lets you keep up with tax record-keeping so that, come tax time, all you have to do is click *prepare* to prepare your taxes, then *file* to send your tax return electronically to the IRS. Financial planning software helps you plan for the future and retirement. Other programs help you keep a home inventory database for insurance purposes. Home *legal advisers* assist you with the creation of a variety of legal documents, from wills to lease agreements. Trip planning software has detailed information on thousands of stops along the route to any destination in the United States.

Home and Personal Software

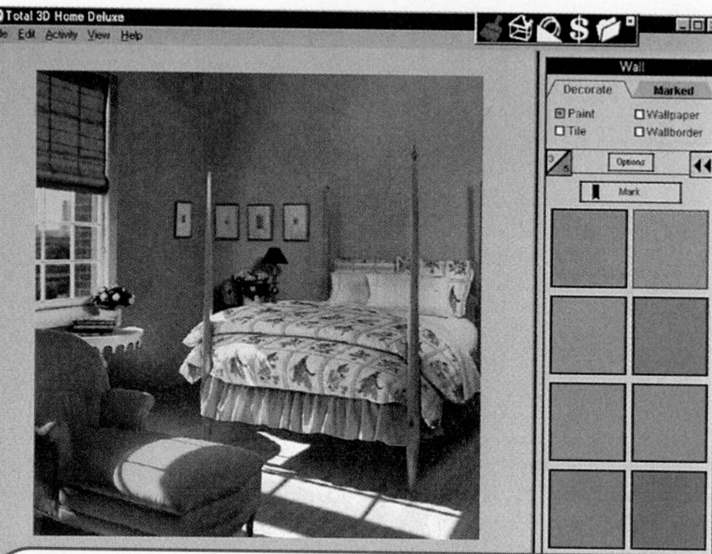

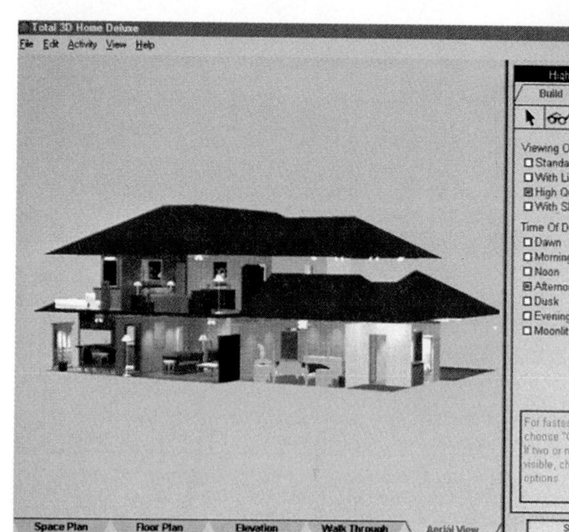

Remodeling or Decorating Your Home? If you want to remodel and decorate your home or you're a professional in the field, *Total 3D Home™ Deluxe* software may be a tool you need to add to your toolbox. With an editable, Interactive Showroom™, you can instantly "try on" colors, fabrics, and textures, all without having to put down a paint drop cloth. Other features include an instant staircase builder and roof builder. Courtesy of Broderbund Software, Inc.

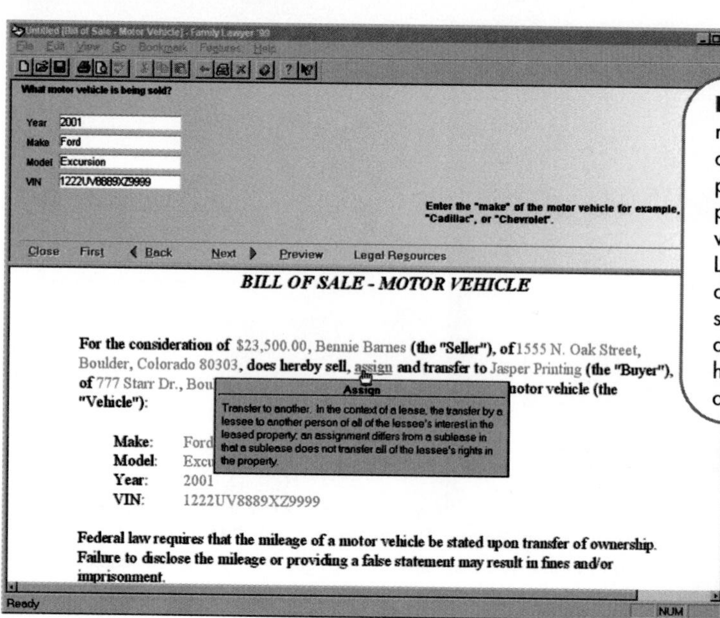

Help with Legal Matters It's possible to create most common legal documents without the assistance of an attorney. You can use Intuit Inc.'s Quicken® Family Lawyer to protect your family and everything you own. The software package includes almost 100 legal documents, letters, and worksheets, all created by a team of attorneys. Family Lawyer documents are customized by state, so you're always assured of having tailored agreements. With this software, you can interactively create wills, powers of attorney, estate planning documents, bills of sale (shown here), real estate leases, and many more legal documents as if you were talking to an attorney.

Become Your Own Printer All too often the local greeting-card store has cards and announcements for everyone except you. When you want something special, try doing it yourself with Corel® Print House™. This software helps you create imaginative banners, greeting cards, business cards, letterheads, certificates, calendars, announcements, invitations (shown here), and more. You select the backdrop, size of paper, graphics, fonts, text box shape, and supply the words.

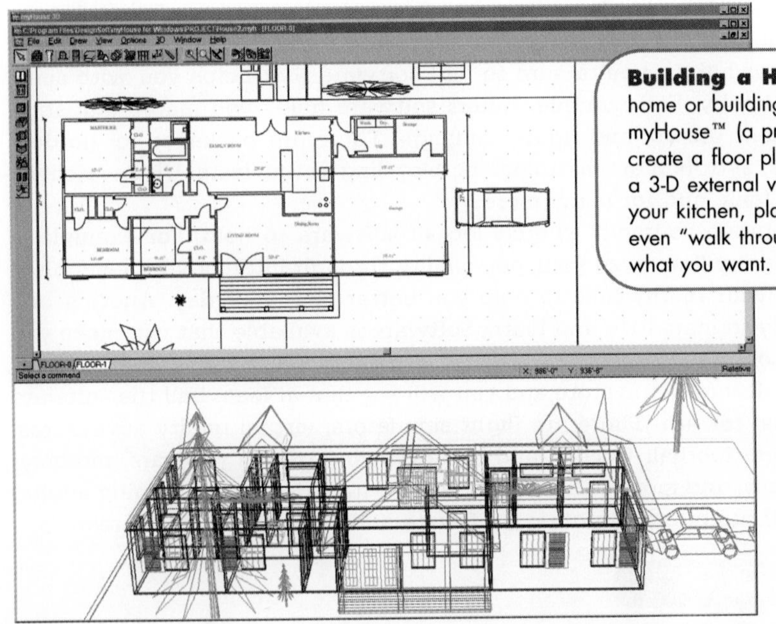

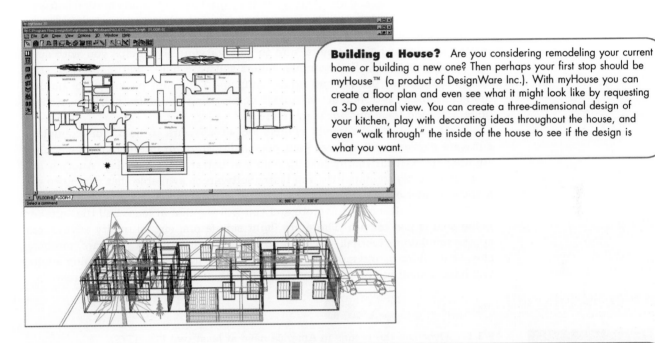

Building a House? Are you considering remodeling your current home or building a new one? Then perhaps your first stop should be myHouse™ (a product of DesignWare Inc.). With myHouse you can create a floor plan and even see what it might look like by requesting a 3-D external view. You can create a three-dimensional design of your kitchen, play with decorating ideas throughout the house, and even "walk through" the inside of the house to see if the design is what you want.

Financial Planning for the Future Quicken® Financial Planner guides you step-by-step through the creation of a personalized financial plan. Use it to plan for retirement, college expenses, buying a new home, and much more. The program assists you in deciding how much you should save and where to invest your savings. It also tracks your progress and can generate a variety of helpful reports and graphs.

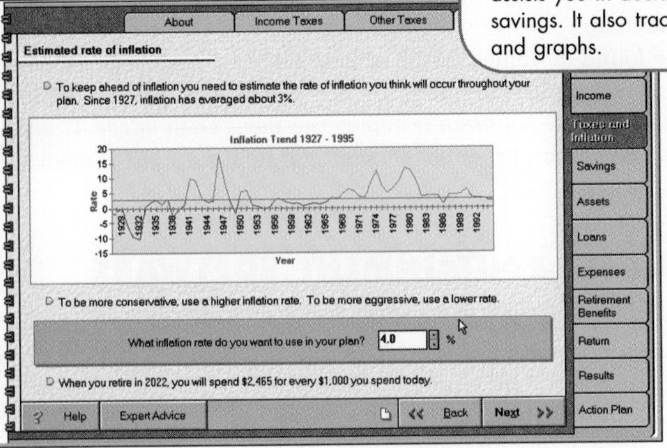

Entertainment The most popular software in any retail store is entertainment software. This collage of screen shots from selected games is representative of the hundreds of games on the market. Clockwise from top left around are *Solitaire* (distributed with Microsoft Windows), *NFL Blitz*™ (Midway Games, Inc.), *Rampage*™ *World Tour* (Midway Games, Inc.), *Tomb Raider*™ *III* (Eidos Interactive), and *Turok*® *Dinosaur Hunter* (Acclaim Entertainment, Inc.)

Medical software is a staple around the home PC. The first medical software purchased usually is a medical encyclopedia that includes emergency medical information. People may expand their medical library to include CD-ROMs with tips for taking alternative medicine, pharmacy systems that check medications for possible adverse interactions, or, perhaps, dieting software that can help you with nutrition and recipes and with the administrative aspects of dieting.

Software is available that is specifically designed for personal advocacy; that is, it helps you make your point to government agencies, political action groups, politicians, and any other organization or individual you wish to influence. There are software packages designed to help college-bound students and their parents find and secure financial aid. And when they graduate, résumé creation software packages can help them put their best foot forward when looking for a job.

Of course, a plethora of software packages have emerged for hobbyists. No matter what your hobby, you're sure to find software that helps you with some aspect of your hobby. For example, tennis software helps you match statistics, create tournament draws, and figure rankings. There are packages for gardeners/landscapers, astronomers, astrologists, bicycling enthusiasts, UFO watchers, golfers, fishing fans, and for many more.

Want to improve yourself? There's lots of software to help. For example, a software package will analyze your personality through interactive questioning. Another tracks your biorhythms to help you better plan your day. Another bolsters your ability to memorize and learn. Software is available that can make you a speed reader or speed typist.

Go to any software retail store and you will see that at least half the software being sold is just for fun. There are flight simulators, virtual reality adventures, sports simulators (football, soccer, and so on), racing games (for cars, motorcycles, boats, horses, and more). The typical home with kids (and/or gaming adults) will have a shelf full of entertainment software and another for all the rest.

SECTION SELF-CHECK

Self-Check

9-3.1 Over half the homes in America have at least two PCs. (T/F)

9-3.2 Tax preparation software lets you file taxes electronically. (T/F)

9-3.3 Software developers are currently creating software for hobbyists. (T/F)

9-3.4 Which of these software applications would not be considered a common application for home use: (a) greeting cards, (b) tax preparation, (c) morphing, or (d) trip planning?

9-3.5 Medical software found in homes might include all but which of the following: (a) medical encyclopedia, (b) pharmacy, (c) medicine law, or (d) dieting?

9-3.6 Which type of home/family software occupies the most shelf space at retail stores: (a) self-improvement, (b) entertainment, (c) hobbyist, or (d) medical-related?

9.4 EDUCATION AND EDUTAINMENT SOFTWARE

Serendipitous Surfing: Hotels and Restaurants

Emerging technologies are prompting fundamental changes in education. The *static, sequential* presentation of books has been the foundation for learning since Gutenberg. Now, however, we are beginning to see *dynamic, linked,* and *interactive technology-based* resources in virtually every discipline. When coupled with online distance learning and personal interaction of the traditional classroom environment, such resources offer a richer learning environment. We need to restate that computer-based education will not replace the classroom or teachers anytime soon, but those who have tried it agree that CBT (computer-based training) will have a dramatic impact on the way we learn.

Educational software is experiencing an explosion of acceptance in our homes and schools. Computer-based educational resources take many forms and are being embraced by young and old alike. Students can learn anatomy by taking vir-

IT Ethics

TERM-PAPER FRAUD

Plagiarism, and more specifically term-paper fraud, has been a problem in higher education throughout this century. However, only during the past few years have for-sale term papers on every common subject been showcased to the world and made readily available over the Internet. Students purchase these papers hoping to pass them off as originals. Typically, they will use a variety of software tools to add a personal touch to these recycled papers.

Many sites on the Internet offer "term-paper assistance" in a variety of topic areas. One site has both off-the-shelf and custom term-paper services, inviting students to "Get a brand-new paper written from scratch according to your exact specifications. Click here." Some states have passed laws prohibiting the sale of prefabricated term papers. However, term-paper mills circumvent these laws by stating that the intended purpose of their term papers is that they be used as models that students can use during the preparation of their own term papers. Students who plagiarize the work of others rob themselves of the knowledge and experience they gain from writing a well-developed paper.

Discussion: What can students do to help deter plagiarism and encourage academic honesty? What can college administrators do? What can professors do? What can government do?

tual tours of the body. Students can travel through the Milky Way to Cassiopeia and other constellations while an electronic teacher explains the mysteries of the universe. Millions of elementary age students are getting one-on-one instruction on keyboarding skills. Chemistry students are doing lab exercises with bits and bytes rather than dangerous chemicals. Some innovative software packages tease the mind by inviting students to learn the power of logic and creativity.

We all have learned at one time or another that learning can, and should, be fun. It didn't take long for education software developers to combine *edu*cation and enter*tainment* into a single learning resource. This *edutainment software* gives students an opportunity to play while learning. Figure 9.12 provides a few examples of education and edutainment software.

SECTION SELF-CHECK

Self-Check

9-4.1 Computer-based training is a failed experiment. (T/F)

9-4.2 Education software can help students learn the power of logic. (T/F)

9-4.3 Which of the following is not a characteristic of education software: (a) linked, (b) sequential, (c) interactive, or (d) dynamic?

9-4.4 Which type of software gives the student an opportunity to play while learning: (a) education, (b) entertainment, (c) edutainment, or (d) fun-and-learn?

9-4.5 In the interactive learning environment, we learn: (a) primarily within workgroups, (b) at our own pace, (c) by the schedule in a syllabus, or (d) only at night?

9.5 REFERENCE SOFTWARE

As soon as the technology gurus figured out that audio CDs could hold 650 MB of digital data, the CD-ROM was born. That observation changed forever how reference information is packaged and distributed. Almost immediately after the introduction of the CD-ROM, books, dictionaries, encyclopedias, newspapers, corporate manuals, and thousands of other printed materials were being translated

Education and Edutainment Software

Where Is Carmen Sandiego? Do you enjoy adventure, travel, and solving mysteries? If so, try chasing Carmen Sandiego, an elegant thief, throughout the countries of the world with this Broderbund® product. Young sleuths follow clues to nab Carmen and her crew while learning geography in *Where in the World Is Carmen Sandiego®*.

The eBook Education will take many twists and turns in the coming years as new hardware and software innovations come to market. This device, the Rocket eBook™, puts a stack of books in the palm of your hand and is sure to reduce the weight of the college student's backpack. The Rocket eBook holds the equivalent of a semester's worth of college textbooks (about 4000 pages of text and images). You can read or study it as you would a print book, making margin notes, underlining special passages, and bookmarking pages. The eBook is searchable, too. Courtesy of NuvoMedia, Inc.

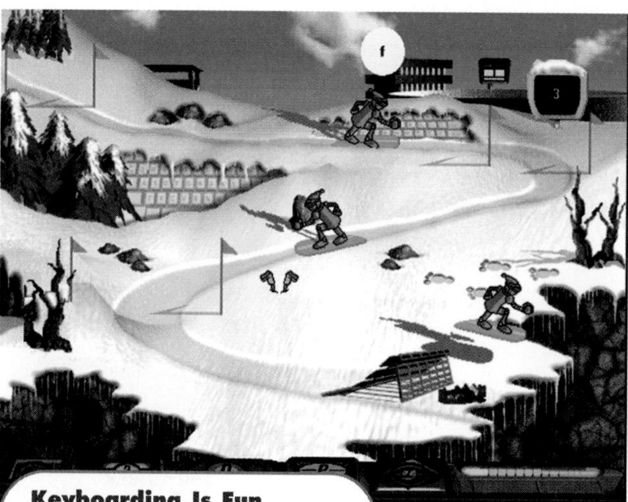

Keyboarding Is Fun JumpStart Typing™ is pure edutainment. It helps young children learn essential typing skills while competing in an extreme keyboarding competition. Students practice their typing skills by taking timed lessons and playing exciting arcade-style games like snowboarding, rock climbing, and skateboarding.
Courtesy of Knowledge Adventure

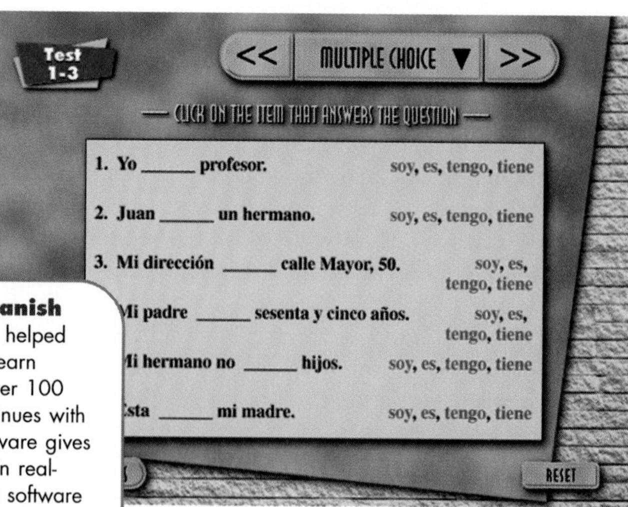

Learn to Speak Spanish The Berlitz Method® has helped over 30 million people learn foreign languages for over 100 years. The tradition continues with Berlitz Spanish. The software gives instruction and practice in real-world conversations. The software has many language activities, tests, audio of native speakers, and speech recognition so that you can build your confidence and speaking, listening, reading, and writing skills.
Courtesy of The Learning Company

to digital media, namely the CD-ROM. Most of the reference material distributed on CD-ROM is commercial (for example, encyclopedias, corporate financial information) or proprietary (for example, corporate sales manuals). However, now that CD-RW (rewritable) is reasonably priced, we at home and in small offices can create our own CD-ROM–based reference material.

Computer-based reference material is much more than simply text on a disk. It's searchable and interactive. Attorneys no longer spend days pouring over scores of cases to prepare for trials. Keyword searches can result in a display of applicable cases within seconds. Also, multimedia content can be integrated with text. Finally, a single CD-ROM, weighing less than an ounce, can store the equivalent of hundreds of books.

Just about any frequently used printed reference material is available on CD-ROM, or it is being considered for CD-ROM publication. We can get detailed geographic information, multilingual dictionaries, state and federal census information, specific entrance requirements for thousands of colleges, Fortune 500 financial information, and much more. Figure 9.13 illustrates a variety of CD-ROM–based reference materials.

FIGURE 9.13

Reference Software

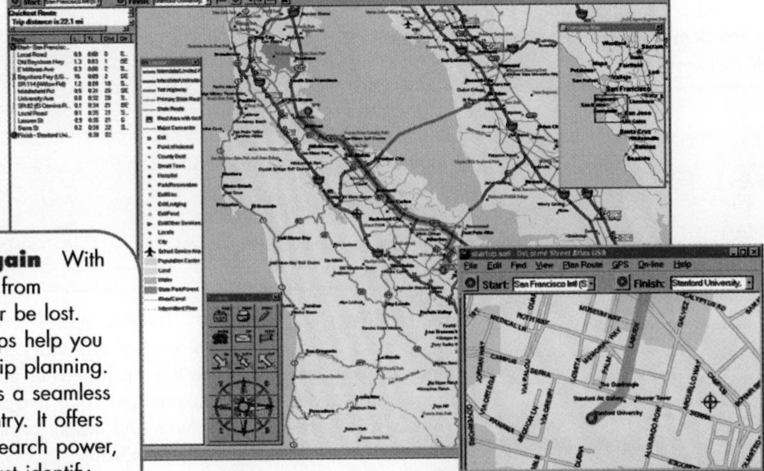

Never Be Lost Again With *Street Atlas USA® 6.0* from DeLorme you will never be lost. Incredibly detailed maps help you take the effort out of trip planning. Street Atlas USA 6.0 is a seamless map of the entire country. It offers detail, street address search power, door-to-door routing. Just identify your start (San Francisco International Airport) and finish (Stanford University) points and the software calculates then displays the best route (in blue). You can zoom in for street-level maps (inset of Stanford campus). The program also interfaces with global positioning systems (GPSs) to pinpoint your location on the map display and to guide you to your destination, prompting you visually and verbally as to when and where to turn.

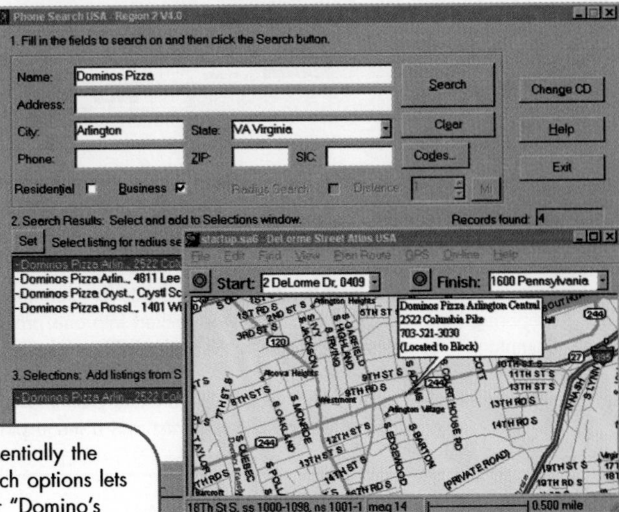

A Circular Phone Book DeLorme's *Phone Search USA™* is essentially the white and yellow pages for the entire United States. A variety of search options lets you find the numbers you want. In the example, the user searched for "Domino's Pizza" in "Arlington," "VA Virginia." The user chose the nearest one, then requested a map to the location. Phone Search requires *Street Atlas* software.

(Figure 9.13 continues on next page)

Figure 9.13 (continued)

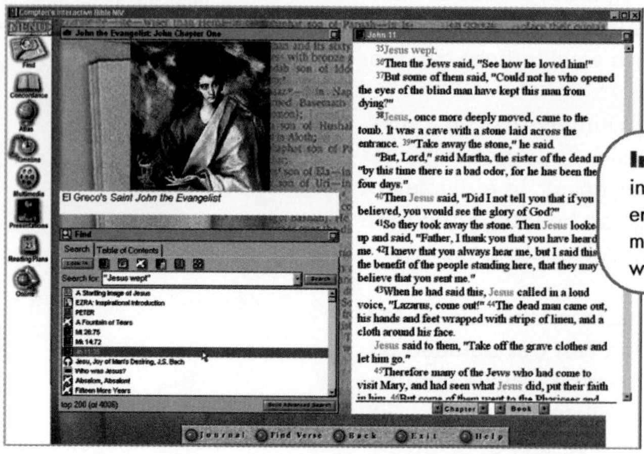

Interactive Bible The best-selling book of all time is now interactive. Compton's® Interactive Bible™ NIV searchable text is enhanced with complementary videos, slide shows, maps, and music. Shown here is the result of a search for the passage "Jesus wept," which was found in the book of John.

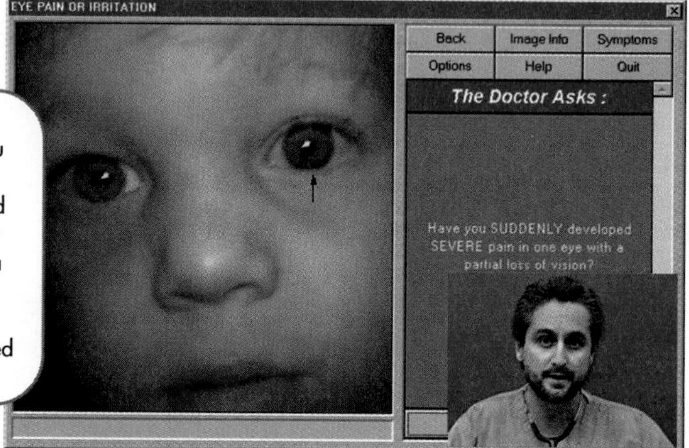

Home Medical Advisor *Home Medical Advisor*™ is a practical guide to symptom diagnosis and preventative care. You can even talk to a "video" doctor to get answers to detailed questions (shown here), and then receive possible diagnoses and treatments. Hundreds of videos show you exactly what to expect if you're scheduling an eye exam, planning surgery, or having a baby. You can analyze potentially harmful interactions of more than 8000 over-the-counter and prescription drugs. Find expert emergency advice and video demonstrations right when you need them—instantly! Courtesy of The Learning Company

A Talking Dictionary *The American Heritage® Talking Dictionary 5.0* is a different kind of dictionary. It has hundreds of thousands of definitions like the much heavier print dictionaries, plus it has audio pronunciations and color images. The software has a variety of search features and instant access to word definitions from any Windows program.
Courtesy of The Learning Company

Interactive Cookbook All the ingredients for planning and preparing perfect recipes and meals are mixed into one program, Compton's® Complete Cookbook™. All of the 2000 plus recipes come with step-by-step instructions, color pictures, detailed nutritional facts, and tips from top chefs. To make planning a snap, the software provides a "smart shopping" list and a menu planner.
Courtesy of The Learning Company

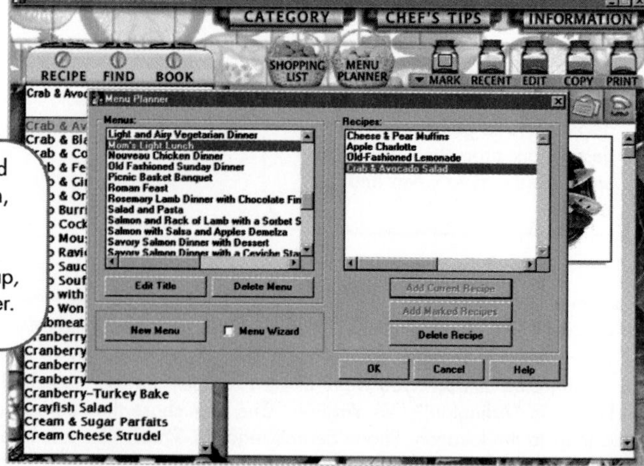

SECTION SELF-CHECK

Self-Check

9-5.1 Mapping systems can interface with global positioning systems to pinpoint your location on a map. (T/F)

9-5.2 Attorneys still prefer law libraries of books and do not use electronic reference material. (T/F)

9-5.3 Which technology prompted the explosion of CD-ROM–based reference software: (a) SDRAM, (b) hard disk, (c) TV, or (d) audio CD?

9-5.4 It's technologically possible for people at home to put their own reference material on CD-ROM by using what technology: (a) CD-RW, (b) audio CD, (c) VHS, or (d) PCMCIA?

9-5.5 Which of the following is not a characteristic of reference material on CD-ROM: (a) searchable, (b) interactive, (c) multimedia, or (d) limited to public domain content?

9.6 BUSINESS AND MANAGEMENT SOFTWARE

With today's PCs having more power than the mainframes of the not-too-distant-past, our PCs are capable of supporting both personal and enterprise-wide computing. Personal computing in the business environment revolves around office suite applications: word processing, spreadsheet, database, presentation, database, and personal information management software. Productivity software is discussed in Chapter 2 and PIM software is discussed earlier in this chapter. Other applications discussed earlier in this chapter and the book, such as computer-aided design (CAD), authoring software, and so on, are helpful in business personal computing. In fact, there are hundreds of helpful programs that can make life around the office a little easier and more productive. For example, one program scans business cards and places the name and address information into a database. Another creates business forms, both online and printed.

There are literally thousands of business-specific software packages that support information processing and management decision making. For example, there are software packages specifically designed for physicians' clinics, city libraries, construction contractors, CPAs, churches, city governments, motels, law offices, general retailing stores, nonprofit organizations, real estate companies, recreation and fitness centers, restaurants, and just about any other business that has administrative information processing needs. Some business-specific software for smaller companies can run on a single PC, and other packages are designed for the LAN client/server environment so information can be shared among workers. Figure 9.14 shows several business software examples, including project management and financial management resources that are applicable to any business.

SECTION SELF-CHECK

Self-Check

9-6.1 Project management software helps you plan and track your projects more effectively. (T/F)

9-6.2 PERT charts would be associated with project management software. (T/F)

9-6.3 Software is available for church administration. (T/F)

9-6.4 Which of these might be considered a "killer app": (a) financial management software, (b) tips for alternative medicine software, (c) simulated golf, or (d) politically correct screen savers?

9-6.5 Which of the following software applications is least likely to be found in a business personal computing environment: (a) database, (b) presentation, (c) multimedia encyclopedia, or (d) spreadsheet?

9-6.6 Which of these software packages would not be considered a business-specific application: (a) physician's clinic, (b) fitness center, (c) real estate, or (d) nationwide telephone directory?

9-6.7 To convert paper archives into usable electronic text and images you might use what type of software: (a) OCR, (b) PIM, (c) CAD, or (d) TSR?

FIGURE 9.14

Business Software

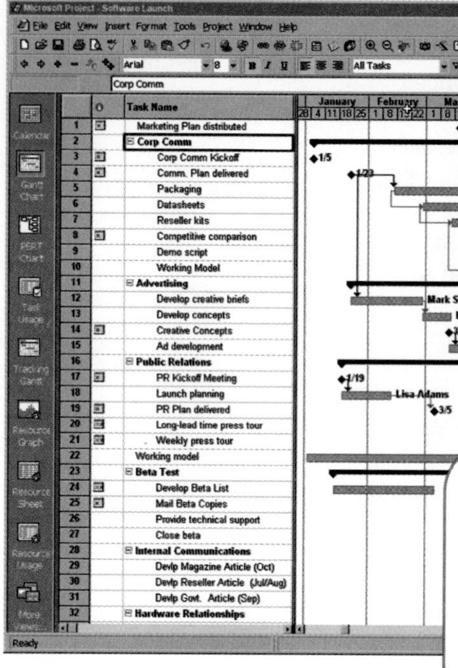

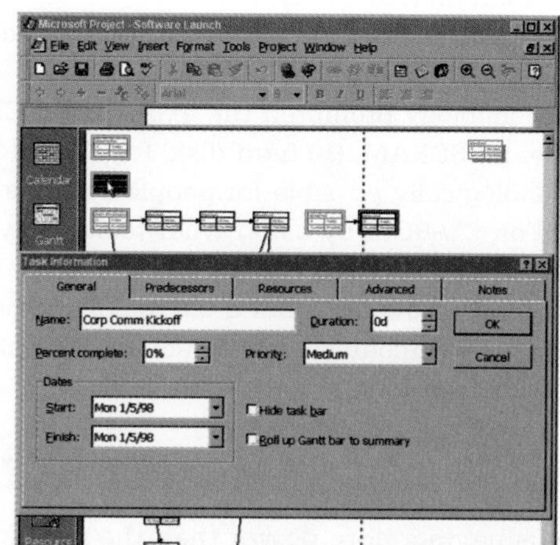

Project Management Microsoft's *Project 98* is a great tool for anyone who oversees a team, plans a budget, juggles schedules, or has deadlines to meet. Project management software helps you plan and track your projects more effectively so you can identify and respond to conflicts before they happen. Shown here are two of the many views that were created for a project to launch a commercial software package. The Gantt chart (left) shows when the various project activities will occur along a calendar scale. The PERT chart lets you review, create, or edit your project tasks and task dependencies as a network diagram (or flowchart). Each box represents each task and a line connecting two boxes represents the dependency between the two tasks.

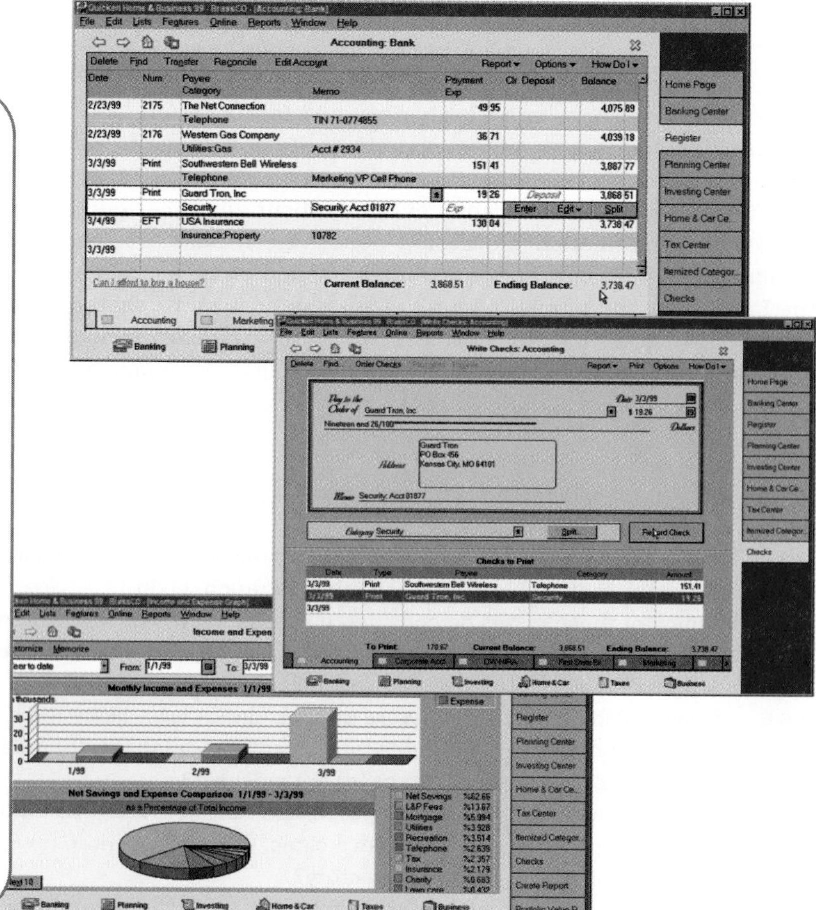

Business and Home Finances Anyone who has attempted to balance a sadly out-of-kilter checkbook or consolidate tax information will appreciate *Quicken® Home and Business Deluxe 99* (*Quicken® 99* software is made and owned by Intuit). Industry analysts refer to Quicken as a "killer app," an application with such useful capabilities that it alone can justify the expense of a computer. This financial-management system helps you or it can help a company manage bills, bank accounts, investments, tax records, assets and liabilities, and much more. And best of all, you don't have to be an accountant to use it. You can even write your checks online and all the details are automatically entered into your checkbook register (see example), thereby eliminating duplicate entries. Just print on check stock (see example) designed for your printer, sign, and send.

Many avid Quicken users keep track of everything from credit-card purchases to stock transactions. The money trail summarized by Quicken gives these people and companies some insight into what's happening at home and in their businesses. For example, one company was surprised to find out that one of its biggest expenses was entertainment. Quicken offers users a variety of reports and graphs (see income/expenses graph example).

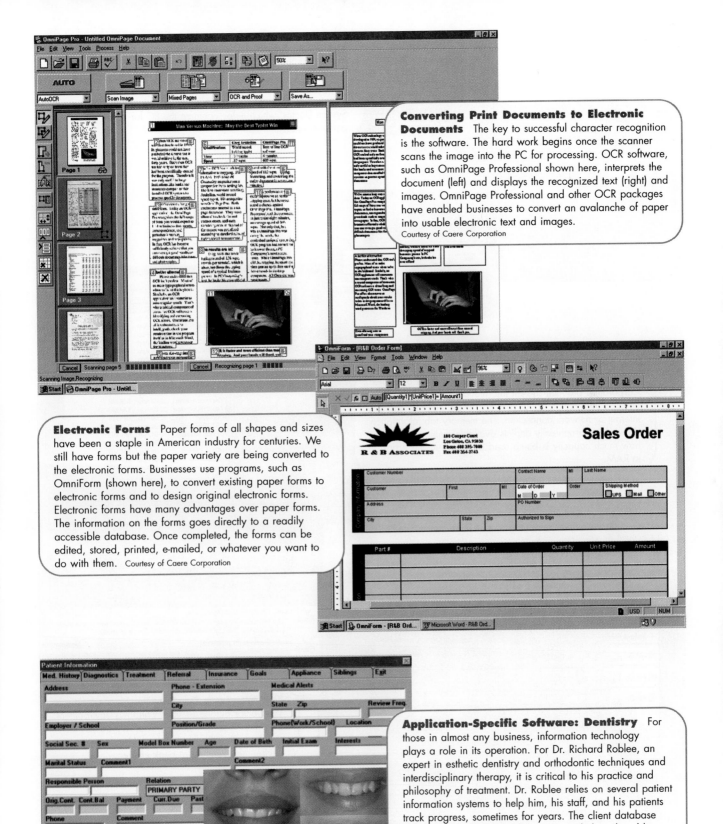

Converting Print Documents to Electronic Documents The key to successful character recognition is the software. The hard work begins once the scanner scans the image into the PC for processing. OCR software, such as OmniPage Professional shown here, interprets the document (left) and displays the recognized text (right) and images. OmniPage Professional and other OCR packages have enabled businesses to convert an avalanche of paper into usable electronic text and images.
Courtesy of Caere Corporation

Electronic Forms Paper forms of all shapes and sizes have been a staple in American industry for centuries. We still have forms but the paper variety are being converted to the electronic forms. Businesses use programs, such as OmniForm (shown here), to convert existing paper forms to electronic forms and to design original electronic forms. Electronic forms have many advantages over paper forms. The information on the forms goes directly to a readily accessible database. Once completed, the forms can be edited, stored, printed, e-mailed, or whatever you want to do with them. Courtesy of Caere Corporation

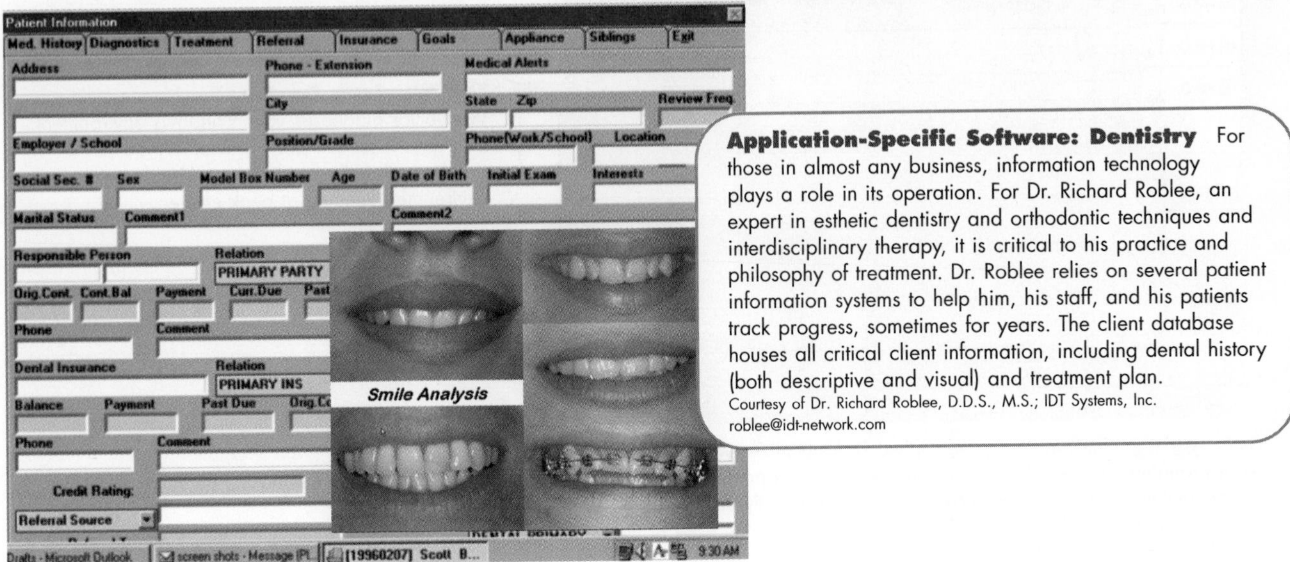

Application-Specific Software: Dentistry For those in almost any business, information technology plays a role in its operation. For Dr. Richard Roblee, an expert in esthetic dentistry and orthodontic techniques and interdisciplinary therapy, it is critical to his practice and philosophy of treatment. Dr. Roblee relies on several patient information systems to help him, his staff, and his patients track progress, sometimes for years. The client database houses all critical client information, including dental history (both descriptive and visual) and treatment plan.
Courtesy of Dr. Richard Roblee, D.D.S., M.S.; IDT Systems, Inc.
roblee@idt-network.com

FIGURE 9.15

Utility Software

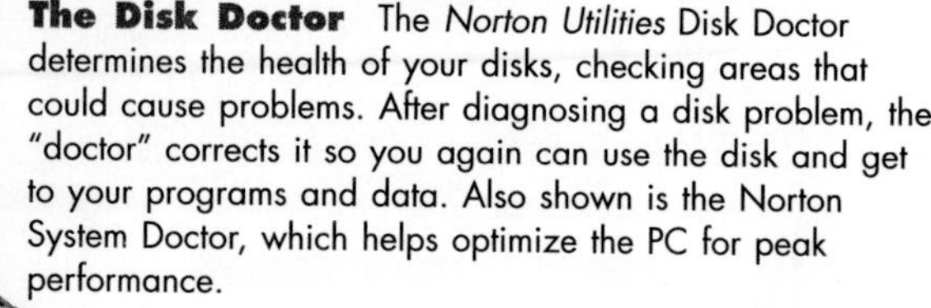

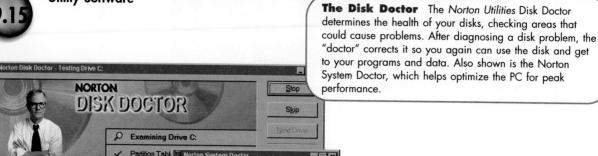

The Disk Doctor The *Norton Utilities* Disk Doctor determines the health of your disks, checking areas that could cause problems. After diagnosing a disk problem, the "doctor" corrects it so you again can use the disk and get to your programs and data. Also shown is the Norton System Doctor, which helps optimize the PC for peak performance.

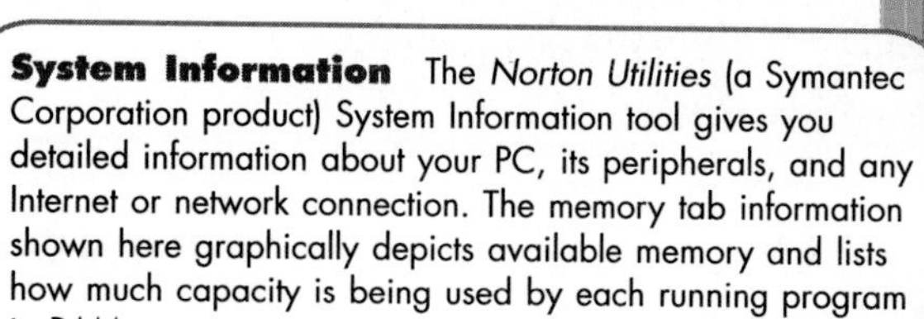

System Information The *Norton Utilities* (a Symantec Corporation product) System Information tool gives you detailed information about your PC, its peripherals, and any Internet or network connection. The memory tab information shown here graphically depicts available memory and lists how much capacity is being used by each running program in RAM.

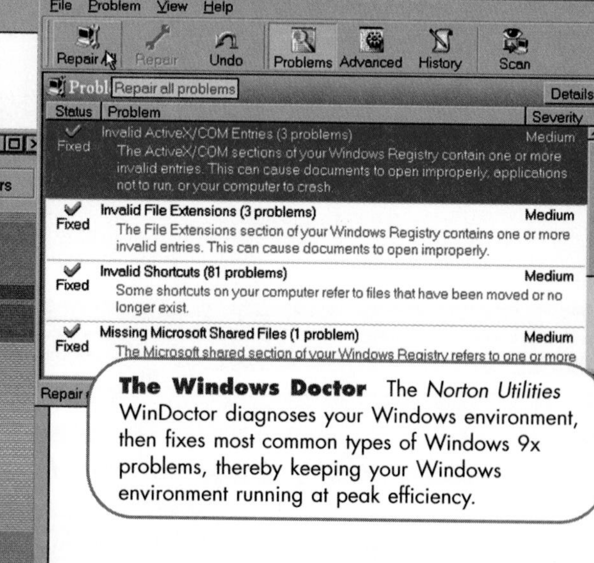

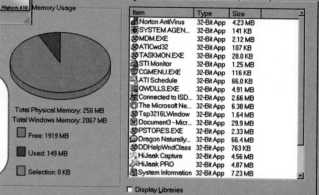

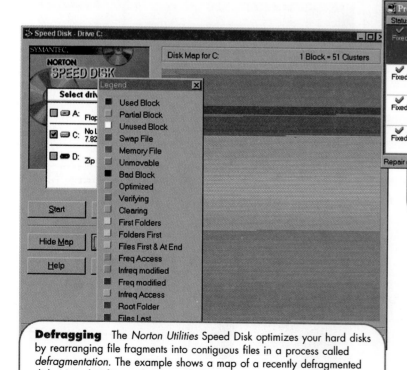

The Windows Doctor The *Norton Utilities* WinDoctor diagnoses your Windows environment, then fixes most common types of Windows 9x problems, thereby keeping your Windows environment running at peak efficiency.

Defragging The *Norton Utilities* Speed Disk optimizes your hard disks by rearranging file fragments into contiguous files in a process called *defragmentation*. The example shows a map of a recently defragmented disk. Note that frequently accessed files are grouped in one area of the disk to minimize movement of the disk-access arm.

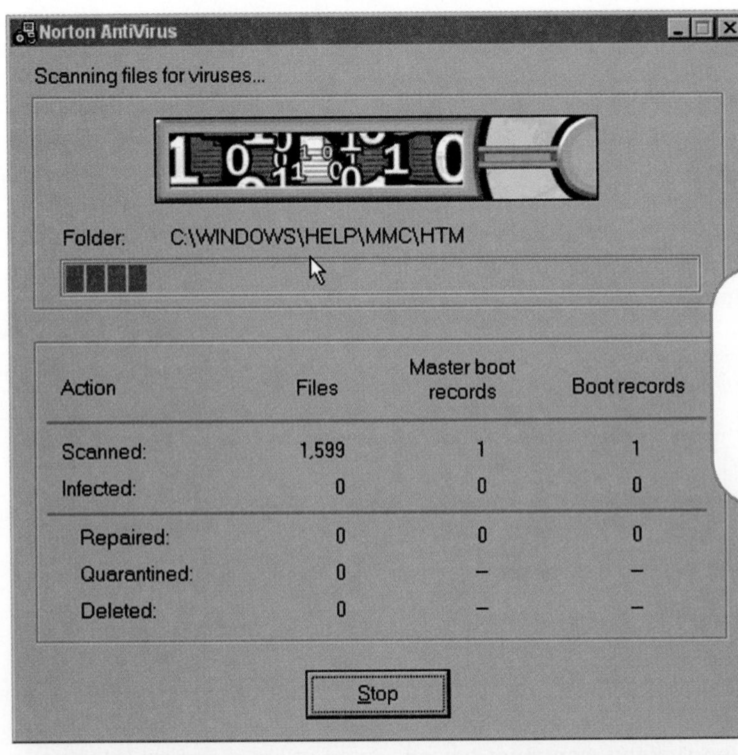

Virus Protection *Norton AntiVirus*, a popular virus vaccine, scans your disk drive(s) for viruses at system start up. Also, it monitors your PC for any activity that might indicate that a virus is at work in your system. It alerts you to problems, then removes the virus. Each month, more viruses are added to a list of hundreds that float around cyberspace. The LiveUpdate feature lets you periodically download protection from new viruses.

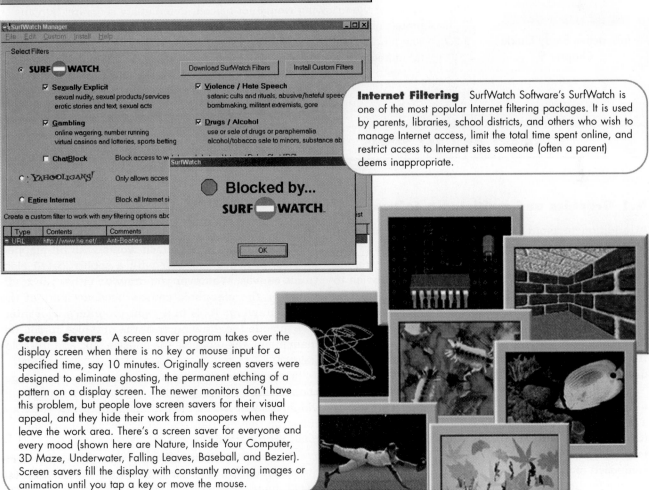

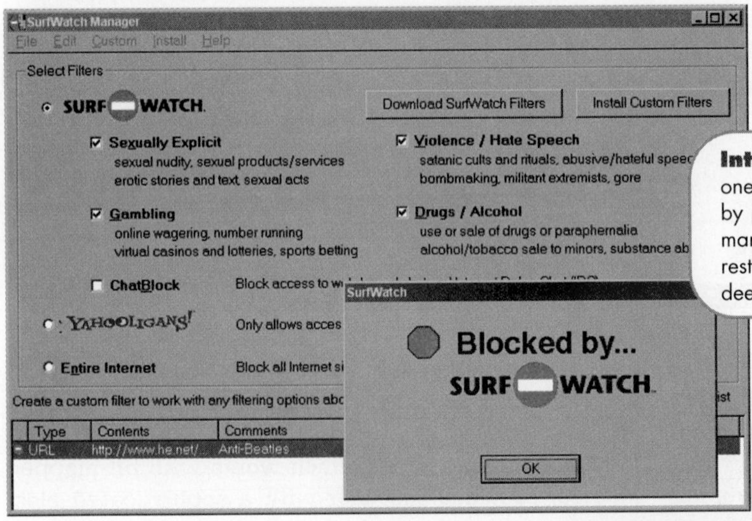

Internet Filtering SurfWatch Software's SurfWatch is one of the most popular Internet filtering packages. It is used by parents, libraries, school districts, and others who wish to manage Internet access, limit the total time spent online, and restrict access to Internet sites someone (often a parent) deems inappropriate.

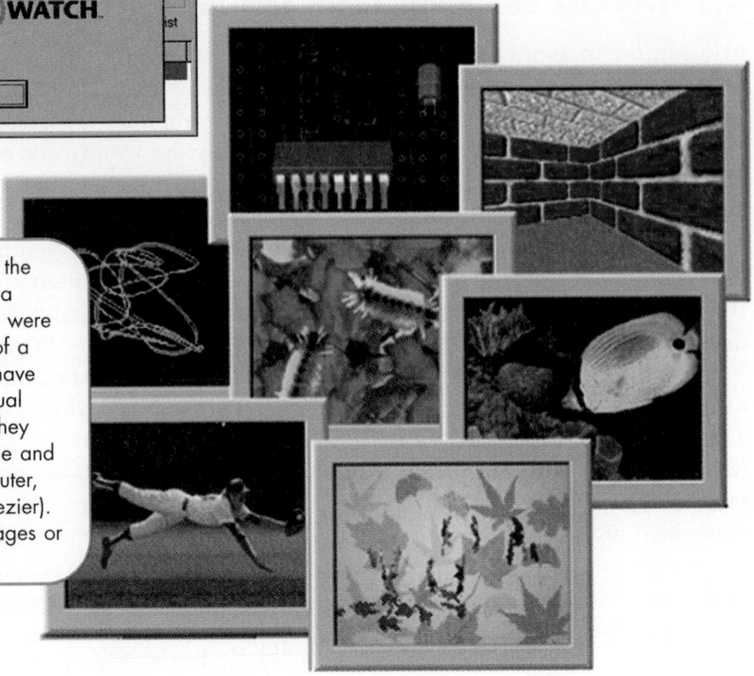

Screen Savers A screen saver program takes over the display screen when there is no key or mouse input for a specified time, say 10 minutes. Originally screen savers were designed to eliminate ghosting, the permanent etching of a pattern on a display screen. The newer monitors don't have this problem, but people love screen savers for their visual appeal, and they hide their work from snoopers when they leave the work area. There's a screen saver for everyone and every mood (shown here are Nature, Inside Your Computer, 3D Maze, Underwater, Falling Leaves, Baseball, and Bezier). Screen savers fill the display with constantly moving images or animation until you tap a key or move the mouse.

9.7 UTILITY SOFTWARE

System software, which includes the operating system and its GUI, is applications-independent. Generally system software supports the operation and maintenance of the PC's hardware, software, and files. A wide variety of system software *utilities* are available to help you with the day-to-day chores associated with personal computing (disk and file maintenance, system recovery, security, backup, virus protection, and so on) and to keep your system running at peak performance. Figure 9.15 gives you a sampling of common utilities you might use to enhance your personal computing environment.

SECTION SELF-CHECK

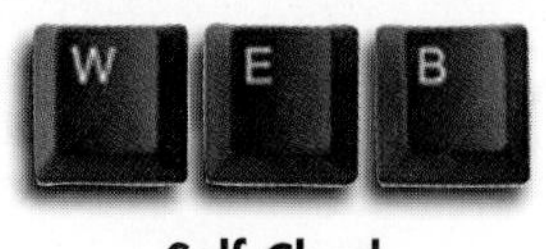

Self-Check

Interactive Study Guide Chapter 9

9-7.1 The proper use of utility software can help keep a PC running at peak efficiency. (T/F)

9-7.2 Software that provides detailed information with regard to available memory and disk space would be considered utility software. (T/F)

9-7.3 The universal use of virus vaccine software over the past decade has done away with the threat of computer viruses. (T/F)

9-7.4 To eliminate the possibility of ghosting on modern monitors, the use of screen savers is essential. (T/F)

9-7.5 Utility software would be considered: (a) applications software, (b) system software, (c) utilitarian software, or (d) operating system software?

9-7.6 Which of the following would not be considered utility software: (a) virus protection, (b) backup, (c) file maintenance, or (d) gaming?

9-7.7 The process that rearranges file fragments into contiguous files is called: (a) unfragging, (b) file filling, (c) folder folding, or (d) defragmentation?

SUMMARY AND KEY TERMS

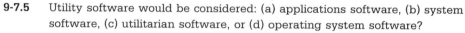

9.1 Graphics and multimedia software

In addition to word processing, desktop publishing, presentation graphics, spreadsheet, database, and browser software, you will want to familiarize yourself with graphics and multimedia software if you wish to add pizzazz to your documents.

Graphics software facilitates the creation, manipulation, and management of computer-based images. Graphics software is discussed within the context of these capabilities: painting, drawing, photo illustration, drag-and-drop, and animation.

Graphic images are presented as **bit-mapped graphics** (4) (**file formats** [5] include **BMP, GIF, TIFF** or **TIF, PCX, PNG,** and **JPEG** or **JPG**) (5), **vector graphics (CGM** and **EPS)** (6), and **metafiles (WMF)** (4). In bit-mapped graphics, or **raster graphics** (5), the image is composed of patterns of dots (pixels). In vector graphics, the image is composed of patterns of lines, points, and other geometric shapes (vectors). The metafile is a class of graphics that combines the components of bit-mapped and vector graphics formats. Specialized *graphics conversion programs* provide dozens of conversion options between file formats.

Paint software (7), which works with bit-mapped images, provides the user with a sophisticated electronic canvas. Whatever you draw on either the traditional or the electronic canvas becomes part of the whole drawing. Tools in a paint program's user interface include the drawing area, the graphics cursor, the main menu, the tool box, the linesize box, and the color palette.

Draw software (8) lets you create a screen image, then isolate and manipulate representations of individual objects within the overall image. Draw software relies on vector graphics, so a specific object can be dealt with independently.

Photo illustration software (9) enables you to create original images as well as to dress up existing digitized images, such as photographs and electronic paintings. Images can be retouched with special effects, such as **morphing** (9), with which you can show the changes that take place as one image is modified to become an entirely different image.

Drag-and-drop software (9) allows users to drag ready-made shapes from application-specific stencils to the desired position on the drawing area. With drag-and-drop software, you can glue the shapes together such that the shapes stay connected even if one of them is moved.

Animation (10) is accomplished by the rapid repositioning of objects on the display screen. Animation software lets you further enhance presentations with such tools as animated bullet build and animated charting features.

Multimedia refers to a computer system that lets users access and interact with computer-based text, high-resolution still graphics, motion visuals, animation, and sound. Three elements in particular distinguish multimedia: sound, motion, and the opportunity for interaction.

The next stage of multimedia growth would include some or all of the following hardware and software: a video camera, a videocassette recorder/player, an audiocassette player, a CD-audio player, a television, a synthesizer, a video capture card, a color scanner, a digital camera, CD-RW, professional applications development software, and a source library.

Multimedia applications draw content material from a number of sources, including text files, database files, sound files, image files, animation files, and motion video files. Sound files are of two types: *waveform* (or **wave file**) (16) and *nonwaveform* (or **MIDI file**) (17). Sources for image files include those the user creates, clip art, scanned images, and photo images.

There is a variety of software packages available to help you create multimedia applications. These include presentation software and multimedia development tools, including **authoring software** (16) and multimedia programming languages.

9.2 Personal information management software

Personal information management, or PIM, refers to messaging and personal information management software. PIM software helps you manage your messages, appointments, contacts, and tasks.

9.3 Home and family software

A wide range of software is available for home PCs that can help us with the many activities of day-to-day living. Popular home applications include greeting cards and banners, tax preparation, home "legal advisers," medical encyclopedias, and entertainment. A variety of software packages is available for self-improvement and hobbyists.

9.4 Education and edutainment software

Over the coming years, the static, sequential presentation of books may be giving way to dynamic, linked, and interactive technology-based resources in education. Edutainment software combines education and entertainment into a single software package.

9.5 Reference software

Most of the reference material distributed on CD-ROM is commercial (for example, encyclopedias) or proprietary. However, with CD-RW we can create our own CD-ROM–based reference material. Computer-based reference material is searchable, interactive, and can contain multimedia components.

9.6 Business and management software

Personal computing in the business environment revolves around office suite applications, including personal information management software. However, there are thousands of business-specific software packages and many other packages, such as project management and financial management resources, that are applicable to any business.

9.7 Utility software

System software, which includes the operating system and utility software, is applications-independent. Utility software is available to help you with disk and file maintenance, system recovery, security, backup, virus protection, and other system-related tasks.

DISCUSSION AND PROBLEM SOLVING

9.1 **a.** Describe the advantages of a multimedia-based encyclopedia over a traditional printed encyclopedia. Describe the advantages of a traditional printed encyclopedia over a multimedia-based encyclopedia.

b. Use paint software, such as Paint (which comes with Windows 9x/2000), to create an image of your choice. Use at least five different paint software features in the creation of the image. Discuss the capabilities and limitations of Paint software.

c. *Multimedia* was the buzzword of the mid-1990s, but its glitter is wearing off. Why?

d. Describe two scenarios for which information kiosks would be applicable.

e. Why do you suppose there are so many different graphics file formats? Why doesn't the graphics industry standardize a single format for bit-mapped graphics and a single format for vector graphics?

f. Speculate on at least one application for drag-and-drop software in your chosen career field. Briefly describe the appearance of the resulting document.

g. Identify and briefly describe at least three situations where you have witnessed the use of computer animation.

h. Would a music composer work with a wave file or a MIDI file? Explain.

9.2 **a.** Describe how you might use personal information management software at home.

b. Describe how you might use personal information management software at work. Which PIM component would be most helpful to you?

9.3 **a.** If you have a PC, list the three home and family software packages in your software portfolio that are most important to you. What home and family packages would you like to add to your portfolio?

b. If you do not own a PC, what home and family software packages would you like to add to your software portfolio during your first year of PC ownership?

c. Would you feel comfortable creating common legal documents, such as wills and bills of sale, with legal software without input from an attorney? Explain.

d. Some children spend more time playing computer-based games than they do attending school. Would you limit your child's time at playing games? If so, how much time each day would be appropriate?

9.4 **a.** For centuries, the book has been the primary resource for learning. How do you feel about exchanging that tradition for computer-based learning resources that are dynamic, linked, and interactive?

b. What do you think about integrating entertainment with education software for elementary age children? How about doing this with education software for adults?

9.5 **a.** Identify at least three printed reference documents you have used in the past that might be improved if made available as CD-ROM–based reference software. Explain why each would be better in electronic format.

b. A diminishing number of attorneys choose to use printed law books. Would you rather retain the services of an attorney who prefers books or one who prefers using electronic media? Explain.

9.6 **a.** If you work in a business, briefly describe the personal computing software (other than office suite software) that is most useful to you in your job.

b. All of us have completed many forms, most with pen and pencil. The trend, however, is toward electronic forms. Describe the advantages of the latter.

9.7 **a.** How often should you run virus vaccine software to scan your PC system for viruses?

b. Discuss the consequences of not performing routine disk maintenance with utility software.

NOTES

Computers in Society: Today

Learning Objectives

10.1 Put society's dependence on computers in perspective.

10.2 Recognize the relationship between career mobility and computer knowledge.

10.3 Identify ergonomic and environmental considerations in the design of the knowledge worker's workplace.

10.4 Explore ethical questions concerning the use of information technology.

10.5 Identify points of security vulnerability for a computer center, an information system, and a PC.

chapter 10

WHY THIS CHAPTER IS IMPORTANT TO YOU

Information technology is not all bits, bytes, and procedures. The IT revolution continually raises difficult questions that beg for answers and serious issues that must be resolved.

We have reached the point of no return with regard to information technology. There is a good chance that you will embrace a career as a professional who relies on computers and IT to do your job. Many who take this course choose a career as an IT professional. This chapter will introduce you to opportunities for both the non-IT specialist with IT competency and the common IT specialist positions.

How we fare as a society depends on how we cope with a continuous stream of information technology issues. Just about any IT issue is fuzzy, and there is no historical perspective from which to derive a solution. Frequently, we must address these issues on an individual basis to determine what course of action to take. This chapter should prepare you to make good decisions on the critical IT issues of the day and to make you sensitive to ethical concerns.

Eventually we will wear our computer systems, but until then, you will seldom be much more than an arm's length from your PC. Reading this chapter will give you a better understanding of the ergonomics (human–machine interaction) of computing and help you build a healthy workplace and avoid some of the health problems associated with the computing environment.

Trillions of bytes of information travel over millions of miles of wires and through the air from computer to computer. This information, which often is sensitive in nature, eventually resides on magnetic storage devices. Whether traveling at the speed of light or spinning on a disk, this information is vulnerable to theft and/or abuse. This chapter will help you to better understand what can be done to minimize the exposure of information and computer systems to the criminal elements of our society.

10.1 THE INFORMATION TECHNOLOGY PARADOX

Monthly Technology Update
Chapter 10

We as a society are caught in an information technology paradox: Information technology is thriving in a society that may not be ready for it.

Are We Ready for Information Technology?

One in every seven VCRs blinks "12:00" because its owner is unable to set the clock. Less than 10% of the working population can claim information technology competency. Many college curricula do not require courses on computers or IT. Corporate executives are seriously concerned that the skill level of workers is not keeping pace with the technology. Worse, millions of workers may not have the foundational skills needed for retraining. Executives throughout the country are concerned about spending money on remedial training just to get their employees to the point that they can give them information technology–related job training. To better prepare the work force for the explosion of information technology applications, we may need to revise curricula and raise standards at all levels of education. Forecasters are concerned that the United States may not be competitive if American industry is saddled with the burden of upgrading the skills of the work force.

Do We Really Want Information Technology?

Some of us want to wrap ourselves in information technology. Some of us want nothing to do with it. Most of us want it, but in moderation. This reluctant acceptance of information technology has resulted in many IT-based opportunities being overlooked or ignored. For whatever reasons, business, government, and education have elected not to implement computer applications that are well within the state of the art of computer technology. Literally thousands of money-saving IT-based systems are working in the laboratory and, on a small scale, in practice. However, society's pace of IT acceptance has placed such applications on the back burner. A few examples follow.

Smart houses feature computer-controlled lighting, temperature, and security systems. Such systems start the coffeemaker so we can awaken to the aroma of freshly brewed coffee. They even help with paying the utility bills and provide perimeter security. This technology is available today and is relatively inexpensive if properly designed and installed during construction. In any case, such a

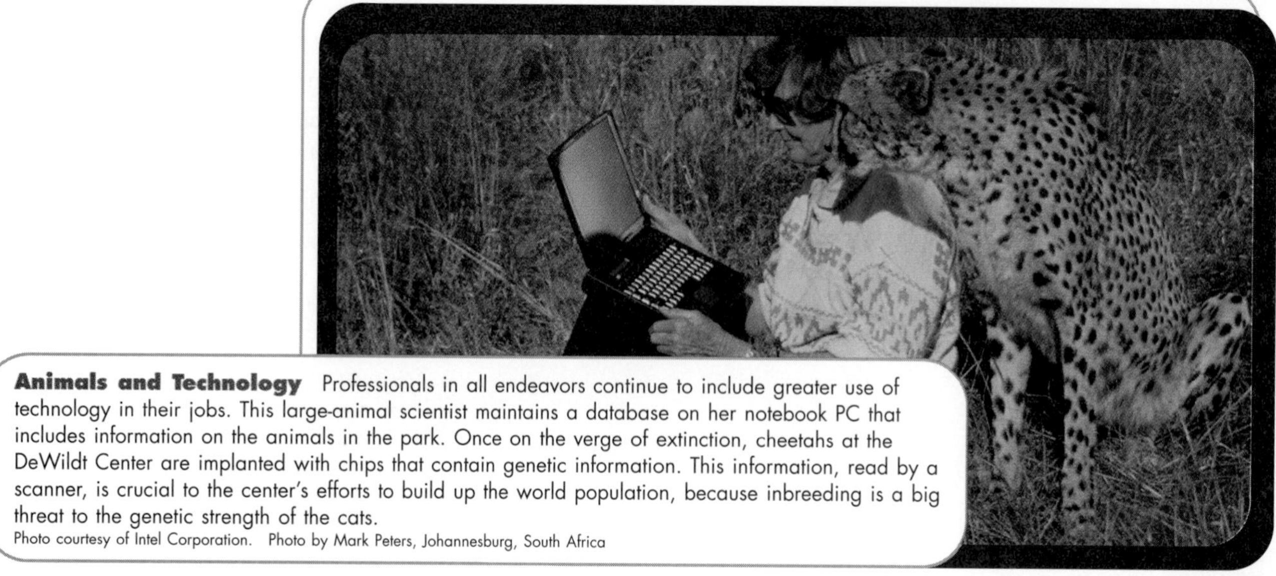

Animals and Technology Professionals in all endeavors continue to include greater use of technology in their jobs. This large-animal scientist maintains a database on her notebook PC that includes information on the animals in the park. Once on the verge of extinction, cheetahs at the DeWildt Center are implanted with chips that contain genetic information. This information, read by a scanner, is crucial to the center's efforts to build up the world population, because inbreeding is a big threat to the genetic strength of the cats.
Photo courtesy of Intel Corporation. Photo by Mark Peters, Johannesburg, South Africa

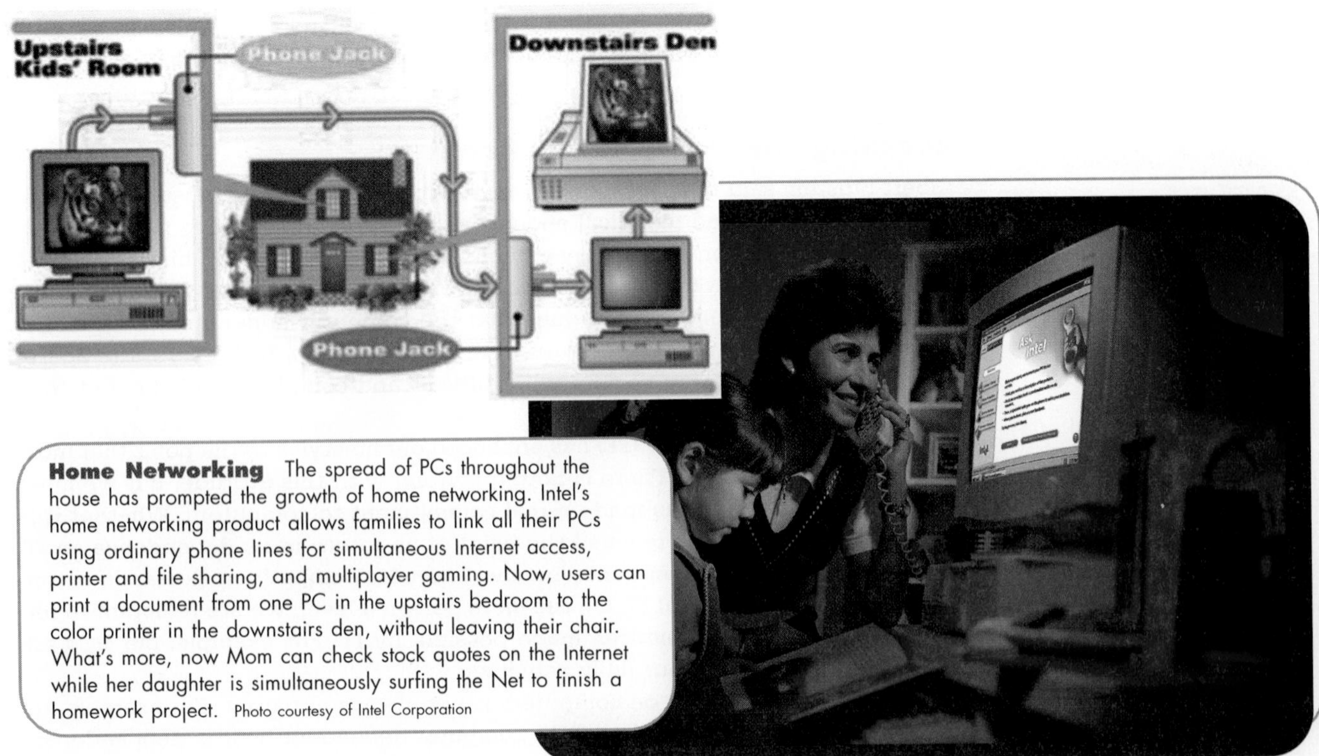

Home Networking The spread of PCs throughout the house has prompted the growth of home networking. Intel's home networking product allows families to link all their PCs using ordinary phone lines for simultaneous Internet access, printer and file sharing, and multiplayer gaming. Now, users can print a document from one PC in the upstairs bedroom to the color printer in the downstairs den, without leaving their chair. What's more, now Mom can check stock quotes on the Internet while her daughter is simultaneously surfing the Net to finish a homework project. Photo courtesy of Intel Corporation

system would pay for itself in a few years through energy savings alone. Generally, neither those in the construction industry nor potential buyers are ready for smart houses, even though they offer tremendous benefits and are cost-effective.

Although some sophisticated computer-controlled medical equipment is now being used, relatively few physicians take advantage of the information-producing potential of the computer to improve patient care. There are expert systems that can help them diagnose diseases, drug-interaction databases that can help them prescribe the right drug, computer-assisted searches that can call up literature pertinent to a particular patient's illness, and online forums through which they can solve health problems. Large groups of physicians are not ready for the age of information, even though these applications have the potential for saving lives.

On a larger scale, society continues to rebuke the concept of a cashless society. A cashless society is technologically and economically possible. In a cashless society, the amount of a purchase is transferred automatically from the purchaser's bank account to the vendor's bank account. Thus, billing, payment, and collection problems are eliminated, along with the need to write checks and to remember to mail them. Properly implemented, a cashless society will result in substantial savings for all concerned—government, business, and individuals. We are on a journey to a cashless society and already are well past halfway there. The remainder of the journey will take a few years because too many of us still like the jingle in our pockets.

Why have these cost-effective and potentially beneficial computer applications not been implemented? Among the reasons are historical momentum, resistance to change, limited education, and lack of available resources. In the case of domestic-control systems, it is probably a matter of education, both of the builder and the homeowner. In the case of computer diagnosis of illness, some physicians are reluctant to admit that the computer is a valuable diagnostic aid. In the case of the cashless society, concerns about invasion of privacy are yet to be resolved.

These and thousands of other "oversights" will not be implemented until enough people have enough knowledge to appreciate their potential. This is where you come in!

Reaching the Point of No Return

Albert Einstein said that "concern for man himself and his fate must always form the chief interest of all technical endeavors." Some people believe that a rapidly advancing information technology exhibits little regard for "man himself and his fate." They contend that computers are overused, misused, and generally detrimental to society. This group argues that the computer is dehumanizing and is slowly forcing society into a pattern of mass conformity. To be sure, the age of information is presenting society with difficult and complex problems, but they can be overcome.

Information technology (IT) has enhanced our lifestyles to the point that most of us take it for granted. There is nothing wrong with this attitude, but we must recognize that society has made a real commitment to computers. Whether it is good or bad, society has reached the point of no return in its dependence on IT, including a growing dependence on the Internet. Competition demands a continued and growing use of IT. On the more personal level, we are reluctant to forfeit the everyday conveniences made possible by IT. For example, our PCs are now an integral part of our daily activities.

Society's dependence on computers is not always apparent. For example, today's automobile assembly line is as computer-dependent as it is people-dependent: An inventory-management system makes sure that parts are delivered to the right assembly point at the right time; computer-controlled robots do the welding and painting; and a process-control computer controls the movement of the assembly line.

Turn off the computer system for a day in almost any company and observe the consequences. Most companies would cease to function. Turn off the computer system for several days, and many companies would cease to exist. It is estimated that a large bank would be out of business in two days if its computer systems were down. A distribution company would last three days, a manufacturing company would last five days, and an insurance company would last six days. A University of Minnesota study examined victims of disasters that disabled computing capabilities. The study concluded that the probability of a victim company's long-term survival was low if it were unable to recover critical operations within 30 hours. Recognizing their dependence on computers, most companies

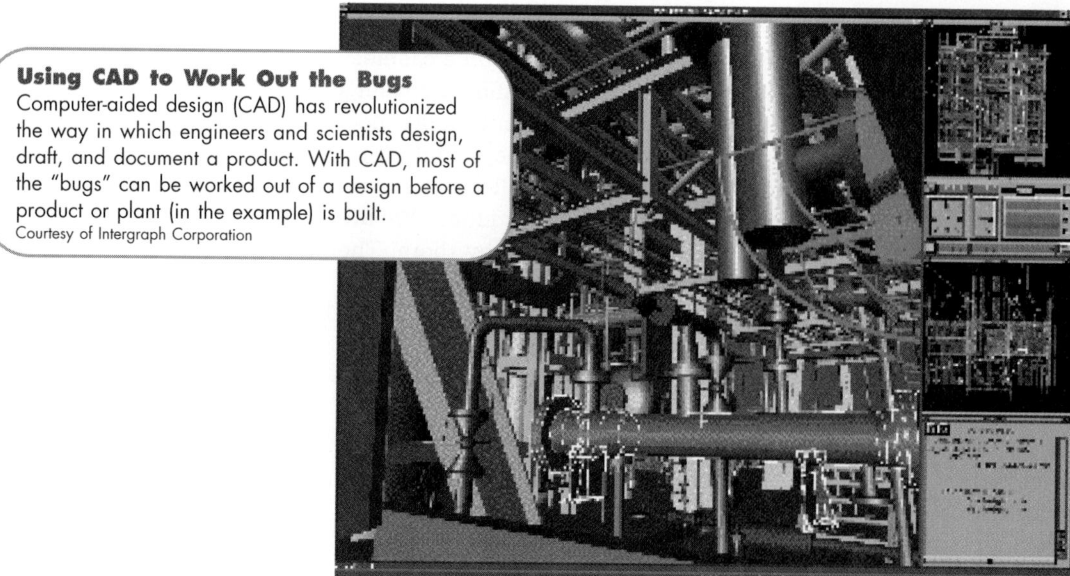

Using CAD to Work Out the Bugs
Computer-aided design (CAD) has revolutionized the way in which engineers and scientists design, draft, and document a product. With CAD, most of the "bugs" can be worked out of a design before a product or plant (in the example) is built.
Courtesy of Intergraph Corporation

have made contingency plans that provide for backup computers in case of disaster.

Dependence on IT is not necessarily bad as long as we keep it in perspective. However, we can't passively assume that information technology will continue to enhance the quality of our lives. It is our obligation to learn to understand computers so that we can better direct their application for society's benefit. Only through understanding can we control the misuse of information technology. As a society, we have a responsibility to weigh the benefits, burdens, and consequences of each successive level of automation.

SECTION SELF-CHECK

Self-Check

10-1.1 We, as a society, are still at least a decade away from dependence on computers. (T/F)

10-1.2 The expert diagnosis system is as much a part of the doctor's medical kit as the stethoscope. (T/F)

10-1.3 A smart house might have all of these computer-controlled features except: (a) lighting, (b) temperature, (c) fertilizing, or (d) security?

10-1.4 Which of these is not a reason that potentially beneficial computer applications have not been implemented: (a) historical momentum, (b) resistance to change, (c) too much education, or (d) lack of available resources?

10.2 WORKING IN THE INFORMATION SOCIETY

Whether you are seeking employment or a promotion as a teacher, an accountant, a writer, a fashion designer, a lawyer, or in any of hundreds of other jobs, someone is sure to ask, "What do you know about computers?" Today, interacting with a PC is part of the daily routine for millions of knowledge workers and is increasingly common for blue-collar workers. No matter which career you choose, in all likelihood you will be a frequent user of computers.

Upon completion of this course, you will be part of the IT–competent minority, and you will be able to respond with confidence to any inquiry about your knowledge of computers. But what of that 90% of our society that must answer "nothing" or "very little"? These people are at a disadvantage.

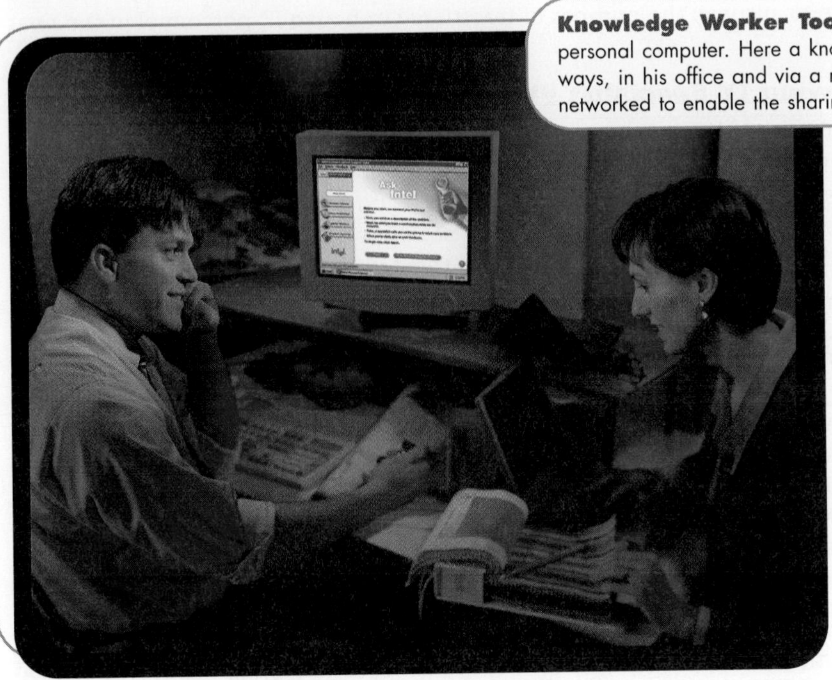

Knowledge Worker Tools The knowledge worker's primary tool is the personal computer. Here a knowledge worker joins another worker in two ways, in his office and via a network link. Properly configured PCs are easily networked to enable the sharing of files and ideas. Photo courtesy of Intel Corporation

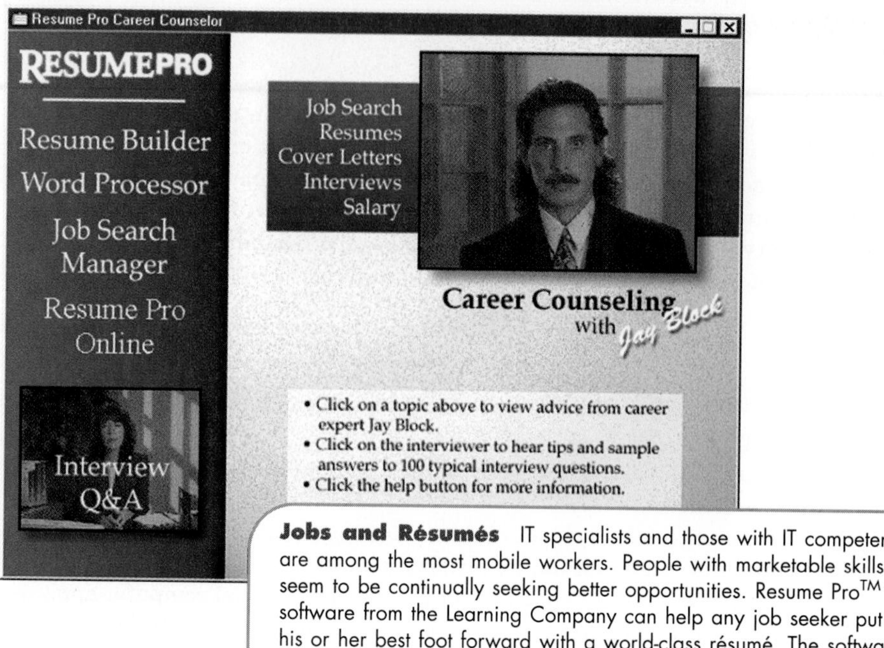

Jobs and Résumés IT specialists and those with IT competency are among the most mobile workers. People with marketable skills seem to be continually seeking better opportunities. Resume Pro™ software from the Learning Company can help any job seeker put his or her best foot forward with a world-class résumé. The software has a built-in contact manager that helps you track your appointments and interviews. Courtesy of The Learning Company

Jobs

Opportunities for IT Specialists

If you are planning a career as an IT specialist, opportunities have never been better. Almost every company, no matter how small or large, employs or contracts with IT specialists, and most of these companies are always looking for qualified information technology people. IT specialists have many doors open to them. If they accept employment in an organization's information services department, they are often given the option of working in a traditional office environment or telecommuting to work at least part of the time. Those who prefer working in a variety of environments are working for consulting firms or working as independent contractors. If the trend toward outsourcing (contracting with external personnel to do in-house work) continues, look for the number of consultants and contractors to surpass the number of traditional in-house IT personnel in the near future.

The Growing IT Specialist Fields

The age of Internet computing came upon us so quickly that there simply aren't enough skilled workers to support this new technology. It's estimated that one in every ten jobs for IT specialists is open, waiting to be filled by a qualified applicant. For the last decade, people with computer and information technology education have been at or near the top of the "most wanted" list. With millions (yes, millions!) of new computers being purchased and installed each year, it is likely that this trend will continue. Of course, the number of people attracted to the booming IT field is also increasing. One of the many reasons for this migration to the IT field is that IT careers are consistently ranked among the most desirable jobs. A recent *Money* magazine ranked 100 jobs in terms of earnings, long- and short-term job growth, job security, prestige rating, and "stress and strain" rating. The magazine called *computer systems analyst* the best job in America, with physician, physical therapist, electrical engineer, and civil engineer rounding out the top five. The systems analyst is but one of dozens of IT specialist careers. These are some of the more visible information technology jobs.

- *Chief information officer.* The director of information services within an organization is often called the **chief information officer (CIO).** This person

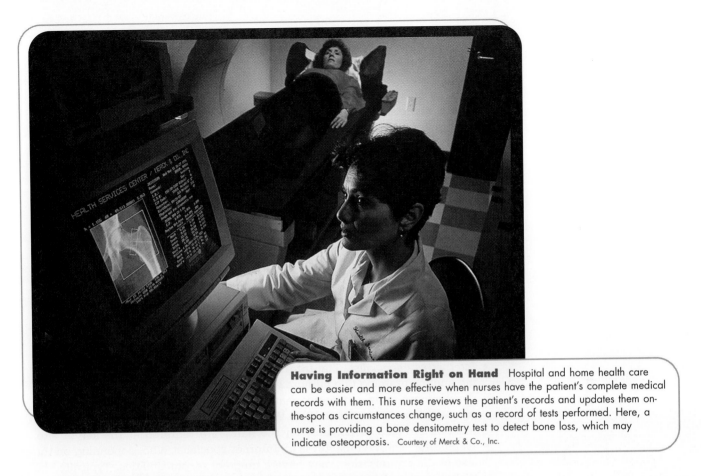

Having Information Right on Hand Hospital and home health care can be easier and more effective when nurses have the patient's complete medical records with them. This nurse reviews the patient's records and updates them on-the-spot as circumstances change, such as a record of tests performed. Here, a nurse is providing a bone densitometry test to detect bone loss, which may indicate osteoporosis. Courtesy of Merck & Co., Inc.

has responsibility for all the information services activity in the company, from the organization's Web page to its inventory control system. The CIO, often a vice president, must be somewhat futuristic, predicting what information technologies will become reality so the company can position itself to use them as they become available.

- *Systems analyst.* **Systems analysts** analyze, design, and implement information systems. They work closely with people in the user areas to design information systems that meet their information processing needs. These

IT in Education This instructor spends much of his workday interacting with students and computers. Courtesy of International Business Machines Corporation. Unauthorized use not permitted.

"problem solvers" are assigned a variety of support tasks, including feasibility studies, system reviews, security assessments, long-range planning, and hardware/software selection.

- *Programmer.* **Applications programmers** translate analyst-prepared system and input/output specifications into programs. Programmers design the logic, then code, debug, test, and document the programs. A person holding a **programmer/analyst** position performs the functions of both a programmer and a systems analyst.
- *Network administrator.* **Network administrators** design and maintain networks: LANs, MANs, and WANs. This work involves selecting and installing appropriate system software and appropriate hardware, such as modems and routers, and selecting the transmission media.
- *System programmer.* **System programmers** design, develop, maintain, and implement system software. System software, such as an operating system, is fundamental to the general operation of the computer; that is, it does not address a specific business or scientific problem.
- *Database administrator.* The **database administrator (DBA)** designs, creates, and maintains the integrated database. The DBA coordinates discussions between user groups to determine the content and format of the database so that data redundancy is kept to a minimum. The integrity and the security of the database are also responsibilities of the database administrator.
- *Internet site specialist.* The **Internet site specialist** is responsible for creating and maintaining one or more Internet sites. This specialist uses Internet development tools and source material from throughout the organization to create and maintain World Wide Web pages. Occasionally, people in this job function are also responsible for the hardware required at the server site.
- *Webmaster.* The **Webmaster** is an Internet specialist who, depending on the size of the organization, may have a range of responsibilities. Typically, the Web server and its software are the responsibility of the Webmaster. The Webmaster monitors Internet traffic on the server computer and responds to external inquiries regarding Web site operations. Some Webmasters are actively involved in the design and update of Web site pages.
- *Computer operator.* The **computer operator** performs those hardware-based activities needed to keep production systems operational in the mainframe

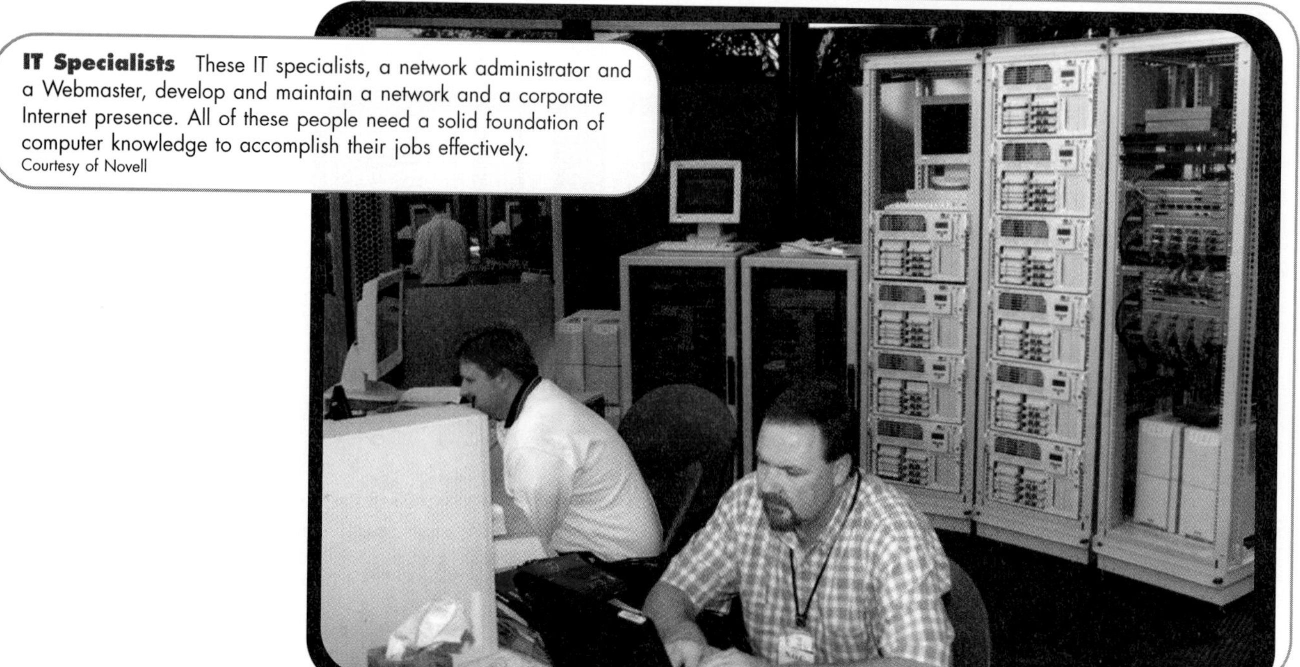

IT Specialists These IT specialists, a network administrator and a Webmaster, develop and maintain a network and a corporate Internet presence. All of these people need a solid foundation of computer knowledge to accomplish their jobs effectively.
Courtesy of Novell

computer and server computer environments. The operator is in constant communication with the computer(s) while monitoring the progress of a number of simultaneous production runs, initiating one-time jobs, and troubleshooting. If the computer system fails, the operator initiates restart procedures to "bring the system up."

- *User liaison.* Computer and information processing activity is very intense in companies that seek to exploit the full potential of information technology. In this environment, someone who is working in a particular functional area (perhaps the marketing department) is told to seek ways to take advantage of available IT resources. More often than not, this person is the user liaison. The **user liaison** is a "live-in" IT specialist who coordinates all computer-related activities within a particular functional area.
- *PC specialist.* **PC specialists** are trained in the function and operation of PCs and related hardware. They are proficient in the use and application of the operating system and all common PC software packages, such as word processing, desktop publishing, Internet browser, spreadsheet, presentation, and database software. Also, they are well-versed in the use of groupware, including e-mail and scheduling applications. Often they have expertise in the installation and maintenance of PC-based local area networks and in establishing links with MANs and WANs. PC specialists help users get on and use the Internet. Frequently, PC specialists staff the organization's help desk. Users throughout an organization rely on help desk personnel to answer a variety of computer-related questions: How do I get a password? How can I import a GIF file into my spreadsheet? Can you recommend a color printer for our department?

Computer-related jobs are not nearly as centralized (for example, an information services department) as they were during the mainframe era (through 1990). The trend toward client/server computing has resulted in the distribution of IT specialists throughout the organization.

The variety and types of IT specialist jobs are ever changing. For example, there's the *information detective.* Companies and individuals call on these high-tech detectives to help them answer such questions as: Has my child's sitter had any driving accidents? Has my materials supplier ever filed for bankruptcy? Did this applicant for the sales manager position really earn an MBA at Harvard? Another related job is the professional *Internet researcher.* Someone who really knows his or her way around the Internet can do in minutes what might take a Net newbie days to do. A good detective or researcher can make in excess of $100 an hour and never leave the comfort of home!

Licensing and Certification

If you are an IT specialist or your chosen career overlaps directly with information technology, you may be in constant contact with sensitive data and may have the power to control events. An implied responsibility to maintain the integrity of the system and its data accompanies such a job. Failure to do so could have a disastrous effect on the lives of individuals and even on the stability of the organization. Trillions of dollars are handled each day by computer-based systems that are created and controlled by IT specialists. The lives of millions of air travelers depend on the responsiveness of the computer-based air traffic control system.

At present, licensing or certification is usually not a requirement for any IT professional; nor is it required for users of computers. Licensing and certification are hotly debated issues. Many professions require demonstration of performance at a certain level of competence before permission is granted to practice. Through examination, the engineer becomes a registered professional engineer, the attorney becomes a member of the bar, and the accountant becomes a certified public accountant. Many people in the trades, including hairdressers, plumbers, and electricians, must be licensed to practice.

Within the computer community, there are a number of certifications. Several professional organizations provide certification options, including by the Institute for Certification of Computer Professionals (ICCP), which awards the *Certified Computing Professional (CCP)* and the *Associate Computing Professional (ACP)*. The CCP and ACP are general certifications in the area of computers and information technology. The ICCP has certified more than 50,000 information technology professionals.

A growing number of companies whose products have become de facto standards offer certifications. For example, software giants Microsoft and Novell sponsor a range of widely accepted certifications. Microsoft offers these certificates for information technology professionals: Microsoft Certified Systems Engineer (MCSE and MCSE+Internet), Microsoft Certified Database Administrator (MCDBA), Microsoft Certified Solution Developer (MCSD), and Microsoft Certified Professional (MCP) with several specialties (MCP + Site Building, MCP + Internet), and Microsoft Certified Trainer (MCT). The Microsoft Office User Specialist (MOUS) program gives you an opportunity to validate your skills in using Microsoft Office, or a specific application, such as PowerPoint or Word.

Novell, a company that specializes in networking products, offers several levels of certification for people who work with their widely used network products: the Certified Novell Administrator (CNA), Novell Authorized CNE (Certified Novell Engineer), Novell Master CNE, and Certified Novell Instructor (CNI). Novell also awards the Novell Certified Internet Professional.

People seeking any of these certifications must pass an array of tests. Generally, such certifications are viewed favorably by recruiters and employers, and often result in higher salaries. However, they are seldom a requirement for employment.

Career Opportunities for the IT-Competent Minority

Information technology competency is becoming a prerequisite for people pursuing almost any career—from actuaries to zoologists. In fact, most professional jobs come with a telephone, a desk, and a PC.

- The terminal or networked PC has become standard equipment at hospital nursing stations and is often found in operating rooms.
- Draftspeople have traded drawing tables for computer-aided design (CAD) workstations.

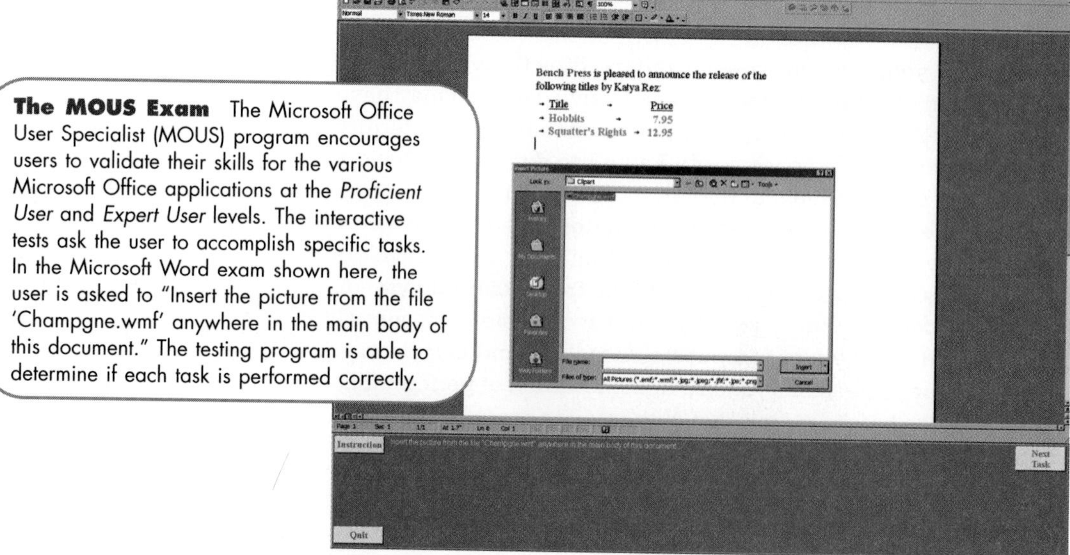

The MOUS Exam The Microsoft Office User Specialist (MOUS) program encourages users to validate their skills for the various Microsoft Office applications at the *Proficient User* and *Expert User* levels. The interactive tests ask the user to accomplish specific tasks. In the Microsoft Word exam shown here, the user is asked to "Insert the picture from the file 'Champgne.wmf' anywhere in the main body of this document." The testing program is able to determine if each task is performed correctly.

- Teachers are integrating the power of computer-based training (CBT) into their courses.
- Economists would be lost without the predictive capabilities of their decision support system (DSS).
- Truck dispatchers query their information systems, which may include the exact location of fleet trucks (via onboard global positioning systems), before scheduling deliveries.
- Construction contractors keep track of on-site inventory on portable laptop computers.
- The PC is the administrative assistant's constant companion for everything from word processing to conference scheduling.
- Stockbrokers often have terminals on both sides of their desks. (Some dedicated brokers have one by their bed at night as well to keep up with Asian markets.)
- An attorney's law library is no longer on the shelf behind the desk, but on CD-ROM and/or the Internet.
- Professional football coaches rely on their play databases to give them insight into what offense or defense to run for given situations.
- Politicians frequently tap Internet-based polls before casting their votes.

Career mobility is becoming forever intertwined with an individual's current and future knowledge of computers and information technology.

Of course, career advancement ultimately depends on your abilities, imagination, and performance, but understanding computers can open doors to opportunities that might otherwise be shut. All things being equal, the person who has the knowledge of and the will to work with computers will have a tremendous career advantage over those who do not.

Our Jobs Are Changing

Automation is causing the elimination of some jobs. For example, the revenue accounting department at a major U.S. airline was reduced from 650 to 350 with the implementation of a new computer-based system. Those remaining had to be retrained to work with the new system. Those displaced had to be retrained for other work opportunities in an increasingly automated society. Fortunately, other jobs are being created by the use of information technology. The explosion of information technology has resulted in thousands of new companies that provide a myriad of previously unknown products and services. Yahoo!, Netscape, America Online, and many other high-tech companies didn't exist a decade ago. Now they employ hundreds, even thousands, of people in high-paying jobs.

As information technology continues to move to the forefront in our society, jobs in every discipline are being redefined. For example, 10 years ago sales representatives carried manuals and

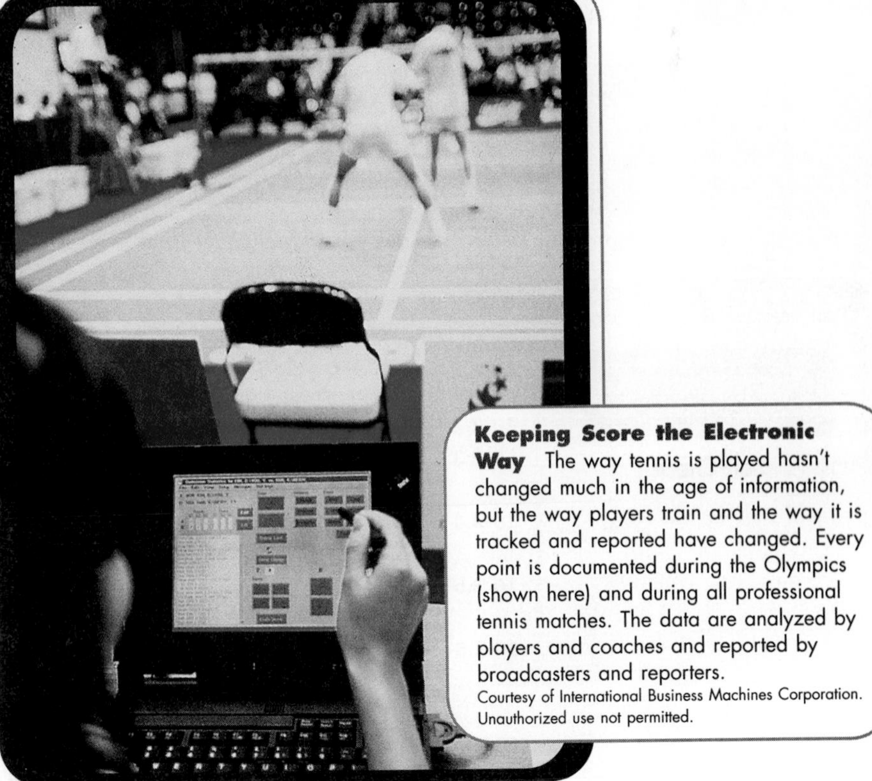

Keeping Score the Electronic Way The way tennis is played hasn't changed much in the age of information, but the way players train and the way it is tracked and reported have changed. Every point is documented during the Olympics (shown here) and during all professional tennis matches. The data are analyzed by players and coaches and reported by broadcasters and reporters.

Tapping the Potential Some say that we are not tapping the full potential of computers in business, these retail clerks being the exception. By using wireless handheld portable devices, they have eliminated the need for intermediate paperwork and the delays associated with inventory control. Courtesy of Symbol Technologies, Inc.

products to the customer site. Today, they still knock on doors, but to a much lesser extent because much of what used to be personal interaction is now electronic interaction (e-mail, fax, and extranets). When they do come calling, they don't carry heavy manuals and products. Instead, they bring their laptops. Thanks to the technology, the sales rep is no longer the sole source of product/service information. Customers can get up-to-date information directly from the vendor via its extranet (an extension of a company's private intranet). Many customers don't deal with sales reps at all. They obtain needed information by browsing the Internet or an extranet, then they place their orders electronically. Radical changes in the way we do our jobs are not limited to the business community. Poets, the clergy, politicians, professors, and others are continually evaluating what they do and how they do it within the context of emerging technology.

Information technology continues to steamroll into our lives. Each of us has a choice: We can resist information technology and hope for the best, or we can embrace it and use it to improve our jobs and our job performance. The fact that you are reading this book indicates that you have chosen the latter.

SECTION SELF-CHECK

Self-Check

10-2.1 Contrary to popular belief, the emergence of information technology does not eliminate jobs. (T/F)

10-2.2 IT careers are consistently ranked among the most desirable jobs. (T/F)

10-2.3 The person with the responsibility for all information services activity is the chief information officer. (T/F)

10-2.4 Professional certification is a requirement for employment in most IT professions. (T/F)

10-2.5 The network administrator's work license permits the design of LANs, but not that of MANs. (T/F)

10-2.6 The person responsible for the security of the database is the: (a) application programmer, (b) PC specialist, (c) network administrator, or (d) database administrator?

10-2.7 Which IT professional analyzes, designs, and implements information systems: (a) Webmaster, (b) DBA, (c) systems analyst, or (d) applications programmer?

10-2.8 What job function serves as an internal consultant to a user area: (a) scheduler, (b) user liaison, (c) network administrator, or (d) CIO?

10-2.9 IT competency is now a prerequisite for lawyers and truck drivers. (T/F)

10-2.10 Which Microsoft certification program gives knowledge workers an opportunity to validate their Microsoft PowerPoint skills: (a) MOUS, (b) CNE, (c) MCSE, or (d) MCP + Internet?

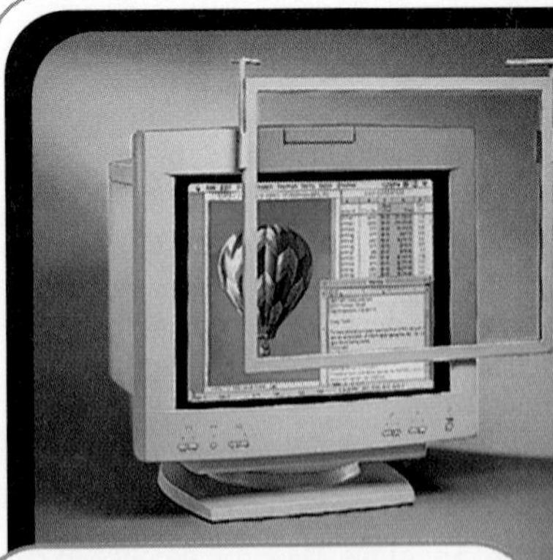

Relief from Eyestrain Working on the computer all day can take its toll on your eyes. Kensington's GlareMaster™ screen filter helps relieve eyestrain by eliminating 99.9% of the glare coming from your computer monitor, without compromising colors or brightness.
Courtesy of Kensington Technology Group

10.3 THE WORKPLACE: ERGONOMICS AND GREEN COMPUTING

Our workplace is changing because we are more attuned to considerations involving human safety and comfort, and we are more sensitive to the growing importance of *green computing.*

Ergonomics and Workplace Design

For close to a hundred years, the design of automobiles was driven by two basic considerations: appearance and functionality. Engineers were asked to design cars that were visually appealing and could go from point A to point B. Surprisingly little attention was given to the human factor. That is, no one considered the connection between the driver and passengers and the automobile. About 25 years ago, automobile executives discovered that they could boost sales and enhance functionality by improving this human connection. Thus began the era of ergonomically designed automobiles. Today, human factors engineers apply the principles of ergonomic design to ensure that the interface between people and cars is *safe, comfortable, effective,* and *efficient.*

Ergonomics is the study of the relationships between people and the things we use. The emergence of ergonomics is beginning to have an impact on the relationship between knowledge workers and their workplaces. Computers are still relatively new in the workplace, and ergonomics has only recently emerged as an important consideration in fitting computers into workplace design.

Just for Feet Give your hands a rest with a programmable Foot Switch. The Kinesis Foot Switch adds input versatility with a three-button keyboard for your feet.
Use Courtesy Kinesis ® Corporation, Bothell, WA

Reasons for Concern

During the 1980s, the knowledge worker's workplace gained attention when workers began to blame headaches, depression, anxiety, nausea, fatigue, and irritability on prolonged interaction with a terminal or PC. These and other problems often associated with extended use of a terminal or PC are collectively called *video operator's distress syndrome,* or *VODS.* Although there was little evidence to link these problems directly with using terminals or PCs (the same problems occurred in other work environments), VODS caused people to take a closer look at the

Ergonomic Products Have You in Mind The Kinesis™ Maxim adjustable keyboard is contoured to fit the shape and movements of the human body. Much more versatile and narrower than "natural-style" keyboards, the Maxim accommodates a wide range of user preferences. The design puts less stress and strain on muscles, reducing the user's risk for fatigue in hands, wrists, and arms. The keyboard also reduces risk factors for developing painful injuries, such as carpal tunnel syndrome, tendinitis, and cumulative trauma disorders (CTDs). Courtesy of Kinesis Corporation

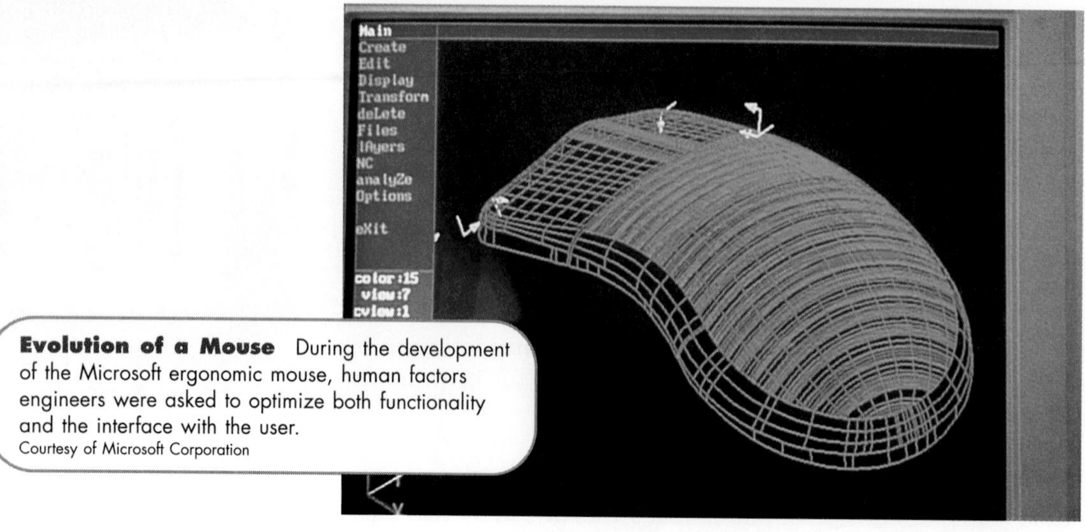

Evolution of a Mouse During the development of the Microsoft ergonomic mouse, human factors engineers were asked to optimize both functionality and the interface with the user.
Courtesy of Microsoft Corporation

workplace and the types of injuries being reported. As the number of *repetitive-stress injuries (RSIs)* increased for knowledge workers, workstation ergonomics became an increasingly important issue for corporate productivity.

A poorly designed workplace has the potential to cause *cumulative trauma disorder (CTD),* a condition that can lead to a permanent disability of motor skills. CTD now accounts for more than half of all work-related problems. It typically occurs when people ignore human factors considerations while spending considerable time at the keyboard. Other workstation-related injuries include mental stress, eyestrain, headaches, muscular injuries, and skeletal injuries. Hand and wrist problems have always been the main complaint, with the repetitive-stress injury called *carpal tunnel syndrome (CTS)* being the most common.

Talk about the radiation emitted by monitors has unduly frightened office workers. A controversial, and apparently flawed, study in the late 1980s concluded that women who are exposed to the radiation emitted from terminals and PCs may have a higher rate of miscarriage than those who are not. A comprehensive four-year federal government study completed in 1991 concluded that women who work with terminals and PCs and those who do not have the same rate of miscarriage.

Stress Reliever The repetitive-stress injuries (RSIs) associated with the keyboard may be eliminated at some time in the future as more people move to speech-recognition technology to interact with their PCs. This executive dictates directly to a computer system using Dragon NaturallySpeaking™ software.
Courtesy of Dragon Systems, Inc.

Workplace Design: An Evaluation

Proper workplace design, whether on the factory floor or in the office, is good business. Any good manager knows that a healthy, happy worker is a more productive worker. A good manager also knows that the leading causes of lost work time are back/shoulder/neck pain and CTD.

The key to designing a proper workplace for the knowledge worker is *flexibility.* The knowledge worker's workplace should be designed with enough flexibility to enable it to be custom-fitted to its worker. Figure 10.1 highlights important considerations in workplace design. Ergonomic problems in the workplace are being addressed in legislation and in proposed regulations from the Occupational Safety and Health Administration (OSHA).

Attention to the overall environment can reduce stress and increase worker performance. For example, equipping impact printers with acoustical enclosures can reduce the noise level. Indirect lighting can reduce glare. Proper ventilation eliminates health concerns caused by the ozone emitted by laser printers. (Excessive exposure to ozone can cause headaches and nausea.)

One of the most important factors in ergonomic programs is employee training. Workers should be shown how to analyze their workstations and make necessary adjustments (such as lowering monitor contrast and brightness or increasing chair lumbar support). Each knowledge worker can then contribute to the quality of his or her workplace by following a couple of simple rules. First, make the adjustments necessary to custom fit your workplace. Second, take periodic mini-breaks. These mini-breaks should involve looking away from your monitor and/or generally altering your body orientation for a few seconds (make a fist, turn your head from side to side, roll your shoulders, walk around your desk, wiggle your toes, wrinkle your nose, and so on).

Ergonomics

Green Computing

The dawning of the age of green computing is upon us. **Green computing** is merely environmentally sensible computing. Computers drain critical resources such as electricity and paper. They also produce unwanted electrical, chemical, and bulk-waste side effects. As a society we are finally adopting a more environmentally sound position with respect to the use and manufacture of computing hardware.

United States government agencies and many businesses have adopted policies that require that all new PCs, monitors, and printers must comply with the Environmental Protection Agency's *Energy Star* guidelines. To comply with Energy Star requirements, monitors and processors in standby mode (not in use) can consume no more than 30 watts of power. Printers are permitted a range of 30 to 45 watts. Computer manufacturers have been moving toward more energy-efficient products in hopes of reducing manufacturing costs and increasing product competitiveness.

It costs about $250 a year to keep a PC and laser page printer running 24 hours a day. We could save a lot of money and fossil fuel if every user were conscientious about turning off PCs and peripheral devices when not in use. Judi-

Ergonomic Considerations in Workplace Design

Knowledge workers, most of whom spend four or more hours each day at a PC or terminal, are paying more attention to the ergonomics (efficiency of the person–machine interface) of the hardware, including chairs and desks.

The Hardware
Monitor location ***(A)***. The monitor should be located directly in front of you at arm's length with the top at forehand level. Outside windows should be to the side of the monitor to reduce glare. *Monitor features.* The monitor should be high-resolution with antiglare screens. *Monitor maintenance.* The monitor should be free from smudges or dust buildup. *Keyboard location* ***(B)***. The keyboard should be located such that the upper arm and forearms are at a 90-degree angle. *Keyboard features.* The keyboard should be ergonomically designed to accommodate better the movements of the fingers, hands, and arms.

The Chair
The chair should be fully adjustable to the size and contour of the body. Features should include: *Pneumatic seat height adjustment* ***(C)***; *Seat and back angle adjustment* ***(D)***; *Backrest height adjustment* ***(E)***; *Recessed armrests with height adjustment* ***(F)***; *Lumbar support adjustment (for lower back support)* ***(G)***; *Five-leg pedestal on casters* ***(H)***.

The Desk
The swing space. Use wraparound work space to keep the PC, important office materials, and files within 18 inches of the chair. *Adjustable tray for keyboard and mouse* ***(I)***: The tray should have height and swivel adjustments.

The Room
Freedom of movement. The work area should permit freedom of movement and ample leg room. *Lighting.* Lighting should be positioned to minimize glare on the monitor and printed materials.

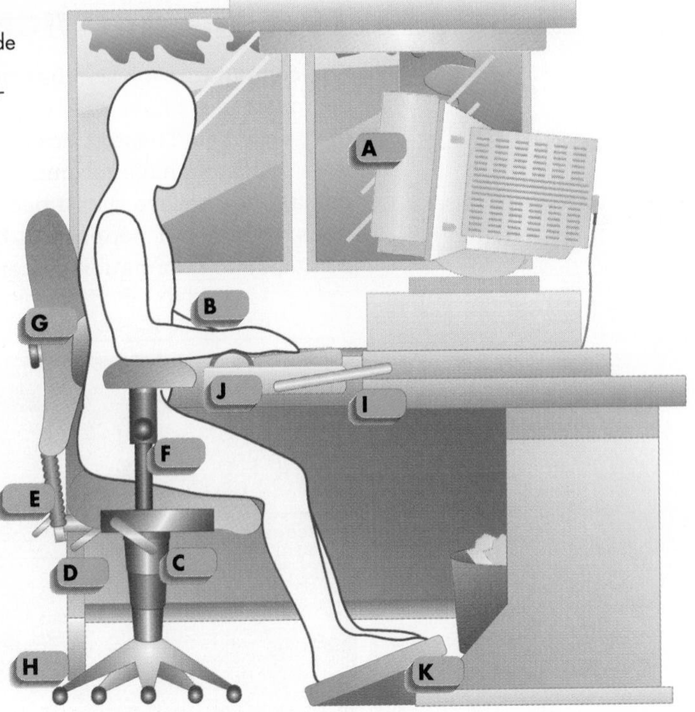

Other Equipment
Wrist rest ***(J)***. The wrist rest is used in conjunction with adjustable armrests to keep arms in a neutral straight position at the keyboard. *Footrest* ***(K)***. The adjustable footrest takes pressure off the lower back while encouraging proper posture.

cious computing can even save trees—why print a letter when e-mail is faster and better for the environment? Green computing means printing only what needs to be printed, saving the paper for more meaningful applications.

Other recommendations by green computing proponents include buying equipment from vendors who are manufacturing environmentally safe products; purchasing recycled paper; recycling paper and toner printer cartridges (which would probably end up in landfills); buying reconditioned components rather than new ones; recycling old PCs and printers; shopping electronically to save gas; and telecommuting at least once or twice a week.

SECTION SELF-CHECK

Self-Check

10-3.1 Attention to the overall workplace design can reduce stress and increase worker performance. (T/F)

10-3.2 Hardware manufacturers that comply with the Environmental Protection Agency's Energy Star guidelines are practicing green computing. (T/F)

10-3.3 A monitor emits radiation. (T/F)

10-3.4 What is the approximate cost of running a PC and a laser printer 24 hours a day for a year: (a) $10, (b) $50, (c) $250, or (d) $2250?

10-3.5 The study of the relationships between people and their machines is called: (a) humanology, (b) human economics, (c) ergology, or (d) ergonomics?

10-3.6 Problems associated with extended use of a PC are collectively: (a) VODS, (b) CTS, (c) CTD, or (d) SOV?

10-3.7 Hand and wrist problems are associated with: (a) ACL, (b) carpal tunnel syndrome, (c) CLA, or (d) SC syndrome?

10-3.8 Laser printers can emit: (a) lead, (b) a harmless water-based compound, (c) sulfur dioxin, or (d) ozone?

10-3.9 Environmentally sensible computing is called: (a) blue computing, (b) green computing, (c) yellow computing, or (d) red computing?

10.4 THE QUESTION OF ETHICS

The computer revolution has generated intense controversy about IT ethics. Many computer users have raised questions about what is and is not ethical with regard to IT activities. These ethics issues are so important to our society that many prominent educators have recommended that IT ethics be integrated into all college curricula. They believe that if people are made aware of the consequences of their actions, then fewer people will be motivated to plant dangerous computer viruses, contaminate information systems with false information, or post pornographic ma-

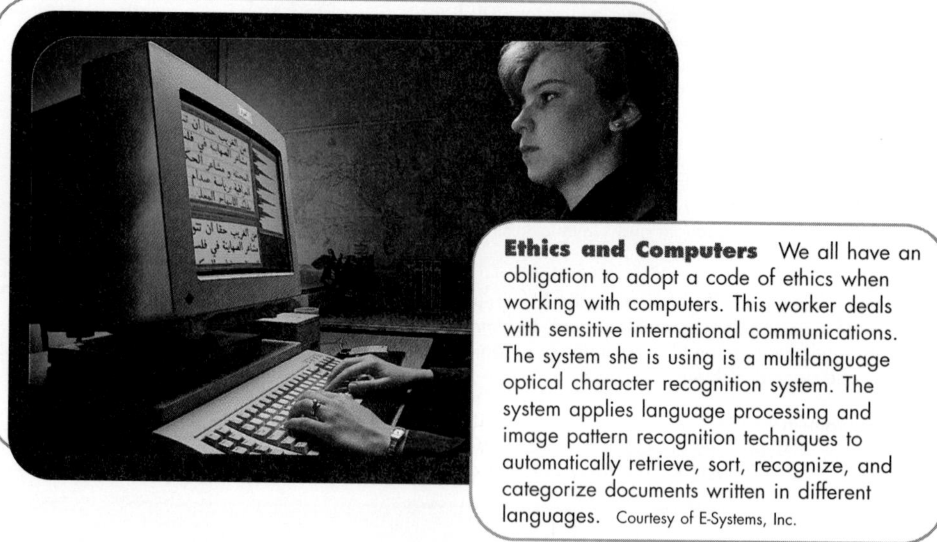

Ethics and Computers We all have an obligation to adopt a code of ethics when working with computers. This worker deals with sensitive international communications. The system she is using is a multilanguage optical character recognition system. The system applies language processing and image pattern recognition techniques to automatically retrieve, sort, recognize, and categorize documents written in different languages. Courtesy of E-Systems, Inc.

terial to the Internet. Ethics-conscientious people will be more likely to protect personal privacy, honor copyright laws, and report unethical activity. Educators warn us of dire consequences should we fail to instill a sense of ethics in future generations. If ethical abuses are left unabated, all roads on the information superhighway will be toll roads for encrypted data; that is, only those who pay for the key to the encrypted information can view it. If this were to happen, we would become a more secretive society, far less willing to share accumulated knowledge.

Standards of Conduct: A Code of Ethics

Most major computer professional societies have adopted a code of ethics. Their codes warn the members, who are mostly professionals in the information technology fields, that they can be expelled or censured if they violate them. Rarely, however, has any action been taken against delinquent members. Does this mean there are no violations? Of course not. A carefully drafted code of ethics provides some guidelines for conduct, but professional societies cannot be expected to police the misdeeds of their members. In many instances, however, a code violation is also a violation of the law.

Ethics in Computing

A code of ethics provides direction for computer professionals and users so that they act responsibly in their application of information technology. The recently updated Association for Computing Machinery (ACM) Code of Conduct summarized in Figure 10.2 provides excellent guidelines for both knowledge workers and for computing and IT professionals. ACM is the largest professional society for computing and IT professionals.

If you follow the ACM code shown in Figure 10.2, it is unlikely that anyone will question your ethics. Nevertheless, well-meaning people routinely violate this

1. General Moral Imperatives
1.1 Contribute to society and human well-being
1.2 Avoid harm to others
1.3 Be honest and trustworthy
1.4 Be fair and take action not to discriminate
1.5 Honor property rights including copyrights and patents
1.6 Give proper credit for intellectual property
1.7 Respect the privacy of others
1.8 Honor confidentiality
2. More Specific Professional Responsibilities
2.1 Strive to achieve the highest quality, effectiveness, and dignity in both the process and products of professional work
2.2 Acquire and maintain professional competence
2.3 Know and respect existing laws pertaining to professional work
2.4 Accept and provide appropriate professional review
2.5 Give comprehensive and thorough evaluations of computer systems and their impacts, including analysis of possible risks
2.6 Honor contracts, agreements, and assigned responsibilities
2.7 Improve public understanding of computing and its consequences
2.8 Access computing and communication resources only when authorized to do so

FIGURE 10.2

A Code of Conduct for Knowledge Workers and IT Professionals The first two sections (shown here) of the Association of Computer Machinery (ACM) Code of Conduct are applicable to all knowledge workers and IT professionals. The full code and detailed explanations can be found at the ACM Web site at <http://acm.org>. The last two sections deal with organizational leadership and code compliance.

simple code because they are unaware of the tremendous detrimental impact of their actions. With the speed and power of computers, a minor code infraction easily can be magnified to a costly catastrophe. For this reason, the use of computers in this electronic age is raising new ethical questions, the most visible of which are discussed in the following sections.

The Misuse of Personal Information

Depending on which poll you accept, about 40% of all white-collar workers are afraid of new technology. Most of these avoid voice mail or refuse to use e-mail. The most common reason they cite for their antitechnology attitude is the fear of loss of privacy.

Sources of Personal Data

The issue with the greatest ethical overtones is the privacy of personal information. Some people fear that computer-based record-keeping offers too much of an opportunity for the invasion of an individual's privacy. There is indeed reason for concern. For example, credit-card users unknowingly leave a "trail" of activities and interests that, when examined and evaluated, can provide a surprisingly comprehensive personal profile.

The date and location of all credit-card transactions are recorded. In effect, when you charge lunch, gasoline, or clothing, you are creating a chronological record of where you have been and your spending habits. From this information, a good analyst could compile a very accurate profile of your lifestyle. For example, the analyst could predict how you dress by knowing the type of clothing stores you patronize. On a more personal level, records are kept that detail the duration, time, and numbers of all your telephone calls. With computers, these numbers easily can be matched to people, businesses, institutions, and telephone services. So each time you make a phone call, you also leave a record of whom or where you call. Enormous amounts of personal data are maintained on everyone by the IRS, colleges, employers, creditors, hospitals, insurance companies, brokers, and so on. A person with access to this information could create quite a detailed profile of almost anyone, including you. The profile could be further fine-tuned by examining your Internet activity, such as what messages you posted to the Internet and the kinds of software you downloaded.

We hope that information about us is up-to-date and accurate. Unfortunately, much of it is not. Laws permit us to examine our records, but first we must find them. You can't just write to the federal government and ask to see your files. To be completely sure you examine all your federal records for completeness and accuracy, you would have to write and probably visit more than 5000 agencies, each of which maintain computer-based files on individuals. The same is true of personal data maintained in the private sector.

Violating the Privacy of Personal Information

Now you know that a lot of your personal information exists on computers, but is this information being misused? Some say yes, and most will agree that the potential exists for abuse. Consider the states that sell lists of the addresses and data on their licensed drivers. At the request of a manager of several petite women's clothing stores, a state provided the manager with a list of all its licensed drivers who were women between the ages of 21 and 40, less than 5 feet 3 inches tall, and under 120 pounds. Is the sale of such a list an abuse of personal information? Does the state cross the line of what is considered ethical practice? You be the judge.

When you visit a Web site, the server may gather and store information about you, both on its system and on your system. Frequently, Web sites will leave a cookie on your hard disk. The **cookie** is a message given to your Web browser by the Web server being accessed. The information in the cookie, which is in the form of a text file, is then sent back to the server each time the browser requests a page from the server. The cookie may contain information about you, including

IT Ethics

MONITORING OF E-MAIL

Many organizations monitor both e-mail and telephone conversations of their employees. These organizations cite productivity and quality control as justification. People who used to chat at the water cooler or snack counter do so now over office e-mail. Monitored e-mail is just as likely to surface "meet you at the gym after work" as "meet you in the conference room."

Realistically, e-mail is monitored to discourage nonbusiness messages and to keep employees focused on job-related activities. We now know that e-mail, when used responsibly, can boost productivity. We also know that, if abused, e-mail can be counterproductive.

Once an organization decides to monitor e-mail, it can do so in a several ways. Individuals can scan e-mail archives for inappropriate transmissions, often a time-consuming process. In large organizations, computers scan e-mail archives for keywords (*baseball, party, boss,* and so on) and kick out messages with questionable content. Already many employees have been fired or disciplined for abusing e-mail.

Employees feel that monitoring of e-mail is an invasion of personal privacy. Many workers view e-mail as just another tool, such as a telephone, and that they should be allowed some reasonable personal use. The issue is being argued in the courts.

Discussion: Does an employer's right to know outweigh the employee's right to privacy?

your name, e-mail address, interests, and personal preferences. Anytime you enter personal information at a Web site, chances are your browser is storing it in a cookie. The main purpose of the cookie is to personalize your interaction with the Web site and to enable the server to present you with a customized Web page, perhaps with your name at the top of the page. This information, however, sometimes is sold to companies that sell e-mail addresses to online marketers, who then send you unsolicited advertisements via e-mail (spam).

Personal information has become the product of a growing industry. Companies have been formed that do nothing but sell information about people. Not only are the people involved not asked for permission to use their data, they are seldom even told that their personal information is being sold! A great deal of personal data can be extracted from public records, both manual and computer-based. For example, one company sends people to county courthouses all over the United States to gather publicly accessible data about people who have recently filed papers to purchase a home. Computer-based databases are then sold to insurance companies, landscape companies, members of Congress seeking new votes, lawyers seeking new clients, and so on. Such information is even sold and distributed over the Net. Those placed on these electronic databases eventually become targets of commerce and special-interest groups.

The use of personal information for profit and other purposes is growing so rapidly that the government has not been able to keep up with abuses. Antiquated laws, combined with judicial unfamiliarity with information technology, make policing and prosecuting abuses of the privacy of personal information difficult and, in many cases, impossible.

Computer Matching

In **computer matching,** separate databases are examined and individuals common to both are identified. The focus of most computer-matching applications is to identify people engaged in wrongdoing. For example, federal employees are being matched with those having delinquent student loans. Wages are then garnished to repay the loans. In another computer-matching case, a $30-million fraud was uncovered when questionable financial transactions were traced to common participants.

The Internal Revenue Service also uses computer matching to identify tax cheaters. The IRS gathers descriptive data, such as neighborhood and automobile type, then uses sophisticated models to create lifestyle profiles. These profiles are matched against reported income on tax returns to predict whether people seem to be underpaying taxes. When the income and projected lifestyle do not match, the return is audited.

Proponents of computer matching cite the potential to reduce criminal activity. Opponents of computer matching consider it an unethical invasion of privacy.

Creating New Applications for Personal Information

The mere fact that personal information is so readily available has opened the door for many new applications of information technology. Some people will praise their merits and others will adamantly oppose them. For example, the White House has proposed that computer-based background checks be done on all airline passengers. The results of the checks would be used to identify which passengers' luggage to search. The proposed system would examine names, addresses, telephone numbers, travel histories, and billing records to search for irregularities that might indicate possible terrorist activity. This application, like many others that involve the use of personal information, has the potential to have a positive impact on society. Protectors of the rights of individuals will argue that the benefits derived may not be great enough to offset this invasion into personal information.

Each new application involving the use of personal information will be carefully scrutinized, but it is inevitable that our personal information will be used for a myriad of applications. These may include systems that locate compatible mates, assign schoolchildren to classes, track sex offenders, identify employees who do not meet company character standards, target sales to likely customers, and so on.

Securing the Integrity of Personal Information

Computer experts feel that the integrity of personal data can be more secure in computer databases than it is in file cabinets. They contend that we can continue to be masters and not victims if we implement proper safeguards for the maintenance and release of this information and enact effective legislation to cope with the abuse of it.

The Privacy Question: No Easy Answers

The ethical questions surrounding the privacy of personal information are extremely complex and difficult to resolve. For example, consider the position of the American Civil Liberties Union. On one hand, the ACLU is fighting to curb abuses of personal information and on the other, it is lobbying the government for greater access to government information, which may include personal information. Are these goals in conflict?

As automation continues to enrich our lives, it also opens the door for abuses of personal information. Research is currently being done that may show that people with certain genetic and/or personality makeups have a statistical predisposition to a physical problem or a mental disorder, such as early heart failure or depression. Will employers use such information to screen potential employees?

By now it should be apparent to you that we may never resolve all of the ethical questions associated with the privacy of personal information. Just as the answer to one question becomes clearer, another is raised by a growing number of applications that deal with personal information.

Computer Monitoring

One of the most controversial applications of information technology is **computer monitoring.** In computer monitoring, computers continuously gather and assimilate data on job activities to measure worker performance, often without the workers' knowledge. Today, computers monitor the job performance of millions

Keeping in Touch with Home With a portable terminal, this trucker is expected to communicate with headquarters. He can send sales information, transaction records, and progress reports quickly, accurately, and wirelessly to the host computer. The host computer can also dispatch instructions, updates, and work orders back out to its work force. Anyone who records transactions on a computer system is a candidate for computer monitoring.
Courtesy of Symbol Technologies, Inc.

of American workers and millions more worldwide. Most of these workers are online and routinely interact with a server computer system via a terminal or PC. Others work with electronic or mechanical equipment linked to a computer system.

Many clerical workers are evaluated by the number of documents they process per unit of time. At insurance companies, computer-monitoring systems provide supervisors with information on the rate at which clerks process claims. Supervisors can request other information, such as time spent at the PC or terminal and the keying-error rate.

Computers also monitor the activities of many jobs that demand frequent use of the telephone. A computer logs the number of inquiries handled by directory-assistance operators. Some companies employ computers to monitor the use of telephones by all employees.

Although most computer monitoring is done at the clerical level, it is also being applied to persons in higher-level positions, such as commodities brokers, programmers, loan officers, and plant managers. For example, CIM (computer-integrated manufacturing) enables corporate executives to monitor the effectiveness of a plant manager on a real-time basis. At any given time, executives can tap the system for productivity information, such as the rate of production for a particular assembly.

Not all computer monitoring is aimed at assessing ongoing job performance. For example, some organizations encourage management scrutiny of employee electronic mail. In this form of monitoring, a robotic scanner "reads" employee e-mail searching for key words and phrases ("party," "skiing," "have a drink," and so on). Questionable e-mail messages are sent to management for review. The purpose of this type of monitoring is to ensure that internal communications are work-related and of a certain level of quality. Many organized worker groups have complained that this form of monitoring is an unnecessary invasion of privacy and can actually be counterproductive.

Workers complain that being constantly observed and analyzed by a computer adds unnecessary stress to their jobs. However, management is reluctant to give up computer monitoring because it has proved itself to be a tool for increasing worker productivity. In general, affected workers are opposing any further intrusion into their professional privacy. Conversely, management is equally vigilant in its quest for better information on worker performance.

IT Ethics

HATE SITES ON THE INTERNET

How do some consumers voice grievances about companies, products, and services? How do some people voice their disgust over a rock group, a political organization, or even a university? They publish their thoughts, warts and all, on the Internet, usually on their own Web page. Just enter the keyword *hate* or *sucks* into an Internet search facility and see how many hits it gets. Anyone or anything is a potential target.

Some of this hate venom may be deserved, but perhaps it isn't. The Internet is a powerful voice that can be used to call attention to flaws in a company's products or services. It can also be used to vilify individuals who may simply be doing their jobs, effectively and legally.

Discussion: Some experts in the field of Internet monitoring say that the best response to hate site venom is no response. Do you believe the experts? If not, how would you respond if one or more Internet sites mounted an unjustified attack on your company's products? How would you respond to an unjustified personal attack?

Computer Crime

Computer Crime

The ethical spectrum for computer issues runs from that which is ethical, to that which is unethical, to that which is against the law—a computer crime. There are many types of computer crimes, ranging from the use of an unauthorized password by a student in a college computer to a billion-dollar insurance fraud. The first case of computer crime was reported in 1958. Since then, all types of computer-related crimes have been reported: fraud, theft, larceny, embezzlement, burglary, sabotage, espionage, and forgery. We know computer crime is a serious problem, but we don't know how serious. Some studies estimate that each year the total money lost from computer crime is greater than the sum total of that taken in all other robberies. In fact, no one really knows the extent of computer crime because much of it is either undetected or unreported. In those cases involving banks, officers may elect to write off the loss rather than announce the crime and risk losing the good will of their customers. Computer crimes involving the greatest amount of money have to do with banking, insurance, product inventories, and securities.

Fortunately, only a small percentage of the people with an inclination toward crime are capable of committing high-tech crimes. Unfortunately, the criminal element in our society, like everyone else, is moving toward information technology competency. Thanks to the improved controls made possible through automation, though, business-related crime, in general, is decreasing. Computers have simply made it more difficult for people to commit business crimes. For the most part, computer crimes are not committed by stereotypical criminals and undesirables. Instead, they are committed by trusted computer users with authorized access to sensitive information.

Computers and the Law

Companies try to employ information technology within the boundaries of any applicable laws. Unfortunately, the laws are not always clear because many legal questions involving the use of information technology are being debated for the first time. For example, is e-mail like a letter or a memo, subject to freedom-of-information laws? Or, is it private, like telephone calls? This question is yet to be resolved. To no one's surprise, IT law is the fastest growing type of law practice.

Laws governing information technology are beginning to take shape. Prior to 1994, federal laws that addressed computer crime were limited because they ap-

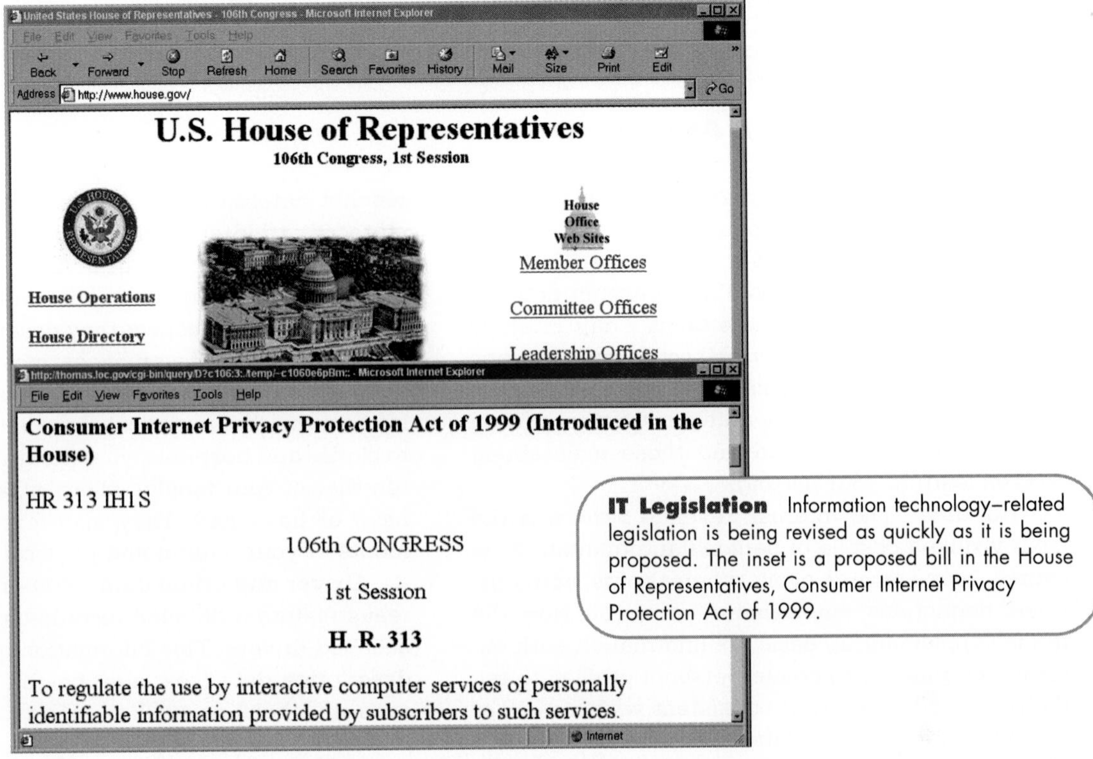

IT Legislation Information technology–related legislation is being revised as quickly as it is being proposed. The inset is a proposed bill in the House of Representatives, Consumer Internet Privacy Protection Act of 1999.

plied only to those computer systems that in some way reflected a "federal interest." The Computer Abuse Amendments Act of 1994 expanded the scope of computer crimes to computers "used in interstate commerce." Effectively, this means any computer, including home PCs, with a link to the Internet. These laws make it a felony to gain unauthorized access to a computer system with the intent to obtain anything of value, to defraud the system, or to cause more than $1000 in damage. Although most states have adopted computer crime laws, current laws are only the skeleton of what is needed to direct an orderly and controlled growth of information technology applications.

Existing federal and state laws concerning the privacy of personal information are being updated every year. At the same time, new laws are being written. Current federal laws outline the handling of credit information, restrict what information the IRS can obtain, restrict government access to financial information, permit individuals to view records maintained by federal agencies, restrict the use of education-related data, and regulate the matching of computer files. States have or are considering laws to deal with the handling of social security numbers, criminal records, telephone numbers, financial information, medical records, and other sensitive personal information.

Computer crime is a relatively recent phenomenon. As a result, legislation, the criminal justice system, and industry are not yet adequately prepared to cope with it. Only a handful of police and FBI agents in the entire country have been trained to handle cases involving computer crime. And when a case comes to court, few judges and even fewer jurors have the background necessary to understand the testimony.

Defrauding the System

Most computer crimes fall under the umbrella of computer fraud. These crimes involve a premeditated or conscious effort to defraud a computer-based system. Here are some examples.

- A U.S. Customs official modified a program to print $160,000 worth of unauthorized federal payroll checks payable to himself and his co-conspirators.

Emerging IT

WHO KNOWS WHAT ABOUT YOU?

Each day your name and personal information are passed from computer to computer over a variety of networks and, of course, over the Internet. Depending on your level of personal and Internet activity, this could happen 100 or more times a day. Literally millions of public- and private-sector organizations maintain data on individuals. The data collection begins before you are born and does not end until all your affairs are settled and those maintaining records learn of your parting.

Tax data The Internal Revenue Service is the most visible stockpile of personal information. It, of course, keeps records of our whereabouts, earnings, taxes, deductions, employment, and so on. Now the IRS is supplementing basic tax information with external information to create personal profiles to tell if a person's tax return is consistent with his or her lifestyle. By law, all IRS data must be made available to about 40 different government agencies.

Education data What you've accomplished during your years in school, such as grades and awards, is recorded in computer-based databases. Included in these databases is a variety of information such as your scores on college entrance exams, data on loan applications that include details of your family's financial status, roommate preferences, disciplinary actions, and so on. In one instance, a Chicago woman was turned down for several government jobs because of a note her third-grade teacher entered in her file. In the note the teacher stated that in her view the girl's mother was crazy.

Medical data Medical files, which contain a mountain of sensitive personal data, are not always treated with the respect they deserve. In many hospitals, hundreds of employees, most of whom do not have a need-to-know, have ready access to patient information. Your medical records list all your visits to clinics and hospitals, your medical history (and often that of your family), allergies, and diseases you have or have had. They also may include assessments of your mental and physical health.

Driver and crime data State motor vehicle bureaus maintain detailed records on over 175 million licensed drivers. This information includes personal descriptive data (sex, age, height, weight, color of eyes and hair) as well as arrests, fines, traffic offenses, and whether your license has been revoked. Some states sell descriptive information to retailers on the open market. The FBI's National Crime Information Center (NCIC) and local police offices maintain databases that contain rap sheet information on 25 million people. This information is readily available to thousands of law-enforcement personnel.

Census data The U.S. Bureau of the Census maintains some very personal data: names, racial heritage, income, the number of bathrooms in our home, and persons of the opposite sex who share

- A 17-year-old high school student tapped into an AT&T computer and stole more than $1 million worth of software.
- One person illegally transferred $10,200,000 from a U.S. bank to a Swiss bank. He probably would have gotten away with this electronic heist if he hadn't felt compelled to brag about it.
- Three data entry clerks in a large metropolitan city conspired with welfare recipients to write over $2 million of fraudulent checks.

These are examples of fraud. Any illegal entry into a computer system, direct or indirect, for the purpose of personal gain is considered fraud.

Computers can be both an invitation to fraud and a tool to thwart fraud. For example, at one time the automated system in place in the pits at the Chicago Board of Trade and the Chicago Mercantile Exchange made it possible for traders to fill personal orders either simultaneously or ahead of their customers to get better prices. A system, involving handheld computer trading devices, could be implemented that would electronically record every trade in sequence, preventing such abuses.

our living quarters. Statistics, however, are released without names.

Insurance data Insurance companies have formed a cooperative to maintain a single database containing medical information on millions of people. This revealing database includes claims, doctors' reports, whether or not you have been refused insurance, how risky you would be as an insuree, and so on.

Lifestyle data A number of cities are installing two-way cable TV that allows the accumulation of information on people's personal viewing habits. When you watch an X-rated movie, or any other movie, your choice is recorded in the family's viewing database. As interactive cable TV matures, you will be able to use it to pay bills, respond to opinion polls, and make dinner reservations. This, of course, will add a greater variety of information to your personal file.

Credit data Credit bureaus routinely release intimate details of our financial well-being. We, of course, hope that the information about us is up-to-date and accurate. However, this is not always the case. About one third of those who ask to review their records (you have the right to do this at any time) challenge their accuracy. Credit bureaus are bound by law to correct inaccuracies within two weeks of being notified of them.

Miscellaneous data Every time you make a long-distance telephone call, the number is recorded. When you make a credit-card purchase, your location at the time and the type of item you buy are recorded. Job-related information is maintained at current and past employers, including the results of performance reports and disciplinary actions. Local and state governments maintain records of property transactions that involve homes, automobiles, boats, guns, and so on. Banks not only keep track of your money, but some monitor the volume and type of transactions you make.

Summary The social security number, now assigned to all citizens, is the link that ties all our personal information together. It doubles as a military serial number, and in many states it serves as your driver's license number. It is the one item, along with your name, that appears on almost all personal forms. For example, your social security number is a permanent entry in hospital, tax, insurance, bank, employment, school, and scores of other types of records.

The few organizations discussed here represent the tip of the iceberg, so to speak. Most organizations handle personal data in a responsible manner. However, abuse continues to give us cause for concern. It's not the technology that abuses the privacy of our personal information, it's the people who use this technology. We as a society must be prepared to meet the challenge with a system of laws that deals realistically with the problem.

Attempts to defraud a computer system require the cooperation of an experienced IT specialist. A common street thug does not have the knowledge or the opportunity to be successful at this type of computer crime. Over 50% of all computer frauds are internal. That is, they are committed by employees of the organization being defrauded. About 30% of those defrauding employees are IT specialists.

Negligence and Incompetence

Not all computer crime is premeditated. Negligence or incompetence can be just as bad for an organization as a premeditated crime. Such crimes are usually a result of poor input/output control. For example, after she paid in full, a woman was sent dunning notices continually and was visited by collection agencies for not making payments on her automobile. Although the records and procedures were in error, the company forcibly repossessed the automobile without thoroughly checking its procedures and the legal implications. The woman had to sue the company for the return of her automobile. The court ordered the automobile returned and the company to pay her a substantial sum as a penalty.

The Cracker Problem

Another problem is the criminal activities of overzealous *hackers,* sometimes called *crackers* for the way they "crack" through network security. These "electronic vandals" have tapped into everything from local credit agencies to top-secret defense systems. The evidence of unlawful entry, perhaps a revised record or access during nonoperating hours, is called a **footprint.**

Many of the millions of Internet sites are vulnerable to attacks by vandals. Vandals have substituted images on home pages with ones that are embarrassing to the organization. Others have bombarded sites with thousands of randomly generated requests for service to preclude their use by legitimate users. Each day hackers and crackers are finding new ways to wreak havoc on the Internet.

The Computer Abuse Amendments Act of 1994 changed the standard for criminal prosecution from "intent" to "reckless disregard," thus increasing the chances of successful prosecution of crackers. Recently, two computer crackers were sentenced to federal prison for their roles in defrauding long-distance carriers of more than $28 million. The crackers stole credit-card numbers from MCI. The cracker who worked at MCI was sentenced to three years and two months, and the other cracker was sentenced to a one-year prison term.

Some people are concerned that the media glorifies criminally oriented hackers, creating heroes for a new generation of computer criminals. This glorification may begin to fade as we read about more and more crackers serving hard time.

Highway Robbery: Crime on the Internet

Security on the Internet, the foundation of the information superhighway, is an ongoing problem. Internet-related intrusions are increasing, averaging over 200 a month. The Internet is so vulnerable that computer science professors have been known to ask their students to break into files at a particular site on the Internet. Successful students bring back proof of system penetration to show they understand the protocols involved.

The Internet's cybercops on the Computer Emergency Response Team (CERT) often work around the clock to thwart electronic vandalism and crime on the Internet. CERT concentrates its efforts on battling major threats to the global Internet. Lesser problems are left to the Internet service providers and to police. A few years ago, the cybercops tracked hackers who were out to prove their ingenuity by breaking into systems just to prove they could. These hackers were mostly harmless, more out to prove their hacking abilities than to act maliciously. Now cyberthiefs are after more than self-esteem: They want to steal something. They intercept credit-card numbers, reroute valuable inventory, download copyrighted software, or make illegal monetary transactions. Fortunately, CERT has found that security incidents generally are decreasing relative to the size of the Internet. Unfortunately, as soon as CERT people plug a hole in the Internet, another is found. The problem won't go away and may become more difficult to cope with as perpetrators gain sophistication.

Security experts say that the best way to deal effectively with crime on the Internet is the universal adoption and use of an international encryption standard. At present, most people and companies are reluctant to adopt such a standard because it would effectively end open worldwide communication. However, if abuse continues, encryption may be the only solution.

Software Piracy and the Theft of Intellectual Property

Federal copyright law automatically protects software from the moment of its creation. This law is the same one that protects other intellectual property (books, audio recordings, films, and so on). The Copyright Law of 1974 gives the owner of the copyright "the exclusive rights" to "reproduce the copyrighted word." Those who purchase copyrighted software have the right to install it to an original computer. Unless specifically stated in the license agreement, the purchasers can install the software to only one computer. The general rule is: one software

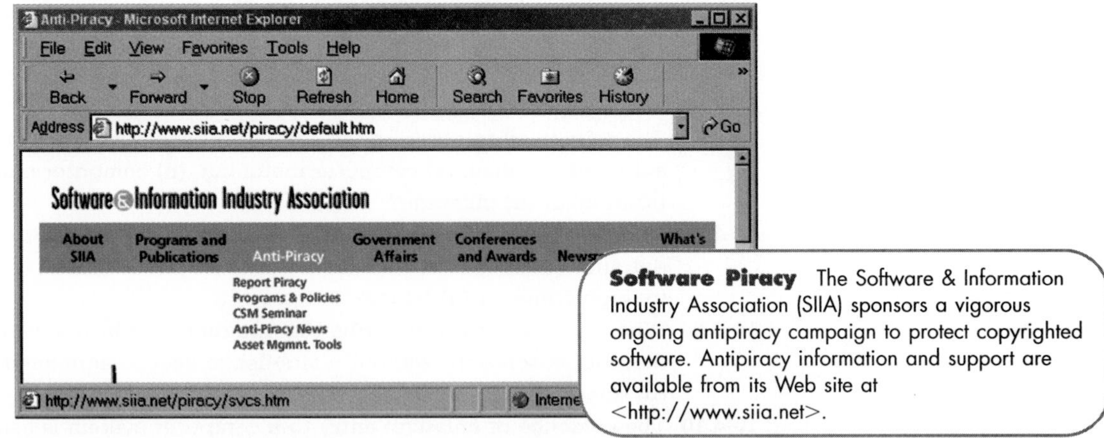

Software Piracy The Software & Information Industry Association (SIIA) sponsors a vigorous ongoing antipiracy campaign to protect copyrighted software. Antipiracy information and support are available from its Web site at <http://www.siia.net>.

package per computer. Any other duplication, whether for sale or for the owner's personal use, is an infringement of copyright law.

It is copyright infringement to allow simultaneous use of a single-user version on a LAN by more than one person. LAN versions of software packages are sold with a *site license* that permits use by a specific number of users. Also, the Software Rental Amendments Act of 1990 prohibits the rental, leasing, or lending of copyright software.

The unlawful duplication of proprietary software, called **software piracy,** is making companies vulnerable to legal action by the affected vendors. The term **pilferage** is used to describe the situation in which a company purchases a software product without a site-usage license agreement, then copies and distributes the software throughout the company. If such piracy is done "willfully and for the purpose of commercial advantage or private financial gain," perpetrators are subject to fines up to $250,000 and 5 years in jail. Software piracy doesn't pay. Two pirates in Canada were forced to walk the plank with a $22,500 fine. This and similar rulings have sent the message loud and clear: Software piracy is no longer tolerated.

Vendors of software for personal computers estimate that for every software product sold, two more are illegally copied. Software piracy is a serious problem, and software vendors are acting vigorously to prosecute people and companies who violate their copyrights. Worldwide, the software industry loses billions of dollars a year to software piracy.

The information superhighway poses big problems for software vendors. How do you keep people from distributing copies of software over the Internet? In all likelihood, software will eventually be encrypted such that the purchaser receives a cryptographic key to decode the program and data files. The key would exist in the program, identifying the owner and the buyer. If the buyer illegally distributes the program over an electronic highway, cybercops will be able to trace the action back to the source of the crime.

Some company managers confront the issue head-on and state bluntly that software piracy is a crime and offenders will be dismissed. This method has proven effective. Some, who are actually accomplices, look the other way as subordinates copy software for office and personal use.

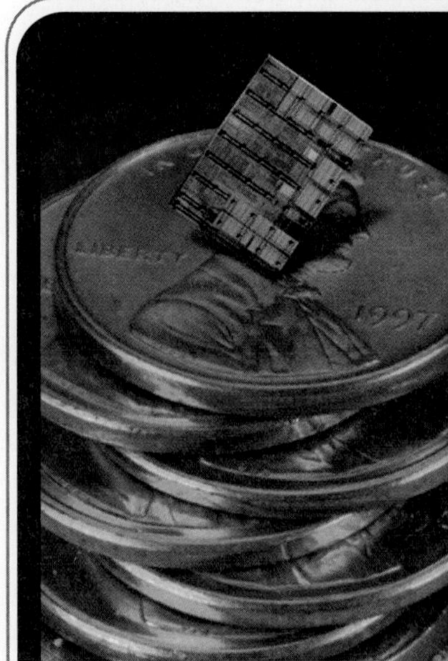

Copyright Law Copyright laws protect literature, music, the design of a silicon chip, and software, to name a few. IBM's innovative copper technology chip design is protected by law.
Courtesy of International Business Machines Corporation. Unauthorized use not permitted.

SECTION SELF-CHECK

Self-Check

10-4.1 Many legal questions involving computers and information processing are yet to be incorporated into the federal laws. (T/F)

10-4.2 The ACM Code of Conduct was recently adopted by the U.S. Senate and is now the law of the land. (T/F)

10-4.3 Over 90 percent of all knowledge workers embrace new technology and seek to incorporate it in their jobs. (T/F)

10-4.4 Current laws are now mature and can foster an orderly and controlled growth of information technology applications. (T/F)

10-4.5 Personal information has become the product of a growing industry. (T/F)

10-4.6 The number of federal government agencies that maintain computer-based files on individuals is between: (a) 50 and 100, (b) 500 and 1000, (c) 5000 and 10,000, or (d) 50,000 and 100,000?

10-4.7 The term used to describe the computer-based collection of data on worker activities is called: (a) computer matching, (b) computer monitoring, (c) footprinting, or (d) pilferage?

10-4.8 Gaining unauthorized access to any computer system with the intent of defrauding the system is a: (a) violation of public ethics, (b) misdemeanor, (c) high crime, or (d) felony?

10-4.9 What term is used to describe the situation in which a company copies and distributes software without a site-usage license agreement: (a) pilferage, (b) thieving, (c) pinching, or (d) filching?

10-4.10 The evidence of unlawful entry to a computer system is called a: (a) bitprint, (b) footprint, (c) handprint, or (d) fingerprint?

10-4.11 What law is violated when an organization duplicates proprietary software without permission: (a) civil rights, (b) antitrust, (c) copyright, or (d) patent?

10.5 COMPUTER, INTERNET, AND SYSTEM SECURITY

According to a recent survey, almost 80 percent of the companies in America have lost critical information on their computer systems during the past two years. Of those who were willing to describe their losses, 14 percent indicated losses over $250,000 and 2 percent had losses in excess of $1,000,000. The problem is serious and will not go away anytime soon. To minimize unethical abuses of information technology and computer crime, individuals and organizations must build an envelope of security around hardware and embed safeguards into the information systems. Security concerns take on added importance now that most business computer systems are interconnected via the Internet. There are too many points of vulnerability, and too much is at stake to overlook the threats to the security of any computer system. These threats take many forms—white-collar crime, computer viruses, natural disasters (earthquakes, floods), vandalism, and carelessness.

In this section we discuss commonly applied measures that can help to neutralize security threats to a computer center, an information system, and a PC.

Computer-Center Security

Enterprise-wide information systems provide information and processing capabilities to workers throughout a given organization. Some systems extend to customers, suppliers, and others outside the organization. Generally, such systems are handled by mainframe computers and/or network server computers located in centralized computer centers. The center can be anything from a secure room for the LAN server to an entire building for the organization's mainframe computers and the information services staff. Whether a room or a building, the computer center has a number of points of vulnerability: *hardware, software, files/databases, data communications (including the Internet),* and *personnel.* We discuss each separately in this section and illustrate them in Figure 10-3.

Hardware

If the hardware fails, the information system fails. The threat of failure can be minimized by implementing security precautions that prevent access by unauthorized personnel and by taking steps to keep all hardware operational.

Common approaches to securing the premises from unauthorized entry include use of closed-circuit TV monitors and alarm systems, as well as computer-controlled devices that check employee badges, fingerprints, or voice prints before unlocking doors at access points. Computer centers also should be isolated from pedestrian traffic. Computer-room fires should be extinguished by a special chemical that douses the fire but does not destroy the files or equipment.

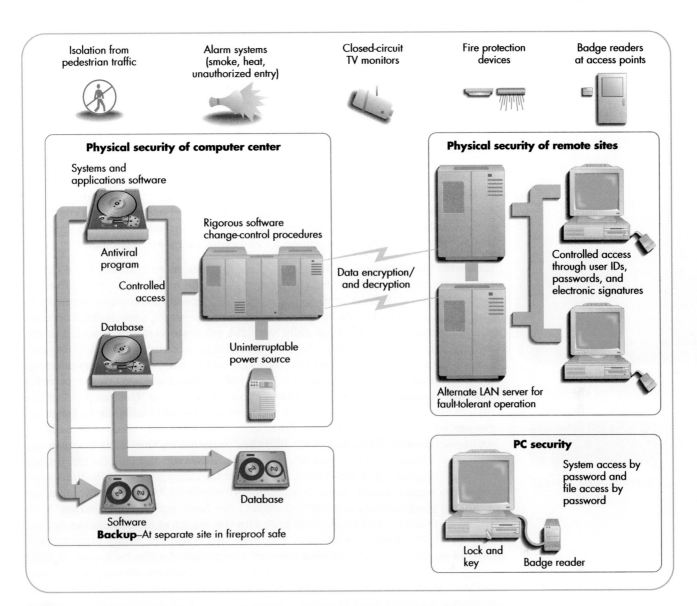

Isolation from pedestrian traffic
Alarm systems (smoke, heat, unauthorized entry)
Closed-circuit TV monitors
Fire protection devices
Badge readers at access points

Physical security of computer center

Systems and applications software
Rigorous software change-control procedures
Antiviral program
Controlled access
Database
Uninterruptable power source
Data encryption/ and decryption

Physical security of remote sites

Controlled access through user IDs, passwords, and electronic signatures
Alternate LAN server for fault-tolerant operation

Database
Software
Backup–At separate site in fireproof safe

PC security

System access by password and file access by password
Lock and key
Badge reader

Security Precautions Some or all of the security measures noted in the figure are in force in most organizations. Each precaution helps minimize the risk of a computer center's, an information system's, or a PC's vulnerability to crime, disasters, and failure.

Any complex system is subject to failure. However, for many organizations, network failure is simply unacceptable. For example, if the network supporting the Hilton Hotel reservation system went down for a couple of hours, thousands of reservations and, perhaps, millions of dollars would be lost. When network downtime is unacceptable, the network must be made **fault-tolerant.** In other words, the network must be designed to permit continuous operation even if important components of the network fail. To accomplish this goal, parts of the system must be duplicated. For example, a LAN might have an alternate LAN server. Fault-tolerant networks are designed to enable alternate routing of messages. Of course, no network can be made totally fault-tolerant. The degree to which a network is made fault-tolerant depends on the amount of money an organization is willing to spend.

Computers must have a "clean," continuous source of power. To minimize the effects of "dirty" power or power outages, each critical computer should draw its power from an **uninterruptible power source (UPS).** Dirty power, with sags and surges in power output or brownouts (low power), causes data transmission errors and program execution errors. A UPS system serves as a buffer between the

Lock It Up The Kensington MemoryLock™ effectively blocks access to the inside of your computer. The hard drive, memory, and all your important information are protected when you lock it up.
Courtesy of Kensington Technology Group

Serendipitous Surfing: Music

external power source and the computer system. In a UPS system, the computer is powered by batteries that deliver clean power, which in turn are regenerated by an external power source. If the external power source fails, the UPS system permits operation to continue for a period of time after an outage. This time cushion allows operators to either "power down" normally or switch to a backup power source, usually a diesel-powered generator. Until recently, UPS systems were associated only with mainframe computer systems and LAN servers. Now they are economically feasible for PCs.

Software

Unless properly controlled, the software for an information system can either be modified for personal gain or vandalized and rendered useless. Close control of software development and the documentation of an information system are needed to minimize the opportunity for computer crime and vandalism.

Unlawful Modification of Software Bank programmers certainly have opportunities to modify software for personal gain. In one case, a couple of programmers modified a savings system to make small deposits from other accounts to their own accounts. Here's how it worked: The interest for each savings account was compounded and credited daily, with the calculated interest rounded to the nearest penny before being credited to the savings account. Programs were modified to round down all interest calculations and put the "extra" penny in one of the programmers' savings accounts. It may not seem like much, but a penny a day from thousands of accounts adds up to a lot of money. The "beauty" of the system was that the books balanced and depositors did not miss the 15 cents (an average of 1/2 cent per day for 30 days) that judiciously was taken from each account each month. Even auditors had difficulty detecting this crime because the total interest paid on all accounts was correct. However, the culprits got greedy and were apprehended when someone noticed that they repeatedly withdrew inordinately large sums of money from their own accounts. Unfortunately, other enterprising programmers in other industries have been equally imaginative.

Operational control procedures built into the design of an information system will constantly monitor processing accuracy. Unfortunately, cagey programmers have been known to get around some of them. Perhaps the best way to safeguard programs from unlawful tampering is to use rigorous change-control procedures. Such procedures require programmers to obtain authorization before modifying an operational program. Change-control procedures make it difficult to modify a program for purposes of personal gain.

Viruses *Melissa, Chernobyl, Michelangelo, Friday the 13th, Stoned,* and *Jerusalem* are phrases that strike fear in PC users. They're names of computer viruses. The infamous Michelangelo virus hits on March 6, the artist's birthday, destroying stored data. Friday the 13th causes its damage on that day. Even though computer viruses have no metabolism of their own, some people are convinced that they fit the definition of a living system because they use the metabolism of a host computer for their parasitic existence.

The growing threat of viruses has resulted in tightening software controls. *Virus software,* which has been found at all levels of computing, "infects" other programs and databases. The virus is so named because it can spread from one system to another like a biological virus. Viruses are written by outlaw programmers to cause harm to the computer systems of unsuspecting victims. Left undetected a virus can result in loss of data and/or programs and even physical damage to the hardware. Viruses are discussed in detail in Chapter 4.

Individuals and companies routinely run antiviral programs, called *vaccines,* to search for and destroy viruses before they can do their dirty work. Many organizations encourage employees to run antiviral programs prior to March 6th and Friday the 13th. IBM researchers are working on an electronic *immune system* that would automatically detect viruses and neutralize them with digital antibodies. The immune system would inoculate other computers on the network, stopping the spread of the virus.

Files/Databases

A database contains the raw material for information. Often the files/databases of a company are its lifeblood. For example, how many companies can afford to lose their accounts receivable file, which documents who owes what? Having several *generations of backups* (backups to backups) to all files is not sufficient insurance against loss of files/databases. The backup and master files should be stored in fireproof safes in separate rooms, preferably in separate buildings. Approaches to system backup are covered in Chapter 4.

Data Communications

The mere existence of data communications/Internet capabilities poses a threat to security. A knowledgeable criminal can tap into the system from a remote location and use it for personal gain. In a well-designed system, such hacking is not an easy task. But it can be and has been done! When one criminal broke a company's security code and tapped into the network of computers, he was able to order certain products without being billed. He filled a warehouse before he eventually was caught. Another tapped into an international banking exchange system to reroute funds to an account of his own in a Swiss bank. In another case, an oil company consistently was able to outbid a competitor by "listening in" on the latter's data transmissions. On several occasions, overzealous hackers have tapped into sensitive defense computer systems. Fortunately, no harm was done.

How do companies protect themselves from these criminal activities? Some companies use **cryptography** to scramble messages sent over data communications channels. Someone who unlawfully intercepts such a message would find meaningless strings of characters. Cryptography is analogous to the code book used by intelligence people during the "cloak-and-dagger" days. Instead of a code book, however, a key is used in conjunction with **encryption/decryption** hardware to unscramble the message. Both sender and receiver must have the key, which is actually an algorithm that rearranges the bit structure of a message.

With the rapid growth of e-commerce, Internet security is beginning to mature. In early 1998, people were reluctant to send their credit-card number over the Internet. Today, people routinely purchase items with their credit cards. The difference is that Web site security has been beefed up with protocols for transmitting data securely over the World Wide Web. One protocol, **Secure Sockets Layer (SSL),** works by using a key to encrypt data that are transferred over the SSL link. Many Web sites use this protocol to transmit sensitive information, such as credit-card numbers, between Web client and Web server.

Most personal transmissions over the Internet are e-mail. Some who send sensitive information are opting to use a digital ID. The **digital ID** serves as an electronic substitute for a sealed envelope. The digital ID becomes part of the browser or e-mail software and allows you to digitally encrypt your e-mail. The digital ID ensures that messages and attachments are protected from tampering, impersonation, and eavesdropping.

Personnel

The biggest threat to a company's security system is the dishonesty and/or negligence of its own employees. Managers should pay close attention to who gets hired for positions with access to computer-based information systems and sensitive data. Many companies flash a message on each networked PC or terminal such as: "All information on this system is confidential and proprietary." It's not very user-friendly, but it gets the message across to employees that they may be fired if they abuse the system. Someone who is grossly negligent can cause just as much harm as someone who is inherently dishonest.

Information Systems Security

Information systems security is classified as physical or logical. **Physical security** refers to hardware, facilities, magnetic disks, and other items that could be illegally accessed, stolen, or destroyed. For example, restricted access to the server or mainframe room is a form of physical security.

Logical security is built into the software by permitting only authorized persons to access and use the system. Logical security for online systems is achieved primarily by using *user IDs* and *passwords.* Only those people with a need to know are given user IDs and told the password. On occasion, however, these security codes fall into the wrong hands. When this happens, an unauthorized person can gain access to programs and sensitive files simply by dialing up the computer and entering the codes.

Keeping user IDs and passwords from the computer criminal is not easy. One approach is to educate employees about techniques used to obtain user IDs and passwords, such as tailgating. The tailgater simply continues a session begun by an authorized user when the user leaves the room. Some companies have added another layer of security with the *electronic signature.* The electronic signature, which is built into hardware or software, can be a number or even a digitized signature of an individual. The host or server computer checks the electronic signature against an approved list before permitting access to the system. This measure thwarts the tailgater who attempts to use illegally obtained passwords on unauthorized PCs or software.

PC Security

Twenty-five years ago, the security problem was solved by wrapping the mainframe-based computer center in an envelope of physical security. Today the security issue is far more complex. PCs more powerful than the mainframes of 25 years ago pepper the corporate landscape. We even carry them with us. It's impractical to apply mainframe standards of security to PCs. If we did, we would all be working in concrete buildings under heavy security, and mobile computing would end.

Mainframe and Internet server security is carefully planned and controlled by security professionals. In contrast, PC security frequently is the responsibility of the individual users who may or may not have security training. As PC users, we have an ongoing obligation to be ever aware of security concerns. Generally, our PCs are readily accessible to other people in the area.

The conscientious PC user has several physical and logical security measures that can be used to safeguard valuable and/or sensitive information. The most frequently used physical tools include the *lock and key* and the *badge reader.* The lock and key, which come standard on most modern PCs, work like an automobile ignition switch. That is, the PC functions only when the lock is turned to the enable position. The badge reader is an optional peripheral device that reads magnetic stripes on badges, such as credit cards. The PC is disabled until an authorized card is inserted and read by the badge reader.

Often the content of your PC's screen bares your soul or perhaps sensitive corporate data. Some people place a special filter over the screen that permits only straight-on viewing. People use it in the office, airplane, or wherever they need to feel secure about their display.

User IDs and passwords remain the foundation of logical security. Users of LAN-based PCs must enter IDs and passwords before being allowed access to LAN resources. Stand-alone PCs also can be set up in a similar manner. Individual files can be secured by assigning them unique passwords. For example, if you were using a word processing package to prepare personnel performance evaluations, you could secure these files by assigning each a password. To recall a file at a later session, you or any other user would have to enter the name of the file and the associated password to gain access to it.

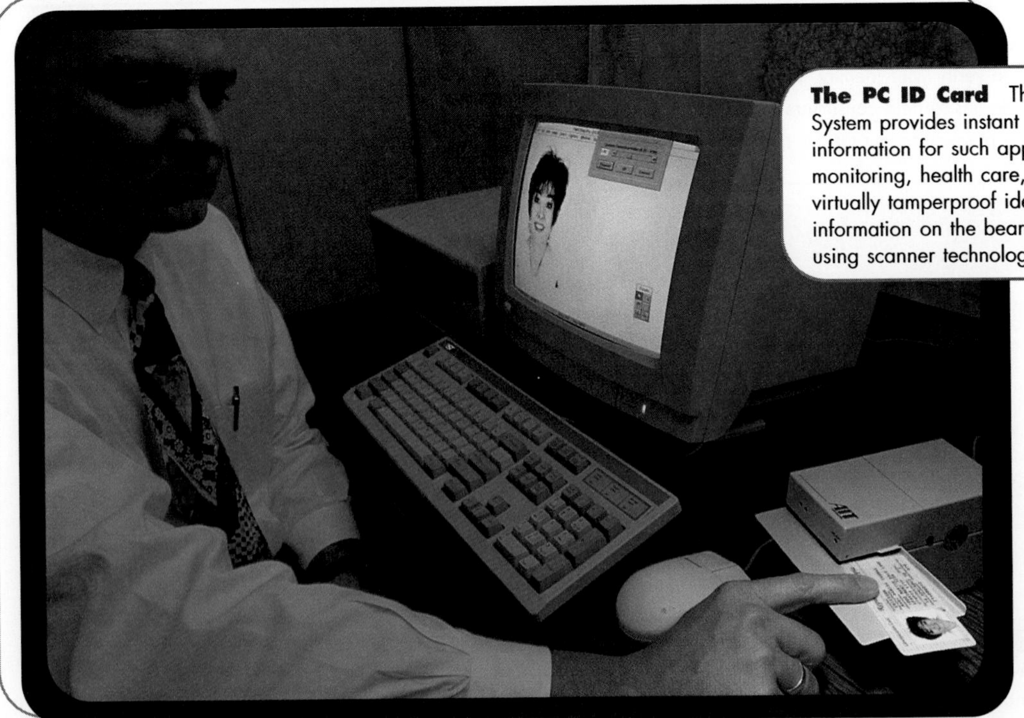

The PC ID Card This Secure ID Document System provides instant access to sensitive real-time information for such applications as border monitoring, health care, and voter registration. A virtually tamperproof identification card includes information on the bearer that can easily be verified using scanner technology. Courtesy of E-Systems, Inc.

The user ID is your electronic identifier and may be known by your friends and colleagues. The password, however, is yours alone to protect and use.

- Never tell anyone your password.
- Never write your password down.
- Change your password frequently.

With biometric identification systems, we don't need to enter a user ID and password. Biometric identification systems detect unique personal characteristics that can be matched against a database containing the characteristics of authorized users. Biometric methods include fingerprint, hand print (hand geometry), voice print, digitized signature, retinal scans (scan of the eye's retina through the pupil), facial thermograms, and facial recognition. Biometric devices (see Figure 10.4) are considered superior to traditional methods because they detect personal characteristics that can't be duplicated.

Level of Risk

No combination of security measures will completely remove the vulnerability of a computer center, an information system, a PC, or a file. Security systems are implemented in degrees. That is, an information system can be made marginally secure or very secure, but never totally secure. Each company must determine the level of risk that it is willing to accept. Unfortunately, some corporations are willing to accept an enormous risk and hope that those rare instances of crime and disaster do not occur. Some of them have found out too late that *rarely* is not the same as *never!*

SECTION SELF-CHECK

Self-Check

10-5.1 Virusology is the study of the assignment of security codes. (T/F)

10-5.2 Although expensive, some companies implement the security measures needed to be totally secure. (T/F)

10-5.3 Normal ceiling-mounted water sprays are installed in all computer centers for fire protection. (T/F)

(Self-Check continues on bottom of page 72.)

Biometric Access Methods Biometrics is a method of measuring unique physical traits or behavioral characteristics. Shown here are three techniques. Your fingerprint, face, palm print, or retina can be used to verify your identity. The security industry has looked to biometric identification technologies to help consumers protect themselves against theft and fraud. Soon we may no longer have passwords or user IDs that can be stolen or forgotten.

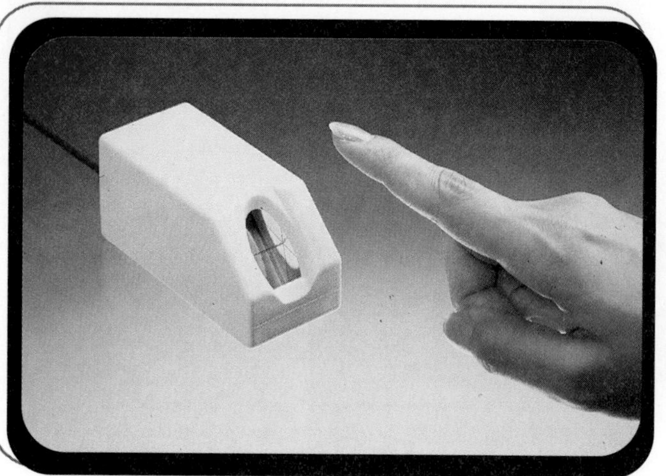

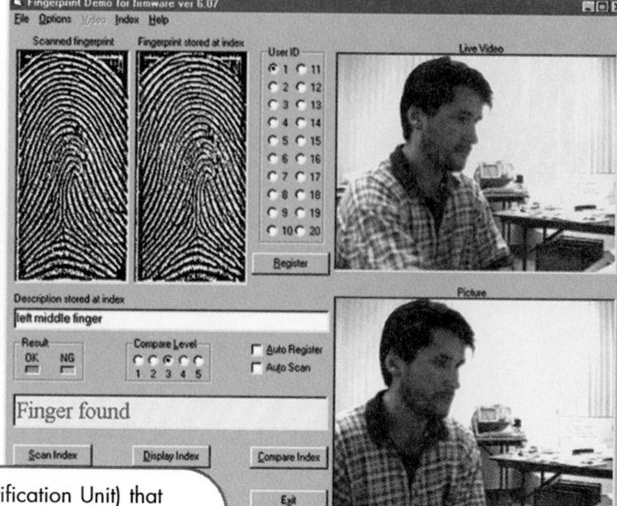

Fingerprint Biometrics Shown here is a Sony FIU (Finger Identification Unit) that contains a biometric sensor that can verify, compare, and store a user's fingerprint template, and all within one second. Courtesy of I/O Software, Inc

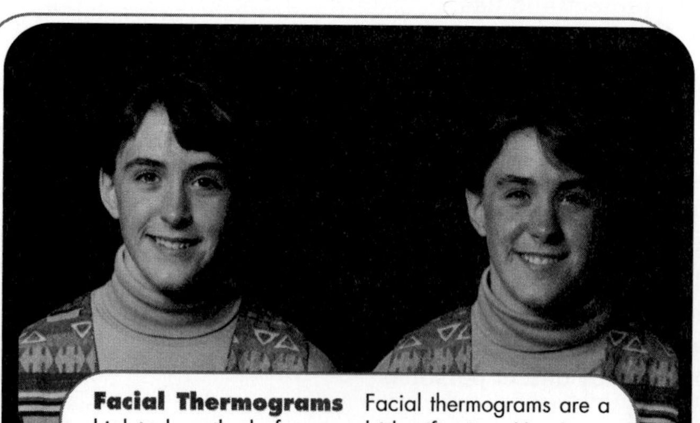

Facial Thermograms Facial thermograms are a high-tech method of personal identification. Here's how it works. There is a system of veins under your skin. Heat travels from these veins through the tissues of your face, creating a unique heat pattern. No two people have the same heat pattern, even the identical twins shown here. When an infrared camera captures a portrait of a face, the image highlights areas, such as blood vessels, that display a higher temperature than the surrounding flesh. A computer compares the infrared portrait to one stored in a database. The program begins by matching general facial features and then moves on to the finer data points.
Courtesy of Technology Recognition Systems

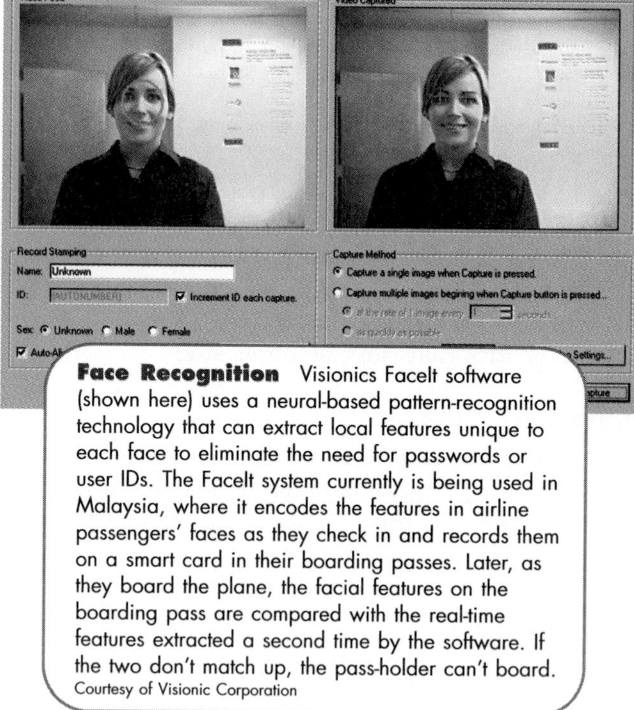

Face Recognition Visionics FaceIt software (shown here) uses a neural-based pattern-recognition technology that can extract local features unique to each face to eliminate the need for passwords or user IDs. The FaceIt system currently is being used in Malaysia, where it encodes the features in airline passengers' faces as they check in and records them on a smart card in their boarding passes. Later, as they board the plane, the facial features on the boarding pass are compared with the real-time features extracted a second time by the software. If the two don't match up, the pass-holder can't board.
Courtesy of Visionic Corporation

10-5.4 What name is given to a program intended to damage the computer system of an unsuspecting victim: (a) virus, (b) bug, (c) germ, or (d) fever?

10-5.5 When network downtime is unacceptable, the network must be made: (a) earthquake ready, (b) faultless, (c) uptime tolerant, or (d) fault-tolerant?

10-5.6 What can be used to scramble messages sent over data communications channels: (a) public keys, (b) encoding, (c) cryptography, or (d) ASCII plus?

10-5.7 Logical security for online systems is achieved primarily by user IDs and: (a) passwords, (b) secret codes, (c) numerical IDs, or (d) social security numbers?

10-5.8 Data can be transmitted securely over the World Wide Web with what protocol: (a) Secure Sockets Layer, (b) ATM, (c) ASCII, or (d) security sheet protocol?

Interactive Study Guide Chapter 10

SUMMARY AND KEY TERMS

10.1 The information technology paradox

We as a society are caught in an information technology paradox: Information technology is thriving in a society that may not be ready for it.

A reluctant acceptance of information technology has resulted in many IT-based opportunities being overlooked or ignored. Among the reasons they are not implemented are historical momentum, resistance to change, limited education, and lack of available resources.

Society has reached a point of no return with regard to dependence on computers. Only through understanding can we control the misuse or abuse of computer technology.

10.2 Working in the information society

People who can include computer knowledge on their résumés will have an advantage over those who can't. Information technology competency is required of employment in many professions, and in a few more years it may well be a requirement in most professions.

The number and type of career paths open to someone entering the computer/information technology field is expanding each year. Some of the most visible career paths are **chief information officer (CIO)** (44), **systems analyst** (45), **applications programmer** (46), **programmer/analyst** (46), **network administrator** (46), **system programmer** (46), **database administrator (DBA)** (46), **Internet site specialist** (46), **Webmaster** (46), **computer operator** (46), **user liaison** (47), and **PC specialists** (47).

At present, licensing or certification is usually not a requirement for any computer professional. However, there are a number of certifications. Some are offered by professional organizations (for example, the CCP and ACP offered by the ICCP, the Institute for Certification of Computer Professionals). Microsoft and Novell sponsor a range of widely accepted certifications, including the Microsoft Certified Systems Engineer (MCSE) and the Novell Authorized CNE (Novell Certified Engineer).

As information technology continues to move to the forefront in our society, jobs in every discipline are being redefined. Some jobs are being eliminated, while others are being created.

10.3 The workplace: Ergonomics and green computing

Human factors engineers are applying the principles of ergonomic design to ensure that the interface between knowledge worker and workplace is safe, comfortable, effective, and efficient. The knowledge worker's workplace should be designed with enough flexibility to enable it to be custom-fitted to its worker. Attention to the overall environment (lighting, noise, and ventilation) can reduce stress and increase worker performance.

Problems associated with extended use of a terminal or PC are collectively referred to as *video operator's distress syndrome,* or *VODS.* As the number of *repetitive-stress injuries (RSIs)* increased for knowledge workers, workstation **ergonomics** (51) became an increasingly important issue for corporate productivity. A poorly designed workplace has the potential to cause *cumulative trauma disorder (CTD),* a condition that can lead to a permanent disability of motor skills.

Green computing (53) adopts a more environmentally sound position with respect to the use and manufacture of computing hardware. The EPA's *Energy Star* guidelines are being used to standardize energy usage for monitors and processors. Good green computing includes sending e-mail (rather than paper); purchasing recycled paper; buying reconditioned components; and telecommuting once or twice a week.

10.4 The question of ethics

A code of ethics provides direction for computer professionals and users so they can apply computer technology responsibly.

The dominant ethical issue is the privacy of personal information. As automation continues to enrich our lives, it also opens the door for abuses of personal information. Personal information has become the product of a growing industry. Not only are the people involved not asked for permission to use their data, they are seldom even told that their personal information is being sold. The mere fact that personal information is so readily available has opened the door for many new applications of information technology. For example, **cookies** (56) containing personal information are passed freely around the Internet. **Computer matching** (57) involves the examination of separate databases to identify individuals common to both. **Computer monitoring** (58) is used to measure worker performance.

Computer crime is a relatively recent phenomenon. Therefore, laws governing information technology are few, and those that do exist are subject to a variety of interpretations. Computer crimes are frequently a result of computer fraud, negligence, or incompetence. Crackers tap into computer systems and sometimes leave evidence of unlawful entry, called a **footprint** (64), or infect the computer system with a virus, which is intended to cause harm to the computer systems of unsuspecting victims.

Security on the Internet is an ongoing problem as Internet-related intrusions are increasing. The Internet's cybercops on the Computer Emergency Response Team are ever vigilant in the fight against Internet crimes.

Software piracy (65) and **pilferage** (65) are computer crimes.

10.5 Computer, Internet, and system security

The threats to the security of computer centers and information systems call for precautionary measures. A computer center can be vulnerable in its hardware, software, files/databases, data communications (including the Internet), and personnel.

Any complex system is subject to failure, but when network downtime is unacceptable, the network must be made **fault-tolerant** (67). That is, the network must be designed to permit continuous operation even if important components of the network fail.

Organizations use a variety of approaches to secure the computer center, including the installation of an **uninterruptible power source (UPS)** (67) and the use of **cryptography** (69) to scramble messages sent over data communications channels. A key is used in conjunction with **encryption/decryption** (69) hardware to unscramble the message.

The **Secure Sockets Layer (SSL)** (69) protocol enables the transmission of data securely over the World Wide Web. The **digital ID** (69) is the equivalent of a sealed envelope for our e-mail.

The growing threat of viruses has resulted in the tightening of software controls. Virus software "infects" other programs and databases. Antiviral programs, called *vaccines,* search for and destroy viruses.

To protect your work, maintain several generations of backups, storing them in fireproof safes in separate rooms or buildings.

Information systems security is classified as **physical security** (70) or **logical security** (70). Logical security for online systems is achieved primarily by using user IDs and passwords. Another security measure is the electronic signature.

In the PC environment, people use several methods to control accessibility, including the *lock and key* and the *badge reader.* Properly equipped PCs can add an extra layer of security by incorporating biometric security methods, such as fingerprints, voice prints, retinal scans, and so on.

Security systems are implemented in degrees, and no computer center, LAN server, PC, or system can be made totally secure.

DISCUSSION AND PROBLEM SOLVING

10.1 a. Describe what yesterday would have been like if you had not used the capabilities of computers. Keep in mind that businesses with which you deal rely on computers and that many of your appliances are computer-based.

b. Two lawyers used the Internet to broadcast thousands of e-mail messages advertising their services. They were subsequently flamed (sent angry e-mail messages) and vilified by Internet users for what they believed to be an inappropriate use of the Net. The attorneys broke no laws. Was the reaction of Internet users justified? Explain.

10.2a. Discuss the differences between the job functions of applications and system programmers.

b. If you are pursuing a career in IT, describe your ideal career path through age 40. If you are pursuing a non-IT specialist career as knowledge worker, describe your ideal career path through age 40.

c. Describe the qualifications for the job of user liaison in a large plant that manufactures automobile parts.

d. Describe the qualifications for the job of chief information officer in a small company (fewer than 40 people).

e. Relatively few computer professionals have any kind of certification. Is it really necessary?

10.3a. Why is green computing important to society?

b. Expand these abbreviations and briefly describe what they mean: VODS, RSI, and CTD.

c. Evaluate your workplace at home, school, or work. Use the guidelines presented in Figure 10.1.

d. What can you do, that you are not doing now, that would be a move toward green computing?

10.4a. Give an example of how computer monitoring might be applied at the clerical level of activity. Give another example for the operational, tactical, or strategic level.

b. The Internal Revenue Service also uses computer matching to identify those who might be underpaying taxes. Is this an invasion of privacy or a legitimate approach to tax collection?

c. In the past, bank officers have been reluctant to report computer crimes. If you were a customer of a bank that made such a decision, how would you react?

d. Why would a judge sentence one person to 10 years in jail for an unarmed robbery of $25 from a convenience store and another to 18 months for computer fraud involving millions of dollars?

e. Discuss what you can do at your college or place of employment to minimize the possibility of computer crime.

f. Discuss the kinds of personal information that can be obtained by analyzing a person's credit-card transactions during the past year.

g. Internet cybercops at CERT are no longer concerned with minor intrusions to Net security. Why is this?

10.5a. What should be done at your college to improve computer security?

b. What should be done at your place of work to improve computer security?

c. Which scenario offers the greatest security for your credit card: paying for a meal at a restaurant, buying a pair of shoes over the Internet, or purchasing a PC via telephone mail order? Explain.

d. What precautions can be taken to minimize the effects of hardware failure?

e. The use of a digital ID provides secure passage for your e-mail and its attachments. How much would you pay for the use of a digital ID per e-mail?

ROBOTS AND ROBOTICS

Our vision of robots may still be in the days of Star Wars' R2D2 or Rosie Jetson's household robot, but things have changed over the past few decades. The field of study that deals with creating robots is called *robotics,* which simply is the integration of computers and robots. Most of us associate robotics with manufacturing and the use of industrial robots. Industrial robots are quite good at repetitive tasks and tasks that require precision movements, moving heavy loads, and working in hazardous areas. However, robots are emerging as major players not only in manufacturing but also in nonmanufacturing industries, such as health care and other service industries. Already we can give robots crude human sensory capabilities and some degree of artificial intelligence. As these capabilities mature over the next decade, look for robots in other areas of the workplace, in our homes, and even on stage and in museums.

Robotics offers the potential for increased productivity and better service. These benefits have not been overlooked by the manufacturing and service industries. Progressive organizations are rushing to install more and more applications of robotics as a means of staying competitive in the global economy. Today, the United States and Japan have the largest robot populations. However, industries throughout the world are looking to robots to help them control costs, respond more quickly to market needs, and reduce labor-related costs.

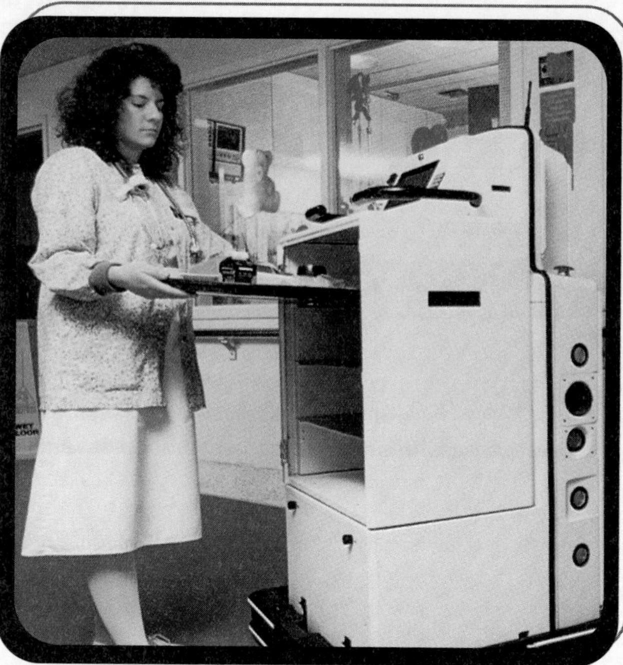

Mobile Robots Can Deliver

What can work 24 hours a day, weighs 575 pounds, stands 4 feet-7 inches tall, always talks politely, blinks a lot, and is extremely dependable? It's HelpMate®, a trackless, robotic courier designed to perform material transport tasks for health-care facilities. This robot can deliver mail, medication, supplies, and meal trays to the nursing units throughout the hospital

Vision and ultrasonic proximity sensors are used to understand the environment and avoid obstacles as they are encountered. It navigates from point to point by using a map of the building to plan the best route and sensory feedback to follow that route. It can even use the elevator! Those using HelpMate say it's really convenient and saves lots of running. They now have more time available for patient care.

Courtesy of Transactions Research Corporation

Refueling That's Fast, Clean, Convenient, and Safe

Without leaving the comfort and safety of their cars, motorists can refuel in minutes using Shell Oil Company's automated SMART Pump system. The new service features groundbreaking technology that uses an automated refueling device, simple robotic customer interface, and a system that identifies the make and model of the car. This allows a robotic arm to open the fuel door and dispense fuel.

Courtesy of Shell Oil Company

Rudimentary Robotics

The "steel-collar" work force is made up of hundreds of thousands of industrial robots. The most common industrial robot is a single mechanical arm controlled by a computer. The arm, called a *manipulator,* has a shoulder, forearm, and wrist and is capable of per-

Pick-and-Place

Computer-controlled industrial robots help insure the flow of work during production. Here a robot transfers materials in a pick-and-place application.

Courtesy of International Business Machines Corporation

forming the motions of a human arm. The manipulator is fitted with a hand designed to accomplish a specific task, such as painting, welding, picking and placing, and so on.

The automotive industry is the largest user of robots (for painting and welding) and the electronics industry (for circuit testing and connecting chips to circuit boards) is second. General Motors, for example, now has a robot base of over 15,000. When companies first started using robots, they would purchase it for a specific operation. When they no longer needed that operation, they would scrap the robot. Today things are different. They can respond to changes in the marketplace by using flexible automation and recycling their robots into needed areas, especially those areas of operation that are difficult or impossible for human workers to perform. For example, robots are used to install windshield glass on cars and trucks. This requires adhesive beads to be applied in a precise and uniform manner—something a robot can perform with high repeatability.

Teaching Robots to Do Their Job

A computer program is written to control the robot just as one is written to print payroll checks. It includes such commands as when to reach, in which direction to reach, how far to reach, when to grasp,

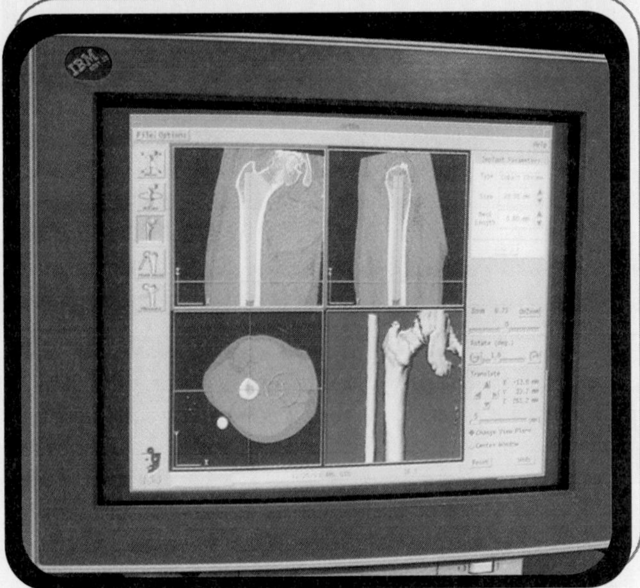

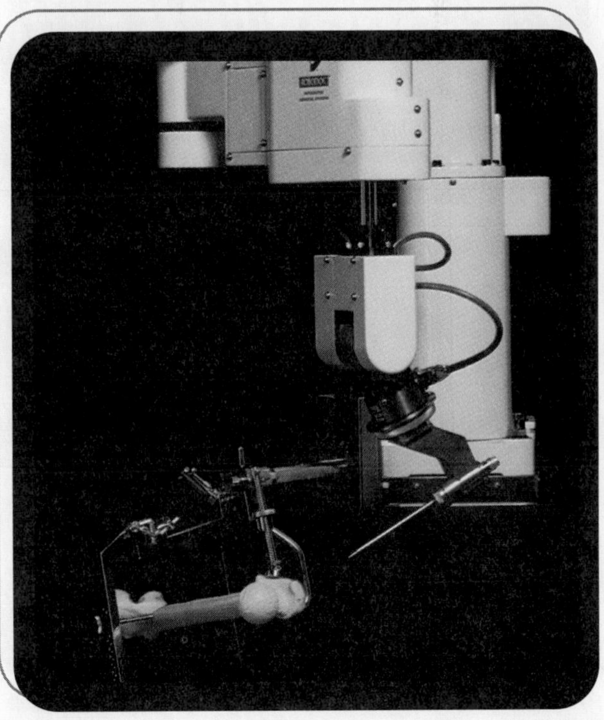

This Doctor's Hand Doesn't Shake

ORTHODOC™ is a computer workstation (above) for preoperative total hip replacement surgery. The system receives data from computed tomography (CT) scans and displays orthogonal and three-dimensional images. These images are used by surgeons for selecting a prosthesis and positioning the implant in the femur model prior to surgery. The ROBODOC Surgical Assistant (right) helps in the hip replacement. With a human surgeon present, ROBODOC machines a cavity in the patient's femur bone before the prosthetic implant is inserted. Courtesy of Integrated Surgical Systems Inc.

The Robot Team

The precise, untiring movement of computer-controlled industrial robots helps assure quality in the assembly of everything from electrical components to automobiles. Here in this Chrysler Motors Corporation plant, 66 industrial robots apply spot welds. About 300 robots weld, seal, train, paint, clean, and handle material at this plant. Chrysler Motors Corporation

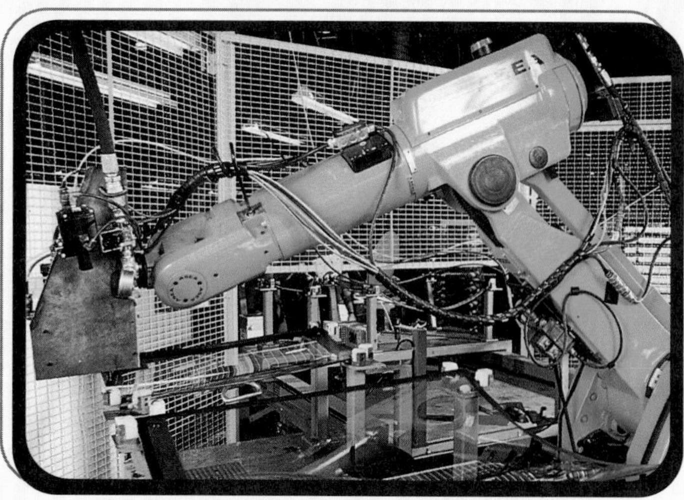

Flexing Muscles

The typical industrial robot has a manipulator arm with a shoulder, forearm, and wrist. Here, an industrial robot at Deere and Company readies a windshield for installation in a tractor's cab. Deere and Company

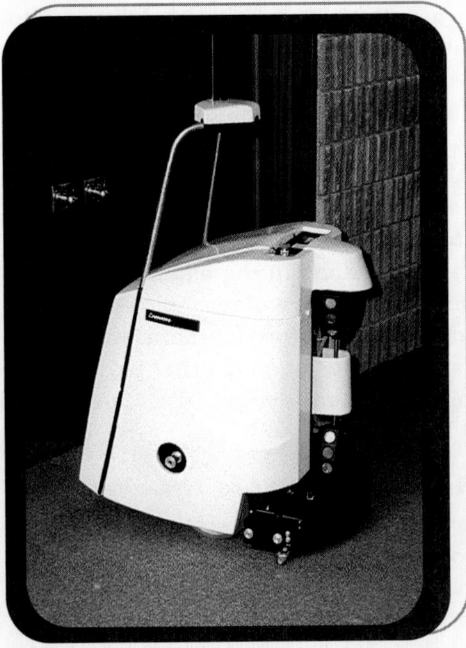

Sweeping the Floor
This modular multifunction service robot can act as a kind of "surrogate body" for a human being. It can be equipped as an autonomous mobile robotic industrial sweeper vacuum cleaner. Or, when outfitted with the surveillance package, it can perform security surveillance and other monitoring tasks.
Courtesy of Cyberworks, Inc.

The Checkout Robot
This CheckRobot Automated Checkout Machine (ACM) assists shoppers during self-checkout at grocery stores as well. The system is faster and less expensive with robot assistance.
CheckRobot Automated Checkout Machines

and so on. Most robots are programmed to reach to a particular location, find a particular item, and then place it somewhere else. This simple application of robotics is called *pick and place.* Instead of a grasping mechanism, other robots are equipped with a variety of industrial tools such as drills, paint guns, welding torches, and so on. Once programmed, robots do not need much attention. One plant manufactures vacuum cleaners 24 hours a day, 7 days a week!

Robots Come to Their Senses

With the exploding developments in sensor technology, roboticists are outfitting robots with artificial intelligence and human sensory capabilities. Of course it will be a very long time before our companions and workmates are robots. Smart sensors, adaptive architectures, microlens imaging, and embedded fiber optic sensors are all part of this technology.

Industrial robots are being equipped with rudimentary sensory capabilities, such as vision, that enable them to simulate human behavior. A robot with

Cut to Order
The automated cutting systems for nonrigid sheet materials used by the apparel, furniture, automotive, and other industries are actually robots. The systems cut patterns based on designs created with CAD (computer-aided design) software.
Gerber Scientific, Inc.

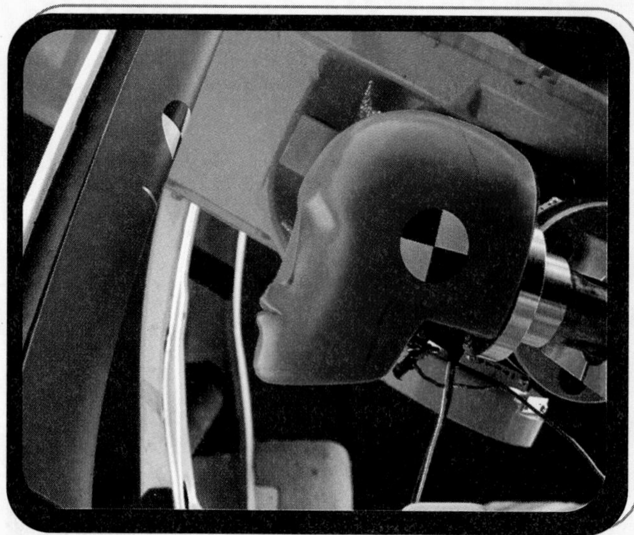

What a Headache

At Ford's Auto Safety Center, a robot directs a crash dummy headform at targets in a vehicle interior. An impactor at the end of a robotic arm fires the headform at speeds up to 15 mph to gather data. The test results are used to improve occupant safety. Courtesy of Ford Motor Company

the added dimension of vision can be given some intelligence. (Robots without intelligence simply repeat preprogrammed motions.) Even though the technology for the vision systems is primitive, a robot can be "taught" to distinguish between dissimilar objects under controlled conditions. With this sensory subsystem, the robot has the capability of making crude but important decisions. For example, a robot equipped with a vision subsystem can distinguish between two boxes approaching on the conveyor. It can be programmed to place a box of particular dimensions on an adjacent conveyer and let all other boxes pass.

As vision system technology continues to improve, more and more robots will have *navigational capabilities* (the ability to move). Now most robots are stationary; those that are not can only detect the presence of an object in their path or are programmed to operate within a well-defined work area where the positions of all obstacles are now. Service industries using mobile-robot technology applications include hospitals, security and patrol, commercial floor care, hazardous waste handling, bomb disposal, nuclear plant cleanup, janitorial services, rehabilitation programs, and the military.

Autonomous robots can make functional decisions without being guided or remotely piloted by a human operator. These robots can react intuitively to real-world stimuli by using the developing technology of image pattern recognition, mobility, agility, and perceptual cognition. Military self-guided cruise missiles are able to make automatic navigational adjustments in response to changing conditions while constantly reviewing their onboard flight maps. Other potential applications for autonomous robots, especially in situations where human workers would be exposed to great risk, include deep underwater exploration (robots helped in the exploration of the *Titanic*), interior surveillance of nuclear reactors (robots helped clean up after the Chernobyl nuclear incident), and surface navigation of other planets (the Sojourner robot scooted around Mars gathering data).

Opportunities for Robots Are Growing

Even surgeons are using robots to help in brain surgery. Robots can be set up to manipulate the surgical drill and biopsy needle with great accuracy, thereby making brain surgery faster, more accurate, and safer. Other surgical applications of robotics include help with hip replacements, knee replacements, and pelvic and spinal surgeries.

Autonomous kinetic sculpture is a new class of robotics and is found in art galleries and in the performing arts. Some robots create works of art, whereas others perform by themselves or with hu-

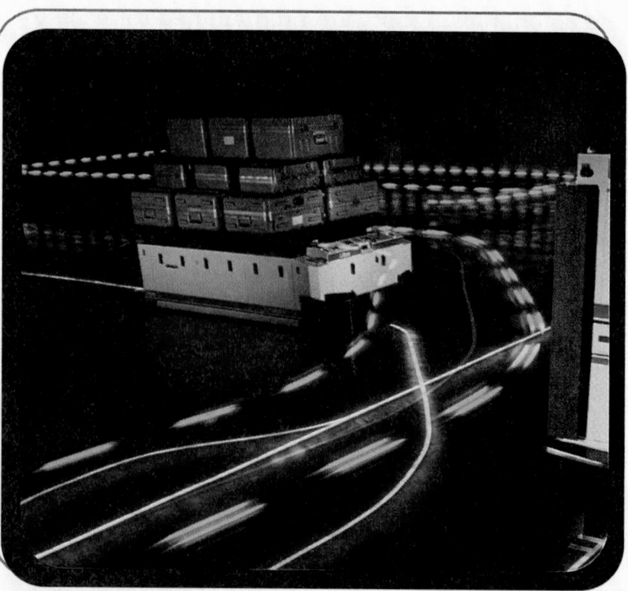

Robot Traffic

These computer-controlled automated guided vehicles (AGVs) are mobile robots. These AGVs are used in plants and warehouses for material and inventory handling. Photo courtesy of Litton Industries, Inc.

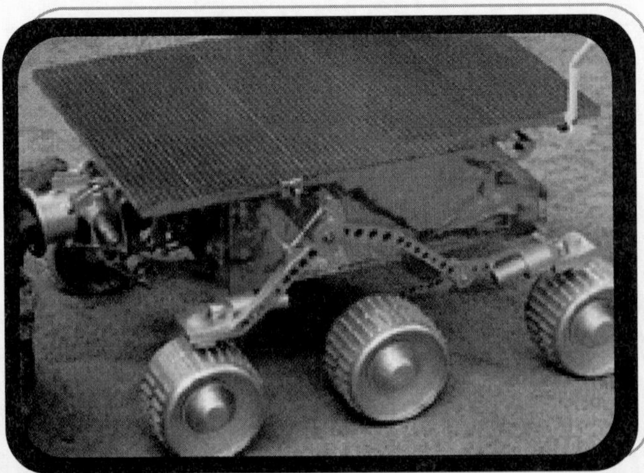

Motoring around Mars

The Mars Pathfinder delivered a stationary lander and a surface rover to the Red Planet on July 4, 1997. The rover vehicle, a mobile robot, was manipulated by controllers some 120,000,000 miles from Earth! The six-wheel rover, named Sojourner, explored the area near the lander, testing the soil and sending back pictures of Mars. This picture was taken from the lander. This mission's primary objective was to demonstrate the feasibility of low-cost landings on the Martian surface. Courtesy NASA

mans. How a performance or robotic sculpture will turn out is often unique because the robots are designed to react in real-time situations and adapt to their environment through their own creative behaviors.

But can I build my own robot? Although the number of robot hobbyists has declined since the mid-1980s, there are those who continue to work on developing home robots with kits or other mechanical and electrical devices. And, of course, there are robot clubs. Several universities have even hosted the Robot Olympics. The Biology, Electronics, Aesthetics, and Mechanics (BEAM) Robot Olympics sponsored by the University of Waterloo in Toronto provides a chance for robot enthusiasts to present their original designs in the spirit of competition. Typical events might include the Solaroller (self-starting robot dragster race), the high jump (robots do the high jump), the legged race (walking robots run for the money), and robot sumo (robots push/bash an opponent out of a ring).

In Summary: Things Are Picking Up

The future of robotics offers exciting opportunities. Companies are sure to take advantage of these opportunities to stay competitive. Robotics suppliers, along with their system integrators, are using Rapid Deployment Automation to expedite the implementation of robotics. This strategy uses computer-aided design to shorten the design-to-build cycle and promotes a user-friendly "no programming" environment for factory floor personnel. Robotics is being implemented in many nonmanufacturing environments as well (see accompanying photos). Who knows, we may someday have robots as helpers around the home and as workmates at the office.

The Third Eye

This technician's third eye is a stationary robot with a vision-input system that can detect tiny, but critical, flaws in circuit boards. The system performs inspections at a speed and precision unattainable with the human eye.

Reprinted with permission of Compaq Computer Corporation. All Rights Reserved.

Computers in Society: Tomorrow

Learning Objectives

11.1 Grasp the significance of the information superhighway at this time in history.

11.2 Be able to conceptualize a futuristic world where IT is an integral part of all we do.

11.3 Describe the major areas of artificial intelligence.

11.4 Identify current and potential applications along the information superhighway.

11.5 Gain insight into the challenges posed by information technology.

chapter 11

Value Learning

WHY THIS CHAPTER IS IMPORTANT TO YOU

Contrasting the timeline of aviation history to that of computing history, computing is about where the Wright brothers were after their first test flight. Just as it was difficult for the Wright brothers to imagine passenger planes that could cross the Atlantic Ocean in three hours or spaceships landing on the moon, it's just as difficult for us to imagine the future of information technology.

The *information technology revolution* is changing our lives in ways humanity has seen only twice before—during the *agricultural revolution* and the *industrial revolution.* You don't have to look very far to see the effects of these revolutions. The cyberworld lets us do things we never imagined just a few years ago. We visit virtual museums, read online newspapers, shop at home online, and "chat" with our senators. Applications and information that were previously reserved for people behind the counter are being made available to customers. You can find and purchase a car, trade stocks, make hotel reservations, and so on. Everything we do is becoming more tightly integrated with computers—robotics in manufacturing, virtual reality in entertainment, and learning without classrooms.

In this chapter you'll learn about state-of-the-art applications, emerging applications, and applications that we can anticipate in the near future. Each new innovation is an invasion of our comfort zone; that is, it invades the familiar. After reading this chapter you'll be better prepared to put each new technological innovation into perspective.

If computing capacity continues to double each year, then we can expect computing capacity to be 1000 times that of today within 10 years. Think about the possibilities. You and everyone else will have access to computing capacity roughly equivalent to all of the computers in New York City during the 1960s! The twenty-first century is going to be very interesting.

11.1 THE VIRTUAL FRONTIER

Monthly Technology Update
Chapter 11

The virtual frontier encompasses the electronic highways that comprise the Internet, thousands of newsgroups, scores of information services, and millions of private networks. The *information superhighway* metaphor is frequently used as a collective reference to these electronic links that have wired our world. This metaphor, though some feel it is inappropriate, is used by many and will probably remain in common usage for some time. There is no official name for our wired world. The government talks about a *National Information Infrastructure (NII),* and the media continues to create more descriptors for the virtual frontier, such as *I-way, infobahn,* and *cyberspace.* Whatever it is or will be called, it eventually will connect virtually every facet of our society. Already this frontier is expanding to embrace other forms of communication, including television, radio, and cellular telephony.

The *virtual frontier* may be the last great frontier. Much of what lies beyond the virtual horizon is uncharted and potentially dangerous territory. Even so, wagon trains filled with brave pioneers set out each day to blaze new electronic trails. The virtual frontier is sometimes likened to the Wild West because there are no rules and new people are arriving every day. Responsible pioneers accept and live by society's traditional rules of behavior, but the seedier elements of society are quick to observe that there is no virtual sheriff.

It's difficult to fathom the hardships endured by nineteenth-century pioneers who headed west for a better life. Imagine a hardy pioneer woman pushing a Conestoga wagon through the mud while her husband coaxes their oxen to pull harder. The hardships along the electronic trails are not as physical or life-threatening, but they exist. We're still sloshing through the virtual mud in the virtual frontier. When we find a road, it's more like a trail or a roadway under construction than a highway. The few highways that exist are narrow, filled with potholes, and have many detours.

The virtual frontier is growing in the same way the Wild West did. In the western frontier, cities grew from nothing overnight. In the virtual frontier, major services or capabilities unheard of a few years ago are becoming mainstream applications in the cyberworld. In the Wild West, many years passed before the ranchers and the farmers could be friends. Similarly, it might be some time before the various telecommunications, hardware, and software industries in the

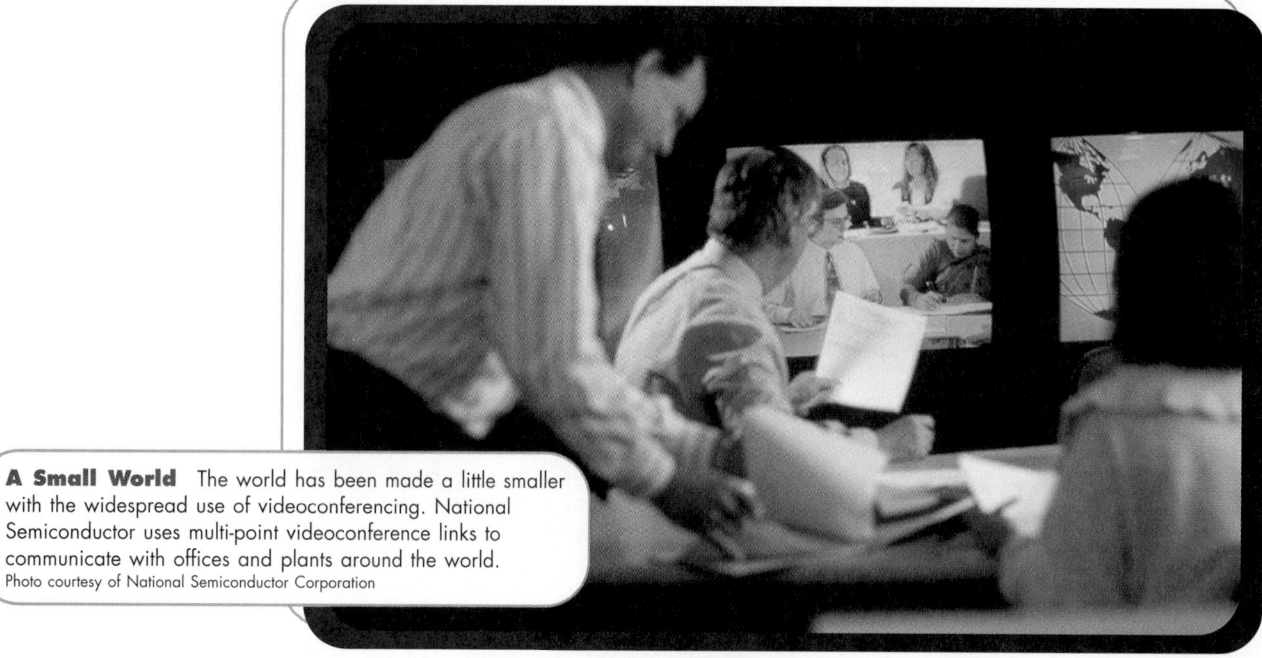

A Small World The world has been made a little smaller with the widespread use of videoconferencing. National Semiconductor uses multi-point videoconference links to communicate with offices and plants around the world.
Photo courtesy of National Semiconductor Corporation

Microminiaturization This IBM Microdrive can store 340 MB. This and other innovations in microminiaturization are changing the shape of things to come. Everything electronic is getting smaller—our digital cameras, video cameras, notebook computers, and so on. PCs will be wristwatch size before long.
Courtesy of International Business Machines Corporation. Unauthorized use not permitted.

virtual frontier can become friends. Outlaws roamed the Wild West, creating havoc until law and order was established. Electronic outlaws may have their way in the virtual frontier, as well, until cybercops armed with strict cyberlaws drive them out of town.

The opportunity for a better life enticed pioneers to risk all and follow the setting sun. Eventually the Wild West was tamed, and they realized their dreams. The modern-day version of the Wild West presents us with the same opportunity. Bear in mind, though, that the information superhighway is truly a frontier that may not be tamed in the foreseeable future. The fact that it is a frontier, with all the associated risks, makes it even more exciting. In this chapter we'll take a closer look at this virtual frontier and speculate about where it is headed. First, let's fast forward to the year 2005.

SECTION SELF-CHECK

Self-Check

11-1.1 The information highway is well-explored and would no longer be considered a frontier. (T/F)

11-1.2 A metaphor frequently used as a reference to the wired world is: (a) cyberway, (b) virtual way, (c) information superhighway, or (d) NINI?

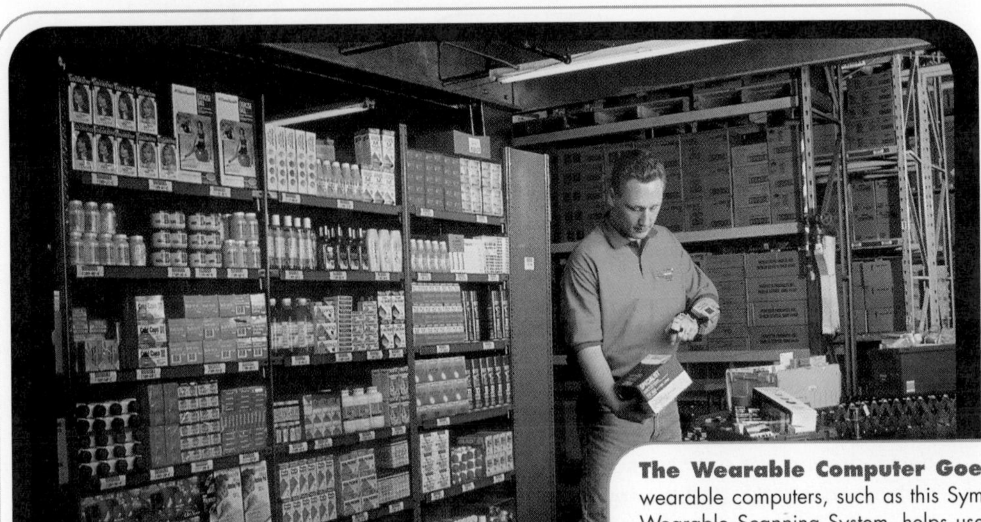

The Wearable Computer Goes Mainstream Using wearable computers, such as this Symbol Technologies' WSS 1000 Wearable Scanning System, helps users improve productivity and accuracy. This warehouse worker uses a miniaturized "aim-and-shoot" ring scanner and wrist-mounted computer to keep his hands free for moving, picking, and packing. Data are transmitted via a wireless link to a server computer. Courtesy of Symbol Technologies, Inc.

11.2 THE WAKE UP CALL

New Technology

The year is 2005. Computers are invisible; that is, they are built into our domestic, working, and external environments. Imagine this scenario: B. J. Rogers' invisible computer can be preprogrammed to awaken him to whatever stimulates him to greet the new day. B. J.'s wake up call, which could just as well be yours, can be any of these and more.

Wake up to your favorite music

Wake up to watching any movie ever produced

Wake up to any live sporting event

Wake up to checking your office p-mail (picture mail) for messages

Wake up to a different sound every day

Wake up to audio or visual weather report

To-Do List

1. Pick up laundry
2. Prepare dinner for Shannon and Pat
3. Teleconference with team members

Wake up to your To-Do list for the day

Wake up to a graphical summary of stock prices

Suppose B. J.'s wake up choice is a *to-do list* for the day. Besides listing the events of the day, his invisible computer, which he calls Rex, might *verbally* emphasize important events (see top left panel on facing page).

In response to B. J.'s request, the nearest video display, which is prominent in every *occupied* room in the house, is filled with a list of possible dishes (see top right panel on facing page). Just as B. J. notices that all dishes are meatless, Rex, the computer, reminds him of an important consideration. Rex might respond to his inquiry about ingredients by checking the home inventory and ordering as needed (all automatic).

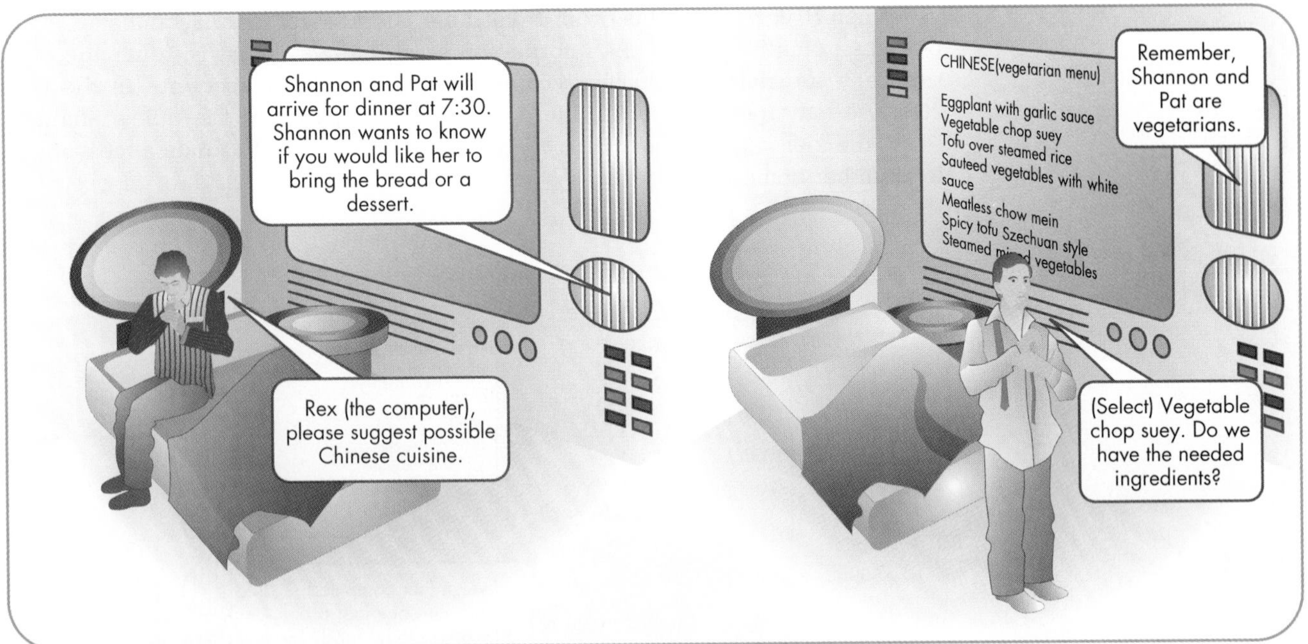

Rex immediately orders the ingredients electronically and asks the retailer to hold them for pickup (see bottom left panel). By 2005, high-speed data communications links will connect you, your invisible computer, the supermarket, and the rest of the country (and the world). Rex the cyberbutler is preprogrammed to prepare a hot, healthy breakfast every day. As B. J. eats breakfast, Rex prompts him again to respond to Shannon's request (see bottom right panel). Before B. J. finishes his next bite, Shannon's computer receives his message.

When B. J. arrives at the supermarket, the store's system identifies his car as he drives to the pickup area and greets him by name. "Good morning, Mr. Rogers. Your order is in Bin 4. Thank you for shopping ElectroMart."

When B. J. removes his order from Bin 4, all monetary transactions are completed automatically over the information superhighway. That is, funds are electronically transferred from his account to an ElectroMart account. (In the year 2005 we may be a cashless society.) Soon after arriving at the office, Shannon reads the messages on her office computer and immediately sends a message to Evelyn, her home computer.

Shannon's (and cybermaid Evelyn's) contribution to the evening meal will be ready at 7:00 P.M. However, even in the year 2005, some tasks will continue to defy total automation. We will still have to rely on our creativity to set the dinner table for the occasion!

Much of this futuristic story is within the grasp of today's technology. Even today, millions of people carry computers with them much of the day. Millions more spend most of their day within arm's reach of a computer. Many of these people routinely use speech-recognition technology to talk to their PCs. Smart homes are now deemed an economically sound investment. You can shop at Wal-Mart, the world's largest retailer from any communications-ready PC. Though expensive, large flat-panel monitors are commercially available. Thousands of high-speed digital lines are being installed in homes every day. Hundreds of radio stations now broadcast over the Internet. So you see, we are well on our way to the day when this fictional scenario emerges as reality.

Few will argue that we are rapidly approaching the age of automation, an era when invisible computers participate in or help us with all we do. However, the way things are going, the future may be here sooner than we think.

SECTION SELF-CHECK

Self-Check

11-2.1 The first smart houses are expected to emerge shortly after the turn of the century. (T/F)

11-2.2 Large, inexpensive flat-panel monitors are currently available, but consumers prefer those that use CRT technology. (T/F)

11-2.3 Which of these is not within the grasp of today's technology: (a) radio broadcasts over the Internet, (b) smart homes, (c) shop online at Wal-Mart, or (d) robot-like domestic help?

11.3 ARTIFICIAL INTELLIGENCE

Artificial Intelligence

Today's computers can simulate many human capabilities, such as reaching, grasping, calculating, speaking, remembering, comparing numbers, and drawing. Researchers are working to expand these capabilities and, therefore, the power of computers, by developing hardware and software that can imitate intelligent human behavior. For example, researchers are working on systems that have the ability to reason, to learn or accumulate knowledge, to strive for self-improvement, and to simulate human sensory and mechanical capabilities. This general area of research is known as **artificial intelligence (AI).**

Artificial intelligence? To some, the mere mention of artificial intelligence creates visions of electromechanical automatons replacing human beings. But as anyone involved in the area of artificial intelligence will tell you, there is a distinct difference between human beings and machines. Computers will never be capable of simulating the distinctly human qualities of creativity, humor, and emotions! However, computers can drive machines that mimic human movements (such as picking up objects and placing them at a prescribed location), provide the "brains" for systems that simulate the human thought process within the domain of a particular area of expertise (tax preparation, medical diagnosis, and so on), and enable us to talk to our computers.

Even though significant strides have been made in the area of artificial intelligence, research is still at the embryonic level. Each year AI researchers come up with new discoveries and innovations that serve to redefine artificial intelligence. Some say that AI is such an abstract concept that it defies definition. It seems as if each new revelation in AI research raises more questions than it answers. "It's a moving horizon," says Marvin Minsky, a pioneer in AI research from MIT.

Categories of Artificial Intelligence

Research in the field of artificial intelligence can be divided into four categories: expert systems, natural languages, simulation of human sensory capabilities, and robotics.

Expert Systems

Expert systems, which are discussed in detail in Chapter 12, rely on a *knowledge base* that is filled with "rules of thumb" (intuition, judgment, and inferences) about a specific application area, such as computer repair. Humans can use the expert system and the IF-THEN rules in the knowledge base to help them solve a particular problem. Once the knowledge of one or more human experts has been entered to an expert system's knowledge base, users can tap this knowledge by interacting with the system in much the same way they would interact with a human expert in that field. Both the user and the computer-based expert system ask and respond to each other's questions until a problem is resolved.

Expert systems are beginning to make a major impact on the way people in the business community make decisions. In recent years, expert systems have been developed to support decision makers in a broad range of disciplines, from medical diagnosis to locomotive repair.

Around tax time most of us are looking for someone to help us prepare our increasingly complex tax forms. Some of us are doing it ourselves with the help of an expert system. Several commercially available PC-based expert systems are designed to assist people in the preparation of their annual tax returns. Taxpayers and tax preparers can have a question-and-answer session with a computerized version of a tax expert. The expert system asks the user questions and, based on the answers provided, asks more detailed questions. The tax preparation expert system contains online facsimiles of the official IRS tax forms onto which users enter their data. The system automatically performs all needed calculations based on the data entered. Official IRS tax schedules can be printed directly by the system for submission to the Internal Revenue Service, or, in some cases, they can be submitted electronically.

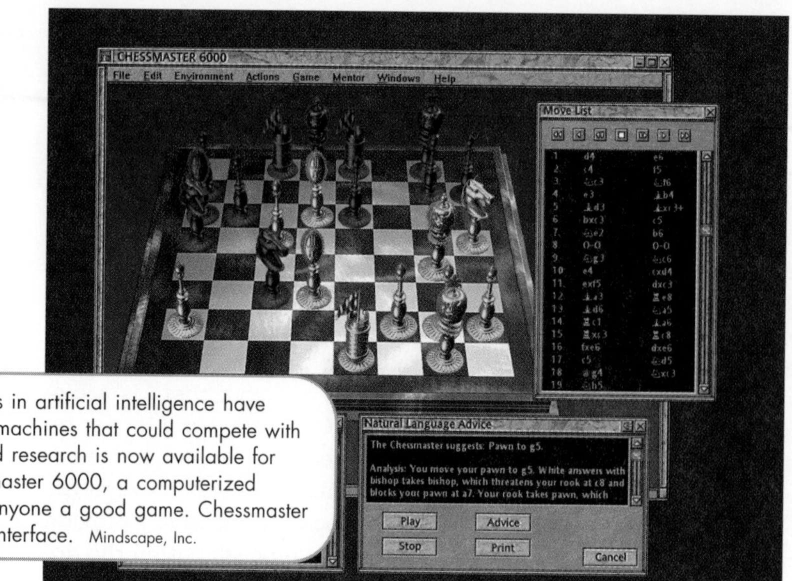

Chess and AI Researchers in artificial intelligence have spent decades trying to build machines that could compete with humans in chess. This AI-based research is now available for your PC in the form of Chessmaster 6000, a computerized chess resource that can give anyone a good game. Chessmaster even has a natural language interface. Mindscape, Inc.

Natural Languages

Natural languages refer to software that enables computer systems to accept, interpret, and execute instructions in the native, or "natural," language of the end user, typically English. For example, the end user uses a natural language when he or she enters brief English commands such as "Show me a pie chart for regional sales" to a computer system. There are, of course, limitations on the complexity of the commands that can be interpreted. The state of the art of natural languages is still somewhat primitive. Most commercial natural languages are designed to provide end users with a means of communicating with a corporate database or an expert system.

Simulation of Human Sensory Capabilities

One area of AI research involves computer simulation of human capabilities. This area focuses on equipping computer systems with the capabilities of seeing, hearing, speaking, feeling (touching), and smelling—yes, smelling. These artificial intelligence capabilities are possible with current technology, to varying degrees.

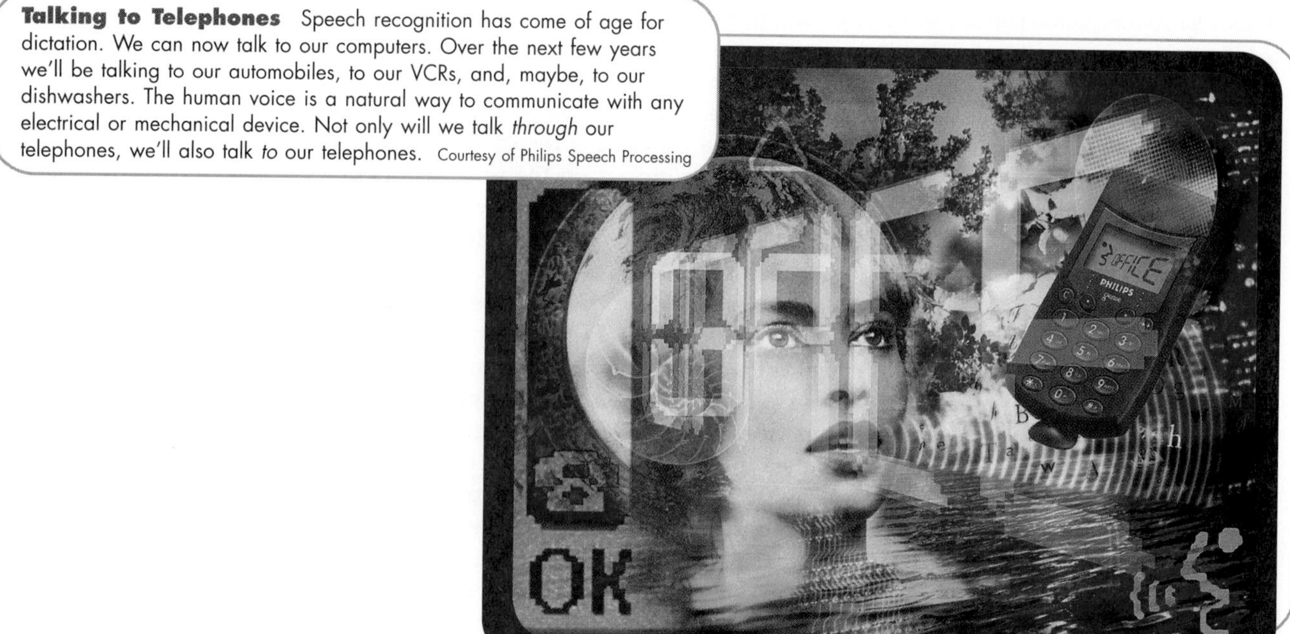

Talking to Telephones Speech recognition has come of age for dictation. We can now talk to our computers. Over the next few years we'll be talking to our automobiles, to our VCRs, and, maybe, to our dishwashers. The human voice is a natural way to communicate with any electrical or mechanical device. Not only will we talk *through* our telephones, we'll also talk *to* our telephones. Courtesy of Philips Speech Processing

For example, some automobiles employ synthesized voice messages to warn the driver and passengers of problems: Have you ever heard, "A door is open"?

One AI area that has advanced rapidly in recent years is speech recognition. Speech-recognition software that can interpret normal speech at close to 100 percent accuracy is now common in the home and the workplace. Industry forecasters are predicting that speech recognition may play an even greater role in our lives. They are predicting that many of our business transactions will take place between a person and an automated personality. If they are correct, then this AI technology will have a huge impact on hundreds of industries and jobs. In 1992, the introduction of a primitive directory-assistance system resulted in the loss of 51,000 jobs at one company. The system was capable of recognizing only five terms: *collect, third party, credit card, person-to-person,* and *operator.* Today, systems are far more sophisticated. Already, United Airlines has developed a speech-recognition system that allows processing of complete travel bookings. Other companies in the securities, retailing, and courier services industries are designing equally advanced systems. Technology will continue to displace workers as our society moves toward greater sophistication in our use of IT; however, history has shown us that displaced workers inevitably are retrained to fill exciting new jobs in information technology.

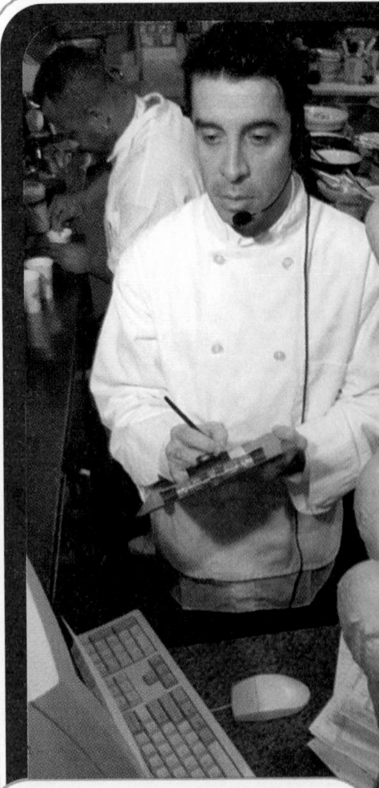

Figures of Speech Peter Corrales, owner of *Barocco to Go* catering in New York City, checks inventory using an IBM-PC computer. The computer translates speech into text using IBM ViaVoice speech-recognition technology.

Robotics

Robotics is the integration of computers and **robots.** Industrial robots, which usually are equipped with an arm and a hand, can be "taught" to perform almost any repetitive manipulative task, such as painting a car, screwing on a bolt, moving material, and even such complex tasks as inspecting a manufactured part for defects. The topic of robotics is addressed in more detail in the *Focus on IT: Robots and Robotics* following Chapter 11.

The Commercialization of Artificial Intelligence

Scientists have been working to build "thinking" machines for a long time, generally paying little attention to the commercial viability of their work. For example, during the formative years of AI, hundreds of researchers were working to develop software that would enable humans to test their chess-playing skills against the skills of a computer. Early chess programs challenged the club player, but today's programs have proven to be formidable opponents for world champions.

For several years, artificial intelligence was the darling of the IT industry. Even though virtually all the companies were experiencing heavy losses, investors remained confident that profits would eventually skyrocket. After two or three years of heavy losses and no profits in sight, most of the companies folded. Reality had set in—people are not willing to buy products that do not contribute to profit. Today, aggressive AI companies are marketing innovative AI products with the potential to have a positive impact on a company's bottom line.

SECTION SELF-CHECK

Self-Check

11-3.1 Artificial intelligence refers to an area of research that uses computers to simulate human capabilities. (T/F)

11-3.2 Computers already are capable of simulating human humor and emotions. (T/F)

11-3.3 A knowledge base may include "rules of thumb." (T/F)

11-3.4 All natural languages are designed for use by IT database professionals. (T/F)

11-3.5 Which term is used to describe the integration of computers and robots: (a) robocomp, (b) androidics, (c) robotics, or (d) automatonics?

11-3.6 Which of these is not an AI category: (a) natural languages, (b) expert systems, (c) robotics, or (d) MIS?

11-3.7 Expert systems are associated with what kind of rules: (a) IF-THEN, (b) bipolar, (c) binary, or (d) robotic?

11.4 DOWN THE ROAD: THE INFORMATION SUPERHIGHWAY

Let's look down the road at what information technology and the information superhighway might have to offer. The text and the images in this section survey a variety of new and emerging IT applications. Bear in mind that information technology and the information superhighway are tools. You and other innovators will ultimately determine what applications are created as well as who and what drive along the information superhighway.

Travelers along the Information Superhighway

Surprisingly, many adult Americans are unaware of the information superhighway, which includes the Internet, and its impact on society. In fact, most people are still waiting at the on ramp. Each day, however, more travelers drive up the ramp and on to the electronic highway. The mode of travel through cyberspace is the computer. A typical Internet session will take you all over the country and often to other countries. The actual traffic along the highway is anything that can be digitized—text (perhaps the morning newspaper), graphic images (an MRI scan of a brain tumor), motion video (a movie), still photographs (a picture of a friend), sound (a radio station), and programs (perhaps multiplayer Internet games that load and run on your PC).

Perhaps the best way to describe the information superhighway is in terms of its current and potential applications. Information services, such as America Online and CompuServe, are growing every day in the scope and variety of services they offer. Features and services of America Online are discussed in detail in Chapter 7. Figure 11.1 gives you a feel for the breadth of services, information, and applications found on the Net. A mind-boggling array of information and telecommunication services have been implemented or are planned for the information superhighway, some of which are described in this section.

Cruising the Net The Internet makes a vast treasure trove of information and services available to people all over the world. This figure contains a sampling of a few of the millions of stops along the Internet.

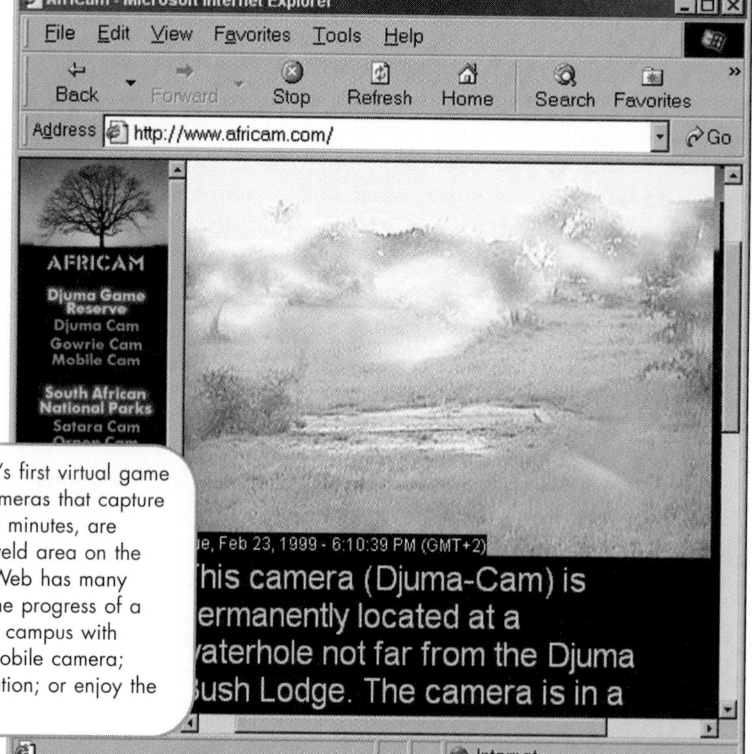

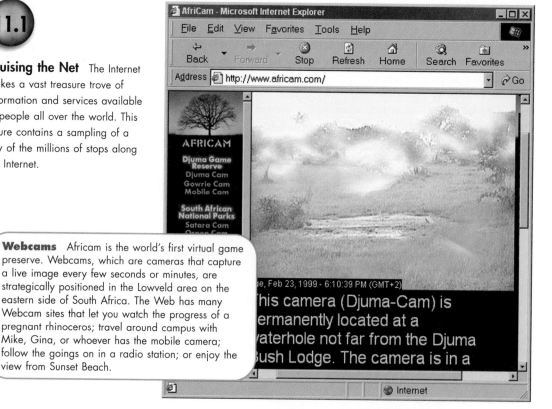

Webcams Africam is the world's first virtual game preserve. Webcams, which are cameras that capture a live image every few seconds or minutes, are strategically positioned in the Lowveld area on the eastern side of South Africa. The Web has many Webcam sites that let you watch the progress of a pregnant rhinoceros; travel around campus with Mike, Gina, or whoever has the mobile camera; follow the goings on in a radio station; or enjoy the view from Sunset Beach.

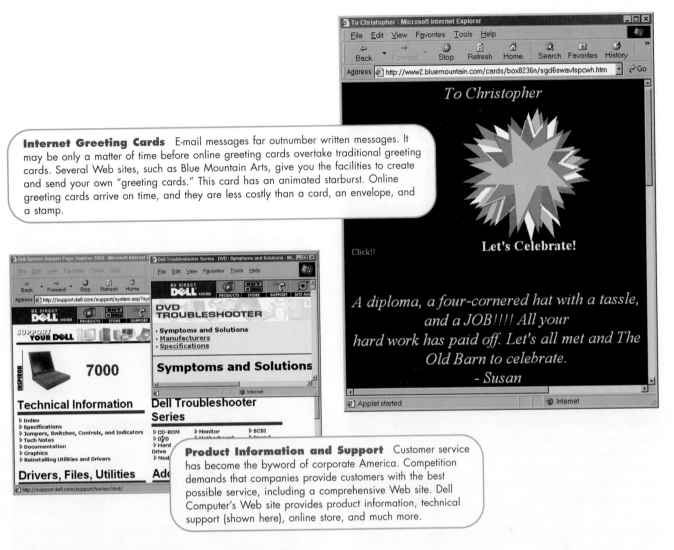

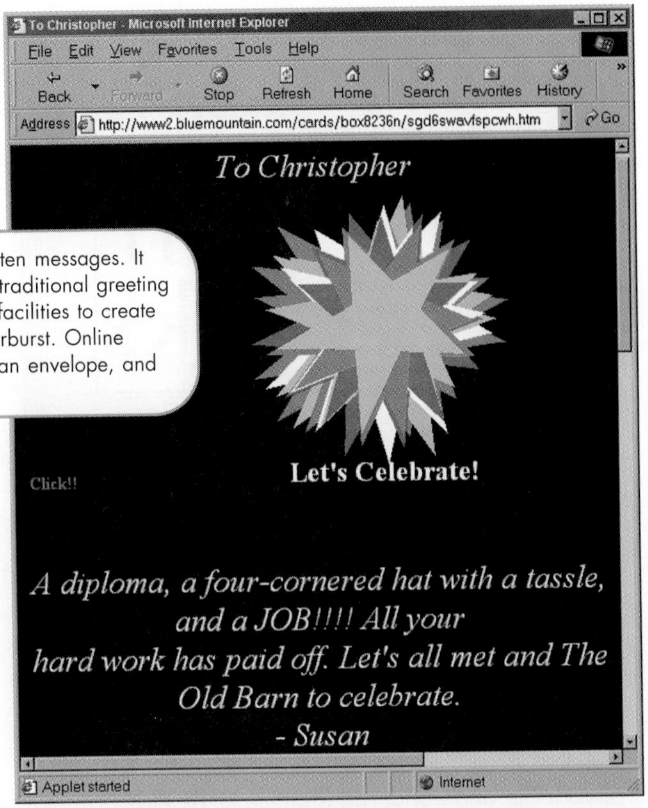

Internet Greeting Cards E-mail messages far outnumber written messages. It may be only a matter of time before online greeting cards overtake traditional greeting cards. Several Web sites, such as Blue Mountain Arts, give you the facilities to create and send your own "greeting cards." This card has an animated starburst. Online greeting cards arrive on time, and they are less costly than a card, an envelope, and a stamp.

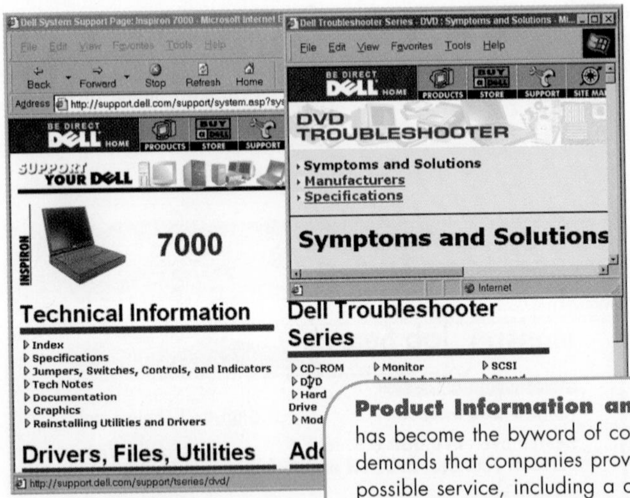

Product Information and Support Customer service has become the byword of corporate America. Competition demands that companies provide customers with the best possible service, including a comprehensive Web site. Dell Computer's Web site provides product information, technical support (shown here), online store, and much more.

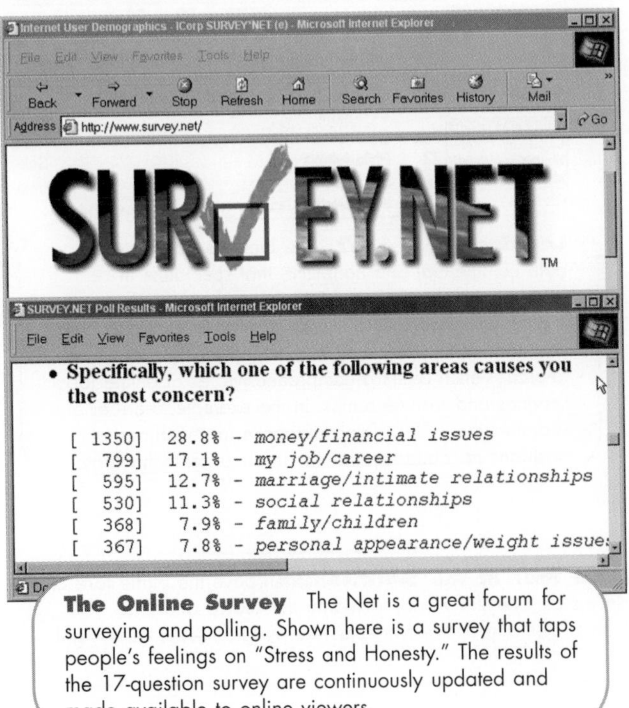

The Online Survey The Net is a great forum for surveying and polling. Shown here is a survey that taps people's feelings on "Stress and Honesty." The results of the 17-question survey are continuously updated and made available to online viewers.

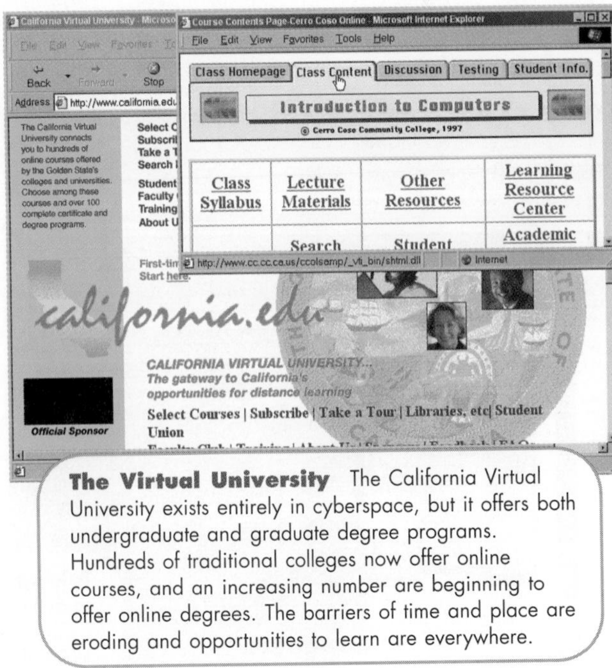

The Virtual University The California Virtual University exists entirely in cyberspace, but it offers both undergraduate and graduate degree programs. Hundreds of traditional colleges now offer online courses, and an increasing number are beginning to offer online degrees. The barriers of time and place are eroding and opportunities to learn are everywhere.

(Figure 11.1 continues on next page)

(Figure 11.1 continued)

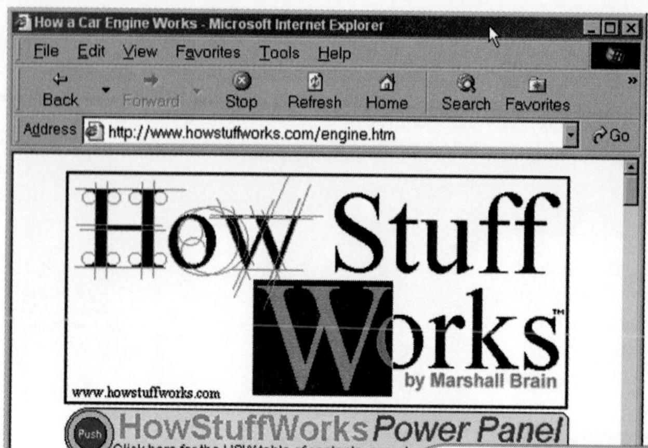

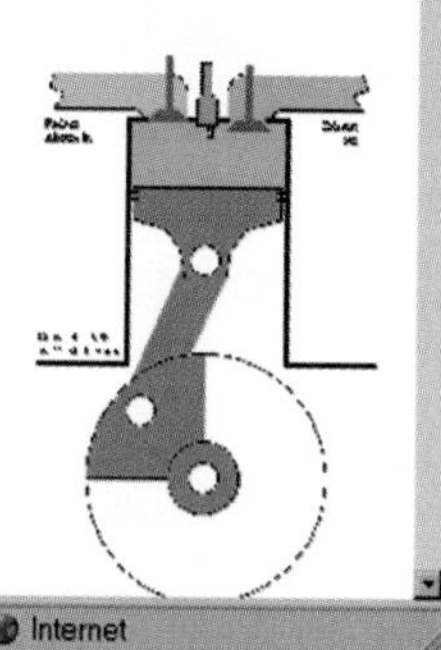

The Best of the Web Cybersurfers are ever vigilant in their search for the best and worst that the Net has to offer. Critics abound on the Internet. People and companies who create Web sites should be aware that cybercritics might eventually pass judgment on the quality of their site, both good and bad. A select few make one of the "best" or "worst" lists. This "How Stuff Works" site was Yahoo's Cool Site of the Year for 1998 (the cylinder graphic is animated).

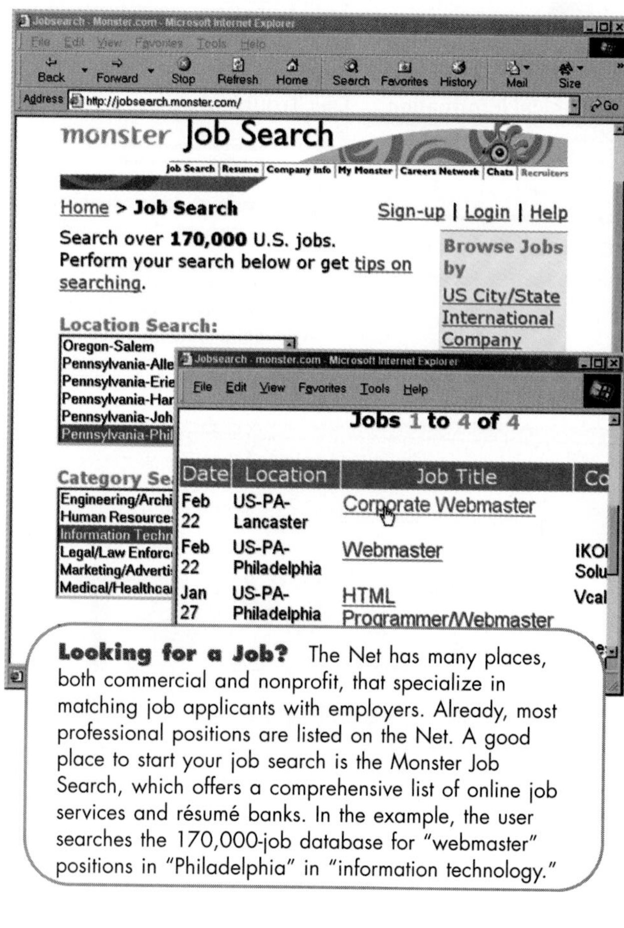

Looking for a Job? The Net has many places, both commercial and nonprofit, that specialize in matching job applicants with employers. Already, most professional positions are listed on the Net. A good place to start your job search is the Monster Job Search, which offers a comprehensive list of online job services and résumé banks. In the example, the user searches the 170,000-job database for "webmaster" positions in "Philadelphia" in "information technology."

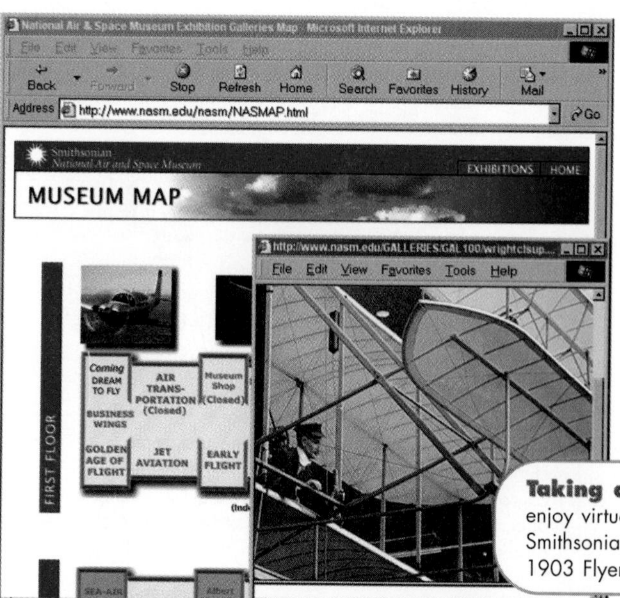

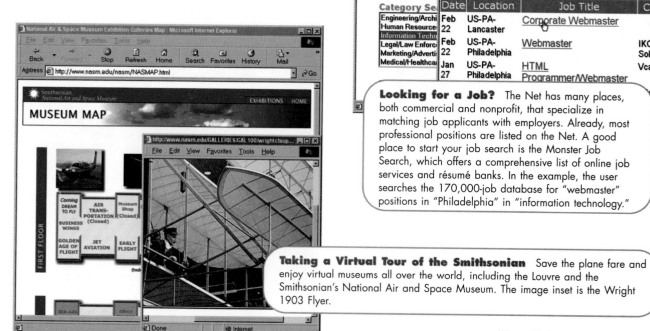

Taking a Virtual Tour of the Smithsonian Save the plane fare and enjoy virtual museums all over the world, including the Louvre and the Smithsonian's National Air and Space Museum. The image inset is the Wright 1903 Flyer.

(Figure 11.1 continues on next page)

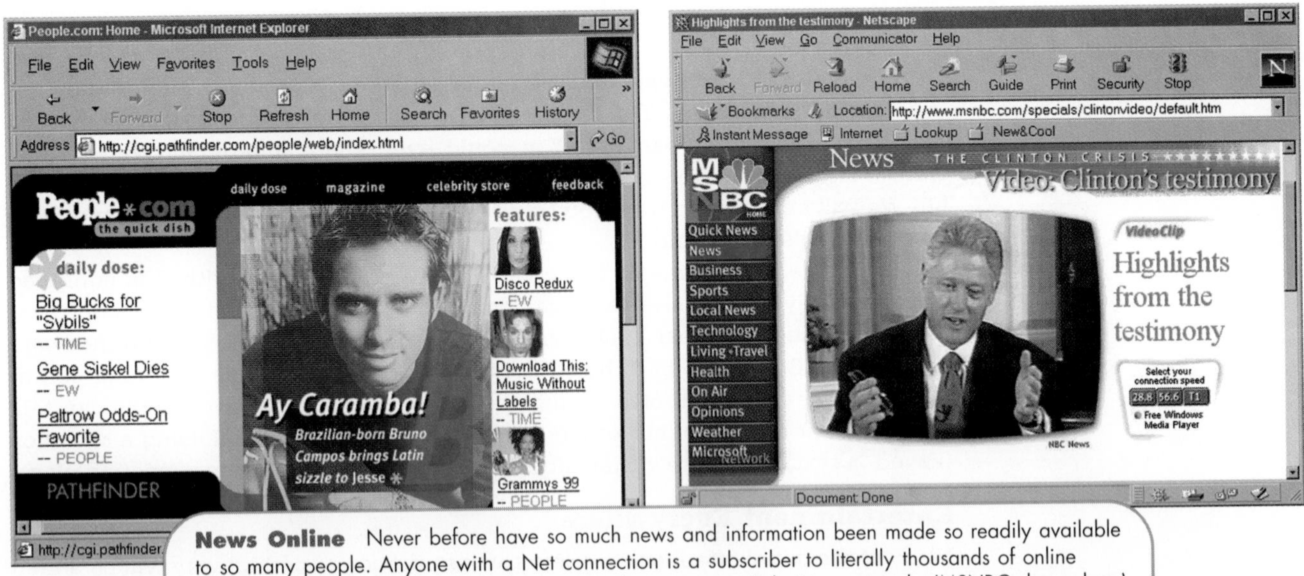

News Online Never before have so much news and information been made so readily available to so many people. Anyone with a Net connection is a subscriber to literally thousands of online magazines (*People* magazine shown here) and newspapers. Television networks (MSNBC shown here) and radio stations also contribute to online news resources. For now, it's free because everyone wants a presence and a readership on the Web. Eventually we may have to subscribe or pay a small fee each time we access online news and information sources.

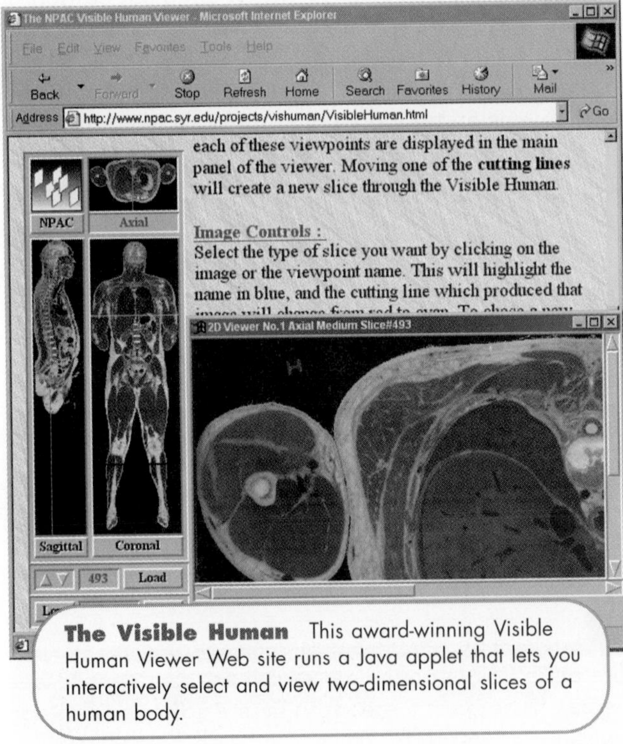

The Visible Human This award-winning Visible Human Viewer Web site runs a Java applet that lets you interactively select and view two-dimensional slices of a human body.

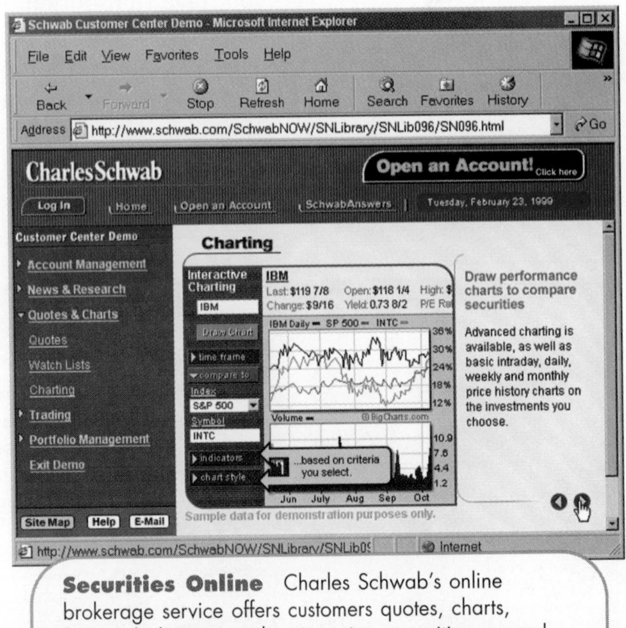

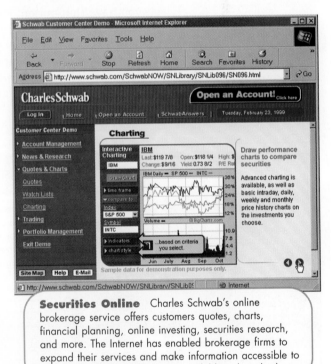

Securities Online Charles Schwab's online brokerage service offers customers quotes, charts, financial planning, online investing, securities research, and more. The Internet has enabled brokerage firms to expand their services and make information accessible to customers that heretofore were available only to brokers.

The Electronic Family Reunion

The telephone as we know it will probably disappear. In the relatively near future, the function of the telephone will be incorporated into videophones, our PCs, our TVs, or perhaps all of these so we can see and hear the person(s) on the other end of the line. The future "telephone" will enable us to pass data and information back and forth as if we were sitting at the same table.

You will be able to use the information superhighway, your television, your PC, and multiple videophone hookups to hold an electronic family reunion. Here is how it would work. You would dial the videophones of your relatives and a real-time video of each family would appear in a window on your wall-size television monitor. The conversation would be in stereo and sound as if all families were in the same room. The members of each family would be able to see the members of the other families. You could even share photos and view family videos. The information superhighway may enable more frequent family reunions, but we will still have to travel on traditional highways to get real hugs and taste grandmother's cherry pie.

Today we have some of these capabilities. Two people with PCs equipped with relatively inexpensive video cameras (under $100) can hold videophone conversations (see and hear each other) over regular telephone line Internet connections (33.6 K bps to 56 K bps). They can even pass pictures and other still or video images back and forth during the conversation. Only two people can talk to each other at a time, but others can join in the conversation using a chat box (keyed-in text) and share visual information, such as directions to a meeting place.

Entertainment Everywhere

Many of the initial offerings traveling the information superhighway will be aimed at entertaining us. We'll have *video-on-demand;* that is, you will be able to choose what television program or movie you want to watch and when you want to watch it. You will be able to watch any movie, from the classic archives to first runs, at your convenience. The same is true of television programming. If you would prefer to watch this week's edition of *60 Minutes* on Monday, rather than Sunday, you have that option. For that matter, you can elect to watch any past edition of *60 Minutes.* As you might expect, video stores and scheduled TV may become only memories in a few years.

The information superhighway opens the door for a more sophisticated form of entertainment. Already major television networks are interweaving on-air and online plots and characters in shows like *The Pretender.* How long will it be be-

The Connected Car The world is changing so quickly that it is difficult to speculate on what it will be like in five years. We know we can expect further integration of computers and cars. Intel, for example, is working with leaders in the automotive, computer, electronics, and communication industries to develop computing platforms that provide drivers and passengers with an environment that is safe, informative (GPS navigation), productive (cellular communications), and entertaining (radio and TV data broadcast, video games).
Photos courtesy of Intel Corporation

In-Dash Windows-Based Computer The Clarion AutoPC, shown here, is an in-dash Microsoft Windows® CE-based computer system that integrates communication, navigation, information, and entertainment within an automobile. A navigator leads you to your destination through both visual and audio prompting. Clarion AutoPC's voice-activated control listens to you, so your eyes never have to leave the road. Courtesy Clarion Corporation of America

IT Ethics

INAPPROPRIATE USE OF THE INTERNET AT WORK

Monitoring Internet use at the workplace has revealed what many workers already know, at least some of the Internet surfing is not job related. Most of this surfing is treated much like nonbusiness telephone calls, such as a call home or to confirm a doctor's appointment. However, management is getting involved when abuse is extensive or "inappropriate" material is viewed or downloaded on company PCs. Although corporate policy on such actions may be nonexistent or unclear, some people are losing their jobs.

Discussion: What would be appropriate punishment, if any, for an employee who, against company policy, downloaded and kept "inappropriate" material on his or her PC? What punishment is appropriate for an employee who abuses his or her Internet connection by doing non-job-related surfing at least one hour per day?

fore we have interactive soap operas? With the inevitable two-way communication capabilities of your future television/terminal, you can be an active participant in how a story unfolds. The soaps will be shot so they can be pieced together in a variety of ways. Imagine—you can decide whether Michelle marries Clifton or Patrick! You say this sounds far-fetched? Not really. Interactive movies are being produced and shown right now.

Your home entertainment center will become a video arcade, with immediate access to all games. You can hone your skills on an individual basis or test them, real time, against the best people in the land. Multiplayer games are already very popular on the Internet. Players in the Professional Gamers League gain celebrity status and make big money playing games like Quake (from Id Software) and Starcraft™ (from Blizzard Entertainment). Spectators can view play online.

The Home Library

As the information superhighway begins to mature during the first decade of the twenty-first century, your home library may look more like that of the Library of Congress. The information superhighway will make it possible for you to browse through virtually any book from your PC or terminal. Then, if you wish to purchase a hard-copy version of a book, it will be charged via e-commerce, then printed and bound on your personal high-speed color printer. The federal government is solidly behind constructing virtual libraries. Already major universities are beginning to create new content and digitize traditional materials so they can be made available over the Net.

Certainly books, magazines, newspapers, and the printed word in general will prevail for casual reading and study during the next few years. However, the information superhighway offers *soft-copy* publishing as an alternative to *hard-copy* publishing. We'll be able to receive virtually any printed matter—books, magazines, newspapers, and reference material—in electronic format. Already you can get newspapers electronically while the news is hot, with no wait for printing and delivery. Your home will become a newsstand in which you can obtain individual issues of any magazine or newspaper. Besides having up-to-the-minute online content, online media have several other advantages over print media. First, they are *linked;* that is, related information is connected via hyperlinks. And second, they are *interactive.* Finally, content can be multimedia with video and audio. If people begin to embrace the convenience of dynamically linked, interactive, and multimedia documents, there may be a trend away from print media to online alternatives. Don't be surprised to see novels written specifically for the online market that give readers the flexibility to follow links rather than pages.

Surf the Net from a Cell Phone Thanks to data communications technology and Kopin's CyberDisplay, we can stay in touch with stock-market developments, send e-mail, surf the Internet, and even participate in videoconferences from almost anywhere. When magnified, the CyberDisplay, which is less than $\frac{1}{4}$-inch (diagonal), provides sharp, bright monochrome or color images.
Courtesy of Kopin Corporation

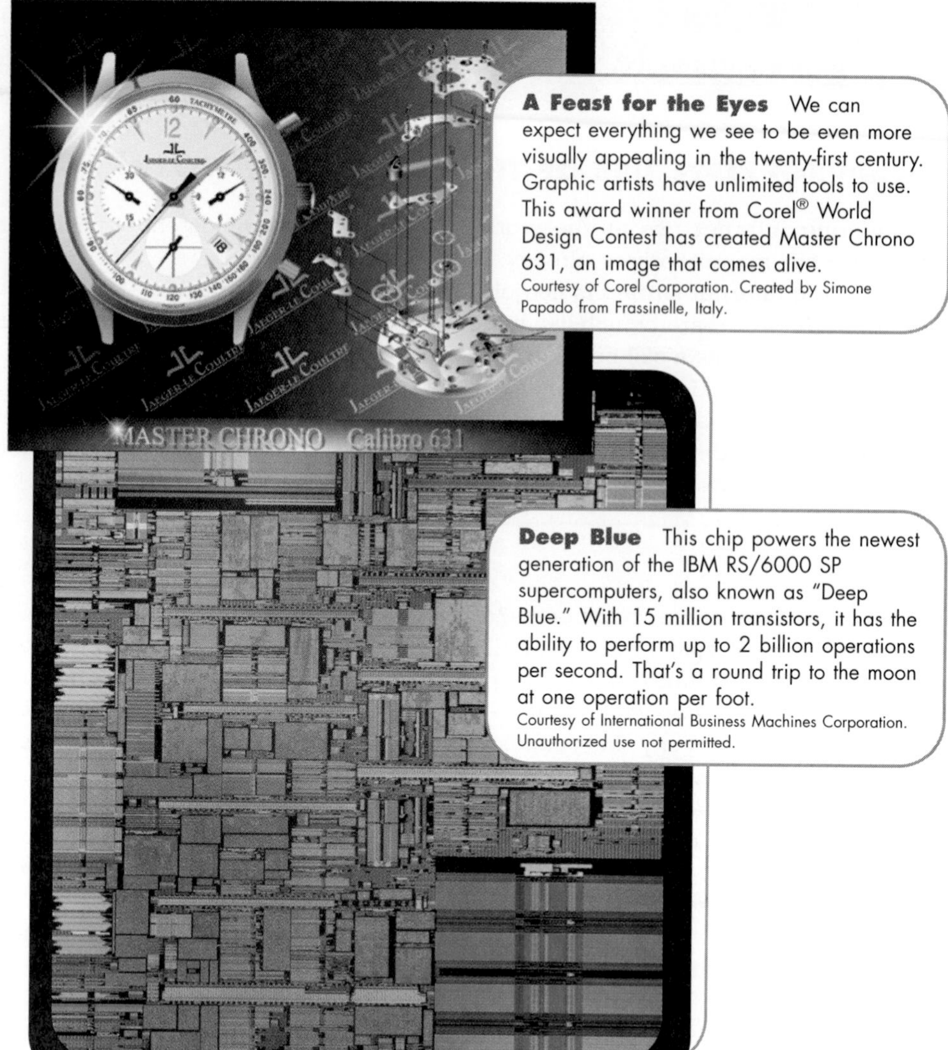

A Feast for the Eyes We can expect everything we see to be even more visually appealing in the twenty-first century. Graphic artists have unlimited tools to use. This award winner from Corel® World Design Contest has created Master Chrono 631, an image that comes alive.
Courtesy of Corel Corporation. Created by Simone Papado from Frassinelle, Italy.

Deep Blue This chip powers the newest generation of the IBM RS/6000 SP supercomputers, also known as "Deep Blue." With 15 million transistors, it has the ability to perform up to 2 billion operations per second. That's a round trip to the moon at one operation per foot.
Courtesy of International Business Machines Corporation. Unauthorized use not permitted.

The transition to soft-copy publishing is well underway. For example, *The Los Angeles Times* makes "almost the whole newspaper" in an interactive and linked format available for free over the Internet, including the classified ads. Other newspapers make their stories available also, either for free or through an online subscription. All or part of many traditional magazines, such as *Time* and *People,* and several new online magazines, such as *Slate,* are available to people with access to the Internet. Frequently, stories incorporate text, audio, and video. The trend to soft copy is evident in other areas also. For example, a number of retailers publish multimedia catalogs on the Internet that are updated almost daily, an option not possible in a print catalog.

Mail at the Speed of Light

Jokes about the pace of postal delivery will gradually disappear as the Internet matures. Most of what we now know as mail will travel electronically over the superhighway. Already, we routinely send e-mail (versus business or personal letters), greeting cards, family photos, and much more over the Internet. The audio-mail (a voice message sent via the Net) application is also becoming popular. And, of course, we will continue to receive our share of electronic junk mail.

The Cashless Society

Each weekday, the financial institutions of the world use electronic funds transfer (EFT) to transfer more than one trillion dollars—that's $1,000,000,000,000! Ap-

IT Ethics

ADDICTION TO THE INTERNET

The Internet has emerged as the centerpiece in the lives of many people, but is it addictive? People who study this issue believe that Internet addiction is as real as alcoholism. People will spend time on anything that is fun to do, but many in the medical community have observed that some people have moved past fun to clinical addiction. These people are said to have Internet addiction disorder (IAD). People with this disorder often lose control and crave surfing the Internet, much as a smoker craves a cigarette. Like others who are addicted to something, whether gambling, cocaine, or exercise, they suffer withdrawal symptoms when they are forced to forgo the Internet.

Millions of Internet users routinely go online without any detrimental effects, but the Internet still takes its toll on a small, but growing, sector of the online community. These people spend from 4 to 10 hours a day on the Internet and will occasionally "binge" for up to 24 hours at a time.

Numerous cases have been reported where the Internet was blamed for broken marriages, for students dropping out of school, and even for illnesses that result in hospital stays. Although most are addicted to the Internet in general, many are addicted to a particular facet of the Net, such as MUD (Multi-User Dungeon), pornography, Internet Relay Chats, newsgroups, or e-mail.

It's ironic, but people with IAD often use the Internet to help them cope with their disorder. Addicts routinely confess their addiction on the Internet. Susie says, "I don't eat . . . I have lost weight . . . I don't sleep . . . I have been sucked into the Internet, hook, line and sinker." Tracey says, "My addiction is so bad I'm flunking most of my classes." John says, "It's ruining my marriage!" Gordon says, "I'm insanely addicted to the Internet and the sad thing about it is that I don't even want to do anything about it."

Discussion: Is it possible for someone to become addicted to the Internet in a clinical sense? If so, have you seen any evidence of Internet addiction disorder (IAD), and what can be done about it?

plications of EFT, such as ATMs and payroll transfer systems, are being implemented all around us. Millions of people now pay utility bills, mortgage payments, and many other bills through automatic electronic bank drafts. The information superhighway may be the first step toward a *cashless society.* It provides the necessary link between individuals, businesses, and financial institutions.

If we should move toward a cashless society, the administrative work associated with handling money, checks, and credit transactions would be eliminated. We would no longer need to manufacture or carry money. Each purchase, no matter how small or large, would result in an immediate transfer of funds between buyer and seller. Think of it—rubber checks and counterfeit money would be eliminated. Moreover, with total EFT you would have a detailed and accurate record of all monetary transactions.

A cashless society is not feasible until mechanisms are in place to accommodate small retail transactions. That's beginning to happen. A federal task force has been formed to plan for the transition to **electronic money,** or **e-money.** Financial institutions are establishing alliances to prepare for the cashless society.

Every day you see more evidence of the move toward e-money. For example, traditional gas pumps are being replaced with ones that accept credit cards—swipe the card and pump the gas. In Phoenix, bus fares can be paid with VISA or MasterCard. All riders have to do is swipe the card and take a seat. Many college students use prepaid debit cards to pay for sodas, photocopying, and concert tickets. One billion U.S. government entitlement checks are distributed electronically each month. Look for the change in your pocket to become collectibles within a very few years.

Shop at Home

The information superhighway already provides a direct visual and electronic link to many mail-order companies and retail/wholesale establishments. More and more people are opting for the convenience and value of electronic shopping. It's no longer necessary to drive from store to store to seek a particular style of sneaker. We can use our personal computer or terminal in conjunction with the Internet to select and purchase almost anything, from paper clips to airplanes. In some cases the items selected will be automatically picked, packaged, and possibly delivered to our doorstep. This type of service will help speed the completion of routine activities, such as grocery shopping, and leave us more time for leisure, travel, and the things we enjoy.

The virtual frontier offers great promise for the retail and wholesale industry. Consider these advantages: a corner bicycle shop in Pomona, California, has access to millions of customers; stores never have to be closed; transactions are handled electronically; and sales and distribution can be done more cost-effectively.

Electronic Cooperation: EDI and Extranets

Companies and organizations are implementing *electronic data interchange (EDI)* and expanding their internal intranets to *extranets.* EDI and extranets can encourage electronic interchange with customers and suppliers and enable all concerned to do business better and more efficiently. EDI and extranets foster intercompany cooperation, which helps all involved save money. Each is a means of electronic cooperation whereby organizations transfer a wide range of information, including e-money, orders, invoices, medical records, real-time POS sales information, and so on via computer networks. EDI and extranets are eliminating the need to produce, send, record, and store billions of paper documents. Many companies still generate orders on their computer systems that are printed and mailed to their suppliers. Many suppliers still re-key the hard-copy data into their computers. This traditional process is time-consuming, costly, and it increases the margin for error. However, companies like Wal-Mart are following the trend toward greater electronic communication with suppliers. When Wal-Mart computers detect low inventory for toothpaste, its computers communicate that need directly to supplier computers. Supplier computers then issue shipping orders to warehouse computers, and the supplier computers send invoices directly to Wal-Mart computers. Payment is issued by electronic funds transfer: computer to computer.

Intercompany electronic links streamline administrative duties by linking supplier to manufacturer, manufacturer to retailer, and field sales and retail outlets to corporate headquarters. They provide solutions to many common business problems: mountains of paperwork, lost orders, unnecessary delays, lost opportunities, staff overheads, postage costs, paper costs, and data security. This type of networking also provides organizations with greater control of the production, distribution, and payment processes. As these benefits become more widely known, EDI and extranets will eventually become standard in most organizations. This is important because intercompany electronic interchange changes the fundamental way that many people do their jobs. By the turn of the century, most organizations, large and small, will be cooperating electronically.

High-Tech Voting and Polling

Local, state, and federal elections might not require an army of volunteers. Politicians might not have to worry about low voter turnout on a rainy Election Day. In the not-too-distant future we will record our votes over the National Information Infrastructure, or whatever our national network will be called. Such a system will reduce the costs of elections and encourage greater voter participation.

Already television newscasters routinely sample the thinking of viewers by asking them to respond over the Internet. Eventually they will be able to tap the

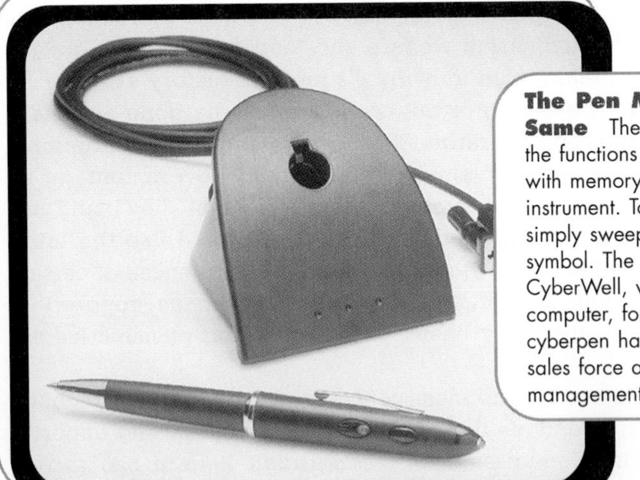

The Pen May Never Be the Same The Symbol CyberPen combines the functions of a contact bar code scanner with memory and an A.T. Cross® writing instrument. To scan a bar code, the user simply sweeps the wand tip across the symbol. The CyberPen is placed in the CyberWell, which is linked to a host computer, for easy data upload. The cyberpen has many applications, including sales force automation and office supply management. Courtesy of Symbol Technologies, Inc.

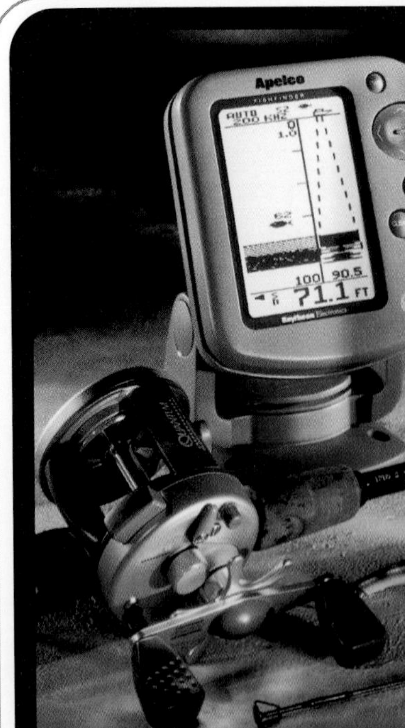

Computer-Aided Fishing Who would have dreamed a decade ago that the computer would become an important part of recreational fishing. These Apelco entry-level Fishfinders help fishermen in their quest for the big one. Courtesy of Raytheon Company

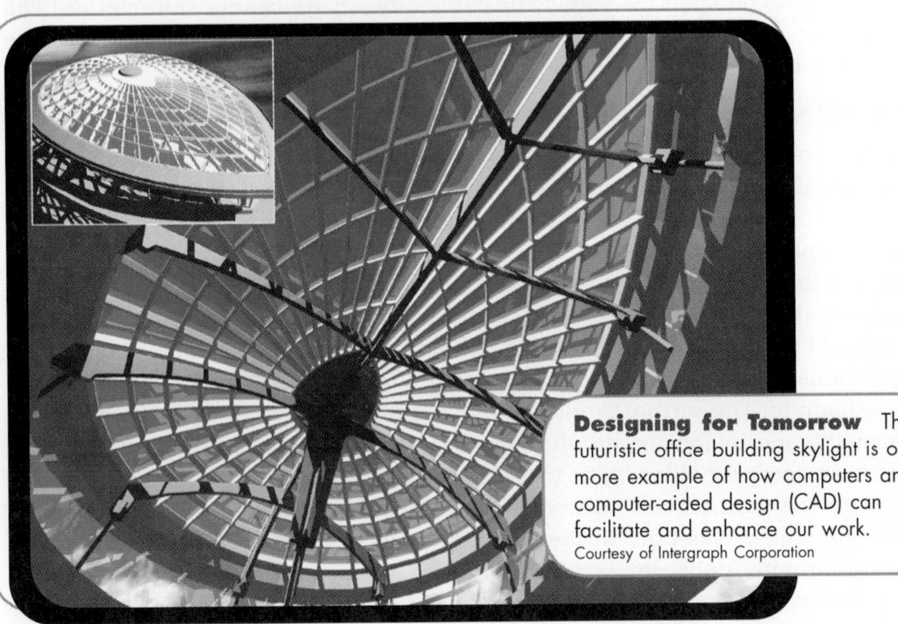

Designing for Tomorrow This futuristic office building skylight is one more example of how computers and computer-aided design (CAD) can facilitate and enhance our work. Courtesy of Intergraph Corporation

collective thinking of tens of thousands, even millions, of people in a matter of minutes. After they ask the questions, we at home will register our responses over the national network. Our responses will be sent immediately to a central computer for analysis, and the results reported almost instantaneously. In this way, television news programs will keep us abreast of public opinion on critical issues and the feeling toward political candidates on a day-to-day basis.

The National Database

The information superhighway will provide the electronic infrastructure needed to maintain a national database. A national database will be a central repository for all personal data for citizens. An individual would be assigned a unique identification number at birth. This ID number would replace the social security number, the driver's license number, the student identification number, and dozens of others. Eventually the ID number probably will be replaced by some kind of unique digital biometric signature, perhaps a fingerprint or retinal scan (eye).

A national database would consolidate the personal data now stored on tens of thousands of manual and computer-based files. It could contain an individual's name, past and present addresses, dependent data, work history, medical history, marital history, tax data, criminal record, military history, credit rating and history, and so on. A national database has certain advantages.

A national database could provide the capability of monitoring the activities of criminal suspects; virtually eliminating welfare and food stamp fraud; quickly identifying illegal aliens; and making an individual's medical history available at any hospital in the country. The taking of the census would be done automatically each year (or even each month), rather than every 10 years. The national database would enable us to generate valuable information. Governments at all levels would have access to up-to-date demographic information they could use to optimize the use of our tax dollars. Medical researchers could use the information to isolate geographical areas with inordinately high incidences of certain illnesses. The Bureau of Labor Statistics could monitor real, as opposed to reported, employment levels on a daily basis. The information possibilities are endless.

The national database is among the most controversial information technology issues in that it offers tremendous benefits to society while posing opportunities for serious abuse. The Commission for Immigration Reform has recommended a national database to Congress. It wants a database with every citizen or legal alien so prospective employers can verify job applicants' information. The proposal has bipartisan support in Congress. Opponents of the national database claim it will lead to abuse and the erosion of personal privacy.

Virtual Reality: Becoming One with Cyberspace

With the increased power of processors and improved sophistication of I/O devices, virtual reality is poised to make a significant impact on how we interact with and what we do with computers. **Virtual reality** is an artificial environment made possible by hardware and software. This artificial environment, sometimes called a *virtual world,* is the electronic equivalent of the real thing. You enter the virtual world by wearing a special *headpiece, gloves,* and *headphones* (see the Emerging IT box "The Promise of Virtual Reality"). The **VR** equipment enables a direct feedback loop between you and a computer system. The audio, visual, and other stimuli for the virtual world vary, depending on what you do. You control the virtual world by looking at what you want to see. Movement of your eyes are tracked causing new video input to the headpiece viewer. You can "touch" something with the data glove to cause a change within the artificial environment.

Virtual reality was born in the late 1960s when the U.S. Air Force began experimenting with flight simulators. From there, the technology was picked up by NASA. Today, NASA and a number of universities and corporations are either developing or using virtual reality systems for a variety of applications.

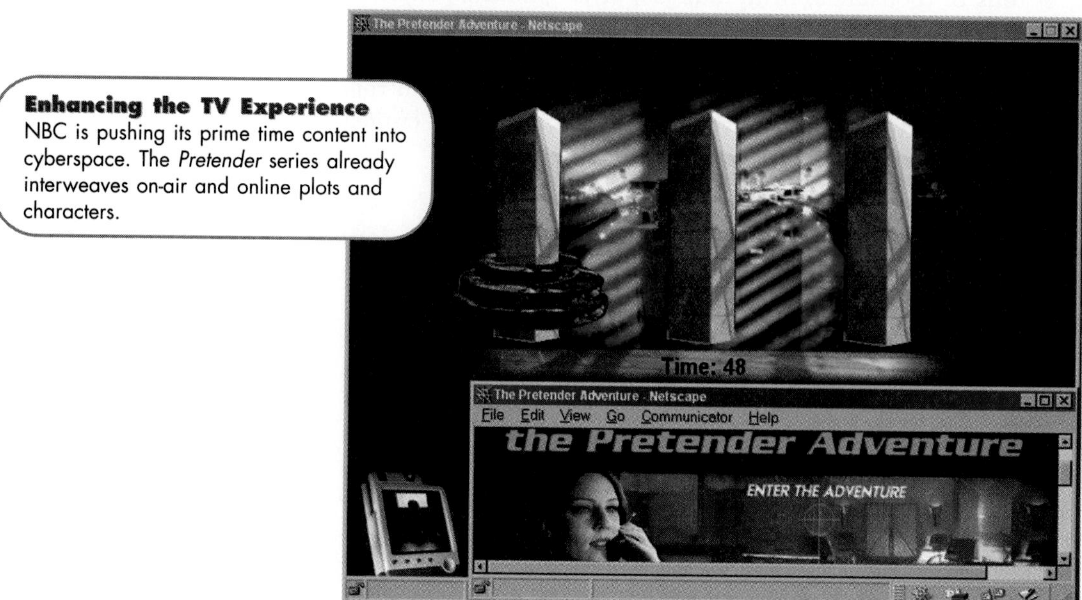

Enhancing the TV Experience
NBC is pushing its prime time content into cyberspace. The *Pretender* series already interweaves on-air and online plots and characters.

VRcades Players occupy individual cockpits as they prepare for a game at Virtual World's theme park. At the controls of your own interdimensional travel vehicle, you and other pilots on your mission are dropped into one of several exciting new dimensions. Courtesy of Virtual World (TM) Entertainment, Inc.

- *Architecture and computer-aided design.* Architects already have access to a number of commercial VR systems that let them conduct electronic "walk-throughs" of proposed buildings.
- *Visualization of data.* NASA has created a virtual wind tunnel that lets a user climb inside an airstream. By gesturing with a data glove, the user can change the airflow and then walk around to view it from different angles.
- *Exploration of hostile environments.* NASA is using raw data to create a VR version of an Antarctic lake bottom that will let researchers study life forms beneath the frigid waters without risk.
- *Sales.* A Japanese department store uses a "virtual kitchen" for planning custom-designed remodeling projects. After store personnel input a kitchen's existing layout and measurements using CAD software, customers don the VR gear and play around with different appliances, open drawers, turn on faucets, and visualize different arrangements.
- *Exercise.* Exercise bikes and massage chairs are finding a place in the virtual world. With the new lighter headgear, you can add adventure to your exercise as you cycle through virtual towns.
- *Training.* Flight training is one of the most sophisticated and oldest applications of VR. Here is found a world that's probably more realistic than the real world. Pilots can take the controls of a fully loaded passenger plane for their first flight because of the training they received in the simulator. In the simulator, a pilot can be exposed to situations that may never be experienced in the real world. VR researchers are creating VR systems training systems for firefighters, police officers, and others. Perhaps someday high school driver's training classes will be conducted in virtual reality.
- *Education.* The learning experience through VR is truly active (versus passive). It allows students to experience firsthand such things as life in a medieval village or walking among dinosaurs.
- *Psychology.* A California psychologist is experimenting with VR therapy for acrophobics (those who fear heights). Wearing a VR headset, a patient walks a plank, crosses a bridge, which spans water and hills, and accomplishes other acts that would instill fear. Over 90% of the patients now feel confident enough to climb ladders and cross the Golden Gate Bridge.

THE PROMISE OF VIRTUAL REALITY

Imagine that your job is to monitor the operation of a vast telecommunications network. Cables snake underground and underwater. Data flows between communications satellites and earth and across wiring inside building walls. Now imagine that a graphic image of this vast grid and its data flows could be laid out below you, as you float above, an "infonaut" looking for the kink that is blocking service to millions of customers. Far below you see a pulsing light. There's the problem. With a gestured command, you fix it—without leaving your office. That's the promise of virtual reality, and it's moving from computer fantasy to computer fact. In fact, US West and a number of other telecommunications firms are already experimenting with such systems.

Virtual reality (VR), a term coined in 1970 by Myron Krueger, combines computer graphics with special hardware to immerse users in *cyberspace,* an artificial three-dimensional world. Instead of passively viewing data or graphics on a screen, users can move about, handle "virtual" representations of data and objects, and get visual, aural, and tactile feedback. In the world of computers, the term *virtual* refers to an environment that is *simulated by hardware and software* (for example, virtual memory, virtual department store).

And what about marriage in cyberspace? A bride, groom, and their minister entered cyberspace by entering pods at the CyberMind Virtual Reality Center in San Francisco. They said their vows amid a virtual re-creation of the lost city of Atlantis. The scene included palaces, chariots, carousels, and even doves.

Dressing for Cyberspace

To enter cyberspace, users don special hardware for the feeling of total immersion in a three-dimensional world.

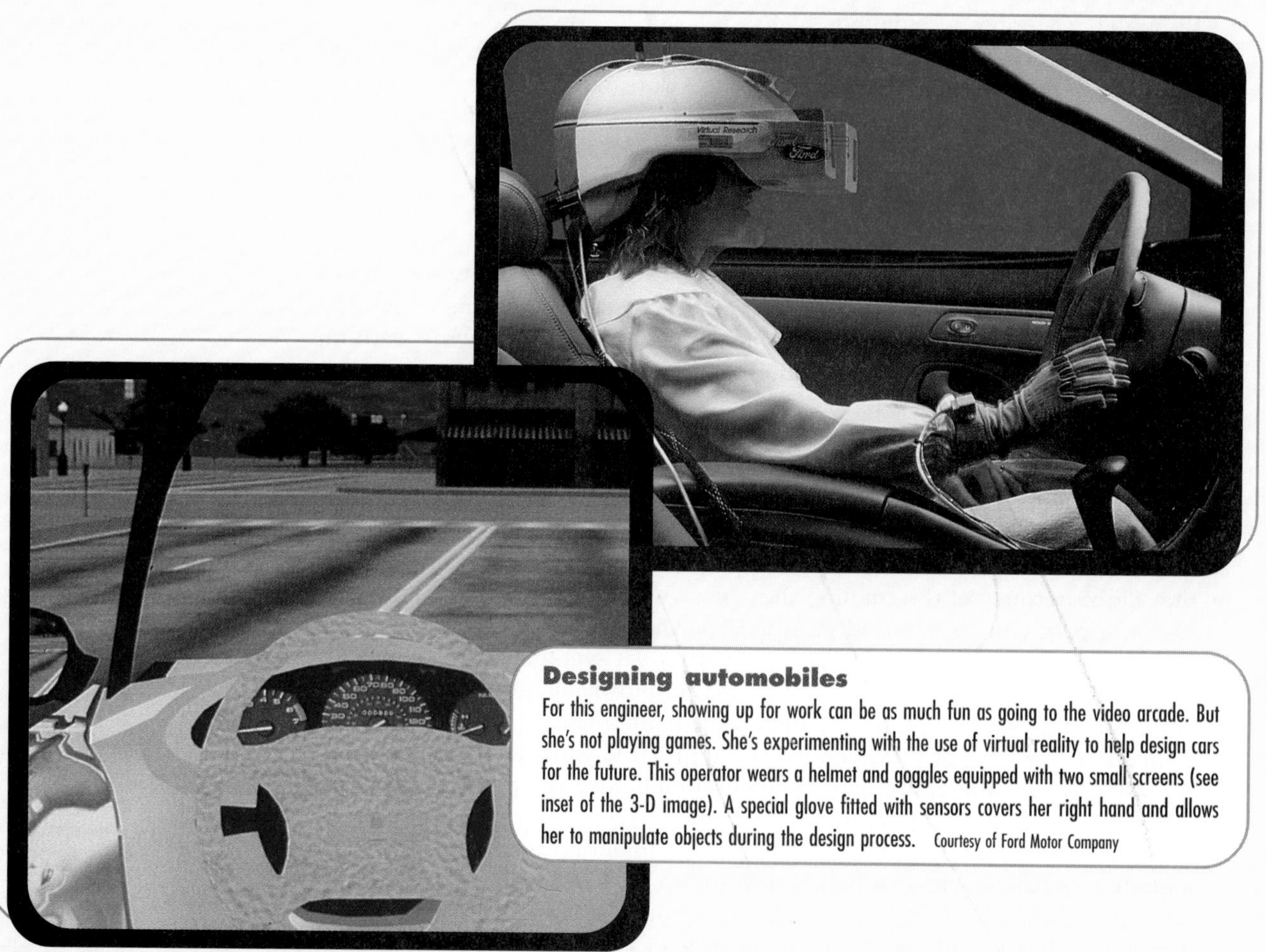

Designing automobiles
For this engineer, showing up for work can be as much fun as going to the video arcade. But she's not playing games. She's experimenting with the use of virtual reality to help design cars for the future. This operator wears a helmet and goggles equipped with two small screens (see inset of the 3-D image). A special glove fitted with sensors covers her right hand and allows her to manipulate objects during the design process. Courtesy of Ford Motor Company

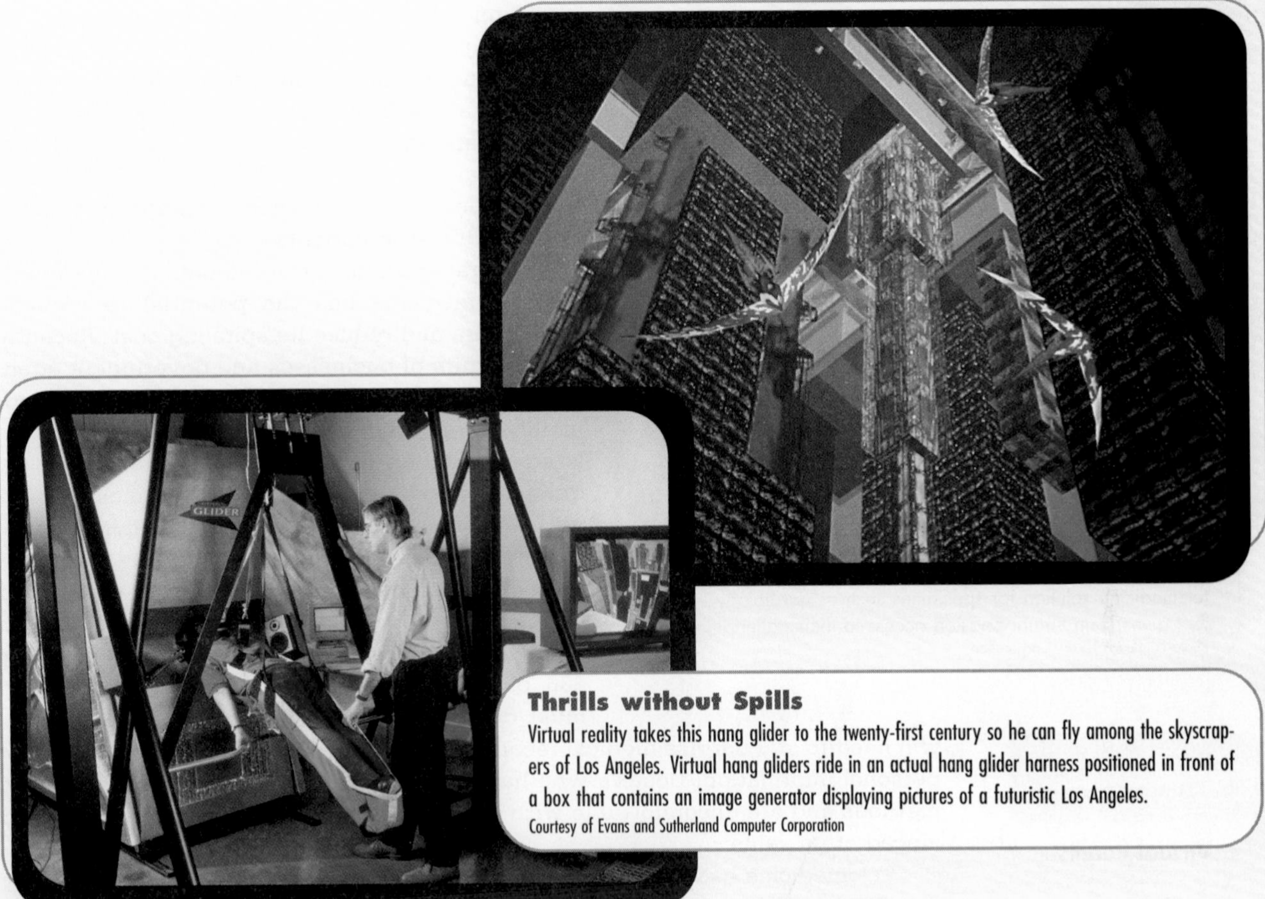

Thrills without Spills

Virtual reality takes this hang glider to the twenty-first century so he can fly among the skyscrapers of Los Angeles. Virtual hang gliders ride in an actual hang glider harness positioned in front of a box that contains an image generator displaying pictures of a futuristic Los Angeles.

Courtesy of Evans and Sutherland Computer Corporation

- *Headpiece.* The goggles-like head-mounted display (HMD) blocks out visual sensations from the real world and substitutes images presented on *two small video screens*—one for each eye, creating a three-dimensional effect. The headpiece also contains *motion,* or *balance, sensors;* move your head and the computer will shift the view presented on the video screens. Just flip up the visor on your headpiece to see what is going on in the real world. Or, flip it down to enter the virtual world.
- *Headphones.* Headphones block out room noise and substitute three-dimensional *holophononic* sounds. Generally the headphones are built into the helmet.
- *Data glove.* The ensemble is completed by a data glove outlined with *fiber optic sensors* and cables. The glove can be used, like a floating mouse, to "gesture" a command or to grasp and move virtual objects about.

Each piece of hardware is tethered to a power pack and to one or more powerful computers via two-way data transfer cables that record the user's movements and provide real-time feedback.

Will the Promise Be Kept?

Virtual reality is still in its infancy, but the breadth and success of existing VR applications have shown us that VR will play an important role in the future. Already, architects can "walkthrough" proposed buildings. Researchers are exploring life forms in virtual worlds. Retailers let customers enter virtual reality for custom design projects. Exercise bikers can cycle through a virtual town. Psychologists are using VR to help patients overcome phobias, such as fear of heights.

Although some VR applications can be run on powerful PCs, the most realistic experiences are created with sophisticated systems that may cost as much as a new Mercedes. Moreover, the equipment is cumbersome and the graphics are often fairly crude. Still, many experts predict that hardware costs will continue to drop and software will become more refined. If so, virtual reality may emerge as the user interface of the future.

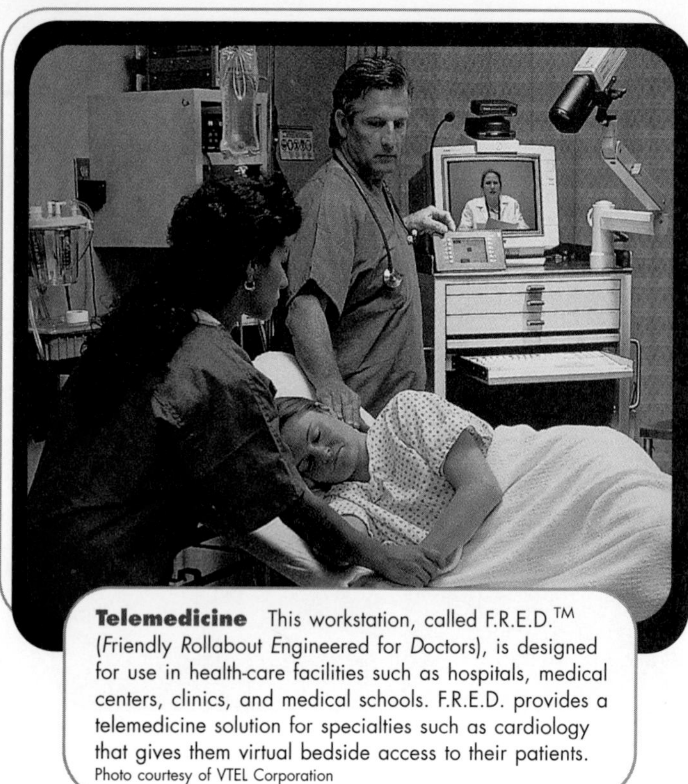

Telemedicine This workstation, called F.R.E.D.™ (*F*riendly *R*ollabout *E*ngineered for *D*octors), is designed for use in health-care facilities such as hospitals, medical centers, clinics, and medical schools. F.R.E.D. provides a telemedicine solution for specialties such as cardiology that gives them virtual bedside access to their patients.
Photo courtesy of VTEL Corporation

Telemedicine: Networked Health Care

The term **telemedicine** was coined to describe any type of health care administered remotely over communications links. Already, many states are practicing telemedicine. Facilities, such as doctors' offices, nursing homes, and prisons, are networked to regional medical centers. Sophisticated input/output hardware at remote sites, such as digital cameras and medical sensing devices, enable medical personnel and equipment to perform diagnostic procedures on patients.

Federal and state governments are optimistic that telemedicine has the potential to improve health care and reduce its spiraling cost. Recently a consortium of businesses and government agencies demonstrated telemedicine technology for members of Congress. The demonstration simulated a situation in which a car crash victim required doctors in different states to quickly examine medical records, X-rays, and other images. Congress was apparently impressed because millions of federal dollars are being targeted to foster telemedicine. Congress is hopeful that high-tech medicine can reduce annual health-care costs by $36 billion. To realize such saving, telemedicine must overcome several hurdles. Medical facilities will need to standardize medical records storage and procedures for protection of personal information. Doctors who have been trained in conventional diagnostic methods and are uncomfortable with the high-tech methods will need to be convinced of its value.

Virtual Reality

Telemedicine has many applications. Mostly it is being used to electronically distribute health-care capabilities to rural areas. It's also used in the cities where many ambulances are equipped to administer telemedicine. By the time the ambulance arrives at the hospital, a doctor may have run preliminary diagnostic procedures via telemedicine. The military uses similar systems in the battlefield. As telemedicine matures, look for it to play a major role in home care of the elderly, eliminating the need for costly hospitalization.

The Education Revolution

Only recently has information technology begun to have an impact on traditional approaches to education. Our approach to education evolved with the industrial revolution—mass production with students (workers) in rows all doing the same thing at a pace dictated by the teacher (manager). Many educators are questioning the wisdom and effectiveness of traditional techniques in light of recent developments in technology-aided education. The computer has proven a marvelous tool for learning at all levels, from preschool to postgraduate continuing education. The advantages are proving too vivid to ignore.

- Learning is interactive.
- Students can work at their own pace.
- Learning can take place anywhere, anytime, via communications links to available resources.
- Learning materials are more sophisticated (animation, 3-D images, hypermedia links, and so on).

Technology-aided education is being introduced rapidly at all levels of education. Many public school systems are looking to technology-aided education to improve the student/teacher ratio, raise test scores, and ease an ongoing budget crunch.

Institutions of higher learning have introduced many ways to leverage information technology in education. Already, the online university is here and growing. You can obtain undergraduate and graduate degrees from reputable colleges and universities through online study. This type of program is sure to appeal to those who are unable to adjust their busy schedules to attend traditional classes. Some universities are using the technology to integrate the teaching of related topics. Rather than teach computers, finance, and ethics in separate courses, they are taught together in concert with applications.

The information superhighway offers the potential for nationwide uniform testing for elementary and secondary students. With uniform learning standards for each subject at each level, students will be able to advance from one grade to the next on the basis of achievement rather than age. Computer-based uniform testing has another advantage. The system will monitor not only student progress but also the effectiveness of individual teachers and schools.

Intelligent Agents at Work for You

Just as we begin to reach electronic saturation with faxes, voice mail, Internet mailing lists, online newspapers, and so on, along come intelligent agents to help cope with information overload. We provide **intelligent agents,** which are software packages, with instructions detailing what to do. We then give them the authority to act on our behalf, just as we would a human agent. Intelligent agents, which are discussed in more detail in Chapter 12, roam around inside our computer systems, ready to help us whenever they can. They can bring urgent faxes to our attention, page us when our spouse leaves a voice-mail message, alert us to mailing-list messages that contain the keywords *kids* and *games,* and search all East Coast newspapers for articles mentioning *forest conservation.* They can remind us of important birthdays and even order the flowers.

Intelligent agents act as intermediaries, filtering the never-ending stream of information to give us only that which we need and want. Today's intelligent agents are still crude, but extremely helpful. We can expect a quantum leap in intelligent agent capabilities in the next five years. In the near future you will be able to ask your intelligent agent to do some comparison shopping, then make recommendations on which digital camera offers the best value and where to buy it. Intelligent agents will alert us when our favorite music artists release a new album and even download a sampling of songs from the album. Within a few

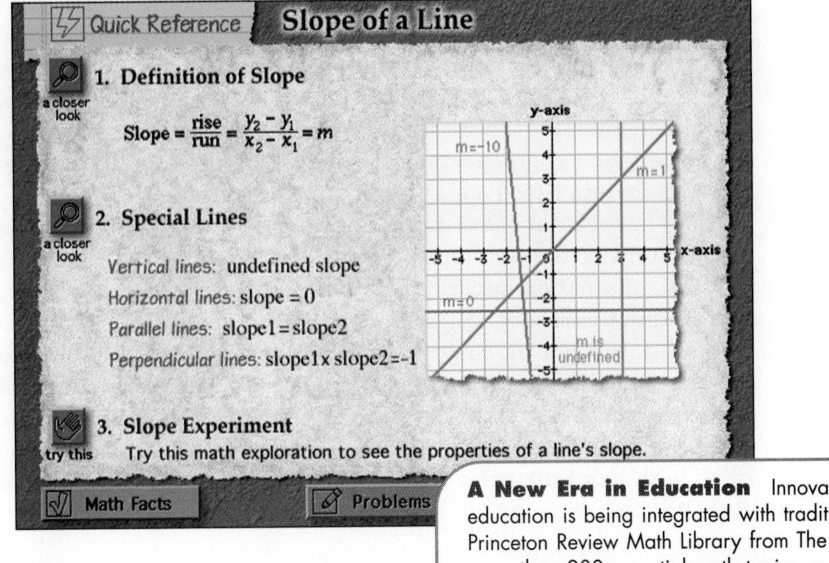

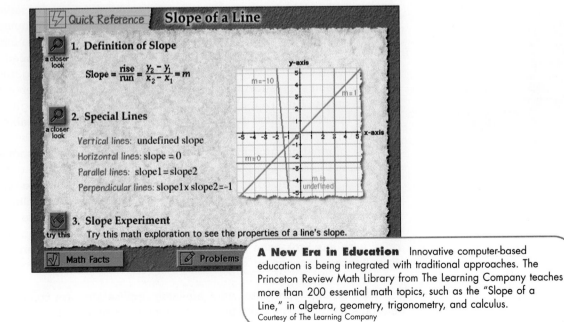

A New Era in Education Innovative computer-based education is being integrated with traditional approaches. The Princeton Review Math Library from The Learning Company teaches more than 200 essential math topics, such as the "Slope of a Line," in algebra, geometry, trigonometry, and calculus.
Courtesy of The Learning Company

years, most of us will begin to rely on these cyberbutlers to bring order to our sometimes-hectic lives.

Build and Buy Your Car Online

It won't be too long before you will be able to shop every showroom and new car lot in the country with a single click of the mouse. You and other consumers will use a *configurator* to identify the exact car and features you want. Such an online system will allow you to pick any car, then select the exact options you desire. Your cost is adjusted as you add and delete options. This inevitable system is more consumer-friendly. The consumer wants information and pricing, but not from a high-pressure salesperson. Dealers who still want that face-to-face opportunity to influence the consumer's decision may fight this approach, but consumerism may again win the day.

Already several Web sites enable consumers to configure cars with dealer-suggested retail pricing. It's a natural extension of the system that will let you simultaneously submit your request to all dealers in a particular region. A fully automated response will include the exact price of the car and when you can expect delivery.

The Information Superhighway: Getting There

Eventually the information highway will enable people of all walks of life to interact with just about anyone else, with institutions, with businesses, and with vast amounts of data and information. The existing information infrastructure, primarily the Internet, needs some improvement before many of the potential applications discussed in this section can be implemented. The Internet has its limits. Never was that more apparent than on the day Independent Counsel Kenneth Starr released his long-awaited report on U.S. President Bill Clinton. The crush of people seeking the report raised Internet activity to an all-time high, bringing many popular sites to their knees. The Internet survived and those running it learned a valuable lesson—today's Internet must expand to meet growing demands.

Upgrades to our information infrastructure will be very expensive and must be implemented in degrees over the next few years. Much of the technology is in place for a modest beginning. For example, many major cities are linked with high-speed fiber optic cable. Millions of homes have personal computers. Thousands of information-based services are made available over the Internet and commercial information services. However, to enable information services such as video-on-demand, high-speed lines must be extended to your home or place of business. At present, when high-speed intercity traffic exits the information superhighway on to a city street, it must travel slowly on low-speed lines. These low-speed lines are the weakest link in the information chain and, therefore, limit the variety and sophistication of applications that can be delivered to your electronic doorstep. However, as you read this, reasonably priced high-speed service is being installed in cities throughout the country, primarily via cable TV hookups and digital twisted-pair lines.

The information superhighway already offers a seemingly endless variety of services, but in reality, these are just the beginning. We can use our PCs to trade securities, but not all companies offer this service. We can take online courses, but not all colleges offer online degrees. We can view many online newspapers and periodicals, but for the most part, they are by-products of the printed version and have little interactivity. In a few years you will be able to buy and sell securities with any brokerage company and pursue any degree at any major university. Printed versions of magazines may well be by-products of the online versions.

We can only speculate what amazing applications are coming to the information superhighway. We'll be able to adjust the temperature at home from any

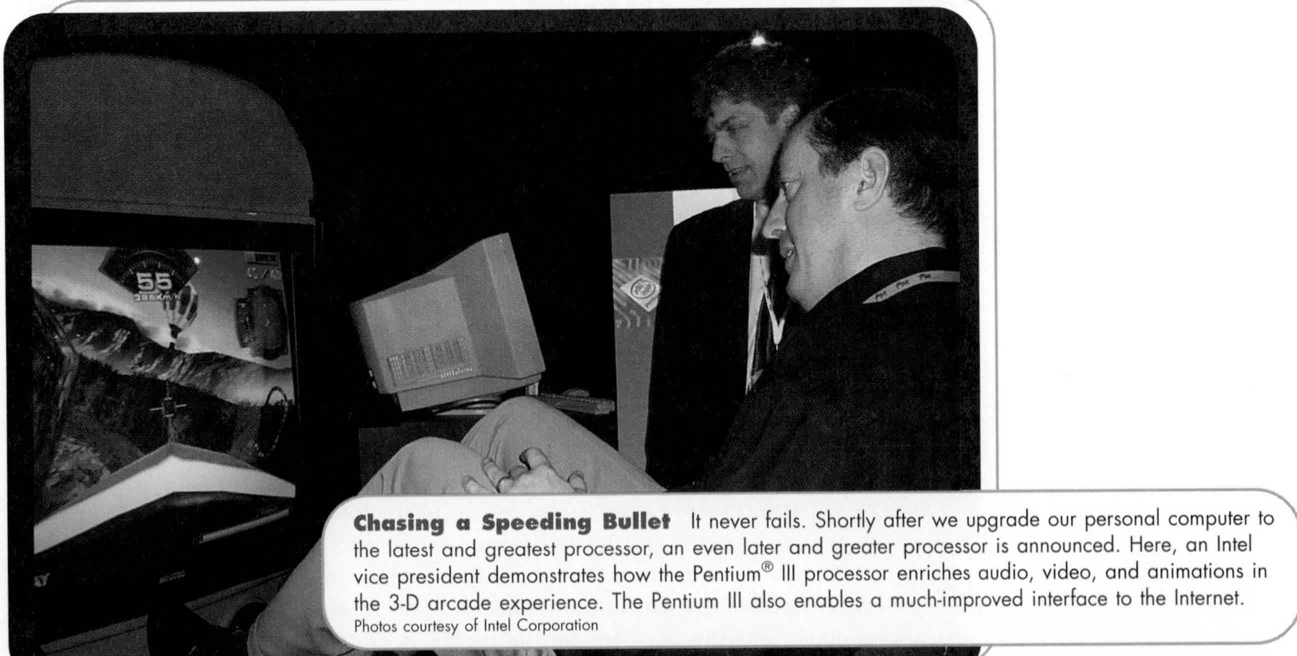

Chasing a Speeding Bullet It never fails. Shortly after we upgrade our personal computer to the latest and greatest processor, an even later and greater processor is announced. Here, an Intel vice president demonstrates how the Pentium® III processor enriches audio, video, and animations in the 3-D arcade experience. The Pentium III also enables a much-improved interface to the Internet.
Photos courtesy of Intel Corporation

remote location. We will be able to view any movie ever made at any time. We'll even be able to talk with someone who is speaking a different language through an electronic interpreter (working prototypes are now in operation). That time may be sooner than you think. Telecommunications, computers, and information services companies are jockeying for position to be a part of what forecasters predict will be the most lucrative industry of the twenty-first century—information technology.

Serendipitous Surfing: Worst and Best

SECTION SELF-CHECK

Self-Check

11-4.1 The volume of traditional mail handled by the postal service is expected to decrease as the information superhighway begins to mature. (T/F)

11-4.2 A national database was approved by Congress and implemented in 1998. (T/F)

11-4.3 The weakest link on the information superhighway is between cities where information must travel at low speeds. (T/F)

11-4.4 What software tool can filter available information to give us only that which we want: (a) an intelligent manager, (b) an intelligent agent, (c) an intelligent diplomat, or (d) an intellectual agent?

11-4.5 When health care is administered remotely over communications links we call it: (a) telemedicine, (b) cybermedicine, (c) health-care magic, or (d) telehealth?

11-4.6 An artificial environment made possible by hardware and software is known as: (a) virtual planet, (b) near reality, (c) virtual reality, or (d) cyberrealism?

11-4.7 Money as we know it may soon be replaced by: (a) e-money, (b) electronic greenbacks, (c) cybercash, or (d) eurodollars?

11-4.8 The application that delivers video upon request is known as: (a) real video, (b) cybervideo, (c) video-on-demand, or (d) at-the-movies?

11-4.9 Intercompany electronic cooperation is made possible with all but which of the following: (a) electronic data interchange, (b) intelligent agents, (c) extranets, or (d) EDI?

11.5 YOUR CHALLENGE

With your newly acquired base of information technology knowledge, you are now positioned to enter the mainstream of our information society. However, the IT learning process is ongoing. The dynamics of rapidly advancing IT demands a constant updating of skills and expertise. By their very nature, computers and IT bring about change. With the total amount of computing capacity in the world doubling every two years, we can expect even more dramatic change in the future. Someday in the not-too-distant future computers will be as commonplace in the home and office as telephones, and as commonplace on our person as wristwatches. English, with its omnipresence on the Internet is emerging as the de facto standard for commerce and global communications. Already, international project teams work together via telecommunications to create and support products (from automobiles to video games) and services (from banking services to legal services). Many business traditions are vulnerable to IT: More people are telecommuting; company hierarchies are flattening out; the worker has greater visibility via the Internet and therefore greater mobility; methods of compensation are placing greater emphasis on innovation and productivity; the laws that govern commerce and intercompany relationships are under constant review; business processes are continually changing to integrate the latest innovations in technology; and the way we communicate is changing dramatically every few years. Are we that far away from **v-mail,** or **video mail,** that's sent as video rather than an electronic document?

So far, the cumulative effects of these changes have altered the basic constructs of society and the way we live, work, and play. Terminals and PCs have replaced calculators and ledger books; e-mail and videoconferencing facilitates communication; word processing has eliminated typewriters; computer-aided design has rendered the drawing table obsolete; e-commerce may eventually eliminate the need for money; online shopping is affecting consumer buying habits; the Internet has opened the doors to virtual universities . . . and the list goes on.

We as a society are, in effect, trading a certain level of computer and IT dependence for an improvement in the quality of life. However, this improvement in the way we live is not a foregone conclusion. Just as our highways play host to objectionable billboards, carjackings, and automobile accidents, the information superhighway is sure to have back roads lined with sleaze, scams, and cyberthiefs. It is our challenge to harness the immense power of information technology and direct it toward the benefit of society.

Interactive Study Guide Chapter 11

Never before has such opportunity presented itself so vividly. This generation, *your generation,* has the technological foundation and capability of changing dreams into reality.

SECTION SELF-CHECK

Self-Check

11-5.1 The total computing capacity in the world is increasing at slightly less than 5% per year. (T/F)

11-5.2 Mail sent as video is called: (a) vidmail, (b) v-mail, (c) e-mail, or (d) z-mail?

SUMMARY AND KEY TERMS

11.1 The virtual frontier

The virtual frontier encompasses the electronic highways that comprise the Internet, thousands of newsgroups, scores of information services, and millions of private networks. It is sometimes likened to the Wild West because there are no rules. The opportunity for a better life is enticing pioneers to explore the virtual frontier.

11.2 The wake up call

During the next decade, computers will be built into our domestic, working, and external environments. Eventually we will talk to our computers within our smart homes. They will even help us perform many duties around the house, even cooking.

11.3 Artificial intelligence

Artificial intelligence (AI) (89) is the area of research that involves creating computer systems with the ability to reason, to learn or accumulate knowledge, to strive for self-improvement, and to simulate human sensory and mechanical capabilities. There are four categories of AI research: **expert systems** (89), which rely on a knowledge base; **natural languages** (90); simulation of human sensory capabilities; and **robotics** (91) (the integration of computers and **robots** [91]).

11.4 Down the road: The information superhighway

The information superhighway is a network of high-speed data communications links that eventually will connect virtually every facet of our society. Traffic on the superhighway will be anything that can be digitized. A wide range of information and telecommunication services are now available and more are planned for the information superhighway. These applications include videophones, video-on-demand, interactive television, virtual libraries, soft-copy publishing (with a hard-copy option), multimedia catalogs, e-mail **electronic money (e-money)** (99), total electronic funds transfer (EFT), electronic shopping, electronic data interchange (EDI) and extranets, electronic voting and polling, a national database, **virtual reality (VR)** (102), **telemedicine** (106), using configurators to buy cars online, and much more. Technology-aided education is being introduced rapidly at all levels of education. **Intelligent agents** (107) act as intermediaries, filtering the never-ending stream of information to give us only that which we need and want.

Eventually the information superhighway will enable people of all walks of life to interact with just about anyone else, with institutions, with businesses, and with vast amounts of data and information. However, it must be significantly improved to realize its promise.

11.5 Your challenge

The computer and IT offer you the opportunity to improve the quality of your life with such applications as **video mail,** or **v-mail** (110). It is your challenge to harness the power of the computer and direct it to the benefit of society.

DISCUSSION AND PROBLEM SOLVING

11.1 a. List as many terms or phrases as you can that have been used to refer to our wired world.

b. Currently the Internet is open and all types of information flow freely, including pornographic text and images. A law enforcement official in Florida calls the Internet a "pedophile's playground." One of the most important issues facing the information superhighway is censorship. Argue for or against censorship.

c. The federal government is calling for "universal service" such that everyone has access to the "information superhighway." Is this an achievable goal?

11.2a. Continue the story line in the "wake up call" scenario described in Section 11.2 by speculating on other futuristic applications.

b. Describe how you think technology-based education will change elementary education by the year 2005. By the year 2010.

c. Describe how you think technology-based education will change college education by the year 2005. By the year 2010.

11.3a. Describe at least three ways in which artificial intelligence applications can help disabled persons cope with the routine of everyday living.

b. AI researchers have spent more time creating a chess-playing computer than on any other project. Why?

c. To varying degrees, computers can see, hear, speak, feel, and smell. Some people think we should continue to pursue this area of AI research with vigor. Some feel that machines should not be given human qualities. Where do you stand and why?

11.4a. Argue for or against a cashless society.

b. Gaming could be one of the most profitable computer applications ever. Americans spent 70 times as much on gambling last year as they spent on movies. Gaming is being proposed as a possible application on the information superhighway. Argue for or against this proposal.

c. Already, thousands of people choose to do their grocery shopping electronically from their PCs. Typically, groceries are selected, packaged, and delivered to their doorsteps for a charge of about $6 to $8. Would you consider virtual grocery shopping under these circumstances? Why or why not?

d. Would you feel comfortable voting in a national election via an online link from your home or would you prefer to do it the old-fashioned way? Explain.

e. A national database would consolidate personal information from hundreds of databases containing information about you (medical, demographic, work history, and so on). Discuss the upside and the downside of implementing a national database.

f. Describe the advantages and disadvantages of video-on-demand, a future information superhighway application.

g. Briefly describe the technology that is expected to replace the telephone over the next few years.

h. Virtual reality enables us to roam around an artificial world. Discuss the upside and the downside of VR.

i. Describe at least one scenario where soft-copy publishing might be expected to replace, at least partially, hard-copy publishing.

j. Describe at least two modern-day applications that support the trend toward a cashless society.

k. Discuss what types of information might be transferred between a retailer and its suppliers via EDI or an extranet.

l. On the Web, there's a saying, "no one knows you're a dog," meaning people can remain anonymous. But in the world of e-commerce, your very business may depend on your ability to discern paying customers from the dogs. What can be done to better target Web marketing efforts?

11.5a. Information technology is touching all aspects of your life. Are you prepared for it? Explain.

Business Information Systems

12 Information Systems

13 Developing Business Information Systems

Information Systems

Learning Objectives

12.1 Demonstrate awareness of the potential impact of information technology on businesses.

12.2 Describe the qualities of information and how information needs vary at each level of the organization.

12.3 Understand the elements, scope, and capabilities of an information system.

12.4 Describe the capabilities of a data processing system.

12.5 Define a management information system (MIS) and describe its capabilities.

12.6 Describe decision support system (DSS) capabilities and tools.

12.7 Demonstrate an overview understanding of expert system concepts and applications.

12.8 Describe the capabilities of intelligent agents.

chapter 12

WHY THIS CHAPTER IS IMPORTANT TO YOU

In the world of computers, systems are everywhere. There are enterprise systems, real-time systems, information systems, expert systems, computer systems, operating systems, and these are just the beginning. Also, many computerese terms and concepts begin with system(s). There's a system this or a system that in just about every office conversation. We've got the system operator, the system board, the system administrator, the system check, the system life cycle, and on and on. At times you'll be convinced that everything is some kind of system. Generally, that's true in information technology (IT).

Most systems involve and/or impact people. That's where you come in. Every day of your life you will be a part of a system, a direct or indirect target of a system, or a user of a system. On most days we're all of these.

In any office there are curious people standing around the perimeter of information technology discussions wondering what's going on. Unfortunately, about all these people can be is curious. They may lack a depth of system understanding to be an active participant. After you read and study this chapter, you'll be more willing to step into the conversation. You'll be more confident about making meaningful contributions at company meetings that revolve around enterprise-based systems. The material in this chapter will help you sort out common systems terminology so you can understand your role within a system better, be more effective as a target of a system, and know when and what kind of system to use.

Value Learning

12.1 AN END TO BUSINESS AS USUAL

Monthly Technology Update Chapter 12

The increased competition of the world market is pressuring corporate managers into a desperate search for solutions—no more business as usual. Those with a genuine desire to make their businesses survive and flourish are doing everything they can to improve profitability. Companies are adopting no-smoking policies to lower the cost of insurance premiums. Unions are accepting wage concessions. Executives are flying coach rather than first class. The days are gone when good management and hard work were considered competitive advantages that would invariably result in success and profits. Now that these corporate qualities are the standard for mere survival, managers are seeking any strategies that can give their companies the competitive advantage. These strategies often involve computers and information technology. In this highly competitive era, intelligent use of available technology can make the difference between profitability and failure.

Every company has plenty of opportunities to use technology to achieve a competitive edge. Information technology can improve product and service quality, reduce costs, increase productivity, aid communication between employees, and even improve company morale. What's more, new and innovative uses of information technology are being discovered and implemented every day.

Money spent on IT yields tremendous returns. A Massachusetts Institute of Technology survey of 400 large companies revealed that the return on the IT dollar exceeded 50%. The best news is that these savings are ultimately passed on to us, the consumers.

Not only are computers and information technology changing the way we do things, they are changing the function and purpose of major companies. As we move into the new century, the distinction between companies will begin to blur. We can expect companies to merge and provide vertical integration of information technology–based products and services. For example, look for banks, bro-

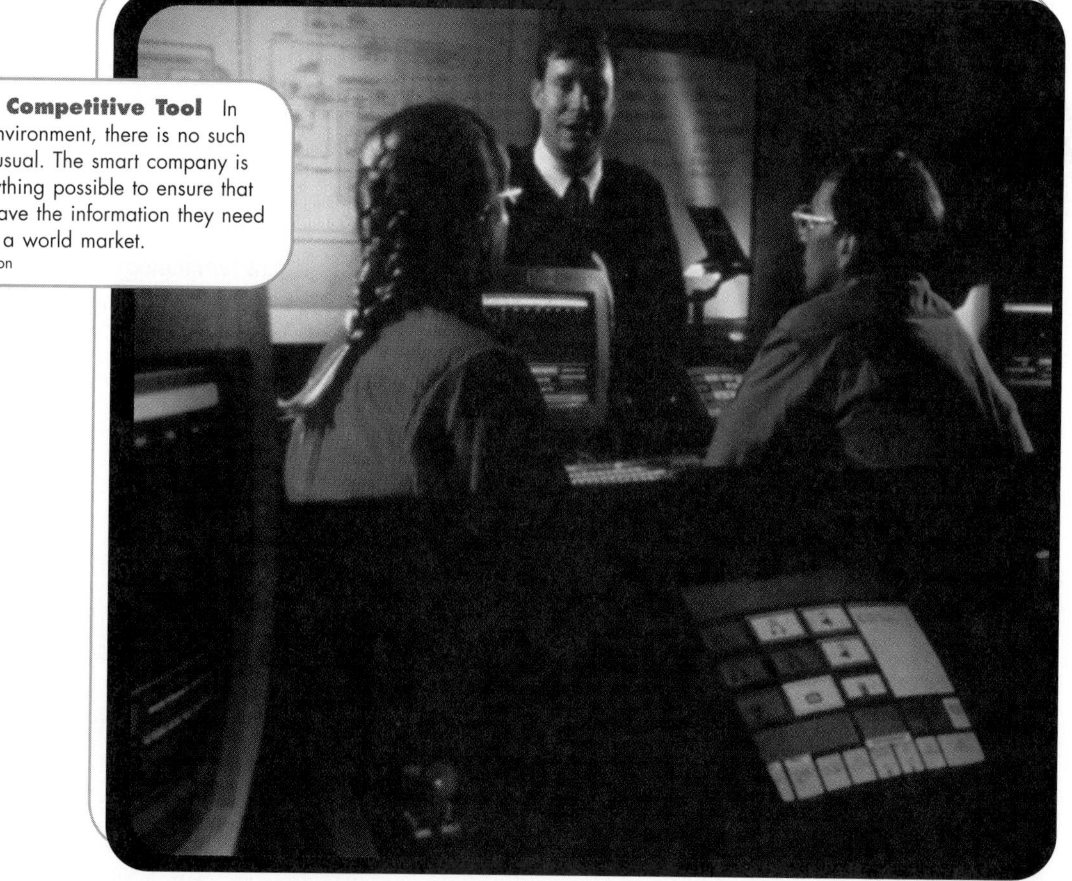

Technology as a Competitive Tool In today's competitive environment, there is no such thing as business as usual. The smart company is dynamic, doing everything possible to ensure that knowledge workers have the information they need to stay competitive in a world market.
Courtesy of Harris Corporation

kerage firms, insurance companies, and other financial services companies to begin offering similar products and services. It only makes sense for companies to leverage their capabilities, and companies in all industries are doing it.

SECTION SELF-CHECK

Self-Check

12-1.1 Money spent on information technology yields positive returns. (T/F)

12-1.2 Relatively few companies have opportunities to use technology to achieve a competitive edge. (T/F)

12.2 INFORMATION AND DECISION MAKING

Serendipitous Surfing: Politics

To be successful, managers must fully understand and use four major resources: money, materials, people, and information. Managers have become skilled at taking full advantage of the resources of *money, materials,* and *people;* but only recently have they begun to tap the potential of the *information* resource.

Qualities of Information

Just as we describe automobiles in terms of features, color, and size, we describe information in terms of its *accuracy, verifiability, completeness, timeliness,* and *relevance.*

Accuracy and Verifiability of Information

The *accuracy* quality of information refers to the degree to which information is free from error. Information is usually assumed to be accurate unless it is presented otherwise. Sometimes it is not economically feasible to collect information that is 100 percent accurate. For example, a market analyst may poll only a fraction of the potential consumers for a proposed product, and then extrapolate the results to all potential consumers.

Accuracy and *verifiability* go hand in hand. A decision maker is reluctant to assume that information is accurate unless it is verifiable. For example, managers usually are comfortable with the accuracy of financial information. Financial information can be verified (usually by auditors) because records are kept of all financial transactions (for example, payments and receipts). Decision makers accept and use unverifiable information, but they do so with caution and skepticism.

Too often managers at all levels are quick to accept computer-generated information as gospel. This can be a mistake. Information is only as good as the data from which it is derived. As the saying goes, "garbage in, garbage out" or **GIGO** (pronounced *"GUY go"*).

Completeness of Information

Information can be completely accurate and verifiable, but it may not tell the whole story. The *completeness* quality of information refers to the degree to which it is free from omissions. There is, of course, no relationship between the amount of information supplied to a decision maker and its completeness. Benefit/cost analysis offers a good example of the importance of considering the completeness of information in the decision-making process. If the benefit information is complete and the cost information is incomplete, the omission of the rest of the costs may result in an unprofitable project being approved. Unfortunately, this very situation is a common occurrence in the business world.

Timeliness of Information

The *timeliness* quality of information refers to the time sensitivity of information. Up-to-date information on today's market trends may be of significant value to an executive. The same information will have less value in a month and probably no value in six months. IT has contributed more toward improving the timeliness quality of information than any of the other information qualities. The power of

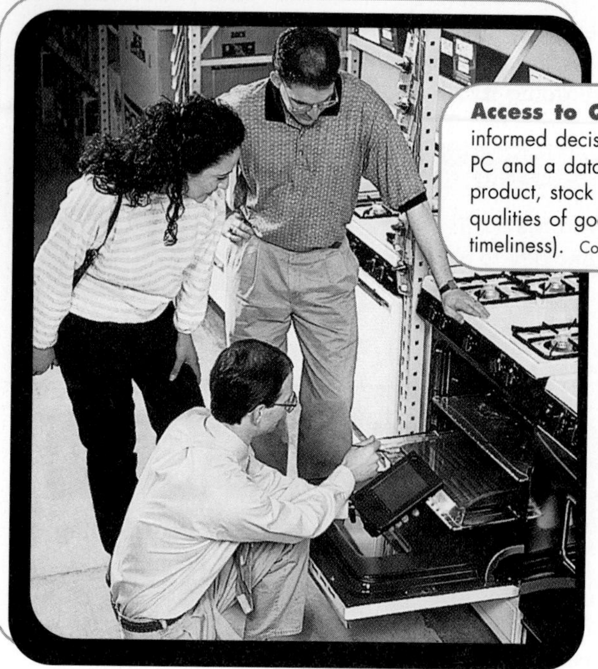

Access to Quality Information A sales assistant is helping this couple make an informed decision about which appliance to put into their new kitchen. With his laptop PC and a database handy, he can respond quickly to customer inquiries relating to the product, stock status, and delivery schedules. The information he provides has all the qualities of good information (accuracy, verifiability, completeness, relevance, and timeliness).

today's computers has made it possible for managers to have not only the right information but also the right information at the right time. Prior to 1980, managers were conditioned to waiting as much as two weeks for relatively simple requests for information. Today, similar requests can be handled in minutes by the person desiring the information.

Relevance of Information

The *relevance* quality of information refers to the appropriateness of the information as input for a particular decision. *Information overload* continues to be a problem for decision makers. Information overload occurs when the volume of available information is so great that the decision maker can't determine which information is relevant and which is not. One of the primary causes of information overload is the accumulation of information that is not relevant to a particular decision. For example, the power requirements for supercomputers are not relevant to decisions involving the acquisition of PCs.

Making Decisions to Produce Products and Services

The four levels of information activity within a company are *strategic, tactical, operational,* and *clerical.* IT-based information systems *process data* at the clerical level and *provide information* for managerial decision making at the strategic, tactical, and operational levels.

- *Strategic.* Strategic-level managers determine long-term strategies and set corporate objectives and policies to be consistent with these objectives. The information available for a strategic-level decision is almost never conclusive. To be sure, information is critical to strategic-level decision making, but virtually all decision makers at this level rely heavily on personal judgment and intuition.
- *Tactical.* Tactical-level managers must implement the objectives and policies made at the strategic level of management by identifying specific tasks that need to be accomplished. The information available for a tactical-level decision is seldom conclusive. That is, the most acceptable alternative cannot be identified from information alone. At this level, most decisions are made by using personal judgment and intuition in conjunction with available information.
- *Operational.* Operational-level managers complete the specific tasks as directed by tactical-level managers. The information available for an operational-level decision is often conclusive. That is, the most acceptable alternative can be clearly identified based on information available to the decision maker. At this level, personal judgment and intuition play a reduced role in the decision-making process.

The business system model shown in Figure 12.1 helps place the decision-making environment in its proper perspective. Managers (the top three levels) must use all the resources at their disposal to meet corporate objectives and perform the management functions of *planning, organizing, leading,* and *controlling.*

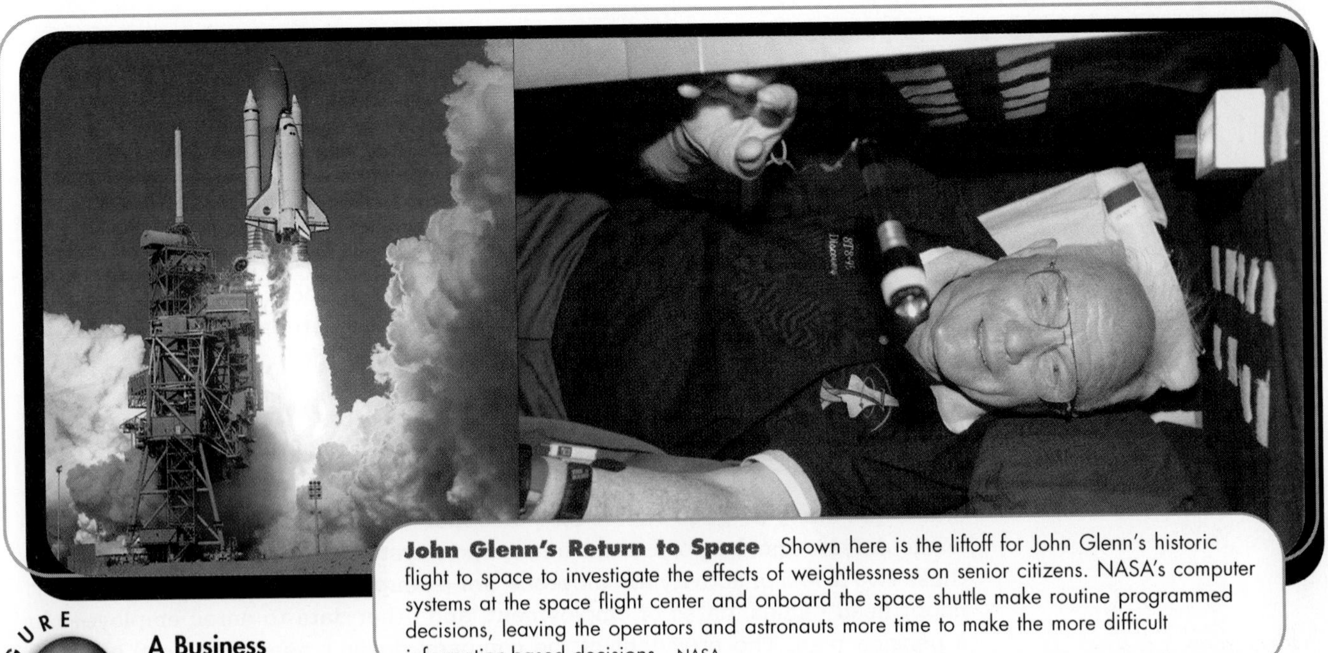

John Glenn's Return to Space Shown here is the liftoff for John Glenn's historic flight to space to investigate the effects of weightlessness on senior citizens. NASA's computer systems at the space flight center and onboard the space shuttle make routine programmed decisions, leaving the operators and astronauts more time to make the more difficult information-based decisions. NASA

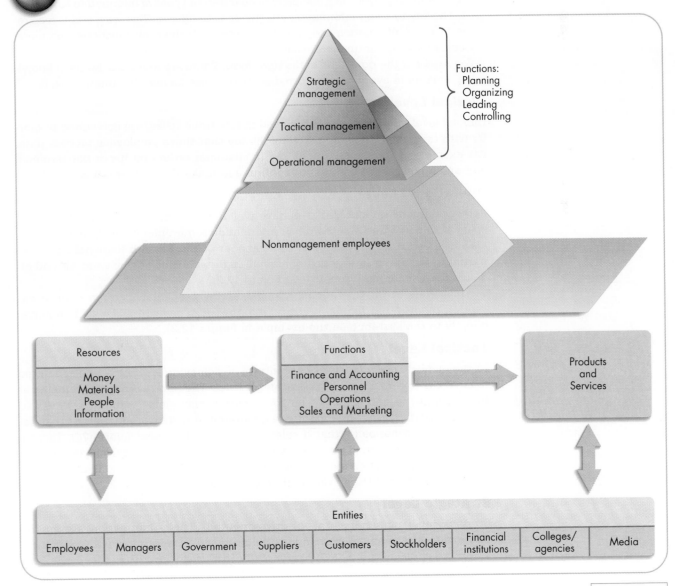

FIGURE 12.1 **A Business System Model**

Figure 12.1 illustrates how the corporate resources of *money, materials* (including facilities and equipment), *people,* and *information* become "input" to the various functional units, such as operations, sales, and accounting. Employees use their talent and knowledge, together with these resources, to produce products and services.

The business system acts together with several *entities,* such as employees, customers, and suppliers (see Figure 12.1). An entity is the source or destination of information flow. An entity also can be the source or destination of materials or product flow. For example, suppliers are a source of both information and materials. They are also the destination of payments for materials. The customer entity is the destination of products and the source of orders.

Filtering Information: Getting the Right Information to the Right Person

The quality of an information system is judged by its output. A system that generates the same 20-page report for personnel at both the clerical and strategic levels defeats the purpose of an information system. The information needs at these two levels of activity are different. For example, an administrative assistant might need names, dates of employment, and other data to enroll employees in a pension plan. The president of the company doesn't need that level of detail but might need information on overall employee pension contributions.

Different employees in a company need different types of information to do their jobs. The key to using information effectively is to *filter* it. This way, employees receive just the information they need to accomplish their job functions—no more, no less. **Filtering** information results in the *right information* reaching the *right decision maker* at the *right time* in the *right form.* There are four basic levels of knowledge workers in every company, and each level has its own information needs.

Clerical Level

Clerical-level personnel, those involved in repetitive tasks, are concerned primarily with *transaction handling.* You might say that these employees process data. For example, a sales clerk might key in customer orders on his or her terminal, and an airline ticket agent might confirm and make flight reservations.

Operational Level

Personnel at the operational level have well-defined short-term tasks that might span as long as three months. Their information requirements often consist of *operational feedback.* For example, the manager of the Eastern Regional Sales Department for Bravo International, a small high-tech firm, might want an end-of-quarter sales summary report (see Figure 12.2).

Managers at the operational, tactical, and strategic levels often request **exception reports** that highlight critical information. They can make such inquiries directly to the system (see the example in Figure 12.2).

Tactical Level

At the tactical level, managers concentrate on achieving a series of goals required to meet the objectives set at the strategic level. The information requirements at this level are usually *periodic,* but on occasion managers require one-time and what-if reports. *"What-if" reports* are generated in response to inquiries that depict what-if scenarios ("What if sales increase by 15% next quarter?"). Tactical managers are concerned primarily with operations and budgets from year to year. In the sales information system, the national sales manager, who is at the tactical level, might want the "Corporate Sales" report of Figure 12.2.

Strategic Level

Strategic-level managers are objective-oriented. Their information system requirements are often *one-time reports, what-if reports,* and *trend analyses.* For example, the president of the company might ask for a report that shows the four-year sales trend for each of the company's four products and overall (Figure 12.2).

FIGURE 12.2

Filtering of Information

A strategic-level sales-trend-by-product report shown in tabular and graphic formats (left). The sales-trend report and bar graph are prepared in response to inquiries from Bravo International's president, a strategic-level manager. Knowing that it is easier to detect trends in a graphic format than in a tabular one, the president requests that the trends be summarized in a bar graph. From the bar graph, the president easily can see that the sales of Alphas and Gammas are experiencing modest growth while the sales of Betas and Deltas are better.

FOUR-YEAR SALES TREND BY PRODUCT($1000)

PRODUCT	1994	1995	1996	1997	4-YEAR AVERAGE
ALPHAS	3,604	3,866	4,001	4,640	4,028
BETAS	1,106	2,240	2,855	3,590	2,448
GAMMAS	2,543	2,587	2,610	2,613	2,588
DELTAS	0	450	2,573	5,846	2,217
TOTALS	7,253	9,143	12,039	16,689	

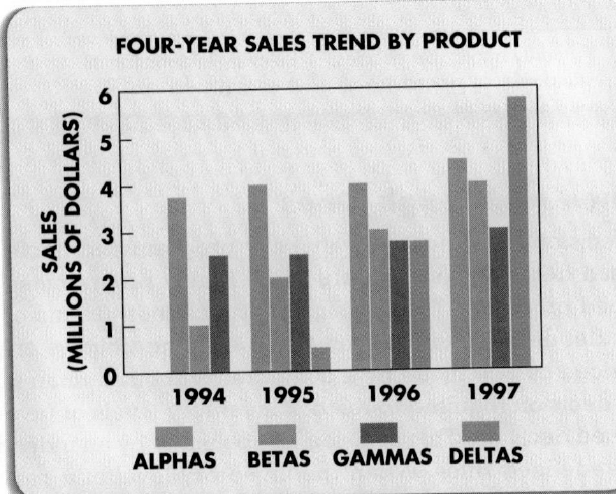

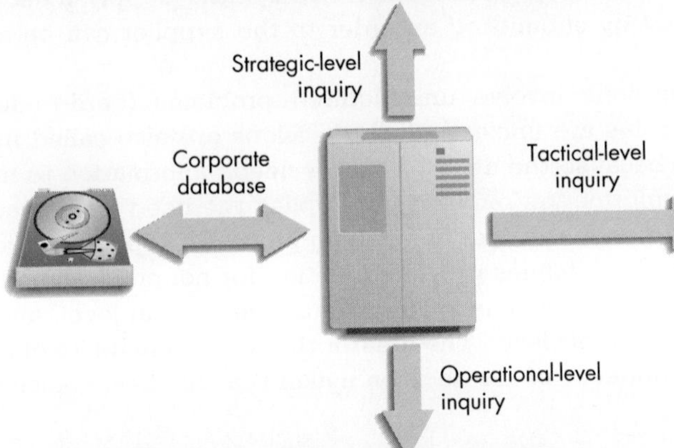

CORPORATE SALES REGIONAL SUMMARY($1000)-1ST QUARTER

REGION	ALPHAS	BETAS	GAMMAS	DELTAS	TOTAL
EASTERN	321	233	224	367	1145
SOUTHERN	180	202	196	308	886
WESTERN	369	250	150	472	1241
NORTHERN	250	170	162	254	836
TOTALS	1120	855	732	1401	4108

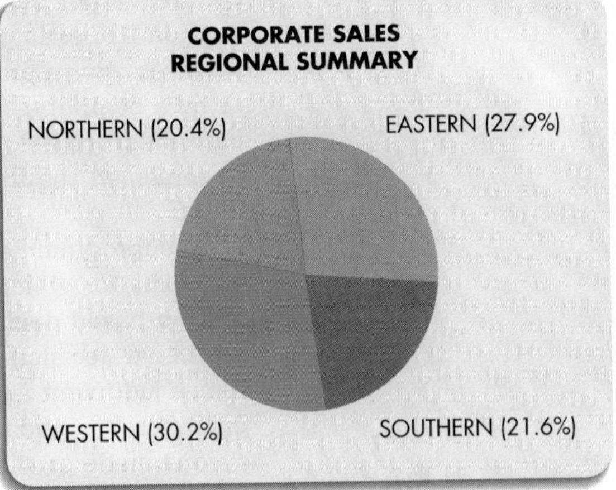

A tactical-level sales summary report shown in tabular and graphic formats (above). The sales summary report and pie graph are prepared in response to inquiries from Bravo International's national sales manager, a tactical-level manager. The report presents dollar-volume sales by sales region for each of the company's four products. To get a better sense of the relative sales contribution of each of the four regional offices during the first quarter, the national sales manager requested that the total sales for each region be presented graphically in a pie graph.

SALES DEPARTMENT - EASTERN REGION
SALES SUMMARY ($1000) - 1ST QUARTER

SALESPERSON	ALPHAS	BETAS	GAMMAS	DELTAS	TOTAL
BAKER	70	10	14	65	159
COOK	60	40	37	77	214
JONES	55	28	40	57	180
LUCAS	20	50	48	68	186
MILLER	45	34	28	48	155
OTT	39	47	29	42	157
RITTER	32	24	28	10	94
TOTALS	321	233	224	367	1145

SALES DEPARTMENT - EASTERN REGION
SALES SUMMARY ($1000) - 1ST QUARTER
SALESPERSONS WITH SALES<$15,000 FOR ANY PRODUCT

SALESPERSON	ALPHAS	BETAS	GAMMAS	DELTAS	TOTAL
BAKER	70	10	14	65	159
RITTER	32	24	28	10	94

An operational-level sales summary and exception report (left). These sales reports are prepared in response to inquiries from an operational-level manager. The top report shows dollar-volume sales by salesperson for each of Bravo International's four products: Alphas, Betas, Gammas, and Deltas. In the report, the sales records of the top (Cook) and bottom (Ritter) performers are highlighted so that managers can use this range as a basis for comparing the performance of the other salespeople.

The eastern regional sales manager used a fourth-generation language to produce the exception report (bottom). The manager's request was: "Display a list of all eastern region salespeople who had sales of less than $15,000 for any product in this quarter." The report highlights the subpar performances of Baker and Ritter.

Types of Decisions

Decision Characteristic	Programmed Decisions	Nonprogrammed Decisions (information-based decisions)
Difficulty	Easy	Tough
Horizon	Short-term	Long-term
Decision-maker level	Clerical	All management levels
Decision problem	Well-defined and structured	Ill-defined and unstructured
Confidence in making the right decision	High	Low to medium
Information requirement	Primarily applicable policies, standards, or procedures	Relevant information in meaningful format

Decisions: Easy Ones and Tough Ones

The two basic types of decisions are the relatively easy **programmed decisions** and tough **nonprogrammed decisions** (see Figure 12.3). Purely programmed decisions address well-defined problems. The decision maker cannot use his or her judgment because the actual decision is determined by existing policies or procedures. Many such decisions can be made by a computer without human intervention. For example, the decision required to restock inventory levels of raw materials is often a programmed decision. This decision can be made by an individual or by a computer using predefined rules. When the inventory level of a particular item drops below the reorder point, perhaps a two months' supply, a decision to replenish the inventory by submitting an order to the supplier can be automatic.

Nonprogrammed decisions involve unstructured problems (hard-to-define problems for which the rules are unclear). Such decisions are also called **information-based decisions** because the decision maker needs information to make a rational decision. The information requirement implies the need for managers to use judgment and intuition in the decision-making process. Corporate policies, procedures, standards, and guidelines provide direction for nonprogrammed decisions made at the operational level, less direction at the tactical level, and little or no direction at the strategic level. The greater the programmability of a decision, the greater the confidence of the decision maker that the best choice was made.

SECTION SELF-CHECK

Self-Check

12-2.1 It is easier for a manager to detect trends presented in a tabular format than in a graphic format. (T/F)

12-2.2 GIGO stands for garbage in, garbage out. (T/F)

12-2.3 Information may be filtered to get it to the right decision maker in a timely manner. (T/F)

12-2.4 Exception reports highlight critical information. (T/F)

12-2.5 Which of these would not be considered a quality of information: (a) verifiability, (b) relevance, (c) weight, or (d) timeliness?

12-2.6 Common corporate resources would include all but which of the following: (a) prestige, (b) money, (c) materials, or (d) information?

12-2.7 Tactical-level managers are charged with the responsibility of implementing the objectives and policies set forth at which level of management: (a) administrative, (b) strategic, (c) operational, or (d) tactical?

12-2.8 Nonprogrammed decisions are also called: (a) computer-oriented decisions, (b) information-based decisions, (c) human decisions, or (c) paranoid actions?

IT Ethics

PREDICTING ELECTION RETURNS

Prior to 1951, people had to wait until the votes were counted to find out who won an election. That changed when a "giant brain," the Univac I computer, predicted Dwight Eisenhower the winner over Adlai Stevenson in the 1951 presidential election with only 5% of the votes counted. Today, computers are as much a part of Election Day as political rhetoric and flag waving. Critics, however, contend that these computer predictions keep many people away from the polls. Voters confess, "Why vote when the winner is already known?" The news media contend that it's the public's right to know.

Discussion: Should the media be allowed to report computer-based elections before the polls close?

12.3 ALL ABOUT INFORMATION SYSTEMS

The Information System: What Is It?

Hardware, software, people, procedures, and *data* are combined to create an *information system* (see Figure 12.4). The term *information system* is a generic reference to a technology-based system that does two things:

Serendipitous Surfing: Distance Learning

- Provides *information processing capabilities* for an individual or, perhaps, an entire company. The processing capability refers to the system's ability to handle and process information (for example, order processing).
- Provides *information people need to make better, more informed decisions.* Information systems provide decision makers with on-demand reports and inquiry capabilities as well as routine periodic reports (daily, weekly, and so on). Information systems routinely make programmed decisions without people being involved.

Creating an Information System

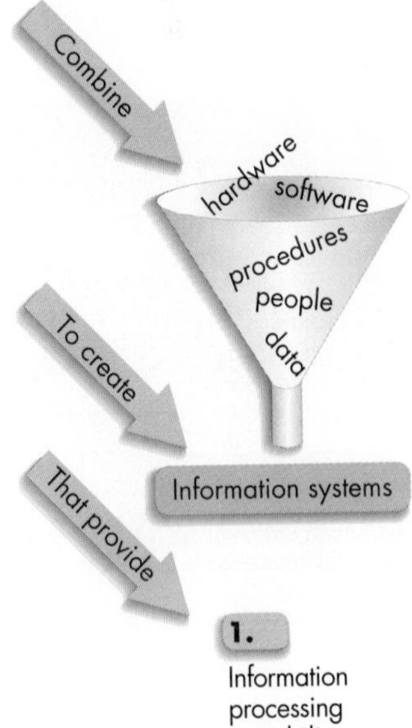

These information system concepts apply to all types of information systems: PC-based systems, LAN-based systems, and enterprise-wide client/server systems.

The Information System: What Can It Do?

Not surprisingly, an information system has the same four capabilities as a computer system: *input, processing, storage,* and *output* (see Figure 12.5).

Input

The information system has the capability to accept various forms of input.

- *Source data.* Source data result from the recording of a transaction or an event (for example, a bank deposit or the receipt of an order).
- *An inquiry.* An inquiry is any request for information.
- *A response to a prompt.* You might enter a Y or an N.
- *An instruction.* "Store file" or "Print invoice" could be instructions.
- *A message* to another user on the system.
- *A change.* When you edit a word processing document, you are entering change data.

Processing

The information system has the capability to perform various types of processing.

- *Retrieving, recording, and updating data in storage.* You can retrieve a customer's record from a database for processing, enter expense data into an

Information System Capabilities

Input

ORDERS
Bickle 8
Ridgets 3
Source data

LAST ORDER?
April 12
Inquiry

Log out now?
Yes
Prompt

Print invoice
Instruction

Meet at the pizzeria for lunch? OK?
Message

Processing

CUSTOMERS
ABC Corp.
Arvell Inc.
Case Stores
Zimco Ent.
Sorting

Zimco Ent.
Hdq. Dallas, TX
Tel. 214-555-8000
Retrieving

BICKLE SALES
-1st Quarter-
Jan 102
Feb 218
Mar 350
Total 770
Summarizing

TOP IN SALES
Mary Main
Eastern Region
Selecting

Price No. Amt.
10 3 $30
8 6 $48
Total $78
Manipulating

Storage

Output

Invoice
Due $78
Hard copy

Soft copy

Control

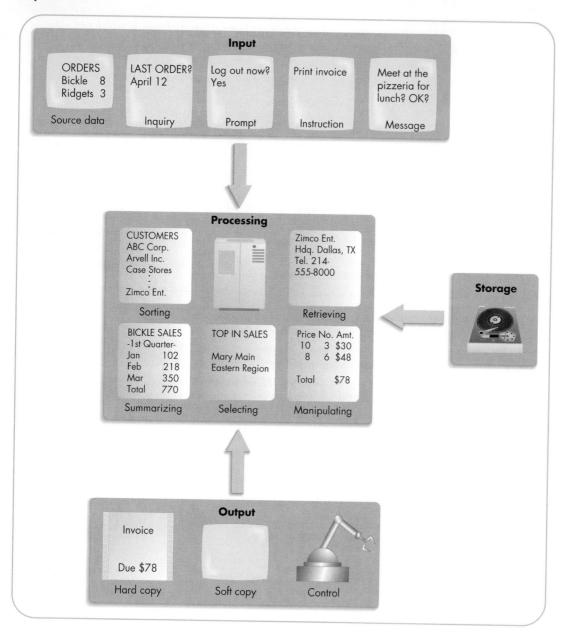

accounting system's database, and change a customer's address on a marketing database, respectively.

- *Summarizing.* You can present information in a condensed format to show totals and subtotals.
- *Selecting.* You can select records by criteria (for example, "Select all employees with 25 or more years of service in the company").
- *Manipulating.* You can perform arithmetic operations (addition, multiplication, and so on) and logic operations (comparing an employee's years of service to 25 to determine if they are greater than, equal to, or less than 25).

Storage

The information system has the capability to store *data, text, images* (graphs, pictures), and *other digital information* (voice messages) so that they can be recalled easily for output or further processing.

Output

The information system is capable of producing output in a variety of formats.

- *Hard copy.* Printed reports, documents, and messages are hard copy.
- *Soft copy.* Temporary displays on monitor displays and voice-mail messages are soft copy.
- *Control.* Instructions to industrial robots or automated processes are also output.

The Manual System: Opportunities for Automation

When we speak of an information system today, we usually mean an automated system. In a *manual system,* the automated elements of an information system (the hardware and software) aren't there. Manual systems consist of people, procedures, and data only. Many information systems in industry, government, and education are still manual, from large organizations with hundreds of computers to two-person companies. Tens of thousands of manual systems have been targeted to be upgraded to IT-based information systems. Ten times that many are awaiting tomorrow's creative users and computer professionals to identify their potential for automation.

Both manual systems and computer-based information systems have an established pattern for work flow and information flow. In a manual payroll system, for example, a payroll clerk receives time sheets from supervisors. The clerk then retrieves each employee's records from folders stored alphabetically in a file cabinet. Next, the clerk uses a calculator to compute gross and net pay, then manually writes (or types) the payroll check and stub. Finally, the payroll clerk compiles the payroll register, which is a listing of the amount paid and the deductions for each employee, on a tally sheet with column totals. About the only way to find and extract information in a manual payroll system is to thumb through employee folders—a painstaking process.

Today most payroll systems have been automated. But look in any office in almost any company and you will find rooms full of filing cabinets, tabbed three-ring binders, circular address files, or drawers filled with 3 by 5 inventory cards. These manual information systems are opportunities to improve a company's profitability and productivity through the application of computer and information technologies.

Function-Based and Integrated Information Systems

An information system can be either function-based or integrated. A **function-based information system** is designed for the exclusive support of a specific application area, such as inventory management or accounting. Its database and procedures are, for the most part, independent of any other system. The databases of function-based information systems probably contain data that are maintained in other function-based systems within the same company. For example, much of the data needed for an accounting system would be duplicated in an inventory management system. It is not unusual for companies with a number of autonomous function-based systems to maintain customer data in 5 to 10 different databases. When a customer moves, the address must be updated in several databases (accounting, sales, distribution, and so on). This kind of data redundancy is an unnecessary financial burden to a company.

During the past decade, great strides have been made in the integration of function-based systems. The resulting **integrated information systems** share a common database. The common database helps minimize data redundancy and allows departments to coordinate their activities more efficiently.

Getting Data into the System: Data Entry Concepts

Online versus Offline

If you'll remember, the four fundamental components of a computer system are input, processing, storage, and output. In a computer system, the input, output, and data storage components receive data from and transmit data to RAM and, eventually, the processor. These hardware components are said to be *online* to the processor. Hardware devices that are not accessible to a processor are said to be *offline.* A peripheral device that is connected to the processor, but not turned on, is considered offline. The concepts of online and offline also apply to data. Data are said to be *online* if they can be accessed and manipulated by the processor. All other data are considered *offline.* For example, when you are logged in to a LAN from a PC, the data on a LAN file server are said to be online. When you log off you are offline.

Source Data

Most data do not exist in a form that can be "read" by the computer. For example, supervisors may record manually the hours worked by the staff on a time sheet. Before the payroll checks can be computed and printed, the data on these time sheets must be *transcribed* (converted) into a *machine-readable format* that can be interpreted by a computer. This conversion is done in an *online* operation by someone at a PC or terminal. The time sheet is the **source document,** and, as you might expect, the data on the time sheet are the **source data.**

Not all source data have to be transcribed. For example, the numbers printed at the bottom of your bank checks are your individual account number and bank

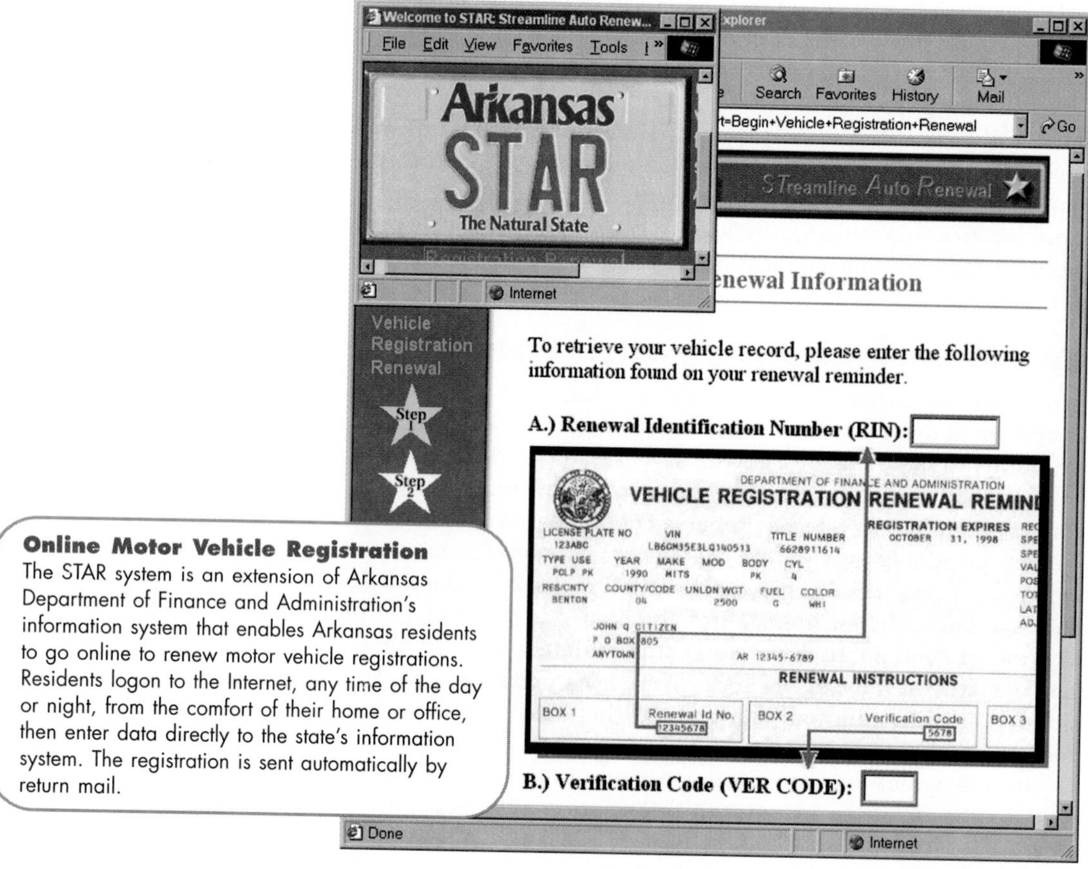

Online Motor Vehicle Registration
The STAR system is an extension of Arkansas Department of Finance and Administration's information system that enables Arkansas residents to go online to renew motor vehicle registrations. Residents logon to the Internet, any time of the day or night, from the comfort of their home or office, then enter data directly to the state's information system. The registration is sent automatically by return mail.

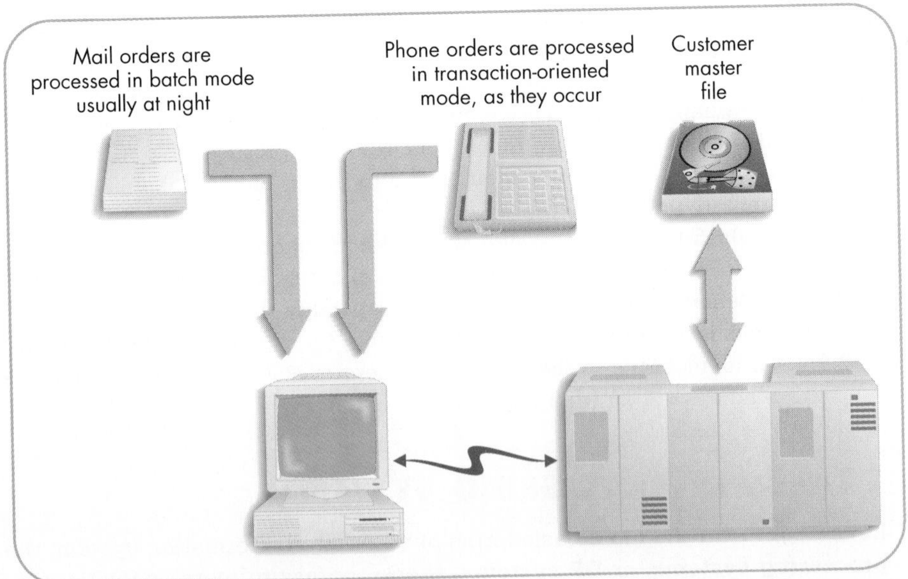
Mail orders are processed in batch mode usually at night
Phone orders are processed in transaction-oriented mode, as they occur
Customer master file

FIGURE 12.6

Batch and Transaction-Oriented Processing The typical order entry system accepts orders by mail and by phone.

number. They are already machine-readable, so they can be read directly by an input device. The UPC bar codes on consumer goods are also machine-readable.

Approaches to Data Entry

The term *data entry* describes the process of entering data into an information system. Information systems are designed to provide users with display-screen prompts to make online data entry easier. The display on the operator's screen, for example, may be the image of the source document (such as a time sheet). A *prompt* is a brief message to the operator that describes what should be entered (for example, "Enter hours worked").

Data entry generally falls into one of these categories.

- *Batch processing.* In **batch processing,** transactions are grouped, or batched, and entered consecutively, one after the other.
- *Transaction-oriented processing.* In **transaction-oriented processing,** transactions are entered to the system as they occur.

To illustrate the difference between batch and transaction-oriented processing, consider the order processing system for Bravo International (see Figure 12.6). The system accepts orders by both mail and phone. The orders received by mail are accumulated, or batched, for data entry—usually at night. Phone orders do not need to accumulate. People taking the phone orders interact with the company information system via PCs or terminals and enter the order data online while talking with the customer. Batch processing is appropriate mainly when information on source documents needs to be transcribed.

The primary advantage of transaction-oriented data entry is that records on the database are updated immediately, as the transaction occurs. With batch data entry, records are batched periodically. In a transaction-oriented environment, the database remains continuously up-to-date and can be queried at any time. Most data entry into enterprise-wide systems or into local area network-based systems is done online, regardless of whether the processing being done is batch or transaction-oriented.

SECTION SELF-CHECK

12-3.1 An integrated information system is designed for the exclusive support of a specific application area. (T/F)

12-3.2 Hardware, software, people, places, and information are combined to create an information system. (T/F)

W E B

Self-Check

12-3.3 An information system can provide information processing capabilities for an individual or an entire company. (T/F)

12-3.4 Source data result from the recording of a transaction or an event. (T/F)

12-3.5 The summarizing activity would be associated with which capability of an information system: (a) input, (b) output, (c) processing, or (d) storage?

12-3.6 A CD-ROM sitting on a shelf is said to be: (a) offline, (b) online, (c) system-oriented, or (d) sealed?

12-3.7 In which type of processing are transactions grouped together for processing: (a) transaction-oriented, (b) bin, (c) batch, or (d) group-driven?

12-3.8 The information system processing capability that encompasses logic operations is: (a) selecting, (b) manipulating, (c) recording, or (d) summarizing?

12-3.9 A brief message to the data entry operator is: (a) a question, (b) a prompt, (c) an answer, or (d) a user query?

12.4 DATA PROCESSING SYSTEMS

Let's begin with the most basic forms of automated information system, the **data processing systems,** or **DP systems,** then progress to more sophisticated information systems. DP systems are concerned with *transaction handling* and *record-keeping,* usually for a particular functional area. Data are entered and stored in a file format, and stored files are updated during routine processing. Periodic outputs include *action documents* (invoices) and *scheduled reports,* primarily for clerical personnel and operational-level managers. The major drawback of data processing systems is that they are inflexible and cannot accommodate data processing or information needs that are not already built into the system. In fact, DP systems are little more than electronic filing cabinets. Most companies have moved beyond the scope of DP systems and now have systems with the flexibility of providing management with information in support of an ever-changing decision-making environment.

SECTION SELF-CHECK

Self-Check

12-4.1 The DP system is considered the most sophisticated information system. (T/F)

12-4.2 The focus of data processing systems is: (a) transaction handling only, (b) record-keeping only, (c) transaction handling and record-keeping, or (d) strategic reporting?

12.5 MANAGEMENT INFORMATION SYSTEMS

MIS/DSS/EIS

In the not-too-distant past, most payroll systems were data processing systems that did little more than process time sheets, print payroll checks, and keep running totals of annual wages and deductions. As managers began to demand more and better information about their personnel, payroll *data processing systems* evolved into human resource **management information systems.** A human resource management information system is capable of predicting the average number of worker sick days, monitoring salary equality between minority groups, making more effective use of available personnel skills, and providing other information needed at all three levels of management—operational, tactical, and strategic.

The Management Information System: What Is It?

If you were to ask any five executives or computer professionals to define a management information system, or **MIS,** the only agreement you would find in their responses is that there is no agreement on its definition. An MIS has been called a method, a function, an approach, a process, an organization, a system, and a subsystem. The following definition is a mouthful, but it captures the essence of the MIS: *An MIS is a computer-based system that optimizes the collection, transfer, and presentation of information throughout an organization by using an integrated structure of databases and information flow.*

The MIS versus the Data Processing System

Here are a few differences between an MIS and a DP system.

- The integrated database of an MIS enables greater flexibility in meeting the information needs of management.
- An MIS integrates the information flow between functional areas (accounting, marketing, inventory management, and so on), whereas DP systems tend to support a single functional area.
- An MIS caters to the information needs of all levels of management, whereas DP systems focus on the clerical and operational levels.
- Management's information needs are supported on a timelier basis with an MIS than they are with a DP system. An MIS, for example, has online inquiry capability for the immediate generation of reports whereas a DP system usually produces only scheduled reports.

Characteristics of Management Information Systems

These are *desirable* characteristics of an MIS.

- An MIS supports transaction handling and record-keeping.
- An MIS uses an integrated database and supports a variety of functional areas.
- An MIS provides operational-, tactical-, and strategic-level managers with easy access to timely but, for the most part, structured information.
- An MIS is somewhat flexible and can be adapted to meet the changing information needs of the organization.
- An MIS can boost system security by limiting access to authorized personnel.

The FedEx Information System Federal Express has one of the world's most sophisticated information systems, providing up-to-minute information for its 150,000 employees. The system uses advanced telecommunications to monitor the status of millions of shipments as they move through key handling points in the system. The FedEx system handles more than 60 million online data transmissions each day.

The MIS in Action

All major airlines rely on management information systems to assist in day-to-day operations and provide valuable information for short-and long-term planning. At the core of such an MIS is the airline reservation subsystem. Airline reservation agents interact with the MIS's integrated database via remote PCs and terminals to update the database the moment a seat on any flight is filled or becomes available.

An airline MIS does much more than keep track of flight reservations. It also closely monitors departure and arrival times so that ground crew activities can be coordinated. The system even compiles and produces many kinds of information needed by management: the number of passenger miles flown, profit per passenger on a particular flight, percent of arrivals on time, average number of empty seats on each flight for each day of the week, and so on.

You may be interested to know that airlines routinely overbook flights. That is, they book seats they do not have. The number of extra seats sold is based on historical "no-show" statistics compiled by the MIS from data in the integrated database. Although these statistics provide good guidelines, occasionally everyone does show up!

The influence of the MIS is just as pervasive in hospitals (patient accounting, point-of-care processing, and so on), insurance (claims-processing systems, policy administration, actuarial statistics, and so on), colleges (student registration, placement, and so on), and other organizations that use computers both for information processing and to gather information for decision making.

SECTION SELF-CHECK

Self-Check

12-5.1 An MIS has the capability to limit access to authorized personnel. (T/F)

12-5.2 An MIS uses an integrated database and supports a variety of functional areas. (T/F)

12-5.3 Which type of information system integrates the information flow between functional areas: (a) DP system, (b) MIS, (c) DSS, or (d) intelligent agent?

12-5.4 MIS is an abbreviation for what term: (a) management information system, (b) mega information system, (c) managing Internet system, or (d) metropolitan IT system?

12.6 DECISION SUPPORT SYSTEMS

The Decision Support System: What Is It?

Decision support systems (DSS) are *interactive* information systems that rely on an integrated set of user-friendly decision support tools (both hardware and software) to produce and present information to support management in the decision-making process. Decisions makers can often rely on their experience to make a quality decision. When they cannot, the information that is readily available from the integrated corporate MIS is usually enough to help them through. However, decision makers, especially at the tactical and strategic levels, are sometimes confronted with complex decisions whose factors are beyond their human abilities to synthesize properly. These types of decisions are "made to order" for decision support systems.

A decision support system can help close the gap between the information they have and the information they need to make quality decisions. By using the latest technological innovations, planning and forecasting models, user-oriented query languages, and even artificial intelligence, DSS hardware and software provide managers with an unparalleled decision-making tool.

Generally, the DSS helps decision makers choose between alternatives. Some DSSs can even automatically rank alternatives based on the decision maker's criteria. Decision support systems can also be used merely to help remove the tedium of gathering and analyzing data. For example, managers no longer have to be burdened with such laborious tasks as manually entering and totaling rows and columns of numbers. They no longer have to be bothered with problems presenting or outputting reports or decision materials because graphics software in the DSS helps managers generate illustrative bar and pie graphs in a matter of seconds. And, with the availability of a variety of user-oriented DSSs, managers can get the information they need without having to depend on direct technical assistance from a computer professional.

The DSS versus the MIS

Management information systems are best at supporting decisions that involve *structured* problems, such as when to replenish raw materials inventory and how much of an inventory item to order. This type of routine operational-level decision is based on production demands, the cost of holding the inventory, and other variables that depend on the use of the inventory item. The MIS integrates these variables into an inventory model and presents specific order information (for example, order quantity and order date) to the manager in charge of inventory management.

In contrast to the MIS, decision support systems are designed to support decision-making processes involving *semistructured* and *unstructured* problems. A semistructured problem might be the need to improve the delivery performance of suppliers. The problem is partially structured in that information comparing the on-time delivery performance of suppliers can be obtained directly from the integrated database supporting the MIS. The unstructured facets of the problem, such as extenuating circumstances, rush-order policy and pricing, and so on, make this problem a candidate for a DSS.

An example of an entirely unstructured problem would be the evaluation and selection of an alternative to a raw material currently being used. A decision maker might enlist the aid of a DSS to provide information on whether it would be advisable to replace a steel component with a plastic or aluminum one. The information requirements for such a decision are diverse and typically beyond the scope of an MIS.

Another distinction we can make between an MIS and a DSS is that an MIS is designed and created to support a set of applications. A DSS is a set of decision support tools that can be adapted to any decision environment.

Characteristics of Decision Support Systems

These are *desirable* characteristics of a DSS.

- A DSS helps the decision maker in the decision-making process.
- A DSS is designed to address semistructured and unstructured problems.
- A DSS supports decision makers at all levels, but it is most effective at the tactical and strategic levels.
- A DSS is an interactive, user-friendly system that can be used by the decision maker with little or no assistance from a computer professional.
- A DSS makes general-purpose models, simulation capabilities, and other analytical tools available to the decision maker.
- A DSS can be readily adapted to meet the information requirements of any decision environment.
- A DSS can interact with the corporate database.
- A DSS is not executed in accordance with a preestablished production schedule (for example, weekly production reports).

The DSS Tool Box

A DSS consists of a set of decision support tools that can be adapted to any decision environment (see Figure 12.7). Together, these tools help managers address

The Decision Support System

A decision support system is a set of software and hardware tools that can be adapted to any decision environment.

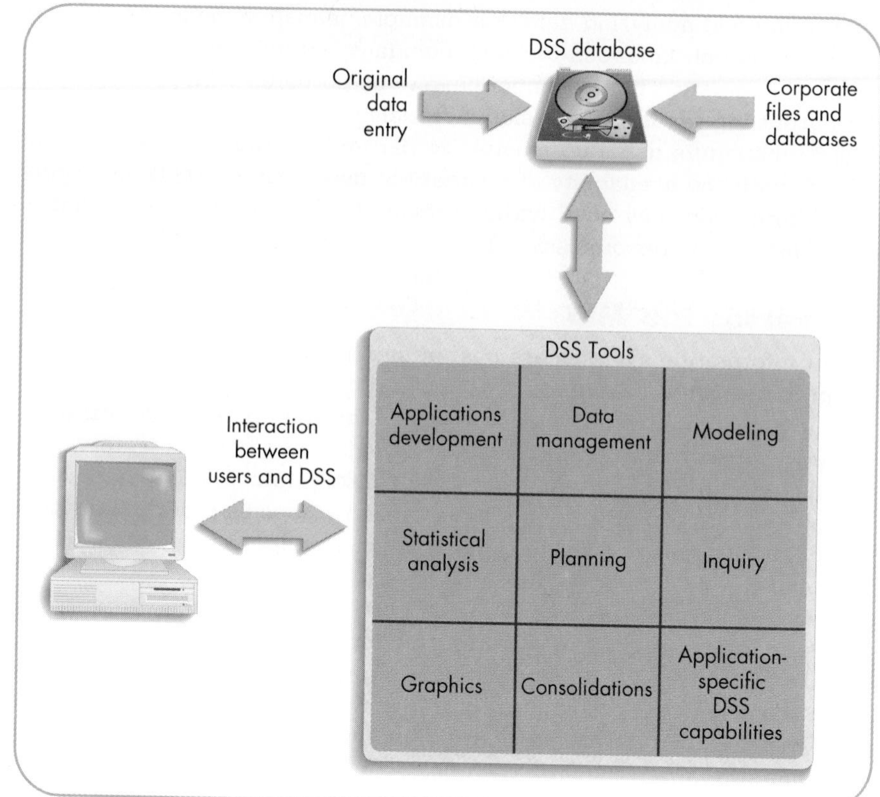

decision-making tasks in specific application areas (the evaluation and promotion of personnel, the acquisition of companies, and so on). DSS includes the following tools.

Applications Development

Some decision support systems provide users with the capability of developing computer-based systems to support the decision-making process. These applications typically involve the input, processing, and storing of data and the output of information. The ease with which DSS applications can be created has spawned a new term—**throwaway systems.** Often DSS applications are developed to support a one-time decision and are then discarded.

Data Management

DSS software packages have many approaches to database management—that is, the software mechanisms for the storage, maintenance, and retrieval of data. Perhaps the most popular DSS data management tool is **data warehousing.** Data warehousing involves moving existing operational files and integrated databases to a **data warehouse.** The data warehouse is a relational database created specifically to help managers get the information they need to make informed decisions.

In many organizations mountains of mission-critical data are compiled during routine data processing, but the data are in cumbersome function-based files and databases. Such data, which are not integrated and may include redundant data, are not easily accessible by management. The DSS data management tool enables scattered data from existing operational corporate files and databases to be collected and copied to a data warehouse. The data in the data warehouse are reorganized into a format that gives decision makers ready access to valuable, time-sensitive information. The operational files and databases may include data about customer buying patterns, inventory supply, seasonal manufacturing trends, and so on and must be constantly updated. This constant change of the operational data means that the data warehouse must be reconstructed periodically, perhaps each day or each week, depending on the volatility of the data.

Once data are consolidated in a data warehouse, managers can make complex queries and do analysis not possible with data spread all over the organization. For example, **data mining,** one of many analytical techniques, involves the analysis of large databases, such as data warehouses. Data mining is essentially getting answers to unasked questions and detecting unanticipated trends from databases. Data mining software is comprised of very sophisticated algorithms that examine large amounts of data for elusive relations or correlations. Data mining has resulted in information that led to increased sales per customer, getting new customers, reducing marketing expenses, identifying cross-selling opportunities, creating customer loyalty, and reducing exposure to fraud. At Coca-Cola, data mining revealed that Diet Coke drinkers buy seven or more books a year, whereas Classic Coke drinkers buy only one or two. This unexpected piece of information resulted in changes to Coca-Cola's marketing campaigns.

This DSS data management tool may be needed to ensure compatibility between a DSS database and an integrated set of DSS tools. Typically, this DSS tool enables access to a wide variety of databases. For example, the DSS data management tool can *import* and use data from a mainframe-based database or a PC-based spreadsheet. The DSS data management tool also can do the reverse; that is, *export* DSS data for use by another program.

Modeling

Decision support systems enable managers to use mathematical modeling techniques to re-create the functional aspects of a system within the confines of a computer. These simulation models are appropriate when decisions involve a number of factors. For example, models often are used when uncertainty and risk are introduced, when several decision makers are involved, and when multiple outcomes are anticipated. In these cases, each decision needs to be evaluated on its own merit.

In the business community, managers use modeling DSS software to simulate sales, production, demand, and much more. Simulation techniques are being applied to other aspects of life as well. Simulations have proven effective in predicting social, environmental, and biological trends.

Statistical Analysis

The DSS statistical analysis capability can handle everything from simple statistics, such as average, median, and standard deviation, to more analytical techniques, such as regression analysis and exponential smoothing, to complex procedures, such as multivariate analysis. Risk analysis and trend analysis are common applications of DSS statistical tools.

Planning

Managers often are faced with making decisions that will be implemented at some time in the future. To help them get a glimpse into the future, they rely on DSS software that permits forecasting, what-if analysis, and goal seeking. In *what-if analysis,* managers make inquiries such as, "What would be the impact on sales if we boost the advertising budget by 30%?" In *goal seeking,* managers make inquiries such as, "How much do we need to increase the advertising budget to achieve a goal of $120 million in sales for next year?"

Inquiry

DSS software helps managers to make online inquiries to the DSS database using English-like commands. For example, a personnel manager may enter this request: "What percentage of employee compensation goes to retirement benefits?" With DSS query capability, users are able to query corporate databases in much the same language that they would use to communicate with their colleagues.

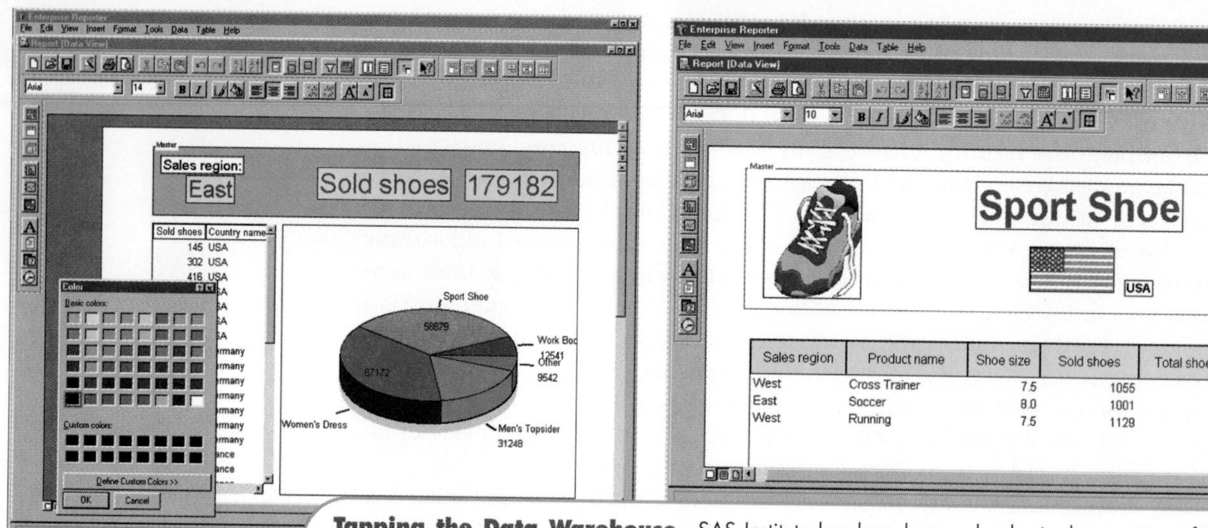

Tapping the Data Warehouse SAS Institute has long been a leader in the creation of DSS and EIS software. The SAS Enterprise Reporter provides decision support by helping nontechnical users tap the resources of a data warehouse and create formatted reports (shown here) that can be distributed on paper or via Internet. Courtesy of SAS Institute Inc.

Graphics

With the graphics DSS tool, managers can create a variety of presentation graphics based on data in the DSS database, including bar graphs, pie graphs, and line graphs. The graphics tool allows you to "drill down" into a graph to uncover additional information. For example, a user viewing a monthly sales bar graph can "drill down" and display a weekly sales bar graph for any given month.

Consolidations

DSS tools are available that enable the consolidation of like data from different sources. A sample use of this DSS tool is the consolidation of financial statements from subsidiary companies into a single corporate financial statement.

Application-Specific DSS Capabilities

DSS tools that support a particular decision environment, such as financial analysis and quality control, are being introduced routinely into the marketplace.

Executive Information Systems: The Executive's DSS

Just when we start to get used to decision support systems, the IT community introduces us to an even more intricate information system: the **executive information system.** As with the terms *MIS* and *DSS,* the term *executive information system,* or **EIS,** has been introduced with fanfare and anticipation but without a common understanding of what it is. The EIS supposedly offers the same decision support tools as the DSS, but each tool is designed specifically to support decision making at the executive levels of management, primarily the tactical and strategic levels. Like the MIS and the DSS, the EIS may eventually gain an identity of its own, but today's commercially available executive information systems look suspiciously like what most managers know as decision support systems.

SECTION SELF-CHECK

Self-Check

12-6.1 Decision support systems are designed to support decision-making processes involving totally structured problems. (T/F)

12-6.2 An MIS is a subset of an EIS. (T/F)

12-6.3 What-if analysis and goal seeking are addressed with the DSS planning tool. (T/F)

12-6.4 Which of the following types of information systems is designed specifically for decision support at the tactical and strategic levels of management: (a) expert systems, (b) executive information systems, (c) DP systems, or (d) management information systems?

12-6.5 Which DSS tool is used to analyze data warehouses to identify possible trends and problems: (a) planning, (b) inquiry, (c) modeling, or (d) data management?

12-6.6 A DSS is most effective at which two levels of management: (a) clerical and operational, (b) operational and tactical, (c) tactical and strategic, or (d) clerical and strategic?

12-6.7 DSS applications that are discarded after providing information support for a one-time decision are called: (a) throwaway systems, (b) toss-out programs, (c) junk systems, or (d) legacy systems?

12.7 EXPERT SYSTEMS

Artificial Intelligence

The kinds of problems that can be solved by computers extend well past those usually associated with computation. Computers can now solve problems requiring the kind of intelligence and reasoning associated with people. Research in *artificial intelligence (AI)* has added a new dimension to computing—the ability to reason and possess crude sensory perceptions. These added abilities enable computers to take on many new tasks. For example, computers have proven to be effective marriage counselors and wise corporate colleagues. The software that gives the computer these human-like capabilities is the expert system.

The Expert System: What Is It?

The **expert system** is a recent addition to the circle of information systems. Like the DSS, expert systems are computer-based systems that help managers resolve problems or make better decisions. However, expert systems do so with a decidedly different twist. An expert system is an interactive system that responds to questions, asks for clarification, makes recommendations, and generally helps the user in the decision-making process. In effect, working with an expert system is much like working directly with a human expert to solve a problem because the system mirrors the human thought process. It even uses information supplied by real experts in a particular field such as medicine, taxes, or geology. Expert systems are particularly good at making critical decisions that we might not be making because of lack of time, interest, resources, knowledge, and so on. In many ways, expert systems re-create the decision process better than humans do. We tend to miss important considerations or alternatives—expert systems don't.

An expert system applies IF-THEN rules to solve a particular problem, such as determining a patient's illness. Like the MIS and DSS, an expert system relies on factual knowledge, but an expert system also relies on *heuristic knowledge* such as intuition, judgment, and inferences. Both the factual knowledge and the heuristic rules of thumb used in an expert system are acquired from one or more real live *domain experts,* human experts in a particular field, such as jet engine repair, life insurance, or property assessment. The expert system uses this human-supplied knowledge to model the human thought process within a particular area of expertise. Once completed, an expert system can approximate the logic of a well-informed human decision maker.

Technically speaking, an *expert system* is the highest form of a **knowledge-based system.** The less sophisticated knowledge-based systems are called **assistant systems.** An assistant system helps users make relatively straightforward decisions. Assistant systems are usually implemented to reduce the possibility that the end user will make an error in judgment rather than to resolve a particular problem. For example, assistant systems are used to help people make on-line charge-card approvals and quote rates for life insurance.

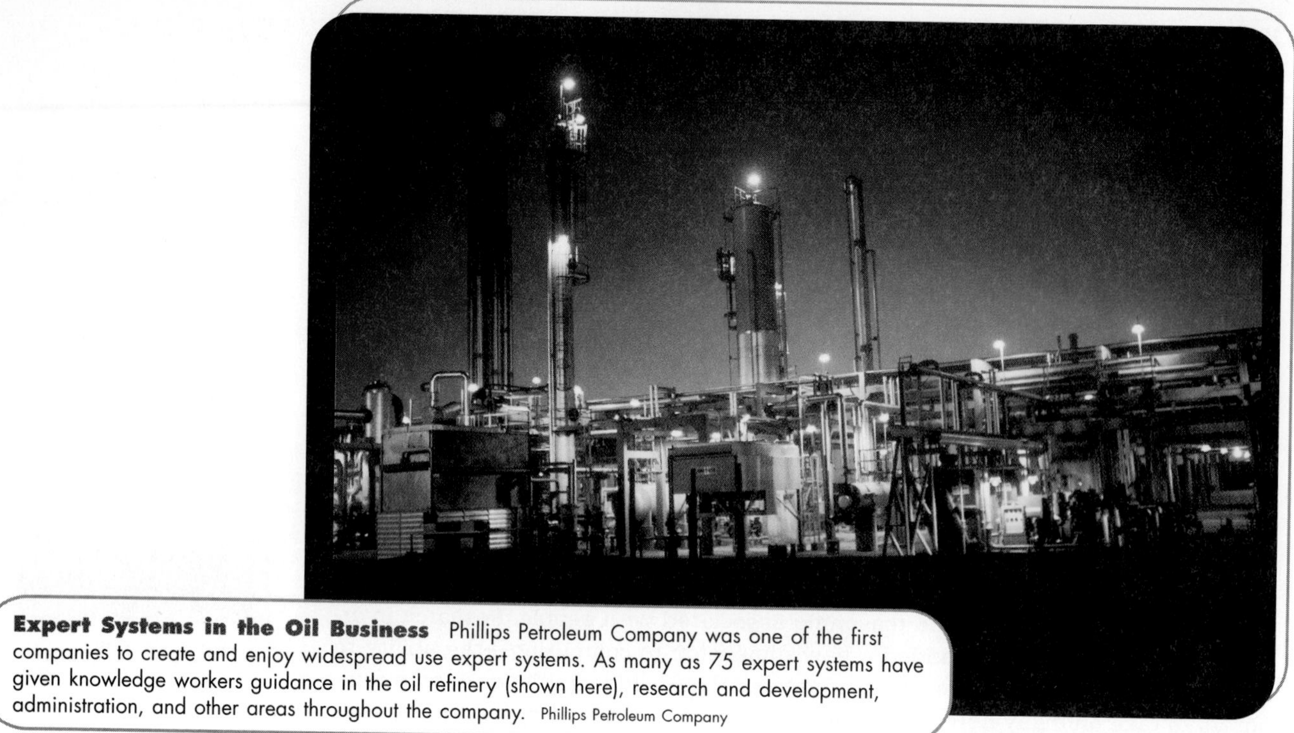

Expert Systems in the Oil Business Phillips Petroleum Company was one of the first companies to create and enjoy widespread use expert systems. As many as 75 expert systems have given knowledge workers guidance in the oil refinery (shown here), research and development, administration, and other areas throughout the company. Phillips Petroleum Company

In effect, expert systems simulate the human thought process. To varying degrees, they can *reason, draw inferences,* and *make judgments.* Let's use medical diagnosis expert systems, which have proven themselves remarkably accurate, for an example. Upon examining a patient, a physician might use an expert diagnosis system to get help in diagnosing the patient's illness or, perhaps, to get a second opinion. First the doctor would relate the symptoms to the expert system: male, age 10, temperature of 103°, and swollen glands about the neck. Needing more information, the expert system might ask the doctor to examine the parotid gland for swelling. Upon receiving an affirmative answer, the system might ask a few more questions and even ask for lab reports before giving a diagnosis. A final question for the physician might be whether the patient had been previously afflicted with or immunized for parotitis. Based on the information, the expert system would diagnose the illness as parotitis, otherwise known as the mumps.

In recent years, expert systems have been developed to support decision makers in a broad range of disciplines, including medical diagnosis, oil exploration, financial planning, tax preparation, chemical analysis, surgery, locomotive repair, weather prediction, computer repair, trouble-shooting satellites, computer systems configuration, nuclear power plant operation, newspaper layout, interpreting government regulations, and many others.

An Expert System Example: Technical Support

Anyone who has owned a printer for any length of time has had it act up or, worse, refuse to act at all. You do not have many alternatives when this happens. You can try to decipher an often-incomplete manual, call a knowledgeable friend, or bite the bullet and call an expensive professional. Now, several printer companies offer a more palatable alternative—an expert system. These expert systems do what call-in technical service people used to do—work users through the problem to a solution. These expert systems have a knowledge base derived from the knowledge of technical service personnel who have handled thousands of such calls. The knowledge base contains:

- Means of identifying the problem(s) to be solved
- Possible solutions to the problem(s)

- How to progress from problem to solution (primarily through facts and rules of inference)

All of this knowledge is integrated in an interactive online expert system that can help users solve most problems in a matter of minutes.

This expert system is probably the beginning of a new trend in technical support. Because technical support tends to be very expensive, hardware and software vendors can't afford very many calls from a customer before their profit from the sale of a product has eroded. Major vendors have hundreds (a few have thousands) of people doing nothing but handling calls for technical support. In some companies, 25% of their employees staff the tech support lines. In a very few years, look for vendors to integrate more and more expert systems into their tech support strategies. The trend to this alternative form of customer service is gathering momentum as more and more people gain access to the Internet.

Information Systems

Data processing (DP) system
- Functional area support
- Transaction handling and record-keeping

Management information system (MIS)
- Integrated database
- DP functions plus management information

Decision support system (DSS)
- Interactive system
- Various tools that support decision making

Executive information system (EIS)
- Subset of DSS
- Decision support at tactical and strategic levels

Expert system
- Interactive knowledge-based system
- Simulates human thought process

Intelligent agent
- Has the authority to act on our behalf
- Performs a variety of tasks

Are Expert Systems in Your Future?

The number and variety of expert system applications have increased dramatically with the advent of powerful, cost-effective PCs. Expert systems advise financial analysts on the best mix of investments; help taxpayers interpret the tax laws; help computer repairpersons diagnose the problems of a malfunctioning computer; and help independent insurance agents select the best overall coverage for their business clients.

In the short period of their existence, expert systems have operated impressively, and they continue to improve. Decision makers in every environment are developing or contemplating developing an expert system. Attorneys will hold mock trials with expert systems to "pre-try" their cases. Doctors routinely will ask a second opinion. Architects will "discuss" the structural design of a building with an expert system. Military officers will "talk" with the "expert" to plan battlefield strategy. City planners will "ask" an expert system to suggest optimal locations for recreational facilities.

Some computer industry observers believe that expert systems are the wave of the future and that each of us will have "expert" help and guidance at home and in our respective professions.

One of the myths surrounding expert systems, though, is that they will actually replace human experts. Although expert systems augment the capabilities of humans and make them more productive, expert systems will never replace people. Expert systems and humans complement one another in the decision-making process. The computer-based expert system can handle routine situations with great accuracy, thereby relieving someone of the burden of a detailed manual analysis. However, humans can combine the insight of an expert system with their flexible intuitive abilities to resolve complex problems.

SECTION SELF-CHECK

Self-Check

12-7.1 An assistant system is the highest form of a knowledge-based system. (T/F)

12-7.2 An expert system relies on factual knowledge and on heuristic knowledge. (T/F)

12-7.3 Expert systems are designed to replace human experts. (T/F)

12-7.4 Which type of information system has the greatest potential to reduce dependencies on critical personnel: (a) MIS, (b) expert system, (c) DP system, or (d) EIS?

12-7.5 Which type of information system would most closely approximate working directly with a human expert to solve a problem: (a) MIS, (b) DSS, (c) DP system, or (d) expert system?

12-7.6 An expert system is the highest form of: (a) assistant system, (b) specialist system, (c) factoid, or (d) knowledge-based system?

Emerging IT

THE MILLENNIUM BUG: Y2K

During this edition of this book, we will move into a new millennium. Relatively, earthlings experience both a change of century and a change of millenniums. Most of us are excited about it, but some aren't. The latter is a community of people who know about and must deal with "the year 2000 problem," commonly known as Y2K. This problem has been brewing throughout the twentieth century and it will fester well into the twenty-first century. If this problem is not adequately addressed, computers may be unable to compute properly in the twenty-first century.

After December 31, 1999, computers with old information systems may not know what year it is. If the Y2K problem is not fixed, there could be chaos—not just in the information technology community, but everywhere in the world. A computer that is confused about the date will be unable to write paychecks, send invoices, replenish inventory, accrue interest, operate traffic signals, calculate employee benefits, honor warranties, operate medical equipment, control airplanes, and on and on.

What Is the Year 2000 Problem?

The year 2000 problem may be one of the biggest challenges, if not the biggest, ever to confront the businesses of the world. The year 2000 problem occurred because analysts and programmers wanted to save keystrokes and storage space. For most of the twentieth century, they designed information systems that use only two digits to represent the year (for example, 99 for 1999). The implication is that all references are to the current century. But what happens when this century ends and a new one begins? At the stroke of midnight on December 31, 1999 (12/31/99), millions of computer systems will interpret January 1, 2000 (1/1/00), as being before the previous day!

The origin of the problem can be traced back to the 1930s, the early days of electromechanical data processing. During this period and into the late 1960s, punched-card technology was used for permanent storage of data. (See "The History of Computing" Focus on IT following Chapter 1.) Each card was able to hold 80 characters of information, not much when you consider that the typical employee record of today has many thousands of characters. With storage space at a premium, programmers of the day opted to abbreviate the year portion of the date field to two digits. The tradition of the two-digit year remained intact during the conversion period from punched-card data processing to computers (from the mid-1950s to the early 1970s).

Computer programmers of the 1950s and 1960s liked the two-digit year because it saved magnetic storage, which was still at a premium, and it reduced data entry time. In perpetuating the "problem," programmers never dreamed that their systems would still be in use in the year 2000. During these decades programmers created literally billions of lines of programming code, all based on the two-digit year. As it turns out, a large number of these mainframe-based legacy systems are still in operation and must be reengineered or converted to modern database technology (four-digit years) prior to the year 2000.

The Year 2000 Problem is all over the Internet, with hundreds of sites emphasizing different facets of the problem.

How Big Is the Problem?

Just how big is the year 2000 problem? Here are some predictions from various sources. (No one really knows the extent of the problem or the consequences of not addressing it, but many industry observers have opinions and many related surveys have been conducted.) Ninety percent of all software applications will be affected and close to 1 million programmer years of effort will be needed to correct the problem. The typical medium-to-large corporation will spend from \$50 million to \$100 million on the problem. The estimated cost to resolve the problem worldwide is \$600,000,000,000—that's \$600 billion! It is projected that from 1% to 5% of the businesses will go bankrupt attempting to fix the problem. Companies that ignore the problem will be liable for millions in lawsuits brought by shareholders when company stock prices begin to fall. Financial institutions that do not attend to the problem will be in chaos. Those reading this book after the millennium don't have to speculate about the results of Y2K. They already know.

Y2K is a problem with embedded systems, too. Embedded systems are the billions of programmable logic controllers, or PLCs, in just about every piece of sophisticated equipment in use today. They are in cars, dishwashers, power plants, and nuclear missiles. All PLCs run programs, but the programs may not be accessible to those who own and operate them. Worse, most people and companies don't even know where their PLCs are located and/or if they are Y2K compliant. Generally, each PLC must be tested separately for compliance. A large utility company might have millions of them.

Why Is the Problem So Difficult to Correct?

The complexity of the year 2000 problem is mind boggling. Not only are millions of programs affected, but also many (some say most) of these programs are poorly documented, nonstructured programs written by people who are no longer around. As a result, many organizations have hundreds, even thousands, of programs whose complex logic must be analyzed, documented, and understood before Y2K modifications can be made. Moreover, these programs have been patched (modified) many times over the years to accommodate changes in the way the organization does business. The accumulation of patches compounds the problem.

Justifying the Cost of Repairing the Problem

Typically, an organization does some kind of cost/benefit analysis to determine whether the investment in a proposed project is justified. For Y2K, though, doing such an analysis may be futile. The cost of addressing the year 2000 problem is very high, but the cost of ignoring it or of waiting too long to fix it is even higher—going out of business. Indeed, the costs associated with fixing the problem are irrelevant when survival in the next millennium is at stake. With less than a year to go at this writing, it's apparent that a significant percentage of companies and government agencies will not be compliant by December 31, 1999. Sadly, some had not yet begun.

How Can Two Digits Make Such a Big Difference?

An example might help you to understand better how such a seemingly small problem (just two digits) could cause such worldwide grief. Let's say you purchase a five-year certificate of deposit on 12/26/98 that will reach maturity on 12/26/03. After December 31, 1999, the computer can't determine how long you've had the CD because it is comparing 01/01/00 to 12/26/98. The result of the comparison is negative!

Nowadays companies and individuals routinely share data via data communications. Data sharing across networks or between users creates the possibility of "contamination" by two-digit data. That means that even if an organization solves the problem internally, it may have to deal with it again if its electronic partners fail to do their part.

If ignored, the Y2K problem will affect any computing environment where date is included in the database. For example, hospital nurses will be given erroneous information about when to administer medication to patients. College transcript programs will show advanced courses taken before basic courses. Everything will be past due!

Y2K Solutions: The Elusive Silver Bullet

At first, managers searched for the silver bullet that would automatically make their existing systems century compliant (four-digit years). Eventually, however, they learned that there is no silver bullet and they would have to address the Y2K problem on a laboriously slow program-by-program basis.

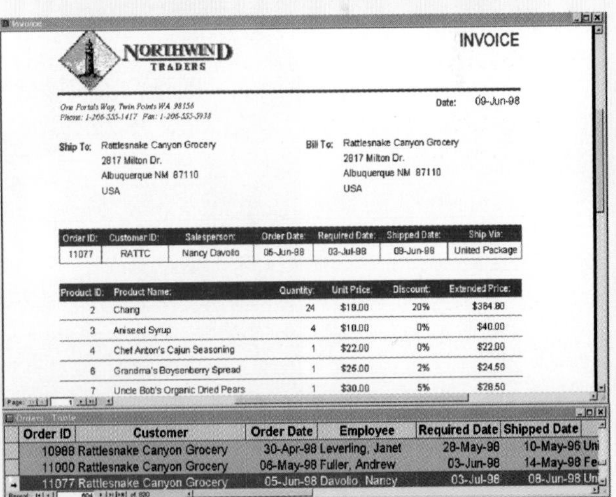

NORTHWIND TRADERS

INVOICE

One Portals Way, Twin Points WA 98156
Phone: 1-206-555-1417 Fax: 1-206-555-5938

Date: 09-Jun-98

Ship To: Rattlesnake Canyon Grocery, 2817 Milton Dr., Albuquerque NM 87110, USA

Bill To: Rattlesnake Canyon Grocery, 2817 Milton Dr., Albuquerque NM 87110, USA

Order ID:	Customer ID:	Salesperson:	Order Date:	Required Date:	Shipped Date:	Ship Via:
11077	RATTC	Nancy Davolio	05-Jun-98	03-Jul-98	08-Jun-98	United Package

Product ID:	Product Name:	Quantity:	Unit Price:	Discount:	Extended Price:
2	Chang	24	$19.00	20%	$364.80
3	Aniseed Syrup	4	$10.00	0%	$40.00
4	Chef Anton's Cajun Seasoning	1	$22.00	0%	$22.00
6	Grandma's Boysenberry Spread	1	$25.00	2%	$24.50
7	Uncle Bob's Organic Dried Pears	1	$30.00	5%	$28.50

Orders : Table

Order ID	Customer	Order Date	Employee	Required Date	Shipped Date
10988	Rattlesnake Canyon Grocery	30-Apr-98	Leverling, Janet	28-May-98	10-May-98
11000	Rattlesnake Canyon Grocery	06-May-98	Fuller, Andrew	03-Jun-98	14-May-98
11077	Rattlesnake Canyon Grocery	05-Jun-98	Davolio, Nancy	03-Jul-98	08-Jun-98

This billing application example is typical of most information systems in that processing and information is time-phased by date. Notice the Order Date, the Required Date, and the Shipped Date fields in the invoice (top) and the database record (bottom). Although the information is formatted to display the year portion of the date field as only two digits (98), the year is maintained internally as four digits (1998). This modern system, based on a Microsoft Access relational database, is not affected by "the year 2000 problem."

12.8 INTELLIGENT AGENTS: WORKING FOR US

In days of yore, well-to-do people had butlers and maids to do their bidding, day and night (and some still do). A recent innovation in information technology may enable a return to the days of yore—sort of. In cyberland, **intelligent agents** will "live" in our computer systems and assist us with the chores of life, both at home and at work. Intelligent agents, like expert systems, are a type of artificial intelligence.

Like all information systems, intelligent agents provide information that can help us make decisions, but they do it in a very different way. An intelligent agent has the authority to act on our behalf, just as a human agent does. We set the information or processing goals for our agents, and the agents act to reach those goals. The agent reacts to meet the demands of a specified goal in several different ways.

- The agent may remain in continuous motion working toward an ongoing goal.
- The agent performs an action when a specified event occurs.
- The agent performs actions needed to accomplish a one-time goal.

For example, you might ask an agent to alert you one week prior to birthdays of selected friends and relatives (an ongoing goal). A week before a birthday, the agent will alert you (an action triggered by an event).

> Linda's 25th birthday is Monday, June 3. Last year you sent a humorous Internet birthday greeting and two dozen red roses from Higdon Floral.

The agent can then be set up to send an e-mail or postal greeting, send flowers (you specify price range), or arrange a party and send out announcements, whichever you tell it to do. If you wish, you can instruct the agent to purchase and deliver a present to Linda (a one-time goal). The agent's response is based on the information contained in Linda's profile (mutual friends, preferences, and so on). If you give an agent the authority to handle all birthdays, you may never have to worry about birthdays again. Of course, if the agent plans a party, you should attend.

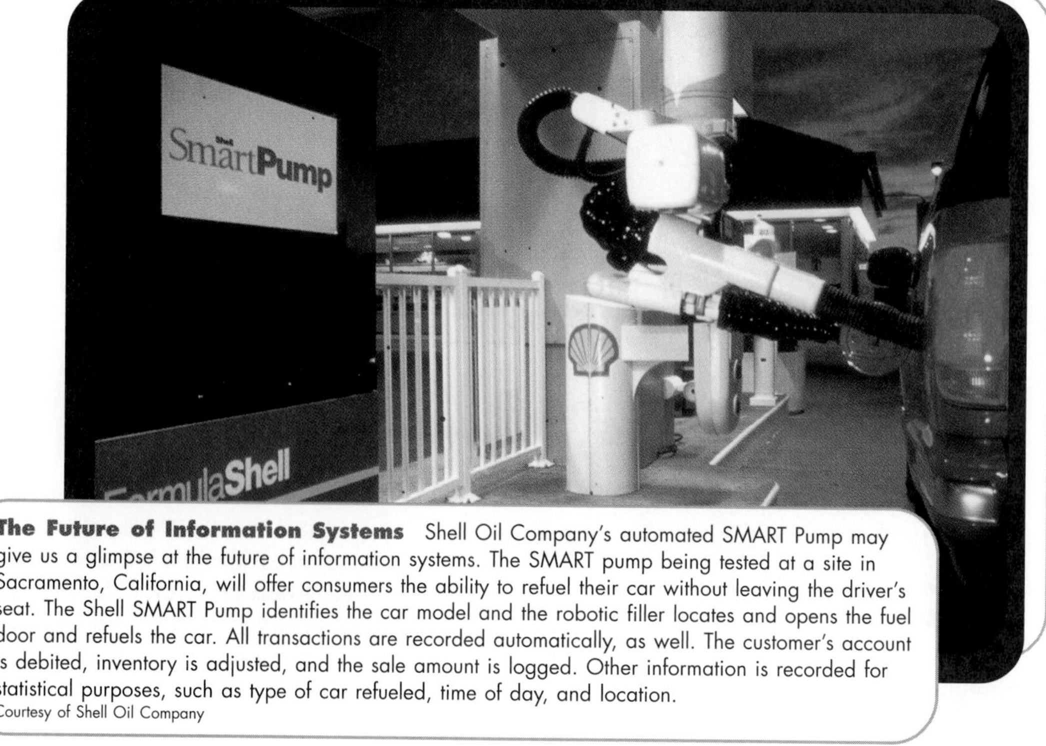

The Future of Information Systems Shell Oil Company's automated SMART Pump may give us a glimpse at the future of information systems. The SMART pump being tested at a site in Sacramento, California, will offer consumers the ability to refuel their car without leaving the driver's seat. The Shell SMART Pump identifies the car model and the robotic filler locates and opens the fuel door and refuels the car. All transactions are recorded automatically, as well. The customer's account is debited, inventory is adjusted, and the sale amount is logged. Other information is recorded for statistical purposes, such as type of car refueled, time of day, and location.
Courtesy of Shell Oil Company

The number and variety of intelligent agents is growing steadily, especially those focusing on the Internet or intranets.

- Intelligent agents can sort through e-mail. The agent scans each message and routes junk e-mail to the electronic equivalent of the trash can.
- Intelligent agents scan online newspapers and magazines for articles in our interest areas (for example, your favorite college basketball, folk music environmental issues).
- Intelligent agents can search the Internet for the best price on a specified product.

In a few years, intelligent agents will be helping us do many more jobs.

- A sailor might instruct an intelligent agent to alert her to favorable wind conditions at the local lake. To achieve this goal, the agent must tap weather information on a regular basis.
- We can tell the intelligent agent the type of vacation we want to book, and it will comb through online databases, looking for the best combination of price and luxury. When the agent reports back, we can make our selection, and the agent will make the reservations.

As you can see, the possibilities for agents are endless. Agents are already at work doing hundreds of tasks and their applications are expected to grow. A number of major companies, including America Online and AT&T, are developing products and services that will accommodate these agents.

It won't be long before our computers are online 24 hours a day to our office, home, college, and the information superhighway. As we evolve to an environment in which PCs are always online, look for intelligent agents to take on an ever-increasing workload. Unlike butlers and maids who had a few days off, intelligent agents never stop working for us.

SECTION SELF-CHECK

12-8.1 Intelligent agent software has the authority to act on our behalf. (T/F)

12-8.2 Intelligent agents already are dated technology and are disappearing from the corporate landscape. (T/F)

12-8.3 Which information system processing capability would be least likely to include logic operation: (a) selecting, (b) manipulating, (c) recording, or (d) sorting?

12-8.4 Which of these types of information systems reacts automatically to meet the demands of a user-specified goal: (a) DSS, (b) intelligent agent, (c) smart manager systems, or (d) EIS?

Self-Check

Interactive Study Guide Chapter 12

SUMMARY AND KEY TERMS

12.1 An end to business as usual

New and innovative uses of information technology are being implemented every day. Each company has a seemingly endless number of opportunities to use technology to achieve a competitive edge. Money spent on information technology yields tremendous returns.

12.2 Information and decision making

Traditionally managers have been very adept at taking full advantage of the resources of money, materials, and people, but only recently have they begun to make effective use of information. The quality of information can be described in terms of its *accuracy, verifiability, completeness, timeliness,* and *relevance*. Information is only as good as the data from which it is derived ("garbage in, garbage out" or **GIGO** [5]). By **filtering** (8) information, the right information reaches the right decision maker at the right time in the right form.

Information systems help process data at the clerical level and provide information for managerial decision making at the operational, tactical, and strategic levels. Managers at the operational, tactical, and strategic levels often request **exception reports** (8) that highlight critical information. For decisions made at the tactical and strategic levels, information is often inconclusive, and managers also must rely on their experience, intuition, and common sense to make the right decision.

The two basic types of decisions are **programmed decisions** (10) and **nonprogrammed decisions** (10). Purely programmed decisions address well-defined problems. Nonprogrammed decisions, also called **information-based decisions** (10), involve ill-defined and unstructured problems.

12.3 All about information systems

Hardware, software, people, procedures, and data are combined to create an information system. An information system provides companies with data processing capabilities and the company's people with information.

An information system has the same four capabilities as a computer system: input, processing, storage, and output. The processing capabilities include sorting; retrieving, recording, and updating data in storage; summarizing; selecting; and manipulating.

An information system can be either function-based or integrated. A **function-based information system** (13) is designed for the exclusive support of a specific application area. **Integrated information systems** (13) share a common database.

Source data (14) on **source documents** (14) must be transcribed into a machine-readable format before they can be interpreted by a computer. Data entry describes the process of entering data into an information system.

When transactions are grouped together for processing, it is called **batch processing** (15). In **transaction-oriented processing** (15), transactions are entered as they occur.

12.4 Data processing systems

Data processing (DP) systems (16) are file-oriented, function-based systems that focus on transaction handling and record-keeping and provide periodic output aimed primarily at operational-level management.

12.5 Management information systems

A **management information system** (16), or **MIS** (16), is a computer-based system that optimizes the collection, transfer, and presentation of information throughout an organization by using an integrated structure of databases and information flow.

An MIS not only supports the traditional data processing functions but also relies on an integrated database to provide managers at all levels with easy access to timely but structured information. An MIS is flexible and can provide system security.

An MIS is oriented to supporting decisions that involve structured problems.

12.6 Decision support systems

Decision support systems (18) are interactive information systems that rely on an integrated set of user-friendly hardware and software tools to produce and present information targeted to support management in the decision-making process.

A **DSS** (18) supports decision making at all levels by making general-purpose models, simulation capabilities, and other analytical tools available to the decision maker. A DSS can be readily adapted to meet the information requirements of any decision environment.

In contrast to the MIS, decision support systems are designed to support decision-making processes involving semistructured and unstructured problems.

A decision support system is made up of a set of software tools and hardware tools. The categories of DSS software tools include applications development (frequently resulting in **throwaway systems**) (20), data management (including the ability to import and export data), modeling, statistical analysis, planning, inquiry, graphics, consolidations, and application-specific DSS capabilities.

Data warehousing (20) involves moving existing operational files and databases from multiple applications to a **data warehouse** (20). The data warehouse is a relational database created specifically to help managers get the information they need to make informed decisions. **Data mining** (21) in data warehouses is used to identify unanticipated trends and problems.

We use the term *import* to describe the process of converting data in one format to a format that is compatible with the calling program, in this case the data management tool. The DSS data management tool also can do the reverse; that is, *export* DSS data for use by another program or, perhaps, a database package.

The **executive information system's (EIS)** (22) is designed specifically to support decision making at the tactical and strategic levels of management.

12.7 Expert systems

Expert systems (23), which are associated with an area of research known as artificial intelligence, help managers resolve problems or make better decisions. They are interactive systems that respond to questions, ask for clarification, make recommendations, and generally help in the decision-making process. An expert system is the highest form of a **knowledge-based system** (23), but in practice the two terms are used interchangeably. The less sophisticated knowledge-based systems are called **assistant systems** (23).

The user interface component of an expert system enables the interaction between end user and expert system needed for heuristic processing. Some computer industry observers believe that expert systems are the wave of the future and that each of us will have "expert" help and guidance at home and in our respective professions.

12.8 Intelligent agents: Working for us

Intelligent agents (28) have the authority to act on our behalf, just as human agents do. We set the goals for our intelligent agents, and they act to reach those goals.

DISCUSSION AND PROBLEM SOLVING

12.1 It is often said that "time is money." Would you say that "information is money"? Discuss.

12.2a. In general, top executives have always treated money, materials, and people as valuable resources, but only recently have they recognized that information is also a valuable resource. Why do you think they waited so long?

b. Pick a type of business (for example, automobile manufacturing, hotels, or city government) and give an example how information may be filtered for use by management.

c. Select an article in the newspaper on a current event and evaluate the information relative to its accuracy, verifiability, completeness, timeliness, and relevance.

d. For each of the three levels of management illustrated in the business system model in Figure 12.1, what would the horizon (time span) be for planning decisions? Explain.

12.3a. Give examples within the context of a corporate information system for these information system processing capabilities: retrieving, summarizing, and manipulating.

b. Reflect on your activities of the past week and identify those activities that generate source data for information systems.

c. A company has five function-based information systems. What would you say to convince management to spend the money necessary to consolidate these systems into a single integrated information system?

12.4 Describe transactions that might be processed by an insurance company's DP system.

12.5a. Describe reports that might be requested by an operational-level manager at a large bank. By a tactical-level manager. By a strategic-level manager.

b. Suppose the company you work for batches all sales data for data entry each night. You have been asked to present a convincing argument to top management about why funds should be allocated to convert the current system to an MIS with transaction-oriented data entry. What would you say?

12.6a. Is it possible for an organization to have both a DSS and an MIS? Explain.

b. How often would the data warehouse need to be updated (reconstructed) in a university? Justify your answer.

c. The upside of data mining is that a company can identify trends early then make adjustments to corporate operations. Is there a downside to data mining? Explain.

d. Give examples of what-if inquiries that the mayor of a large city might make to a DSS.

e. The IT community regularly introduces buzz words, especially for tools designed to provide information for management. Frequently these terms are not clearly defined when introduced (for example, DSS and EIS). Would having more concrete definitions help or hinder IT progress? Explain.

12.7a. Describe a specific decision environment that would be appropriate for the implementation of an expert system.

b. Describe a specific decision environment that would be appropriate for the implementation of an assistant system.

12.8a. Give an example of how an intelligent agent might be able to help you at home.

b. Give an example of how an intelligent agent might be able to help you at work.

Developing Business Information Systems

Learning Objectives

13.1 Describe the four stages of the system life cycle.

13.2 Demonstrate an awareness of basic system development techniques and concepts.

13.3 Describe the scope and capabilities of CASE tools.

13.4 Describe the concepts and phases of prototyping, including the general activities that take place during system analysis and design.

13.5 Describe approaches to system conversion.

13.6 Demonstrate an overview understanding of programming concepts, programming languages, and the programming process.

chapter 13

Value Learning

WHY THIS CHAPTER IS IMPORTANT TO YOU

Throughout the day we interact with information systems. Information systems let us deposit and withdraw money from an ATM. Each month information systems calculate what we are owed for wages and what we owe to our creditors. Everywhere we go, we run into an information system—at the point-of-sale terminal in a department store, when making an airline reservation with our travel agent, or while enrolling at college.

Information systems don't just happen. They are either purchased or developed from scratch. In either case those who will use the system frequently are involved in development and/or implementation of the system. If you are part of the system, and there is a good chance you will be, it is to your advantage to provide input into the development process. Ultimately, the quality of an information system depends on the input and feedback from you and other users. Too often, life at work is a joy or a pain depending on the quality and effectiveness of the information system being used.

Information systems are dynamic, ever changing, and must be constantly upgraded to meet your changing needs and those of your organization. You will be the user of an information system, and as such, it's your responsibility and duty to provide feedback on its operation and effectiveness.

This chapter acquaints you with the system development life cycle so that you can be an effective contributor to any IT project team, whether for a new development project or during a system upgrade. A good effort on a high-profile information system project team is a great way to gain corporate visibility and earn points for an early promotion.

13.1 THE SYSTEM LIFE CYCLE

Monthly Technology Update
Chapter 13

During the early years of automation, information systems were built to handle the basic flow of information within an organization: general accounting data and reports, inventory management, and human resource applications. Typically, they were custom systems built in-house to meet specific organization needs. Most were batch systems where transactions were accumulated or batched prior to processing. Data entry, reporting, and computation were done in or near a central computer center. After a couple of decades in this mode, technology specialists began to seek out new ways to improve existing information systems. First, they integrated separate function-based information systems eliminating system redundancy. Second, they began to incorporate telecommunications capabilities into system design, thus moving information processing activities closer to the action (for example, in the accounting office or on the shop floor).

Today, information systems are being implemented at a fever pitch. Corporate executives, users, and IT specialists are continually seeking new ways to employ technology to improve productivity and product quality. For example, for 30 years, trucking companies knew when their trucks departed and when they arrived (assuming the driver called the dispatcher upon arrival). Modern trucking companies use global positioning systems (GPS) to track trucks wherever they go. This GPS information system constantly feeds dispatchers the exact geographic location (and speed) of company trucks. This and all other information systems have a well-defined system life cycle.

Stages of the Life Cycle

Human beings and *information systems* have life cycles. We are born; information systems are born in the form of an idea. We grow from tiny babies and eventually enter the world on our own; information systems grow from an idea to become ready-to-use software. Through adulthood we make contributions to society in our own special ways; once operational, information systems contribute to organizations by processing data and providing information. We grow old and pass on; information systems grow old and pass on. The life cycle for information systems is called the **system life cycle.** The four stages of this life cycle (birth, development, production, and death) are illustrated in Figure 13.1. The emphasis in this chapter is on the *development stage* of the life cycle.

Applications Software: Whether to Make It or Buy It

An organization can progress through the development stage of the system life cycle and satisfy its information processing needs in two basic ways.

1 *Purchase an information system.* An organization can purchase and install a **proprietary software package.** Proprietary software is developed by a software vendor to sell to a number of potential buyers.

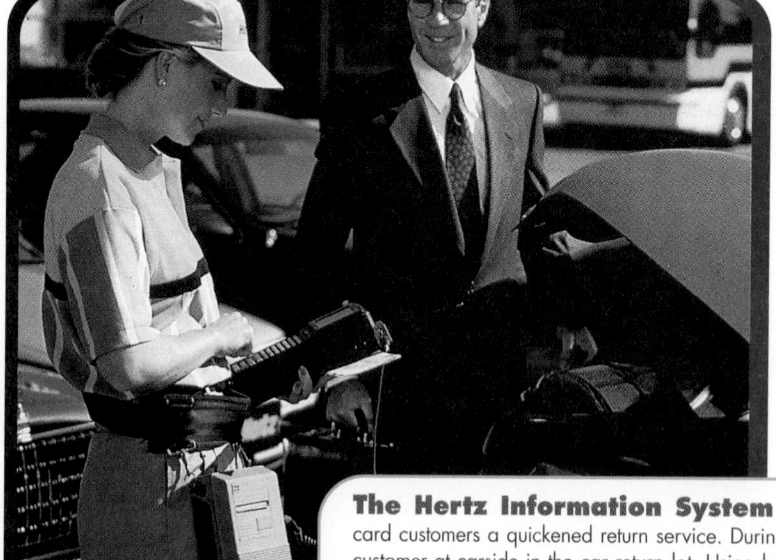

The Hertz Information System Hertz's Instant Return information system offers credit-card customers a quickened return service. During peak hours, a Hertz service representative meets the customer at carside in the car return lot. Using handheld computers, which are linked to a server by radio frequency, the representative processes the return and issues an itemized receipt for the rental in under a minute. This information system makes rental return easier for customers by bringing the service to them.

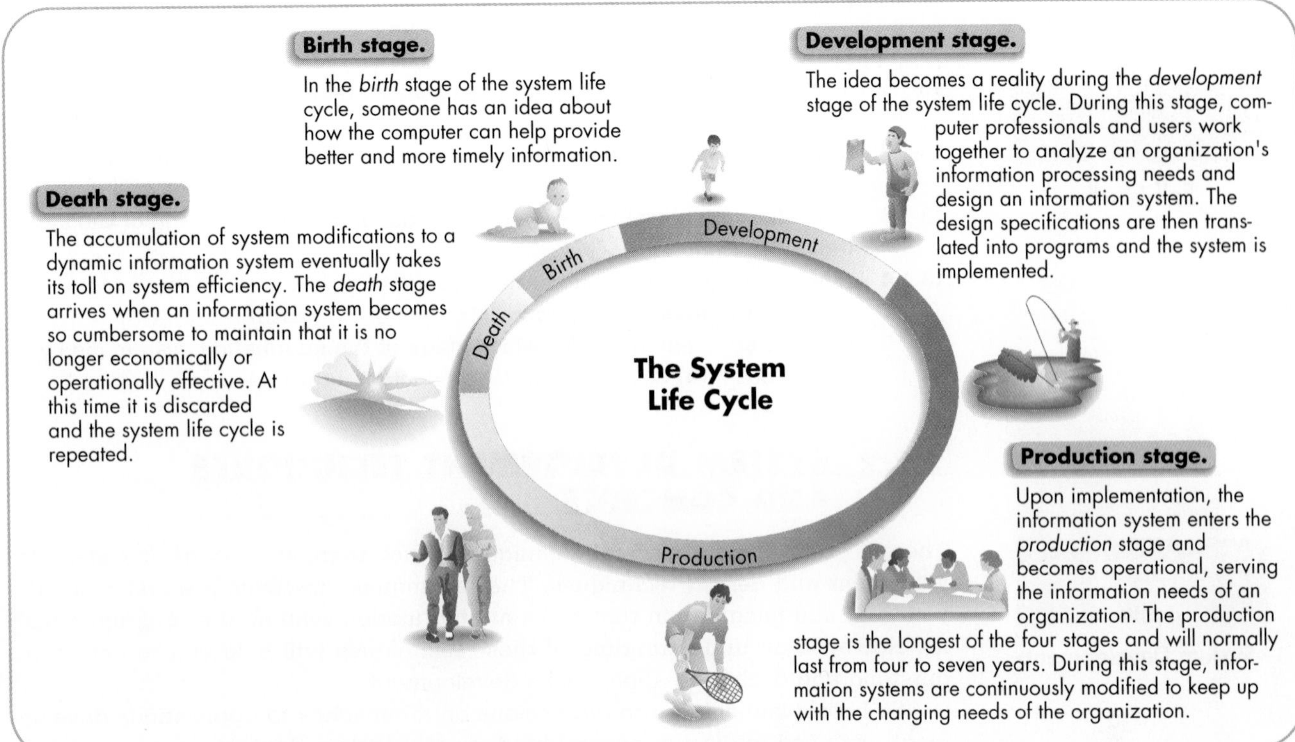

Birth stage.
In the birth stage of the system life cycle, someone has an idea about how the computer can help provide better and more timely information.
Development stage.
The idea becomes a reality during the development stage of the system life cycle. During this stage, computer professionals and users work together to analyze an organization's information processing needs and design an information system. The design specifications are then translated into programs and the system is implemented.
Death stage.
The accumulation of system modifications to a dynamic information system eventually takes its toll on system efficiency. The death stage arrives when an information system becomes so cumbersome to maintain that it is no longer economically or operationally effective. At this time it is discarded and the system life cycle is repeated.
Development
Birth
Death
The System Life Cycle
Production stage.
Upon implementation, the information system enters the production stage and becomes operational, serving the information needs of an organization. The production stage is the longest of the four stages and will normally last from four to seven years. During this stage, information systems are continuously modified to keep up with the changing needs of the organization.
Production

The Life Cycle: System and Human

2 *Develop a custom information system.* Here, employees and/or outside consultants create a customized information system that meets the unique needs of the organization.

These two options pose to managers the classic "make-versus-buy" decision. Each approach has its pros and cons. The best *application portfolios* (an organization's applications software) contain an optimal mix of the two.

Purchasing Proprietary Software

Virtually all installed system software (operating system software) and PC productivity software (spreadsheet, word processing, and so on) are proprietary. There are literally thousands of proprietary applications software packages on the market, from billing systems for veterinarians to general-ledger accounting systems for billion-dollar multinational companies. If there is a market for a software product, chances are that some entrepreneur has developed a package to meet the need. Given the choice, corporate management will typically opt for proprietary software over in-house development.

In-house Development of Custom Information Systems

Most organizations maintain IT professionals who can develop custom information systems, sometimes referred to simply as *applications.* As a rule of thumb, organizations choose in-house development when the operational characteristics of the proposed system are unique to that particular organization. In these cases, there's no proprietary software available for the task anyway.

The material in this chapter describes the process an organization might go through to create an information system. However, the discussion also is applicable to the selection and installation of proprietary software.

SECTION SELF-CHECK

Self-Check

13-1.1 The best corporate application portfolios contain only proprietary software packages. (T/F)

13-1.2 System software, such as operating systems, normally is proprietary software. (T/F)

13-1.3 The information system becomes operational in the birth stage of the system life cycle. (T/F)

13-1.4 In which stage of the information system life cycle are systems maintained: (a) birth, (b) development, (c) production, or (d) death?

13-1.5 Systems are created during which stage of the information system life cycle: (a) birth, (b) development, (c) production, or (d) death?

13.2 SYSTEM DEVELOPMENT TECHNIQUES AND CONCEPTS

System Development

There is no one best analytical technique. In fact, there are dozens of system development and design techniques. The techniques, however, are just tools. It's your skill and imagination that make an information system or a program a reality. However, an understanding of these techniques will help you to better understand approaches to applications development.

So before launching into discussions on approaches to applications development, we need to discuss several fundamental system development techniques, including *structured system design, data flow diagrams, entity relationship diagrams,* and *flowcharting.*

Structured System Design

Information systems, even small ones, can be complex to analyze, design, and implement. It is easier to address the design of a complex information system in small, manageable modules than as one big task. Information systems are designed using the principles of **structured system design.** The structured approach to system design encourages the top-down design technique: That is, the project team divides the system into independent modules for ease of understanding and design. The **structure chart** in Figure 13.2 illustrates how a payroll system can be conceptualized as a hierarchy of modules. Eventually the logic for the mod-

FIGURE 13.2

Structure Chart This structure chart breaks a payroll system down into a hierarchy of modules.

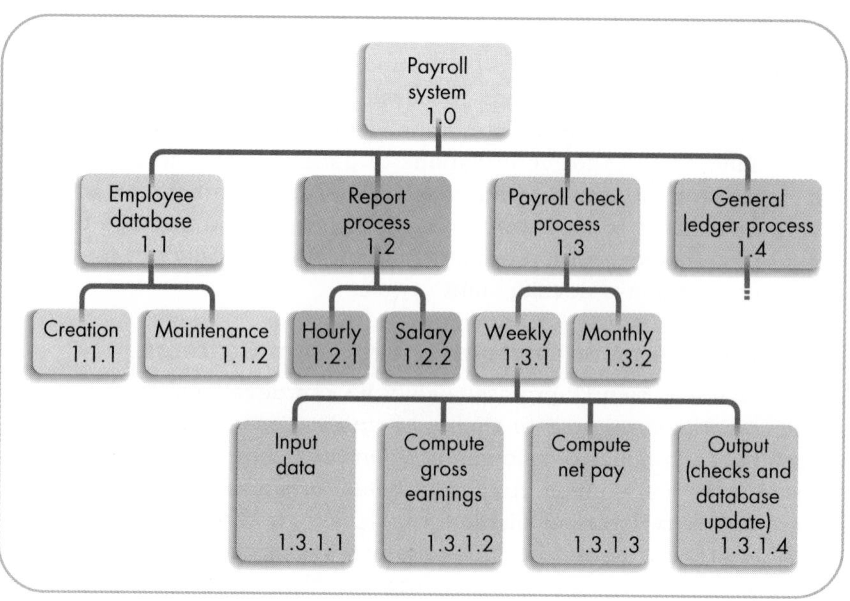

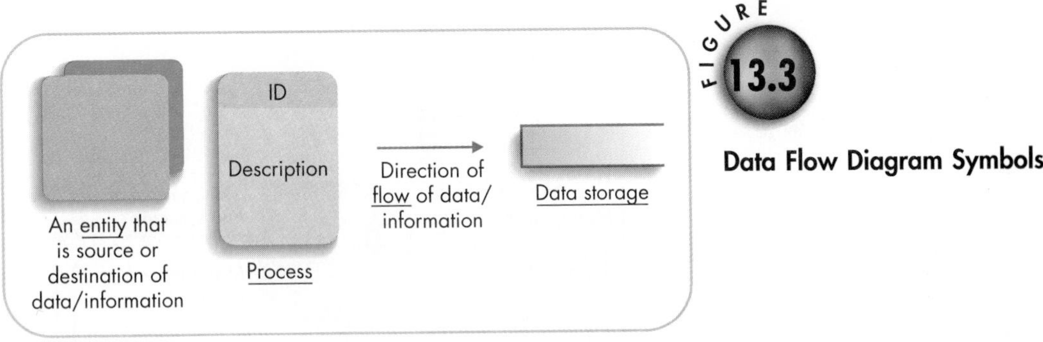

FIGURE 13.3

Data Flow Diagram Symbols

ules is represented in detail in step-by-step diagrams that illustrate the interactions between input, processing, output, and storage activities for a particular module.

Data Flow Diagrams

Data flow diagrams enable systems analysts to design and document systems using the structured approach to system development. Only four symbols are needed for data flow diagrams: entity, process, flow line, and data storage. The symbols are identified in Figure 13.3 and their use is illustrated in Figure 13.4.

- *Entity symbol.* The entity symbol is the source or destination of data or information flow. An entity can be a person, a group of people (for example, customers or employees), a department, or even a place (such as a warehouse).
- *Process symbol.* Each process symbol contains a description of a function to be performed. Process symbols also can be depicted as circles. Typical processes include enter data, calculate, store, create, produce, and verify. Process-symbol identification numbers are assigned in levels (for example, Processes 1.1 and 1.2 are subordinate to Process 1).
- *Flow line.* The flow lines indicate the flow and direction of data or information.
- *Data storage.* Data storage symbols identify storage locations for data, which could be a file drawer, a shelf, a database or file on magnetic disk, and so on.

The data flow diagram shown in Figure 13.4 is for an enterprise-wide MIS at BrassCo, a manufacturing company with about 1200 employees at its corporate headquarters and four plant sites. The data flow diagram in Figure 13.4 provides an overview of BrassCo's MIS, showing information flow between its functional components and the integrated database. The functional components of BrassCo's MIS are:

Process 1 Finance and Accounting
Process 2 Personnel
Process 3 Operations
Process 4 Sales and Marketing

All the MIS component systems share a common database.

In Figure 13.5, the Personnel Process (2) of the BrassCo MIS (Figure 13.4) is *exploded* to show greater detail. The Personnel Process (2) is essentially a personnel accounting system that maintains pertinent data on employees. The major processes within this human resources component are Recruiting (2.1), Pay and Benefits Administration (2.2), and Training and Education (2.3). Process 2.1 could be exploded to a third level of processes to show even greater detail (for example, 2.1.1, 2.1.2, and so on).

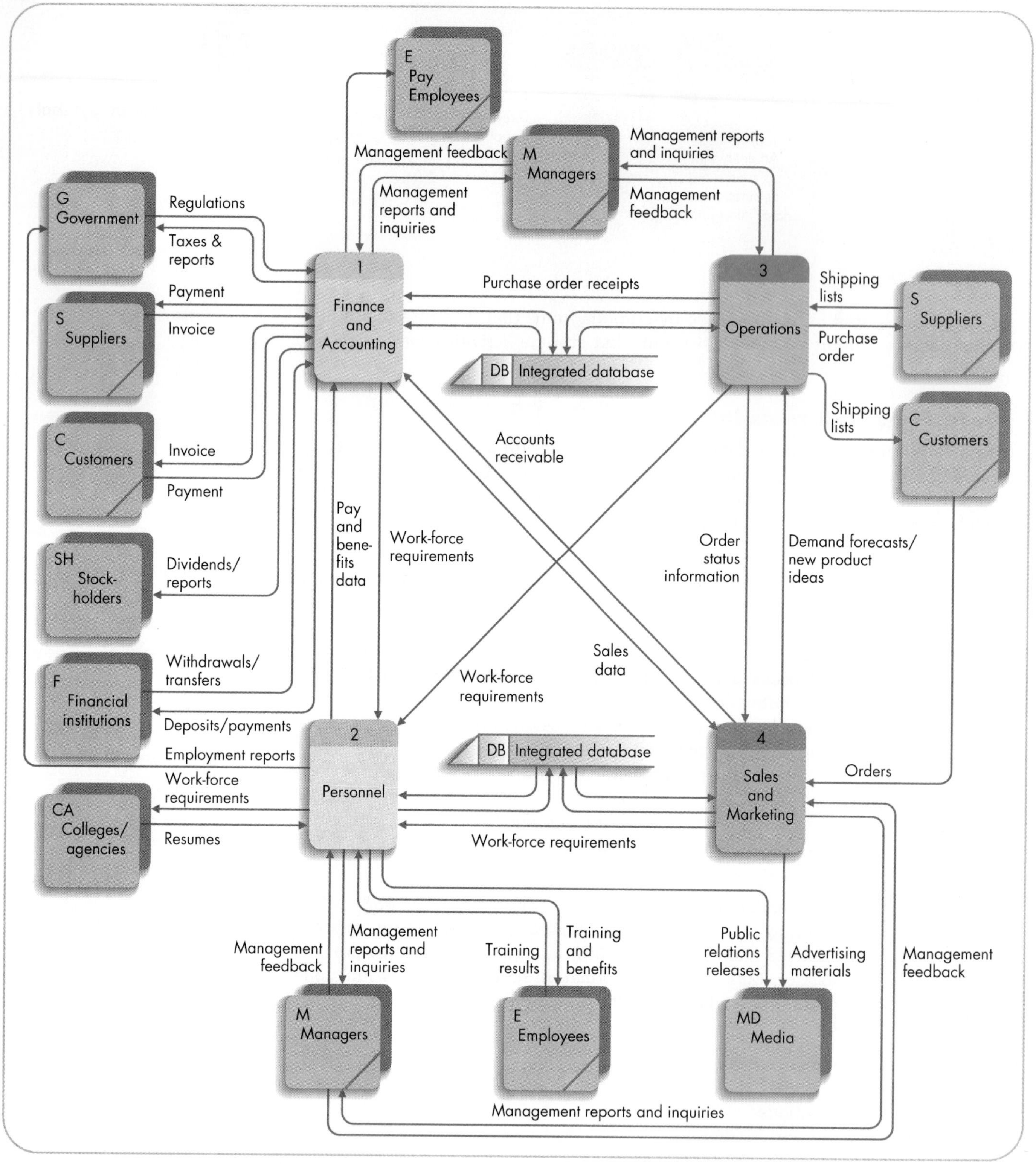

E
Pay Employees
M
Managers
Management feedback
Management reports and inquiries
Management reports and inquiries
Management feedback
G
Government
Regulations
Taxes & reports
S
Suppliers
Payment
Invoice
C
Customers
Invoice
Payment
SH
Stock-holders
Dividends/ reports
F
Financial institutions
Withdrawals/ transfers
Deposits/payments
1
Finance and Accounting
Purchase order receipts
DB Integrated database
3
Operations
Shipping lists
S
Suppliers
Purchase order
Shipping lists
C
Customers
Accounts receivable
Pay and bene-fits data
Work-force requirements
Order status information
Demand forecasts/ new product ideas
Sales data
Work-force requirements
2
Personnel
DB Integrated database
4
Sales and Marketing
Orders
Employment reports
Work-force requirements
Resumes
CA
Colleges/ agencies
Work-force requirements
Management feedback
Management reports and inquiries
Training results
Training and benefits
Public relations releases
Advertising materials
Management feedback
M
Managers
E
Employees
MD
Media
Management reports and inquiries

MIS Overview for BrassCo Enterprises This MIS overview data flow diagram shows the general flow of information within BrassCo. The database symbol and several entities are repeated to simplify the presentation of the data flow diagram. The diagonal line on the left end of the data storage symbols and the diagonal line in the corner of the entity symbols indicate that these symbols are repeated elsewhere in the data flow diagram.

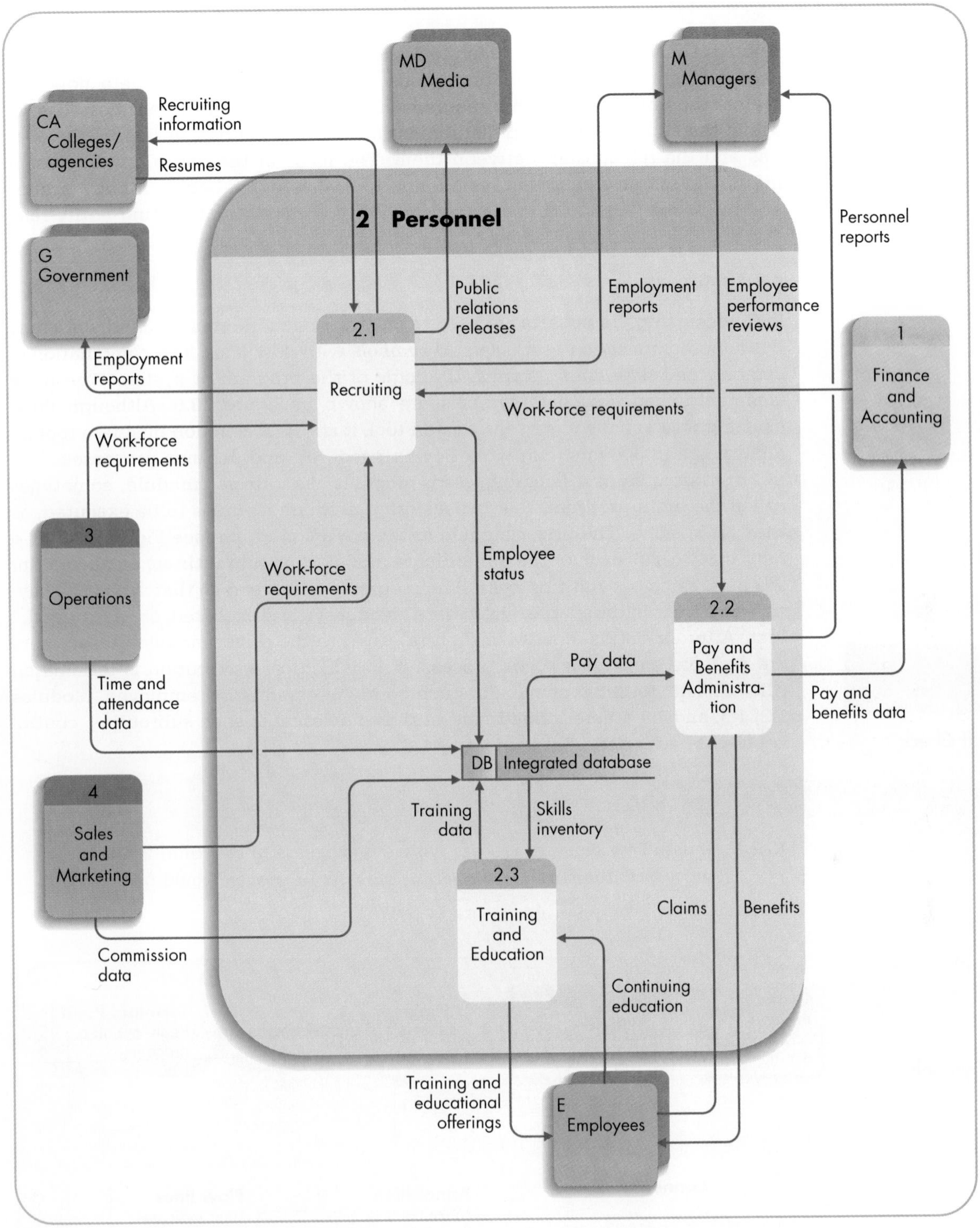

MD
Media

M
Managers

CA
Colleges/
agencies

Recruiting
information

Resumes

G
Government

2 Personnel

Public
relations
releases

Employment
reports

Employee
performance
reviews

Personnel
reports

2.1
Recruiting

Employment
reports

Work-force requirements

1
Finance
and
Accounting

Work-force
requirements

3
Operations

Work-force
requirements

Employee
status

2.2
Pay and
Benefits
Administra-
tion

Pay data

Pay and
benefits data

Time and
attendance
data

DB Integrated database

4
Sales
and
Marketing

Training
data

Skills
inventory

2.3
Training
and
Education

Claims

Benefits

Commission
data

Continuing
education

Training and
educational
offerings

E
Employees

BrassCo's Personnel Resource System This data flow diagram is the explosion of Process 2 (Personnel) of the MIS overview data flow diagram of Figure 13.4.

Entity Relationship Diagrams

Another similar business modeling tool, the **entity relationship diagram,** is widely used for defining the information needs of a business. Like the data flow diagrams, the entity relationship diagram involves identifying the entities. The focus of the entity relationship diagram is the *attributes* (a description) of the entities and the *relationship* between them. The focus of the data flow diagram is *information flow,* which may also define the relationship between both entities and processes. Also in contrast to data flow diagrams, the resulting entity relationship model is independent of any data storage or access method.

Flowcharting

In **flowcharting, flowcharts** are used to illustrate data, information, and work flow by the interconnection of *specialized symbols* with *flow lines.* The combination of symbols and flow lines portrays the logic of the program or system. The more commonly used flowchart symbols are shown in Figure 13.6. Although flowcharting was initially a program design tool, it is now a common business tool for analyzing and documenting work flow, procedures, and decision processes.

In structured programming, each program has a **driver module,** sometimes called the **main program,** that causes other program modules to be executed, as they are needed. The driver module in the payroll program (see Figure 13.7) is a **loop** that "calls" each of the subordinate modules, or **subroutines,** as needed for the processing of each employee. The program is designed so that when the payroll program is initiated, the "input data" module (1.1) is executed, or "performed," first. After execution, control is then returned to the driver module unless there are no more employees to be processed, in which case execution is terminated (the "Finish" terminal point). For each hourly or commission employee, Modules 1.2, 1.3, and 1.4 are performed, and at the completion of each subroutine, control is passed back to the driver module.

Self-Check

SECTION SELF-CHECK

13-2.1 If data flow diagram Process 3.4 were exploded to two third-level processes, the numerical labels of the new processes would be 3.4.1 and 3.4.2. (T/F)

Flowchart Symbols

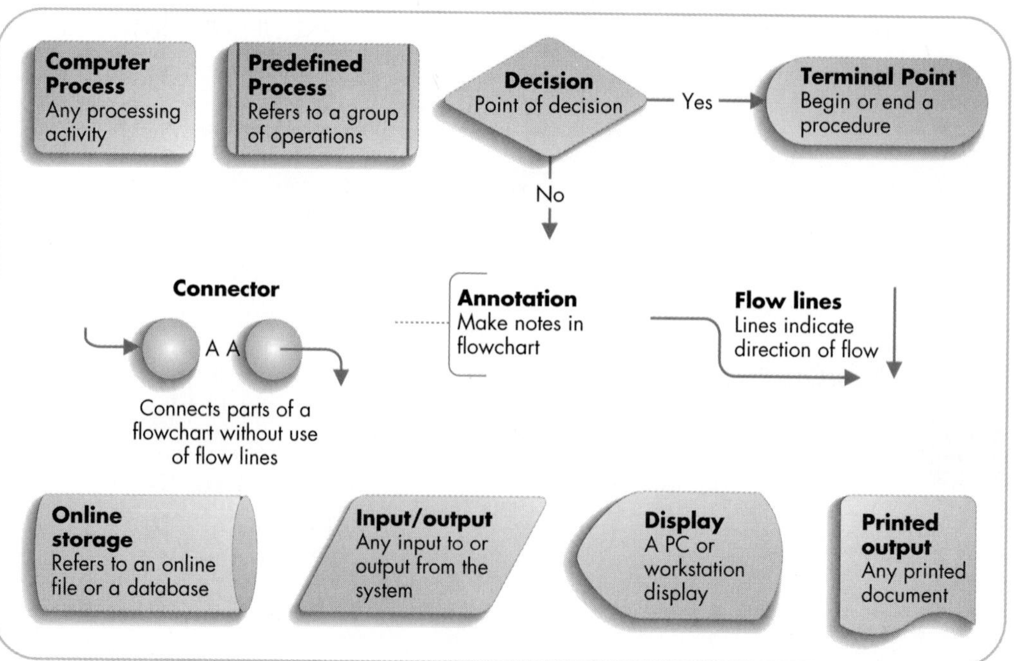

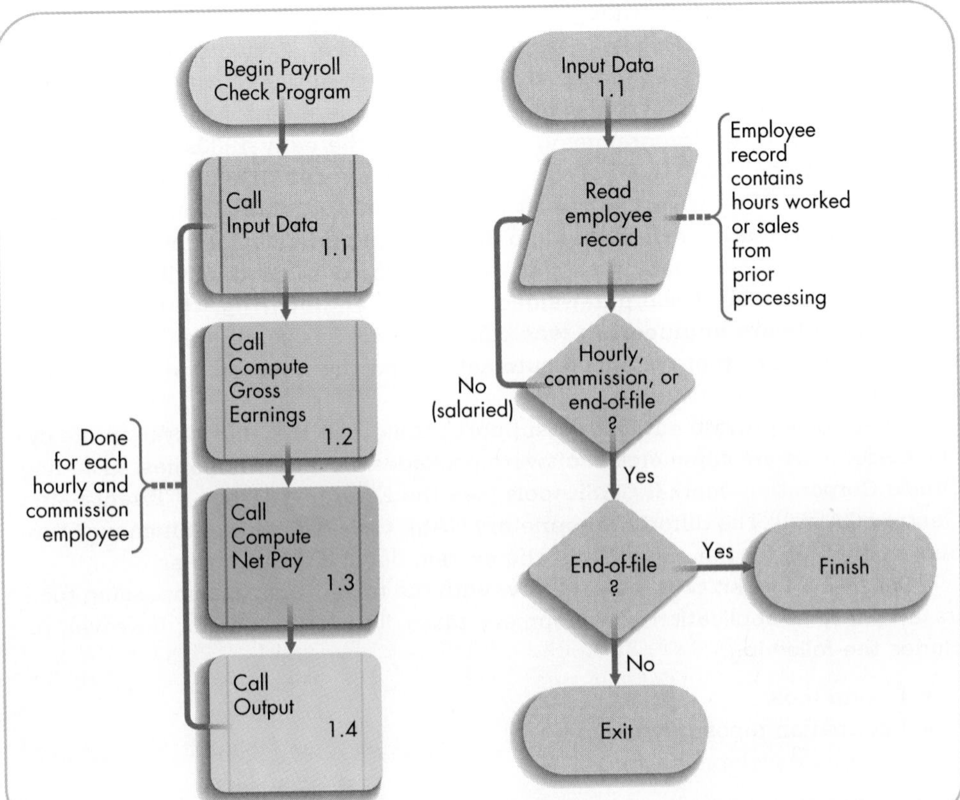

FIGURE 13.7

Program Flowchart The flowchart presents the logic of a payroll program to compute and print payroll checks for hourly and commission employees. The logic is designed so that a driver module calls subroutines as they are needed to process each employee. Only the "Input Data" subroutine is shown.

13-2.2 In structured programming, each program is designed with a driver module. (T/F)

13-2.3 The data flow diagram process symbol is the source or destination of data flow. (T/F)

13-2.4 Flowcharts can be used to illustrate both information and work flow. (T/F)

13-2.5 Which of the following is not a design technique: (a) flowcharting, (b) data flow diagrams, (c) RE charts, or (d) entity relationship diagrams?

13-2.6 What is the design philosophy called that enables complex design problems to be addressed in small, manageable modules: (a) planned design, (b) structured design, (c) ordered design, or (d) controlled design?

13-2.7 In a structured program, subordinate modules that are called as needed are called: (a) subroutines, (b) sub par routines, (c) program pieces, or (d) instruction slices?

13-2.8 Which of these is not one of the four symbols used in data flow diagrams: (a) entity, (b) process, (c) data storage, or (d) decision?

13.3 COMPUTER-AIDED SOFTWARE ENGINEERING: THE CASE TOOL KIT

The system development process is a cooperative effort of users and IT professionals. On one hand, IT professionals are familiar with the technology and how it can be applied to meet a business's information processing needs. On the other, users have in-depth familiarity with their respective functional areas (marketing, manufacturing, personnel, and so on) and the information processing needs of the organization. Over the past decade the methods and tools used to create information systems have changed dramatically. Newer methods, generally referred to as *CASE* (Computer-Aided Software Engineering), take full advantage of the technology to coordinate and automate the applications development process.

For years most people thought the best way to improve productivity in system development was to make it easier for programmers to create programs. *Very high-level programming languages* are an outgrowth of this quest for better programmer productivity. In essence, these languages were designed to let the computer do much of the programming. However, in the early 1980s people began asking, "Why can't the power of the computer be applied to analysis and design work as well?" Now we know that it can. Many of the time-consuming manual tasks, such as creating a database and documenting information flow, can be automated. This general family of software development productivity tools falls under the umbrella of **computer-aided software engineering,** or **CASE,** tools. The term **software engineering** was coined to emphasize an approach to software development that combines automation and the rigors of the engineering discipline.

CASE tools provide automated support throughout the entire system life cycle. CASE tools are commercial software packages. Several companies, including Oracle Corporation, market CASE tools (see the Emerging IT box, "Twenty-First Century CASE"). The different proprietary CASE tools use different nomenclature and techniques for the elements of the system development process.

The CASE tool kit continues to grow with the technology, encompassing tools for a variety of applications development tasks. The basic tool kit, however, includes the following:

- Design tools
- Information repository tools
- Program development tools

Each tool is discussed in the following sections. Note that there is some overlap in the functions of the various CASE tools.

Software engineers are developing software products to bridge the gap between design and executable program code. In a two-step process, these tool kits enable project teams to use automated software packages to help them complete the logic design (information flow, input/output) and the database organization; then the CASE software translates the logical design into the physical implementation of the system (executable program code or the software). Some CASE-developed applications emerge ready to implement with little or no actual programming required. CASE tools, however, are seldom that efficient. An operational information system may require anywhere from a little to a considerable amount of **custom programming** (the writing of original programs) to achieve full implementation.

Design Tools

Prior to the introduction of CASE technologies, the tool kit for the systems analyst and programmer consisted of flowcharting and data flow diagram templates, lettering templates, rulers, scissors, glue, pencils, pens, and plenty of erasers and "whiteout." The CASE *design tools* provide an automated alternative. They help analysts and programmers prepare schematics that graphically depict the logic of a system or program (for example, data flow diagrams, entity relationship diagrams, structure charts). These automated design tools are to a systems analyst as word processing software is to a writer.

Automated design tools enable an analyst or programmer to select and position symbols, such as the data flow diagram process and entity symbols, and to connect these symbols with flow lines. Both symbols and flow lines can be labeled. Because all the design techniques supported by CASE products are structured design techniques, systems ultimately are depicted in several levels of generality.

CASE design tools also help designers prepare the user interface and generate screen and report layouts. The *user interface* capability enables the project team to design and create the system's user interface. The *screen generator* capability provides systems analysts with the capability of generating a mockup, or layout, of a screen while in direct consultation with the user. The **layout** is a detailed output and/or input specification that graphically illustrates exactly where information should be placed, or entered, on a screen or on a printer output. The *report generator* permits the calculation of summary totals by criteria and overall, the creation of graphs and charts, and the editing of output. For example, a report generator can produce a sales report that includes summary totals for each sales region and for overall, plus a bar graph of the information.

Information Repository Tools

The **information repository** is a central computer-based storage facility for all design information. For example, in an information repository, each field in a database is cross-referenced to all other components in the system. That is, the field *customer number* would be cross-referenced to every screen, report, graph, record/file, database, program, or any other design element in which it occurred. Cross-references are also made to processes in data flow diagrams and entity relationship diagrams. Once the company has had the information repository in place for a while, cross-references can be extended between information systems. The information repository permits all system documentation to be packaged electronically. That is, any part of the system—layouts, database design, notes, project schedules, and so on—can be recalled and displayed for review or modification. In effect, the information repository is the "database" for the system development project.

Program Development Tools

Program development tools focus on the programming aspect of the system development effort. There are a variety of CASE program development tools, but the **application generators** make the biggest contribution to productivity. Instead of actually coding programs, programmers use application generators in conjunction with the design specifications and the structure of a database to generate software for a particular application. Another program development tool helps the project team with the generation of text data, one of the more laborious tasks associated with applications development.

SECTION SELF-CHECK

Self Check

13-3.1 Many of the manual tasks in system development, such as creating a database and documenting information flow, can be automated. (T/F)

13-3.2 The application generator is one of the CASE program development tools. (T/F)

13-3.3 Custom programming involves the writing of original programs. (T/F)

13-3.4 Which CASE tool is a central computer-based storage facility for all design information: (a) design tool, (b) information repository tool, (c) program development tool, or (d) prototype tool?

13-3.5 Which CASE tool provides systems analysts with the capability of generating a mockup of a screen: (a) design tool, (b) information repository tool, (c) program development tool, or (d) prototype tool?

13-3.6 A detailed output and/or input specification is: (a) a layout, (b) an I/O outline, (c) a screen image spec, or (d) a GUI?

13.4 PROTOTYPING: CREATING A MODEL OF THE TARGET SYSTEM

Serendipitous Surfing: Business

The CASE tool kit enables the system development project team to work with users to develop a **prototype system,** a model of a full-scale system. This approach to applications development is called **prototyping.** In effect, a prototype system permits users a "sneak" preview of the completed system. A typical prototype system does the following:

- Handles the main transaction-oriented procedures
- Produces common reports
- Permits typical inquiries to the database

Throughout the twentieth century, manufacturers have built prototypes of everything from toasters to airplanes. Automobile manufacturers routinely build prototypes according to design specifications. Scaled-down clay models are made to evaluate aesthetics and aerodynamics. Ultimately, a full-size, fully functional prototype is created that enables the driver and passengers to test all aspects of the car's functionality. If engineers see possibilities for improvement, the prototypes are modified and retested until they meet or exceed all specifications. Today, building *scalable* prototype systems is standard procedure in software development. A **scalable system** is one whose design can handle any size database or any number of users. Scalable systems are desirable because they can be implemented at one level, then expanded to keep up with corporate growth by simply adding more hardware (server, PCs, and so on).

The Emergence of Prototyping

Most managers have a *good idea* of what they want in an information system, but they do not know *exactly* what they want. This is a problem when it comes to developing information systems. Systems analysts and programmers need precise specifications to give the users what they want in an information system. Prior to the emergence of automated system development tools, users were asked to commit themselves to **system specifications** long before they felt comfortable with the specifications. These **specs** include everything from the functionality of the system to the format of the system's output screens and reports. In this traditional approach, the project team would use feedback from user interviews to formulate **functional specifications** for system input, processing, and output requirements (information needs). The functional specifications describe the logic of the system (input/output, work, and information flow) from the *user's perspective.*

Realistically, though, users cannot know exactly what they want, nor can they recognize the potential of a system, until they have had an opportunity to work with it. In the traditional approach to system development, user familiarity comes

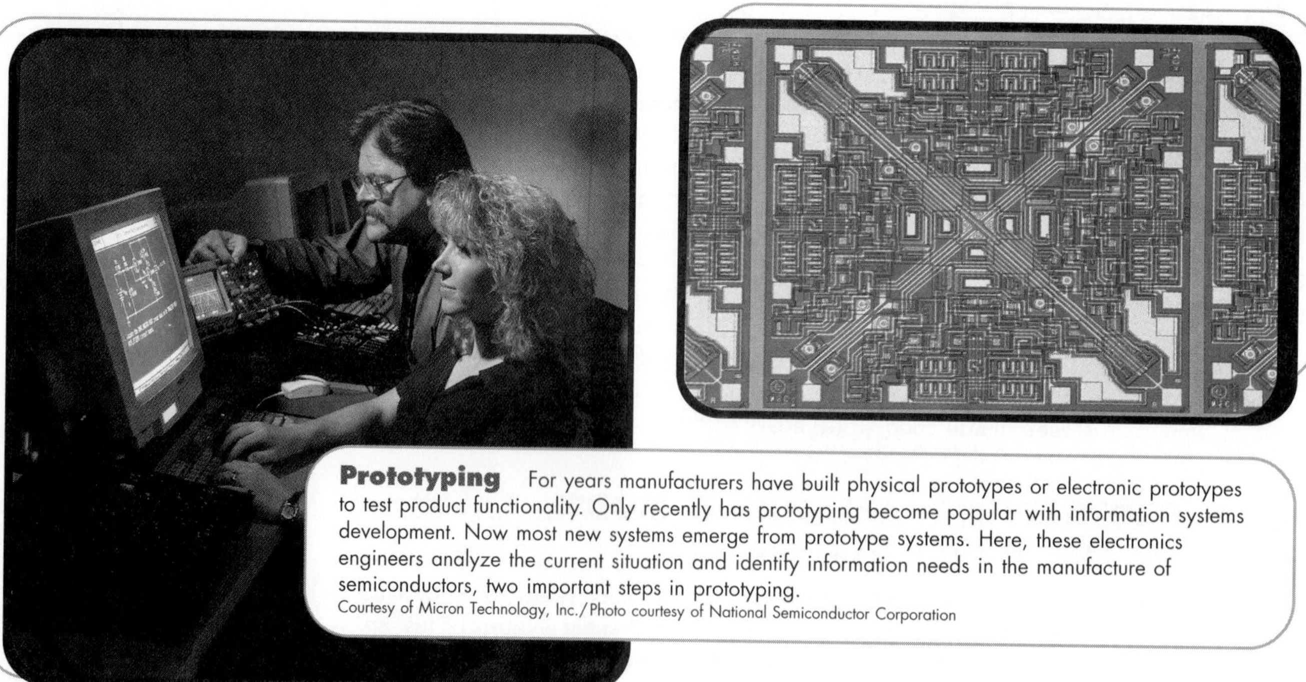

Prototyping For years manufacturers have built physical prototypes or electronic prototypes to test product functionality. Only recently has prototyping become popular with information systems development. Now most new systems emerge from prototype systems. Here, these electronics engineers analyze the current situation and identify information needs in the manufacture of semiconductors, two important steps in prototyping.
Courtesy of Micron Technology, Inc./Photo courtesy of National Semiconductor Corporation

after the fact and too late for quick fixes and inexpensive modifications. After system implementation, even small changes to an information system can be time-consuming and expensive.

Today, project team members are able to use CASE tools to create prototype systems that, to the user at a terminal or PC, appear and act very much like the finished product.

The Prototype System

The three objectives of prototyping are

- To analyze the current situation
- To identify information needs
- To develop a model of the proposed system, often called the **target system**

The prototype system gives users an actual opportunity to work with the functional aspect of the proposed system long before the system is implemented. Once users gain hands-on familiarity with the prototype system, they can relate more precise information processing needs to the project team.

A prototype system can be anything from a nonfunctional demonstration of the input/output of a proposed information system to a full-scale operational system. These models are tested and refined until the users are confident that what they see is what they want. In some cases, the prototype is a scalable system that can be expanded to become a fully operational information system. However, in most cases, the prototype system provides a vehicle for compiling the design specifications.

Rapid Application Development

Rapid application development (RAD) results in information systems of varying degrees of sophistication. RAD has emerged to be a generic reference to using software tools (CASE) to design, develop, and implement information systems. At the low end, there's the "quick and dirty" RAD prototype, which gives users an opportunity to experiment with the look and feel of a system. This resulting system is just for show and doesn't permit interaction with a database. At this level, RAD focuses on three aspects of the design: the user interface, data entry displays, and system outputs.

At the other end of the RAD spectrum is the fully functional prototype system. This type of prototype system lets users try out the features of the target system during interactive practice sessions. The prototype is modified and refined based on user feedback. Some prototype systems are scalable systems and can be implemented directly at the enterprise level when complete. For example, Wal-Mart information systems are scalable such that all they do is add more computing capacity as stores are opened. Some fully functional systems are for design only and provide specifications for the system development process.

The Prototyping Process

Both the prototyping and the traditional approaches to system development depend on the efforts of a project team. The composition of the project team is essentially the same for both approaches. The team consists of *systems analysts, programmers,* perhaps the *database administrator,* users who will eventually use the system, and perhaps one or more managers. All work together to develop the system design specifications. The database administrator assists the team in designing and creating the database.

The development of an information system via prototyping is done in four phases (see Figure 13.8).

- Phase I—Define System Specifications
- Phase II—Create Prototype System
- Phase III—Refine Prototype System
- Phase IV—Develop Operational System

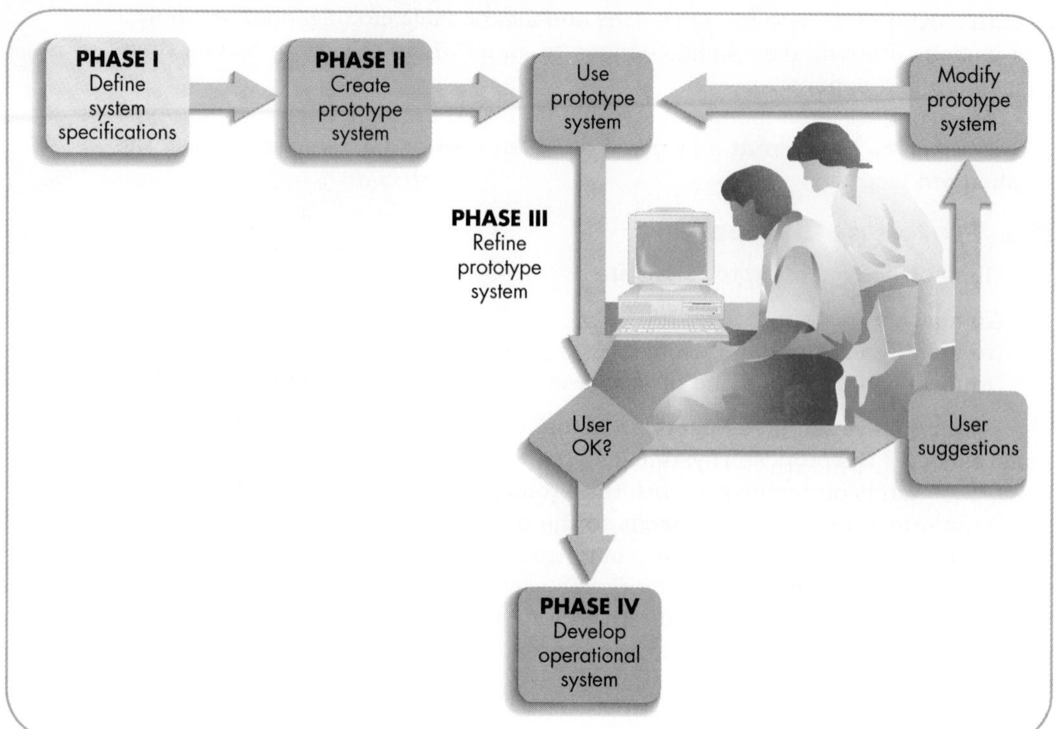

13.8 The Four Phases of the Prototyping Process

Phase I—Define System Specifications

In the traditional approach to system development, system specifications are "frozen" early in the project. That means that no more changes can be made to the specs. In prototyping, the specs do not need to be frozen because the prototype system is easily modified to meet changing needs. It is during this phase (see Figure 13.8) that the current system is analyzed (system analysis) and the target system is designed (system design). What results is the specifications (database structure, input/output layouts, and so on) needed to develop the prototype system. Typically these specifications are determined during interactive sessions with users. During the sessions, the team will define system specifications for graphical user interfaces, menus, reports, various input/output screens, and the database.

System Analysis: Understanding the System System analysis produces the following results.

- *Existing system review.* Before designing a new or enhanced information system, the members of the project team must have a good grasp of the existing work and information flow, be it manual or computer-based. Here the team documents the work and information flow of the system by reducing it to its basic components—input, processing, and output. The use of CASE technologies usually encourages a detailed examination of business processes, often resulting in reengineering of existing processes to achieve greater effectiveness and efficiency.
- *System objectives.* Once the existing system is documented, the project team can begin to identify the obvious and not-so-obvious problem areas (for example, procedural bottlenecks, duplication of effort, and so on). This knowledge is formalized as system objectives.
- *Design constraints.* The target system will be developed subject to specific constraints. The purpose of this activity is to detail, at the onset of the system development process, any costs, hardware, schedule, procedural, software, database, and operating constraints that may limit the definition and design of the target system.

- *Requirements definition.* In this activity the project team completes a needs analysis that results in a definition of the information and information processing requirements for the target system.

System Design: Putting It All Together During system design, the project team takes information from the system analysis and develops a system design for the target system. The design of an information system is more of a challenge to the human intellect than it is a procedural challenge. Just as an author begins with a blank page and an idea, the members of the project team begin with empty RAM and the information requirements definitions. From here they must create what sometimes can be a very complex information system. The number of ways in which a particular information system can be designed is limited only by the imaginations of the project team members.

The system design process involves continuous communication between members of the project team and all affected users. After evaluating several alternative approaches, the project team translates the system specifications into a system design. The documentation completed in the system design stage might include the following:

- A graphic illustration that depicts the fundamental operation of the target system (for example, using data flow diagrams)
- A written explanation of the graphic illustration
- Descriptions of the outputs to be produced by the system, including display screens and hard-copy reports and documents

Eventually the system design documentation depicts the relationship between *all processing activities* and the *input/output associated with them.*

The database must be defined during system design, as well. The database is the common denominator of any system. It contains the raw material (data) necessary to produce the output (information). In manufacturing, for example, you decide what you are going to make, then you order the raw material. In the process of developing an information system, you decide what your output requirements are, and then you determine which data are needed to produce the output. In a sense, output requirements can be thought of as input to database design.

The system design is the cornerstone of the system development process. It is here that the relationships between the various components of the system are defined. The system specifications are transformed with the project team's imagination and skill into an information system. The system design is the *blueprint* for all project team activities that follow.

Phase II—Create Prototype System

To create a prototype system, project team members rough out the logic of the system and how the elements fit together, and then work with the user to define the I/O interfaces (the system interaction with the user). The next challenge is to translate the system design and specifications into instructions that can be interpreted and executed by the computer. This, of course, involves software development.

During this phase (see Figure 13.8), the creation of software becomes the dominant activity. Project team members use CASE tools to create the screen images (menus, reports, inquiries, and so on), to create a database, and to generate much of the programming code (software). Typically programmers will need to write custom programs to complement automatically generated programs. Programming is discussed later in the chapter. The system specifications resulting from system analysis and design are all that is necessary for programmers to write, or *code,* the necessary programs. The custom programming task is made easier with the well-documented specifications from the design stage. The subsequent programs result in a physical representation of a target system.

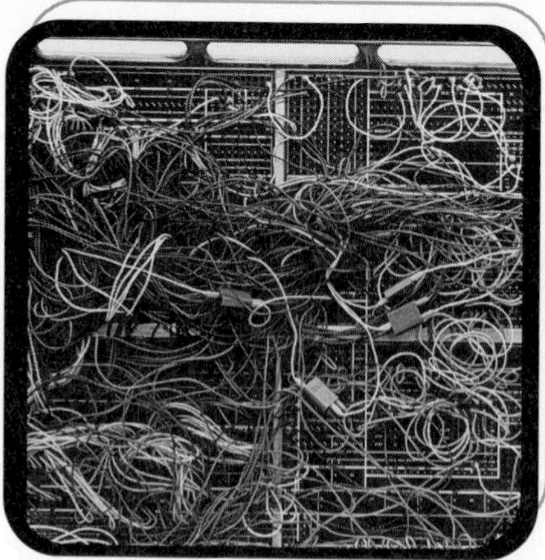

Programming Then and Now If you ever feel intimidated by the idea of programming a computer, just remember how much easier it is today than in the computer's early days. Prior to the invention of the electronic digital computer, companies relied on electromechanical accounting machines (EAM) for automated data processing. The act of programming these devices was referred to as "wiring the program." Early programmers literally created the circuitry for the devices by inserting wires into interchangeable removable control panels (top left).

The quantum leap in technology brought about by the invention of the ENIAC (1946), the first large-scale fully operational electronic digital computer, was offset by the cumbersome method of programming the machine. For each program to be run, switches had to be set and wires inserted into a series of panels (top right).

Today CASE tools are able to generate much of the software for an information system. For custom programming, programmers choose the best programming language for the job, then use high-level instructions to interactively create and debug the program. Amsterdam's Schiphol Airport in the Netherlands uses software designed to help meet the growing demands of air traffic control by using a modern-day airport approach and departure control system called Standard Terminal Automation Replacement System (STARS).

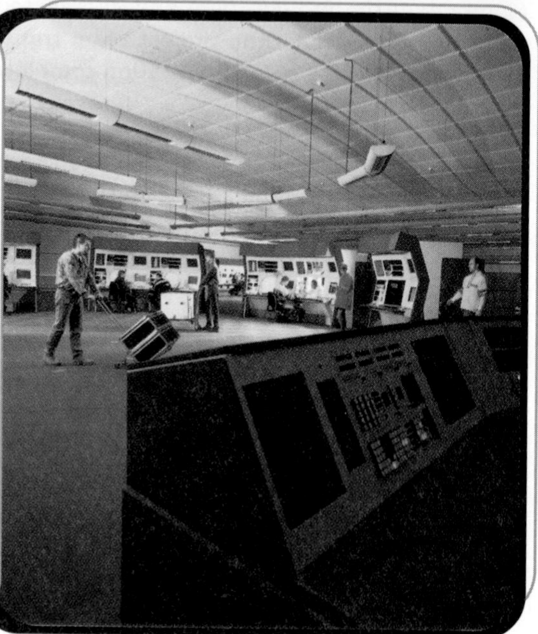

Phase III—Refine Prototype System

In this phase (see Figure 13.8), users actually sit down at a terminal or PC and evaluate portions and, eventually, all of the prototype system. Invariably, users have suggestions for improving the user interfaces and/or the format of the I/O. And, without fail, their examination reveals new needs for information. In effect, the original prototype system is the beginning. From here, the system is expanded (if needed) and refined to meet the users' total information needs. The use-and-modify cycle depicted in Figure 13.8 is repeated until users are satisfied with the prototype system.

Phase IV—Develop Operational System

At this point in the prototyping process (see Figure 13.8), users have a system that looks and feels like what they want. If the system is other than a fully functional scalable prototype, the system must be enhanced or another system, based on the prototype system, must be developed. In the latter case, the prototype system is discarded once the specs have been determined. From these specs, the software for an operational information system capable of handling the required volume of work is developed.

Fully functional scalable prototypes are working models of the target information system that can be scaled to meet the information processing needs of the organization. Scalable systems are implemented directly.

Self Check

13-4.1 A fully functional prototype system is essentially a complete information system, but without the capability to access a database. (T/F)

13-4.2 Modern prototyping tools enable the development of a scalable system that can be used by any number of users. (T/F)

13-4.3 A needs analysis results in a definition of the information and information processing requirements for the target system. (T/F)

13-4.4 A model of a full-scale information system is: (a) an archetype, (b) a prototype, (c) a system instance, or (d) a blueprint?

13-4.5 Which results are realized during the system design: (a) database design, (b) existing system review, (c) design constraints, or (d) final system documentation?

13-4.6 Functional specifications include requirements for system input, output, and: (a) timing, (b) processing, (c) benefits, or (d) feedback?

13-4.7 The target system's specifications are done in which of the four phases of prototyping: (a) Phase I, (b) Phase II, (c) Phase III, or (d) Phase IV?

13-4.8 Which of these includes all processing activities and the input/output associated with them for a target information system: (a) driver module flowchart, (b) blueprint, (c) system design documentation, or (d) system review results?

13-4.9 The functional specifications describe the logic of a target system from whose perspective: (a) systems analyst, (b) CEO, (c) programmer, or (d) user?

13.5 SYSTEM CONVERSION AND IMPLEMENTATION: MAKING THE TRANSITION

Once an information system has been developed and approved by those who will use it, it must be implemented within the organization.

Systems and Acceptance Testing

The first step of the system conversion and implementation process is systems testing. This testing encompasses everything that makes up the information system—the hardware, the software, the end users, the procedures (for example, online help documents), and the data. If needed, the interfaces between the system and other systems are tested as well.

During Phase II, Create Prototype System, programs are generated or written according to system specifications and are individually tested. Although the programs that make up the software for the system have undergone **unit testing** (individual testing) and have been debugged, there is no guarantee that the programs will work together as a system. To ensure that the software can be combined into an operational information system, the project team performs integrated **systems testing.**

To conduct the system test, the project team compiles and thoroughly tests the system with *test data.* In this first stage, tests are run for each subsystem (one of the functional aspects of the system) or cycle (weekly or monthly activities). The test data are compiled so all program and system options and all error and validation routines are tested. The tests are repeated and modifications are made until all subsystems or cycles function properly. At this point the entire system is tested as a unit. Testing and modifications continue until the components of the system work as they should and all input/output is validated.

The second stage of systems testing is done with *live data* by several of the people who will eventually use the system. Live data have already been processed through the existing system. Testing with live data provides an extra level of assurance that the system will work properly when implemented.

The system is now subjected to the scrutiny of the user managers whose departments will ultimately work with the system. The managers accept the system as ready for implementation or they send it back for further modification and testing.

Approaches to System Conversion

Once systems testing is complete, the project team can begin to integrate people, software, hardware, procedures, and data into an operational information system. This normally involves a conversion from the existing system to the new one. An organization's approach to system conversion depends on its *willingness to accept risk* and the *amount of time available* for the conversion. Four common approaches are parallel conversion, direct conversion, phased conversion, and pilot conversion. These approaches are illustrated in Figure 13.9.

Parallel Conversion

In **parallel conversion,** the existing system and the new system operate simultaneously, or in parallel, until the project team is confident the new system is working properly. Parallel conversion has two important advantages. First, the existing system serves as a backup if the new system fails to operate as expected. Second, the results of the new system can be compared to the results of the existing system.

There is less risk with this strategy because the present system provides backup. However, it doubles the workload of personnel and hardware resources during the conversion. Parallel conversion usually takes one month or a major system cycle. For a public utility company, this might be one complete billing cycle, which is usually a month.

Direct Conversion

As companies improve their systems testing procedures, they begin to gain confidence in their ability to implement a working system. Some companies forego parallel conversion in favor of a **direct conversion,** where the old system is terminated when the new system goes online. Direct conversion involves a greater risk because there is no backup in case the system fails.

Companies select this "cold-turkey" approach when there is no existing system or when the existing system is substantially different. For example, all online hotel reservations systems are implemented cold turkey.

Phased Conversion

In **phased conversion,** an information system is implemented one module at a time by either parallel or direct conversion. For example, in a point-of-sale system, the first phase might be to convert the sales-accounting module. The sec-

Common Approaches to System Conversion

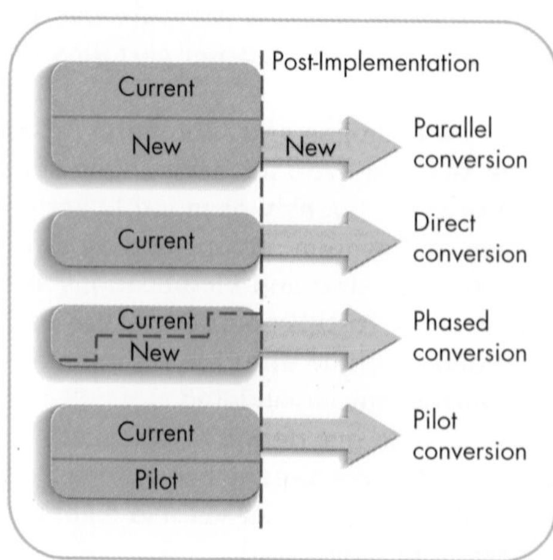

IT Ethics

COLLECTING AND DISTRIBUTING PERSONAL INFORMATION

Online information services and systems not only provide information, they collect information—sometimes from you. Anytime you interact with a corporate server online via the Internet or through any other online source, it's possible that it may be compiling data on you, including your social security number, credit-card number, demographic information, and interest areas. This information is sometimes made available to others. Sometimes, it's even published in print or placed on the Web.

Discussion: Would you be for or against legislation that would require all telecommunications companies, including online information services and companies with a presence on the Web, to tell people what information is being collected on them and how it's being used?

ond phase could involve the inventory-management module. The third might be the credit-check module.

Phased conversion has the advantage of spreading the demand for resources to avoid an intense demand. The disadvantages are that the conversion takes longer and an interface must be developed between the existing system and the new one.

Pilot Conversion

In **pilot conversion,** the new system is implemented by parallel, direct, or phased conversion as a pilot system in only one of the areas for which it is targeted. Suppose a company wants to implement a manufacturing resources planning system in its eight plants. One plant would be selected as a pilot, and the new information system would be implemented there first.

The advantage of pilot conversion is that the inevitable bugs in a system can be removed before the system is implemented at the other locations. The disadvantage is that the implementation time for the total system takes longer than if the entire system were implemented at one time.

The System Becomes Operational

Once the conversion has been completed, the information system enters the production stage of the system life cycle (see Figure 13.1). During the production stage the system becomes operational and is turned over to the users. Once an information system is implemented and goes online, the emphasis switches from *development* to *operations.* In a payroll system, supervisors begin to enter hours worked on their PCs or terminals, and the computer center produces and issues payroll checks. Once operational, an information system becomes a cooperative effort between users and IT professionals.

Just as a new automobile will need some screws tightened after a few hundred miles, an information system will need some fine-tuning just after implementation. Thereafter, and throughout the production stage of the system life cycle, the system will be modified many times. An information system is dynamic and must be responsive to the changing needs of the company and those who use it. The process of modifying an information system to meet changing needs is known as **system maintenance.**

Prior to the emergence of CASE technology, making modifications to operational systems were time-consuming and expensive. CASE tools, however, permit flexibility in system design. For example, when fields are added to the database or screen formats are modified, affected programs are automatically updated to reflect the changes.

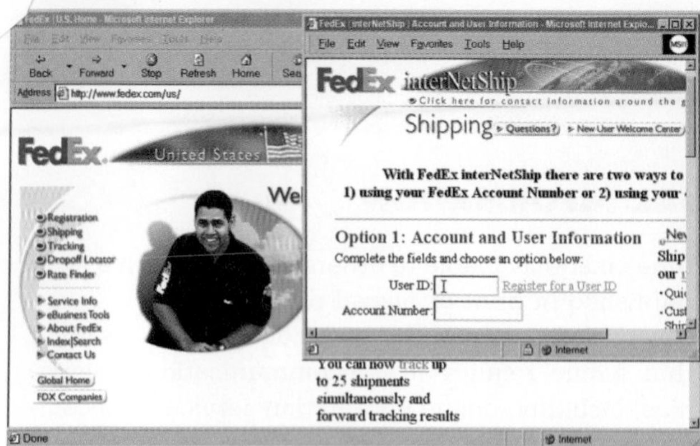

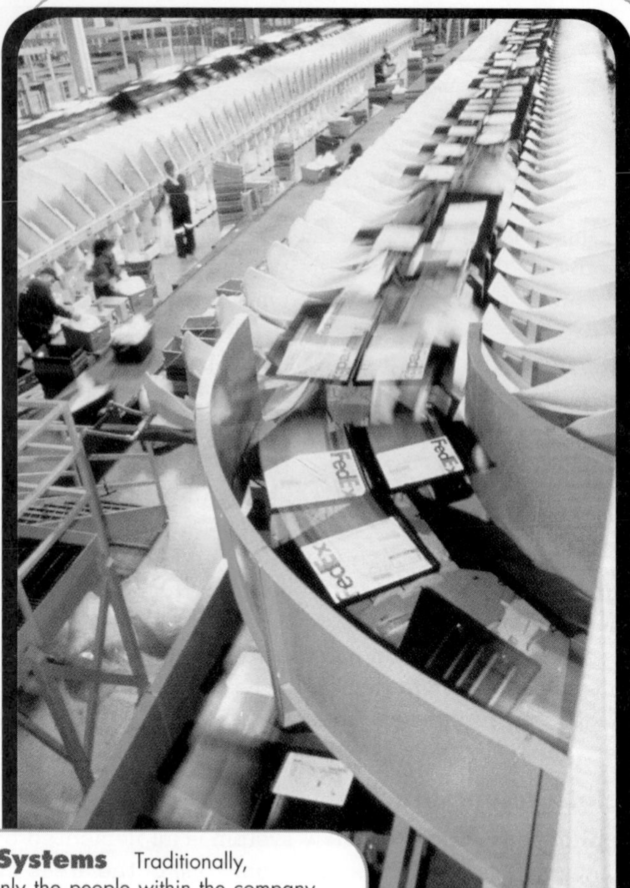

FedEx Information Systems Traditionally, information systems involved only the people within the company they service. However, more and more companies are expanding the reach of their information systems to include customers as well. Federal Express Corp. (FedEx) is actively developing new information systems for a new era of electronic commerce and Internet accessibility. FedEx customers in more than 200 countries can access a FedEx home page that displays shipping, tracking, and customer service options available in the country where the customer is located.

An information system cannot live forever. The accumulation of modifications and enhancements eventually will make any information system cumbersome and inefficient. Minor modifications are known as **patches.** Depending on the number of patches and enhancements, an information system will remain operational—that is, be in the production stage of the system life cycle (see Figure 13.1)—from four to seven years.

Computers at Work

Toward the end of the useful life of an information system, it is more trouble to continue patching the system than it is to redesign the system completely. The end of the production stage signals the death stage of the system life cycle (see Figure 13.1). A new system is then "born" of need, and the system development process is repeated.

SECTION SELF-CHECK

Self-Check

13-5.1 Greater risk is associated with direct conversion than with phased conversion. (T/F)

13-5.2 Systems testing is always completed prior to unit testing. (T/F)

13-5.3 Companies may select the direct conversion approach when there is no existing system. (T/F)

13-5.4 In pilot conversion, the new system always is implemented by parallel conversion. (T/F)

13-5.5 Individual program testing is known as: (a) unit testing, (b) module testing, (c) hierarchical testing, or (d) bullet testing?

13-5.6 In which approach to system conversion do both the full existing system and the full new system operate simultaneously: (a) direct, (b) parallel, (c) pilot, or (d) phased?

13-5.7 Once an information system is implemented, the emphasis is switched from development to: (a) testing, (b) operations, (c) training, or (d) programming?

13.6 PROGRAMMING: MAKING IT HAPPEN

Once the system has been designed, the software must be created before the system can go online. Some, and sometimes all, of the programs are created as a by-product of the CASE prototyping process. However, most systems require considerable amounts of custom programming by programmers, people who write programs.

Programs are made up of instructions that are logically sequenced and assembled through the act of programming. Programmers use a variety of **programming languages,** such as C++, Visual BASIC, and Java, to communicate instructions to the computer. Twenty years ago, virtually all programmers were computer specialists. Today, office managers, management consultants, engineers, politicians, and people in all walks of life write programs to meet business and domestic needs. And, some people do it for fun. Unless you plan on becoming a computer professional, it is unlikely that you will write programs in support of an enterprise-wide information system. You may, however, write programs to perform many personal tasks, such as preparing graphs from spreadsheet data and sequencing displays for multimedia presentations. As you develop expertise and confidence you may tackle more challenging programming tasks.

Programming

Many languages have emerged over thousands of years of spoken communication. Although computers have existed for only a short while, there are already as many programming languages as there are spoken languages. In this section, we will sort out these languages and explain what they mean to you, but first, let's put software into perspective.

Software in Perspective

Suppose you are sick in bed and you ask a friend to get you a glass of ice water. Your friend then instinctively goes to the kitchen, opens the cabinet door and selects a glass, opens the refrigerator, gets some ice, turns on the tap, fills the glass with water, returns to your bedside, and hands you the water. Now imagine making the same request to a computer. You would have to tell the computer not only where to get the water but also how to get there, which end of the glass to fill, when to shut off the water, and much, much, more. Now you know why software has to have so many instructions!

We use programming languages to write programs. A single program addresses a particular problem—to compute grades, to monitor a patient's heart rate, and so on. In effect, when you write a program, you are solving a *problem,* which requires you to use your powers of *logic* to develop a procedure for solving the problem. Creating a program is like constructing a building. Much of the brainwork involved in the construction goes into the blueprint. The location, appearance, and function of a building are determined long before the first brick is laid. With programming, the design of a program, or its *programming logic* (the blueprint), is completed before the program is written.

Each programming language has an instruction set with a variety of instructions. For example, input/output instructions direct the computer to "read from" or "write to" a peripheral device. Computation instructions direct the computer to perform arithmetic operations. Control instructions can alter the sequence of

Emerging IT

TWENTY-FIRST CENTURY CASE

During the last few years, the manner in which we develop information systems has undergone radical change. This change can be attributed to two important technological events.

- *Transition to client/server systems.* We are in transition from a traditional environment in which enterprise-wide information systems were developed to run on mainframe-based networks. For the most part, users interacted with these systems via character-oriented terminals. The trend in development is toward client/server systems where client computers (usually PCs and workstations) work together with one or more server computers to process data and produce information. Also, momentum is growing to create Internet and intranet-based systems. These client/server systems are called *Web applications.* GUI-based client/server systems are more sophisticated and require software for both client computers and server computers.
- *Emergence of CASE tools.* The emergence of computer-aided software engineering (CASE) tools has made it possible to automate much of the coordination and work associated with system development. The use of CASE tools can result in higher-quality information systems, reduced cost and time to create information systems, and the elimination of much of the laborious work associated with system development.

To talk about system development in other than general terms, you must do so within the context of a particular set of proprietary CASE tools. CASE tools are created as entrepreneurial ventures; therefore, each has its own methods, procedures, capabilities, and terminology. This Emerging IT box takes an overview look at several of Oracle Corporation's CASE tools. Oracle Corporation is an established leader in CASE technology. It offers a complete suite of CASE tools that can be used to develop client/server and Web applications. It also offers tools that enable system users to obtain critical information from the corporate database. The example screen shots in this box are taken from Oracle's Designer, Developer, and Discoverer.

Oracle's tightly integrated CASE tools have a shared repository in which technology-independent definitions of applications and business logic are stored. The automated repository makes up-to-date documentation, from entity relationship diagrams to screen layouts, readily available to those working on the project. This shared multiuser repository is the key to enabling the creation of enterprise-scale applications where large numbers of people are involved.

Oracle's application development software offers organizations tremendous flexibility in implementation; that is, a system can be simultaneously developed for implementation on several platforms. Once the design is complete, the application can be generated for an enterprise client/server environment or the Web.

Designer

Designer is an integrated set of system modeling tools that empowers systems analysts, users, and others involved in the application development process to work together to create a formal design for an application. Designer's information and function modeling diagrammers are used to construct models that capture business and user needs. These needs are portrayed as the logical and physical structures required in business systems. The modeling done with Designer results in the automatic

The Designer Process Modeler

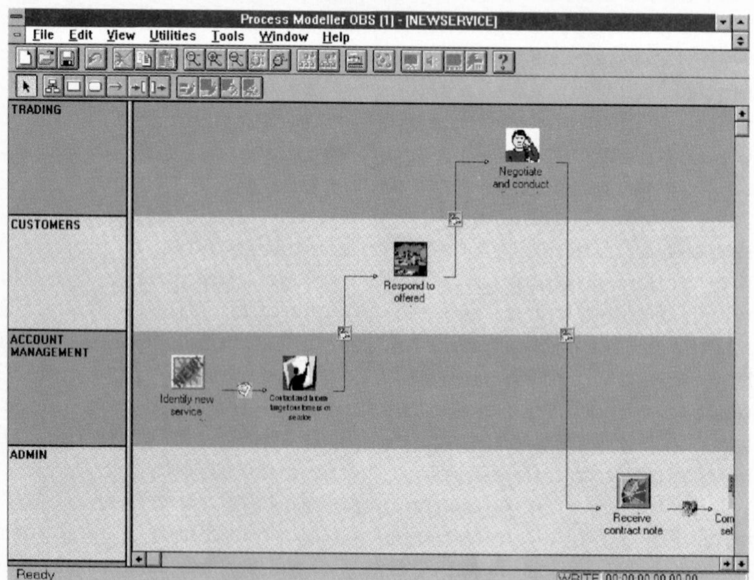

creation of the graphical user interfaces, database access, server logic, and application logic needed for the development stage. This design tool makes extensive use of *templates* (existing design elements that can be used in the target system) and *wizards* (dialog boxes that lead you through the preparation of a particular design element).

Designer's drag-and-drop process modeling capabilities (see example) give designers a better understanding of interorganizational dependencies and process-cycle durations. Proposed and existing multilevel organization units can be viewed in an easily understood form. During the design and development stages, the repository tool promotes a shared vision of the project among team members.

Designer enables the online creation of entity relationship diagrams (see example) to capture the structure and interrelationships of all entities associated with the system. WYSIWYG (what you see is what you get) editors are used by designers to better visualize and create the system interfaces.

Developer

Developer incorporates an integrated set of "builders" for creating forms (see example), reports, charts, queries, databases, and procedures. Wizards (see example) help developers build applications. These components generate the software for applications from Designer specifications and database definitions, all without writing a single line of program code. The features of Developer let developers create scalable systems to accommodate from 5 to 5000 users. The resultant system can be anything from a simple decision support system for a couple of managers to a complex client/server enterprise-wide information system.

(continues on next page)

The Designer Entity Relationship Diagrammer

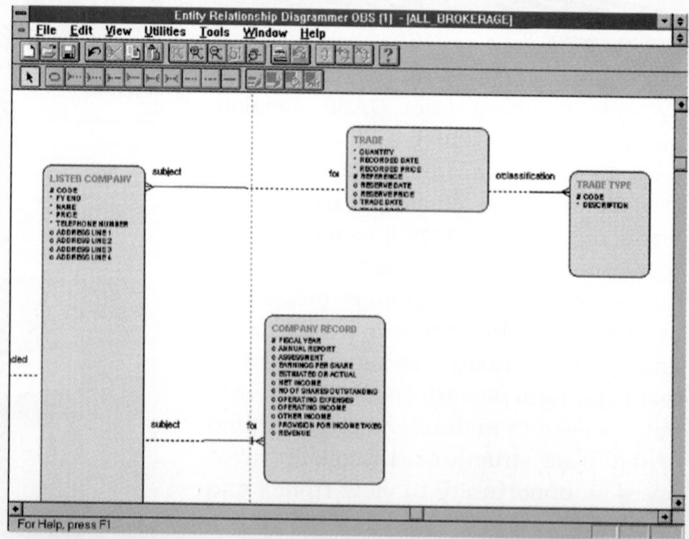

Building a Form for an Employee Directory

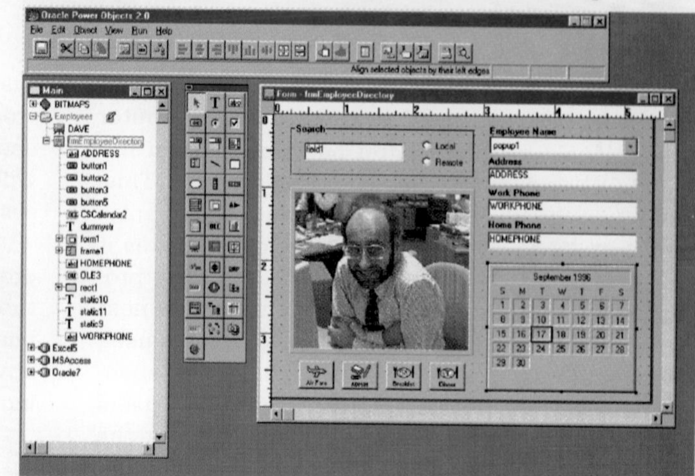

A Layout Wizard

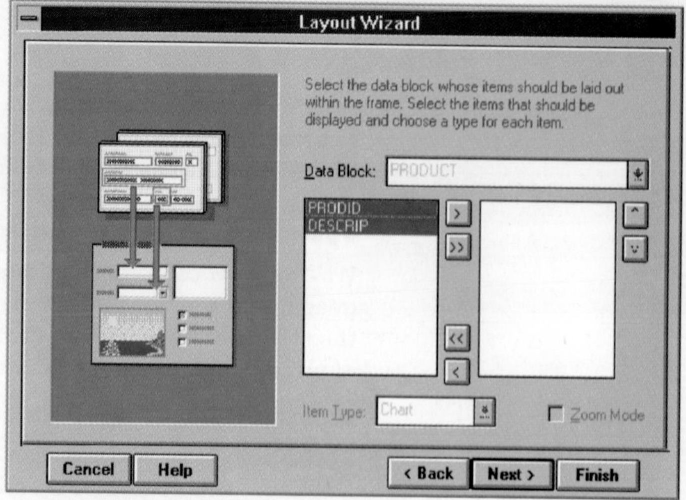

Emerging IT *continued*

Discoverer

Discoverer works with the information systems resulting from CASE development to permit intuitive ad hoc query, reporting, exploration, and Web publishing. Discoverer enables business users at all levels of the organization to gain access to information from databases, data warehouses, or online transaction processing systems. Oracle Discoverer empowers end users to create queries and reports, and to perform powerful exploration without the need to understand programming or database structures. Discoverer gives users an opportunity to view trends and problems by displaying data as graphs and charts (see example).

A Business Chart

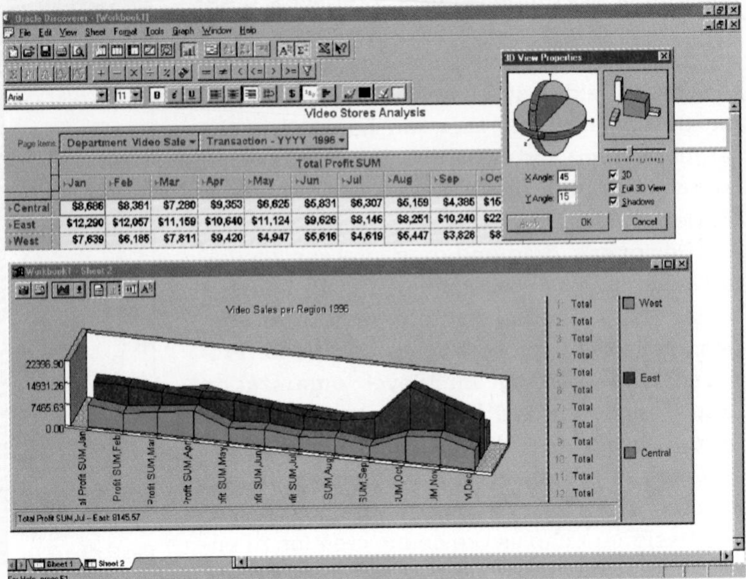

The Future of CASE

The creation of an information system is a cooperative effort between those who use it and computer professionals, with the latter handling most of the technical aspects of systems development. This, however, may change as we move into the twenty-first century. Each year, CASE technology makes it possible for us to assign more of the hard-core programming and design work to computers. The next generation of CASE technology may be for the user, giving the user a new level of technical independence. User-friendly CASE software will allow users to describe, in general terms, what they want the system to accomplish. The CASE software will then create a prototype system that can be refined by the user. Once refined, the *user-oriented* CASE software will generate the necessary programs and install the system.

Most of us who work have become, to some degree, slaves to technology. We need computers and their information processing capabilities to accomplish our jobs. Ultimately, it may be CASE technology that frees us from technological bondage, making us masters of technology and our information.

the program's execution. With these and a few other types of instructions, you can create software to model almost any business or scientific procedure, whether it is sales forecasting or guiding rockets to the moon.

Types of Programming Languages

We "talk" to computers within the framework of a particular programming language, and the selection of a programming language depends on who is doing the talking and the nature of the "conversation." There are many different types of programming languages in use today.

Machine Language: Native Tongue

In Chapter 3 we learned that all programs are ultimately executed in machine language, the computer's native language. Creating programs in machine language is a cumbersome process, so we write programs in more programmer-friendly programming languages. However, our resulting programs must be translated into machine language before they can be executed.

Procedure-Oriented Languages

The introduction of more user-friendly programming languages (in 1955) resulted in a quantum leap in programmer convenience. Programmers could write a single instruction instead of several cumbersome machine-language instructions. These early languages were **procedure-oriented languages,** which require programmers to solve programming problems using traditional programming logic. *COBOL,* shown in Figure 13.10, is a good example of a procedure-oriented language.

Object-Oriented Languages and OOP

In procedure-oriented languages, the emphasis is on *what* is done (the procedure). In **object-oriented languages,** the emphasis is on the *object* of the action. The structure of **object-oriented programming (OOP)** makes programs easier to design and understand. Also, OOP (rhymes with *"hoop"*) handles images, videos, and sound better than do procedure-oriented languages. Examples of object-oriented languages include *Smalltalk* and *C++.*

The Fourth Generation: 4GLs

Most of the programming in procedure- and object-oriented languages is done by computer specialists. Programming in user-friendly **fourth-generation languages (4GLs)** is done by computer specialists and also a growing legion of end users. Fourth-generation languages use high-level English-like instructions to retrieve

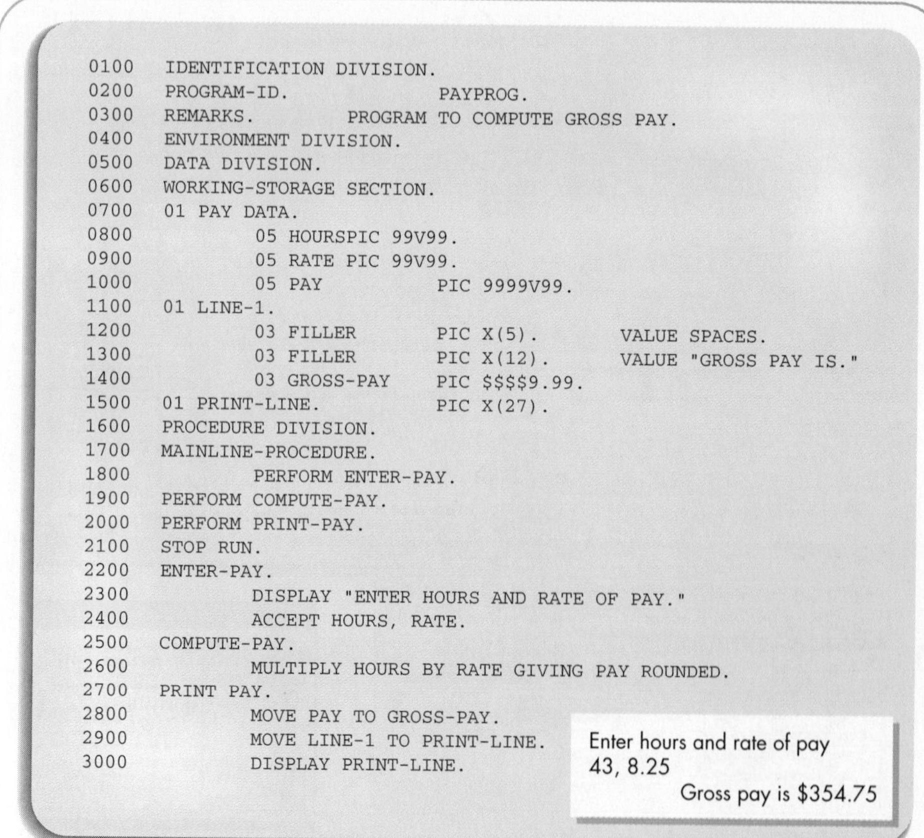

```
0100  IDENTIFICATION DIVISION.
0200  PROGRAM-ID.             PAYPROG.
0300  REMARKS.        PROGRAM TO COMPUTE GROSS PAY.
0400  ENVIRONMENT DIVISION.
0500  DATA DIVISION.
0600  WORKING-STORAGE SECTION.
0700  01 PAY DATA.
0800          05 HOURSPIC 99V99.
0900          05 RATE PIC 99V99.
1000          05 PAY          PIC 9999V99.
1100  01 LINE-1.
1200          03 FILLER       PIC X(5).        VALUE SPACES.
1300          03 FILLER       PIC X(12).       VALUE "GROSS PAY IS."
1400          03 GROSS-PAY    PIC $$$$9.99.
1500  01 PRINT-LINE.          PIC X(27).
1600  PROCEDURE DIVISION.
1700  MAINLINE-PROCEDURE.
1800          PERFORM ENTER-PAY.
1900  PERFORM COMPUTE-PAY.
2000  PERFORM PRINT-PAY.
2100  STOP RUN.
2200  ENTER-PAY.
2300          DISPLAY "ENTER HOURS AND RATE OF PAY."
2400          ACCEPT HOURS, RATE.
2500  COMPUTE-PAY.
2600          MULTIPLY HOURS BY RATE GIVING PAY ROUNDED.
2700  PRINT PAY.
2800          MOVE PAY TO GROSS-PAY.
2900          MOVE LINE-1 TO PRINT-LINE.
3000          DISPLAY PRINT-LINE.
```

Enter hours and rate of pay
43, 8.25
Gross pay is $354.75

A COBOL Program This COBOL program accepts the number of hours worked and the pay rate for an hourly wage earner, then computes and displays the gross pay amount. The interactive session below the program listing shows the input prompt, the values entered by the user, and the result.

and format data for inquiries and reporting. In 4GLs, the programmer specifies what to do, *not* how to do it. A few simple 4GL instructions are all that are needed to respond to the following typical management requests:

- Which employees have accumulated more than 20 sick days since May 1?
- Which deluxe single hospital rooms, if any, will be vacated by the end of the day?
- List departments that have exceeded their budgets alphabetically by the department head's name.

Visual Languages: Icons for Words

As they say, a picture is worth a thousand words, and so it is in programming. **Visual programming** takes object-oriented programming to the next level, replacing text-based instructions with symbolic icons, each of which represents an object or a common programming function (see Figure 13.11). Microsoft's **Visual BASIC** is one of the most popular visual languages for both the casual user and the professional software developer.

Writing the Program

The challenge to programmers is to translate the system design and specifications created during the prototyping process into instructions that can be interpreted and executed by the computer. To do so, they follow these steps.

System Specifications Review

The system specifications completed during the systems analysis and design are all that is necessary for programmers to write, or *code,* the programs to implement the target information system. But before getting started, programmers should review and study the system specifications (layouts, design, and so on) until they thoroughly understand what needs to be accomplished.

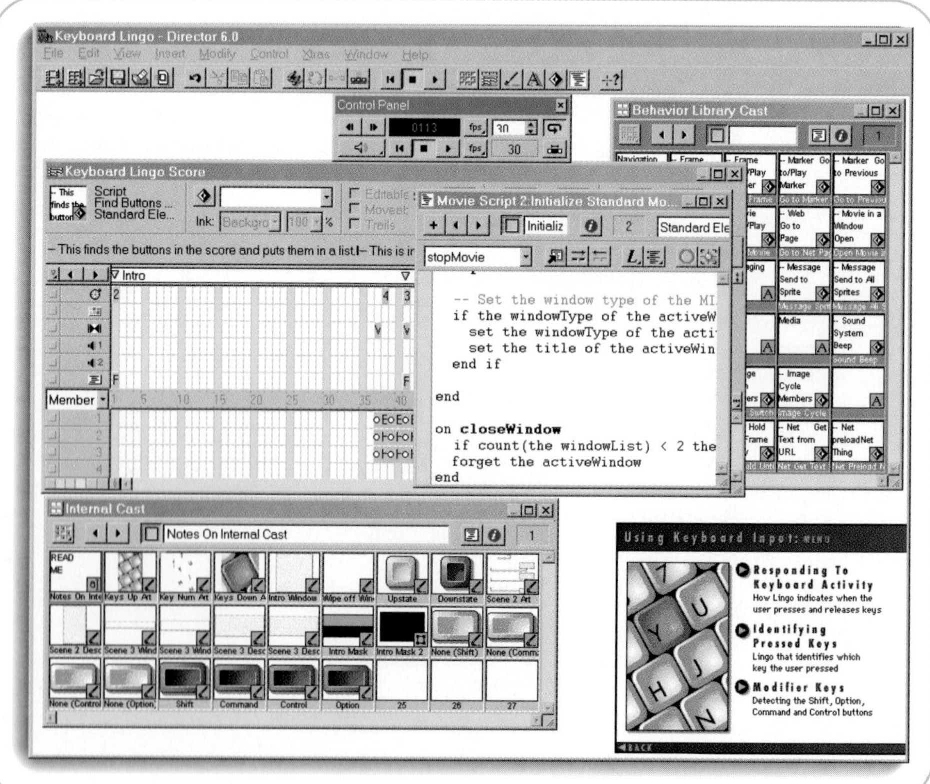

Visual Programming
Macromedia Director "movies," which are interactive multimedia images, are the result of a scripting program. A variety of Director visual programming enables the creation of the program (see center of example). When played, the resulting "Using Keyboard Input" (lower right) demonstrates interactively, with sound and motion, the use of a keyboard. The Score window (top left) graphically illustrates the sequencing and play attributes of the elements in the Director "movie." The Internal Cast window (bottom left) shows the member of the cast (elements under program control). Members of the cast can be assigned a particular type of behavior using the Behavior Library Cast window.

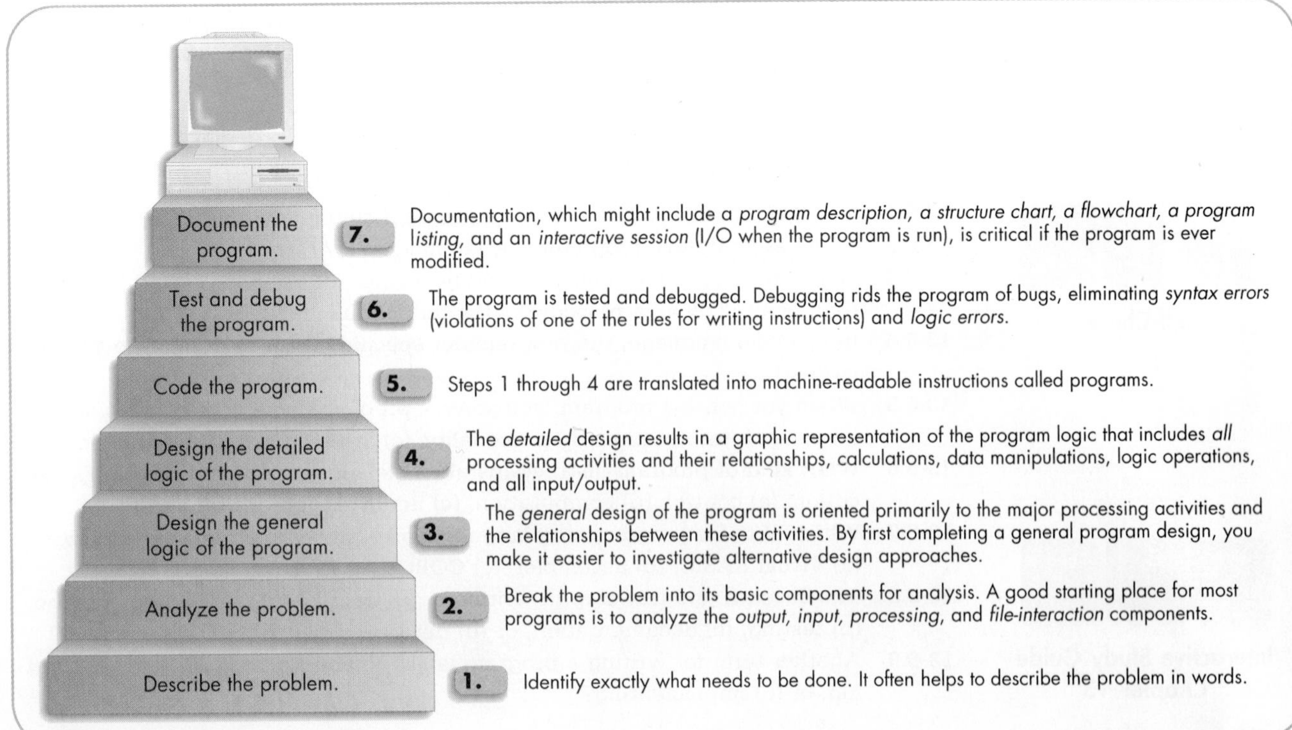

Document the program.
7.
Documentation, which might include a program description, a structure chart, a flowchart, a program listing, and an interactive session (I/O when the program is run), is critical if the program is ever modified.
Test and debug the program.
6.
The program is tested and debugged. Debugging rids the program of bugs, eliminating syntax errors (violations of one of the rules for writing instructions) and logic errors.
Code the program.
5.
Steps 1 through 4 are translated into machine-readable instructions called programs.
Design the detailed logic of the program.
4.
The detailed design results in a graphic representation of the program logic that includes all processing activities and their relationships, calculations, data manipulations, logic operations, and all input/output.
Design the general logic of the program.
3.
The general design of the program is oriented primarily to the major processing activities and the relationships between these activities. By first completing a general program design, you make it easier to investigate alternative design approaches.
Analyze the problem.
2.
Break the problem into its basic components for analysis. A good starting place for most programs is to analyze the output, input, processing, and file-interaction components.
Describe the problem.
1.
Identify exactly what needs to be done. It often helps to describe the problem in words.

FIGURE 13.12 **Steps in Writing a Program**

Program Identification and Description

An information system needs an array of programs to create and update the database, print reports, permit online inquiry, and so on. Depending on the scope of the system and how many programs can be generated using applications development tools, as few as three or four or as many as several thousand programs may need to be written before the system can be implemented. At this point, all programs necessary to make the system operational are identified and described (tasks to be performed, input, output, and so on).

Program Coding, Testing, and Documentation

Armed with system specifications and program descriptions, programmers can begin the actual coding of programs. The development of a program is actually a project within a project. Just as there are certain steps the project team takes to develop an information system, there are certain steps a programmer takes to write a program. These seven steps are summarized in Figure 13.12. Several techniques, such as flowcharting, are available to help programmers analyze a problem and design the program.

Programming and You

As you continue to gain experience with PCs and PC software, you, like so many before you, will probably begin to seek greater speed, power, and efficiency from your PC and its software. To gain speed and power, you will need to upgrade your hardware with the latest technology. To improve efficiency, you might wish to consider learning to write programs—yes, programs. You do not have to be a professional programmer—most people who program are not. They are users who write programs to accomplish personal processing objectives, often resulting in time savings of up to 15 hours a week!

SECTION SELF-CHECK

Self-Check

13-6.1 C++, Visual BASIC, and Java are programming languages. (T/F)

13-6.2 There are only five programming languages. (T/F)

13-6.3 Object-oriented programming handles images, videos, and sound better than does COBOL, a procedure-oriented language. (T/F)

13-6.4 In machine language, the programmer specifies what to do, not how to do it. (T/F)

13-6.5 When you write a program, you solve a problem using your powers of: (a) visual interpretation, (b) personality, (c) common sense, or (d) logic?

13-6.6 What kind of program instructions alter the sequence of the program's execution: (a) control, (b) computation, (c) input/output, or (d) format?

13-6.7 Which of these programming languages is a procedure-oriented language: (a) Visual BASIC, (b) assembler, (c) COBOL, or (d) LISP?

13-6.8 The seventh and last step in writing a program is: (a) problem description, (b) testing, (c) documentation, or (d) detailed design?

13-6.9 Another term for writing a program is: (a) coding, (b) logicizing, (c) converting, or (d) implementing?

Interactive Study Guide
Chapter 13

SUMMARY AND KEY TERMS

13.1 The system life cycle

The four stages of a computer-based information system comprise the **system life cycle** (34). They are birth, development, production, and death.

There are two basic approaches to satisfying a company's information processing needs. The first is to purchase and install a **proprietary software package** (34). The alternative is to use company employees and/or outside consultants to create an information system customized to meet user specifications.

13.2 Systems development techniques and concepts

The system's design includes all processing activities and the input/output associated with them. When adhering to **structured system design** (36), designers divide the system into independent modules for ease of understanding and design. The **structure chart** (36) enables system designers to conceptualize a system in a hierarchy of modules.

Data flow diagrams (37) enable analysts to design and document systems using the structured approach to system development. The four symbols used in data flow diagrams are entity, process, flow line, and data storage. The focus of the data flow diagram is information flow. Another similar business modeling tool is the **entity relationship diagram** (40). The focus of the entity relationship diagram is the attributes of the entities and the relationship between them.

Flowcharting (40) is another popular technique for portraying system and programming logic. **Flowcharts** (40) illustrate data, information, and work flow by the interconnection of specialized symbols with flow lines. In structured programming, each program is designed with a **driver module** (40) (which might include a **loop** [40]), or **main program** (40), that calls **subroutines** (40) as they are needed.

13.3 Computer-aided software engineering: The CASE tool kit

The general family of automated software development productivity tools falls under the umbrella of **computer-aided software engineering** (42), or **CASE** (42), tools. The term **software engineering** (42) was coined to emphasize an approach to software development that combines automation and the rigors of the engineering discipline. The basic CASE tool kit includes design tools, information repository tools, and program development tools.

CASE design tools help analysts, programmers, and other project team members prepare schematics that graphically depict the logic of a system. Project team members use CASE design tools to create a physical representation of a target information system. CASE design tools also help designers prepare the user interface and generate screen and report **layouts** (43). The **information repository** (43) is a central computer-based storage facility for all design information. In an information repository, each piece of system documentation is cross-referenced to all other components in the system. The CASE program development tools, which include **application generators** (43), use the system design to generate the software for the system. Occasionally, **custom programming** (42) is required to complete the system. **Software engineers** (42) develop software products to bridge the gap between design and executable program code.

13.4 Prototyping: Creating a model of the target system

The CASE tool kit enables the system development project team to work with users to develop a **prototype system** (43). This approach to applications development is called **prototyping** (43). Modern prototyping tools enable the development of a **scalable system** (44), one whose design can handle any size database or any number of users.

In the traditional approach to system development, the project team would formulate **functional specifications** (44) for system input, processing, and output requirements, but these specs were inaccurate because users had not had an opportunity to work with the **target system** (45).

The three objectives of prototyping are to analyze the current situation, to identify information needs, and to develop a scaled-down model of the target system.

Ideally, users should experiment and familiarize themselves with the operation of a target system as early in the development process as possible. The prototyping process enables users to relate accurate information processing needs to the project team during the early phases of the project and throughout the project.

Rapid application development (RAD) (45) results in information systems of varying degrees of sophistication.

During Phase I, Define System Specifications, of prototyping, the current system is analyzed (system analysis) and the target system is designed (system design). During system analysis, the team does the existing system review where it documents the work and information flow of the system. Team members also formalize the system objectives, identify design constraints, and complete a needs analysis that results in a requirements definition.

During system design, the project team takes information from the system analysis and develops a system design for the target system. The design documentation, the **system specification** (44), might include the following: a graphic illustration of the target system, a written explanation of the graphic illustration, and descriptions of the outputs to be produced by the system. The database is defined during system design, as well.

During Phase II, Create Prototype System, the project team translates the system design and **specs** (44) into instructions that can be interpreted and executed by the computer. During this phase, the creation of CASE-generated and custom software becomes the dominant activity.

During Phase III, Refine Prototype System, a use-and-modify cycle is repeated until users are satisfied with the prototype system.

During Phase IV, Develop Operational System, software capable of handling the required volume of work for an operational information system is developed.

13.5 System conversion and implementation: Making the transition

Once an information system has been developed, it must be implemented within the organization. Although the programs that make up the software for an information system have been debugged on an individual basis **(unit testing)** (49), they must be combined and subjected to integrated **systems testing** (49) prior to implementation.

The four common approaches to system conversion are **parallel conversion** (50), **direct conversion** (50), **phased conversion** (50), and **pilot conversion** (51). The approach that an organization selects depends on its willingness to accept risk and the amount of time available for the conversion.

An information system is dynamic and must be responsive to the changing needs of the company and those who use it. The process of modifying, or **patching** (52), an information system to meet changing needs is known as **system maintenance** (51).

13.6 Programming: Making it happen

Programmers use a variety of **programming languages** (53) to communicate instructions to the computer. The design of a program, or its *programming logic,* is completed before the program is written. Each language uses several types of instructions.

All programming languages are ultimately translated into *machine language* in order to be executed. In **procedure-oriented languages** (57), such as COBOL, programmers code the instructions in the sequence in which they must be executed to solve the problem.

Object-oriented languages (57), such as Smalltalk and C++, emphasize the *object* of the action. The hical structure of **object-oriented programming** (57) makes programs easier to design and understand.

In **fourth-generation languages (4GLs)** (57), the programmer need only specify *what* to do, not *how* to do it. One feature of 4GLs is the use of English-like instructions.

In **visual programming** (58), text-based instructions are replaced with symbolic icons, each of which represents a common programming function. An example of this is **Visual BASIC** (58).

Programmers translate the system design and specifications created during the prototyping process into instructions for programs. First, they do a system specifications review. Then they describe all programs necessary to make the system operational. Finally, they write the programs, test them, and document them.

DISCUSSION AND PROBLEM SOLVING

13.1 a. Would it be possible for a company with 600 employees to maintain a skeleton information services division of about five IT professionals and use commercially available packaged software for all its computer application needs? Explain.

b. In general, is it better to change internal procedures to fit a particular proprietary software package or to modify the software to fit existing procedures? Discuss.

13.2 a. Give a system-oriented example, perhaps relating to the registration system at your college, of when you might use each of the flowcharting symbols in Figure 13.6.

b. Name one way in which data flow diagrams and entity relationship diagrams are alike and one way in which they are not.

c. Discuss the rationale for the "divide and conquer" approach to system analysis and design.

d. Break down the registration system at your college into a simple structure chart. Discuss each box in the chart.

e. Complete a flowchart to illustrate the programming logic for a program that accepts three quiz grades from each of any number of students. The program should compute and display the average for each student. Include a driver module in your logic.

f. Put yourself in the role of a systems analyst. Draw a first-level data flow diagram depicting your college's student registration system.

g. Expand on the above question and explode one of the processes in the data flow diagram to show detail.

13.3 a. Twenty years ago, IT professionals didn't have CASE. Discuss how CASE has changed the traditional approach to system development.

b. Explain how using a CASE information repository during the system development process can have a positive impact on target system quality.

c. Much of the programming code for an information system can be generated with CASE tools. Nevertheless, the demand for programmers in all areas is high. Explain.

13.4 a. One of the objectives of prototyping is to develop a scaled-down model of the target system. However, some prototype systems are fully functional. Describe how a functional prototype system is scaled down.

b. What is meant by the remark "Garbage in, garbage out" as applied to system specifications?

c. Design a screen layout for an online hospital admittance system. Design only that screen with which the hospital clerk would interact to enter basic patient data. Distinguish between input and output by underlining the input.

d. Software tools are available for rapid application development (RAD), yet many companies continue to use traditional approaches to system development even though system development costs may be greater and project times may be longer. Explain.

13.5 a. Why do information systems need patches? What is accomplished when we patch an information system?

b. What is the downside of testing a system only with test data and not with live data, too?

c. What advantage does direct conversion have over parallel conversion? Parallel over direct?

13.6a. During the last fifty years, hundreds of programming languages have been developed, with over a hundred used widely throughout the world. Why do we need so many programming languages?

b. Discuss the steps you must take to turn on your TV and select the ESPN channel. Be very specific as you would in a computer program.

c. Discuss the difference between a procedure-oriented language and a fourth-generation language.

d. Do you believe that you may eventually write computer programs in your chosen profession? If so, what kind of programs? If not, why?

NOTES

Answers to the Section Self-Checks

1–1.1 F
1–1.2 T
1–1.3 T
1–1.4 A
1–1.5 B
1–1.6 A
1–2.1 F
1–2.2 T
1–2.3 C
1–2.4 B
1–2.5 A
1–3.1 T
1–3.2 T
1–3.3 F
1–3.4 F
1–3.5 B
1–3.6 B
1–3.7 C
1–4.1 F
1–4.2 F
1–4.3 F
1–4.4 T
1–4.5 A
1–4.6 B
1–4.7 D
1–4.8 C
1–5.1 F
1–5.2 T
1–5.3 T
1–5.4 T
1–5.5 A
1–5.6 A
1–5.7 D
1–6.1 T
1–6.2 T
1–6.3 D
1–6.4 C
1–6.5 A
2–1.1 F
2–1.2 T
2–1.3 A
2–2.1 F
2–2.2 T
2–2.3 T
2–2.4 T
2–2.5 T
2–2.6 T
2–2.7 D
2–2.8 D
2–2.9 A
2–2.10 C
2–3.1 T
2–3.2 F
2–3.3 T
2–3.4 T
2–3.5 C
2–3.6 A
2–3.7 B
2–4.1 T
2–4.2 F
2–4.3 T
2–4.4 T
2–4.5 C
2–4.6 B
2–4.7 A
2–4.8 C
2–4.9 A
2–5.1 T
2–5.2 F
2–5.3 T
2–5.4 F
2–5.5 T
2–5.6 B
2–5.7 C
2–5.8 C
2–5.9 C
2–5.10 D
2–6.1 T
2–6.2 F
2–6.3 F
2–6.4 T
2–6.5 D
2–6.6 A
2–6.7 A
2–6.8 B
2–6.9 D
2–6.10 C
2–6.11 D
3–1.1 F
3–1.2 T
3–1.3 T
3–1.4 A
3–1.5 A
3–1.6 D
3–1.7 B
3–1.8 B
3–2.1 T
3–2.2 F
3–2.3 T
3–2.4 T
3–2.5 B
3–2.6 D
3–2.7 A
3–2.8 C
3–2.9 B
3–2.10 B
3–2.11 A
3–3.1 F
3–3.2 T
3–3.3 T
3–3.4 B
3–3.5 A
3–3.6 A
3–4.1 T
3–4.2 T
3–4.3 F
3–4.4 C
3–4.5 B
3–4.6 C
4–1.1 F
4–1.2 T
4–1.3 T
4–1.4 F
4–1.5 F
4–1.6 B
4–1.7 C
4–1.8 D
4–1.9 A
4–2.1 F
4–2.2 F
4–2.3 T
4–2.4 F
4–2.5 F
4–2.6 T
4–2.7 F
4–2.8 T
4–2.9 T
4–2.10 D
4–2.11 C
4–2.12 B
4–2.13 A
4–2.14 A
4–2.15 D
4–2.16 C
4–2.17 C
4–3.1 T
4–3.2 T
4–3.3 F
4–3.4 A
4–3.5 D
4–3.6 B
4–4.1 T
4–4.2 T
4–4.3 T
4–4.4 T
4–4.5 T
4–4.6 F
4–4.7 A
4–4.8 A
4–4.9 D
4–5.1 T
4–5.2 F
4–5.3 B
5–1.1 T
5–1.2 F
5–1.3 C
5–2.1 T
5–2.2 F
5–2.3 F
5–2.4 A
5–2.5 B
5–2.6 A
5–3.1 F
5–3.2 T
5–3.3 F
5–3.4 T
5–3.5 T
5–3.6 F
5–3.7 D
5–3.8 A
5–3.9 B
5–3.10 C
5–3.11 A
5–3.12 D
5–3.13 A
5–3.14 B
5–3.15 A
5–4.1 T
5–4.2 F
5–4.3 F
5–4.4 F
5–4.5 T
5–4.6 B
5–4.7 A
5–4.8 C
5–4.9 D
5–4.10 A
5–4.11 A
5–4.12 C
5–4.13 C
5–4.14 B
5–4.15 C
5–4.16 A
5–5.1 T
5–5.2 T
5–5.3 T
5–5.4 T
5–5.5 B
5–5.6 B
5–5.7 D
6–1.1 T
6–1.2 F
6–1.3 F
6–1.4 A
6–1.5 B
6–2.1 T
6–2.2 F
6–2.3 T
6–2.4 T
6–2.5 A
6–2.6 D
6–2.7 C
6–2.8 A
6–3.1 T
6–3.2 T
6–3.3 T
6–3.4 T
6–3.5 F
6–3.6 F
6–3.7 B
6–3.8 A
6–3.9 C
6–3.10 A
6–4.1 F
6–4.2 T
6–4.3 T
6–4.4 C
6–4.5 C
6–4.6 B
6–4.7 B
6–5.1 F
6–5.2 F
6–5.3 T
6–5.4 T
6–5.5 A
6–5.6 C
6–5.7 D
6–5.8 B
7–1.1 T
7–1.2 A
7–2.1 F
7–2.2 T
7–2.3 C
7–2.4 B
7–2.5 C
7–3.1 F
7–3.2 F
7–3.3 F
7–3.4 F
7–3.5 F
7–3.6 A
7–3.7 A
7–3.8 B
7–3.9 A
7–3.10 B

.11 A
-3.12 B
7–4.1 F
7–4.2 T
7–4.3 F
7–4.4 B
7–4.5 C
7–4.6 D
7–4.7 B
7–4.8 A
7–4.9 D
7–5.1 T
7–5.2 T
7–5.3 T
7–5.4 F
7–5.5 T
7–5.6 T
7–5.7 B
7–5.8 C
7–5.9 C
7–5.10 C
7–5.11 D
7–5.12 B
7–5.13 B
7–5.14 A
7–6.1 F
7–6.2 C
7–6.3 A
8–1.1 F
8–1.2 T
8–1.3 F
8–1.4 B
8–1.5 B
8–1.6 D
8–2.1 F
8–2.2 F
8–2.3 T
8–2.4 B
8–2.5 C
8–2.6 A
8–2.7 C
8–3.1 T
8–3.2 T
8–3.3 T
8–3.4 F
8–3.5 F
8–3.6 F
8–3.7 F
8–3.8 A
8–3.9 D
8–3.10 C
8–3.11 D
8–3.12 C
8–3.13 D
8–3.14 C
8–4.1 F
8–4.2 T
8–4.3 T
8–4.4 A
8–4.5 D
8–4.6 C
8–5.1 T
8–5.2 F
8–5.3 F
8–5.4 F
8–5.5 B
8–5.6 A
8–5.7 B
9–1.1 T
9–1.2 T
9–1.3 T
9–1.4 F
9–1.5 F
9–1.6 C
9–1.7 B
9–1.8 A
9–1.9 B
9–1.10 A
9–1.11 B
9–1.12 A
9–1.13 B
9–1.14 A
9–1.15 C
9–2.1 T
9–2.2 T
9–2.3 T
9–2.4 D
9–2.5 B
9–2.6 B
9–3.1 F
9–3.2 T
9–3.3 T
9–3.4 C
9–3.5 C
9–3.6 B
9–4.1 F
9–4.2 T
9–4.3 B
9–4.4 C
9–4.5 B
9–5.1 T
9–5.2 F
9–5.3 D
9–5.4 A
9–5.5 D
9–6.1 T
9–6.2 T
9–6.3 T
9–6.4 A
9–6.5 C
9–6.6 D
9–6.7 A
9–7.1 T
9–7.2 T
9–7.3 F
9–7.4 F
9–7.5 B
9–7.6 D
9–7.7 D
10–1.1 F
10–1.2 F
10–1.3 C
10–1.4 C
10–2.1 F
10–2.2 T
10–2.3 T
10–2.4 F
10–2.5 F
10–2.6 D
10–2.7 C
10–2.8 B
10–2.9 F
10–2.10 A
10–3.1 T
10–3.2 T
10–3.3 T
10–3.4 C
10–3.5 D
10–3.6 A
10–3.7 B
10–3.8 D
10–3.9 B
10–4.1 T
10–4.2 F
10–4.3 F
10–4.4 F
10–4.5 T
10–4.6 C
10–4.7 B
10–4.8 D
10–4.9 A
10–4.10 B
10–4.11 C
10–5.1 F
10–5.2 F
10–5.3 F
10–5.4 A
10–5.5 D
10–5.6 C
10–5.7 A
10–5.8 A
11–1.1 F
11–1.2 C
11–2.1 F
11–2.2 F
11–2.3 D
11–3.1 T
11–3.2 F
11–3.3 T
11–3.4 F
11–3.5 C
11–3.6 D
11–3.7 A
11–4.1 T
11–4.2 F
11–4.3 F
11–4.4 B
11–4.5 A
11–4.6 C
11–4.7 A
11–4.8 C
11–4.9 B
11–5.1 F
11–5.2 B
12–1.1 T
12–1.2 F
12–2.1 F
12–2.2 T
12–2.3 T
12–2.4 T
12–2.5 C
12–2.6 A
12–2.7 D
12–2.8 B
12–3.1 F
12–3.2 F
12–3.3 T
12–3.4 T
12–3.5 C
12–3.6 A
12–3.7 C
12–3.8 C
12–3.9 B
12–4.1 F
12–4.2 C
12–5.1 T
12–5.2 T
12–5.3 B
12–5.4 A
12–6.1 F
12–6.2 F
12–6.3 T
12–6.4 B
12–6.5 D
12–6.6 C
12–6.7 A
12–7.1 F
12–7.2 T
12–7.3 F
12–7.4 B
12–7.5 D
12–7.6 D
12–8.1 T
12–8.2 F
12–8.3 C
12–8.4 B
13–1.1 F
13–1.2 T
13–1.3 F
13–1.4 C
13–1.5 A
13–2.1 T
13–2.2 T
13–2.3 T
13–2.4 T
13–2.5 C
13–2.6 B
13–2.7 A
13–2.8 D
13–3.1 T
13–3.2 T
13–3.3 T
13–3.4 B
13–3.5 A
13–3.6 A
13–4.1 F
13–4.2 T
13–4.3 T
13–4.4 B
13–4.5 A
13–4.6 B
13–4.7 A
13–4.8 C
13–4.9 D
13–5.1 T
13–5.2 F
13–5.3 T
13–5.4 F
13–5.5 A
13–5.6 B
13–5.7 B
13–6.1 T
13–6.2 F
13–6.3 T
13–6.4 F
13–6.5 D
13–6.6 A
13–6.7 C
13–6.8 C
13–6.9 A

Glossary

Absolute cell address A cell address in a spreadsheet that always refers to the same cell.

Access arm The disk drive mechanism used to position the read/write heads over the appropriate track.

Access time The time interval between the instant a computer makes a request for a transfer of data from disk storage and the instant this operation is completed.

Accumulator The computer register in which the result of an arithmetic or logic operation is formed. (Related to *arithmetic and logic unit.*)

Active window The window in Microsoft Windows® with which the user may interact.

Address (1) A name, numeral, or label that designates a particular location in RAM or disk storage. (2) A location identifier for nodes in a computer network.

Address bus Pathway through which source and destination addresses are transmitted between RAM, cache memory, and the processor. (See also *data bus.*)

ADSL (Asymmetric Digital Subscriber Line) A digital telecommunications standard for data delivery over twisted-pair lines with downstream transmission speeds up to 9 M bps.

AGP (Accelerated Graphics Port) board A graphics adapter that permits interfacing with video monitors.

Alpha A reference to the letters of the alphabet. (Compare with *numeric* and *alphanumeric.*)

Alphanumeric Pertaining to a character set that contains letters, digits, punctuation, and special symbols. (Related to *alpha* and *numeric.*)

America Online (AOL) An online information service.

Analog signal A continuous waveform signal that can be used to represent such things as sound, temperature, and velocity. (See also *digital signal.*)

Animation The rapid repositioning of objects on a display to create movement.

Anonymous FTP site An Internet site that permits FTP (file transfer protocol) file transfers without prior permission.

ANSI The American National Standards Institute is a nongovernment standards-setting organization that develops and publishes standards for "voluntary" use in the United States.

Applet A small program sent over the Internet or an intranet that is interpreted and executed by Internet browser software.

Application generator A system development tool used to actually generate the system programming code based on design specifications.

Application icon A miniature visual representation of a software application on a diplay.

Application window A rectangular window containing an open, or running, application in Microsoft Windows.

Applications programmer A programmer who translates analyst-prepared system and input/output specifications into programs. Programmers design the logic, then code, debug, test, and document the programs.

Applications software Software designed and written to address a specific personal, business, or processing task.

Argument That portion of a function that identifies the data to be operated on.

Arithmetic and logic unit That portion of the computer that performs arithmetic and logic operations. (Related to *accumulator.*)

Arithmetic operators Mathematical operators (add [+], subtract [−], multiply [*], divide [/], and exponentiation [^]) used in programming and in spreadsheet and database software for computations.

Artificial intelligence (AI) The ability of a computer to reason, to learn, to strive for self-improvement, and to simulate human sensory capabilities.

ASCII [*A*merican *S*tandard *C*ode for *I*nformation *I*nterchange] A 7-bit or 8-bit encoding system.

ASCII file A generic text file that is stripped of program-specific control characters.

Assembler language A programming language that uses easily recognized symbols, called mnemonics, to represent instructions.

Assistant system This knowledge-based system that helps users make relatively straightforward decisions. (See also *expert system.*)

Asymmetric Digital Subscriber Line See *ADSL.*

Asynchronous transmission A protocol in which data are transmitted at irregular intervals on an as-needed basis. (See also *synchronous transmission.*)

Attached file A file that is attached and sent with an e-mail message.

Audio file A file that contains digitized sound.

Audio mail An electronic mail capability that lets you speak your message instead of typing it.

Authoring software Software that lets you create multimedia applications that integrate sound, motion, text, animation, and images.

Automatic teller machine (ATM) An automated deposit/withdrawal device used in banking.

Backbone A system of routers and the associated transmission media that facilitates the interconnection of computer networks.

Back-end applications software This software on the server computer performs processing tasks in support of its clients, such as tasks associated with storage and maintenance of a centralized corporate database. (See also *front-end applications software.*)

Background (1) That part of RAM that contains the lowest priority programs. (2) In Windows, the area of the display over which the foreground is superimposed. (Contrast with *foreground.*)

Backup Pertaining to equipment, procedures, or databases that can be used to restart the system in the event of system failure.

kup file Duplicate of an existing file.
adge reader An input device that reads data on badges and cards.
Bar code A graphic encoding technique in which printed vertical bars of varying widths are used to represent data.
Bar graph A graph that contains bars that represent specified numeric values.
Batch processing A technique in which transactions and/or jobs are collected into groups (batched) and processed together.
Baud (1) A measure of the maximum number of electronic signals that can be transmitted via a communications channel. (2) Bits per second (common-use definition).
Binary A base-2 numbering system.
Bit A *bi*nary digi*t* (0 or 1).
Bit-mapped graphics Referring to an image that has been projected, or mapped, to a screen based on binary bits. (See also *raster graphics.*)
Bits per second (bps) The number of bits that can be transmitted per second over a communications channel.
BMP A popular format for bit-mapped files.
Boilerplate Existing text in a word processing file that can in some way be customized to be used in a variety of word processing applications.
Bold A font presentation attribute that thickens the lines of a character.
Boot The procedure for loading the operating system to RAM and readying a computer system for use.
Bridge A protocol-independent hardware device that permits communication between devices on separate local area networks.
Browsers Programs that let you navigate to and view the various Internet resources.
Bug A logic or syntax error in a program, a logic error in the design of a computer system, or a hardware fault. (See also *debug.*)
Bus An electrical pathway through which the processor sends data and commands to RAM and all peripheral devices.
Bus topology A computer network that permits the connection of terminals, peripheral devices, and microcomputers along an open-ended central cable.
Button bar A software option that contains a group of pictographs that represent a menu option or a command.
Byte A group of adjacent bits configured to represent a character or symbol.

C A transportable programming language that can be used to develop software.
C++ An object-oriented version of the C programming language.
Cache memory High-speed solid-state memory for program instructions and data.
CAD See *computer-aided design.*
Carrier Standard-sized pin connectors that permit chips to be attached to a circuit board.
Cascading menu A pop-up menu that is displayed when a command from the active menu is chosen.
Cascading windows Two or more windows that are displayed on a computer screen in an overlapping manner.
Cathode-ray tube See *CRT.*
CBT See *computer-based training.*
CD production station A device used to duplicate locally produced CD-ROMs.
CD writer A peripheral device that can write once to a CD-R disk to create an audio CD or a CD-ROM.
CD-R [*C*ompact *D*isk-*R*ecordable] The medium on which CD writers create CDs and CD-ROMs.
CD-ReWritable (CD-RW) This technology allows users to rewrite to the same CD media.
CD-ROM disk [*C*ompact-*D*isk *R*ead-*O*nly *M*emory disk] A type of optical laser storage media.
CD-ROM drive A storage device into which an interchangeable CD-ROM is inserted for processing.
Celeron A line of Intel® microprocessors designed for low-cost PCs.
Cell The intersection of a particular row and column in a spreadsheet.
Cell address The location—column and row—of a cell in a spreadsheet.
Central processing unit (CPU) See *processor.*
Centronics connector A 36-pin connector that is used for the electronic interconnection of computers, modems, and other peripheral devices.
CGM A popular vector graphics file format.
Channel The facility by which data are transmitted between locations in a computer network (e.g., terminal to host, host to printer).
Channel capacity The number of bits that can be transmitted over a communications channel per second.
Chief information officer (CIO) The individual responsible for all the information services activity in a company.
Chip See *integrated circuit.*
Chipset A motherboard's intelligence that controls the flow of information between system components connected to the board.
Choose To pick a menu item or icon in such a manner as to initiate processing activity.
CISC [*C*omplex *I*nstruction *S*et *C*omputer] A computer design architecture that offers machine language programmers a wide variety of instructions. (Contrast with *RISC.*)
Click A single tap on a mouse's button.
Client application (1) An application running on a networked workstation or PC that works in tandem with a server application. (See also *server application.*) (2) In object linking and embedding, the application containing the destination document.
Client computer Typically a PC or a workstation that requests processing support or another type of service from one or more server computers. (See also *server computer.*)
Client program A software program that runs on a PC

and works in conjunction with a companion server program that runs on a server computer. (See also *server program.*)
Client/server computing A computing environment in which processing capabilities are distributed throughout a network such that a client computer requests processing or some other type of service from a server computer.
Clip art Prepackaged electronic images that are stored on disk to be used as needed in computer-based documents.
Clipboard An intermediate holding area in internal storage for information en route to another application.
Clone A hardware device or a software package that emulates a product with an established reputation and market acceptance.
Cluster The smallest unit of disk space that can be allocated to a file.
Coaxial cable A shielded wire used as a medium to transmit data between computers and between computers and peripheral devices.
COBOL [*C*ommon *B*usiness *O*riented *L*anguage] A third-generation programming language designed to handle business problems.
Code (1) The rules used to translate a bit configuration into alphanumeric characters and symbols. (2) The process of compiling computer instructions into the form of a computer program. (3) The actual computer program.
Command An instruction to a computer that invokes the execution of a preprogrammed sequence of instructions.
Common carrier A company that provides channels for data transmission.
Communications channel The facility by which data are transmitted between locations in a computer network.
Communications protocols Rules established to govern the way data in a computer network are transmitted.
Communications server The LAN component that provides external communications links.
Communications software (1) Software that enables a microcomputer to emulate a terminal and to transfer files between a micro and another computer. (2) Software that enables communication between remote devices in a computer network.
Compact disk-recordable See *CD-R.*
Compatibility Pertaining to the ability of computers and computer components (hardware and software) to work together.
Compile To translate a high-level programming language into machine language in preparation for execution.
Compiler A program that translates the instructions of a high-level language to machine language instructions that the computer can interpret and execute.
Compound document A document, such as a word processing document, that contains one or more linked objects from other applications.
CompuServe An online information service.
Computer An electronic device capable of interpreting and executing programmed commands for input, output, computation, and logic operations.
Computer competency A fundamental understanding of the technology, operation, applications, and issues surrounding computers.
Computer literacy See *computer competency.*
Computer matching The procedure whereby separate databases are examined and individuals common to both are identified.
Computer monitoring Observing and regulating employee activities and job performance through the use of computers.
Computer network An integration of computer systems, terminals, and communications links.
Computer operator One who performs those hardware-based activities needed to keep production information systems operational in the mainframe environment.
Computer system A collective reference to all interconnected computing hardware, including processors, storage devices, input/output devices, and communications equipment.
Computer virus See *virus.*
Computer-aided design (CAD) Use of computer graphics in design, drafting, and documentation in product and manufacturing engineering.
Computer-aided software engineering (CASE) An approach to software development that combines automation and the rigors of the engineering discipline.
Computer-based training (CBT) Using computer technologies for training and education.
Computerese A colloquial reference to the language of computers and information technology.
Configuration The computer and its peripheral devices.
Connectivity Pertains to the degree to which hardware devices, software, and databases can be functionally linked to one another.
Context-sensitive Referring to an on-screen explanation that relates to a user's current software activity.
Control unit The portion of the processor that interprets program instructions, directs internal operations, and directs the flow of input/output to or from RAM.
Cookie A message given to your Web browser by the Web server being accessed. The cookie is a text file containing user preference information.
Cooperative processing An environment in which organizations cooperate internally and externally to take full advantage of available information and to obtain meaningful, accurate, and timely information. (See also *intercompany networking.*)
Coprocessor An auxiliary processor that handles a narrow range of tasks, usually those associated with arithmetic operations.
CPU See *processor.*
Cracker An overzealous hacker who "cracks" through network security to gain unauthorized access to the network. (Contrast with *hacker.*)

Cross-platform technologies Enabling technologies that allow communication and the sharing of resources between different platforms.
CRT [*C*athode-*R*ay *T*ube] The video monitor component of a terminal.
Cryptography A communications crime-prevention technology that uses methods of data encryption and decryption to scramble codes sent over communications channels.
CSMA/CD access method [*C*arrier *S*ense *M*ultiple *A*ccess/*C*ollision *D*etection] A network access method in which nodes on the LAN must contend for the right to send a message.
Current window The window in a GUI in which the user can manipulate text, data, or graphics.
Cursor control device (CCD) Any point-and-draw device, such as a mouse or touchpad, that moves the cursor around the computer screen.
Cursor, graphics Typically an arrow or a cross hair that can be moved about a monitor's screen by a point-and-draw device to create a graphic image or select an item from a menu. (See also *cursor, text.*)
Cursor, text A blinking character that indicates the location of the next keyed-in character on the display screen. (See also *cursor, graphics.*)
Cursor-control keys The arrow keys on the keyboard that move the cursor vertically and horizontally.
Custom programming Program development to create software for situations unique to a particular processing environment.
Cyberphobia The irrational fear of, and aversion to, computers.
Cylinder A disk-storage concept. A cylinder is that portion of the disk that can be read in any given position of the access arm. (Contrast with *sector.*)

Data Representations of facts. Raw material for information. (Plural of *datum.*)
Data bits A data communications parameter that refers to a timing unit.
Data bus A common pathway between RAM, cache memory, and the processor through which data and instructions are transferred. (See also *address bus.*)
Data cartridge Magnetic tape storage in cassette format.
Data communications The collection and distribution of the electronic representation of information between two locations.
Data compression A method of reducing disk-storage requirements for computer files.
Data entry The transcription of source data into a machine-readable format.
Data file This file contains data organized into records.
Data flow diagram A design technique that permits documentation of a system or program at several levels of generality.
Data mining An analytical technique that involves the analysis of large databases, such as data warehouses, to identify possible trends and problems.
Data path The electronic channel through which data flows within a computer system.
Data processing (DP) Using the computer to perform operations on data.
Data processing (DP) system Systems concerned with transaction handling and record-keeping, usually for a particular functional area.
Data transfer rate The rate at which data are read/written from/to disk storage to RAM.
Data/voice/fax/modem A modem that permits data communication with remote computers via a telephone-line link and enabling telephone calls and fax machine simulation via a PC.
Data warehouse A relational database created from existing operational files and databases specifically to help managers get the information they need to make informed decisions.
Data warehousing An approach to database management that involves moving existing operational files and databases from multiple applications to a data warehouse.
Database The integrated data resource for a computer-based information system
Database administrator (DBA) The individual responsible for the physical and logical maintenance of the database.
Database software Software that permits users to create and maintain a database and to extract information from the database.
Debug To eliminate bugs in a program or system. (See also *bug.*)
Decision support system (DSS) An interactive information system that relies on an integrated set of user-friendly hardware and software tools to produce and present information targeted to support management in the decision-making process. (Contrast with *management information system* and *executive information system.*)
Decode To reverse the encoding process. (Contrast with *encode.*)
Decoder That portion of a processor's control unit that interprets instructions.
Dedicated keyboard port A port built into the system board specifically for the keyboard.
Dedicated mouse port A port built into the system board specifically for the cursor-control device.
Default options Preset software options that are assumed valid unless specified otherwise by the user.
Defragmentation Using utility software to reorganize files on a hard disk such that files are stored in contiguous clusters.
Density The number of bytes per linear length or unit area of a recording medium.
Desktop The screen in Windows upon which icons, windows, a background, and so on are displayed.
Desktop PC A nonportable personal computer that is designed to rest on the top of a desk. (Contrast with *laptop PC* and *tower PC.*)
Desktop publishing software (DTP) Software that allows users to produce near-typeset-quality copy for

newsletters, advertisements, and many other printing needs, all from the confines of a desktop.

Destination application, clipboard The software application into which the clipboard contents are to be pasted. (Contrast with *source application.*)

Detailed system design That portion of the systems development process in which the target system is defined in detail.

Device controller Microprocessors that control the operation of peripheral devices.

Device driver software Software that contains instructions needed by the operating system to communicate with the peripheral device.

Dialog box A window that is displayed when the user must choose parameters or enter further information before the chosen menu option can be executed.

Dialup connection Temporary modem-based communications link with another computer.

Dial-up line See *switched line.*

Digital A reference to any system based on discrete data, such as the binary nature of computers.

Digital camera A camera that records images digitally rather than on film.

Digital convergence The integration of computers, communications, and consumer electronics, with all having digital compatibility.

Digital ID A digital code that can be attached to an electronic message that uniquely identifies the sender.

Digital signal Electronic signals that are transmitted as in strings of 1s and 0s. (See also *analog signal.*)

Digital videodisk (DVD) The successor technology to the CD-ROM that can store up to about 10 gigabytes.

Digitize To translate data or an image into a discrete format that can be interpreted by computers.

Digitizer tablet and pen A pressure-sensitive tablet with the same *x-y* coordinates as a computer-generated screen. The outline of an image drawn on a tablet with a stylus (pen) or puck is reproduced on the display.

DIMM [*D*ual *I*n-line *M*emory *M*odule] A small circuit board, capable of holding several memory chips, that has a 64-bit data path and can be easily connected to a PC's system board. (Contrast with *SIMM.*)

Dimmed A menu option, which is usually gray, that is disabled or unavailable.

Direct access See *random access.*

Direct conversion An approach to system conversion whereby operational support by the new system is begun when the existing system is terminated.

Direct-access storage device (DASD) A random-access disk storage.

Disk address The physical location of a particular set of data or a program on a magnetic disk.

Disk caching A hardware/software technique in which frequently referenced disk-based data are placed in an area of RAM that simulates disk storage. (See also *RAM disk.*)

Disk density The number of bits that can be stored per unit of area on the disk-face surface.

Disk drive, magnetic A magnetic storage device that records data on flat rotating disks. (Compare with *tape drive, magnetic.*)

Disk, magnetic A storage medium for random-access data storage available in permanently installed or interchangeable formats.

Disk optimizer A program that reorganizes files on a hard disk to eliminate file fragmentation.

Diskette A thin interchangeable disk for secondary random-access data storage (same as *floppy disk*).

Docking station A device into which a notebook PC is inserted to give the notebook PC expanded capabilities, such as a high-capacity disk, interchangeable disk options, a tape backup unit, a large monitor, and so on.

Document A generic reference to whatever is currently displayed in a software package's work area or to a permanent file containing document contents.

Document file The result when work with an applications program, such as word processing, is saved to disk storage.

Document icon A pictograph used by Windows within an application to represent a minimized document window.

Document window Window within an application window that is used to display a separate document created or used by that application.

Domain expert An expert in a particular field who provides the factual knowledge and the heuristic rules for input to a knowledge base.

Domain name That portion of the Internet URL following the double forward slashes (//) that identifies an Internet host site.

DOS [*D*isk *O*perating *S*ystem] See *MS-DOS.*

Dot pitch The distance between the centers of adjacent pixels on a display.

Dot-matrix printer A printer that arranges printed dots to form characters and images.

Double-click Tapping a button on a point-and-draw device twice in rapid succession.

Download The transmission of data from a remote computer to a local computer.

Downsizing Used to describe the trend toward increased reliance on smaller computers for personal as well as enterprise-wide processing tasks.

Downstream rate The data communications rate from server computer to client computer.

Downtime The time during which a computer system is not operational.

DP See *data processing.*

Drag A point-and-draw device procedure by which an object is moved or a contiguous area on the display is marked for processing.

Drag-and-drop software Software that lets users drag ready-made shapes from application-specific stencils to the desired position on the drawing area to do drawings for flowcharting, landscaping, business graphics, and other applications.

Draw software Software that enables users to create electronic images. Resultant images are stored as vector graphics images.

Driver The software that enables interaction between the operating system and a specific peripheral device.
Driver module The program module that calls other subordinate program modules to be executed as they are needed (also called a *main program*).
DTP See *desktop publishing.*
Dual in-line memory module See *DIMM.*
DVD See *digital videodisk.*

EBCDIC [*E*xtended *B*inary *C*oded *D*ecimal *I*nterchange *C*ode] An 8-bit encoding system.
Echo A host computer's retransmission of characters back to the sending device.
E-commerce (electronic commerce) Business conducted online, primarily over the Internet.
EDI See *electronic data interchange.*
Edutainment software Software that combines *edu*cation and enter*tainment.*
EFT [*E*lectronic *F*unds *T*ransfer] A computer-based system allowing electronic transfer of money from one account to another.
Electronic commerce See *e-commerce.*
Electronic data interchange (EDI) The use of computers and data communications to transmit data electronically between companies.
Electronic dictionary A disk-based dictionary used in conjunction with a spelling-checker program to verify the spelling of words in a word processing document.
Electronic document See *online document.*
Electronic funds transfer See *EFT.*
Electronic mail A computer application whereby messages are transmitted via data communications to "electronic mailboxes" (also called *e-mail*). (Contrast with *voice message switching.*)
Electronic messaging A workgroup computing application that enables electronic mail to be associated with other workgroup applications.
Electronic money (e-money) A payment system in which all monetary transactions are handled electronically.
Electronic publishing The creation of electronic documents that are designed to be retrieved from disk storage and viewed.
E-mail See *electronic mail.*
E-mail server A host or network that services e-mail.
E-money See *electronic money.*
Encode To apply the rules of a code. (Contrast with *decode.*)
Encoding system A system that permits alphanumeric characters and symbols to be coded in terms of bits.
Encryption/decryption The encoding of data for security purposes. Encoded data must be decoded or deciphered to be used.
Enhanced television A TV presentation combining video and general programming from broadcast, satellite, and cable networks.
Enterprise-wide information system Information systems that provide information and processing capabilities to workers throughout a given organization.
Entity relationship diagram A business modeling tool used for defining the information needs of a business, including the attributes of the entities and the relationship between them.
EPS (*E*ncapsulated *P*ost*S*cript) A vector graphics file format used by the PostScript language.
Ergonomics The study of the relationships between people and machines.
Ethernet A local-area-net protocol in which the nodes must contend for the right to send a message. (See also *token access method.*)
E-time See *execution time.*
Exception report A report that has been filtered to highlight critical information.
Executable program file A file that contains programs that can be executed and run on a computer.
Execution time The elapsed time it takes to execute a computer instruction and store the results (also called *E-time*).
Executive information system (EIS) A system designed specifically to support decision making at the executive levels of management, primarily the tactical and strategic levels.
Exit routine A software procedure that returns you to a GUI, an operating system prompt, or a higher-level applications program.
Expansion board These add-on circuit boards contain the electronic circuitry for many supplemental capabilities, such as a fax modem, and are made to fit a particular type of bus (also called *expansion cards*).
Expansion bus An extension of the common electrical bus that accepts the expansion boards that control the video display, disks, and other peripherals. (See also *bus.*)
Expansion card See *expansion board.*
Expansion slots Slots within the processing component of a microcomputer into which optional add-on circuit boards may be inserted.
Expert system An interactive knowledge-based system that responds to questions, asks for clarification, makes recommendations, and generally helps users make complex decisions. (See also *assistant system.*)
Export The process of converting a file in the format of the current program to a format that can be used by another program. (Contrast with *import.*)
Extranet An extension of an intranet such that it is partially accessible to authorized outsiders, such as customers and suppliers. (See also *intranet.*)

Facsimile (fax) The transferring of images, usually of hard-copy documents, via telephone lines to another device that can receive and interpret the images.
FAQ A frequently asked question.
Fault-tolerant Referring to a computer system or network that is resistant to software errors and hardware problems.
Fax See *facsimile.*
Fax modem A modem that enables a PC to emulate a facsimile machine. (See also *modem.*)
Feedback loop A closed loop in which a computer-controlled process generates data that become input to the computer.

Fetch instruction That part of the instruction cycle in which the control unit retrieves a program instruction from RAM and loads it to the processor.
Fiber optic cable A data transmission medium that carries data in the form of light in very thin transparent fibers.
Field The smallest logical unit of data. Examples are employee number, first name, and price.
File (1) A collection of related records. (2) A named area on a disk-storage device that contains a program or digitized information (text, image, sound, and so on).
File allocation table (FAT) MS-DOS's method of storing and keeping track of files on a disk.
File compression A technique by which file size can be reduced. Compressed files are decompressed for use.
File format The manner in which a file is stored on disk storage.
File server A dedicated computer system with high-capacity disk for storing the data and programs shared by the users on a local area network.
File Transfer Protocol (FTP) A communications protocol that is used to transmit files over the Internet.
Filtering The process of selecting and presenting only that information appropriate to support a particular decision.
Firewall Software that is designed to restrict access to an organization's network or its Intranet.
Fixed magnetic disk See *hard disk.*
Flaming A barrage of scathing messages from irate Internet users sent to somebody who posts messages out of phase with the societal norms.
Flash memory A type nonvolatile memory that can be altered easily by the user.
Flat files A file that does not point to or physically link with another file.
Flat-panel monitor A monitor, thin from front to back, that uses liquid crystal and gas plasma technology.
Floating menu A special-function menu that can be positioned anywhere on the work area until you no longer need it.
Floppy disk See *diskette.*
Floppy disk drive A disk drive that accepts either the 3.5-inch or 5.25-inch diskette.
FLOPS [Floating Point Operations Per Second] A measure of speed for supercomputers.
Flowchart A diagram that illustrates data, information, and work flow via specialized symbols, which, when connected by flow lines, portray the logic of a system or program.
Flowcharting The act of creating a flowchart.
Folder An object in a Windows® graphical user interface that contains a logical grouping of related files and subordinate folders.
Font A typeface that is described by its letter style, its height in points, and its presentation attribute.
Footprint (1) The evidence of unlawful entry or use of a computer system. (2) The floor or desktop space required for a hardware component.
Foreground (1) That part of RAM that contains the highest priority program. (2) In Windows, the area of the display containing the active window. (Contrast with *background.*)
Formatted disk A disk that has been initialized with the recording format for a specific operating system.
FORTRAN [*FOR*mula *TRAN*slator] A high-level programming language designed primarily for scientific applications.
Fourth-generation language (4GL) A programming language that uses high-level English-like instructions to retrieve and format data for inquiries and reporting.
Frame A rectangular area in a desktop publishing–produced document into which elements, such as text and images, are placed.
Frames (Web page) The display of more than one independently controllable section on a single Web page.
Front-end applications software Client software that performs processing associated with the user interface and applications processing that can be done locally. (See also *back-end applications software.*)
Front-end processor A processor used to offload certain data communications tasks from the host processor.
Full-duplex line A communications channel that transmits data in both directions at the same time. (Contrast with *half-duplex line.*)
Function A predefined operation that performs mathematical, logical, statistical, financial, and character-string operations on data in a spreadsheet or a database.
Function key A special-function key on the keyboard that can be used to instruct the computer to perform a specific operation.
Functional specifications Specifications that describe the logic of an information system from the user's perspective.
Function-based information system An information system designed for the exclusive support of a specific application area, such as inventory management or accounting.

Gb See *gigabit.*
GB See *gigabyte.*
General system design That portion of the system development process in which the target system is defined in general.
General-purpose computer Computer systems that are designed with the flexibility to do a variety of tasks, such as CA, payroll processing, climate control, and so on.
Geosynchronous orbit An orbit that permits a communications satellite to maintain a fixed position relative to the surface of the earth.
GFLOPS A billion FLOPS. (See *FLOPS.*)
GIF A popular format for bit-mapped files.
Gigabit (Gb) One billion bits.
Gigabyte (GB) One billion bytes.
GIGO Garbage in, Garbage out.
Gopher A type of menu tree to "go for" items on the Internet, thus bypassing complicated addresses and commands.

Graceful exit Quitting a program according to normal procedures and returning to a higher-level program.

Grammar and style checker An add-on program to word processing software that highlights grammatical concerns and deviations from effective writing style in a word processing document.

Graphical user interface (GUI) A user-friendly interface that lets users interact with the system by pointing to processing options with a point-and-draw device.

Graphics adapter A device controller that provides the electronic link between the motherboard and the monitor.

Graphics conversion program Software that enables files containing graphic images to be passed between programs.

Graphics file A file that contains digitized images.

Graphics software Software that enables you to create line drawings, art, and presentation graphics.

Gray scales The number of shades of a color that can be presented on a monochrome monitor's screen or on a monochrome printer's output.

Green computing Environmentally sensible computing.

Groupware Software whose application is designed to benefit a group of people. (Related to *workgroup computing.*)

Hacker A computer enthusiast who uses the computer as a source of recreation. (Contrast with *cracker.*)

Half-duplex line A communications channel that transmits data in one direction at the same time. (Contrast with *full-duplex line.*)

Half-size expansion board An expansion board that fits in half an expansion slot.

Handheld PC Any personal computer than can be held comfortably in a person's hand (usually weighs less than a pound). (See also *personal digital assistant.*)

Handshaking The process by which both sending and receiving devices in a computer network maintain and coordinate data communications.

Hard copy A readable printed copy of computer output. (Contrast with *soft copy.*)

Hard disk A permanently installed, continuously spinning magnetic storage medium made up of one or more rigid disk platters. (Same as *fixed magnetic disk*; contrast with *interchangeable magnetic disk.*)

Hard disk drive See *hard disk.*

Hardware The physical devices that comprise a computer system. (Contrast with *software.*)

Help command A software feature that provides an online explanation of or instruction on how to proceed.

Help desk A centralized location (either within an organization or outside of it) where computer-related questions about product usage, installation, problems, or services are answered.

High-level language A language with instructions that combine several machine-level instructions into one instruction. (Compare with *machine language* or *low-level language.*)

Home page The Web page that is the starting point for accessing information at a site or in a particular area.

Horizontal scroll bar A narrow screen object located along the bottom edge of a window that is used to navigate side to side through a document.

Host computer The processor responsible for the overall control of a computer system.

Hot plug A universal serial bus (USB) feature that allows peripheral devices to be connected to or removed from the USB port while the PC is running.

Hotkey A seldom used key combination that, when activated, causes the computer to perform the function associated with the key combination.

HTML (HyperText Markup Language) The language used to compose and format most of the content found on the Internet.

Http (HyperText Transfer Protocol) The primary access method for interacting with the Internet.

Hub A common point of connection for computers and devices in a network.

Hyperlinks Clickable images or text phrase that let you link to other parts of a document or to different documents together within a computer system or on the Internet.

IBM Personal Computer (IBM PC) IBM's first personal computer (1981). This PC was the basis for PC-compatible computers.

Icons Pictographs used in place of words or phrases on screen displays.

iMac An Apple Computer personal computer.

Image processing A reference to computer applications in which digitized images are retrieved, displayed, altered, merged with text, stored, and sent via data communications to one or several remote locations.

Image scanner A device that can scan and digitize an image so that it can be stored on a disk and manipulated by a computer.

Impact printer A printer that uses pins or hammers that hit a ribbon to transfer images to the paper.

Import The process of converting data in one format to a format that is compatible with the calling program. (Contrast with *export.*)

Information Data that have been collected and processed into a meaningful form.

Information repository A central computer–based database for all system design information.

Information resource management (IRM) A concept advocating that information be treated as a corporate resource.

Information service A commercial network that provides remote users with access to a variety of information services.

Information society A society in which the generation and dissemination of information becomes the central focus of commerce.

Information superhighway A metaphor for a network of high-speed data communication links that will eventually connect virtually every facet of our society.

Information system A computer-based system that provides both data processing capability and information for managerial decision making.
Information technology (IT) A collective reference to the integration of computing technology and information processing.
Information technology competency (IT competency) Being able to interact with and use computers and having an understanding of IT issues.
Information-based decision See *nonprogrammed decision.*
Infrared port See *IrDA port.*
Ink-jet printer A nonimpact printer in which the print head contains independently controlled injection chambers that squirt ink droplets on the paper to form letters and images.
Input Data entered to a computer system for processing.
Input/output A generic reference to input and/or output to a computer.
Input/output-bound application An IT application in which the amount of work that can be performed by the computer system is limited primarily by the speeds of the I/O devices.
Instruction A programming language statement that specifies a particular computer operation to be performed.
Instruction register The register that contains the instruction being executed.
Instruction time The elapsed time it takes to fetch and decode a computer instruction (also called *I-time.*)
Integrated circuit (IC) Thousands of electronic components that are etched into a tiny silicon chip in the form of a special-function electronic circuit.
Integrated information system An information system that services two or more functional areas, all of which share a common database.
Integrated Services Digital Network (ISDN) A digital telecommunications standard for data delivery over twisted-pair lines with transmission speeds up to 128 K bps.
Intelligent agent Artificial intelligence–based software that has the authority to act on a person's or thing's behalf.
Interactive Pertaining to online and immediate communication between the user and the computer.
Interchangeable magnetic disk A magnetic disk that can be stored offline and loaded to the computer system as needed. (Contrast with *hard disk*, or *fixed magnetic disk.*)
Intercompany networking Companies cooperating with customers and other companies via electronic data interchange and extranets.
Internet Relay Chat (IRC) An Internet protocol that allows users to join and participate in group chat sessions.
Internet service provider (ISP) Any company that provides individuals and organizations with access to or presence on the Internet.
Internet site specialist A person responsible for creating and maintaining one or more Internet sites.
Internet, the (the Net) A global network that connects more than tens of thousands of networks, millions of large multiuser computers, and tens of millions of users in more than one hundred countries.
Interoperability The ability to run software and exchange information in a multiplatform environment.
Intranet An Internet-like network whose scope is restricted to the networks within a particular organization. (See also *extranet.*)
Invoke Execute a command or a macro.
I/O [Input/Output] Input or output or both.
IRC See *Internet Relay Chat.*
IrDA port Enables wireless transmission of data via infrared light waves between PCs, printers, and other devices (also called *infrared port*).
ISA bus An expansion bus for PC compatibles.
ISDN See *Integrated Services Digital Network.*
ISDN modem A modem that enables data communication over an ISDN line.
ISP See *Internet service provider.*
I-time See *instruction time.*

Jaz cartridge An interchangeable 3.5-inch hard-disk cartridge that can store up to 1 GB of information.
Jaz drive A disk drive that uses interchangeable Jaz cartridges.
Joystick A vertical stick that moves the cursor on a screen in the direction in which the stick is pushed.
JPEG A bit-mapped file format that compresses image size.
JPG The Windows-based extension for JPEG files, a bit-mapped file format that compresses image size.
Jukebox A storage device for multiple sets of CD-ROMs, tape cartridges, or disk modules enabling ready access to vast amounts of online data.

Kb See *kilobit.*
KB See *kilobyte.*
Kernel An operating system program that loads other operating system programs and applications programs to RAM as they are needed.
Key field The field in a record that is used as an identifier for accessing, sorting, and collating records.
Keyboard A device used for key data entry.
Keypad That portion of a keyboard that permits rapid numeric data entry.
Kilobit (Kb) 1024, or about 1000, bits.
Kilobyte (KB) 1024, or about 1000, bytes.
Knowledge base The foundation of a knowledge-based system that contains facts, rules, inferences, and procedures.
Knowledge engineer Someone trained in the use of expert system shells and in the interview techniques needed to extract information from a domain expert.
Knowledge worker Someone whose job function revolves around the use, manipulation, and dissemination of information.

ge-based system A computer-based system, ssociated with artificial intelligence, that helps s make decisions by enabling them to interact with knowledge base.

LAN operating system The operating system for a local area network.

LAN server A high-end PC on a local area network whose resources are shared by other users on the LAN.

Landscape Referring to the orientation of the print on the page. Printed lines run parallel to the longer side of the page. (Contrast with *portrait.*)

Laptop PC Portable PC that can operate without an external power source. (Contrast with *desktop PC* and *tower PC;* see also *pocket PC.*)

Large-format ink-jet printer See *plotter.*

Laser printer A page printer that uses laser technology to produce the image.

Layout A reference to the positioning of the visual elements on a display or page.

Leased line See *private line.*

Linux An open source spinoff of the UNIX operating system that runs on a number of hardware platforms and is made available for free over the Internet.

Listserv A reference to an Internet mailing list.

Load To transfer programs or data from disk to RAM.

Local area network (LAN or local net) A system of hardware, software, and communications channels that connects devices on the local premises. (Contrast with *wide area network.*)

Local bus A bus that links expansion boards directly to the computer system's common bus.

Local net See *local area network.*

Log off The procedure by which a user terminates a communications link with a remote computer. (Contrast with *logon.*)

Logic error A programming error that causes an erroneous result when the program is executed.

Logical operators AND, OR, and NOT operators can be used to combine relational expressions logically in spreadsheet, database, and other programs. (See also *relational operators.*)

Logical security That aspect of computer-center security that deals with user access to systems and data.

Logon The procedure by which a user establishes a communications link with a remote computer. (Contrast with *log off.*)

Loop A sequence of program instructions executed repeatedly until a particular condition is met.

Low-level language A language comprising the fundamental instruction set of a particular computer. (Compare with *high-level language.*)

Mac OS The operating system for the Apple family of microcomputers.

Machine cycle The cycle of operations performed by the processor to process a single program instruction: fetch, decode, execute, and place result in memory.

Machine language The programming language that is interpreted and executed directly by the computer.

Macintosh An Apple Computer personal computer.

Macro A sequence of frequently used operations or keystrokes that can be invoked to help speed user interaction with microcomputer productivity software.

Macro language Programming languages whose instructions relate specifically to the functionality of the parent software.

Magnetic disk drive See *disk drive, magnetic.*

Magnetic stripe A magnetic storage medium for low-volume storage of data on badges and cards. (Related to *badge reader.*)

Magnetic tape See *tape, magnetic.*

Magnetic tape cartridge Cartridge-based magnetic tape storage media.

Magnetic tape drive See *tape drive, magnetic.*

Magnetic-ink character recognition (MICR) A data entry technique used primarily in banking. Magnetic characters are imprinted on checks and deposits, then scanned to retrieve the data.

Magneto-optical technology An erasable recording technology that incorporates attributes of both magnetic and optical storage technologies.

Mail merge A computer application in which text generated by word processing is merged with data from a database (e.g., a form letter with an address).

Mailing list An Internet-based capability that lets people discuss issues of common interest via common e-mail.

Main menu The highest-level menu in a menu tree.

Main program Same as *driver module.*

Mainframe computer A large computer that can service many users simultaneously in support of enterprise-wide applications.

MAN See *Metropolitan Area Network.*

Management information system (MIS) A computer-based system that optimizes the collection, transfer, and presentation of information throughout an organization, through an integrated structure of databases and information flow. (Contrast with *decision support system* and *executive information system.*)

Mass storage Various techniques and devices used to hold and retain electronic data.

Massively parallel processing (MPP) An approach to the design of computer systems that involves the integration of thousands of microprocessors within a single computer.

Master file The permanent source of data for a particular computer application area.

Mb See *megabit.*

MB See *megabyte.*

Megabit (Mb) 1,048,576, or about one million, bits.

Megabyte (MB) 1,048,576, or about one million, bytes.

Megahertz (MHZ) One million hertz (cycles per second).

Memory See *RAM.*

Menu A display with a list of processing choices from which a user may select.

Menu bar A menu in which the options are displayed across the screen.

Menu tree A hierarchy of menus.

Message A series of bits sent from a terminal to a computer, or vice versa.
Metafile A class of graphics that combines the components of raster and vector graphics formats.
Metropolitan Area Network (MAN) A data network designed for use within the confines of a town or city.
MHZ See *megahertz.*
MICR See *magnetic-ink character recognition.*
Microcomputer (or micro) A small computer. (See also *PC.*)
Microprocessor A computer on a single chip. The processing component of a microcomputer.
Microsecond One millionth of a second.
Microsoft Network (MSN) An information service provider sponsored by Microsoft Corporation.
Microwave signal A high-frequency line-of-sight electromagnetic wave used in wireless communications.
MIDI [*M*usical *I*nstrument *D*igital *I*nterface] An interface between PCs and electronic musical instruments, like the synthesizer.
MIDI file A nonwaveform file result for MIDI applications.
Millisecond One thousandth of a second.
Minicomputer (or mini) A midsized computer.
Minimize Reducing a window on the display screen to an icon.
MIPS Millions of instructions per second.
Mnemonics A memory aid often made up from the initials of the words in a term or process.
Modem [*MO*dulator-*DEM*odulator] A device used to convert computer-compatible signals to signals that can be transmitted over the telephone lines, then back again to computer signals at the other end of the line.
Monitor A televisionlike display for soft-copy output in a computer system.
Morphing Using graphics software to transform one image into an entirely different image. The term is derived from the word *metamorphosis.*
Motherboard See *system board.*
Mouse A point-and-draw device that, when moved across a desktop a particular distance and direction, causes the same movement of the cursor on a screen.
Mouse cursor A symbol that indicates the positioning of the point-and-draw device cursor on the screen.
MS-DOS [*M*icro*S*oft–*D*isk *O*perating *S*ystem] The pre-Windows PC operating system.
Multifunction expansion board An add-on circuit board that contains the electronic circuitry for two or more supplemental capabilities (for example, a serial port and a fax modem).
Multifunction printer Multifunction machines that can handle several paper-related tasks such as computer-based printing, facsimile, scanning, and copying.
Multimedia application Computer applications that involve the integration of text, sound, graphics, motion video, and animation.
Multimedia projector An output peripheral device that can project the screen image (display) onto a large screen for group viewing.
Multiplatform environment A computing environment that supports more than one platform.
Multiplexor A communications device that collects data from a number of low-speed devices, then transmits the combined data over a single communications channel. At the destination, it separates the signals for processing.
Multitasking The concurrent execution of more than one program at a time.
Multiuser PC A microcomputer that can serve more than one user at any given time.

Nanosecond One billionth of a second.
National Information Infrastructure (NII) Refers to a futuristic network of high-speed data communications links that eventually will connect virtually every facet of our society. See also *information superhighway.*
Natural language A programming language in which the programmer writes specifications without regard to the computer's instruction format or syntax—essentially, using everyday human language to program.
Navigation Movement within and between a software application's work areas.
Net PC Same as *network computer (NC).*
Network address An electronic identifier assigned to each computer system and terminal/PC in a computer network.
Network administrator A data communications specialist who designs and maintains local area networks (LANs) and wide area networks (WANs).
Network bus A common cable in a bus topology that permits the connection of terminals, peripheral devices, and microcomputers to create a computer network.
Network, computer See *computer network.*
Network computer (NC) A single-user computer, usually diskless, that is designed to work with a server computer to obtain programs and data (also called *Net PC*).
Network interface card (NIC) A PC expansion card or PCMCIA card that facilitates and controls the exchange of data between the PC and its network.
Network topology The configuration of the interconnections between the nodes in a communications network.
Neural network A field of artificial intelligence in which millions of chips (processing elements) are interconnected to enable computers to imitate the way the human brain works.
Newbie A new user of the Internet.
Newsgroup The electronic counterpart of a wall-mounted bulletin board that enables Internet users to exchange ideas and information via a centralized message database.
Node An endpoint in a computer network.
Nondestructive read A read operation in which the program and/or data that are loaded to RAM from disk storage reside in both RAM (temporarily) and disk storage (permanently).
Nonimpact printer A printer that uses chemicals, lasers, or heat to form the images on the paper.

…grammed decision A decision that involves an …ned and unstructured problem (also called *infor…ion-based decision*).

Nonvolatile memory Solid-state RAM that retains its contents after an electrical interruption. (Contrast with *volatile memory.*)

Non-Windows application A computer application that will run under Windows but does not conform to the Windows standards for software.

Notebook PC A notebook-size laptop PC.

Numeric A reference to any of the digits 0–9. (Compare with *alpha* and *alphanumeric.*)

Object A result of any Windows application, such as a block of text, all or part of a graphic image, or a sound clip.

Object linking and embedding See *OLE.*

Object program A machine-level program that results from the compilation of a source program. (Compare with *source program.*)

Object-oriented language A programming language structured to enable the interaction between user-defined concepts that contain data and operations to be performed on the data.

Object-oriented programming (OOP) A form of software development in which programs are built with entities called objects, which model any physical or conceptual item. Objects are linked together in a top-down hierarchy.

OCR See *optical character recognition.*

Offline Pertaining to data that are not accessible by, or hardware devices that are not connected to, a computer system. (Contrast with *online.*)

OLE [*O*bject *L*inking and *E*mbedding] The software capability that enables the creation of a compound document that contains one or more objects from other applications. Objects can be linked or embedded.

Online Pertaining to data and/or hardware devices accessible to and under the control of a computer system. (Contrast with *offline.*)

Online document Documents that are designed to be retrieved from disk storage (locally or over a network) and viewed on a monitor. (Same as *electronic document.*)

Online thesaurus Software that enables a user to request synonyms interactively during a word processing session.

Open application A running application.

Open source software Referring to software for which the actual source programming code is made available to users for review and modification.

Operating system The software that controls the execution of all applications and system software programs.

Optical character recognition (OCR) A data entry technique that permits original source data entry. Coded symbols or characters are scanned to retrieve the data.

Optical laser disk A storage medium that uses laser technology to score the surface of a disk to represent a bit.

Output The presentation of the results of processing.

Packet Strings of bits that contain information and a network address that are routed over different paths on the Internet according to a specific communications protocol.

Page (Web) The area in which information is presented on the World Wide Web.

Page printer A printer that prints a page at a time.

Paint software Software that enables users to "paint" electronic images. Resultant images are stored as raster graphics images.

Palmtop PC See *pocket PC.*

Parallel conversion An approach to system conversion whereby the existing system and the new system operate simultaneously prior to conversion.

Parallel port A direct link with the microcomputer's bus that facilitates the parallel transmission of data, usually one byte at a time.

Parallel processing A processing procedure in which one main processor examines the programming problem and determines what portions, if any, of the problem can be solved in pieces by other subordinate processors.

Parallel transmission Pertaining to the transmission of data in groups of bits versus one bit at a time. (Contrast with *serial transmission.*)

Parameter A descriptor that can take on different values.

Parity checking A built-in checking procedure in a computer system to help ensure that the transmission of data is complete and accurate. (Related to *parity error.*)

Parity error Occurs when a bit is dropped in the transmission of data from one hardware device to another. (Related to *parity checking.*)

Password A word or phrase known only to the user. When entered, it permits the user to gain access to the system.

Patch A modification of a program or an information system.

PC [*P*ersonal *C*omputer] A small computer designed for use by an individual. See also *microcomputer.*

PC card Same as *PCMCIA card.*

PC specialist A person trained in the function and operation of PCs and related hardware and software.

PCI local bus [*P*eripheral *C*omponent *I*nterconnect] Intel's local bus. (See *local bus.*)

PCMCIA card A credit-card-sized module that is inserted into a PCMCIA-compliant interface to offer add-on capabilities such as expanded memory, fax modem, and so on (also called *PC card*).

PCX A bit-mapped file format.

PDF See *portable document format.*

Peer-to-peer LAN A local area network in which all PCs on the network are functionally equal.

Pen-based computing Computer applications that rely on the pen-based PCs for processing capability.

Pen-based PC Same as *slate PC.*

Pentium® An Intel microprocessor.

Pentium®Pro Successor to the Intel® Pentium microprocessor.

Pentium® II Successor to the Intel® Pentium Pro microprocessor.

Pentium® III Successor to the Intel® Pentium II microprocessor.

Peripheral device Any hardware device other than the processor.

Personal computer (PC) See *PC.*

Personal computing A computing environment in which individuals use personal computers for domestic and/or business applications.

Personal digital assistant (PDA) Handheld personal computers that support a variety of personal information systems.

Personal identification number (PIN) A code or number that is used in conjunction with a password to permit the user to gain access to a computer system.

Personal information management (PIM) system Software application designed to help users organize random bits of information and to provide communications capabilities, such as e-mail and fax.

Phased conversion An approach to system conversion whereby an information system is implemented one module at a time.

Photo illustration software Software that enables the creation of original images and the modification of existing digitized images.

Physical security That aspect of computer-center security that deals with access to computers and peripheral devices.

Picosecond One trillionth of a second.

Picture element See *pixel.*

Pie graph A circular graph that illustrates each "piece" of datum in its proper relationship to the whole "pie."

Pilferage A special case of software piracy whereby a company purchases a software product without a site-usage license agreement, then copies and distributes it throughout the company.

Pilot conversion An approach to system conversion whereby the new system is implemented first in only one of the several areas for which it is targeted.

Pixel [*Pi*cture element] An addressable point on a display screen to which light can be directed under program control.

Platform A definition of the standards by which software is developed and hardware is designed.

Plotter A device that produces high-precision hard-copy graphic output (also called *large-format ink-jet printer*).

Plug-and-play Refers to making a peripheral device or an expansion board immediately operational by simply plugging it into a port or an expansion slot.

PNG A license-free bit-mapped file format, similar to GIF.

Pocket PC A handheld personal computer (also called *palmtop PC*).

Point-and-draw device An input device, such as a mouse or trackpad, used to *point* to and select a particular user option and to *draw.*

Pointer The highlighted area in a spreadsheet display that indicates the current cell.

Polling A line-control procedure in which each terminal is "polled" in rotation to determine whether a message is ready to be sent.

POP (point-of-presence) An access point to the Internet.

Pop-out menu A menu displayed next to the menu option selected in a higher-level pull-down or pop-up menu.

Pop-up menu A menu that is superimposed in a window over whatever is currently being displayed on the monitor.

Port An access point in a computer system that permits communication between the computer and a peripheral device.

Port replicator A device to which a notebook PC can be readily connected to give the PC access to whatever external peripheral devices are connected to its common ports (keyboard, monitor, mouse, network, printer, and so on).

Portable document An electronic document that can be passed around the electronic world as you would a print document in the physical world.

Portable Document Format (PDF) A standard, created by Adobe Corporation, creating portable documents.

Portal A Web site or service that offers a broad array of Internet-based resources and services.

Portrait Referring to the orientation of the print on the page. Printed lines run parallel to the shorter side of the page. (Contrast with *landscape.*)

Post Office Protocol (POP) Refers to the way an e-mail client software gets e-mail from its server.

POTS Short for *p*lain *o*ld *t*elephone *s*ervice, the standard voice-grade telephone service common in homes and business.

Power up To turn on the electrical power to a computer system.

PowerPC processor A RISC-based processor used in Apple iMac and other computers.

Presentation software Software used to prepare information for multimedia presentations in meetings, reports, and oral presentations.

Prespecification An approach to system development in which users relate their information processing needs to the project team during the early stages of the project.

Print server A LAN-based PC that handles LAN user print jobs and controls at least one printer.

Printer A device used to prepare hard-copy output.

Private line A dedicated communications channel provided by a common carrier between any two points in a computer network. (Same as *leased line.*)

Procedure-oriented language A high-level language whose general-purpose instruction set can be used to sequence of instructions to model scientific ness procedures.

...ssor The logical component of a computer sys-...n that interprets and executes program instructions.

Processor-bound operation The amount of work that can be performed by the computer system is limited primarily by the speed of the computer.

Program (1) Computer instructions structured and ordered in a manner that, when executed, causes a computer to perform a particular function. (2) The act of producing computer software. (Related to *software.*)

Program register The register that contains the address of the next instruction to be executed.

Programmed decision Decisions that address well-defined problems with easily identifiable solutions.

Programmer One who writes computer programs.

Programmer/analyst The title of one who performs both the programming and systems analysis function.

Programming The act of writing a computer program.

Programming language A language programmers use to communicate instructions to a computer.

PROM [*P*rogrammable *R*ead-*O*nly *M*emory] ROM in which the user can load read-only programs and data.

Prompt A program-generated message describing what should be entered.

Proprietary software package Vendor-developed software that is marketed to the public.

Protocols See *communications protocols.*

Prototype system A model of a full-scale system.

Prototyping An approach to systems development that results in a prototype system.

Pseudocode Nonexecutable program code used as an aid to develop and document structured programs.

Pull technology Technology where data are requested from another program or computer, such as with an Internet browser. (Contrast with *push technology.*)

Pull-down menu A menu that is "pulled down" from an option in a higher-level menu.

Push technology Technology where data are sent automatically to an Internet user. (Contrast with *pull technology.*)

Query by example A method of database inquiry in which the user sets conditions for the selection of records by composing one or more example relational expressions.

Radio buttons Circle bullets in front of user options that when selected include a dot in the middle of the circle.

Radio signals Signals that enable data communication between radio transmitters and receivers.

RAM [*R*andom-*A*ccess *M*emory] The memory area in which all programs and data must reside before programs can be executed or data manipulated.

RAM disk That area of RAM that facilitates disk caching. (See also *disk caching.*)

Rambus DRAM See *RDRAM.*

Random access Direct access to records, regardless of their physical location on the storage medium. (Contrast with *sequential access.*)

Random processing Processing data and records randomly. (Contrast with *sequential processing.*)

Random-access memory See *RAM.*

Range A cell or a rectangular group of adjacent cells in a spreadsheet.

Rapid application development (RAD) Using sophisticated development tools to create a prototype or a functional information system.

Raster graphics A method for maintaining a screen image as patterns of dots. (See also *bit-mapped graphics.*)

RDRAM (Rambus DRAM) A new RAM technology capable of very high-speed transfer of data (600 MHz) to/from the processor.

Read The process by which a record or a portion of a record is accessed from the disk-storage medium and transferred to RAM for processing. (Contrast with *write.*)

Read-only memory (ROM) A memory chip with contents permanently loaded by the manufacturer for read-only applications.

Read/write head That component of a disk drive or tape drive that reads from and writes to its respective storage medium.

Record A collection of related fields (such as an employee record) describing an event or an item.

Register A small high-speed storage area in which data pertaining to the execution of a particular instruction are stored.

Relational database A database, made up of logically linked tables, in which data are accessed by content rather than by address.

Relational operators Used in formulas to show the equality relationship between two expressions (= [equal to], < [less than], > [greater than], <= [less than or equal to], >= [greater than or equal to], <> [not equal to]). (See also *logical operators.*)

Relative cell address Refers to a cell's position in a spreadsheet in relation to the cell containing the formula in which the address is used.

Resolution Referring to the number of addressable points on a monitor's screen or the number of dots per unit area on printed output.

RGB monitor Color monitors that mix red, green, and blue to achieve a spectrum of colors.

Ring topology A computer network that involves computer systems connected in a closed loop, with no one computer system the focal point of the network.

RISC [*R*educed *I*nstruction *S*et *C*omputer] A computer design architecture based on a limited instruction set machine language. (Contrast with *CISC.*)

Robot A computer-controlled manipulator capable of locomotion and/or moving items through a variety of spatial motions.

Robotics The integration of computers and industrial robots.

ROM [*R*ead-*O*nly *M*emory] RAM that can be read only, not written to.

Root directory The directory at the highest level of a hierarchy of directories.

Routers Communications hardware that enables communications links between LANs and WANs by performing the necessary protocol conversions.

RS-232C connector A 9-pin or 25-pin plug that is used for the electronic interconnection of computers, modems, and other peripheral devices.

Ruler bar In the document window, a line that shows appropriate document measurements.

Run To open and execute a program.

Scalable system A system whose design permits expansion to handle any size database or any number of users.

Scalable typeface An outline-based typeface from which fonts of any point size can be created.

Scanner A device that scans hard copy and digitizes the text and/or images to a format that can be interpreted by a computer.

Scheduler Someone who schedules the use of hardware resources to optimize system efficiency.

Screen saver A utility program used to change static screens on idle monitors to interesting dynamic displays.

Screen-capture programs Memory-resident programs that enable users to transfer all or part of the current screen image to a disk file.

Scroll arrow Small box containing an arrow at each end of a scroll bar that is used to navigate in small increments within a document or list.

Scroll box A square object that is dragged along a scroll bar to navigate within a document or list.

Scrolling Using the cursor keys to view parts of a document that extend past the bottom or top or sides of the screen.

SCSI bus [*S*mall *C*omputer *S*ystem *I*nterface] This hardware interface allows the connection of several peripheral devices to a single SCSI expansion board (or adapter).

SCSI controller The add-on circuitry needed for a SCSI port.

SCSI port A device interface to which up to 15 peripheral devices can be daisy-chained to a single USB port. (Contrast with *USB port.*)

SDRAM (Synchronous dynamic RAM) RAM that is able to synchronize itself with the processor enabling high-speed transfer of data (600 MHz) to/from the processor.

Search engine An Internet resource discovery tool that lets people find information by keyword(s) searches.

Sector A disk-storage concept of a pie-shaped portion of a disk or diskette in which records are stored and subsequently retrieved. (Contrast with *cylinder.*)

Sector organization Magnetic disk organization in which the recording surface is divided into pie-shaped sectors.

Secure Sockets Layer (SSL) A protocol developed by Netscape for transmitting private documents via the Internet.

Select Highlighting an object on a windows screen or a menu option.

Sequential access Accessing records in the order in which they are stored. (Contrast with *random access.*)

Sequential files Files containing records that are ordered according to a key field.

Sequential processing Processing of files that are ordered numerically or alphabetically by a key field. (Contrast with *random processing.*)

Serial port A direct link with the microcomputer's bus that facilitates the serial transmission of data.

Serial representation The storing of bits one after another on a storage medium.

Serial transmission Pertaining to processing data one bit at a time. (Contrast with *parallel transmission.*)

Server A LAN component that can be shared by users on a LAN.

Server application (1) An application running on a network server that works in tandem with a client workstation or PC application. (See also *client application.*) (2) In object linking and embedding, the application in which the linked object originates.

Server computer Any type of computer, from a PC to a supercomputer, that performs a variety of functions for its client computers, including the storage of data and applications software. (See also *client computer.*)

Server program A software program on the server computer that manages resources and can work in conjunction with a client program. (See also *client program.*)

Shortcut icon A graphic icon that represents an application or document that when chosen causes the application to be run or the document to be opened.

Shortcut key A key combination that chooses a menu option without the need to display a menu.

Shut down The processes of exiting all applications and shutting off the power to a computer system.

SIMM [*S*ingle *I*n-line *M*emory *M*odule] A small circuit board, capable of holding several memory chips, that has a 32-bit data path and can be easily connected to a PC's system board. (Contrast with *DIMM.*)

Simultaneous click Tapping both buttons on a point-and-draw device at the same time.

Slate PC A portable personal computer that enables input via an electronic pen in conjunction with a pressure-sensitive monitor/drawing surface.

Slides One of the images to be displayed in presentation software.

Smalltalk An object-oriented language.

Smart card A card or badge with an embedded microprocessor.

Soft copy Temporary output that can be interpreted visually, as on a monitor. (Contrast with *hard copy.*)

Soft font An electronic description of a font that is retrieved from disk storage and downloaded to the printer's memory.

Soft keyboard A keyboard displayed on a touch-sensitive screen such that when a displayed key is touched with a finger or stylus, the character or command is sent to memory for processing.

Software The programs used to direct the functions of a computer system. (Contrast with *hardware*; related to *program.*)

…ngineer A person who develops software …s to bridge the gap between design and exe…ble program code.

…ftware engineering A term coined to emphasize an approach to software development that embodies the rigors of the engineering discipline.

Software installation The process of copying the program and data files from a vendor-supplied master disk(s) to a PC's hard disk.

Software package One or more programs designed to perform a particular processing task.

Software piracy The unlawful duplication of proprietary software. (Related to *pilferage.*)

Software suite An integrated collection of software tools that may include a variety of business applications packages.

Sort The rearrangement of fields or records in an ordered sequence by a key field.

Source application, clipboard The software application from which the clipboard contents originated. (Contrast with *destination application.*)

Source data Original data that usually involve the recording of a transaction or the documenting of an event or an item.

Source document The original hard copy from which data are entered.

Source program The code of the original program (also called *source code*). (Compare with *object program.*)

Source program file This file contains high-level instructions to the computer that must be compiled prior to program execution.

Source-data automation Entering data directly to a computer system at the source without the need for key entry transcription.

Spam Unsolicited junk e-mail.

Spammer A person who distributes spam.

Speech synthesis Converting raw data into electronically produced speech.

Speech synthesizers Devices that convert raw data into electronically produced speech.

Speech-recognition system A device that permits voice input to a computer system.

Spelling checker A software feature that checks the spelling of every word in a document against an electronic dictionary.

Spreadsheet file A file containing data and formulas in tabular format.

Spreadsheet software Refers to software that permits users to work with rows and columns of data.

Star topology A computer network that involves a centralized host computer connected to a number of smaller computer systems.

Start button Permanent button on the Windows® task bar.

Stop bits A data communications parameter that refers to the number of bits in the character or byte.

Structure chart A chart that graphically illustrates the conceptualization of an information system as a hierarchy of modules.

Structured system design A systems design technique that encourages top-down design.

Subroutine A group or sequence of instructions for a specific programming task that is called by another program.

Supercomputer The category that includes the largest and most powerful computers.

Superdisk A disk-storage technology that supports very high-density diskettes.

Switched line A telephone line used as a regular data communications channel (also called *dial-up line*).

Switching hub A type of hub that accepts packets of information sent within a network, then forwards them to the appropriate port for routing to their network destination based on the network address contained in the packet.

Synchronous dynamic RAM (SDRAM) RAM that is able to synchronize itself with the processor enabling faster throughput.

Synchronous transmission A communications protocol in which the source and destination points operate in timed alignment to enable high-speed data transfer. (See also *asynchronous transmission.*)

Syntax The rules that govern the formulation of the instructions in a computer program.

Syntax error An invalid format for a program instruction.

System Any group of components (functions, people, activities, events, and so on) that interface with and complement one another to achieve one or more predefined goals.

System board A microcomputer circuit board that contains the microprocessor, electronic circuitry for handling such tasks as input/output signals from peripheral devices, and memory chips (same as *motherboard*).

System check An internal verification of the operational capabilities of a computer's electronic components.

System life cycle A reference to the four stages of a computer-based information system—birth, development, production, and death.

System maintenance The process of modifying an information system to meet changing needs.

System programmer A programmer who develops and maintains system programs and software.

System prompt A visual prompt to the user to enter a system command.

System software Software that is independent of any specific applications area.

System specifications (specs) Information system details that include everything from the functionality of the system to the format of the system's output screens and reports.

System unit An enclosure containing the computer system's electronic circuitry and various storage devices.

Systems analysis The examination of an existing system to determine input, processing, and output requirements for the target system.

Systems analyst A person who does systems analysis.
Systems testing A phase of testing where all programs in a system are tested together.

T-1 line A high-speed digital link to the Internet (1.544 M bps).
T-3 line A high-speed digital link to the Internet (44.736 M bps).
TAN See *tiny area network.*
Tape backup unit (TBU) A magnetic tape drive designed to provide backup for data and programs.
Tape drive, magnetic The hardware device that contains the read/write mechanism for the magnetic tape storage medium. (Compare with *disk drive, magnetic.*)
Tape, magnetic A storage medium for sequential data storage and backup.
Target system A proposed information system that is the object of a systems development effort.
Task The basic unit of work for a processor.
Taskbar In a Windows session, the bar shows what programs are running and available for use.
TCP/IP [*T*ransmission *C*ontrol *P*rotocol/*I*nternet *P*rotocol] A set of communications protocols developed by the Department of Defense to link dissimilar computers across many kinds of networks.
Telecommunications The collection and distribution of the electronic representation of information between two points.
Telecommuting "Commuting" via a communications link between home and office.
Telemedicine Describes any type of health care administered remotely over communication links.
Telephony The integration of computers and telephones.
Telnet A terminal emulation protocol that allows users to work from a PC as if it were a terminal linked directly to a host computer.
Template A model for a particular microcomputer software application.
Terabyte (TB) About one trillion bytes.
Terminal Any device capable of sending and receiving data over a communications channel.
Terminal emulation mode The software transformation of a PC so that its keyboard, monitor, and data interface emulate that of a terminal.
Text cursor A symbol controlled by the arrow keys that shows the location of where the next keyed-in character will appear on the screen.
TFLOPS A trillion FLOPS. (See *FLOPS.*)
Thesaurus, online See *online thesaurus.*
Third-generation language (3GL) A procedure-oriented programming language that can be used to model almost any scientific or business procedure. (Related to *procedure-oriented language.*)
Thread (newsgroup) An original Internet newsgroup message and any posted replies to that message.
Throughput A measure of computer system efficiency; the rate at which work can be performed by a computer system.
Throwaway system An information system developed to support information for a one-time decision, then discarded.
Thumbnail A miniature display of an image or a page to be viewed or printed.
TIF The Windows-based extension for TIFF files, a bit-mapped file format often used in print publishing.
TIFF A bit-mapped file format often used in print publishing.
Tiled windows Two or more windows displayed on the screen in a nonoverlapping manner.
Tiny area network (TAN) A term coined to refer to very small local area networks, typically installed in the home or small office.
Title bar A narrow Windows screen object at the top of each window that runs the width of the window.
Toggle The action of pressing a single key on a keyboard to switch between two or more modes of operation, such as insert and replace.
Token access method A local-area-net protocol in which an electronic token travels around a network giving priority transmission rights to nodes. (See also *Ethernet.*)
Toolbar A group of rectangular graphics in a software package's user interface that represent a frequently used menu option or a command.
Touch-screen monitors Monitors with touch-sensitive screens that enable users to choose from available options simply by touching the desired icon or menu item with their finger.
Tower PC A PC that includes a system unit that is designed to rest vertically. (Contrast with *laptop PC* and *desktop PC.*)
Track, disk That portion of a magnetic disk-face surface that can be accessed in any given setting of a single read/write head. Tracks are configured in concentric circles.
Track, tape That portion of a magnetic tape that can be accessed by any one of the tape drive's read/write heads. A track runs the length of the tape.
Trackball A ball mounted in a box that, when moved, results in a similar movement of the cursor on a display screen.
Trackpad A point-and-draw device with no moving parts that includes a touch-sensitive pad to move the graphics cursor.
Trackpoint A point-and-draw device that functions like a miniature joystick but is operated with the tip of the finger.
Tracks per inch (TPI) A measure of the recording density, or spacing, of tracks on a magnetic disk.
Transaction A procedural event in a system that prompts manual or computer-based activity.
Transaction file A file containing records of data activity (transactions); used to update the master file.
Transaction-oriented processing Transactions are recorded and entered as they occur.
Transmission medium The central cable along which terminals, peripheral devices, and microcomputers are connected in a bus topology.

...t A reference to a procedure or activity that [illegible] ...utomatically and does not have to be considered ...by the user.

...R [*T*erminate-and-*S*tay-*R*esident] Programs that remain in memory so they can be instantly popped up over the current application by pressing a hotkey.

Turnaround document A computer-produced output that is ultimately returned to a computer system as a machine-readable input.

Twisted-pair wire A pair of insulated copper wires twisted around each other for use in transmission of telephone conversations and for cabling in local area networks.

Typeface A set of characters that are of the same type style.

ULS (User Location Service) An Internet-based listing of Internet users who are currently online and ready to receive Internet telephone calls.

Unicode A 16-bit encoding system.

Uniform Resource Locator (URL) An Internet address for locating Internet elements, such as server sites, documents, files, bulletin boards (newsgroups), and so.

Uninterruptible power source (UPS) A buffer between an external power source and a computer system that supplies clean, continuous power.

Unit testing That phase of testing in which the programs that make up an information system are tested individually.

Universal product code (UPC) A 10-digit machine-readable bar code placed on consumer products.

Universal Serial Bus (USB) A bus standard that permits up to 127 peripheral devices to be connected to an external bus.

UNIX A multiuser operating system.

Upload The transmission of data from a local computer to a remote computer.

Upstream rate The data communications rate from client computer to server computer.

Uptime That time when the computer system is in operation.

URL See *uniform resource locator.*

USB port (*U*niversal *S*erial *B*us port) A high-speed device interface to which up to 127 peripheral devices can be daisy-chained to a single USB port. (Contrast with *SCSI port.*)

USENET A worldwide network of servers, often hosting newsgroups, that can be accessed over the Internet.

User The individual providing input to the computer or using computer output.

User interface A reference to the software, method, or displays that enable interaction between the user and the software being used.

User liaison A person who serves as the technical interface between the information services department and the user group.

User Location Service (ULS) Internet-based listing of Internet users who are currently online and ready to receive Internet telephone calls.

User-friendly Pertaining to an online system that permits a person with relatively little experience to interact successfully with the system.

Utility software System software programs that can assist with the day-to-day chores associated with computing and maintaining a computer system.

Vaccine An antiviral program.

VDT [*V*ideo *D*isplay *T*erminal] A terminal on which printed and graphic information are displayed on a televisionlike monitor and into which data are entered on a typewriterlike keyboard.

Vector graphics A method for maintaining a screen image as patterns of lines, points, and other geometric shapes.

Vertical scroll bar A narrow screen object located along the right edge of a window that is used to navigate up and down through a document or list.

VGA [*V*ideo *G*raphics *A*rray] A circuit board that enables the interfacing of very high-resolution monitors to microcomputers.

Video display terminal See *VDT.*

Video file This file contains digitized video frames that when played rapidly produce motion video.

Video mail (V-mail) Mail that's sent as video rather than as an electronic document.

Video RAM (VRAM) RAM on the graphics adapter.

Videophone An Internet-based capability that permits two parties to both see and hear one another during a conversation.

Virtual file allocation table (VFAT) Windows® method for storing and keeping track of files on a disk.

Virtual machine The processing capabilities of one computer system created through software (and sometimes hardware) in a different computer system.

Virtual reality An artificial environment made possible by hardware and software.

Virus A program written with malicious intent and loaded to the computer system of an unsuspecting victim. Ultimately, the program destroys or introduces errors in programs and databases.

Vision-input systems A device that enables limited visual input to a computer system.

Visual Basic A visual programming language.

Visual C++ A visual programming language.

Visual programming An approach to program development that relies more on visual association with tools and menus than with syntax-based instructions.

V-mail See *video mail.*

Voice message switching Using computers, the telephone system, and other electronic means to store and forward voice messages. (Contrast with *electronic mail.*)

Voice-response system A device that enables output from a computer system in the form of user-recorded words, phrases, music, alarms, and so on.

Volatile memory Solid-state semiconductor RAM in which the data are lost when the electrical current is turned off or interrupted. (Contrast with *nonvolatile memory.*)

WAIS [*W*ide *A*rea *I*nformation *S*erver] A database on the Internet that contains indexes to documents that reside on the Internet.
WAN See *wide area network.*
Wand scanner Handheld OCR scanner.
Wave file A windows sound file.
Web pages A document on the Web that is identified by a unique URL.
Web, the See *World Wide Web.*
Webcast The broadcasting of real-time audio and/or video streams over the Internet.
Webmaster An individual who manages a Web site.
Wheel mouse A mouse with a "wheel" to facilitate scrolling.
Whiteboarding An area on a display screen that permits a document or image to be viewed and worked on simultaneously by several users on the network.
Wide area network (WAN) A computer network that connects nodes in widely dispersed geographic areas. (Contrast with *local area network.*)
Window A rectangular section of a display screen that is dedicated to a specific document, activity, or application.
Windows® A generic reference to all Microsoft Windows operating system products.
Windows® 95 An operating system by Microsoft Corporation.
Windows® 98 An operating system by Microsoft Corporation (the successor to Windows 95).
Windows® 2000 Professional The client-side portion of the Windows 2000 operating system.
Windows® 2000 Server The server-side portion of the Windows 2000 operating system.
Windows® application An application that conforms to the Windows standards for software and operates under the Microsoft Windows platform.
Windows® CE A Microsoft operating system, whose GUI is similar to Windows 9x operating systems, that is designed to run on handheld PCs, PDAs, and other small computers.
Windows® NT Server The server-side portion of the Windows NT operating system that evolved to Windows 2000 Server.
Windows® NT Workstation The client-side portion of the Windows NT operating system that evolved to Windows 2000 Professional.
Windows® terminal An intelligent terminal that can run Windows operating systems, but is not designed for stand-alone operation.
Wintel PC A personal computer using a Microsoft Windows® operating system in conjunction with an Intel® or Intel-compatible processor.
Wireless transceiver Short for *transmitter-receiver,* a device that both transmits and receives data via high-frequency radio waves.
Wizard A utility within an application that helps you use the application to perform a particular task.
WMF (Windows metafile) A popular format for metafiles.
Word For a given computer, an established number of bits that are handled as a unit.
Word processing software Software that uses the computer to enter, store, manipulate, and print text.
Workgroup computing Computer applications that involve cooperation among people linked by a computer network. (Related to *groupware.*)
Workspace The area in a window below the title bar or menu bar containing everything that relates to the application noted in the title bar.
Workstation A high-performance single-user computer system with sophisticated input/output devices that can be easily networked with other workstations or computers.
World Wide Web (the Web, WWW, W3) An Internet server that offers multimedia and hypertext links.
Worm A program that erases data and/or programs from a computer system's memory, usually with malicious intent.
WORM disk [*W*rite-*O*nce *R*ead-*M*any disk] An optical laser disk that can be read many times after the data are written to it, but the data cannot be changed or erased.
WORM disk cartridge The medium for WORM disk drives.
Write To record data on the output medium of a particular I/O device (tape, hard copy, PC display). (Contrast with *read.*)
WYSIWYG [*W*hat *Y*ou *S*ee *I*s *W*hat *Y*ou *G*et] A software package in which what is displayed on the screen is very similar in appearance to what you get when the document is printed.

X terminal A terminal that enables the user to interact via a graphical user interface (GUI).

Yahoo An Internet portal.
Year 2000 problem (Y2K) An information systems problem brought on by the fact that many legacy information systems still treat the year field as two digits (98) rather than four (1998).

Zip disk The storae medium for Zip drives.
Zip drive A storage device that uses optical technology together with magnetic technology to read and write to an interchangeable floppy-size 100 MB Zip disk.
Zoom An integrated software command that expands a window to fill the entire screen.

Index

omputers, seventh edition, is a modular book that is custom published to meet curriculum needs. This book contains the *Information Technology Concepts* module (noted as *I* in the index) with none or any combination of the other two optional modules: *Living in an Information Society* (noted as *S* in the index), or *Business Information Systems* (noted as *B* in the index). One of the module indicators (*I, S,* or *B*) is included with each page entry in the index. When an index entry has several page references, the main reference(s) is in boldface type (for example: Data mining, **B21**, B30).

Abacus, I40
ABC, I43
Accumulator, **I91**, I94, I96, I106
ADSL, **I191**, I195–96, I208, I211, I216, I220–21, I225, I247
AGP board, I89, **I99**, I106, I163, I173, I262
Aiken, Howard, I44
Alphanumeric
  characters, I67, I75, I80, **I85**, I87
  keyboard, **I149**, I177
ALT key, I260
Altair 8800, I47
America Online (AOL), I6, **I10–11**, I34, I37, I182, I216–20, I222, I225, I247
Americans with Disabilities Act of 1990, I165
Analog, I10, **I84**, I87, I105, I134, I163, I172–73, I186–87, I189–91
Analytical engine, I41
Animation, I23, I33, I35, I38, S4, **S10**, S13–14, S16–17, S19, S33–35
Anonymous FTP site, **I234**, I248
ANSI, I85, **I87**, I105
Apple Computer Corporation, I47
  Apple II, I47
  iMac, **I19–20**, I37, I121, I281
  Macintosh, I19, I37, **I48**, I139, I151, I239, I256–58, S15
Applet, **I226**, I229, I248, S95
Application generator, **B43**, B61
Applications
  airline, I10, I16, I25, I32, I150, I174, I176, I188, I215, S49, S58, S72, B8, B18, B33
  architecture, I106, I109, I230, I256, S101
  art, I61, I64, I116, I230, I234, I240, S11–12, S16–17, S40, S80, S90
  automotive, S77, S79, S96
  education, I34–35, I38, I40, I51–52, I57, I73, I76, I78, I286, S24–26, S35, S43–44, S103, S106–7, S111
  entertainment, I18, I27, I32, I35–36, I38, I51, I84, I175, I183, I230, I262, S18, S23–25, S30, S35, S83, S96–97, S102
  financial and banking, I16–17, I157, I175, I184, I218, S22–23, S60, S69, S95, S99, S110, B5, B27
  genealogy, I219
  geology, B23
  government, I4, I11, I26, I32, I41–42, I57, I131, I135, I183, I202, I210, I217–19, I261, S24–25, S29, S40–41, S52–53, S56–58, S61–63, S66, S81, S84, S97, S99, S106, B13–14, B24, B27
  health care, I28, I32, I34, I52, I76, I78, I110, I156–57, I159, I164, I175, I183, I209, I216, I274, S11–12, S24, S28–29, S32, S35, S40–41, S43, S45, S48, S61–63, S71, S76, S89, S97, S99–102, S106, S109, S111, B23–24, B26–27, B58
  insurance, I10, I52, I156–57, S22, S42, S56–57, S59–60, S63, B4–5, B18, B23, B25
  legal, S10, S22, S43
  library, I84, I134, I141, I235, I245, S16–17, S24, S35, S49, S97
  manufacturing, I45, I85, I92, I108–10, I140, I155, S12, S42, S53–54, S59, S76, S79, S83, B20, B37, B41, B47, B51
  marketing, I74, I79, I108, I137, I183, S10–11, S47, S91, B12, B17, B21, B41
  music, I18, I35, I52, I84, I98, I99, I105, I134, I138, I172, I226, I234, I238–39, S13, S16–17, S28, S65, S107, B29
  order entry, I74, B15
  order processing, B11, B15
  payroll, I28–30, I91, I168, S61, S77, S99, B13–14, B16, B27, B36, B40–41, B51
  petroleum, I60, S69, B24
  publishing, I33, I36, I60–62, I74, I79, I135, I137, S5, S18, S97–98, S111, B56
  real estate, I6, I57, S22, S29
  retail sales, I16–18, I150
  traffic-control, S47, B48
  transportation, I105, I139, I148, I203, B34
  videoconferencing, I10, I242, I248, I286, S84, S110
  video-on-demand, I183, S96, S108–9, S111
  weather, I10, I11, I27, I37, I215, I236, B24, B29
Arithmetic and logic unit, **I89–91**, I93–94, I96, I100–1, I106
ARPANET, **I217–19**, I225, I247
Artificial intelligence (AI), I159, S76, S79, S82, **S89–91**, S111, B18, B23, B28–30
ASCII encoding system, **I85–87**, I105, I116–19, I143, I185, I225, I237, S72–73
Asynchronous transmission, **I200–1**, I212

AT&T, I44, I195, I202, I221, I222, S62, B29
Atanasoff, John V., I43
ATM (automatic teller machine), I7, I116, **I148–49**, I157–58, I175–76
Audio mail, I236, **I239**, I241–42, I248

Babbage, Charles, **I41–42**, I44
Backbone, **I189**, I191, I211, I219
Background, **I254**, I263, I269, I277–78
Backup, I24, **I31**, I38, I96, I116, I121, I127, I130, **I131–33**, I143, I176, I208, I287, S34–35, S68–69, B50
Badge reader, **I158**, I176–77, S70, S74
Bar code, **I154–55**, I158, I162, I177, B15
Batch processing, **B15**, B30
Baud rate, **I190**, I211
Berry, Clifford E., I43
Binary, I41, I44, **I84–87**, I95, I105, I138, I185, I187, S4, S91
  numbering system, **I84**, I105
Bit, **I84–87**, I96, I105, I123, I138, I201, S69
Bits per second (bps), **I190**, I211
Boot procedure, **I276–77**, I279
Bridge (data communications), I186
Browsers, I49, I51–52, I58–59, I79, I117, I136–37, I214, **I216**, I222–23, **I225–30**, I232, I234–35, I247–48, S3–4, S21, S34, S47, S56–57
  navigation, I227–29
Bug, I3, **I45**, I258, B26
Bus, I82–83, **I89**, I91–92, I96, I117, I163, I187, S99
  expansion, **I98–99**, I106
  ISA, **I98**, I106
  local, **I98–100**, I106
  network, **I197–98**, I201, I205, I207, I211
  PCI local, I89, **I98–100**, I106
  SCSI, **I98–100**, I106
  topology, **I197–98**, I205, I207, I211
Byte, I3, **I86–87**, I93, I103, I200

Cache memory, I89, **I93**, I102–3, I106, I282
Carpal tunnel syndrome, **S51–52**, S54
Cashless society, **S41**, S88, S98–99
Cathode-ray tube (CRT), I168
CD production station, **I140**, I144
CD writer, **I140**, I142, I144
CD-Recordable (CD-R), **I140–142**
CD-ReWritable (CD-RW) I134, **I140–42**, I144, I161, I268, I282, I284–85, S16, S27, S35
CD-ROM, **I23**, I134, I138–41, I144
  disk, **I139**, I144
  drive, I19, **I23**, I38, I138, I140, I142, I144, I275, I282, I287
  jukebox, **I139**, I144
  pits, I85, **I134**
Celeron microprocessor, I19, **I90**, I106
Cell, **I67–71**, I79–80
  absolute addressing, I68
  address, **I67–68**, I80
  current, **I67**, I70–71
  range, I67
  relative address, I68
Central processing unit (CPU), **I90–91**, I106
Centronics connector, **I96**, I106
Channel Bar (Windows), I263
Charts
  organization, **I64**, I80
  text, S10
Chip, making of, I108–13
Chipset, **I89**, I105
Client
  application, **I270**, I278
  computer, **I29**, I32, I38, **I198–99**, I201, I211, B54
  program, **I222–23**, I247
Client/server computing, I180, I189, **I198–99**, I201, I211, I256–57, I277, S29, S47, B11, B54–55
Clip art, **I61–62**, I64, I66, I75, I80, I117, S4, S17, S35
Clipboard, **I270–71**, I273, I278, S7
Clock cycle, **I102**, I104
Cluster, **I124–25**, I130, I143
Coaxial cable, **I191**, I193, I195, I204–5, I210–11
Color palette, **I266**, S7, S19, S34
Common carrier, **I195–96**, I201, I204, I211–12, I222
Communications, **I10**, I181–225, I237–249 (*see also* Data communications)
  channel, I188, **I190–91**, I195–96, I199, I204
  channel capacity, **I190–91**, I194–96
  protocols, **I189**, I222, I225, I247
  software (*see* Software, communications)
Compact disk-recordable (CD-R), I130, I134, **I140–42**
Compatibility, I115, I182, **I256–57**, I263, I272, I281
  upward, I46
  backward, I139, I263, I272
Compiler, **I45**, I157, S56
Complex Instruction Set Computer (CISC), **I103–6**
CompuServe, **I34**, I182, I216–17, I219–20, I222, I247, I286, S92
Computation operation, I12, **I30**, I32
Computer, **I12**, I37
  accuracy of, I31
  backup, **I31**, I38, S43
  capacity, **I13**, I15, I27, I35–37, I104, I198, S83, S110, B45
  certification, **S47–48**, S73
  crime, **S60–66**, S68, S74
  dedicated, I253
  electromechanical, I44
  general-purpose, **I26**, I41, I253
  history of, I40–49
  host, I12, **I25**, I28, I38, I186–88, I247–48
  licensing, **S47–48**, S73
  mainframe, **I13–14**, I25–27
  matching, **S57–58**, S66, S74
  monitoring, **S58–59**, S66, S74

...ontinued
...rk, I2, **I9–10,** I12, I37, I128, I143, I182–212
...gramming, I95
reliability, I31
speed of, **I31**, I106
stand-alone, **I26**, I95
system, **I12–16**, I88–106
uses, I32–36
wearable, **I274**, S85
Computer system
configuration, **I19**, I21, I23, I85, I197, I257, I275, B24
Computer-aided design (CAD), **I25**, I34, I38, I103, I108, I167, I286, S5–6, S12, S29, S42, S48, S79, S81, S103, S110
Computer-aided software engineering (CASE), B32, **B41–48**, B51–56, B60–61
Computer-based training (CBT), **I35–36**, I53, S13, S24, S49
Computerese, I14
Computing-Tabulating-Recording Company, I42
Connectivity, I180, **I183**, I185, I188
Context-sensitive help, **I149**, I233, I266, I276–79
Control unit, **I89–91**, I93–94, I96, I100–1, I106
Conversion (system)
direct, **B50**, B52
parallel, **B50**, B53
phased, **B50–52**
pilot, **B50–51**, B53
Cookie, **S56–57**, S74
Cooperative processing, **I184**, I211
Crackers, S64
Crosshair device, I24, **I151–52**
Cross-platform technologies, **I258**, I278
Cryptography, S64, **S69**, S72–74
Crystal oscillator, I102
Cumulative trauma disorder (CTD), **S51–52**, S73
Cursor
control device (CCD), **I260**, I266
graphics, I269, I271, S6, S34
mouse, **I151**, I177
text, **I149**, I177
Cursor-control keys, **I149**, I177, I266
Custom programming, **B42**, B47–48, B53
Cyberspace, **I5**, I240, S33

Data, I7
demographic, I67
entering, I19, **I48–62**, B15–16, B26, B45
live, B49
source, **B14**, B30
test, B49
Data cartridge, I114, **I131**, I143
Data communications, I37, I180–81, **I185–87**, I192–204
channels, **I190–96**, I211
hardware, **I185–89**, I211
Data compression, I130
Data flow diagram, **B36–43**, B47, B60
Data mining, **B21**, B30
Data path, **I92**, I256
Data processing (DP) system, **B16–18**, B23, B25
Data transfer rate, **I127**, I143
Data warehousing, **B20–23**, B30, B56
Database, I10, I33, **I72 -78**
attribute, I54
integrated, S4, **B17–20**, B30, B37
national, **S101–2**, S109, S111
relational, **I73**, I80, B20, B27, B30
structure, I75–76, B46, B56
table, I73–80
Debug, S46, **B48**
Decision support system (DSS), S49, B2, **B18–23**, B25, B29–30
Decisions
information-based, B7, **B10**
nonprogrammed, **B10**
programmed, B7, **B10–11**
Decode, I86, I91
Decoder, **I91**, I106
Default options, I53, I60, I79, **I275**, I277, I279
Defragmentation, **I125**, I130, I143, I287, S32–34
Desktop (Windows), I254, **I262–68**, I276, I278
Desktop mainframe, I13
Desktop publishing (DTP), **I33**, I38, I50–52, I60–62, I74, I77, I79–80, S4, S7, S34, S47
Destination application, **I270–71**, I278
Device controller, **I89**, I105, I163
Dialog box, I225, **I266–67**, I269, I278, B55
Dial-up line, **I195–96**, I211
Dialup connection, **I220–22**, I227, I247
Dictionary (electronic), **I54**, I60, I79, I139, S28
Difference engine, I41
Digital camera, I8, I10, I64, I96, **I160–63**, I242, S4, S15–17, S35, S85, S106–7
Digital convergence, **I182–83**, I185–86, I211
Digital ID, **S69**, S74
Digital signals, **I84**, I163, I186–90, I194
Digitize, I8, I11, I37, **I84**, I116–17, I134, I138, I141, **I156–57**, I159–63, I183, I185, I237, S34, S70–71
Digitizer tablet and pen, **I152–53**, I177, S11
Dimmed, **I265**
Direct access, I119
Disk, I12
access arm, **I122–24**, I127, I129–30, I134, I143
access time, I112, **I127**, I138, I141–143
address, **I124**, I130, I143
caching, I127
cylinder organization, I122, **I124**, I130, I143
density, **I121**, I124
drive, **I23**
fixed, **I119–22**, I128
fixed magnetic, **I119**, I143
floppy, I20, **I23**, I38, I120–23, I130, I143

Disk, *continued*
floppy drive, **I23**, I38, I121
format, **I125–26**, I143
hard, I58, I100, I116, **I118–19**, I121, I122–28, I130–135, I142–43, I207, I275, I279, S17, S29, S32, S56
interchangeable, I12, **I119–22**, I143
Jaz cartridge, **I122**, I130, I143
Jaz drive, **I122–23**, I143
magnetic, I12, I30, I85–87, I114, I116, **I119–128**, I130–34
read/write head, I120, **I122–25**, I127, I129–30, I287
sector organization, **I124**, I126, I138, I143
SuperDisk, I20, **I120–21**, I129, I131–32, I287
WORM, I134, **I141–42**, I144
WORM cartridge, **I141–42**, I144
Zip, I88, I115, **I120–21**, I129, I131–32, I287–88
Zip drive, I88, **I121**, I132, I143, I268
Diskette, **I23**, I38, I120–22
Docking station, **I19**, I23, I28, I37
Document
compound, **I270**, I272, I278
file, **I32**, I38
layout, I61, I78, **B42–3**
online, I58–59, **I135–37**
source, I270, **B14–15**, B30
Document-composition process, **I61–62**, I80
Domain name, **I224**, I227, I248
Dot pitch, **I166**, I172–74
Dots per inch (dpi), I169
Download, I9, **I11**, I217, I219, I232, I234, I244, S33, S64
Downsizing, I119
Downstream rate, **I191**, I211
Downtime, **I31**, I38
Drag-and-drop, I225, **S9–10**
Driver (peripheral device), **I262**, I278
Driver module, **B40–41**, B49, B60
Dual in-line memory module (DIMM), **I92**, I106
DVD, I83, I88–89, I134–35, **I137–139**, I141–42, I282, I288
Dynamic RAM (DRAM), **I92–93**, I106

EAM, I43, B48
Eckert, J. Presper, I44
E-commerce, I17, **I246**, I249, S69, S97, S110
Electronic data interchange (EDI), **I184–85**, I211, S100, S109, S111
Electronic funds transfer (EFT), S98–100, **S98–99**, S111
Electronic messaging, I257
Electronic signature, **S70**, S74
E-mail, **I6**, **I236–39**, I241–43, B28–29
attached file, **I237**, I248
message, I236–39
E-money (electronic money), **S99–100**, S109
Emoticons, I240
Enabling technology, **I5**, I10, I159, I64–65
Enhanced television, **I262**, I278
Encoding system, **I85–87**, I105
Encryption/decryption, S64, **S69**, S72, S74
End user (*see* User)
ENIAC, **I44**, I49, I108, I264, B48
Entering commands, I254
Entity relationship diagram, **B40**, B60
Ergonomics, I151, S39, **S51–54**, S73
Ethernet access method, **I205**, I212
Ethics (in computing), I8, I59, I131, I175, I194, I223, I258, I288, S12, **S54–65**, S73, S97, S99, S107, B11, B51
Exception report, **B8–9**, B30
Execution time (e-time), **I95–96**, I100
Executive information system (EIS), **B22–23**, B25, B29–30
Exit routine, **I276–77**, I279
Expansion board, I82, I88–89, **I97–100**, I106, I130, I173, I186–87, I256, I259, I287, S16, S18
network interface card (NIC), **I100**, I186–89, I209–12
sound, **I99**, I173, I241, I287
video capture, S35
Expansion slot, I19, I89, **I98–100**
Expert system, I252, S41, **S89–91**, B2–3, **B23–25**, B28–31
assistant system, **B23**
domain expert, B23
Export, **I64**, I118, I137, I143, B21, B30
Extranet, **I184**, I211

FAQ (frequently asked question), **I232**, I248
Fault tolerant **S67**, S74
Fax, I21, **I172**
Feedback loop, S102
Fiber optic cable, I85, I87, I185, **I191–95**
Field, **I57**, I73–80
key, **I72**, I76, I78–80
name, **I57**, I75, I76
size, **I75**, I79
type, I75
File, I116
archiving, I143
ASCII, **I117–19**, I143
audio, **I117–18**, I143
backup, I132
compression, **I118**, I143
data, **I117–18**, I143, I273, I275, I287, S65
document, I57, **I117–18**, I143
executable program, **I117–18**, I143
format, I118, **S5**, S7, S18–19, S34
graphics, **I117–19**, I126, I143, S6–7
master, **I8**, I30, I37, I130, S69
MIDI, **S17**, S19, S35
naming, **I224**
portability, I143
print, I207
source program, **I117–18**, I143
spreadsheet, **I117–18**, I143

...nued
..., I61, **I80**, S35, S56
...ansfer, I230
video, **I117–18**, I143, S18, S35
wave, **S16**, S35
File allocation table (FAT), I124–26
File Transfer Protocol (FTP), I224–25, I227, I232, **I234**
File type
BMP, **S5–6**, S19, S34
CGM, **S6**, S34
GIF, I234, **S5–7**, S19, S34, S47
JPEG *or* JPG, **S5–6**, S34
TIF *or* TIFF, **S5**, S34
WMF (metafile), **S4**, S6, S34
Filtering,
information, **B8–9**, S107
Internet, S33
Firewall, **I246**, I249
Flamed, **I246**, I249
FLOPS, **I101–2**, I104
Flowchart, S9, S30, B36, **B40–42**
Fonts, **I53–54**
Footprint, **S64**
Forecasting, **B18**, B21
Foreground
RAM, **I254**
Window, **I269**, I277–78
Frame
desktop publishing, **I60–62**, I80,
Web page, **I233**, I248
Full duplex, I241

Garbage in, garbage out (GIGO), **B5**
Gates, Bill, **I47**, I245, I256
Gateway, **I220–22**, I247
Geosynchronous orbit, **I193**, I211
Gigabyte, **I102–3**
Global positioning system (GPS), **I100**, I106, I148, S27, S29, S49, S96, B34
Global village, **I9–10**, I37
Goal seeking, B21–22
Gopher, I234–35
Grammar and style checker, **I55–56**, I60, I79
Graphical user interface (GUI), I48, **I151–54**, **I254–55**
Graphics
bit-mapped, **S4–8**, S18–19
conversion program, S6–7
drag-and-drop, **S9**
draw program, **S8–9**, S11
glass block effect, S9
morphing, **S9**, S19, S24
paint program, I271, S4, **S6–9**
photo illustration, **S8–9**
raster, **S5**, S34
vector, **S4–6**, S8–9, S18–19
Graphics adapter, I106, **I163**, I172–73
Graphs
bar, **I57–58**
line, **I64**
pie, **I64**
Gray scales, **I166**, I172
Green computing, S51, **S53–54**, S73
Groupware, I203, **I209–12**

Half duplex, I241
Handshaking, **I188–89**, I211
Hardcopy output, **I12**, I37
Hard-disk drive, **I23**
Hardware, **I-5**
data communications, I185–89
peripheral devices, **I12**, I23–24, I116–76
Help command, **I276**
Help desk, S47
Heuristic knowledge, B23–25
Hollerith, Herman, I42
Home office, I202–203, S19, S53
Home page, I59, **I227–28**, I230, I248, S64, B52
Honeywell, Inc., I45
Hopper, Grace, I45
Hot plug, **I99**, I106
Hot swap, I100
Hotkey, **I260**, I278
Hyperlink, **I58–60**, I62, I228–33
Hypermedia, S106
Hypertext, **I227**, I230, I246, I248
HyperText Markup Language (HTML), I136–37, **I224–26**, I230, I232–33, I248, I262
HyperText Transport Protocol (HTTP), **I223**, I248

Icon, **I255**, I261
application, I263, I265, **I267**
disk drive, **I268**
document, **I267–68**
shortcut, **I267**
Image processing, I141, I144, **I156–57**
Import (a file), **I63–64**, I66, I118–19, I143, S47, B21, B30
Information, I7
Information network, I11
Information repository, **B43**, B60–61
Information service, I4, **I10–12**, I33–37, I49, I214–17
Information society, **I4–8**, I11–12, S110
Information superhighway, **I6**, S95–97, S99–101, S107–11, B29
Information system, **I31–32**, S31, S66–71, B2–29, B33–60
enterprise-wide, **I25**, B53–55
function-based, **B13**, B30
integrated, **B13**
Information technology (IT), **I4**, S40–43
competency, **I4**, S48–50
Infrared port (IrDA), **I98**, S72
Input, I4

Input devices, I19, **I148–62**
Input/output (I/O), **I14–15**
Input/output-bound applications, **I26**, I38
Instruction time (i-time), **I95–96**
Instructions
  execution of, I102
  input/output, B53
  program, **I30**, I91–93, B60
Integrated circuit (chip), **I12**, I37, I45–46, I49, I85, **I89–93**, I105, **I108–13**, S65, S98
Intel Corporation, **I18**, I22, I49, I110, I203
Intelligent agent, **S107**, S109, B2, B18, **B28–29**, B31
Interactive book (i-book), I226, **S18**
Interactive kiosk, **I134**, S14
International Business Machines (IBM), **I18**, I20, I37, I40, I42–44, I46–48, I59, I90, I108, I120, I159, I256, I274, I286, S65, S68, S85, S91, S98
Internet, I6, I8, **I10–11**, I16–18, I51–52, I58–59, I116–18, I135–37, I181–85, I190–94, **I215–47**, S8, S13–17, S32–33, S46–74, S92–100, S107–11, B14, B18, B22, B25–29, B48, B51–54
  address, I223–25
  browsers, I225–30
  connecting to, I220–23
  defined, I217
  history of, I217–19
  issues, I246–247
  using, I230–43
Internet Protocol (IP), **I222**
Internet relay chat (IRC), **I239**
Internet service provider (ISP), **I10**, **I220–22**
Interoperability, I251, **I258**
Intranet, I135, **I184–85**, I211, I246, I249, S50
ISDN, **I189–91**, I195–96, I211, I216, I220–21, I225, I247
  modem, **I190**, I211

Jacquard, Joseph-Marie, I41–42
Java, S95, **B53**, B60
Jobs (computer related)
  applications programmer, **S46**, S50
  chief information officer (CIO), **S44–45**, S51
  computer operator, **S46**
  database administrator (DBA), **S46**, S50
  Internet site specialist, **S46**
  network administrator, I222, **S46**, S50, S51
  PC specialist, **S47**, S50
  programmer, I42, I45, I202, **S46**, S50, B26, B42, B49, B57–62
  programmer/analyst, **S46**
  software engineers, **B42**, B61
  system operator, B3
  systems analyst, **S44**, S46, S50, B37, B42–45, B49, B54
  systems programmer, **S46**
  user liaison, **S47**, S51
  Webmaster, **I46**, I73
Jobs, Steven, I47
Joystick, I98–99, **I152–54**, I177, I283

Kapor, Mitchell, I48
Kemeny, John, I46
Kernel, **I252**, I255, I277
Key
  function, I25, **I149–50**, I154, I177
Keyboard, **I12**, I19, I21–24, **I147–54**
  QWERTY, I147, **I149–50**, I177
  soft keyboard, **I162**, I177
  special-function, **I149**, I177
Keypad, I25, **I148–50**
Kilby, Jack, I45
Kilobit, I103–4
Kilobyte, I102–3
Knowledge base, I104, **S89**, S91, S111, B24
Knowledge engineer, I252
Knowledge worker, I4
Knowledge-based system, **B23–25**, B30
Kurtz, Thomas, I46

Local area network (LAN), **I29**, **I204–12**, I221, S20–21, S66–68, B14–15
  operating system, I208–9
  peer-to-peer, **I208–9**, I210
  software, I208
Landscape format, **I167–68**, I173, I177
LCD, I24, I62, **I167–68**, I172–73
Leased line, **I195**, I211
LED, I169
Logic error, I31
Logon, **I216**, I247
Logic operations, **I12**, I30, I37–38, I91, I104–06, B12, B16
Loop, **B40**, B60
Lotus Development Company, **I48**, I52, I66
Lovelace, Lady Ada Augusta, I42

Machine cycle, **I95**, I100, I106
Machine-readable format, I36, **B14**
Macros, I149
Magnetic stripe, I7, **I157–58**, I162–63, S70
Magnetic tape, I96, I116, **I130–33**, I143
  cartridge, **I130**, I133, I284
  drive, **I116**, I130–31, I143
Mailing list, I236, **I238–39**
Main program, **B40**, B60
Mainframe computer system, **I13–15**, I25–27, S46–47, S66, S68, S70
Management information system (MIS), S76, S78, S81, S91, B2, **B16–19**, B22–23, B25, B27, B30, B37–39
Management levels
  clerical, B6
  operational, **B6**, B8
  strategic, B6
  tactical, **B6**, B8

144–45
...ively parallel processing (MPP), **I104**, I107
...uchly, John W., I44
Megabit, I103–4
Megabyte, I102–3
Megahertz (MHz), I106
Memory, **I12**, I88–89, **I92–96**, I100–8
capacity, **I101–3**
flash, **I93**, I100, I106, I142, I161–63
main, I100
nonvolatile, **I93**, I106, I158,
programmable read-only memory (PROM), **I93**, I106
random-access, **I12** (*see also* RAM)
read-only memory (ROM), **I93**, I106, I205, I212, I276, I279
volatile, **I92**, I106
Menu, **I149**, I177
bar, S6
floating, **I266**
hierarchy of, I266
main, I55, I79, I218, I276, **S6**, S34
pop-out, I263, **I265**
pop-up, **I266**
pull-down, I228, **I265–66**, I270
tree, I224, **I229–31**, I234
Message, **I188**, I211
Message frame, I205
Metropolitan area network (MAN), **I204**, I212
Microcomputer, **I13** (*See also* Personal computer)
Micron, I31
Microprocessor, I49, **I90**, I100, I105, I108
Microsecond, **I31–32**
Microsoft Access, I52, **I72–74**, I205–6
Microsoft Corporation, **I47**, I131, I259
Microsoft Excel, **I52**, I64, **I66–74**, I273, S13
Microsoft Internet Explorer, I59, I136–37 **I228–29**, I248, I261–62, I268
Microsoft Office, **I51–52**, I59, I260, S3, S48
Microsoft Outlook, **I237**, I262, S19–21
Microsoft PowerPoint, I52, **I62–66**, I74–75, I80, I254, S18
Microsoft Window (*see* Windows)
Microsoft Word, I32–33, **I51–61**, I64, I74–75, I79, I270–72, S4
Microwave radio signal, **I191–93**, I195
Millions of instructions per second (MIPS), I101–4
Millisecond, **I31**
Minicomputer, **I25**, I38, I45
Mnemonic, **I266**, I278
Modem, I83, I89, **I98–99**, I106, I181, I186–87, I189–91, I195, I200, I204, I211, I216, I220, I247, I282, I288
cable, **I99**, I106
data/voice/fax, **I99–100**, I106
external, I96, **I187**
fax, I56, I89, **I99–100**, I187, I287
internal, I187
ISDN, **I190**, I211
Monitors, **I12,** I163, I166–68
color, I25, **I166**
flat-panel, **I167–68**, I173, S88
head-mounted, S105
monochrome, **I166**, I177
pixels, **I166**, I168, I172–73, I177, S4–5, S7
RGB, **I166**, I177
resolution, **I25**, I38, **I166**, I177
touch screen, I162, **I167–68**, I177
Motherboard, I82–83, **I88–90**, I92, I95, I96–100, I105–6, I163, I187, I282, B3
Motorola Corporation, **I19**, I37, I90, I257
Mouse, **I12**, **I151–52**
click, **I151–52**, I267–69
double-click, **I152**, I267–69
drag, I101, **I152**, I154, I268–69
wheel, **I151**
MS-DOS (*see* Operating systems, MS-DOS)
Multimedia, I25, **S13–19**, S97–98, S111
applications, **I23**, I49, I123, I134, I139, I144, **S16–19**
projector, I172
Multiplatform environment, **I258**, I278
Multiplexor, **I186–89**, I193, I207
Multitasking, **I254–55**, I263

Nanosecond, I31
NASA, **I32**, S81, S102–3, B7
National Information Infrastructure (NII), **I219**, S84, S100
Netscape Communicator, I136, **I223**, I228–29
NetWare, I209
Network
address, **I188–89**, I211
network interface card (NIC), I100, **I186–89**, I209–12
node, **I196–98**, I211
portable, I210
topologies, I180, **I197–98**, I201
Network computer (NC), **I21–23**, I38, I104, I281
Networking
intercompany, I184
intracompany, I184
Neural network, I104–5
Newbie, I215, **I221**
Newsgroup, I224, I232, **I238–39**, I243
Novell Corporation, I209, **S48**, S73
Numeric characters, I85

Object, **I33**, I38, **I270**, I278
Object linking and embedding (OLE), **I270**, I273
Object-oriented programming (OOP), **B57–58**, B62
Offline, **I11**, I37, B14
Online, **I10**, I37, B14
shopping, I16–18
Online service, I216, I286
Open application, **I264**, I278

Operating systems, **I18–19**, I208–10, I251–79, I287, S7, S14, S34–35, S46–47, B35–36
LAN, **I208–9**, I211
Linux, **I256–57**, I278
Mac 0S, **I257**, I278
MS-DOS, I47, **I254–56**, I276–77
platform, **I18–19**, I37, I137, I256–58
UNIX, **I257–58**, I278
Windows CE, **I256–57**
Windows 3.1, I260
Windows 95, I18, I48, I209, **I256–57**, I259, I260–62, I267–69, I277–78
Windows 98, **I18**, I48, I209, I239, I252, I255–63, I267–69, I273, I277–78, I282, S6
Windows 9x, **I18**, I37, I259–61, I267–69, I275–78, S32
Windows NT, **I18**, I48, I209, I252, I256–59, I277–78
Windows NT Server, I209
Windows 2000, **I256–57**
Operators
arithmetic, I69
logical, I76
relational, I76
Optical character recognition (OCR), I32, I147, **I155**, I157, I162–63, S29, S31, S54
Output, I4
Output device, I26, I146–49, **I163–178**, S16

Packets, I222
Pages per minute (ppm), I169
Parallel processing, **I104–6**, I163
Parallel transmission, **I96**, I98, I100
Parameters, I266
Parity checking, I210
Pascal, Blaise, I40
Pascaline, I40
Password, I157, I175, **I216–18**, I222, I234, I247, S47, S60, S70–71
Patching (system), **B52**, B61
PCMCIA (PC) card, I82–83, **I100**, I106, I187–88
PDF (portable document format), I136–37
PDP-8, I45
Pentium®, I19
Pentium® II, I19, I49, **I89–90**, I101, I281, I287, S109
Pentium® III, **I90**, I101
Pentium® Pro, I49, I102
Personal computer, **I5–7**, I18–24, I37–38, I47–48, I95, I102–3, I273–79, S108–9
buyer's guide, I280–88
compatible, I18–19
desktop, **I19–21**, I37, I100–1,
handheld, I21
IBM PC-compatible, **I18**, I37, I47–48
iMac, **I19–20**, I37, I121, I281
laptop, **I19–20**, I22, I37, I101, I120, I142, I153, I154, B6
Macintosh, I19, I37, **I48**, I139, I256–58, S15
notebook, **I19**, I23, I28–29,
palmtop, **I19**, I23, I37, I120
pen-based, **I21**, I23, I37, I281
pocket, **I19–20**, I37, I256, I257, I277
portable, **I19–21**, I100, I164, I210
slate, **I21**, I37, I162, I281
tower, **I19–21**, I29, I37
wearable, I153, I162, **I274**
Wintel, **I18**, I37
Personal computing, I6, **I32**, I38, I254–57, S3, S19, S29, S34
Personal digital assistant (PDA), **I21**, I23, I100
Personal identification number (PIN), I157–58
Personal information, privacy of, I21, I37, I51, I237, S2, S19, S29, S35, **S56–63**, S73–74, S106
Personal information management (PIM) system, **I21**, **I37–38**
Picosecond, I31
Pixel, **I166**, I168, I172–73, I177, S4–5, S7
Plain old telephone service (POTS), **I190–91**, I195–96, I211
Platforms (*see* Operating systems, platforms)
Plotter, **I171**, I178, I204
Plug-and-play, **I256**, I259, I262–63
Point-and-draw devices, I12, **I151–54**, S6
Pointer, **I67**, I71, I79–80, I227, I270, I278
Point-of-presence (POP), **I222**, I247
Port, **I19**, I28, I37, I96–98, I187, I190, I256
IrDA, **I98**, I106
keyboard, I89, I96
mouse, I96
parallel, I89, **I96**, I100, I106, I282
SCSI, **I96–98**, I106
serial, I89, **I96–97**, I106, I193, I282
USB, I89, I96, I98, I99, I106, I282
Port replicator, **I19**, I37
Portal, **I229–32**, I238, I248
Post Office Protocol (POP), **I237–38**, I248
Portrait format, **I168–69**, I173, I177
Power down/up, **I276**, I279, S68
PowerPC, **I19**, I37
PPP connection, **I222**, I237, I247
Printers, **I12**, I15, I21, I23–24, **I168–72**, I267–69, I282–87, S53–54, S97, B24, B43
desktop page, I62, **I168–72**
dot-matrix, **I170–73**, I178
impact, **I171–72**, I178, S52
ink-jet, **I169–73**, I178
laser, **I169**, I173, I177, S52, S54
large-format ink-jet, **I171**, I178
multifunction, I169
nonimpact, I172–73
page, I26, **I169–71**, I177
serial, I200
Private line, **I195–96**, I211
Processing operation, **I29**, I52

...r, **I12,** I13, I15, I18–20, I26–27 I37–38, I82–83, **I88–96**, I99–109, I165–66, I188–89, I210–11, I252–56, I281–82, S6–7, S109, B14
description, I101-03
design, I103-05
front-end, **I186–200**, I211
Intel, I18–19, **I90**, I102
special-function, I187, I253
Processor-bound application, **I27**, I38
Program, **I5** (*See also* Software)
Programmable read-only memory (PROM), I93, I106
Programming, I42, **I45–47**, I51, I72–73, I103–6, B32, B40–43, B47–48, **B53–62**
code, B26, B47
logic, B53, B57, B60–61
Programming languages, I42, I45–47, I93, S18, S35, B32, **B53–58**, B61–62
Ada, I42
C++, I95, S18, B53, **B57**, B60–61
COBOL, I45, B27, **B57**, B60–61
fourth-generation language (4GL), B9, **B57–58**, B62
high-level, B42
machine, **I95–96**, I103, I106, I117, B56–57, B60–61
natural, **S89–91**, S111
object-oriented, **B57**, B61–62
procedure-oriented, **B57**, B60–61
visual, **B58**, B62
Visual Basic, B53, **B58**, B60, B62
Prompt (system), I71, I93, I188, I209, I234, I254, B11, **B15–16**
Protocols
communications, **I189**, I199–201, S64, S69
contention, I210
polling, **S93**, S111
Prototype system, I173, **B43–49**, B56, B61
Prototyping, B32, **B43–49**, B53, B58, B61–62
Pull technology, **I235–36**
Punched cards, I42–43
Push technology, **I235–36**

Query by example (QBE), **I76–77**, I79–80

Radio button, **I233**, I248, I266–67, I269
RAM, **I12**, I23, I37–38, **I88–94**, I124–25, I141–43, I173–74, I207–10, I276–79
address, **I93**, I106
Rambus dynamic RAM (RDRAM), **I92–93**, I106
Rapid application development (RAD), **B45**, B61
Record, **I-8**, I72–79, B14, B16
Reduced-instruction-set computer (RISC), **I103**, I105–6
Register, **I91**, I93
instruction, **I91**, I96, I106
program, **I91**, I106
Repetitive-stress injuries, S52
Report generator, B43
Resolution, **I25**, I38, **I166**, I177
Ring topology, **I197**, I211
Robotics, I4, S76–81, **S91**, S111
manipulator, S76–78
pick and place, S79
Robots, **S76–81**, S91, S111
Router, I186, **I189**, I211, I222
RS-232C connector, **I96**, I100, I106
Ruler bar, I264, **I266**

Satellite, **I191–93**, I198, I216, I262–65
Scalable system, **B44–45**, B49, B55, B61
Scanners, I97, I147, **I154–56**
document, **I154**, I163
image, I23, I61, I62, **I156–57** , I282
label, I155
laser, I154–55
optical mark, I155
page, I156–57
stationary label, I163
wand, **I155**, I163
Screen generator, B42
Screen image projector, I63
Screen saver, S33–34
Scroll bar**, I69**, I80, I264–67
arrow, **I69**, I80, I265
box, **I69**, I80, I265
Scrolling, **I69**, I80
SCSI
adapter, I89, I97, **I99–100**
bus, **I98**
interface card, **I100**, I106
port, **I96**
Search engine, I18, I224, **I226–27**, I230–32, I243, I248
Secure Sockets Layer (SSL), **S69**, S74
Security, S66–71
logical, **S68–70**
physical, S66–68, **S70**
Sequential
access, **I143**, S19
processing, I130
Serial
representation, **I123**, I143
transmission, **I96**, I98
Server
application, **I270**, I273, I278
communications, **I207–8**, I210, I212
computer, I21, I23, **I29**, I187–88, **I198–99**, I222–23, I225–26, I256–57, S46–47
dedicated, **I208–10**, I212
e-mail, **I237**, I243, I248
file, **I207**, I209–10, I212, B14
LAN, **I208**, I210, I261, S66–68
print, **I207–8**, I210, I212
program, **I222–23**, I247
Windows 2000, I257
Shareware, I286

Shortcut Bar (Windows), I263
Shortcut key, **I260**, I265, I269, I278
Shut down procedure, **I276**, I279
Signature (electronic), **S70–71**, S74
Silicon wafers, I109
Single in-line memory module (SIMM), **I92**, I106
Site license, S65
Smalltalk, **B57**, B61
Smart card, **I157–58**, I162–63, S72
Smart house, S40–41, S43, S88
Soft copy, **I12**, I15, I37, S98, B13
Soft key, **I162**, I177
Software, **I5**
  applications, **I15**
  authoring, I286, **S16**, S18–19, S29, S35
  back-end applications, **I199**, I211
  business, S29–35
  copyrighted, S65
  command-driven, I254
  communications, **I33**, I38, I216–17, I225
  database, **I33**, I38, I50–52, **I72–80**, S4, S47
  desktop publishing, **I33**, I38, I50–52, **I60–62**, S34, S47
  document-composition, I61
  education, **S24–28**, S35
  edutainment, I35–36, S2, **S24–28**
  front-end applications, **I199**, I201
  general-purpose, I209
  graphics, I79, I152, **S4–13**, S17, S19, S34–35
  home, S19–24
  installing, **I273**, I275–77
  license agreement, **I275**, S64–66
  multimedia, S4, **S13–18**, S34
  personal information management (PIM), I15, **S19**
  pilferage, S65–66
  piracy, S65
  portfolio, S3, B35, B36
  presentation, **I33**, I38, **I62–66**
  productivity, I15, **I32–33**, I258, B35
  proprietary, I128, S65–66, **B35–36**, B60
  spreadsheet, **I33**, I50, I52, I62, **I66–72**, I78, I80, S4
  suites, **I51–52**, I140, I286, S3
  system, **I14–15**, I252, I255, S34, S46, B35
  utility, **I125–26**, **S32–34**
  word processing, **I32–33**, I50, **I52–61**, B42
Software engineering, **B42**, B54, B60
Sorting, **I57**, I78–80, B30
Source application, **I270–71**, I273
Source data, **B14**, B30
Source-data automation, I146, **I154–63**, I177
Source document, **B14**, B30
Source program, **I117–19**, I143
Spam, I8, **I246–47**, I249, S57
Spammer, I246–47
Specifications (specs)
  functional, **B44**, B49, B61
  system, **B44**, B61
Speech synthesis, I165, **I172–73**, I178
Speech-recognition, **I21**, I147, **I158–60**, I274, S52, S88, S91
Spelling checker, **I54**, I56
Spreadsheet
  column range, **I67**, I71
  formulas, **I67–71**, I80
  functions, I70
  range, **I67–69**, I80
Star topology, **I197**, I211
Start button, **I263**, I278
Start/stop transmission, **I200**, I212
Storage
  data, I30, **I116–42**, B60
  devices, I26, I30, **I116–42**
  mass, I116–42
Structure chart, **B36**, B42, B60
Subroutine, **B40–41**, B60
Super VGA, I282
Supercomputer, **I13–14**, I26–27, I29, I197–98
Switched line, I195–96
Switching hubs, I186
Synchronous dynamic RAM (SDRAM), I89, **I92–93**, S29
Synchronous transmission, **I200**, I212
Syntax, I45, **I254–55**
System check, **I276**, I279, B3
System life cycle, B3, B32, **B34–36**, B42, B51–52
System maintenance, B51
System prompt, I75, **I276–77**, I279
System specifications, **B44**, B46, B47, B49, B58–59, B62
System unit, **I88**
Systems design, B34, B36, **B45–49**, B51, B58, B60–62
  program, B40
  structured, **B36**, B60
  tools, B42, B60–61

T-1 line, **I221**, I225
T-3 line, **I221**, I225
Tabulating Machine Company, I42
Tailgating, S70
Tape backup unit (TBU), I99, **I130–32**, I143
Target system, **B45–47**, B49, B55, B61
Taskbar (Windows), I259, **I263**, I265, I267
TCP/IP, I200, **I222**, I225, I247
Telecommunications, **S92**, S111
Telecommuting, I194, **I202–3**, I215, I283, S44, S54, S73, S110
Teleconferencing, I195
Telemedicine, **S106**, S111
Telephony, **I175**, I177–78, I262, S84
Telnet, I232, **I234–35**, I243, I248
Templates, **I63**, I66–71, I74–75
Terabyte, **I102**, I106
Terminal, **I25**
  dumb, **I176**, I178, I198
  point-of-sale (POS), **I176–78**, B33

…, *continued*
…cial-function, **I175–76**, I178
…DT, **I174**, I176–78
Windows, **I174**, I178
Testing
systems, **B49–50**, B61
unit, **B49**, B52–53, B61
Texas Instruments, I45
Thesaurus (online), **I55–56**, I59–60
Thread, I41, **I238–39**, I246, I248
Throughput, **I93**, I100, I103–4, I106, I121
Throwaway system, **B20**, B23, B30
Thumbnail, **I65**, I80
Tiny area network (TAN), I201, **I204**, I210, S19
Title bar (Windows), **I264–65**, I268–69
Token access method, **I205–206**, I212
Toolbar, I228–30, I248, **I264–66**
Track, **I122–25**, I130, I138
density, **I124**, I130
number, I119, **I124**
tracks per inch, **I124**, I129
Trackball, **I152–53**, I165
Trackpad, **I152–54**, I177, I255
Transaction-oriented processing, **B15**, B30
Transfer rate, **I127**, I139
Transistor, **I45**, I108
Transmission Control Protocol (TCP), **I222**, I247
Transparent, I191
TSR, S29
Turnaround document, **I156**, I177
Twisted-pair wire, **I190–91**, I211
Typefaces, **I53**, I79, I280

Unicode, **I87**, I105
Uniform Resource Locator (URL), I6, **I223–25**, I227–30, I233, I247–48
Uninterruptible power source (UPS), I21, **S67–68**, S74
UNIVAC I, I40, **I44**
Universal product code (UPC), **I155**, B15
Universal Serial Bus (USB), I89, **I96–100**, I106, I262–63, I278, I282, I288
Upload, **I11**, I37, I118, I143, I199, I226, I234, I248
Upstream rate, **I191**, I211
Uptime, I31, S72
USENET, **I238**, I248
User, I7
User ID, S70–74
User Location Service (ULS), I230, **I241**, I246, I248

Vacuum tube, **I43–44**, I108
VGA, I97, I99
Video mail, S110–11
Video operator's distress syndrome (VODS), **S51**, S54, S73
Video RAM (VRAM), **I163**, I177
Videophone, **I10**, I33, I147, I167, I215, S95–96
Virtual file allocation (VAT), **I124**, I143
Virtual reality, S24, S83, **S102–5**, S109, S111
data glove, **S102–3**, S105
Virus (computer), **I128–29**, S68–69
antiviral program, **S33–34**, S68
vaccines, **I128**, I143, S68
Vision-input system, **I160**, S81
Visual programming, **B58**, B62
Voice prints, S66, S71, S74
Voice-response system, **I148–49**, I163, I172–77

Watson, Thomas J., I42
Webcasting, **I235–36**
Webmaster, **S46**, S73, S94
What-if analysis, I73, **B21**
Whiteboarding, **I242**, I248
Wide area network (WAN), **I201**, I210
Windows
active, **I263–65**, I269
applications, I87, **I260**, I268–71
cascading, I268–69
concepts, I259–69
document, **I264**, I266, I268–69
Explorer, **I267**, I278
features, I270–77
non-Windows application, **I260**, I268–69
platforms, I255–258
terminal, **I174**, I178
tiled, I268
wizard, **I261–62**, I278, I287, B55
workspace, I264–65
Wireless transceivers, I187, **I193–95**, I204
Word processing
boilerplate, **I56–57**, I75
Word size, I82, **I101**, I103, I106
WordPerfect, **I52**, I118
Workgroup computing, I15, I121, **I209–10**, I212
Workstation, I13–14
World Wide Web, I16, I49, **I58**, I61, I79, I117, I136–37, I217, I225, I227–28, I231–34, I242–44, I248, I259, I261–63, S13, S46, S56–57, S69, S73–74, S94–95, B51, B54
page, **I58**, I79, **I227**
Wozniak, Steve, I47
WYSIWYG, **I54**, I79, I225, B55

Yahoo, **I229–31**, I243, S49, S94
Year 2000 problem, B26–27

Zoom, S7